BIOGRAPHICAL DICTIONARY OF PSYCHOLOGY

BIOGRAPHICAL DICTIONARY OF PSYCHOLOGY

Edited by
Noel Sheehy
Antony J. Chapman
Wendy A. Conroy

London and New York

First published 1997
by Routledge
11 New Fetter Lane, London EC4P 4EE
29 West 35th Street, New York, NY 10001

© 1997 Routledge

Typeset in Franklin Gothic Demi and Times
by Mathematical Composition Setters, Salisbury, Wiltshire

Printed and bound in Great Britain by
TJ International (Padstow) Ltd, Padstow, Cornwall

British Library Cataloguing in Publication Data

A catalogue record for this book is available from the British Library

Library of Congress Cataloging in Publication Data

Biographical dictionary of psychology/edited by N.P. Sheehy, A.J.
Chapman, and W.A. Conroy
    p.   cm.
    Includes bibliographical references and indexes.
    1. Psychologists--Biography--Dictionaries. 2. Psychology-
-History. I. Sheehy, Noel II. Chapman, Antony J.
III. Conroy, W. A.
BF109.A1B56 1997
150'.92'.2
[B]--DC20   96-343333
                                        CIP

ISBN 0-415-09997-8

CONTENTS

EDITORIAL ADVISORY BOARD

INTRODUCTION

Our aim was to compile a reference volume containing basic information and analysis, including descriptions of influences and reception concerning some 500 individuals whose work is of significance in psychology. The *Dictionary* represent the practice of psychology worldwide and includes entries on psychologists whose influence may not be particularly well-known to North American and European psychologists. It also includes entries on those who might not regard themselves as psychologists, such as Chomsky or Sperry, but whose work has had a profound impact on developments within the discipline.

In compiling this dictionary we have used a method which attempts to minimize sources of bias due to our familiarity with particular topic areas, cultures and periods of history. Like Edwin G. Boring (Annin, Boring and Watson, 1968) our approach is based on a combination of quantitative and qualitative judgements. Boring and Robert I. Watson compiled a list of 1,040 deceased individuals who had made a significant impact in the evolution and development of psychology between 1600 and 1967. The list was circulated among seven other eminent psychologists and a rating scale devised to rank order the names. One point was awarded if a name was recognized, two points if the person's major contribution was recognized and three points if it was felt that the person should be included in a list of 500 most prominent psychologists. Using a cut-off score of 11 a final list of 538 names was drawn up. Boring died before the project could be completed but Leonard Zusne had been working on a very similar project and was encouraged by Watson to complete a list of Names in the History of Psychology using the method devised by Boring (Zusne, 1976). Zusne's biographical sourcebook contained entries on 526 deceased psychologists, and surveys a longer time period, from the Greek philosophers to the twentieth century.

Unlike Boring and Zusne we have not used a rating scale to determine who should be included in the *Dictionary* and we have not required that those included should be dead. The time period surveyed in this biographical dictionary differs from the studies by Boring and by Zusne. Our survey covers the period from the emergence of experimental psychology in the mid-nineteenth century – the earliest entry considers the work of Flourens (1796–1867) – through to the late twentieth century.

Methodology

In compiling the *Dictionary* we have used a three step method. First, we compiled a list of just over 2,000 names who might be included in the *Dictionary*. Second, by rank ordering on a combination of criteria we reduced the list to about 770 names. Third, we circulated the list among 15 colleagues, including the Editorial Advisory Board, and asked them to identify ways of further reducing the length of the list and, more importantly, to spot important omissions. An emphasis on substantial publication or reception up to the early 1990s means that there are some psychologists whose work is not referenced in this *Dictionary* but who may qualify for inclusion in a later revision.

The major historical figures were identified as those who are included in most of the main histories of psychology of the period. We surveyed a sample of 16 histories of psychology published between 1950 and 1990 and the names of all those referenced, including the total number of references to each person in the Name Index was recorded. This list of 1,721 names was rank ordered using the total number of references to each person.

The contents of four encyclopedias of psychology, published between 1960 and 1993, was surveyed. Particular attention was paid to the reference listings – the assumption being that entries appearing in substantive reference volumes will probably include references to key contributions. This produced a list of 1,090 names which was rank ordered using the total number of references to each person. Not surprisingly, there was considerable overlap between this list and the list compiled from the histories of psychology.

The reference listings in 31 introductory textbooks, published between 1960 and 1990, were surveyed. We considered for inclusion the works of those whose names recurred most often. We assumed that citations to these individuals reflected their significance in the discipline through the transmission of key ideas and texts from one generation to another. The 1,800 names were rank ordered using the cumulative references to each person.

Citation analysis is a complex and controversial methodology (e.g. Lindholm-Romantschuk and Warner, 1996). However we used it cautiously to identify significant contributions by modern and contemporary psychologists. This was done by referring to both the citation count on an individual and weighting this using the citation impact factor of the journals in which the cited work was published. This was a laborious task because the ISI Science and Social Science citation indexes do not identify authors by discipline. For example, computer-based citation analysis on 'M. Lewis' cannot distinguish between the psychologist Michael Lewis and other psychologists, sociologists, economists and physicians of the same name. Cumulative citations to commonly occurring names are usually spurious. Thus, the citation counts on almost 500 living psychologists identified through the surveys of histories, reference volumes and introductory texts were checked manually to ensure that the computer-based citation analysis was identifying only those individuals who had made a contribution to psychology. This laborious task (undertaken by Dr Siriol David) also allowed us to check for high levels of self-citation.

Sources such as the major library catalogues (Books in Print, Books out of Print and Psychological Abstracts) of published works were surveyed in order to identify other potentially significant contributions to psychology – such as books and monographs – which tend to be under-represented in the ISI citation indexes. It was not proposed to include anyone merely because of the number of books or monographs they had published.

A number of societies, notably the APA and BPS, make awards annually in recognition of significant contributions to the discipline. We sampled from these listings since the inception of an award category. The listings proved useful in identifying contributions in professional activities other than publication and dissemination in conventional media.

Reducing the list

The 2,050 names were rank ordered using a combination of citations in histories of psychology, reference volumes, introductory texts and ISI citation indexes. The rank ordering of the top half of the list – the top 1,000 names – was more precise than the lower half. Twenty-one

psychologists who had received awards for significant contributions other than through publication were not included in this ranking. The 1,300 names appearing towards the bottom of the list were excluded from further considering. This left 750 names, plus the 21 psychologists who had attracted awards for distinguished contributions to professional practice.

An alphabetical listing of the 771 names was circulated to 15 colleagues including members of the Editorial Advisory Board. It was explained that entries on each name could be longer (2,000 words) or shorter (1,300 words or 700 words). Alongside each name was a brief description (using the titles of the APA Divisions) of the principal areas in which the person had made a contribution and the proposed length of entry for each person. The length of entry was based on the rank order (which was not given to these advisors). There were 50 entries of 2,000 words, 100 entries of 1,500 words and the remainder were entries of 700 words. Advisors were invited to comment on the list: to suggest names who did not appear (23 names were suggested), identify individuals who they considered should probably not be included (eight names were identified), comment on the proposed length of entry and suggest individuals who might be approached to write an entry on the contribution of the person listed. Informed by their advise and comments the list was further shortened by the Editors to 550 names. Entries for around 500 individuals appear in this first edition of the *Biographical Dictionary of Psychology*. Some individuals did not respond to an invitation to supply biographical details and a curriculum vitae, and it was not possible to prepare a substantive entry on their contribution.

Format of entries

Biographers were invited to supply entries and those who replied within the time permitted by the production schedule adhered to the following standard format:

> Name
> Date and place of birth and death as appropriate
> Nationality
> Main area of interest in psychology with reference to the Divisions of the APA
> Education
> Principal appointments, honours and awards

Principal publications

Further reading (i.e. sources of critical, appreciative or analytic accounts of the person's main work)

Intellectual development and main ideas including an assessment of influence

Key terms against which the person's contributions should be indexed

The name of the biographer appears at the end of each entry. Where there is no name the entry has been prepared by the Editors.

References

Annin, E.L., Boring, E.G. and Watson, R.I. (1968) Important psychologists, 1600–1967. *Journal of the Behavioral Sciences*, 4, 303, 315.

Lindholm-Romantschuk, Y. and Warner, J. (1996) The role of monographs in scholarly communication: An empirical study of philosophy, sociology and economics. *Journal of Documentation*, 52, 389–404.

O'Connell, A.N. and Russo, N.F. (1990) (eds) *Women in Psychology: A Bio-bibliographic Sourcebook.* Greenwood Press.

Zusne, L. (1976) *Names in the History of Psychology.* Halstead and Wiley.

PROFESSOR NOEL SHEEHY
PROFESSOR ANTONY J. CHAPMAN
WENDY A. CONROY

HOW TO USE THE DICTIONARY

Structure of an entry

The *Dictionary* contains alphabetically-arranged entries on around 500 psychologists, each of which is designed in the same way. Below the name heading are up to six subheadings with biographical details of birth (**Born:**) and death (**Died:**), nationality (**Nat:**), professional interests (**Ints:**), education (**Educ:**) and appointments and awards or honours (**Appts & awards:**). This last section includes professional and academic posts, membership of societies and other psychological associations such as the APA or the BPS, or of editorial boards of journals, honorary degrees and appointments and other awards.

This is followed by a bibliographical section split into two elements. **Principal publications** gives information on the major works of the entrant, listed chronologically by date of publication and including (where available) date and title, journal details for an article or publisher details for a book. **Further reading** lists critical materials, in alphabetical order of the author/ editor, about the work of the entrant or the entrant's field of interest. A short biographical and critical appreciation forms the rest of the entry. The contributor's name is given underneath the entry; where no name is given, the entry is the work of the Editors.

Indexes

There are four indexes to help readers use the *Dictionary*. Each lists surnames only for entrants, except where this would lead to ambiguity.

Index of Names

This contains names of entrants cross-referenced with others who also have an entry. Within the main body of the text, names of other entrants are indicated in bold type.

Index of Interests

This allows a reader to identify the broad areas within psychology in which an entrant's work has had a significant impact. This index is structured around the Divisions of the APA, with some additions (e.g. artificial intelligence, cognitive science), and reflects the information given in the **Ints:** field of the entry.

Index of Key Terms

This index is more specific than the Index of Interests. The key terms identified by contributors can be used to link concepts and terms in psychology to the people who have been closely associated with them.

Index of Institutions

Identifies the individuals linked with the academic and professional institutions and institutional associations mentioned in the *Dictionary*.

CONTRIBUTORS

Archer, John
University of Central Lancashire

Ancona, Leonardo
University of Rome

Amsel, K.W.S.
University of Texas at Austin

Baker, Leo

Beloff, John
University of Edinburgh

Bennett, N.J.M.

Bevans, H. Gordon
University of Leeds (retd)

Brennan, James F.
University of Massachusetts at Amherst

Bridgeman, B.
University of California at Santa Cruz

Carroll, Douglas
University of Birmingham

Child, Irvin L.
Yale University

Clifford, B.R.
University of East London

Colley, Ann
University of Leicester

Cooper, Colin
The Queen's University of Belfast

Cox, Cate
The Queen's University of Belfast

Crozier, W.R.
University of Wales, Cardiff

Dabbs, Alan
University of Leeds

Davies, Roy

Dickins, David
University of Liverpool

Dry, Avis M.
Trinity and All Saints University College of Leeds

Faber, Diana
University of Liverpool

Foot, H.C.
University of Strathclyde

Fullerton, Clare
University of East London

Funk, Rainier
University of Tübingen

Hanks, Helga
University of Leeds

Hargreaves, David J.
Leicester University

Hartnett, Oonagh
University of Wales

Harvey, Jonathan G.
The Queen's University of Belfast

Helson, R.M.
University of California at Berkeley

Henle, E.B.T.

Hogan, John D.
St John's University, New York

Iaccino, William
St John's University, New York

Kline, Paul
University of Exeter

Kovach, Joseph K.
The Menninger Clinic, Kansas

Logvinenko, A.

Lorion, Raymond P.
University of Maryland

Lovie, A.D.
University of Liverpool

Lovie, Patricia
University of Keele

Lundin, Robert W.
University of the South at Sewanee, Tennessee

Maguire, Moira
University of Luton

Marks, David F.
Middlesex University

Massaro, Dominic W.
University of California at Santa Cruz

Milner, A.D.
University of St Andrews

Moran, Aidan
University College Dublin

Morgan, Michelle
The Queen's University of Belfast

Morss, John
University of Otago

Murray, D.

Nucci, L.P.
University of Illinois

Oborne, David
University College Swansea

Peyser, Charles
University of the South at Sewanee, Tennessee

Pickersgill, Mary J.
Royal Holloway, University of London

Priestnall, R.
University of Ulster

Richards, Graham
University of East London

Rudmin, F.W.
Queen's University Kingston

Schmeidler, Gertrude R.
City College, City University of New York

Sherrard, Carol
University of Leeds

Smith, John L.
University of Sunderland

Smith, Leslie
Lancaster University

Sokolskaya, T.
The Queen's University of Belfast

Sonnentag, Sabine
University of Amsterdam

Staudt-Sexton, Virginia
St John's University, New York

Stedmon, Jackie
Plymouth Hospital NHS Trust

Still, Arthur
University of Durham

Stratton, P.
Leeds Family Therapy and Research Centre, University of Leeds

Swan, Des
University College Dublin

Terry, W. Scott
University of North Carolina at Charlotte

Thompson, D.
Georgia State University

Timberlake, William
Indiana University

Tizard, Barbara
Thomas Coram Research Unit

Trew, Karen
The Queen's University of Belfast

Valentine, Elizabeth R.
Royal Holloway, University of London

Verleger, Rolf
Medical University of Lübeck

Wallis, Donald
University of Wales

Wapner, Seymour

Wesley, Frank
Portland State University

Wetherick, N.E.
University of Aberdeen (retd)

Wilkinson, Robert
Open University, UK

Wilson, Richard M.S.
Loughborough University

Wolfe, R.N.
State University of New York at Geneseo

Zusne, Leonard

ACRONYMS

The following acronyms are used in the text for institutions connected with psychology and associated disciplines.

AAA&S	American Academy of Arts and Science
AAAS	American Association for the Advancement of Science
AERA	American Education Research Association
AMA	American Medical Association
APA	American Psychological Association
APF	American Psychological Foundation
APS	American Psychological Society
ARPA	American Research Projects Agency
ASA	American Sociological Association
BMA	British Medical Association
BPS	British Psychological Society
CPA	Canadian Psychological Association
ESRC	Economic and Social Research Council
NAS	National Academy of Sciences
NASP	National Association of School Psychology
NIH	National Institute of Health
NIMH	National Institute for Mental Health
NRC	National Research Council
NSF	National Science Foundation
SRC	Science Research Council
SSRC	Social Science Research Council

A

Abeles, Norman

Born: 1928, Vienna, Austria *Nat:* Austrian *Ints:* Clinical neuropsychology, clinical psychology, counselling psychology, psychotherapy, psychology and law *Educ:* BA New York University, 1949; MA University of Texas, 1952; PhD University of Texas, 1958 *Appts & awards:* Fulbright Professor, University of Utrecht, The Netherlands, 1968–9; Professor of Psychology, Michigan State University, 1968– ; Fellow, APA Divisions 8, 12, 17, 29, 31, 39, 40; President, Michigan Psychological Association, 1971–2; Fellow, APA, 1973– ; Distinguished Psychologist Award, Michigan Psychological Association, 1974; Trustee, American Board of Professional Psychology, 1975–8; Editorial Board, *Psychotherapy: Theory, Research and Practice*, 1975– ; Editor, *Academic Psychology Bulletin*, 1978–82; Director, Psychological Clinic, 1978– ; Consulting Editor, *Journal of Professional Psychology*, 1979–82, 1989– ; Recording Secretary, APA, 1980–6; Editor, *Professional Psychology: Research and Practice*, 1983–8; Consulting Editor, *Journal of Personality Assessment*, 1988– ; President, APA Division 12 (Clinical psychology), APA Division 29 (Psychotherapy), 1990; Consulting Editor, *Clinical Psychology: Science and Practice*, 1994–

Principal publications

1967   Liking for clients: Its relationship to therapist's personality: Unexpected findings. *Psychotherapy: Theory, Research and Practice*, 4, 19–21.

1971   The relationship of liking, empathy and therapist's experience to outcome in therapy. *Journal of Counseling Psychology*, 18, 39–43.

1975   Client therapist complementarity and therapeutic outcome. *Journal of Counseling Psychology*, 22, 264–72.

1979   Psychodynamic theory. In H. Burks and B. Stefflre (eds), *Counseling Theory*. New York: McGraw-Hill.

1980   Teaching ethical principles by means of value confrontations. *Psychotherapy: Theory, Research and Practice*, 7, 384–91.

1984   Congruence of perception on client symptoms and post therapy outcome. *Professional Psychology: Research and Practice*, 15, 846–55.

1986   Clients' pretherapy interpersonal attitudes and psychotherapy outcome. *Professional Psychology: Research and Practice*, 17, 217–22.

1988   Therapeutic alliance and outcome: Impact of treatment length and pretreatment symptomatology. *Psychotherapy*, 25, 536–542 (with T. Eaton and J. Gutfreund).

1993   Negative indicators, therapeutic alliance and therapy outcome. *Psychotherapy Research*, 3, 115–23 (with D.M. Rubin and R.T. Muller).

1994   Ethical issues and dilemmas in the mental health organization. *Administration and Policy in Mental Health*, 22, 7–17 (with B. Clark).

Further reading

Garrison, E.G. (1987) Psychological maltreatment of children – an emerging focus for inquiry and concern. *American Psychologist*, 42, 2, 157–9.

Klineberg, O. (1984) Public opinion and nuclear war. *American Psychologist*, 39, 11, 1245–53.

Markey, E.J. (1985) The politics of arms control. *American Psychologist*, 40, 5, 557–60.

Melton, G.B. and Garrison, E.G. (1987) Fear, prejudice and neglect discrimination against mentally disabled persons. *American Psychologist*, 42, 11, 1007–26.

The academic career of Norman Abeles has always involved teaching and research, particularly of graduate students seeking careers in research and professional practice. Together with his students, he has been involved in a variety of research projects designed to investigate how psychotherapy works. The now classic volume authored by M.L. Smith, Gene V. Glass and Thomas I. Miller titled *The Benefits of Psychotherapy*, based on a meta-analysis of 475 psychotherapy studies, dispelled any lingering doubts about the effectiveness of psychotherapy. Thus, Abeles argued that the focus of research enquiry should be on determining the efficacy of the various psychotherapeutic methods. With his colleagues he has constructed a data archive based on more than 300 patients, including pre and post data on patients, ratings elicited from therapists and patients, and audio recordings of patient–therapist sessions. This is the single largest psychotherapy tape library for outpatients in the United States, and probably in the world.

A second strand of research activity has addressed the interaction between mood and memory in older adults. This has involved a combination of fundamental investigations of psychological processes and the development and evaluation of intervention programmes (cognitive behavioural workshops and meditation workshops).

In addition, Abeles has been concerned with the development of professional psychology in the United States and in other countries. This has included forays into such areas as professional and research ethics, competence of psychologists and the education and credentialling of psychologists. In this he is regularly involved in contemporary debates (e.g. see Further reading) on ethical, legal and political challenges for psychology.

Adler, Alfred

Born: 1870, Vienna, Austria **Died:** 1937, Aberdeen, Scotland **Nat:** Austrian **Ints:** Educational psychology, health and medical psychology, personality and social psychology, psychoanalysis, psychotherapy, teaching psychology **Educ:** MD University of Vienna 1895 **Appts & awards:** Professor in Medical Psychology, Long Island College of Medicine; Founder and President, Vienna Psychoanalytical Association; Founder of the Society of Free Analytic Research (later the School of Individual Psychology); Co-editor, *Zentralblatt für Psychologie*; Founding Editor, *Internationale Zeitschrift für Individual-Psychologie*, 1914; Founding Editor, *Journal of Individual Psychology*, 1936

Principal publications

1898 *Health Book for the Tailor Trade.*
1907 *Study of Organ Inferiority and its Psychological Compensation: A Contribution to Clinical Medicine* (Studie über Minderwertigkeit von Organen). Nervous and Mental Diseases Publishing.
1912 *The Neurotic Constitution* (Über den nervösen Charakter). Mead (with B. Bergman and W. Dodd).
1913 *Traum und Traumdeutung* (Dreams and dream interpretation). *Zentralblatt für Psychologie*, 3, 574–83.

1914 *Heilen und Bilden.* Reinhardt.
1917 The problem of homosexuality. *Zeitschrift für Individuale-Psychologie.*
1920 *Praxis und Theorie der Individual-Psychologie: Vorträge zur Einführung in die Psychotherapie für Ärzte, Psychologen und Lehrer.* Bergmann.
1927 *The Practice and Theory of Individual Psychology.* (*Praxis und Theorie der Individual-Psychologie*). Harcourt Brace.
1927 *Understanding Human Nature.* Leipzig.
1929 *Problems of Neurosis: A Book of Case Histories.* Kegan Paul.
1929 *Science of Living.* Greenberg.
1930 *The Education of Children.* Greenberg.
1931 *What Life Should be to You.* Little and Brown.
1933 *The Other Side.* Vienna.
1933 *Social Interest: A Challenge to Mankind.* Faber and Faber.
1956 *Presentation in Selections from his Writings.* Basic Books (with H.L. and R.R. Ansbacher).

Further reading

Ansbacher, H.L. (1971) Alfred Adler and humanistic psychology. *Journal of Humanistic Psychology*, 11, 53–63.
—— and Ansbacher, R. (1956) (eds) *The Individual Psychology of Alfred Adler.* Basic Books.
Colby, K.M. (1951) On the disagreement between Freud and Adler. *American Imago*, 8, 229–38.

Alfred Adler started as a medical practitioner who had a keen interest in the social and political structure of society. He explored the effects of environmental and psychological influences on the symptomatology of physical disorders. Early in his life he was influenced by political theory, especially that of Marx, though this interest lapsed. By 1898 he had made a specific impact on education, and wrote his first paper on the subject. He had established the first Child Guidance Clinic in Vienna; by the time the clinics were closed down in 1933, there were thirty. Sigmund **Freud** asked Adler to join his small group in 1902, recognizing his talent, specifically to discuss psychology and neurosis. He was named Freud's successor, becoming President of the Vienna Psychoanalytical Society.

However, it quickly became apparent that the two men had developed different theoretical perspectives. For example, Adler argued that behaviour is determined by expectations about what we hope to achieve in the future, not by what we have done in the past, or what others have done to us. He resigned from the Psychoanalytical Society in 1911. He founded the Society for Free Psychoanalytical Research (later called Individual Psychology), and in 1914 the *Zeitschrift für Individuale-Psychologie*. Adler was a theoretician and therapist of considerable stature. A number of his theories are still influential in current thinking. He is best known for his stress on power as the individual goal (cf. Freud's focus on sex). He posited that each individual develops 'guiding fictions'. These are based on the child's experience of impotence and humiliation, resulting in the creation of a self-ideal, the expression of which is linked for the individual with feelings of strength and power, and hence overcoming feelings of helplessness and inferiority. His therapeutic approach concentrated on current difficulties and is concretely based on a social and cultural context. In his later years, having established himself in America, he travelled, teaching widely in Europe. His ideas have been pervasive throughout social and developmental psychology but rarely explicitly attributed to him. He influenced analytical thought including the work of **Sullivan**, **Horney** and **Fromm** and, indirectly, contemporary cognitive and existential therapies. He died in Aberdeen while on a lecture tour.

H. HANKS AND P. STRATTON

Ainsworth, Mary Dinsmore (Salter)

Born: Mary Dinsmore Salter, 1913, Glendale, Ohio, USA **Nat:** American **Ints:** Clinical psychology, cross-cultural psychology, developmental psychology **Educ:** BA University of Toronto, 1935; MA University of Toronto, 1936; PhD University of Toronto, 1939; Hon. DSc, University of Toronto, 1990 **Appts & awards:** Superintendent of Women's Rehabilitation, Department of Veteran Affairs, Ottawa, Canada, 1945–6; Assistant Professor and Research Fellow, Institute of Child Study, University of Toronto, 1945–50; Senior Research Psychologist, Tavistock Clinic, London, 1950–4; Senior Research Fellow, Makrere College, Kampala, Uganda, 1954–5; Lecturer, 1956–8, Associate Professor, 1958–63, and Professor, 1963–75, in Psychology, Johns Hopkins University; Fellow at Center for Advanced Studies, 1957–77; Professor, 1975–6, and Commonwealth Professor, 1976–84, in Psychology, University of Virginia; Professor Emeritus, University of Virginia, 1984– ; recipient of seven Distinguished Scientific Contribution Awards from

various national scientific organizations, including the G. Stanley Hall Award from APA

Principal publications

1952 Psychodiagnostic assessment of a child after prolonged separation in early childhood. *British Journal of Medical Psychology*, 25, 169–201 (with M. Boston).

1954 Research strategy in the study of mother–child separation. *Courier de la Centre International de l'Enfance*, 4, 105–113 (with J. Bowlby).

1958 *Measuring Security in Personal Adjustment*. World Books (with L.H. Ainsworth).

1965 *Child Care and the Growth of Love*. Penguin Books (with J. Bowlby).

1967 *Infancy in Uganda: Infant Care and the Growth of Love*. Johns Hopkins University Press.

1983 Infant attachment, with some preventive and clinical implications. *Dialogue*, 6, 41–9.

1985 Patterns of infant–mother attachments: Antecedents and effects on development. *Bulletin of the New York Academy of Medicine*, 61, 771–91.

1989 Attachment beyond infancy. *American Psychologist*, 44, 709–16.

1991 An ethological approach to personality development. *American Psychologist*, 46, 333–41 (with J. Bowlby).

Further reading

Bowlby, J. (1969) *Attachment and Loss*, vol. 1. Basic Books.
—— (1973) *Attachment and Loss*, vol. 2. Basic Books.
—— (1980) *Attachment and Loss*, vol. 3. Basic Books.

Ainsworth's doctoral dissertation, sponsored by William E. Blatz, set her on a course of basic research that would have probably focused on Blatz's theory of 'security' in the context of personality development. But the outbreak of the war interrupted her career. She joined the Canadian Women's Army Corps in 1942. Serving as a consultant to the Director of Personnel Selection, she reached the rank of major by the time she was decommissioned in 1945. The intense psychological work of the war years helped to put her career on a new research track, which was once again interrupted when she married L.H. Ainsworth and followed his academic track to London. However, once there, she again managed to turn the change in her work situation into an advantage: she found her way to John Bowlby's research project at the Tavistock Clinic. **Bowlby** became first a mentor, then a lifelong collaborator on her burgeoning research of the role of emotional security in early mother–infant attachment. Ainsworth's interest and research experience also added a much-needed new dimension to Bowlby's attempt to synthesize a set of ethological concepts (imprinting, genetically influenced developmental predispositions, sensitive-stage-dependent early learning) with psychoanalytic theory. She helped translate Bowlby's then emerging conceptualization of early infantile attachment into testable hypotheses and experimentation. Unlike Blatz, she was comfortable with such psychodynamic concepts as defence mechanisms and separation anxiety, but agreed with Bowlby about the need to anchor them in biological data and experimental instead of introspective or hermeneutic verification. In Uganda, Ainsworth studied the effects of maternal separation on infant behaviours and the related processes of early acculturation. By 1970 she developed the concept of secure base attachment and translated it into studies of infant exploratory behaviours and responses to separation in a strange situation. Her data negated the Freudian conception of passive, narcissistic and purely receptive oral phase and diffuse libidinal impulses in infancy. On the contrary, the infants she studied exhibited behaviours that elicited and reciprocated attachment responses from mother or caretaker (smiling, crying, approaching, avoiding, exploring, etc.), and the variations of these behaviours were fully predictable under her experimental conditions of 'strange situation'.

The picture of early attachment that emerged from Ainsworth's work is widely accepted by developmental psychologists today and the attachment theory continues to generate significant research. But Ainsworth's work has met mostly silence from the quarters that would seem most affected by it; from psychoanalytic and social learning theorists. Others more hospitable to the attachment theory (see especially Michael **Lamb**) call for attention to the great complexities of the attachment process, wherein mother–infant reciprocities may be facilitated or thwarted by supportive or disruptive influences from the larger environment. There is also the problem of individually variable temperamental predispositions children bring into this world, which has not been adequately addressed by Ainsworth. But most importantly, the causal role of early attachment in personality development, which is a funda-

mental tenet of attachment theory, has not yet been substantiated.

JOSEPH KOVACH

Ajzen, Icek
Born: 1942, Chelm, Poland **Nat:** Polish/American **Ints:** Consumer, health, personality and social **Educ:** BA Hebrew University, Jerusalem, 1966; MA University of Illinois, Urbana-Champaign, 1967; PhD University of Illinois, Urbana-Champaign, 1969 **Appts & awards:** Professor, Department of Psychology, University of Massachusetts, Amherst; Fellow, American Psychological Society; Member, Society for Personality and Social Psychology, Society of Experimental Social Psychology, New England Social Psychological Association

Principal publications
1971 Attitudinal vs. normative messages: An investigation of the differential effects of persuasive communications on behavior. *Sociometry*, 34, 263–80.

1973 Attitudinal and normative variables as predictors of specific behaviors. *Journal of Personality and Social Psychology*, 27, 41–59 (with M. Fishbein).

1974 Effects of information on interpersonal attraction: Similarity versus affective value. *Journal of Personality and Social Psychology*, 29, 374–80.

1974 Attitudes toward objects as predictors of single and multiple behavioral criteria. *Psychological Review*, 81, 59–74 (with M. Fishbein).

1975 A Bayesian analysis of attribution processes. *Psychological Bulletin*, 82, 261–77 (with M. Fishbein).

1975 *Belief, Attitude, Intention, and Behavior: An Introduction to Theory and Research*. Addison-Wesley (with M. Fishbein).

1977 Attitude–behavior relations: A theoretical analysis and review of empirical research. *Psychological Bulletin*, 84, 888–918 (with M. Fishbein).

1977 Intuitive theories of events and the effects of base-rate information on prediction. *Journal of Personality and Social Psychology*, 35, 303–314.

1980 *Understanding Attitudes and Predicting Social Behavior*. Prentice-Hall (with M. Fishbein).

1981 Acceptance, yielding, and impact: Cognitive responses to message content. In R.E. Petty, T.M. Ostrom and T.C. Brock (eds), *Cognitive Responses in Persuasion*. Erlbaum (with M. Fishbein).

1985 From intentions to actions: A theory of planned behavior. In J. Kuhl and J. Becksman (eds), *Action Control: From Cognition to Behavior*. Springer-Verlag.

1988   *Attitudes, Personality and Behavior*. Open University Press and Dorsey Press.

1991   Attitudes and thought systems. In T.S. Srull and R.R. Wyer Jr (eds), *Advances in Social Cognition*. Erlbaum.

1992   Accessibility and stability of predictors in the theory of planned behavior. *Journal of Personality and Social Psychology*, 63, 754–65.

Further reading

Doll, J. and Orth, B. (1993) The Fishbein and Ajzen theory of reasoned action applied to contraceptive behavior: Model variants and meaningfulness. *Journal of Applied Social Psychology*, 23, 395–415.

Madden, T.J., Ellen, P.S. and Ajzen, I (1992) A comparison of the theory of planned behavior and the theory of reasoned action. *Personality and Social Psychology Bulletin*, 18, 3–9.

Netemeyer, R.G., Burton, S. and Johnston, M. (1991) A comparison of two models for the prediction of volitional and goal-directed behaviors: A confirmatory analysis approach. *Social Psychology Quarterly*, 54, 87–100.

Ajzen has made fundamental contributions to the theory and measurement of attitude and the relationship between attitude and behaviour. When he began researching in this area in the late 1960s, the attitude concept was under attack by contemporary social psychologists. Numerous studies had observed little, if any, correspondence between verbal expressions of attitude and overt (observable) behaviour. Ajzen worked with Martin **Fishbein** to reconceptualize the nature of the attitude–behaviour relation, and developed the theory of reasoned action, later called the theory of planned behaviour. Ajzen and Fishbein's analysis of attitudes is formulated around an expectancy-value model which, at its simplest, states that a person's attitude to an issue or a person is a function of his or her evaluative beliefs about the attributes of the issue or person. These evaluative components have an expectancy component (e.g. the probability that the issue or person possesses the perceived attribute) and a value component – the evaluation of that attribute. One implication of adopting this approach is that attitude is regarded as an outcome of expected value (cognition) and behaviour is considered an outcome of attitude. A limitation of the model is that it would seem to preclude the possibility that affect (e.g. mood and emotion) and behav-

iour can directly influence attitude independently of belief.

According to the theory of planned behaviour the immediate determinant of any behaviour is the person's intention to perform the behaviour, which, in turn, is a function of attitude towards the behaviour and of perceived social pressure (subjective norm). In combination with the efforts of other social psychologists, this work has helped to reinstate attitude as a central concept in the field. There is a substantial volume of empirical evidence that people do in fact act in accordance with their expressed attitudes, provided that the investigator has measured attitudes appropriate to the behaviour of interest. A fundamental assumption in the theory of reasoned action is that the behaviour to be predicted is under volitional control. Attitudes and subjective norms can explain why a person decides to perform or not to perform a given behaviour. However, many behaviours are not completely under a person's volitional control, and in such cases other factors also influence achievement of a behavioural goal. Ajzen and Fishbein's theory has been successfully used to predict behaviour in a wide range of situations and has informed the development of intervention programmes in health psychology (e.g. smoking, drinking, dental care and family planning). Ajzen's current efforts are directed towards developing and testing the theory, which is widely regarded as the leading account of attitude–behaviour relationships.

Albee, George W.

Born: 1921, St Mary's, Pennsylvania, USA **Nat:** American **Ints:** Clinical psychology, Society for Community Research and Action **Educ:** BA Bethany College, West Virginia, 1943; MS University of Pittsburgh, 1947; PhD University of Pittsburgh, 1949 **Appts & awards:** Associate Professor, Professor, and George Trumbell Ladd Distinguished Professor of Psychology, Case Western Reserve University, Cleveland, Ohio, 1954–71; President, APA Division of Clinical Psychology, 1968; APA, President, 1970; Professor of Psychology, University of Vermont, Burlington, Vermont, 1971–92; Distinguished Professional Contribution Award, American Psychological Association, 1975; Distinguished Contribution Award, APA Division 27 (Community Psychology), 1980; University Scholar Award in the Social Sciences and the Humanities, University of Vermont, 1986; President, American Association for

Applied and Preventive Psychology, 1990–2; Gold Medal Award for Lifetime Contribution in the Public Interest, APF, 1993; George W. Albee Invited Lectureship in Primary Prevention, Annual Meeting of the World Federation for Mental Health

Principal publications

1959 *Mental Health Manpower Trends.* Basic Books.

1968 Conceptual models and manpower requirements in psychology. *American Psychologist*, 23, 317–320.

1970 The uncertain future of clinical psychology. *American Psychologist*, 25, 1071–80.

1977 *The Primary Prevention of Psychopathology: The Issues.* University Press of New England (ed. with J.M. Joffe).

1982 Preventing psychopathology and promoting human potential. *American Psychologist*, 37, 1043–57.

1986 Toward a just society: Lessons from observations on the primary prevention of psychopathology. *American Psychologist*, 41, 891–7.

1988 *Prevention, Powerlessness and Politics: A Book of Readings on Social Change.* University Press of New England (ed. with J.M. Joffe and L. Dusenbury).

1992 *Improving Children's Lives: Global Perspectives on Prevention.* Sage (ed. with L.A. Bond and T.V. Monsey).

Further reading

Kessler, M., Goldston, S.E. and Joffe, J.M. (eds) (1992) *The Present and Future of Prevention: In Honor of George W. Albee.* Sage.

George W. Albee was born in 1921 and raised in St Mary's, Pennsylvania. He received his undergraduate education in Psychology from Bethany College in West Virginia in 1943. After a three-year tour of duty with the United States Air Force, he entered the University of Pittsburgh's doctoral programme in Clinical Psychology as one of the first trainees supported by the Veterans' Administration Clinical Psychology Program. Albee received his doctorate in 1946 and subsequently accepted a Research Associate position at the Western Psychiatric Institute. During his career, he has contributed to the development of mental health theory and practice through his research, his writing and his leadership of professional, national and international organizations.

Albee has held distinguished academic posi-

tions at Case Western Reserve University (1954–71), where he was named the George Trumbull Ladd Distinguished Professor of Psychology, and at the University of Vermont (1971–92), where he remains a Professor Emeritus. In 1975 he established the Vermont Conference on the Primary Prevention of Psychopathology (VCPPP). Annually thereafter, Albee and his colleagues have brought together the leading researchers, theorists and practitioners of prevention science. Through its meetings and related published proceedings, VCPPP has been a substantive contributor to the pace and success with which developments have occurred in the prevention of psychopathology and the promotion of emotional health.

In 1951, as one of four professional staff of the APA, Albee established and set the direction for the APA public information efforts. As director of the Task Force on Manpower of the Joint Commission on Mental Illness and Health, Albee oversaw a comprehensive analysis of professional resources in the mental health professions. Subsequently reported in *Mental Health Manpower Trends* (1959), the Task Force's findings made clear the seriousness of existing and projected shortages in mental health service delivery resources resulting from continued adherence to established methods of responding to emotional and behavioural needs. Because of its timing and the clarity of its argument, this report was seminal to ongoing debates about the need to address mental health needs through proactive, preventive rather than traditional, reactive treatment approaches. Echoing the public health truism that disease has never been controlled through treatment but only through prevention, Albee's findings influenced the decision to incorporate concepts of consultation and prevention into the Joint Commission's recommendations to establish the community mental health centre system.

Underlying his lifelong commitment to the development of prevention theory and practice have been Albee's contributions to: (1) psychology's sense of itself as a profession; (2) the debate over the applicability of the illness model to mental and emotional disorder; and (3) the role of injustice and inequality in the development and maintenance of psychopathology. In his capacity as President of the Ohio Psychological Association, Albee called for the independence of psychology from the methods, models and professional definitions of psychiatry. In his 1963 presidential address to this group, he argued for the establishment of unique, discipline-specific sites for training clinical psychologists. In Albee's view, such sites would free the discipline from its restricting identification with psychiatry, from its views on how disorder is defined, and from the limits it has set on the nature and timing of interventions.

Throughout his career, Albee urged psychology to reflect on the costs for the discipline and for the recipients of its services of relying on individual psychotherapy and other forms of involvement only after the establishment of disorder. Albee continuously emphasized an alternative, i.e. involvement prior to or early in the genesis of disorder through preventive and health promotion activities. In his 1982 paper entitled 'Preventing psychopathology and promoting human potential', Albee offered a heuristically valuable alternative to the predominant view of mental and emotional disorder as analogous to other medical illnesses. Albee's model pointed out the important mediating effects of environmental factors such as social support, self-esteem and coping skills. Singly and in combination, these mediators offered avenues for prevention and promotion efforts.

Expanding on that model, Albee emphasized the insidiously pathogenic quality of the effects of racism, sexism, ageism and other forms of social inequality on emotional and mental health. In his writings and speeches throughout the world, Albee made explicit in recent years the disproportionate influence of such injustices on the incidence and prevalence of emotional disorder. His words have affected mental health policy makers and citizens throughout the world, raising their consciousness of the emotional impact of political and economic conditions. Albee's legacy is that the truth of his themes will grow more evident in the years and decades ahead.

RAYMOND P. LORION

Alexander, Franz Gabriel

Born: 1891, Budapest, Hungary **Died:** 1954, California, America **Nat:** Hungarian **Ints:** Clinical psychology, personality and social psychology, psychoanalysis, psychotherapy **Educ:** MD University of Budapest, 1913 **Appts & awards:** Military physician, 1914–18; Fellow, American Medical Association, Merit Cross (Hungary), 1917; Assistant at the Neuropsychiatric Clinic, Budapest University, 1919–20; Clinical Associate and Lecturer, Berlin Psychoanalytic Institute, 1920–30; Freud Prize, International Psychoanalysis Association,

1921; Visiting Professor of Psychoanalysis, University of Chicago, 1931–2; First Director, Chicago Institute Psychoanalysis, 1932–56; Associate Professor, University of Illinois, 1935–8; Physician, Cook County Psychopathic Hospital, Chicago, 1935–56; President, APA, 1938; Founding Editor, *Journal of Psychosomatic Medicine*, 1939; President, American Society for Research in Psychosomatic Problems, 1947; Head, Psychiatry Department, Mount Sinai Hospital, Los Angeles, 1956–64; Semmelweis Medal, American Hungarian Medical Association, 1957; Clinical Professor of Psychiatry, University of Southern California, 1957–64; Samuel Rubin Foundation Award, 1958; Member Editorial Board, *Behavioural Science*

Principal publications

1923   The castration complex in the formation of character. *International Journal of Psychoanalysis*, 4, 11–42.
1927   *The Psychoanalysis of the Total Personality*. Nervous and Mental Disease Publishing.
1935   The logic of emotions and its dynamic background. *International Journal of Psychoanalysis*, 1, 399–413 (with T.M. French *et al.*).
1935   The problem of psychoanalytic technique. *Psychoanalytic Quarterly*, 4, 588–611.
1936   Psychoanalysis and social disorganization. *American Journal of Sociology*, 42, 781–813.
1940   Psychoanalysis revised. *Psychoanalytical Quarterly*, 9, 1–36.
1943   Fundamental concepts of psychosomatic research: Psychogenesis, conversion, specificity. *Psychosomatic Medicine*, 5, 205–10.
1946   *Psychoanalytic Therapy*. Ronald.
1948   Educative influence of personality factors in the environment. In C. Kluckholn and H.A. Murray (eds), *Personality in Nature, Society and Culture*. Knopf.
1948   *Fundamentals of Psychoanalysis*. Norton.
1950   *Psychosomatic Medicine*. Norton.
1950   Analysis of the therapeutic factors in psychoanalytic treatment. *Psychoanalytic Quarterly*, 19, 482–500.
1956   *Psychoanalysis and Psychotherapy*. Norton.
1964   Social significance of psychoanalysis and psychotherapy. *Archives of General Psychiatry*, 11, 235–44.
1964   Neurosis and creativity. *American Journal of Psychoanalysis*, 24, 116–130.

Further reading

Kopp, M. and Shrabshi, A. (1989) What does the legacy of Hans Selye and Franz Alexander mean to-day? The psychophysiological approach in medical practice. Founding session of the working group of psychophysiology, Hungarian Psychiatric Society (1988, Budapest, Hungary). *International Journal of Psychophysiology*, 8, 99–105.

Wolberg, A. (1989) Pilgrims progress through the psychoanalytic maze. *Psychoanalysis and Psychotherapy*, 7, 18–26.

Alexander's contributions lie in the areas of psychoanalytic research, psychotherapy and psychosomatics. He was the most prominent representative of the neo-Freudian Chicago School of psychoanalysis. This school, which centred on the Chicago Institute of Psychoanalysis became known more for its application of psychoanalysis to new situations than for its contributions to theory. Early in his career, for instance, Alexander sought to apply psychoanalysis to criminology. He de-emphasized the origin of neuroses in early experiences and in sexual problems, stressing actual difficulties of the patient whose causes are beyond his or her control.

He defined neurosis as a relationship between personality and social setting, and the aim of psychoanalysis as 'to increase the patient's ability to find gratification for his subjective needs in ways acceptable both to himself and to the world he lives in, and thus to free him to develop his capacities'. Alexander's principle of surplus energy states that sexuality is a specific discharge of unused excitation in the organism. The therapeutic emphasis is on 'corrective emotional experience' to release this surplus energy, a process central to therapy as practised in the Chicago School. Planning and flexibility are two additional adaptations of the classical psychoanalytical procedure.

Therapy is planned in accordance with the diagnosis and the personality of the patient, and may change depending on the outcome of therapy, so that different methods may be used with different patients and with the same patient during a course of treatment. Alexander pioneered the use of a shortened, 'brief' course of therapy. He is also considered to be one of the founding fathers of psychosomatic medicine. Already in the late 1930s, he was showing that chronic emotional tension was correlated with such disorders as gastric ulcers, colitis, hypertension, asthma, thyrotoxicosis and rheumatoid arthritis, and proposed a theory relating specific emotional factors to specific organic disorders. He wrote some 120 articles and eighteen books.

LEONARD ZUSNE

Allport, Floyd Henry

Born: 1890, Milwaukee, Wisconsin, USA **Died:** 1978, Syracuse, New York, USA **Nat:** American **Ints:** Experimental psychology, personality and social psychology, philosophical and theoretical psychology, Society for the Psychological Study of Social Issues **Educ:** AB Harvard University, 1913; PhD Harvard University, 1919; Hon. Doc., Syracuse University, 1974 **Appts & awards:** Instructor of Psychology, Harvard University and Radcliffe College, 1919–22; Editor, *Journal of Abnormal and Social Psychology*, 1921–4; Associate Professor of Psychology, University of North Carolina, 1922–4; Professor of Social and Political Psychology, Syracuse University, 1924–56; Board of Directors, APA, 1928–30; President, Society for the Study of Social Issues, 1939–40; Emeritus Professor, Syracuse University, 1956–78; APA Distinguished Scientific Contribution Award, 1965; APF Gold Medal Award, 1968

Principal publications

1919 Behavior and experiment in social psychology. *Journal of Abnormal Psychology*, 14, 297–306.

1921 Personality traits: Their classification and measurement. *Journal of Abnormal and Social Psychology*, 16, 6–40 (with G.W. Allport).

1924 *Social Psychology*. Houghton Mifflin.

1924 The group fallacy in relation to social science. *American Journal of Sociology*, 29, 688–706.

1927 'Group' and 'institution' as concepts in a natural science of social phenomena. *Publications of the American Sociological Society*, 22, 83–99.

1927 The nature of institutions. *Social Forces*, 6, 167–79.

1927 Political science and psychology. In W.F. Ogburn and A. Goldenwieser (eds), *The Social Sciences and their Interrelations*. Houghton Mifflin.

1933 *Institutional Behavior*. Houghton Mifflin.

1934 The J-curve hypothesis of conforming behavior. *Journal of Social Psychology*, 5, 141–83.

1942 Methods in the study of collective action phenomena. *Journal of Social Psychology*, 15, 165–85.

1954 The structuring of events: Outline of a general theory with applications to psychology. *Psychological Review*, 281–303.

1962 A structoronomic conception of behavior: Individual and collective: 1. Structural theory and the master problem of social psychology. *Journal of Abnormal and Social Psychology*, 64, 3–30.

Further reading

Brooks, G.P. and Johnson, R.W. (1978) Floyd Allport

and the master problem of social psychology. *Psychological Reports*, 42, 295–308.

Floyd Allport has been called the father of experimental social psychology. He was the second of four sons born to John and Nellie (Wise) Allport, and his youngest brother, **Gordon Allport**, became another famous social psychologist. Floyd Allport had an early interest in the piano and, while an undergraduate at Harvard, thought of majoring in music. His graduate education at Harvard was interrupted by World War I, during which he served as a second lieutenant in the field artillery. While an instructor at Harvard, Allport was asked to edit the *Journal of Abnormal and Social Psychology*, which had recently been expanded to include social psychology. The first issue of the newly expanded journal had as its lead article a paper titled 'Personality traits: Their classification and measurement'. This article, co-authored with his brother Gordon, had a major impact on the early development of personality psychology. His major book was the influential *Social Psychology*, which appeared in 1924. While at the University of North Carolina, Allport was asked to teach at the newly established Maxwell Graduate School of Citizenship and Public Affairs at Syracuse University. Here he was given the title of Professor of Social and Political Psychology, taught the first courses ever offered in political psychology, and directed the first doctoral programme in social psychology. Allport remained at Syracuse until his retirement in 1956.

Allport's early work concerned the effects of the group on the individual, and his work in this area led him to coin the term 'social facilitation'. He set out to correct such fictions as the 'group mind', in which group concepts were given personality attributes. His pioneering research in field settings helped to alter such misconceptions. Most of Allport's important theoretical work appeared in *Social Psychology*, which was well received at the time of its publication. Here Allport stressed the psychological rather than the sociological aspects of social psychology. He translated the Freudian concept of conflict into behaviouristic terms and made use of Freudian mechanisms in relation to social problems. This work also represented one of the first conceptual integrations of these two approaches, setting the stage for future attempts.

In *Social Psychology* Allport also presented some of his own classic research on group

influence, which led to the establishment of group experimentation as the norm in social psychology. Finally, he provided the field with a number of useful concepts for research, such as social increment and decrement, prepotent reflexes and habits, circular and linear social behaviour, co-acting and interacting groups, and attitudes of conformity. Allport's later interests were in the field of institutional behaviour. His book *Institutional Behavior* was based on his theoretical study of the accepted doctrines of the time regarding social institutions, as well as his students' research on legal compliance, conformity in industrial settings, ceremonial religious activities, and the factors which cause normative behaviour in a small community. However, the influence of this volume was not far-reaching. Allport's interest in social prejudice and ethnic conflict led him to produce a statement from the social science community on the effects of segregation during the *Brown v. Board of Education* Supreme Court Case. Later in his career, Allport became interested in the problems of relationships and social structure. He spent the latter part of his academic life trying to develop a workable theory of the structure of action on a behavioural level, in which he incorporated theory and research from physics, genetics and microbiology. His somewhat abstruse theoretical work in this area never gained widespread appeal. Floyd Allport's contributions have been said to have had two major consequences. First, he shaped the field of social psychology so that it became primarily concerned with social influence and the measurement of human behaviour. Second, he provided the rationale and empirical examples for the behavioural trend in social psychology.

JOHN D. HOGAN AND VIRGINIA STAUDT-SEXTON

Allport, Gordon Willard

Born: 1897, Montezuma, Indiana, USA **Died:** 1967, Cambridge, Massachusetts, USA **Nat:** American **Ints:** General psychology, humanistic psychology, personality and social psychology, psychology and religion, teaching of psychology **Educ:** AB Harvard University, 1919; PhD Harvard University, 1922 **Appts & awards:** Assistant Professor, Dartmouth College, 1926–30; Assistant Professor, 1930–42, Professor, 1942–67, Department of Psychology, Harvard University; President, APA, 1939; Editor, *Journal of Abnormal and Social Psychology*, 1937–49; APA Distinguished Scientific Contribution Award, 1964

Principal publications

1921 Personality traits: Their classification and measurement. *Journal of Abnormal and Social Psychology*, 16, 6–40 (with F.H. Allport).

1927 Concepts of trait and personality. *Psychological Bulletin*, 24, 284–93.

1933 *Studies in Expressive Movement*. Macmillan (with P.E. Vernon).

1937 *Personality: A Psychological Interpretation*. Holt.

1937 The functional autonomy of motives. *American Journal of Psychology*, 50, 141–56.

1954 *The Nature of Prejudice*. Addison-Wesley.

1955 *Becoming: Basic Considerations for a Psychology of Personality*. Yale University Press.

1960 The open system in personality theory. *Journal of Abnormal and Social Psychology*, 61, 301–10.

1961 *Pattern and Growth in Personality*. Holt, Rinehart & Winston.

1962 The general and the unique in psychological science. *Journal of Personality*, 30, 405–22.

1966 Traits revisited. *American Psychologist*, 21, 1–10.

A complete list of Allport's writings may be found in G.W. Allport (1968) *The Person in Psychology: Selected Essays*. Beacon Press.

Further reading

Allport, G.W. (1967) Autobiography. In E. Boring and G. Lindzey (eds), *A History of Psychology in Autobiography*. Beacon Press.

Hall, C.S. and Lindzey, G. (1957) *Theories of Personality*. Wiley.

Holt, R.R. (1962) Individuality and generalization in the psychology of personality. *Journal of Personality*, 30, 377–404.

Gordon Allport was the youngest of four brothers. His father was a country physician, and the family moved to Ohio shortly after Gordon's birth. Allport was educated in Cleveland and described his family life as one based on trust, affection and the Protestant work ethic. His decision to study at Harvard University was partly due to the influence of his brother, **Floyd Allport**, who was a graduate student in psychology at that university. Allport took a number of courses in psychology but majored in economics and philosophy. After graduating he taught English and sociology at Robert College, Constantinople, Turkey, and in 1920 won a fellowship to study psychology at Harvard. Allport completed his PhD (on personality traits – the first such study conducted in the

United States) under Herbert S. Langfield (1879–1958), who strongly influenced his general approach to psychology. Langfield had studied under **Stumpf** (1848–1936) at the University of Berlin and subscribed to a motor theory of consciousness (the idea that sensations, emotions and thoughts are all linked to motor processes). Personality, according to Allport, similarly involves complex linkages between physiological and mental processes.

Allport regarded personality as an integrated evolving system of habits, attitudes and traits. In his first book authored alone, *Personality: A Psychological Interpretation*, he classified fifty different definitions of personality and concluded that they had in common a concern for determining 'what a man really is'. Allport's own definition of personality is 'the dynamic organization within the individual of those psychological systems that determine his characteristic behavior and thought'. No two people are completely alike, and Allport explained this using the concept of trait, which he defined as a predisposition to act in the same way in a wide range of situations. He suggested that traits, like habits, generalize to individuals and situations. Thus, there are traits that are specific to individuals and ones that are shared by most individuals. In 'Traits revisited', he proposed that certain criteria define a personality trait: a trait has more than nominal existence; a trait is more generalized than a habit; a trait's existence can be established empirically; traits are only relatively independent of one another; a trait is not synonymous with moral or social judgements; a trait may be considered in the context of either the personality that contains it or its distribution in the general population; acts that are inconsistent with a trait are not proof of the non-existence of the trait. In his early work Allport distinguished between common/dimensional/ nomothetic traits – characteristics shared by a number of people in a particular culture – and individual/morphological traits – characteristics peculiar to individuals that do not allow comparisons among people. Later he considered that using the term 'trait' in connection with both individual and common characteristics caused unnecessary confusion, and he called individual traits 'personal dispositions' and common traits simply 'traits'. He distinguished between three types of personal disposition: cardinal dispositions (so pervasive that almost everything a person does can be traced to its influence), central dispositions (generalized characteristics of a person – the 'building blocks' of personality), and secondary dispositions (less consistent and generalized, e.g. food and fashion preferences).

For Allport the unifying core of the personality is the self ('the proprium'), which strives to realize its potentialities and life goals. Allport regarded the person as motivated more by social than by physiological influences and as constantly striving to become something new and different. The core of his personality theory, the self, he saw as an awesome enigma, but with characteristic tenacity he set this concept within trait theory and then proceeded to define 'the proprium'. The latter consisted of seven subjective aspects of the self: the sense of bodily self, self-identity, self-esteem, self-image, the extension of the self, the sense of striving and the self as a rational being. This, together with a theory of motivation which overcame the limitations of homeostatic explanations, enabled Allport to formulate a detailed theory of personality based on the ideas of an earlier book, *Becoming: Basic Considerations for a Psychology of Personality*. Allport took the view that a person's basic convictions about what is and is not of real importance in life are founded on values, and he proceeded to identify and measure basic value dimensions. This lead to the development of the widely used multidimensional personality test, the Study of Values.

Gordon Allport's collection of essays entitled *The Person in Psychology* provides a good indication of his wide field of interest, not only in personality, but in mental health, prejudice, religion and fundamental methodological problems of psychology. He attempted to grasp the complexity of human beings set in the context of a social environment, and in so doing he resolutely refused to settle for the fashionable dogmas of his profession. He demonstrated a firm belief in an 'imaginative and systematic eclecticism'. His most influential work, *Personality: A Psychological Interpretation*, offered a survey of what he called 'the most important fruits of psychological research', and is distinguished by its attempt to provide a theory embracing the results of this research. It appeared later in a much revised form as *Pattern and Growth in Personality*, in which he once again demonstrated an undogmatic but relentless concern for precision and finesse in pursuit of the intricacies of human personality. In his own words, he refused 'to close off or discourage any avenue of approach to the investigation of human nature'. Although he is often referred to as 'the dean of American personality study', his theory of personality has attracted a modest degree of research interest. There are two reasons for this: first, the theory makes extensive use of somewhat loosely defined concepts (e.g. propriate striving, personal disposition), and second, the linkages between traits and the development of the proprium are not clearly specified. Nevertheless Allport's ideas have had a profound impact in promoting idiographic methods for studying people.

The idea of 'Becoming' as contrasted to 'Being' is central to Allport's work, and this aligned him with the so-called 'third force' or humanistic psychologists, although his thoughtful eclecticism allowed him to accept parts of both the psychoanalytic and behaviourist viewpoints in his developing framework. This open system, as he called it, mapped out and refined in twelve books and 228 other publications, laid the basis for a psychology of the human being. Perhaps of all his publications, the most fascinating is his departure from 'abstractions about personality-in-general' to an attempt to explain a 'single concrete life'. In the idiographic *Letters from Jenny* (1965), he provided a unique teaching instrument for subsequent generations of students.

Altman, Irwin

Born: 1930, New York City, USA *Nat:* American *Ints:* Personality and social psychology, population and environmental psychology, psychological study of social issues *Educ:* BA New York University, 1951; MA University of Maryland, 1954, PhD University of Maryland, 1957 *Appts & awards:* Editorial Board, *Comparative Group Studies (Small Groups)*, 1970–8, *Sociometry*, 1973–6, *Journal of Applied Social Psychology*, 1973– , *Journal of Personality and Social Psychology*, 1974– , *Contemporary Psychology*, 1975– , *Environment and Behavior*, 1975– , *Environmental Psychology and Nonverbal Behavior*, 1976–9, *Journal of Social Issues*, 1977– , *American Journal of Community Psychology*, 1978–81, *Journal of Environmental Psychology*, 1980– , *Review of Personality and Social Psychology*, 1980– , *Population and Environment*, 1981– , *Computers in Human Behavior*, 1984– , series on Advances in Environment, Behavior and Design, 1984– , monograph series on Environment, Behavior and Design, 1984– , *International Journal of Applied Social Psychology*, 1985– ; Vice-President for Academic

Affairs, University of Utah, Salt Lake City, David P. Gardner Research Fellowship, University of Utah, 1976; Distinguished Research Award, University of Utah, 1978; President, APA Division 8, 1979–80, Division 34, 1981–2; Distinguished Service Award in the Social Sciences, Utah Academy of Sciences, Arts and Letters, 1981; Career Award, Environmental Design Research Association, 1982; APA Award for Distinguished Education and Training Contributions, 1994; Co-editor, Monograph series in Environmental Psychology

Principal publications

1966 *Small Group Research: Synthesis and Critique of the Field*. Holt, Rinehart & Winston (with J.E. McGrath).

1975 *Environment and Social Behavior: Privacy, Personal Space, Territory and Crowding*. Brooks/Cole. Irvington, 1981.

1977 Personal space: An analysis of E.T. Hall's proxemics framework. In I. Altman and J. Wohwill (eds), *Human Behavior and Environment: Advances in Theory and Research*, vol. 2. Plenum.

1977 Research on environment and behavior: A personal statement of strategy. In D. Stokols (ed.), *Psychological Perspectives on Environment and Behavior: Conceptual and Empirical Trends*. Plenum.

1980 *Culture and Environment*. Brooks/Cole (with M.M. Chemers).

1981 Dialectic conceptions in social psychology: An application to social penetration and privacy regulation. In *Advances in Experimental Social Psychology*, vol. 4. Academic Press (with A. Vinsel and B.B. Brown).

1983 Homes and social change: A cross-cultural analysis. In N.R. Feimer and E.S. Geler (eds), *Environmental Psychology: Directions and Perspectives*. Praeger (with M. Gauvain and H. Fahim).

1985 *Home Environments, vol. 8: Human Behavior and Environment*. Plenum (co-ed. with C.M. Werner).

1985 Temporal aspects of homes: A transactional perspective. In I. Altman and C.M. Werner (eds), *Home Environments, vol. 8: Human Behavior and Environment*. Plenum.

1989 *Public Places and Spaces*. Plenum (co-ed. with E.H. Zube).

1992 A transactional perspective on transitions to new environments. *Environment and Behavior*, 24, 268–80.

1993 Dialectics, physical environments, and personal relationships. *Communication Monographs*, 60, 26–34.

1994 *Women and the Environment*. Plenum (co-ed. with A. Churchman).

Further reading

APA Awards for Distinguished Education and Training Contributions: 1994. Irwin Altman. *American Psychologist*, 50, 256–8.

Bell, P.A., Fisher, J.D. and Loomis, R.J. (1978) *Environmental Psychology*. W.B. Saunders.

Along with **Proshansky**, **Stokols** and **Barker**, Irwin Altman is associated with defining the field of environmental psychology: the study of human behaviour in its physical (and by implication social and cultural) contexts. Altman's principal contributions have been in interpersonal relationships, home environments, environmental psychology, privacy theory, and dialectical and transactional approaches to psychological phenomena. Altman is probably best known for his work on the ecology of interpersonal relationships – the mutual interaction between people and their environments. Central to his model of this interaction is the definition of the situation in which interactants find themselves. The model predicts that when people engage in face-to-face interaction they define 'the situation' in terms of two kinds of antecedent factor: environmental characteristics and interactant characteristics. Environmental characteristics refer to factors external to the interactants, such as light, available space, temperature and so on. Interactant characteristics refer to attributes of people themselves, such as physiological factors (e.g. fatigue, elation), physical factors (e.g. height, weight), social factors (e.g. role, status), and interpersonal factors (e.g. previous encounters between the interactants). These two categories of antecedent factor allow interactants to form expectations of the interaction and to form judgements about the appropriateness of behaviour. The model has made, and continues to make, a significant contribution to the development of innovative research designs in laboratory and field settings.

Ames, Louise B.

Born: 1908, Portland, USA *Nat:* American *Ints:* Adult development and ageing, developmental, evaluation and measurement, projective techniques, school *Educ:* AB University of Maine, 1930; MA University of Maine, 1933; PhD Yale University, 1936; *Appts & awards:* Associate Director, Gesell Institute of Human Development; USA President of the Corporate Board,

President, Society for Projective Techniques, 1969–71; Member, Sigma XI; Editor, *Journal of Genetic Psychology*, *Journal of Learning Disabilities*, *Education Digest*; Bruno Klopfer Distinguished Contribution Award, 1974; University of Maine Alumni Career Award, 1974; Deborah Morton Award, Westbrook College, 1980

Principal publications

1940 The ontogenetic organization of prone behavior. *Journal of Genetic Psychology*, 56, 247–63 (with A. Gesell).

1943 *Infant and Child in the Culture of Today.* Harper and Row (with A. Gesell, F.L. Ilg and J. Learned Rodell).

1946 *The Child from Five to Ten.* Harper and Row (with A. Gesell, F.L. Ilg and G. Bullis).

1946 Imaginary companions. *Journal of Genetic Psychology*, 69, 14–168 (with J. Learned).

1956 *Youth: The Years from Ten to Sixteen.* Harper and Row (with A. Gesell and F.L. Ilg).

1956 *Child Rorschach Responses.* Hoeber (with J. Learned Rodell, R. Metraux and R.N. Walker).

1963 *The Gesell Incomplete Man.* Genetic Psychology Monographs, 103, 75–91.

1964 The developmental point of view with special reference to the principle of reciprocal neuromotor interweaving. *Journal of Genetic Psychology*, 105, 195–209.

1965 *School Readiness.* Harper and Row (with F.L. Ilg).

1966 *Children's Stories.* Genetic Psychology Monographs, 74, 337–96.

1966 Rorschach responses of Negroes and whites compared. *Journal of Genetic Psychology*, 109, 297–309.

1975 Are Rorschach responses influenced by society's change? *Journal of Personality Assessment*, 39, 439–52.

1984 Calibration of aging. *Journal of Personality Assessment*, 38, 507–29.

Further reading

Ames, L.B. (1989) *Arnold Gesell: Themes of his Work.* Human Sciences Press.

The earliest work of Louise Ames included the development of motor behaviour in infants, and involved gathering data both by direct observation and by cinema analysis. She published numerous papers in this area in the 1930s and 1940s before moving on to study individual differences in young children, and editing films on visual fixation, twinning, postural behaviour, feeding behaviour and laterality.

In 1943, in collaboration with Arnold **Gesell** and Francis Ilg, she began longitudinal research on behaviour changes with age, resulting in a series of books for parents. In 1950, when Gesell retired from Yale, she left Yale, and with colleagues founded the Gesell Institute, New Haven, Connecticut. In 1952 she began an influential daily newspaper column, 'Child behavior'. This continued for approximately twenty-five years and was carried by some sixty-five major newspapers. In 1953, she started a weekly live television series with WBZ in Boston. This continued for several years and was followed by a weekly series in Cleveland and later a daily series on all Westinghouse stations, titled *Playmates/Schoolmates: A Nursery School on the Air.* From the 1950s her principal interests were in school placement, and she wrote and lectured extensively on this topic. She also became involved in the use of the Rorschach technique and the Lowenfeld Mosaic. Ames's contributions are closely linked with her work with Gesell on developmental norms. They remain the basis of many early assessments of behavioural functioning. Like Gesell's, her influence as a theorist has been less direct.

Anastasi, Anne

Born: 1908, New York, USA **Nat:** American **Ints:** Clinical psychology, educational psychology, evaluation and measurement, general psychology, industrial and organizational psychology, personality and social psychology **Educ:** BA Barnard College, 1928; PhD Columbia University, 1930 **Appts & awards:** President, Eastern Psychological Association, 1946; Professor of Psychology, Graduate school of Arts and Sciences, Fordham University, 1947; Hon. DLitt University of Windsor, Canada, 1967; APA Distinguished Scientific award, 1971; Hon. PaedD Villanova University, 1971; President, APA, 1971; Hon. SciD Cedar Crest College, 1971; Education Testing Service Award, 1977; Hon. SciD Fordham University, 1979; Hon. SciD LaSalle University, 1979; APA E.L. Thorndike Medal, 1983; APF Gold Medal, 1984

Principal publications

1937 *Differential Psychology.* Macmillan.

1954 *Psychological Testing.* Macmillan.

1958 Heredity, environment and the question 'how'. *Psychological Review*, 65, 197–208.

1964 *Fields of Applied Psychology.* McGraw-Hill.

1981 Sex differences: Historical perspectives and

methodological implications. *Developmental Review*, 1, 187–206.

1991 The gap between experimental and psychometric orientations. *Journal of the Washington Academy of Sciences*, 81, 61–73.

Further reading

Anastasi, A (1988) Autobiography. In A.N O'Connell and N.F. Russo (eds), *Models of Achievement: Reflections of Eminent Women in Psychology*, Vol. 2. Erlbaum.

Gavin, E. (1987) Prominent women in psychology, determined by ratings of distinguished peers. *Psychotherapy in Private Practice*, 5, 53–68.

Anne Anastasi's father died when she was one year old. Soon afterwards her maternal relatives became estranged from her father's family and she never met any of them. Anastasi was educated at home by her grandmother. She started attending public school at the age of nine and graduated at the top of her class. When she enrolled at Barnard College, New York, in 1924 she had intended to major in mathematics but was attracted to psychology partly through her reading of **Spearman**'s work on correlation coefficients. After graduating she enrolled for a PhD at Columbia University under the supervision of H.E. Garrett.

There she met her future husband, John Porter Foley Jr, who was also completing a PhD. They were married in 1933 and and a year later she was diagnosed with cancer, the treatment for which left her unable to have children. Jobs being scarce at the time Anastasi took a position at Barnard College and Foley worked in Washington. Later Foley secured a position with the Psychological Corporation in New York City, where they have lived ever since.

The name 'Anastasi' has come to be synonymous with 'psychometrics' for several generations of students and professionals because of the immense popularity of the many editions of her standard texts on psychometrics. These grew out of courses that she taught throughout her academic career, and are characterized by their engaging style, their attempt to explain complex statistical terms as simply as possible, and their broad, eclectic approach to psychology. For example, Anne Anastasi's treatment of the formation of psychological traits draws upon models of animal experimentation, infant behaviour and educational psychology, as well as the more obvious forms of psychological research. *Fields of Applied Psychology* similarly introduces a wide range of applications of psychological principles. Anastasi was interested in understanding the underlying causes of ability long before such process models were widely popular. She made seminal contributions to our understanding of the origins of traits and the relationship between life history, intelligence and variables as diverse as family size, creativity and the content of drawings of hospitalized psychiatric patients.

This generalist approach has a number of benefits. Perhaps the major one is that Anastasi does not become mesmerized by psychometric minutiae, but instead pays due attention to the psychological content of psychometric measures, the link between psychometric tests and other areas of psychology, and the social context of mental testing. Her books tell a compelling story of how properly constructed, well-validated and psychologically well-founded mental tests can prove valuable in both theoretical and applied fields provided that the underlying sociocultural, developmental and cognitive processes are well understood. Through them she has made a real and substantial contribution to the science of psychometrics and to good testing practice.

COLIN COOPER

Anderson, John Robert

Born: 1947, Vancouver, Canada *Nat:* Canadian *Ints:* Cognitive science and artificial intelligence, experimental psychology *Educ:* BA University of British Columbia, 1968; PhD Stanford University, 1972 *Appts & awards:* APA's Early Career Award, 1978; Member, Society of Experimental Psychologists, 1981– ; Professor, Department of Psychology, Carnegie Mellon University, Professor, Department of Computer Science, Carnegie Mellon University, 1983– ; President, Cognitive Science Society, 1988–9; Research Scientist Award, NIMH, 1989–94; APA's Distinguished Scientific Career Award, 1994; Member, Psychonomic Society, Cognitive Science Society; Consulting Editor, Cognitive Science Series, *Cognitive Science, Cognitive Psychology, Human–Computer Interaction, International Journal for Intelligent Systems, Machine Learning*

Principal publications

1972 Recognition and retrieval processes in free recall. *Psychological Review*, 79, 97–123 (with G.H. Bower)

1973 *Human Associative Memory*. Winston and Sons (with G.H. Bower).

1976 *Language, Memory and Thought.* Erlbaum.

1978 Arguments concerning representations for mental imagery. *Psychological Review*, 85, 249–77.

1979 An elaborative processing explanation of depth of processing. In L.S. Cermak and F.I.M. Craik (eds), *Levels of Processing in Human Memory.* Erlbaum (with L.M. Reder).

1980 *Cognitive Psychology and its Implications.* Freeman. (2nd edn 1985.)

1981 *Cognitive Skills and their Acquisition.* Erlbaum.

1982 Acquisition of cognitive skill. *Psychological Review*, 89, 369–403.

1983 *The Architecture of Cognition.* Harvard University Press.

1983 A spreading activation theory of memory. *Journal of Verbal Learning and Verbal Behavior*, 22, 261–95.

1987 Skill acquisition: Compilation of weak-method problem solutions. *Psychological Review*, 94, 192–210.

1987 Cognitive principles in the design of computer tutors. In P. Morris (ed.), *Modeling Cognition.* Wiley (with C.F. Boyle, R. Farrell and B.J. Reiser).

1989 Skill Acquisition and the LISP tutor. *Cognitive Science*, 13, 467–506 (with F.G. Conrad and A.T. Corbett).

1989 *Transfer of Cognitive Skill.* Harvard University Press (with M.K. Singley).

1990 *The Adaptive Character of Thought.* Erlbaum.

1990 Cognitive modelling and intelligent tutoring. *Artificial Intelligence*, 42, 7–49 (with C.F. Boyle, A. Corbett, A. Lewis and M.W. Lewis).

1991 Reflections of the environment in memory. *Psychological Science*, 2, 396–408 (with L.J. Schooler).

1991 The adaptive nature of human categorization. *Psychological Review*, 98, 409–29.

1992 Explorations of an incremental, Bayesian algorithm for categorization. *Machine Learning*, 9, 275–308 (with M. Matessa).

1993 *Rules of the Mind.* Erlbaum.

1995 *Learning and Memory.* Wiley.

Further reading

Kolodner, J.L. (1983) Reconstructive memory – a computer model. *Cognitive Science*, 7, 281–328.

Reder, L.M. and Ross, B.H. (1983) Integrated knowledge in different tasks – the role of retrieval strategy on fan effects. *Journal of Experimental Psychology – Learning, Memory and Cognition*, 8, 66–72.

Simon, H.A. (1981) Information-processing models of cognition. *Journal of the American Society for Information Science*, 32, 364–77.

John Anderson was born in Vancouver, British Columbia in 1947. From the seventh grade he began to pursue scholastic interests, and wrote novels as a hobby. Despite being an excellent student during his high school days, on arrival at the University of British Columbia, he found himself poorly prepared for the scholarly demands of college. It was during his early academic struggles with university demands that Anderson developed his first deep intellectual interests. He developed an intense interest in the issues of learning theory and became committed to a precise, quantitative approach to psychological research. He worked with Arthur Rebur on the perception of clicks in linguistic messages, and the work formed part of his senior thesis. His commitment to psychology was demonstrated in his dramatic improvement in academic performance. In 1968 he graduated at the head of his class in arts and sciences.

Anderson went to Stanford in 1968, intending to pursue graduate studies in mathematical psychology and psycholinguistics. Membership of the faculty included **Richard Atkinson**, Gordon Bower, **Herbert Clark**, Roger Shepard and Edward Smith. In this environment, Anderson developed an enthusiasm for the information-processing approach to cognitive psychology. With Edward **Feigenbaum**, he came to realize the opportunities inherent in computer simulation to achieve precision in theory while maintaining the complexity of interesting cognitive phenomenon. Anderson worked very closely with Gordon Bower, their research involving a series of experiments and theoretical analyses of item memory and sentence memory, in relation to categorical structure in free recall. They developed the 'free recall in an associative net' (FRAN) simulation of free recall. As the research went on they realized the need for a complete model of the structure of human memory with emphasis on meaningful structure. In 1973, they published the book *Human Associative Memory*, which expressed the HAM theory. HAM was a complete model of the structures and processes of human memory, having as its central construct a propositional network representation. It had been developed with extensive use of computer simulation and dealt in detail with the way human memory processes linguistic material.

Anderson graduated from Stanford in 1972 and went to Yale University as an assistant professor. He taught undergraduate and graduate courses in thinking and his consideration of broader issues in cognitive psychology, such as cognitive processes and structures, intensified. He remained there for a year before leaving to become a Junior Fellow at the University of Michigan, where his wife, Lynne Reder, was a graduate student. They married in 1973, and formed a close intellectual partnership. Anderson spent three years at Michigan, where he developed his interests in language and learning, and designed a computer simulation model of language acquisition. Through his association with James Greeno he also became interested in the applications of cognitive psychology to education. Both of these developments were to become significant later in his career. While at Michigan, Anderson developed the theory and experiments which were to lead to the ACT (adaptive control of thought) theory. ACT was, like HAM, based upon a computer simulation program, but with the important extension of a subtheory dealing with the way cognitive procedures interact with memory. Where HAM had concentrated upon a theory of the declarative system in knowledge, ACT employed a production system in order to interpret a propositional network. Production systems are essentially an analogy for condition–action pairs, which theoretically underlie human cognition. The condition specifies some data patterns, and if elements matching these patterns are in working memory, then the production can apply. The working memory is defined as the active portion of the long-term memory network. Anderson and colleagues extended the production of ACT to include ACTE, a computer simulation of ACT where it was possible to program production sets that modelled various tasks. In addressing the issues of learning theory for production systems, ACTF was developed, which was the first production system to contain an extensive theory of production acquisition.

In 1976, Anderson returned to Yale as an associate professor. He wrote the book *Language, Memory and Thought*, which described ACT theory. He was promoted to full professor in 1977. At Yale he continued to research and test the ACT theory, and examined the way past knowledge interacts with and facilitates the acquisition of knowledge. The theory proposed human cognition as an interaction between declarative and procedural knowledge structures, and was intended as a comprehensive theory of higher-level cognition. In the autumn of 1978, Anderson and Reder moved to Carnegie Mellon University. He continued his research, with greater emphasis on computer

simulation of problem solving. Resident at CMU were Herbert **Simon** and Alan Newell, who had developed problem-solving computer simulation and were researching production system ideas.

In 1980, Anderson published the textbook *Cognitive Psychology and its Implications*, which is now in its fourth edition. This was followed in 1983 by the research monograph *The Architecture of Cognition*, which illustrated the fully evolved theory, ACT* (ACT star). Anderson described it as a theory of the basic principles of operation built into cognitive systems. It addressed higher-level cognition, the elements that give direction to thought, and how production systems serve to delineate the adaptive processing choices in the human cognitive system.

In 1980 and 1985 Lynne Reder and John Anderson had two sons. Anderson became intrigued by the development of their cognitive abilities. An early simulation of his eldest son's language acquisition appeared in *The Architecture of Cognition*. His earlier interest in the application of cognitive psychology to education rekindled and he became involved in their schooling by tutoring them in mathematics. He began to develop computer-based systems for instruction, intelligent tutors, based on the ACT theory. The approach to their development was called model-tracing, and involved generating a cognitive model of the skill that was to be learned. It emphasized the use of real-time cognitive modelling in instruction, employing a set of production rules that solve the class of problems in the way that students should solve them.

Anderson continued pursuing applications of ACT; then, following a sabbatical at the Flinders University in Australia, he began looking at how cognition might be adapted to statistical structure in the environment. In 1990, he published *The Adaptive Character of Thought*, which described what Anderson called 'rational analysis'. This approach presented a theory which proposed the understanding of the statistical structure of problems as key to understanding human cognition, rather than its cognitive mechanisms. It was particularly applied to the development of theories of human memory and categorization.

Since 1990, Anderson has been diversely involved with the development of ACT, rational analysis and intelligent tutoring systems, publishing research and a further edition of *Cognitive Psychology and its Implications*.

Aided by knowledge derived from his tutoring work, he developed a new theory of procedural learning, incorporating rational analysis in defining versions of subsymbolic activation processes. This, the ACT-R theory, was published in *Rules of the Mind* (1993), with an accompanying ACT-R simulation on personal computer disk. In recent years, Anderson has been largely occupied with teaching and developing ACT-R applications to a wide range of cognitive phenomena.

CATE COX

Andreyeva, Galina Michailovna

Born: 1924, Kazan, Russia *Nat:* Russian *Ints:* Social cognition, social psychology *Educ:* Dr Philosophical Sciences, Moscow State University, 1965 *Appts & awards:* Head, Department of Methodology of Social Sciences, Moscow State University, 1968–71; Head, Department of Social Psychology, Moscow State University, 1971–89; Honor Scientists of Russia, 1984; Lomonosov Prize, 1984; Member, Russian Academy of Education, 1993

Principal publications

1965 *Contemporary American Empirical Sociology.* Mysl Publishers (in Russian).

1972 *Lectures in Methodology of Social Sciences.* Moscow University Press (in Russian).

1978 *Contemporary Social Psychology in the West (Theoretical Orientations).* Moscow University Press (in Russian) (with L. Petrovskaya and N. Bogomolova).

1980 *Social Psychology: A Textbook.* Moscow University Press (in Russian).

1988 *Actual Problems of Social Psychology.* Moscow University Press (in Russian).

Further reading

Andreyeva, G.M. (1990) *Social Psychology.* Progress Publishers.

—— and Janoushek, J.(1981) *Communication and Activity.* Prague.

—— and —— (1987) *Communication and Optimisation of Common Activity.* Moscow University Press (in Russian).

Duck, S. and Gilmour, N. (1981) *Personal Relationships.* Academic Press.

Strickland, L.H. (1979) *Soviet and Western Perspectives in Social Psychology.* Pergamon.

Galina Michailovna Andreyeva was born on 13 June 1924 in Kazan into the family of a doctor. After Germany's invasion in 1941 she volunteered for the Red Army, where she spent all four war years (1941–5). After the end of the war she went to Moscow University Department of Philosophy, where she obtained her first scientific degree in 1953, that of Candidate of Philosophical Sciences (equivalent to a PhD). In 1968 Andreyeva established at Moscow University the first Department of Sociology in the former USSR. There she started to deliver a course in social psychology. In 1971 she moved to the new, growing faculty of psychology, where she took the Chair in Social Psychology, and she became the Head of the School up to 1989. This School became the centre for the development of social psychology in the USSR. An important role in this process was played by *Social Psychology: A Textbook*, which was the first textbook on this subject in the former USSR. It has since been republished four times and translated into eight foreign languages.

The conception of social psychology as a science was, at the time, original. It was based on the activity theory of **Leont'ev** and other Soviet psychologists belonging to the **Vygotsky** school. At the same time it relied on some fundamental ideas popular in European social psychology. It was generally typical for her scientific activity to make a bridge between Western, particularly American, and Soviet social psychology, which had been in isolation and under strong ideological pressure during the Cold War period. For the first since the beginning of Krushchev's thawing of the political climate and elementary enlightenment, work was desperately needed, and it was done in Andreyeva's books *Contemporary American Empirical Sociology* and *Contemporary Social Psychology in the West*. For the last decade she has been working on social cognition and interpersonal perception.

T. SOKOLSKAYA AND A. LOGVINENKO

Antonovsky, Aaron

Born: 1923, New York City, USA *Died:* 1994, Beer-Sheva, Israel *Nat:* American-Israeli *Ints:* Health psychology, public health, sociology *Educ:* BA Brooklyn College, 1945; MA Yale University, 1952; PhD in Sociology, Yale University, 1955; Hon. Doc., Nordic School of Public Health, Göteborg, Sweden, 1993 *Appts & awards:* Lecturer in Sociology, Brooklyn College, 1955–9; Director of Research, New York State Commission Against Discrimination, 1956–9; Teaching Fellow, Associate Professor, Hebrew University-Hadassa Medical School,

1969–72; Kunin-Lunenfeld Professor of Medical Sociology and Chair, 1972–93, Professor Emeritus, 1993–4, Department of the Sociology of Health, Ben-Gurion University of the Negev, Israel

Principal publications

1960 Identity, anxiety and the Jews. In A. Vidich, M. Stein and D.M. White (eds), *Identity and Anxiety*. Free Press.

1965 Epidemiologic study of multiple sclerosis in Israel. An overall review of methods and findings. *Archives of Neurology*, 13, 183–93.

1967 Social class, life expectancy and overall mortality. *Midbank Memorial Fund Quarterly*, 43, 31–73.

1969 *Poverty and Health: A Sociological Analysis.* Harvard University Press (with J. Kosa and I.K. Zola).

1977 Social class and infant mortality. *Social Science and Medicine*, 11, 453–70 (with J. Bernstein).

1979 *Stress and Coping: New Perspectives on Mental and Physical Well-being.* Jossey-Bass.

1984 The sense of coherence as a determinant of health. In J.D. Matarazzo (ed.), *Behavioral Health: A Handbook of Health Enhancement and Disease Prevention*. Wiley.

1987 *Unraveling the Mystery of Health: How People Manage Stress and Stay Well*. Jossey-Bass.

1990 Personality and health: Testing the sense of coherence model. In H.S Friedman (ed.), *Personality and Disease*. Wiley.

1991 The structural sources of salutogenic strengths. In C.L. Cooper and R. Payne (eds), *Individual Differences: Personality and Stress*. Wiley.

1993 The structure and properties of the sense of coherence scale. *Social Science and Medicine*, 36, 725–33.

Further reading

Lenderking, W.R. and Levine, S. (1995) In Memory of Aaron Antonovsky. *Advances: The Journal of Mind–Body Health*, 11, 69–71.

Aaron Antonovsky was born and educated in the USA and served in the US Army in World War II. After completing his education and working in various positions, including a year at the University of Tehran as a Fulbright Professor, he emigrated to Israel in 1960. Trained as a sociologist, Antonovsky did not consider himself a psychologist. However, Antonovsky made major contributions to sociology, to the field of health psychology, and to public health more generally. With his influential constructs of 'salutogenesis' and 'sense of coherence', Antonovsky defined new ways of thinking about health, and significant new research lines were developed as a result.

Antonovsky's early research career was dedicated to the study of discrimination, inequality, immigration and minority ethnic groups, especially the Jews. His theoretical ideas were founded on the sociology of social class, culture, subculture and social stratification. He then developed the concept of 'salutogenesis': the study of how people stay healthy and alive in spite of 'myriad immanent pathogens (varying from microbiological through social) constantly confronting them'. One salutogenetic factor of some significance appeared to be 'sense of coherence'.

Antonovsky defined this as: 'a global orientation that expresses the extent to which one has a pervasive, enduring though dynamic feeling of confidence that (1) the stimuli deriving from one's internal and external environments in the course of living are structured, predictable, and explicable; (2) the resources are available to meet the demands posed by these stimuli; and (3) these demands are challenges worthy of investment and engagement'. Antonovsky's scale measured the construct along three dimensions – comprehensibility, manageability and meaningfulness – and an international network of researchers tested and improved its validity and disseminated their findings. Linking well-being with the sense of coherence construct became an active area of empirical research along with studies of the social and working conditions favouring their development.

Antonovsky was an idealist, believing in a better, more just world. He strongly opposed social injustice, discrimination and intolerance and was deeply interested in teasing out the relationships between social class, poverty and health years before the research community and most governments gave these issues the prominence they deserve. Scholars, policy makers and all those interested in public health owe Antonovsky a great debt. His works will live after him for a very long time.

DAVID F. MARKS

Apter, Michael John
Born: 1939, Stockton on Tees, England *Nat:* British *Ints:* Clinical and psychotherapy, general, personality and social, philosophical and theoretical *Educ:* BSc Bristol University, 1960; Princeton University, 1961; PhD Bristol Univer-

sity, 1964 **Appts & awards:** Fellow, Nuffield Social Science Study, 1977; Fellow, BPS, 1978; Member, BPS Council, 1984– ; Visiting Fellow, Yale University, 1993– ; Visiting Professor, University of Chicago, Northwestern University, Loyola University of Chicago, Purdue University Indiana, University of Chicago, University of Barcelona, Georgetown University Washington, 1994–

Principal publications

1965   Cybernetics and development, 1. Information theory. *Journal of Theoretical Biology*, 8, 244–57.

1966   *Cybernetics and Development*. Pergamon.

1973   *The Computer Simulation of Behaviour.* Hutchinson, 1970; Harper and Row, 1971.

1977   Humour and the theory of psychological reversals. In A.J. Chapman and H.C. Foot (eds), *It's a Funny Thing Humour*. Pergamon (with K.C.P. Smith).

1978   The development of the Telic Dominance Scale. *Journal of Personality Assessment*, 42, 519–28 (with S. Murgatroyd, C. Rushton and C. Ray).

1979   Human action and the theory of psychological reversals. In G. Underwood and R. Stevens (eds), *Aspects of Consciousness*, vol. 1. Academic Press.

1981   The possibility of a structural phenomenology: The case of reversal theory. *Journal of Phenomenological Psychology*, 12, 173–87.

1982   *The Experience of Psychological Reversals.* Academic Press.

1982   Colour preference, arousal and the theory of psychological reversals. *Motivation and Emotion*, 6, 193–215 (with J. Walters and S. Svebak).

1983   Negativism and the sense of identity. In G. Breakwell (ed.), *Threatened Identities*. Wiley.

1984   Reversal theory and personality: A review. *Journal of Research in Personality*, 18, 265–88.

1985   Experiencing personal relationships. In M.J. Apter, D. Fontana and S. Murgatroyd (eds), *Reversal Theory Applications and Developments.* University College Cardiff Press (with K.C.P. Smith).

1991   Reversal theory and the structure of emotional experience. In C. Spielberger, Z. Kulcsar, J. Strelau and G.L. Van Heck (eds), *Stress and Emotion.* Hemisphere.

1993   Sixty consecutive days: Telic and paratelic states in everyday life. In J.H. Kerr, S. Murgatroyd and M.J. Apter (eds), *Advances in Reversal Theory*. Swets and Zeitlinger.

Further reading

Lachenicht, L. (1988) A critical introduction to reversal theory. In M.J. Apter, D. Fontana and S.

Murgatroyd (eds), *Reversal Theory: Applications and Developments*. University College Cardiff Press.

Scott, C.S. (1985) The theory of psychological reversals – a review and critique. *Journal of Guidance and Counselling*, 21, 139–46.

The apparently diverse interests of Michael Apter's career, which included work in automata theory, morphogenesis, computer simulation and educational technology, are in fact united by an enthusiasm for the cybernetic, or systems theoretic, approach to the understanding and control of complex systems. As his interests turned increasingly from computational to purely psychological problems, this general orientation remained, but it was added to by what some would regard as a contradictory influence: phenomenology. Apter took the view that a full understanding of human behaviour and psychological processes would never be possible without taking concomitant mental states into account. He attempted to synthesize these two broad orientations, and developed a general approach which he termed 'structural phenomenology'. This novel approach, and a belief that there was a need for general integrative theories in psychology, led to collaboration with Dr K.C. Smith (a British psychiatrist), and to the construction of a new general theory of motivation, affect and personality which he called 'reversal theory'. Based on such concepts as multistability, meta-motivation, reversal and cognitive synergy, it proved possible to give a unitary account of a wide variety of seemingly disparate and unrelated psychological (including social psychological, psychophysiological and clinical) phenomena. The theory attempts to explicate the structure of experience, and because a person might construe a given mental state of arousal (for example) as excitement or as fear it argues that it is important to find out what it is an individual is experiencing. The theory places considerable importance on pairs (four) of meta-motivational states where, at any one time, (1) one member of each pair is operational and provides some part of the meaning of an experience, and (2) each pair exhibits multistability (i.e. each state is stable but a switch is always possible to the other relatively stable state). The theory has stimulated a considerable body of empirical research by psychologists working in a number of different branches of the subject; and an increasing number of practitioners, especially therapists, have found it useful to adopt it in their work. Challenges posed by the empirical analysis of the 'reversals' postulated by the theory are attracting greater attention in recent times. A Reversal Theory Society has been formed, and several international conferences have been held on the theory and its uses.

Argyle, John Michael

Born: 1925, Nottingham, England **Nat:** British **Ints:** Consulting psychology, industrial and organizational psychology, personality and social psychology **Educ:** BA University of Cambridge, 1950; MA University of Cambridge, 1952; MA University of Oxford, 1952 **Appts & awards:** Fellow, Center for Advanced Study in the Behavioral Sciences, 1958–9; Fellow, BPS; Member of Council, BPS; Chairman of Social Psychology Section, BPS, 1964–7, 1972–4; Fellow, Wolfson College, 1965; Fellow, European Association of Experimental Social Psychology; Fellow, International Society for the Study of Social and Personal Relationships; Social Psychology Editor, *British Journal of Social and Clinical Psychology*; Editor, Social Psychology series for Penguin, Science of Behavior monographs, 1967–74; DSc University of Oxford, 1979; International Series in Experimental Social Psychology, 1979– ; DLitt University of Adelaide, 1982; Hon. DSc. Psych., University of Brussels, 1982; Emeritus Reader, University of Oxford, 1992; Emeritus Professor, Oxford Brookes University, 1992; Distinguished Career Contribution Award, International Society for the Study of Personal Relationships, 1990; Hon. FBPsS, 1992; Consulting Editor, *British Journal of Social and Clinical Psychology*, *Journal for the Theory of Social Behaviour*, *Review of Personality and Social Psychology*, *Language and Communication*, *Journal of Social and Clinical Psychology*, *Journal of Social and Personnel Relationships*, *Applied Social Psychology Annual*, *Basic and Applied Social Psychology*, *International and Intercultural Communication Annual*, *Social Indicators Research*, *International Journal for the Psychology of Religion*

Principal publications

1967 The experimental analysis of social performance. In L. Berkowitz (ed.), *Advances in Experimental Social Psychology*, vol. 3. Academic Press (with A. Kendon).
1969 *Social Interaction.* Methuen/Atherton Press.
1972 Do personality traits apply to social behaviour? *Journal for the Theory of Social Behaviour*, 2, 1–35 (with B. Little).
1975 *Bodily Communication.* Methuen/International Universities Press.
1983 *The Psychology of Interpersonal Behaviour.* 4th edn. Penguin.
1984 The rules of friendship. *Journal of Social and Personal Relationships*, 1, 211–37 (with M. Henderson).
1985 *The Anatomy of Relationships.* Heinemann/Penguin (with M. Henderson).
1987 *The Psychology of Happiness.* Methuen.
1993 *Experiments in Social Interaction.*

Further reading

Greenbaum, C.W. (1972) Social psychology – retreat from the laboratory? *Contemporary Psychology*, 17, 202–3.
Secord, P.F. (1982) Social psychologists preach it, Argyle and colleagues do it. *Contemporary Psychology*, 27, 848–9.

On leaving Nottingham High School Argyle joined the RAF (1943–7), and after World War II took a degree in psychology at the University of Cambridge. He was a research student at Cambridge (1950–2) and was then appointed University Lecturer in Social Psychology (1952–68) at the University of Cambridge, and later Reader (1969–92). From 1958 to 1959 he was a Fellow at the Center for Advanced Study in the Behavioral Sciences. Argyle was a leading figure in the development of social psychology in Britain. He helped to found and was the first social psychology editor (1961–7) of the *British Journal of Social and Clinical Psychology*, helped build up the Social Psychology Section of the BPS to an active body, and started its annual conferences.

Argyle is a social psychologist who, from his earliest work, demonstrated a concern with examining social behaviour at a more detailed level than hitherto, and with understanding exactly how it went wrong for some people. His formulation of a social skills model provided a robust conceptual framework for his efforts, with an emphasis on interpersonal feedback via gaze, the use of non-verbal signals and their coordination with speech. This led to some of the first laboratory studies of these topics. Later he tried to develop less contrived though still rigorous research methods, and carried out numerous studies outside laboratory contexts over a wide range of topics, moving into new areas of research on social interaction, such as the analysis of situations, social skills, conversational analysis, long-term relationships, and happiness and work, together with cross-cultural studies of these topics. The main application of his research has been to social skills training (SST) and he was always concerned to facilitate the transfer of research advances to SST. Argyle is a prolific writer (170 papers, nineteen authored books with translations in many languages, and eight edited books) with a talent for writing for research psychologists, practitioners and the wider public: *The Psychology of Interpersonal Behaviour* has sold more than half a million copies.

Argyris, Chris

Born: 1923, Newark, New Jersey, USA *Nat:* American *Ints:* Consulting psychology, industrial and organizational psychology, personality and social psychology *Educ:* AB Clark University, 1947; MA Kansas University, 1949; PhD Cornell University, 1951 *Appts & awards:* James Bryant Conant Professor, Graduate Schools of Business Administration and of Education, Harvard University, Soldiers Field, Boston; Hon. Doctorates: in Law, McGill University, 1977; in Psychology and Pedagogy, University of Leuven, Belgium, 1978, in Economics, Stockholm School of Economics, 1979, of Letters, IMCB, 1987, in Law, De Paul University, 1987, William B. Groat Alumni Award, Cornell University; American Board of Professional Psychology, Distinguished Contribution Award, 1977; Irwin Award, Academy of Management; Fellow, Academy of Management; Fellow, International Academy of Management, National Academy of Human Resources, 1994; McKinsey Prize, 1994; Distinguished Lifetime Contributions to Management; Financial Times Handbook of Management, 1994; Board of Editors, *Accounting Organization Society, British Journal of Management, Administrative Science Quarterly, Journal of Applied Social Sociology, Journal of Management Studies, Journal of Occupational Behavior, Journal of Organizational Management, Journal of Voluntary Action Research, Organizational Dynamics, Qualitative Organizational Studies, Sage Professional Administrative Sciences*

Principal publications

1952 Diagnosing defenses against the outsider. *Journal of Social Issues*, 8, 1–10.
1957 The individual and organization: Some problems of mutual adjustment. *Administrative Science Quarterly*, 2, 1–24.
1960 Individual actualization in complex organization. *Mental Hygiene*, 44, 2, 226–37.
1965 Explorations in interpersonal competence I. *Journal of Applied Behavioral Science*, 1, 58–84.
1967 On the future of laboratory education. *Journal of Applied Behavioural Science*, 3, 143–210.
1974 *Theory in Practice.* Jossey-Bass (with D. Schön).
1975 Problems and new directions for industrial psychology. In M. Dunnette (ed.), *Handbook of Industrial and Organizational Psychology.* Rand McNally.
1976 Theories of action that inhibit individual learning. *American Psychologist*, 31, 638–54.
1978 Is capitalism the culprit? *Organizational Dynamics*, Spring, 21–37.
1983 Action, science and intervention. *Journal of Applied Behavioral Science*, 19, 115–35.
1985 *Strategy, Change and Defensive Routines.* Ballinger.
1989 Strategy implementation: An experience in learning. *Organizational Dynamics*, 18, 5–15.
1991 Inappropriate defenses against the monitoring of organization development practice. *Journal of Applied Behavioral Science*, 26, 299–312.
1992 *On Organizational Learning.* Blackwell.
1993 *Actionable Knowledge: Especially for Changing the Status Quo.* Jossey-Bass.
Numerous other books, book chapters and articles in learned journals.

Further reading

Friedman, V.J. and Lipshitz, R. (1992) Teaching people to shift cognitive gears: Overcoming resistance on the road to Model II. Special Issue: Intervention with groups in organizations. *Journal of Applied Behavioral Science*, 28, 118–36.
Hawkins, P. (1991) The spiritual dimension of the learning organisation. Special Issue: Joining forces. *Management Education and Development*, 22, 172–87.

Chris Argyris began with the study of the impact of organizational structure, control systems and leadership on individuals, especially at the middle and lower levels of organizations. Next, he focused on research to change the negative impact. This led him to the study of the top management, arguing that without commitment at this level there could be little change. He suggests that most organizations are managed to inhibit learning. He conducted a series of studies related to: (1) how organizations can learn to detect and correct errors; (2) how they can learn when they are unable to learn how to detect and correct their errors; and (3) how they can design policies and actions that are implemented effectively. Out of this research activity emerged a new finding: human beings would tend to inhibit their own and others' learning if they used their minds correctly and if they adhered to a theory of action most of them learn early in life as to how to deal with complexity and threat. Argyris suggests that human beings are programmed to produce a paradox. If they behaved correctly and skilfully they would succeed and fail. Moreover, they would tend to be unaware of their causal responsibility for these consequences; and others (especially subordinates) would act to keep them blind. People tend to resist switching from an automatic, unproblematic, socially immersed level of awareness to a conscious, reflective mode of thinking under conditions of ambiguity and threat. With Daniel Schön, he developed a theory to explain this resistance and a method for 'unfreezing' automatic reasoning processes so that people can learn this more reflective kind of thinking. His research also focuses on how to help people to overcome these factors in order to be reflective practitioners. In 1994 Yale University established the Chris Argyris Chair in the Social Psychology of Organizations.

Arnheim, Rudolf

Born: 1904, Berlin, Germany **Nat:** American **Ints:** General psychology, history of psychology, philosophical and theoretical psychology, psychology and the arts **Educ:** PhD University of Berlin, 1928 **Appts & awards:** Guggenheim Fellow, 1942–3; President, APA Division 10, 1957, 1965, 1971; President, American Society for Aesthetics, 1959, 1979; Professor Emeritus of the Psychology of Art, Harvard University, 1974; Fellow, AAA&S, 1976– ; Distinguished Service Award, National Art Education Association, 1976– ; Hon. doctorates from Rhode Island School of Design, 1976, Bates College, 1981, Marquette University, 1984, Kansas City Art Institute, 1985, Sarah Lawrence College, 1985

Principal publications

1949 The *Gestalt* theory of expression. *Psychological Review*, 56, 156–71.

1954, 1966, 1974 *Art and Visual Perception*. University of California Press.

1966 *Toward a Psychology of Art*. University of California Press.

1969 *Visual Thinking*. University of California Press.

1977 *The Dynamics of Architectural Form*. University of California Press.

1986 *New Essays on the Psychology of Art*. University of California Press.

1989 Zum Thema von Zufall und Gesetzlichkeit (On the topic of chance and lawfulness). *Gestalt Theory*, 11, 268–70.

1989 Die verschwindende Welt und Kohlers Tintenfass (The disappearing world and Kohler's ink-well). *Gestalt Theory*, 11, 191–8.

1991 Beyond the double truth. *New Ideas in Psychology*, 9, 1–8.

1994 Consciousness: An island of images. *Journal of Theoretical and Philosophical Psychology*, 14, 121–7.

1994 Artistry in retardation. *Arts in Psychotherapy*, 21, 329–32.

Further reading

Franklin, M.B. (1994) A feeling for words: Arnheim on language. Special issue: Rudolf Arnheim's life and work. *Arts in Psychotherapy*, 21, 261–7.

McNiff, S. (1994) Rudolf Arnheim: A clinician of images. Special issue: Rudolf Arnheim's life and work. *Arts in Psychotherapy*, 21, 249–59.

Winner, E. (1982) *Invented Worlds: The Psychology of the Arts*. Harvard University Press.

When he completed his PhD (an experimental investigation of visual perception) Arnheim worked for five years (1928–33) as assistant editor of a cultural affairs magazine published in Berlin. He then moved to the International Institute for Educational Film, League of Nations, in Rome, where he worked in a similar capacity until 1938. A year later found him in London, working as a translator for the BBC (Overseas Service), where he remained for just a year. In 1940 he emigrated to the USA, where he was employed as a research officer (on radio research) at Columbia University, New York. He became an American citizen in 1946. From 1943 to 1968 he was on the Psychology Faculty, Sarah Lawrence College, Bronxville, New York, and was Lecturer and Visiting Professor (Graduate Faculty), at the New School for Social Research, New York. From 1968 until his retirement in 1974 he was Professor of Psychology at the Department of Visual and Environmental Studies at Harvard University, and Visiting Professor at the University of Michigan.

Arnheim's contributions are in three areas: art perception, art therapy, and visual cognition and problem solving. His approach to psychology was formulated on the thesis that during the

Middle Ages, the narrative facts on which Western religions were based at the time of their foundation began to come into conflict with the knowledge of philosophers and later with the discoveries of the natural sciences. This generated a doctrine of the 'double truth' – a psychological split between belief and knowledge that persists in modern times. Reconciliation of the split between knowledge and belief can be approached through artistic experience. In his psychology of art Arnheim provided a framework for understanding the theory and practice of expressive arts therapies. He developed a view of artistic behaviour as an aesthetically and cognitively grounded activity that is characterized by a complex interplay between use of a medium and articulation of themes or ideas. Representation rests on the invention of forms that are structurally or dynamically equivalent to an object. Artistic representation does not aim for one-to-one correspondence with an original object. The drawing medium with its specific tools tends to encourage shapes made of lines and contours, and these shapes are the constituents from which a complex graphic language develops. Arnheim drew extensively on *Gestalt* psychology in the development of this conceptual framework and thereby offered an alternative to neo-behaviourist, cognitive-developmental and psychoanalytic approaches to the arts. His psychology of art provided a conceptual framework which could be extended to accommodate cognition and problem solving more generally. For example, he argued that problem solving proceeds not as a sequence of static stages, but as a process of dynamic changes leading either from an original matrix through deviations, deformations or variations to a more complex structure, or from a distorted structure to a more adequate, simple shape. Thus, problem solving involves the fixating power of percepts: the better the *Gestalt*, the more firmly a percept will impose itself on the memory, thinking and learning of a percipient.

Aronson, Elliot

Born: 1932, Revere, Massachusetts, USA *Nat:* American *Ints:* Applied social psychology, media psychology, social psychology, society for the psychological study of social issues *Educ:* BA Brandeis University, 1954; MA Wesleyan University, 1956; PhD Stanford University, 1959 *Appts & awards:* Professor of Psychology, University of California at Santa Cruz; AAAS, Award for Distinguished Research in Social Psychology, 1970; National Media Award, APA 1973– ; Distinguished Teaching Award, University of Texas, 1973; APA Distinguished Teaching Award in Psychology, APA, 1980; Guggenheim Fellowship, 1981–2; President, Western Psychological Association, 1989–90; Elected to the American Academy of Arts and Sciences, 1992; Distinguished Scientific Career Award, Society of Experimental Social Psychology, 1994; Fellow, Center for Advanced Study in the Behavioural Sciences, 1970–1, 1977–8, APA, APS; American Academy of Arts and Sciences, APA Division 9, Society for the Psychological Study of Social Issues, International Association of Applied Social Science, APA Division 8, Society of Personality and Social Psychology; Editorial Board, *Contemporary Psychology*, *British Journal of Social Psychology*; Advisory Editor, *Journal of Personality and Social Psychology*, *Journal of Experimental Social Psychology*

Principal publications

1959 The effect of severity of initiation on liking for a group. *Journal of Abnormal and Social Psychology*, 59, 177–81 (with J. Mills).

1965 Gain and loss of esteem as determinants of interpersonal attractiveness. *Journal of Experimental Social Psychology*, 1, 156–71 (with D. Linder).

1966 The effect of a pratfall on increasing interpersonal attractiveness. *Psychonomic Science*, 4, 227–8. (with B. Willerman and J. Floyd).

1968 *Handbook of Social Psychology*. Random House (with G. Lindzey). Reprinted 1985.

1968 My enemy's enemy is my friend. *Journal of Personality and Social Psychology*, 8, 8–12 (with V. Cope).

1968 Dishonest behavior as a function of differential levels of induced self esteem. *Journal of Personality and Social Psychology*, 9, 121–7. (with D.R. Mettee).

1968 Dissonance theory: Progress and problems. In R.P. Abelson, E. Aronson, W.J. McGuire, T.W. Newcomb, M.J. Rosenberg and P.H. Tannenbaum (eds), *Theories of Cognitive Consistency: A Sourcebook*. Rand McNally.

1969 Experimentation in social psychology. In G. Lindzey and E. Aronson (eds), *Handbook of Social Psychology*, 2nd edn, vol. II. Addison-Wesley (with J.M. Carlsmith).

1972 *The Social Animal*. W.H Freeman. Reprinted 1976, 1980, 1984.

1978 *The Jigsaw Classroom*. Sage.

1978 *Methods of Research in Social Psychology.*
Addison-Wesley (with P.C. Ellsworth and J.M.
Carlsmith).

1981 *Burnout.* Free Press (with A. Pines).

1982 Modifying the environment of the
desegregated classroom. In A.J. Stewart (ed.),
Motivation and Society. Jossey-Bass.

1983 A social psychological perspective on
energy conservation in residential buildings.
American Psychologist, 38, 435–44 (with S.
Yates).

1984 *Energy Use: The Human Dimension.* W.H.
Freeman (with P.C. Stern).

1985 *The Handbook of Social Psychology.* Random
House (3rd edn, with G. Lindzey).

1988 *Career Burnout.* Free Press (with A. Pines).

1990 *Methods of Research in Social Psychology.*
McGraw-Hill (with P.C. Ellsworth, J.M. Carlsmith
and Gonzale).

1992 *Age of Propaganda.* W.H. Freeman (with
A.R. Pratkanis).

1993 *Social Psychology*, vols 1, 2, 3. Elgar (with
A.R. Pratkanis).

1994 *Social Psychology: The Heart and the Mind.*
HarperCollins (with T. Wilson and R. Akert).

Further reading

Wicklund, R. and Brehm, W. (1976) *Perspectives on
Cognitive Dissonance.* Erlbaum.

Aronson started in graduate school in the same
year as Leon **Festinger** published his *Theory of
Cognitive Dissonance.* Reading that set Aronson
on a course to study social psychology. Stimulated by dissonance theory's heuristic elegance,
he generated some intriguing questions about
human motivation, cognition and behaviour –
and found the answers to those questions
through laboratory experimentation. The first of
these experiments showed that exerting effort in
order to gain admission to a group increases the
attractiveness of that group. The research led to
a modification of dissonance theory and the
conclusion that what really produced dissonance
was behaviour that was inconsistent with a
person's self-concept. This emerged most
clearly in an experiment carried out with
Mettee, showing that temporarily raising (or
lowering) self-esteem would reduce (or
increase) dishonest behaviour. He attempted to
design experiments that were simultaneously
rigorous and meaningful. Without quite realizing it, he was finding solutions to problems that
had puzzled researchers for decades. He became
interested in research methodologies and in
1969 he published an influential *Handbook*

chapter (with Carlsmith) on how to do experiments in psychology.

In 1971, while he was experimenting on self-
esteem and interpersonal attraction, the local
schools desegregated, producing riots, violence
and turmoil, and he was called in as a consultant. It became clear that the highly
competitive atmosphere dominating most
American classrooms was exacerbating an
already difficult situation. He introduced a
model structure based on the principle of interdependence (jigsaw structure), which led to
reduced prejudice, increased self-esteem and
improved academic performance. This process
has been adopted by hundreds of schools
throughout North America with similar,
encouraging results. The success of these
'action' experiments in public school produced a
major change in the direction of Aronson's
research. This led to involvement in the application of social psychology to national policy
issues such as racism, energy conservation and
the treatment of the elderly.

Asch, Solomon

Born: 1907, Warsaw, Poland **Nat:** Polish/
American **Ints:** Personality and social psychol-
ogy, experimental psychology **Educ:** BS
(Literature and Science), City College, New
York, 1928; MA Columbia University, 1930;
PhD Columbia University, 1932 **Appts & awards:**
Instructor and Assistant Professor, Brooklyn
College, 1932–41; Associate Professor, New
School for Social Research, 1944–7; Professor,
Swarthmore College, 1947–66; Professor, Insti-
tute for Cognitive Studies, Rutgers State
University, 1966–72; Professor, University of
Pennsylvania, 1972–9; APA Distinguished
Scientific Contribution Award, 1967

Principal publications

1946 Forming impressions of personality. *Journal
of Abnormal Social Psychology*, 41, 258–90.

1948 Studies in space orientation: 1. Perception of
the upright with displaced visual fields. *Journal of
Experimental Psychology*, 38, 325–37 (with H.A.
Witkin).

1948 Studies in space orientation: II. Perception of
the upright with displaced visual fields and with
body tilted. *Journal of Experimental Psychology*,
38, 455–77 (with H.A. Witkin).

1948 Studies in space orientation: III. Perception of
the upright in the absence of a visual field. *Journal
of Experimental Psychology*, 38, 603–14 (with
H.A. Witkin).

1948 Studies in space orientation: IV. Further

experiments on perception of the upright with displaced visual fields. *Journal of Experimental Psychology*, 38, 762–82 (with H.A. Witkin).

1952   *Social Psychology*. Prentice-Hall (Oxford University Press, 1987).

1955   Opinions and social pressure. *Scientific American*, 193, 31–5.

Further reading

Gergen, K.J. (1994) *Realities and Relationships*. Harvard University Press.

Gibson, J.J. and Mowrer, O.H. (1938) Determinants of the perceived vertical and horizontal. *Psychological Review*, 45, 300–23.

Rock, I. (ed.) (1990) *The Legacy of Solomon Asch: Essays in Cognition and Social Psychology*. Erlbaum.

Saussure, F. (1967) *Cours de Linguistique Generale*. Hatier.

Warr, P.B. and Knapper C. (1968) *The Perception of People and Events*. Wiley.

Asch was born in Poland but emigrated to North America in 1920. He was a graduate student at Columbia University and later taught at Brooklyn College and Swarthmore College. In 1966 he became one of the founding members of the Institute for Cognitive Studies at Rutgers University. In 1972 he went to the University of Pennsylvania as Professor of Psychology, where he remained until he retired in 1979. A fuller and more personal account of Asch's biography is provided in the festschrift edited by Rock.

Asch's interests and influences were wide-ranging but they centred on a number of themes in social psychology. Asch's research *modus operandi* was primarily experimental, but this predilection should not be used to tag him as a behaviourist. As a graduate student he became interested in *Gestalt* psychology and was critical of both behaviourism and psychoanalytic theory. He worked to develop a social psychology that would contribute to the solution of the major problems in society. In flying the colours of this liberal intellectual mission, he exemplifies the modernist psychology characteristic of the post-World War II era.

It is fascinating to read Asch from the standpoint of the post-experimental critical social psychology of the 1990s. On the one hand he stands for all that the post-positivists dislike and, on the other, many of his ideas resonate well with post-modern psychology. For example, his caveat not to take for granted local social practices as if they were natural givens provides a strong link with the social construc-

tionism and cultural relativism of the 1990s. He writes as one who is worried by the fact that psychology has striven to emulate the quantitative exactness of the natural sciences without thinking the matter through sufficiently. He does not appear overjoyed by the fact that others within the discipline seem content to use the behaviour of the lower organisms as a model for human conduct. Furthermore, he takes the view that psychology needs to relate to the social sciences of economics, history or politics just as much as it does to the natural and biological sciences. All these concerns he shares with the critical social psychologists of the post-modern era. From the standpoint of contemporary critical social psychology, he seems to have been ahead of his time. It is possible, however, that this positive evaluation has been clouded by the ethical criticisms which some of his experiments have aroused, and I shall comment on that aspect of his work later.

A student used to the modern register and style of North American texts, with their colourful boxes, photographs, glossaries and marginal notes, may be surprised by the straightforward way in which Asch's (1952) textbook is written; his intellect comes through directly to the reader, unhindered by the paraphernalia of modern marketing. The book stands the test of time well, except for some rather obvious problems with sexist language, and, indeed, it was much later reissued as a paperback with a new preface. Rather than attempting to match the breadth of this general text in social psychology, I have chosen to focus upon research in three areas which have had considerable influence. Asch is probably most famous for the experiments he conducted into conformity, but his work on impression formation and field dependence was also of great interest, and it is to the latter topic that I now turn.

In the late 1940s Asch and Witkin published a series of experiments on the perception of the upright in four related papers. These experiments were designed to clarify an apparent contradiction between earlier work carried out by **Gibson** and **Mowrer**, who believed that our orientation in space is anchored mainly to postural factors, and **Max Wertheimer**, who, on the basis of his mirror experiment, felt that visual field factors outweighed the postural. In the first experiment, subjects viewed a scene (the laboratory in which they were located) by looking at it through a cardboard tube aimed at its reflection in a tilted mirror. In the room, there was a rod which the subjects had to align with true vertical as it was slowly moved by the (unseen) experimenter. Because this scene was viewed through the tilted mirror, it provided a framework which was itself tilted away from true vertical by about 30°. This sounds more complex than it actually was, and subjects had little difficulty in understanding what they had to do. The results confirmed the importance of the surrounding visual field, as opposed to the postural cues, since the settings were found to be much closer to the apparent (tilted) axes generated by the scene in the mirror than to the true settings. The effect of this was noticeable when the subjects viewed a restricted portion of the scene through the tube, but was most marked when they stood directly in front of the mirror and looked at the scene without the tube. The researchers explain this in terms of the more lifelike quality of the scene when the subject looked into the mirror without the tube, despite the subject's more accurate knowledge of the true conditions. They also reported large individual differences in this study.

In summarizing this work (mainly drawing on the first series of experiments), it has been necessary to omit much methodological detail. This is a shame in some respects, since the descriptions in the original papers evoke strongly the atmosphere of laboratory work prior to electronic recording and the ubiquitous microchip. This is a world in which subjects in darkened rooms have to close their eyes whilst the luminous paint on the stimulus rod is refreshed by exposure to daylight. Blindfolded subjects are led into laboratories only to peer through cardboard tubes at tilted mirrors; their chairs are tilted this way and that. Here, make-believe rooms are knocked up out of plywood and propped up on saw horses.

Apart from his work on field dependence, Asch also carried out some pioneering experiments on person perception. His strategy was to present subjects with lists of personality characteristics (one list, for example, contained these items: warm, intelligent, skilful, industrious, determined, practical, cautious) and then to obtain further judgements or ratings on the subject's impressions of the hypothetical person so described. By giving different subject groups lists which were identical save for one key item (the most famous switch was to substitute 'cold' for 'warm' in the second stimulus list), it was possible for him to get some idea about the effect the target trait had on the impression formed. He established that some traits were more central than others, in the sense that a change in the key trait had quite a marked effect in the subject's overall impression of the stimulus person. He also concluded from this research that people tend to form an impression of the whole person and do not simply add together independent trait judgements in an entirely separate fashion. Thus any two traits that are understood to belong to someone cease to do so as isolated units. 'The two [traits] come into immediate dynamic interaction. The subject perceives not this and that quality, but the two entering into a particular relation.' This is similar to de Saussure's (1967) position that the meaning of one linguistic symbol comes alive partly through the distinctions it makes in terms of what it excludes or opposes; the meaning is determined not by the relationship between the word and an objective underlying reality, so much as by the way it is used within localized sociolinguistic language games. This stance would be very much at home in the discursive psychology of the 1990s. Asch is aware of the danger of forcing subjects to judge artificially isolated traits, but he nevertheless does precisely this. The temptation is, perhaps, to dismiss this work as lacking ecological validity (this problem has been subsequently redressed to a large extent by the experiments reported by Warr and Knapper).

I come finally to the work for which, probably, Asch is most widely known: a relatively simple series of experiments he conducted on conformity to group pressure. He invited naive subjects into the laboratory to participate in an experiment requiring perceptual judgements to be made. The subjects had to state which of three lines of differing lengths matched exactly a stimulus line (and there always was, in fact, an exact match). When the subjects arrived to do this task they found that there were others already waiting to do the experiment. Unbeknown to them, the others were confederates of the experimenter. On certain key trials the confederates unanimously stated that an incorrect comparison line matched the stimulus. The naive subjects always gave their judgement last, so they were therefore exposed to the influence of the opposing unanimous majority. Many yielded to this pressure and Asch was thus able to demonstrate, in a laboratory setting, the effect of conformity in a totally unambiguous perceptual task. This was a startling, worrying and attention-grabbing piece of research. It has also been regarded as the epitome of deceptive research. Asch could not have run his experiments without lying to his subjects about the purpose of the study.

In sum, Asch has wide-ranging interests; he writes in a clear and challenging style; and has conducted some of the best-known experiments in social psychology. Whilst there have been fierce attacks made against experimental psychology since the days when Asch was a leading figure in the field, it would be a shame to dismiss his work merely on the grounds that some of his experiments lacked ecological validity and others involved deception. His theoretical background in *Gestalt* psychology ensures that his writing goes beyond any naive acceptance of the doctrine of the objective experiment and, indeed, provides many interesting links to the post-experimental critical social psychology of the 1990s.

JOHN L. SMITH

Atkinson, John William

Born: 1923, New Jersey, USA **Nat:** American **Ints:** Motivational psychology, personality and social psychology **Educ:** BA Wesleyan, 1947; MA University of Michigan, 1948; PhD University of Michigan, 1950; Dr Phil HC Ruhr-Universitat Bochum, 1980 **Appts & awards:** Instructor, University of Michigan, 1948–9; Assistant Professor, Wesleyan University, 1949–50; Assistant Professor, University of Michigan, 1950–5; Fellow, Social Science Research Council, 1952–5, Center for Advanced Study in Behavioral Sciences, 1955–6; Associate Professor, 1955–59, Guggenheim Fellow, 1960–1; Professor of Psychology, 1960–88 (Retired), University of Michigan, Ann Arbor; Special Research Fellow, USPHS, 1969–70; APA Distinguished Scientific Contribution Award, 1979

Principal publications

1948 The effect of different intensities of the hunger drive on thematic apperception. *Journal of Experimental Psychology*, 38, 643–58 (with D.C. McClelland).
1949 The effect of the need for achievement on thematic apperception. *Journal of Experimental Psychology*, 39, 242–55 (with D.C. McClelland, R.A. Clark and T.B. Roby).
1953 *The Achievement Motive*. Appleton-Century-Crofts (with D.C. McClelland, R.A. Clark and E.L. Lowell).
1957 Motivational determinants of risk-taking behavior. *Psychological Review*, 64, 359–72.
1958 Towards experimental analysis of human

motivation in terms of motives, expectancies and incentives. In J.W. Atkinson (ed.), *Motives in Fantasy, Action and Society*. Van Nostrand.
1960 Achievement motive and test anxiety conceived as motive to approach success and motive to avoid failure. *Journal of Abnormal and Social Psychology*, 60, 52–63 (with G.H. Litwin).
1964 *An Introduction to Motivation*. Van Nostrand.
1964 Some neglected variables in contemporary conceptions of decision and performance. *Psychological Reports*, 14 (monograph supp., 5-14), 575–90 (with D. Cartwright).
1966 *A Theory of Achievement Motivation*. Wiley (with N.T. Feather).
1970 *The Dynamics of Action*. Wiley (with D. Birch).
1974 Strength of motivation and efficiency of performance. In J.W. Atkinson and J.O. Raynor (eds), *Motivation and Achievement*. Winston.
1974 Motivational determinants of intellective performance and cumulative achievement. In J.W Atkinson and J.O. Raynor (eds), *Motivation and Achievement*. Winston.
1977 Explorations using computer simulation to comprehend thematic apperceptive measurement of motivation. *Motivation and Emotion*, 1, 1–27 (with K. Bongort and L.H. Price).
1981 Studying personality in the context of an advanced motivational psychology. *American Psychologist*, 36, 117–28.
1983 *Personality, Motivation and Action: Selected Papers*. Praeger.

Further reading

Smith, C.P., Atkinson, J.W., McClelland, D.C. and Veroff, J. (eds) (1992) *Motivation and Personality: Handbook of Thematic Content Analysis*. Cambridge University Press.

John Atkinson grew up in the small town of Oradell. He graduated (1941) from Dwight Morrow High School, Englewood, New Jersey with Mary Jane Wanta, and they were married three years later. He completed three semesters at Wesleyan University before serving as a pilot and flight instructor in the Army Air Corps. He returned to Wesleyan in October 1945 and completed his BA two years later. He conducted his doctoral research under the guidance of Donald G. Marquis and Edward L. Walker. That was completed while Atkinson was filling in for David C. **McClelland** (on leave at Harvard) at Weslyan University (1949–50).

John Atkinson has been a key figure in the psychology of motivation. His early work (1948–53) with D.C. McClelland demonstrated that hunger and experimentally induced achievement motivation are expressed in the content of imaginative stories. This validation of 'thematic apperception' as a measure of motivation formed the basis for subsequent investigations of individual differences in motivation. Atkinson's theory of achievement motivation and research at the University of Michigan helped to identify expectations of consequences as the cognitive alternative to the earlier conception of drive and habit in the treatment of motivation. Studies showing how combinations of motives influence performance in different situations (e.g. alone versus audience) contributed to the empirical analysis of the inverted-U-shaped relationship between strength of motivation and efficiency of performance. What he considered to be inadequacies in the traditional episodic framework of psychology were overcome in realizing that initiation of action and persistence are not two separate motivational problems but two aspects of a single basic problem – a change in activity. New principles, advanced in *The Dynamics of Action* with David Birch, dealt with the temporal continuity of behaviour and the underlying processes of motivation which govern the waxing and waning of tendencies that are expressed in the stream of behaviour. The development of a computer program of the dynamics allowed simulation of complex motivational problems such as the thematic apperceptive measurement of motivation, which shows that its validity (as a measure of motive strength) does not depend on internal consistency (reliability) as critics had claimed.

Atkinson, Richard Chatham

Born: 1929, Oak Park, Illinois, USA *Nat:* American *Ints:* Cognitive psychology, educational psychology, experimental psychology, mathematical psychology *Educ:* PhB University of Chicago, 1948; PhD Indiana University, 1955 *Appts & awards:* Chancellor, University of California at San Diego; Distinguished Scientific Contribution Award, APA, 1977; Member, Society of Experimental Psychologists, National Academy of Sciences, American Academy of Arts and Sciences, National Academy of Education, Institute of Medicine, American Philosophical Society

Principal publications

1963 Stimulus sampling theory. In R.D. Luce, R.R. Bush and E. Galanter (eds), *Handbook of Mathematical Psychology*, vol. 2. Wiley.

1964 *Studies in Mathematical Psychology*. Stanford University Press.

1965 *An Introduction to Mathematical Learning Theory*. Wiley (with G.H. Bower and E.J. Crothers).

1965 A learning model for forced-choice detection experiments. *British Journal of Mathematical and Statistical Psychology*, 18, 184–206 (with R.A. Kinchla).

1968 Human memory: A proposed system and its control processes. In K.W. Spence and J.T. Spence (eds), *The Psychology of Learning and Motivation: Advances in Research and Theory*, vol. 2. Academic Press (with R.M. Shiffrin).

1968 Computerized instruction and the learning process. *American Psychologist*, 23, 114–29.

1971 Human memory and the concept of reinforcement. In R. Glazer (ed.), *The Nature of Reinforcement*. Academic Press (with T.D. Wickens).

1972 Ingredients for a theory of instruction. *American Psychologist*, 27, 921–31.

1974 *Contemporary Developments in Mathematical Psychology, vol. I: Learning, Memory and Thinking, vol. II: Measurement, Psychophysics and Neural Information Processing*. Freeman (with D.H. Krantz, R.D. Luce and P. Suppes).

1974 Search and decision processes in recognition memory. In *Contemporary Developments in Mathematical Psychology, vol. I: Learning, Memory and Thinking*. Freeman (with J.F. Juola).

1975 Mnemotechnics in second-language learning. *American Psychologist*, 30, 821–8.

1976 Fact retrieval processes in human memory. In W.K. Estes (ed.), *Handbook of Learning and Cognitive Processes*, vol. 4. Erlbaum (with K.T. Wescourt).

1983 *Introduction to Psychology*, 8th edn. Harcourt Brace Jovanovich (with R.L. Atkinson and E.R. Hilgard).

1984 A comparison of paired-associate learning models having different acquisition and retention axioms. *Journal of Mathematical Psychology*, 1, 285–315 (with E.J. Crothers).

Further reading

Krasner, L. and Houts, A.C. (1984) A study of the value systems of behavioral scientists. *American Psychologist*, 39, 8, 840–50.

Paivio, A. and Desrochers, A. (1981) Mnemonic techniques in second language learning. *Journal of Educational Psychology*, 73, 6, 780–95.

Richard Atkinson attended grade school and the first two years of high school in Oak Park. Instead of completing high school he entered the

University of Chicago in 1944 and graduated four years later. After a brief period at the University of Louisville he enrolled for his PhD at Indiana University, where he worked closely with William K. **Estes**. From 1954 to 1956 he worked at the Human Resources Research Unit at Fort Ord, California. When he joined Stanford University in 1956 he expected to pursue a career in applied mathematics and statistics. However, academic positions were scarce at the time and Atkinson took up an offer of a post as assistant professor of psychology at UCLA.

In the 1950s and early 1960s, Atkinson based his research on mathematical models for learning and perception. During this time, he became interested in the development of systems for computer-assisted instruction, one of which was a program in reading for young children. By the mid-1960s, he had turned to cognitive psychology, particularly theories of memory and their control processes. This work proved to have implications for optimizing the instructional process, and led to the development of mathematical models for optimization. These models were remarkably effective when implemented as part of a program for computer-assisted instruction. From 1956 to 1975 he was part of the faculty at Stanford University. In 1975 he was appointed as the Deputy Director of the National Science Foundation by President Ford, and in 1977, Director of the Foundation by President Carter. He has served as Chancellor of the University of California, San Diego, since 1980.

Atkinson combined mathematics with the emerging techniques of computer science and information processing, and applied experimental techniques in the advancement of psychological theory and its applications. His long-term collaboration with Patrick **Suppes** yielded the first extensive application of learning theory to multiperson interactions. With Richard M. Shiffrin he developed a cognitive model that influenced two decades of research on human short-term memory, and with James Juola and other colleagues he developed an almost equally influential family of models for recognition and search processes. In applying cognitive psychology to computer-guided instruction he anticipated later demands for problem-directed, applications-oriented research.

Azrin, Nathan H.

Born: 1930, Boston, Massachusetts, USA ***Nat:*** American ***Ints:*** Behavioural therapy, clinical psychology, experimental analysis of behaviour ***Educ:*** BA (cum laude) Boston University, 1951; MA Boston University, 1952; PhD Harvard University, 1956 ***Appts & awards:*** Director, Department of Treatment Development, Anna Mental Health and Development Center, 1958–60; Lecturer, Department of Psychology, Southern Illinois University, 1958–66; Executive Editor, *Journal of the Experimental Analysis of Behavior*, 1963–6; President, Society for the Experimental Analysis of Behavior, 1963–6; Founder, *Journal of Applied Behavior Analysis*, 1966; Professor, Rehabilitation Institute, Southern Illinois University, 1966–80; Board of Directors, Society for the Experimental Analysis of Behavior, 1966–89; Fellow, APA Divisions 12, 25, President Division 25, 1967–70; Council of Representatives, APA, 1967–70, 1979–82; Distinguished Contributions for Applications in Psychology Award, APA, 1975; Association for Advancement of Behavior Therapy, 1976; President, Association for Behavioral Analysis, 1977; President, Midwestern Psychological Association, 1977; Professor of Psychology, Nova Southeastern University, 1980– ; Vice-president, Society for the Experimental Analysis of Behavior, 1989–92; First Annual Award for Scientific Applications of Psychology, American Psychological Society, 1993; President, Cambridge Center for Behavioral Sciences

Principal publications

1956 Reinforcement of cooperation between children. *Journal of Abnormal and Social Psychology*, 52, 100–2 (with O.R. Lindsley).
1959 Punishment and recovery during fixed-ratio performance. *Journal of the Experimental Analysis of Behavior*, 2, 301–5.
1960 Sequential effects of punishment. *Science*, 131, 605–6.
1961 Time-out from positive reinforcement. *Science*, 133, 382–3.
1965 Conditioned punishment. *Journal of the Experimental Analysis of Behavior*, 8, 279–94 (with D.F. Hake).
1966 Punishment. In W.K. Honig (ed.), *Operant Behavior: Areas of Research and Application*. Prentice-Hall (with W.C. Holz).
1966 Conditioning human verbal behavior. In W.K. Honig (ed.), *Operant Behavior: Areas of Research and Application*. Prentice-Hall (with W.C. Holz).
1968 *The Token Economy: A Motivational System for Therapy and Rehabilitation*. Appleton-Century-Crofts (with T. Ayllon).

1973 Required relaxation: A method of inhibiting agitative-disruptive behavior of retardates. *Behavior Research and Therapy*, 11, 67–78 (with D.R. Webster).

1976 Improvements in the community-reinforcement approach to alcoholism. *Behavior Research and Therapy*, 14, 339–48.

1981 An operant reinforcement method of treating depression. *Journal of Behavior Therapy and Experimental Psychiatry*, 12, 145–51 (with V.A. Besalel).

1988 Comparative study of behavioral methods of rating severe self-injury. *Behavioral Residential Treatment*, 3, 119–49 (with V.A. Besalel, J.P. Jamner and J.N. Caputo).

1994 Behavior therapy for drug abuse: A controlled outcome study. *Behavior Research and Therapy*, 32, 857–66 (with P. McMahon, V.A. Besalel, B.C. Donahue, R. Acierno and E.S. Kogan).

Further reading

Barber, J.G. (1992) Relapse prevention and the need for brief social interventions. *Journal of Substance Abuse Treatment*, 9, 157–8.

Woods, D.W. and Miltonberg, R.G. (1995) Habit Reversal: a review of applications and variations. *Journal of Behavior Therapy and Experimental Psychiatry*, 26, 123–31.

Nathan Azrin has combined a record of solid basic research, in the tradition of B.F. **Skinner**'s radical behaviourism, with consistent applications of behavioural principles to clinical as well as social issues. Coupled with his clever methodological contribution, Azrin has maintained a prodigious record of achievements in the academic and clinical arenas. While a graduate student at both Boston University and Harvard University, he displayed an early inclination towards a wide range of applications of behavioural principles. For example, he studied psychosis in children, then worked with Skinner on an automated procedure for teaching arithmetic to primary school children.

Azrin's work under Skinner proved significant. Skinner's positivism advocated a methodological emphasis that valued the study of behaviour defined in terms of peripheral events, and he consistently eschewed speculation about central mediating agencies of behaviour, whether physiological or cognitive. Behaviour, for Skinner, was completely subject to environmental determinacy. If the environment is controlled, behaviour is controlled. The basis of Skinner's research approach was the study of operant behaviour. In contrast to respondent behaviour, where responses are elicited by specific stimuli, operant behaviour is ongoing without any apparent stimulus. Learning occurs when the operant behaviour comes under the control of reinforcement from the environment.

After two postdoctoral years as a research psychologist, first at the Institute of Living, with Karl **Pribram**, and then with the US Army Ordinance studying human factors in fatigue, in 1958 Azrin became Director of the Department of Treatment Development at the Anna Mental Health and Development Center in Anna, Illinois. During that time, he also maintained a strong affiliation with Southern Illinois University, which he continues as an adjunct professor at Southern Illinois's Rehabilitation Institute. Since 1980, Azrin has been at Nova Southeastern University as Professor of Psychology, and he served also as Clinical Director from 1981 to 1986. During his professional career, Azrin has been quite active in the editorship of journals. He served as executive editor (1963–6) of the main Skinnerian journal, the *Journal of the Experimental Analysis of Behavior*, and in 1966 he was a founder of the *Journal of Applied Behavior Analysis*. He has served on the editorial board of fifteen academic and applied journals.

Azrin's contributions are categorized into basic science and applied areas, and in both he has been notably successful and creative. His work on operant behaviour controlled by aversive stimuli and punishment was seminal and continues to be cited. Similarly, his applications of operant principles in the closed context of a token economy and in areas of behavioural therapy have been widely received and earned him a considerable following in the popular media as well. Azrin's work may be summarized in terms of its empirical foundation – namely, as results well founded in sophisticated experimental methodology.

Azrin's work, like that of Skinner, has drawn the criticism of those who take exception to the mechanical conception of human nature inherent to the model of behaviour. However, this view derives support from the basic positivism of the approach and the empirical referents of the findings. Azrin has thus been notably successful in bridging the academic and applied.

JAMES F. BRENNAN

B

Back, Kurt W.

Born: 1919, Vienna, Austria *Nat:* Austrian *Ints:* Adult development and ageing, history of psychology, personality and social, philosophical and theoretical psychology, population and environment *Educ:* BA New York University, 1940; MA University of California, Los Angeles, 1941; PhD Massachusetts Institute of Technology, 1949 *Appts & awards:* James B. Duke Professor of Sociology and Professor of Medical Sociology, Department of Psychiatry, Duke University; Helen J. Deroy Award, Society for Study of Social Problems, 1956 (with R. Hill and J.M. Stycos); Burgess Award of the National Council on Family Relations, 1961 (with R. Hill and J.M. Stycos); Editorial Boards, *Journal of Applied Behavioral Science*, 1965–7; *Journal of Experimental Social Psychology*, 1965–7, *American Journal of Sociology*, 1966–71, *Sociometry*, 1966–72, Council, Society for the Psychological Study of Social Issues, 1967–9; Rockefeller University, 1967–8; Special Research Fellow, NIH, St Johns College Cambridge, 1973–4; American Association for Public Opinion Research: Council, 1970–2, Chairman, Dissertation Award Committee, 1972–4; American Sociological Association: Fellow, Chairman, Methodology Section, 1972; Council, 1974–6; Chairman, *Psychology Today* Dissertation Award Committee, 1977–9; Fellow, AAAS, 1978, President, AAAS, Section K, 1979; Committee, Distinguished Contribution to Sociology, 1979–82; President, Sociological Research Association, 1981–2; Chairman, Social Psychology Section, 1986–7; Guest Editor, *Journal of Social Issues*, 30, 4 (with J. Fawcett); Contributing Editor, *Social Psychology*, *In Search of Community: Encounter Groups and Social Change*, *The Life Course: Integrative Theories and Model Populations*

Principal publications

1950 *Social Pressures in Informal Groups*. Harpers (with L. Festinger and S. Schachter).

1951 Influence through social communication. *Journal of Abnormal and Social Psychology*, 46, 9–23.

1959 *The Family and Population Control*. University of North Carolina Press (with R. Hill and J.M. Stycos).

1962 *Slums Projects and People*. Duke University Press.

1968 *The June Bug: A Study of Hysterical Contagion*. Appleton-Century-Crofts (with A.C. Kerckhoff).

1972 *Beyond Worlds: The Story of Sensitivity Training and the Encounter Movement*. Russell Sage Foundation.

1979 The small groups: Tightrope between sociology and personality. *Journal of Applied Behavioral Science*, 15, 283–94.

1980 The role of social psychology in population control. In L. Festinger (ed.), *Retrospections in Social Psychology*. Oxford University Press.

1981 Small groups. In M. Rosenberg and R. Turner (eds), *Sociological Perspectives on Social Psychology*. Basic Books.

1982 Clapham to Bloomsbury: Life course analysis of an intellectual aristocracy. *Biography*, 5, 39–51.

1982 Response effects of role-restricted respondent characteristics. In W. Dijkstra and J. Van der Zouwen (eds), *Response Behavior in the Survey Interview*. Academic Press (with T. Cross).

1983 Cohort analysis: Modal logic and possible worlds in life course analysis. *Interdisciplinary topics in Gerontology*, 17, 170–81.

1983 Teenage pregnancy: Science and ideology in applied social psychology. In R.F. Kidd and M.J. Saks (eds), *Advances in Applied Social Psychology*, vol. 2. Erlbaum.

1983 Compliance and conformity in an age of sincerity. In M. Rosenbaum (ed.) *Compliant Behavior*. Human Science Press.

1984 Psychology and sociology. In M.H Bornstein (ed.), *Psychology and its Allied Disciplines*, vol. 2. Erlbaum.

Further reading

Malatesta, C.Z. (1981) Affective development over the lifespan – involution or growth. *Merrill-Palmer Quarterly – Journal of Developmental Psychology*, 27, 145–73.

Pepitone, A. (1981) Lessons from the history of social psychology. *American Psychologist*, 36, 972–85.

Tziner, A. and Vardi, Y. (1982) Effects of command style and group cohesiveness on the performance effectiveness of self selected task crews. *Journal of Applied Psychology*, 67, 769–75.

Kurt Back's contributions have been in social psychology, where he has made theoretical, methodological and applied advances and also contributed to cultural analyses of social processes. His theoretical contributions stem from early work on group dynamics, specifically on cohesion and conformity, and this led to the formulation of a general scheme of conceptual expression of interpersonal variables, such as communication and the individual and community conditions, and especially the place of small groups. His methodological contributions stem from a perspective in which he considered research methods in social psychology as social occasions. For instance, interviewing is a social occasion requiring interactants to conduct themselves according to certain rules and roles, and this research technique can be considered as a communication problem. More generally he regarded the research process as a communications process, and he offered logical and mathematical methods to represent it and improve it. As an applied psychologist he integrated method and theory across a wide range of social issues including fertility control, housing, ageing, life-course analysis, encounter groups and studies of the self. He has also applied social psychology to the study of culture and to the study of itself as a cultural phenomenon, and thereby explored the ideological and philosophical basis of the social history of the current period.

Backman, Carl W.

Born: 1923, New York, USA **Nat:** American **Ints:** Adult development and ageing, personality and social psychology **Educ:** BA Oberlin College, 1948; MA Indiana University, 1950; PhD Indiana University, 1954 **Appts & awards:** Professor, Department of Sociology, University of Nevada; Editorial Board, *Sociometry*, 1968–70, *Journal of Applied Social Psychology*, 1970–82, *Journal for the Theory of Social Behaviour*, 1971– , *Sociological Quarterly*, 1973– , *Sociological Perspectives in Social Psychology*, 1978–80, *Annual Review of Social Psychology*, 1979– , *Journal of Social and Personal Relationships*, 1982– ; President, Pacific Sociology Association, 1969–70; Chairman, Executive Committee, Society of Experimental Social Psychology, 1970–1; Editor, *Sociometry*, 1970–3; Chairperson, Social Psychology Section, American Sociological Association, 1979–80

Principal publications

1956 Sampling mass media content: The use of the cluster design. *American Sociological Review*, 6, 730–1.

1961 Personality theory and the problem of stability and change in individual behavior: An interpersonal approach. *Psychological Review*, 68, 21–32 (with P.F. Secord).

1962 Liking, selective interaction and misperception in congruent interpersonal relations. *Sociometry*, 25, 321–35 (with P.F. Secord).

1963 Resistance to change in the self concept as a function of consensus among significant others. *Sociometry*, 20, 102–11 (with P.F. Secord and J.R. Peirce).

1964 *Social Psychology*. McGraw-Hill, 2nd edn 1974 (with P.F. Secord).

1965 An interpersonal approach to personality. In B. Maher (ed.), *Progress in Experimental Personality Research*, vol. 2. Academic Press.

1966 *Problems in Social Psychology*. McGraw-Hill (with P.F. Secord).

1968 *A Social Psychological View of Education*. Harcourt, Brace and World (with P.F. Secord).

1968 The self and role section. In C. Gordon and K. Gergen (eds), *The Self in Social Interaction*. Wiley (with P.F. Secord).

1976 *Understanding Social Life: An Introduction to Social Psychology*. McGraw-Hill (with P.F. Secord).

1976 Explorations in psycho-ethics: The warranting of judgements. In R. Harré (ed.), *Life Sentences: Aspects of the Social Role of Language*. Wiley.

1981 Attraction in interpersonal relationships. In R. Turner and M. Rosenberg (eds), *Sociological Perspectives on Social Psychology*. Basic Books.

1983 Towards an indisciplinary social psychology. In L. Berkowitz (ed.), *Advances in Social Psychology*, vol. 16. Academic Press.

1985 Identity, self-presentation and the resolution of moral dilemmas: Toward a social psychological theory of moral behavior. In B. Schenkler (ed.), *The Self and Social Life*. McGraw-Hill.

Further reading

Sirgy, M.J. (1987) Toward a general systems theory of social behavior – a psychocybernetic perspective. *Systems Research*, 4, 93–110.

Swann, W.B., Delaronde, C. and Hixon, J.G. (1994) Authenticity and positivity strivings in marriage and courtship. *Journal of Personality and Social Psychology*, 66, 857–69.

Taylor, M.C. and Johnson, M.D. (1986) Strategies for linking individual psychology and social structure – interdisciplinary and cross-disciplinary social psychology rejoinder. *British Journal of Social Psychology*, 25, 197–8.

In addition to co-authoring and co-editing (with P.F. **Secord**) a number of books widely used as text materials throughout the world, Backman has researched and written for the most part in three areas: interpersonal attraction and the development of relationships, self-theory, and moral judgement and behaviour. The first two topics are linked by a theory that views the development of identity and formation of relationships as interrelated processes. He argues that relationships and identities therein can be viewed as dialectical products of a variety of intrapersonal and interpersonal social psychological processes. His ideas and arguments influenced a considerable corpus of empirical and theoretical enquiry into many different kinds of interpersonal relationship. The third topic is guided by a theory of moral judgement and behaviour which specifies the conditions under which people are able to violate moral norms and at the same time maintain a favourable view of themselves. His approach links situational and personal variables to features of negotiated definitions of situations as they relate to goal achievement and self-esteem in circumstances involving moral choice. In addition to these contributions Backman has written on a number of issues of professional concern, particularly those that emerged during debates in the 1970s and 1980s about the methodological basis of social psychology.

Baddeley, Alan D.

Born: 1934, Leeds, England **Nat:** British **Ints:** Clinical neuropsychology, experimental psychology, general psychology **Educ:** BA University College London, 1956; MA Princeton, 1957; PhD Cambridge, 1963; BPS President's Award 1982 **Appts & awards:** Director, Medical Research Council, Applied Psychology Unit; Myers Lecturer, BPS, 1980; Member, British Neuropsychology Committee, ESRC Psychology Committee, MRC Neurosciences Board, Member 1981–5; MRC Neurosciences Board, Chairman, 1987–9;

President, Experimental Psychology Society, 1982–4; President, Experimental Psychology Society, 1984–6; President, European Society for Cognitive Psychology, 1986–90; Bartlett Lecturer, Experimental Psychological Society, 1988; Fellow, Royal Society, 1993; Editorial Board, *Applied Cognitive Psychology* (Special Editorial Advisor), *Cognition and Emotion, Cognitive Neuropsychiatry, Consciousness and Cognition: Essays in Cognitive Psychology (Erlbaum), European Journal of Cognitive Psychology, Learning and Individual Differences, Learning and Memory, Neuropsychological Rehabilitation, Psychological Review.*

Principal publications

1966 Short-term memory for word sequences as a function of acoustic, semantic and formal similarity. *Quarterly Journal of Experimental Psychology*, 18, 362–5.

1966 Influence of depth on the manual dexterity of free divers: A comparison between open sea and pressure chamber testing. *Journal of Applied Psychology*, 50, 81–5.

1970 Amnesia and the distinction between long- and short-term memory. *Journal of Verbal Learning and Verbal Behavior*, 9, 176–89 (with E.K. Warrington).

1974 Working memory. In G. Bower (ed.), *Recent Advances in Learning and Motivation*, vol. VIII. Academic Press (with G.J. Hitch).

1975 Word length and the structure of short-term memory. *Journal of Verbal Learning and Verbal Behavior*, 14, 575–89 (with N. Thomson and M. Buchanan).

1976 *The Psychology of Memory.* Basic Books.

1978 The trouble with levels: A re-examination of Craik and Lockhart's framework for memory research. *Psychological Review*, 85, 139–52.

1981 *Attention and Performance IX.* Erlbaum (with J.B. Long).

1981 The cognitive psychology of everyday life. *British Journal of Psychology*, 72, 257–69.

1982 *Your Memory: A User's Guide.* Sedgwick and Jackson, (Penguin, 1983).

1982 Implications of neuropsychological evidence for theories of normal memory. *Philosophical Transactions of the Royal Society, London B*, 298, 59–72.

1982 Domains of recollection. *Psychological Review*, 89, 708–29.

1983 Working memory. *Transactions of the Royal Society, London B*, 302, 311–24.

1986 *Working Memory.* Clarendon Press.

1990 *Human Memory: Theory and Practice.* Erlbaum.

1993 *Your Memory: A User's Guide*, 2nd edn.
Lifecycle Publications.
1993 *Working Memory and Language*. Erlbaum.

Further reading

Gibson, A.J. (1981) A further analysis of memory
loss in dementia and depression in the elderly.
British Journal of Clinical Psychology, 20,
179–85.
Johnson, J.C. (1981) Effects of advance precuring of
alternatives on the perception of letters alone and in
words. *Journal of Experimental Psychology,
Human Perception and Performance*, 7, 560–72.
Smith, S.L. (1981) Exploring compatability with
words and pictures. *Human Factors*, 23, 305–15.
Wetherell, A. (1981) The efficacy of some auditory
vocal subsidiary tasks as measures of the mental
load on male and female drivers. *Ergonomics*, 24,
197–214.

Alan Baddeley began his research career in
Princeton working on a cognitive approach to
secondary reinforcement in rats. On returning to
Britain he joined the Applied Psychology Unit
financed by the Post Office, which at the time
was interested in the design of postal codes, and
this led to an interest in human memory and in
the application of psychology outside the laboratory. While a graduate student, he became
interested in diving and was intrigued by the
problems of measuring diver performance in the
open sea; he continues to work in this area. An
interest in short-term and working memory came
from a project where he tried, unsuccessfully, to
develop ways of evaluating the quality of telephone lines. In one study he used immediate
memory for similar and dissimilar words, and
was struck by the robustness of the phonological
similarity effect. He discovered that similarity of
meaning had a much less powerful effect than
phonological similarity in immediate memory,
while for long-term learning exactly the opposite
occurred, with phonological similarity being
unimportant and semantic similarity dominant.
This result led him to regard memory as having
separate long-term (LTM) and short-term (STM)
components. A similar conclusion came from
collaborative work with Elizabeth Warrington on
amnesic patients, who appeared to have normal
performance on STM tasks, but grossly impaired
LTM.

During the 1970s the dichotomous view
became unpopular, being replaced by the 'levels
of processing' interpretation of memory in terms
of depth of encoding. While regarding this as a
useful reconceptualization of earlier findings on

the role of coding in memory, Baddeley's approach was to accept the limitations of the earlier
concept of STM, and to elaborate it into a multi-
component model of working memory. The
model has proved both robust and fruitful,
being applied to a range of situations from the
analysis of adult reading to the breakdown of
memory in aphasic patients, and from the
development of memory in children to the
memory deficit of patients suffering from senile
dementia. The model works well, since it allows
continuous theoretical development based on
empirical research, and offers a sufficiently
broad and robust model to be applicable to a
wide range of real-world problems.

Bain, Alexander

Born: 1818, Aberdeen, Scotland ***Died:*** 1903,
Aberdeen, Scotland ***Nat:*** British ***Ints:*** General
psychology ***Educ:*** MA University of Aberdeen,
1840 ***Appts & awards:*** Gray Mathematical
Bursary, Marischal College, 1839; Assistant in
Moral Philosophy, University of Aberdeen,
1841–4; Professor of Mathematics and Natural
Philosophy, Andersonian University of Glas-
gow, 1845–6; Lecturer in Mental and Moral
Philosophy, Bedford College, London, 1851–4;
Professor of Logic and Rhetoric, University of
Aberdeen, 1860–80; Honorary Doctorate of
Laws, University of Edinburgh, 1871; Rector,
University of Aberdeen, 1881–4, 1884–7

Principal publications

1855 *The Senses and the Intellect*. Parker.
1859 *The Emotions and the Will*. Parker.
1861 *The Study of Character*. Parker.
1868 *Mental and Moral Science*. Longmans Green.
1872 *Mind and Body: The Theories of their
Relation*. King.
1879 *Education as a Science*. Kegan Paul.
1879 *Logic*. Longmans.
1903 *Dissertations on Leading Philosophical
Topics*. Longmans.

Further reading

Bain, A. (1904) *Autobiography*. Longmans.
Boyle, D.G. (1993) *Psychology – the Aberdeen
Connection*. University of Aberdeen.
Cardno, J.A. (1955) Bain and physiological
psychology. *Australian Journal of Psychology*, 7,
108–20.
—— (1956) Bain as a social psychologist. *Australian
Journal of Psychology*, 8, 66–76.
Davidson, W.L. (1904) Professor Bain. *Mind*, 13,
151–5.

—— (1910) Alexander Bain. In H. Chisholm (ed.), *Encyclopaedia Brittanica*, 11th edn, vol. 3, 221–2.

Fisch, M.H. (1954) Alexander Bain and the genealogy of pragmatism. *Journal of the History of Ideas*, 15, 413–44.

Greenway, A.P. (1973) The incorporation of action into associationism: The psychology of Alexander Bain. *Journal of the History of the Behavioural Sciences*, 9, 42–52.

Habu, Y. (1995) Alexander Bain as an integrator of ideas in modern psychology. Paper presented at the conference on Aberdeen in the History of Psychology, University of Aberdeen.

Knight, R. (1956) A Bain centenary. *Aberdeen University Review*, 36, 160–3.

Still, A. (1995) Alexander Bain and the evolution of trial and error: a missed opportunity in the history of psychology? Paper presented at the conference on Aberdeen in the History of Psychology, University of Aberdeen.

Alexander Bain was born in and associated for much of his life with Aberdeen. His father was a weaver of Calvinist persuasion. Bain had a hard youth, leaving school at 11. He attended evening classes at the Mechanics Institute but was largely self-taught. In 1836 he entered Marischal College, where he studied classics, mathematics, science and philosophy. He was awarded a bursary and graduated joint top in 1840.

His agnosticism made it difficult for him to get a job. He found employment in London, as an Assistant Secretary at the Board of Health. Here he became acquainted with J.S. Mill (whom he helped to edit Mill's father's work), George Grote, G.H. Lewes, Thomas Carlyle, Herbert Spencer and Charles **Darwin** and contributed articles to the *Westminster Review*. In Paris, he met Comte and **Ribot**, and, in Leipzig, **Wundt**, **Cattell**, **Ebbinghaus** and **Helmholtz**. From 1851 to 1854 he lectured on psychology and geography at Bedford College, London. Finally in 1860, when King's and Marischal Colleges formed a united University of Aberdeen, he obtained the newly created Chair of Logic, which involved teaching grammar, composition and rhetoric as well as mental and moral philosophy.

In 1876, he founded the journal *Mind*, undertaking the publishing risks, serving as its proprietor for sixteen years. It was the first journal to publish psychological articles and played an important role in establishing psychology as a profession. Following his retirement in 1880, he was active in university and public life.

He was twice elected Rector of the University of Aberdeen, on the second occasion defeating Lord Randolph Churchill. He lectured on education all over Britain, campaigned for curriculum reform, and was a staunch supporter of the local Mechanics Institute and free public libraries.

Bain wrote on topics as diverse as electricity, astronomy, meteorology, travel, wit, toys and cruelty to animals, but his major works were *The Senses and the Intellect* and *The Emotions and the Will*, later combined into a single volume. This is generally regarded as the first systematic, properly psychological text, and became the standard authority for half a century. The scope of psychology was more clearly defined than previously and the treatment comprehensive. The discussion of habit formed the basis of **James**'s famous chapter on the topic. The text contained a wealth of careful observations (e.g. of a suckling infant and movements of day-old lambs) and detailed analysis (ranging from that of coughing and sneezing to artistic creation and scientific discovery). Bain's observation that pungency can diminish odour has recently been experimentally confirmed and extended.

Bain is in many ways a transitional figure, representing the culmination of the empiricist-associationist tradition on the one hand, yet anticipating many ideas which proved seminal. His writings did much to establish psychology as a positive observational science, the requirements of scientific method being better understood. (Spalding, on hearing him lecture, was inspired to carry out experiments on instinctive behaviour.) In part this was because Bain stressed the importance of physiological foundations for psychology. His textbooks contained a thorough treatment of the nervous system. Bain had attended Sharpey's lectures at University College London. His claim that 'For every act of memory, every exercise of bodily aptitude, every habit, recollection, train of ideas, there is a specific grouping, or co-ordination of sensations and movements, by virtue of specific growths in the cell junctions' has a peculiarly modern ring.

Bain set out to maintain and elaborate the doctrine of association of ideas but in the process quite transformed it. He held two principles of association: continuity and resemblance, but association was not considered a complete explanation. The most fundamental property of the intellect was discrimination; primitive, innate responses were allowed; feelings and the will were thought to play a part in determining the passage of ideas in our minds; and motivation was not restricted to pursuit of pleasure and avoidance of pain.

Probably Bain's most important contribution was the stress he placed on movement and activity. The nervous system was credited with spontaneous, inherent activity, thus enabling action rather than reaction. Bain was particularly interested in the development of voluntary behaviour and the way in which the infant's undifferentiated movements led to the development of connections between feelings, sensations and actions. He applied the concept of feedback (found in a mathematics textbook) to psychology. These ideas were greatly influential in **Dewey**'s subsequent treatment of the reflex arc, **Baldwin**'s circular reaction and **Piaget**'s genetic psychology. Taine and **Binet** developed the idea of the intellect as active and autonomous, incorporating motor elements into perceptual representations. Binet transformed Bain's motor associations into motor images, and also based a work on the relation between mind and brain on Bain's treatment of the topic, in which he had introduced the theory of psychophysical parallelism.

The effects of action were also considered criterial of belief, defined as 'that upon which a man is prepared to act' (the evolutionary flavour is not without significance). This was subsequently developed by **Peirce** and **James** into the doctrine of pragmatism, described by Peirce as 'scarce more than a corollary' to Bain's theory.

Bain introduced the term 'trial and error' but in the context of voluntary control over spontaneous action as opposed to behaviour based on prior knowledge and practised skill. His usage of the term was much more flexible than in the subsequent polarization between rational and random processes, where it became identified exclusively with the latter. He was the first to formulate what became the law of effect, influencing Lloyd **Morgan** and thence **Thorndike** and the tradition of American learning theory. His distinction between molar and molecular, introduced in a lecture at the Royal Institution in 1867, was taken up by Spencer.

Bain also anticipated the modern treatment of social-psychological questions, dealing not only with will, belief, conscience and sympathy, but also with interpersonal behaviour, social norms and the relation of psychology to ethics. He helped to advance the reference of the discussion from a moral faculty to social norms. He was also interested in social influences and applied psychology, and anticipated developments in occupational psychology, aptitude testing, and training in industry, sport and the military.

Bain played a formative role in establishing psychology as a scientific discipline and profession, as well as being the originator of many seminal ideas, often unrecognized, perhaps because he failed to realize their significance or to develop them. He was eclipsed by William James, who wrote so much more engagingly, by C.S. Peirce and by Charles Darwin. Even James Mill's work on logic and Herbert Spencer's on evolutionary psychology are more likely to be remembered. Though Bain was an astute psychologist with a powerful analytical mind, his writing is ponderous, verbose and lengthy. Nevertheless, Anglo-American psychology owes him an enormous dept. One cannot help marvel at the breadth of his contribution. Current psychology might benefit by reflecting on his integration, incorporating elements of associationist and act psychology, behaviourist and cognitive psychology.

E.R. VALENTINE

Baldwin, James Mark

Born: 1861, Columbia, South Carolina, USA **Died:** 1934, Paris, France **Nat:** American **Ints:** Developmental psychology, educational psychology, history, personality and social, philosophical and theoretical psychology **Educ:** BA Princeton University, 1884; MA Princeton University, 1887; PhD Princeton University, 1889; Hon. DSc University of Oxford, 1900; Hon. DSc University of Geneva, 1909; Hon. LLD University of Glasgow, 1901; Hon. LLD South Carolina College, 1905 **Appts & awards:** Instructor in French and German, Princeton University, 1886–7; Professor of Philosophy, Lake Forest University, 1887–9; Professor of Logic and Metaphysics, Toronto University, 1889–93; Professor of Psychology, Princeton University, 1893–1903; President American Psychological Association, 1897; Professor of Philosophy and Psychology, Johns Hopkins University, 1903–9; Advisor, National University of Mexico, 1909–13; Professor, L'École des Hautes Études Sociales, Paris, 1919

Principal publications

1895 *Mental Development in the Child and the Race*. Macmillan.
1897 *Social and Ethical Interpretations in Mental Development*. Macmillan.

1889–91   *Handbook of Psychology*, vols 1 and 2. Holt.
1901–6   (ed.) *Dictionary of Philosophy and Psychology*, vols 1–4. Macmillan.
1902   *Development and Evolution*. Macmillan.
1906–11   *Thought and Things or Genetic Logic*, vols 1–3. Macmillan.
1913   *History of Psychology*, vols 1 and 2. Watts.
1915   *Genetic Theory of Reality*. Plenum.

Further reading
Baldwin, J.M. (1926) *Between Two Wars, 1861–1921*, vols 1, 2. Stratford.
—— (1930) James Mark Baldwin. In C. Murchison (ed.), *A History of Psychology in Autobiography*, vol. 1. Clark University Press.
Russell J. (1978) *The Acquisition of Knowledge*. Macmillan.

Baldwin represents the rather interesting case of a researcher whose early career neatly tracked the empirical path that American psychology took during the years bridging the nineteenth and twentieth centuries, but who then seemed to revert to the more philosophical interests and approaches of an earlier time. He gained an early reputation as a peripatetic laboratory builder, founding the experimental psychology laboratories in Toronto (1889), Princeton (1893) and Johns Hopkins (1903), and also as an experimentalist with work on reaction time 'types' and visual illusions, topics which were then representative of the everyday output of the typical psychological laboratory. He had also published translations, introductions and surveys on the new empirical psychology, including its sensory and experimental bases and its history.

However, in 1903, and apparently echoing the despair of William **James** at the seeming inability of any laboratory to tackle really serious psychological questions, Baldwin's adherence to the empirical enterprise appeared to wane in favour of a more philosophical and sociological approach to psychology. Even during his apparently more conventional period, in fact, Baldwin was exploring areas of psychology and approaches to it which were actually far from conventional. Thus we see that his important and challenging writings on child development and social psychology predate 1903, while much of his work on what is now termed 'genetic epistemology' overlaps his last years in Princeton and then at Johns Hopkins. Baldwin was essentially a philosopher for whom the new and vigorous form of empirical

psychology seemed to offer a promising way forward, both for philosophy and psychology. Alas, that was not to be, and his abrupt departure from the American academic scene in 1909 pretty well marks the end of his creative involvement with American psychology.

What exactly were Baldwin's views on psychology? Although many commentators have assumed that he was a developmental psychologist as that is understood today, he was really moved only by deeper philosophical issues, particularly ones concerned with the relationship between the acquisition and form of knowledge. This lead him to an epistemology which mixed individual development with nineteenth-century evolutionary concepts. The main thrust of this work is captured by Baldwin's notion of the 'circular reaction', which posits a continuously adapting and reciprocal interaction between the organism and its environment. From this, Baldwin evolved a form of developmental social psychology even more radical than that adopted by near contemporaries such as G.H. **Mead** and Cooley: 'the individual is a social outcome not a social unit'. Thus, epistemology was described as a 'social heritage' and thinking as a selective process drawing on such a socially defined knowledge base. Perhaps the most ambitious exploitation of this notion is to be found in his last major work, published between 1906 and 1915, which modestly attempts to recast logic and rhetoric in psychogenetic terms.

Baldwin became a neglected figure in psychology long before his death in 1934. However, the discipline's recent unease over its conceptual and philosophical foundations has returned his ideas to the centre stage.

A.D. LOVIE AND PATRICIA LOVIE

Bales, Robert Freed
Born: 1916, Ellington, Missouri, USA *Nat:* American *Ints:* Evaluation and measurement, family psychology, industrial and organizational psychology, personality and social psychology, psychotherapy *Educ:* BA University of Oregon, 1938; MS 1941; MA Harvard University, 1943; PhD, 1945 *Appts & awards:* Research Associate, Yale University, 1944–5; Harvard University, Department of Sociology, 1945–7, Department of Psychology and Social Relations, 1947–57, Professor of Social Relations, 1957–86, Emeritus Professor, 1986– ; Affiliate, Boston Psychoanalytic Society and Institute, 1956; President, Eastern Sociological Society, 1962–3;

Distinguished Career Award, American Association of Specialists in Group Work, 1982; Cooley–Mead Award, American Sociological Association, Social Psychology Section, 1983; APF Award for Distinguished Teaching of Group Processes, 1984; Member AAAS; Fellow, APA; ASA

Principal publications

1950 *Interaction Process Analysis: A Method for the Study of Small Groups.* Addison-Wesley (University of Chicago Press, 1976).

1951 Phases in group problem solving. *Journal of Abnormal and Social Psychology*, 46, 485–95 (with F.L. Strodtbeck).

1953 *Working Papers in the Theory of Action.* Free Press (ed. with T. Parsons and E.A. Shils).

1955 Role differentiation in small decision-making groups. In R.F. Bales, S.P. and S.A. Williamson (eds), *The Family, Socialization and Interaction Process.* Free Press (with P.E. Slater).

1965 The equilibrium problem in small groups. In A.P. Hare, E.F. Borgetta and R.F. Bales (eds), *Small Groups: Studies in Social Interaction.* Knopf.

1970 *Personality and Interpersonal Behavior.* Holt, Rinehart and Winston.

1979 *SYMLOG: A System for the Multiple Level Observation of Groups.* Free Press (with S.P. Cohen).

1980 *SYMLOG. Case Study Kit: With Instructions for a Group Self Study.* Free Press.

1984 The integration of social psychology. *Social Psychology Quarterly*, 47, 98–101.

1985 The new field theory in social psychology. *International Journal of Small Group Research*, 1, 1–18.

Further reading

Polley, R. B., Hare, P.A. and Stone, P.J. (1988) *The SYMLOG Practitioner: Applications of Small Group Research.* Praeger.

Srodbeck, F.L., (1984) Cooley–Mead award 1983: Robert F. Bales *Social Psychology Quarterly*, 47, 1, 95–101.

Following his introduction to social psychology at the University of Oregan, Bales entered Harvard with the conviction that the observation of interaction in small groups was the best way to untangle the semantic problems he encountered as an undergraduate student. Gradually he developed Interaction Process Analysis (IPA), which was the first practical observational system developed intentionally for general theoretical purposes. As Strodbeck notes: 'His system was a meld of role theory, phenomenology and problem solving all enmeshed … in a social system perspective'. Using this coding system, Bales and his co-workers made a number of discoveries which are now the taken-for-granted foundations of group research. His findings included evidence of: a typical role differentiation between task leaders and social leaders; typical gradients of amount of interaction between members arranged in an 'interaction matrix'; and a tendency under optimum conditions for a pattern of phases in group problem solving to appear within a single meeting, and a pattern of developmental phases to appear over a series of meetings.

Early in his career, Bales had inherited a course for undergraduate students at Harvard in human relations devoted to 'case discussion'. He transformed it, over many years, into what he called an 'academic self-analytic group', which by the mid-1980s had become a computer-based laboratory course in 'group psychology'. The growth of this course reflected changes in Bales's concepts and practice of leadership, teaching and therapy and the development of a more holistic approach to group behaviour known as SYMLOG (systematic multiple level observation of groups). This computerized system involved taking account of attitudes and values, and of participants' definitions of situations as well as that of the researcher. It has generated a new series of hypotheses and methods of application, which have been widely tested in the real world. SYMLOG has applications in multiple settings (e.g. industrial management, classroom management, social work, international relations and psychotherapy) and across cultures.

Both IPA and SYMLOG benefit from easily grasped graphical representations of group relationships, which have been widely adopted as methods for assessing and communicating group functioning. SYMLOG is a powerful conceptual and methodological tool, which enables the trained practitioner to understand the dynamics of group processes. Bales considered that social psychologists must do more of their work in complex, real-life situations, and his work continues to be most influential in these settings.

KAREN TREW

Baltes, Paul B.

Born: 1939, Saarlouis, Germany *Nat:* German *Educ:* Diploma University of Saarbrucken,

1963; PhD, 1967; Hon. PhD University of
Jvyäskylä, Finland, 1990 **Appts & awards:**
Senior Scientist, Max Planck Institute for
Human Development and Education; Profes-
sor, Free University of Berlin, 1981– ;
President, APA Division 20; Fellow, APA,
American Psychological Society, Gerontologi-
cal Society of America, German Society for
Psychology; Cattell Award, 1975; Gerontologi-
cal Book Foundation Prize, 1987; APA
Distinguished Scientific Contribution to Psy-
chology Award, 1990; Gerontological Society
of America, Distinguished Mentorship Award,
1990

Principal publications

1977 *Life-span Developmental Psychology:
Introduction to Research Methods.* Erlbaum (with
H.W. Reese and J.R. Nesselroade).

1990 Interpreting correlations between children's
perceived control and cognitive performance:
Control, agency, or means–ends beliefs?
Developmental Psychology, 26, 246–53 (with M.
Chapman and E.A. Skinner).

1990 Wisdom-related knowledge: Age/cohort
differences in response to life-planning problems.
Developmental Psychology, 26, 494–505 (with J.
Smith).

1990 On the locus and process of magnification of
age differences during mnemonic training. Special
section: Cognitive training in later adulthood.
Developmental Psychology, 26, 894–904 (with R.
Kliegl and J. Smith).

1990 *Successful Aging: Perspectives from the
Behavioral Sciences.* Cambridge University Press.
(ed. with M.M. Baltes).

1991 Perceived controllability of expected
psychological change across adulthood and old age.
Journal of Gerontology, 46, 165–73 (with J.
Heckhausen).

1991 The many faces of human ageing: Toward a
psychological culture of old age. *Psychological
Medicine,* 21, 837–54.

1992 Further testing of limits of cognitive plasticity:
Negative age differences in a mnemonic skill are
robust. *Developmental Psychology,* 28, 121–5
(with R. Kliegl).

1993 The aging mind: Potential and limits.
Gerontologist, 33, 580–94.

1993 Resilience and levels of reserve capacity in
later adulthood: Perspectives from life-span
theory. Special issue: Milestones in the
development of resilience. *Development and
Psychopathology,* 5, 541–66 (with U.M.
Staudinger and M. Marsiske).

1994 Sensory functioning and intelligence in old

age: A strong connection. *Psychology and Aging,*
9, 339–55.

1995 Agency, control, and means–ends beliefs
about school performance in Moscow children:
How similar are they to beliefs of Western
children? *Developmental Psychology,* 31, 285–99
(with A. Stetsenko, T.D. Little and G. Oettingen).

Further reading

Berg, C.A. (1990) What is intellectual efficiency over
the life course? Using adults' conceptions to
address the question. In J. Rodin, C. Schooler and
K.W. Schaie (eds), *Self Directedness.* Erlbaum.

Raykov, T. (1989) Reserve capacity of the elderly in
aging sensitive tests of fluid intelligence: A
reanalysis via a structural equation modelling
approach. *Zeitschrift für Psychologie,* 197, 263–.

Sternberg, R.J. (1990) *Encyclopedia of Human
Intelligence.* Macmillan.

While an undergraduate at the University of
Saarbrucken Paul Baltes spent a year (1963–4)
as an exchange student at the University of
Nebraska. After completing his PhD he spent
four years (1968–72) at West Virginia University. From 1972 to 1974 he was Associate
Professor at Pennsylvania State University,
Director of Individual and Family Studies
(1972–8) and Professor of Human Development (1974–80). In 1980 he was appointed to
the staff of the Max-Planck Institute.

Baltes is known principally for his work on
life-span development, particularly intellectual
development, and his approach places particular
emphasis on: the multidirectionality in ontogenetic change; the importance of both age-
dependent and age-independent developmental
factors; the dynamic and continuous interplay
between growth and decline; the role of historical and other contextual factors; the plasticity of
developmental processes; and the idea that every
developmental process involves a gain as well
as a loss of adaptive capacity. In his work on
wisdom he developed a research framework in
which wisdom is considered as expert knowledge about fundamental life matters. The
criteria for defining wisdom are: rich factual
and procedural knowledge; life-span contextualism; relativism; and the recognition and
management of uncertainty. Baltes draws a
distinction between the mechanics (memory)
and the cognitive pragmatics (wisdom) of mind
and uses this to illustrate a profound dynamic
associated with biological and cultural streams
of inheritance. In drawing this distinction he
extends the theory of fluid and crystallized

intelligence developed by R.B. **Cattell** and colleagues. Fluid intelligence reflects an individual's ability to solve novel problems, whereas crystallized intelligence reflects the acquisition and use of culturally valued knowledge. Baltes links 'fluid' intelligence to the evolutionarily guided neurophysiological architecture of the mind, and 'crystallized' pragmatic cognition to culturally mediated cognition. In terms of cognitive mechanics, people are guided by genetically driven evolution and generally suffer a decline with age. However, cognitive pragmatics is culturally driven and a decline does not necessarily have to occur. He argues that the potential for future enhancement of the ageing mind is considerable despite the biological limits, because old age is culturally young (i.e. it is only during the last century that people have reached old age). Thus, there has not been much opportunity for the development and refinement of a culture for and of old age. He suggests that such a culture has the potential to compensate for biological decline.

Bandura, Albert

Born: 1925, Mundare, Alberta, Canada **Nat:** Canadian **Ints:** Developmental psychology, experimental psychology, personality and social **Educ:** BA University of British Columbia, 1949; MA University of Iowa, 1951; PhD University of Iowa, 1952 **Appts & Awards:** David Starr Jordan Professor of Social Science in Psychology, Stanford University, Stanford, 1953– ; Editorial Board, *Behaviour Research and Therapy*, 1963, *Behaviour Therapy*, 1970–3, *Child Development*, 1971–7, *Journal of Abnormal Psychology*, 1973, *Journal of Mental Imagery*, 1978, *Psychological Review*, 1980–2, *Journal of Personality and Social Psychology*, 1963–77, *Journal of Experimental Social Psychology*, 1967–77, *Journal of Experimental Child Psychology*, 1967–82, *Journal of Applied Behavior Analysis*, 1968–72, 1975–8, 1980–1, *Journal of Behavior Therapy and Experimental Psychiatry*, 1970, *Aggression: An International Interdisciplinary Journal*, 1974–82, *Cognitive Therapy and Research*, 1977–9, 1982, *Review of Personality and Social Psychology*, 1979, *Anxiety, Stress and Coping*, 1988– , *Social Behavior and Personality: An International Journal*, 1992– ; Guggenheim Fellow, 1972; Fellow, American Academy of Arts and Sciences; Distinguished Scientific Achievement Award, CPA, 1973;

President, APA, 1974, WPA, 1980; Hon. Dr. University of British Columbia, 1979, Distinguished Contribution Award, International Society for Research on Aggression, 1980; Distinguished Scientific Contributions Award, 1980; University of Lethbridge, 1983; University of New Brunswick, 1985; William James Award, American Psychological Society 1989; Member, Institute of Medicine of the National Academy of Sciences, 1989

Principal publications

1959 *Adolescent Aggression*. Ronald Press (with R.H. Walters).

1962 Social learning through imitation. In M.R. Jones (ed.), *Nebraska Symposium on Motivation*. University of Nebraska Press.

1963 *Social Learning and Personality Development*. Holt, Rinehart and Winston (with R.H. Walters)

1969 *Principles of Behavior Modification*. Holt, Rinehart and Winston.

1971 *Psychological Modeling: Conflicting Theories*. Aldine-Atherton Press.

1973 *Aggression: A Social Learning Analysis*. Prentice-Hall.

1974 Behavior theory and the models of man. *American Psychologist*, 29, 859–869.

1977 *Social Learning Theory*. Prentice-Hall.

1977 Self efficacy: Toward a unifying theory of behavioral change. *Psychological Review*, 84, 91–215.

1978 Psychological modeling: Theory and practice. In, S.L. Garfield and A.E Bergin (eds), *Handbook of Psychotherapy and Behavior Change*, 2nd edn. Wiley (with T.L. Rosenthal).

1979 Psychological mechanisms of aggression. In M. von Cranach, K. Foppa, W. LaPenies and D. Ploog (eds), *Human Ethology: Claims and Limits of a New Discipline*. Cambridge University Press.

1981 Self-referent thought: A developmental analysis of self-efficacy. In J.H. Flavell and L. Ross (eds), *Social Cognitive Development: Frontiers and Possible Futures*. cambridge University Press.

1982 The self and mechanisms of agency. In J. Suls (ed.), *Psychological perspectives on the Self*. Erlbaum.

1986 *Social Foundations of Thought and Action: A Social Cognitive Theory*. Prentice-Hall.

1995 *Self-Efficacy in Changing Societies*. Cambridge University Press.

1995 *Self-Efficacy: The Exercise of Control*. Freeman.

Further reading

Hall, C.S. and Lindzey, C. (1957) *Theories of Personality*. Wiley.

Albert Bandura grew up in Mundare, Northern Alberta, Canada. He spent his elementary and high-school years in the village's one and only school. At the University of Iowa he studied with Kenneth **Spence** (an associate of Clark **Hull**) and earned a doctorate in clinical psychology. In 1952 he moved to Wichita, Kansas, to a one-year internship at the Wichita Guidance Center. He then moved to Stanford University.

At the start of his career, Bandura focused on learning. Most of the research at that time was concerned with learning as a consequence of direct experience. It was widely assumed that learning could only occur through performing responses and experiencing their effects. Bandura felt that this line of theorizing was at odds with informal evidence that virtually all learning phenomena resulting from direct experience occur on a vicarious basis through observing other people's behaviour and its consequences for them. This interest led to a programme of research on the determinants and mechanisms of observational learning and abstract modelling of rule-governed behaviour. With the enormous advances in the technology of communication through the century, the symbolic environment is playing an increasingly powerful role in shaping human thought, attitudes and styles of behaviour, and Bandura's work has considerable relevance to contemporary developments. He gave special attention to the paramount role of symbolic modelling in the social diffusion of new behaviour patterns and social practice.

Another major line of interest for Bandura is designed to clarify the different mechanisms of personal agency. This work is concerned with how people exercise control over their own motivation and behaviour and over their environment. The focus of some of this research is on how human behaviour is motivated and regulated by internal standards and anticipatory self-evaluative reactions. Among the mechanisms of personal agency, none is more central or pervasive than people's perceived efficacy to exert control over different aspects of their lives.

His studies of familial causes of aggression with his first graduate student, Richard Walters, promoted an increasing emphasis on the central role of modelling influences in personality development. Like Walter **Mischel**, he has developed a social cognitive theory which considers the person as an active agent using cognitive processes to represent experiences of the world and to make decisions and plan behaviour. This contrasts with views in which the person is considered as a more or less passive respondent to environmental circumstances or a victim of unconscious drives. Bandura argues that behaviour can be explained in terms of an interaction between the person and the environment, a position he calls 'reciprocal determinism'. The person both is responsive to environmental conditions and actively constructs and influences situations. Social cognitive theory sees the adaptively functioning person as a well-tuned organism capable of adapting the environment and of changing parts of the environment to suit himself or herself. Social cognitive theory sees the self not as a fixed structure but as a set of cognitive processes. In other words the person does not have a structure called the 'self' but self-processes that are part of the person. Self-efficacy, or the perceived ability to cope with specific situations, occupies a central position in Bandura's thinking. People's perceptions of what they are capable of influence behaviour in many ways. For example, they affect which activities people will tend to engage in, how much effort they will expend, how long they will persist when faced with obstacles, how they solve problems, and their emotional reactions. Bandura considers behaviour to be essentially goal-directed activity. Goals are fundamental in the ways people attempt to anticipate the future.

Barber, Theodore Xenophon
Born: 1927, Martins Ferry, Ohio, USA ***Nat:*** American ***Ints:*** General psychology, hypnosis, personality, physiological and comparative psychology, psychotherapy, social psychology ***Educ:*** BA American University, Washington DC, 1954; PhD American University, Washington DC, 1956 ***Appts & awards:*** Senior Research Associate, 1959–68, Director of Psychological Research, 1968–78, Medfield Foundation, Medfield; President, APA Division 30, 1972–3; President, Massachusetts Psychological Association, 1974–5

Principal publications
1961 Antisocial and criminal acts induced by 'hypnosis': A review of clinical and experimental findings. *Archives of General Psychiatry*, 5, 301–12.
1965 Experimental analysis of 'hypnotic' behavior: A review of recent empirical findings. *Journal of Abnormal Psychology*, 70, 132–54.
1969 *Hypnosis: A Scientific Approach*. Van Nostrand Reinhold (Jason Aronson, 1995).
1970 *LSD, Marihuana, Yoga and Hypnosis*. Aldine.

1973 Experimental hypnosis. In B.B. Wolman (ed.), *Handbook of General Psychology*. Prentice-Hall.

1974 *Hypnosis, Imagination, and Human Potentialities*. Pergamon.

1983 The fantasy-prone personality: Implications for understanding imagery, hypnosis, and parapsychological phenomena. In A.A. Sheikh (ed.), *Imagery: Current Theory, Research, and Applications*. Wiley.

1984 Changing 'unchangeable' bodily processes by (hypnotic) suggestions: A new look at hypnosis, cognitions, imagining, and the mind–body problem. In A.A. Sheikh (ed.), *Imagination and Healing*. Baywood.

1985 Hypnosuggestive procedures as catalysts for all psychotherapies, In S.J. Lynn, and J.P. Garske (eds), *Contemporary Psychotherapies*. Charles E. Merrill.

1993 Hypnosuggestive approaches to stress reduction. In P.M. Lehree and R.L. Woolfolk (eds), *Principles and Practice of Stress Management*, 2nd edn. Guilford Press.

Further reading

Dienstfrey, H. (1991) *Where the Mind Meets the Body*. HarperCollins.

Gauld, A. (1992) *A History of Hypnotism*. Cambridge University Press.

Sheehan, P.W. and Perry, C.W. (1976) *Methodologies of Hypnosis*. Erlbaum.

Theodore X. Barber grew up in Ohio and received both his bachelor and doctoral degrees at American University in Washington DC. As an undergraduate in biology, with a special interest in physiology, and then as a graduate student in psychology, 'Ted' Barber felt that hypnosis was an important but neglected topic. He became deeply interested in questions such as: 'How is it possible by hypnosis to produce blisters, remove warts, and induce hallucinations, anaesthesia and amnesia?' After three years as a post-doc at Harvard University, he joined the Medfield Foundation, where he conducted intensive research on hypnosis. In the 1950s, when Barber began his ground-breaking research, it was generally assumed that hypnosis produces a unique, trance state of consciousness.

Barber's hypnosis research was in two distinct stages. In stage 1, research with hypnotic and non-hypnotic, 'task-motivated' participants suggested that hypnotic induction procedures are unnecessary for the production of hypnotic phenomena and that the concepts of 'trance' and 'hypnosis' are misleading, since the phenomena

can be explained by known psychological principles. The person who responded well to the hypnotist's suggestions was motivated to respond and had positive attitudes and expectancies towards the hypnotic situation. Hypnotic behaviour across a diverse range of effects, including amnesia, age regression, deafness, enhancement of recall, visual and auditory hallucination and pain reduction, could all be understood in ordinary cognitive and social terms such as 'thinking' and 'imagining'. Barber's ideas led to the cognitive behavioural approach to hypnosis, an approach which is linked historically with a similar movement in psychotherapy led by Albert **Bandura**.

In the 1970s Barber's interests shifted towards behavioural medicine and biofeedback: he edited an influential book series. In the 1980s his hypnosis research took a new turn and entered stage 2 with the description of what he and Sheryl Wilson called the 'fantasy-prone' person, a seemingly well-adjusted individual reporting a lifelong history of profound imaginative involvement, including paranormal, creative and transformative imaginative experience. In this light, more extreme forms of dissociative experience such as multiple personality disorder can be seen as creations of fantasy while the sufferer is under the influence of auto-suggestion and/or a self-deceiving hypnotherapist.

Barber's new ways of thinking about hypnosis transformed the field. Thus 'ordinary' cognitive and social processes were found to be capable of some highly significant and interesting psychological phenomena when associated with both suggestion and high fantasy-proneness. Largely because of Barber's work, the boundary between trance and non-trance theories of hypnosis initially strengthened but then disappeared, leaving the field in a more advanced state.

DAVID F. MARKS

Bardon, Jack Irving

Born: 1925, Cleveland, Ohio, USA **Died:** 1993, Greensboro, North Carolina, USA **Nat:** American **Ints:** Community and counseling, consulting, educational, school **Educ:** BA Western Reserve University, Ohio, 1949; MA University of Pennsylvania, Philadelphia, 1951; PhD University of Pennsylvania, Philadelphia, 1956 **Appts & awards:** School Psychologist, Princeton Borough, New Jersey, 1952–60; Director, Doctoral Programme in School

Psychology, Rutgers University, 1960–8; APA Council of Representatives, 1966–70, 1974–7; Excellence Foundation Professor of Education and Psychology, School of Education, University of North Carolina at Greensboro, 1969–76; APA Division 16 Distinguished Service Award, 1976; APA Board of Professional Affairs, 1978–80, Chairman, 1969–71, 1980; APA Award, Distinguished Contributions to Applied Psychology as Professional Practice, 1981; Board of Directors, American Orthopsychiatric Association, 1981–4; American Board of Professional Psychology, Distinguished Service and Outstanding Contributions Award, 1987; NASP Lifetime Contributions to the Profession of Psychology, 1991; Lifetime Achievement Award, North Carolina School Psychology Association, 1991; Chairman, Task Force on the Structure of APA, 1985; APA Policy and Planning Board, 1984–5; Editor, *Journal of School Psychology*, 1968–71; Editorial Board, *Journal of School Psychology*, 1971–84, *Professional Psychology: Research and Practice, 1979–84, School Psychology Monograph*, 1971–6; *School Psychology Digest*, 1971–6, and many other journals; Guest Editor, *Journal of School Psychology* vol. 3, no. 2, *Journal of School Psychology*, vol. 5, no. 3, *Measurement and Evaluation in Guidance*, vol. 15, no. 1, *Professional Psychology*, vol. 13, no. 4

Principal publications

1963 Mental health education: A framework for psychological services in the school. *Journal of School Psychology*, 1963, 1, 20–7.

1967 School psychology and school psychologists: An approach to an old problem. *American Psychologist*, 1967, 23, 187–94.

1970 Your present is our past: Implications for the future of school psychology. *Professional Psychology*, 1, 8–13.

1974 *School Psychology*. Prentice-Hall (with V.C. Bennett).

1974 Achievement motivation among Negro adolescents in regular and special education classes. *American Journal of Mental Deficiency*, 20–6 (with R.J. Zito).

1977 The effects of a school program on teenage mothers and their children. *American Journal of Orthopsychiatry*, 1977, 47, 671–8.

1982 The psychology of school psychology. In C.R. Reynolds and T.B. Gutkin (eds), *A Handbook for the Practice of School Psychology*. Wiley.

1982 School psychology's dilemma: A proposal for its resolution. *Professional Psychology and Research*, 13, 955–68.

1983 Psychology applied to education: A speciality in search of an identity. *American Psychologist*, 38, 185–96.

Further reading

Awards for Distinguished Professional Contributions: (1981)/(1982) Jack I. Bardon. *American Psychologist*, 37, 60–4.

Reilly, D.H. (1994) Jack I. Bardon (1925–93). *American Psychologist*, 49, 813–14.

Jack I. Bardon served with the US Army in Burma during World War II and after returning from the war obtained a BA in psychology (education minor), an MA in experimental psychology and a PhD with a major in clinical psychology. During his time at Rutgers University (1960–8) there was a rapid expansion in school psychology training programmes at a national level, and acceptance within the profession and the APA as a psychological speciality. These developments were due in no small part to the influence and efforts of Jack Bardon. He was one of the founders and editor of the *Journal of School Psychology*.

Throughout his career Bardon was concerned with how school psychologists can best serve schools and how the body of scientific knowledge and theory in psychology can be applied to problems in schooling. In his early writings he used a 'mental health' approach, relying mainly on theory and findings in clinical psychology. His major focus was on role and function, efficacy of service position, and clarification of how training in school psychology might be differentiated from training in other areas of professional psychology. Because of the highly applied nature of school psychology and its relatively low status in American psychology, much of his effort was directed towards raising standards of practice and training, and towards assisting school psychology to gain entrance into the mainstream of professional psychology. He did this by writing, researching in the field, and engaging in professional activities aimed at the enhancement of professional psychology, with particular attention to school psychology. As the field developed and matured, he shifted focus from mental health/clinical problems to how school psychology can serve schools, teachers, parents and the community in general, through a greater emphasis on its unique opportunity to use educational psychology knowledge as a basis for applied research and practice. Application to problems of schooling, wherever they may occur, and specialization in how psychology can be applied to problems of teaching and learning in educational settings of all kinds, seemed to him to be important problems that school psychology could address better than other specialities in psychology. His writings, speeches and professional activities were sometimes viewed as controversial, but that helped to bring new ways of viewing the speciality to the attention of psychologists and educators. His primary contributions have been those of helping school psychology take its place as a major American psychological professional speciality and providing new and provocative ideas for its development and expansion.

Barker, Roger Garlock

Born: 1903, Macksburg, Iowa, USA *Died:* 1990, Oskaloosa, Kansas, USA *Nat:* American *Ints:* Developmental, philosophical and theoretical, population and environmental, psychological study of social issues, rehabilitation psychology *Educ:* BA Stanford University, 1928; MA Stanford University, 1930; PhD Stanford University, 1934 *Appts and Awards:* General Education Board Fellowship, University of Iowa, 1935–7; Instructor, Harvard University, 1937–8; Assistant Professor (Child Psychology), University of Illinois, 1938–42; Associate Professor, Stanford University, 1942–6; G. Stanley Hall Professor of Genetic Psychology, Clark University, 1946–7; Professor and Emeritus Professor of Psychology, University of Kansas, 1947–72; President, APA Division 7, 1952–3; APA Committee on Child Development, 1956–8; Fellow, Center for Advanced Study in the Behavioral Sciences, 1957–8; President, National Research Council, 1957–9; APA Committee on Primary Records in the Behavioral Sciences, 1957–61; APA Distinguished Scientific Contribution Award, 1963; NIMH Research Career Award, 1963–72; APA Committee for the Distinguished Contributions Award, 1964–6; APA G. Stanley Hall Award, 1969; APA Division 9, Kurt Lewin Award, 1969

Principal publications

1939 The attitudes and interests of premenarcheal and postmenarcheal girls. *Journal of Genetic Psychology*, 54, 257–66 (with C.P. Stone).
1941 Frustration and regression: A study of young children. *University of Iowa Studies of Child Welfare*, 18, No. 1 (with T. Dembo and K. Lewin).
1942 An experimental study of the resolution of conflict by children. In Q. McNemar and M.A. Merrill (eds), *Studies in Personality*. McGraw-Hill.
1946 An experimental study of the relationship between certainty of choice and the relative valence of the alternatives. *Journal of Personality*, 15, 41–52.
1955 *Midwest and its Children.* Harper & Row (with H.F. Wright).
1960 Ecology and motivation. In *Nebraska Symposium on Motivation, 1960.* University of Nebraska Press.
1963 On the nature of the environment. *Journal of Social Issues*, 19, 17–38.
1964 *Big School, Small School.* Stanford University Press (with P.V. Gump).
1965 Explorations in ecological psychology. *American Psychologist*, 20, 1–14.
1968 *Ecological Psychology.* Stanford University Press.
1973 *Qualities of Community Life.* Jossey-Bass (with P. Schoggen).
1978 *Habitats, Environments, and Human Behavior.* Jossey-Bass (with associates).
1978 Prospecting in environmental psychology. In D. Stokols and D. Altman (eds), *Handbook of Environmental Psychology.* Wiley.
1979 Settings of a professional lifetime. *Journal of Personality and Social Psychology*, 37, 2137–57.
1990 Recollections of the Midwest Psychological Field Station. Special issue: The Midwest Psychological Field Station: A celebration of its founding. *Environment and Behavior*, 22, 503–13.

Further reading

Fox, K.A. (1985) *Social System Accounts.* Reidel.
Houston, U. (1990) Inside Midwest and its field station: The Barker Effect. Special issue: The Midwest Psychological Field Station: A celebration of its founding. *Environment and Behavior*, 22, 468–91.
Schoggen, P. (1992) Roger Garlock Barker (1903–90) *American Psychologist*, 47, 77–8.

After a period of experimental research with animals and children in the 1930s and 1940s under the influence of Lewis **Terman** and Kurt **Lewin**, Barker became interested in the dearth of scientific information about the behaviour of children outside laboratories and clinics. The major part of his career was devoted to investigating the everyday lives of children and adults, with emphasis upon identifying, describing and measuring the environments in which they live. In 1947 he established the Midwest Psychological Field Station in the small town of Oskaloosa, Kansas, to investigate the everyday lives of the children of the town; what happens to them (their environments) and how they react (their behaviour). The Station operated for twenty-five years and the findings are reported in seven books and about sixty journal publications and theses. All of these materials – original data, analyses and reports – are deposited in the Spencer Research Library of the University of Kansas. Two kinds of datum resulted from the two methods he used: specimen record data and behaviour setting data. Specimen records are day-long, minute-by-minute, narrative accounts of the personal environments and behaviour of individual children as seen and recorded on the spot by teams of skilled observers. Behaviour settings are the stable, environmental enclaves (e.g. the doctors' offices, the basketball games) a community provides for its inhabitants. These settings are 'geo-physical-behavioural' entities with characteristic standing patterns of activity and strong forces which coerce the behaviour of individuals appropriately. Behaviour settings theory provides a multidimensional model of behaviour that includes consideration of place, time, social organization, actions and goals. Specimen record data were explained using psychological concepts, but Barker did not consider psychology capable of explaining behaviour setting data, and so he explored alternative 'eco-behavioural' concepts and theories. His work has had a major influence within the field of environmental psychology (e.g. on the work of **Altman**, **Proshansky** and **Stokols**) and beyond (e.g. on social systems analysis), and a lesser impact on theories of child development.

Barlow, David Harrison
Born: 1942 Needham, Massachusetts, USA *Nat:* American *Ints:* Clinical *Educ:* AB University of Notre Dame, 1964; MA Boston College, 1966; PhD University of Vermont, 1969; MA (*ad eundum*) Brown University, 1976 *Appts & awards:* Professor of Psychology, State University of New York; Fellow, APA Divisions 12, 25; President, Association for the Advancement of Behavior Therapy, 1978–9; Chair, Section 111, APA Division 12; Editorial Board, *Psychological Reports*, 1970–7, *Perceptual and Motor Skills*, 1970–8, *Journal of Applied Behavior Analysis*, 1972–7, *Behavior Therapy*, 1973–8, *Archives of Sexual Behavior*, 1975–7, *Journal of Behavior Therapy and Experimental Psychiatry*, 1976– , *Behavior Modification*, 1976–82, *Behavioral Assessment*, 1979– ,

Clinical Behavior Therapy Review, 1978–81, *Clinical Psychology Review*, 1980– , *Journal of Consulting and Clinical Psychology*, 1980– , *Professional School Psychology*, 1985– , *Behavior Change*, 1985– ; Editor, *Journal of Applied Behavior Analysis*, 1980–3, *Behavior Therapy*, 1983– ; Associate Editor, *Journal of Applied Behavior Analysis*, 1973–7, *Journal of Consulting and Clinical Psychology*, 1978–80.

Principal publications
1969 Experimental control of sexual deviation through manipulation of the noxious scene in covert sensitization. *Journal of Abnormal Psychology*, 74, 596–601 (with H. Leintenberg and W. Agras).
1973 Gender identity change in a transsexual. *Archives of General Psychiatry*, 28, 569–79 (with E.J. Reynolds and W.S. Agras).
1973 Single case experimental designs: Uses in applied clinical research. *Archives of General Psychiatry*, 29, 319–25 (with M. Hersen).
1976 *Single Case Experimental Designs: Strategies for Studying Behavior Change*. Pergamon (with M. Hersen). (2nd edn 1984.)
1978 *The Prevention of Sexual Disorders: Issues and Approaches*. Plenum (ed. with C.B. Qualls, J.P. Wincze).
1980 Behavior therapy: The next decade. *Behavior Therapy*, 11, 315–28.
1981 (ed.) *Behavioral Assessment of Adult Disorders*. Guilford Press.
1981 *Phobia: Psychological and Pharmacological Treatment*. Guilford Press (ed. with M. Mavissakalian).
1981 On the relation of clinical research to clinical practice: Current issues, new directions. *Journal of Consulting and Clinical Psychology*, 49, 147–56.
1981 Behavioral approaches to anxiety disorders: A report on the NIMG–SUNY Albany research conference. *Journal of Consulting and Clinical Psychology*, 49, 448–55 (with B.E. Wolfe).
1983 Anxiety increase sexual arousal. *Journal of Abnormal Psychology*, 92, 49–55 (with D.K. Sakheim and J.G. Beck).
1983 Couples treatment of agrophobia. *Behavior Therapy*, 15, 41–59 (with G.T. O'Brien and C.G. Last).
1984 Panic and generalized anxiety disorders: Nature and treatment. *Behavior Therapy*, 15, 431–49 (with A.S. Cohen, M.T. Waddell, B.B. Vermilyea, J.S. Klosko, E.B. Blanchard and P.A. DiNardo).
1984 The Scientist Practitioner. *Research and Accountability in Clinical and Educational Settings*. Pergamon (with S.C. Hayes and R.O. Nelson)

1990 The etiology of posttraumatic stress disorder. *Clinical Psychology Review*, 10, 299–328 (with J.C. Jones).

1991 Behavioral treatment of panic disorder: A two-year follow-up. *Behavior Therapy*, 22, 289–304 (with M.G. Craske and T.A. Brown).

1993 Efficacy and specific effects data on new treatments: A case study strategy with mixed anxiety–depression. *Journal of Consulting and Clinical Psychology*, 61, 412–20 (with K. Moras and L.A. Telfer).

1994 Psychological interventions in the era of managed competition. *Clinical Psychology Science and Practice*, 1, 109–22.

1994 The empirical basis of generalized anxiety disorder. *American Journal of Psychiatry*, 151, 1272–80 (with T.A. Brown and M.R. Liebowitz).

1994 Comorbidity in social phobia: Implications for cognitive-behavioral treatment. *Bulletin of the Menninger Clinic*, 58, A43–A57.

Further reading

Barlow, D.H. and Mark, V.M. (1995) *Abnormal Psychology: An Integrative Approach*. Brooks/Cole.

Eysenck, H.J. (1991) Neuroticism, anxiety, and depression. *Psychological Inquiry*, 2, 75–6.

During the 1960s clinical psychology struggled, with little success, to bring together the roles of the scientist and practitioner, but Barlow was a leader in achieving a productive and enduring integration between the two. During his doctoral training he encountered as role models experimentalists who were interested in clinical issues, a psychiatrist who was interested in clinical issues, and a psychiatrist who was interested in experimental ones. Joseph Cautella at Boston College and Harold Leitenberg at the University of Vermont were the psychiatrists. Out of this collaboration grew an interest in applying and rigorously evaluating the principles of experimental psychology to clinical psychological problems. Aided by a clinical traineeship with Joseph **Wolpe**, another experimentally oriented psychiatrist, he developed an enduring interest in uncovering the nature of anxiety and sexual disorders and developing new and more effective treatments for these problems.

During the late 1960s when he was still in graduate school, his clinical research focused on evaluating therapeutic procedures with single subjects. He would replicate single-case findings on additional subjects or patients. These therapeutic procedures were derived from laboratory-based studies of operant psychology and used in the evaluation of clinical problems,

resulting in his first book, published with Michael **Hersen** in 1976. His 1984 book with Hayes and Nelson describes a model emanating from the single-case approach where the individual practitioner can fully participate in the research process, while retaining his or her emphasis on and interest in the individual.

Later he returned to an early interest in anxiety disorders and panic, which had been lying somewhat dormant since graduate school days. In this research he has attempted to establish the psychological basis of panic and to develop more efficient and more effective treatments for all of the anxiety disorders, based on a re-evaluation of the underlying nature of generalized anxiety and panic. His approach to treatment for the control of panic focuses on the panic attacks themselves rather than on agoraphobic avoidance, involving systematic, structured exposure to feared physical and related cognitive symptoms. When the feared symptoms have been identified, they are targeted for treatment. He has developed and evaluated a cognitive behavioural group therapy for social phobia structured around six components: (1) a cognitive behavioural explanation of the social phobia; (2) the identification and analysis of problematic thoughts using structured exercises; (3) exposure to simulated anxiety-provoking situations; (4) cognitive restructuring procedures intended to teach clients how to control maladaptive thinking before, during and after simulated exposure; (5) homework assignments for actual naturalistic exposure; and (6) self-administered cognitive restructuring for use before and after behavioural homework.

More recently he has identified etiological and phenomenological similarities between anxiety disorders and post-traumatic stress disorder (PSTD). This has led to a new model of PSTD based on his theoretical and empirical studies of the process and origins of anxiety and panic. The model includes a consideration of the role of biological and psychological vulnerabilities, negative life events, fear reactions, perceptions of control, social support and coping strategies. This work continues a theoretical emphasis that concentrates on the application of the principles of experimental psychology to clinical problems, which is a broadly conceived definition of 'behaviour therapy'. While particular theoretical approaches are somewhat blurred in his work, the emphasis on rigorous empirical approaches to clinical problems is distinctive and testament to one of the lasting contributions of behaviour therapy.

Baron, Robert Alan

Born: 1943, New York City, USA *Nat:* American *Ints:* Industrial and organizational, personality and social psychology *Educ:* BS Brooklyn College, 1964; MA University of Iowa, 1967; PhD University of Iowa, 1968 *Appts & awards:* Award in Teaching Excellence, Purdue University, 1974; Fellow, American Psychological Association, 1978; Member of Council, International Society for Research in Aggression, 1981; Award in Teaching Excellence, Purdue University, 1982; MCL Award in Teaching Excellence, Purdue University, 1984; Best Paper Award (Organizational Conflict) International Association for Conflict Management Fairfax, 1987; Professor of Management, Professor of Psychology, Rensselaer Polytechnic Institute, 1987– ; Topic Editor, *Journal of Personality and Social Psychology*, 1976–9; Editorial Board, *Journal of Personality and Social Psychology*, 1979–85, *Journal of Applied Social Psychology*, 1971– , *Aggressive Behavior*, 1982– ; *Motivation and Emotion*, 1989–

Principal publications

1977 *Human Aggression*. Plenum.

1977 Sexual arousal and aggression by males: Effects of type and erotic stimuli and prior provocation. *Journal of Personality and Social Psychology*, 35, 79–87 (with P.A. Bell).

1978 Aggression inhibiting influence of sexual humour. *Journal of Personality and Social Psychology*, 36, 189–97.

1978 Ambient temperature and collective violence: The long hot summer revisited. *Journal of Personality and Social Psychology*, 36, 351–60 (with V.M. Ransberger).

1978 Invasions of personal space and helping: Mediating effects of the invader's apparent need. *Journal of Experimental Social Psychology*, 14, 304–12.

1983 The control of human aggression: An optimistic overview. *Journal of Social and Clinical Psychology*, 1, 97–119.

1983 The 'sweet smell of success'? The impact of pleasant artificial scents on evaluations of job applicants. *Journal of Applied Psychology*, 68, 709–13.

1984 *Social Psychology*, 4th edn. Allyn and Bacon (with D. Byrne). (1st edn 1974.)

1984 Reducing organizational conflict: An incompatible response approach. *Journal of Applied Psychology*, 69, 272–9.

1985 *Understanding Human Relationships*. Allyn and Bacon.

1985 Reducing organizational conflict: The role of attributions. *Journal of Applied Psychology*, 70, 434–41.

1985 Negative ions and behavior: Impact on mood, memory and aggression among Type A and Type B persons. *Journal of Personality and Social Psychology*, 48, 746–54 (with G.W. Russell and R.L. Arms).

1986 *Behavior in Organizations*, 2nd edn. Allyn and Bacon. (1st edn 1983.)

1992 *Psychology: The Essential Science*, 2nd edn. Allyn and Bacon. (1st edn 1989.)

1995 *Psychology*, 3rd edn. Allyn and Bacon.

Further reading

Atlas, R. (1984) Violence in prison – environmental influences. *Environment and Behavior*, 16, 275–306.

Isen, A.M. (1987) Positive affect, cognitive processes and social behavior. *Advances in Experimental Social Psychology*, 20, 203–53.

Wiggins, J.A. (1983) Family violence as a case of interpersonal aggression. A situational analysis. *Social Forces*, 62, 102–23.

Several 'themes' emerge in Baron's career that organize his principal contributions to psychology. He began with a basic interest in human aggression, especially in various means for reducing or controlling this dangerous form of behaviour. Within this context, he investigated the potential aggression-inhibiting impact of such factors as humour, empathy and mild sexual arousal. On the basis of this research he formulated the incompatible response theory – a principle viewed as one of his major contributions. Continuing work on aggression led him to consider the impact of various aspects of the physical environment on this form of behaviour. This led to several productive years of investigation on the impact of heat, crowding, noise and negative ions on human aggression. More recently his interests have shifted once more, and now are mainly around the task of applying the findings and principles of social psychology to many practical problems. Specifically, he has moved increasingly into the area of organizational behaviour, where much attention has been focused on applying current knowledge about human aggression to the development of effective techniques for minimizing organizational conflict.

Barron, Frank Xavier

Born: 1922, Lansford, Pennsylvania, USA *Nat:* American *Ints:* Clinical psychology, general,

personality and social, philosophical and theoretical psychology, psychology and the arts
Educ: BA La Salle College, 1942; MA University of Minnesota, 1948; PhD University of California at Berkeley, 1950 **Appts & awards:** Professor of Psychology and Chief, Laboratory for the Study of Lives, University of California at Santa Cruz; Fellow, Center for the Advanced Study in the Behavioral Sciences, 1958–9; Fellow, Social Science Research Council, 1965; Guggenheim Fellow, 1967–8; APA Richardson Creativity Award, 1969; Outstanding Research Award, American Personnel and Guidance Association, 1970; President, APA Division 10, 1972; Silver Psi Award, California Psychological Association, 1972; Hon ScD, La Salle University, 1978; Editorial Board, *Psychedelic Review*, 1963–8, *Journal of Aesthetic Education*, 1970–5, *Journal of Creative Behavior*, 1969–70, *Acta Genetic Medicae et Gemellolgiae*, 1972–9

Principal publications

1952 Personality style and perceptual choice. *Journal of Personality*, 20, 385–401.

1953 An ego-strength scale which predicts response to psychotherapy. *Journal of Consulting Psychology*, 17, 327–33.

1953 Some test correlates of response to psychotherapy. *Journal of Consulting Psychology*, 18, 235–41.

1953 Complexity–simplicity as a personality dimension. *Journal of Abnormal and Social Psychology*, 48, 163–72.

1953 Some personality correlates of independence of judgement. *Journal of Personality*, 21, 287–97.

1955 Threshold for the perception of human movement in inkblots. *Journal of Consulting Psychology*, 19, 33–8.

1958 The psychology of imagination. *Scientific American*, 199, 150–6.

1961 Freedom as feeling. *Journal of Humanistic Psychology*, 1, 91–100.

1963 *Creativity and Psychological Health*. Van Nostrand. (Revised and expanded as *Creativity and Personal Freedom*, 1968).

1963 *Scientific Creativity*. Wiley.

1969 *Creative Person and Creative Process*. Holt, Rinehart and Winston.

1970 Heritability factors in creativity and judgement. *Acta Genetic Medicae et Gemellogiae*, 1, 91–114.

1972 *Artists in the Making*. Seminar.

1972 Toward an ecology of consciousness. *Inquiry*, 15, 95–113.

1979 *The Shaping of Personality*. Harper & Row.

Further reading

Harrington, D.M. and Andersen, S.M. (1981) Creativity, masculinity, femininity and three models of psychological androgeny. *Journal of Personality and Social Psychology*, 41, 4, 744–57.

Rashin, R. and Hall, C.S. (1981) The narcissistic personality inventory alternate form reliability and further evidence of construct validity. *Journal of Personality Assessment*, 45, 2, 159–62.

Schwartz, H.S. (1983) Maslow and the hierarchical enactment of organizational reality. *Human Relations*, 36, 933–55.

Simonton, D.K. (1992) Gender and genius in Japan – feminine eminence in masculine culture. *Sex Roles*, 27, 101–19.

Frank Barron's interest in creativity began during his undergraduate years at La Salle College. It had its roots more in philosophy than in psychology: he had started to write his senior thesis on Bergson's 'creative evolution', but his analysis of Bergson's distinction between intellect and intuition led back into the origins of dynamic psychology and he became interested in altered states of consciousness, the eventual topic of his thesis. F.W.H. Myers's *Human Personality*, especially the chapters on genius, hypnosis and subliminal perception, particularly influenced his thinking. A brief period of study after World War II with Sir Frederick **Bartlett** at Cambridge gave an empirical and experimental slant to his interests in higher mental processes. Once again, he started on a thesis (for his PhD) with one topic but then moved into another: he devised an experiment on stereotypic thinking, but was deflected from this into a concern with the break-out from stereotype into a creative mode of thought, feeling and action through psychotherapy. This led to a series of studies to discover hidden strengths of the ego not only in patients but in everyone. He devised measures of ego strength, aesthetic preferences, independence of judgement, complexity of outlook and originality, most of which were assembled into the 'Inventory of Personal Philosophy'. These measures were applied in numerous investigations and to elucidate the characteristics of creative people. Much of his work has drawn equally from psychology and philosophy, and has involved looking at the problems of freedom and of human choice, which he sees as being at the heart of the psychology of creativity.

Bar-Tal, Daniel

Born: 1946, Stalinbad, USSR *Nat:* Israeli *Ints:* Developmental psychology, educational psychology, personality and social psychology, philosophical and theoretical psychology, political psychology. *Educ:* BA Tel Aviv University, 1970; MS University of Pittsburgh, 1973; PhD University of Pittsburgh, 1974 *Appts & awards:* Learning Associate, Learning Research and Development Center, University of Pittsburgh, 1974–5; Lecturer, School of Education, Tel-Aviv University, 1975–89, Professor, 1989– ; Visiting Professor, Dept of Psychology, Brandeis University 1987–8; Visiting Professor, Ecole des Hautes Etudes en Sciences Sociales, Paris, 1991– ; Otto Klineberg Intercultural and International Relations Prize of SPSSI, 1991; Vice-president of the International Society of Political Psychology, 1994–

Principal publications

1976 *Prosocial Behavior: Theory and Research.* Halsted.

1978 Attributional analysis of achievement-related behaviour. *Review of Educational Research*, 48, 259–271.

1978 Social outcomes of schooling process and their taxonomy. In D. Bar-Tal and L. Saxe (eds), *Social Psychology of Education: Theory and Research.* Halsted.

1979 Consistency of helping behaviour measures, *Child Development*, 50, 1235–8 (with A. Raviv).

1982 A cognitive-learning model of helping behavior development: Possible implications and applications. In N. Eisenberg-Berg (ed.), *The Development of Prosocial Behavior.* Academic Press (with D. Raviv).

1982 Sequential development of helping behavior. *Developmental Review*, 2, 101–24.

1988 A new perspective for social psychology. In D. Bar-Tal and A.W. Kruglanski (eds), *Social Psychology of Knowledge.* Cambridge University Press (with Y. Bar-Tal).

1989 Conflict termination: An epistemological analysis of international cases. *Political Psychology*, 10, 233–55 (with A.W. Kruglanski and Y. Klar).

1989 Delegitimization: The extreme case of stereotyping and prejudice. In D. Bar-Tal, C. Graumann, A.W. Kruglanski and W. Stroebe (eds), *Stereotyping and Prejudice: Changing Conceptions.* Springer-Verlag.

1990 *Group Beliefs: A Conception for Analyzing Group Structure, Processes and Behaviour.* Springer-Verlag.

1990 Causes and consequences of delegitimization:

Models of conflict and ethnocentrism. *Journal of Social Issues*, 46, 65–81.

1990 Israeli–Palestinian conflict: A cognitive analysis. *International Journal of Intercultural Relations* 14, 7–29.

1992 Beliefs about negative intentions of the world: A study of the Israeli siege mentality. *Political Psychology*, 13, 633–45 (with D. Antebi).

1994 Formation and change of ethnic and national stereotypes: An integrative model. *Psicologia Politica*, 9, 21–50.

1995 Security feelings among Jewish settlers in the occupied territories: A study of communal and personal antecedents. *Journal of Conflict Resolution.* 39, 353–77 (with D. Jacobson and T. Freund).

Further reading

Billig, M. (1993) Patriotism and forms of community: A comment. *Politics and the Individual*, 3, 63–6.

Kurtines, W.M. and Gewirtz, J.L. (eds) (1991) *Handbook of Moral Behavior and Development.* Erlbaum.

Daniel Bar-Tal has been interested in the nature of human knowledge and its effects on human behaviour since his graduate studies in social psychology. His early scientific career focused on understanding the cognitive antecedents of helping behaviour and the effects of beliefs regarding successes or failures on achievement behaviour. His research on prosocial behaviour explored the development of motives for helping behaviour, conceptualized as reasons to act. The research dealt mainly with: (1) the differences in the repertoire of motives among children of different ages, and (2) the relationship between helping motives and helping behaviour. This research highlighted the effectiveness of external rewards in encouraging prosocial behaviour in younger children who had not acquired internal motives for helping; and the view that altruism grows with age as children come to see things from another person's perspective.

During recent years, Bar-Tal's theoretical and empirical interests in the relationship between human knowledge and behaviour have widened to include general problems of the acquisition and change of knowledge and its influence on affective, cognitive and behavioural reactions. His present work is located within a framework of lay epistemology theory, which is concerned with the process whereby people acquire knowledge. One line of research has focused on the nature of accumulated knowledge in social psychology. Another set of studies focuses on political beliefs. In this line, he has written a series of articles about group beliefs, on conflict, delegitimization, patriotism and siege syndrome, describing the content of these beliefs, their functions, and their implications for group behaviour. Bar-Tal's diverse research interests and extensive publications are unified by his primary concern with the social psychology of knowledge and the applied nature of much of his research and writing.

KAREN TREW

Bartlett, Frederick Charles

Born: 1886, Stow-on-the-Wold, Gloucestershire, England **Died:** 1969, Cambridge, England **Nat:** British **Ints:** Anthropological psychology, experimental psychology **Educ:** MA (Sociology and Ethics) University Correspondence College, University of London; MA (Moral Sciences) University of Cambridge **Appts & awards:** Assistant Director, Psychology Laboratory, Cambridge, 1914–22, Reader, 1922, Director, 1922; First Professor of Experimental Psychology, Cambridge University, 1931, Professor Emeritus, 1952–69; Consultant to the Medical Research Council's Applied Psychology Unit, 1952–69; LLD, DSc., DPhil, DPsych, FRS, 1932; CBE, 1941, Royal Society Baly and Huxley medals, 1943; Knighted, 1948; Royal Medal, 1952; Hon. Doctorates from the universities of Athens, Princeton, Louvain, London, Edinburgh, Oxford and Padua; Editor, *British Journal of Psychology*, 1924–48

Principal publications

1916   An experimental study of some problems of perceiving and imaging. *British Journal of Psychology*, 8, 222–66.
1923   *Psychology and Primitive Culture*. Cambridge University Press.
1929   Experimental method in psychology. *Nature*, 124, 341–5.
1932   *Remembering: A Study in Experimental and Social Psychology*. Cambridge University Press.
1934   *The Problem of Noise*. Cambridge University Press.
1937   Psychological methods and anthropological problems. *Africa*, 10, 401–20.
1958   *Thinking: An Experimental and Social Study*. Allen and Unwin.

Further reading

Broadbent, D.E. (1970) Sir Frederick Bartlett: An appreciation. *Bulletin of the British Psychological Society*, 23, 1–3.
Murcheson, C. (ed.) (1936) Frederic Charles Bartlett. *History of Psychology in Biography*, vol. 3. Clark University Press.
Oldfield, R.C. (1972) Frederick Charles Bartlett. *American Journal of Psychology*, 85, 133–40.
For a full listing of Bartlett's publications: see R.B. Buzzard (1971) *Occupational Psychology*, 45, 1–11.

In childhood Bartlett was largely self-educated, supported by his father and the library of a local nonconformist minister. After an early start in social anthropology he became Assistant Director of the Psychology Laboratory at Cambridge (1914), Reader in Experimental Psychology (1922) and Director in the same year on the retirement of C.S. Myers. Bartlett twice switched his interests from lively academic fields to ones where there were practical problems to be solved. The first was a switch from sociology and anthropology to the experimental psychology of perception and remembering, and the second from academic psychology to ergonomics and to the application of psychology in occupational settings.

Bartlett is best known for his investigations into memory and social psychology and in particular for his book *Remembering* (1932), which examined experimentally the influences of social factors on memory. In contrast to contemporary practices of using nonsense syllables, Bartlett used meaningful stimuli to study the effects of past experiences on the assimilation of new material. This marked a break with the German tradition in its use of methods that did not rely on the use of introspection. This work is all the more remarkable in that it presented data that had been collected and analysed some fifteen years earlier. Bartlett demonstrated that people would rework the new material in the light of prior experiences. He is credited with the theory of schemata. A schema is constantly changing in the light of new experiences, but it also provides a dynamic framework or model into which new experiences are interpreted and into which they are structured. Bartlett rarely referred to this theory in his later work, and it was left to others to exploit its theoretical power.

With the outbreak of World War II Bartlett, a member of the Air Ministry's Flying Personnel Research Committee, was drawn into the analysis of psychological problems revealed by the expansion of the RAF. His close association with Kenneth Craik, who joined the Cambridge laboratory in 1936, was indispensable in this work. Later Bartlett adapted the methods used to investigate remembering to the analysis of thought processes. As a practical activity he considered that thinking involved the completion (by interpolation or extrapolation) of some previously incomplete state of affairs, and he devised experimental procedures to explore this idea systematically. His book *Thinking* is less remarkable than the earlier *Remembering*, although in many ways it reveals more of his personal attitudes and thinking (e.g. his involvement with anthropology, sociology and philosophy) than any of his earlier published work. Bartlett occupies a pre-eminent position in the development of psychology in Britain. Starting with just one laboratory assistant in 1922, he was guiding the efforts of more than seventy staff and researchers some thirty years later, and most of the important psychological appointments in Britain during the middle of the twentieth century were made from among those who had been trained under him.

Bass, Bernard M.

Born: 1925, New York, USA *Nat:* American *Ints:* Evaluation and measurement, industrial and organizational psychology, military psychology, humanistic psychology, personality and social psychology *Educ:* BA Ohio State University, 1946; MA Ohio State University, 1947; PhD Ohio State University, 1949 *Appts & awards:* Distinguished Professor of Management, School of Management, State University of New York; APA Council, 1965–8; President, Division of Organizational Psychology, International Association of Applied Psychology, 1978–82; Executive Committee, International Association of Applied Psychology, 1980– ; APA Committee on Women Psychologists, 1983–5; Consulting Editor, *Journal of Applied Psychology*, 1972–6, 1983– , *European Training*, 1983– , *Journal of Cross Cultural Psychology* 1975–7, *Organizational Behavior and Human Performance*, 1976–8

Principal publications

1954 The leaderless group discussion. *Psychological Bulletin*, 51, 465–92.
1960 *Leadership, Psychology and Organizational Behavior*. Harper.
1965 *Organizational Psychology*. Allyn and Bacon.
1967 The anarchist movement and the t-group: Some possible lessons for organizational development. *Journal of Applied Behavioral Science*, 3, 211–30.

1967 Social behavior and the orientation inventory: A review. *Psychological Bulletin*, 68, 260–92.
1974 The substance and the shadow. *American Psychologist*, 29, 870–86.
1975 Management styles associated with organizational task, personal and interpersonal contingencies. *Journal of Applied Psychology*, 60, 720–9 (with H.R. Valenzi, D.L. Farrow and R.J. Solomon).
1976 Prosper – training and research for increasing management awareness about affirmative action in race relations. *Academy of Management Journal*, 19, 353–69 (with W.F. Cascio, J.W. McPherson and H.J. Tragash).
1977 Utility of managerial self-planning on a simulated production task with replications in twelve countries. *Journal of Applied Psychology*, 62, 506–9.
1978 Lifespace variables and managerial success. *Journal of Applied Psychology*, 63, 81–8 (with F. Vicino).
1979 *Assessment of Managers: An International Comparison*. Free Press (with P.A. Burger, G.V. Barrett and R. Doctor)
1981 *Stodgill's Handbook of Leadership*. Free Press.
1982 Individual capability, team response and productivity. In E.A. Fleishman and M.D. Dunnette (eds), *Human Performance and Productivity, vol. 1: Human Capability Assessment*. Erlbaum.
1983 *Organizational Decision Making*. Irwin.
1985 *Leadership and Performance Beyond Expectations*. Free Press.
1993 Transformational Leadership and Performance: A longitudinal investigation. *Leadership Quarterly*, 4, 81–102 (with F.J. Yammarino and W.D. Spangler).
1994 *Improving Organizational Effectiveness through Transformational Leadership*. Sage (ed. with B.J. Avolio).

Further reading

Barnett, G.V., Caldwell, M.S. and Alexander, R.A. (1985) The concept of dynamic criteria – a critical re-analysis. *Personnel Psychology*, 38, 41–56.
Chemers, M.M. and Ayman (eds) (1993) *Leadership Theory and Research: Perspectives and directions*. Academic Press.
Heaven, D.C.L. (1983) Authoritarianism or acquiescence – South African findings. *Journal of Social Psychology*, 119, 11–15.
Isenberg, D.J. (1981) Some effects of time-pressure on vertical structure and decision-making accuracy in small groups. *Organizational Behavior and Human Performance*, 27, 119–34.

Bernard Bass's early work was on the use of

leaderless group discussion in assessment (1948–54) and on small groups and leadership (1952–67). During the early 1960s he collaborated with Harold Leavitt (who coined the term 'organizational psychology' in 1962) and in 1965 he published the first hardback text with the title *Organizational Psychology*. He developed a small group exercise for each of the chapters to generate phenomena dealing with the book's contents. Translated into fifteen languages, the exercises have been used for training and research in more than twenty countries since then. *Assessment of Managers: An International Comparison* reviews the research results with the exercises. With colleagues Valenzi, Farrow and Miller he developed and applied a systems approach to leadership and managerial style. His later work is partially summarized in *Leadership and Performance Beyond Expectations*, which deals with a new understanding of leadership – transformational leadership. In this his thinking was influenced by James MacGregor Burns's book *Leadership* (1978) and Abraham Zaleznik's subsequent writings on the subject.

From the perspective of subordinates, transactional leaders: (1) recognise what it is we want to get from our work and try to see that we get what we want if our performance warrants; (2) exchange rewards and promises of rewards for our effort; and (3) are responsive to our immediate self-interests if they can be and by getting the work done. The transactional leader pursues a cost-benefit economic exchange to meet subordinate material and psychological needs in return for 'contracted' services. The transformation leader goes further and attempts to elevate subordinates from a lower to a higher level of need according to **Maslow**'s hierarchy of need.

Bateson, Gregory

Born: 1904, Grantchester, England **Died:** 1980, San Francisco, USA **Nat:** British **Ints:** Family psychology, physiological and comparative psychology, philosophical and theoretical psychology, psychotherapy **Educ:** BA University of Cambridge, 1924; MA University of Cambridge, 1930 **Appts & awards:** Ethnologist, Veterans Administration Hospital, Palo Alto, 1949–62; Board of Regents, University of California, 1976–80

Principal publications

1936   *Naven: A Survey of the Problems Suggested by a Composite Picture of the Culture of a New*

Guinea Tribe Drawn from Three Points of View. Cambridge University Press.

1942   Social planning and the concept of deutero-learning. (Reprinted in *Steps to an Ecology of Mind*).

1942   *Balinese Character: A Photographic Analysis.* New York Academy of Sciences (with M. Mead).

1951   *Communication: The Social Matrix of Psychiatry.* Norton (with J. Ruesch).

1956   Toward a theory of schizophrenia. *Behavioral Science*, 1, 251–4 (with D. Jackson, J. Haley and J. Weakland). (Reprinted in *Steps to an Ecology of Mind*).

1964   The logical categories of learning and communication. *Psychiatry*, 34, 1–18. (Reprinted in *Steps to an Ecology of Mind*).

1971   The cybernetics of 'self': A theory of alcoholism. (Reprinted in *Steps to an Ecology of Mind*).

1972   *Steps to an Ecology of Mind.* Chandler.

1979   *Mind and Nature: A Necessary Unity.* Dutton.

Further reading

Bateson, M.C. (1984) *With a Daughter's Eye: A Memoir of Margaret Mead and Gregory Bateson.* Morrow.

Lipset, D. (1980) *Gregory Bateson: The Legacy of a Scientist.* Prentice-Hall.

Gregory Bateson had an extraordinary career, comprised of a series of research projects into the cybernetics of social life. He held no permanent teaching or research post, moving from one location to another as opportunity beckoned or as necessity demanded. This itinerant career generated an enormous wealth of ideas, observations and insights into the nature of complexity in human (and animal) activity – into the interconnecting patterns and the formal structures of communicating minds. Bateson's writings remain a rich resource for present-day psychologists jaded by narrow-minded experimentalism or baffled by discourse analysis.

Born into an academically aristocratic Cambridge family, Bateson first studied zoology, with particular attention to formal analysis. He was most interested in such issues as anatomical symmetry and other morphological topics. At the same time, he displayed a Darwin-like delight in studying wildlife in its natural habitats. Bateson's turn to anthropology appears to have been something of a chance one, although it supplied exactly the opportunity he needed to investigate the interconnections of mind and nature. He carried out fieldwork in New Britain and in New Guinea, attempting to find new

ways of describing tribal society and its structures – in particular, patterns of conflict and
other interactions between groups. He married
the anthropologist Margaret Mead, and co-
authored with her the account of Balinese child-
rearing. Here it was argued that paradoxical
forms of interaction with the infant both reflect
and prepare the way for the characteristic adult
personality in Bali.

Anthropological fieldwork was followed,
after World War II, by focused attention on the
implications for social science of the new
developments in cybernetics and information
theory. Through a series of influential conferences and through his writings, Bateson
explored the structures and functions of communication in humans and in other animals.
Interests in animal and human learning crystallized in the notion of deutero-learning, an
archetypal Batesonian notion combining logical
and empirical analysis, and following and
extending Russell's theory of logical types (an
analysis of the distinctiveness of hierarchical
categories).

JOHN MORSS

Baumrind, Diana

Born: 1927, New York, USA **Nat:** American
Ints: Clinical, developmental, personality and
social, philosophical and theoretical **Educ:** BA
Hunter College, New York, 1948; MA Univer-
sity of California at Berkeley, 1951; PhD
University of California at Berkeley, 1955
Appts & awards: Research Psychologist, Uni-
versity Of California at Berkeley; APA Fellow;
Consulting Editor, *Developmental Psychology*,
Child Development, Research Scientist Award,
NIMH, 1984–8; G. Stanley Hall Award, Ameri-
can Psychological Association, Division 7.

Principal publications

1964   Some thoughts on ethics of research: After
reading Milgram's *Behavioral Study of Obedience*.
American Psychologist, 19, 421–23.

1966   Effects of authoritative parental control on
child behavior. *Child Development*, 887–907.

1967   *Child Care Practices Anteceding Three
Patterns of Preschool Behavior*. Genetic
Psychology Monograph 75.

1967   Socialization practices associated with
dimensions of competence in preschool boys and
girls. *Child Development*, 255–71 (with A.E
Black).

1971   Current patterns of parental authority.
Developmental Psychology Monograph 4, 1, Pt. 2.

1975   Early socialization and adolescence
competence. In S.E Dragastin and G. Elder Jr
(eds), *Adolescence in the Life Cycle*. Hemisphere.

1978   A dialectical materialist's perspective on
knowing social reality. *New Direction for Child
Development*, 2, 61–82.

1978   Parental disciplinary patterns and social
competence in children. *Youth and Society*, 9,
239–76.

1980   New directions in socialization research.
American Psychologist, 35, 639–52.

1983   Specious causal attributions in the social
sciences: The reformulated stepping-stone theory of
heroin use as exemplar. *Journal of Personality and
Social Psychology*, 45, 1289–98.

1985   Research using intentional deception on
adolescent drug abuse. *Advances in Alcohol and
Substance Abuse*, 4, 41–67 (with K. Moselle).

1990   Doing good well. In C.B. Fisher and W.W.
Tryon (eds), *Ethics in Applied Development
Psychology: Emerging Issues in an Emerging
Field*. Ablex.

1995   *Child Maltreatment and Optimal Caregiving
in Social Contexts*. Garland.

Further reading

Fisher, C.B. and Tryon, W.W. (eds) (1990) *Ethics in
Applied Development Psychology: Emerging Issues
in an Emerging Field*. Ablex.

Puka, B. (ed.) (1994) Caring voices and women's
moral frames: Gilligan's view. *Moral development:
A Compendium*, vol 6. Garland.

Diana Baumrind has been concerned with
accounting for individual differences in (1) competence (defined as socially responsible self-
assertive behaviour), and (2) moral outlook and
behaviour. Her work focuses on the role of
the family in the development of character,
personality and competence in children and
adolescents. The unifying theme in her work is
an examination of individual reciprocal rights
and responsibilities in relationships of unequal
power (such as the adult–child relationship).
She has published a substantial body of work on
parent–child socialization throughout childhood
and adolescence; a series of essays on informed
consent and deceit in social psychological
experiments, beginning with an important
critique of the **Milgram** obedience experiments;
and several papers on moral development. The
longitudinal database of the Family Socialization and Developmental Competence Project
which Baumrind directs has also supported
studies of gender-differentiated socialization
effects and the causes and consequences of

adolescent drug abuse. Her methodological approach emphasizes minimal experimental manipulation, ecologically valid observations, and typological analyses which preserve the coherence of the individual.

The moral norm of reciprocity figures strongly in her analysis of both parent–child and investigator–subject relationships. In any relationship there must be an exchange of rights and responsibilities appropriate to the roles and stages of development of the participants. Thus, authoritative child-rearing balances high demands with high responsiveness, whereas authoritarian child-rearing is demanding but not responsive, and permissive child-rearing is responsive but not demanding. She argues that both an authoritative (in contrast to an authoritarian or permissive) parent–child relationship, and a respectful and non-deceitful investigator–subject relationship (which does not obtain, for example, in the Milgram obedience studies), embody the moral norm of reciprocity which should be operative in all relationships.

In more recent work she argues that much of our information about family functioning is derived from studies of healthy middle-class families concerned with their promoting children's development. However, the majority of families identified as abusive are poor, and their children are endangered by crime, substandard living conditions, and lack of adequate medical care. She argues that the primary cause of child maltreatment is poverty rather than psychological factors.

Bayley, Nancy

Born: 1899, The Dalles, Oregon, USA *Nat:* American *Ints:* Developmental psychology *Educ:* BS University of Washington, 1922; MS University of Washington, 1924; PhD University of Iowa, 1926 *Appts & awards:* Institute for Human Development, University of California at Berkeley; APA Associate, 1928, Fellow, 1937; APA division 7, President 1953–4; Western Psychological Association, President 1953–4; APA division 20, President 1957–8; APA Distinguished Scientific Contribution Award, 1966; Distinguished Contributions Award, Institute of Human Development, University of California at Berkeley, 1967; APA division 7G, Stanley Hall Award, 1971; California State Psychological Association, Distinguished Contributions to Psychology Award, 1976; APF Gold Medal Award, 1982

Principal publications

1926   Performance tests for three-, four- and five-year-old children. *Journal of Genetic Psychology*, 33, 435–54.

1932   A study of the crying of infants during mental and physical tests. *Journal of Genetic Psychology*, 40, 306–29.

1933   *The California First-year Mental Scale.* University of California Press.

1935   The development of motor abilities during the first three years: A study of sixty-one infants tested repeatedly. Monographs of the Society for Research in Child Development, 1, 26–61.

1936   *The California Infant Scale of Motor Development.* University of California Press.

1937   Environmental correlates of mental and motor development: A cumulative study from infancy to six years. *Child Development*, 8, 329–41.

1939   Mental and motor development from two to twelve years. *Review of Educational Research*, 9, 18–37.

1940   *Studies in the Development of Young Children.* University of California Press.

1943   Skeletal maturing in adolescence as a basis for determining percentage of completed growth. *Child Development*, 14, 1–46.

1946   Tables for predicting adult height from skeletal age and present height. *Journal of Pediatrics*, 28, 49–64.

1946   The assessment of somatic androgyny. *American Journal of Physical Anthropology*, 4, 433–61.

1949   Consistency and variability in the growth of intelligence from birth to eighteen years. *Journal of Genetic Psychology*, 75, 165–96.

1950   Motor development and decline. *Review of Educational Research*, 14, 381–9 (with A. Espenchade).

1956   Individual patterns of development. *Child Development*, 27, 45–74.

1965   Comparisons of mental and motor test scores for ages 1–15 months by sex, birth order, race, geographical location, and education of parents. *Child Development*, 36, 379–411.

1968   Behavioral correlates of mental growth: Birth to thirty-six years. *American Psychologist*, 23, 1–17.

Further reading

Lipsitt, L.P. and Eichorn, D.H. (1990) Nancy Bayley (1899–). In A.N. O'Connell and N.F. Russo (eds), *Women in Psychology: A Bio-bibliographic Sourcebook.* Greenwood Press.

Rosenblith, J.F. (1992) A singular career: Nancy Bayley. *Developmental Psychology*, 28, 747–58.

Nancy Bayley's father headed the grocery department of a department store while her mother cared for the family (four girls and one boy) and was also heavily involved in supporting other families in the community. She was not a particularly healthy child and did not attend public school until she was eight. After completing High School she had intended to become an English teacher and enrolled at the University of Washington. An introductory course in psychology (with E.R. **Guthrie**) sparked an interest which reorientated her career.

Nancy Bayley's contributions are in three main areas: growth and skeletal maturation, body build and androgyny, and motor and mental development. In her studies of growth in body size Bayley showed that the greatest correlations from one time to another were head circumference, length and stem length. Bayley was the first to publish correlations that related infants' size to their adult size. In 1946 she published the first of a series of famous tables for predicting adult height from measures of a child's present height and skeletal range. In the same year Bayley and Bayer published a scheme for classifying the photographs of the backs of males and females and described which characteristics covaried with sex. Eight items that were reliably rated and with bimodal distributions were used to determine maleness, femaleness and androgynous characteristics. Bayley and Bayer argued that the tool could be used to examine the relationships between sex, body type and personality. This work anticipated much of the later (1980s) interest in psychological androgyny. Bayley is also well known for the development of the California Infant Scale of Motor Development. With this instrument she demonstrated that motor development proceeds rapidly in the first twenty-one months, followed by an abrupt decrease. The development of gross motor co-ordination appeared to grow more quickly during the first two years than did other mental abilities, but the situation was reversed in the third year.

Later in her career she extended her investigations of motor development into adulthood and its decline. Her name is most frequently used in connection with the Bayley Scales of Infant Development, the origins of which can be traced back to her master's thesis. The scales were revised in 1965 when they were selected for the assessment of 50,000 children in the National Collaborative Perinatal Project. The scales were administered to more than 1400 infants, aged from one to fifteen months. The findings replicated her earlier reports of no difference relating to sex, birth order or educational level on either the motor or mental parts of the scales. Throughout her career Bayley demonstrated a commitment to methodological innovation and measurement precision which set her work apart and which continues to distinguish her contributions in contemporary longitudinal prospective studies of development.

Békésy, Georg von

Born: 1899, Budapest, Hungary **Died:** 1972, Hawaii, USA **Nat:** Hungarian/American **Ints:** Engineering psychology, experimental, physiological and comparative **Educ:** PhD University of Budapest, 1923 **Appts & awards:** Laboratory, Royal Hungarian Institute for Research in Telegraphy Systems, 1924–46; Professor, University of Budapest, 1940; Ordinarius, Physical Institute, University of Budapest, 1946; Senior Research Fellow, Psycho-acoustic Laboratory, Harvard University, 1946–66; Research Professor, Royal Institute of Technology, Stockholm 1947; Hon. MD, universities of Münster, 1955, Berne, 1959, Padua, 1962; Hon. DSc, University of Pennsylvania, 1965; Nobel Prize in Medicine and Physiology, 1961; Professor of Sensory Sciences, University of Hawaii, 1966–72; ten medals from Scientific Societies

Principal publications

1928   Zur Theorie des Hörens: Die Schwingungsforme der Basilarmembran (Hearing theory: Vibrations of the basilar membrane). *Physicalische Zeitschrift*, 29, 793–810.

1935   Über akustische Reizung des Vestibularapparates (Acoustic stimulation of the vestibular mechanism). *Pflügers Archiv für die gesamte Physiologie*, 236, 59–76.

1938   Psychologie und Fernsprechtechnik (Psychology and telephone technique). *Forschung und Fortschritte*, 14, 342–4.

1939   Über die Vibrationsempfindung (The vibratory sense). *Akustische Zeitschrift*, 4, 316–34.

1947   A new audiometer. *Acta Oto-laryngologica*, 35, 411–22.

1956   Current status of theories of hearing. *Science*, 145, 834–35.

1960   *Experiments in Hearing*. McGraw-Hill.

1964   Duplexity theory of taste. *Science*, 145, 834–5.

1967   *Sensory Inhibition*. Princeton University Press.

Further reading
Newman, E.B. (1973) Georg von Békésy:
1899–1972. *Journal of American Psychology*, 86,
4, 855–7.
New York Times (1972) Dr Georg von Békésy. 15
June, 44, 4.

Georg von Békésy was born in Budapest, where
he received a Gymnasium education. Since his
father was in the diplomatic service of the
Austro-Hungarian Empire he spent part of his
youth in several foreign countries. He first
studied chemistry in Berne and later took his
PhD in experimental physics at the University of
Budapest. He spent a year in the laboratory of
the engineering firm Simens and Halske in
Berlin, and thereafter went back to Budapest to
supervise the linkage of the Hungarian telephone system with the trans-European network.
It became part of his task to design and evaluate
various types of wire and wireless transmission
systems. However, some of the technical improvements of these systems did not lead to a
better perception on the listener's side. This
finding convinced Békésy that the mechanism
of the inner ear and our tonal perceptions must
be more fully understood before advanced
technical transmission equipment could be
designed. With this thought he started on a
lifelong research career investigating the physical mechanism and the psychophysical aspects
of hearing and other senses.

With his skills in chemistry, physics and
engineering Békésy examined the histology,
anatomy and the function of the cochlea and the
basilar membrane. He designed most of his own
sound source and detection equipment. In his
text *Experiments in Hearing*, he summarizes the
results of eighty-three of his own experiments,
as well as the work of others, involving the
vibrations and the resonance which occur in the
ear during stimulation. Békésy developed intri-
cate experimental procedures such as injecting
silver crystals into the cochlear fluid to observe
the motion of the basilar membrane in response
to stimulations by different frequencies and
amplitudes. Using a microscope and strobos-
copic illumination, he could see that sounds set
the entire basilar membrane in vibration. High
tones would generate waves towards the base of
the membrane and low tones towards the apex.
Contrary to previous beliefs he found that
sounds do not produce tension in the hair cells
of the basilar membrane.

After his work on telephone transmission
systems Békésy was concerned with noise, the
unwanted stimulations and echoes which
interfere with perceptions. He wanted to know
how the ear and other sense organs keep out
unwanted information. Experimenting on sound
location, he found that the humans can localize
a sound when it reaches one ear as little as one
millisecond earlier than the other. Békésy found
that this capacity is due to 'lateral inhibition', a
central phenomenon which inhibits the reception
on the contra-lateral side, as soon as one side
is stimulated. Since sense organs developed
embryonically from the skin, Békésy suspected
similarities and began to examine other senses.
In his book *Sensory Inhibition*, he reports on
experimental findings which showed the existence of lateral inhibition in skin sensation, taste
and smell.

Békésy's work opened the way to major
advances in the diagnosis and correction of
damaged hearing. His Nobel Prize citation read:
'There is hardly any problem concerning the
physical mechanism of acoustic stimulation to
which Dr Békésy did not add clarity and
understanding.'

FRANK WESLEY

Bellak, Leopold

Born: 1916, Vienna, Austria **Nat:** American
Ints: Clinical psychology, psychiatry, psy-
choanalysis **Educ:** Matura University of Vienna
Medical School, 1935–8; MA Boston Univer-
sity, 1939; MA Harvard University, 1942; MD
New York Medical College, 1944 **Appts &
awards:** Clinical Professor of Psychiatry, Albert
Einstein College of Medicine; Clinical Professor
of Psychology, Postdoctoral Programme in
Psychotherapy, New York University; Private
practice of psychiatry and psychoanalysis,
Larchmont, New York; Secretary, Academic
Association for Medical Psychology, University
of Vienna, 1937; Austin and Rantoul Fellow,
Harvard University, 1941–2; President, NY
Society for Projective Technique, 1954, Society
for Projective Techniques and Rorschach
Institute, 1958, Westchester Psychoanalytic
Institute, 1962–3; Award for Contribution to
the Theory and Practice of Community Psy-
chiatry, Psychiatric Outpatient Centers of
America, 1976; Award of Excellence, Society
of Technical Communication, 1980

Principal publications
1948 *Dementia Praecox: The Past Decade's Work
and Present Status: A Review and Evaluation.*
Grune and Stratton.

1954   A study of limitations and 'failures': Toward an ego psychology of projective techniques. *Journal Projective Techniques*, 18, 279–93.

1956   An experimental exploration of the psychoanalytic process: Exemplification of a method. *Psychoanalysis Quarterly*, 25, 385–414 (with M. Brewster Smith).

1960   The rehabilitation of psychotics in the community. *American Journal of Orthopsychiatry*, 30, 346–55 (with B. Black).

1963   Acting out: Some conceptual and therapeutic considerations. *American Journal of Psychotherapy*, 17, 375–89.

1964   An approach to the evaluation of drug effects during psychotherapy: A double-blind study of a single case. *Journal of Nervous and Mental Disorders*, 139, 20–30 (with J.B. Chassen).

1969   A systematic study of ego functions. *Journal of Nervous and Mental Disorders*, 148, 569–85 (with M. Hurvich).

1974   *A Concise Handbook of Community Psychiatry and Community Mental Health*. Grune and Stratton.

1974   Contemporary character as crisis adaptation. *American Journal of Psychotherapy*, 28, 46–58.

1977   Psychiatric states in adults with minimal brain dysfunction. *Psychiatric Annals*, 7, 575–98.

1978   *Emergency Psychotherapy and Brief Psychotherapy*. Grune and Stratton/CPS (with L. Small).

1979   Schizophrenic syndrome related to minimal brain dysfunction: A possible neurologic subgroup. *Schizophrenia Bulletin*, 5, 480–89.

1981   *Reading Faces*. Holt, Rinehart & Winston (with S.S. Baker).

1983   *The Broad Scope of Ego Function Assessment*. Wiley (with L. Goldsmith).

1983   *Handbook of Intensive Brief and Emergency Psychotherapy (BEP)*. CPS (with H. Siegel).

Further reading

Alexander, P.A., Jetto, T.L., White, J.L. *et al.* (1994) Young children's creative solutions to realistic and fanciful story patterns. *Journal of Creative Behavior*, 28, 89–106.

Fewtrell, W.D. and O'Connor, L.P. (1988) Dizziness and depersonalization. *Advances in Behavior Research and Therapy*, 10, 201–18.

Lake, B. (1985) Concept of ego strength in psychotherapy. *British Journal of Psychiatry*, 147, 471–8.

Sanua, V.D. (1991) The etiology of schizophrenia as perceived by psychiatrists in Europe and the United States. *Current Psychology: Research and Reviews*, 9, 4, 355–71.

Leopold Bellak's career can be divided into three interrelated parts, as a psychologist, a psychiatrist and a psychoanalyst. He was a life fellow in the professional organizations for all three areas. His first publication, for example, concerned itself with a psychoanalytic interpretation of IQ variability at different ages, and from there he moved on to become involved in an experimental demonstration of the concept of projection. His first book, *Dementia Praecox*, became a standard reference text for psychiatrists, as did his third book on the Thematic Apperception Test.

Having created the idea for a centre for research in schizophrenia at the NIMH, he managed to survive the political battles which ensued and ensured the success of the centre functioning along his guidelines. He has published and worked extensively in community mental health, drug therapy and brief psychotherapy, and done research in ego functions.

The later part of his career focuses on the study of attention deficit disorder (ADD) in adults. He wanted to show the effect of what is essentially a neurophysiological disorder on personality formation in psychoanalytic terms, demonstrating the defects by neuropsychological testing and establishing a new psychiatric diagnosis of the outcome of severe cases of ADD, leading to what he defines as the ADD psychosis, which he considers to be often misdiagnosed as schizophrenia.

Bem, Daryl J.

Born: 1938, Denver, Colorado, USA *Nat:* American *Ints:* Personality and social, Society for the Psychological Study of Social Issues *Educ:* BA Reed College, Oregon, 1960; PhD University of Michigan, 1964 *Appts & awards:* Professor of Psychology, Cornell University, Ithaca, New York; Member-at-Large, Division of Behavioral Sciences, National Research Council; Council Member, APA Division 9, 1971–3; National Academy of Sciences, 1971–4; Member, Secretary's Advisory Commission on Women, United States Department of Health, Education and Welfare, 1972–3; Fellow, APA, 1976– ; Personality Editor, *Journal of Personality and Social Psychology*, 1976–8; Consulting Editor, *Journal of Personality*, 1982–4, *Journal for the Theory of Social Behavior*, 1982–5; *Psychological Review*, 1982–

Principal publications

1962   Group influence on individual risk taking. *Journal of Abnormal and Social Psychology*, 65, 75–86 (with M.A. Wallace and N. Kogan).

1965   *A Laboratory Manual for the Control and Analysis of Behavior*. Brooks Cole.

1965   An experimental analysis of self-persuasion. *Journal of Experimental Social Psychology*, 1, 199–218.

1967   Self-perception: An alternative interpretation of cognitive dissonance phenomena. *Psychological Review*, 74, 183–200.

1970   *Beliefs, Attitudes and Human Affairs*. Brooks Cole.

1972   Self-perception theory. In L. Berkowitz (ed.), *Advances in Experimental Social Psychology*, vol. 6. Academic Press.

1974   Predicting some of the people some of the time: The search for cross-situational consistencies in behavior. *Psychological Review*, 81, 506–20 (with A. Allen).

1978   Predicting more of the people more of the time: Assessing the personality of situations. *Psychological Review*, 85, 485–500 (with D. Funder).

1983   Toward a response style theory of persons in situations. In R.A. Dienstbier and M. Page (eds), *Nebraska Symposium on Motivation 1982: Personality – Current Theory and Research*, vol. 30. University of Nebraska Press.

1989   Continuities and consequences of interactional styles across the life course. Special issue: Long-term stability and change in personality. *Journal of Personality*, 57, 375–406 (with A. Caspi and G.H. Elder).

1993   The Ganzfeld experiment. Special issue: A tribute to Charles Honorton. *Journal of Parapsychology*, 57, 101–10.

1994   Does psi exist? Replicable evidence for an anomalous process of information transfer. *Psychological Bulletin*, 115, 4–18 (with C. Honorton).

Further reading

Adams, J.F. and Sprenkle, D.H. (1990) Self-perception and personal commitment: A challenge to current theory of marital dissolution and stability and implications for marital therapy. *American Journal of Family Therapy*, 18, 131–40.

Olson, J.M. (1992) Self-perception of humor: Evidence for discounting and augmentation effects. *Journal of Personality and Social Psychology*, 62, 369–77.

Pervin, L.A. (ed.) (1990) *Handbook of Personality: Theory and Research*. Guilford Press.

Daryl Bem's contributions fall into three thematic areas. First, he proposed a theory of self-perception which offers an account of the way people come to know their internal states. This was a precursor to more general attribution theories. Second, and somewhat related, he has considered long-term continuities in personality and its relationship to styles of interaction. Third, he has recently rekindled a debate about the position of parapsychology within mainstream psychology.

Bem's theory of self-perception states that people come to know their internal states 'partially by inferring them from observations of their own overt behavior and/or the circumstances in which the behavior occurs'. For example, this means that people know their own attitudes not by introspection but rather by noticing regularities in their behaviour. Environmental factors are also important because they can give clues to the relationship between a self-perceived behaviour and a cognitive or emotional state. For instance, if someone knows she or he is peeling an onion she or he also knows that her or his crying behaviour should not be taken to mean emotional upset. Bem distinguished between manded behaviour (controlled by environmental stimuli) and tacted behaviour (not due to environmental stimuli and therefore indicative of a person's internal state). In effect Bem is stating that the procedures we invoke to infer internal states in others are based on the same principle we apply to guess our own internal states. This is the most fundamental and controversial aspect to his theory, articulated from a rigorous behaviourist standpoint. The theory accounts reasonably well for self-perception in circumstances where one's behaviour is consistent with prior attitudes, but not when there are inconsistencies.

On a related theme, he argues that there are long-term continuities of personality in interactional styles that are sustained both by the progressive accumulation of their own consequences over time (what he calls cumulative continuity) and by their contemporary, evocative consequences in reciprocal social interaction (what he terms interactional continuity). This theory has yet to be properly tested.

More recently he has turned his attention to research in extrasensory perception, a topic which is generally regarded with considerable scepticism by most academic psychologists. He argues that the replication rates and effect sizes achieved by one particular experimental method, the Ganzfeld procedure, are now sufficient to warrant bringing this body of data to the attention of the wider psychological community. His arguments are compelling and there is a suspicion that the resistance to the inclusion of any aspect of parapsychology into mainstream science sometimes results as much from prejudice as from rational argument.

Bem, Sandra (Lipsitz)

Born: 1944, Pittsburgh, USA *Nat:* American *Ints:* Developmental psychology, personality and social psychology, psychological study of social issues, psychology of women *Educ:* BA Carnegie Mellon University, 1965; PhD University of Michigan, 1968 *Appts & awards:* Professor of Psychology and Women's Studies, Cornel University, Ithaca, New York; Distinguished Scientific Award for an Early Career Contribution to Psychology, APA, 1976; Distinguished Publication Award, Association for Women in Psychology, 1977; Young Scholar Award, American Association of University Women, 1980; Hon. Doctor of Science, Wilson College Chambersburg, Penna, 1985; Editorial Board, *Journal of Consulting and Clinical Psychology, Journal of Applied Social Psychology, Signs: Journal of Women in Culture and Society, Psychology of Women Quarterly, Journal of Homosexuality, Sex Roles: A Journal of Research*

Principal publications

1970   Case study of a non-conscious ideology: Training the women to know her place. In D.J. Bem (ed.), *Beliefs, Attitudes and Human Affairs.* Brooks Cole.

1974   The measurement of psychological androgyny. *Journal of Consulting and Clinical Psychology*, 42, 155–62.

1975   Sex role adaptability: One consequence of psychological androgyny. *Journal of Personality and Social Psychology*, 31, 634–43.

1976   Sex typing and androgyny: Further exploration of the expressive domain. *Journal of Personality and Social Psychology*, 34, 1016–23 (with W. Martyna and C. Watson).

1981   Gender schema theory. *Psychological Review*, 88, 354–64.

1981   *Bem Sex Role Inventory Professional Manual.* Consulting Psychologists Press.

1981   Sex typing and the avoidance of cross-sex behaviour. *Journal of Personality and Social Psychology*, 33, 48–54 (with E. Linney).

1985   Androgyny and gender schema theory: A conceptual and empirical integration. In T.B. Sonderegger (ed.), *Motivation 1984: The Psychology of Gender.* University of Nebraska Press.

1985   If you're gender-schematic, all members of the opposite sex look alike. *Journal of Personality and Social Psychology*, 49, 459–68 (with D.E.S. Frable).

1987   Gender schema theory and the romantic tradition. In R. Shaver and C. Hendrick (eds), *Sex and Gender. Review of Personality and Social Psychology*, vol. 7. Sage.

1993   *The Lenses of Gender: Transforming the Debate on Sexual Inequality.* Yale University Press.

Further reading

Jacklin, C.N. (ed.) (1992) *The Psychology of Gender*, vol. 3. Edward Elgar.

Roth Walsh, M. (ed.) (1987) *The Psychology of Women: Ongoing Debates.* Yale University Press

Sandra Lipsitz's father was a postal clerk, and her mother was a secretary. She has one sister seven years younger. During elementary school she was one of three girls in a class of twelve at Hillel Academy. She attended Carnegie-Mellon University where she met a new assistant professor in the department, Daryl Bem whom she later married. For her PhD at the University of Michigan she worked in developmental psychology; her dissertation dealt with cognitive processing and problem solving in young children. Soon after completing her PhD her interests were channelled into women's liberation, and in the early 1970s she turned her attention to establishing a solid empirical basis for her feminist convictions.

Bem's research on gender began in the early 1970s with the articulation of the concept of psychological androgyny, the development of the Bem Sex Role Inventory, and empirical research on the behavioural correlates of sex types and androgynous self-concepts. At that time the view was widely in psychology, and society generally, that being sex typed was not only the normal but also the desirable outcome of human development. The idea of an androgynous individual – someone who does not rely on gender as a cognitive organizing principle, and whose personality combines both masculine and feminine elements – was undefined and unarticulated. Thus, from the beginning Bem challenged unproblematic concepts and exposed the assumptions on which they were based. At the beginning she tended to emphasize the surface attributes of the androgynous individual rather than the underlying psychological process that permitted both stereotypically masculine and feminine attributes to coexist within the same person. There was a shift in her research interests, about the late 1970s, to the study of the cognitive processes mediating sex typing and androgyny and to an articulation of what is now termed gender schema theory.

The first proposition of gender schema theory is that children become sex typed, in part, because they come to perceive, evaluate and regulate their own behaviour (and the behaviour of others) in terms of the prevailing cultural definition of gender appropriateness. This proposition has been tested empirically in many studies with adults, the results of which support the view that sex-typed individuals have a greater readiness than others to organize information in general, and their self-concepts in particular, in terms of gender. The second proposition of gender schema theory is that children come to use gender as a cognitive organising principle not because of any property intrinsic to sex itself, but because the culture communicates to the child both implicitly and explicitly that sex is the most important category in human social life. From an early age children are taught that, unlike other social categories which are significant in some contexts and not in others, the dichotomy between male and female has and ought to have intensive and extensive relevance to virtually every domain of human experience. There is a good deal of empirical support for this proposition too.

Parts of gender schema theory have been difficult to test because of the difficulty of observing parents and others sex typing children in the way that it suggests. Nevertheless the theory enjoys strong empirical support and dominates contemporary debates on sex typing.

Benton, Arthur Lester

Born: 1909, New York, USA *Nat:* American *Ints:* Clinical neuropsychology, clinical psychology, developmental psychology, physiological and comparative *Educ:* BA Oberlin College, 1931; MA Oberlin College, 1933; PhD Columbia University, 1935 *Appts & awards:* Professor Emeritus of Psychology and Neurology, University of Iowa; President, American Orthopsychiatric Association, 1964–5, International Neuropsychological Society, 1970–1; Secretary General, Research Group of Aphasia, World Federation of Neurology, 1972–8; Distinguished Professional Contribution Award,

APA, 1978; Hon. DSc, Cornell College, 1978; Directeur Associé, Ecole des Hautes Etudes, 1979; Outstanding Scientific Contribution Award, International Neuropsychological Society, 1981; Samuel Torrey Orton Award, 1982; Editorial Boards, *American Journal of Orthopsychiatry*, 1958–63, *Neurology*, 1960–72, *American Journal of Mental Deficiency*, 1962–6, *Neuropsychologia*, 1963– ; *Cortex*, 1964– , *Journal of Abnormal Psychology*, 1974–80, *Archives of Neurology*, 1976–80, *Journal of Clinical and Experimental Neuropsychology*, 1979–

Principal publications

1945 A visual retention test for clinical use. *Archives of Neurology and Psychiatry*, 54, 212–216.
1959 *Right–Left Discrimination and Finger Localization*. Hoeber-Harper.
1959 Reaction time in unilateral cerebral disease. *Confinia Neurologica*, 19, 247–56 (with R.J. Joynt).
1961 The fiction of the 'Gerstman syndrome'. *Journal of Neurology, Neurosurgery and Psychiatry*, 24, 176–81.
1966 *Problemi di Neuropsicologia*. Editrice Universitaria G. Barbera.
1967 Constructional apraxia and the minor hemisphere. *Confinia Neurologica*, 29, 1–16.
1968 Impairment in facial recognition in patients with cerebral disease. *Cortex*, 4, 344–58.
1970 *Behavioral Change in Cerebrovascular Disease*. Harper and Row.
1978 Visuospatial judgment: A clinical test. *Archives of Neurology*, 35, 364–8 (with N.R. Varney and K. des Hamsher).
1979 Facial recognition in patients with focal brain lesions. *Archives of Neurology*, 36, 837–9 (with K. des Hamsher and H.S. Levin).
1982 *Neurobehavioral Consequences of Closed Head Injury*. Oxford University Press (with H.S. Levin and R.G. Grossman).
1983 *Contributions to Neuropsychological Assessment*. Oxford (with K. des Hamsher, N.R. Varney and O. Spreen).

Further reading

des Hamsher, K. (1985) The Iowa Group. *International Journal of Neuroscience*, 25, 295–305.

Benton's interest in neuropsychology dates back to the pre-World War II era, when he studied closed head injury, the mental development of prematurely born children, and the developmental aspects of right–left orientation and finger recognition. Clinical experience with brain-wounded men in naval hospitals during World War II provided the opportunity to work with neurologists and neurosurgeons and thereby strengthened his interests. In 1950, he established a neuropsychological laboratory in the Department of Neurology at the University of Iowa Hospital. Many graduate and postgraduate students came to study there, establishing it as a major centre of training and research in neuropsychology. He directed a comprehensive programme of research, including reaction time, body schema performances (right–left orientation and finger recognition), clinical application of the method of double sensory stimulation, motor impersistence in brain-diseased adults and children, constructional praxis, hemispheric asymmetry in the mediation of visual, auditory and somesthetic performances and aphasic disorders. On his retirement in 1978, the center was renamed the Benton Laboratory of Neuropsychology in his honour.

Berkowitz, Leonard

Born: 1926, New York, USA *Nat:* American *Ints:* Social psychology, industrial and organizational psychology *Educ:* BA New York University, 1948; PhD University of Michigan, 1951 *Appts & awards:* Research Psychologist, Human Resources Research Center, San Antonio, 1951–5; Department of Psychology, University of Wisconsin, Madison, Assistant Professor, 1955–9, Associate Professor, 1959–62, Professor, 1962– ; Vilas Research Professor, 1969–93; Fellow, Center for the Advanced Study in Behavioral Sciences, Stanford, 1970–1, AAAS, 1977– ; President, APA Division 8, 1971–2; Overseas Fellow, Churchill College, University of Cambridge, 1974, 1976; Hon. Dr, University of Louvain-la-Neuve, 1977; Chair, APA Publications Board, 1981–2; International Society for Research on Aggression, 1981–3; APA Distinguished Scientific Award for the Application of Psychology, 1988; SESP Distinguished Scientific Award, 1989

Principal publications

1954 Group standards, cohesiveness and productivity. *Human Relations*, 7, 509–19.

1957 Liking for the group and the perceived merit of the group's behavior. *Journal of Abnormal and Social Behaviour*, 54, 353–7.

1958 The expression and reduction of hostility. *Psychological Bulletin*, 55, 257–83.

1960 Judgmental processes in personality functioning. *Psychological Review*, 67, 130–42.

1962 *Aggression: A Social Psychological Analysis.* McGraw-Hill.

1963 Effects of film violence on inhibitions against subsequent aggression. *Journal of Abnormal and Social Psychology*, 66, 405–12 (with E. Rawlings).

1964 Aggressive cues in aggressive behavior and hostility catharsis. *Psychological Review*, 71, 104–22.

1965 Some aspects of observed aggression. *Journal of Personality and Social Psychology*, 2, 359–69.

1967 Weapons as aggression-eliciting stimuli. *Journal of Personality and Social Psychology*, 7, 202–7 (with A. LePage).

1968 Impulse, aggression and the gun. *Psychology Today*, 2, 18–22.

1969 (ed.) *Roots of Aggression: A Re-examination of the Frustration–Aggression Hypothesis.* Atherton.

1970 *Altruism and Helping Behavior.* Academic Press (ed. with J. Macaulay).

1971 The contagion of criminal violence. *Sociometry*, 34, 238–60 (with J. Macaulay).

1972 *Social Psychology.* Scott Foreman.

1972 Social norms, feelings, and other factors affecting helping and altruism. In L. Berkowitz (ed.), *Advances in Experimental Social Psychology*, vol. 6. Academic Press.

1972 Frustrations, comparisons, and other sources of emotional arousal as contributors to social unrest. *Journal of Social Issues*, 28, 77–91.

1973 The meaning of an observed event as a determinant of its aggressive consequence. *Journal of Personality and Social Psychology*, 28, 206–17 (with J.T. Alioto).

1974 Some determinants of impulsive aggression: The role of mediated associations with reinforcements for aggression. *Psychological Review*, 81, 165–76.

1977 The stimulating and inhibiting effects of weapons on aggressive behavior. *Aggressive Behavior*, 3, 355–78 (with C.W. Turner, L.S. Simon and A. Frodi).

1978 Whatever happened to the frustration–aggression hypothesis? *American Behavioral Science*, 21, 691–708.

1981 The concept of aggression. In P. Brain and D. Benton (eds), *Multidisciplinary Approaches to Aggression Research*. Elsevier.

1981 Physical pain and the goal of aversively stimulated aggression. *Journal of Personality and Social Psychology*, 40, 687–700 (with S. Cochran and M. Embree).

1982 External validity is more than skin deep: Some answers to criticisms of laboratory experiments.

American Psychologist, 37, 245–57 (with E. Donnerstein).

1983   Aversively stimulated aggression: Some parallels and differences in research with animals and humans. *American Psychologist*, 38, 1135–44.

1984   Some effects of thoughts on anti- and pro-social influences of media events: A cognitive neoassociationist analysis. *Psychological Bulletin*, 95, 410–27.

1987   Pay equity, job gratification and comparisons in pay satisfaction. *Journal of Applied Psychology*, 72, 544–51 (with C. Fraser, F.P. Treasure and S. Cochrane).

1987   Mood, self-awareness, and willingness to help. *Journal of Personality and Social Psychology*, 52, 721–9.

1989   Frustration–aggression hypothesis: Examination and reformulation. *Psychological Bulletin*, 106, 59–73.

1989   On the construction of the anger experience: Aversive events and negative priming in the formation of feelings. In L. Berkowitz (ed.), *Advances in Experimental Social Psychology*, vol. 22. Academic Press (with K. Heimer).

1990   On the formation and regulation of anger and aggression: A cognitive-neoassociationistic analysis: American Psychological Association Distinguished Scientific Award for the Application of Psychology. *American Psychologist*, 45, 494–503.

1993   *Aggression: Its Causes, Consequences and Control*. McGraw-Hill.

1993   Frustration–aggression hypothesis: Examination and reformulation. *Psychological Bulletin*, 106, 59–73.

1993   Pain and aggression: Some findings and implications. *Motivation and Emotion*, 17, 277–93.

Further reading

Berkowitz, L. (1995) A career on aggression. In G.G. Brannigan and M.R. Merrens (eds), *The Social Psychologists: Research Adventures*. McGraw-Hill.

Cooper, J. and Fazio, R.H. (1989) Research traditions, analysis, and synthesis: Building a faulty case around misinterpreted theory. *Personality and Social Psychology Bulletin*, 15, 519–29.

Huesmann, L.R. (eds) (1994) *Aggressive Behavior: Current Perspectives*. Plenum.

Wyer, R.S. Jr and Srull, T.K. (eds) (1993) *Perspectives on Anger and Emotion*. Erlbaum.

Leonard Berkowitz was born in New York City, where he completed his primary and secondary education. Following military service, he graduated from New York University. In 1948 he started graduate work in psychology at the University of Michigan, where he specialized in social psychology. A research assistantship on a project investigating decision-making conferences was the basis for his doctoral dissertation on conference leadership, which he completed in June 1951 with the guidance of Dan Katz.

He spent from 1951 to 1955 at the Crew Research Laboratory of the US Air Force's Human Resource Research Center at San Antonio. In 1955, he was offered a position at the University of Wisconsin, Madison, and has remained a member of that department. He has had visiting appointments at both Oxford and Cambridge universities in England and at the University of Western Australia, as well as at Stanford and Cornell universities in the United States.

His interest in aggression led him to include this topic in an advanced undergraduate course in social psychology when he started working at the University of Wisconsin. His class lecture notes became the basis for a *Psychological Bulletin* article (1958) and subsequently his 1962 book, which was one of the first modern books to review the quantitative research on humans and aggression. These reviews raised many questions which led to a successful seventeen-year programme of research on aggression funded by the NIMH. Berkowitz conducted some of the pioneering research on the impact of media violence. His research included laboratory studies (1966) as well as field studies carried out during his time in Europe as well as in the United States. Berkowitz's research and writing on aggression have been conducted within a cognitive neo-associationistic framework, which he developed to account for the relationships between environmental factors, negative affect and the display of emotional aggression. He summarized his understanding of the nature of aggression in his 1993 book *Aggression: Its Causes, Consequences and Control*.

At the same time as Berkowitz was studying aggression he was also one of the first social psychologists to become interested in prosocial behaviour. His research developed out of his original interest in group dynamics and his observations that, under certain circumstances, people worked hard on behalf of dependent others even if they did not directly gain any reward themselves. His research programme, supported by the National Science Foundation for many years, investigated when and why people were motivated to aid others who needed their assistance.

Berkowitz founded and edited *Advances in Experimental Social Psychology* in 1964. He subsequently edited a total of twenty-two volumes of this series, which continues today under the editorship of Mark Zanna. In the preface to volume 1, Berkowitz saw the *Advances* as enabling social psychologists to do more than accumulate facts. The series was built on the belief that the scientist must 'integrate the available data in such a way that the observed events can be shown to be special cases of more general phenomena'. In other words, he was concerned to promote theoretical integration of findings in a particular research area which he considered might be useful in stimulating further research. As he also noted in the editorial to volume 1, 'There is no claim … that the theoretical statements presented in these volumes are the last word and will remain unaltered as additional information is obtained … by presenting their hypotheses, the writers have contributed to the data collection and the development that will question their own formulations. Their theoretical statement will help social psychology go further.' The content of subsequent volumes reflects not only Berkowitz's bias towards the experimental method (although he believed too that social psychology must conduct field research in naturalistic settings) but also his commitment to promoting exchanges of social-psychological information across national boundaries.

Berkowitz is one of the world's experts on human aggression and has provided the theoretical and empirical framework for one of the major strands in current understanding of its nature. According to Berkowitz, aggression is an externally elicited drive to harm or injure others. Most of his research and writings in the area of aggressive behaviour have attempted to demonstrate how aggressive actions can be influenced involuntarily by stimuli in the surrounding environment. Berkowitz and LePage (1967) carried out a classic study which demonstrated that the mere physical presence of a weapon facilitated aggression in an angry subject even though he or she did not use the gun. As Berkowitz noted in a much-cited statement, 'Guns not only permit violence, they can stimulate it as well. The finger pulls the trigger, but the trigger may also pull the finger.' Subsequent research has shown that the effect demonstrated by Berkowitz and LePage is found only under restricted conditions, but nevertheless this study had a major impact in demonstrating that aggression is determined by external as well as internal factors. The other stimuli which Berkowitz and his colleagues have studied extensively include the observed aggressive behaviour of others and, more generally, stimuli associated either with previously obtained reinforcements for aggression or with aversive events. All of these stimuli are considered, by definition, to produce negative affect.

Berkowitz's cognitive neo-associationistic view of aggression focused attention on affect at a time when social psychology tended to be predominantly cognitive. According to this view, negative affect produced by aversive stimuli (e.g. pain, heat, frustration, attack) automatically activates tendencies towards both aggression and avoidance, as well as thought and memories associated with these experiences. Whether aggression or avoidance follows an aversive stimulus is seen as associated with both the situation and the networks of associations which the individual has developed between anger and these activities, including appropriate behaviour in these circumstances. The experience of anger is therefore viewed as a prime for aggressive behaviour rather than a direct instigator. Berkowitz argued that the priming effect was bidirectional, and empirically demonstrated that thinking about aggressive behaviour can also prime feelings of anger. More recently, he extended the frustration–aggression hypothesis, which overstated the relationship between frustration and aggression by arguing that frustrations evoke an instigation to aggression primarily because they are aversive occurrences and that aversive stimulation is basically the root of 'angry' aggression.

Berkowitz's analysis of aggression is more hopeful than theories which locate aggression in biological terms or in reaction to inner characteristics. The cognitive neo-associationist model suggests that violence can be controlled by reducing aversive stimuli such as inadequate food, strengthening social norms which promote non-aggressive actions, and reducing overall availability of aggressive models.

Leonard Berkowitz was awarded the Distinguished Scientific Award for the Applications of Psychology in 1988. The value of his research and writing on aggression, emotions and helping behaviour, as well as his role as an editor and author, were recognized, but the citation specifically noted 'his integrative work in combining experimental and social psychology theoretically and methodologically'.

KAREN TREW

Berlucchi, Giovanni

Born: 1935, Pavia, Italy **Nat:** Italian **Ints:** Clinical neuropsychology, experimental psychology, physiological and comparative psychology **Educ:** MD (cum laude) University of Pavia, School of Medicine, 1959 **Appts & awards:** Institute of Physiology, University of Pisa, 1960–74, Full Professor, 1976–83; Joint Prize of Italian Society for Electroencephalography and Clinical Neurophysiology, 1963; Member, EBBS Committee, 1971–3, 1986–9, ENA Council, 1976–83, Programme Committee, 1994– , ETP Council, 1979–84, NATO Panel on Human Factors, 1979–83, Chairman, 1981, INS Committee, 1983–6, Società Italiana di Fisiologia, Council, 1984–7, IBRO Governing Council, 1992– ; Member, Accademia dei Fisiocritici, Siena, 1975, EEG Deutsche Gesellschaft, 1983, Academia Rodinensis pro Remediatione, Stockholm, 1988, Academia Europaea, 1990, New York Academy of Sciences, 1990, Accademia Nazionale dei Lincei, 1992, Accademia Nazionale Virgiliana di Scienze, Lettere ed Arti, 1995; Director, Institute of Human Physiology, University of Verona, 1983–93, Department of Neurological and Visual Sciences, University of Verona, 1994–; Special JM Sprague Lecturer, University of Pennsylvania, 1990; Gordon Holmes Lecturer, London, 1995; Section Editor for Neuropsychology and Behavioural Sciences, *Experimental Brain Research*, 1981–9. Editor in chief, *Neuropsychologia*, 1992: Editorial Board, *Brain Research*, 1974–9, *Behavioural Brain Research*, 1980–8, *Human Neurobiology*, 1981–7, *International Journal of Psychophysiology*, 1983–8, *Excerpta Medica Physiology*, 1983– , *Functional Neurology*, 1986– , *Consciousness and Cognition*, 1990–3, *Cognitive Brain Research*, 1991– , *Journal of Physiology*, 1993– , *Journal of Neuroscience*, 1994–

Principal publications

1967 Microelectrode analysis of transfer of visual information by the corpus callosum. *Archives Italiennes de Biologie*, 105, 583–96 (with M.S. Gazzaniga and G. Rizzolatti).

1968 Binocularly driven neurons in visual cortex of split chiasm cats. *Science*, 159, 308–10 (with G. Rizzolatti).

1971 Simple reaction time of ipsilateral and contralateral hand to lateralized visual stimuli. *Brain*, 94, 419–30 (with W. Heron *et al.*).

1971 Opposite superiorities of the right and left cerebral hemispheres in discriminative reaction time to physiognomical and alphabetical material.

Brain, 94, 431–42 (with G. Rizzolatti and C. Umiltà).

1972 The pretectum and superior colliculus in visually guided behavior, and in flux and form discrimination in the cat. *Journal of Comparative and Physiological Psychology*, 78, 123–72 (with J.M. Sprague *et al.*).

1972 Anatomical and physiological aspects of visual functions of corpus callosum. *Brain Research*, 37, 371–92.

1977 Influence of spatial stimulus-response compatibility on reaction time of ipsilateral and contralateral hand to lateralized light stimuli. *Journal of Experimental Psychology, Human Perception and Performance*, 3, 505–17 (with F. Crea *et al.*).

1979 *Structure and Function of the Cerebral Commissures*. Macmillan (with I.S. Russell and M.W. van Hof).

1981 Recent advances in the analysis of the neural substrates of interhemispheric communication. In O. Pompeiano and C. Ajmone-Marsan (eds), *Brain Mechanisms of Perceptual Awareness and Purposeful Behavior*. Raven Press.

1983 Interhemispheric transmission of information in manual and verbal reaction-time tasks. *Human Neurobiology*, 2, 77–85 (with G. Tassinari and M. Morelli).

1983 Physiological organization of callosal connections of a visual lateral suprasylvian cortical area in the cat. *Journal of Neurophysiology*, 49, 903–21 (with A. Antonini and F. Lepore).

1989 Spatial distribution of the inhibitory effect of peripheral non-informative cues on the simple reaction time to non-fixated targets. *Neuropsychologia*, 27, 201–21 (with G. Tassinari *et al.*).

1995 Corpus callosum and simple visuomotor integration. *Neuropsychologia*, 33, 923–36 (with S. Aglioti *et al.*).

Further reading

Milner, A.D. (1994) Interhemispheric pathways for visual integration. In M. Lassonde and M.A. Jeeves (eds), *Callosal Agenesis: The Natural Split Brain*. Plenum.

—— and Rugg, M.D. (1989) Interhemispheric transmission times. In J.R. Crawford and D.M. Parker (eds), *Developments in Clinical and Experimental Neuropsychology*. Plenum.

Giovanni Berlucchi was born and educated in the ancient University city of Pavia, in Lombardy, northern Italy. After graduating in medicine at the university, he moved to Pisa, where he has spent the major part of his scientific career. He gained his initial research training from Giuseppe Moruzzi, one of the greatest neuroscientists of all time. In this period as a postdoctoral fellow, Berlucchi (with Moruzzi and Strata) confirmed the existence of sleep centres in the caudal medulla and showed that during rapid eye movement (REM) sleep the activity of a major output of the cortex, the pyramidal tract, increases tonically while the pupillary and middle ear muscles contract phasically in association with REMs.

Berlucchi spent the year 1964–5 at the California Institute of Technology, working with Roger **Sperry**. It was at this time that his principal research interests moved in the direction of inter-hemispheric relations and cerebral asymmetries, the area in which he has made his major scientific contributions. Another stay in the USA, at the University of Pennsylvania during 1968, allowed him to apply the 'split-brain' approach to problems concerning the cortical and subcortical substrates of vision in the cat. In seminal work with Giacomo **Rizzolatti** and Michael **Gazzaniga**, he provided two independent physiological demonstrations of the selective relation of the callosal connections of the visual cortices with the vertical meridian of the visual field. In this work, done in Pisa, he was able to document the orderly convergence of intra- and inter-hemispheric visual afferents onto single cortical neurones. In further highly original work done partially in collaboration with James Sprague at Pennsylvania, he showed that in the cat the superior colliculus played an important role in form discrimination, and in separate studies he explored the role of extrastriate visual cortex in form vision. In these and later studies, he showed how harnessing behavioural techniques could powerfully complement physiological studies in probing the function of the visual system and its commissural links. In subsequent physiological studies, especially with his students Carlo Marzi and Antonella Antonini, Berlucchi went on to demonstrate that the superior colliculus participates in the integration of visual information across the vertical midline of the visual field by receiving an indirect input through the cortical callosum.

At this time in the late 1960s, Berlucchi was also among the first investigators to apply physiological reasoning to problems of inter-hemispheric interactions in normal human subjects, by combining reaction-time measurements with lateralized stimulus presentation. Along with Rizzolatti and Carlo Umiltà, he demonstrated opposite hemifield (and therefore hemispheric) superiorities for discriminative reaction time to letters and faces. In an influential series of subsequent studies, mainly in collaboration with Marzi and Giancarlo Tassinari, he was able to show that the time required for inter-hemispheric transmission to determine manual responses is constant irrespective of changes in visual stimulation conditions and stimulus–response compatibility. This work has more recently been extended to the study of patients with lesions of the corpus callosum (both congenital and surgically induced), in collaboration especially with Tassinari and Salvatore Aglioti. These studies are revealing important hints as to the contribution of different parts of the callosum to the mediation of visuomotor behaviour. In a separate, still continuing, series of important studies on human subjects, Berlucchi and his colleagues have been exploiting the paradigms developed by Michael **Posner** to examine systematically the facilitatory and inhibitory effects of non-informative cueing on visuomotor responses.

Berlucchi's research is characterised by high standards of scientific rigour, allied with elegant and incisive experimental techniques, often innovatively and imaginatively applied. He has brought to neuropsychology the physiologist's distaste for grand theoretical edifices, and instead concentrated on studies designed to advance the field, one step at a time, within well-defined areas where experimental questions can yield clear answers. His standing in the field of contemporary neuropsychology (and neuroscience generally) is clear from a glance at his editorial positions on many of the highest-ranking journals in his field.

A.D. MILNER

Berlyne, Daniel Ellis

Born: 1924, Salford, Lancashire, England **Died:** 1976, Toronto, Ontario, Canada **Nat:** British/Canadian **Ints:** Experimental, general, physiological and comparative, psychology and the arts **Educ:** BA Cambridge University, 1947; MA Cambridge University, 1949; PhD Yale University, 1953 **Appts & awards:** Professor of Psychology, University of Toronto, 1962–76; Teaching positions, Brooklyn College, New York City, Universities of St Andrews, Aberdeen, Boston, and other visiting posts in Europe and North America; Fellow, Royal Society of Canada; President, Canadian Psychological Association, 1971–2, APA General Psychology

Section, 1973–4, APA Psychology and the Arts Section, 1974–5, International Association of Empirical Aesthetics, 1974–6

Principal publications

1957 Conflict and information theory as determinants of human perceptual curiosity. *Journal of Experimental Psychology*, 53, 399–404.

1960 *Conflict, Arousal and Curiosity*. McGraw-Hill.

1965 *Structure and Direction in Thinking*. Wiley

1970 Novelty, complexity and hedonic value. *Perception and Psychophysics*, 8, 279–86.

1971 *Aesthetics and Psychobiology*. Appleton-Century-Crofts.

1973 *Pleasure, Reward and Preference*. Academic Press (with K.B. Madsen).

1974 *Studies in the New Experimental Aesthetics*. Hemisphere.

1976 The new experimental aesthetics and the problem of classifying works of art. *Scientific Aesthetics*, 1, 85–106.

Further reading

Konecni, V.J. (1978) Daniel E. Berlyne: 1924–76. *American Journal of Psychology*, 91, 133–7.

Machotka, P. (1980) Daniel Berlyne's contributions to empirical aesthetics. *Motivation and Emotion*, 4, 113–21.

Daniel Berlyne was born in Salford, England, and was educated at Manchester Grammar School and the University of Cambridge before taking his doctoral degree at Yale University in 1953. He spent most of his working life as Professor of Psychology at the University of Toronto, until his untimely death at the age of 52. Berlyne had an unusually encyclopaedic knowledge not only of a wide range of areas of psychology, but also of other sciences and humanities. His scholarship was characterised by drawing on this breadth and depth of knowledge in a tireless and energetic pursuit of particular theoretical ideas to their logical limits.

This is most obviously and clearly seen in his attempt to explain diverse aspects of animal and human behaviour in terms of a small number of motivational principles, and formed part of the new approach to motivation in the 1960s, which moved away from an emphasis on physiological drives and towards one on curiosity and exploratory behaviour. Berlyne's investigations of why people and animals explore their environments, displaying curiosity, interest and liking for objects such as art works, formed the basis of what became known as the 'new experimental aesthetics'; Berlyne was primarily responsible for proposing a sound theoretical and empirical basis for this.

Berlyne's theory of collative motivation seeks to explain what he called the 'hedonic value' of stimuli in terms of fluctuations in the organism's level of arousal, and this is in turn affected by three classes of stimulus variables, namely collative, ecological and psychophysical ones. A central concept in the theory, which has antecedents in the work of Aristotle as well as that of Wilhelm **Wundt**, is that an inverted-U relationship obtains between the hedonic value of stimuli and the observer's lack of arousal: stimuli are most liked when they create intermediate levels of arousal in the observer, because of the levels of activity which are evoked in the reticular activating system. Berlyne tested this theory by experimental investigations of the relationship between aesthetic preferences and particular stimulus properties, by investigating changes in preferences over time, and by conducting specific manipulations of levels of arousal. Towards the end of his life, Berlyne began to employ multidimensional scaling techniques in the systematic analysis of real-life stimuli such as pieces of music and paintings.

The strength of Berlyne's theory lies in its potential to explain a very wide range of aesthetic phenomena in terms of basic, biologically founded principles. More recent research in experimental aesthetics has begun to question the range of application of these principles, and to develop complementary models: a recent focus is upon the prototypicality of objects in relation to the classes of which they form a part. The implication of these new approaches for Berlyne's theory are still being worked out. He would undoubtedly be gratified to know that the International Association of Experimental Aesthetics, which he worked so hard to promote, is playing a major role in these developments.

DAVID J. HARGREAVES

Berscheid, Ellen S.

Nat: American *Ints:* Personality and social psychology *Educ:* BA University of Nevada, 1959; MA University of Nevada, 1960; PhD University of Minnesota, 1965 *Appts & awards:* Professor, Department of Psychology, University of Minnesota; Editorial Board, *Journal of Experimental Social Psychology*, 1970–90, *Sociometry*, 1971–2, *Journal of Personality and Social Psychology: Interpersonal Relations and Group Processes*, 1979– , *Journal of Personality*, 1981–3, *International Journal of Social and Personal Relationships*, 1982–5, *Journal of Social and Clinical Psychology*, 1982–5, *Review of Personality and Social Psychology*, 1985–90, *Sage Monographs in Interpersonal Relationships*, 1989–91, *Personal Relationships*, 1993– ; Executive Board, Society of Experimental Social Psychology, 1971–4, 1977–80, 1985–9; Chair, Membership Committee, 1973, 1985–8; NRC Assembly of Behavioural and Social Sciences, 1973–7; APA Division 8, D.T Campbell Award, 1984; President, APA Division 8, 1984, International Society for the Study of Interpersonal Relationships, 1991–2; Society of Experimental Social Psychology, Senior Distinguished Scientific Awards Committee, 1984–6; NRC Committee on Basic Research in the Behavioural and Social Sciences, Workgroup on Social Interaction, 1985; Fellow, APA, APA Division 9; APA Council of Editors, 1985–91; Editor, *Contemporary Psychology*, 1985–91; Distinguished Scientist Award, Society of Experimental Social Psychology, 1993; Editorial roles in numerous other journals; International Network for the Study of Interpersonal Relationships named research award: The Ellen Berscheid and Elaine Hatfield Award for Distinguished Scholarship in Interpersonal Relationships

Principal publications

1967   When does a harm-doer compensate a victim? *Journal of Personality and Social Psychology*, 6, 435–41 (with E. Walster).

1969   *Interpersonal Attraction*. Addison-Wesley (with E. Walster).

1971   Physical attractiveness and dating choice: A test of matching hypothesis. Journal of *Experimental Social Psychology*, 7, 173–89 (with K. Dion, E. Walster and G.W. Walster).

1974   Physical attractiveness and social perception among children. *Sociometry*, 37, 1–12 (with K. Dion).

1974   Physical attractiveness. In L. Berkowitz (ed.), *Advances in Experimental Social Psychology*, vol. III. Academic Press (with E. Walster).

1976   Gain/loss theory and 'the law of infidelity': Mr. Doting vs the Admiring Stranger. *Journal of Personality and Social Psychology*, 33, 709–18 (with T. Brothon and W. Graziano).

1977   Privacy: A hidden variable in experimental social psychology. *Journal of Social Issues*, 33, 85–101.

1978   *Equity: Theory and Research*. Allyn and Bacon (with W. Walster and G.W. Walster).

1982   Intimate relationships. In C. Offir (ed.), *Human Sexuality*. Harcourt, Brace, Jovanovich.

1983   *Close Relationships*. Freeman (with H.H. Kelly, A. Christensen, J. Harvey, T. Huston, G. Levinger, E. McClintock, A. Peplau and D. Petersen).

1983   Interpersonal attraction. In G. Lindzey and E. Aronson (eds), *Handbook of Social Psychology*. Addison-Wesley.

1986   Emotion and interpersonal communication. In G. Miller and M. Roloff (eds), *Explorations in Interpersonal Communication*. Sage.

1989   The Relationship Closeness Inventory: Assessing the closeness of interpersonal relationships. *Journal of Personality and Social Psychology*, 57, 792–807.

1991   Interpersonal attraction. In R. Dulbecco (ed.), *Affect and Social Behavior*. Cambridge University Press.

1994   Interpersonal relationships. In L.W. Porter and M.R. Rosenzweig (eds), *Annual Review of Psychology*: Annual Reviews.

Further reading

Hendrick, S.S. and Hendrick, C. (1992) *Romantic Love*. Sage.

Sternberg, R.J. (1987) Liking versus loving: A comparative evaluation of theories. *Psychological Bulletin*, 102, 331–45.

—— and Barnes, M.L. (eds) (1988) *The Psychology of Love*. Yale University Press.

Ellen Berscheid's work on interpersonal relationships is closely linked with the contributions of her colleague Elaine Walster (**Hatfield**). They argued that there are fundamental differences between the feelings of liking and loving. To account for these differences Berscheid used Seymour **Schacter**'s theory of emotion, which states that the interpretations and labels people attach to feelings of arousal are determined by external factors. For example, two people working in a busy, emotionally demanding environment may endure long work hours and high levels of physiological arousal. They begin to feel emotionally and physically attracted to one another and explain this in terms of their similar lifestyles and interests. If their arousal levels remain high they are likely to begin to label their mutual attachment as love. Berscheid and Walster argue that there are two types of love: passionate and compassionate. Passionate love is associated with sexual attraction and emotional turbulence and usually occurs earlier in a relationship, whereas compassionate love is rather like an extension and intensification of liking.

Equity theory says that a person will try to maximize his or her 'profits', which means everyone will pursue the rich and beautiful.

Bickhard, Mark H.

Born: 1945, Chicago, USA *Nat:* American *Ints:* Developmental psychology, personality and social psychology, philosophical and theoretical psychology, psychotherapy *Educ:* internship in clinical psychology, 1969–71, and PhD, 1973, University of Chicago *Appts & awards:* Professor of Educational Psychology, University of Texas, Austin, 1972–90; Henry R. Luce Professor in Cognitive Robotics and the Philosophy of Knowledge, Lehigh University, Bethlehem, Pennsylvania, 1990–

Principal publications

1978   The nature of developmental stages. *Human Development*, 21, 217–33.

1980   Functionalism in Adlerian psychology. *Journal of Individual Psychology*, 33, 66–74.

1980   *Cognition, Convention and Communication.* Praeger.

1983   *On the Nature of Representation: A Case Study of James Gibson's Theory of Perception.* Praeger (with D.M. Richie).

1988   Piaget on variation and selection models. *Human Development*, 31, 274–312.

1989   The nature of psychopathology. In L. Simek-Downing (ed.), *International Psychotherapy: Theories, Research and Cross-Cultural Implications.* Praeger.

1991   A pre-logical model of rationality. In L. Steffe (ed.), *Epistemological Foundations of Mathematical Experience.* Springer-Verlag.

1992   Commentary on the age 4 transition. *Human Development*, 35, 182–92.

1992   Some foundational questions concerning language studies. *Journal of Pragmatics*, 17, 401–33, (with R.L. Campbell).

1995   Intrinsic constraints on language: Grammar and hermeneutics. *Journal of Pragmatics*, 23, 541–54.

1995   *Foundational Issues in Artificial Intelligence and Cognitive Science: Impasse and Solution.* Elsevier Scientific (with L. Terveen).

Further reading

Kirkeby, O.F. (1992) Dual textuality and the phenomenology of events: On some conceptual problems in the article by M.H. Bickhard and R.L. Campbell. *Journal of Pragmatics*, 17, 483–90.

Steffe, L.P. and Gale, J.E. (eds) (1995) *Constructivism in Education.* Erlbaum.

Yngve, V.H. (1992) Criteria of acceptance: Comments on M.H. Bickhard and R.L. Campbell, 'Some foundational questions concerning language studies' *Journal of Pragmatics*, 17, 549–55.

Mark Bickhard was educated at the University of Chicago, initially in mathematics and statistics, but switched to an internship in clinical psychology and a PhD deriving from and extending **Piaget**'s theory of human development. He has published widely on Piagettian theory, on **Gibson**'s perceptual theory and on **Adler**ian individual psychology, and practised as a psychotherapist from 1975 to 1990. Recently he has turned his attention to the general theory of human behaviour, taking a constructivist position equally applicable in human development and in AI and cognitive science. He is currently working with Donald T. **Campbell** on developments of the latter's well-known 'blind variation and selective retention' paradigm.

Bickhard argues for a version of naturalism, holding that if a model of a particular psychological phenomenon makes it impossible for that phenomenon to have come into existence, then the model must be wrong. He shows how current models fail that test because the individual organism can evaluate its supposed models only against other models; it is allowed no well-grounded point of origin for the models. Such errors follow the adoption of a false and outdated metaphysic. What Bickhard calls 'substance metaphysics' was taken for granted from the earliest times; new substances were postulated to explain any new phenomenon under investigation. 'Caloric' was, for example, postulated as the substance accounting for heat by its presence or absence. In modern physical science such ideas have been abandoned in favour of a 'process metaphysics'; heat is now regarded as a process (kinetic energy), not a substance. Substance metaphysics has not been abandoned in psychology; 'mind' is still commonly treated as a substance even though most of the psychologists who do so would hotly deny that they were mind–body dualists. That mind is so treated appears from the very wide adoption of theories of representation that, as Bickhard has shown, cannot account for the origin of the representations. He advocates a move towards a process metaphysic (in which psychology would be doing only what the other sciences had already done) and has offered process models of various psychological functions including perception, rationality and language. He comes to the task with a wider background of relevant knowledge and experience than is commonly found among psychologists, and his work promises much for the future.

N.E. WETHERICK

Binet, Alfred

Born: 1857, Nice, France **Died:** 1911, Paris, France **Nat:** French **Ints:** Developmental psychology, educational psychology, evaluation and measurement, mental retardation, personality and social **Educ:** Licence (Law), Paris, 1878; Doctorate, 1894 **Appts & awards:** Lauréat, Academy of Moral and Political Sciences, 1887; Director, Psychology Laboratory, Ecole Pratique des Hautes Etudes, 1894; Founder and First Editor, *L'Année Psychologique*, 1894–1911, *Bulletin of the Société Libre pour l'Étude Psychologique de l'Enfant*, 1900–11; Elected to Société de Biologie, 1895; Visiting Professor, University of Bucharest, 1895; Invited Member, later 'Assesseur', Société Libre pour l'Étude Psychologique de l'Enfant, 1899

Principal publications

1887 *Le Magnétisme Animal*. Alcan (with C. Féré).
1890 Perceptions d'Enfants. *Revue Philosophique*, 30, 582–611.
1892 *Les Altérations de la Personnalité*. Alcan.
1893 Les Grandes Mémoires: Résumé d'une enquête sur les joueurs d'échecs. *Revue des Deux Mondes*, June, 826–60.
1894 *Introduction à la Psychologie Expérimentale*. Alcan (with J. Philippe, J. Courtier and V. Henri).
1895 La Mémoire des phrases. *L'Année Psychologique*, 1, 24–59 (with V. Henri).
1896 La Psychologie individuelle. *L'Année Psychologique*, 2, 411–65 (with V. Henri).
1898 *La Fatigue Intellectuelle*. Schleicher Frères (with V. Henri).
1898 La Mesure en psychologie individuelle. *Revue Philosophique*, 46, 113–23.
1900 *La Suggestibilité*. Schleicher Frères.
1903 *L'Etude Expérimentale de l'Intelligence*. Schleicher Frères.
1905 Sur la nécessité d'établir un diagnostic scientifique des états inférieurs de l'intelligence. *L'Année Psychologique*, 11, 163–90 (with Th. Simon).
1905 Méthodes Nouvelles pour le diagnostic du niveau intellectuel des anormaux. *L'Année*

Psychologique, 11. 191–244 (with Th. Simon).
1905 Application des méthodes nouvelles du diagnostic du niveau intellectuel chez des enfants normaux et anormaux d'hospice et d'école primaire. *L'Année Psychologique*, 11, 245–336 (with Th. Simon).
1908 *Les Idées Modernes sur les Enfants*. Flammarion. (New edn 1911.)
1908 Le développement de l'intelligence chez les enfants. *L'Année Psychologique*, 14, 1–94.
1911 Nouvelles recherches sur la mesure du niveau intellectuel chez les enfants d'école. *L'Année Psychologique*, 14, 145–201.

Further reading

Avanzini, G. (1969) *Alfred Binet et la Pédagogie Scientifique*. Vrin.
Fancher, R. (1985) *The Intelligence Men*. Norton.
Wolf, T. (1973) *Alfred Binet*. Norton.

Alfred Binet was born in Nice, France, in 1857, but in the year 1869 his family moved to Paris, where he spent the rest of his life. He attended the prestigious lycée Louis-le-Grand, and later obtained a degree in law (1878), but law was a profession which he despised. As he was of independent means, Binet was able to pursue his own interests. He read widely in the Bibliothèque Nationale over a few years, and after an introduction in 1882 to Jean-Martin **Charcot**, the neurologist at the Salpêtrière Hospital, Binet worked under him for the next eight years. The outcome of this work was seventeen publications on the topics of animal magnetism, hypnosis and hysteria. Starting late in 1887 or early 1888 Binet attended courses at the embryological laboratory of Balbiani, where he also became familiar with botany and zoology; there he learned of experimental methods and the importance of careful observation. His doctoral thesis on the subintestinal nervous system of insects secured for him a Doctorate in Natural Science in 1894. In the meantime Binet had also started work with Beaunis, the Director of the psychological laboratory at the Sorbonne University, and became its Director in 1894. In the same year Binet founded and became the first editor of *L'Année Psychologique*, the first journal in France to be devoted to the discipline of psychology. By this time Binet's wide-ranging interests had also resulted in many publications on the following topics: fetishism, hallucinations, animal magnetism, hypnotism, hysteria, suggestion, perception, visual imagery, extraordinary memories, blindfold chess-players, music, theatre, fear, religion, the physical correlates of normality versus abnormality, dementia, manic depression, mental fatigue, handwriting and deaf mutes.

In the summer of 1895 Binet lectured at the University of Bucharest as a visiting professor, but declined the offer made to him of a permanent chair. From 1894 onwards, in collaboration with Victor Henri, he conducted experiments on school children in Paris. These children (usually boys) provided them with subjects which were not forthcoming in the psychological laboratory. In addition Binet became both an advocator and promoter of what he termed 'psychologie individuelle' and methods of measuring individual differences. In 1899 Binet made the acquaintance of Théodore Simon, a clinician who became his important collaborator over the next eleven years. Binet became a member of the Société Libre pour l'Etude Psychologique de l'Enfant. His skills and knowledge were recognized within this society, in which he tried to convince the members of the importance of observation and experimental method in pedagogy. At the end of 1904 Binet headed a Ministerial Commission which was required to track down the 'abnormal' children in the schools of Paris, i.e. those who were unable to learn adequately in the regular school system. Binet and Simon saw that this commission required a psychological and experimental method. By May 1905 they produced sufficient test items which, in hierarchical order of difficulty, constituted what was immediately recognized as the first workable scale of intelligence. In 1908 this scale was revised by Binet and Simon, and Binet, still unsatisfied, made a final revision in 1911, the year of his death.

The most likely influences on Binet's life came from his wide reading, which included that of the English Empiricists John Locke and J.S. Mill. He probably gained his knowledge of German psychology through the work of **Ribot** and through his collaboration with Henri, who had studied under **Külpe** at Wurzburg. As a psychologist and later in his career as a pedagogue, Binet was convinced that the only valuable method was that of observation and experimentation. His preferred stance was atheoretical, particularly as he saw that preconceived ideas biased both method and results in experimentation. His interest in child development can be traced to 1890, when he tried out some simple tests of reaction times and perception on a few young children. He could observe his own daughters' development, and

they became his subjects – as Marguérite and Armande – between the years 1900 and 1903; he investigated their thinking processes, and observed distinct personality differences and cognitive styles. It was this latest set of experiments, together with others carried out on school children on perception, memory, judgement, etc., that formed the groundwork for him and Simon by providing test items for their scale of intelligence. Binet had no systematic theory of intelligence, but saw that comprehension, judgement, common sense and to some extent memory manifested themselves in many ways. Unlike Francis **Galton**, J. McKeen **Cattell** and Wissler in the so-called mental testing movement, Binet was convinced that individual differences in intelligence lay in the higher mental processes. His developmental view provided a further insight: he saw that a child's level of functioning could be assessed with reference to what most children of that age could do. These two beliefs formed the logical basis of a scale of tasks of increasing difficulty in which a child's intellectual level could be identified. Binet did not use the term 'mental age', and expressed a reluctance to attach a label to an individual child. These first scales of intelligence are generally considered to represent the breakthrough in intelligence testing, and Binet's principal contribution to psychology. However, only a much wider reading of his work can provide an adequate idea of the quality and originality of one of France's earliest experimental psychologists.

DIANA FABER

Bisiach, Edoardo Leandro

Born: 1932, Venegono, Italy *Nat:* Italian *Ints:* Clinical Neuropsychology; Experimental psychology; Philosophical and theoretical psychology *Educ:* MD, Università di Milano, 1956; Specialization in Clinical Neurology, Università di Milano 1959 *Appts & awards:* Clinica Neurologica, Università di Milano, 1959–83, Università di Padova, 1991–4, Università di Torino, 1994– ; many invited lectures, including the twentieth Sir Frederick Bartlett Lecture, Queen's College, Oxford, 1992, State of the Art Lecture at the XXVth International Congress of Psychology, Brussels, 1992; Special Lecture at the eighteenth Annual Meeting of the Japanese Society of Aphasiology and Higher Brain Function, Nagoya, 1994, Special Lecture to the Keio Medical Society, Tokyo, 1994

Principal publications

1976 Halving a horizontal segment: A study on hemisphere-damaged patients with cerebral focal lesions. *Archives Suisses de Neurologie, Neurochirurgie et de Psychiatrie*, 118, 199–206 (with E. Capitani, A. Colombo and H. Spinnler).

1978 Unilateral neglect of representational space. *Cortex*, 14, 129–33 (with C. Luzzatti).

1979 Unilateral neglect, representational schema and consciousness. *Brain*, 102, 609–618 (with C. Luzzatti and D. Perani).

1980 Loss of mental imagery: A case study. *Neuropsychologia*, 18, 435–42 (with A. Basso and C. Luzzatti).

1981 Brain and conscious representation of outside reality. *Neuropsychologia*, 19, 543–51 (with E. Capitani, C. Luzzatti and D. Perani).

1983 Line bisection and cognitive plasticity of unilateral neglect of space. *Brain and Cognition*, 2, 32–8 (with E. Bisiach, C. Bulgarelli, R. Sterzi and G. Vallar).

1984 Disorders of perceived auditory localization after lesions of the right hemisphere. *Brain*, 107, 37–52 (with L. Cornacchia, R. Sterzi and G. Vallar).

1987 Dyschiria: An attempt at its systematic explanation. In M. Jeannerod (ed.), *Neurophysiological and Neuropsychological Aspects of Spatial Neglect*. North-Holland (with A. Berti).

1988 *Consciousness in Contemporary Science* Oxford University Press (ed. with A.J. Marcel).

1988 Hemineglect in humans. In F. Boller and J. Grafman (eds), *Handbook of Neuropsychology*, vol. 1. Elsevier (with G. Vallar).

1989 Influence of response modality on perceptual awareness of contralesional visual stimuli. *Brain*, 112, 1627–36 (with G. Vallar and G. Geminiani).

1990 Perceptual and premotor factors in unilateral neglect. *Neurology*, 40, 1278–81 (with G. Geminiani, A. Berti and M.L. Rusconi).

1991 Anosognosia related to hemiplegia and hemianopia. In G. Prigatano and D. L. Schacter (eds), *Awareness of Deficit after Brain Injury*. Oxford University Press (with G. Geminiani).

1992 Understanding consciousness: Clues from unilateral neglect and related disorders. In A.D. Milner and M.D. Rugg (eds), *The Neuropsychology of Consciousness*. Academic Press.

1993 Mental representation in unilateral neglect and related disorders. The twentieth Bartlett Memorial Lecture. *Quarterly Journal of Experimental Psychology*, 46A, 435–61.

1994 Consciousness in dyschiria. M.S. Gazzaniga (ed.), *The Cognitive Neurosciences*. MIT Press (with A. Berti).

Further reading

Jeannerod, M. (ed.) (1987) *Neurophysiological and Neuropsychological Aspects of Spatial Neglect*. Elsevier.

Robertson, I.H. and Marshall, J.C. (eds) (1993) *Unilateral Neglect: Clinical and Experimental Studies*. Erlbaum.

Most of Edoardo Bisiach's early publications were in various aspects of clinical neurology. He became fascinated with psychological aspects of brain damage, however, during the early 1960s, and this interest led him to take an opportunity to spend a year (1963–4) in the former USSR, training with the great pioneer of neuropsychology, Alexander R. **Luria**, at the University of Moscow. Although Bisiach continued his work as a neurologist for many years afterwards, this experience undoubtedly confirmed him in his career course in neuropsychology, and was a major influence on his intellectual development. Perhaps Bisiach's most famous research finding was first reported in his 1978 paper with Luzzatti, in which he reported a simple but dramatic experiment in two right-brain-damaged patients with unilateral visual neglect. Each patient was asked to imagine standing facing the facade of Milan Cathedral from the other side of the Piazza del Duomo, and to describe the buildings and other landmarks around the Piazza. The patients described almost entirely items lying on the right side. Yet when asked to imagine standing in front of the cathedral and facing the other way, the patients described mainly items lying on the previously unreported side. These patients, in other words, demonstrated that unilateral neglect can operate at the very highest levels of mental representation. In 1981 Bisiach and his colleagues confirmed that this 'imaginal neglect' was quite common, though not universal, among neglect patients. In a similarly elegant experiment, Bisiach and his colleagues showed in 1979 that leftward neglect could be observed in a task where patients were presented with a nonsense shape moving behind a vertical slit. In this case the whole shape had never been seen at once, so that the neglect was of a constructed percept, not of an actual spatial array; furthermore, all parts of the figure, including the neglected ones, had been seen in central vision.

These and other influential papers confirmed that neglect was a potentially fascinating and fruitful area for neuropsychological research, and led directly to the enormous expansion of research in the area that we see today. There were, for example, only an average of 42 papers published on neglect or inattention each year between 1981 and 1985, but between 1991 and 1995 the average had become an amazing 470. Bisiach has proceeded to carry out many other elegant experimental studies, but also to put forward a series of theoretical proposals in which he has tried to exploit neuropsychological findings within a wider philosophical framework, in order to develop a fuller understanding of the nature of consciousness. In developing his ideas he has pursued the implications of various mental dissociations seen in patients with neglect (or 'dyschiria') and anosognosia (the unawareness of sensory or motor disorders), implications missed by many less acute observers. He has been unafraid to dwell on the puzzles created by these phenomena, and has enriched the literature by combining a detailed knowledge of the philosophical literature with his extensive clinical and scientific expertise. Along with Weiskrantz and others, Bisiach has brought the study of consciousness back into serious psychological and neuropsychological thought.

Bisiach's standing in the field of contemporary neuropsychology (and psychology generally) is clear from a glance at his editorial positions on many of the highest-ranking journals in the field. These include the editorial boards of *Brain*, *Consciousness and Cognition*, *Cortex*, *Neuropsychologia* and *Cognitive Neuropsychiatry*.

A.D. MILNER

Bleuler, Paul E.
Born: 1857, Zollikon, Switzerland **Died:** 1939, Zollikon, Switzerland **Nat:** Swiss **Ints:** Clinical pathology and psychotherapy **Educ:** MD University of Zurich **Appts & awards:** Psychiatric Hospital Rheinau, Zurich, Doctor 1986; Professor of Psychiatry, University of Zurich; Director, Burgholzli Psychiatric Clinic and the University Hospital, 1898–1927

Principal publications
1906 *Affektivitat, Suggestibilitat, Paranoia* (*Affectivity, Suggestibility, Paranoia*). Marhold (State Hospitals Press 1912).
1908 *Die schizophrenen Geistesstorungen im Lichte langjahriger Kranken- und Familegeschichten* (*Schizophrenic Disorders in the Light of Long-term Case and Family Histories*). Thieme (trans., 1972).
1911 *Dementia praecox; oder, Gruppe der Schizophrenien* (*Dementia Praecox: Or, The Group of Schizophrenias*). F. Deutiche (1960, International Universities Press).
1916 *Lehrbuch der psychiatrie.* (*Textbook of psychiatry*). J. Springer (1924, Macmillan).
Bleuler published more than one hundred and fifty psychiatric papers and books.

Further reading
Brill, A.A. (1939) In memoriam: Eugen Bleuler. *American Journal of Psychiatry*, 96, 513–16.
Zilboorg, G. (1939) Eugen Bleuler. *Psychoanalytic Quarterly*, 382–4.

Bleuler is known in part because he was the first prominent psychiatrist outside of Austria to recognize the importance of the work of Sigmund **Freud**. Indeed, around 1904 he encouraged Carl **Jung** (his assistant from 1900 to 1909) to apply Freud's theories to patients, thereby leading to an important Jung paper and Jung's association with Freud.

In his own right he was responsible for a drastic change in the conceptualization of what is now known by his term of schizophrenia. He led the rejection of Kraepelin's term 'dementia praecox' as it implied an irreversible condition rather than a treatable one. Bleuler conceptualized the schizophrenias as a loosening of associations that cause the personality to disintegrate, although not uniformly, but only at certain times and to some types of question. His search beyond the surface symptoms added descriptive vocabulary including 'neologism', 'word salad' and 'negative speech'. Bleuler added the category of simple schizophrenia to Krapelin's three (hebephrenic, paranoid, catatonic). By 1916 he had added the concepts of autism (loss of contact with reality) and ambivalence (mutually exclusive contradictions existing concurrently – at the intellectual, emotional and/or volitional level) to the understanding of the schizophrenias.

Some consider Bleuler's writings to anticipate the existential movement, with a direct link through his student Binswanger. Other prominent figures at Burgholzli during Bleuler's time include **Rorschach**, **Piaget**, Adolf Meyer and Karl Abraham. In his early days Bleuler studied hypnosis briefly with **Charcot** at Salpetrière.

CHARLES PEYSER

Block, Ned Joel
Born: 1942, Chicago, USA **Nat:** American **Ints:** Philosophical and theoretical psychology **Educ:** MIT, graduated 1964; Oxford University,

1964–6; PhD Harvard, 1971 **Appts & awards:** MIT, 1971; Professor, 1983– ; Voted One of the 'Ten Best Philosophers', 1983, 1990.

Principal publications

1977 *The IQ Controversy: Critical Readings.* Quartet Books (with G. Dworkin).

1980 (ed.) *Readings in the Philosophy of Psychology.* vols I and II. Methuen.

1981 (ed.) *Imagery.* MIT Press.

Further reading

Block, N. (1995) On a confusion about a function of consciousness. *Behavioral and Brain Sciences*, 18, 227–87.

Ned Block has a high reputation in the USA, having been named one of the ten best philosophers in 1983 and again in 1990. He has published numerous articles in philosophy and psychology journals and edited and introduced three books on philosophical issues in psychology.

The IQ Controversy contains a representative selection of papers by participants in the controversy, which was notable for its violence (intellectual and sometimes physical). **Jensen**, following **Burt**, had suggested that the lower average IQ scores of the American black population are genetically determined and this was unacceptable to the political left, e.g. Kamin and Lewontin. Unfortunately IQ measurement was not (and is not) a sufficiently exact science to allow the issue to be resolved. In his introduction, Block concludes that the investigation of genotypic racial differences in IQ should not be banned and those who conduct such research should not be persecuted, but that scientists 'should voluntarily refrain'.

Readings in the Philosophy of Psychology includes an introduction by Block, 'What is the philosophy of psychology?', which is of great value. It shows how it is that conceptual issues about mind are nearly the same for philosophy and psychology, though, in the case of philosophy and the physical sciences, the issues are different because the physical sciences (unlike psychology) have introduced 'strikingly new concepts'. Block also contributes an introductory section, 'What is functionalism?', and a concluding article, 'Troubles with functionalism', which are among the best critiques available. These contributions (the latter in particular) are not easy to read but worth the effort: vol. I is philosophically oriented and vol. II more concerned with empirical psychological issues.

In *Imagery* the issue is whether images are fundamentally pictorial or descriptional in character. Empirical evidence shows that images can be scanned like percepts, that they occupy much the same neural machinery and that imaged objects can be mentally rotated – the time required being dependent on the degree of rotation. However, it is clear that images cannot be stored as pictures in the brain; the storage code must be more propositional in character. The evidence for pictorial storage is controverted by protagonists of AI, since computers employ descriptional (propositional) storage and there is no obvious way in which they could imitate the pictorial strategy that appears to be available to brains. Block provides a valuable analysis of the conceptual issues involved.

More recently Block has been concerned with the problems of consciousness. In the *Behavioral and Brain Sciences* article cited and in his commentary on earlier articles he attacks the view that phenomenal consciousness (consciousness as experienced) has anything to do with 'availability for use in reasoning etc.' (i.e. access consciousness). Phenomenal consciousness may still be present independent of any mental function it may have, or it may be required by a central executive even though not required by cognitively impenetrable modular functions.

Block performs a valuable service in trying to keep psychologists on the conceptual straight and narrow path, but he has not so far become associated with an approach of his own to philosophical issues.

N.E. WETHERICK

Boden, Margaret Ann

Born: 1936, London, England **Nat:** British **Ints:** Developmental psychology, general psychology, history of psychology, philosophical and theoretical psychology **Educ:** BA (Natural Sciences for Medicine) University of Cambridge, 1958; MA (History of Modern Philosophy) University of Cambridge, 1959; AM Harvard Graduate School, 1964; PhD Harvard University, 1968; ScD University of Cambridge, 1990 **Appts & awards:** Assistant Lecturer/Lecturer (Philosophy), University of Birmingham, 1959–62, 1962–5; Lecturer/Reader (Philosophy and Psychology), University of Sussex, 1965–72, 1973–80; Hon. Secretary, British Social Philosophical Science Committee, 1960–8; AISB Program Committee, International Joint Conference on Artificial Intelligence, 1960s; Harkness Fellow, 1962–4; Leslie McMichael

Premium of Institute of Electronic and Radio Engineers, 1978; Professor (Philosophy and Psychology), University of Sussex, 1980– ; Executive Committee, Mind Association, 1982–7; Chairperson, BPS Section on History and Philosophy of Psychology, 1983; Fellow, British Academy, 1983 (Council, 1988–91, Vice-president, 1989–91), Royal Society of Arts, 1992; Editorial Board of several journals

Principal publications

1972 *Purposive Explanation in Psychology.* Harvard University Press.

1977 *Artificial Intelligence and Natural Man.* Basic/Harvester.

1979 *Piaget.* Collins-Fontana/Viking-Penguin.

1981 *Minds and Mechanisms.* Cornell University Press/Harvester.

1982 Is equilibration important? A view from artificial intelligence. *British Journal of Psychology*, 73, 165–173.

1983 Educational implications of artificial intelligence. In W. Maxwell (ed.), *Thinking: The Frontier Expands.* Franklin.

1983 Interdisciplinary epistemology. In S. Mogdil and G. Brown (eds), *Jean Piaget: An Interdisciplinary Critique.* Routledge Kegan Paul.

1983 Artificial intelligence and animal psychology. *New Ideas in Psychology*, 1, 11–33.

1984 What is computational psychology? *Proceedings of the Aristotelian Society*, Supplement, 43, 17–35.

1984 Fame is not the spur. In, O.G. Selfridge, E.L. Rislland and M. Arbib (eds), *Adaptive Control in Ill Defined Systems.* Plenum.

1984 Artificial intelligence and biological reductionism. In M. Wan-Ho and P. Saunders (eds), *Beyond Neo-Darwinianism: An Introduction to the New Evolutionary Paradigm.* Academic Press.

1988 *Computer Models of Mind: Computational Approaches in Theoretical Psychology.* Cambridge University Press.

1990 *The Creative Mind: Myths and Mechanisms.* Weidenfeld and Nicolson.

1992 Understanding creativity. *Journal of Creative Behavior*, 26, 213–17.

1994 (ed.) *Dimensions of Creativity.* MIT Press.

Further reading

Boden, M.A. (1994) Précis of *The Creative Mind: Myths and Mechanisms. Brain and Behavioral Sciences*, 17, 519–70.

Casey, G. and Moran, A. (1989) The computational metaphor and cognitive psychology. Special issue: Cognitive science. *Irish Journal of Psychology*, 10, 143–61.

Margaret Boden's early interest in the mind – what it is, how it works, and how it relates to the body – led her to medicine, philosophy, psychology and artificial intelligence (AI). She first encountered computational ideas through *Plans and the Structure of Behavior*. She was convinced that computer modelling was profoundly relevant to theoretical psychology and the philosophy of mind. In a paper on **McDougall** (1963), she argued that this approach is not dehumanizing and that even humanist theories of personality might be understood in computational terms. Concepts such as purpose, instinct, sentiment, belief, self, dissociation, freedom and consciousness could be reconciled with neurophysiology without necessarily being reduced to it. This theme was further explored in *Purposive Explanation in Psychology*, which adopted a programming paradigm throughout. In *Artificial Intelligence and Natural Man* she described and evaluated the achievements of AI – what had been done (and how), and what had not been done and why. As the title suggests, comparisons were continually made with human psychology: Boden commented, 'in my own mind, I thought of this book on AI as an extended clarificatory footnote to my earlier work on purposive explanation'. Because of her synoptic vision of the mind she became interested in **Piaget**'s work. In a short book on Piaget (1981), she argued that his psychology can be understood only in the context of his biological and philosophical interests, and that his formalist structuralism had much in common with subsequent attempts at computer modelling. Her later work has focused on creativity and on the specific influences computer modelling has had on theoretical psychology. Here Boden argues that the ostensibly intractable concept of creativity can be scientifically understood with the help of computational concepts: computers can sometimes do creative things, and a computational approach can give the psychologist a way of exploring more clearly the subtleties of the human mind. She has remained true to her early conviction that a scientific understanding of creativity neither threatens, destroys nor dehumanizes it, but demystifies it while increasing our sense of wonder towards it.

Bohr, Niels

Born: 1885, Copenhagen, Denmark **Died:** 1962, Copenhagen, Denmark **Nat:** Danish **Ints:** Philosophical and theoretical psychology **Appts**

& awards: Lecturer in Physics, University of Copenhagen, 1913; Schuster Reader, University of Manchester, 1914–16; Professor, University of Copenhagen, 1916–62; Director, Copenhagen Institute for Theoretical Physics, 1921–62; Hughes Medal (Royal Society), 1921; Nobel Prize for Physics, 1922; President, Royal Danish Academy of Sciences, 1939

Principal publications

1934 *Atomic Theory and the Description of Nature.* Cambridge University Press. (Reprinted, 1961).

1958 *Atomic Physics and Human Knowledge.* Wiley.

1963 *Essays (1958–62) on Atomic Physics and Human Knowledge.* Wiley.

Publications in physical science are not listed.

Further reading

Bohr, N. (1985) *Niels Bohr: A Centenary Volume.* Harvard University Press (with A.P French and P.J. Kennedy).

Folse, H.J. (1985) *The Philosophy of Niels Bohr: The Framework of Complementarity.* North-Holland.

Niels Bohr was born in Copenhagen in 1885. In 1913 he showed that the model of the atom proposed by Rutherford (in which electrons revolved in random orbits around a nucleus) could not be reconciled with what was known about atomic spectra, and must be replaced by a model in which only certain fixed orbits were available and electrons somehow 'jumped' from one to another. This was the first hint that electrons did not behave like classical Newtonian particles. For this work he was awarded the Nobel Prize in 1922. In 1926–7 Heisenberg showed further that it was not possible to measure both the position and the momentum of an electron at the same time. Other physicists developed a mathematical theory (known as quantum theory) that related these findings and proved (still proves) overwhelmingly successful in the solution of practical problems, but that left open the question of whether the electron was a particle that had position or a wave that could have momentum but no precise position. In 1927 Bohr proposed what is now called the 'Copenhagen interpretation' of quantum theory: whatever is identified by experimental observation as 'wave' or 'particle' cannot be asserted to exist except at the moment of observation and in the form observed. This interpretation is unacceptable to any physicist (Einstein was one) who wishes to insist that particles have a continuing existence. For them, quantum theory is either wrong or incomplete – but the fact remains that it is a very successful theory.

Bohr proposed that 'wave' and 'particle' are alternative but 'complementary' ways of viewing the electron. Jointly (but not individually) they give us exhaustive knowledge of the phenomenon. He was from his youth concerned above all with the conditions for conceptual communication – with language. A conceptual framework may at any time prove too narrow for what we want to express: mathematics may be regarded as an extension of language that gives access to wider though more specialized conceptual frameworks. He once remarked, 'We are suspended in language in such a way that we cannot say what is up and what is down.' – His theory of complementarity was implicit in his thinking long before quantum theory and, after 1927, for the remainder of his life, he insisted that the theory was relevant and indeed fundamental outside physics. Free will/determinism, mechanism/finalism, nature/nurture, etc., were all, in his view, complementary opposites that could, jointly but not individually, give us exhaustive knowledge of the phenomena. Unfortunately he never published a clear account of his meaning in making such assertions and no-one has done so since his death.

Bohr does not appear to have been worried by ontology. In his arguments with Einstein the question at issue was the real existence (or lack of it) of subatomic particles. This was a burning issue for Einstein but not for Bohr. To many people, it appears self-evident that one or the other of free will/determinism, etc. must be true, not both complementarily. It is certainly conceivable that different methods of investigation, even different investigators, may generate results (in psychology, anthropology, etc.) that appear to be incommensurable – beyond reconcilement. But does it then follow necessarily that there is no real existent that is the object of the investigations? Acceptance of Bohr's position would require a radical reorientation of our principal (realist) conceptual framework in science that shows no signs of being about to occur.

N.E. WETHERICK

Boring, Edwin Garrigues

Born: 1886, Philadelphia, USA **Died:** 1968, Massachusetts, USA **Nat:** American **Ints:** Experimental psychology, history of psychology, philosophical and theoretical, teaching **Educ:** Master of Engineering Cornell University, 1908; PhD Cornell University, 1914 **Appts**

& awards: Instructor, Cornell University, 1914–17; Captain, US Army, 1917–19; Graduate School Appointment, Clark University, 1920–22; Associate Professor, 1922, Director, Psychology Laboratory, 1924, Professor, 1928, Edgar Pierce Professor Emeritus, 1949, Harvard University; President, APA, 1928; Member, National Academy of Sciences, 1932; Editorial Board, *Contemporary Psychology*, *American Journal of Psychology*

Principal publications

1920–1   The stimulus error. *American Journal of Psychology*, 32, 449–71.
1927   The problem of originality in science. *American Journal of Psychology*, 39, 70–90.
1929   *The History of Experimental Psychology*. Appleton Century. (2nd edn, 1950.)
1933   *The Physical Dimensions of Consciousness*. Appleton Century.
1939   *Introduction to Psychology*. Wiley (with H.S. Langfeld and H.P. Weld).
1942   *Sensation and Perception in the History of Experimental Psychology*. Appleton Century.
1945   Symposium on operationism. *Psychological Review*, 52, 241–9.
1953   A history of introspection. *Psychological Bulletin*, 50, 169–86.
1954   The nature and history of experimental control. *American Journal of Psychology*, 67, 573–89.

Further reading

Boring, E.G. (1961) *Psychologist at Large, an autobiography and selected letters*. Basic Books.
Jaynes, J. (1969) Edwin Garrigues Boring. *Journal of History of the Behavioral Sciences*, 5, 99–112.
Mace, A. (1969) Edwin Garrigues Boring: An appreciation. *Bulletin of the British Psychological Society*, 22, 99–100.
Stevens, S.S. (1968) Edwin Garrigues Boring. *American Journal of Psychology*, 81, 589–606.

Edwin Boring trained as an engineer and subsequently switched to psychology, becoming a student and fervent admirer of **Titchener**, and through him, of the tradition in psychology stemming from **Wundt**. He published much experimental psychology which was significant in its time, but is now chiefly remembered for his work on the history of psychology, particularly on issues like the 'stimulus error' that were significant but are no longer at the forefront of interest. His first major work, *The History of Experimental Psychology*, was a resounding success; it chronicled an epoch that was about to end but was still fresh in the minds of his contemporaries. He was bitterly disappointed by the relative failure of his second, *The Physical Dimensions of Consciousness*. He took this failure as evidence of deterioration in his own mental faculties as a consequence of ageing, and the resulting depression caused him to embark on a personal psychoanalysis – from which, however, he did not benefit much. In fact the book espoused a view of consciousness that had just gone out of fashion, Titchener's view that 'all conscious content is sensory'; but it also adumbrated what is now called mind–brain identity theory which is probably the dominant view at the present time. As regards the effects of ageing, Boring need not have worried since he continued to publish until his death in 1968 and was the active Head of Psychology at Harvard until his retirement in 1949.

He published a textbook of psychology in 1939 (with Langfield and Weld) that was widely used and, in 1942, his second major work in history, *Sensation and Perception in the History of Experimental Psychology* – which was followed by several invaluable shorter pieces on what were then becoming historical topics. Boring is the main point of access for English-language readers to the tradition in psychology that was ousted by behaviourism. His work will continue to be important for that reason.

N.E. WETHERICK

Bornstein, Marc H.

Born: 1947, Boston, USA **Nat:** American **Ints:** Developmental, experimental, population and environmental psychology, psychology and the arts **Educ:** BA Columbia College, 1969; MS Yale University, 1973; PhD Yale University, 1974 **Appts & awards:** NIH National Institute of Child Health and Human Development, Section on Child and Family Research; C.S. Ford Cross-Cultural Research Award, Human Relations Area Files, 1972; Prize Teaching Fellowship, Yale University, 1972–3; Editorial Boards, *Psychological Research*, 1976, *Child Development*, 1977–84, *Developmental Psychology*, 1981, *Jewels Journal of Developmental Psychology* (India), 1984, *Journal of Experimental Child Psychology*, 1984–5; APA B.R. McCandless Young Scientist Award, 1978; Editor in Chief, Cross-Currents in Contemporary Psychology Series, 1979– ; J.S. Guggenheim Foundation Fellow, 1983–4; Research Career Development Award, National Institute of Child Health and Human Development, 1983–88

Principal publications

1975   The influence of visual perception on culture. *American Anthropologist*, 77, 774–98.

1976   The categories of hue and infancy. *Science*, 191, 201–2 (with W. Kessen and S. Weiskopf).

1979   *Psychological Development from Infancy: Image to Intention*. Erlbaum (with W. Kessen).

1979   Perceptual development. In M.H. Bornstein and W. Kessen (eds), *Psychological Development from Infancy*. Erlbaum.

1980   *Comparative Methods in Psychology*. Erlbaum.

1980   Cross-cultural developmental psychology. In M.H. Bornstein (ed.), *Comparative Methods in Psychology*. Erlbaum.

1981   Two kinds of perceptual organization near the beginning of life. In W.A. Collins (ed.), *Minnesota Symposia on Child Psychology*, vol. 14. Erlbaum.

1984   *Developmental Psychology: An Advanced Textbook*. Erlbaum (with M.E. Lamb).

1984   *Psychology and Its Allied Disciplines, vol. I: Psychology and the Humanities, vol. II: Psychology and the Social Sciences, vol. III: Psychology and the Natural Sciences*. Erlbaum.

1984   A descriptive taxonomy of psychological categories used by infants. In C. Sophian (ed.), *Origins of Cognitive Skills*. Erlbaum.

1984   Psychology and art. In M.H. Bornstein (ed.), *Psychology and Its Allied Disciplines, vol. I: Psychology and the Humanities*. Erlbaum.

1985   Habituation of attention as a measure of visual information processing in human infants: Summary, systemization and synthesis. In G. Gottlieb and N.A. Krasnegor (eds), *Measurement of Audition and Vision in the First Year of Postnatal Life: A Methodological Overview*. Ablex.

1985   Infant color vision and color perception. In L.B. Cohen and P. Salapatek (eds), *Handbook of Infant Perception*. Academic Press.

1987   Perceptual categories in vision and audition. In S. Harnad (ed.), *Categorical Perception: The Groundwork of Cognition*. Cambridge University Press.

1988   Mothers, infants, and the development of cognitive competence. In H.E. Fitzgerald, B.M. Lester and M.W. Yogman (eds), *Theory and Research in Behavioral Pediatrics*, vol. 4. Plenum.

1990   Language, play, and attention at one year. *Infant Behavior and Development*, 13, 85–98 (with C.S. Tamis-LeMonda).

1992   Maternal responsiveness to infants in three societies: The United States, France, and Japan. *Child Development*, 63, 808–21 (with C.S. Tamis-LeMonda, J. Tal *et al.*).

1994   Antecedents of information-processing skills in infants: Habituation, novelty responsiveness, and cross-modal transfer. *Infant Behavior and Development*, 17, 371–80 (with C.S. Tamis-LeMonda).

1994   Specificity in mother–toddler language-play relations across the second year. *Developmental Psychology*, 30, 283–92. (with C.S. Tamis-LeMonda).

Further reading

Bornstein, M. and Lamb, M.E. (eds) (1992) *Developmental Psychology: An Advanced Textbook*, 3rd edn. Erlbaum

At Columbia College Bornstein studied problems of visual perception in humans and pigeons; he continued at Yale, but altered direction to engage in developmental questions. His approach was to synthesize two traditions – the experimental analysis of animal behaviour and visual psychophysics – in an examination of visual development in human infancy. His studies of early perceptual development addressed colour and pattern vision and intersensory organization, and have led to the formulation of a new view of perceptual organization in infancy. This work culminated in the APA B.R. McCandless Young Scientist Award for Distinguished Contributions to Developmental Psychology.

In the 1980s his research work addressed a new set of questions concerned with the readiness of the human infant to process information. This led to a focus on the assessment and prediction of cognitive functioning from the first half-year of life, and with defining and operationalizing interaction techniques through which caretakers promote cognitive development. This work embraced both laboratory and field (home-based) investigations, and broadened to include information processing and temperament in the infant as well as patterns of parent–infant interaction. He suggests that habituation of attention in the infant reflects underlying individual differences that may carry modest predictive validity for mental development in the child. This work has been recognized in a Research Career Development Award, various grants and a Guggenheim fellowship.

In more recent work he has examined the contributions of maternal stimulation to toddlers' language and play. This has included comparative analyses of maternal responsiveness to infant activity in New York City, Paris and Tokyo. Infants behaved similarly; mothers also behaved similarly with regard to a hierarchy of response types; and mothers and infants manifested both specificity and mutual appropriateness in their interactions. However, differences in maternal responsiveness between cultures were observed for infant looking and in mothers' emphasizing of dyadic loci of interaction. With Tamis-LeMonda he examined the relationship between language production, language comprehension, play competence and attention span in toddlers. He suggests that there may be two important factors at work in language and play development: a play-language factor and a play-attention factor, each reflecting different underlying mental capacities in the young child.

Bowlby, Edward John Mostyn

Born: 1907, London, England *Nat:* British *Ints:* Developmental, family, child, youth and family services, psychoanalysis, psychotherapy *Educ:* BA University of Cambridge, 1928; MA University of Cambridge, 1932; BCh University of Cambridge, 1933; MD University of Cambridge, 1939 *Appts & awards:* Hon. Consultant Psychiatrist, Tavistock Clinic; British Psychoanalytical Society, Training Secretary, 1944–7, Deputy President, 1956–7, 1958–61; Fellow, Center for Advanced Study in the Behavioral Sciences, 1957–8; Chairman, Association for Child Psychology and Psychiatry, 1958–9; ACPP Hon. Member, 1959– ; President, International Association for Child Psychology and Psychiatry, 1962–6; Editorial Board, *Journal of Child Psychology and Psychiatry*, 1963– ; Hon. DLitt, University of Leicester, 1971; CBE, 1972; James Spence Medal, British Paediatric Association, 1974, APA G. Stanley Hall Medal, 1974; Hon. ScD, University of Cambridge, 1977; Council, Royal College of Psychiatrists, Hon. Fellow, 1980– ; Foreign Hon. Member, American Academy of Arts and Science, 1981– ; SRCD Distinguished Scientific Contribution Award, 1981; Blanch Ittleson Award, American Orthopsychiatric Association, 1981; Salmon Medal, New York Academy of Medicine, 1984

Principal publications

1946 *Forty-four Juvenile Thieves*. Balliere, Tindall and Cox.
1951 *Maternal Care and Mental Health*. WHO.
1953 *Child Care and the Growth of Love*. Penguin.
1953 Some pathological processes set in train by early mother–child separation. *Journal of Mental Science*, 99, 265–72.

1958 The nature of the child's tie to his mother. *International Journal of Psychoanalysis*, 39, 350–73.
1960 Separation anxiety. *International Journal of Psychoanalysis*, 41, 89–113.
1961 Processes of mourning. *International Journal of Psychoanalysis*, 42, 317–40.
1970 *The Making and Breaking of Affectional Bonds*. Methuen.
1975 Attachment theory, separation anxiety and mourning. In D.A. Hamburg and H.K. Brodie (eds), *American Handbook of Psychiatry*, 2nd edn, vol. 6. Basic.
1979 Psychoanalysis as art and science. *International Review of Psychoanalysis*, 6, 3–14.
1979 On knowing what you are not supposed to know and feeling what you are not supposed to feel. *Canadian Journal of Psychiatry*, 24, 403–8.
1980 By ethology out of psychoanalysis: An experiment in interbreeding. *Animal Behavior*, 28, 649–56.
1981 Psychoanalysis as a natural science. *International Review of Psychoanalysis*, 8, 243–56.

Further reading

Bowlby, J. (1969–80) *Attachment and Loss*, vols. 1, 2, 3. Basic Books.

As a specialist in child and family psychiatry Bowlby was concerned to treat disturbed children and their families and especially to prevent disturbances developing. Following Cambridge, where he studied some psychology, he spent a year in a school for maladjusted children, which decided his future career. By 1939 he had completed formal training and became interested in the part played by a child's experience within his or her family in influencing personality development. For research purposes, he focused on the effects of long separations from mother during the early years. A study of forty-four juvenile thieves, in which he attributed psychopathic development to maternal deprivation, was in draft in 1940 when he became an army psychiatrist. Five years' service, mostly in research and training centres for officer selection, provided a postgraduate education in psychology. From 1946 he worked at the Tavistock Clinic as Chairman of the Department for Children and Parents, and developed a programme of research into the effects of placing a young child in a strange place with strange people. In collaboration with James Robertson, he described the phases of protest, despair and detachment, followed on return by intense separation anxiety. Dissatisfied with traditional psychoanalytic theory, he turned to ethology as promising a better conceptual framework for understanding socioemotional development and psychopathology. This led to the formulation of the theory of attachment as a distinctive behavioural system having the biological function of protection. He applied these concepts to clinical problems, e.g. separation anxiety, mourning, ambivalence, depression, violence and defensive processes, thereby reformulating psychoanalytic theory. In the hands of colleagues, notably Mary **Ainsworth**, attachment theory has been fruitful in guiding research and in understanding patterns of child–mother interaction during the early years.

Brainerd, Charles

Born: 1944, Lansing, USA **Nat:** American **Ints:** Developmental psychology, experimental psychology, philosophical and theoretical psychology **Educ:** BSc Michigan State University, 1966; MA Michigan State University, 1968; PhD Michigan State University, 1970 **Appts & awards:** Henry Marshall Tory Professor of Social Sciences, University of Alberta; Fellow, APA, Canadian Psychological Association; Coordinator, Developmental Division, Canadian Psychological Association, 1986

Principal publications

1973 Judgements and explanations as criteria for the presence of cognitive structures. *Psychological Bulletin*, 79, 172–79.
1978 *Piaget's Theory of Intelligence*. Prentice-Hall.
1978 The stage question in cognitive developmental theory. *Behavioural and Brain Sciences*, 1, 207–13.
1979 *The Origins of the Number Concept*. Praeger.
1979 Markovian interpretations of conservation learning. *Psychological Review*, 181–213.
1981 Working memory and the developmental analysis of probability judgement. *Psychological Review*, 88, 463–502.
1982 (ed.) *Children's Logical and Mathematical Cognition*. Springer-Verlag.
1982 The General Theory of Two Stage Learning: A mathematical review with illustrations from memory development. *Psychological Bulletin*, 91, 634–65 (with M.L. Howe and A. Desrochers).
1983 (ed.) *Recent Advances in Cognitive-developmental Theory*. Springer-Verlag.
1983 Young children's mental arithmetic errors: A

working memory analysis. *Child Development*, 54, 812–30.
1984 Do children have to remember to reason? A fuzzy trace theory of transitivity development. *Developmental Review*, 4, 311–77 (with J. Kingma).
1985 (ed.) *Basic Processes in Memory Development*. Springer-Verlag.
1993 Memory independence and memory interference in cognitive development. *Psychological Review*, 100, 42–67.
1995 Fuzzy-trace theory: An interim synthesis. *Learning and Individual Differences*, 7, 1–75 (with V.F. Reyna).

Further reading
Chapman, M.L. and Lindenberger, U. (1992) How to detect reasoning-remembering dependence (and how not to). *Development Review*, 12, 187–98.
A symposium on fuzzy-trace theory. *Learning and Individual Differences*, no. 2 (special issue).

As a graduate student, Brainerd became interested in cognitive development theory, especially **Piaget**'s work. During that time and for several years thereafter, his theoretical contributions focused on certain issues in Piagetian cognitive developmental theory. The bulk of this work was on measurement questions (e.g. the judgements–explanations controversy), the stage question, and the question of sequentiality in concept development. On the empirical side, his earliest research report dealt with the laboratory learning of logical concepts such as conservation. Subsequent experiments were concerned with the learning of other logical concepts and with sequences in concept development. In later work he concerned himself with the role of basic memory and learning processes in cognitive development. The overriding feature of these theoretical efforts has been the use of stochastic models to measure various theoretical processes in working memory and in long-term memory. His research work has included studies of working-memory variables that affect children's performance on thinking and reasoning problems, and studies of long-term memory variables that affect children's performance on traditional episodic memory tasks. In more recent work he has addressed the development of forgetting from long-term memory; the application of mathematical models of memory development to special child populations (e.g. retardates and the learning disabled) is currently in progress.

Bray, Douglas Weston

Born: 1918, Springfield, Massachusetts, USA
Nat: American **Ints:** Adult development and
ageing, industrial and organizational, personal-
ity and social **Educ:** BA American International
College, 1940; MA Clark University, 1941; PhD
Yale University, 1948; Hon. DSc American
International College, 1990 **Appts & awards:**
Research Associate, Princeton University,
1948–50; Research Associate, Columbia Uni-
versity, 1950–5; AT&T, 1956–90; President,
APA Division 14, 1971–2; Distinguished
Scholar Award, Hofstra University, 1975; APA
Division 14 Professional Practice Award, 1977;
APA Distinguished Professional Contribution to
Applied Psychology Award, 1980; President,
American Board of Professional Psychology,
1982–3; APA Division 13 Perry L. Rohrer
Award, 1986; Society of Psychologists in Man-
agement Outstanding Contribution Award,
1986; Distinguished Service and Outstanding
Contribution Award, 1988; Academy of Man-
agement George R. Terry Award, 1989;
Chairman, Development Dimensions Inter-
national, Pittsburgh, 1990– ; APF Gold Medal
Award, 1991

Principal publications

1950   The prediction of behavior from two attitude
scales. *Journal of Abnormal and Social
Psychology*, 45, 64–84.

1953   *The Uneducated*. Columbia University Press
(with E. Ginzberg).

1954   *Issues in the Study of Talent*. Kings Crown.

1966   The assessment center in the measurement of
potential for business management. Psychological
Monographs, 80, whole no. 625 (with D.L. Grant).

1968   Selection of salesmen by means of an
assessment center. *Journal of Applied Psychology*,
52, 36–41 (with R.J. Campbell).

1974   *Formative Years in Business: A Long Term
AT&T Study of Managerial Lives*. Wiley (with R.J.
Campbell and D.L. Grant).

1976   The assessment center method. In R.L. Craig
(ed.), *Training and Development Handbook*,
McGraw-Hill.

1980   Career success and life satisfactions of
middle-aged managers. In L. Bond and J.C. Rosen
(eds), *Coping and Competence During Adulthood*.
University Press of New England (with A. Howard).

1982   The assessment center and the study of lives.
American Psychologist, 37, 180–9.

1983   An AT&T longitudinal study of managers. In
K. Schaie (ed.), *Longitudinal Studies of Adult
Psychological Development*. Guilford Press (with
A. Howard).

1983   *Producing Useful Knowledge for
Organizations*. Praeger.

1991   *Working with Organizations and their People:
A Guide to Human Resources Practice*. Guilford
Press.

1993   Use of an assessment center as an aid in
management selection. Special issue: Innovations
in research methods for field settings. Personnel
Psychology, 46, 691–9.

Further reading

APA Awards for Distinguished Professional
Contributions: 1980. Douglas W. Bray. (1981)
American Psychologist, 36, 52–5.

APF Gold Medal Award: Douglas W. Bray. (1991)
American Psychologist, 46, 780–2.

Douglas Bray grew up during the Depression.
His parents had a modest education but his
father encouraged Bray to enrol in the American
International College, where scholarships were
available. He graduated with a BA in sociology
and took up a post as a graduate assistant (there
were studentships in psychology) at Clark
University, where he completed his MA in
abnormal psychology. During World War II
Bray was drafted in the aviation psychology
programme of the Air Corps. After the war
he was accepted for graduate work in Carl I.
Hovland's department at Yale University,
where he completed his PhD and took a minor
in industrial psychology.

Bray is best known for his longitudinal
research on management careers and for originating and developing management assessment
centres. Both of these achievements took place
while Bray was with American Telephone and
Telegraph Co. (AT&T). In 1969 he co-founded
(with W.C. Byham) Development Dimensions
International, a leading firm in management
selection and development programmes. The
AT&T longitudinal research included two
major studies. The Management Progress
Study, begun in 1956, tracked the careers of
422 managers as their lives unfolded, and
included extensive psychological evaluation of
the participants at various points along the way.
In 1977 Bray began, with Dr Anne Howard, a
parallel study, called the Management Continuity Study, to follow a new generation of
managers through time. These studies have led
to important insights into the abilities, motivations and personality characteristics essential to
managerial success, and more generally into the
course of adult life. Changes and stabilities in
individual characteristics have been charted and

related to management level attained and to overall psychological adjustment. Other studies have thrown light on generational differences. Taking these in conjunction with the longitudinal data, Bray showed that the ranks of management are in constant flux due to age and societal changes. He argued that although a substantial core of stability exists, the differences between managers of different ages and different levels warrant careful attention by organizations. He devised the first management assessment centre in 1956 as a research tool in his longitudinal studies. It was quickly adopted, however, as a practical method for use in management selection and development. As it spread in the Bell System, he promoted its uptake in other organizations, and by the 1970s assessment centres, had become a general movement. Recently (1993) Bray completed an evaluation of assessment centres indicating that they have had a beneficial effect on the performance of managers.

Broadbent, Donald Eric

Born: 1926, Birmingham, England **Died:** 1993, Oxford, England **Nat:** British **Ints:** Engineering psychology, experimental psychology, industrial and organizational psychology **Educ:** BA University of Cambridge, 1949; MA University of Cambridge, 1951; ScD University of Cambridge, 1965 **Appts & awards:** Applied Psychology Unit, University of Cambridge, 1949–58, Director, 1958–74; Fellow, Acoustical Society of America, 1963, BPS, 1957; Royal Society, 1968, Human Factors Society, 1968, Hon. Dr, University of Southampton, 1973, University of York, 1979, University of Loughborough, 1982, City University, London, 1983, University of Brussels, 1985; Experimental Psychology Society, BPS, 1964–5; Psychology Section, British Association for the Advancement of Science, 1967, President, 1973–4, CBE, 1974; Medical Research Council External Staff Member, Department of Experimental Psychology, University of Oxford, 1974–91; Hon. Fellow (Faculty of Occupational Medicine), Royal College of Physicians, 1981, Royal College of Psychiatrists, 1985; Hon DSc University of Wales, 1992; Editorial Board: *Journal of Experimental Psychology: Human Perception and Performance*, 1975–93, *Journal of Applied Psychology*, 1977–93 and *Psychological Medicine*, 1980–93; Editorial Panel (Psychology), Oxford University Press, 1979–93.

Principal publications

1957   A mechanical model for human attention and immediate memory. *Psychological Review*, 64, 205–15.

1958   *Perception and Communication*. Pergamon.

1961   *Behaviour*. Eyre and Spottiswood.

1963   Vigilance considered as a statistical decision. *British Journal of Psychology*, 54, 309–23 (with M.H.P. Gregory).

1967   The word frequency effect and response bias. *Psychological Review*, 74, 1–15.

1967   The perception of emotionally toned words. *Nature*, 215, 581–84 (with M.H.P. Gregory).

1971   *Decision and Stress*. Academic Press.

1973   *In Defence of Empirical Psychology*. Methuen.

1977   Levels, hierarchies, and the locus of control. *Quarterly Journal of Experimental Psychology*, 29, 181–201.

1984   The Maltese Cross: A new simplistic model for memory. *Brain and Behavioral Sciences*, 7, 55–94.

1985   The clinical impact of job design. *British Journal of Clinical Psychology*, 24, 33–4.

1986   Implicit and explicit knowledge in the control of complex systems. *British Journal of Psychology*, 77, 33–50 (with P. Fitzgerald and M.H.P. Broadbent).

1986   Performance correlates of self-reported cognitive failures and of obsessionality. *British Journal of Clinical Psychology*, 25, 285–99 (with M.H.P. Broadbent and J.L. Jones).

1988   Interactive tasks and the implicit–explicit distinction. *British Journal of Psychology*, 79, 251–72 (with D.C. Berry).

Further reading

Baddeley, A. and Weiskrants, L. (eds) (1993) *Attention: Selection, Awareness, and Control: A Tribute to Donald Broadbent*. Clarendon Press/ Oxford University Press.

British Journal of Psychology (1991) Special issue to mark the retirement of D.E. Broadbent. 82, Part 3.

Swets, J.A. and Kristofferson, A.B. (1970) Attention. *Annual Review of Psychology*, 21, 329–66.

Donald E. Broadbent was born in Birmingham but grew up in Wales. He was educated at Winchester College and planned to read engineering at the University of Cambridge. His RAF flying training was undertaken in North America, where he first encountered the subject of psychology – then largely unheard of by most young people in England. He was drawn to considering the problems that can arise when people are required to work with complex technologies, and this motivated a switch from engineering to psychology. Thus, he was originally attracted to the area by, and remained primarily concerned about, the need to design technological environments suitable for human use. The Cambridge Department of Psychology, headed by Sir Frederick **Bartlett**, was a particularly appropriate place for someone with such interests. Wartime work on developing applications of cognitive psychology for resolving user–technology problems had led in 1944 to the foundation of the Medical Research Council's Applied Psychology Unit at Cambridge. On graduation Broadbent joined that unit and commenced work on topics relating to the influence of environmental stressors on human cognitive performance. This was to be an enduring theme throughout his career. In 1958 he became Director and over the next sixteen years he shaped the unit, creating an enduring blend of pure and applied research. In 1974 Broadbent moved to Oxford to pursue his own work without the administrative responsibilities of the unit. Much of this work was conducted in collaboration with his second wife, Margaret H.P. Gregory. In the following year he received the APA Distinguished Scientific Contribution Award. Broadbent served on the national committees of the Social Science Research Council, Medical Research Council, Science and Engineering Research Council.

Broadbent was trained in Cambridge at a time when the influences of A. Turing and K.J.W. Craik created an atmosphere which was sympathetic to his interests in designing technological environments suitable for human use, and to the idea of explaining human behaviour in terms of the computational processes that must be undertaken by any system that behaves as people do. During the 1950s he worked on a variety of applied problems, first on the effects of noise on cognitive performance and then on the difficulties of handling a large number of speech messages simultaneously. These problems were readily handled in terms of the conceptual frameworks due to Craik, Turing, Bartlett and other influences on the Cambridge group; but problematic to handle in the terminology current in psychology laboratories at that time. Consequently he encountered some difficulty in publishing early work in the mainstream academic journals. His work on auditory selective attention was seminal for two reasons. First, it provided a methodology for investigating the psychology of attention at a time when behaviourism had rejected attempts to investigate such phenomena. Second, it exploited new

information-processing concepts being developed in mathematics and engineering to develop a model of human cognition that proved both theoretically sound and useful in practical matters.

Perception and Communication summarised many of the results obtained in his laboratory and in a variety of others. In it Broadbent adopted an information-processing framework and argued for its advantages over statements in terms of stimulus and response. The publication of the book proved timely and became widely quoted by psychologists turning to a cybernetic, information-processing or cognitive approach to explaining human behaviour. The book set the agenda for what subsequently became known as cognitive psychology, and it is probably the contribution for which he is best known. It is often not fully recognized that the perspective proposed in the book was a by-product of research undertaken for applied reasons. This reflects an important feature of the individuality of his contribution: he demonstrated that psychological theory is best when grounded in the empirical analysis of practical problems: as he wrote, 'The test of intellectual excellence of a psychological theory, as well as its moral justification, lies in its application to concrete practical considerations.'

A central theme of *Perception and Communication* is that a person undertaking several tasks might experience interference between the central processes involved in each of them, that it could be reduced by practice, and that in some cases certain tasks are selected rather than others by a 'filtering' mechanism. The conception was, however, determinate and, like many psychologists at that time, Broadbent thought of one internal event succeeding another in a straightforward causal fashion. During the 1960s he and others produced a great deal of evidence to indicate that the central processes are not like that; on the contrary, each momentary event 'inside' a person is only statistically related to the things that have happened before; so that stable and efficient behaviour depends on the averaging or cumulation of a lot of separate processes. From this perspective, errors become very important as a way of sorting out the details of the process; it is also in principle impossible ever to eliminate human error totally. These arguments altered conceptualizations of attention and workload quite considerably and raised a number of questions about the role of probability and motivation in perception. The revised views were presented in *Decision and*

Stress, but this had considerably less impact than *Perception and Communication*. Broadbent attributed this to a failure of presentation and communication and not to problems with the underlying arguments and evidence. In subsequent work he continued to be concerned to argue against psychological theories that assume determinate and separate mechanisms of cognition. He argued that it was hopeless to attempt to find 'the' mechanism by which any particular psychological task is performed. Different people perform the same task differently, and the same person may perform it differently on different occasions. This led to his arguing for two lines of attack in psychology. First, one needs to study the implications of one strategy of cognition rather than another: which ways of thinking show which kinds of advantage and disadvantage? Second, one should look at the external circumstances that cause one strategy to be adopted rather than another.

This change of emphasis coincided with a change in the practical needs of society; no longer for 'quick fix' cures for problems created by particular technological devices that have been badly made, but rather for extended planning and designing of devices that might not be completed for a long time ahead. Thus, his move from the Applied Psychology Unit to Oxford afforded opportunities to demonstrate that the gradual accumulation of evidence from laboratory experiments on different styles of attention and memory could be linked to lengthy life experiences of the individual in the world outside. These efforts took him through the 1970s and into the 1980s and produced a number of important detailed findings, including evidence that people in certain kinds of job develop certain psychiatric symptoms. The kinds of symptom that develop depend on the particular characteristics of the job, and the process is linked to particular individual patterns of selective attention that the person can be shown to display in the laboratory. Thus, in later years he addressed the effects of powerful, pervasive social stressors in the working environment. As part of this work he developed the Cognitive Failures Questionnaire, a widely used measure of absent-mindedness. His breadth of research interests – attention and memory, perception, stress, individual differences in temperament, occupational health, and copying styles – address problems and applications which are related through an underlying theoretical fabric. In lighter moments, he would suggest that he was trying to contribute to establishing a new topic

called 'Dyccop': dynamic cognitive clinical occupational psychology. The value of his contribution is appropriately summarized in the following extract from the citation accompanying the APA Distinguished Scientific Contribution Award: 'For offering experimental and applied psychology a new view of their subject matter that has been profoundly influential on both sides of the atlantic. His *Perception and Communication* was the first systematic treatment of the organism as an information-processing system, with a specific structure that could be investigated by experiment. To this end, he devised many ingenious new methods for the study of perception, attention and memory. His consistent emphasis on the interrelation of theory and application has strengthened both.'

Bromley, Dennis Basil

Born: 1924, Stoke-on-Trent, England ***Nat:*** British ***Ints:*** Adult development and ageing, developmental psychology, personality and social, philosophical and theoretical, psychology and the law. ***Educ:*** BA University of Manchester, 1950; PhD University of Liverpool, 1952 ***Appts & awards:*** Department of Psychology, University of Liverpool, Lecturer and Reader, 1950–75, Professor, 1975–90, Emeritus Professor, 1990– ; Fellow, British Psychological Society, 1962, Gerontological Society of America, 1972; Acting Head, Medical Research Control Unit for Research into Occupational Aspects of Ageing, 1964–5; Visiting Research Scientist, Philadelphia Geriatric Center, 1968; Founding Member, British Society of Gerontology, Chairperson, 1971–6; Board, BPS Scientific Affairs, 1983

Principal publications

1953 Primitive forms of response to the matrices test. *Journal of Mental Science*, 14, 374–93.

1956 Research prospects in the psychology of ageing. *Journal of Mental Science*, 102, 272–279.

1956 Some experimental tests of the effect of age on creative intellectual output. *Journal of Gerontology*, 11, 74–82.

1957 Some effects of age on the quality of intellectual output. *Journal of Gerontology*, 12, 318–23.

1958 Some effects of age on short term learning and remembering. *Journal of Gerontology*, 13, 398–406.

1963 Age differences in conceptual abilities. In R.H. Williams, C. Tibbitts and W. Donahue (eds), *Processes of Ageing: Social and Psychological Perspectives*, vol. 1. Atherton.

1966 Rank order cluster analysis. *British Journal of Mathematics and Statistical Psychology*, 19, 105–23.

1966 *Psychology of Human Ageing*. Penguin. (2nd edn, 1974).

1967 Age and sex differences in the serial production of creative conceptual responses. *Journal of Gerontology*, 22, 32–42.

1968 Conceptual analysis in the study of personality and adjustment. *Bulletin of the British Psychological Society*, 21, 155–60.

1970 An approach to theory construction in the psychology of development and ageing. In L.R. Goulet and P.B. Baltes (eds), *Life Span Developmental Psychology: Research and Theory*. Academic Press.

1973 *Person Perception in Childhood and Adolescence*. Wiley (with W.J. Livesley).

1976 Geriatrics in relation to the social and behavioral sciences. *Age and Ageing*, 5, 205–13.

1977 *Personality Description in Ordinary Language*. Wiley.

1978 Natural language and the development of the self. In C.B. Keasey (ed.), *Nebraska Symposium on Motivation 1977: Social and Cognitive Development*. University of Nebraska Press.

1986 *Case Study Method in Psychology and Related Disciplines*. Wiley.

1988 Approaching the limits. *Social Behavior*, 3, 71–84.

1988 *Human Ageing: An Introduction to Gerontology*. Penguin.

1990 Aspects of written language production over adult life. *Psychology and Ageing*, 6, 229–308.

1993 *Reputation, Image and Impression Management*. Wiley.

Further reading

Birren, J. and Schaie, K.W. (1980) Handbook of the Psychology of Ageing, 3rd edn. Academic Press.

Botwinick, J. (1978) *Ageing and Behavior*. Spinger-Verlag.

Dennis Bromley first became interested in psychology during the last year of his service with the RAF in 1946. He graduated from the University of Manchester in 1950 and was appointed to the staff of the Department of Psychology at the University of Liverpool, where he spent the whole of his academic career apart from two sabbatical years abroad. While his first teaching responsibilities were in social psychology and personality, his interest soon shifted to the cognitive aspects of normal ageing, a newly emerging area of research at that time. His doctoral thesis in 1952 described a number of investigations using some established and some new methods of assessment. After publishing a series of articles in the *Journal of Gerontology* and elsewhere, he published his first book, *The Psychology of Human Ageing*, in 1966. This was revised in 1974 and more recently in 1988 under the title *Human Ageing: An Introduction to Gerontology*. In his early work in gerontology, Bromley addressed the issues of intelligence, creativity, problem solving and concept formation. Among his publications at that time, he presented evidence based on cross-sectional data that growth and decline of problem solving follow the same developmental pattern as do changes in IQ. In one of the most often-cited experiments from this period, 'Some effects of age on the quality of intellectual output', he argued that not only do older people seem to prefer tasks that are concrete rather than those that are abstract, but they more than younger adults tend also to perform in concrete fashion. In this experiment, Bromely gave subjects aged 17 to 82 years two types of proverb task which required interpretation. In the first, the subject's interpretations of a series of proverbs were scored on a continuum from the principle being abstracted and generalized to a concrete response. The second task was one of multiple choice, and consisted of ten proverbs each with three explanations. Subjects were asked to record the 'best', 'next best' and 'worst' explanations. It was found that increased age was associated with a decrease in the tendency to form higher-order generalizations as in the first test, or to choose these when given an opportunity to do so as in the second test. While the results were based on cross-sectional data, they stimulated widespread discussion for many years. His more recent work in the field has tended to concentrate on theory building and on conceptual issues. In an important paper, 'An approach to theory construction in the psychology of development and ageing', he argued that progress in developmental psychology is hampered by administrative obstacles such as the time, cost, and manpower needed for conducting longitudinal studies or of gaining adequate samples, and by value judgements which dictate research priorities independently of their theoretical importance. As a result, what passes for theory construction is the discovery of rule relationships, or the development of classification schemes which seem to bring order to data, or to permit inference that previously could not be made. He suggested that these problems are basically the same as those in other scientific disciplines.

Over the course of his career Bromley's attention turned to other areas. With W.J. Liversley, he wrote *Person Perception in Childhood and Adolescence*. The techniques of qualitative data analysis used in that research were subsequently developed and used in connection with research into the language of personality description, leading to the publication of *Personality Description in Ordinary Language*. His interests in the study of individual cases, 'judicial' methods of enquiry, and the nature of scientific method in the social and behavioural sciences led to the publication of *The Case Study Method in Psychology and Related Disciplines*. By 1990 he had completed a new textbook on ageing, entitled *Behavioral Gerontology: Central Issues in the Psychology of Ageing*. In this book, he emphasized the affective aspects of human ageing and the importance of small-scale, intensive research methods. Following this publication, Bromley returned to his interest in social psychology and personality description. In 1993, *Reputation, Image and Impression Management* was published. In his view, reputation is to social psychology what personality is to the study of individual differences, and at least as important. His book explores group factors influencing how people are perceived, including an analysis of the media and the perpetuation of fads and stereotypes. Also included is a discussion of image and impression management at the personal level.

At the present time, Emeritus Professor Bromley is retired but teaches part-time and continues his research into the effects of ageing, on the language of personality and self-description, and into the social psychology of reputation. While perhaps best known for his work in the field of ageing, his contributions to psychology are wide and varied, and he is often cited in works on personality and social psychology.

D. THOMPSON

Brooks-Gunn, Jeanne

Born: Jeanne Brooks, 1946, Bethesda, Maryland, USA *Nat:* American *Ints:* Child, youth and family services: developmental psychology *Educ:* BA Connecticut College, 1969; EdM Harvard University, 1970; PhD University of Pennsylvania, 1975 *Appts & awards:* Educational Testing Service, Associate Director, Institute for the Study of Exceptional Children, 1977–82, Research Scientist, Center for Research in Human Development, 1978–83, Senior Research Scientist, Division of Education Policy Research, 1983–93; William

Goode Book Award for *Adolescent Mothers in Later Life* (with F.F. Furstenberg and P. Morgan), American Sociological Association, 1988; Virginia and Leonard Marx Professor in Child Development and Education, Teachers College, Columbia University, 1991–

Principal publications

1977   *He and She: How Children Develop their Sex-Role Identity*. Prentice-Hall (with W. Mathews).

1977   College women's attitudes and expectations concerning menstrual-related changes. *Psychosomatic Medicine*, 39, 288–98 (with D.N. Ruble and A. Clarke).

1979   *Social Cognition and the Acquisition of Self*. Plenum (with M. Lewis).

1980   The menstrual attitude questionnaire. *Psychosomatic Medicine*, 42, 503–12 (with D.N. Ruble).

1982   Methods and models of menstrual research: A sociocultural approach. In A.M. Voda, M. Dinnerstein and S.R. O'Donnell (eds), *Changing Perspectives on Menopause*. University of Texas Press.

1987   *Adolescent Mothers in Later Life*. Cambridge University Press (with F.F. Furstenberg and P. Morgan).

1989   Pubertal processes and the early adolescent transition. In W. Damon (ed.), *Child Development Today and Tomorrow*. Jossey-Bass.

1989   Adolescents as daughters and as mothers: A developmental perspective. In I.E. Sigel and G.H. Brody (eds), *Methods of Family Research: Biographies of Research Projects, Volume I: Normal Families*. Erlbaum.

1990   Overcoming barriers to adolescent research on pubertal and reproductive development. *Journal of Youth and Adolescence*, 19, 425–40.

1990   Identifying the vulnerable young child. In D.E. Rogers and E. Ginzberg (eds), *Improving the Life Chances of Children at Risk*. Westview Press.

1991   How stressful is the transition to adolescence in girls? In M.E. Colten and S. Gore (eds), *Adolescent Stress: Causes and Consequences*. Aldine de Gruyter.

1992   Growing up female: Stressful events and the transition to adolescence. In T. Field, P. McCabe and N. Schneiderman (eds), *Stress and Coping in Infancy and Childhood*. Erlbaum.

1994   Economic deprivation and early childhood development. *Child Development*, 65, 296–318 (with G.J. Duncan and P.K. Klebanov).

Further reading

Bornstein, M.H. (ed.) (1995) *Handbook of Parenting*. Erlbaum.

Chase-Lansdale, P.L. and Brooks-Gunn, J. (eds)
(1995) *Escape from Poverty: What makes a
Difference for Children?* Cambridge University
Press.
Cicchetti, D. and Cohen, D.J. (eds) (1995)
*Development Psychopathology, Vol. 2: Risk,
Disorder, and Adaptation.* Wiley.
Kujawaki, J. and Bower, T.G. (1993) Same-sex
preferential looking during infancy as a function of
abstract representation. *British Journal of
Developmental Psychology*, 11, 201–9.

Jeanne Brooks was born to Richard and Mary
Brooks on 9 December 1946. She received her
undergraduate training from Connecticut College, earning a BA in psychology in 1969. The
following year Brooks earned an EdM degree
from Harvard University in human learning and
development. It was also during this year that
she married Robert W. Gunn.

Her earliest research interests were in the
development of visual self-recognition in
infancy, as well as infant social perception and
peer group interaction. She also performed
research during this period on attitudes and
expectations about the menstrual cycle, and
developed the Menstrual Attitude Questionnaire, with Diane Ruble. Some major findings
in this area were that female children have
specific expectations about menstruation as
early as the fifth grade, and that early symptom
expectations are positively related to later menstrual distress. While performing research in
these areas she continued her graduate training,
earning her PhD in 1975 from the University
of Pennsylvania, also in human learning and
development. In the late 1970s, Brooks-Gunn
helped establish an Early Childhood Institute at
the Educational Testing Service and St Luke's-
Roosevelt Hospital in New York City for the
purpose of developing diagnostic and assessment instruments, and creating a curriculum for
at-risk children.

Over the years, some of Brooks-Gunn's most
significant research has been done in the area of
transition to adolescence among females. She
has argued that the transition to adolescence
is multidimensional, and that problems which
develop during this period, such as depression,
aggressive affect and eating disorders, derive
more from social events than from hormonal
changes. Brooks-Gunn has also performed a
considerable amount of research on the development of low-birth-weight, premature infants.
She has reported findings which suggest that
family income and poverty status are powerful
correlates of the cognitive development and
behavior of such children.

One of Brooks-Gunn's most noteworthy
contributions came from her collaboration with
Frank Furstenberg on a follow-up to a study on
300 adolescent mothers in the Baltimore area.
These young women, all African-American,
were first interviewed in the mid-1960s, and
their transition to adulthood was documented
over a five-year period. The seventeen-year
follow-up of the study examined the directions
which these young mothers' lives took in adulthood. The book *Adolescent Mothers in Later Life*
described the results of the study, and earned the
William Goode Book Award from the American
Sociological Association. A significant finding
was the diversity in long-term adaptation to early
motherhood, and a strong case was made for
carefully designed social programmes to ameliorate the problem. Brooks-Gunn has produced
over 250 journal articles, chapters and books in
her relatively brief career, and continues to be a
very prolific scholar.

J.D. HOGAN AND W. IACCINO

Brown, Ivan D.

Born: 1927, Cambridge, England *Nat:* British
Ints: Evaluation and measurement, experimental
analysis of behaviour, experimental psychology,
industrial and organizational, psychology and
law *Educ:* BSc University of London, 1961;
PhD University of London, 1967 *Appts &
awards:* Assistant Director, Medical Research
Council, Applied Psychology Unit; Transport and
Road Research Laboratory Advisory Groups,
1960–83; Editorial Board, *Accident Analysis
and Prevention*, 1970– , *Ergonomics Abstracts*,
1983; UK Ergonomics Society Council, 1971–5,
Chairman, 1980–2, President, 1982–4, Lecturer, 1985; *Ergonomics*, Editor, 1975–80,
Board, 1980– ; Psychologist Member of Medical Commission on Accident Prevention,
1976– ; Chairman, Parliamentary Advisory
Council for Transport Society, Roaduser Group
1981– ; Director, Human Factors Society,
Europe Chapter, 1984–6; Deputy Chairman of
MCAP Transport Committee, 1984–

Principal publications

1964 The measurement of perceptual load and
reserve capacity. *Transactions of the Association of
Industrial Medical Officers*, 14, 44–9.
1972 *Human Factors for Designers of Naval
Equipment.* Medical Research Council (with M.D.
Elliott, M.D. Joel, A.M. Keeling, J.F. Milton,

H.C.W. Stockbridge, R.J. Whitney, J.H. Williams, B. Hoskins and F.E. Smith).

1975   Driver's attitudes to the seriousness of traffic offences considered in relation to the design of sanctions. *Accident Analysis and Prevention, 7,* 15–26 (with A.K. Copeman).

1979   Can ergonomics improve primary safety in transport systems? *Ergonomics,* 22, 109–16.

1982   The traffic offence as a rational decision: exposure of a problem and suggested countermeasures. In S.M. Lloyds-Bostock (ed.), *Psychology in Legal Contexts: Applications and Limitations.* Wiley.

1982   Driver behaviour. In A.J. Chapman, F.M. Wade and H.C. Foot (eds), *Pedestrian Accidents.* Wiley.

1982   Measurement of mental effort: Some theoretical and practical issues. In E.G. Ainsworth-Harrison (ed.), *Energy and Effort.* Taylor and Francis.

1982   Driving fatigue. *Endeavour,* 6, 83–90.

1982   A psychophysiological investigation of system efficiency in public telephone switchrooms. *Ergonomics,* 25, 1013–40 (with D.G. Wastell and A.K. Copeman).

1983   *Human Factors and Information Technology.* National Electronics Council (ed. with D.D. O'Brien and P. Wilson).

1985   *Ergonomics International* '85. Taylor and Francis (with R. Goldsmith, K.E. Coombes and M.A. Sinclair).

1986   *Occupational Fatigue.* Wiley.

Further reading

Wilson, J.R. and Corlett, E.N. (eds) (1995) *Evaluation of Human Work: A Practical Ergonomics Methodology.* Taylor and Francis.

There are two clear influences on the contributions to psychology of Ivan Brown: (1) a previous seven-year career in electrical measurement and control, and (2) a late developer in his formative years spent under the guiding influence of F.C. **Bartlett**'s followers at Cambridge. Inevitably, he was drawn to methods of measuring human performance and the study of sociotechnological systems. The application of information theory to psychology in the 1960s shaped this early interest in 'dual task' techniques for the measurement of 'mental load' and 'reserve capacity'. Published work in this field, his 'engineering psychology' background and a job at APU Cambridge made Brown a natural recipient of queries from designers and operators of technological systems.

Perhaps because everyone is a potential user

and the ergonomics issues are therefore rather challenging, he divided his attention mainly between telecommunications and transport systems. In both areas, the need to develop appropriate methodology for human performance measurement was as much a motivating factor as an engineer's interest in new system designs, or a psychologist's interest in the causes of human error. This may help to explain why his bibliography of some eighty publications includes writings on such diverse topics as fatigue effects, the design of postage stamps, traffic offences, information technology, hazard perception, and the determinants of mood fluctuations among telephone switchboard operators.

Ergonomics is about the design of interfaces between people, hardware and software, and the selection and training of system users. Brown's contributions to the applied psychology aspects of ergonomics have covered this full range and have been directed to both psychologists and non-psychologists. This is true both for his publications and for his membership of committees, advisory and professional groups. It reflects his interpretation of the Medical Research Council's view that its research should be carried to the point of application rather than terminating in an academic publication.

DAVE OBORNE

Brown, Roger William

Born: 1925, Detroit, Michigan, USA *Nat:* American *Ints:* Developmental psychology, personality and social psychology *Educ:* BA University of Michigan, 1948; MA University of Michigan, 1949; PhD University of Michigan, 1952 *Appts & awards:* Instructor, Harvard University, 1952–3, Assistant Professor, 1953–7; Associate Professor, Massachusetts Institute of Technology, 1957–60, Professor, 1960–2; Professor of Social Psychology, Harvard University, 1962– ; President, New England Psychological Association, 1965–6, Eastern Psychological Association, 1971–2; Outstanding Achievement Award, University of Michigan, 1969; Doctor of the University Award, University of York, 1970; Distinguished Scientific Achievement Award, APA, 1971; G. Stanley Hall Prize in Developmental Psychology of the APA, 1973; International Prize of the Foundation Fyssen, Paris, 1985

Principal publications

1954   A study in language and cognition. *Journal of*

Abnormal and Social Psychology, 49, 454–62 (with E.H. Lenneberg).

1955 Phonetic symbolism in natural languages. *Journal of Abnormal and Social Psychology*, 50, 388–93 (with A.H. Black and A.E. Horowitz).

1958 *Words and Things*. Free Press.

1960 The pronouns of power and solidarity. In T. Sebeok (ed.), *Aspects of Style in Language* MIT Press (with A. Gilman).

1965 *Social Psychology*. Free Press.

1966 Personality and style in Concord. In M. Simon and T.H. Parsons (eds), *Transcendentalism and its Legacy*. University of Michigan Press (with A. Gilman).

1966 The 'tip of the tongue' phenomenon. *Journal of Verbal Learning and Verbal Behavior*, 5, 325–37 (with D. McNeill).

1970 Derivational complexity and order of acquisition in child speech. In R. Hayes (ed.), *Cognition and the Development of Language*. Wiley (with C. Hanlon).

1973 *A First Language: The Early Stages*. Harvard University Press.

1974 *Psychology*. Little, Brown (with R. Herrnstein).

1977 Flashbulb memories. *Cognition*, 5, 73–99 (with J. Kulik).

1983 The psychological causality implicit in language. *Cognition*, 14: 237–73 (with D. Fish).

1985 *Social Psychology*, 2nd edn. Free Press.

1986 Linguistic relativity. In S.H. Hulse and B.F. Green, Jr. (eds), *One Hundred Years of Psychological Research in America*. Johns Hopkins University Press.

Further reading

Lindzey, G. (1989) *A History of Psychology in Autobiography*, vol. VII. Stanford University Press.

Roger Brown graduated from Edwin Denby High in 1943 intending to become a novelist of social protest. He attended the University of Michigan for one year but soon entered the Navy at the end of World War II. While on a ship which carried food and medical supplies for the United Nations from Shanghai, Brown read John B. **Watson**'s *Behaviorism*. From that point on, Brown knew he wanted to become a psychologist. He returned to the University of Michigan, earning a BA degree in 1948, an MA in 1949, and a PhD in 1952. While a graduate student, Brown taught a number of courses, including sensation and perception, and history and systems. His dissertation topic was in social psychology, and concerned the constructs of rigidity and authoritarianism.

Brown's academic interests became clearer during his post-doctoral year at the University of Michigan. He attended a lecture by linguist Charles Fries and was immediately fascinated with the field of linguistics, with which he had not been familiar. Until that point, Brown was not particularly motivated to do his part in helping to solve the 'ancient questions' of psychology. The science of linguistics, he later wrote, 'pulled me together as a person.' While Brown's interest in social psychology remained, as the publication of his two texts on the subject indicates, his research interests for the remainder of his career became focused on the psychology of language. His first work in the area was 'A stimulus-response analysis of language and meaning', an article ultimately published in 1958.

In 1952, Brown joined Jerome **Bruner**'s cognition research project at Harvard, and began a six-year stint as an Instructor of Social Psychology and the Psychology of Language. In 1957 he was appointed Associate Professor of Social Psychology at the Massachusetts Institute of Technology, where he had contact with the noted psycholinguist Noam **Chomsky**. Brown's research interests became focused on children's acquisition of their first language. In 1962 he returned to Harvard as Professor of Social Psychology. At this time he obtained support from the NIMH for a five-year study of language acquisition. This ground-breaking study involved the intensive analysis of samples of spontaneous verbalizations of three children, referred to in the literature as Adam, Eve and Sarah. Support for the project was extended to ten years, and the results were finally published in 1973, in *A First Language: The Early Stages*. This volume did not elucidate how language is acquired, but did produce generalizable results which have held up empirically over the years. Brown never completed a planned second volume on the study, stating his belief that he had not observed anything remotely generalizable on the order of what the first volume had yielded. Claiming only a 'prodigious polyglot' could keep up with the fast pace of research in psycholinguistics, he abandoned the study of language acquisition.

Brown also wrote two textbooks on psychology: *Social Psychology*, and *Psychology* with R. Herrnstein. This latter volume did not gain wide-spread appeal, as it was 'more searching and more difficult' than most introductory texts. It has been used widely in its German translation, however. His *Social Psychology*, published in 1965, has become a citation classic, though its 1985 revision has not been used widely.

Brown's classic studies on flashbulb memories and the 'tip of the tongue' phenomenon are examples of the rich information to be learned from phenomenon-centred studies. He expressed his preference for this type of research over theory-driven research as one of temperament, since it requires a degree of combativeness to defend a theoretical formulation. Brown's brand of research, as he has described it, 'aims at understanding, not at *p* values', and it is likely that for this reason his work has enjoyed a high degree of replicability.

J.D. HOGAN AND W. IACCINO

Bruce, V.

Born: 1953, Essex, England **Nat:** British and Canadian **Ints:** Experimental psychology; cognitive psychology; clinical psychology **Educ:** University of Cambridge, 1974; MA University of Cambridge, 1978 **Appts & awards:** Sarah Smithson Studentship, Newnham College, 1976–7; BPS Standing Conference Committee, 1980–4; Fellow, Royal Society of Edinburgh, Experimental Psychology Society, Member 1980– , Committee, 1986–9; Associate Editor, *British Journal of Psychology*, 1983–8, *Quarterly Journal of Experimental Psychology*, 1989–93; Editorial Advisory Board, *Psychological Research*, 1988– ; Member, European Society for Cognitive Psychology, 1987– , Committee Member; Member, Psychonomic Society, 1988– ; Editorial Board, *European Journal of Cognitive Psychology*, 1988– , *Visual Cognition*, 1993– ; Fellow and Chartered Psychologist, BPS, 1989– ; Chair, BPS Scientific Affairs Board, 1989–92; Spearman Medal and Presidents' Award Committees, 1989–92; Committee for Ethics of Research with Human Participants, 1989–92, Council, 1989–92, Finance and General Purposes Committee, 1989–92; Guest Editor, Special issue on face recognition, *European Journal of Cognitive Psychology*, 1991; Executive Committee Member, Association of Learned Societies in the Social Sciences, 1991–3; Co-editor, Philosophical Transactions of the Royal Society, 1992, Visual Cognition on Object and Face Recognition, 1994; Professor of Psychology, University of Stirling, 1992– ; Member, Advisory Council, Attention and Performance, 1994– ; Consulting Editor, *Journal of Experimental Psychology: Applied*, 1994– ; Editor, *British Journal of Psychology*, 1995–

Principal publications

1982 Changing faces: Visual and non-visual coding processes in face recognition. *British Journal of Psychology*, 73, 105–16.

1983 Recognizing faces. *Philosophical Transactions of the Royal Society of London*, Series B, 302, 423–36.

1985 *Visual Perception: Physiology, Psychology and Ecology*. Erlbaum (with P. Green).

1985 Identity priming in the recognition of familiar faces. *British Journal of Psychology*, 76, 373–83 (with T. Valentine).

1986 Understanding face recognition. *British Journal of Psychology*, 77, 305–27 (with A. Young).

1988 *Recognising Faces*. Erlbaum.

1989 *Visual Cognition: Computational, Experimental and Neuropsychological Perspectives*. Erlbaum (with G. Humphreys).

1990 Understanding face recognition with an interactive activation model. *British Journal of Psychology*, 81, 361–80 (with R.A. Johnston).

1991 Remembering facial configurations. *Cognition*, 38, 109–44 (with T. Doyle, N. Dench and A.M. Burton).

1993 Naming faces and naming names. *Memory*, 1, 457–80.

1994 Stability from variation: the case of face recognition. M.D. Vernon memorial lecture. *Quarterly Journal of Experimental Psychology*, 47 A, 5–28.

1995 Facial identity and facial speech processing: Familiar faces and voices in the McGurk effect. *Perception and Psychophysics*, 57, 1124–33 (with S. Walker and C. O'Malley).

Further reading

Bredart, S. and Bruyer, R. (1994) The cognitive approach to familiar face processing in human subjects. Special issue: Individual and social recognition. *Behavioural Processes*, 33, 213–32.

de Haan, E.H., Young, A.W. and Newcombe, F. (1991) A dissociation between the sense of familiarity and access to semantic information concerning familiar people. Special issue: Face recognition. *European Journal of Cognitive Psychology*, 3, 51–67.

Young, A.W. (1993) Recognising friends and acquaintances. In G.M. Davies and R.H. Logie (eds), *Memory in Everyday Life*. North-Holland/Elsevier Science.

Vicki Bruce completed her PhD ('Processing and remembering pictorial information') under A.D. **Baddeley**. Her early interests in the cognitive processing of pictures led to subsequent interests in the extent to which there may be special processing 'modules' for the recognition of different classes of visual object. Her most significant work relates to recognition of human faces, for which there exists neuropsychological and experimental evidence indicating that recognition occurs via special brain structures and processes. She has developed a model of face recognition which has attracted particular interests because it explicitly posits functional relationships between special 'face recognition units' and other components of face perception, such as the analysis of expression and naming.

Bruce points out that, like pictures of other visual objects, pictures of faces are categorized semantically (e.g. 'politician', 'sportsman') more quickly than they can be named (e.g. 'Paul', 'Anne'). This suggests that faces, like visual objects, access semantic codes directly, and names only indirectly via the semantic system. The similarity between faces and other visual objects, in terms of the functional organization of semantic access and name retrieval, is important for two reasons. First, it suggests that although there may be face-specific processes, there may not necessarily be unique processes involve in face perception and recognition. Second, given the similarity in functional organization, faces are an important type of visual object in which it is possible to process physical and semantic properties independently. For example, a person might look like a sportsman but actually be a famous actor. The identity of a face cannot be known from its particular configuration, and in this sense faces are more like words than other visual objects, but they are processed more like objects than words. Thus, face recognition seems to proceed within a specialized processing 'module' that is organized in a similar way to the modules used to recognize other kinds of visual object. The model accounts quite successfully for cases of prosopagnosia (selectively impaired face recognition) and has stimulated a considerable corpus of empirical and theoretical enquiry into visual object recognition as it applies to faces.

Bruner, Jerome Seymour

Born: 1915, New York, USA **Nat:** American **Ints:** Developmental psychology, general psychology, philosophical and theoretical psychology **Educ:** AB Duke University 1937; AM Harvard University, 1939; PhD Harvard University, 1941 **Appts & awards:** Fellow, New York Institute for the Humanities; Editor, *Public Opinion Quarterly*, 1934–44; Associate Director, Office of Public Opinion Research, 1942–4; Member, Institute for Advanced Study, 1951, White House Panel on Educational Research and Development; Lecturer, Salzburg Seminar, 1952; Professor of Psychology, Harvard University, 1952–72; Guggenheim Fellow, Cambridge University, 1955; Director, Centre for Cognitive Studies, 1961–72; Fellow, American Psychological Association (President, 1964–5, Distinguished Scientific Contribution Award, 1962), American Academy of Arts and Sciences, Swiss Psychological Society (Hon.), Social Psychology Study Social Issues (past president), American Association University Professors, Puerto Rican Academy of Arts and Sciences (Hon.); Syndic, Harvard University Press, 1962–3; Hon. DHL, Lesley College, 1964; Bacon Professor, University of Aix-en-Provence, 1965; Hon. DSc, Northwestern University, 1965, University of Sheffield, 1970, University of Cincinnati, 1966, University of New Brunswick, 1969; University of Bristol, 1975, Hon. DLitt, North Michigan University, 1969, Duke University, 1969; Hon. Dr, Sorbonne, 1974, University of Leuven, 1976, University of Ghent, 1977, University of Madrid, 1987, Free University Berlin, 1988, Columbia University, 1988, University of Stirling, 1990, University of Rome, 1992; Watts Professor of Psychology, University of Oxford, 1972–80; G.H. Mead University Professor, New School for Social Research, 1980–8; Research Professor of Psychology, New York University, 1987– ; International Balzan Prize, 1987

Principal publications

1956   *A Study of Thinking*. Wiley (with J. Goodnow and G. Austin).

1960   *The Process of Education*. Harvard University Press.

1962   *On Knowing: Essays for the Left Hand*. Belknap.

1965   The growth of mind. *American Psychologist*, 20, 1007–17.

1966   *Studies in Cognitive Growth*. Wiley (ed. with R.R. Olver, P.M. Greenfield *et al.*).

1966   *Toward a Theory of Instruction*. Belknap.

1968   *Processes of Cognitive Growth*. Clark University Press.

1970   *Poverty and Childhood*. Merrill-Palmer Institute.

1973   *Beyond the Information Given: Studies in the Psychology of Knowing*. Norton (ed. with Anglin).

1983   *Child's Talk*. Norton.
1983   In Search of Mind: Essays in Autobiography.
  Harper & Row.
1986   *Actual Minds, Possible Worlds*. Harvard
  University Press.
1990   *Acts of Meaning*. Harvard University Press.
1990   Culture and human development: A new look.
  Human Development, 33, 344–55.

Further reading
Fiske, S.T. (1992) Thinking is for doing: Portraits of
  social cognition from Daguerreotype to laserphoto.
  Journal of Personality and Social Psychology, 63,
  877–89.
Greenfield, P. (1990) Jerome Bruner: The Harvard
  years. *Human Development*, 33, 327–33.
Gopnik, A. (1990) Knowing, doing, and talking: The
  Oxford years. *Human Development*, 33, 334–8.
Olson, D.R. (1990) Possible minds: Reflections on
  Bruner's recent writings on mind and self. *Human
  Development*, 33, 339–43.

Jerome Bruner's contributions can be anchored
in three concepts which are concerned with how
we learn to mean and to understand others'
meanings. These are intentionality, thinking and
culture. Intentionality is a central concept in all
of Bruner's work. In his studies of infancy he
showed that the ontogenesis of action begins
with the goal and ends with the means to achieving it. For example, in his examination of
poverty and childhood he argued that children of
poverty and their parents characteristically lack
confidence in means–end relations in intentional, goal-oriented behaviour. In his studies
of language he showed that the development of
communication ante-dates the development of
language. Children can share meanings long
before they use language. He considers language
as a tool of thought – a problem-solving device
which can be used in the creation of meaning. In
other words, children make language rather than
simply acquire or learn it. In formulating this
functionalist view of language he can be
credited with instigating interest in the field of
developmental pragmatics.

  His contributions to the development of
thinking are based on the notion that the major
activity of human beings involves extracting
meanings from their encounters with the world.
Modes of representation are crucial here – they
are the tools through which the child learns
meaning. The ordered development of three
modes of representation (enactive, iconic and
symbolic) is central to Bruner's theory of cognitive development. While later modes depend on

earlier ones, they do not comprise developmental stages. As we grow older we do not lose or
outgrow earlier representational forms for making and interpreting meaning; we retain them
and can use all three in different situations.
Bruner's is an active view of mind which
contrasts with nativist positions (knowledge
matures and is triggered by events and
experiences) and information-processing ones
(knowledge is acquired as developmental constraints are lifted and as memory and language
expand). Knowledge is active and functional,
and it requires a social or cultural context.

  For Bruner, culture provides amplification
systems for each mode of representation. Thus,
he talks about amplifiers of action (e.g. ham-
mers, levers, wheels), amplifiers of senses –
ways of looking (e.g. pictures, diagrams), and
amplifiers of thinking (e.g. language, logic,
mathematics). Culture and cognitive development are closely linked, and a theory of
development must include a theory of instruction that can relate the ordering of cultural
amplifiers to the developmental sequence of the
three representational modes. In exploring the
social and cultural origins of the self, he has
developed a perspective on folk psychology in
which he argues that each culture generates
narratives about how people are, how and why
they act, and how they deal with trouble. These
narratives typically depict a canonical state of
things and a deviation from that state, and
are useful in making these deviations
comprehensible.

  Although the worlds we live in are symbolic
constructions, and there are many possible
worlds, Bruner regards the constructive activities themselves as reflecting universal
properties of mind. This position sets him apart
from traditional cognitive psychology which,
he argues, has failed to address the concept of
the self adequately; self-concept is inseparable
from an elaboration of human meaning.
Cultural context – the symbolic world of
shared meaning – is composed of the vocabulary and linguistic peculiarities of the self in
context.

Bühler, Charlotte B.
Born: Charlotte Malachowski, 1893, Berlin,
Germany ***Died:*** 1974, Stuttgart, West Germany
Nat: German ***Ints:*** Developmental, evaluation
and measurement, humanism, personality and
social, psychotherapy ***Educ:*** BS University
of Berlin, 1915; PhD University of Munich,

1918 **Appts & awards:** Rockefeller Exchange Fellowship, 1923; Series Editor, Quellen und Studien zur Jugendkunde, 1925–37; President, Association for Humanistic Psychology, 1965–6

Principal publications

1929   *Das Seekenleben des Jugendlichen*, 5th edn. Fisher.
1933   *Der menschliche Lebenslauf als psychologisches Problem*. Hirzel.
1950   The concept of integration and the Rorschach test as a measurement of personality integration. *Journal of Projective Techniques*, 14, 315–19.
1951   Maturation and motivation. *Personality*, 1, 184–211.
1951   The World Test, a projective technique. *Journal of Child Psychiatry*, 2, 4–23.
1954   The reality principle. *American Journal of Psychotherapy*, 8, 626–47.
1954   The process-organization of psychotherapy. *Psychiatry Quarterly*, 28, 287–311.
1959   Theoretical observations about life's basic tendencies. *American Journal of Psychotherapy*, 13, 561–81.
1962   *Psychologie im Leben unserer Zeit*. Droemer.
1968   Psychotherapy and the image of man. *Psychotherapy*, 5, 2.
1971   Basic theoretical concepts of humanistic psychology. *American Psychologist*, 26, 378–86.

Further reading

Bühler, C. and Allen, M. (1972) *Introduction to Humanistic Psychology*. Brooks-Cole.
—— and Massarik, F. (1968) *The Course of Human Life: A Study of Goals in the Humanistic Perspective*. Springer-Verlag.

Charlotte Malachowski born in 1893 in Berlin, the elder of two children. Her father was an architect and her mother an accomplished musician.

Completing her undergraduate studies at the University of Berlin, Charlotte Malachowski went to Munich to work under Oswald **Külpe**, where, after a whirlwind courtship, she married Karl Bühler. With her PhD finished in 1918, the next twenty years saw the Bühlers build a reputation for developing new research methods. In 1923, Charlotte was awarded a Rockefeller Exchange fellowship, and went to work with **Thorndike** at Columbia University. From there she returned to Vienna, where with her husband she founded a highly respected child psychology department.

Using the innovative life biography approach,

in 1922 Bühler published *Das Seelenleben des Jugendlichen*, a study of adolescents that established her reputation as a psychologist. Eleven years later, the publication of *Der menschliche Lebenslauf als psychologisches Problem* reflected her broader interest in developmental psychology. This productive sojourn in Vienna came to an end in 1938, with the arrival in Austria of the Nazis. Karl was imprisoned for his anti-Nazi sentiments. In 1939, Charlotte negotiated his release.

Forced to leave the country, the Bühlers went first to Norway. Karl went to live in America later that same year and Charlotte followed a year later. They finally settled in Los Angeles in 1945, where Charlotte Bühler worked first as chief clinical psychologist at the Los Angeles County Hospital, and then as clinical professor of psychiatry at the University of Southern California School of Medicine. She started a successful private psychotherapy practice, and in 1962 published *Psychologie im Leben unserer Zeit*, considered to be one of her most important books.

With **Maslow**, **Rogers** and Frankl, she organized the Old Saybrook Conference in 1964, which led to the establishment of the Association for Humanistic Psychology, of which she was president from 1965 to 1996. Her publications of 1968 and 1972 (listed under Further reading above) reflect her central role in the humanistic movement. Failing health saw her return to Germany in 1972, where she died in her sleep in 1974.

ALAN DABBS

Bühler, Karl

Born: 1879, Meckesheim, Germany **Died:** 1963, Los Angeles, California **Nat:** German **Ints:** General, developmental, personality and social, philosophical and theoretical, humanistic. **Educ:** MD University of Freiburg, 1903; PhD University of Strasbourg, 1904 **Appts & awards:** Editorial Board, *The Journal of General Psychology*, 1928–64; Hon. President, 16th International Congress in Psychology, 1960; Wilhelm Wundt Medal, 1960

Principal publications

1907   Tatsachen und Probleme zu einer Psychologie der Denkvorgange. I: Über Gendanken. *Arch. Psychologie*, 9.
1908   II: Über Gedenkenzusammenhange. *Arch. Psychologie* 12; III: Über Gedenkenerinnerungen. *Arch. Psychologie* 12.
1927   *Die Krise der Psychologie*. Fisher.

1934   *Ausdruckspsychologie*. Fisher.
1952   The skywise and neighbours' navigation of
        ants and bees. *Acta Psychologie* 8, 225–63.
1953   The breathing factor in scent trails of animals.
        Jahrbuch für Psychologie und Psychotherapie, 1,
        479–83.
1954   Essentials of contact navigation. *Acta
        Psychologica*, 10, 278–316.
1954   Human distance orientation (discussion with
        reference to Columbus and Lindbergh). *Jahrbuch
        für Psychologie und Psychotherapie*, 2, 242–58.
1958   *Menschen und Tiere*. Hans Huber.

Further reading

Bolgar, H. (1964) Karl Bühler. *American Journal of
    Psychology*, 77, 674–8.

In 1906, after a spell at the University of Berlin,
Bühler joined the **Külpe** Group in Würzburg. His
contribution concerned development of a method
of observing and interpreting thought that involved
asking subjects a series of questions requiring
subsequent explanation. The result, Bühler's
Ausfragemethod, resembled the now familiar
structured interview employed by some clinicians.

Bühler became Professor of Psychology at
the University of Bonn in 1909, developing an
interest in *Gestalt* phenomena. His work on
Gestalt perception was published in 1913,
coinciding with a move to the University of
Munich as Professor of Psychology.

In 1918, Bühler published what has been
considered to be the first attempt at a comprehensive treatment of child psychology, and was
appointed Professor of Psychology at Dresden.
Four years later, he accepted the offer of
the Chair of Psychology at the University of
Vienna, from which point Bühler, with his wife
Charlotte, developed Vienna's Department of
Psychology into one of the leading centres for
research into child psychology.

His disenchantment with American behaviourism, and commitment to a holistic approach to the
study of personality provoked Bühler to address
the methodological problems implicit in the two
approaches. In *Die Krise der Psychologe*, published in 1927, Bühler does not totally reject any
one school of thought, but rather aims his criticism
at the claims made by each to absolute truth.

In 1931, Bühler turned to linguistics, introducing the notion of control factors into the
stimulus-response model of the time, and applying the principles of *Gestalt* psychology to the
study of language.

With the arrival of the Nazis in Vienna in
1938, Bühler was forced to leave first for Nor-

way, then America. Because of the behaviouristic nature of psychology in America his latter
work concerning information theory and communications did not come to be appreciated until
much later.

ALAN DABBS

Buros, Oscar Krisen

Born: 1905, Lake Nebagamon, Wisconsin,
USA **Died:** 1978, New Brunswick, New Jersey,
USA **Nat:** American **Ints:** Clinical psychology,
educational   psychology,   evaluation   and
measurement, industrial and organizational
psychology, military psychology, personality
and social psychology **Educ:** BS University of
Minnesota, 1925; MA Teachers College,
Columbia University, 1928 **Appts & awards:**
Associate Professor, Professor, Rutgers Univer-
sity, 1932–65; Director, Buros Institute for
Mental Measurement; Citation, APA, 1953;
Senior Fulbright lectureship, 1956–57. Phi
Delta Kappa research award, 1965; Hon. DSc,
Uppsala College, 1973; Educational Testing
Service Award for Distinguished Service to
Measurement, 1973; Fellow, American Psy-
chological Association, American Statistical
Association

Principal publications

1938   *The 1938 Mental Measurements Yearbook*.
        Gryphon.
1940   *The 1940 Mental Measurements Yearbook*.
        Gryphon.
1949   *The Third Mental Measurements Yearbook*.
        Gryphon.
1953   *The Fourth Mental Measurements Yearbook*.
        Gryphon.
1959   *The Fifth Mental Measurements Yearbook*.
        Gryphon.
1965   *The Sixth Mental Measurements Yearbook*.
        Gryphon.
1970   *Personality Tests and Reviews*. Gryphon.
1972   *The Seventh Mental Measurements Yearbook*.
        Gryphon.
1974   *Tests in Print*. Gryphon.
1978   *The Eighth Mental Measurements Yearbook*.
        Gryphon.

Further reading

Plake, B.S. *et al*. (1991) The Buros Institute of Mental
    Measurements: Commitment to the tradition of
    excellence. *Journal of Counselling and
    Development*, 69, 449–55.

Oscar Buros's life work was entirely focused on

the area of applied psychological measurement. In particular, he and his late wife Luella devoted their lives to ensuring that test users were able to identify all published psychological tests that existed to measure a particular topic, and to select the most appropriate instrument for their particular application. This was achieved through the *Mental Measurement Yearbooks*, *Tests in Print* and other publications of the Gryphon Press – the publishing organization that Buros founded for this purpose. The publication of such works continues today under the aegis of the Buros Institute for Mental Measurement and continues to expand in scope – e.g. through a presence on the Internet, where the index to the *Yearbooks* is freely available.

It is difficult to imagine how the science of mental testing might have developed without Buros's influence. He foresaw that the widespread use of psychometrically dubious psychological tests would set back the emerging disciplines of educational, occupational and clinical psychology, and would have a disastrous effect on the scientific credibility of differential psychology. What was clearly needed was a sort of 'consumers' guide' to mental tests that would allow potential test users to scan what was available, and select the most appropriate instrument for their needs on the basis of detailed reviews by distinguished experts in the field of mental testing.

The first *Mental Measurement Yearbook* was published in 1938, and the basic formula continues almost unchanged to this day. Its appearance was not without controversy: according to a newspaper clipping cited by the Buros Institute, a test publisher begged Buros to discontinue the project 'in the name of common decency'. Each *Yearbook* contains scholarly and impartial reviews of a wide range of tests together with details of publishers, prices and a classified index of test topics. Some editions also contain book reviews and bibliographic information, allowing scholars to identify papers and books that cite individual tests. Buros insisted on high standards of scholarship and evaluation from his distinguished panel of reviewers, and some of the reviews (such as Rorer on the Gough Adjective Checklist and Lee on the Lüscher) have become classics. The drawback to this project is that only tests that are commercially published are included: those that appear in appendices to journal articles (particularly in the areas of social and clinical psychology) are excluded – although these tests are often both widely used and psychometrically flawed.

Buros also made a substantial contribution to applied psychology through his wartime work as head of testing for the US Army, and subsequently through his input to leadership assessment at West Point, although little has been published in this area. If Buros had concentrated more on such applied interests and less on educating the rest of us about the necessity for rigorous standards in psychological testing, my suspicion is that psychometric theory would have had far less impact on testing practice. Today the only real excuse for investigators using an inappropriate or invalid test is because they are ignorant of the legacy of Oscar Krisen Buros.

COLIN COOPER

Burt, Cyril Ludowic

Born: 1883, London, England **Died:** 1971, London, England **Nat:** British **Ints:** Educational psychology, evaluation and measurement, mental retardation, personality and social psychology, school psychology **Educ:** BA Oxford, 1907; MA Oxford, 1909, DSc Oxford, 1923 **Appts & awards:** John Locke Scholarship, Oxford, 1908; Psychologist to London County Council (Education Department), 1913–32; Professor of Education, University of London, 1924–31; Professor of Psychology, University College London, 1931–50; Hon. LlD, Aberdeen, 1939; President, BPS, 1941–3; Hon. DLitt, Reading, 1948; Fellow, British Academy, 1950; APA Thorndike Award, 1971

Principal publications

1909 Experimental tests of general intelligence. *British Journal of Psychology*, 3, 94–177.
1917 *The Distribution and Relations of Educational Abilities*. King.
1921 *Mental and Scholastic Tests*. King.
1925 *The Young Delinquent*. University of London Press.
1937 *The Backward Child*. University of London Press.
1940 *The Factors of Mind*. University of London Press.

Further reading

Hearnshaw, L.S. (1979) *Cyril Burt: Psychologist*. Hodder and Stoughton.
Joynson, R.B. (1989) *The Burt Affair*. Routledge.
Mackintosh, N.J. (1995) *Cyril Burt: Fraud or Framed?* Oxford University Press.

Following contact with Francis **Galton** early in

his life, Cyril Burt's first academic appointment was to Charles **Sherrington**'s Department of Physiology in the University of Liverpool. In 1913 he moved to London as psychologist to the London County Council: the first educational psychologist appointment in Britain. Here he produced much of his most important applied work into the distribution and correlates of intelligence, and the underlying causes of low educational attainment and delinquency. He also founded child and vocational guidance services. On succeeding **Spearman** as Professor of Psychology at University College London, Burt expanded these interests and produced a number of still-influential papers in the fields of psychometric theory, and a book on factor analysis. Many of these papers were published in the *British Journal of Mathematical Psychology*, which he co-edited from 1948 to 1960. Burt nominally retired from academic life in 1951 but continued to publish extensively until his death in 1971.

As an applied psychologist Burt sought to explain complex phenomena in terms of a few basic physiological, psychological and social processes. For example, he traced offenders' family trees to examine the possibility of a genetic influence and sought to determine the impact of environmental factors such as parental behaviour, disease, poverty, family relationships, and the consequences of being reared in a 'vicious home' on children's later behaviour. He also explored fields as diverse as infant development, personality, ability and physiognomy in order to evaluate their influence on the children with whom he dealt, and made important contributions to factor analysis, test construction and other branches of psychometrics. Thus Burt identified a number of important subdisciplines of psychology and performed seminal research in several of them. It is important to remember this, since it emerged that there were some irregularities in the data that were published in a 1966 paper on the genetics of intelligence.

Burt's work on the genetics of intelligence involved comparing the intelligence of pairs of identical twins who were separated shortly after birth and reared in different environments. Tracking down and testing such individuals is a difficult and time-consuming process, and Burt's data were highly regarded because his sample of twins was so large. Following Burt's death a British journalist, Oliver Gillie, was alerted to some curious features of Burt's reported correlations. The subsequent investiga-

tions and re-evaluation of this work strongly suggests that the sample of twins was not as large as had been claimed by Burt, although it is not clear whether this reflects a deliberate attempt at scientific fraud or an old man's carelessness at checking typescript. More recently, other scientifically impeccable studies have been performed based on different samples of twins. Like Burt they conclude that intelligence has a very substantial genetic component, so whatever Burt's scientific failings, the data that he presented are in almost exact accord with subsequent replications.

The 'Burt affair' (as it is known) has become notorious and eclipses Burt's other contributions to psychology. There seems to be an unfounded assumption that all of Burt's work is in some way 'unsafe'. The many contributions of this leading pioneer of individual differences research are thus largely unrecognized.

COLIN COOPER

Byrne, Donald G.

Born: 1948, Broken Hill, Australia *Nat:* Australian *Ints:* Clinical, health, personality and social, psychotherapy, rehabilitation *Educ:* BA University of Adelaide, 1971; PhD University of Adelaide, 1975 *Appts & awards:* Reader in Clinical Psychology, Australian National University, Member, APS Registration Committee, 1979– , National Heart Foundation of Australia Committees 1979– ; Editorial Board, *Australian and New Zealand Journal of Psychiatry*, 1979– ; Director, Mental Health Foundation of Australia, 1982– ; Councillor and Board Member, International College of Psychosomatic Medicine, 1983– ; Deputy Chairman, Mental Health Advisory Committee, 1984–

Principal publications

1976   Choice reaction times in depressive states. *British Journal of Social and Clinical Psychology*, 15, 149–56.

1976   Vigilance and arousal in depressive states. *British Journal of Social and Clinical Psychology*, 15, 167–74.

1978   Dimensions of illness behavior in survivors of myocardial infection. *Journal of Psychosomatic Research*, 22, 485–91 (with H.M. Whyte).

1979   Severity of illness and illness behavior: A comparative study of coronary care patients. *Journal of Psychosomatic Research*, 23, 57–62 (with H.M. Whyte).

1980   Life events and myocardial infarction revisited: The role of measures of individual impact. *Psychosomatic Medicine*, 42, 1–10 (with H.M. Whyte).

1980   Social relationships, adversity and neurosis: A study of associations in a general population sample. *British Journal of Psychiatry*, 136, 574–83 (with A.S. Henderson and P. Duncan-Jones).

1981   *Neurosis and the Social Environment.* Academic Press (with A.S. Henderson and P. Duncan-Jones)

1981   Illness behavior and outcome following myocardial infarction: A prospective study. *Journal of Psychosomatic Research*, 25, 97–107 (with H.M. Whyte and K.L. Butler).

1981   Type A behavior, life events and myocardial infarction: Independent or related risk factors? *British Journal of Medical Psychology*, 54. 371–8.

1982   Psychological responses to illness and outcome after survived myocardial infarction: A long-term follow-up. *Journal of Psychosomatic Research*, 26, 105–12.

1985   *The Behavioral Management of the Cardiac Patient.* Ablex. (2nd edn 1987.)

1985   Consistency and variation among instruments purporting measure the Type A behavior pattern. *Psychosomatic Medicine*, 47, 1–20.

1992   *Psychology for Nurses: Theory and Practice.* MacMillan.

1994   *Counselling Skills for the Health Care Professions.* MacMillan.

Like many academic clinical psychologists, Byrne began his career with an enthusiasm for the relevance of experimental methodologies to the solution of clinical problems. This is reflected in some early work on psychomotor and psychophysiological disturbances in depression. Ultimately, however, the laboratory came to be too limited an environment for enquiry, particularly since the environment itself was becoming an attractive focus for research as a contributor to and mediator of symptoms. This emerging interest initiated a continuing series of studies involving the definition and measurements of the noxious elements in the social environment and the associations which these had with the development of states of psychological distress. The methodological challenges of such work, together with the unfolding data, continue to provide great stimulation. The first phase of this work culminated in the publication, with two colleagues, of the book *Neurosis and the Social Environment.*

During this time Byrne's interest in physical as well as psychological symptoms was growing and, in particular, the area of coronary heart disease became a primary focus of investigation.

It is now clear that the social environment influences both onset of coronary heart disease and recovery from it, though the multitude of ways in which this can happen will provide research hypotheses well into the future. Byrne's interests have encompassed three areas in this field: (1) the role of the social environment in precipitating clinical episodes of myocardial infarction; (2) the influence of psychological responses to illness on recovery and rehabilitation; and (3) the interaction between Type A behaviour and the environment in creating vulnerability to heart disease. The medical emphasis of this work reflects his belief that clinical psychology can contribute to the many processes of health care to an extent far beyond its traditional links with psychiatry, and this belief is reflected in more recent publications directed to cognate professional groups.

Byrne, Donn

Born: 1931, Austin, Texas, USA *Nat:* American *Ints:* Personality and social, population and environmental psychology *Educ:* BA California State University at Fresno, 1953; MA California State University at Fresno, 1956; PhD Stanford University, 1958 *Appts & awards:* Professor of Psychology and Chairman, Dept. of Psychology, State University of New York at Albany; Editorial Board, Psychological Monographs, 1962–4, *Journal of Experimental Social Psychology*, 1967–70, *Journal of Research in Personality*, 1968–77, *Personality: An International Journal*, 1969–72, *Journal of Applied Social Psychology*, 1970–6, *Psychonomic Science*, 1971–2, *Sociometry*, 1972–6, *Journal of Personality*, 1973–5, *Memory and Cognition*, 1973–8, *Motivation and Emotion*, 1975– , *Journal of Sex Research*, 1977, *Inter American Journal of Psychology*, 1983– ; Fellow, Divisions 8, 34, Society for the Scientific Study of Sex, AAAS; President, Midwestern Psychological Association, 1978–81; Co-editor, Sexual Behavior Series, State University Press, 1982–9.

Principal publications

1961   Interpersonal attraction and attitude similarity. *Journal of Abnormal and Social Psychology*, 62, 713–15.

1961   The repression–sensitization scale: Rationale, reliability and validity. *Journal of Personality*, 29, 334–9.

1964   Attitude statements as positive and negative

reinforcements. *Science*, 176, 798–9 (with C. Golightly).

1965   Attraction as a linear function of proportion of positive reinforcements. *Journal of Personality and Social Psychology*, 1, 659–63 (with D. Nelson).

1966   *An Introduction to Personality*. Prentice-Hall (with K. Kelley).

1967   Attraction and similarity of personality characteristics. *Journal of Personality and Social Psychology*, 5, 82–90 (with W. Griffitt and D. Stefaniak).

1967   Effective arousal and attraction. *Journal of Personality and Social Psychology*, 6, 638 (with G.L. Clore).

1970   A reinforcement model of evaluative responses. *Personality: An International Journal*, 1, 103–28 (with G.L. Clore).

1970   Continuity between the experimental study of attraction and real life computer dating. *Journal of Personality and Social Psychology*, 16, 157–65 (with C.R. Ervin and J. Lamberth).

1971   *The Attraction Paradigm*. Academic Press.

1974   *Social Psychology*. Allyn & Bacon (with R.A. Baron).

1977   Social psychology and the study of sexual behavior. *Personality and Social Psychology Bulletin*, 3, 3–30.

1983   *Adolescents, Sex and Contraception*. Erlbaum (with W.A. Fisher).

1984   The mediating role of cognitive processes in self-reported sexual arousal. *Journal of Research in Personality*, 18, 54–63 (with D.P.J. Przybyla).

1985   *Approaches to Human Sexual Behavior*. Erlbaum (with K. Kelley).

1990   Personality dispositions as mediators of sexual responses. *Annual Review of Sex Research*, 1, 93–117 (with L. Schulte).

Further reading

Sternberg, R.J. and Barnee, M.L. (eds) (1988) *The Psychology of Love*. Yale University Press.

During his graduate years at the California State University at Fresno and at Stanford, Byrne gradually changed his interests from clinical psychology to research in personality and social psychology. Among his earliest graduate student publications were works on two themes which have remained dominant in his subsequent career: interpersonal attraction and approach-avoidance responses to anxiety-evoking stimuli.

The work on attraction has been the most important aspect of contributions to date. Working within a consistent empirical and theoretical paradigm, he constructed and elaborated on a framework that has impressive predictive and explanatory power. An interesting, and quite unanticipated, aspect of the work on attraction has been the series of challenges over the years by those who question one or more aspects of this body of research. Though such 'attacks' are momentarily annoying, they provided the opportunity for Byrne to explain, clarify and inform others about the meaning of this work. They also provided an opportunity for him to write in a less solemn fashion than is ordinarily provided by the traditional journal format.

The more recent phase of his research career has centred on human sexual behavior. Though the theoretical framework has developed directly from that utilized in attraction research, there is not yet the feeling of a tight, coherent body of findings. As we learn more about sexual attitudes, the power of fantasy, and the role of belief systems, he is quite hopeful that we will be as successful as in the previous instance.

C

Calkins, Mary Whiton

Born: Hartford, Connecticut, USA, 1863 **Died:** Newton, Massachusetts, USA, 1930 **Nat:** American **Ints:** Experimental psychology **Educ:** PhD Harvard University, 1895

Principal publications

1894 Association: I. *Psychological Review*, 1, 476–83.

1896 Association: II. *Psychological Review*, 3, 32–49.

1896 Association: An essay analytical and experimental. *Psychological Review Monograph Supplements*, 1, no. 2.

1898 Short studies in memory and in association from the Wellesley College Psychological Laboratory: 1. A study of immediate and delayed recall of the concrete and of the verbal. *Psychological Review*, 5, 451–6.

Further reading

Calkins, M.W. (1930) Mary Whiton Calkins. In C. Murchison (ed.), *A History of Psychology in Autobiography*, vol. 1. Clark University Press.

Furumoto, L. (1979) Mary Whiton Calkins (1863–1930): Fourteenth President of the American Psychological Association. *Journal of the History of the Behavioral Sciences*, 15, 346–56.

Mary Calkins obtained her first position as an instructor of Greek at Wellesley College in 1887. Despite policies that excluded women from graduate programmes, she was able to join William **James**'s graduate seminar in 1890. This graduate training was taken unofficially, as was her work with Hugo Münsterberg in 1892–4, which formed the basis of her research and publications on association and memory.

Calkins's main findings on memory concerned the influence of primacy, recency, frequency and vividness. She found that vividness was by far the strongest influence: in general a repeated pairing of words overrode the influence of a vivid or a recent one. She is arguably the first psychologist to have used the 'paired associates' method to investigate memory, although she never used the term in her early writing. Calkins's work was met by an immediate disappointment. In 1895, she took the equivalent of a doctoral examination at Harvard University. Although the award of the doctoral degree was strongly recommended by **James**, **Royce** and **Münsterberg**, the university did not act on their recommendation and she was not awarded a degree. She returned to Wellesley in 1895 as an associate professor and was appointed full professor in 1898. In 1902 she declined the offer of a doctorate from Radcliffe College. Twenty-five years later a petition to the university from Harvard degree holders to award Calkins the PhD was once again rejected. After this Calkins published little in the area of memory but focused her efforts on investigations of introspection and the concept of self.

Campbell, Donald Thomas

Born: 1916, Michigan, USA **Nat:** American **Ints:** Personality and social, Society for the Psychological Study of Social Issues, philosophical and theoretical psychology **Educ:** AB University of California, Berkeley, 1939; PhD University of California, Berkeley, 1947 **Appts & awards:** Professor, Department of Psychology and Social Relations, Lehigh University; National Academy of Sciences, Distinguished Scientific Contribution Award, 1970; Member, 1973, 1975; APA, President, APA Kurt Lewin Memorial Award, 1974; Society for the Psychological Study of Social Issues, Myrdal Prize in Science, 1977; Hon. DSS, Claremont Graduate School, 1978; Hon. LLD, University of Michigan, 1974; Hon. ScD, University of Florida, 1975; Hon. DHL, University of Chicago, 1978; Hon. DS, University of Southern California, 1979; Evaluation Research Society Award for Distinguished Contributions to Research in Education, 1981; Hon. DS, Northwestern University, 1983

Principal publications

1959 Convergent and discriminant validation by the multitrait–multimethod matrix. *Psychological Bulletin*, 56, 81–105 (with D.W. Fiske).

1963 Social attitude and other acquired behavioural dispositions. In S. Koch (ed.), *Psychology: A Study of a Science, vol. 6: Investigations of Man as Socius*. McGraw-Hill.

1966 *Experimental and Quasi-Experimental Designs for Research*. Rand-McNally (with J.C. Stanley).

1966 *The Influence of Culture on Visual Perception*. Bobbs-Merril. (with M.H. Segall and M.J. Herskovits)

1966 Pattern matching as an essential in distal knowing. In K.R. Hammon (ed.), *The Psychology of Egon Brunswick*. Holt, Rinehart and Winston.

1967 Stereotypes and the perception of group differences. *American Psychologist*, 22, 817–29.

1969 Variation and selective retention in socio-cultural evolution. In L. von Bertalanffy, A. Rapoport and R.L. Meier (eds), *General Systems: Yearbook of the Society for General Systems Research*.

1969 Reforms as experiments. *American Psychologist*, 24, 309–429.

1973 *Ethnocentrism: Theories of Conflict, Ethnic Attitudes and Group Behaviour*. Wiley (with R.A. Levine).

1974 Evolutionary epistemology. In P.A. Schilpp (ed.), *The Philosophy of Karl R. Popper. vol. 14: The Library of Living Philosophers*. Open Court.

1981 *Non-reactive Measures in the Social Sciences*. Houghton Mifflin (with E.J. Webb, R.D. Schwartz, L. Sechrest and J.B. Grove).

1981 *Quasi-Experimentation: Design and Analysis for Field Settings*. Houghton Mifflin (with T.D. Cook).

1983 Two distinct routes beyond kin selection to ultrasociality: Implications for the humanities and social sciences. In D.L. Bridgeman (ed.), *The Nature of Prosocial Development: Theories and Strategies*. Academic Press.

1984 Can we be scientific in applied social science? In R.F. Conner *et al.* (eds), *Evaluation Studies Review Annual*, vol. 9. Sage.

Further reading

Millsap, R.E. (1995) The statistical analysis of method effects in multitrait-multimethod data: A review. In P.E. Shrout and S.T. Fiske (eds) *Personality Research, Methods, and Theory*. Erlbaum.

Originally, Campbell would have been regarded as a social psychologist: he worked on social attitudes and their relations to principles of perception and learning. Interest in ethnic prejudice and intergroup conflict led him to a preponderant emphasis on social-organizational factors, combined with an emphasis on the universals of biological human nature, rather than upon individual differences in attitudes. This merged with interest in group selection in biological and cultural evolution. However he is primarily known for methodological contributions such as the multitrait, multimethod matrix and quasi-experimental designs. Independently he was interested in the 'blind-variation-and-selective retention' (b-v-s-r) algorithm. These two lines of interest eventually came together in his interest in 'evolutionary epistemology' and in a sociology of scientific validity. The b-v-s-r algorithm has its most elaborated exemplification in biological evolution, and Campbell has attempted to extend it to cultural evolution, in a model in which culturally induced behavioural dispositions can override biological ones.

Cannon, Walter Bradford

Born: 1871, Prairie du Chein, Wisconsin, USA
Died: 1945, Franklin, New Hampshire, USA
Nat: American **Ints:** Physiology **Educ:** MA Harvard College, 1897; MD Harvard Medical School, 1900 **Appts & awards:** Professor of Physiology, Harvard Medical School, 1906–42; President of the American Physiological Society, 1914–16

Principal publications

1909 The influence of emotional states on the functions of the alimentary canal. *American Journal of the Medical Sciences*, 137, 480–7.

1912 An explanation of hunger. *American Journal of Physiology*, 29, 363–6 (with A.L. Washburn).

1914 The emergency function of the adrenal medulla in pain and other major emotions. *American Journal of Physiology*, 33, 356–72.

1914 The interrelations of emotions as suggested by recent physiological researches. *American Journal of Psychology*, 15, 256–82.

1918 The physiological basis of thirst. *Proceedings of the Royal Society of London*, B90, 283–301.

1919 Studies on the conditions of activity in endocrine glands: V. The isolated heart as an indicator of adrenal secretion induced by pain, asphyxia and excitement. *American Journal of Physiology*, 50, 399–432.

1927 The James–Lange theory of emotions: A critical examination and an alternative. *American Journal of Psychology*, 39, 106–24.

1929 *Bodily Changes in Pain, Hunger, Fear and Rage*. Branford.

1932 *The Wisdom of the Body*. Norton (revised and enlarged 1960).

1935 Stress and strains of homeostasis (Mary Scott Newbold lecture). *American Journal of the Medical Sciences*, 189, 1–14.

1935 *Autonomic Neuro-effector Systems*. Macmillan (with A. Rosenbleuth).

1942 'Voodoo' death. *American Psychologist*, 44, 169–81.

Further reading

Benison, S., Barger, A.C. and Wolfe, E.L. (1987) *Walter B. Cannon: The Life and Times of a Young Scientist*. Harvard University Press.

Cannon, W.B. (1945) *The Way of the Investigator: A Scientist's Experiences in Medical Research*. Norton.

Walter Cannon grew up, the son of a chief clerk for the St Paul and Pacific Railroad, in St Paul, Minnesota. He entered Harvard College in 1892, to follow a programme in arts and sciences, preparatory to medical training. It was during his undergraduate days that Cannon first encountered William **James**. James, then head of the philosophy department at Harvard, so stimulated Cannon's interest that he considered forsaking medicine for graduate studies in philosophy and psychology. James's counsel was concise: 'Don't do it, you may be filling your belly with the East wind.' Cannon clearly heeded the advice, entering Harvard Medical School in 1896.

His talent for innovative physiological research was quickly demonstrated. As early as his first semester, Cannon, along with a second-year student colleague, Albert Moser, was the first to apply Roentgen's X-rays to the study of physiological phenomena: in this case, activity in the alimentary canal. The peristaltic waves that Cannon and Moser observed in a cat's stomach were the first such observations made by X-ray in an unanaesthetized mammal. Cannon's interest in the gastrointestinal tract continued after his graduation in medicine and his appointment as an instructor in physiology at Harvard. Following studies on adrenal secretions, Cannon turned to the topic of hunger and with Arthur L. Washburn, one of his students, published a classic study demonstrating the simultaneity of felt hunger pangs and stomach contractions. Evidently, students in the first-year physiology class were both concerned and fascinated by the sight of Washburn with a tube, one end of which was attached to a balloon in his stomach, sticking out of his mouth and tied to one of his ears. This distal end was reattached to the kymograph once the lecture was over.

Work on thirst followed, and for both motivational states Cannon emphasized the importance of local mechanisms.

Cannon's interest in the digestive system led him to the discovery of the gastrointestinal effects of strong emotions, and to chart the various adaptive changes that occur during emotional stress. It is this work and Cannon's interpretation of it that make him an important figure in psychology. His critique of William James's theory of emotions, the then dominant account, and Cannon's alternative, now known as the Cannon–Bard theory of emotions, led to one of the great debates of twentieth-century psychology. It is a debate that has yet to be resolved properly, but Cannon's criticisms certainly did damage to James's notion that bodily activity, once perceived, was a sufficient condition for emotional experience. In contrast, Cannon regarded strong emotion and the contingent changes in bodily systems as constituting an emergency reaction: the marshalling of available resources for 'fight or flight'. In doing so, he shifted much of the research emphasis from the phenomenology of internal states to the central and autonomic mechanisms that controlled them, as well as to the eliciting of environmental conditions. With regard to the former, Cannon was early in identifying the key roles played by the hypothalamus, the adrenal glands and their secretions.

However, it is Cannon's formulation of stress and homeostasis, described in *The Wisdom of the Body* which will probably remain his most telling contribution. Cannon was among the first to use the term 'stress' in a non-engineering context. He regarded it as a disturbing force, something which disrupts the usual balance or equilibrium. It was to this balance or equilibrium that he applied the term 'homeostasis'. Few currently researching the psychophysiology of stress depart much from Cannon's approach. Sixty years on, they may not acknowledge the debt explicitly, but it is plain in the way they conceptualize psychophysiological systems under challenge.

In a later article on serendipity in science, Cannon cited the early American physicist, Joseph Henry, as saying that 'The seeds of great discoveries are constantly floating around us, but they only take root on minds well prepared to receive them.' Psychology is fortunate indeed that Walter Cannon had such a mind.

DOUGLAS CARROLL

Carmichael, Leonard

Born: 1898, Philadelphia, USA *Died:* 1973, Washington, DC *Nat:* American *Ints:* Developmental, experimental, military, physiological and comparative, teaching. *Educ:* BS, Tufts University Medford; PhD, Harvard University, 1924 *Appts & awards:* Professor, Brown University, 1923–36; Sheldon Fellowship, Harvard University, 1924–5; Princeton University, 1925–7; Dean of the Faculty, University of Rochester, 1936–8; President, Tufts University, 1938–52; Director, National Roster of Scientific and Specialized Personnel, 1939–45; APA, President, 1940; Army Scientific Advisory Panel, 1947–52; Naval Research Advisory Committee, 1947–52; Chairman, American Council of Education, 1947–53; Secretary, Smithsonian Institution, 1953–64; Vice-Chairman, Harvard Foundation for Advanced Study and Research, National Advisory Committee for Aeronautics, 1956–8; Vice President, American Philosophical Society, 1962–5; Vice President and Chairman, Committee for Research and Exploration, National Geographic Society, 1964–73; Editorial Advisor in Psychology, Houghton Mifflin; Editor, *Manual of Child Psychology*; Twenty-three Honorary Degrees; Presidential Citations from Presidents Truman and Eisenhower

Principal publications

1925   Heredity and environment: Are they antithetical? *Journal of Abnormal Social Psychology*, 20, 245–60.
1926   The development of behavior in vertebrates experimentally removed from the influence of external stimulation. *Psychological Review*, 33, 185–217.
1930   *Elements of Human Psychology*. Houghton Mifflin (with H.C. Warren)
1932   An experimental study of the effect of language on the reproduction of visually perceived form. *Journal of Experimental Psychology*, 15, 73–86 (with H.P. Hogan and A.A. Walter).
1933   Origin and prenatal growth of behavior. In C. Murchison (ed.), *A Handbook of Child Psychology*. Clark University Press.
1934   An experimental study in the prenatal guinea pig of the origin and development of reflexes and patterns of behavior in relation to the stimulation of specific receptor areas during the period of active fetal life. *Genetic Psychology Monographs*, 16, 337–491.
1935   Electrical potentials from the intact human brain. *Science*, 89, 51–3 (with H.H. Jasper).
1938   Learning which modifies an animal's subsequent capacity for learning. *Journal of Genetic Psychology*, 52, 159–63.
1941   The experimental embryology of mind. *Psychological Bulletin*, 38, 1–28.
1946   (ed.) *Manual of Child Psychology*. Wiley.
1946   *Reading and Visual Fatigue*. Houghton Mifflin (with W.F. Dearborn).
1951   Ontogenetic development. In S.S. Stevens (ed.), *Handbook of Experimental Psychology*. Wiley.
1956   *The Making of Modern Mind*. Elsevier.
1957   *Basic Psychology*. Random House.
1964   The early growth of language capacity in the individual. In E.H. Lenneberg (ed.), *New Directions in the Study of Language*. MIT Press.

Further reading

Boring, E.G. and Lindzey, G. (eds) (1967) *A History of Psychology in Autobiography*, vol. 5. Appleton-Century-Crofts.

During his college days Carmichael committed himself to experimental zoology and psychology, although his dissertation was a theoretical analysis of the history of technical thought about human and animal instincts. At Princeton University he conducted his classic work on the behaviour of larval amblystoma and frog tadpoles, reared under anaesthetic. To his surprise the findings showed that genetic determinants were more important in development than environmental ones. His conviction in this view inspired his later work on the foetal development of organized behaviour.

At Brown University he fulfilled his ambition to study the prenatal development of foetal mammals, and displayed for the first time a whole repertory of 'species-specific' responses. He discovered that most specific foetal responses could be stimulated experimentally before the time that they would serve a biologically adaptive function in the normal development of the organism. He also worked on the righting reflex in cats.

In 1935, with H.H. **Jasper**, he reported the first human electroencephalographic work in America. He also developed a device for the electrical recording of the eye movements of animals. This method enabled him to perform elaborate research with W.F. Dearborn on eye movements, reading and visual fatigue while at Tufts, despite his main responsibilities as an administrator.

During World War II Carmichael recruited psychologists for the war effort and contributed research on the validation of synthetic training devices and the development of selection procedures. He became involved with numerous committees in an advisory capacity.

Carmichael had a long-term personal interest in primate research. He was also extraordinarily energetic as a teacher, and was proud that at Princeton, Brown and Rochester his laboratories ran morning, afternoon and evenings, including weekends. Particularly while at the Smithsonian Institute, he presented psychology to the public, and wrote his book *Basic Psychology* for the 'educated' general reader.

JACKIE STEDMON

Carterette, Edward Calvin

Born: 1921, Mount Tabor, USA **Nat:** American **Ints:** Auditory perception, experimental psychology, music perception, psychophysics, speech synthesis. **Educ:** AB University of Chicago, 1949; AB Harvard University, 1952; MA Indiana University, 1954; PhD Indiana University, 1957 **Appts & awards:** NSF, Scientific Instrumentation Program, 1954–65, Special Reviewer, Division of Psychobiology, 1961– ; Awards Panel, 1962–70, APA Division 3, Program Committee, 1962–5, Chairman, 1964–8, Membership Committee, 1974–7; APA Visiting Scientist, 1964–6, 1968; NIMH, Special Review, 1967– ; Professor of Psychology, University of California, Los Angeles 1968; NCR; NAS, 1968–72; Western Psychological Association Convention Program, Chair, 1970; NCR Canada, Special Reviewer, 1976; Society of Experimental Psychologists, Chairman, 1977–8, Secretary-Treasurer, 1982– ; AAAS, Electorate Nominating Committee, Chair, 1983–4; APA Fellow; AAAS Fellow; Fellow of the Acoustical Society of America

Principal publications

1958 Message repetition and receiver confirmation of messages in noise. *Journal of the Acoustical Society of America*, 30, 846–85.

1963 Repetition and confirmation of messages received by ear and eye. *Quarterly Journal of Experimental Psychology*, 15, 15–172 (with M. Cole).

1966 (ed.) *Brain Function, vol. III: Speech, Language and Communication*. University of California Press.

1968 Comparisons of some learning models for response bias in signal detection. *Perception and Psychophysics*, 3, 5–11 (with M. Friedman, L. Nakatani and A. Ahumada).

1969 Mach bands in hearing. *Journal of the Acoustical Society of America*, 45, 986–98 (with M. Friedman and J. Lovell).

1974 *Informal Speech: Alphabetic and Phonemic texts with Statistical Analysis*. University of California Press (with M. Jones).

1974–8 *Handbook of Perception*, vols I–X. Academic Press (with M. Friedman).

1975 Recognition memory for voices. In A. Cohen and S. Nooteboom (eds), *Structure and Process in Speech Perception*. Springer-Verlag (with A. Barnebey).

1975 Perceptual space for musical structures. *Journal of the Acoustical Society of America*, 58, 711–20 (with J. Miller).

1978 Some historical notes on research in hearing. In E. Carterette and M. Friedman (eds), *Hearing, vol. IV: Handbook of Perception*. Academic Press.

1979 Bisection of loudness. *Perception and Psychophysics*, 26, 265–80 (with N. Anderson).

1981 Applications of signal theory to problems of neuropsychology. In R. Malathesa and L. Hartlage (eds), *Neuropsychology and Cognition*, vol. II. Sitjhoff and Noordhoof.

1984 On synthesising animal speech: The case of the cat. In G. Bristow (ed.), *Electronic Speech Synthesis*. McGraw-Hill (with C. Shipley and J. Buchwald).

1986 Similarities among transformed melodies: The abstraction of invariants. *Music Perception*, 3(4), 393–409 (with D. Kohl and A. Pitt).

1987 A comparison of the musical scales of the ancient Chinese bronze bell ensemble and the modern bamboo flute. Special issue: Understanding melody and rhythm. *Perception and Psychophysics*, 41(6), 547–62 (with R. Yu-an and W. Yu-kui).

1987 The effect of melodic and temporal contour on recognition memory for pitch change. Special issue: Understanding melody and rhythm. *Perception and Psychophysics*, 41(6), 576–600 (with C. Monahan and R. Kendall).

1987 Setting straight the record. *Perception and Psychophysics*, 42(4), 409–10 (with N. Anderson).

1988 Hearing impairment among orchestral musicians. *Music Perception*, 5(3), 261–84. (with D. Woolford).

1989 Interactive factors in consonant confusion patterns. *Journal of the Acoustical Society of America*, 85(1), 339–46 (with T. Bell and D. Dirks).

1990 Communication of musical expression. *Music Perception*, 2, 129–63 (with R. Kendall).

1991 Perceptual scaling of simultaneous wind instrument timbres. *Music Perception*, 8(4), 369–404 (with R. Kendall).

1993 Verbal attributes of simultaneous wind instruments I: Von Bismarck's adjectives. *Music Perception*, 10(4), 445–67 (with R. Kendall).

1993 Verbal attributes of simultaneous wind instruments II: Adjectives induced from Pisoni's orchestration. *Music Perception*, 10(4), (with R. Kendall).

Professor Carterette began studying neurology at Yale before defecting to mathematical psychology and finally ending up in perceptual psychology. He has focused on the theoretical and experimental problems of hearing and speech perception and their interactions. In his own words, he likes to 'solve problems and to understand the basis of mechanisms and concepts'. This approach is reflected in such projects as the *Handbok of Perception*, a work that he considers to have pointed the way to many others.

He has had a considerable influence on the areas of speech and perception through both his research and his students, many of whom have gone on to applied research in places such as NASA and the Bell laboratories. He has also forged many foreign connections through the large number of postdoctoral fellows and visiting scientists that have come to work with him.

Professor Carterette enjoys both his work and position in the university: as he says, 'The University is a good home for one like me who wishes to try everything but from the security of the monastery. There is a vast panoply of intellectual and aesthetic delights to be had which even the richest cannot afford. Yet the exotic world (the marketplace) is open for brief forays into reality, with always the haven of the campus at one's back.'

MORIA MAGUIRE

Cattell, James McKeen

Born: 1860, Easton, Pennsylvania, USA **Died:** 1944, Lancaster, Pennsylvania, USA **Nat:** American **Educ:** BA Lafayette College, 1880; PhD University of Leipzig, 1886 **Appts & awards:** Chair of Psychology (first in the world), Professor, University of Pennsylvania, 1887–91; Columbia University, 1891; APA, President, 1895; Editor, *Psychological Review*, 1894–1903, *Popular Science Monthly*, 1900–15, *Science*, 1904–44, *American Naturalist*, 1907–44, *School and Society*, 1915–39; *Scientific Monthly*, 1915–43, Psychological Corporation, Founder and President, 1917; President, Ninth International Congress of Psychology, 1929

Principal publications

1885 Über die Zeit der Erkennung und Benennung von Schriftzeichen Bildern und Farben. *Philosophical Studies*, 2, 635–50. (abridged, *Mind* (1886), 11, 635–50).

1885 Über die Trägheit der Netzhaut und des Sehcentrums. *Philosophical Studies*, 3, 94–127. (also *Brain*, 8, 295–312).

1886 Psychometrische Untersuchungen. *Philosophical Studies*, 3, 305–35, 452–92; (1887), 4, 241–50. (Also *Mind* (1886), 11, 220–42, 377–92, 524–38; (1887), 12, 68–74.)

1890 Mental tests and measurements. *Mind*, 15, 373–81.

1893 On errors of observation. *American Journal of Psychology*, 5, 285–93.

1894 On reaction-times and the velocity of the nervous impulse. *Psychological Review*, 1, 159–68.

1895 Measurements of the accuracy of recollection. *Science*, 2, 761–6.

1896 Physical and mental measurements of the students of Columbia University. *Psychological Review*, 3, 618–48.

1902 The time of perception as a measure of differences in intensity. *Philos. Stud.*, 19, 63–8.

1906 *American Men of Science*. Science Press. (6 edn, 1938.)

1906 A statistical study of American men of science. *Science*, 32, 633–48, 672–88.

Further reading

Wells, F.L. (1944) James McKeen Cattell. *American Journal of Psychology*, 57, 270–5.

Woodworth, R.S. (1944) James McKeen Cattell. *Psychological Review*, 51, 201–9.

Cattell's early interests were in literature, and he graduated from the college of which his father was president (1863–83). He travelled to Europe to study philosophy, where he was influenced by **Wundt** (at Leipzig) and Lotze (at Göttingen). A paper on Lotze lead to a fellowship in philosophy at Johns Hopkins University (1882–3), with **Dewey** and Jastrow as fellow students. At this time Charles S. **Peirce** was conducting experiments in psychophysics and Stanley **Hall** was establishing a major psychological laboratory. Cattell completed several investigations of the timing of various psychological processes and then returned to work with Wundt (1883–6) as his first research assistant. Although Cattell's studies of reaction time fitted well with the established programme of investigation on this topic, his theoretical position was different from that of Wundt. Wundt's investigations of reaction time included introspection as a control variable, whereas Cattell found it difficult to carry out the required subjective controls and was doubtful of the ability of others to do so. Somewhat later he conducted psychophysical studies; his approach was guided by the argument that psychophysics should be concerned with examining the accuracy of observation under different conditions. He hypothesized that observational error should increase as the square root of the observed magnitude, rather than in direct proportion to that magnitude (as stated in **Weber**'s Law).

After leaving Leipzig, Cattell met Francis **Galton**, and this inspired a long series of investigations into individual differences. This was to lead to an interest in mental tests (Cattell coined the phrase in his 1890 *Mind* article), although his 'anthropometric test' movement was overtaken by interest in the techniques and theory espoused by **Binet**. His interests in psychophysics and individual differences led Cattell to develop a method of ranking that was used extensively in psychophysics, aesthetics and value-judgements. He applied the method to assess the relative eminence of scientists, and this influenced his publication of the *Directory of American Men of Science*.

Cattell is not associated with a particular school or theory of psychological thought, and was not a prolific writer, but he was responsible for promulgating quantitative methods and techniques in psychology, principally within a functionalist framework, and thereby changed the face of the discipline. Thus, he is regarded as a leading figure in the 'second generation' of American psychologists along with **Titchener**, **Baldwin**, **Münsterberg** and others.

Cattell, Raymond Bernard

Born: 1905, Hill Top, Staffordshire, England **Nat:** British **Ints:** Clinical, educational, evaluation and measurement, experimental, personality and social **Educ:** BSc University of London, 1924; PhD University of London, 1929; DSc University of London, 1939 **Appts & awards:** Professor Emeritus, School of Professional Psychology, University of Illinois; APA, Fellow; Darwin Fellowship, 1935; Wenner Gren Prize, New York Academy of Science, 1950; President, Society of Multivariate Experimental Psychology, 1961; BPS, Hon. Member, 1981– ; APA Award for Psychometrics, 1983; US Department of Education Award for Contributions, 1984; Editorial Consultant, *Multivariate Behaviorial Research*; Co-editor, *Multivariate Experimental Clinical Research*; Consultant on various journals

Principal publications

1928 The significance of the actual resistances in GSR experiments. *British Journal of Psychology*, 19, 34–48.

1936 Is material intelligence declining? *Eugenics Review*, 27, 18–203.

1944 An objective text of character and temperament. *Journal of Social Psychology*, 19, 99–114.

1950 The main personality factors in questionnaire material. *Journal of Social Psychology*, 31, 3–38.

1951 P-technique: A new method for analysing personal motivation. *Transactions of the New York Academy of Sciences*, 14, 29–34.

1952 A confirmation of the ergs and self sentiment patterns among dynamic traits by R technique. *British Journal of Psychology*, 43, 280–94.

1960 The multiple abstract variance analysis equations and solutions. *Psychological Review*, 67, 353–72.

1966 Refinement and test of the theory of fluid and crystallized intelligence. *Journal of Educational Psychology*, 57, 253–70.

1971 *Abilities: Their Structure, Growth and Action.* Houghton Mifflin.

1971 Estimating modulation indices and state liabilities. *Multivariate Behavioral Research*, 6, 7–32.

1973 *Personality and Mood by Questionnaire.* Jossey-Bass.

1979 *Personality and Learning Theory*, vols 1 and 2. Springer-Verlag.

1979 Ethics and the social sciences – the Beyondist Solution. *Management Science Quarterly*, 19, 298–310.

1982 *The Inheritance of Personality and Ability.* Academic Press.

1987 *Beyondism: Religion from Science.* Praeger.

1987 *Intelligence: Its Structure, Growth and Action.* North Holland.

1990 Advances in Cattellian personality theory. In L.A. Pervin (ed.), *Handbook of Personality: Theory and Research*. Guilford Press.

1992 Human motivation objectively, experimentally analysed. *British Journal of Medical Psychology*, 65, 237–43.

1994 Finding personality structure when ipsative measurements are the unavoidable basis of the variables. *American Journal of Psychology*, 107, 261–74 (with J. Brennan).

Further reading

Cattell, R.B. (1974) Travels in psychological

hyperspace. In T.S. Krawiec (ed.), *The Psychologists*, vol. 2. Oxford University Press.

Goldberg, L.R. (1990) An alternative 'description of personality': The Big-Five factor structure. *Journal of Personality and Social Psychology*, 59, 1216–29.

Krug, S.E. and John, E.F. (1990) The 16 Personality Factor Questionnaire. In C.E. Watkins Jr and V.L. Campbell (eds), *Testing in Counseling Practice*. Erlbaum.

Schultz, D.P. and Schultz, S.E. (1994) *Theories of Personality* (5th edn). Brooks Cole.

Raymond B. Cattell was the second of three sons, and his father and grandfather were owner-managers of several manufacturing plants. By the age of 19 he had secured a university degree in chemistry. Later he heard of the work of Sir Cyril **Burt**, and this influenced his decision to study psychology. On completion of his PhD he secured a position as lecturer at Exeter University and in 1932 he became Director of the City Polytechnic Clinic at Leicester, England. In 1937 E.L. **Thorndike** offered him a research position and the following year he was offered the G. Stanley **Hall** professorship at Clark University. In 1941 he moved to a lectureship at Harvard, which brought him into contact with **Allport**, **Murray** and others, and three years later he was offered a research professorship at the University of Illinois. Later he moved to a professorship at the University of Hawaii.

Raymond Cattell has made fundamental contributions to our understanding of the architecture of personality and of ability. He defines personality as that which predicts what a person will do in a given situation. The implication in this definition is that we cannot define personality more fully until we define the concepts we plan to use in our investigations. He distinguishes three methods for studying personality: bivariate, multivariate and clinical. Cattell is critical of the bivariate approach because it cannot adequately address the complexity of relationships among the many factors that make up personality. The clinical approach he regards as useful because it permits observation of important behaviours as they occur. In combination the multivariate and clinical approaches can describe and help us understand complex patterns of behaviour. In his investigations of personality he developed four research techniques: (1) P-technique, in which a person's scores on a number of measures are compared across different situations and over time; (2) Q-technique, where two people are correlated on a large number of different measures; (3) R-technique, in which a large number of people are compared in terms of their scores or performance on a large number of specific measures; and (4) Differential-R technique, in which measures are repeated on different occasions and the changes between them correlated.

Traits (predispositions) are fundamental to Cattell's theory of personality, and he makes two kinds of distinction between traits. The first is between ability traits, temperament traits and dynamic traits, and the second is between surface traits and source traits. Ability traits relate to skills and abilities, and this group includes intelligence. Temperament traits relate to the emotional life of a person, and dynamic traits to the motivational life. Surface traits refer to behaviours that appear to covary at a superficial level but which do not necessarily have a common cause. Source traits refer to behaviours that covary and form a unitary, independent dimension of personality. Surface traits can be identified by clinical investigation and by asking people which characteristics they think go together, but source traits can only be discovered using multivariate statistical techniques. Cattell began by applying his experience of factor analysis (with C.E. **Spearman**) to the problems of personality structure using three kinds of datum: ratings, questionnaires and objective behavioural measures. This work resulted in the 16PF questionnaire series (16PF, HSPQ, CPQ, ESXO) and in the OA (Objective Analytic) personality battery. In support of his structural account of personality Cattell cites several sources of evidence: factor analysis of different kinds of datum, replicability across cultures, similarity of findings across age groups, usefulness in predicting behaviour, and evidence for a genetic contribution to many traits. In order to explicate the contributions of genetic and environmental factors to personality he developed multiple abstract variance analysis (MAVA, 1960), which was a significant advance on traditional techniques of the time.

In the 1960s he commenced a line of research into the nature and structure of ability. According to Cattell abilities are organized hierarchically. At the top of the hierarchy is g or general ability. Below g are successive levels of gradually narrowing abilities, terminating with Spearman's specific abilities. Cattell argued, with supporting empirical evidence, that there are twenty primary abilities and six secondaries. In addition he drew a distinction between fluid and crystallized ability. Fluid intelligence reflects an individual's ability to solve novel problems, whereas crystallized intelligence reflects the acquisition and use of culturally valued knowledge. With J.L. Horn (1966) he argued that crystallized ability increases over the life-span whereas fluid ability increases in childhood and adolescence but decreases in later years.

Although his work and theories have been received with enthusiasm, the derivation of so much from factor analytic and advanced mathematical models has stood as a barrier to acceptance and discussion by the majority of psychological practitioners. More recently Cattell has been applying dynamic calculus (a system of mathematical formulae to assess motivational factors in behaviour) to a quantitative psychoanalysis whereby psychiatrists can measure patients' unitary drives ('ergs') and states through the administration of such tests as the Motivation Analysis Test. This research has provided some statistical support for concepts such as drives and ego structure.

Chapanis, Alphonse

Born: 1917, Meriden, USA **Nat:** American **Ints:** Experimental psychology, Society of Engineering Psychologists **Educ:** BA University of Connecticut, 1937; MA Yale University, 1942; PhD Yale University, 1943 **Appts & awards:** President, Alphonse Chapanis Industrial and Human Factors Consulting Services, Society of Engineering Psychologists; APA Division 21, 1959–60; President, Human Factors Society, 1963–4; Franklin V. Taylor Award for 'outstanding contributions to the field of engineering psychology', 1963; Paul M. Fitts Award for 'outstanding contributions to human factors education', 1973; President, International Ergonomics Association, 1976–9; APA Distinguished Contribution for Applications in Psychology Award, 1978; Outstanding Scientific Contributions to Psychology Award, Maryland Psychological Association, 1981

Principal publications

1949 *Applied Experimental Psychology.* Wiley (with W.R. Garner and C.T. Morgan).
1949 How we see: A summary of basic principles. In Panel on Psychology and Physiology, *Committee on Undersea Warfare: A Survey Report on Human Factors in Undersea Warfare*, 1, 3–60. National Research Council.
1959 *Research Techniques in Human Engineering.* Johns Hopkins University Press.

1961 Men, machines and models. *American Psychologist*, 16, 113–31.
1963 *Human Engineering Guide to Equipment Design.* McGraw-Hill (with C.T. Morgan, J.S. Cook and M.W. Lund).
1965 *Man–Machine Engineering.* Brooks Cole.
1965 Words, words, words. *Human Factors*, 7, 1–17.
1967 The relevance of laboratory studies to practical situations. *Ergonomics*, 10, 557–77.
1971 The search for relevance in applied research. In W.T. Singleton, J.G. Fox and D. Whitfield (eds), *Measurement of Man at Work*. Taylor and Francis.
1971 Prelude to 2001: Explorations in human communication. *American Psychologist*, 26, 949–61.
1975 (ed.) *Ethnic Variables in Human Factors Engineering.* Johns Hopkins University Press.
1981 Tutorials for the first-time computer user. *Institute of Electrical and Electronics Engineers Transactions on Professional Communication*, PC-24, 30–5 (with J. Al-Award and W.R. Ford).
1981 Interactive human communication: Some lessons learned from laboratory experiments. In B. Shackel (ed.), *Man–Computer Interaction: Human Factors Aspects of Computers and People*. Sitjhoff and Noordhoff.
1982 What do professional persons think about computers? *Behaviour and Information Technology*, vol. 1, 55–68.
1984 Psychology and engineering. In M.H. Bornstein (ed.), *Psychology and its Allied Disciplines. vol. 3: The Natural Sciences* Erlbaum.

Further reading

Oborne, D.J. (ed.) (1995) *Ergonomics and Human Factors*. Elgar.

In 1942, immediately after he had completed his thesis but before graduation, Chapanis joined the Army Air Force's Aero Medical Laboratory at Wright-Patterson Air Force Base, Dayton, Ohio, as the first psychologist to be employed there. Research there was at the forefront of physiological and psychological science, investigating phenomena – anoxia, aeroembolism, explosive decompression, high G forces, night flying – that at the time were poorly understood. That experience made him acutely aware of the many immensely important practical problems to be solved in the world and how much more difficult it was to work on them than on abstract problems in an academic environment.

At the conclusion of the war, he moved to Johns Hopkins and was continually associated with that university until his retirement in June 1982. Those were fruitful years. With **Garner** and **Morgan** he wrote the first textbook in human factors; it set the pattern for subsequent books and for the development of the field. He also directed laboratories supported at various times by research contracts and grants from the Department of the Navy, National Aeronautics and Space Administration, National Science Foundation, International Business Machines Corporation and GTE Laboratories. His last laboratory, the Communications Research Laboratory, was a large and productive organization that he reluctantly closed after his retirement.

His immersion in human factors became almost total following his formal 'retirement'. As President of his own consulting firm, he faced an almost unending series of new problems, which stretched his imagination and forced him to use his science and knowledge to make an increasingly technological world a better and safer place in which to live.

DAVE OBORNE

Charcot, Jean Martin

Born: 1825, Paris, France **Died:** 1893, Paris, France **Nat:** French **Ints:** Anatomy, hypnosis, hysteria, nervous system, physiology **Educ:** MD University of Paris, 1853 **Appts & awards:** Professor of Anatomy, La Salpetriere Hospital, 1860; Neurological Clinic at La Salpetriere; 1862–93. President (Honorary), First International Congress of Psychology, 1889

Principal publications

1889   *Clinical Lectures on the Diseases of the Nervous System.* New Sydenham Society.
1890   *Complete Works* (especially vol. 1). Fourmville.

Further reading

Mackey, F.H. and Legrand, E. (1935) Jean Marie Charcot (1825–1893). *Archives of Neurology and Psychiatry*, 34, 390–400.
Zilborg, G. and Henry, G. (1951) *A History of Medical Psychology.* Norton.

After receiving his MD degree at the University of Paris, Charcot founded the first neurological clinic at La Salpetriere Hospital in Paris. This became the best-known neurological clinic in its time throughout the world. Both Pierre **Janet** and Sigmund **Freud** came to study with him. Charcot became interested in studying pati-

ents who were suffering from the disorder then known as hysteria. This consisted of a variety of symptoms ranging from paralysis, anaesthesias, and loss of visual, auditory and memory functions, as well as dissociated syptoms such as amnesia and seizures. Today these disorders are listed in the *Diagnostic and Statistical Manual of the American Psychiatric Association* (DSM IV) under the headings of somatoform and dissociated disorders.

Charcot observed that these symptoms conformed more to what the patients thought them to be neurologically than their real neurological pattern. For example, a patient could have a glove anesthesia or a stocking anesthesia conforming to the part of the skin which would be covered only by a glove or stocking. He also observed patients with epileptic-like seizures, which he referred to as hysterical epilepsy, and that the symptoms involved sexual matters. Here, he antedated Freud on the importance of sexuality in the disorder.

Charcot attempted to treat his patients with hypnosis. Since Mesmer's time in the eighteenth century, hypnosis (then known as Mesmerism) had gone out of fashion, but eventually it regained popularity and was acceptable by the medical profession. So Charcot attempted to treat his hysterical patients with hypnosis, with some success. He believed that the hypnotic process went through three stages: lethargy, catalepsy and somnambulism. This order is also followed in the formation of hysterical symptoms. He thus concluded that hysterical symptoms could be brought on through hypnosis. They both involved the modification of muscular states, reflex movements and sensory responses. He reported these findings to the French Academie des Sciences in 1882. The Academie had previously rejected the findings of Mesmer, but later accepted the work of Charcot, since by that time hypnosis had become respectable. However, Charcot still maintained that hysteria was a predisposed disorder of the nervous system and so had neurological origins of some kind, perhaps a weakened nervous system.

The school of Nancy, France, led by Bernheim and Liébeault, had a different theory, so Charcot's position became known as the Paris School and Liébeault and Bernheim's as the Nancy school. The latter maintained that hysteria was nothing more than self-hypnosis, or auto-suggestion.

In Vienna, around 1885, Sigmund Freud heard about Charcot's work with hysteria, and went to Paris to study with him for a period of about six months. During a lecture Charcot was treating a man (he originally thought hysteria was limited to women), whose symptoms involved a paralysis. As the story goes, Charcot said, 'This has to do with sexual zones, always, always, always.'

Charcot's school in Paris became very popular for its study of not only hysteria but other forms of neurosis. As a neurologist it was difficult for him to give up the notion that hysteria had some neurological foundations; although he did not completely abandon the idea that psychological implications were involved, he opposed the hypothesis of Bernheim and Liébeault that hypnosis and hysteria were purely psychological.

Eventually the theories of the Nancy school won out: hysteria was merely a matter of suggestion or self-hypnosis. Part of the success of both schools was that hypnosis had a therapeutic effect. In some cases, merely suggesting away the symptoms actually worked. In general, the psychoneuroses which Freud espoused were disturbances of the psyche.

Perhaps the final step in the self-hypnosis (suggestion) theory came in the work of Emil Coué in the early part of the twentieth century, also in Paris. He became known for the saying: 'Every day, in every way I am becoming better and better.'

ROBERT W. LUNDIN

Chiland, Collette

Born: 1928, Paris, France **Nat:** French **Ints:** Clinical psychology, psychology of women, psychoanalysis, psychotherapy, teaching of psychology **Educ:** Agrégé de Philosophie; Docteur en Médecine; Docteur en Lettres et Sciences Humaines **Appts & awards:** Professeur de Psychologie Clinique, Université René Descartes; Médecin au Centre Alfred Binet; President, International Association for Child and Adolescent Psychiatry and Allied Professions; Editorial Board, *Psychologie Française*, International Journal of Psychoanalysis Series; Co-editor, *The Child in his Family*

Principal publications

1971   Le statut du fantasme chez Freud. *Revue Française de Psychanalyse*, 35, 203–16.

1972   Des apories de toute reflexion sur la normalité. *Revue Française de Psychanalyse*, 36, 411–19.

1974   Chemins de l'Oedipe à l'anti-Oedipe. In *Chemins de l'Anti-Oedipe*. Privat.

1975   La psychanalyse des enfants en 1920 et en 1974. *La Psychiatrie de l'Enfant*, 18, 211–18.

1976   A propos de la négation (Freud 1925). *Bulletin de Psychologie*, 29, 8–13, 439–44.

1977   Borderline or prepsychotic conditions in childhood. In P. Hartocollis (ed.), *Borderline Personality Disorders*. International Universities Press (with A.S. Lebovici).

1978   L'enfant de six ans devenu adolescent. *Revue de Neuropsychiatrie Infantile*, 26, 697–707.

1979   The Child and his Family, 5 vols. Wiley, 1979–82;

1979   Reflexions d'une psychanalyste en 1979 sur la sexualite femininé. *Psychanalyse à l'Université*, 4, 341–7.

1980   Winnicott au present. Situation de Winnicott dans la psychiatrie et la psychanalyse contemporaines. *La Psychanalyse à l'Université*, 5, 541–52.

1983   *L'Entretien Clinique*. PUF.

1988   The child in his family, vol. 8: Perilous development: Child raising and identity formation under stress. *Yearbook of the International Association for Child Adolescent Psychiatry and Allied Professions*. Wiley (co-ed. with E.J. Anthony).

1988   Enfance et transsexualisme (Childhood and transsexualism). *Psychiatrie de l'Enfant*, 31, 313–73.

1989   Le monde interieur et la visée de l'autre (The inner world and the other's goals). *Revue Française de Psychanalyse*, 53, 405–8.

1990   Why children reject school: Views from seven countries. vol. 10 and *Yearbook of the International Association for Child and Adolescent Psychiatry for Allied Professions*. Yale University Press (co-ed with J.G. Young).

1990   Jouissance sexuelle et identité sexuée. (Sexual pleasure and sexualized identity.) *Revue Française de Psychanalyse*, 54, 197–208.

1992   Etre fou ou n'etre pas fou (To be insane or not to be insane.). *Psychiatrie de l'Enfant*, 35, 454–79

1993   Actualité de 'Malaise dans la Civilisation' (Topicality of 'Civilization and its Discontents'). *Revue Française de Psychanalyse*, 57, 1217–21.

1993   Dans la tête de l'autre (Inside the head of the other). *Revue Française de Psychanalyse*, 57, 1631–40

1994   Children and violence. In *The Child in the Family*. Aronson (co-ed. with J.G. Young and D. Kaplan).

1994   Homosexualité feminine et identité sexuelle (Female homosexuality and sexual identity). *Revue Française de Psychanalyse*, 58, 147–56.

Chiland's contributions have been in child and adolescent psychiatry and in human sexuality. She addresses these issues from a psycho-analytic and psychotherapeutic perspective, although all of her work conveys a sense of the value she attaches to interdisciplinary collaboration. In her work on human sexuality Chiland argues that transsexualism is not a purely sexual phenomenon, but has social and cultural implications. In her clinical and research work she has attempted to clarify the relationship between female homosexuality and sexual identity. For example, women (biological females) who request to be transformed into men often share a refusal to consider themselves as homosexuals. She argues that their quest for a partner of the same sex demonstrates the flaws in their relationship with their mother and identification with an idealized father. Her work in child psychiatry has been concerned with understanding what violence is, how it affects children, how children can be helped to be resilient in the face of various types of violence, and what factors in the child's family, community and culture might spawn violence in the developing child. As a theoretician Chiland has made important contributions to definitional issues; for example, in relation to transsexualism, she has exposed how medicine, psychology and psychoanalysis differ on matters of terminology, and she has also explored cultural differences – how definitions in French and English differ. She has been concerned to explicate psychoanalytic concepts; for example, the concept of object as it relates to sexuality and love.

Chomsky, Noam

Born: 1928, Philadelphia, Pennsylvania, USA **Nat:** American **Ints:** Linguistics **Educ:** PhD University of Pennsylvania, 1955 **Appts & awards:** Institute Professor, MIT, 1976– ; Institute for Advanced Study at Princeton, 1958–9; Fellow, American Academy of Arts and Science; Member, National Academy of Science; Distinguished Scientific Contribution Award of the APA; Linguistics Society of America; American Philosophical Association; Hon. degrees, University of London, 1967, University of Chicago, 1967, Loyola University of Chicago, 1970, Swarthmore College, 1970, Bard College, 1971, Delhi University, 1972, University of Massachusetts, 1973, University of Pennsylvania, 1974

Principal publications

1957 *Syntactic Structures.* Mouton.
1959 Review of Skinner, 'Verbal Behavior'. *Language*, 35, 26–57.
1964 *Current Issues in Linguistic Theory.* Mouton.
1966 *Cartesian Linguistics: A Chapter in the History of Rationalist Thought.* Harper & Row.
1968 *Language and Mind.* Harcourt, Brace Jovanovitch. (Reprinted 1972.)
1968 *The Sound Pattern of English.* Harper & Row (with M. Halle).
1972 *Studies of Semantics in Generative Grammar.* Mouton.
1975 *The Logical Structure of Linguistic Theory.* Plenum.
1980 *Rules and Representations.* Blackwell.
1988 *Language and Problems of Knowledge: The Managua Lectures.* MIT Press.

Further reading

Alexander, G. (ed.) (1990) *Reflections on Chomsky.* Blackwell.
Bruner, J. (1983) *Child's Talk.* Norton.
Lyons, J. (1977) *Chomsky.* Harvester.
Modgil, S. and Modgil, C. (eds) (1987) *Naom Chomsky: Consensus and Controversy.* Falmer.

Chomsky's early education was in an experimental progressive school. At the University of Pennsylvania he studied mathematics, philosophy and linguistics. He also received his PhD in linguistics from Pennsylvania, although most of the work was conducted at Harvard between 1951 and 1955. Chomsky has made three fundamental and enduring contributions. First, he moved the emphasis in linguistics away from the descriptive, inductive level to an explanatory level; second, he stimulated a reconsideration of language learning; and third, his distinction between competence and performance has proved a useful metaphor for structural investigations and explanations throughout psychology.

Initially Chomsky set out to explain how an ideal or theoretical language user could generate and understand new and unique grammatical sentences which had never been encountered before. This set him on a course which led him to show how a limited and describable set of transformational rules defined the 'competence' of the ideal language learner. 'Performance' refers to the finite number of grammatical sentences realized by language users. This is the corpus of data from which competence models can be built and tested. Central to Chomsky's account is the notion of a generative grammar. Crudely stated, this is an elementary system of rules that recursively define and give rise to sentence transformations. Thus, according to Chomsky, 'A generative grammar may be said to generate a set of structural descriptions, each of which, ideally, incorporates a deep structure, a surface structure, a semantic interpretation (of the deep structure) and a phonetic interpretation (of the surface structure).' The structure of a grammar may be of three basic types: finite state grammar (a linear grammar whereby sentences are generated by simple choices at each step); phrase structure grammar (which corresponds to traditional parsing); and transformational grammar (a way of deriving a new constituent structure, e.g. from active to passive form, from a set of rules). The transformational grammar is equivalent to Chomsky's concept of 'deep structure'.

Chomsky takes the view that language acquisition and language competence cannot be explained inductively, and he was highly critical of behaviourist efforts to so do. Chomsky argues for the existence of an innate, specifically human, language capacity as a way of explaining the nature of human language. He suggests that human beings have a language acquisition device (LAD), and he uses this to explain why children throughout the world develop language at the same pace and according to a similar developmental sequence.

Chomsky's contributions stand as one of the intellectual achievements of the twentieth century. Nevertheless his theory of language has been criticized in three respects. First, there is a problem with the notion of an idealized language speaker. The problem is not that competence is defined as virtual but that this competence is identified with a non-linguistic component – the speaker – rather than the language itself. This criticism is more often made by linguists than psycholinguists, who do not see a problem with the notion that language is an individual cognitive capacity.

Second, there is a problem with the emphasis placed on the competence of the speaker as the model speaker of a language. It could be argued that the native speaker is not necessarily the ideal language speaker. The ideal language speaker should, in principle, be able to acquire competence in several languages rather than one. It could also be argued that an essential feature of any language is that it should be possible to translate it. This aspect is overlooked in Chomsky's emphasis on the competence of the native speaker.

Third, Chomsky's rationalist position is something of an overreaction to the behaviourist

and empiricist traditions. Many psycholinguists argue that language is not suddenly 'switched on' and that there is a large body of evidence to show that learning is crucial (e.g. Bruner, 1983).

Cialdini, Robert Beno

Born: 1945, Milwaukee, Wisconsin, USA *Nat:* American *Ints:* Consumer psychology, health, personality and social *Educ:* BS University of Wisconsin, 1967; MS University of North Carolina, 1969; PhD University of North Carolina, 1970; NSF Postdoctoral Fellow, 1970–1 *Appts & awards:* Regents' Professor of Psychology, Arizona State University; Society for Experimental Social Psychology; Arizona State University Graduate Distinguished Research Professor, 1985–6; Editorial Board, *Applied Social Psychology Annual*, *Journal of Personality and Social Psychology*; Associate Editor, *Journal of Personality and Social Psychology*, *Representative Research in Social Psychology*

Principal publications

1973   Transgression and altruism: A case for hedonism. *Journal of Experimental Social Psychology*, 9, 502–16.

1975   Reciprocal concessions procedure for inducing compliance: The door-in-the face technique. *Journal of Personality and Social Psychology*, 31, 206–15.

1976   Basking in reflected glory: Three (football) field studies. *Journal of Personality and Social Psychology*, 34, 366–75.

1976   Elastic shifts of opinion: Determinants of direction and durability. *Journal of Personality and Social Psychology*, 36, 663–72.

1978   The low-ball procedure for inducing compliance: Commitment then cost. *Journal of Personality and Social Psychology*, 36, 463–76.

1980   Full cycle social psychology. *Applied Social Psychology Annual*, 1, 21–47.

1981   Attitudes and attitude change. *Annual Review of Psychology*, 32, 41–53.

1984   *Influence: How and Why People Agree to Things.*

1985   *Influence: Science and Practice.* Scott, Foresman. (1993, HarperCollins).

1987   Consistency-based compliance: When and why do children become vulnerable? *Journal of Personality and Social Psychology*, 52, 1174–81 (with N. Eisenberg, H. McCreath and R. Shell).

Further reading

Cialdini, R.B. (1995) A full-cycle approach to social psychology. In G.G. Brannigan and M.R. Merrens (eds), *The Social Psychologists: Research Adventures.* McGraw-Hill.

As an undergraduate psychology student Cialdini worked on the behaviour of lower animals. However, his primary interest lay more with people – the everyday, normal behaviour of people. To pursue this, he applied for graduate training in social psychology at the University of North Carolina, where he concentrated mostly on the psychology of persuasion. He received a fellowship to study at Columbia University, where he continued to develop interests in the factors that enable one individual to influence another. At the completion of his postgraduate training at Columbia, he took a position on the psychology department faculty at Arizona State University, where he continues to research on the topic of personal influence. Cialdini suggests that his work in this area probably stems from his interest in how certain individuals can so consistently arrange for the rest of us to say yes to them. To satisfy his curiosity, he began to research the question as a university-based social psychologist. He realized that the investigations he was conducting – mostly in laboratory settings with college students – would not be sufficient to understand fully the powerful tactics and procedures that lead to 'yes'. This realization led to a wider programme of systematic observation of the compliance professions – those individuals whose livelihoods depend on getting other people to comply (e.g. salespeople, advertisers, fund-raisers). For the most part, he has sought to observe the compliance professionals from the inside by taking training or employment, incognito, in a range of naturally occurring compliance settings. From this perspective he has learned the tactics that are most frequently taught and most successfully and widely used to gain compliance by the various professionals. It is with the insights derived from this programme of naturalistic observation that he has continued with experimental studies, with adults and children, into the influence process.

Claparède, Edouard

Born: 1873, Geneva, Switzerland ***Died:*** 1940, Geneva, Switzerland ***Nat:*** Swiss ***Ints:*** Applied psychology, developmental, educational, general, mental retardation ***Educ:*** MD University of Geneva, 1897 ***Appts & awards:*** Founder and Joint Editor, *Archives de Psychologie,* 1901–40; General Secretary, Second International Congress of Psychology, 1904; General Secretary, Sixth International Congress of Psychology, 1909; Professor of Psychology, University of Geneva, 1915–40; Permanent Secretary, International Congress of Psychology; Life President, Comité de l'Association Internationale des Conferences de Psychotechnique

Principal publications
1903 *L'Association des Idées.* Doin.
1905 *Psychologie de l'Enfant et Pedagogie Experimentale.* Delachaux.
1905 Esquisse d'une théorie biologique du sommeil. *Archives de Psychologie,* 4, 245–9.
1917 La psychologie de l'intelligence. *Scientia,* 11, 353–67.
1918 La conscience de la ressemblance et de la différence chez l'enfant. *Archives de Psychologie,* 17, 67–78.
1930 Autobiography. In C. Murchison (ed.), *History of Psychology in Autobiography,* vol. 1. Clark University Press.
1931 *L'Education Fonctionelle.* Delachaux.
1933 La genèse de l'hypothèse: Etude experimentale. *Archives de Psychologie,* 24, 1–155.

Further reading
American Journal of Psychology (1941) 54, 296–9.
Pillsbury, W. (1941) Edouard Claparède. *Psychological Review,* 48, 271–8.

Edouard Claparède was born and spent most of his life in Geneva. After studying science and medicine he concentrated on psychology, studying, and later collaborating, with Theodore Fluornoy, to whom he was closely related. Claparède succeeded Fluornoy as Professor of Psychology at the University of Geneva in 1915, a post he held until his death. His psychological interests were broad, including such topics as sleep, intelligent action, problem solving and education. He also maintained interests in neurology and psychiatry. As well as theoretical, experimental and applied work in psychology, Claparède devoted considerable time to professional and organizational activities. He co-founded with Flournoy the journal *Archives de Psychologie,* and contributed significantly to the international co-operation of psychologists through the International Congress of Psychology. In addition he founded (in 1912) the Institute J.J. Rousseau as a centre for innovative research and practice in education, and subsequently home to much of the work of Jean **Piaget**.

Throughout his wide range of interests, Claparède insisted on the importance of function. For example, his approach to the topic of sleep was to treat it as a positive state, interrelated with the need for the organism to protect itself against fatigue. He argued that there must be an active inhibition of activity, under neural control. Withdrawal of contact with the sensory world – a condition that he suggested was also the case in hysteria – must take place for functional reasons. Indeed the notion of contact between the organism and its environment was central to Claparède's thinking, linking it conceptually to the ideas of the pragmatist approach, as illustrated by his 'Law of Becoming Conscious'. This proposal was a complex one which made a number of different predictions. It stated that mental activity does not emerge into consciousness so long as it is succeeding in its function. Like the instincts, cognitive processing may be effective without resource to consciousness so long as it is succeeding in its function. Only if some new demand is imposed by the environment will the mental processes be 'grasped' by consciousness. Acquired experience may then be brought to bear on the problem and appropriate adjustments of action made. This dynamic approach to consciousness owed something to Claparède's long-standing interest in the claims of psychoanalysis as well as the findings of comparative psychology. It gave rise to an experimental method in which the research subject provided verbal protocols as problem solving took place. This method gave Claparède's research some of the characteristics of the cognitive psychology of more recent times.

A second aspect of the 'Law of Becoming Conscious' is the developmental one. Claparède argued that processes which are employed earliest in development, without the necessity for conscious awareness of them, are the latest to be grasped by consciousness. That is to say, 'the earlier and the longer a relation has been in use, the later it is consciously perceived'. His own chief example was resemblance. Thus the infant acts on the basis of resemblance between objects and situations, but becomes consciously aware of resemblance long after becoming conscious of difference. This developmental hypothesis, like many other aspects of Claparède's Law and of his other claims, received careful attention from Piaget. Its corollary seems particularly provocative, for if we

could agree on what the latest (most mature) developmental achievements might be, this would offer fascinating possibilities for the understanding of infancy. Logical implication, for example, might be thought of as a late achievement in conscious awareness. If so, the corollary of Claparède's Law would predict that non-conscious employment of logical implication must be among the earliest of cognitive capabilities. It should be stressed that Piaget's work does not exhaust the potential of Claparède's Law of Becoming Conscious, or of his other suggestions. Indeed Claparède often seems to have taken a more dynamic, open-ended approach to cognitive development than his younger colleague. Claparède's approach was always open-minded, constantly attempting to recognize the fluidity of human action in its relationship with the environment.

JOHN MORSS

Clark, Eve V.

Born: 1942, Camberley, England **Nat:** British **Ints:** Language acquisition, semantics of natural languages **Educ:** MA University of Edinburgh, 1965; Dipl. in General Linguistics University of Edinburgh, 1966; PhD University of Edinburgh, 1969 **Appts & awards:** Professor of Linguistics, Department of Linguistics, Stanford University Fellow, Center for Advanced Study in Behavioral Sciences, Stanford, 1979–90; Fellow, Guggenheim Foundation, 1983–4; Editorial Board, *Journal of Linguistics and Philosophy*, *Journal of Language and Memory*, *Journal of Child Language*, *Cognition*, *Cahiers de Psychologie Cognitive*, *Language and Cognitive Processes*; Associate Editor, *Language*

Principal publications

1973 What's in a word? On the child's acquisition of semantics in his first language. In T.E. Moore (ed.), *Cognitive Development and the Acquisition of Language*. Wiley.

1973 Non-linguistic strategies and the acquisition of word meanings. *Cognition*, 2, 161–82.

1977 *Psychology and Language*. Harcourt Brace Jovanovich (with H.H. Clark).

1978 Strategies in the acquisition of deixis. *Journal of Child Language*, 5, 457–75 (with C.J. Sengul).

1979 *The Ontogenesis of Language*. Athenaion.

1979 When nouns surface as verbs. *Language*, 55, 767–811 (with H.H. Clark).

1982 Language change during language acquisition. In M.E. Lamb and A.L. Brown (eds), *Advances in Developmental Psychology*, vol. 2. Erlbaum.

1982   Learning to coin agent and instrument nouns. *Cognition*, 12, 1–24 (with F.B. Hecht).

1983   Meanings and concepts. In J.H. Flavell and E.M. Markman (eds), *Cognitive Development.* Wiley.

1984   Structure and use in the acquisition of word formation. *Language*, 60, 542–90 (with R.A. Berman).

1985   Noun compounds and category structure in young children. *Child Development*, 56, 84–94 (with S.A. Gelman and M. Lane).

1988   On the logic of contrast. *Journal of Child Language*, 15, 317–35.

1989   Learning to use compounds for contrast: Data from Hebrew. *First Language*, 9, 247–70.

1990   On the pragmatics of contrast. *Journal of Child Language*, 17, 417–31.

1993   The lexicon in acquisition. In *Cambridge Studies in linguistics*, vol. 65. Cambridge University Press.

1995   Language acquisition: The lexicon and syntax. In J.L. Miller and P.D. Eimas (eds), *Speech, Language, and Communication: Handbook of Perception and Cognition*, 2nd edn, vol. 11. Academic Press.

Further reading

Miller, J.E. and Eimas, P.D. (eds) (1995) *Speech, Language, and Communication. Handbook of Perception and Cognition*, 2nd edn, vol. 11. Academic Press.

Eve Clarke has made important contributions to our understanding of the ontogenesis of language. The semantic feature's hypothesis and semantic overextensions are prominent contributions in her early work. The former states that the meaning of a word is composed of semantic features associated with it (e.g. four-legged, purrs, tail, etc.). The child initially tends to notice more conspicuous features of an object and applies the word when one or more features are extended (e.g. all four-legged, tailed creatures are cats). For words that are used as nouns, meanings can be overextended or underextended. Clark uncovered a large number of overextensions in early language development but pointed out that underextensions are often not detected and their frequency is underestimated.

In her later work Clarke argues for the centrality of the lexicon to language and language acquisition. She regards the general principles of conventionality and contrast as being at the core of language acquisition. She starts with children's emerging knowledge of conventional words and their meanings, the ontological categories they rely on for early meanings, and their strategies for mapping meanings onto forms. She then takes up their growing knowledge of word structure as reflected in their formation of new words, and shows that children learning different languages follow similar paths as they learn about words and word structure. The principle of contrast (that different words have different meanings) is readily apparent in adult language use; Clark has examined its development through childhood. Specifically, she has queried whether children rely on the principle from the start, or whether they assume that new words may have the same meaning until they discover otherwise. If the latter is true it places a heavy burden on language learners, and it seems unlikely. She suggests that children could discover the principle of contrast as part of their experience of language, cognition and social interaction, and has provided important evidence that the contrast principle is pervasive in children's speech from an early age. Clark argues that the principle of contrast (POC) is a pragmatic one that accounts for the acquisition of irregular forms in morphology and plays a crucial role in the acquisition of allomorphy. Along with the principle of conventionality, the POC accounts for the pre-emption of novel words by well-established ones. The distinctive characteristics of her approach are her use of a large, varied and unusual corpus of data from a wide range of languages, her emphasis on the general principles children rely on as they analyse complex word forms, and the broad perspective she adopts on the issues of lexical acquisition.

Clark, Herbert H.

Born: 1940, Deadwood, South Dakota, USA **Nat:** American **Ints:** Cognitive psychology, experimental psychology, psycholinguistics. **Educ:** BA Stanford University, 1962; MA Johns Hopkins University, 1964; PhD Johns Hopkins University, 1966 **Appts & awards:** NSF Graduate Fellowship, 1963–6; Assistant Professor, Carnegie-Mellon University, 1966–9; Associate Professor, Stanford University, 1969–75, Professor, Stanford University, 1975– ; Guggenheim Fellowship, 1975–6; Fellow, APA Division 3, 1978– ; Fellow, Center for Advanced Study in the Behavioral Sciences, 1978–9; Fellow, American Academy of Arts and Sciences, 1982– ; Society of Experimental Psychologists, 1984–

Principal publications

1969 Linguistic processes in deductive reasoning. *Psychological Review*, 76, 387–404.

1972 On the process of comparing sentences against pictures. *Cognitive Psychology*, 3, 472–517 (with W.G. Chase).

1973 Space, time, semantics, and the child. In T. Moore (ed.), *Cognitive Development and the Acquisition of Language*. Academic Press, 27–63.

1973 The language-as-fixed-effect fallacy: A critique of language statistics in psychological research. *Journal of Verbal Learning and Verbal Behavior*, 12, 335–59.

1977 Comprehension and the given-new contract. In R.O. Freedle (ed.), *Discourse Production and Comprehension*. Erlbaum (with S.E. Haviland).

1979 Responding to indirect speech acts. *Cognitive Psychology*, 11, 430–77.

1979 When nouns surface as verbs. *Language*, 55, 767–811 (with E.V. Clark).

1981 Definite reference and mutual knowledge. In A.K. Joshi, B. Webber and I. Sag (eds), *Linguistics Structure and Discourse Setting*. Cambridge University Press (with C. Marshall).

1982 Hearers and speech acts. *Language*, 58, 332–73 (with T.B. Carlson).

1985 Language use and language users. In G. Lindzey and E. Aronson (eds), *The Handbook of Social Psychology*, 3rd edn. Harper & Row.

1987 Collaborating on contributions to conversations. *Language and Cognitive Processes*, 2, 19–41 (with E.F. Schaefer).

1989 Contributing to discourse. *Cognitive Science*, 13, 259–94.

1990 Ostensible invitations. *Language in Society*, 19, 493–509.

1990 Referring as a collaborative process. In P.R. Cohen, J. Morgan and M.E. Pollack (eds), *Intentions in Communication*. MIT Press (with D. Wilkes-Gibbs).

1991 Grounding in communication. In L.B. Resnick, J.M. Levine and S.D. Teasley (eds), *Perspectives on Socially Shared Cognition*. APA (with S.E. Brennan).

1991 Words, the world, and their possibilities. In G.R. Lockhead and J.R. Pomerantz (eds), *The Perception of Structure: Essays in Honor of Wendell R. Garner*. APA.

1992 *Arenas of Language Use*. University of Chicago Press.

1992 Asking questions and influencing answers. In J.M. Tanur (ed.), *Questions about Questions: Inquiries into the Cognitive Bases of Surveys*. Russell Sage Foundation (with M.F. Schober).

1993 Reproduction and demonstration in quotation. *Journal of Memory and Language*, 32, 805–19 (with E. Wade).

1994 Managing problems in speaking. Special issue: Spoken dialogue. *Speech Communication*, 15, 243–50.

1994 Discourse in production. In M.A. Gernsbacher (ed.), *Handbook of Psycholinguistics*. Academic Press.

Throughout his research career, Herbert Clark has studied how language is used and understood. His work has increased our knowledge of ways in which the social context of language use advances the intentions of the speaker and the understanding of the addressee. He first began to investigate memory for utterances, but soon concluded that this strategy was not leading to the processes of understanding. In this, Clark was moving towards a major role in the emergence of psycholinguistics, which places emphasis on the cognitive bases of language and memory. In contrast to the associationist approach first proposed by **Ebbinghaus** in the nineteenth century, which dominated the study of verbal learning until after World War II, psycholinguistics derived inspiration from the developmental studies of Jean **Piaget** and the model of language acquisition proposed by Noam **Chomsky**. Instead of accepting the unit of verbal communication as the word, psycholinguists began to examine the structure of language in terms of grammar and semantics as reflective of mental or cognitive organization of communication. Psycholinguistics emphasizes the study of communication and the characteristics of the person communicating. Thus, it considers the child as possessing innate mechanisms for interpreting and organizing speech from the environment, and the child's acquisition of grammatical syntax as reflecting an individual sense of language, supporting the child's mediation of the linguistic environment.

Since psycholinguistic theory points to the major function of language as central to the formation of ideas, conceptions and thoughts as expressed in sentence structures, Clark turned to studies of reasoning with language and to the verification of descriptions of pictures as true or false. For example, subjects were asked to describe a picture of one object above another and then asked to judge brief descriptions about the pictures. Clark found that subjects followed preference rules in describing objects, and the rules were dependent upon the characteristics of the pictures and the demands of the task. These experiments led Clark to recognize how understanding consists of taking as known what speakers take for granted, and of adding to memory what they take to be new information. In this context, understanding is a process of drawing exactly those inferences that the speakers intended.

Clark then proceeded to studies about what inferences are present in speech and how addressees, and even overhearers, draw them. He proposed several models that attempt to accommodate how people in conversation co-ordinate references. Generally, these experiments suggest that people engage in an interactive process that allows them to modify jointly the meaning of word phrases until they agree on a version. Thus, the social character of conversation points to a mutual responsibility that participants in a conversation assume towards the understanding of each other. In addition, Clark has studied how speakers' actions make their intentions manifest.

Clark has also pursued related themes in his pursuit of the study of cognitive processes. In particular, he has investigated how people use language in describing space and time. He has studied how a word may have identical conventional meaning in difference descriptions, but be understood as denoting very different objects or events. He found that word denotations are highly specific to individual situations and contexts. In another vein, Clark has been concerned with the need to correct what he argues is widespread abuse of certain statistical practices in research on language. For example, he has argued that studies of words, sentences and other language units rarely provide statistical evidence that the findings may be generalized beyond the particular sample of language materials chosen. Yet often these same studies make wide claims and draw conclusions about language processes in general. Clark has called for use of the appropriate statistics within proper experimental designs, relying on systematic sampling procedures.

Through his research articles, books and chapter reviews, Clark presents a coherent approach to language as it is used to foster understanding, a process that is individual and cognitive as well as social. His work has emphasized language processes within a comprehensive cognitive model. Language is thus viewed as an expression among modes of communication, including semantic memory, sentence comprehension, and concept formation. Clark's importance in studying the social processes involved in understanding is based upon elegantly designed and creative experiments that integrate the varying influences of the individual's context in language as used. His work and that of his students on the effects of interactions in the pursuit of understanding between speaker and addressee has opened new lines of investigation and advanced our knowledge of both language and memory.

JAMES F. BRENNAN

Coles, Michael G.H.

Born: 1944, England ***Nat:*** British ***Ints:*** (in order of significance) Psychophysiology, experimental psychology (human perception and performance) ***Appts & awards:*** Professor of Psychology, University of Illinois, 1984– ; Editor, *Psychophysiology*, 1987–93; President, Society for Psychophysiological Research, 1988

Principal publications

1985   A psychophysiological investigation of the continuous flow model of human information processing. *Journal of Experimental Psychology: Human Perception and Performance*, 11, 529–53 (with G. Gratton, T.R. Bashore, C.W. Eriksen and E. Donchin).

1988   Detecting early communication: Using measures of movement-related potentials to illuminate human information processing. *Biological Psychology*, 26, 69–89 (with G. Gratton and E. Donchin).

1988   Pre- and post-stimulus activation of response channels: A psychophysiological analysis. *Journal of Experimental Psychology: Human Perception and Performance*, 14, 331–44 (with G. Gratton, E.J. Sirevaag, C.W. Eriksen and E. Donchin).

1989   Modern mind-brain reading: Psychophysiology, physiology, and cognition. *Psychophysiology*, 26, 251–69.

1993   A neural mechanism for error detection and compensation. *Psychological Science*, 4, 385–90 (with W.J. Gehring, B. Goss, E. Donchin and D.E. Meyer).

1995   Where did you go wrong? Errors, partial errors, and the nature of human information processing. *Acta Psychologica*, 90, 129–44 (with M.K. Scheffers and L. Fournier).

1995   Strategies and mechanisms in nonselective and selective inhibitory motor control. *Journal of Experimental Psychology: Human Perception and Performance*, 21, 498–511 (with R. de Jong and G.D. Logan).

Further reading

Jennings, J.R. and Coles, M.G.H. (eds) (1991)

Handbook of Cognitive Psychophysiology: Central and Autonomic Nervous System Approaches. Wiley.

Kramer, A.F. *et al.* (eds) (1996) *Converging Operations in the Study of Visual Selective Attention.* American Psychological Association.

Rugg, M.D. and Coles, M.G.H. (eds) (1995) *Electrophysiology of Mind: Event-Related Brain Potentials and Cognition.* Oxford University Press.

Michael Coles studied psychology and philosophy in Exeter, England, 1964–70. In 1970, he went to the USA to work with **Donchin** at the University of Illinois, where he was appointed full professor in 1984. In Donchin's lab, Coles first focused on cardiovascular psychophysiology but later abandoned this area in favour of research in event-related potentials (ERPs) of the EEG. It is there that he brought three remarkable developments under way.

First, in 1985 he showed how a delay of overtly visible response times (induced by incompatible flankers in the 'Eriksen task') can be accounted for up to the nearest millisecond by the sum of delays of two psychophysiological measures (the delay of P3 latency reflecting the stimulus-related portion, and the lengthening of the interval between EMG onset and the actual response reflecting the delay due to response competition). Second, in 1988 his group showed that response tendencies can be measured by means of the 'lateralized readiness potential' (LRP) The LRP is the difference potential (contralateral minus ipsilateral) of the two motor cortices, measured at central scalp sites. Coles and co-workers described a short-lived lateralization of the 'wrong' motor cortex with incompatible flanking stimuli; i.e. they demonstrated a momentary tendency in their subjects' brains to respond in the way suggested by the flanking stimuli. Third, in 1993, Coles described an error-related negativity; i.e. a component of the ERP that was evoked by stimuli that were incorrectly responded. Here was an objective sign of subjects' knowing that their overt response was incorrect.

Coles's 1985 paper marks a turning point in the relationship between psychophysiology and experimental psychology. Up to that time, psychophysiology was busy defining its variables and adopting the standards set by experimental psychology. In contrast, the 1985 paper made a contribution to experimental psychology that could not have been made by experimental psychology alone. This tendency was continued by Coles's introduction of the LRP to experimental psychology.

Of course, these developments are too recent to make the conclusion unavoidable that all experimental psychologists should record EEG potentials. For example, Coles's 1985 equation 'P3 delay + EMG lengthening = RT delay' has not been replicated so far. Nor has it become unambiguously clear so far what parameters of the response process are reflected by the LRP and whether the LRP sometimes reflects other overlapping processes (e.g. lateralized visual attention).

ROLF VERLEGER

Combe, George

Born: 1788, Edinburgh, Scotland **Died:** 1858 **Nat:** British **Ints:** Phrenology, 'science of man' **Educ:** No academic posts or qualifications, although attended lectures at the University of Edinburgh for two years. **Appts & awards:** Founder, Phrenological Society, 1820; Founder, *Phrenological Journal*, 1823

Principal publications

1819 *Essays on Phrenology: Or an Inquiry into the Principles and Utility of the System of Drs. Gall and Spurzheim, and into the Objections made against it.* Mclachlan, Stewart and Anderson. (Subsequent editions were retitled *A System of Phrenology: Or an Inquiry* …. 5th edn, 2 vols, 1843).

1824 *Elements of Phrenology.* Anderson. (4th edn, 1836.)

1827 *Essay on the Constitution of Man and its Relations to External Objects.* Neill. 'Corrected and enlarged', 1835; 9th edn, 1860; generally reprinted as *The Constitution of Man*).

1833 *Lectures on Popular Education.* John Anderson Jr.

1840 *Moral Philosophy: Or, the Duties of Man Considered in his Individual, Social, and Domestic Capacities.* Mclachlan and Stewart.

1846 *Phrenology – its Nature and Uses: An Address to the Students of Anderson's University.* Maclachlan and Stewart.

1855 *Phrenology applied to Painting and Sculpture.* Simpkin and Marshall. (See also: Andrew Combe (1830). *Observations on Mental Derangement.* J. Anderson Jr.)

Further reading

Cooter, R. (1984) *The Cultural Meaning of Popular Science: Phrenology and the Organization of Consent in Nineteenth-century Britain.* Cambridge University Press.

De Giustino, D. (1975) *Conquest of Mind: Phrenology and Victorian Social Thought*. Croom Helm.

Gibbon, C. (1878) *The Life of George Combe*. Macmillan.

Richards, G. (1992) *Mental Machinery: The Origins and Consequences of Psychological Ideas. Part One: From 1600 to 1850*. Athlone Press.

Walsh, A.A. (1971) George Combe: A Portrait of a Heretofore Generally Unknown Behaviorist. *Journal of the History of the Behavioral Sciences*, 7, 269–78.

Young, R.M. (1970) *Mind, Brain and Adaptation in the Nineteenth Century: Cerebral Localization and its Biological Context from Gall to Ferrier*. Clarendon. (Reprinted 1990.)

Combe's significance for psychology is twofold: as the leading British phrenologist, and as author of the best-selling *The Constitution of Man*. Early nineteenth-century Scotland provided a receptive environment for the phrenological doctrines of Franz Josef Gall and his disciple J.G. Spurzheim, who first visited Scotland in 1815. The classification of 'Powers' proposed by the dominant Scottish Realist philosophers Thomas Reid and Dugald Stewart closely resembled the phrenologists' list of functions. Phrenologists held these to be served by localized cerebral 'organs', the relative sizes and powers of which were ascertainable by external cranial examination. Young (1970) identifies this as the first attempt at empirically identifying psychological functions. Cooter (1984) sees an analogy between this image and emerging forms of industrial factory organization and 'division of labour', to which much of phrenology's appeal to the expanding upper working and lower middle classes was due, as ostensibly offering a 'scientific' route for obtaining self-knowledge congruent with this new industrial culture. Combe modified and expanded Gall's faculties, significantly rendering his phrenology more normative and hierarchical. Assisted by his brother Andrew, Combe zealously promoted phrenology as an applicable scientific theory of human nature from the mid-1820s. In 1846, he even gained access to Buckingham Palace and the heads of the royal children, as well as examining George Eliot (whom he highly regarded until her relationship with G.H. Lewes became known). Combe's historical role would, none the less, be less significant were it not for *The Constitution of Man*. This expounded, in a theistical fashion, the physical, psychological and moral laws governing human nature, again having affinities with Scottish philosophical doctrines, which by the 1830s and 1840s were being widely disseminated in Britain and the US as 'mental and moral philosophy'.

More narrowly, Combe has a place in the history of the oscillating fortunes of localization of brain function theories. Beyond this, though, he promulgated an image of human nature which for a period caught the popular mood. It moved beyond traditional philosophical and religious accounts, appeared congruent with new physiological discoveries, promoted the notion of a 'science of man' accessible to the educated citizen, reflected prevailing values of self-improvement and moral earnestness, and presented a more secular image of humanity's cosmological place. Combe's self-promotional skills earned him public eminence and influence, but Darwinian and, especially, Spencerian evolutionary approaches rapidly rendered his views outdated after the mid-1850s. Psychology's canonical British founders, Herbert Spencer and Alexander **Bain**, nevertheless began their psychological careers in phrenology. While disciplinary historians were traditionally dismissive of phrenology ('an embarrassing *faux pas*' according to J.C. Flügel), this attitude is rejected by more recent writers. Many now see phrenology as a preparatory 'dry run' for the psychology which eventually emerged following phrenology's demise as a serious project around 1850. Between the 1820s and 1850s Combe thus played a crucial role in integrating the scattered modes of psychological discourse into a putatively scientific discipline. He bequeathed his papers, which he considered an invaluable repository of wisdom, to the University of Edinburgh. We yet await, however, a full modern biographical study of Combe's own 'psychology' – on which his skull sheds far less light than he imagined!

GRAHAM RICHARDS

Conger, John J.
Born: 1921, New Brunswick, New Jersey, USA
Nat: American *Ints:* Clinical, developmental, experimental, physiological and comparative psychology *Educ:* BA Amherst College, 1943; MS Yale University, 1947; PhD Yale University 1949 *Appts & awards:* Professor of Clinical Psychology, University of Colorado Health Sciences Centre; Chairman, Professional Advisory Group, Colorado Mental Health Association, 1953–4; President, Colorado Psycho-

logical Association, 1958–9; Editorial Board, *Journal of Medical Education*, 1965–70, *Traffic Safety Research Review*, 1963–8; Secretary's Advisory Committee on Traffic Safety, Department of Health, Education and Welfare, 1966–8; Vice President, Board of Trustees, Center for Continuing Medical Education, 1966–70; Vice-chairman, National Motor Vehicle Safety Advisory Council, Department of Transportation, 1967–70; APA Policy and Planning Board, 1967–70; Board of Directors and Recording Secretary, 1974–82, Member, Presidential Task Force on Highway Safety, 1969–70; R.L. Stearns Award, University of Colorado, 1970; Fellow, APA, AAAS, Center for Advanced Study in the Behavioral Sciences, Stanford, 1970–1; Member, President's Commission on Mental Health, 1977–8; Member, Program Committee, 1972, 1974–5; SRCD Publications Committee, 1977–81, Award for Distinguished Service to Psychology and the Nation, American Board of Examiners in Professional Psychology, 1979; Member, National Advisory Council, Hogg Foundation for Mental Health, 1979–82; APA President, 1981; Hon. DSc, Ohio University, 1981, Amherst College, 1983; Member, Academy of Behavioral Medicine Research, 1982– ; Member, US Commission for UNESCO, 1983– ; Member, Institute of Medicine, NAS, 1983– ; APF President, 1986–, Board of Trustees, 1983– ; Award for Outstanding Contribution to Health Psychology, APA Division 38, 1986; Distinguished Service Awards, Denver Medical Society, Colorado Medical Society, Colorado Dental Society

Principal publications

1950   An experimental investigation of the role of psychological factors in the production of gastric ulcers in rats. *Journal of Comparative and Physiological Psychology*, 49, 452–61 (with W.L. Sawrey and E.S. Turrell).

1951   Effects of alcohol on conflict behavior in the albino rat. *Quarterly Journal of Studies on Alcholol*, 12, 1–29.

1956   *Child Development and Personality*. Harper (with P.H. Mussen and J. Kagan). (6th edn, 1984.)

1956   Reinforcement theory and the dynamics of alcoholism. *Quarterly Journal of Studies on Alcohol*, 17, 291–324.

1958   The role of social experience in the production of gastric ulcers in hooded rats placed in a conflict situation. *Journal of Abnormal Social Psychology*, 214–19 (with W.L. Sawrey and E.S. Turrell).

1960   An objective method of grouping profiles by

distance functions and its relation to factor analysis. *Journal of Educational and Psychological Measures*, 20, 651–73 (with W.L. Sawrey and L. Keller)

1965   *Readings in Child Development and Personality*. Harper & Row (with P.H. Mussen and J. Kagan). (reprinted 1970.)

1965   Psychological and psychophysiological factors in motor vehicle accidents. In W. Haddon Jr, E. Suchman and D. Klein (eds), *Accident Research*. Harper & Row (with H.S. Gaskill, D.D. Gland, L. Hassell, R.V. Rainey and W.L. Sawrey).

1966   Effects of alcohol on conflict behavior in the albino rat. *Perspectives in Psychopathology*, 174–95.

1971   A world they never knew: The family and social change. *Daedalus*, 1105–38.

1973   *Adolescence and Youth: Psychological Development in a Changing World*. Harper & Row (with A.C. Peterson).(reprinted 1979.)

1980   *Essentials of Child Development and Personality*. Harper & Row (with P.H. Mussen and J. Kagan).

1980   *Readings in Child and Adolescent Psychology: Contemporary Perspectives*. Harper and Row (with P.H. Mussen and J. Kagan).

1981   Freedom and commitment: Families, youth and social change. *American Psychologist*, 36, 1475–84.

Further reading

Parke, R.D. *et al.* (eds) (1994) *A Century of Developmental Psychology*. American Psychological Association.

Rolf, J.E. *et al.* (eds) (1990) *Risk and Protective Factors in the Development of Psychopathology*. Cambridge University Press.

If there has been a common thread running through the rather varied career of Conger as a developmental and clinical psychologist, it has been an abiding curiosity about human nature and a concern for the optimal development of children and adolescents. Because he is convinced that we become the kinds of person that we do as a consequence of the continuing interaction of nature and nurture, he believes that only by abandoning narrow disciplinary boundaries can we hope to understand the nature of human development. Consequently, he has looked for clues in many disciplines – psychology, anthropology, sociology, psychiatry, neuropsychology, philosophy. This approach can be traced to the early influences of an undergraduate education in the liberal arts at Amherst College and graduate work in psychology at Yale's interdisciplinary Institute of Human Relations in the late 1940s. His books and most of his research, teaching and clinical work reflect his interests in children and adolescents. His *Child Development and Personality* (with **Kagan** and **Mussen**) was a highly influential text and introduced two or more decades of undergraduates to developmental psychology. Perhaps less obviously, these same concerns have strongly influenced most of his other activities, whether as government advisor, administrator, foundation officer, APA President, or board member of a local home for emotionally troubled adolescents. As a result, he has been troubled by what appears to be a retreat from the increased concern for others in society that characterized the 1960s, to an increased narcissistic preoccupation with the self and with material values. He warns that in such a society, those most likely to be hurt are those least able to defend themselves politically or economically: children, adolescents, the elderly, minorities, the poor. He points to the argument that a society's degree of civilization can be judged by the way it treats its children, and concludes that if actions speak louder than words, we have a considerable way to go.

Converse, Philip Ernest

Born: 1928, Concord, New Hampshire, USA **Nat:** American **Ints:** Population and environmental psychology, psychological study of social issues **Educ:** BA Denison University, 1949; MA State University of Iowa, 1950; Certificat des Etudes Françaises, University of Paris, 1956; MA University of Michigan, 1956; PhD University of Michigan, 1958; Dr Humane Letters, Denison University, 1974; Dr Humane Letters, University of Chicago, 1979 **Appts & awards:** Horace H. Rackham Fellow, 1955–6; Fulbright Fellow, 1959–60; University of Michigan, Assistant Professor of Sociology, 1960–3, Associate Professor of Political Science, 1963–5, Professor of Sociology and Political Science, 1965–89, Program Director, Survey Research Center, 1965–82, Robert C. Angell Professor of Political Sciences and Sociology, 1975–89, Director, Center for Political Studies, 1982–6, Director, Institute for Social Research, 1986–9; NSF Senior Postdoctoral Fellow, 1967–8; Elected Member, NAA and S, 1968; Elected Member, NAS, 1973; Guggenheim Fellow, 1975–6; AAAS Fellow, 1977; Fellow, Center for Advanced Study in the Behavioral Sciences, Stanford, 1979; President,

International Society of Political Psychology, 1980–1, American Political Science Association, 1983–4; Trustee, Russell Sage Foundation, 1982– ; Stanford University, Director, Center for Advanced Study in the Behavioral Sciences, 1989–95

Principal publications

1958 The shifting role of class in political attitudes and behaviour. In E.E. Maccoby, T.M. Newcomb and E.L. Hartley (eds), *Readings in Social Psychology*. Rinehart and Winston.

1960 *The American Voter*. Wiley (with A. Campbell, W.E. Miller and D.E. Stokes).

1964 The nature of belief systems in mass publics. In D.E. Apter (ed.), *Ideology and Discontent*. The Free Press.

1965 *Social Psychology: The Study of Human Interaction*. Holt, Rinehart and Winston (with T. Newcomb and R. Turner).

1969 Of time and partisan stability. *Comparative Political Studies*, 2, 139–71.

1969 Survey research and the decoding of patterns in ecological data. In M. Dogan and S. Rokkan (eds), *Quantitative Ecological Analysis in the Social Sciences*. MIT Press.

1970 Attitudes and nonattitudes: Continuation of a dialogue. In E.R. Tufte (ed.), *The Quantitative Analysis of Social Problems*. Addison-Wesley.

1975 Measures of the perceived overall quality of life. *Social Indicators Research*, 2, 127–52 (with W. Rodgers).

1975 Some mass–elite contrasts in the perception of political space. *Social Science Information*, 14, 49–83.

1976 *The Quality of American Life*. Russell Sage Foundation (with A. Campbell and W. Rodgers).

1979 Societal growth and the quality of life. In A.H. Hawley (ed.), *Societal Growth: Processes and Applications*. Free Press.

1986 *Political Representation in France*, Harvard University Press (with R. Pierce).

1986 Assessing the accuracy of polls and surveys. *Science*, 234, 1094–8 (with M.W. Traugott).

1990 Attitudinal sources of protest behaviour in France: Differences between before and after measurement. *Public Opinion Quarterly*, 54, 295–316 (with R. Pierce).

1992 Partisanship and the party system. *Political Behaviour*, 14, 239–59 (with R. Pierce).

Further reading

Petty, R.E. and Krosnik, J.A. (eds) (1995) *Attitude Strength, Antecedents and Consequences: Fourth Ohio State University Volume on Attitudes and Persuasion*. Erlbaum.

Philip Converse's initial interest was in English literature. Following his masters degree at the University of Iowa, he was drafted into the Korean war. This gave him time to think and read about the human condition. Upon his release from the army he spent a year based in Paris following the *cours pour l'étranger* at the Sorbonne. Returning to the United States, matriculation at the University of Michigan enabled him to develop his interest in the social sciences so that he could enter the university's graduate social psychology programme. This eclectic course was a launching pad for his subsequent career, which spanned the social sciences. He had been interested in politics from an early age but unusually, for a future professor of sociology and political science, he did not complete a single course in political science. His lifetime professional involvement with survey research and the political process began when, as a graduate student, he went to work with Angus Campbell on the 1956 election study, one of a series of national surveys of the American electorate begun in 1952, covering presidential and mid-term elections. Converse became one of the principal investigators of these 'Michigan' Election Studies, which in 1976 were transformed into the American National Election Studies.

In his initial job interview with Campbell, Converse mentioned that he had an ambition to carry out a national survey of a major French election, which would provide a comparison with the surveys of the American electorate. In 1959–60 he spent a Fulbright year in France doing that. In 1986 he published, with Roy Pierce, the findings of an immense study carried out in France between 1967 and 1969, which was designed to examine the nature of representative government in an apparently unstable political context. The study initially involved interviews with both representative samples from selected electoral districts and the political candidates in these districts. Following political unrest in France in 1968, the project expanded to establish the impact of popular disturbances on both voters and political elites.

Converse's theoretical research and writings on political attitudes, ideology, non-attitudes, quality of life and the use of time are all firmly based on his analyses of large scale survey data from representative samples of American and international populations. His 1964 work on ideology has been seen as the culmination of the traditional positivist approach in social science, which views ideology as a coherent set of political beliefs and values embraced by formal political parties. Using large-scale survey evidence, Converse concluded that the American public display little internal consistency in their political attitudes and do not develop a coherent belief system which enables valid predictions of their attitudes to be made according to a simple yardstick, such as the liberal–conservative continuum. He also noted that a longitudinal study of the American electorate revealed that whereas those with an interest in, and knowledge about, a topic showed stable responses to policy issues, the majority displayed little stability in attitudes over time.

Converse used the term 'nonattitudes' to describe the apparently random responses given by some people to repeated measures of their attitudes to specific policy issues. As he noted in his foreword to a volume of papers on attitude strength 'three decades ago, it never occurred to me that there could be any controversy over the proposition that not everybody has preformed attitudes about all possible attitude objects. But as controversy has emerged, it is clear researchers do not like to contemplate the possibility of hidden nonattitudes.'

The controversy of non-attitudes would seem to have been resolved by viewing the concept in terms of the coherent body of research and theory which has emerged in recent years on the reality of attitude strength effects. In contrast, Converse's work on ideology has grown more controversial over time, as the use of the concept of ideology has been extended to encompass far more than formal political belief systems.

Converse's writings are only a small part of his contribution to research. There are now available extensive databases which derive from his commitment to survey research. This may be because, as one of the pioneers in this field, he admits that from an early stage in his career he 'became very enamoured of using the new methodology of scientifically-clean survey research to elicit national-level information on all sorts of aspects of human life that had never been researchable in a systematic way in earlier human history'.

KAREN TREW

Coombs, Clyde Hamilton

Born: 1912, Paterson, New Jersey, USA **Died:** 1988, Ann Arbor, Michigan, USA **Nat:** American **Ints:** Evaluation and measurement, experimental psychology **Educ:** BA University of California at Berkely, 1935; MA University of California at Berkeley, 1937; PhD University of Chicago, 1940 **Appts & awards:** Daniel Katz Distinguished University Professor, University of Michigan; Psychometric Society, Secretary; President, 1955–6; Fulbright Research Professor, University of Amsterdam, 1955–6; APA Division 5, President, 1958–9; APA Board of Scientific Affairs, 1960–2, Chair, 1962; Social Science Research Council, Committee on Application of Mathematics in the Behavioral Sciences, 1961; National Research Council, Division of Psychology and Anthropology, 1962–3; National Institute of General Medical Sciences, Behavioral Sciences Training Committee, 1962–8; Guggenheim Fellowship, 1970; NIMH, Committee on Epidemiology and Biometry, 1971–3; Hon. Dr, University of Leiden, 1975; Fulbright-Hayes Award, Central University of Caracas, 1975; Fellow, American Academy of Arts and Sciences, 1977; Society for Mathematical Psychology, Chair, 1977–8; Psychological Association of Spain, Honorary Member, 1979; Distinguished Senior Faculty Lecturer, University of Michigan; 1980; National Academy of Sciences, Member, 1982; APA Distinguished Scientific Contribution Award, 1985; Professor Emeritus of Psychology, University of Michigan

Principal publications

1950 Psychological scaling without a unit of measurement. *Psychological Review*, 57, 145–58.

1954 *Decision Processes*. Wiley (co-ed. with R.M. Thrall and R.C. Davis).

1954 Some views on mathematical models and measurement theory. *Psychological Review*, 61, 132–44 (with H. Raiffa and R.M. Thrall).

1958 On the use of inconsistency of preferences in psychological measurement. *Journal of Experimental Psychology*, 55, 1–7.

1964 *Theory of Data*. Wiley.

1967 Testing expectation theories of decision making without measuring utility or subjective probability. *Journal of Mathematical Psychology*, 4, 72–103 (with T.G.G. Bezembinder and F.M. Goode).

1970 *Mathematical Psychology: An Elementary Introduction*. Prentice-Hall (with A. Tversky and R. Dawes).

1973 On the detection of structure in attitudes and developmental processes. *Psychological Review*, 80, 337–51 (with J.E.K. Smith).

1975 Preference scales for number and sex of children. *Population Studies*, 29, 273–98 (with L.C. Coombs and G.H. McClelland).

1977 Single peaked functions and the theory of preference. *Psychological Review*, 84, 216–30 (with G.S. Avrunin).

1983 *Psychology and Mathematics: An Essay on Theory*. University of Michigan Press.

1984 Conjoint design and analysis of the bilinear model: An application of judgements of risk. *Journal of Mathematical Psychology*, 28, 1–42 (with P.E. Lehner).

1984 An empirical study of some election systems. *American Psychologist*, 39, 140–57.

Further reading

Jacoby, W.G. (1991) *Data Theory and Dimensional Analysis*. Sage.

Link, S.W. (1992) *The Wave Theory of Difference and Similarity*. Erlbaum.

Clyde Coombs made significant contributions to a theory of data that advanced the scientific study of psychology, particularly in terms of scaling methods and the measurement of subjective values. His earliest interests were in physiological psychology, particularly focused on neurophysiology and the physiochemical basis of biological processes. He was deeply affected by L.L. **Thurstone**'s ideas in *Vectors of the Mind*, and he went to the University of Chicago to study with Thurstone and with N. Rashevsky in mathematical biophysics. His work at the University of Chicago was mostly in mathematics.

After six years in the military during World War II, Coombs returned to academia and spent the majority of his professional career at the University of Michigan. Throughout these years, he was committed to advancing the methodological foundations of behavioural science and the quantification of subjective variables. This concern led to his theory of data and the development of non-metric methods of scaling preferences and subjective values.

An experiment on the stochastic properties of preferential choice, done in 1955–6 while supported by a Fulbright Fellowship at the University of Amsterdam, had a tremendous impact on the direction of Coombs's theoretical work. Up until then, the complexities of preferential choice had received little attention. Views tended to centre on psychophysics, dominated by the monotonicity of sensation with physical variables. Coombs believed that preference is more complex than sensation, involving trade-offs among variables, thus violating monotonicity. The Amsterdam experiments strengthened his interest in single peaked functions as a representation of such trade-offs.

Single peaked functions, however, do not always occur, and this lead Coombs to seek the conditions for their occurrence. In collaboration with George Avrunin, Coombs developed a simple mathematical theory based on behavioural science principles which accounted for the occurrence and non-occurrence of peaked functions. This theory suggested that the critical point was the structure on the options and not the decisions processes in the individual.

If a choice between options must be made when an option does not dominate the other, the individual is torn between incompatible goals; the person must make a trade-off, which involves resolving conflict. The theoretical developments of this theory became a basis for Coombs's formal study of social conflict, which occupied his attention in the latter part of his career. Thus, Clyde Coombs is important to behavioural science for advancing its methodological sophistication in determining subtle measures of subjective states, and for offering theoretical guidance for scaling strategies that moved beyond the linear constraints of traditional psychophysical approaches.

JAMES F. BRENNAN

Cooper, Cary Lynn

Born: 1940, Los Angeles, California, USA
Nat: American/British **Ints:** Health psychology, humanistic psychology, industrial and organizational psychology, psychology of women
Educ: BS University of California, Los Angeles, 1962; MBA University of California, Los Angeles, 1964; PhD University of Leeds, 1969; MSc University of Manchester, 1979
Appts & awards: Professor of Organizational Psychology, University of Manchester; 1975– ; Chairman, (American) Academy of Management's MED Division, 1979–80; Fellow, BPS, 1980– , Royal Society of Arts, 1990; Advisor, WHO, 1981–3, ILO, 1983; Leverhulme Trust Fellowship, 1982–3; Founding President, British Academy of Management, 1986–90; Book Series Editor, Individual, Groups and Organizations, 1978– , Studies in Occupational Stress, 1978– , Applied Management, 1980– ; Editor in Chief, *Journal of Occupational Behavior*, 1980– ; Co-editor, *Stress Medicine*, 1988– ; Editorial Boards, *Stress Medicine*, 1985– , *Leadership and Organizational Development Journal*, 1981– , *Portuguese Journal of Applied Psychology*, 1982–

Principal publications

1978   Identifying sources of occupational stress among dentists. *Journal of Occupational Psychology*, 51, 227–34 (with M. Mallinger and R. Kahn).

1979   A cybernetic framework for studying occupational stress. *Human Relations*, 32, 395–419 (with T. Cummings).
1981   *The Stress Check*. Prentice-Hall.
1982   *Executive Families under Stress*. Prentice-Hall.
1982   Stress in the police service. *Journal of Occupational Medicine*, 24, 30–6.
1983   Identifying stressors at work: Recent research. *Journal of Psychosomatic Research*, 27, 369–76.
1983   Occupational stress among international interpreters. *Journal of Occupational Medicine*, 25, 889–95 (with R. Davies-Cooper).
1983   *High Pressure: Working Lives of Women Managers*. Fontana (with M.J. Davidson).
1983   (ed.) *Stress Research: Issues for the 80s*. Wiley.
1984   (ed.) *Psychological Stress and Cancer*. Wiley.
1984   Executive stress and health: Differences between men and women. *Journal of Occupational Medicine*, 26, 99–104.
1984   The social psychological precursors to cancer. *Journal of Human Stress*, 10, 4–11.
1985   *The Changemakers: Successful Careers in Business and Industry*. Harper & Row.
1985   Occupational and psychosocial stress among commercial aviation pilots. *Journal of Occupational Medicine*, 27, 570–6.
1985   Occupational stress among word processor operators. *Stress Medicine*, 1, 87–92 (with A. Cox).
1988   *Living with Stress*. Penguin (with L. Eaker).
1990   *Understanding Stress: A Psychological Perspective for Health Professionals*. Chapman and Hall (with V. Sutherland).
1991   *Stress and Accidents in the Offshore Oil and Gas Industry*. Gulf.
1992   *The Stress Survivors*. HarperCollins (with M. Davidson).
1993   *Stress in the Dealing Room*. Routledge (with H. Kahn).
1994   *Business Elites: The Psychology of Entrepreneurs and Intrapreneurs*. Routledge (with R. Jennings and C. Cox).

Further reading

Cooper, C. (ed.) (1996) *Handbook of Stress, Medicine, and Health*. CRC Press.
Zeidner, M. and Endler, N.S. (eds) (1996) *Handbook of Coping: Theory, Research, Applications*. Wiley.

Most of Cary Cooper's original research was in the field of group psychology. Initial scholarly research articles and books concentrated on an evaluation of experimental learning group techniques. It became apparent that although experiential techniques were partially influential in changing people in industry, the stresses and strains of worklife were far more predominant. It was in the middle 1970s, therefore, that his emphasis changed to exploring occupation stress, an area in which he has published dozens of books and hundreds of articles. Since then, he has developed a team of researchers who have carried out in-depth studies on a variety of white- and blue-collar occupations. This has also led to a concern for health promotion in organizations. Much of his empirical work has suggested that the way in which an organization is managed and structured is responsible for the job satisfaction and health of its employees. He considered it is the responsibility of occupational psychologists to heighten awareness, both empirically and pragmatically, about the way the workplace can adversely affect its constituents; and what can be done to create more liveable work environments. In addition, he carried out a great deal of research on the plight of working women. It would appear that the health, well-being and productivity of many working women are being adversely affected by male-dominated corporate personnel policies and actions. Although in most Western societies nearly two-thirds of all women work, little effort has been devoted to acknowledging and responding to this important social change. The dual-career family has arrived, but there have been inevitable negative consequences. Cooper has attempted to highlight the problems of working women, in an effort to seek practical and effective solutions in the workplace.

Cooper, Lynn Ann

Born: 1947, Toledo, Ohio, USA *Nat:* American *Educ:* BA University of Michigan, 1969; PhD Stanford University, 1972 *Appts & awards:* University of California at San Diego, 1972–6; APA Member, 1975; Cornell University, 1976–80; APA Award, 1980; Learning Research and Development Center, University of Pittsburgh, 1980–

Principal publications

1972 Coming of age with the Delboeuf illusion: Brightness contrast, cognition, and perceptual development. *Developmental Psychology*, 6, 187–97 (with D.J. Weintraub).

1973 The time required to prepare for a rotated stimulus. *Memory and Cognition*, 1, 246–50.

1973 Chronometric studies in the rotation of mental images. In W.G. Chase (ed.), *Visual Information Processing*. Academic Press.

1975 Mental rotation of random two-dimensional shapes. *Cognitive Psychology*, 7, 20–43.

1975 Mental transformations in the identification of right and left hands. *Journal of Experimental Psychology: Human Perception and Performance*, 1, 48–56.

1976 Individual differences in visual comparison processes. *Perception and Psychophysics*, 19, 433–44.

1978 Spatial comprehension and comparison processes in verification tasks. *Cognitive Psychology*, 10, 391–421.

1978 Transformations on representations of objects in space. In E.C. Carterette and M.P. Friedman (eds), *Handbook of Perception. Vol. 8: Perceptual Coding*. Academic Press.

Further reading

Kosslyn, S.M. (1980) *Image and Mind*. Harvester University Press.

Pylyshyn, Z. (1981) The imagery debate: Analogue media versus tacit knowledge. *Psychological Review*, 88, 16–45.

When Lynn Cooper entered the University of Michigan she had not planned to study psychology, but her interests in the subject developed during her second and third years there. Staff included Eric **Lenneberg** and Rachel Kaplan, both of whom had a strong influence on her intellectual development. She worked closely and co-authored papers with her thesis supervisor, Daniel J. Weintraub, and she was awarded the University's Pillsbury Prize for distinguished undergraduate research. While completing her doctoral research at Stanford she developed a strong research partnership with her thesis advisor, Roger N. **Shepard**. Her interests changed from psychophysical investigations of visual perception to cognition aspects of visual processing, where Shephard devised an ingenious serious of chronometric studies on the 'mental rotation' of objects. With Shephard she demonstrated qualitative differences in holistic as opposed to analytical processing of visual information. This work led to fundamental advances in our understanding of the mechanisms underlying the representation and transformation of what is seen. Her work challenged the prevailing view that mental processes and representations could be most appropriately characterized as discrete and symbolic. Instead she demonstrated that people could perform analogical mental operations on cognitive representations of visual objects. Her theories of mental imagery attracted considerable criticism in the 1980s and have undergone considerable modification since that time.

Corsini, Raymond J.

Born: 1914, Vermont, USA *Nat:* American *Ints:* Experimental, general psychology, personality and social psychology, school psychology, psychotherapy *Educ:* BA City College of New York, 1939; MSEd City College of New York, 1941; PhD University of Chicago, 1955 *Appts & awards:* Professor Corsini has a private practice; James McKeen Cattell Award; Sentoma Education Award; Former Editor, *Journal of Individual Psychology*; Editorial Board, *Journal of Social Behavior and Personality*

Principal publications

1947   Non-directive vocational guidance of prison inmates. *Journal of Clinical Psychology*, 3, 96–100.

1951   On the theory of change resulting from group therapy. *Group Psychotherapy*, 4, 179–80.

1955   Mechanisms of group psychotherapy. *Journal of Abnormal and Social Psychology*, 51, 406–11. (with B. Rosenberg).

1956   The blind man and the elephant. *ETC*, 245–7.

1956   Understanding and similarity in marriage. *Journal of Abnormal and Social Psychology*, 52, 327–32.

1959   *Methods of Group Psychotherapy*. McGraw-Hill.

1959   Appearance and criminality. *American Journal of Sociology*, 45, 49–51.

1971   Logic and the scientific method reconsidered. *Wormrunners Digest*, 13, 111–12.

1973   *Current Psychotherapies*. Peacock. (Reprinted 1979, 1989.)

1974   Dispositional sets. *Journal of Individual Psychology*, 30, 163–78. (with N. Kefir).

1977   Individual education. *Journal of Individual Psychology*, 33, 295–349.

1981   (ed.) *Handbook of Innovative Psychotherapies*. Wiley.

1982   *Individual Psychology*. Peacock (with G. Manaster).

1984   (ed.) *Encyclopaedia of Psychology*. Wiley.

Further reading

MacKenzie, K.R. (ed.) (1992) *Classics in Group Psychotherapy*. Guilford.

Zeig, J.K. and Munion, W.M. (eds) (1990) *What is Psychotherapy?: Contemporary Perspectives*. Jossey-Bass.

Raymond Corsini started work as a psychologist

at the Vocational Adjustment Bureau for Girls, and worked for ten years in various locations, including a Negro Agency and Prison where he was involved in vocational counselling. His guidance was based mostly on tests, but his own research showed that not one of his fifty inmates interviewed consecutively had followed his advice; so he gave up and became a non-directive counsellor, trained originally by Carl **Rogers** (by post!) in the early 1940s. When he eventually returned to studying at the age of 38 to complete his PhD, it was to work with Rogers – in person this time. Following his PhD he became an industrial psychologist, where he was very successful but unhappy, feeling he had to compromise his ethics in order to succeed. He moved into teaching, working at the Illinois Institute of Technology and at the University of California, but disliked the pressures of students grades, faculty rivalries and so on.

Eventually he moved to Hawaii, where he was able to spend 50 per cent of his time writing and editing and the rest as a counsellor and psychotherapist in private practice. He has over a hundred publications, including some twenty-five books. He considers himself to be a 'scientist working with people' and his most satisfying personality theory as the 'Individual Psychology of Alfred Adler'. He regards his most important contribution as being in the School System, called first 'Individual Education' and then the 'Corsini Four-R School System'. Used in the USA, Holland, Canada and Israel, it seems to be vastly superior to the traditional system in achieving the usual goals of education. At 72 he condensed his four-volume *Encyclopaedia of Psychology* into one volume, and he continues publishing and editing.

Craik, Fergus I.M.

Born: 1935, Edinburgh, Scotland *Nat:* British *Ints:* Experimental and adult development and ageing *Educ:* BSc University of Edinburgh, 1960, PhD; University of Liverpool, 1965 *Appts & awards:* Professor of Psychology, University of Toronto; Fellow, Royal Society of Canada; Killam Research Fellowship, 1982–4; Fellow, Center for Advanced Study in the Behavioural Sciences, 1982–3, Chairman, Governing Board, Psychonomic Society, 1984–5; Editor, *Journal of Verbal Learning and Verbal Behavior*, 1980–4; Editorial Board, *Journal of Verbal Learning and Verbal Behavior*, 1973– , *Journal of Experimental Psychology*, 1973–6, *Memory* and Cognition, 1973–6, Canadian Journal of Psychology, 1974–9, Quarterly Journal of Experimental Psychology, 1975–6, Journal of Gerontology, 1979–81, Canadian Journal on Aging, 1982–3

Principal publications

1970 The fate of primary memory items in free recall. *Journal of Verbal Learning and Verbal Behavior*, 9, 143–8.

1972 Levels of processing: A framework for memory research. *Journal of Verbal Learning and Verbal Behavior*, 11, 671–84 (with R.S Lockhart).

1975 Depth of processing and the retention of words in episodic memory. *Journal of Experimental Psychology: General*, 104, 268–94 (with E. Tulving).

1976 The concept of primary memory. In W.K. Estes (ed.), *Handbook of Learning and Cognitive Processes*. Erlbaum (with B. A Levy).

1977 Age differences in human memory. In J.E. Birren and K.W. Scaie (eds), *Handbook of the Psychology of Aging*. Van Nostrand Reinhold.

1979 *Levels of Processing in Human Memory*. Erlbaum (with L.S. Cermak).

1982 *Aging and Cognitive Processes*. Plenum (with S.E. Trehub).

1983 On the transfer of information from temporary to permanent memory. *Philosophical Transactions of the Royal Society*, Series B, 302, 341–59.

Further reading

Baddeley, A.D. (1990) *Human Memory: Theory and Practice*. Erlbaum

Parkin, A.J. (1993) *Memory: Phenomena, Experiment and Theory*. Blackwell.

Craik's initial interests in psychology, as an undergraduate, were in perception and cognition viewed from a functional, biological perspective, and he retained this general orientation while working on various more specialized topics. His first publications were on adult age differences in information processing, examining such issues as dichotic listening performance and various aspects of short-term memory. In the late 1960s he spent a year as a visitor at the University of Toronto, and he returned there as a faculty member in 1971. Contacts with colleagues at Toronto (especially perhaps Robert Lockhart and Endel **Tulving**) have influenced his thinking. In the late 1960s and early 1970s his research was on short-term retention in humans, carried out within the framework of information-processing models, but he became increasingly dissatisfied with the structural,

mechanistic limitations of such models. In 1972, Lockhart and Craik published an influential article on levels of processing, which proposed a more flexible, functional, process-oriented account of remembering. They argued that the strength and persistence of a memory trace was a product of the perceptual processing that occurred when something was being remembered. Perceptual processing was thought to vary in depth. Shallow processing would involve superficial or incidental details – for example, the shape of the letters of a word. Deeper processing would involve the sound of the word, and deeper still would be the denotation and connotation of the word. Essentially, the deeper the processing the better the memory. These ideas – principally that memory performance largely reflected the type of initial processing carried out – were backed up by a series of empirical studies published with Endel Tulving in 1975.

Two kinds of criticism have been levelled against the 'levels of processing' theory. First, it became clear that it did not fit with emerging theories of perceptual processing which suggested that analysis of information does not proceed from structure to meaning, but that 'theory-driven' or 'top-down' predictions of probable meaning can aid perceptions, and that analysis can proceed at several levels simultaneously. Second, it proved extremely difficult to measure the levels of processing independently – poor performance was taken as evidence of shallow encoding and better performance as evidence of deep encoding. However, later studies successfully addressed this criticism. A residual criticism remains: the levels of processing theory overemphasizes encoding, and does not pay sufficient attention to the importance of the specific nature of the encoding process and the conditions pertaining at the time of retrieval. Nevertheless the theory offers a useful heuristic for predicting how effective an encoding task will be.

About 1975 Craik was asked by James Birren to write a chapter on memory for his revision of the *Handbook of the Psychology of Aging*; this review rekindled an early interest in ageing. Since then his empirical work has been a mixture of studies on age differences in memory and attention, and experiments examining the interactions between encoding and retrieval processes in memory generally. With respect to theory, he continued to think in functional, process-oriented terms, with increasing sympathy for the notion (put forward by **Bartlett** and later by Paul Kolers) that perceiving, thinking and remembering should be thought of as skilled activities.

Cronbach, Lee Joseph

Born: 1916, Fresno, California, USA **Died:** 1994, Atherton, California, USA **Nat:** American **Ints:** Educational psychology, evaluation and measurement, personality and social psychology **Educ:** BA Fresno State College, 1934; MA University of California at Berkeley, 1937; PhD University of Chicago, 1940 **Appts & awards:** Instructor to Associate Professor, State College, Washington, 1940–6; Associate Psychologist, University of California Division of War Research, 1944–5; Assistant Professor, University of Chicago, 1946–8; Associate Professor, then Professor of Educational Psychology, University of Illinois, 1948–64; Scientific Liaison Officer, Office of Naval Research, London, 1955–6; Member, Institute for Advanced Study, Princeton, 1960–1; Fellow, Centre for Advanced Study in Behavioral Studies, 1963–4; Stanford University, Professor of Education, 1964–6, Vida Jacks Professor of Education, 1966–80, Professor Emeritus, 1980; Fulbright Lecturer, University of Tokyo, 1967–8; Hon. LHD, Yeshiva University, 1967, University of Chicago, 1979, University of Illinois, 1982; Hon. PhD, University of Gothenburg, 1977, U. Autónoma, Madrid, 1985; President, APA, 1955–7; APA Distinguished Scientific Contribution Award, 1994

Principal publications

1949 *Essentials of Psychological Testing.* Harper and Row. (5th edn, 1990.)
1949 Statistical methods applied to Rorschach scores: A review. *Psychological Bulletin*, 46, 393–429.
1951 Coefficient alpha and the internal structure of tests. *Psychometrika*, 16, 297–334.
1954 *Educational Psychology.* Harcourt, Brace. (3rd edn, 1977.)
1955 Construct validity in psychological tests. *Psychological Bulletin*, 52, 281–302 (with P.E. Meehl).
1957 The two disciplines of scientific psychology. *American Psychologist*, 12, 671–84.
1957 *Psychological Tests and Personnel Decisions.* University of Illinois Press (with G.C. Gleser). (2nd edn, 1965.)
1970 Test validation. In R.L. Thorndike (ed.), *Educational Measurement.* American Council on Education.
1972 *The Dependability of Behavioral*

Measurements: Theory of Generalizability for Scores and Profiles. Wiley (with G.C. Gleser, H. Nanda and N. Rajaratnam).
1975 Five decades of public controversy over mental testing. *American Psychologist*, 30, 1–14.
1975 Beyond the two disciplines of scientific psychology. *American Psychologist*, 30, 116–27.
1982 *Designing Evaluations of Educational and Social Programs.* Jossey-Bass.

Further reading

Snow, R.E. and Wiley, D.E. (eds) (1991) *Straight Thinking: A Volume in Honor of Lee J. Cronbach.* Erlbaum.

From an early age, Lee J. Cronbach's life was part of the history of psychological testing. In 1921 he was found to have an exceptionally high IQ on the Stanford–**Binet**, and became one of the gifted children whose lives were traced in **Terman**'s *Genetic Study of Genius*. It is ironic, or perhaps natural, that his career was largely devoted to questioning and sharpening, and sometimes undermining, the tools of the trade pioneered by Terman.

In spite of this start, Cronbach came to testing quite late, and took little formal training in psychology before graduating. At Fresno State College he set out to become a chemist. He majored in chemistry and mathematics, and took a course on 'tests and measurements', where he was 'entranced' by **Thurstone** and Chave on the measurement of attitudes. He studied the history of American education, an arts subject which suited his sharp analytical skills and steered him towards educational research. He began with an MA at Berkeley, which he combined with student high-school teaching. His dissertation was on understanding vocabulary in algebra. Influenced by **Dewey**, he devised tests which allowed for a variety of possible uses for a word, rather than simple criteria of right or wrong.

For his PhD in psychology Cronbach went to the University of Chicago. He took a course on laboratory methods with Judd's student Guy Buswell, and for a dissertation refined Judd and Cowling's 1907 study on children's replications of nonsense squiggles by recording eye fixations. He was one of the group monitoring local progressive schools under Ralph Tyler, and he shared their determination to view the student and instruction in context, rather than in isolation from social and political background. Cronbach was responsible for applying the latest work on test reliability by Kuder and Richardson, both colleagues at Chicago. This was to lead to an important generalization of their formulae for reliability based on item correlation in his 'coefficient alpha', which he published in 1951.

In 1940 he became instructor in psychology at Washington State College, and began work on *Essential of Psychological Testing*, to replace the textbooks he found available for his course on mental measurement. In 1944 he worked on military training projects, including one for anti-submarine personnel. There he confirmed his interest in instructional research, and discovered that the **Weber–Fechner** law does not hold well for sonar detection – as he later characteristically put it, 'in the presence of Frequency × Tonal Quality interaction it no longer accounted for appreciable variance'.

In 1946 he returned to Chicago as Assistant Professor of Education. There he came to know Thurstone – earlier he had been too busy meeting requirements to attend his lectures. He took over Tyler's course on educational psychology, which led to the writing of his *Educational Psychology*. In 1948 he was given tenure, and as a 'marginal man' (his own phrase for himself), straddling education, psychology and statistics, he became in demand as a consultant and as a member of committees and working groups locally, nationally and internationally. In this way he cultivated his very broad interdisciplinary sympathies. He was appointed president of the APA in 1955, and during the same busy time enjoyed thirteen months visiting researchers throughout Europe as liaison scientist at the Office of Naval Research in London. Later he became advisor on research grants to the NIMH and chaired the Committee on Learning and the Educational Process for the Social Science Research Council. The important work with Paul **Meehl** on construct validity originated in discussions in the Committee on Test Standard, of which he was chairman.

During the second half of his career, now at Stanford, he returned to problems of evaluation, characteristically favouring a 'formative' approach, in which the evaluator is an enquirer fully involved in assessment and feedback throughout the course of instruction. He recognized that precision, however good in itself, may only be gained at the cost of ignoring context and diversity.

Cronbach was a great writer of textbooks, and his *Essentials of Psychological Testing* and *Educational Psychology* were widely used. He also made important contributions to our understanding of validity and reliability, with his extraordinary alertness to the potential discrepancy between mathematical assumptions and psychological plausibility. But he was a cautious man who avoided shouting about great truths or joining sides in public debates. He refused to be drawn by the **Jensen** affair. He had no intention of being forced into a quarrel whose terms, as he saw it, had been dictated by the mass media. Instead he worked to put the debate in historical perspective, and showed how it generated its own momentum, which had little to do with the wishes or considered opinions of the protagonists. The episode reflected much broader social issues than the presence of racism in mental testing.

Most importantly Cronbach was a relativist about truth who believed in method, and tried to put his relativism into mathematical form. As a college student he had recognized, through studying Hilbert and Klein on the foundation of mathematics, that even the most rigorous conclusions are relative to an implicit model framing the enquiry. This, together with his reading of Dewey, made him ready for a crucial moment of insight, triggered by a chance remark that the demarcation of species involves *decisions* on the part of the taxonomist. This drove home for him that the scientist is a construer of nature rather than just a discoverer. This constructionism is reflected in his *American Psychologist* papers on the two disciplines of scientific psychology. Both were critical of laboratory psychology, the first when this was unfashionable, the second when it had become a platitude. In both cases he described the problem in statistical terms. By controlling as many conditions as possible we ignore possible interactions with the factors deemed irrelevant. Thus instruction by one method may be better than another, but will the same difference hold for different age groups or different tasks? The problem of unacknowledged interactions has obvious practical implications, and he had worked on it with Goldine Glaser in their work on interactions between aptitude and treatment (ATIs).

Cronbach's solution for the laboratory was to use correlation rather than to dismiss experimental studies for their lack of generalizability, but he recognized that there is no end to this, no good logical reason for stopping at first-order interactions. Time itself is an important factor and what holds in 1970 may be reversed 100 years later. He was a true pragmatist for whom evaluation cannot be separated from public policy and the current *Zeitgeist*. There are no absolutes, but enquiry can guide contemporary policy and individual choice, and theoretical concepts can help people to think. Perhaps this generalization at least will stand the test of time.

ARTHUR STILL

Crowne, Douglas Prescott

Born: 1928, Brooklyn, New York, USA *Nat:* American *Ints:* Clinical neuropsychology, physiological and Comparative, personality and Social *Educ:* BA Antioch College, 1951; EdM University of Rochester, 1956; PhD Purdue University, 1959 *Appts & awards:* Professor, Department of Psychology, University of Waterloo; Fellow, APA, 1967, Canadian Psychological Association

Principal publications

1960 A new scale of social desirability independent of psychopathology. *Journal of Consulting Psychology*, 24, 349–54 (with D. Marlowe).

1963 Conformity under varying conditions of personal commitment. *Journal of Abnormal and Social Psychology*, 66, 547–55 (with S. Liverant).

1964 *The Motive for Approval: Studies in Evaluative Dependence.* Wiley (with D. Marlowe).

1964 Instigation to aggression, emotional arousal and defensive emulation. *Journal of Personality*, 32, 163–79 (with L.K. Conn).

1975 Some characteristics and functional relations of the electrical activity of the primate hippocampus and an hypothesis of hippocampal function. In R.L. Isaacson and K.H. Pribram (eds), *The Hippocampus: A Comprehensive Treatise.* Plenum (with D.D. Radcliffe).

1979 *The Experimental Study of Personality.* Erlbaum.

1983 The frontal eye field and attention. *Psychological Bulletin*, 93, 232–60.

1983 Brief deprivation of vision after unilateral lesions of the frontal eye field prevents contralateral inattention. *Science*, 220, 527–30 (with C.M. Richardson and G. Ward).

1987 Lateralization of emotionality in right parietal cortex of the rat. *Behavioral Neuroscience*, 101, 134–8 (with C.M. Richardson and K.A. Dawson).

Further reading

Robinson, J.P., Shaver, P.R. and Wrightsman, L.S. (eds) (1991) Measures of personality and social psychological attitudes. *Measures of Social Psychological Attitudes, Vol. 1.* Academic Press.

It is possible to discern three distinct phases in Crowne's career. In the first of them, he

addressed some critical problems in personality measurement centring on self-evaluative style. His work on social desirability established that this response set represents an important personality dimension in its own right, one with behavioural implications for conformity, susceptibility to social influence, responsiveness in psychotherapy, and defensiveness. In the second and third phases, his work turned to the study of brain and behaviour. In the decade beginning in 1968, he worked on the functions of the hippocampus, investigating the role of the limbic structure in orienting and studying its electrical activity. Research with primates sought to bridge the gap between animal and human functions. The third phase, from 1978 on, continued the concern with cross-species homologies of function. The research during this period has asked anew a question going back at least 300 years: do homologies of function follow from homologies of structure? His work has included studies of deficits arising from unilateral cortical lesions, as well as lateralization of function in non-human species. More recent work is concerned with investigating the lateralization and localization of such functions as emotionality, spatial orientation and spatial learning.

Crutchfield, Richard

Born: 1912, Pittsburgh, USA *Died:* 1977, Berkeley, California, USA *Nat:* American *Ints:* Experimental, personality and social, Society for the Psychological Study of Social Issues, teaching *Educ:* BA California Institute of Technology, 1934; PhD University of California, at Berkeley, 1938 *Appts & awards:* APA Council of Representatives, 1950–3; APA Division of Personality and Social Psychology, President, 1953–4; Professor, University of California at Berkeley, 1953–77; Fellow, Institute for Advanced Study, 1958–9, Miller Institute for Research in Basic Science, 1962–3; Chairman, University of California at Berkeley, 1964–5; Director, Institute of Personality Assessment and Research, 1970–3; Berkeley Citation (from University of California), 1976.

Principal publications

1948 *Theory and Problems of Social Psychology.* McGraw-Hill (with D. Krech).

1955 Conformity and character. *American Psychologist*, 10, 191–8.

1958 *Elements of Psychology.* Knopf (with D. Krech).

1966   *The Productive Thinking Program.* Brazelton
(with M.V. Covington and L.B. Davis).

1970   *Elements of Psychology: A Briefer Course.*
Knopf (with D. Krech and N. Livson).

1970   Creative types in mathematics. *Journal of
Personality*, 38, 177–97 (with R. Nelson).

1973   The creative process. In M. Bloomberg (ed.),
Creativity: Theory and Research. College and
University Press.

Further reading

Bornstein, R.F. (1992) The dependent personality:
Developmental, social, and clinical perspectives.
Psychological Bulletin, 112, 3–23.

Forsuth, D.R. (ed.) (1987) *Social Psychology.*
Brooks/Cole.

In the 1930s Crutchfield was a pioneer in moving psychology from a tradition of single-factor
experiments to an experimental design based on
analysis of variance and covariance. During
World War II he contributed to the developing
methodology of opinion surveys. With David
Krech, he co-authored two influential texts,
Theory and Problems of Social Psychology and
Elements of Psychology, the second of which
had numerous editions and derivatives. In the
1950s his work helped to establish the linkage
between cognitive-perceptual processes and
significant facets of personality. His best-known
research was a seminal series of investigations
of the nature of conformity in the interpersonal
sphere, published during the height of the
'conformity era' in the US. In the late 1950s and
1960s he collaborated with several colleagues to
develop a programme of automated instruction
in productive thinking. Crutchfield was an
excellent teacher. He was a student of **Tolman**
and remained a generalist in an era of specialization. He combined rigour and precision with
humanitarian concerns and artistic sensibility.

R.M. HELSON

Cummings, Nicholas Andrew

Born: 1924, Monterey County, California, USA
Nat: American **Ints:** Clinical, health, innovative
health delivery systems, psychotherapy, short-
term psychotherapy methods **Educ:** BA
University of California at Berkeley, 1948;
MA Claremont Graduate School, 1954; PhD
Adelphi University, 1957 **Appts & awards:**
Chairman and Chief Executive Officer, Ameri-
can Biodyne, Inc., Biodyne Institute; Hon. Litt
D, California School of Professional Psychol-
ogy, 1976; Distinguished Psychologist Award,

APA Division 29, 1976; Distinguished Practi-
tioner Award, American Association of
Psychologists in Practice, 1978; APA, Presi-
dent, 1979, Fellow, Divisions 12, 13, 29, 31,
37, 42; President, National Academies of Prac-
tice, 1981– ; Distinguished Practitioner Award,
National Academies of Practice, 1981;
Associate Editor, *American Psychologist*; Guest
Editor, Special issue, *American Psychologist*,
Special issue, *Professional Psychology*; Edi-
torial Board, *American Psychologist*, *American
Journal of Psychotherapy*, *Professional
Psychology*, *Rural Community Psychology*,
Psychotherapy: Research and Practice, *Psycho-
therapy in Private Practice*, *Computers and
Human Behavior*; APA Distinguished Profes-
sional Contributions Award, 1985; Silver PSI
Award, NIMH

Principal publications

1967   Psychiatry and medial utilization in a prepaid
health plan setting. *Medical Care*, 5, 25–35 (with
W.T. Follette).

1968   Psychiatry and medical utilization: Part II.
Medical Care, 6, 31–41 (with W.T. Follette).

1976   Brief psychotherapy and medical utilization:
An 8-year follow up. In H. Dorken (ed.), *The
Professional Psychologist Today.* Jossey-Bass
(with W.T. Follette).

1977   Prolonged (ideal) versus short-term (realistic)
psychotherapy. *Professional Psychology*, 8,
491–505.

1979   *Psychology and National Health Insurance.*
APA (with C.A. Kiesler and G.R. Vandenbos).

1979   The anatomy of psychotherapy under national
v health insurance. *American Psychologist*, 32,
711–18.

1979   The dismantling of our health system.
American Psychologist, 41, 426–31.

1979   The general practice of psychology.
Professional Psychology, 10, 430–40 (with G.R.
Vandenbos).

1983   *The Biodyne Training Manual.* Biodyne
Institute Press.

1986   The emergence of the mental health complex.
Psychiatric Annals, 16, 1–17 (with L.J. Duhl).

1986   The new delivery systems. *Psychiatric Annals*,
16, 93–100 (with L.J. Duhl).

1987   *The Future of Mental Health Services:
Coping with Crisis.* Springer-Verlag (with L.J.
Duhl).

1987   *Brief, Intermittent Therapy throughout the
Life Cycle.* Aronson.

1995   *Focused Psychotherapy: A casebook of Brief,
Intermittent Psychotherapy Throughout the Life
Cycle.* Brunner/Mazel (with M. Sayama).

Further reading

Bersoff, D.N. (ed.) (1995) *Ethical Conflicts in Psychology.* American Psychological Association.

Lowman, R.L. and Resnick, R.J (eds) (1994) *The Mental Health Professional's Guide to Managed Care.* American Psychological Association.

The primary contribution of Nicholas Cummings has been to articulate the cutting edge of professional psychology in the United States for thirty years. At times this was unpopular; at other times it was a rallying point. This lifetime of professional activity began with the implementation and design of the first pre-paid comprehensive Mental Health Plan in the USA. Then, because the universities were not utilizing practitioners on their faculties, he spearheaded the Professional School movement by founding the California School of Professional Psychology, which grew to four campuses. As the first Chairman of the APA's Committee on Health Insurance, he initiated and developed the struggle that resulted in the universal recognition of American psychologists as autonomous providers of comprehensive mental health services under private insurance plans. He was only the second private practitioner to be elected as President of the APA. His term of office is credited (or blamed, depending on one's point of view) with ending the domination of APA governance by academic psychologists. Cummings has had considerable influence on the evolution of the private sector practice of psychology in the United States, by establishing and implementing actual models which served as demonstrations of what could be done.

D

Dallenbach, Karl M.

Born: Champaign, Illinois, USA, 1887 **Died:** Austin, Texas, USA, 1971 **Nat:** American **Ints:** Experimental psychology **Educ:** PhD Cornell University, 1913 **Appts & awards:** Professor, University of Oregon, 1913–14; Professor, Ohio State University, 1915–16; Professor, Cornell University, 1916–47; Co-operating Editor, *American Journal of Psychology*, 1921–5; Editor, *American Journal of Psychology*, 1926–68; Professor, Department of Psychology, University of Texas, 1948–71

Principal publications

1913   The relation of memory error to time interval. *Psychological Review*, 20, 323–37.

1913   The measurement of attention. *American Journal of Psychology*, 24, 465–507.

1920   Introspection and general methods. *Psychological Bulletin*, 17, 313–21.

1921   'Subjective' perceptions. *Journal of Experimental Psychology*, 4, 143–63.

1922   Haptical illusions of movement. *American Journal of Psychology*, 33, 277–84 (with W.A. Andrews).

1925   The determination of memory span by the method of constant stimuli. *American Journal of Psychology*, 36, 621–8 (with J.P. Guilford).

1926   Attention. *Psychological Bulletin*, 23, 1–18.

1932   A comparative study of the errors of localization on the finger-tips. *American Journal of Psychology*, 44, 327–31.

1936   The adaptation of pain aroused by cold. *American Journal of Psychology*, 48, 307–15 (with B. Edes).

1939   Pain: History and present status. *American Journal of Psychology*, 52, 331–47.

1944   'Facial vision': The perception of obstacles by the blind. *American Journal of Psychology*, 57, 133–83 (with M. Supa and M. Cotzin).

1946   The effect of activity upon learning and retention in the cockroach. *American Journal of Psychology*, 59, 1–58 (with H. Minami).

1953   'Facial vision': The perception of obstacles out of doors by blindfolded and blindfolded-deafened subjects. *American Journal of Psychology*, 66, 519–53.

Further reading

Boring, E.G. (1958) Karl M. Dallenbach. *American Journal of Psychology*, 71, 1–40.

Evans, R.B. (1972) Karl M. Dallenbach. *American Journal of Psychology*, 85, 463–76.

Karl Dallenbach was the second of three sons of John Jacob Dallenbach and Anna Caroline Mittendorf. At school he was constantly in mischief. Football consumed much of his energy for four years at the University of Illinois and for a year at the University of Pittsburgh; but at Illinois he was strongly influenced by John Wallace Baird. In 1909 Baird left Illinois for Clark University, and with the opportunity of a fellowship at Pittsburgh Dallenbach left too. A fellowship at Cornell under **Titchener** (who had earlier taught Baird) followed and led to a doctorate.

Dallenbach was an experimental psychologist in the strictest sense – the term excluded for him, as it did for **Wundt** and Titchener, social, child, abnormal and animal psychology (although he published work with Minami on learning in the cockroach). For Dallenbach experimental psychology concerned the laboratory investigation of the normally functioning adult mind, a view which influenced his editorial policy for the *American Journal of Psychology*, which he purchased from G. Stanley **Hall** in 1920. He was the owner of the journal for the next forty-eight years and the editor for forty-two.

Dallenbach's 94 core publications (from a total of 234) can be organized around seven themes: attention, cutaneous sensitivity, somesthetic perception, taste, visual perception, 'facial' vision, and memory and cognitive processes. His studies of attention are probably the most important of these contributions. He introduced the double-task method: instead of having an object of attention with distractors, he arranged two tasks so that each was a distraction for the other. Using this method, he obtained clearer measures than had hitherto been published. The technique was taken up and widely used by others. His experimental investigations of 'facial' vision – a sense attributed to the blind – is also important and a model of experimental method. He demonstrated how facial vision is a product of complex auditory and even thermal or olfactory cues.

Darwin, Charles Robert

Born: 1809, Shrewsbury, England *Died:* 1882, Downe, England *Nat:* British *Ints:* Physiological and comparative psychology *Educ:* MA Cambridge, 1831 *Appts & awards:* Gentleman companion to Captain Robert Fitzroy during the voyage on the HMS *Beagle* on the continuance of the Royal Navy Survey of the coasts of South America, 1831–6; Hon. Secretary Geological Society, 1838–41; Fellow, Royal Society, 1839; Fellow, Zoological Society, 1839; Royal Medal of the Royal Society, 1853; Wollaston Medal of the Geological Society, 1859; Copley Medal of the Royal Society, 1864; Order, Pour la Mérité, Prussia, 1867; Daly Medal of the Royal College of Physicians, 1879; Prize, Bressa, Reale Accademia della Scienze, Turin, 1879; Hon. Fellow, about forty-three societies in Europe and thirteen in the Americas

Principal publications

1839 *Journal of Researches into the Geology and Natural History of the Various Countries visited by H.M.S. Beagle, Under the Command of Captain Fitzroy R.N. from 1832 to 1836.* Henry Colburn.

1859 *The Origin of Species by means of Natural Selection or The Preservation of Favoured Races in the Struggle for Life* John Murray.

1871 *The Descent of Man, and Selection in Relation to Sex.* John Murray.

1872 *The Expression of the Emotions in Man and Animals.* John Murray.

1876 *The Movements and Habits of Climbing Plants.* John Murray.

1877 A biographical sketch of an infant. *Mind*, 2, 285–94.

1880 *The Power of Movement in Plants.* John Murray.

1881 *The Formation of Vegetable Mould through the Action of Worms, with Observations on their Habits.* John Murray.

Further reading

Boakes, R.A. (1984) *From Darwin to Behaviourism: Psychology and the Minds of Animals.* Cambridge University Press.

Dennett, D.C. (1995) *Darwin's Dangerous Idea: Evolution and the Meanings of Life.* Penguin.

Desmond, A. and Moore, J. (1992). *Darwin.* Penguin.

Ghiselin, M.T. (1969) *The Triumph of the Darwinian Method.* University of Chicago Press.

Gruber, H.E. (1981). *Darwin on Man: A Psychological Study of Scientific Creativity*, 2nd edn. University of Chicago Press.

Ruse, M. (1982) *Darwinism Defended: A Guide to the Evolution Controversies.* Addison-Wesley.

Charles Darwin was the second son of a wealthy and eminent physician. He went to Edinburgh to study medicine, but gave this up and went to Cambridge to take a BA degree in 1831, with a view to becoming a country parson. The crucial point in Darwin's life was his appointment that year as gentleman companion to Captain Robert Fitzroy on HMS *Beagle* on a round-the-world surveying voyage (27 December 1831–2 October 1836). This enabled him to study, particularly in South America, the geology, the fauna and flora, and the people. He kept diligent notes, and collected innumerable specimens.

On his return he soon acquired a scientific reputation for his work on his specimens, and the accounts of his voyage and of the origin of coral reefs. He began to speculate systematically and privately in notebooks on the 'Transmutation of Species' and 'Man, Mind, and Materialism'.

In September 1839 he achieved his principal insight into the mechanism of the evolution of all forms of life, namely the principle of natural selection, but he delayed publication for two decades. Instead he launched himself into an eight-year study of barnacles. In 1858 he received a letter from Alfred Russel Wallace, 'anticipating' the essential argument of natural selection. Papers by both men were read at the Linnaean Society, followed rapidly by publication of *The Origin of Species*.

In the *Origin* Darwin compellingly collated the evidence for the fact of evolution, and presented natural selection as the main mechanism through which evolution had come about. He made scant mention of the human species. The main section relevant to psychology is the chapter on 'Instinct'. While habits acquired by a particular individual cannot be inherited, instincts can be, and small variations provide the raw material for natural selection to operate upon. Darwin speculated about the evolutionary stages through which examples of such behaviours may have passed, making comparisons between species.

Darwin's main published views on human psychology came later, in *The Descent of Man* and *The Expression of the Emotions in Man and Animals*, although he began preparatory, private notes in 1838. These emphasize continuity between humans and other animals. Rather than being a special problem, humans were a special opportunity to study the possible central role of intelligence in evolutionary change. Darwin was at that time in quest of a scientific psychology, based on evolutionary and materialist principles.

In *The Descent of Man* Darwin listed gradations between the 'mental powers' of humans and other animals. Complex instincts and high intelligence were interconvertible, but instincts more often evolved into more complex instincts. Many anthropomorphic anecdotes from observers of reputation were related. On the evolution of language he anticipated virtually all of the issues current today – song-learning and dialects in songbirds, vocalizations used as labels by parrots, warning calls for specific predators, evolution of the vocal apparatus and of the brain, concept formation in animals, language in thought, and the philological complexity of all languages and their evolution towards simplicity. The origin of language he attributes to our ancestors' imitation of natural sounds in song, in the context of inter- and intra-sexual selection. This last topic occupies the second half of *Descent*, with little connection with the first half of the book. Moral sense is the most distinctive feature of ourselves, though prosocial behaviour of animals must be its precursor. Only humans have the intellectual capacity to review how they resolved a conflict between immediate gratification and loftier aims, and feel, if need be, remorse, risking social disapprobation. The religious sense is likewise unique to humans: beliefs dependent on high civilization transcend the repellent superstitions of simpler societies.

In *The Expression of the Emotions* Darwin again sought homologies between ourselves and other species. He enunciated three principles, of 'serviceable associated habits' (behaviours that have habitually accompanied an emotion), 'antithesis' (as the opposite sets of postures in an aggressive versus a friendly dog), and 'actions due to the constitution of the Nervous System' (for the physical accompaniments of felt emotion), which were innate, though capable of imitation, and served in communication.

Apart from 'A biographical sketch of an infant', based on his old notes on his first child, William, Darwin moved away from the consideration of human behaviour and that of 'higher' animals. Instead he tackled the directed movements of plants, and continued his lifelong study of earthworms, the subject of his last book.

Darwin married his cousin Emma Wedgwood in 1839, and they soon left London to live at Down House in the quiet Kent village of Downe, and raised seven children. Darwin was plagued with perpetual debilitating ailments, which have been the subject of speculation, but he managed to be immensely productive. He had long been a respected figure in the scientific community, which accepted his evolutionary arguments soon after publication. He did have influential enemies, such as the anatomist Richard Owen, but also many influential friends, including the botanist Henslow and the geologist Sedgwick from his days at Cambridge, and later Lyell, whose *Principles of Geology* Darwin read during his *Beagle* voyage, the botanist Hooker, and Thomas Huxley, Darwin's 'bulldog'. Darwin corresponded voluminously with other scientists and, using questionnaires, interrogated animal breeders on heredity, and travellers on ethnography.

The perceived challenge of evolution to orthodox Christian belief correlated with Darwin's own increasing agnosticism, always muted out of consideration for the beliefs of his wife, and his fear of Victorian intolerance and of the political implications hotheads were always contriving to discern. Like the heliocentric theory of the solar system, the animal origins of humans were a blow to the self-esteem of our species, but no compensating sense of an overall Grand Design was provided: the tree of life as a conglomeration of purely chance events is a key feature of Darwinism which took longer to accept. Nevertheless, by the time of Darwin's death much of the conflict had subsided, and his eminence was recognized by his burial in Westminster Abbey.

The discovery of the particulate nature of heredity, not generally known until the start of the twentieth century, removed the main logical flaw in Darwin's theory, and the need for the principle of the inheritance of acquired characteristics. This led to a better understanding of population genetics (Sewall Wright, Haldane). The full implications for behaviour and psychology were not grasped, however, until the principle of selection at the level of the gene was clarified by Hamilton in 1964. Further insights into the consequences for human society and morality were gained by applying the theory of games (Maynard Smith) and the notion (Trivers, Axelrod) of reciprocal as well as nepotistic altruism.

If Darwin is not a founding father of psychology *per se*, he provided the unifying theory for biology which extends to all features of the behaviour of the human species. The simple elegance of the principle of natural selection is compelling, but this does not mean its implications are so easily understood. For a long time it was the evolutionary continuity between humans and other species, and the quest for the development of human intellectual functions in particular, that underpinned comparative psychology, in the behaviourist tradition in the USA and among the Russian reflexologists leading to **Pavlov**. Despite some rebuffs from psycholinguists, and some recasting of laboratory phenomena in more cognitive terms, the insights of these studies remain. Darwin's other radical strand of 'mind and materialism' continues to inspire physiological psychology and its sister neurosciences, with work on the neural basis of behaviour in animals of all kinds. Computer analogues of 'neural' networks offer a *rapprochement* between 'cognitive science' and this biological reductionism.

For a long time natural selection was largely ignored by psychologists and biologists alike. Whilst seen as a plausible, sufficient explanation of the occurrence of evolution, the fine details of its workings over time were thought inaccessible to research. Recent work, e.g. on Darwin's finches on the Galapagos, is correcting this impression. Niko **Tinbergen**'s insight into the adaptive functions of behaviour in the natural habitat, combining with Konrad **Lorenz** in the detailed study of the the evolution of specific behaviours in related sets of species like ducks and geese, or gulls, led to the rival science of behaviour, known as ethology. With its own crude ideas of motivation, not unlike those of Freud, and an emphasis on the interplay of instinct and learning in ontogeny, ethology became synthesized with psychology, and emphasized the systematic observation of behaviour as a complement to experimental studies. Measuring the Darwinian fitness costs and benefits of behaviour in the field led to behavioural ecology, whilst the implications of selection at the level of the gene gave rise to sociobiology. Most recently a group of evolutionary or Darwinian psychologists has declared itself specifically in search of biological adaptations and constraints in human mentation, which comparative laboratories had adjusted to half a generation before.

All these developments are at root Darwinian, and historical research on the immense corpus of books, papers and letters created by Darwin is as active now as it ever has been. In the learned as in the popular press, Charles Darwin continues to be 'news'.

DAVID DICKINS

Davis, James Henry

Born: 1932, Effingham, Illinois, USA **Nat:** American **Ints:** Evaluation and measurement, experimental, industrial and organizational, personality and social, psychology and the law **Educ:** BS University of Illinois, 1954, MA Michigan State University, 1958; PhD Michigan State University, 1961 **Appts & awards:** Professor of Psychology, University of Illinois; Chairman, Society of Experimental Social Psychology, 1976–7; APA Division 8, Fellow, Executive Committee, 1976–9; Topic Editor, *Journal of Personality and Social Psychology*, 1975–7; Editorial Board, *Journal of Experimental Social Psychology*, *British Journal of Social Psychology*, *Journal of Applied Social Psychology*, *Review of Personality and Social Psychology*, Co-editor, *International Journal of Applied Social Psychology*

Principal publications

1962 Success and speed of problem solving by individual and groups. *Psychological Review*, 69, 520–36.

1963 The preliminary analysis of emergent social structure in groups. *Psychometrika*, 28, 189–98.

1968 *Group Performance*. Addison-Wesley

1973 Effects of audience status, evaluation and time of action on performance with hidden word problems. *Journal of Personality and Social Psychology*, 27, 74–85 (with J. Cohen).

1973 Group decision and social interaction: A theory of social decision schemes. *Psychological Review*, 80, 97–125.

1974 Social decision schemes under risk. *Journal of Personality and Social Psychology*, 30, 248–71 (with N. Kerr, M. Sussman and A. Rissman).

1975 The decision process of 6- and 12-person juries assigned unanimous and 2/3 majority rules. *Journal of Personality and Social Psychology*, 32, 1–14 (with N. Kerr, R. Atkin, R. Holt and D. Meek).

1976 The social psychology of small groups: Cooperative and mixed motive interaction. *Annual Review of Psychology*, 27, 501–41 (with P. Laughlin and S. Komorita).

1978 *Dynamics of Group Decisions*. Sage (with H. Brandsetter and H. Schuler).

1980 Group decision and procedural justices. In M. Fishbein (ed.), *Progress in Social Psychology*. Erlbaum.

1981   Group decision making with social influence: A social interaction sequence model. *Psychological Review*, 88, 523–51 (with G. Stasser).

1981   *Progress in Applied Social Psychology*, vol. 1. Wiley (with G.M. Stephenson).

1982   *Group Decision Making*. Academic Press (with H. Brandetter and G. Stocker-Kreichgauer).

1983   Group decision making and jury verdicts. In H. Blumberg, P. Hare, V. Kent and G. Stocker-Kreichgauer (eds), *Small Groups and Social Interaction*, vol. 2. Wiley (with S. Tindale).

1984   *Progress in Applied Social Psychology*, vol. 2. Wiley (with G.M. Stephenson).

1989   Psychology and law: The last fifteen years. *Journal of Applied Social Psychology*, 19, 199–230.

1991   Enhancing team performance. In R. Bjork and D. Druckman (eds), *In the Mind's Eye: Understanding the Basics of Human Performance*. National Academy Press (with J. Singer).

1992   Group Decision Making. Special issue: *Organizational Behavior and Human Decision Processes*, 52, 1–13.

(In press)   Group decision making and quantitative judgments: A consensus model. In E. Witte and J.H. Davis (eds), *Understanding Group Behavior: Consensual Action by Small Groups*, vol. 1. Erlbaum.

Further reading

Paulus, P.B. (ed.) (1989) *Psychology of Group Influence*. Erlbaum.

Davis's fundamental research objective has been to study how a set of individuals collaborate in some way to solve a problem, reach a decision, or arrive at a consensus on some issue or judgement about which there may initially be some disagreement, ignorance or uncertainty. In the process of studying task-oriented groups of this sort, questions of social influence, competition–co-operation, interpersonal information processing, personal judgement and decision and the like arise naturally. At the outset, attention was focused upon individual and group problem solving, and the primary achievement here was a probabilistic model of how individuals solved word problems, and a model of how individuals combined contributions to achieve a group solution. Subsequently, a rather different model was derived to predict, under a variety of social and task conditions, how individuals combine or aggregate choices and preferences (explicitly or implicitly during interaction) to reach a consensus decision. It was the success of this Social Decision Scheme Model that allowed some

useful applications to problems of jury size, assigned decision rule, and various other questions associated with the law – especially courtroom trials. An extension of the model (the Social Interaction Sequence Model) to address social dynamics was stimulated by empirical observations of members changing decision preferences during interaction, thereby creating different factions or subgroups over time. Although various empirical findings, ranging from very applied questions (e.g. optimal jury size, effects of agenda-item order) to issues of a more fundamental concern, are important in their own right, development of theoretical models of group performance has been his major concern.

Day, Ross Henry

Born: 1927, Albany, Western Australia ***Nat:*** Australian ***Ints:*** Developmental, experimental, history, philosophical and theoretical reaching ***Educ:*** BSc University of Western Australia, 1949; PhD University of Bristol, 1954 ***Appts & awards:*** Fulbright Fellow, Brown University, 1961–2; Australian Psychological Society, Constitutions Committee, 1964–5, Council, 1965–76, President, 1966–7, Fellow, 1968– ; Professor and Chairman, Department of Psychology, Monash University, Australia 1965– ; Fellow, Academy of the Social Sciences in Australia, 1967– ; Co-founder, Australian Experimental Psychology Conferences, 1973; Editorial Board, *Perceptual and Motor Skills*, 1956– , *Perception*, 1978– , *British Journal of Psychology*, 1983– , *Australian and New Zealand Journal of Psychiatry*, 1973–9; Associate Editor, *Australian Journal of Psychology*, 1966–72; Editor-in-Chief, *Australian Journal of Psychology*, 1978–81

Principal publications

1958   On interocular transfer and the central origin of visual after-effects. *American Journal of Psychology*, 71, 784–9.

1965   Apparent reversal (oscillation) of rotary motion in depth: An investigation and a general theory. *Psychological Review*, 72, 117–27 (with R.P. Power).

1966   *Perception*. W. C. Brown.

1967   *Perception: A Laboratory Manual*. New South Wales University Press (with G. Singer and A. Bennett).

1967   Sensory adaptation and behavioral compensation with spatially transformed vision and hearing. *Psychological Bulletin*, 67, 307–22 (with G. Singer).

1969 *Human Perception.* Wiley.
1969 Mechanisms involved in visual orientation constancy. *Psychological Bulletin,* 71, 33–42 (with N.J Wade).
1971 Reduction or disappearance of visual after-effect of movement in the absence of a patterned surround. *Nature,* 230, 55–6 (with E.R Strelow).
1976 The components of the Poggendorff Illusion. *British Journal of Psychology,* 67, 537–52 (with R.G. Dickinson).
1977 *Studies in Perception.* University of Western Australia Press (with G.V. Stanley).
1978 Subjective contours, visual acuity and line contrast. In J.C. Armington, J. Krauskopf and B.R. Wooten (eds), *Visual Psychophysics: Its Physiological Basis.* Academic Press (with M.K. Jory).
1981 Infant perception of the invariant size of approaching and receding objects. *Developmental Psychology,* 17, 670–7 (with B.E. McKenzie).
1984 On the nature of perceptual illusions. *Interdisciplinary Science Reviews,* 9, 47–58.
1984 Localization of events in space: Young infants are not always egocentric. *British Journal of Developmental Psychology,* 2, 1–19 (with B.E. McKenzie and E. Ihsen).

Further reading
Gorden, I.E. (1989). *Theories of Visual Perception.* Wiley.
Murch, G.M. (1973). *Visual and Auditory Perception.* Bobbs-Merrill.

Ross Day's first interest in research and the one that has continued unabated since graduation days is the nature of human perception – the manner in which the external world of objects and events comes to be represented to the individual in consciousness. His papers on sensory after-effects in the visual kinaesthetic and tactile modalities, on a wide range of non-veridical perceptual effects (apparent reversal of rotary motion, induced movement, geometrical distortions, and illusory contours) and on perception in early infancy are reflections of this general concern with the nature of perception.

He considered the perceptual phenomena which he investigated, and in one or two cases discovered, to be simply means of probing the characteristics of perception and of revealing its operating principles. While perceptual illusions are intriguing, beguiling and fascinating in their own right, it is his view that they stand to tell us something about how normal, veridical perception works. His first main interest was in sensory after-effects consequent on protracted stimulation by a particular object property – orientation, size, direction of movement. The most interesting observation to emerge from that welter of work was made with Strelow on the visual movement after-effect. They found that this does not occur in the absence of a stationary patterned background. This revealed the 'relational-tuning' of perceptual mechanisms; some mechanisms are activated only by the relationship between the components of a stimulus array. Another important principle emerged from his work with Power on the apparent reversal of rotary motion in depth – the Ames effect. They concluded that rotary motion is by itself ambiguous and that the perceptual ambiguity can only be resolved in perception by stimulus information for orientation. This is another instance of the importance of relationships – in this case between direction of movement and object orientation – in stable, veridical perception of objects. Wade and Day found this to be so in their work on body tilt and visual orientation. McKenzie and Day worked intensively on perceptual constancy of shape, size and position in early infancy. It now seems clear that these stable forms of perception in the face of continuously varying patterns of sensory stimulation are operating well within the first year of life.

De Charms, Richard
Born: 1927, Wilkes Barre, Philadelphia, USA *Nat:* American *Ints:* Human motivation, personality and social *Educ:* BA Swarthmore College, 1952; MA Wesleyan University, 1954; PhD University of North Carolina, 1956 *Appts & awards:* Professor of Psychology and Education, Washington University

Principal publications
1962 Values expressed in American children's readers: 1800–1950. *Journal of Abnormal and Social Psychology,* 64, 136–42.
1965 The 'origin–pawn' variable in person perception. *Sociometry,* 28, 241–58 (with V. Carpenter and A. Kuperman).
1968 *Personal Causation: The Affective Determinants of Behavior.* Academic Press.
1976 *Enhancing Motivation: Change in the Classroom.* Irvington (reprinted 1985).
1976 Beyond attribution theory: The human conception of motivation and causality. In L.H. Strickland, F.E. Aboud and K.J. Gergen (eds), *Social Psychology in Transition.* Plenum (with D.J. Shea).

1978 Motivation: Social approaches. *Annual Review of Psychology*, 29, 91–113 (with M.S. Muir).

1979 Personal causation and perceived control. In L.C. Perlmuter and R.A. Monty (eds) *Choice and Perceived Control*. Erlbaum.

1980 The origins of competence and achievement motivation in personal causation. In L.J. Fyans Jr (ed.), *Achievement Motivation: Recent Trends in Theory and Research*. Plenum.

1981 Personal causation and locus of control: Two different traditions and two uncorrelated measures. In H.M. Lefcourt (ed.), *Research with the Locus of Control Construct*, vol. 1. Academic Press.

1982 That's not psychology: Some implications of McClelland's approach to motivation. In A.J. Stewart (ed.), *Motivation and Society*. Jossey-Bass.

1984 Motivation enhancement in educational settings. In R.E. Ames and C. Ames (eds), *Research on Motivation in Education*, vol. 1. Academic Press.

Further reading

Smith, C.P. *et al.* (eds) (1992) *Motivation and Personality: Handbook of Thematic Content Analysis*. Cambridge University Press.

Young-Eisendrath, P. and Hall, J.A. (eds) (1987) *The Book of the Self: Person, Pretext, and Process*. New York University Press.

In his predoctoral years De Charms was influenced by contact with Wolfgang **Köhler**, David C. **McClelland** and John W. **Thibaut**. In a sense his career has been an attempt to reconcile the philosophical and *Gestalt* orientations (Köhler) with the learning theory and clinical approach to motivation (McClelland) with social psychology and Lewinian group dynamics (Thibaut). De Charms's primary interest has always been in the analysis of human motivation and personal causation. For ten years he took the inner-city elementary school classroom as his laboratory. An abiding interest in philosophy of science and methodology led him in 1985 to a concentration on the contrasting models of human beings implicit in American and European psychology. His interest in personal causation and human agency contrasts with the trend towards depicting human beings as nothing but rational information processors.

De Renzi, Ennio

Born: 1924, Cremona, Italy *Nat:* Italian *Ints:* Experimental psychology, clinical neuropsychology *Educ:* MD University of Pavia School of Medicine, 1950 *Appts & awards:* University of Pavia, 1950–5; University of Milan, 1958–69; Professor of Neurology, University of Trieste, 1969–71; Professor of Neurology, University of Milan, 1971–4; Professor and Head, Department of Neurology, University of Modena, 1974– ; Honorary Visiting Professor, University of Aberdeen, 1996; President European Brain and Behaviour Society, 1969–71; Member by Election, Academia Europaea, American Neurological Association, Academy of Aphasia, Research Group on Aphasia of the World Federation of Neurology, International Neuropsychological Symposia

Principal publications

1962 The token test: A sensitive test to detect receptive disturbances in aphasics. *Brain*, 85, 665–78 (with L.A. Vignolo).

1969 Perceptual and associative disorders of visual recognition. *Neurology*, 19, 634–42 (with G. Scotti and H. Spinnler).

1970 Hemispheric contribution to exploration of space through the visual and tactile modality. *Cortex*, 6, 191–203 (with P. Faglioni and G. Scotti).

1975 Verbal and non-verbal short-term memory impairment following hemispheric damage. *Cortex*, 11, 341–54 (with P. Nichelli).

1977 Topographical amnesia. *Journal of Neurology, Neurosurgery and Psychiatry*, 40, 498–505 (with P. Faglioni and P. Villa).

1980 Imitating gestures: A quantitative approach to ideomotor apraxia. *Archives of Neurology*, 37, 6–10 (with F. Motti and P. Nichelli).

1982 Conjugate gaze paresis in stroke patients with unilateral damage: An unexpected instance of hemispheric asymmetry. *Archives of Neurology*, 39, 482–6 (with A. Colombo, P. Faglioni and M. Gibertoni).

1982 *Disorders of Space Exploration and Cognition*. Wiley.

1985 Disorders of spatial orientation. In J.A.M. Frederiks (ed.), *Handbook of Clinical Neurology I (45): Clinical Neuropsychology*. Elsevier.

1986 Current issues on prosopagnosia. In H.D. Ellis, M.A. Jeeves *et al.* (eds), *Aspects of Face Processing*. Martinus Nijhoff.

1988 Ideational apraxia. *Brain*, 111, 1173–85 (with F. Lucchelli).

1989 Attentional shift towards the rightmost stimuli in patients with left visual neglect. *Cortex*, 25, 231–7 (with M. Gentilini *et al.*).

1989 Apraxia. In F. Boller and J. Grafman (eds), *Handbook of Neuropsychology*, vol. 2. Elsevier.

1991 Apperceptive and associative forms of

prosopagnosia. *Cortex*, 27, 213–21 (with P. Faglioni *et al.*).

1994 Prosopagnosia can be associated with damage confined to the right hemisphere: An MRI and PET study and a review of the literature. *Neuropsychologia*, 32, 893–902 (with D. Perani *et al.*).

Further reading

Boller, F. and Grafman, J. (1988–9) *Handbook of Neuropsychology*, vols. 1 and 2. Elsevier.

Ennio De Renzi has been one of the most influential of post-war neuropsychologists, and a member of an international group who were responsible for transforming the study of brain-damaged patients from an art into a science. Along with Hans-Lucas Teuber, Brenda Milner, Henry Hécaen and others, he inspired a generation of neuropsychologists, and indeed helped define the nature of neuropsychology. A major influence on his scientific development was Arthur L. **Benton**, whom he met in the early sixties, and who became both a good friend and mentor. During a series of meetings with Benton, as well as several months spent in Iowa City as a Fulbright Professor, De Renzi acquired the methodological discipline he needed to add to his already extensive neurological knowledge and experience.

Benton's influence is perhaps evident in one of De Renzi's most important guiding principles in his research during the 1960s and 1970s: the need for the study of consecutive, unselected clinical cases when studying a particular behavioural or cognitive task, rather than the traditional strategy of examining intensively a small group of patients selected for a particular impairment or syndrome. Studies of this kind allowed him and his colleagues to make clear inferences about the incidence of impairment in patients with left- versus right-hemisphere damage, and to establish how any asymmetry interacted with the anterior/posterior location of the damage (typically indexed by the presence/ absence of visual field defects). Another important colleague during this period was Piero Faglioni, a fellow neurologist with an unusually strong interest and expertise in statistical analysis. Faglioni greatly influenced De Renzi's approach to experimental design, and was a collaborator in many of his research papers.

From the beginning of his scientific career, De Renzi has had an unusually broad range of interests. He has made major contributions, for example, to our understanding of spatial disorders, disorders of language, apraxia, hemispatial neglect, sensory extinction, prosopagnosia, topographical amnesia, and disorders of eye movements. This breadth of interest made De Renzi an ideal person to succeed Dr G. Gastaldi as Chief Editor of the journal *Cortex* in 1973, a position he continues to hold with distinction. He was closely involved with the journal from its inception in 1964, one year after the first appearance of *Neuropsychologia*, at a time when neuropsychology was still very much a minority interest and a belief in its future was largely a matter of faith. This foresight had been well vindicated by the time De Renzi took over. *Cortex* occupies a major (and even increasing) proportion of his time, because he continues to read every single submitted paper himself before deciding whether to send it to external reviewers.

In 1982, De Renzi published his influential book *Disorders of Space Exploration and Cognition*, which is still the best in the literature. It combines insightful reviews of relevant animal research with exhaustive discussions of the human neuropsychological literature, and is a mine of information for the researcher across a wide range of perceptual and visuomotor disorders. As well as his influential empirical papers, he has also published some very highly cited methodological papers on the assessment of aphasic impairments. Neuropsychologists look forward with keen anticipation to the publication of a second edition of his book.

A.D. MILNER

Deaux, Kay

Born: 1941 Warren, Ohio USA *Nat:* American *Ints:* Personality and social, psychology of women, Society for the Psychological Study of Social Issues *Educ:* BA North-western University, 1963; PhD University of Texas at Austin, 1967 *Appts & awards:* Professor of Psychology, CUNY Graduate School, Ford Foundation Fellowship in Women's Studies, 1973–4; Ford Foundation Member, 1973–4; Fellow, APA Divisions 8, 9, and 35, American Psychological Society; American Association for the Advancement of Sciences; President, Midwestern Psychological Association, 1981–2; Chair of Executive Committee, Society of Experimental Social Psychology, 1983–4; Fellow, Center for Advanced Study in the Behavioral Sciences, 1983–4; Center for Advanced Study in the Behavioral Sciences, Stanford, 1983–4, 1986–7; NIMH Training Grant Review Panel,

1983–7; APA Publication and Communications Board, 1983–8; AAAS Nominating Committee, Electorate J, 1984–6; Carolyn Wood Sherif Award, Division 35 of APA 1987; Heritage Research Award, Division 35 of APA 1993; Editorial Board, *Journal of Experimental Social Psychology*, 1975–8, *Journal of Personality*, 1975–83, *Journal of Applied Social Psychology*, 1975– , *Personality and Social Psychology Bulletin*, 1977–82, *Journal of Personality*, 1977–84, *Social Psychology*, 1979–81, *Sex Roles* 1980–3, *Contemporary Psychology*, 1985–

Principal publications

1973   When women are more deserving than men: Equity, attribution and perceived sex differences. *Journal of Personality and Social Psychology*, 28, 360–7 (with J. Taynor).

1974   Explanations of successful performance in sex-linked tasks: What is skill for the male is luck for the female. *Journal of Personality and Social Psychology*, 29, 80–5 (with T. Enswiller).

1976   *The Behavior of Women and Men.* Brooks Cole.

1976   Sex: A perspective on the attribution process. In J. Harvey, W.J. Ickes and R.F. Kidd (eds), *New Directions in Attribution Research*, vol. 1. Erlbaum.

1977   Sex differences. In T. Blass (ed.), *Personality Variables in Social Behavior.* Erlbaum.

1977   Attributing causes for one's own performance: The effects of sex, norms and outcome. *Journal of Research in Personality*, 11, 59–72 (with E. Farris).

1978   Skill vs. luck: Field and laboratory studies of male and female preferences. *Journal of Personality and Social Psychology*, 32, 629–36 (with L. White and E. Farris).

1983   *Women of Steel.* Praeger (with J.C. Ulman).

1984   *Social Psychology in the 80s*, 3rd edn. Brooks Cole (with L.S. Wrightsman).

1984   From individual differences to social categories: Analysis of a decade's research on gender. *American Psychologist*, 39, 105–16.

1984   The structure of gender stereotypes: Interrelationships among components and gender label. *Journal of Personality and Social Psychology*, 46, 991–1004 (with L.L. Lewis).

1985   Sex-roles in contemporary American society. In G. Lindzey and E. Aronson (eds), *Handbook of Social Psychology.* Random House (with J.T. Spence and R.L. Helmreich).

1985   Sex and gender. In M.R. Rosenzweig and L.W. Porter (eds), *Annual Review of Psychology.* Annual Reviews.

1987   Psychological constructions of masculinity and feminity. In J.M. Reinisch, L.A. Rosenblum and S.A. Sanders (eds), *Masculinity/Femininity: Basic Perspectives.* Oxford University Press.

1993   Reconstructing social identity. *Personality and Social Psychology Bulletin*, 19, 4–12.

In Press   Gender and social behavior. In G. Lindzey, D. Gilbert and S.T. Fiske (eds), *Handbook of Social Psychology*, 4th edn. Random House.

Further reading

Curtis, R. (ed.) (1991) *The Relational Self: Theoretical Convergences in Psychoanalysis and Social Psychology.* Guilford Press.

Denmark, F.L. and Paludi, M.A. (eds) (1993) *Psychology of Women: A Handbook of Issues and Theories.* Greenwood.

After predoctoral and a few years of postdoctoral work in the area of attitude change, Deaux shifted her interests to questions related to sex and gender. What could be construed as initial curiosity as to whether findings obtained with male samples could be replicated with females gave way to more systematic enquiry. Then as now, she tried to see how social psychological principles and theories could shed light on gender-related phenomena. In the early 1970s, for example, she used equity theory and attribution theory to predict judgements of male and female performance, and the explanations for those performances. Later she invoked principles of social cognition to explore the beliefs and stereotypes that are held about women and men. Other work explores the ramifications of expectancy confirmation sequences and self-presentation processes, with the aim of developing a truly social psychological understanding of gender-based interactions. Thus, her analysis of identity is in terms of social categories in which an individual claims membership, as well as the personal meaning associated with those categories. Deaux identified four key issues: first, a need for better understanding of the structure and interrelationships among multiple identities; second, the several functions that identities serve; third, the importance of context to the development and enactment of identities; and fourth, the need for longitudinal studies of identity change. In all of these endeavours, her contributions are bi-directional. She has demonstrated that not only can theories of social psychology aid in the analysis of gender-related questions, but the findings from these research efforts can contribute in significant ways to a more comprehensive social psychology. Finally, nearly two decades of undergraduate students have benefited from the highly regarded text *Social Psychology in the 80s* (now *Social Psychology in the 90s*, co-authored with L.S. Wrightsman *et al.*).

Decarie, Thérèse Gouin

Born: 1923, Montreal, Canada *Nat:* Canadian *Ints:* Developmental psychology, ethology, teaching psychology *Educ:* BA Université de Montreal, 1945; LPh Université de Montreal, 1947; PhD Université de Montreal, 1960 *Appts & awards:* Member, Societé Royale du Canada; Office, Ordre du Canada; Member, National Research Council of Canada, 1970–6; Professor, Université de Montreal; Hon. Dr, Université d'Ottawa, 1981; Member, Conseil de l'Université; Member, Comité Executif; Member, Assemblée Universitaire; Hon. President, Canadian Psychological Society, 1984–5

Principal publications

1953 Le développement psychologique de l'enfant, 2nd edn. Fides.

1962 L'intelligence et l'affectivité chez le jeune enfant. Préface de Jean Piaget. Delachaux and Niestle.

1966 Intelligence sensori-motrice et psychologie du premier age. *Psychologie et epistemologie genetiques*, 1, 229–305.

1968 A study of the mental and emotional development of the thalidomide child. In B.M. Foss (ed.), *Determinants of Infant Behaviour*. Methuen.

1971 The effects of three kinds of perceptual-social stimulation on the development of institutionalized infants. *Early Child Development and Care*, 1, 111–30 (with M. Brossard).

1972 La réaction du jeune enfant à la personne étrangere. Les Presses de l'Université de Montréal.

1974 Modifications du rythme cardiaque chez des enfants de 9–12 mois au cours de la rencontre avec la personne étrangere. *Canadian Journal of Behavioural Science*, 6, (2) (with M. Provost).

1976 Fear of strangers: A developmental milestone or an overstudied phenomenon? *Canadian Journal of Behavioural Science*, 8, 351–61 (with R. Solomon).

1977 An ethology-based catalogue of facial/vocal behaviors in infancy. *Animal Behaviour*, 25, 95–107 (with G. Young).

1979 Cognition and perception in the object concept. *Canadian Journal of Psychology*, 33, 396–407 (with K. Simoneau).

1980 Les origines de la socialisation dans l'enfant:

Explorations récentes en psychologie du developpement. Monographie sous la direction de Jean-François Saucier. Les Presses de l'Université de Montréal.

1985 L'objet et la personne, un probleme de repertoire et de mesure des comportements. In P.M. Baudonniere (ed.), *Etudier l'enfant de 0 a 3 ans: Les grands courants methodologiques actuels*. CNRS (with M. Ricard).

Further reading

Vyt, A. *et al.* (eds) (1994) *Early Child Development in the French Tradition: Contributions from Current Research*. Erlbaum.

As early as 1954 Decarie began to collaborate with **Piaget**, which led to a number of meetings and publications. The University of Montreal Piagetian Group was instrumental in introducing Piaget's theory to Canada and to many American universities. In 1964 Decarie led a research team to evaluate the mental and affective development of a group of thalidomide children. Her contribution in this field has modified some of our conceptions of handicapped children. She was the first psychologist to become a member of the Research Council of Canada and the first women psychologist in the Royal Society of Canada.

Deci, Edward L.

Born: 1942, Clifton Springs, New York, USA *Nat:* American *Ints:* Developmental, humanistic, industrial and organizational, personality and social, psychotherapy *Educ:* AB Hamilton College, New York, 1964; MBA University of Pennsylvania, 1967; MS Carnegie-Mellon University, 1968; PhD Carnegie-Mellon University, 1970 *Appts & awards:* Professor, Department of Psychology, University of Rochester, APA Fellow; Editor, *Journal of Personality and Social Psychology*; Editor, *Journal of Experimental Social Psychology*; Editor, *Journal of Applied Psychology*; Editor, *Journal of Educational Psychology*

Principal publications

1970 *Management and Motivation*. Penguin (ed. with V.H. Vroom).

1971 Effects of externally mediated rewards on intrinsic motivation. *Journal of Personality and Social Psychology*, 18, 105–15.

1972 Intrinsic motivation, extrinsic reinforcement and inequity. *Journal of Personality and Social Psychology*, 22, 113–20.

1975   Cognitive evaluation theory and some comments on the Calder, Staw Critique. *Journal of Personality and Social Psychology*, 31, 81–5 (with W. Cascio and J. Krusell).

1975   *Intrinsic Motivation*. Plenum.

1977   *Industrial and Organizational Psychology*. McGraw-Hill (with B.v.H. Gilmer).

1978   On the importance of self-determination for intrinsically motivated behavior. *Personality and Social Psychology Bulletin*, 4, 443–6 (with M. Zuckerman, J. Porac, D. Lathin and R. Smith).

1980   *The Psychology of Self-determination*. Lexington.

1981   Characteristics of the rewarder and intrinsic motivation of the rewardee. *Journal of Personality and Social Psychology*, 40, 1–10 (with J. Nezlek and L. Sheinman).

1981   When trying to win: Competition and intrinsic motivation. *Personality and Social Psychology Bulletin*, 7, 79–83 (with G. Betley, J. Kahle, L. Abrams and J. Porac).

1982   The effects of performance standards on teaching styles: The behavior of controlling teachers. *Journal of Educational Psychology*, 74, 852–9 (with N. Speigel, R. Ryan, R. Koestner and M. Kauffman).

1985   *Intrinsic Motivation and Self-determination in Human Behavior*. Plenum (with R.M. Ryan).

1991   Ego-involved persistence: When free-choice behavior is not intrinsically motivated. *Motivation and Emotion*, 15, 185–205 (with R.M. Ryan and R. Koestner).

1992   Beyond the intrinsic–extrinsic dichotomy: Self-determination in motivation and learning. Special issue: Perspectives on intrinsic motivation. *Motivation and Emotion*, 16, 165–85 (with C.S. Rigby, B.C. Patrick and R.M. Ryan).

1994   Facilitating internalization: The self-determination theory perspective. *Journal of Personality*, 62, 119–42 (with H. Eghrari, B.C. Patrick and D.R. Leone).

1994   Promoting self-determined education. *Scandinavian Journal of Educational Research*, 38, 3–14 (with R.M. Ryan).

Further reading

Koestner, R. and Zuckerman, M. (1994) Causality orientations, failure, and achievement. *Journal of Personality*, 62, 321–46.

Kristjansson, M. (1993) Deci and Ryan's cognitive evaluation theory of intrinsic motivation: A set of common sense theorems. *Scandinavian Journal of Psychology*, 34, 338–52.

Mawhinney, T.C. (1990) Decreasing intrinsic 'motivation' with extrinsic rewards: Easier said than done. Special issue: Promoting excellence through performance management. *Journal of Organizational Behavior Management*, 11, 175–91.

Valas, H. and Sovik, N. (1993) Variables affecting students' intrinsic motivation for school mathematics: Two empirical studies based on Deci and Ryan's theory on motivation. *Learning and Instruction*, 3, 281–98.

All of Deci's work has dealt with issues related to human motivation. He began by doing social psychological laboratory experiments exploring the effects of various initiating and regulatory events on intrinsic motivation, and made the first published study that demonstrated the undermining of intrinsic motivation by extrinsic rewards. To account for the results of those studies, he developed Cognitive Evaluation Theory, which has been frequently tested and used to integrate many published studies on the topic. Later his work expanded to include personality research on the motivational variables called causality orientations, and research on the development of both intrinsic and extrinsic motivation. With Richard Ryan he formulated a theory of self-determination in which the concepts of intrinsic motivation and extrinsic motivation are explicated and the innate psychological needs for competence, autonomy and relatedness are considered. This theory posits the existence of four types of motivation (intrinsic, self-determined extrinsic, non self-determined extrinsic, and amotivation) that are assumed to have a number of consequences for adaptation and well-being. Laboratory experiments and field studies indicate that (1) social contexts that facilitate satisfaction of three basic needs (by providing optimal challenge, informational feedback, interpersonal involvement, and autonomy support) promote both intrinsic motivation and self-determined forms of extrinsic motivation, and (2) intrinsic motivation and self-determined extrinsic motivation are positively associated with high-quality learning and personal adjustment. Applied to educational outcomes, this means that students who are intrinsically motivated for doing schoolwork are more likely to stay in school, to behave, to show conceptual understanding, and to be well-adjusted than other students. Supports for competence (e.g. optimal challenges and performance feedback) and for relatedness (e.g. parental involvement and peer acceptance) facilitate motivation. The degree to which teachers are autonomy supportive vs. controlling also affects student motivation and self-determination.

Delago, Jose Manuel Rodriguez

Born: 1915, Ronda, Malaga, Spain *Nat:* Spanish *Ints:* Experimental psychology, neuropsychology, psychopharmacology *Educ:* MD Madrid University, 1940; DSc Madrid University, 1942; MA Yale University, 1967 *Appts & awards:* Director, Centro de Estudios Neurobiologiocos, Madrid; Ramon y Cajal Prize, 1962; Guggenheim Fellow, 1963; Salmon Lecturer, NY Academy of Science, 1968; Gold Medal, American Psychiatric Association, 1971; Alfonso X El Sabio Medal, 1972; Gold Medal, International Society of Biological Psychiatry, 1974; Adolph Meyer Lecturer, American Psychiatric Association, 1979

Principal publications

1969 *Physical Control of the Mind: Toward a Psychocivilized Society*. Harper and Row.

1973 *Control Fisico de la Mente: Hacia una Sociedad Psicocivilizada*. Espasa-Calpe.

1977 *Behavioral Neurochemistry*. Spectrum (ed. with F. DeFeudis).

1977 Therapeutic programmed stimulation of the brain in man. In W. Sweet (ed.), *Neurosurgical Treatment in Psychiatry, Pain and Epilepsy*. University Park Press.

1981 Brain stimulation and neurochemical studies on the control of aggression. In P.F. Brain and D. Benton (eds), *The Biology of Aggression*. Sitjthoff and Noordhoff.

1982 Embryological changes induced by weak, extremely low frequency electromagnetic fields. *Journal of Anatomy*, 134, 533–51 (with J. Leal, J.L. Monteagudo and M. Garcia Gracia).

1983 Psychophysiology of freedom. *Political Psychology*, 4, 355–74.

Further reading

Grossman, S.P. (1967) *A Textbook of Physiological Psychology*. Wiley.

Myers, R.D. (ed.) (1971) *Methods in Psychology*, vol. 1. Academic Press.

In 1950, working at the Yale Medical School, Delago developed a technique for the implantation of intracerebral electrodes in cats and monkeys. The technique was adopted in laboratories around the world. He demonstrated in these animals that electrical stimulation of specific points within the brain evoked a wide variety of behavioural effects indistinguishable from spontaneous activities. Cats and monkeys were induced to yawn, lie down, sleep, eat, drink, stand up, turn around, walk, climb, hide, attack or stop motionless. Changes in respiration, heart rate, pupillary size and other autonomic functions could also be produced. These results were analysed with respect to stimulation parameters, fatigability, chronic excitation, spontaneous and evoked electrical activity, spatiotemporal characteristics of induced seizure discharges, etc. Other studies demonstrated that fearful behaviour, conditioning, trial-and-error learning, and instrumental responses could be induced by stimulation of specific areas of the brain. Later methods were developed to perfuse cerebral structures using permanently implanted double cannulas, which also had contacts for electrical studies. This 'chemitrode' technique was used in awake monkeys under restraint or completely free while forming colonies. In addition to simple motor responses, many types of socially significant behaviour were evoked including aggression, inhibition, sexual activity and social conditioning. Delago conducted a series of studies in which electrodes were implanted in the brains of human patients for diagnostic and therapeutic purposes. During tape-recorded interviews, brain stimulations produced effects traditionally related to the psyche, such as sensations, hallucinations, changes in mood or in sexual orientation, memories, increase in conversation, friendly behaviour, hostility, fear and pleasure. In recent years he has developed methods for non-invasive stimulation of the brain, using weak electromagnetic fields and very high-voltage pulses of microsecond duration. More generally, Delago has also investigated the psychological, educational and philosophical implications of physical, chemical and sensory methods which may influence brain functions. The aim of these studies was to establish neurobiological bases for the education of human beings with greater intelligence, personal freedom and happiness.

Dember, William N.

Born: 1928, Waterbury, Connecticut, USA *Nat:* American *Ints:* Experimental psychology, motivation and emotion, vision *Educ:* AB Yale College, 1950; MA University of Michigan, 1951; PhD University of Michigan, 1955 *Appts & awards:* Phi Beta Kappa, 1950; Sigma Xi, 1950; Assistant Professor of Psychology, Yale University, 1956–9; Visiting Lecturer in Psychology, Connecticut College, 1959; University of Cincinnati, Assistant Professor, 1959–62, Associate Professor and Director of Graduate Training, 1962–5, Assistant Dean, Graduate School of Arts and Sciences, 1965–7; Visiting

Associate Professor of Psychology, Indiana University, 1963; University of Cincinnati Chapter Annual Award for Distinguished Research, 1964; Professor of Psychology, 1965–, Head, Department of Psychology, 1968–76, 1979–81, Dean, McMicken College of Arts and Sciences, 1981–6; Eastern Psychological Association, Member of Council; Midwestern Psychological Association, Member of council, 1971–4, President, 1976; Graduate Fellow, University of Cincinnati, Chair, 1972–4; Professional Accomplishment Award, Engineering Society of Cincinnati, 1984; AAAS, Fellow, Secretary Section J, 1984–94; APA, Fellow; Honorary Member Golden Key, 1989; Distinguished Research Professor, University of Cincinnati, 1989; Society of Cosmetic Chemists Award, 1992; American Psychological Society, Fellow; Psychonomic Society, Member

Principal publications

1955 The relation between free choice alcohol consumption and susceptibility to audiogenic seizures. *Quarterly Journal of Studies on Alcohol*, 16, 86–95 (with A. Kristofferson).

1957 The relation of decision-time to stimulus similarity. *Journal of Experimental Psychology*, 53, 69–72.

1958 Stimulus alternation in peripherally-blinded rats. *Canadian Journal of Psychology*, 12, 219–21.

1958 Spontaneous alternation behavior. *Psychological Bulletin*, 55, 412–28 (with H. Fowler).

1960 *The Psychology of Perception*. Holt. (2nd edn, 1979, with J.S. Warm.)

1964 (ed.) *Visual Perception: The Nineteenth Century*. Wiley.

1965 The new look in motivation. *American Scientist*, 53, 409–27.

1967 Recovery of masked visual targets by inhibition of the masking stimulus. *Science*, 157, 1335–6 (with D.G. Purcell).

1970 *General Psychology: Modeling Behavior and Experience*. Prentice-Hall (with J.J. Jenkins; Italian trans., 1977).

1972 Backward enhancement? *Science*, 175, 93–5 (with M. Stefl).

1974 Perception. *Encyclopaedia Britannica*, 15th edn, 14, 38–45.

1974 Motivation and the cognitive revolution. *American Psychologist*, 29, 161–8.

1985 A history of perception. In G. Kimble and K. Schlesinger (eds), *Topics in the History of Psychology*, 1. Erlbaum (with M. Bagwell).

1989 *Spontaneous Alternation Behavior*. Springer-Verlag (ed. with C.L. Richman).

1991 Cognition, motivation, and emotion: Ideology revisited. In R.R. Hoffman and D.S. Palerma (eds), *Cognition and the Symbolic Processes*. Erlbaum.

Further reading

Bruce, V. and Green, P. (1990) *Visual Perception: Physiology, Psychology and Ecology*. Erlbaum.

William Dember has made significant contributions to the psychology of perception, especially in terms of emotionality. After completing his PhD in experimental psychology at the University of Michigan in 1955, he joined the Department of Psychology at Yale University for three years. From 1959, he has been associated with the University of Cincinnati in various faculty and administrative positions.

In addition to carrying out substantial research, Dember has been an effective communicator of psychology through his texts on perception and on general psychology. Both works highlight his clear writing and insightful syntheses of complicated issues. His text on *The Psychology of Perception* became a central feature of the undergraduate and graduate curricula of many institutions and introduced students to this area of psychology, which effectively launched the discipline in the nineteenth century. Dember effectively underscored this point through his 1964 work on vision as the issue that helped to define psychology as a discipline independent of physiology and philosophy in European universities, particularly within the intellectual climate of nineteenth-century German universities.

Dember has also made important contributions to research on spontaneous alternation behaviour in animals. In particular, he has examined such behaviour as a product of perceptual cues, including vision and olfaction. Moreover, he has called for research on various factors affecting this behaviour, including age, gender and species-specific factors, as well as the numerous neuroanatomical and neurochemical variables. His own work has underlined the importance of odour cues controlling this behaviour.

Dember holds a sweeping view of psychology that is both refreshing and stimulating. While perception in terms of its subjective properties occupies a central place in his purview of psychology, he has been able to focus on specific behavioural characteristics through well-designed and programmatic experimentation. His combination of a historical appreciation of psychology's past and his activity as a scientist emphasizes the relevance of his writing. Consistently, he has advocated a view of behaviour that accommodates not only the many organismic variables that impinge from the environment, but the essential fact that behaviour is both motivated and emotionally active.

JAMES F. BRENNAN

Denmark, Florence Harriet (Levion)

Born: 1932, Philadelphia, Pennsylvania, USA **Nat:** American **Ints:** History, personality and social, psychology of women, Society for the Psychological Study of Social Issues, teaching psychology **Educ:** AB University of Pennsylvania, 1952; AM University of Pennsylvania, 1954; PhD University of Pennsylvania, 1958 **Appts & awards:** President, NY State Psychological Association 1972–3, Eastern Psychological Association, 1985–6, APA, 1980–1; National President, NY Psi Chi, 1978–80; Vice President, NY Academy of Sciences, 1984– ; Hon. DHL, Massachusetts School of Professional Psychology, 1985; Fellow, APA Divisions 1, 2, 8, 9, 31, 35, 44; APA Award for Distinguished Education and Training Contributions, 1987; Hon DHL Cedar Crest College, 1988; APA Award for Distinguished Contribution to Psychology in the Public Interest, 1992; Hon. PsyD, Illinois School of Professional Psychology, 1995; Robert Scott Pace Professor and Chair, Department of Psychology, Pace University; Associate Editor, *International Journal of Group Tensions*, 1971–84, Editorial Board, *Sex Roles*, 1975– , *Psychology of Women Quarterly*, 1975–7, *Mind and Behavior*, 1980– , and several other leading journals

Principal publications

1975 *Dependent or Independent Variable?* Psychological Dimensions (with R. Unger).

1976 *Woman: Volume 1 (A Professional Research Annual)*. Psychological Dimensions.

1977 The psychology of women: An overview of an emerging field. *Personality and Social Psychology Bulletin*, 3, 356–67.

1977 Styles of leadership. *Psychology of Women Quarterly*, 2, 99–113.

1978 A second look at adolescence theories. *Sex Roles: A Journal of Research*, 4, 375–9 (with H.M. Goodfield).

1979 *The Psychology of Women: Future Directions in Research*. Psychological Dimensions (with J.A. Sherman).

1979 Affiliation, achievement and power. In J.

Shearman and F.L. Denmark (eds), *The Psychology of Women: Future Directions in Research*. Psychological Dimensions (with S.S. Tangri and S. McCandless).

1979 Women in psychology in the United States. In A.M. Bruscor and S.M. Pfafflin (eds), Expanding the role of women in the sciences. *Annals of the New York Academy of Sciences*, 323, 65–78.

1980 Psyche: From rocking the cradle to rocking the boat. *American Psychologist*, 35, 1057–65.

1983 Integrating the psychology of women into introductory psychology. In C.J. Scheirer and A.M. Rogers (eds), *The G. Stanley Hall Lecture Series*. Washington APA.

1984 Women's worlds: Ghetto, refuge or power base? Published as part of an edited collection for Praeger Publishing Co. In M. Safir, and N. Mednick (eds).

1992 The thirty-something woman: To career or not to career. In B.R. Wainrib (ed.), *Gender Issues Across the Life Cycle*. Springer-Verlag.

1992 Women in consulting: Three perspectives. *Consulting Psychology Journal Practice and Research*, 44, 1–13 (with J.S. Blanton, J.E. Adams and A.M. O'Roark).

1993 Women, leadership, and empowerment. *Psychology of Women Quarterly*, 17, 343–56.

Further reading

Denmark, F.L. and Paludi, M.A. (eds) (1993) *Psychology of Women: a Handbook of Issues and Theories*. Greenwood.

Florence Harriet Levion grew up in a large extended family. Her mother was a musician and her father an attorney. She attended Roxborough High School in Philadelphia, and entered the Women's College of the University of Pennsylvania in 1948 majoring in history. She married Stanley Denmark in 1953 and continued her graduate training at the University of Pennsylvania.

Florence Denmark received her AB from the University of Pennsylvania in 1952, the only person until that time in the history of that institution to graduate with honours in both history and psychology. In 1972, Denmark was appointed Executive Officer of the City University of New York Graduate School's Doctoral Program in Psychology, serving in the capacity for seven years, right up until her election as the fifth woman President of the APA. Denmark is known as a pioneer in the field of the psychology of women. Her work on leadership, authoritarian behaviour and discrimination against women was published at a time when there was little interest in these topics. She has long been in the vanguard of work in the field of the psychology of women and minority-group achievement, and as such has served as a mentor and a role model for many students in these areas. For example, as Director of a programme for high-risk students at Hunter College and as President of Division 35 of the APA, among many other affiliations, she found herself in a position to implement much of the knowledge and skill acquired over years of education and research. Denmark was the first person to serve as both the President of the APA and the National President of Psi Chi, the Honor Society in Psychology.

Dennett, Daniel Clement

Born: 1942, Boston, USA *Nat:* American *Ints:* Philosophical and theoretical psychology *Appts & awards:* University of California, Irvine, 1965–71; Tufts University, Medford, Massachusetts, 1971–85; Visiting Professor, Harvard University, 1973; Visiting Professor, University of Pittsburgh, 1975; John Locke Lecturer, Oxford University, 1983; Visiting Professor, Ecole Nationale Superieure Paris, 1985; Tufts University, Distinguished Professor of Arts and Sciences, Director of the Centre for Cognitive Studies, 1985–

Principal publications

1969   *Content and Consciousness.* Routledge and Kegan Paul.
1978   *Brainstorms: Philosophical Essays on Mind and Psychology.* Harvester.
1984   *Elbow Room: The Varieties of Free Will Worth Wanting.* Oxford University Press.
1987   *The Intentional Stance.* MIT Press.
1991   *Consciousness Explained.* Little, Brown.
1995   *Darwin's Dangerous Idea.* Allen Lane.

Further reading

Dahlbom, B. (1993) *Dennett and his Critics.* Blackwell.

Daniel Dennett was a student of Gilbert Ryle at Oxford in the 1960s. Like Ryle he is often described as a behaviourist but rejects the label. Instead of a label he offers a slogan, 'Once you have explained everything that happens you have explained everything.' ('Everything that happens' here includes everything that happens in the central nervous system.) His position is best understood in the light of his concept of 'heterophenomenology'. 'Phenomenology' is here used in its original (non-philosophical)

sense, meaning the sum-total of our knowledge about something – its origins, effects etc., 'Homophenomenology' would, if it was used, be more or less equivalent to 'phenomenology' in the technical, philosophical sense (the sum-total of knowledge possessed by one person). Dennett's heterophenomenology applies phenomenology in its original sense to persons (including oneself) as known by observation of their behaviour – once you have explained everything about them, and its origins, effects etc., you have explained all there is to explain. The only thing that could be left is what is not open to any kind of scientific explanation – in other words, mystery. Dennett distinguishes several heterophenomenological stances, a stance being a strategy that one might adopt in order to explain or predict something. Other persons may be regarded from a 'physical' stance (as physical objects having a certain weight, a certain value in the slave market, etc.) or from a 'design' stance (their susceptibility to perceptual illusions may be explained by the fact that they never, in the course of evolution, encountered situations in which liability to the illusions posed any threat to survival), or, more importantly, from an 'intentional' stance (they may be interacted with on a normal, person-to-person basis). The intentional stance requires, in Dennett's view, the assumption of rationality in them, since otherwise their behaviour cannot be explained or predicted.

Dennett maintains that from his view it follows that nothing that is even potentially explicable by science can be postulated to exist 'in the mind': no 'mental models', no 'language of thought', no 'mental logic'. Any evidence seeming to justify such a postulation can be explained better in terms of publicly observable events. He extends his view to biology generally and to evolution. Biology differs fundamentally from physics because it has to postulate function. Evolution cannot legitimately postulate purposes – even purposes set, in some sense, by the evolving organisms themselves. Though insisting on the primacy of the environment in explanation and prediction, Dennett does not regard social factors as specially significant in the differentiation of human mental capacity from that of lower animals.

Cognitive psychology has long since superseded behaviourism in the affections of most psychologists, and the only current challenge is from so-called 'discursive' psychology, which emphasizes solely the social factors that Dennett has rejected. It happens to be the case that we all have direct access to what may appear to be 'mental objects' (images, ideas, models, etc.). The temptation to incorporate these into psychological science has not been resisted, but Dennett makes a strong case for the view that they are scientifically worthless and should not be postulated as having any kind of 'real' existence. Much good might follow from regarding them as no more than hypotheses *pro tem* to guide the investigations of the neurophysiologist.

N.E. WETHERICK

Deutsch, Morton

Born: 1920, New York, USA *Nat:* American *Ints:* Conflict, distributive justice, personality and social, psychology and prevention of war, social issues *Educ:* BS City College of New York, 1939; MA University of Pennsylvania, 1940; PhD MIT, 1948 *Appts & awards:* E.L. Thorndike Professor of Psychology and Education, Teachers College, Columbia University, USA President, Society for the Psychological Society of Social Issues, 1960–1, APA Division 8, 1964–5; New York State Psychological Association 1965–6, Eastern Psychological Association, 1968–9, International Society of Political Psychology, 1981–2, Soci-Psychological Prize, AAAS, 1961; Hovland Memorial Award, Yale University, 1967; Kurt Lewin Memorial Award, Society for the Psychological Study of Social Issues, 1968; Gordon Allport Prize, Society for the Psychological Study of Social Issues, 1973; Nevitt Sanford Award, International Society of Political Psychology, 1984; Research Award, Society of Experimental Social Psychology, 1985; Editorial Board, *Political Psychology, Journal of Conflict Resolution, Contemporary Psychology, Contemporary Psychoanalysis, Journal of Personality and Social Psychology, Journal of Applied Social Psychology, Journal of Experimental Social Psychology, Journal of Peace Research*

Principal publications

1949 A theory of co-operation and competition. *Human Relations*, 2, 129–51.
1949 An experimental study of the effects of co-operation and competition. *Human Relations*, 2, 199–232.
1951 *Interracial Housing*. University of Minnesota Press (With M.E. Collins).
1951 *Research Methods in Social Relations*. Holt-Dryden (1958).

1954 Field theory in social psychology. In G. Lindzey (ed.), *Handbook of Social Psychology*. Addison-Wesley.
1955 A study of normative and social influence. *Journal of Abnormal and Social Psychology*, 51, 629–36 (with H.B. Gerrard).
1958 Trust and suspicion. *Journal of Conflict Resolution*, 2, 265–79.
1962 *Preventing World War III*. Simon and Schuster (with Q. Wright and W.M. Evan).
1965 *Theories in Social Psychology*. Basic Books (with R.M. Krauss).
1969 Conflicts: Productive and destructive. *Journal of Social Issues*, 25, 7–41.
1973 *The Resolution of Conflict*. Yale University Press.
1975 Equity, equality and need: What determines which value will be used as the basis of distributive justice? *Journal of Social Issues*, 31, 137–49.
1980 Fifty years of conflict. In L. Festinger (ed.), *Retrospections on Social Psychology*. Oxford University Press.
1982 Interdependence and psychological orientation. In V. Denlega and J.L. Grzelak (eds), *Co-operation and Helping Behavior: Theories and Research*. Academic Press.
1983 Preventing World War III: A psychological perspective. *Political Psychology*, 3, 3–31.
1985 *Distributive Justice*. Yale University Press.

Further reading

Bunker, B.B. and Rubin, J.Z. (1995) *Conflict, Cooperation, and Justice: Essays Inspired by the Work of Morton Deutsch*. Jossey-Bass.

Deutsch's principle contributions have been in the interrelated areas of co-operation, competition, conflict and bargaining, and distributive justice. His 1948 dissertation was an investigation of the effects of co-operation and competition upon groups. It analysed the psychological processes involved in these relations as well as their effects upon performance, member interrelations and self-attitudes. The research was done with classroom groups, which were graded on a co-operative or competitive basis. Many others have followed up with studies of co-operative learning, with the consequence that a major change has occurred in many classrooms. Next, with his students, he studied (under various headings) what determines whether a mixed-motive relationship will become co-operative or competitive, e.g. trust and suspicion, bargaining and negotiation, and conflict resolution. Much of the research employed experimental 'games', created to induce the conditions they wished to study. Along with others, they helped to create a methodology of 'gaming'. Their research also contributed to the basic understanding of what determines whether a conflict will take a constructive or destructive course. They discovered that the typical effects of a co-operative process will induce a co-operative process: similarly for a competitive process.

Further, they found that a co-operative process leads to constructive conflict resolution while a competitive process leads to destructive conflict. This knowledge has been useful to people concerned with the practical; management of various sorts of conflict: marital, labour-management, intergroup and international. The results of the research on mixed-motive situations were generalized into 'Deutsch's crude law of social relations': the typical effects of a given social relation tend to induce that social relation. This crude law was employed to develop a framework for conducting research on distributive justice. This research indicates that each distributive principle – for example, 'equity' or 'equality' – has distinctive psychological orientations associated with it: once induced, these also produce a preference for the related principle.

Dewey, John

Born: 1859, Burlington, Vermont USA **Died:** 1952, New York, USA **Nat:** American **Ints:** Educational psychology, philosophical and theoretical psychology, school psychology **Educ:** BA University of Vermont, 1879; PhD (Philosophy) Johns Hopkins University, 1884 **Appts & awards:** High School Teacher, 1879–82; Fellow, Johns Hopkins University, 1883; University of Michigan Instructor, 1884–8, Professor of Philosophy, 1889–94; Professor of Philosophy, University of Chicago, 1894–1904; President, APA, 1899–1900; President, American Philosophical Society, 1905–06; Hon. LLD, University of Wisconsin, 1904, University of Vermont, 1910; Professor of Philosophy, Columbia University, 1905–1939; Hon. Doctorate, University of Paris, 1930

Principal publications

1886 Psychology and philosophical method. *Mind*, 11, 1–19.
1887 *Psychology*. Harper and Brothers.
1894 *The Study of Ethics: A Syllabus*. Register, Inland Press.

1896 The reflex arc concept in psychology. *Psychological Review*, 3, 357–70.
1899 *The School and Society*. University of Chicago Press.
1900 Some stages of logical thought. *Philosophical Review*, 9, 465–89.
1900 Psychology and social practice. *Psychological Review*, 7, 105–24.
1906 Reality as experience. *Journal of Philosophy*, 3, 253–7.
1910 *How We Think*. D.C. Heath.
1920 *The Influence of Darwin on Philosophy*. Holt.
1922 *Human Nature and Conduct*. Holt.
1922 *Reconstruction in Philosophy*. Holt.
1925 *Experience and Nature*. Open Court.
1938 *Logic – The Theory of Enquiry*. Holt.

Further reading

Marcell, D.W. (1974) *Progress and Pragmatism*. Greenwood Press.
Schilpp, P.A. (1951) *The Philosophy of John Dewey*, 2nd edn. Tudor.

John Dewey grew up in Burlington, Vermont, the son of a tobacconist. He did not initially study philosophy but became interested in the subject while working as a school teacher. Philosophy was not at that time sharply distinguished from psychology, and he published a textbook in the latter subject in 1887, but his interests shifted in the direction of the application of philosophy to public affairs – in his own words, towards 'science in the cause of social welfare'. He taught mainly philosophy at Michigan, Chicago (where he was head of a combined department of philosophy, psychology and education) and Columbia, retiring as professor emeritus in 1939 at the age of 80. While at Chicago, he and his wife had opened an experimental primary school, and it was a disagreement with the University Principal over the conduct of the school that led to his move to Columbia.

His (1896) article in the *Psychological Review* opposed the mechanistic interpretation of the terms 'stimulus' and 'response', which, in his own words, 'leaves us with a disjointed psychology'. (This was twenty years before the advent of **Watson**ian behaviourism.) Dewey wished to emphasize that stimulus and response ought rightly to be regarded as the two ends of a functional relationship, operating as part of the process of adjustment of the organism to its environment. Education was (ought to be) a process in which the child learned how to solve problems (as distinct from learning by rote).

Dewey defined philosophy as 'the general theory of education' and developed a psychology of thinking and a formal logic out of this initial insight.

He was continuously involved in public affairs at a local, national and international level, always in opposition to upholders of left- and right-wing political views who believed that they had *a priori* valid policies for social betterment that ought to be implemented. He was a founder of the New School of Social Research in New York, which, in the 1930s offered a home to many refugee scholars from Europe. In 1937 he chaired a commission which exonerated Trotsky from Stalin's charges of plotting the downfall of the Soviet Union, and he actively opposed the refusal of the US authorities to admit Bertrand Russell to take up a post at the City University of New York. When, in 1930, he was awarded an honorary doctorate at the University of Paris, he was aptly described in the citation as 'the most profound and complete expression of the American genius'.

The best introduction to Dewey's thought is his *Reconstruction in Philosophy* – lectures delivered in Tokyo in 1919 and published in 1922. When the book was reissued in 1948 he provided a new introduction, which reaffirmed the ideals he had striven for throughout his life, the need to 'carry over into any enquiry into human and moral subjects the kind of method (the method of observation, theory as hypotheses, and experimental test) by which understanding of physical nature has been brought to its present pitch'. Purveyors of *a priori* certainty in human and moral subjects are not noticeably less active now than they were in Dewey's time, but his ideal was none the less a noble one. His influence has been felt mainly in the field of education. Lesser minds have interpreted his emphasis on problem solving as a need to require every child to rebuild the whole edifice of human knowledge from scratch, which was far from Dewey's intention. His theory was, however, a valuable corrective in its time, even though the pendulum now appears to be swinging back.

N.E. WETHERICK

Dohrenwend, Bruce Philip

Born: 1927, New York, USA **Nat:** American **Ints:** Community psychology, health psychology, psychological study of social issues **Educ:** BA Columbia College, 1950; MA Columbia University, 1951; PhD Cornell University, 1955

Appts & awards: Columbia University, Professor of Social Science, 1970– , Professor of Public Health, 1973– , Foundations' Fund for Research in Psychiatry, 1976– ; New York NIMH Research Scientist Award, 1971–6, 1976–81, 1981–6; APA Division 27 Distinguished Contributions Award (with B.S. Dohrenwend), 1980; APHA Rema Lapouse Mental Health Epidemiology Award (with B.S. Dohrenwend), 1981; AAAS Prize for Behavioral Science Research, 1990; Fellow, APA, AAS, APHA; President, APHA, 1993–4; Society for the Study of Social Problems (Psychiatric Sociology Division) Distinguished Contributions Award, 1994; American Psychopathology Association Hamilton Medal, 1994; Editorial Board, *American Journal of Community Psychology*, 1984–9; *Journal of Traumatic Stress*, 1987–92; Advisory Board, *Journal of Nervous and Mental Disease*, 1985– ; Consulting Editor, *Journal of Abnormal Psychology*, 1987– ; Advisory Editor, *Psychiatry*, 1993–7

Principal publications

1961 The social psychological nature of stress: A framework for causal inquiry. *Journal of Abnormal and Social Psychology*, 62, 294–302.

1965 The problem of validity in field studies of psychological disorder. *Journal of Abnormal Psychology*, 70, 52–69 (with B.S. Dohrenwend).

1966 Social status and psychological disorder: An issue of substance and an issue of method. *American Sociological Review*, 31, 14–35 (with B.S. Dohrenwend).

1969 *Social Status and Psychological Disorder: A Causal Inquiry*. Wiley (with B.S. Dohrenwend).

1980 *Stressful Life Events: Their Nature and Effects*. Wiley (ed. with B.S. Dohrenwend).

1980 Measures of nonspecific psychological distress and other dimensions of psychopathology in the general population. Archives of General Psychiatry,37, 1229–36 (with P.E. Shrout, G. Ergi and F.S. Mendelsohn).

1981 Socioenvironmental factors, stress and psychopathology – Part 1: Quasi-experimental evidence on the social causation–social selection issue posed by class differences. *American Journal of Community Psychology*, 9, 129–46 (with B.S. Dohrenwend).

1981 Socioenvironmental factors, stress and psychopathology – Part 2: Hypotheses about stress processes linking social class to various types of psychopathology. *American Journal of Community Psychology*, 9, 146–59 (with B.S. Dohrenwend).

1983 *Stressful Life Events and their Contexts*. Neale

Watson Academic/Rutgers University Press (ed. with B.S. Dohrenwend).

1990 Measuring life events: The problem of variability within event categories. Special issue: II–IV. Advances in measuring life stress. *Stress Medicine*, 6, 179–87 (with B.G. Link, R. Kern, P.E. Shrout, S. Schwartz, G. Naveh, B.G. Link, A.E. Skodol and A. Stuvee).

1990 Socioeconomic status (SES) and psychiatric disorders: Are the issues still compelling? *Social Psychiatry and Psychiatric Epidemiology*, 25, 41–7.

1992 Socioeconomic status and psychiatric disorders: The causation–selection issue. *Science*, 255, 946–52 (with I. Levtav, P.E. Shrout, S. Schwarz *et al.*)

1993 An epidemiological study of mental disorders in a 10-year cohort of young adults in Israel. *Psychological Medicine*, 23, 691–707 (with I. Levav, R. Kohn, P.E. Shrout *et al.*).

1993 Socioeconomic status and depression: The role of occupations involving direction, control, and planning. *American Journal of Sociology*, 98, 1351–87 (with B.G. Link and M.C. Lennon).

1994 Psychology, psychologists, and psychiatric epidemiology. *Acta Psychiatrica Scandinavica Supplementum*, 90, 13–20.

Further reading

Jablensky, A. (1994) Discussion of B. P. Dohrenwend: 'Psychology, psychologists, and psychiatric epidemiology'. *Acta Psychiatrica Scandinavica Supplementum*, 90, 23–4.

McQuaid, J.R. *et al.* (1992) Toward the standardization of life stress assessment: Definitional discrepancies and inconsistencies in methods. *Stress Medicine*, 8, 47–56.

Rehm, J., Witzke, W., Fichter, M. *et al.* (1988) Was messen psychiatrische Skalen? Ein empirischer Vergleich. (What do psychiatric scales measure? An empirical comparison.) *Diagnostica*, 34, 227–43.

Starting with journal publications in 1965 and 1966, Bruce Dohrenwend, his wife Barbara Dohrenwend and their colleagues presented analyses of epidemiological studies of the true prevalence of psychiatric disorders conducted since the turn of the century. These analyses focused on what might be considered the first (pre-World War II) and second generation (post-World War II) of epidemiological studies that attempted to estimate not only treated but also untreated cases of psychiatric disorders in community populations in various parts of the world; a third generation, using more rigorous methods, commenced during the mid-1980s and continues. Dohrenwend is associated with the measures of stressful life events that bear his name, but has been principally concerned with evaluating the proposition that socioenvironmental factors, especially environmentally induced stress, are important in causing various types of psychiatric disorder and distress. He has focused on so-called 'functional disorders' that have been shown by epidemiological studies to be inversely related to social class and/or to vary with gender. These include schizophrenia, major depression and non-specific distress, which he prefers to describe as 'demoralization'. His epidemiological investigations suggest that social selection may be more important for schizophrenia, and that social causation may be more important for depression in women and for antisocial personality and substance-use disorders in men. He put forward a social causation explanation for the association between socioeconomic status (SES) and depression/distress. The model links SES, occupational direction, control and planning, personality factors and depression/distress in a causal sequence. Empirical studies from a variety of sources support the social causation model and warrant further research on the links between occupational conditions and mental disorder.

Dollard, John

Born: 1900, Menasha, Wisconsin, USA **Died:** 1980, Yale, Connecticut, USA **Nat:** American **Ints:** Experimental analysis of behaviour, military psychology, personality and social psychology, psychoanalysis, psychotherapy **Educ:** AB University of Wisconsin, 1922; PhD University of Chicago, 1931; training in psychoanalysis, Berlin, 1931–2 **Appts & awards:** Researcher, Institute of Human Relations, Yale University, 1932; Professor of Psychology, Yale University, 1952.

Principal publications

1935 *Criteria for the Life History.* Yale University Press.

1938 Hostility and fear in social life. *Social Forces*, 17, 15–29.

1939 *Frustration and Aggression.* Yale University Press (with J.W. Doob, N.E. Miller, O.H. Mowrer and R.R. Sears).

1939 Culture, society, impulse and socialization. *American Journal of Sociology*, 45, 50–63.

1941 *Social Learning and Imitation.* Yale University Press (with N.E. Miller).

1943   *Fear in Battle*. Yale University Press.
1949   'Do we have a science of child rearing?. In
    *Anniversary Papers of the Community Service
    Society: The Family in a Democratic Society.*
    Columbia University Press.
1949   Exploration on morale factors among combat
    air crew men – memorandum to research branch,
    information and education division. *Psychological
    Service Center Journal*, 1, 79–89.
1950   *Personality and Psychotherapy: An Analysis
    in Terms of Learning, Thinking and Culture.*
    McGraw-Hill (with N.E. Miller).
1953   *Steps in Psychotherapy*. Macmillan (with F.
    Auld and A. White).

Further reading

Berkowitz, L. (1989) The frustration–aggression
    hypothesis: An examination and reformulation.
    Psychological Bulletin, 106, 59–73.

John Dollard was above all a pioneer in the
interdisciplinary integration of the social and
behavioural sciences. Originally working as a
sociologist, he is perhaps best known within the
psychological community as a member of the
distinguished group of young researchers at
Yale University in the 1930s who, inspired
initially by **Hull**, sought to combine learning
theory and psychoanalysis. The group's first
major publication, *Frustration and Aggression*,
has become a classic which is still widely cited
in introductory texts. It outlined a view, now
referred to as the frustration–aggression
hypothesis, which formed the basis for later
developments such as Len **Berkowitz**'s *Aggression: A Social Psychological Analysis* (1962)
and the animal research on frustration and
aggression in the 1960s and 1970s.

Dollard wrote or co-authored ten books in all,
on subjects ranging from the study of life
history to fear in battle to the social position of
southern blacks in the 1930s. The book which
Dollard himself regarded as his best was *Personality and Psychotherapy* (co-authored with
Neal **Miller**). In this, they sought to take central
issues in **Freud**ian theory, such as dependency,
aggression, identification and conscience
formation, and to reformulate developmental
explanations of these in terms of learning theory
principles. Dollard and Miller were particularly
interested in constructing a psychotherapy based
on social learning theory, a subject which Dollard explored more in the 1950s. A decade
earlier, in *Social Learning and Imitation*, they
had first introduced the concept of imitation into
social learning accounts, thus providing the

groundwork for the social learning theory of the
1960s. Neal Miller summed up Dollard's
contribution thus: 'If trying to bring together
contributions from sociology, anthropology,
psychology, and psychotherapy no longer seems
so novel, it is because Dollard and other pioneers had the courage and tenacity to break
through traditional barriers.'

JOHN ARCHER

Donaldson, Margaret Caldwell

Born: 1926, Paisley, Scotland ***Nat:*** British
Ints: Developmental, educational, general,
philosophical and theoretical ***Educ:*** MEd
University of Edinburgh, 1947; D University of
Edinburgh, 1953 ***Appts & awards:*** Professor of
Developmental Psychology (Emeritus), Univer-
sity of Edinburgh; David H. Russell Award for
distinguished research in the teaching of
English, 1956; Donald H. Russell Award
(USA), 1983. Hon. Life Member, United King-
dom Reading Association, 1991; Hon. Fellow,
BPS, 1993; Editorial Boards, *Journal of Child
Language*, 1974–84, *Cognition*, 1978–80,
Educational Psychology, 1981;

Principal publications

1963   *A Study of Children's Thinking*. Tavistock.
1968   Less is more: A study of language
    comprehension in young children. *British
    Journal of Psychology*, 59, 461–71 (with
    G. Balfour).
1970   Developmental aspects of performance with
    negatives. In G.B. Flores D'Arcais and W.J.M.
    Levelt (eds), *Advances in Psycholinguistics*. North-
    Holland.
1971   Preconditions of inference. In J.K. Cole (ed.),
    Nebraska Symposium on Motivation. Nebraska
    University Press.
1974   Sentences and situations: Children's
    judgements of match and mismatch. In F. Bresson
    (ed.), *Problems Actuels en Psycholinguistique*.
    Centre National de la Recherche Scientifique (with
    P. Lloyd).
1974   Some clues to the nature of semantic
    development. *Journal of Child Language*, 1,
    185–94 (with J. McGarrigle).
1976   Constraints on classificatory skills in young
    children. *British Journal of Psychology*, 67,
    89–100 (with R. Campbell and B. Young).
1977   L'erreur et la prise de conscience de l'erreur.
    Bulletin de Psychologie, 30, 181–6.
1979   *Children's Minds*. Fontana, 1978. (American
    edn, W.W. Norton, 1979, and numerous
    translations.)

1982   Conservation: What is the question? *British Journal of Psychology*, 73, 199–207.
1983   *Early Childhood Development and Education*. Blackwell (with R. Grieve and C. Pratt). (American edn, Guilford Press).
1984   Speech and writing and modes of learning. In H. Goelman, A. Oberg and F. Smith (eds), *Awakening to Literacy*. Heinman Educational.
1992   *Human Minds: An Exploration*. Penguin. (American edn, 1993, Viking Penguin).

Further reading

Flavell, J. (1993) *Cognitive Development*. Prentice-Hall.
Grieve, R. and Hughes, M. (eds) (1990) *Understanding Children: Essays in Honour of Margaret Donaldson*. Basil Blackwell.

When, as a student, Donaldson learned about the construction of intelligence tests, she was troubled by the lack of theory to guide the choice of test items. This led to an interest in the mental processes by which children tackle such problems and to a study of the nature of the errors made, which proved to be a pathway to a more general concern with the nature and course of cognitive development. A term spent in Geneva made her, for a time, an enthusiastic **Piaget**ian. Later, however, work undertaken in Edinburgh caused her to question some of Piaget's central claims, especially those concerning the nature of the shift from pre-operational to concrete operational thinking. Around this time she became interested in language, and particularly in the question of how context influences children's interpretations of the words they hear. By 'context' she refers to both the physical and interpersonal setting. She argues that it is essential to take account of contextual effects in the widest sense when we base theories of cognitive development on children's answers to the questions we put to them. This conviction led her to an interest in the difference between spoken language and the decontextualized written word; and hence to a concern with the effects of literacy on the developing mind. She came to believe that the nature of the intellectual demands made by 'Western' schooling has not been widely understood and that this has significant practical consequences.

Donchin, Emanuel

Born: 1935, Tel Aviv, Israel ***Nat:*** Israeli ***Ints:*** (in order of significance) Psychophysiology, experimental psychology (learning, memory and cognition), experimental psychology (human perception and performance), human factors, multivariate analysis ***Appts & awards:*** University Illinois, Professor of Psychology, 1972– , Head of the Department of Psychology, 1980–94; President, Society for Psychophysiological Research, 1980; SPR Award for Distinguished Contributions to Psychophysiology, 1994

Principal publications

1969   *Average Evoked Potentials: Methods, Results and Evaluations (NASA SP-191)*. US Government Printing Office (with D.B Lindsley).
1977   Augmenting mental chronometry: The P300 as a measure of stimulus evaluation time. *Science*, 197, 792–5 (with M. Kutas and G. McCarthy).
1978   Cognitive psychophysiology: The endogenous components of the ERP. In E. Callaway, P. Tueting, and S.H. Koslow (eds), *Event-related Brain Potentials in Man*. Academic Press (with W. Ritter and W.C. McCallum).
1978   Multivariate analysis of event-related potential data: A tutorial review. In D. Otto (ed.), *Multidisciplinary Perspectives in Event-related Brain Potential Research*. US Government Printing Office (with E.F Heffley).
1979   Event-related brain potentials: A tool in the study of human information processing. In H. Begleiter (ed.), *Evoked Brain Potentials and Behavior*. Plenum.
1980   Preparation to respond as manifested by movement-related potentials. *Brain Research*, 202, 95–115 (with M. Kutas).
1981   A metric for thought: A comparison of P300 latency and reaction time. *Science*, 211, 77–80 (with G. McCarthy).
1981   Surprise! ... Surprise? *Psychophysiology*, 18, 493–513.
1983   Performance of concurrent tasks: A psychophysiological analysis of the reciprocity of information-processing resources. *Science*, 221, 1080–1082 (with C. Wickens, A. Kramer, and L. Vanasse).
1988   Is the P300 component a manifestation of context updating? *Behavioral and Brain Sciences* 11, 357–74 (with M.G.H. Coles).
1991   The truth will out: Interrogative polygraphy ('lie detection') with event-related potentials. *Psychophysiology*, 28, 531–47 (with L.A Farwell).

Further reading

Coles, M.G.H. (1995) SPR award, 1994, for distinguished contributions to psychophysiology: Emanuel Donchin. *Psychophysiology*, 32, 101–7.

Näätänen, R. (1969) Anticipation of relevant stimuli and evoked potentials: A reply to Donchin and Cohen. *Perceptual and Motor Skills*, 29, 233–4.

Ragot, R. and Renault, B. (1985) P300 and S-R compatibility: A reply to Magliero *et al*. *Psychophysiology*, 22, 349–52.

Verleger, R. (1988) Event-related potentials and cognition: A critique of the context updating hypothesis and an alternative interpretation of P3. *Behavioral and Brain Sciences*, 11, 343–56.

Emanuel Donchin studied psychology and statistics in Jerusalem, 1957–61. In 1961, he went to the USA, first as a doctoral student in Los Angeles, later at Stanford, and since 1968 at the University of Illinois. During his doctoral study, he became acquainted with the approach of measuring event-related potentials (ERPs) of the EEG, and it is to this area of research that he devoted his scientific life. He stressed psychological methodology in ERP research, including reliance on experimentally induced variation and the use of multivariate techniques for data analysis. His own research focused on the P300 component of the ERP. His 'context updating' hypothesis says that P300 is a manifestation of the brain's 'strategical' response to a stimulus, i.e. P300 reflects not a process needed for the present response to a stimulus but one needed by the subject for integrating the recently perceived stimulus into a schema of the entire situation. Second, he promoted the use of the peak latency of P300 as a measure of mental chronometry, by arguing that P300 latency is relatively insensitive to response-related processes, and thus might provide a suitable measure for the stimulus-related portion of total response time. Besides the P300, his work on movement-related potentials anticipated the use of the 'lateralized readiness potential' (for example, as reflected in the work of M. **Coles**) as a measure of response tendencies. He constantly looked for the use of ERP measures in applied settings, including ergonomy and lie detection.

Donchin is one of the founders of research in ERPs, and he is probably the one that did and accomplished the most for its integration with psychology. His impact on the field can hardly be overestimated. Many ERP researchers, not only from the US, spent some time in his lab. He likes the scientific dispute, as may be easily understood from the above selection of further readings.

His 'context updating' is still the dominant hypothesis on P300. It is presumably more adequate than believed by his critics, but due to a reason that runs somewhat counter to Donchin's original intentions. Whereas he tried to keep considerations about the ERPs' physiological substrates out of the focus of interest, the main argument in favor of 'context updating' is physiological: no alternative hypothesis can so easily accommodate the fact that the dominant intracranial activity coincident with the scalp-P300 occurs in the hippocampus.

ROLF VERLEGER

Dreikurs, Rudolf

Born: 1897, Vienna, Austria **Died:** 1972, Chicago, USA **Nat:** Austrian **Ints:** Clinical psychology, counselling psychology, educational psychology, psychotherapy, family psychology **Educ:** MD University of Vienna, 1923 **Appts & awards:** Internship, Vienna General Hospital, 1924; Residency in Psychiatry and Neurology, University of Vienna Neurological Institute and the Psychiatry Clinic, 1928; Founder, Society of Individual Psychology of Rio de Janeiro, 1937; Professor of Psychiatry, Chicago Medical School 1942–72; Vice President, American Humanist Association, 1944–51; Alfred Adler Institute of Chicago, Founder, 1950, President, 1950–72; American Psychological Society, Founder Member, 1952, President, 1955–6; President, American Society of Group Psychotherapy and Psychodrama, 1954; International Association of Individual Psychology, Founder Member, 1954, Vice President, 1957–60; Vice President, American Academy of Psychotherapy, 1959; Founding Editor, *Individual Psychology Newsletter*, 1940–1, *Individual Psychology Bulletin*, 1941–51; Editor, *American Journal of Individual Psychology*, 1952–6; Editorial Board, *Journal of Individual Psychology Editorial*, 1957–72

Principal publications

1933 *Fundamentals of Adlerian Psychology*. Hirzel. (Kegan Paul, 1935; Alfred Adler Institute of Chicago, 1950, 1955; revised edn, in German, Klett 1969).

1946 *The Challenge of Marriage*. Duell Sloan and Pearce.

1947 The four goals of the maladjusted child. *Nervous Child*, 6, 321–8.

1950 Guilt feelings as an excuse. *Individual Psychology Bulletin*, 8, 12–21.

1950 Techniques and dynamics of multiple psychotherapy. *Psychiatric Quarterly*, 24, 788–99.

1951 Family group therapy in the Chicago
Community Child Guidance Centers. *Mental
Hygiene*, 35, 291–301.
1954 The psychological interview in medicine.
American Journal of Individual Psychology, 10,
99–122.
1956 The contribution of psychotherapy to
psychiatry. *Group Psychotherapy*, 9, 115–25.
1957 *Psychology in the Classroom*. Harper. 1968.
1957 Psychotherapy as correction of faulty social
values. *Journal of Individual Psychology*, 13,
150–8.
1959 The impact of the group for music therapy and
music education. *Music Therapy*, 9, 93–106.
1960 Are psychological schools of thought outdated?
Journal of Individual Psychology, 16, 3–10.
1964 *Children: The Challenge*. Hawthorne (with V.
Soltz).
1971 *Social Equality: The Challenge of Today*.
Regency. (reprinted 1984, Alfred Adler Institute of
Chicago.)
1972 Technology of conflict resolution. *Journal of
Individual Psychology*, 28, 203–6.
1972 'Equality: The life-style of tomorrow'.
Futurist, 6, 153–5. (Published posthumously.)

Further reading

MacKenzie, K.R. (ed.) (1992) *Classics in Group
Psychotherapy*. Guilford.
Mozdzierz, G.J. (1990) Adlerian psychology and the
challenge of hypnosis. *Individual Psychology
Journal of Adlerian Theory, Research and Practice*,
46, 544–57.

Dreikurs's writing centred on therapy, education, philosophy, child development and
social processes. As a major figure in **Adler**ian
circles, and as leader following the death of
Alfred Adler in 1937, Dreikurs founded the
Adlerian Journal in the USA. He was involved
in the setting up of the American and International Societies of Adlerian Psychology in the
Chicago area. He taught and trained many
professionals in clinical practice and counselling
techniques, whether involved in medicine,
education or the correction system.

He is probably best known for his formulation
of 'four goals of misbehaviour' and 'four steps
of conflict resolution'. He introduced psychodrama and group therapy into his private
psychiatric practice in the early stages of the
development of such therapies. He applied the
social-teleological and cognitive-dynamic ideas
of Adler to music therapy, and he encouraged
his wife and colleague Sadie Dreikurs to apply
them to art therapy.

His later years were devoted increasingly to
applying his concepts of social equality and
democratic living to all social settings. He
sought to extend the concepts he had successfully applied in his clinical practice into the
field of business and large organizations. He
was convinced that common principles and
techniques of conflict resolution and human
relationships applied to all these areas. His
professional life was taken up with spreading the ideas of Adlerian psychology, and to
that end he was involved in journals and
bulletins including the *Journal of Individual
Psychology*.

H. HANKS

Drenth, Pieter Johan Diederik

Born: 1935, Appelscha, Friesland, The Netherlands **Nat:** Dutch **Ints:** Educational psychology,
evaluation and measurement, industrial and
organizational psychology, personality and
social psychology **Educ:** Candidate Psychology
Free University, 1955; Doctoral Examination
Psychology Free University, 1958; PhD Free
University, 1960 **Appts & awards:** Chairman,
Test Research Committee, Netherlands Institute
of Psychologists, 1966–69, Human Factors
Panel, NATO Science Committee, 1974–5,
1982–3, Supervisory Board, Center for Edu-
cational Research in Developing Countries, Den
Haag, 1976–84, Annual Conference, Dutch
Psychological Association, 1982; Royal Nether-
lands Academy of Arts and Science, 1980– ;
Hon. Dr, State University of Ghent, 1981;
President, IAAP, Division Organizational
Psychology, 1982– ; Free University, Amster-
dam, Professor of Work and Organizational
Psychology, Rector Magnificus (Vice Chancel-
lor), 1983–7; President, Royal Netherlands
Academy of Arts and Sciences, Amsterdam,
1990–; Editorial Board, *Journal of Applied
Psychology*, 1969–83, *Didakometrisch en
Psychometrisch Onderzoek van het Nederlands
Tijdschrift voor Psychologie*, 1968–75,
Tijdschrft voor Onderwijsresearch, 1975–6,
International Journal of Intercultural Relations,
1976– ; Consulting Editor, *International
Review of Applied Psychology*, 1975– ,
Journal of Cross-Cultural Psychology,
1975–84, *Journal of Management*, 1983– ;
International Consulting Editor, *Journal of
Occupational Psychology*, 1983– ; Co-editor,
Bedrijfskundig Lexicon, sectie Bedrijfspy-
chologie, 1968–83, *Onderwijfskundig Lexicon*
1975–

Principal publications

1967 *De Psychologische Test.* Van Loghum Slaterus.

1970 *Bedrijfspsychologie, Onderzoek en Evaluatie.* Kluwer.

1971 Theory and methods of selection. In P.B. Warr (ed.), *Psychology at Work.* Penguin.

1972 *Mental Tests and Cultural Adaptation* (ed. with L.J. Cronbach).

1974 The Works' Council in The Netherlands: An experiment in participation. In *Participation and Self-management, vol. 5: Social System and Participation.* E. Pusic *et al.*

1977 Prediction of school performance: School grades or psychological tests? *Journal of Cross-cultural Psychology* 8, 49–68.

1980, 1983 *Handbook Arbeids – en Organisatiepsychologie,* vols. 1 and 2. Van Loghum Slaterus (1989, Wiley) (ed. with Hk. Thierry, P.J. Willems and Ch.J. de Wolff).

1981 MOW-International research team member. *The meaning of working: a cross-national study.* Academic Press.

1981 *Industrial Democracy in Europe,* vols. 1 and 2. Oxford University Press (ed. with IDE International Research Group).

1983 Cross-cultural organizational psychology: challenges and limitations. In S.H. Irvine and J. Berry (eds.), *Human Assessment and Cultural Factors.* Plenum.

1983 A contingency model of participative decision making: an analysis of 56 decisions on the three Dutch organizations. *Journal of Occupational Psychology,* 56, 1–18 (with P.L. Koopman, F.A. Heller and V. Rus).

1983 Educational selection in Tanzania. *Evaluation in Education,* 7, 93–217 (with H. van der Flier and I.M. Omari).

1990 Industrial democracy in Europe: Cross-national comparisons. *European Perspectives in Psychology,* 3, 115–31.

1992 Work meanings: A conceptual, semantic and developmental approach. *European Work and Organizational Psychologist,* 1, 125–33.

Further reading

Bleichrodt, N. and Drenth, P. (eds) (1991) *Contemporary Issues in Cross-Cultural Psychology.* Swets and Zeitlinger.

Drenth, P.J.D., Sargeant, J.A. and Takens, R.J. (eds) (1990) *European Perspectives in Psychology, Vol. 3: Work and Organizational, Social and Economic, Cross-Cultural.* Wiley.

Drenth began his career in the Selection and Personnel Department of the Royal Dutch Navy (1955–60). He spent a year in North America as a Fulbright Fellow (1960–1) and returned to the Netherlands to work as a Research Fellow at Vrije Universiteit, Amsterdam. He was promoted to Lecturer in 1962 and Professor of Work and Organizational Psychology in 1967.

Drenth's primary contributions have been in three areas: psychometrics and test development, organizational psychology, and the psychology of work. In psychometrics and test development he developed a large number of tests for use in school and organizational settings. Several of these (e.g. the African Child Intelligence Test) have been developed with particular reference to the cultural relativity of what it means to be intelligent. His introductory textbook on test theory was widely used at Dutch universities and by practitioners, and may have helped to develop a more scientific attitude in psychodiagnostics and selection. His interest in the effects of culture on experience is also apparent in his contributions to organizational psychology: Drenth was one of the first to identify the challenges of cross-cultural organizational psychology. In work psychology he is principally known for his contributions to the analysis of organizational decision making and for theoretical and empirical investigations into the meaning of work. He published two books on industrial and organizational psychology, followed by the two-volume *Handbook of Work and Organizational Psychology,* in which a more European view and approach are defended as opposed to the often prevailing American orientation in this particular field.

Dunnette, Marvin D.

Born: 1926, Austin, Minnesota, USA **Nat:** American **Ints:** Counselling, differential Psychology and human abilities, evaluation and measurement, industrial and organizational **Educ:** B ChE University of Minnesota, 1948; MA University of Minnesota, 1951; PhD University of Minnesota, 1954 **Appts & awards:** Professor, Department of Psychology, University of Minnesota, 1964– ; James McKeen Cattell Award for Outstanding Research Proposal, 1965; James A. Hamilton Outstanding Book Award (American College of Hospital Administration); President, APA Division 14, 1966–7; Fellow, APA Divisions 5 14; Outstanding Scientific Contributions Award, APA Division 14, 1985; Chairman and Director of Research, Personnel

Decisions Research Institute, 1989– ; Editorial Board, *Annual Review of Psychology*, 1965–70; Past Consulting Editor, *Contemporary Psychology*, *Organisational Behavior and Human Performance*, *Journal of Applied Psychology; Consulting Editor, American Psychologist*, *Journal of Applied Psychology*, *Psychological Bulletin*, *Psychological Review*

Principal publications

1953   The MN Engineering Analogies Test. *Journal of Applied Psychology*, 37, 170–5.

1956   Influence of scale administrator on employee attitude responses. *Journal of Applied Psychology*, 40, 73–7 (with G.G. Heneman Jr.).

1961   Driver opinions and reported performance under various interchange marking and night-time visibility conditions. *Journal of Applied Psychology*, 45, 170–4.

1962   Personnel management. *Annual Review of Psychology*, 13, 285–314.

1963   A modified model for test validation and selection research. *Journal of Applied Psychology*, 47, 317–23.

1963   The effect of group participation on brainstorming effectiveness for two industrial samples. *Journal of Applied Psychology*, 47, 30–7 (with J.P. Campbell and K. Jaastad).

1965   *Psychology Applied to Industry*. Appleton-Century-Crofts (with W.K. Kirchner).

1966   *Personnel Selection and Placement*. Wadsworth.

1967   The role of financial compensation in industrial motivation. *Psychological Bulletin*, 66, 94–118 (with R.L. Opsahl).

1967   Factors contributing to job satisfaction and job dissatisfaction in six occupational groups. *Organizational Behavior and Human Performance*, 2, 143–74 (with J.P. Campbell and M. Hakel).

1967   Development of moderator variables to enhance the prediction of managerial effectiveness. *Journal of Applied Psychology*, 51, 50–64 (with R. Hobert).

1968   The effectiveness of T-Group experiences in managerial training and development. *Psychological Bulletin*, 70, 73–104 (with J.P. Campbell).

1968   Laboratory education: Impact on people and organizations. *Industrial Relations*, 8, 1–27 (with J.P. Campbell).

1969   People feeling: Joy, more joy and the slough of despond. *Journal of Applied Behavioral Science*, 5, 25–45.

1970   *Managerial Behavior, Performance and Effectiveness*. McGraw-Hill (with J.P. Cambell, E.E. Lawler and K.E. Weick).

1971   Multiple assessment procedures in identifying and developing managerial talent. In P. Reynolds (ed.), *Advances in Psychological Assessment 11*. Science and Behavior Books.

1971   *Validity Study Results for Jobs Relevant to the Petroleum Industry*. Technical report. Personnel Decisions (with R.D. Arvey and J.A. Arnold).

1973   *Work and Non Work in the Year 2001*. Brooks Cole.

1973   The development and evaluation of behaviorally-based rating scales. *Journal of Applied Psychology*, 57, 15–22 (with J.P. Campbell, R.D. Arvey and L.W. Hellervik).

1974   Personnel selection and classification systems. In H.L. Fromkin and J.J. Sherwood (eds), *Integrating the Organization*. Free Press.

1976   *Handbook of Industrial and Organizational Psychology*. Rand McNally.

1979   Personnel selection and classification systems. In L.W. Porter and M.R. Rosenzweig (eds), *Annual Review of Psychology*, 30, 477–525 (with W.C. Borman).

1982   *Human Performance and Productivity: vol. 1. Human Capability Assessment*. Erlbaum (with E.A. Fleishman).

1982   Estimating benefits and costs of anti-sexist training programs in organizations. In H.J. Bernardin (ed.), *Women in the Work Force*. Praeger (with S.J. Motowidlo).

Further reading

Dunnette, M.D. and Hough, L.M. (1990) *Handbook of Industrial and Organizational Psychology*, Vol 1, 2nd edn. Rand McNally.

Shortly after obtaining his PhD Dunnette joined 3M as Manager of Employee Relations Research. During his years at 3M, he developed new procedures for selecting and appraising sales personnel, research scientists and clerical employees. He left 3M in 1960 to become Associate Professor of Psychology at Minnesota.

He founded Personnel Decisions Inc., a management consulting firm, in 1967 and served as its president until 1975. In that year he founded a non-profit research organization, the Personnel Decisions Research Institute. The Institute carries out behavioural science research in areas related to the improved and more productive utilization of human resources.

Over the years, Dunnette either singly or through research organizations has developed improved selection procedures for occupations as diverse as those of police officers, lawyers, managers, firefighters, navy recruiters, salesmen, prison guards and power plant operators.

Other research activities have involved the motivation, morale and job satisfaction of army personnel, production workers and salesmen; the antecedents and consequences of adolescent drug use; interpersonal perception or empathy; and improved methods of job analysis and job performance appraisal.

He has influenced the development of the field of industrial and organizational psychology through both his teaching and his publications. He has served as academic advisor to forty-three students who have received their PhD degrees in the fields of industrial psychology, counselling psychology and psychometrics. He has published nearly 200 articles, technical reports, chapters and books. He is probably best known for his influential *Handbook of Industrial and Organizational Psychology*, published in 1976, with a second edition being published in four volumes, the first in 1990.

JONATHAN G. HARVEY

E

Eagly, Alice H.

Born: 1938, Los Angeles, California, USA **Nat:** American **Ints:** Personality and social, psychology of women, Society for Psychological Study of Social Issues **Educ:** BA Harvard University, 1960; MA University of Michigan, 1963; PhD University of Michigan, 1965 **Appts & awards:** APA Division 8, Executive Committee, 1973–6, 1981–83, Secretary-Treasurer, 1975–7, President, 1981; Division 35, Fellows Committee, 1993–6; Chair, 1993–4; APA Council of Representatives, 1975–7; Social Psychology Editor, Journal Supplement Abstract Service of APA, 1973–4; Associate Editor, *Journal of Personality and Social Psychology*, 1974–6; Consulting Editor, *Psychology of Women Quarterly*, 1978; *Personality and Social Psychology Bulletin*, 1978–9, 1982–4, *Journal of Personality and Social Psychology*, 1979– ; Gordon Allport Intergroup Relations Prize of Society for Psychological Study of Social Issues, 1976; Distinguished Publication Award of Association for Women in Psychology, 1978; Professor of Psychology, Purdue University, 1980–95; Citation as Distinguished Leader for Women in Psychology from Committee on Women in Psychology of APA, 1994; Donald Campbell Award for Distinguished Scientific Contribution to the field of social psychology (Division 8 APA Award), 1994; Editorial Board, *Review of Personality and Social Psychology*, 1980–9, *Current Psychological Research and Reviews*, 1985– , *European Review of Social Psychology*, 1990– , *Journal of Experimental Social Psychology*, 1990–

Principal publications

1974 *Readings in Attitude Change* (with S. Himmelfarb). Wiley.

1974 Comprehensibility of persuasive arguments as a determinant of opinion change. *Journal of Personality and Social Psychology*, 29, 758–73.

1978 Casual inferences about communicators and their effect on opinion change. *Journal of Personality and Social Psychology*, 36, 424–35.

1981 Sex of researchers and sex-typed communicators as determinants of sex differences in influenceability: A meta analysis of social influence studies. *Psychological Bulletin*, 90, 1–20 (with L.L. Carli).

1983 Communication modality as a determinant of persuasion: The role of communicator salience. *Journal of Personality and Social Psychology*, 45, 241–56 (with S. Chaiken).

1983 Gender and social influence: A social psychological analysis. *American Psychologist*, 38, 971–81.

1984 Gender stereotypes stem from the distribution of women and men into social roles. *Journal of Personality and Social Psychology*, 46, 735–54 (with V.J. Steffen).

1986 Gender and helping behavior: A meta-analytic review of the social psychological literature. *Psychological Bulletin*, 100, 283–308 (with M. Crowley).

1986 Gender and aggressive behavior: A meta-analytic review of the social psychological literature. *Psychological Bulletin*, 100, 309–30.

1987 *Sex Differences in Social Behavior: A Social Role Interpretation*. Erlbaum.

1990 Involvement and persuasion: Types, traditions and the evidence. *Psychological Bulletin*, 107, 375–84 (with B.T. Johnson).

1992 Gender and the evaluation of leaders: A meta-analysis. *Psychological Bulletin*, 111, 3–22.

1993 *The Psychology of Attitudes*. Harcourt Brace Jovanovich.

Further reading

Mareck, J. (1995) Gender, politics, and psychology's ways of knowing. *American Psychologist*, 50, 162–3.

Petty, R.E. and Cacioppo, J.T. (1990) Involvement and persuasion: Tradition versus integration. *Psychological Bulletin*, 107, 367–74.

Zanna, M.P., Olson, J.M. and Herman, C.P. (eds) (1987) *Social Influence: The Ontario Symposium*, vol. 5. Erlbaum.

Alice Eagly is noted for her contributions in two areas – attitudes and sex differences in social behaviour. The study of attitudes represents the earlier of these two interests. As a graduate student she completed a dissertation on an attitudinal topic, and as a postgraduate she continued this interest and focused on the cognitive mediation of persuasion. She worked on several aspects of cognitive mediation, including the comprehension of messages and attributions about communicators. More recently her work reflects her efforts to synthesize available studies in various areas of attitude research.

Her interest in sex differences arose from work on attitudes where she investigated whether women were more easily influenced than men. In looking at this question she studied the quantitative methods of research integration ('meta-analysis'), and subsequently applied these methods to the research literatures on sex differences in helping behaviour, aggressive behaviour and leadership. In addition, she developed a theory of sex differences that gives primacy to adult social roles as the causes of sex differences. In *Sex Differences in Social Behavior* she interprets a large corpus of fundings from this theoretical perspective. Because sex differences are linked closely to the issue of what people think are the differences between the sexes, she has investigated gender stereotypes. She proposed natural setting differences in the distribution of women and men into social roles as being the cause of gender stereotypes. The link between gender stereotypes and actual sex differences continues as a focus of concern in her current work.

Ebbinghaus, Hermann

Born: 1850, Barmen, Germany **Died:** 1909, Breslau, Germany (now Wrocław, Poland) **Nat:** German **Ints:** Experimental psychology, human memory **Educ:** Doctor of Philosophy, University of Bonn, 1873 **Appts & awards:** Dozent, University of Berlin, 1880–6; Ausserordentlicher Professor, University of Berlin, 1886–94; Co-founder and Editor, *Zeitschrift für Psychologie und Physiologie der Sinnesorgane*, 1890; Professor, University of Breslau, 1894–1909

Principal publications

1885   *Über das Gedächtnis.*
1887   *Die Gesetzmässigkeit des Helligkeits-Contrastes.* Sitzungsber preuss. Acad. Wiss.
1889   Über den Grund der Abseichungen vom dem Weberschen Gestez bei Lichtempfindungen (Pfluger's). *Arch. ges Physiol.*, 45, 113–33.
1893   Theorie des Farbensehens. *Zeitschrift für Psychologie und Physiologie der Sinnesorgane*, 5, 145–238.

1897   Über eine Methode zur Prüfung geistiger Fähigkeiten und ihre Andwendung bei Schulkindern. *Zeitschrift für Psychologie und Physiologie der Sinnesorgane*, 13, 401–59.
1902   *Grundzüge der Psychologie*, vol. 1.
1908   *Abriss der Psychologie.*
1913   *Grundzüge der Psychologie*, vol. 2.

Further reading

Ebbinghaus, H. (1948) Memory. In W. Dennis (ed.), *Readings in the History of Psychology.* Appleton-Century-Crofts.
Postman, L. (1968) Hermann Ebbinghaus. *American Psychologist*, 23, 149–57.
Shakow, D. (1930) Hermann Ebbinghaus. *American Journal of Psychology*, 43, 505–18.

An innovative researcher, productive experimentalist, and very important force in nineteenth-century German psychology, Ebbinghaus was educated at the University of Bonn, where he wrote a doctoral dissertation based upon the views of Eduard von Hartmann on the unconscious. At the completion of his degree, Ebbinghaus spent seven years in England and in France, studying at various universities and tutoring students to support himself. Towards the end of this period, he studied intensively Gustav **Fechner**'s pioneering work, *Elemente der Psychophysik*, which presented objective measurement of subjective sensations. Impressed by the methodological impact of psychophysics, Ebbinghaus set out to study memory in the same manner as Fechner had studied sensations. That is, his goal was to examine memory as a higher mental process under the scrutiny of objective experimentation. From his exposure to the British associationist philosophers, Ebbinghaus valued repetition as the principle key to the measurement of memory. He employed the 'nonsense syllable' which typically consists of a vowel separating two consonants as the main task unit. Thus, he studied his own memory processes and those of subjects by presenting lists of nonsense syllables, deliberately composed to avoid meaning, which Ebbinghaus believed would confound his goals in the study of memory.

His seminal work *Über das Gedächtnis*, translated into English as *On Memory*, described Ebbinghaus's methodology and results, including retention curves showing forgetting over time. This work received wide acclaim for its range of topical coverage, the sophistication of the methodology and completeness of the results, and the clarity of presentation. In addition, it challenged the prevailing views of Wilhelm **Wundt** that higher mental processes could not be studied experimentally.

Ebbinghaus established laboratories at the Universities of Berlin and Breslau, and he also taught at Halle, attracting many students at all three institutions. His journal *Zeitschrift für Psychologie und Physiologie der Sinnesorgane* (*New Writing for the Psychology and Physiology of Sense Organs*) was directed at a national audience. From his studies on memory, Ebbinghaus addressed experimental questions in colour vision, and he also developed early versions of intelligence tests, including his design of the 'completion test'. His text of general psychology, *Grundzüge der Psychologie* (*Foundations of Psychology*), became the standard introduction to psychology in German universities during the early part of the twentieth century. The second volume of this sweeping treatment of psychology and its research basis was published posthumously.

Ebbinghaus's work on memory has been criticized, especially in light of studies over the last fifty years that deliberately focus on meaning in memory and the linguistic basis of verbal memory. In the mid-1980s, his life and work received favourable attention through publications and symposia in his honour. Although noted for his work on memory, he should be remembered as an exponent of careful experimentation in psychology. As such, Hermann Ebbinghaus expanded the subject matter of the new discipline in academic research and deserves a prominent place as a founder of modern experimental psychology.

JAMES F. BRENNAN

Eibl-Eibesfeldt, Irenäus

Born: 1928, Vienna, Austria **Nat:** Austrian **Ints:** Biology of behaviour, ethology, experimental, general, human ethology, personality and social, physiological and comparative **Educ:** DPhil, Biological Station, Wilhelminenberg, 1949; Venia Legendi, University of Munich, 1963; Goldene Bolsche-Medaille of the Kosmos Society for Human Ethology, 1971 **Appts & awards:** Head of the Research Unit for Human Ethology, Max Planck Institute for Behavioural Physiology; President, Charles Darwin Foundation for the Galapagos Islands, Member of Executive Board, 1958– ; International Society for Human Ethology; President 1985–; Editorial Board, *Aggressive Behavior*, 1973– , *Journal of Social and Biological Structures*, 1976,

Partnerberatung, 1977, *Ethology and Sociobiology*, 1978– , *Language and Communication*, 1980– , *Abstracts on German Anthropology*, *Encyclopedia Cinematographica*; Editorial Advisory Board, *Behavioral Processes*; Board of Editorial Commentators, *Behavioral and Brain Sciences*, *Current Anthropology*, *Laboratoria di Scienze dell 'Umo*; Review Board, *Journal of Human Evolution*; Editorial Committee, *Prometeo Revista Trimestrale di Scienze e Storia*

Principal publications

1970 *Ethology – The Biology of Behavior*. Holt, Rinehart and Winston.

1972 *Love and Hate*. Holt Rinehart and Winston.

1973 *Der vorprogrammierte Mensch Das Ererbte als bestimmender Faktor im menschlichen Verhalten*. Molden. (1986, Orion Heimreiter.)

1973 The expressive behavior of the deaf and blind-born. In I. Vine and M. von Cranach (eds), *Social Communication and Movement*. Academic Press.

1974 The myth of the aggression-free hunter and gatherer society. In R.L. Holloway (ed.), *Territoriality and Xenophobia: A Comparative Perspective*. Academic Press.

1976 *Menschenforchung auf neuen Wegen*. Molden.

1979 *The Biology of Peace and War*. Viking Penguin Press.

1979 Functions of rituals, ritual and ritualization from a biological perspective. In M.V. Cranach, K. Foppa, W. Lepenies and D. Ploog (eds), *Human Ethology: Claims and Limits of a New Discipline*. Cambridge University Press.

1980 Strategies of social interaction. In R. Plutchik (ed.), *Emotion: Theory, Research and Experience, Volume 1: Theories of Emotion*. Academic Press.

1981 Human ethology: Concepts and implications for the sciences of man. *Behavioral and Brain Sciences*, 2, 1–57.

1982 Warfare, man's indoctrinability and group selection. *Zeitschrift für Tierpsychologie*1, 60, 177–98.

1983 Patterns of parent–child interaction in a cross-cultural perspective. In A. Oliverio and M. Zapela (eds), *The Behavior of Human Infants*. Plenum.

1983 The comparative approach in human ethology. In D.W. Rajecki (ed.), *Comparing Behavior: Studying Man, Studying Animal*. Erlbaum.

1984 *Die Biologie des Menschlichen Verhaltens – Grundriss der Humanethologie*. Piper.

Further reading

Dewsbury, D.A. (ed) (1985) *Studying Animal Behavior: Autobiographies of the Founders*. University of Chicago Press.

Lamb, M.E. and Keller, H. (eds) (1991) *Infant Development: Perspectives from German-speaking Countries*, Erlbaum.

For the first eighteen years of his career Eibl-Eibesfeldt focused on the study of animal behaviour along two lines. The first dealt with questions of the ontogeny of behaviour, with the particular goal of finding out to what extent behaviour appeared to be programmed by phylogenetic adaptation and in which way particular learning experiences contributed to functional maturity. His work with mammals clarified disputed questions as to the role of the innate in mammalian behavior. The second line of interest was the study of processes of communication: how do signals, including expression movements, control the changes of social interactions, and how did those signals come about? He became interested in the processes of ritualization and showed that the invention of maternal behaviour was a turning point in the evolution of social behaviour. He pointed out that patterns of courting and other behaviours of bonding are derived from the repertory of mother–child signals. This type of study demanded a comparative approach and it allowed him to pick up problems as they occurred.

These animal studies started when he was a student together with a group in a workshop situation. They were based in a barracks in the Viennese Forest and built a biological laboratory under the supervision of Otto Koenig. The field station, Biologische Station Wilhelminenberg, still exists. In 1951 he joined with Konrad **Lorenz** and moved to his Institute in Altenberg. During his zoological career, he established a biological station on the Galapagos Islands, which is still there today. In the late 1960s his interest shifted from animal to human behavior and the basic questions relating to communication and ontogeny arose. An extensive programme for the cross-cultural documentation of unstaged human social interactions was established, using a special method of unobtrusive filming. More than 250 km of film are currently stored in the Institute resulting from this research.

He published the first textbook on human ethology in 1984, an area he was keen to pioneer. With others, he found that verbal and nonverbal interactions alike are controlled by a universal system of rules which structured these events. His Institute, the Ludwig Boltzmann Institute of Urban Ethology in Vienna, continues this research.

Eisdorfer, Carl

Born: 1930, Bronx, New York, USA **Nat:** American **Ints:** Adult development and ageing, clinical, community, health, psychopharmacology **Educ:** BA New York University, 1951; MA New York University, 1953; PhD New York University, 1959; MD Duke University, 1964 **Appts & awards:** Professor, Department of Psychiatry and Neuroscience, Albert Einstein College of Medicine; Robert W. Kleemeier Award, Gerontological Society, 1969; President, Gerontology Society of America, 1971–2; Chair, APA Division 20 Task Force on Aging, 1971–3; Edward B. Allen Award, American Geriatrics Society, 1974; Member, NAS, 1975; National Advisory Council, National Institute on Aging, 1975–6; Social Science Award and Kesten Award, Ethel Percy Andrus Center, University of South Carolina, 1976; AAAS Fellow, 1977; World Congress of Psychiatry Section of Geriatric Psychiatry, Secretary, 1977–83, Vice Chairman, 1983; Member, Academy of Behavioral Medicine, 1978; Joseph Freeman Award, Division of Clinical Medicine, Gerontological Society, 1979; Hon. Fellow, American Association of Psychoanalytic Physicians, 1979; President, Western Gerontological Society, 1980–2; APA Award for Distinguished Professional Contributions to Knowledge, 1981; American Federation for Aging Research, Vice President 1981–4, President Elect, 1985; Potamkin Prize for Outstanding Contributions to Research in Dementia, 1982; Distinguished Scholar Award, Harlem Valley Psychiatric Center, 1983; Board of Directors, Foundation for Geriatric Medical Education, 1983– ; Jack Weinberg Memorial Award for Excellence in Geriatric Psychiatry, American Psychiatric Association, 1984; Distinguished Alumnus, Duke University School of Medicine, 1985; Fellow, Society of Behavioral Medicine, 1985, New York Academy of Medicine, 1981; Chair, APA Division 20, 1970–1; Editor in Chief, *Annual Review of Gerontology and Geriatrics*, 1978– ; Consulting Editor, *Encyclopedia of Aging*, 1984– , *Contemporary Psychology*, 1969–74; Contributing Editor, *Postgraduate Medicine*, 1969–74; Editorial Board, *Alzheimer's Disease and Related Disorders – An International Journal*, 1985– , *Aging and Human Development*, *Neurobiology of Aging*, *Experimental and Clinical Research*, *Experimental Aging*, *Geriatric Medicine*, *Gerontological Abstracts*, *Community Psychology*, *Community Mental Health*, *Law and Contemporary Problems*

Principal publications

1967 Geropsychiatry: The psychiatry of senescence. *Geriatrics*, 22, 139–49 (with A. Verwoerdt).

1971 Intelligence and blood pressure in the aged. *Science*, 172, 959–62 (with F. Wilkie).

1977 Evaluation of the quality of psychiatric care for the aged. *American Journal of Psychiatry*, 134, 315–7.

1980 *Annual Review of Gerontology and Geriatrics*, vols I–VII. Springer-Verlag.

1980 *Psychopharmacology of Aging*. Spectrum (with W. Fann).

1981 Management of the patient and family coping with dementing illness. *Journal of Family Practice*, 12, 831–7 (with D. Cohen).

1982 *Stress and Human Health*. Springer-Verlag (with M. Fann).

1983 Conceptual models of aging: The challenge of a new frontier. *American Psychologist*, 38, 197–202.

1986 *Loss of Self*. Norton (with D. Cohen).

1989 An analysis of intrusive error types in Alzheimer's disease and related disorders. *Developmental Neuropsychology*, 5, 115–26 (with D.A. Lowenstein, F. Wilkie, A. Guterman *et al.*).

1990 Caring for relatives with Alzheimer's disease: The mental health risks to spouses, adult children, and other family caregivers. *Behavior Health and Aging*, 1, 171–82 (with D. Cohen, D. Luchins, J. Gregory *et al.*).

1992 An empirical evaluation of the Global Deterioration Scale for staging Alzheimer's disease. *American Journal of Psychiatry*, 149, 190–4 (with D. Cohen, G.J. Paveza, J. Ashford *et al.*).

1993 Psychopathology associated with Alzheimer's disease and related disorders. *Journal of Gerontology*, 48, M255–M260 (with D. Cohen, P. Goreick, G. Paveza *et al.*).

Further reading

Cerella, J., Rybash, J., Hoyer, W. and Commons, M.L. (eds) (1993) *Adult Information Processing: Limits on Loss*. Academic Press.

Kukull, W.A., Larson, E.B., Reifler, B.V. *et al.* (1990) The validity of three clinical diagnostic criteria for Alzheimer's disease. *Neurology*, 40, 1364–9.

Carl Eisdorfer is associated with scientific investigations of the ageing process with the goal of disentangling myth from fact. He has also been at the forefront of attempts to elucidate implicit models of ageing and to develop alternative, explicit models based on the facts as we know them.

Eisdorfer's analysis starts from the position that our ideas about human ageing mediate psychological theories of ageing as well as perception of needs, values and benefits of activity related to the aged. Ageing, he argues, often provokes deep-rooted fears and anxieties. The aged are often regarded as non-productive, incapable, and economically and socially peripheral to the main focus and goal of society. Psychological theories and professional activities cannot stand in isolation from the cultural and historical context in which they are developed, and society's wider views of ageing and the aged often permeate psychological theory and practice.

Eisdorfer distinguishes between several models of ageing. This first is an economic model which defines those elderly who are not in the labour market as economically and functionally dependent on others who are economically independent and highly functional. While not a psychological model, it influences policy on the distribution of resources and therefore impacts on the aged and their carers. The professional health model emphasizes the heightened vulnerability of the aged; the social model attends to the family and community contexts; and the biological model emphasizes the degenerating organism and its systems. These different models are interrelated, not systematically but through implicit fears and misunderstandings of the ageing process. Eisdorfer's principal contribution has been to raise awareness of these models and argue for a fundamental reconceptualization of ageing and the roles for older people, and their carers, in society.

Ekman, Paul

Born: 1934, Washington, D.C., USA **Nat:** American **Ints:** Personality and social, psychological study of social issues **Educ:** BA New York University, 1954; MA Adelphi University, 1955; PhD Adelphi University, 1958 **Appts & awards:** Professor, University of California, San Francisco, 1958; NIMH, Research Scientist Award, 1972, 1976, 1981; Series Co-editor, Emotion and Social Interaction, 1979; Fulbright Senior Professor, Leningrad STATC University, 1983; Faculty Research Lecturer, University of California, San Francisco, 1983

Principal publications

1969 The repertoire of nonverbal behavior. *Semiotica*, 1, 49–98 (with W.V. Friesen).

1969 Nonverbal leakage and clues to deception. *Psychiatry*, 32, 88–105 (with W.V. Friesen).

1969 Pan-cultural elements in facial displays and emotion. *Science*, 164 (3875), 86–8 (with W.V. Friesen and E.R. Sorenson).

1971 Constants across cultures in the face and emotion. *Journal of Personality and Social Psychology*, 17, 124–283 (with W.V. Friesen).

1972 Universals and cultural differences in facial expressions of emotion. In J. Cole (ed.), *Nebraska Symposium on Motivation, 1971*. University of Nebraska Press.

1973 *Darwin and Facial Expression*. Academic Press.

1975 *Unmasking the Face*. Prentice-Hall (with W.V. Friesen).

1976 Measuring facial movement. *Journal of Environmental Psychology and Nonverbal behavior*, 1, 56–75 (with W.V. Friesen).

1978 *Facial Action Coding Systems*. Friesen Consulting Psychologists Press.

1981 *Face of Man*. Garland.

1983 Autonomic nervous system activity distinguishes between emotions. *Science*, 221, 1208–10 (with W.V. Friesen and R.W. Levenson).

1985 *Telling Lies*. Norton.

1985 Is the startle reaction an emotion? *Journal of Personality and Social Psychology*, 49 (5), 1416–21 (with W.V. Friesen and R.C. Simmons).

1985 *Telling Lies: Clues to Deceit in the Marketplace, Marriage and Politics*. Norton.

1988 *Gesichtsausdruck und Gefühl: 20 Jahre Forschung von Paul Ekman*. Junfermann-Verlag.

1991 *Why Kids Lie*. Charles Scribners Sons.

Ekman became interested in non-verbal behaviour at a time when it was largely neglected in clinical, personality and social psychology. His first accomplishment (1969) was to develop an overall taxonomy of non-verbal behaviours, drawing from both semiotics and ethology. This article reported his first findings of universality in facial expression, and these findings, in particular the studies in New Guinea, and the formulation of the concept of 'display rules' to account for cultural differences in the control of expression became well known. At the same time he began to focus on how non-verbal behaviour can betray deceit, publishing his first theoretical and empirical findings, and coining the term 'leakage'. He developed the first and only comprehensive technique for measuring facial movement, and that tool (the Facial Action Coding System) is now widely used to measure facial movement objectively. He continues to be interested in deceit and has published a book on that topic.

Ekman considers himself no longer a student of non-verbal behaviour but instead one of emotion. His more recent work has focused on two old questions in the field: What is an emotion? Is autonomic nervous system activity emotion specific? To begin to answer the first of these he carried out a study of the startle, which he claims to be a model of what emotion is not. On the second, he carried out a series of studies on the relationship between expression and physiology which shows evidence of emotion-specific patterns of physiological activity.

Elkind, D.

Born: 1931, Detroit, Michigan, USA **Nat:** American **Ints:** Developmental, educational and clinical **Educ:** BA University of California at Los Angeles, 1952; PhD University of California at Los Angeles, 1955 **Appts & awards:** Hon. Dr Sci., Rhode Island College, 1987; Professor of Child Study, Senior Resident Scholar, Tufts University; NSF Senior Postdoctoral Fellow, Geneva; President, National Association for the Education of Young Children; G. Stanley Hall Lecturer; Scandinavian Lecturer; Editorial Board, *Computers and Human Behavior*, *Bulletin of the Menninger Clinic*, *Journal of Youth and Adolescence*

Principal publications

1967 Effects of perceptual training at three age levels. *Science*, 137, 3732–7.

1967 Middle-class delinquency. *Mental Hygiene*, 50, 80–4.

1967 Egocentrism in adolescence. *Child Development*, 38, 1025–34.

1967 Early education and formal education: A necessary difference. *Phi Delta Kappan*, May, 631–6.

1969 Piagetian and psychometric approaches to intelligence. *Harvard Educational Review*, 39, 319–37.

1970 Erik Erikson: The ages of man. *New York Times Magazine*, 5 April.

1975 Perceptive development in children. *American Scientist*, 63, 535–41.

1979 *The Child and Society*. Oxford University Press.

1981 *Children and Adolescents*. Oxford University Press.

1981 *The Hurried Child*. Addison Wesley.

1984 *All Grown Up and No Place to Go*. Addison-Wesley.

1987 *Miseducation: Preschoolers at Risk*. Knopf.

1991 (ed.) *Perspectives on Early Childhood Education: Growing with Young Children toward the 21st Century.* National Education Association.

1991   Instrumental narcissism in parents. *Bulletin of the Menninger Clinic*, 55, 299–307.

1994   *Ties that Stress: The New Family Imbalance.* Harvard University Press.

Further reading

Kagan, S.L. and Zigler, E.F. (eds) (1987) *Early Schooling: The National Debate.* Yale University Press.

Lapsley, D.K. (1993) Toward an integrated theory of adolescent ego development: The 'new look' at adolescent egocentrism. *American Journal of Orthopsychiatry*, 63, 562–71.

Miler, P.H. (1989) Theories of adolescent development. In J. Worell and F. Danner (eds), *The Adolescent as Decision-maker: Applications to Development and Education.* Academic Press.

Elkind's father was a machinist who worked in a small factory serving the car industry. Elkind describes his clearest memories of childhood as listening to his father complain when he returned from work about the engineers who had drawn the blueprints he worked from. Although the engineers had more education than he, they knew nothing about running a lathe, so that they often drew plans of metal parts that could not be machined. These experiences made a deep impression on Elkind and account in part for his abiding concern with the relation of theory to practice.

Throughout his career he tried to investigate particular issues – conceptual development, perceptual development, reading, religious development – but also to interpret what the findings meant for practical endeavours such as education and therapy. In this connection, he has produced a large amount of 'popular' writing in an effort to provide for the general public some of the important child-rearing and educational implications of child development theory and research.

Elkind is probably best known for his work on the psychology of adolescence and in particular adolescent egocentrism – adolescents' failure to differentiate between their own mental preoccupations and what others are thinking. According to Elkind, adolescents are prone to commit three kinds of egocentric error. The first involves an inability to distinguish between transient and abiding thoughts, as, for example, when embarrassed adolescents declare that they will never again be able to show their face in public. The second involves an inability to differentiate the objective from the subjective. Adolescent self-

consciousness is a product of this error, as is the imaginary audience of interested onlookers. The third egocentric error entails an inability to differentiate the unique from the universal. For example, young adolescents, experiencing new feelings or thoughts for the first time, may regard their experiences of the world as unique and never before experienced by others. Elkind refers to this as the 'personal fable'.

A different theme of Elkind's work has been the importance of variety as a critical factor in healthy learning and development. In his doctoral dissertation, 'Resistance to extinction as a function of variety of need satisfaction during training', he found that with a number of reinforcements constant the effect was greater when a variety of need satisfactions (hunger and thirst) were used rather than one or the other in isolation. With respect to learning he emphasized that horizontal enrichment (a variety of experiences at the same level) is more beneficial than vertical acceleration (moving to more and more difficult tasks without first developing a firm base). It is this conviction regarding the importance of the breadth and variety of experience for healthy development that underlies his concern about children being hurried to grow up too fast, too soon. Hurrying prevents the richness of experience which he believes is essential for learning in the deepest and most profound sense of that word. Thus more recently he has examined instrumental narcissism, a syndrome manifested by parents who feel compelled to transform their infants and young children into geniuses. The parents' effort devalues the child's own abilities and exaggerates the parents' self-perceived powers.

Ellis, Albert

Born: 1913, Pittsburgh, Pennsylvania, USA ***Nat:*** American ***Ints:*** Clinical, family, rational-emotive therapy, sex therapy, psychotherapy ***Educ:*** BBA City College of New York, 1934; MA Columbia University, 1943; PhD Columbia University, 1947 ***Appts & awards:*** Executive Director, Institute for Rational-Emotive Therapy; Humanist of the Year, American Humanist Association; Distinguished Psychologist Award, APA Division 29; Distinguished Psychologist Award, Academy of Psychologists in Marital and Family Therapy; Distinguished Sexologist Award, Society for the Scientific Study of Sex; Distinguished Sex Educator and Therapist Award, American Society of Sex Educators, Counselors and Therapists; APA Distinguished

Award for Professional Contributions to Knowledge; Member, National Academy for Practice in Psychology; Editorial Board, *Journal of Rational-Emotive Therapy, Journal of Marriage and the Family, International Journal of Sexology, Journal of Sex Education and Therapy, Psychological Reports, Existential Psychiatry, Journal of Contemporary Psychotherapy, Journal of Sex Research, Voices, Art and Science of Psychotherapy, Cognitive Therapy and Research, Individual Psychology, Journal of Child and Adolescent Psychotherapy, Journal of Marital and Family Therapy*

Principal publications

1953   Is the vaginal orgasm a myth? In A.P. Pillay and A. Ellis (eds), *Sex, Society and the Individual.* International Journal of Sexology.

1958   *Sex Without Guilt.* Lyle Stuart.

1962   *Reason and Emotion in Psychotherapy.* Citadel Press.

1971   A 23-year-old girl, guilty about not following her parents' rules. In A. Ellis (ed.), *Growth through Reason.* Science and Behavior Books.

1975   *A New Guide to Rational Living.* Wilshire (with R.A. Harper).

1979   Rational-emotive therapy: Research data that support the clinical and personality hypotheses of RETX and other modes of cognitive-behavior therapy. In A. Ellis and J. Whiteley (eds), *Theoretical and Empirical Foundations of Rational-emotive Therapy.* Brooks Cole.

1982   Rational-emotive group therapy. In G.M. Gaxda (ed.), *Basic Approaches to Group Psychotherapy and Group Counselling.* Thomas.

1982   Rational-emotive family therapy. In A.M. Horne and M.M. Ohlsen (eds), *Family Counseling and Therapy.* Peacock.

1983   An overview of rational-emotive approaches to the problems of childhood. In A. Ellis and M. Bernard (eds), *Rational-emotive Approaches to the Problems of Childhood.* Plenum.

1984   Rational-emotive therapy. In R.J. Corsini (ed.), *Current Psychotherapies.* Peacock.

1985   *Resistance: Rational-emotive Therapy with Difficult Clients.* Springer-Verlag.

1985   Expanding the ABCs of rational-emotive Therapy. In M.J. Mahoney and A. Freeman (eds), *Cognition and Psychotherapy.* Plenum.

1985   Jealousy: Its etiology and treatment. In D.C. Goldberg (ed.), *Contemporary Marriage: Special Issues in Couples Therapy.* Dorsey.

1985   Love and its problems. In A. Ellis and M. Bernard (eds), *Clinical Applications of Rational-emotive Therapy.* Plenum.

1996   *Better, Deeper, and more Enduring Brief Therapy: The Rational Emotive Behavior Therapy Approach.* Brunner/Mazel.

Further reading

Dryden, W. (1994) Reason and emotion in psychotherapy: Thirty years on. *Journal of Rational Emotive and Cognitive Behavior Therapy,* 12, 83–99.

Franks, C.M. (1995) RET, REBT and Albert Ellis. *Journal of Rational Emotive and Cognitive Behavior Therapy,* 13, 91–5.

Kendall, P.C., Haaga, D.A.F. *et al.* (1995) Rational-emotive therapy in the 1990s and beyond: Current status, recent revisions, and research questions. *Clinical Psychology Review,* 15, 169–85.

Albert Ellis's early interests were in the fields of sex, love and marital relationships, in which he did considerable research (including that recorded in *Psychology of Sex Offenders*) and published many popular books which sold millions of copies in hard and paperback form, including *The Folklore of Sex, The Art and Science of Love, Sex Without Guilt,* and the *Encyclopedia of Sexual Behavior.* Along with Alfred C. Kinsey, he was one of the main promulgators of the modern sex revolution in the 1950s and 1960s, and gave a large number of talks and workshops on sexual liberalism and anti-censorship in the United States and throughout the world. He also appeared on many radio and TV shows and was one of the first outspoken therapists who espoused liberal sex ideas in down-to-earth language. He was the leading promulgator of so-called obscene language in his public talks, as well as at professional meetings, such as those of the APA.

He was trained in psychoanalysis and practised it from 1947 to 1953. However, he became quite disillusioned with psychoanalysis, thought that it was anti-scientific and a most ineffective form of psychotherapy, and became a revisionist writer on it. He researched other modes of therapy and as a result published a monograph in 1955, *New Approaches to Psychotherapy Techniques,* as well as a follow-up article, 'Psychotherapy techniques for use with psychotics'. Consequently, at the beginning of 1955, he started to practise rational-emotive therapy (RET), the pioneering form of what is now called cognitive or cognitive behaviour therapy.

At first, RET was extremely unpopular, and Ellis was vilified by the vast majority of therapists and critics. But using the principles of RET on himself, he convinced himself that there was no reason why other people must approve of him and that it was highly inconvenient, but hardly terrible and awful, when they did not; and he stubbornly persisted to promulgate the theory and practice of RET. At first he had only a few devoted followers, but by the late 1960s and early 1970s many outcome studies supporting the efficacy of RET and cognitive behaviour therapy began to appear. Innumerable other therapists were attracted to RET, so that it is primarily employed by a sizeable minority of today's practitioners.

Ellis, Havelock

Born: 1859, Croydon, Surrey, England **Died:** 1939, Hintlesham, East Anglia, England **Nat:** British **Ints:** APA **Educ:** Licentiate in Medicine, Surgery and Midwifery, Society of Apothecaries, London, 1889– **Appts & awards:** Physician's licence, St Thomas's Hospital, London, 1889

Principal publications

1894 *Man and Woman.* Walter Scott.
1897 *Sexual Inversion.*
1898–1928 *Studies in the Psychology of Sex*, 7 vols. F.A. Davis.
1910 *Sex in Relation to Society.*
1918 *The Erotic Rights of Women.*
1921 *The Play Function of Sex.*
1923 *The Dance of Life.*
1929 *Marriage Today and Tomorrow.*
1931 *More Essays on Love and Virtue.* Constable.

Further reading

Ellis, H. (1936) *Studies in the Psychology of Sex.* Random House.
—— (1940) *My Life.* Heinemann.
Grosskurth, P. (1981) *Havelock Ellis.* Quartet Books.

Havelock Ellis, while writing extensively on other subjects also, was a major pioneer in the endeavour to dispel the rigidity and secrecy regarding sexual matters which held sway in Western Europe, not least in Britain, during the later nineteenth and early twentieth centuries. His upbringing in a pious middle-class household was probably remarkable only in being more heavily weighted on the female side than most, his father (a sea captain) necessarily being absent during the greater part of every year. Ellis attended several not very satisfactory private schools of the type used by those with somewhat limited resources, left at 16, and, being uncertain of his future career, was sent on his father's ship to Australia – the colonies, as

they were then called, frequently being regarded as a solution in such circumstances. He regarded the fourth and final year of his sojourn in Australia as the most formative in his life. As a young schoolmaster – on incredibly little training – in the outback, he had time and solitude to reflect on religious problems, which he solved by adopting a rather vague pantheism, and on sexual questions, which came upon him forcefully. According to his own account he had never before in waking life experienced sexual feelings, but one afternoon, lying on his bed, he became aware of a delightful sensation which he recognized intuitively as orgasm, and to which he reacted by deciding to become a doctor in order to devote himself to the study of sexual phenomena. Returning to England in 1879, he enrolled as a medical student at St Thomas's Hospital in London.

The years which followed were exceptionally full. Medical studies were largely uncongenial, and after a period of relative stimulus deprivation in Australia he found much else to do, editing the plays of a group of Elizabethan dramatists and becoming acquainted with many figures in literary and social reformist circles. That he took seven years instead of the customary five to complete the unprestigious Licentiate of the Society of Apothecaries is not surprising. That he did complete indicates the strength of his resolve. The circumstance that even the most technical papers in his major work, *Studies in the Psychology of Sex*, hardly require full medical training might raise the question of the necessity for all this toil. However, the closed nature of the medical world, a hundred years ago especially, and the pre-eminence in this field accorded to it by society, meant that Ellis was right – nothing else could have conferred even partial respectability. He always retained membership of the BMA, and greatly appreciated election to a Fellowship of the Royal College of Physicians in 1936.

Considering his contributions, he himself declared his claim to originality to have been greatly reduced through work then recently published by German psychiatrists – Krafft-Ebing, Westphal and others – from which he often quoted: 'Any originality can only lie in the bringing together of elements from diverse fields.' This he did extensively, including comparisons with non-human species and customs gathered from anthropological studies without close consideration of their cultures; thus the *Studies in the Psychology of Sex* sometimes resembles a more recent *Anatomy of Melancholy*.

Occasionally, as in his paper on 'Inversion', or homosexuality, case studies are introduced, but not in detail. Unlike his contemporary **Freud**, the great bulk of whose writings consist of his own case material and comments or hypotheses derived therefrom, Ellis obtained much of his material from reports by friends or from correspondence, which he seldom followed up by interview. Frequently his handling was quite superficial; e.g. he stated, without producing evidence or defining terms, that in all respects other than inversion these individuals were normal. Topics for investigation there are, such as the assertion that inversion is largely innate; however, to attempt investigation one would find oneself considering hypotheses derived from Freud concerning relationships in early life; there is little sign in Ellis's own work of a systematic body of hypothesis or – a characteristic which indeed he shares with Freud – of close attention to their testing. In consequence even those branches of present-day psychology – developmental, social, personality – which link up with his work most readily have come about with very little influence from him.

There is much ambivalence in Ellis's attitude to Freud's psychology. Ellis acknowledged that infantile sexuality exists, but added that such 'sexual precocity' is not universal. (There is even one passage in which he speaks of 'a boy's pure passion' with 'no physical desires and voluptuous emotions', as though, after all, sexuality was not so pure.) Similarly with attraction to the parent of the opposite sex – it does not form a normal or universal stage in personality development but may well be evoked by the behaviour of the parent; also with therapy, in which he discounted the use of transference as a tool, leaving himself more dependent on what the patient can or will report; and with dreams, which he regarded as more often wish-fulfilling in 'the abnormal'. A *modus vivendi* is in fact attempted by describing Freud's work as having particular relevance to 'the abnormal' and his own as more applicable to 'the normal', again without definition of the terms. Unfortunately all that is known of personality nullifies so clear-cut a distinction.

On the other hand, there may have been a positive element in Ellis's remarks. Freud was, after all a practising psychiatrist – he did not have the freedom of a freelance littérateur. In Ellis's favour, it might be said that to assist in removing homosexuality from the spheres exclusively of 'insanity' and criminality; to dispel the bogey of masturbation, which haunted many thousands, by insisting on its universality; and to write with compassion on such subjects as the sexual ignorance in which many women of his time were kept, are contributions not to be despised. It is also possible that even his hesitations and ambivalence had their place, making work on sexuality more palatable at a time when that was needed. Or, as Ellis wrote to Freud himself, 'many English people after reading my books are prepared to receive your doctrines, whereas if they had gone directly to your books they would have failed to understand them and have been repelled'. In short, Havelock Ellis in relation to Freud might be described as having a 'John the Baptist' role.

AVIS M. DRY

Endler, Norman Solomon

Born: 1931, Montreal, Canada *Nat:* Canadian *Ints:* Clinical, health, personality and social, philosophical and theoretical, social issues *Educ:* BSc McGill University, 1953; MSc McGill University, 1954; PhD University of Illinois, Urbana, 1958 *Appts & awards:* Professor, Department of Psychology, York University; Editorial Consultant, *Journal of Research in Personality*, 1977, *Journal of Personality Disorders*, 1985; Canadian Silver Jubilee Medal (Queen Elizabeth II), 1978

Principal publications

1975   A person–situation interaction model of anxiety. In C.D. Spielberger and I.G. Sarason (eds), *Stress and Anxiety*, vol. I. Wiley.

1976   *Contemporary Issues in Developmental Psychology*. Holt, Rinehart and Winston (with R.L. Bouter and H. Osser).

1976   *Interactional Psychology and Personality*. Wiley (with D. Magnusson).

1976   An S-R inventory of anxiousness. *Psychological Monographs*, no. 17 (whole no. 636), 1–33 (with J.McV. Hunt and A.J. Rosenstein).

1976   Personality and person situational interactions. In N.S. Endler and D. Magnusson (eds), *Interactional Psychology and Personality*. Wiley (with D. Magnusson).

1976   Toward an interactional psychology of personality. *Psychological Bulletin*, 83, 956–74 (with D. Magnusson).

1977   *Personality at the Crossroads: Current Issues in Interactional Psychology*. Erlbaum (with D. Magnusson).

1977   The role of person by situation interactions in personality theory. In C. Uzgiris and F. Weizmann (eds), *The Structuring of Experience*. Plenum.

1981   Persons, situations and their interactions. In A.I. Rabin, J. Aronoff, R.M. Barclay and R.A. Zucker (eds), *Further Explorations in Personality*. Wiley.

1981   Situational aspects of interactional psychology. In D. Magnusson (ed.), *Toward a Psychology of Situations: An Interactional Perspective*. Erlbaum.

1982   *Holiday of Darkness*. Wiley.

1982   Interactionism comes of age. In M.P. Zanna, E.T. Higgins and C.P. Herman (eds), *Consistency in Social Behavior: The Ontario Symposium*, vol. 2. Erlbaum.

1983   Interactionism: A personality model, but not yet a theory. In M.M. Page (ed.), *Nebraska Symposium on Motivation: Personality – Current Theory and Research*. University of Nebraska Press.

1984   *Personality and the Behavioral Disorders*. Wiley (with J.McV. Hunt).

1984   Interactionism. In N.S. Endler and J.McV. Hunt (eds), *Personality and the Behavioral Disorders*. Wiley.

1988   The origins of electroconvulsive therapy. *Convulsive Therapy*, 4, 5–23.

1990   State and trait anxiety, depression and coping styles. *Australian Journal of Psychology*, 42, 207–20.

1996   *Handbook of Coping: Theory, Research Applications*. Wiley.

Further reading

Zeidner, M. and Endler, N.S. (eds) (1996) *Handbook of Coping: Theory, Research, Applications*. Wiley.

For a number of years, in his late teens and early twenties, Endler was a counsellor and head counsellor at a summer camp. He was puzzled by the fact that various counsellors discussed each camper in a different manner. When he started his PhD graduate training at the University of Illinois in clinical psychology (after completing the master's degree), he had the opportunity to be puzzled while involved in practical training and internship. Often, during a case conference, he discovered that the psychiatrist, the psychologist and the social worker all described the patient in ways different from one another's and different from his, when he had assessed the patients via the assistance of various psychological tests. At about the same time he took a graduate course in Personality from J.McV. **Hunt** in which he presented a logical analysis of what can be meant by saying that one individual manifests more than another of a given, adjectively designated common trait

(e.g. anxiety). One of the things discussed, in class, was that observers do not always agree about the extent to which any given trait or characteristic is exhibited in a person or sample of persons. One of the sources of disagreement among observers or raters is that they may observe subjects' responses in different situations or contexts. For example, therefore, Bill the camper may be anxious in the swimming situation, but not in the snake-handling situation. The disagreement between the two counsellors regarding Bill's anxiety resides in the fact that they observed Bill in two different situations. From this early interest, the work on the interaction model of personality has continued to evolve. The multidimensional interaction model of anxiety that Endler developed distinguishes between state and trait anxiety, proposes that both are multidimensional, and suggests that both person and situation factors must be considered in predicting state anxiety response.

Entwistle, Noel J.

Born: 1936, Bolton, England **Nat:** British **Ints:** Educational psychology, evaluation and measurement **Educ:** BSc University of Sheffield, 1960; PhD University of Aberdeen, 1967 **Appts & awards:** Bell Professor of Education and Director of the Godfrey Thomson Unit for Educational Research, University of Edinburgh, Withers Memorial Prize, Manchester, 1961; Owen's Club Prize, University of Manchester, 1961; *British Journal of Educational Psychology*, Editor, 1975–9, Higher Education Co-ordinating Editor, 1993–; Fellow, BPS, 1977; President, European Association for Research on Learning and Instruction, 1991–3

Principal publications

1968   Neuroticism and school attainment – a linear relationship? *British Journal of Educational Psychology*, 38, 123–32 (with S. Cunningham).

1971   The academic performance of students II – Types of successful students. *British Journal of Educational Psychology*, 41, 268–76 (with T. Brennan).

1974   Complementary paradigms for research and development work in higher education. In W.A. Verreck (ed.), *Methodological Problems in Research and Development in Higher Education*. Swets and Zeitlinger.

1977   *Degrees of Excellence: The Academic Achievement Game*. Hodder and Stoughton (with J.D. Wilson).

1977   Approaches to teaching and learning: Guidelines from research. In N.J. Entwistle (ed.), *Strategies for Research and Development in Higher Education*. Swets and Zeitlinger.

1977   Choice of science courses in secondary school: Trends and explanations. *Studies in Science Education*, 4, 68–82 (with D. Duckworth).

1979   Stages, levels, styles or strategies: Dilemmas in the description of thinking. *Educational Review*, 31, 123–32.

1981   *Styles of Learning and Teaching*. Wiley.

1982   Learning from the student's perspective. First Vernon Wall Lecture. BPS.

1983   *Understanding Student Learning*. Croom Helm (with P. Ramsden).

1984   Changing conceptions of learning and research. In F. Morton, D.J. Hounsell and N.J. Entwistle (eds), *The Experience of Learning*. Scottish Academic Press (with F. Morton).

1984   *The Experience of Learning*. Scottish Academic Press (ed. with F. Morton and D.J. Hounsell).

1985   Relationships between school motivation approaches to studying and attainment among British and Hungarian adolescents. *British Journal of Educational Psychology*, 55, 124–37 (with B. Kozéki).

1985   Explaining individual differences in school learning. In *Proceedings of the First European Conference on Research in Learning and Instruction, University of Leuven, Belgium, June*.

1987   A model of the teaching–learning process. In J.T.E. Richardson, M.W. Eysenck and D. Warren (eds), *Student Learning: Research in Education and Cognitive Psychology*. Open University Press.

Further reading

Reiff, J.C. (1992) *Learning styles*. National Education Association.

Schmeck, R.R. (ed.) (1988) *Learning Strategies and Learning Styles: Perspectives on Individual Differences*. Plenum.

Entwistle started his career as a school teacher, where he began research into the transfer from primary to secondary education. This highlighted the effects of personality and motivation on school attainment, which led to a study of the relationship at school and university levels and how children are affected by a wide range of intervening variables – age, sex, ability level, area of study and teaching methods. His research was directed towards higher education, where his interests are both methodological and substantive. In *Degrees of Excellence*, he explored the application of both factor and cluster analysis to date describing the psychological and educational characteristics of students. These analyses presented a misleading view of student learning, as they ignored the process of learning and the situational effects. In *Understanding Student Learning*, the advantages of alternating between quantitative and qualitative research methodologies were demonstrated. *The Experience of Learning* explains a rigorous technique of analysing students 'experiences' of learning, which produce concepts describing a 'recognizable reality' of the teaching–learning process in higher education. The main concept, 'approaches to learning', describes a fundamental difference in tackling academic tasks between seeking personal understanding and minimally fulfilling perceived task requirements. In *Styles of Learning and Teaching*, Entwistle argued that students seek understanding in characteristically different ways, using preferred learning styles which are an expression of their cognitive styles and personality, and that teachers adopt teaching styles which reflect their own learning styles. The approach to learning adopted by a student on a particular occasion depends partly on the relatively stable individual characteristic of predominant motivation and partly on the situationally variable features of the student's perceptions of the learning environment. Although Entwistle maintained his interest in personality and motivation, he became more interested in the processes of learning which are also strongly affected by the teacher and the institution, and he moved on to work on the development of a model of the teaching–learning process which incorporates these three main interactions.

Epstein, Alan Neil

Born: 1932, New York City, USA **Nat:** American **Ints:** Behavioural neuroscience of ingestive behaviour of mammals: feeding, drinking, sodium appetite, swelling and ontogeny of ingestive behaviour of mammals **Educ:** BA 1954; MA Johns Hopkins University, 1954; MD Johns Hopkins University, 1958 **Appts & awards:** AAAS, Member, 1958; Fellow, APA, 1973; Professor of Behavioral Neurosciences, Department of Biology, University of Pennsylvania 1977– ; Education Committee Society of Neuroscience, Member, 1979–81; Biological Sciences Training Review Committee, Society of Neuroscience, Member, 1979–81; Neuropsychology Research Review Committee, NIMH, Member, 1979–81; Javitz Award, NINEDS, 1985; Consulting Editor, *Behavioural Neuro-sciences*, *Journal of Comparative and Physiological Psychology*, 1962–74; Associate Editor, *Journal of Neuroscience*, 1981–4; Editorial Board, APA, 1968–75; Series Co-editor, Progress in Psychobiology and Physiological Psychology

Principal publications

1962   Regulation of food intake in the absence of taste, smell and other oropharyngeal sensations. *Journal of Comparative Physiological Psychology*, 55, 753–95 (with P. Teitelbaum).

1970   Drinking induced by injection of angiotensin into the brain of the rat. *Journal of Physiology (London)*, 210, 457–75 (with J.T. Fitzsimons and B.J. Simons).

1975   The cerebral ventricles as the avenue for the dipsogenic action of intracranial angiotensin. *Brain Research*, 86, 399–418 (with A.K. Johnson).

1978   Localisation of dipsogenic receptors for angiotensin in the subfornical organ. *Journal of Comparative Physiological Psychology*, 92, 768–95 (with J.B. Simpson and J.S. Camardo).

1980   Arousal of a specific and persistent sodium appetite with continuous intracerebroventricular angiotensin II. *Journal of Physiology*, 301, 365–82 (with R.W. Bryant, J.T. Fitzsimons and S.J. Fluharty).

1981   Biobehavioral determinants of evaporative water loss in the rat. *Behavioral and Neural Biology*, 33, 101–16 (with B.A. MacFarlane).

1982   Differential effects of gastrointestinal fill on milk ingestion and nipple attachment in the sucking rat. *Journal of Developmental Psychobiology*, 15, 309–30 (with D. Lorenz and S. Ellis).

1983   The behavioral neuroscience of drinking behavior. In *Handbook of Behavioral Neurobiology*. Plenum.

1983   Sodium appetite elicited by intracerebroventricular infusion of angiotensin II in the rat; II. Synergistic interaction with systemic mineralocorticoids. *Behavioral Neuroscience*, 97, 746–58 (with S.J. Fluharty).

1984   The involvement of the renin-angiotensin system in captopril induced sodium appetite. *Journal of Physiology (London)*, 354, 11–27 (with R.M. Elfont and J.T. Fitzsimons).

1988   *Progress in Psychobiology and Physiological Psychology*, vol. 13. Academic Press (ed. with A.R. Morrison).

1989   Ontogeny of renin-induced salt appetite in the rat pup. *Developmental Psychobiology*, 22, 437–45.

1991   Transient and lasting effects of reproductive episodes on NaCl intake of the female rat. *Appetite*, 16, 193–204 (with S.P. Frankmann and P. Ulrich).

1992   *Progress in Psychobiology and Physiological Psychology*, vol. 15. Academic Press (ed. with A.R. Morrison).

1993   Salt appetite consequent on sodium depletion in the suckling rat pup. *Developmental Psychobiology*, 26, 97–114 (with M. Leshem and J. Langberg).

Further reading

Stricker, E.M. (1990) *Handbook of Behavioral Neurobiology*, vol. 10. Plenum.

Professor Epstein is an empiricist interested in how the brain governs behaviour. His formal training was in medicine, where the emphasis is on the analysis of phenomens (disease in the special instance of medicine). As a student of Stellar and Teitelbaum he was introduced to behavioural phenomena and spent his research career analysing them. Work in a biology department encouraged him to place his work in a biological context, and as a result of this he was less interested in the traditional psychological problems than in the neurological and endocrinological mechanisms of the spontaneous behaviour of animals, and in how they permit the animal to make its living.

He began by studying the phenomena of (1) recovery from lateral hypotualamic damage with emphasis on feeding and drinking, (2) the elicitation of behaviour by direct chemical manipulations of the brain, and (3) salt appetite, all in the rat. This inaugural work lead to studies of the functions of the salivary glands in behavioural thermoregulation and in ingestion of food, and to an interest in the dipsogenic section of the hormone angiotensin. He later studied the endocrine basis of salt appetite, and the ontogony of feeding and drinking in the suckling rat.

Epstein's work on salt appetite emphasized the actions of aldosterone and angiotensin, which are the hormones of aural sodium conservation and, he discovered, also the hormones of salt ingestion. Working with his students, S. Flaherty and P. Saksi, he found that a robust, realistic and rapid salt appetite can be aroused in the salt-replete rat by treatment of it with doses of aldosterone and angiotensin, which when used alone do not increase salt intake. Moreover, the salt appetite that is elicited by sodium depletion can be completely suppressed with drugs that block the sections of endogenous aldosterone and angiotensin. The hormones arouse the appetite by acting in synergy on the brain.

This work on the ontogeny of ingestive behaviours has revealed an early and complex competence of the suckling act for adult-like feeding and drinking, including sensitivity of the suckling for the dipsogenic section of angiotensin and for the erexigenic action of norepincphrinc. Epstein, his team and others found that these neural mechanisms for feeding and drinking, which can be activated in the neonatal brain, do not control suckling. They do not effect intake of mother's milk by newborn rat pups suckling it from their dam. Epstein believes that there are two parallel and separate neural systems for ingestion in the newborn mammal, one for suckling, which is used shortly after birth, and another for adult feeding and drinking, which is present in the suckling and controls behaviour at weaning.

Erikson, Erik Homburger

Born: 1902, Germany **Died:** 1994, Harwich, Massachusetts, USA **Ints:** Psychoanalysis, developmental psychology, personality and social psychology **Educ:** Vienna Psychoanalytic Institute, graduated 1933 **Appts & awards:** Harvard Medical School; University of California, Berkeley; Austen Riggs Center, Massachusetts; Harvard, 1960–70

Principal publications

1958 *Young Man Luther*. Norton.
1959 Identity and the life cycle. *Psychological Issues*, Monograph 1, 1 (1). International Universities Press.
1963 *Childhood and Society*. Norton.
1964 *Insight and Responsibility*. Norton.
1968 *Identity, Youth and Crisis*. Norton.
1969 *Gandhi's Truth*. Norton.
1974 *Dimensions of a New Identity*. Norton.
1975 *Life History and the Historical Moment*. Norton.
1977 *Toys and Reasons*. Norton.
1982 *The Life Cycle Completed: A Review*. Norton

Further reading

Coles, R. (1970) *Erik H. Erikson: The Growth of his Work*. Little, Brown.
Erikson, K.T. (1975) *In Search of Common Ground: Conversations with Erik H. Erikson and Huey P. Newton*. Norton.

Erik Erikson's Danish parents separated before he was born, and during his childhood he assumed his stepfather, a pediatrician, was his real father. After leaving gymnasium he had loosely formulated plans for a career as an artist. He travelled – or wandered – through Europe for a year, sketching and writing about his observations. He enrolled at an art school, left soon afterwards, entered another school of art and began exhibiting some of his work (woodcuts and etchings). In 1927 he began a career in teaching in Vienna, at a school for American children. Many of the children's parents had travelled to Vienna for analysis with Sigmund **Freud** or his colleagues, and it was not long before Erikson met Freud and his family. Erikson enrolled at the Vienna Psychoanalytic Institute and began a personal analysis with Anna **Freud**. He was highly regarded at the Institute and graduated in 1933. In autobiographical pieces he says that much of his theoretical work was influenced by early feelings of confusion and alienation, a theme that emerges in his work on identity crisis. In 1933, aware of the worsening political climate in Austria and Germany, he moved to the USA with his wife, Joan Serson, and their children, Kai and Jon (Susan, their third child, was born in America). They settled in Boston, where he opened the city's first child psychoanalyst's practice. Erikson secured appointments at the Harvard Medical School and Massachusetts General Hospital, and affiliate status with the Harvard Psychological Clinic. At Harvard he came in to contact with numerous academics, including Gregory **Bateson**, Henry **Murray** and Kurt **Lewin**, who were to shape his attempts to integrate psychoanalysis with psychology and anthropology, with particular success in his studies of child development. He moved to the University of California, Berkeley, from which he later resigned in protest at the university's dismissal of staff who refused to sign an oath of loyalty and disclose political affiliations. He then moved to the Austen Riggs Center in Massachusetts, and from there returned in 1960 to Harvard, where he remained until his retirement in 1970.

Erikson is associated with the psychoanalytic tradition of ego psychology, one of whose major innovations was the inclusion within psychoanalytic theory of the influences of the external environment. The ego is considered to develop and function through a combination of internal processes and external events. Thus, Erikson built on the work of Sigmund and Anna Freud and emphasized the creative qualities of the ego, which strives to adapt to its environment and to find creative solutions to each new problem that confronts it.

Erikson developed a theory of ego development using concepts from embryology, especially the principle of epigenesis. This states that a new living organism develops from an undifferentiated entity that is programmed to develop all of the organism's parts in sequence. The ego is thought to develop in a planned sequence of stages, each consisting of a unique developmental task that confronts individuals in the form of a crisis or challenge that must be faced. For Erikson, this crisis is not a catastrophe but a turning point of increased vulnerability and enhanced potential. The more an individual resolves the crises successfully, the healthier the development will be.

Erikson defines eight developmental stages, of which trust–mistrust is the first. It is experienced in the first year of life. A sense of trust requires a feeling of physical comfort and a minimal amount of fear and apprehension about the future. Trust in infancy sets the stage for a lifelong expectation that the world will be a good and pleasant place to live.

Autonomy versus shame and doubt is the second stage of development. It occurs in late infancy (1–3 years). After developing a sense of trust in their caregivers, infants begin to discover the impact of their behaviour on others. They start to assert their sense of independence and autonomy. Erikson's theory suggests that if infants are restrained too much or punished too harshly for expressing this sense of freedom, they are likely to develop a sense of shame and doubt.

Initiative versus guilt is the third stage of development, and it occurs during the pre-school years. As pre-school children encounter a widening social world, they are challenged more than when they were infants. Active, purposeful behaviour is needed to cope with the challenges. As they mature, children are encouraged to assume responsibility for their bodies, their behaviour, their toys and their pets. Developing a sense of responsibility increases initiative. Uncomfortable guilt feelings may arise, though, if the child is irresponsible and is made to feel too anxious. Erikson suggests that most guilt is quickly compensated for by a sense of accomplishment.

Industry versus inferiority is the fourth developmental stage, occurring approximately in the early primary school years. Children's initiative brings them in to contact with a wealth of new experiences. As they move into middle and late childhood, they direct their energy towards mastering cognitive skills. Thus, at no other time is the child more enthusiastic about learning that at this stage. One danger in the primary school years resides in the potential for developing of a sense of inferiority – of feeling relatively incompetent.

Identity versus identity confusion is the fifth developmental stage, encountered during adolescence. At this time, individuals are faced with finding out who they are and where they are going in life, and with many new adult roles. If these are explored in a healthy manner, the adolescent arrives at a positive path to follow in life and a positive identity will be achieved. If an identity is forced on the adolescent by parents or peers, if the adolescent does not adequately explore many roles, and if a positive future path is not defined, then identity confusion is likely to result.

Intimacy versus isolation is the sixth development stage. It characterizes development during the early adult years. At this time, individuals face the developmental task of forming intimate relationships with others. If the young adult forms healthy friendships and an intimate, close relationship with another individual, intimacy will be achieved; if not, isolation will result.

Generativity versus stagnation is the seventh developmental stage, which individuals experience during middle adulthood. A chief concern for this stage of development is to assist the younger generation in developing and leading useful lives – this is what Erikson means by 'generativity'. The feeling of having done nothing to help the next generation is referred to as stagnation.

Integrity versus despair is the final developmental stage, which individuals experience during late adulthood. In the later years of life, we look back and evaluate what we have done with our lives. Through many different routes, the older person may have developed a positive outlook in most or all of the previous stages of development. If so, the retrospective glances will reveal a picture of a life well spent, and the person will feel a sense of satisfaction. A sense of completeness may be achieved. If the older adult resolved many of the earlier stages negatively, the retrospective glances will be likely to yield doubt or gloom and may be experienced as a sense of incompleteness and despair.

Four kinds of criticism have been directed against Erikson's theory. First, whereas Freud could be considered to be overly pessimistic of the human condition Erikson is often considered to be overly optimistic. He has countered that this is not true and that for each psychosocial stage there is a crisis and a specific negative ego quality (e.g. shame, mistrust) which may be a lifelong source of potential anxiety. Second, it has been said that Erikson has exaggerated the role of the ego at the expense of the id and the unconscious. This is probably true, but it does not seriously impact on the integrity of his position. Third, it is sometimes argued that Erikson's theory places too great an emphasis on the need for the individual to adjust to the norms and expectations of society. However, his argument is that our sense of identity develops within the possibilities offered by society, and these may include stability or change. For example, in *Gandhi's Truth* he demonstrates a profound interest in people who create and sustain a healthy sense of identity through radical social upheaval. Finally, Erikson has been criticized for the nature of his research designs, which (except for some studies of children's play) are primarily based on personal observation rather than controlled experimentation. Thus, while Erikson offers a considerable corpus of empirical evidence in support of his theory, much of the evidence has been collected in ways that favour support for his position.

Despite these criticisms Erikson's contributions are significant: he emphasized the psychosocial as well as the instinctual basis for behaviour and development; his account of development embraces the whole life-cycle; and his theoretical position explicitly acknowledges that the individuals often look as much to their future as to their past.

Eron, Leonard David

Born: 1920, Newark, New Jersey, USA **Nat:** American **Ints:** Clinical psychology, developmental psychology, personality and social psychology **Educ:** BS City College of New York, 1941; MA Columbia University, 1946; PhD University of Wisconsin, 1949 **Appts & awards:** Fulbright Senior Scholar, 1976–7; Emeritus Professor, University of Illinois, APA Distinguished Contributions to Knowledge Award, 1980; James McKeen Cattell Foundation Award, 1984; President, Midwestern Psychological Association, 1985–6; Editor, *Journal of Abnormal Psychology*, 1973–80; Editorial Board, *Nursing Research*, 1979–82, *Clinical Psychology Review*, 1980– , *Contemporary Psychology*, 1980–4, *Aggressive Behavior*, 1982– , *Violence in America*, 1985–

Principal publications

1950   A normative study of the Thematic Apperception Test. *Psychological Monographs*, 64, no. 9 (2).

1954   The use of the Rorschach method in medical student selection. *Journal of Medical Education*, 29, 34–9.

1958   The effect of medical education on attitudes: A follow up study. *Journal of Medical Education*, 33, 23–33.

1963   The relationship of TV viewing habits and aggressive behavior in children. *Journal of Abnormal and Social Psychology*, 67, 193–6.

1965   *An Experimental Approach to Projective Techniques*. Wiley (with J. Zubin and F. Schumer).

1969   *Relation of Theory to Practice in Psychotherapy*. Aldine (ed. with R. Callaghan).

1970   Prescription for reduction of aggression. *American Psychologist*, 35, 244–52.

1971   *The Learning of Aggression in Children*. Little, Brown (with L. Walder and M. Lefkowitz).

1972   Parent–child interaction, television violence and aggression in children. *American Psychologist*, 27, 197–211.

1972   Does television violence cause aggression? *American Psychologist*, 27, 253–63 (with L.R. Huesmann, M.M. Lefkowitz and L.O. Walder).

1977   *Growing Up to Be Violent*. Pergamon (with M. Lefkowitz, L. Walder and L.R. Huesmann).

1979   (ed.) *Classification of Behavioral Disorders*. Aldine.

1984   The relation of prosocial behavior to the development of aggression and psychopathology. *Aggressive Behavior*, 10, 201–11.

1984   Intervening variables in the television violence–aggression relation: Evidence from two countries. *Developmental Psychology*, 20, 746–55 (with L.R. Huesmann and K.C. Lagerspetz).

1985   The stability of aggressive behavior over time and generations. *Developmental Psychology*, 26, 1120–34 (with L.R. Huesmann).

Further reading

Eron, L.D. *et al.* (eds) (1994) *Reason to Hope: A Psychosocial Perspective on Violence and Youth*. American Psychological Association, Washington.

Huesmann L.R. (ed) (1994) *Aggressive behavior: Current Perspectives*. Plenum.

Eron's early research was concerned with personality assessment, and he demonstrated that a number of widely used psychodiagnostic techniques had dubious reliability and validity. This led him to consider the predictability of personality over time, and throughout his career he made extensive use of longitudinal designs in order to demonstrate both continuity and change. His first large-scale longitudinal study was with an entire class of medical students whom he followed over four years, demonstrating among them an increase in cynicism and anxiety and a decrease in humanitarianism. The same was not true of comparable classes of law students and graduate students of nursing followed over a similar period. The changes in personality over time which were demonstrated in these young adults led to further longitudinal studies, and he turned his attention to younger subjects.

He was interested in how children learn to be aggressive, and in 1960 studied a large group of 8-year-old children (the entire population of 857 third-graders in a semi-rural county in New York) and interviewed three-quarters of their parents. He demonstrated that the aggressive behaviour of these children in school was related to the conditions of learning in their home environment; specifically, the extent of frustration rewards, and punishment, for aggressive behaviour, and available models of aggressive behaviour. The children were seen again at age 19 and 30. At age 30, 410 of the original subjects were interviewed as well as 165 of their spouses and 82 of their children. Also available were New York State Criminal Justice and Traffic data. Some follow-up data were available on 632 of the original subjects. The most remarkable finding was the stability of aggressive behaviour over time and across three generations. The more aggressive the children were at age 8, the more crimes they committed by age 30; the more traffic violations and convictions for drunken driving; the more abusive they were rated by their spouses; the more severely they punished their own children and the more aggressive were their own children. Eron has developed structural and process models simulating the causes of aggression over time, and his is now one of the most important databanks in developmental psychology in the USA. In much of his later work he collaborated with Rowell Huesmann; their studies are widely cited in debates concerning the effects of media violence on children.

Escalona, Sibylle K.
Born: 1915, Berlin, Germany **Nat:** German **Ints:** Clinical psychology, developmental psychology, personality and social psychology, psychoanalysis **Educ:** MA University of Iowa, 1938; PhD Teachers College, Columbia University, 1947 **Appts & awards:** Professor Emeritus, Department of Psychiatry (Psychology), Albert Einstein College of Medicine; Board Member and Chairman, Foundation's Fund for Research in Psychiatry, 1956–9; Research Scientist Award, 1972

Principal publications

1949 Unusual sensitivities in very young children. *Psychoanalytic Study of the Child*, 3/4, 333–52 (with P. Bergman).

1959 *Prediction and Outcome: A Study of Child Development*. Basic Books (with G. Heider).

1961 The prediction of school age intelligence from infant tests. *Child Development*, 32, 597–605.

1962 The study of individual difference and the problem of state. *Journal of the American Academy of Child Psychiatry*, 1, 11–37.

1965 Some determinants of individual differences in early ego development. *Transactions of the New York Academy of Sciences*, 27, 802–16.

1968 *The Roots of Individuality: Normal Patterns of Development in Infancy*. Aldine.

1974 Early life experience and the development of competence. *International Review of Psychoanalysis*, 1, 151–68 (with H.H. Corman).

1982 Growing up with the threat of nuclear war. *Journal of Orthopsychiatry*, 52, 600–7.

1982 Babies at double hazard: Early development of infants at biologic and social risk. *Pediatrics*, 70, 570–6.

1986 *Early Arrivals: A Study of Premature Infants and their Families*. Yale University Academic Press.

Further reading
Inhelder, B. *et al.* (1987) *Piaget Today*. Erlbaum.

Escalona's primary interest was in the analysis of the processes of human development, especially during the early years of life. When her professional career began the field was long on theory and short on facts, and this has led her to undertake phenomenological studies of infants and young children, which demonstrated the importance of individual differences beginning on day one for both personality and cognitive development. Organismic predispositions have different consequences depending on the sociocultural conditions and interpersonal experiences to which the young organism must adapt. In order to understand manifold developmental patterns within a coherent conceptual framework, Escalona was among the first to propose a model of development that eliminates the nature–nurture dichotomy and emphasizes the more direct link between patterns of experience and developmental course and outcome (cf. *The Roots of Individuality*). Her subsequent studies of healthy infants, disturbed children, children in poverty and premature infants were based on this approach.

Estes, William K.

Born: 1919, Minneapolis, Minnesota, USA *Nat:* American *Ints:* Experimental *Educ:* BA University of Minnesota, 1940; PhD University of Minnesota, 1943 *Appts & awards:* President, Midwestern Psychological Association, 1957; President, APA Division of Experimental Psychology, 1959; Psychonomic Society, Governing Board, 1960–72, Chair, 1972; APA Distinguished Scientific Contribution Award, 1962; Warren Medal, Society of Experimental Psychologists, 1963; NRC Mathematical Social Sciences Board, Member, 1972–6, Chair, 1974–6; Commission on Human Resources, NRC, 1974–7; Hon. DSc, Indiana University, 1976; Hon. MA, Harvard University, 1979; Chair, NRC, 1982; Executive Committee, Society for Mathematical Psychology, 1982; Senior Consultant and Chair, Advisory Committee, Office of Scientific and Engineering Personnel, NRC, 1983–5; Society for Mathematical Psychology, Chairman, 1984; Professor, Department of Psychology, Harvard University, USA Guggenheim Fellow, 1985–6; NAS Fellow; AAA&S Honorary Life Member; New York Academy of Arts and Sciences; Editor, *Journal of Comparative and Physiological Psychology*, 1963–8, *Psychological Review*, 1977–82

Principal publications

1950 Toward a statistical theory of learning. *Psychological Review*, 57, 94–107.
1954 *Modern Learning Theory*. Appleton-Century-Crofts (with S. Koch).
1957 Of models and men. *American Psychologist*, 12, 609–17.
1959 The statistical approach to learning theory. In S. Koch (ed.), *Psychology: A Study of Science*. McGraw-Hill.
1959 *Studies in Mathematical Learning Theory*. Stanford University Press (with R.R. Bush).
1960 Learning theory and the new 'mental chemistry'. *Psychological Review*, 67, 207–23.
1967 *Stimulus Sampling Theory*. Holden-Day (with E.D. Neinmark).
1969 Reinforcement in human learning. In J. Tapp (ed.), *Reinforcement and Behavior*. Academic Press.
1972 Interactions of signal and background variables in visual processing. *Perception and Psychophysics*, 12, 278–86.

1975 Some targets for mathematical psychology. *Journal of Mathematical Psychology*, 12, 263–82.
1976 The cognitive side of probability learning. *Psychological Review*, 83, 37–64.
1977 *Learning Theory and Mental Development*. Academic Press.
1980 Is human memory obsolete? *American Scientist*, 68, 62–9.
1982 *Models of Learning, Memory and Choice*. Praeger.
1982 Similarity interactions in visual processing. *Journal of Experimental Psychology: Human Perception and Performance*, 8, 353–82.

Further reading

Estes, W.K. (1991) *Statistical Models in Behavioral Research*. Erlbaum.
Geissler, H.G. *et al.* (eds) (1992) *Cognition, Information Processing and Psychophysics: Basic Issues*. Scientific Psychology Series. Erlbaum.

William K. Estes's graduate research training included working as assistant to S.R. Hathaway in the development of the Minnesota Multiphasic Personality Inventory. He also worked with B.F. **Skinner** studying animal learning and conditioning, in which, with Skinner, he developed the method that has become standard for tracing the emotional reactions related to fear ('conditioned emotional responses'). Estes served briefly with the National Defence Research Council on a research project, and then enlisted in the US Army. Initially he served in the Air Force Flexible Gunnery Research Program, then as a Clinical Psychologist and Medical Administrative Officer in the Asiatic-Pacific Theatre. In 1945, he joined Skinner once again, at Indiana University. He joined the faculty as an instructor, then attained positions successively as Assistant Professor (1947–50), Associate Professor (1950–5), Professor (1955–60) and Research Professor of Psychology (1960–2).

Up until the late 1940s Estes published variously in the field of animal learning. However, he is best known for his work in mathematical psychology, particularly the stimulus sampling theory. In 1950, he developed a statistical theory of elementary learning, predicated on **Guthrie**'s principal of contiguity: learning, complete in one trial, is a learned response, a condition which is a sample of all possible stimulus elements reaching the individual on subsequent trials. This was followed in subsequent decades by the development of mathematical models for human learning and decision making, visual information processing (as in the recognition of letters and words during reading), and various aspects of memory.

In the original version of 'Towards a statistical theory of learning', learning is considered as a statistical process which occurs in discrete jumps. The basic tenet of the theory lies in the concept of the stimulus as as a set of stimulus elements. On any given trial the organism will sample some proportion of the total set of elements available. If an element is sampled on a trial, and some response terminates the trial, that particular element is regarded as conditioned or connected to that response as a result of that single pairing. A stimulus element can be connected to only one response at a time. Extinction occurs whenever the stimulus elements become connected to some other response than the previously reinforced one. The response measure is the probability of its occurrence, the gradual increase observed, due to the appearance of only a sample of the stimulus population on a given trial. Successive samples from the population may not always contain enough elements that are conditioned to the response to make it occur. Estes developed a basic learning equation which provided a fit to acquisition data obtained from rats in runways, T-mazes and bar-pressing experiments.

One of the most impressive features of the theory was the extension into different areas of learning behaviour and its ability to stimulate a large amount of empirical research. Associated lines of research yielded a comprehensive analysis of motivational and cognitive factors contributing to the way human beings profit or fail to profit from experience with rewards and punishments. It lead to Estes's involvement with the identification of some of the principal sources of capacity limitation on human learning of categories and concepts. His approach continued to evolve alongside considerations of the relationships within learning and retention.

In 1962, Estes moved to Stanford University as Professor of Psychology and member of the Institute for Mathematical Studies in the Social Sciences. During his years at Stanford University, he worked in association with Richard C. **Atkinson**, Gordon H. Bower and Patrick **Suppes**. Among their joint activities, in varying combinations, was the systematization of the foundations of statistical learning theory, early work on the theoretical basis for computer-assisted instruction, and the development of a programme of graduate training in mathematical psychology through which passed many of the individuals who are now leaders in the field.

Among Estes's broad range of professional activities, he founded the Psychonomic Society and the Society for Mathematical Psychology. He worked with commissions and committees of the National Academy of Sciences/National Research Council on such matters as assessing the current state of research in cognitive science, problems of supply and demand for scientific and engineering personnel, and mobilizing the potential contributions of the behavioural and social sciences to problems of international security and the prevention of nuclear conflict.

CATE COX

Evans, Richard I.

Born: 1922, Chicago, Illinois, USA **Nat:** American **Ints:** Behavioural medicine, health psychology, research and prevention, social psychology **Educ:** BS University of Pittsburgh, 1946; MS University of Pittsburgh, 1947; PhD Michigan State University, 1950 **Appts & awards:** Professor, then Distinguished University Professor, University of Houston, 1958– ; President, APA Division 38, 1985; Fellow, APA Divisions 2, 8, 9, 16, 26 and 38; APA and American Psychological Foundation National Media Award, 1989; Outstanding Contributions to Health Psychology Award, APA, 1992; Distinguished Senior Research Award, Division 38, APA, 1992

Principal publications

1955 The planning and implementation of a psychology series on a non-commercial educational television station. *American Psychologist*, 10, 602–5.

1963 The 'radical right': A threat to the behavioral sciences. *Journal of Social Issues*, 19 (2), 86–106.

1964 *Conversation with Carl Jung*. Van Nostrand.

1966 *Dialogue with Erich Fromm*. Harper and Row.

1968 *B.F. Skinner: The Man and his Ideas*. Dutton.

1968 *Resistance to Innovation in Higher Education: A Social Psychological Exploration Focused on Television and the Establishment*. Jossey-Bass.

1973 *Jean Piaget: The Man and his Ideas*. Dutton.

1975 *Carl Rogers: The Man and his Ideas*. Dutton.

1976 *R.D. Laing: The Man and his Ideas*. Dutton.

1980 *The Making of Social Psychology*. Gardner Press.

1980 Deterring smoking in adolescents: A social-psychological perspective. In R.M. Lauer and R.E. Shekelle (eds), *Childhood Prevention of Atherosclerosis and Hypertensive Diseases*. Raven Press.

1981 Social modeling films to deter smoking in adolescents: Results of a three-year field investigation. *Journal of Applied Psychology*, 66, 399–414 (with C.A. Dill, A.H. Henderson, P.C. Hill, T.S. Guthrie, S.E. Maxwell, B.E. Racines and S.E. Rozelle).

1988 Health promotion – science or ideology? *Health Psychology*, 7, 203–19.

1989 *Albert Bandura: The Man and his Ideas.* Praeger.

(In press) Social influences in biology and prevention of smoking in children and adolescents. In A. Baum, T. Revenson and J. Singer (eds), *Handbook of Health Psychology.* Erlbaum.

Further reading

Baum, A., Revenson T. and Singer, J. (eds) (in press) *Handbook of Health Psychology.* Erlbaum.

Matarazzo, J.D. (eds) (1994) *Behavioral Health: A Handbook of Health Enhancement and Disease Prevention.* Wiley.

Evans has been associated with two major developments in the social and behavioural sciences. The first is the oral/visual history project supported by the Ford Foundation and National Science Foundation, having pioneered educational television with the first college course on television in 1953. Evans recorded dialogues in both the electronic and print media with some of the world's notable contributors to the behavioural sciences. This ambitious project began in 1957 with a filmed dialogue with the late C.G. **Jung** and an associated book. Further dialogues were completed with **Piaget**, **Fromm**, **Erikson**, **Lorenz**, **Allport**, **Skinner**, **Murray**, **Bandura**, **Hilgard**, **Murphy**, **Jones**, **Sanford**, **Cattell**, **Eysenck**, Frankl, **Laing**, May, **Tinbergen** and **Rogers** (among others). These have been widely disseminated as invaluable historical records of many of the major contributors to psychological science in the twentieth century.

Evans's other major involvement has been in the fields of behavioural medicine and health psychology, especially the application of social psychological theory to the prevention of the use of harmful substances by children and adolescents. In the 1970s, Evans began to explore two critical questions: 'If young people are aware of the risks to their health in using cigarettes, alcohol, illegal drugs, and engaging in unsafe sexual behaviour, why do they nevertheless engage in in such behaviours?' and 'How can theories in social psychology be applied to prevent such self-destructive behaviours?'

Social influences on the initiation of self-destructive behaviours investigated by Evans include direct or perceived peer pressure, role models provided by parents, siblings and friends, and representations in the media. Evans developed programmes based on 'social inoculation theory' to equip children and adolescents with the skills to resist these social pressures. For example, with 'low' peer pressure, simply learning how to say 'Just say no' might be sufficient. With stronger pressures, 'Just say no' would be insufficient, even though Nancy Reagan's campaign in the 1980s called attention to the importance of providing children and teenagers with such resistance skills. The social inoculation concept has been utilized in almost all abuse prevention programmes in the United States and several other countries.

DAVID F. MARKS

Eysenck, Hans Jurgen

Born: 1916, Berlin, Germany *Nat:* British *Ints:* Clinical psychology, evaluation and measurement, experimental psychology, personality and social psychology, psychological study of social issues *Educ:* BA University of London, 1938; PhD University of London, 1940 *Appts & awards:* Director, Psychological Department, Maudsley Hospital, 1946–83; Visiting Professor, University of Pennsylvania, 1949–50, University of California, Berkeley, 1954; Institute of Psychiatry, University of London, Reader in Psychology, 1950–4, Professor of Psychology, 1955–83, Emeritus Professor, 1983– ; Fellow, British Psychological Association, APA; Hon. Dsc, University of London, 1962; President, International Society for the Study of Individual Differences, 1983–5; APA Presidential Citation for Outstanding Contributions to Psychology, 1993; Founding Editor, *Behaviour Research and Therapy*, 1963; Editor, *Personality and Individual Differences*, 1980–

Principal publications

1947 *Dimensions of Personality.* Routledge and Kegan Paul.

1952 The effects of psychotherapy: An evaluation. *Journal of Consulting Psychology*, 16, 319–24.

1953 *The Uses and Abuses of Psychology.* Penguin.

1960 (ed.) *Behavior Therapy and the Neuroses.* Pergamon.

1964 *Crime and Personality.* Routledge and Kegan Paul.

1967 *The Biological Basis of Personality.* C.C. Thomas.

1972   (ed.) *Handbook of Abnormal Psychology*, 2nd edn. Pitman.

1976   *Sex and Personality*. Open Books.

1979   *The Structure of Intellect and Measurement of Intelligence*. Springer-Verlag.

1979   The conditioning model of neurosis. *Behavioral and Brain Sciences*, 2, 155–99.

1980   *The Causes and Effects of Smoking*. Temple Smith (with L.J. Eaves).

1980   *The Great Intelligence Debate*. Lifecycle (with L.J. Kamin).

1989   *Genes, Culture and Personality: An Empirical Approach*. Academic Press (with L.J. Eaves and N.G. Martin).

Further reading

Eysenck, H.J. (1979) The conditioning model of neurosis. *The Behavioral and Brain Sciences*, 2, 155–99 (including peer commentary).

—— (1982) *Personality, Genetics, and Behavior: Selected Papers*. Praeger.

Gibson, H.B. (1981) *Hans Eysenck: The Man and his Work*. Peter Owen.

Modgil, S. and Modgil, C. (eds) (1986) *Hans Eysenck: Consensus and Controversy*. Taylor and Francis.

Both of Hans J. Eysenck's parents were actors; they divorced when he was 2. He was raised by his Catholic grandmother, who subsequently died in a concentration camp during World War II. After attending various private schools in Europe, Eysenck left Germany in 1934 to study physics at the University of London. Disappointed at finding that he did not have the proper prerequisites, he enquired about other scientific subjects he was eligible to take. By this quirk of fate, psychology acquired one of its most eminent, prolific and controversial contributors. Eysenck completed his BA with first class honours, and then his PhD under Sir Cyril **Burt**. Eysenck's first publication described a factor analytic study of mental ability tests in which he replicated **Thurstone**'s primary mental abilities, but also showed that there was a general factor which accounted for a larger share of the variance, thus supporting **Spearman**'s notion of a general intelligence, or *g*. Eysenck was later to return to this finding in his Structure of Intellect (1979), in which he advocated a hierarchical model of general and specific intellectual factors.

Eysenck was treated with suspicion during the early war years in Britain, although he had nothing but hatred for Hitler and Nazism. He finally received an appointment to study abnormal psychology, of which he knew little at the time, at the Mint Hill Hospital and then the **Maudsley** Hospital, the foremost psychiatric institute in Britain. Sir Aubrey Lewis, its director, eventually appointed Eysenck to be in charge of clinical psychology, and later head of the Psychology Department at the Institute of Psychiatry of the University of London. During these early years Eysenck developed the two themes with which his name is most prominently linked: his criticism of psychoanalysis, and his theory of personality.

Undoubtedly Eysenck's premier empirical contribution was his conceptualization of personality as a small number of dimensional traits. Applying the methods of factor analysis, Eysenck first derived the two major factors of extraversion–introversion and neuroticism–stability. (A third factor, psychoticism, was added a few years later but has not gained widespread acceptance.) Our popular conceptions of extraversion and anxiety, which have origins in **Jung**'s typologies and Greek humoral theory, are due to Eysenck, who gave these traits contemporary empirical meanings. The robustness of the two primary factors of extraversion and neuroticism can be demonstrated by their discovery in the factor analysis of other personality tests (such as **Cattell**'s 16 Personality Factor Inventory); their appearance within the 'Big Five' factor model of personality now in vogue; their replicability cross-culturally; and in the demonstration of personality differences by behavioural and physiological measures. Eysenck developed several widely used standardized tests: the Maudsley Personality Inventory in 1959; the Eysenck Personality Inventory in 1963; and, with his wife Sybil B.G. Eysenck, the Eysenck Personality Questionnaire in 1975.

Not being content simply to describe these personality traits, Eysenck demonstrated the construct validity of the concepts in several ways. Working both sides of **Cronbach**'s 'two psychologies' (i.e. the correlational and the experimental), Eysenck sought to demonstrate differential effects of personality variables in behavioural tasks, particularly classical conditioning and verbal learning. His son Michael Eysenck continues this work today within the context of cognitive and memory research. Although the major personality factors were meant to apply to the normal range of individual differences, Eysenck early on suggested that certain personality types would be more prone to certain kinds of psychopathology; for example, neurotic introverts would become depressed and neurotic extraverts would become hysterics. He returned to this theme years later in considering personality predispositions to certain diseases, such as lung cancer.

Eysenck's description of personality was elaborated significantly as he postulated an underlying biological basis for the two major traits. He first drew parallels with **Pavlov**'s notions of cortical inhibition and **Hull**'s concept of drive. More generally accepted was his later conceptualization of extraversion as being modulated by the lowered arousal levels of the cortical-reticular activating system, thus leading to stimulation seeking and other extraverted behaviours, whereas neuroticism was determined by lability in limbic arousal, as manifested by autonomic overreactivity and fear. Eysenck's suggestion that personality is ultimately genetically determined led to studies of personality in twins and families, and the selective-breeding experiments conducted by his colleagues to produce the Maudsley Reactive and Nonreactive strains of rats. Eysenck was vociferously criticized by those who advocated environmental determinism, and even those in agreement with him thought he overstated the degree of genetic influence. Given the current swing of the pendulum from nurture back towards nature, Eysenck seems to have been ahead of his time.

There have been challenges over the years to the adequacy of postulating these two factors as basic to human personality. Are the factors too molar or, for example, could extraversion be subdivided parsimoniously into traits of sociability and impulsivity? Are two (or three, including psychoticism) major factors sufficient? Does the biology of the brain really separate the arousal systems of neuroticism from introversion, or can they be integrated through a single, alternative system?

The personality theory was the foundation of much of Eysenck's work in other realms. According to his theory, extraverts are under-aroused relative to introverts and thus seek stimulation; and neurotics acquire fears faster than do stable personalities. With these ideas, Eysenck subsequently related personality differences to marital satisfaction and sexual behaviour, criminal tendencies, cigarette smoking and political attitudes, and even considered their relationship to ESP and psychic abilities.

Another early and significant facet of Eysenck's work has been his outspoken opposition to psychoanalytic (particularly **Freud**ian)

theory, and his advocacy of behavioural psychotherapy. In his now-classic 1952 review of the efficacy of psychoanalytic therapy, Eysenck found no evidence for its effectiveness beyond what could be expected by the passage of time alone. Although his conclusion has subsequently been challenged as possibly too extreme, even current reviews conclude that psychoanalysis is no more effective than other forms of therapy. It is of continuing importance that he demonstrated the need to apply scientific methods to the validation of any psychotherapeutic method. In rejecting the domination of psychiatrists over psychologists at the Institute of Psychiatry, Eysenck moved clinical psychology from diagnostics to active therapeutic treatment. Though not a therapist or clinician himself, he nevertheless may be said to have founded clinical psychology in Britain. His department provided a home for the developing behavioural psychotherapy, and a refuge for its practitioners. The flavour of his approach is nicely captured by the subtitle of two of his edited volumes, 'Readings in Modern Methods of Treatment ... Derived from Learning Theory'. Ironically, in promulgating behavioural therapy Eysenck first bore the brunt of criticism from the psychoanalysts; later his stance was criticized by cognitive therapists for his excessive reliance on behavioural therapy and theory.

In recent decades Eysenck has renewed his work on the topic of intelligence, in which he has served as a reviewer and arbiter for the general reader, as well as a theorizer and active contributor. Arthur **Jensen** cites several themes in Eysenck's recent work: the fractionation of general intelligence; seeking more basic measures of intelligence, for example reaction times and evoked potentials; and the consideration of the genetic basis for intelligence.

Eysenck's work spans both sides of the nature–nurture question. As noted above, he has conducted extensive empirical work on the biological basis of his postulated personality factors. In addition, a persistent theme is that the biologically genetically determined trait (e.g. personality or intelligence) influences what may be learned though experience. Whereas genes predispose, it is the environment that shapes the outcome. For example, classical conditioning is said to be the mechanism for acquiring fears, and anxious (or high-neurotic) individuals are more susceptible to fear conditioning than are the low anxious, given comparable learning experiences. Interestingly, Kenneth **Spence**'s extensive research on anxiety and learning rate, conceived of within a completely different theoretical framework, is generally congruent with Eysenck's theory. Eysenck's 'The conditioning theory of neurosis' (1989) updates the **Watson–Mowrer** theory of phobia conditioning and avoidance behaviour on the basis of current research on learning, and thus further elaborates his beliefs in environmental determinism. In other places, he has suggested that criminal behaviour develops because some individuals, due to their personality configurations, fail to acquire a conscience that could inhibit certain actions. Eysenck suggests a diathesis–stress model for the development of cigarette smoking: smoking is partially determined by genetic dispositions related to personality (primarily motivated by boredom among extraverts and emotional strain among neurotics), and environmental factors such as stress and peer pressure.

Eysenck has frequently been the centre of intense controversies to a degree exceptional even among well-known academic psychologists. Interestingly, he has provoked opposition in several areas: his criticism of psychoanalysis and his advocacy of behavioural therapy as an alternative; his criticism of the evidence for the link between smoking and cancer; his advocacy of the genetic basis for personality and intelligence, and his discussion of possible racial differences in the latter; and his willingness at least to consider the evidence for ESP and other psychic abilities. The reasons for controversy are sometimes less what Eysenck has said than what others have said he said; less how radical his opinions are than their timing with respect to the *Zeitgeist*; and less his science than the political implications of his views. For example, Eysenck joined a small group of scientists, which included the distinguished statistician Sir Ronald Fisher, who went against the orthodoxy of the medical and scientific establishment in arguing that a causal link between cigarette smoking and lung cancer or coronary disease remained unproven. Simply put, correlational findings within self-selected samples of people have not demonstrated (and cannot demonstrate) that cigarette smoking is either a necessary or a sufficient cause for all cases of lung cancer. The social responsibility of a scientist demands an unbiased and objective (as far as humanly possible) analysis of the methods and data, particularly in areas where the conclusion may be unpopular. Eysenck noted the inconsistency by which scientists rigorously criticize the methods and data relating to some topics (such as paranormal and psychic phenomena) and not to others (in this case, the smoking–disease link). Granting these arguments, one might still wonder whether Eysenck places excessive trust in the validity of our 'facts', given that we know that truth in science is often relative and changeable. The title of Eysenck's recent autobiography (*Rebel with a Cause*, 1990) indicates that he is not naive regarding the ideological implications of the stances he takes.

Eysenck has been the conveyor of popular psychology to the general reader through a series of books dating back to *Uses and Abuses of Psychology* (1953), through works such as *Know Your Own IQ* (1964) and *Know Your Own psi-Q* (1984), and up to *I DO: How to Choose Your Mate and Have a Happy Marriage* (1985). In books such as these Eysenck presents his own views on personality, genetics, intelligence and psychological measurement; his criticisms of psychoanalysis; and his views on science and pseudoscience. He has consistently tried to present a view of psychology as being fully the science that physics, his original vocation, is.

Eysenck's impact can be documented by any number of measures. To say he has been prolific is an understatement. A conservative count shows over sixty authored or edited books, and over 600 articles or chapters. In research on citation frequency reported in the *American Psychologist*, a 1970 study placed Eysenck in the 98th percentile among cited authors, and he was the fifth most-cited psychologist in the year 1975. Gibson's biography cites other studies from the mid-1970s showing that Eysenck was the second most-cited living psychologist (after **Piaget**), and the most-cited British psychologist. A survey among historians of psychology and department chairs in 1991 placed him in the top ten among contemporary psychologists. Eysenck has influenced a large number of graduate and postdoctoral students, many of whom have continued to investigate the problem areas they started with as his students. This now worldwide proliferation of scientists and scholars has been referred to, not as an empire, but appropriately as the Eysenck Commonwealth.

W. S. TERRY

F

Fancher, Raymond Elwood

Born: 1940, Waterbury, Connecticut, USA **Nat:** American **Ints:** General psychology, history of psychology, personality and social psychology, psychoanalysis **Educ:** BA Wesleyan University, 1962; MA Harvard University, 1964; PhD Harvard University, 1967 **Appts & awards:** University of Rochester (New York), Assistant Professor of Psychology, 1966–70; York University (Ontario), Assistant Professor of Psychology 1970–79, Professor 1980– , Director, Graduate Programme in Psychology, 1990–3; Fellow, APA Divisions 1, 26

Principal publications

1973 *Psychoanalytic Psychology: The Development of Freud's Thought.* Norton.

1979 *Pioneers of Psychology* (3nd edn, 1996). Norton.

1985 *The Intelligence Men: Makers of the IQ Controversy.* Norton.

1993 Galton and the Darwins. *General Psychologist,* 29, 1–5.

Further reading

Smith, J.D. (1988) Fancher on Gould, Goddard, and historical interpretation: A reply. *American Psychologist,* 43, 744–5.

Raymond Fancher was born in Waterbury, Connecticut, and educated at Wesleyan University and Harvard, obtaining a PhD in clinical psychology. His early work was concerned with the problem of making accurate predictions about and writing valid conceptualizations of individual case histories, in which he was influenced by Gordon **Allport** and Robert White, his teachers at Harvard, and by his own interest in biography. In the early 1970s he became interested in **Freud**ian psychology, and his first book was essentially concerned with the relationship between Freud's biography and the development of his theory, in particular with the influence exerted by his early training in neurology. The relationship between the biography of a theorist in psychology and the theory he or she develops became a general theme of his work as his inter-

ests expanded to cover other major figures in psychology. His second book dealt with a number of pioneers from Descartes to **Skinner**, and his third with the main protagonists in the controversy that raged in the 1970s and 1980s around IQ and the relative effects of nature and nurture on its development. Fancher takes the view that 'personal experience and background seem often to have outweighed scientific evidence in determining individual positions'. It is certainly true that the controversy was conducted with greater venom (and sometimes violence) than would appear to be justified by what should have been an academic issue and that this seems to have come about owing to what were perceived as implications for policy on political and racial questions. In most human individuals such questions occupy a place of more central importance than questions of scientific validity. Even the scientist usually spends more time out of her or his laboratory than in it.

Fancher has written (and continues to write) extensively on **Galton** and on the history of statistics, and in the early 1980s he was instrumental in setting up one of the most successful PhD programmes in the history and theory of Psychology.

N.E. WETHERICK

Fantino, Edmund

Born: 1939, New York City, USA **Nat:** American **Ints:** Experimental analysis of behaviour, experimental psychology, health physiological and comparative **Educ:** BA Cornell University, 1961; PhD Harvard University, 1964 **Appts & awards:** Professor of Psychology and Member of the Group in the Neurosciences, University of California at San Diego, 1967– ; Society for the Experimental Analysis of Behavior, Board, 1972–80, 1982–90, 1991– , Secretary, 1975–6, President, 1985–7; Member, APA Division 6, Psychonomic Society, Association of Behavior Analysis, American Psychological Society (Charter member), Japanese Psychological Association; Associate Editor, *Behavioral Processes,* 1984– ; Editorial Board,

Behavioral Processes, 1984– , *Behavioral Analysis Letters*, 1980–4, *Behaviorism*, 1984, *Journal of Economic Psychology*, 1985– ; Editor, *Journal of the Experimental Analysis of Behavior*, 1987–91

Principal publications

1969   Choice and rate of reinforcement. *Journal of the Experimental Analysis of Behavior*, 12, 163–91.

1972   The psychological distance to reward. *Journal of the Experimental Analysis of Behavior*, 18, 23–34 (with B. Duncan).

1973   Stimulus change contemporaneous with food presentation maintains responding in the presence of free food. *Science*, 182, 1038–9 (with R.F. Wallace, S. Osborne and J. Norborg).

1974   Stochastic transitivity and undimensional behavior theories. *Psychological Review*, 81, 426–41 (with D. Navarick).

1975   *Introduction to Contemporary Psychology.* Freeman (with G.S. Reynolds).

1976   Self-control and general models of choice. *Journal of Experimental Psychology: Animal Behavior Process*, 2, 75–87 (with D. Navarick).

1977   Conditioned reinforcement: Choice and information. In W. Honig and J. Staddon (eds), *Handbook of Operant Psychology*. Prentice-Hall.

1979   *The Experimental Analysis of Behavior: A Biological Perspective.* Freeman (with C. Logan).

1981   Self-punitive behavior in humans: Effects of a self-fulfilling prophecy. *Learning and Motivation*, 12, 212–38 (with J.E. Rose).

1983   The delay-reduction hypothesis: Extension to three-alternative choice. *Journal of Experimental Psychology: Animal Behavior Processes*, 9, 132–46 (with R. Dunn).

1983   Observing reward-informative and un-informative stimuli by normal children of different ages. *Journal of Experimental Child Psychology*, 36, 437–52 (with D.A. Case and D. Altrus).

1985   Choice, optimal foraging and the delay-reduction hypothesis. *Behavioral and Brain Sciences*, 8, 315–62 (with N. Abarca).

1987   A molecular analysis of choice on concurrent-chains schedules. *Journal of the Experimental Analysis of Behavior*, 47, 145–59 (with P. Royalty).

1988   Effects of reinforcement context on choice. *Journal of the Experimental Analysis of Behavior*, 49, 367–81 (with T.C. Jacob).

1989   Instructions and reinforcement in the observing behavior of adults and children. *Learning and Motivation*, 2, 373–412 (with D.A. Case).

1990   Unification of models for choice between delayed reinforcers. *Journal of the Experimental Analysis of Behavior*, 53, 189–200 (with P.R. Killeen).

1993   The delay-reduction hypothesis: Effects of informative events on response rates and choice. *Quarterly Journal of Experimental Psychology*, 46B, 145–61 (with D.A. Case).

Further reading

Commons, M.L., Kacelnik, A. and Shettleworth, S.J. (eds) (1987) *Foraging*. Erlbaum.

—— Mazur, J.E., Nevin, J.E. and Rachlin, H. (eds) (1987) *The Effect of Delay and of Intervening Events on Reinforcement Value*. Erlbaum.

Luco, J.E. (1990) Matching, delay-reduction, and maximizing models for choice in concurrent-chains schedules. *Journal of the Experimental Analysis of Behavior*, 54, 53–67.

Behaving organisms are continually making choices and Fantino has always been interested in the factors determining those choices. His early work developed the delay-reduction hypothesis (DRH), which states that the effec-tiveness of a stimulus as a conditioned reinforcer may be predicted by calculating the reduction in the length of time to primary rein-forcement correlated with the onset of that stimulus relative to the length of time to primary reinforcement measured from the onset of the preceding stimulus. Expressed differently, the greater the improvement, in terms of temporal proximity or waiting time to reinforcement, correlated with the onset of a stimulus, the more reinforcing that stimulus will be. The work showed that the proportions of delay-reduction correlated with each outcome. The DRH has been extended to areas such as elicited respond-ing and self-control. Currently the emphasis is on extensions to observing and foraging.

The observing studies carried out by Fantino and his team investigate what maintains atten-tional responses in human adults and children. Making these attentional responses produces stimuli that are correlated with either reward ('good news') or non-reward ('bad news') outcomes, but they do not themselves influence the occurrence of the rewards. In a variety of experiments Fantino and his co-workers have shown that stimuli maintain observing only if correlated with a reduction in time to reinforce-ment or if correlated with a reduction in effort. These results support the DRH and are inconsistent with information and uncertainty-reduction hypotheses (since 'bad news' is avoided rather than produced).

Recently the theoretical and empirical study

of choice by behavioural ecologists and behavioural psychologists has converged on the area of foraging. Fantino and his colleagues have shown that the DRH generates optimal solutions in decision-making procedures and that it is also consistent empirically with decision making in situations sharing important properties with naturally occurring foraging.

Fantz, Robert Lowell

Born: 1925, Muncie, Indiana, USA **Died:** 1981, Cleveland, Ohio, USA **Nat:** American **Ints:** Cognitive development, comparative psychology, developmental psychology, experimental psychology, infancy, perceptual development **Educ:** PhB University of Chicago, 1947; PhD University of Chicago, 1954 **Appts & awards:** Research Assistant, University of Chicago, 1949–53; Assistant, Yerkes Laboratories of Primate Biology 1953–5; Research Associate, Institute for Child Welfare, University of California at Berkeley, 1956; Case Western Reserve University, Cleveland, Ohio, Research Associate, 1957, from Assistant Clinical Professor to Associate Clinical Professor, 1958–71, Associate Professor, 1971–81

Principal publications

1957 Form preferences in newly hatched chicks. *Journal of Comparative and Physiological Psychology*, 50, 422–30.

1958 Pattern perception in young infants. *Psychological Record*, 8, 43–7.

1961 A method for studying depth perception in infants under six months of age. *Psychological Record*, 11, 27–32.

1961 The origin of form perception. *Scientific American*, 204, 66–72.

1962 Maturation of pattern visualization in infants during the first six months. *Journal of Comparative and Physiological Psychology*, 55, 907–17 (with J.M. Ordy and M.S. Udelf).

1963 Pattern vision in newborn infants. *Science*, 140, 296–7.

1964 Visual experience in infants: Decreased attention to familiar patterns relative to novel ones. *Science*, 146, 668–70.

1965 Visual perception from birth as shown by pattern selectivity. In H.E. Whipple (ed.), New issues in infant development. *Annals of the New York Academy of Science*, 118, 793–814.

1967 Pattern preferences and perceptual cognitive development in early infancy. *Merrill-Palmer Quarterly*, 13, 77–108 (with S. Nevis).

1975 Early visual selectivity. In L.B. Cohen and P.

Salapatek (eds), *Infant perception: From Sensation to Cognition*, vol. 1. Academic Press (with J. Fagan and S.B. Miranda).

1975 Newborn infant attention to form of contour. *Child Development*, 46, 224–8 (with S.B. Miranda).

Further reading

Nash, J. (1978) *Developmental Psychology: A Psychobiological Approach*. Prentice-Hall.

Walk, R. (1981) *Perceptual Development*. Brooks Cole.

Robert L. Fantz was born on 25 September 1925 in Muncie, Indiana. He served in the United States Army during World War II, and was awarded the Bronze Star for courage in battle. Following the war he attended the University of Chicago, where he was awarded his PhB in 1947 and his PhD in psychology in 1954. He was trained as a comparative psychologist, studying under Eckhard Hess. His dissertation consisted of a series of experiments which demonstrated the existence of form perception in newly hatched chicks, which, presented with a variety of stimuli, can discriminate shape, size and three-dimensionality without reward. This interest in early visual perception was continued during his postdoctoral years, first at the Yerkes primate laboratories, and later at the Institute for Child Welfare at the University of California at Berkeley. In a series of articles beginning in 1958, Fantz developed the visual interest task as a means for exploring visual perception in the human infant. Fantz argued that if a baby looked preferentially at one stimulus over another, in a paired choice design, and the baby's choice was consistent, that preference could be taken to indicate discrimination. In the years following the development of this technique, Fantz's procedure came to be regarded as the foundation of many infant research techniques.

In 1961 Fantz published an influential article in *Scientific American* in which he presented some of the discoveries made with the visual interest test up to that time. By that time, he had, in this and his other publications, established that infants visually prefer faces over non-facial configurations of the same stimuli, and prefer some pattern organizations over others, as well as some colours over others.

In 1962 Fantz extended this preference technique to examine visual form perception and visual acuity during the first year. In this study, Fantz and his co-workers based their rationale on the observation that infants prefer heterogeneous patterns over homogeneous ones. The researchers displayed pairs of patterns in which one member was always grey and the other a set of stripes. As stripe widths were varied to finer and finer patterns, the stripe width that failed to evoke a response from the baby represented the limits of the baby's ability to discriminate stripes from solid grey, and thus became a measure of acuity. By this measure, newborns showed 20/400 vision (in Snellon notation) reaching 20/100 vision by six months.

The origin of visual perception was explored in a study using neonates published in *Science* in 1963. This study was an extension of results using somewhat older infants published in the *Psychological Record* in 1961. In these experiments, Fantz was interested in the infant's ability to distinguish the human face. The general procedure was to present the infant with flat objects the size and shape of the head. One resembled a human face, another presented facial features (hair, eyes, nose, mouth, etc.) in a scrambled fashion, and a third consisted of a head shape with black shading equivalent in extent to the others, but presented as a solid block. In both experiments there was preference for the human face. In his analysis of the results, Fantz stated that it would be unwarranted to assume that infants have 'instinctive recognition' of a human face. What it does suggest, he argued, is that a pattern with similarities to social objects has stimulus properties for the infant, and this may facilitate the development of social responsiveness.

The infant's ability to retain visual information was documented in a second article that was published in *Science* in 1964. In 1967 he published a longitudinal study on pattern preferences and perceptual cognitive development in early infancy. In that study the possibility was raised that individual differences in early perceptual development might have value for the prediction of later cognitive functioning. To a large extent, his life's work climaxed in a book chapter which was at once a general review, a presentation of original data, and a theoretical statement. The chapter, published in Cohen and Salapatek's *Infant Perception: From Sensation to Cognition*, has been regarded as his magnum opus.

In many ways Fantz was a reclusive scientist. He had few of his own students and held no firm academic position, supporting himself solely on the basis of research grants. In the lab he often arrived at late hours, and worked at night. He did not hold office in any scientific organization, and rarely attended conventions. Yet he influenced many, first by developing a methodology, and second by devising a set of issues to be explored.

D. THOMPSON

Farquhar, John W.

Born: 1927, Winnipeg, Manitoba, Canada **Nat:** American **Ints:** Behavioural medicine, health communication, health psychology, social psychology **Educ:** AB University of California at Berkeley, 1949; MD University of California School of Medicine, San Francisco, 1952 **Appts & awards:** Stanford University School of Medicine, Assistant Professor, 1962–6, Associate Professor, 1966–73, Professor of Medicine, 1973– , Professor of Family, Community and Preventive Medicine, 1978–88, Professor of Health Research and Policy, 1988– ; Director, Stanford Center for Research in Disease Prevention; James D. Bruce Memorial Award for Excellence in Preventive Medicine, American College of Physicians, 1983; Myrdal Prize for Contributions to Evaluation Practice, American Evaluation Association, 1986; Academy of Behavioral Medicine Research, Member, 1990; Charles A. Dana Foundation Award for Pioneering Achievements in Health, 1991; National Cholesterol Award for Public Education, National Cholesterol Education Program, 1991–2; President, Society of Behavioral Medicine, 1992; American Heart Association Research Achievement Award, 1992; Fellow, United States–China Educational Institute, 1992

Principal publications

1977 Community education for cardiovascular health. *Lancet*, 1, 1192–5 (with N. Maccoby *et al.*).

1978 *The American Way of Life Need Not Be Hazardous to Your Health.* Norton (revised edn, 1987).

1978 The community-based model of lifestyle intervention trials. *American Journal of Epidemiology*, 108, 103–11.

1980 Skills training in a cardiovascular health education campaign. *Journal of Consulting and Clinical Psychology*, 48, 129–42 (with A. Meyer, J.D. Nash, A. McAlister and N. Maccoby).

1980 Changing cardiovascular risk factors in entire communities: The Stanford Three Community Project. In R.M. Lauer and R.B. Shekelle (eds), *Childhood Prevention of Atherosclerosis and Hypertension*. Raven Press.

1984   Community applications of behavioral
        medicine. In W.D. Gentry (ed.), *Handbook of
        Behavioral Medicine*. Guilford Press (with N.
        Maccoby and D.S. Solomon).
1990   The Stanford Five-City Project: Effects of
        community-wide education on cardiovascular
        disease risk factors. *Journal of the American
        Medical Association*, 264, 359–65 (with S.P.
        Fortmann, J.A. Flora, C.B. Taylor, W.L. Haskell,
        P.T. Williams, N. Maccoby and P.D. Wood).
1990   *The Last Puff*. Norton (with G.A. Spiller).
1996   A functional interpretation of a health
        campaign's effects. *Health Communication* (in
        press, with S.H. Chaffee, C. Roser and J. Flora).

Further reading

Baum, A., Revenson, T. and Singer, J. (eds) (in press)
    Handbook of Health Psychology. Erlbaum.
Matarazzo, J.D. (eds) (1984) *Behavioral Health: A
    Handbook of Health Enhancement And Disease
    Prevention*. Wiley.

John W. Farquhar was born in Canada but educated in the United States, where he was first in his class at the University of California School of Medicine, San Francisco. As an Assistant Professor at the Stanford University School of Medicine, Farquhar's first interests were in the metabolism of lipids with specific reference to heart disease. However, a sabbatical year spent studying epidemiology and medical statistics at the London School of Hygiene and Tropical Medicine in 1968–9 convinced him that significant progress against the cardiovascular 'epidemic' would come only from efforts to educate the public about the risk factors for heart disease, and to provide them with the tools for self-directed change of diet and lifestyle. The roots of cardiovascular disease were to be found in cultural and environmental factors that can best be addressed by change at the individual and community level – not in the doctor's office.

In the late 1960s and 1970s these ideas were new, and on his return to Stanford University, Farquhar brought together distinguished psychologists, educators, epidemiologists and medical scientists to develop an experimental approach for changing the health habits of entire communities that was the first of its type in the world. The consensus of prominent social psychologists at that time (D. Cartwright, H. Hyman, P. Sheatsley and R. Bauer) was that mass media campaigns generally failed to make major changes in the behaviour of free-living populations. In collaboration with a team of social and medical scientists and applying to community populations many of the ideas for behaviour change embodied in the social cognitive theory of Albert **Bandura**, Farquhar developed and implemented the Three-Community Study (1972–5), the first in a number of large-scale behaviour modification trials. Matched farming communities were given different 'treatment' for heart disease prevention, with one receiving only messages delivered by mass media and the direct mail; one receiving additional intensive instruction for those considered at high risk; and one acting as a control. The innovative aspects of the Three-Community Study included creation of a team approach, use of a public health model of reaching entire communities, and use of methods based on advanced social science theories and testing whether success in achieving a 'community effect' by a media-only approach required additional face-to-face instruction.

The finding – that the mass media were generally as effective as direct instruction in making a significant reduction in heart disease risk – spurred the development of many similar projects throughout the world, including Switzerland, South Africa and Australia. This finding is now described in almost all major texts in public health, health promotion or health communication. The study results reinforced Farquhar's conviction that the key to health improvement lay in community-based approaches. Since the success of the first study, Farquhar's Stanford group has conducted many other projects, including the Five-City Project, which achieved success not only through the use of mass media but by mobilizing the community's own resources for change. The group has also expanded its work beyond cardiovascular disease with projects involving health promotion in many different population groups, including suicide prevention among young Native Americans, women's health, violence prevention and substance abuse prevention, including especially prevention of tobacco use.

In recent years, John Farquhar has turned his attention to the need for disease prevention on a global scale, working through the World Health Organization and the 'Victoria Declaration' Advisory Group, which he chairs. The aim is to promote international actions to reduce cardiovascular disease world-wide, and the group convenes regular international conferences to encourage the prevention of heart disease in developing or economically disadvantaged countries, where it is climbing steeply, even as it is declining in the developed world. Based on his own experience with community-directed change, Farquhar has encouraged the Advisory Group to adopt recommendations that call not only for the richer countries and the international organizations to make resources available to the poorer, but for countries themselves to apply principles of community change as they consider their own cultural, political and economic barriers to the adoption of new customs or processes, and take steps to change them.

Schools of public health and medicine, many social science departments including psychology and communication, and training programmes for health education and health psychology have been considerably influenced by the research findings of Farquhar and colleagues. His citation with the James D. Bruce Memorial Award from the American College of Physicians was 'in recognition of outstanding accomplishments and contributions in the field of preventive medicine'. The American Heart Association Research Achievement Award citation of 1992 stated in reference to the Three-Community Study: 'this landmark study … became a model for other community intervention projects, and established the Stanford Center for Research in Disease Prevention as an international resource and training center for prevention of chronic disease'.

The World Health Organization's InterHealth Project, which is carrying out community programmes in chronic disease prevention in twenty-seven countries, uses many of the methods developed by John Farquhar and colleagues. Although he trained in medicine, Farquhar's achievements lie squarely within the overlapping interdisciplinary fields of behavioural medicine and health psychology. His successes have resulted from the systematic application across entire populations of methods of self-directed behaviour change based on social cognitive theory and the cognitive behavioural approach. The approach has been applied in a multilevelled fashion with attention to health-related behaviours at individual, institutional, national and, now, international levels. The focus upon community-based behaviour change provides both high impact and high cost-effectiveness, emphasizing 'collective efficacy' at the community level as much as self-efficacy at the level of the individual.

DAVID F. MARKS

Farrington, David Philip
Born: 1944, Ormskirk, Lancashire, England *Nat:* British *Ints:* Developmental psychology, evaluation and measurement, personality and social psychology, psychology and law, psychological study of social issues *Educ:* BA University of Cambridge, 1966; MA University of Cambridge, 1970; PhD University of Cambridge, 1970 *Appts & awards:* Professor of Psychological Criminology, Cambridge University Institute of Criminology 1969– ; ASA (Criminology Section) Prize for Distinguished Scholarship, 1986; Sellin-Glueck Award, American Society of Criminology, 1984; Fellow, BPS, American Society of Criminology; Associate Editor, *Criminology*, 1984–7; Associate Editor, *Criminal Behaviour and Mental Health*, 1989–; Editorial Board, *British Journal of Social Psychology*, 1981–3, *Criminal Justice and Behaviour*, 1981–92, *Law and Human Behavior*, 1983– , *Journal of Quantitative Criminology*, 1984– , *Social Behaviour*, 1985–90, *Behavioural Sciences and the Law*, 1990– , *British Journal of Criminology*, 1992– , *Psychology, Crime and Law*, 1992– , *Legal and Criminolgical Psychology*, 1994–

Principal publications
1977   *The Delinquent Way of Life*. Heinemann (with D.J. West).
1979   Delinquent behaviour modification in the natural environment. *British Journal of Criminology*, 19, 353–72.
1980   Prison size, overcrowding, prison violence and recidivism. *Journal of Criminal Justice*, 8, 221–31 (with C.P. Nuttall).
1980   Four studies of stealing as a risky decision. In P.D. Lipsitt and B.D. Sales (eds), *New Directions in Psycholegal Research*. Van Nostrand Reinhold (with B.J. Knight).
1981   The Cambridge Study in Delinquent Development. In S.A. Mednick and A.E. Baert (eds), *Prospective Longitudinal Research*. Oxford University Press (with D.J. West).
1981   An experimental study of sentencing by magistrates. *Law and Human Behavior*, 5, 107–21 (with A. Kapardis).
1982   *Abnormal Offenders, Delinquency and the Criminal Justice System*. Wiley (ed. with J. Gunn).
1982   Longitudinal analyses of criminal violence. In M.E. Wolfgang and N.A. Weiner (eds), *Criminal Violence*. Sage.
1982   Naturalistic experiments on helping behaviour. In A.M. Colman (ed.), *Cooperation and Competition in Humans and Animals*. Van Nostrand Reinhold.

1983 Sex, sentencing and reconviction. *British Journal of Criminology*, 23, 229–48 (with A.M. Morris).

1983 Randomized experiments on crime and justice. In M. Tonry and N. Morris (eds), *Crime and Justice*, vol. 4. University of Chicago Press.

1984 An observational study of shoplifting. *British Journal of Criminology*, 24, 63–73 (with A. Buckle).

1985 *Aggressions and Dangerousness*. Wiley (ed. with J. Gunn).

1986 *Understanding and Controlling Crime: Toward a New Research Strategy*. Springer-Verlag (with L.E. Ohlin and J.Q. Wilson).

1991 Predicting participation, early onset, and later persistence in officially recorded offending. *Criminal Behaviour and Mental Health*, 1, 1–33.

1992 Criminal career research: Lessons for crime prevention. *Studies on Crime and Crime Prevention*, 1, 7–29.

1994 (ed.) *Psychological Explanations of Crime*. Dartmouth.

Further reading

Feldman, P. (1993) *The Psychology of Crime*. Cambridge University Press.

Hollan, C.R. (1992) *Criminal Behaviour*. Falmer.

Stephenson, G.M. (1992) *The Psychology of Criminal Justice*. Blackwell.

David Farrington was trained as an experimental psychologist, and shortly after completing his PhD (in human learning) he began to work at Cambridge with D.J. West on a major longitudinal survey of crime and delinquency, the Cambridge Study in Delinquent Behaviour (commenced 1961 with a cohort of 411 8–9-year-old boys, published in four books and more than sixty journal articles). He is also Co-principal Investigator of the Pittsburgh Youth Survey, a prospective study of 1500 males aged from 7 to 20. Throughout his career, he has applied rigorous controlled research methods – experimental, longitudinal and observational – to investigate criminological and legal problems. He is best known for his work on the developmental course of criminal careers and for his contributions to psychological theories of criminal behaviour. Apart from continuing the longitudinal survey to the present day, he: (1) conducted a series of experimental studies of stealing, mostly with B.J. Knight; (2) supervised experimental studies of sentencing and linked them to other kinds of sentencing research; and (3) conducted observational studies of shoplifting. He has also published important work on prison overcrowd-

ing, on police cautioning and on crime rates (comparing police records and results from victim surveys); however, his continuing aim is to apply the best available methods (experimental, longitudinal, observational) to advance knowledge about why people commit crimes, about crime prevention, and about reactions to crime by police, courts and prisons. In addition, his work for the BPS indicates a long-term commitment to developing criminological and legal psychology as a recognized area of academic scholarship and professional activity.

Feather, Norman Thomas

Born: 1930, Sydney, Australia **Nat:** Australian **Ints:** Developmental, industrial and organizational, personality and social, psychology of women, society for the psychological study of social issues **Educ:** BA University of Sydney, 1951; DipEd University of Sydney, 1952; MA University of New England, 1958; PhD University of Michigan, 1960 **Appts & awards:** Fulbright Scholarship, University of Michigan, 1958, 1967; Professor, Department of Psychology, Flinders University of South Australia; Marquis Award, University of Michigan, 1961; Fellow, Academy of the Social Sciences in Australia, Australian Psychological Society; President, Australian Psychological Society, 1978–9; Editorial Board, *Journal of Personality and Social Psychology*, *Journal of Personality*, *Administrative Science Quarterly*, *European Journal of Social Psychology*, *Motivation and Emotion*, *Journal of Occupational Psychology*, *Applied Social Psychology Annual*; Associate Editor, *Australian Journal of Psychology*

Principal publications

1959 Subjective probability and decision under uncertainty. *Psychological Review*, 66, 150–64.

1961 The study of persistence. *Psychological Bulletin*, 59, 94–115.

1966 *Theory of Achievement Motivation*. Wiley (with J.W. Atkinson).

1967 A structural balance approach to the analysis of communication effects. In L. Berkowitz (ed.), *Advances in Experimental Social Psychology*, vol. 3. Academic Press.

1967 An expectancy-value model of information-seeking behavior. *Psychological Review*, 74, 342–60.

1969 Attribution of responsibility and valence of success and failure in relation to initial confidence and task performance. *Journal of Personality and Social Psychology*, 13, 129–44.

1971   Organization and discrepancy in cognitive structures. *Psychological Review*, 78, 355–79.

1975   *Values in Education and Society*. Free Press.

1979   Values, expectancy and action. *Australian Psychologist*, 14, 234–60.

1980   Values in adolescence. In J. Adelson (ed.), *Handbook of Adolescent Psychology*. Wiley.

1981   Unemployment and depressive affect: A motivational and attributional analysis. *Journal of Personality and Social Psychology*, 41, 422–36.

1982   (ed.) *Expectations and Actions: Expectancy-Value Models in Psychology*. Erlbaum.

1984   Masculinity, femininity, psychological androgyny, and the structure of values. *Journal of Personality and Social Psychology*, 47, 604–20.

1985   (ed.) *Australian Psychology: A Review of Research*. Allen and Unwin.

1986   A longitudinal analysis of the effects of different patterns of employment and unemployment on school-leavers. *British Journal of Psychology*, 77, 459–79.

1990   *The Psychological Impact of Unemployment*. Springer-Verlag.

1993   Authoritarianism and attitudes toward high achievement. *Journal of Personality and Social Psychology*, 65, 152–64.

Further reading

Higgins, E.T. and Sorrentino, R.M. (eds) (1990) *Handbook of Motivation and Cognition: Foundations of Socal Behavior, Vol 2*. Guilford.

Sparks, P. *et al.* (1991) Expectancy-value models of attitudes: A note on the relationship between theory and methodology. *European Journal of Social Psychology*, 21, 261–71.

Norman Feather has maintained an interest in the expectancy-value approach to human motivation throughout his career, believing that what a person does is related to the attractiveness and aversiveness of perceived consequences and to the person's expectations that these consequences might or might not occur. Earlier studies applied this model to the analysis of choice, persistence and performance in experimental situations. Later he explored the relevance of the theory to applied problems such as the psychological impact of unemployment. He also related causal attributions for outcomes to the expectations that a person holds prior to engaging in a task or activity. He tried to understand the role of needs and values as variables that affect the attractiveness and aversiveness of events and outcomes. Feather believes that the expectancy-value approach helps to bridge the gap between cognition and behaviour and that there are many areas that still await its application. His 1982 book sums up a lot of this work.

Feather has also investigated the way people resolve discrepancies between information input and underlying cognitive structures. His early research on dissonance theory and his later research on cognitive balance, communication effects, and organization and discrepancy in cognitive structures reflects that interest. It also appears in his studies on value discrepancies. He has made contributions as well to the psychology of values, attribution theory and sex roles, and he attempted to break new ground in these areas. The 'values' work was brought together in his 1975 book. Interests in attribution processes and sex-role variables (e.g. masculinity, femininity and psychological androgyny) mainly appear in journal articles.

Fechner, Gustav Theodor

Born: 1801, Gross-Sarchen, Germany **Died:** 1887, Leipzig, Germany **Nat:** German **Ints:** Experimental, psychology and the arts **Educ:** Degree in Medicine from University of Leipzig, 1822 **Appts & Awards:** Professor of Physics, University of Leipzig, 1834–9

Principal publications

1838   Über die subjectiven complementer Farben. *Poggendorffs Annalen der Physik und Chemie*, 44, 513–35.

1838   Über eine Scheibe zur Erzeugung subjectiver Farben. *Poggendorffs Annalen der Physik und Chemie*, 45, 227–32.

1851   *Zend-Avesta oder über die Dinge des Himmels und des Jenseits*. Voss.

1860   *Elemente der Psychophysik*, vols 1 and 2. Breitkopf and Härtel. (Trans. H. Alder as *Elements of Psychophysics*, vol. 1, eds E.G. Boring and D.H. Howes, Holt, Rinehart and Winston, 1966.)

1865   Über die Frage des goldenen Schnittes. *Archiv für die zeichnenden Künste*, 11, 100–12.

1866   *Das Büchlein vom Leben nach dem Tode*. Voss (1st edn, 1835).

1876   *Vorschule der Ästhetik*. Breitkopf and Härtel.

1882   *Revision der Hauptpunkte der Psychophysik*. Breitkopf and Härtel.

Further reading

Arnheim, R. (1992) The other Gustav Theodor Fechner. In S. Koch and D.E. Leary (eds), *A Century of Psychology as Science*. APA.

Berlyne, D.E. (ed.) (1974) *Studies in the New Experimental Aesthetics*. Wiley.

Heidleberger, M. (1993) *Die innere Seite der Natur:*

Gustav Theodor Fechners wissenschaftlich-philosophische Weltauffassung. Vittorio Klostermann.

Höge, H. (1995) Fechner's experimental aesthetics and the golden section hypothesis today. *Empirical Studies of the Arts*, 13, 131–48.

Link, S.W. (1994) Rediscovering the past: Gustav Fechner and signal detection theory. *Psychological Science*, 5, 335–40.

Murray, D.J. (1993) A perspective for viewing the history of psychophysics. *Behavioral and Brain Sciences*, 16, 115–37.

Fechner was one of a small number of German scientists whose work in the nineteenth century laid the foundation for modern experimental psychology. Their contributions can be understood in the context of the growth of science in Germany beginning in the eighteenth century, particularly studies of physiology that were based upon experimental methods. Changes in the university curriculum in Germany are also significant, in particular the emergence of philosophy as a discipline, encouraging 'pure' research rather than preparation for the professions. Finally, the *Zeitgeist* of 'romanticism' with its quest for understanding the totality of human nature should be taken into account too. These trends provide the background to Fechner's research interests and methods; however, his lasting influence on psychology reflects the search for a creative synthesis of experimental investigations of the mind and metaphysical theories that preoccupied him throughout his career.

After graduating in medicine, with physics and chemistry, from Leipzig in 1822, Fechner devoted several years to the study of mechanics and electricity and to the translation of French scientific papers into German. Largely on the basis of his studies of the galvanic battery, he was appointed to the chair of physics at Leipzig in 1834. While he held this post he published work on subjective colours and after-images. Simultaneously, he continued his interests in metaphysics, and his speculative book, *Das Büchlein vom Leben nach dem Tode* (*The Little Book of Life After Death*), was published under the pseudonym 'Dr. Mises'. He resigned his chair in 1839 because of ill health (which seems to have been a combination of what is now called a nervous breakdown and problems with his eyesight induced by looking at the sun in pursuit of his research into positive after-images). His major contributions were carried out in retirement. Apparently, it was while lying awake in bed on 22 October 1850 that he

intuitively arrived at his formulation of the logarithmic relationship between the magnitude of sensation and physical stimulation, which he was to term Weber's Law but which has since become known as Fechner's Law, and which founded the study of psychophysics. His first discussion of this relationship is in his philosophical book *Zend-Avesta*. Subsequently, Fechner discovered that an increase in stimulus intensity that is just noticeably different is a constant fraction of stimulus intensity, and he conducted extensive empirical studies to test these generalizations. He provided an account of this research in his best-known work, *Elemente der Psychophysik*.

Fechner next turned his attention to the application of experimental methods to the study of aesthetics. He argued that questions of beauty could be expressed in scientific form, and he offered his own principles of beauty. However, his lasting contributions have been methodological rather than theoretical and the principles that he elucidated are now of only historical interest. He recommended the use of empirical methods that included the study of reactions to works of art and to specially constructed simplified stimuli. When two versions of Holbein's painting *Madonna* were exhibited side by side in Dresden, Fechner investigated the preferences of visitors to the exhibition, a study that represents the first attempt to base aesthetics on sampling the judgements of lay persons rather than on the introspections of a small number of experts. He proposed three methods for the study of aesthetics: those of choice, production and use. The three methods were applied to the study of the golden section, or the ratio of Phidias, 1 : 1.618. This ratio has exerted fascination for centuries. In response to a proposal made by Zeising in 1855 that it provided a fundamental law of aesthetic judgement, Fechner applied the method of choice in a series of investigations, systematically varying the ratios of sides of rectangular cards and eliciting judgements of how pleasing they were. In the method of production, subjects drew the rectangles that they found most pleasing; in the method of use, the sides of paintings were measured to ascertain whether their ratio approximated the golden section. The design of these experiments would not seem out of place today, and a very large literature has been devoted to showing that the golden section has some special significance in aesthetic judgement. Despite this attention, its significance is, perhaps, no clearer than in Fechner's time.

Fechner occupied a special place in the history of experimental psychology and it is arguable whether he or **Wundt** should be recognized as the founder of the discipline. The problems that he addressed are still the subject of investigation. His theories took precise mathematical form and he pioneered the systematic application of experimental methods to issues in perception. He made several methodological advances that strongly influenced the development of psychophysics; his approach influenced signal detection theory and his 'inner psychophysics' has been interpreted by some as anticipating contemporary connectionist approaches in cognitive science. Fechner's law has had wide application wherever the scaling of psychological judgements is studied; for example, the Fechner–Thurstone utility function in decision theory. Within aesthetics, the research strategy introduced by Fechner, of producing simple analogues of complex figures and examining the relationship between properties of these simpler forms and aesthetic judgements ('aesthetics from below'), remains the dominant approach in the psychology of art. The strategy was adopted by later researchers like Birkhoff, who proposed a mathematical relationship between aesthetic value and the order and complexity of works of art, and **Berlyne**, who interpreted order and complexity in terms derived from information theory and arousal theory in investigating the 'new' experimental aesthetics.

Of greater significance than these specific contributions, perhaps, is the fact that his theoretical principles and empirical work were presented in such rigorous fashion that they attracted similar empirical investigation from contemporaries such as **Helmholtz**, Mach and Volkmann, and hence demonstrated that questions about mental processes could conform to the conventions of scientific discourse. This process provided the foundation for a scientific psychology.

W.R. CROZIER

Feigenbaum, Edward A.

Born: 1936, Weehawken, New Jersey, USA **Nat:** American **Ints:** Artificial intelligence, cognitive science **Educ:** BS Carnegie Institute of Technology, 1956; PhD Carnegie Institute of Technology, 1960 **Appts & awards:** Fulbright Research Scholar, 1959–60; Professor, Department of Computer Science, Stanford University, 1965; Editor, Computer Science Series, 1965–79; Computer and Biomathematical Sciences, Member of Study Section, NIH, 1968–72; Committee on Mathematics in the Social Sciences, SSRC, 1977–8; Computer Science Advisory Committee, NSF, 1977–80; National Computer Conference Award, Best Technical Paper, 1978; Cognitive Science Society, Governing Board, 1979–82; American Association for Artificial Intelligence, Council, 1979–82, President, 1980–1, Fellow, 1990; Fellow, AAAS, 1983, American College of Medical Informatics, 1984; Member, National Academy of Engineering, 1986; Elected to Productivity Hall of Fame, Republic of Singapore, 1986; Hon. Sci, Aston University, 1989; Member, American Academy of Arts and Sciences, 1991; Career Achievement Medal, World Congress on Expert Systems ('Feigenbaum Medal' named in his honour), 1991; Fellow, American Institute of Medical and Biological Engineering, 1994; Editorial Board, *Journal of Artificial Intelligence*, 1970, *Journal of Parallel and Distributed Computing*, 1984; Editorial Advisory Board, Science Citation Index 151, 1978

Principal publications

1961   The distinctiveness of stimuli. *Psychological Review*, 69, 285–8 (with H.A. Simon).

1961   *Information Processing Language V Manual*. Prentice-Hall (with A. Newell, F. Tonge, G. Mealy *et al.*).

1962   A theory of the serial position effect. *British Journal of Psychology*, 53, 307–20 (with H.A. Simon).

1963   *Computers and Thought*. McGraw-Hill (with J. Feldman).

1965   Memory mechanism and EPAM Theory: Monologue and interchange at the First Conference on Remembering, Learning and Forgetting. In D. Kimble (ed.), *The Anatomy of Memory*. Science and Behavior Books.

1968   Mechanization of inductive inference in organic chemistry. In B. Kleinmuntz (ed.), *Formal Representations for Human Judgment*. Wiley.

1970   Toward an understanding of information processes of scientific inference in the context of organic chemistry. In B. Meltzer and D. Michie (eds), *Machine Intelligence*. Edinburgh University Press.

1972   Information processing. In *Readiness to Remember: Proceedings of the Third Conference on Remembering, Learning and Forgetting*. Gordon and Breach.

1977   A correlation between crystallographic computing and artificial intelligence research. *Acta*

Crystalographia, A33, 13–18 (with R.S. Englemore and C.K. Johnson).

1979 Knowledge engineering for medical decision making: A review of computer-based clinical decision aids. *Proceedings of the IEE*, 67, 1207–24 (with E.H. Shortliffe and B.G. Buchanan).

1980 *Applications of Artificial Intelligence of Organic Chemistry: The DENDRAL Project.* McGraw-Hill (with K. Lindsay, B.G. Buchanan and J. Lederberg).

1981 *Handbook of Artificial Intelligence*, 3 vols. Kaufman (with A. Barr and P. Cohen).

1983 *The Fifth Generation: Artificial Intelligence and Japan's Computer Challenge to the World.* Addison-Wesley (with P. McCorduck).

1984 Knowledge engineering: The applied side of artificial intelligence. *Annals of the New York Academy of Sciences*, 426, 91–107.

1984 Computer assisted decision making in medicine. *Journal of Philosophy and Medicine*, 9, 135–60 (with J. Kunz, E.H. Shortliffe and B.G. Buchanan).

1989 What hath Simon wrought? In D. Klahr and K. Kotovsky (eds), *Complex Information Processing: The Impact of Herbert A. Simon.*

Further reading

Richman, H.B., Staszewski, J.J. and Simon, H.A. (1995) Simulation of expert memory using EPAM IV. *Psychological Review*, 102, 305–30.

Edward Feigenbaum was born in New Jersey on 20 January 1936. He received his Bachelor of Science degree in electrical engineering in 1956, from the Carnegie Institute of Technology, and his PhD in 1960 from the Graduate School of Industrial Administration, Carnegie Institute of Technology, where he was a student of Herbert **Simon**. In the September of 1960 Feigenbaum moved to the University of California at Berkeley as an assistant professor, and remained until January 1965. While there he was recruited by the Advanced Research Projects Agency (ARPA) to work on a time-sharing system at Berkeley. He then moved to Stanford University in 1965, where he continued to do ARPA-sponsored research in artificial intelligence.

Feigenbaum's twenty-nine-year career at Stanford University has included numerous positions and associated distinctions in the field of artificial intelligence. In 1959, he developed and programmed for computer EPAM, a theoretical process model of human perception and memory, which has proved an excellent fit to experimental data from a wide variety of psychological tasks. In subsequent years EPAM has been progressively extended and adapted to new domains without radical changes in its central mechanisms. The most recent version, EPAM IV (1994), has been adapted to deal with various short-term and long-term memory tasks and for expert memory tasks. The main modifications include a retrieval structure or a long-term memory schema, created by the expert's learning and the addition of an associative search process in long-term memory. Feigenbaum founded the Heuristic Programming Project (HPP) within the Knowledge Systems Laboratory (KSL), a leading laboratory for work in knowledge engineering and expert systems, in 1965.

As an architect of artificial intelligence, Feigenbaum has contributed both to academia and to industry with pioneering work both in expert systems, which perform super-intelligently in narrow ranges of human behaviour, and in the development of knowledge systems or intelligent problem-solving systems. He has co-founded three springboard firms in applied artificial intelligence and has served on the board of directors of several companies. His research interests are focused on developing a general framework for modelling physical devices that support reasoning about their designed structure, function and actual behaviour. He is also involved in studying the structure, dynamics and technological industry trends in software production, as part of the Stanford Computer Industry Project.

In addition, Edward Feigenbaum is the chief scientist of the US Air Force, Washington, DC, and has served as the chief scientific advisor to the Chief of Staff and the Secretary.

Feshbach, Seymour

Born: 1925, New York, USA *Nat:* American *Ints:* Clinical psychology, developmental, personality and social, social issues *Educ:* BS City College of New York, 1947; MA Yale University, 1948; PhD Yale University, 1951 *Appts & awards:* NIMH Study Section, Member 1964–8; NIMH Psychology Training Committee, Member, 1968–71, Chair, 1971–2; President, Western Psychological Association, 1977; Division 9 Rep to APA Council, 1980–2; Distinguished Scientist Award, California Psychological Association, 1983; Chair, APA Committee on Graduate Education, 1984–5; President, International Society for Research on Aggression, 1985–7; Editorial Board, *Journal of Abnormal Psychology, Journal of Personality* and Social Psychology, Developmental Psychology, Journal of Social Issues, Current Psychological Research, 1981–2, Current Psychological Reviews, 1981–2, Current Psychological Research and Reviews, 1984– , Aggressive Behavior, Imagination, Cognition and Personality

Principal publications

1955   The drive reducing function of fantasy behavior. *Journal of Abnormal and Social Psychology*, 50, 8.
1964   The function of aggression and the regulation of aggressive drive. *Psychological Review*, 71, 257–72.
1967   *Cognition, Personality and Clinical Psychology.* Jossey-Bass (ed. with R. Jessor).
1970   *Television and Aggression.* Jossey-Bass (with R. Singer).
1970   Aggression. In P. Mussen (ed.), *Carmichael's Manual of Child Psychology*, vol. 11. Wiley.
1971   The dynamics and morality of violence: Some psychological considerations. *American Psychologist*, 26, 281–92.
1972   Reality and fantasy in filmed violence. In J.P. Murray, E.A. Rubinstein and G.A. Comstock (eds), *Television and Social Behavior*, vol. 11: Television and Social Learning. US Government Printing Office, Washington.
1974   The development and regulation of aggression: Some research gaps and a proposed cognitive approach. In W.W. Hartup and J. DeWit (eds), *Determinants and Origins of Aggressive Behavior.* Mouton.
1974   The remediation of learning problems among the disadvantaged. *Journal of Educational Psychology*, 66, 16–28 (with H. Adelman).
1977   The prediction of reading and related academic problems. *Journal of Educational Psychology*, 69, 299–308 (with H. Adelman and W. Fuller).
1979   *Aggression and Behavior Change: Biological and Social Processes.* Praeger (ed. with A. Fraczek).
1980   Must the child be the victim of political violence? An issue in adult moral consciousness. *Journal of Clinical Child Psychology*, 9, 123–7.
1982   *Personality.* Heath (with B. Weiner).
1983   *Educating for Empathy: Classroom Activities for Social Development.* Scott, Foresman (with N. Feshbach, M. Fauvre and M. Campbell).
1986   *Personality.* (2nd edn). Heath (with B. Weiner).
1989   The bases and development of individual aggression. In J. Groebel and R. Hinde (eds),

Aggression and War: Their Biological and Social Bases. Cambridge University Press.
1991   *Personality* (3rd edn). Heath (with B. Weiner).

Further reading

Griebel, J. and Hinde, R.A. (1989) *Aggression and War: Their Biological and Social Bases.* Cambridge University Press.
Huesmann, L.R. (ed.) (1994) *Aggressive Behavior: Current Perspectives.* Plenum.

Although he trained as a clinical psychologist, Feshbach's early work was in personality, and he participated for several years in a major project on attitude change. The diversity and breadth of this training, possible only at a time when psychology had not yet expanded into major areas of specialization, has had a marked influence on his academic career. The research issue that has provided the principle focus of his research career – the dynamics and regulation of aggression – has reinforced the crossing of area boundaries, although his primary identification is still with clinical work. A theme which permeates his theoretical and empirical work on aggression is the issue of aggressive drive. Research on the effects of violence in the mass media, on aggressive play and aggressive fantasy, on the connection between the aggressive and sexual domains, and on the projection of aggression is influenced by this construct, as are the theoretical papers on catharsis, on the distinction between anger, instrumental aggression and aggressive drive, and on the cognitive basis of aggressive drive. The perspectives of clinical, personality and social psychology that are variously brought to bear on his scholarly work are reflected and integrated in the text that he co-authored on *Personality*.

A second motif in his research has been an interest in children's psychological problems and children's welfare. Work on the early identification of learning problems, on children's rights, and on the development of programmes for the modification of aggression in children fall into this category. Finally, his concern with social issues is most recently reflected in a series of studies addressed to the determinants of attitudes towards nuclear armament–disarmament policies. The two motifs – aggression and psychodynamics, and children's problems and social issues – are joined in several papers examining the relationship between psychological research and social advocacy and cultural influences on research results and their interpretation.

Festinger, Leon

Born: 1919, New York City, USA **Died:** 1989, New York, USA **Nat:** American **Ints:** Cognition, communication and social influence, statistics **Educ:** BS City College of New York, 1939; MA State University of Iowa, 1940; PhD State University of Iowa, 1942 **Appts & awards:** Hon. Dr, University of Mannheim, 1978; Else and Hans Staudinger Professor of Psychology, New School of Social Research, Stanford, 1955–89; Member of National Academy of Science; APA Distinguished Scientist Award, 1959; Fellow, AAAS, 1945; Member of Society of Experimental Psychologists; Distinguished Senior Scientists Award; Society of Experimental Social Psychology, 1980; Einstein Visiting Fellow, Israel Academy of Sciences and Humanities, 1980–1

Principal publications

1943   A quantitative theory of decision. *Psychological Review*, 50, 595–621 (with D. Cartwright).

1950   Informal social communication. *Psychological Review*, 57, 271–82.

1951   Interpersonal communication in small groups. *Journal of Abnormal Social Psychology*, 46, 92–9 (with J. Thibaut).

1954   A theory of social comparison processes. *Human Relations*, 117–40.

1957   *A Theory of Cognitive Dissonance*. Row, Peterson.

1961   The psychological effects of insufficient reward. *American Psychologist*, 16, 1–12.

1962   *Deterrents and Reinforcement: The Psychology of Insufficient Reward*. Stanford University Press (with D.H. Lawrence).

1964   *Conflict, Decision and Dissonance*. Stanford University Press.

1968   Eye movements and decrement in the Müller-Lyer illusion. *Perception and Psychophysics*, 3, 376–82 (with C.W. White and M.R. Allyn).

1974   Inferences about the efferent system based on a perceptual illusion produced by eye movements. *Psychological Review*, 81, 44–58 (with A.M. Easton).

1976   Visual perception during smooth pursuit eye movements. *Vision Research*, 16, 1377–86 (with H.A. Sedgwick and J.D. Holtzman).

1978   Retinal image smear as a source of information about magnitude of eye movement. *Journal of Experimental Psychology: Human Perception and Performance*, 4, 573–85 (with J. Holtzman).

1980   (ed.) *Retrospections on Social Psychology*. Oxford University Press.

1981   Human nature and human competence. *Social Research*, 48, 306–21.

Further reading

Aronson, E. (1992) The return of the repressed: Dissonance theory makes a comeback. *Psychological Inquiry*, 3, 303–11.

Festinger, L., Schachter, S. and Gazzaniga, M. (eds) (1989) *Extending Psychological Frontiers: Selected Works of Leon Festinger*. Russell Sage Foundation.

Kunda, Z. (1992) Can dissonance theory do it all? *Psychological Inquiry*, 3, 337–9.

What have each of the following got in common: decision making, communication, level of aspiration, food deprivation, persuasion, deindividuation in groups, pursuit eye movement and the technology of prehistoric hunting tools? The answer is Leon Festinger, and that gives some indication of the breadth of his intellect. Leon Festinger's work includes many landmarks in the history of social psychology, and he must be credited with major contributions to its intellectual and methodological development. His principal contributions relate to the analysis of self and specifically to self-evaluation and to the maintenance of cognitive consistency (cognitive dissonance theory).

Leon Festinger was born the son of an embroidery manufacturer. After completing his PhD he was employed as a research associate at the University of Iowa, and between 1943 and 1945 he was a statistician for the Committee on Selection and Training of Aircraft Pilots at the University of Rochester. In 1945 he joined Kurt **Lewin** at MIT. When the Research Center for Group Dynamics moved to the University of Michigan Festinger moved too, to a position as Associate Professor and Program Director of the Center. He moved to the University of Minnesota in 1951 and to Stanford in 1955.

Festinger argues that people make sense of themselves through comparisons with others. Many skills, attitudes and values can be assessed by comparisons with others. To account for this process he developed social comparison theory, which states that in the absence of an objective standard people will evaluate themselves with reference to others. Self-evaluation through social comparison is more fruitful when people choose to make comparisons with people who are generally similar to themselves. Comparisons generally reflect a bias towards unidirectional upward comparison. In other words, people tend to evaluate themselves with others who are perceived to be similar to but somewhat better than themselves. This 'similarity hypothesis' is somewhat controversial. People sometimes make comparisons on attributes that are irrelevant to performance or skill; they sometimes prefer comparisons with dissimilar others; and comparisons are often forced on people by others. Moreover comparisons can be relatively straightforward when it comes to skill but far less clear cut for attitudes, values and beliefs.

Festinger's theory of cognitive dissonance has its historical origins in *Gestalt* psychology, and specifically it makes use of Kurt Lewin's ideas about conflict, decision making and the changes that follow decisions. The basic assumptions of the theory are these. First, cognitions (e.g. attitudes, beliefs, thoughts) can be relevant ('I'm forgetful', 'I'm often late for appointments') or irrelevant ('I'm forgetful', 'I am religious') to one another. Second, two relevant cognitions may be consonant – in agreement – or dissonant – in disagreement. Cognitive dissonance is said to exist when a person has two relevant cognitions (e.g. thoughts, attitudes, beliefs) that contradict each another. Third, cognitive dissonance creates a motivational state to reduce or eliminate the dissonance and restore the *Gestalt*. The degree of cognitive dissonance depends on two factors: the ratio of dissonant to consonant cognitions and the importance of each cognition to the person. Motivation to reduce cognitive dissonance is great when important beliefs or attitudes are at stake. Festinger suggests that dissonance can be reduced in several ways. One can reduce the number or importance of the dissonant cognitions or increase the number and importance of the consonant cognitions. Another method involves changing one of the dissonant cognitions and thereby making it consistent. For instance, a woman might forget her father's birthday, she might convince herself that celebrations are pretty meaningless, or she might decide that her father would prefer not to be reminded of his advanced age. Alternatively she might change her self-perception and decide that she is not the thoughtful person she once imagined. This example underpins an important feature of cognitive dissonance theory. The theory states that any psychological element in a relationship can change, and this allows one to treat the attitude–behaviour relationship from either the attitude-to-behaviour direction or vice versa. A

change in a person's cognitions about herself or himself may change behaviour, or a change in behaviour may cause a change in attitudes.

The general applicability of Festinger's theory of cognitive dissonance was an important factor in its popularity, and this explains the enormous body of associated empirical literature. An important limitation of the theory stems from the fact that it cannot predict when a person will change the interaction between any of the elements in a cognitive behaviour relationship. In other words it came to be regarded as a retrospective or *post hoc* account its accuracy was restricted to telling when cognitive dissonance had caused a change.

Festinger's theory of cognitive dissonance is a general model of motivation based on the consequences of inconsistency. It is also regarded as offering an alternative approach to the analysis of attitude change developed by Carl **Hovland** and the Yale school. Whereas the Yale School (e.g. **Insko**) focused on the analysis of communication variables, Festinger offered a cognitive analysis of attitude change. His theory revitalized social psychology with its deft blend of cognition and motivation. By the mid-1970s, the popularity of the theory began to wane as interest in the topic of motivation faded and interest in cognitive approaches (e.g. cognitive attribution theory) to social psychology expanded.

Fiedler, Fred E.

Born: 1922, Vienna, Austria **Nat:** Austrian **Ints:** Industrial and organizational, military psychology **Educ:** AM University of Chicago, 1947; PhD University of Chicago, 1949 **Appts & awards:** Professor of Psychology and of Management and Organization, University of Washington; Research Award, APA Division 13, 1971; Associate, Center for Advanced Studies, University of Illinois, 1969; APA Ralph M. Stogdill Distinguished Scholarship Award in the Field of Leadership, 1978; APA Division 19, Award for Outstanding Scientific and Professional Contribution to Military Psychology, 1979; Consulting Editor, *Organizational Behavior and Human Performance*, 1971– ; *Academy of Management Journal*, 1971–83; *Leadership and Organisational Development Journal*, 1979–

Principal publications

1955 The influence of leader–keyman relations on combat crew effectiveness. *Journal of Abnormal and Social Psychology*, 51, 227–35.

1959 Quasitherapeutic relations in small college and military groups. *Psychological Monographs*, 73, 1–28 (with E.F. Hutchins and J.S. Dodge).

1965 Engineer the job to fit the manager. *Harvard Business Review*, 43, 116–22.

1971 *Leadership*. General Learning Press.

1972 A theory of leadership effectiveness. In W.S. Sahakian (ed.), *Social Psychology*. International Textbook Company, 1972.

1974 *Leadership and Effective Management*. Scott Foresman (with M.M. Chemers)

1978 *Managerial Control and Organizational Democracy*. Winston (ed. with B. King and S. Streufert).

1979 The effectiveness of contingency model training: A review of the validation of Leader Match. *Personnel Psychology*, 32, 45–62 (with L. Mahar).

1979 Organizational stress and the use and misuse of managerial intelligence and experience. *Journal of Applied Psychology*, 64, 635–47 (with E.H. Potter III, M.M. Zais and W. Knowlton Jr).

1984 *Improving Leadership Effectiveness: The Leader Match Concept*. Wiley (with M.M. Chemers).

1987 *Leadership: Cognitive Resources and Performance*. Wiley (with J.E. Garcia).

Further reading

Bass, B. (1981) *Stodgill's Handbook of Leadership*. Free Press.

Chemers, M.M. and Ayman (eds) (1993) *Leadership Theory and Research: Perspectives and Directions*. Academic Press.

Guest, D.E. (1987) Leadership and management. In P. Warr (ed.), *Psychology at Work*, 3rd edn. Penguin Books.

Peters, L.H., Harthe, D.D. and Pohlmann, J.T. (1985) Fiedler's contingency theory of leadership: An application of the meta-analysis procedures of Schmidt and Hunter. *Psychological Bulletin*, 97, 274–85.

Rosenbach, W.E. and Taylor, R.L. (eds) (1993) *Contempory Issues in Leadership* (3rd ed.). Westview.

Although his initial training at the University of Chicago was in clinical psychology, Fiedler has always been interested in industrial and organizational psychology. His research focus since 1951 has single-mindedly been on leadership effectiveness. His five books and over 180 publications deal with this topic, with a few exceptions (e.g. 'Port noise complaints'; 'Verbal and behavioral reactions to airport-related noise'). Most of his effort has gone into the development, validation and extension of the Contingency Model of Leadership.

The Contingency Model is based on the assumption that individuals possess relatively stable personality traits which predispose them towards a leadership style. That style will be primarily concerned either with the interpersonal relations or with the task. From this Fiedler developed a means of assessing an individual's style using a semantic differential measure of a person's 'least preferred co-worker' (LPC). A low LPC indicates a style more concerned with the task whilst a high LPC indicates one more concerned with maintaining good interpersonal skills. Success is said to depend on three aspects of the environment: (1) leader–group member relations (trust and liking of the leader); (2) task structure (how well defined goals and performance criteria are); (3) leader's power position (the extent to which he or she controls reward). This results in eight possible combinations.

A number of important problems have been suggested regarding this model. These relate to its basic structure, the contingency variables themselves and the empirical testing of the model. With regard to basic structure: (1) it is assumed that the LPC measures a stable personality trait, but there is evidence that this is not the case and that an individual may move from a high to a low LPC and vice versa; (2) there seems to be a lack of consistent linking between a particular LPC score and the expected style of leadership, suggesting problems with the reliability and validity of the measure; (3) conceptually it has been criticized, as it dichotomizes behaviour as either task- or person-centred. With regard to the contingency variables: it is not clear how they are measured, how they should combine, how they should be weighted, or why these dimensions are the most important contingent variables, either individually or in combination. With regard to the empirical testing of the theory: it is not clear what constitutes an adequate test, nor whether it is necessary to test across the eight factors in the model within one study. However, most studies tend to use small samples, and therefore have problems with tests of significance (Guest 1987).

One review in 1978 concluded that there is little empirical support for the theory. More recent use of meta-analysis has served only to fuel the debate again, with a review concluding that although the original formulation is a valid derivation from Fiedler's early studies, subsequent research has been less supportive. This also found that additional contingent variables seem necessary to explain some of the results (Peters *et al.* 1985). Perhaps most importantly, field studies have been much less supportive than laboratory ones.

Responding to these criticisms, Fiedler has built on his earlier work (Fiedler and Garcia, 1987). His Cognitive Resource Theory (CRT) incorporates important elements of the Contingency Model and identifies the specific conditions under which leader and/or member cognitive resources contribute to leadership performance. He argues that in situations of low interpersonal stress (perhaps equivalent to high favourability), leaders use their intelligence more than their experience. In situations of high stress (low favourability), they use their experience more than their intelligence; in fact, in such situations intelligence can be a positive disadvantage. It would appear that stress disturbs cognitive functioning, and perhaps those who are accustomed to high-level thinking find this disruption hardest to deal with.

The debate on the basis of leadership will no doubt continue, and Fiedler must be seen as one of the most significant contributors to it. The ongoing development of the cognitive resource theory suggests that this discussion has much still to offer.

JONATHAN G. HARVEY

Fischhoff, Baruch

Born: 1946, Detroit, Michigan, USA **Nat:** American **Ints:** Environmental management, judgement and decision making, public policy **Educ:** BS Wayne State University, Michigan, 1967; MA (magna cum laude) Hebrew University of Jerusalem 1972; PhD Hebrew University of Jerusalem, 1975 **Appts & awards:** APA Divisions 3 and 37, Phi Beta Kappa, 1967; Research Associate, Decision Research, Oregon, 1974–85; APA Distinguished Scientific Award for Early Career Contribution to Psychology, 1980; Visiting Scientist, Medical Research Council Applied Psychology Unit, 1981–2; Visiting Scientist, Department of Psychology, University of Stockholm, 1982–3; Eugene Research Institute, Research Associate, 1984–90, President, 1984–7; Professor, Department of Social and Decision Sciences, Department of Engineering and Public Policy, Carnegie Mellon University, 1987– ; APA Award for Early Career Contribution to Psychology in the Public Interest, 1990; President, Society for Judgement and Decision Making,

1990; Society for Risk Analysis, Distinguished Achievement Award, 1991; Member, Institute of Medicine of National Academy of Sciences, 1993

Principal publications

1975 Hindsight/foresight: The effect of outcome knowledge on judgement under uncertainty. *Journal of Experimental Psychology: Human Perception and Performance*, 104, 288–99.

1977 Knowing with certainty: The appropriateness of extreme confidence. *Journal of Experimental Psychology: Human Perception and Performance*, 3, 552–64 (with P. Slovic and S. Lichtenstein).

1978 How safe is safe enough? A psychometric study of attitudes towards technological risks and benefits. *Policy Sciences*, 8, 127–52 (with P. Slovic, S. Lichtenstein, S. Read and B. Combs).

1981 *Acceptable Risk*. Cambridge University Press (with S. Lichtenstein, P. Slovic, S.L. Derby and R.L. Keeney).

1983 Hypothesis evaluation from a Bayesian perspective. *Psychological Review*, 90, 239–60 (with R. Beyth-Marom).

1984 Defining risk. *Policy Sciences*, 17, 123–39 (with S. Watson and C. Hope).

1986 Assessing uncertainty in physical constants. *American Journal of Physics*, 54, 791–8 (with M. Henrion).

1988 Measuring values: A conceptual framework for interpreting transactions. *Journal of Risk and Uncertainty*, 1, 147–84.

1991 Value elicitation: Is there anything in there? *American Psychologist*, 46, 835–47.

1992 Giving advice: Decision theory perspectives on sexual assault. *American Psychologist*, 47, 577–88.

1993 Risk perception and communication. *Annual Review of Public Health*, 14, 183–203 (with A. Bostrom and M.J. Quadrel).

1994 What forecasts (seem to) mean. *International Journal of Forecasting*, 10, 387–403.

(in press) The real world: What good is it? *Organizational Behavior and Human Decision Processes.*

Baruch Fischhoff was born in the post-war baby boom. He benefited from the fine academic and social education available in the 1950s and 1960s in the Detroit Public School system. Although those were optimistic times in the United States, they were passed in the shadow of persistent social problems, including racial injustice, economic inequality and McCarthyism, creating formative and significant undercurrents in Fischhoff's intellectual development. Although

American anti-Semitism was in decline, the Jewish community was still dealing with its precarious recent history and the tragedy of the Holocaust. Gradually, the Vietnam War posed direct challenges to Fischhoff's own generation. Fischhoff sought some balance between these social issues and his academic predilection for mathematics. While pursuing a mathematics degree at Wayne State University, he devoted his extracurricular energies to Hashomer Hatzair, a youth movement advocating kibbutz life.

In 1967, Fischhoff emigrated to Israel, dividing the next three years between two kibbutzim, Gal-On and Lahav, working primarily in agricultural jobs. The lifestyle had many attractions, but cultural differences with kibbutz veterans led Fischhoff and his wife, Andi, to leave for Jerusalem to study at the Hebrew University. Fischhoff joined the research group of Daniel **Kahneman** and Amos **Tversky** when they were formulating their heuristics-and-biases approach to judgement and uncertainty. The group included a remarkable cohort of graduate students, including Maya Bar Hillel, Gershon Ben-Shahar, Ruth Beyth-Marom, Ruma Falk, David Navon, Zur Shapira and Monica Shapiro. Like some of the others, Fischhoff found a bias to make his own, the 'hindsight bias', a tendency to exaggerate the predictability of past events. Although related to his political interests, the systematic study of how people extract lessons from history seemed far removed from concerns of the day, and he maintained a parallel life of activism in Israel's 'peace left'.

The real opportunity to integrate his two lives came during a period with Paul **Slovic** and Sarah Lichtenstein at Decision Research in Eugene, Oregon. Their studies helped create the field of risk-perception research, revealing a more complicated situation than the common claim that social conflicts reflect confrontations between ignorant, hysterical lay people and arrogant, self-serving experts. While often in error, lay concerns were seldom ill-founded, in the sense that lay people typically make sensible inferences, albeit on imperfect information. This prompted studies of risk communication, designed to reduce misunderstandings and not just describe them.

Attention to lay concerns also revealed that people wanted to know not just how large risks were, but also how risks are created and controlled. Such knowledge allows people to monitor risks, to feel more competent in judging risks, and to devise control strategies exercised through personal or political action. Fischhoff's methodology focused on people's 'mental models' of risks, initially by evaluating the technical and scientific knowledge, proceeding with interviews designed to characterize lay beliefs and followed by the development and empirical testing of communications. This research was encouraged by the interdisciplinary atmosphere at Carnegie Mellon University, where Fischhoff has worked from 1987. The research addressed diverse risks, including sexual assault, climate change, radon, nuclear energy and sexually transmitted diseases. Important colleagues included Cindy Atman, Ann Bostrom, Paul Fischbeck, Lita Furby, Zvi Lanir, Michael Maharik, Jon Merz, Granger Morgan, Claire Palmgren, Marilyn Quadrel and Ola Svenson.

Interacting with experts from other fields led Fischhoff to realize that each field rests on fundamental but typically unrecognized behavioural assumptions. As a result, he has written expository analyses applying a psychological perspective to fields such as resource economics, risk assessment, survey research and policy analysis. At times, this has led to empirical studies of expert judgement. With Max Henrion, Fischhoff studied the confidence of particle physicists in their estimates of physical constants. The wish to see a psychological perspective in policy making led Fischhoff to accept national advisory assignments on AIDS risk communication, chemical toxicity testing, drug labelling, global environmental change, and federal research-and-development funding.

His involvement with 'real-world' issues also created some discomfort with the necessarily stylized settings created by experimental research. Fischhoff addressed these concerns in two complementary ways. One is with empirical research designed to extract the salient features of actual problems in a systematic way, hoping to identify basic research questions suitable for experimental study. For example, the work on risk perceptions prompted studies of how people use quantitative response modes and how they estimate risk accumulation over time. Open-ended interviews with adolescents engendered studies challenging the belief that adolescents take risks because they view themselves as invulnerable. A complementary strategy for connecting the world to the lab is to analyse systematically the contexts created in experimental studies. Although there may be no substitute for the painstaking process of gradually discovering the implicit constraints of existing experimental tasks, such analyses might guide those with an immediate need to utilize psychological results. Fischhoff adopted both strategies in research into evaluating environmental changes and setting priorities among competing demands for controlling societal risks.

At Carnegie Mellon, Fischhoff helped to organize one of the first public meetings of Israeli and Palestinian leaders, at the beginning of the peace process. Earlier, he served on the Eugene Commission on the Rights of Women. Generally, though, his policy interests have produced work that is not overtly political. While social concerns can and should govern the choice of research topic, Fischhoff believes that empirical results should be allowed to speak for themselves, sometimes supporting, sometimes contradicting political preconceptions. Baruch Fischhoff's unusual combination of energy, scientific rigour, commitment to social issues and concern for the environment has significantly influenced the new fields of risk analysis and environmental management.

DAVID F. MARKS

Fishbein, Martin

Born: 1936, New York, USA **Nat:** American **Ints:** Consumer psychology, evaluation and measurement, health, population and environmental, personality and social **Educ:** AB Reed College, Oregon, 1957; PhD University of California at Los Angeles, 1961 **Appts & awards:** Professor of Psychology, 1970; Research Professor, Institute of Communications Research; Coordinator of Social, Organizational, Industrial and Individual Differences Division, Department of Psychology, University of Illinois, 1980–7; Guggenheim Fellow, 1967–8; Center for Advanced Study, University of Illinois, 1974–5; AMA, Attitude Research Hall of Fame, 1981– ; AMA, Paul D. Converse Award for Outstanding Contribution to Theory and Science in Marketing, 1981; National Association of Recording Merchandisers, Special Recognition Award, 1982; Editorial Board, *Journal of Consumer Behavior*, 1974–84, *Journal of Applied Social Psychology*, 1979– , *British Journal of Social Psychology*, 1981–4

Principal publications

1962 The AB scales: An operational definition of belief and attitude. *Human Relations*, 15, 35–44 (with B.H. Raven).

1963 An investigation of the relationships between beliefs about an object and the attitude toward that object. *Human Relations*, 16, 233–40.

1965 *Current Studies in Social Psychology*. Holt, Rinehart and Winston (ed. with I.D. Steiner).

1967 (ed.) *Readings in Attitude Theory and Measurement*. Wiley.

1970 The prediction of behavior from attitudinal and normative variables. *Journal of Experimental Social Psychology*, 6, 466–87 (with I. Ajzen).

1972 Attitudes and opinions. In P. Mussen and M. Rosenzweig (eds), *Annual Review of Psychology*, vol. 23. Annual Reviews (with I. Ajzen).

1974 Attitudes toward objects as predictors of single and multiple behavioral criteria. *Psychological Review*, 81, 59–74 (with I. Ajzen).

1975 *Belief, Attitude, Intention and Behavior: An Introduction to Theory and Research*. Addison-Wesley (with I. Ajzen).

1976 Persuasive communication: A social-psychological perspective influencing communication effectiveness. In A.E. Bennett (ed.), *Communication Between Doctors and Patients*. Oxford University Press.

1977 Attitude–behavior relations: A theoretical analysis and review of empirical research. *Psychological Bulletin*, 84, 888–918 (with I. Ajzen).

1980 A theory of reasoned action: Some applications and implications. In H. Howe and M. Page (eds), *Nebraska Symposium on Motivation, 1979*. University of Nebraska Press.

1980 (ed.) *Progress in Social Psychology*, vol. 1. Erlbaum.

1980 *Understanding Attitudes and Predicting Social Behavior*. Prentice-Hall (with I. Ajzen).

1981 Acceptance, yielding and impact: Cognitive processes in persuasion. In R.E. Petty, T.M. Ostrom and T.C. Brock (eds), *Cognitive Responses in Persuasion*. Erlbaum (with I. Ajzen).

1981 Attitudes and voting behavior: An application of the theory of reasoned action. In G.M. Stephenson and J.H. Davis (eds), *Progress in Applied Social Psychology*, vol. 1. Wiley (with I. Ajzen).

Further reading

Doll, J. and Orth, B. (1993) The Fishbein and Ajzen theory of reasoned action applied to contraceptive behavior: Model variants and meaningfulness. *Journal of Applied Social Psychology*, 23, 395–415.

Madden, T.J., Ellen, P.S. and Ajzen, I. (1992) A comparison of the theory of planned behavior and the theory of reasoned action. *Personality and Social Psychology Bulletin*, 18, 3–9.

Netemeyer, R.G., Burton, S. and Johnston, M. (1991)
A comparison of two models for the prediction of
volitional and goal-directed behaviors: A
confirmatory analysis approach. *Social Psychology
Quarterly*, 54, 87–100.

Martin Fishbein's work has focused upon the
relationships among beliefs, attitudes, intentions
and behaviours in both laboratory and field
settings. Starting with an attempt to distinguish
operationally between beliefs and attitudes, his
interests turned to the study of their relationships. This work led to the development of an
expectancy-value model of attitudes. Simply
stated, the model predicts that a person's attitude
toward any object is a function of his or her
salient beliefs about the object and the evaluative aspects of those beliefs [A = f(**E**b$_i$e$_i$)]. The
next stage of his research was directed at understanding the role of attitudes in behavioural
prediction. With **Ajzen**, he argued that traditional measures of attitudes (toward objects)
were, at best, very poor predictors of behaviour,
and they showed that the single best predictor
was a person's intention to perform that behaviour. Thus, Fishbein's interest turned to an
attempt to understand the determinants of intention. Empirical work on this problem led to a
theory of reasoned action and a model for the
prediction of intentions and behaviour. According to the model, a person's intention to perform
any behaviour is a function of (1) his or her
attitude towards performing the behaviour and
(2) his or her subjective norm concerning the
performance of that behaviour. The model has
now been used to predict a variety of behaviours
in both laboratory and field settings. Much of
this work is summarized in *Understanding
Attitudes and Predicting Social Behavior*.

Fitts, Paul Morris

Born: 1912, Martin, Tennessee, USA **Died:**
1965, Ann Arbor, Michigan, USA **Nat:** Ameri-
can **Ints:** Experimental psychology, industrial and
organizational psychology, military psychology,
Society of Engineering Psychologists **Educ:** AM
Brown University 1936; PhD University of
Rochester, 1938 **Appts & awards:** Research
Assistant, University of Tennessee, 1938–42; US
Army Air Force, Assistant Chief of the Psychol-
ogy Branch (Office of Air Surgeon) 1942–9;
Chief, Psychology Branch, Air Force Aeromedi-
cal Laboratory, 1945–9; Professor, Ohio State
University, 1949–58; Professor, University of
Michigan, 1958–63; Director, Human Perfor-

mance Centre, University of Michigan, 1963–5;
Franklin V Taylor Award for contributions to
engineering psychology; Air Force Exceptional
Service Award for contributions to the effectiveness of research and development in the Air
Force; President, Division for Military Psychology, APA; President, Society of Engineering
Psychologists; Human Factors Society, Council
Member, 1958–60, President, 1962–3; Member,
numerous US Government panels and Boards,
including Research and Development Board of
the Department of Defense, Air Force Scientific
Advisory Board, Defense Science Board,
National Research Council, Executive Committee
on Bioastronautics

Principal publications
1947 (ed.) *Psychological Research on Equipment
Design.*
1951 *Human Engineering for an Effective Air
Navigation Traffic Control System.*
1951 Engineering psychology and equipment
design. In S.S. Stevens (ed.), *Handbook of
Experimental Psychology.* Wiley.
1953 S-R Compatibility: Spatial characteristics of
stimulus and response codes. *Journal of
Experimental Psychology*, 46, 199–210 (with C.M.
Seeger).
1954 The information capacity of discrete motor
responses. *Journal of Experimental Psychology*,
47, 381–91.
1954 S-R Compatibility: Spatial characteristics of
stimulus and response codes. *Journal of
Experimental Psychology*, 48, 483–92 (with R.L.
Deininger).
1957 *Stimulus Correlates of Visual Pattern
Recognition – A Probability Approach* (with J.A.
Leonard).
1958 Engineering psychology. *Annual Reviews of
Psychology*, 9, 267–94.
1959 (ed.) *Human Engineering Concepts and
Theory.*
1962 Cognitive aspects of information processing: I.
The familiarity of S-R sets and sub-sets. *Journal of
Experimental Psychology*, 63, 321–9 (with G.
Switzer).
1963 Cognitive aspects of information processing:
II. Adjustments to stimulus redundancy. *Journal of
Experimental Psychology*, 65, 423–32 (with J.R.
Peterson and G. Wolpe).
1964 Information capacity of discrete motor
responses. *Journal of Experimental Psychology*,
67, 103–12 (with J.R. Peterson).
1966 Cognitive aspects of information processing:
III. Set for speed versus accuracy. *Journal of
Experimental Psychology*, 71, 849–57.

1966   Information capacity of discrete motor responses under different cognitive sets. *Journal of Experimental Psychology*, 71, 475–82 (with B.K. Radford).
1967   *Human Performance*.

Further reading

Holding, D.H. (ed.) (1989) *Human Skills* (2nd edn). Wiley.
Oborne, D.J. (ed.) (1995) *Ergonomics and Human Factors*. Elgar.

Fitts's contribution to psychology was avowedly within the area of applying psychological theories and principles to practical problems in working situations, particularly those faced within an aviation setting. His work helped to define a new field in psychology – engineering psychology – which he characterized pragmatically as the application of psychological knowledge to the design and manipulation of practical systems. Fitts's contribution, however, extended beyond simply applying human performance principles derived by others; his argument was always that engineering psychology would never be able to prosper as a respectable technology unless it rested firmly on a much broader base of knowledge and theory of human performance. This he helped to produce.

Thus, during World War II and after, not only did Fitts contribute to such applied and pressing problems as cockpit design, radar operator training, etc., but his research also included more basic work on visual form perception and information processing, as well as motivation, attitudes and the environment. Towards the end of his life, Fitts became occupied with the development of an information-based human performance theory that integrated our knowledge of human sensation, motivation, learning, thinking and problem solving.

DAVE OBORNE

Flament, Claude

Born: 1930, Paris, France **Nat:** French **Ints:** Experimental, measurement, social **Educ:** Doctorat des Sciences Humaines, Sorbonne, 1971 **Appts & awards:** Professor of Social Psychology, University of Provence; President, European Association of Social Psychology, 1972–4; Editorial Board, *Journal of Experimental Social Psychology*, 1964–70, *Progress in Mathematical Social Sciences*, 1973–6, *Social Networks*, 1979–82, *Mathematiques et Sciences Humaines*, 1980– , *Mathematical Social Sciences*, 1980–

Principal publications

1963   *Applications of Graph Theory to Group Structure*. Prentice-Hall.
1965   *Réseaux de Communication et Structures de Groupe*. Dunod.
1976   *L'Analyse Booléenne de Questionnaire*. Mouton.
1970   Equilibre d'un graphe: Quelques resultats algebriques. *Mathematiques et Sciences Humaines*, 8, 5–10.
1971   Social categorization and intergroup behaviour. *European Journal of Social Psychology*, 1, 149–78 (with H. Tajfel *et al.*).
1972   The cognitive structures of the scientist. In J. Israel and H. Tajfel (eds), *The Context of Social Psychology*. Academic Press.
1979   Independent generalizations of balance. In P.W. Holland and S. Leinhardt (eds), *Perspectives on Social Network Research*. Academic Press.
1982   Ordered sets and social sciences. In I. Rival (ed.), *Ordered Sets*. Reidel (with J.P. Barthelemy and B. Montjardet).
1983   On incomplete preference structures. *Mathematical Social Sciences*, 5, 61–72.
1984   From the bias of structural balance to the representation of the group. In R.M. Farr and S. Moscovici (eds), *Social Representations*. Cambridge University Press.
1985   Comparability graph with constraint. *Discrete Mathematics*, 53, 79–89.

Further reading

Rabbie, J.M. and Schot, J.C. (1990) Group behavior in the minimal group paradigm: Fact or fiction? In P.J.D. Drenth *et al.* (eds), *European Perspectives in Psychology, Vol. 3: Work and Organizational, Social and Economic, Cross-Cultural*. Wiley.

Flament's early interests were in the experimental study of communication networks. He used graph theory to model the results. From this starting point, he developed two relatively independent series of research programmes. He applied mathematics to varied structures in psychology, sociology, anthropology, decision-making theory (using graphs, ordered sets, lattices) and used the same discrete mathematics, instead of statistics, to analyse data. He also studied social influence on attitude change, developed some interests in cognitive psychology, and was influenced by Serge Moscovici's work on social representations. He showed experimentally that the cognitive schema of structural balance is not a primitive fact, but results from a more general cognitive structure; namely, the representation of the 'ideal group', which is characterized by equality and friendship. He now considers social representation theory to be an adequate framework for the coordination of the various theories' of schemata (such as script theory). Through experimental and field work, he studies the structure and dynamics of social representations considered as systems of schemata; for example, with colleagues he studied the mentality changes of Cameroon peasants confronted with new agricultural techniques.

Flanagan, John C.

Born: 1906, Armour, South Dakota, USA **Nat:** American **Ints:** Counselling, educational, evaluation and measurement, industrial, military **Educ:** BS University of Washington, 1929; MA University of Washington, 1932; PhD Harvard University, 1934 **Appts & awards:** Chairman, Board of Directors, American Institute for Research; Legion of Merit, USAAF 1946; Raymond Flongacre Award of the Acro Medical Association 1954; APA Thorndike Award, 1972; APA Distinguished Contribution Award, 1976; APA Professional Practice Award, 1982; Distinguished Professional Service Award, Education Testing Service, 1978; Meritorious Contribution Award, Phi Beta Kappa, 1977; Vice President, AERA, 1973; Vice President, New York Academy of Sciences, 1936; President, APA Divisions 1, 4, 15, 19

Principal publications

1935   *Factor Analysis in the Study of Personality.* Stanford University Press.

1941   A preliminary study of the validity of the 1940 edition of the National Teacher Examinations. *School and Social*, 54, 59–64.

1943   The Aviation Psychology Program of the Army Air Forces. *Psychological Bulletin*, 40, 759–69.

1946   *The Aviation Psychology Program in the Army Air Forces.* US Government Publishing Office.

1954   The critical incident technique. *Psychological Bulletin*, 51, 327–58.

1957   The Flanagan aptitude classification tests. *Personnel and Guidance Journal*, 25, 495–507.

1962   *Measuring Human Performance.* American Institute for Research.

1962   *Design for a Study of American Youth.* Houghton Mifflin.

1964   Project TALENT: Some early findings from a national survey. *NEA Journal*, 53, 8–10.

1970   Individualizing education. *Education*, 90, 191–206.

1971   The psychologist's role in youth's quest for fulfillment. *Educational Psychologist*, 8, 21–5.

1973   Education: How and for what. *American Psychologist* 28, 551–6.

1973   The first fifteen years of project TALENT: Implications for career guidance. *Vocational Guidance Quarterly*, 22, 874.

1975   Education's contribution to the quality of life of a national sample of 30 year olds. *Educational Researcher*, 4, 13–16.

1977   American Institute for Research: The first thirty years. *Education*, 97, 307–17.

1978   *Perspectives on Improving Education.* Praeger.

1978   A research approach to improving our quality of life. *American Psychologist*, 33, 138–47.

Further reading

APF Gold Medal Award: John C. Flanagan. *American Psychologist*, 1993, 48, 717–19.

Because of the lasting effects of the depression period, it was very difficult for Flanagan to find a suitable position after receiving a doctoral degree from Harvard in 1934. However, after doing odd jobs around the university for a year under the supervision of J. Lee Kelly, a position opened up as Assistant for Measurement and Statistics with Benjamin D. Wood, Director of the Co-operative Test Service of the American Council on Education.

In the summer of 1941 the Army Air Corps was growing rapidly and wanted a psychologist to assist with the problems in selecting and classifying personnel for air-crew duty and other assignments. Because of contacts made in a previous study, Flanagan was invited to direct this new programme. The Aviation Psychology Program grew to involve 150 of the USA's best psychologists as officers and 1500 graduate students as psychological assistants. The major contribution to the war effort made by this programme, which Flanagan planned and supervised, was documented in nineteen volumes.

After the war, in the summer of 1946, Flanagan was invited to join the faculty of the University of Pittsburgh as a professor of psychology, with the understanding that time and space would be made available to establish an independent, non-profit, personnel research organization. Later that year the American Institute for Research (AIR) was incorporated. Under Flanagan's leadership, AIR was able to implement all aspects of his twenty-year plan for improving many social programmes.

With financial support from industry, the foundations and government, these plans have resulted in important contributions, including: (1) increased military effectiveness in many areas; (2) the improved selection, training and performance of personnel in business and industry; (3) the development of more valid examining procedures for licensing physicians, nurses and other professional specialists; (4) the improvement of the educational programmes in schools; (5) the development of a programme to assist students in planning their career goals; and (6) the identification and description of the major contributors to the overall quality of life of Americans at ages 30, 50 and 70.

Flavell, John H.

Born: 1928, Rockland, Massachusetts, USA **Nat:** American **Ints:** Developmental and cognitive psychology **Educ:** BA Northeastern University, 1951; MA Clark University, 1952; PhD Clark University, 1954 **Appts & Awards:** Professor, Department of Psychology, Stanford University, 1976; SRCD President, 1979–81; SRCD Governing Council, 1975–83; APA Division 7 President, 1969; APA Distinguished Scientific Contribution Award, 1984; Consulting Editor, *Cognitive Psychology*

Principal publications

1963 *The Developmental Psychology of Jean Piaget.* Van Nostrand.

1966 Spontaneous verbal rehearsal in a memory task as a function of age. *Child Development,* 37, 283–99 (with D.R. Beach and J.M. Chinsky).

1969 *Studies in Child Development: Essays in Honour of Jean Piaget.* Oxford University Press (ed. with D. Elkind).

1969 Formal and functional aspects of cognitive development. In D. Elkind and J. Flavell (eds), *Studies in Cognitive Development: Essays in Honour of Jean Piaget.* Oxford University Press (with J.F. Wohlwill).

1970 Developmental studies of mediated memory. In H.W. Reese and L.P. Lipsitt (eds), *Advances in Child Development and Behavior,* vol. 5. Academic Press.

1971 Stage-related properties of cognitive development. *Cognitive Psychology,* 2, 421–53.

1972 An analysis of cognitive-developmental sequences. *Genetic Psychology Monographs,* 86, 279–350.

1974 The development of inferences about others. In T. Mischell (ed.), *Understanding Other Persons.* Blackwell and Mott.

1975 An interview study of children's knowledge about memory. *Monographs of the Society for Research in Child Development,* 40 (1, serial no. 159) (with M.A. Kreutzer and C. Leonard).

1977 Metamemory. In R.V. Kail and J.W. Hagen (eds), *Perspectives on the Development of Memory and Cognition.* Erlbaum (with H.M. Wellman).

1977 *Cognitive Development.* Prentice-Hall.

1979 Metacognition and cognitive monitoring: A new area of cognitive-development inquiry. *American Psychologist,* 34, 906–11.

1983 Development of the appearance–reality distinction. *Cognitive Psychology,* 15, 95–120 (with E.R. Flavell and F.L. Green).

1983 *Handbook of Child Psychology: Cognitive Development.* Wiley (with E.M. Markman).

1985 *Cognitive Development,* 2nd edn. Prentice-Hall.

1990 Inferring false beliefs from actions and reactions. *Child Development,* 61, 929–45 (with L.J. Moses).

1991 What young children know about the mind. *Contemporary Psychology,* 36, 741–2.

1993 *Cognitive Development,* 3rd edn. Prentice-Hall.

John Flavell's early childhood coincided with the Great Depression, which caused his parents (his father was a civil engineer) and two sisters considerable hardship. After high school he spent two years in the army. In 1947 he entered Northeastern University, and after graduating was offered positions in the psychology programmes at Clark and Harvard. He chose Clark for financial reasons. At that time the dominant theories at Clark University were psychoanalysis and Heinz **Werner's** organismic developmental psychology. After completing his doctoral dissertation, Flavell first took a position as a clinical psychologist at a veteran Administration hospital in Colorado, and a year later (1955) accepted a teaching position at the University of Rochester. There he began work on a book summarizing prominent developmental theories, but abandoned that in favour of a major work on Jean **Piaget**.

While at Rochester, Flavell began an important programme of work on children's role-taking and communication skills and on their developing use of memory strategies. In his work on role taking he argues that to be able to take the role of another the child must draw upon four cognitive skills. These involve (1) recognizing that a different point of view exists; (2) an appreciation of the need to consider another person's perspective in order to sustain successful social interaction; (3) inferring attributes in others that are relevant to the social task; and (4) the application of the inferences, the monitoring of the application and the simultaneous engagement in the ongoing social activity. Flavell has not specified when these skills emerge. However, by identifying them he defined the multitude of information-processing demands on children and provided a framework for their systematic investigation.

In 1965 Flavell left Rochester for a position at the University of Minnesota's Institute of Child Development, where his work on children's metacognition developed rapidly. His involvement in memory research arose indirectly. Research on discrimination learning indicated that, in early childhood, children do not use verbal mediators between a stimulus and a response. Flavell reasoned that this could be due either to the fact that the young child produced verbal mediators, but they failed to work in the way they do for older children (mediation deficiency); or that young children fail to produce any mediators at all (production deficiency). To determine what was happening, he studied children's verbal rehearsal on short-term memory tasks. At this time the memory task was not the object of interest for Flavell. He found that young children were able to rehearse – they could be induced into doing so – but they did not do this spontaneously and could not be encouraged to maintain the strategy even when they had used it. In other words, children have a production deficiency and it further indicated that children's awareness of a strategy might be crucial for them to use it spontaneously. This prompted Flavell to investigate the processes that control the use of memory strategies. He argued that the development of knowledge about memory might be an important factor in age-related improvements in memory performance, knowledge which he referred to as metamemory. This line of research was to develop and expand into metacognition: the knowledge children have accumulated about the human mind and how its works. We still know relatively little about the development of metacognition, but Flavell is a pioneer in providing insights into the ways children think about thinking.

Flourens, Marie Jean Pierre

Born: 1794, Maureilhen, France **Died:** 1867, Montgeron, France **Nat:** French **Ints:** Physiological and comparative psychology **Educ:** MD University of Montpelier, 1813; **Appts & awards:** Montyon prize, 1824, 1825; Academie

des Sciences, 1828; Permanent Secretary, Academie des Sciences, 1833; Academie de France, 1840

Principal publications

1824   *Recherches experimentales sur les proprietés et fonctions du systeme nerveux dans les animaux vertebres*. Crevot.
1836   *Cours sur la génération, l'ovologie et l'embryologie*. Trinquart.
1842   *Recherches sur le dévelopment des os et des dents*. Gide.
1844   *Memoires d'anatomie et de physiologie comparées*. Balliere.
1856   *Cours de physiologie comparée*. Balliere.

Further reading

Wade, N. (1995) *Psychologists in Word and Image*. MIT Press.
Young, R.M. (1990) *Mind, Brain and Adaptation in the Nineteenth Century: Cerebral Localization and its Biological Context from Gall to Ferrier*. Oxford University Press.

Flourens's early investigations of the localization of function within the central nervous system were a landmark in the history of physiology and influenced much of the early research in neuropsychology. His methods and ideas were a significant advance on those used by the phrenologists, of whom he was highly critical. He worked principally on the excitability of the cerebral hemispheres and spinal cord. Using the technique of ablation on a variety of species, he divided the nervous system into six anatomically and functionally differentiated units: the cerebral lobes, responsible for perception, intelligence and will; the cerebellum, for co-ordination of locomotory movements; the medulla oblongata, for conservation (an integrative centre); the corpora quadrigemina, for sight; the spinal cord, for conduction; and the nerves, for excitation. He also demonstrated that opium suppressed the functioning of the cerebral hemispheres, belladonna suppressed the corpora quadrigemina and alcohol affected the cerebellum. Flourens suggested that there was not only diversification of function within the central nervous system (which he termed 'action propre') but also unity ('action commune'), the parts working together as a unitary system. These ideas anticipated **Lashley**'s concepts of mass action and equipotentiality. Flourens also discovered that lesions in the semicircular canals of the inner ear induced compulsive movements of the head and disturbances of equilibrium.

He is credited too with the location of the respiratory centre in the medulla oblongata, the reunion of nerves, the role of periosteum in the formation and growth of bone, and the anaesthetic properties of chloroform in animals.

Flugel, John Carl

Born: 1884, Liverpool, England **Died:** 1955, London, England **Nat:** British **Ints:** Experimental psychology, history of psychology, personality and social psychoanalysis, psychology **Educ:** John Locke Scholar in Mental Philosophy; BA University of Oxford, 1908; DSc University of London, 1929; Hon. FBPsS **Appts & awards:** University College, London, Demonstrator, 1909, Assistant, 1910, Senior Lecturer, 1920, Assistant Professor, 1929–55; BPsS, Hon. Secretary, 1911–20, Hon. Librarian, 1921–32, President, 1932–5; Hon. Secretary, International Psychoanalytical Association, 1920–2; Carpenter Medallist, University of London, 1931; Conway Memorial Lecturer, 1941; Chairman, Programme Committee, International Congress on Mental Health, 1948; President, British Association Section J, 1950; Hon. Member, Indian Psychological Association

Principal publications

1909 Further observations on the variation of the intensity of visual sensation with the duration of the stimulus. *British Journal of Psychology*, 3, 178–207 (with W. McDougall).

1913 Some observations on local fatigue in illusions of reversible perspective. *British Journal of Psychology*, 6, Pt I.

1913 The influence of attention in illusions of reversible perspective. *British Journal of Psychology*, 357.

1921 *The Psycho-analytic Study of the Family.* Hogarth.

1929 On mental attitude to present day clothes – report on a questionnaire. *British Journal of Medical Psychology*, 9, Pt 2.

1929 Clothes symbolism and clothes ambivalence. *International Journal of Psycho-Analysis.*

1930 *The Psychology of Clothes.* Hogarth.

1933 *A Hundred Years of Psychology (1833–1933): Parts 1–4.* Duckworth.

1934 *Some Recent Studies of Mental Oscillation from the Psychological Laboratory.* University College, London.

1934 *Men and their Motives.* Kegan Paul.

1936 The Tannhäuser motif. *British Journal of Medical Psychology*, 15, Pt 4.

1945 *Man, Morals and Society.* Kegan Paul.

1945 *Careers in Psychology and Certain Allied Fields.* BPS.

1947 *A Hundred Years of Psychology: Parts 1–5.* Duckworth.

1947 *Population, Psychology and Peace.* Duckworth.

1955 *Studies in Feeling and Desire.* Duckworth.

1963 *A Hundred Years of Psychology: Parts 1–5 Revised.* Duckworth.

Further reading

British Psycho-Analytical Society 50th Anniversary Publication, 1963.

Jones, E. (1956) *International Journal of Psychoanalysis*, 37, 103–97.

Pear, T.H. (1948) *British Journal of Psychology*, 47, 1–4.

Russell, R.W. (1956) *American Journal of Psychology*, 69, 328–9.

Sutherland, J.D. (1956) *British Journal of Medical Psychology*, 29.

Jack Flugel studied at both Balliol College, Oxford, and the University of Würzburg. Brought up in the tradition of experimental psychology and using the new statistical methods introduced by **Spearman**, he directed the psychological laboratory of the University of London for more than twenty years. Combining, possibly uniquely at that time, the academic psychologist with the psychoanalyst, Flugel devoted a great part of his life to the development of Sigmund **Freud**'s ideas. His interest in human behaviour and his wide educational background enabled him to present psychoanalysis in a more objective and acceptable way than most other adherents of Freud. On 30 October 1913, Ernest **Jones**, Jack Flugel and friends founded the London Psycho-Analytical Society. Later, in February 1919, the British Psycho-Analytical Society was founded, at a meeting at Ernest Jones's house attended by Jack Flugel and a few other colleagues. A large and distinguished Special Committee was set up by the British Medical Association in 1927, to investigate and report on the subject of psychoanalysis; this included J.C. Flugel, who also gave evidence. The end report was seen as the magna carta of psychoanalysis.

Flugel's first book, *The Psychoanalytic Study of the Family*, attracted much attention and introduced the concept of the Oedipus complex to a wider public. Flugel was a leading British writer on psychoanalysis and contributed many articles to psychological journals. It was his third book, *The Psychology of Clothes*, which really came to the attention of non-academics and is still published in many languages today. It was a learned and entertaining treatise using Freudian theory to explain and speculate on the vagaries of dress and fashion. His *Hundred Years of Psychology* was the first of the Hundred series to appear, and his last book, *Studies in Feeling and Desire*, received wide praise, including that of the *Times Literary Supplement*. Throughout his career Flugel used his persuasive and entertaining writing style to encourage further the study of psychology and its acceptance as a science.

N.J.M. BENNETT AND D. MURRAY

Fodor, Jerry Alan

Born: 1935, New York, USA **Nat:** American **Ints:** Philosophical and theoretical psychology, experimental psychology **Appts & awards:** Professor at MIT and currently Professor at Rutgers University

Principal publications

1968 *Psychological Explanation*. Random House.
1975 *The Language of Thought*. Harvard University Press.
1983 *The Modularity of Mind*. MIT Press.
1987 *Psychosemantics: The Problem of Meaning*. MIT Press.
1990 *A Theory of Content*. MIT Press.
1994 *The Elm and the Expert*. MIT Press.

Further reading

Loewer, B. and Rey, G. (1991) *Meaning in Mind: Fodor and his Critics*. Blackwell.

Fodor is widely regarded as the most significant contemporary philosopher of psychology – particularly by psychologists. There are a number of reasons for this. He has been personally involved in some highly regarded empirical work in psychology, which most philosophers have not. His first book, *Psychological Explanation*, had as its opening chapter a spirited defence of the possibility of scientific psychology. More important, however, may be the fact that in his *Language of Thought* and subsequently, he postulates real mental existents – propositions couched in the 'language of thought' (or 'mentalese') – as the subject matter of psychology. Psychologists are thereby reassured that they are engaged in the investigation of things that do really exist. Fodor avoids postulating any kind of Cartesian mind-stuff but also denies the possibility of direct reduction of

psychological entities to neurophysiology. The former view is now a matter of general agreement among scientifically inclined persons, and the latter is forced upon psychologists by the impossibility of effecting any such reduction in the present or likely future state of our knowledge.

Fodor's mental existents represent in the mind states of affairs in the real world outside us, and participate as elements in the mental computations that constitute thinking as he sees it. Coded symbols in the brain lock onto various properties of the real world (their broad content) but are in general inclined to lock only onto a subset of these properties (their narrow content). Broad content allows the possibility of individual error (in a particular case a cow may be misperceived as a horse); narrow content allows the possibility of a communality of properties permitting 'horse' to function as a symbol in intra- and inter-personal communication. There is asymmetrical dependency of meaning, in the sense that incorrect use of the word 'horse' may be supposed to depend on correct use (that is how it is known to be incorrect) but correct use does not depend on incorrect.

Symbols may be linked in mentalese as propositions (e.g. 'horses are four-legged animals'), which are stored in what Fodor sometimes calls the belief-box, and these propositions may be computationally linked with other propositions to yield propositional attitudes (beliefs, hopes, fears, etc., that 'horses may be...'). The business of psychology is, in Fodor's view, to state laws relating these propositions/propositional attitudes, and such laws will be true (if they are true) by virtue of the ultimate neurophysiological mechanisms that implement the linkages. They will not, however, be reducible to these mechanisms. Different mechanisms may implement similar linkages and vice versa. (Fodor refers to cognitive neuroscience as that 'paradigm of oxymorons'.)

In *The Modularity of Mind* Fodor maintains, contrary to **Bruner**'s 'new look' approach, that perception is cognitively impenetrable. It was (and is) widely held that perception is saturated by cognition, that we see what we are cognitively prepared to see, and further, that our scientific theories determine what observations we make and are in turn determined by broad social and economic factors. Our very metaphysics has been held to be determined by the structure of the language we speak. Fodor characterizes these views as 'relativistic holism'. If we accept them we are precluded from getting outside the framework; we can criticize only from within. Hatred of relativism is a recurring theme in Fodor's work because it denies what he calls the 'fixed structure of human nature'. Human perceptual capacity is, in part at least, independent of cognition. We are ultimately obliged to perceive what there is, even if we harbour a theory suggesting that no such thing can be. Here too, Fodor comes to the aid of the hard-pressed empirical psychologist, beset on all sides as he or she is by relativists from the other humane disciplines.

Fodor's intentional realism is, I have suggested, a properly articulated and rationally defensible version of the view that most philosophically naive psychologists take for granted in any case. It allows easy commerce with work in artificial intelligence and related types of investigation but it does not follow that it will, in the final analysis, prove satisfactory. There are a number of objections to it which seem fatal in the eyes of some critics (notably Daniel **Dennett**). Dennett espouses an alternative, neo-behaviourist view that is as sympathetic to psychology but not as congenial to the philosophically unsophisticated. The argument is really only accessible to specialists (do not be misled by the bantering tone adopted by both parties to the argument). The principal objections to Fodor's language of thought are as follows. (1) If there is a belief-box containing real mental entities couched in mentalese, it must be supposed to contain an immense number of highly unlikely beliefs; e.g. that it is farther from the earth to the sun than from here to the corner shop. This is undoubtedly true but the fact may never have occurred to anybody. If we add in true and false negative beliefs – e.g. that is not farther … than …, the number is greater still. Neo-behaviourism does not postulate the existence of mental entities, so there is no problem. (2) Suppose a neurosurgeon managed to insert the belief 'I have a brother in Cleveland' into my belief-box. If asked, I should then reply 'I have a brother in Cleveland' but would be unable to give any other information about him. It would appear that I can hold such a belief only in the context of other beliefs. But to admit that opens the way to holism (in which, in a given individual, every belief depends more or less on every other). This in turn leads to relativism, which Fodor wishes to avoid at all costs.

Avoiding postulation of more than the minimum number of entity types required is a principle observed as a matter of course by most

modern philosophers. The need to do so is not, however, apparent to most lay people, or to many psychologists. (It is perhaps worth noting that behaviourism flourished only at a time when virtually all psychologists had received some training in philosophy as part of their education.) Fodor believes that the facts of the case require the postulation of mental entities and tries to deal with the difficulties that follow. The neo-behaviourists believe that no such postulation is required, but in this they come into conflict with some of our most ingrained (realist) habits of thinking.

N.E. WETHERICK

Foss, Donald J.

Born: 1940, Minneapolis, Minnesota, USA **Nat:** American **Ints:** Developmental, engineering, experimental **Educ:** BA University of Minnesota, 1962; PhD University of Minnesota, 1966 **Appts & awards:** Professor and Chair, Department of Psychology, University of Texas at Austin; AAAS Fellow; Fellow, APA Division 3; Chair, APA Council of Editors, 1984–5; Member, APA Publications and Communications Board, 1985– ; Editor, *Contemporary Psychology*, 1980–5; Associate Editor, *Contemporary Psychology*, 1974–9; Editorial Board, *Psychonomic Science*, 1970–2, *Memory and Cognition*, 1972–7, *Journal of Verbal Learning and Verbal Behavior*, 1972–80, *Journal of Experimental Psychology: Learning Memory and Cognition*, 1981–

Principal publications

1968 An analysis of learning in a miniature linguistic system. *Journal of Experimental Psychology*, 76, 450–9.
1969 Decision processes during sentence comprehension: Effects of lexical item difficulty and position upon decision times. *Journal of Verbal Learning and Verbal Behavior*, 8, 457–62.
1973 Some effects of context on the comprehension of ambiguous sentences. *Journal of Verbal Learning and Verbal Behavior*, 12, 577–89 (with C.J. Jenkins).
1975 Memory for sentences: Implications for human associative memory. *Journal of Verbal Learning and Verbal Behavior*, 14, 1–16 (with D.A. Harwood).
1978 *Psycholinguistics: An Introduction to the Psychology of Language*. Prentice-Hall (with D.T. Hakes).
1980 Identifying the speech codes. *Cognitive Psychology*, 12, 1–31 (with M.A. Blank).

1982   A discourse on priming. *Cognitive Psychology*, 14, 590–607.

1983   Great expectations: Some effects of context on sentence processing. In G.B. Flores d'Arcais and R.J. Jarvella (eds), *The Process of Language Understanding*. Wiley (with J.R. Ross).

1983   Breaking the dual code: A unitary model of phoneme identification. *Journal of Verbal Learning and Verbal Behavior*, 22, 609–32 (with M. Gernsbacher).

1987   Vowels as islands of reliability. *Journal of Memory and Language*, 26, 564–73 (with R. Diehl, K. Kluender and E. Parker).

1987   On comprehending a computer manual: Analysis of variables affecting performance. *International Journal of Man–Machine Studies*, 26, 277–300 (with P. Smith-Kerker and M.B. Rosson).

1987   Technology transfer: On learning a new computer-based system. In J.M. Carroll (ed.), *Interfacing Thought: Cognitive aspects of Human–Computer Interaction*. MIT Press (with M. De Ridder).

1988   Experimental psycholinguistics. *Annual Review of Psychology*, 39, 301–48.

1990   *Mental Health Research in Texas: Retrospect and Prospect*. Hogg Foundation for Mental Health (ed. with C.M. Bonjean).

1991   Global and local context effects in sentence processing. In R.R. Hoffman and D.S. Palermo (eds), *Cognition and the Symbolic Processes: Applied and Ecological Perspectives*. Erlbaum (with S.R. Speer).

1995   Effects of global and local context on lexical processing during language comprehension. *Journal of Experimental Psychology General*, 124, 62–82 (with D.J. Hess and P. Carrol).

Further reading

Hoffman, R.R. and Palermo, D.S. (eds) (1991) *Cognition and the Symbolic Processes: Applied and Ecological Perspectives*. Erlbaum.

Donald Foss's graduate school career began with postdoctoral work at what was then the only Center for Cognitive Studies, at Harvard University. His principal research interests have been focused on two themes. The first concerns understanding apparently rule-governed yet creatively varying behaviour, as expressed by language. Early work with James J. Jenkins on mediation and miniature linguistic systems reflected that concern. A second theme involved the examination of complex rule-governed processes while they were occurring. In 1969, Foss developed the 'phoneme monitoring'

technique. Developed to focus on linguistic units in comprehension processing, this involved the timed detection of a predetermined phoneme presented in the context of a sentence. In terms of a serial view of processing, the decision (i.e. detection) made at a point of ambiguity governed the following interpretation, until shown by subsequent context to be incorrect. It was among the first of many such techniques applied to comprehension processing and persists as a research theme. Now there are many 'on-line' methods from which to choose. More recent work in the area of linguistic processing has included context effects in sentence processing and semantic integration. Foss's work has also developed into the areas of organization of the mental lexicon, flow of information and lexical access.

Foss has diversified his research interests into the domain of applied problems in human–computer interaction. His interest in the topic was prompted by the desire to assist students in the job market. His work in the area is concerned with the cognitive aspects of transfer of training and the design and usability of user interfaces.

CATE COX

Fraisse, Paul

Born: 1911, St Etienne, France **Nat:** French **Ints:** Developmental psychology, experimental psychology, general psychology, physiological and comparative psychology **Educ:** License de philosophie, University of Lyons, 1935; Docteur en philosophie, University of Louvain, 1943; Docteur en Lettres, Paris, 1956 **Appts & awards:** Professor Emeritus, Université René Descartes, Paris; l'Ecole les Hautes Etudes, Directeur adjoint, 1941–52, Directeur, 1952–79, President, 1976–9; l'Institut de Psychologie, Université de Paris, Directeur adjoint, 1947–61, Directeur, 1961–9; Professor of Experimental Psychology, Sorbonne, 1952–79; Secretary General, French Psychological Society, 1949–59; Secretary General, Association de Psychologie Scientifique Française, 1952–70; Member, Psychonomic Society, 1965; Foreign Member, National Academy of Sciences of the USA, 1982

Principal publications

1937   Etudes sur la memoire immediate. *L'Année Psychologique*, 38, 38–85 (with R. Fraisse).

1949   Les aptitudes rythmiques: Etude comparée des Oligophrenes et des enfants normaux. *Journal de*

Psychologie Normale et Pathologigue, 3, 309–30
(with P. Pichot and G. Clairouin).

1956   *Les Structures Syltiniques*. Editions
Universitaise de Louvain.

1957   *La Psychologie du Temps*. Presse Université
de France.

1961   Influence de la durée et de la fréquence des
changements sur l'estimation du temps. *L'Année
Psychologique*, 61, 325–39.

1962   Vers une psychologique complète.
Psychologie Française, 7, 165–77.

1963–6   *Fraite de Psychologie Experimentale*, 9
vols. Presse Université de France (ed. with J.
Piaget).

1964   Relations entre le seuil de reconnaissance
perceptive et le temps de réaction verbale.
Psychologie Française, 9, 77–85.

1966   L'anticipation de stimulus rythmiques, vitesse
d'etablissment et precision de la synchronisation.
L'Année Psychologique, 66, 15–36.

1970   Reconnaissance de l'identité physique et
semantique de dessins et de noms. *Revue Suisse de
Psychologie*, 29, 76–84.

1973   Temporal isolation, activity, rhythms and time
estimation. In J.E. Ramussen (ed.), *Man in
Isolation and Confinement*. Aldine.

1974   *Psychologie du Srythire*. Presse Université de
France.

1975–6   Psychologie: Science de l'homme ou
science du comportment. Adresse Presidentielle au
XXIe Congres International de Psychologie.
Bulletin de Psychologie, 29, 929–37.

1981   Cognition of time in human activity. In G.
d'Ydewalle and W. Lens (eds), *Cognition of
Human Motivation and Learning*. Erlbaum.

1982   (ed.) *La Psychologie et Demain*. Presse
Université de France.

Further reading

Aschersleben, G. and Prinz, W. (1995) Synchronizing
actions with events: The role of sensory information. *Perception and Psychophysics*, 57, 305–17.

Macar, F. *et al.* (eds) (1992) *Time, Action and
Cognition: Towards Bridging the Gap*. Kluwer.

While completing his License de philosophie at
the University of Lyons, Paul Fraisse was persuaded by A.E. **Michotte** to work on rhythm,
perception and movement. He did this for his
doctorate under the guidance of Michotte at
Louvain. The study of rhythm led him to
examine the perception of time, and he focused
on the development of time perception in
children. Debates with Jean **Piaget** stimulated
much of this work. The study of immediate
memory has also been central to his work. Much

of his work in this field was conducted within
the framework of information processing; for
example, he conducted experimental studies of
the speed of perception and recall of words to
those of drawings. After World War II, Fraisse
was virtually the only French experimental
psychologist, and consequently he trained many
of the leading French psychologists of the post-
war era. His interests broadened and included
studies in psychopathology, psychoneurology
and social psychology. But besides his experimental work, Fraisse was interested in
theoretical problems and particularly the unity
of psychology. He has worked tirelessly to
promote the international growth of psychology
through professional organizations like the
Societé Françcaise de Psychologie and the
International Union of Scientific Psychology,
through the creation of independent departments
of psychology in France, and as an editor of
scientific journals and books.

Frank, Jerome David

Born: 1909, New York, USA ***Nat:*** American
Ints: Psychological study of social issues,
psychotherapy ***Educ:*** BA Harvard University,
1930; PhD Harvard University, 1934; MD
Harvard University, 1939 ***Appts & awards:***
Professor Emeritus of Psychiatry, Johns
Hopkins University School of Medicine; Presi-
dent, American Psychopathological Associa-
tion, 1963–4; President, Society for the
Psychological Study of Social Issues, 1965–6;
Vice-Chairman, Federation of American Scient-
ists, 1975–7; Kurt Lewin Memorial Award,
Society for the Psychological Study of Social
Issues, 1972; McAlpin Research Achievement
Award, National Mental Health Association,
1981; Special Research Award, Society for
Psychotherapy Research, 1981; Advisory
Board, *Journal of Nervous and Mental Disease*

Principal publications

1953   *Group Psychotherapy: Studies in
Methodology of Research and Therapy*. Harvard
University Press (with F. Powdermaker).

1959   The dynamics of the psychotherapeutic
relationship: Determinants and effects of the
therapist's influence. *Psychiatry*, 22, 17–39.

1960   Breaking the thought barrier: Psychological
challenges of the nuclear age. *Psychiatry*, 23,
245–66.

1961   *Persuasion and Healing: A Comparative
Study of Psychotherapy*. Johns Hopkins University
Press.

1964   Systematic preparation of patients for
psychotherapy: I. Effects on therapy behavior and
outcome. *Journal of Psychiatric Research*, 2,
267–81 (with R. Hoehn-Saric, D.D. Imber, B.L.
Liberman and A.R. Stone).

1977   Nature and functions of belief systems:
Humanism and transcendental religion. *American
Psychologist*, 32, 555–9.

1977   The two faces of psychotherapy. *Journal of
Nervous and Mental Disease*, 164, 3–7.

1978   *Effective Ingredients of Successful
Psychotherapy*. Bruner/Mazel (with R. Hoehn-
Saric, S.D. Imber, E.H. Nash, A.R. Stone and C.C.
Battle).

1978   *Psychotherapy and the Human Predicament:
A Psychosocial Approach*. Schocken Books.

1979   Mental health in a fragmented society: The
shattered crystal ball. *American Journal of
Orthopsychiatry*, 49, 397–408.

1981   Holistic medicine – a view from the fence.
Johns Hopkins Medical Journal, 149, 222–7.

1982   *Sanity and Survival in the Nuclear Age*.
Random House.

1982   Therapeutic components shared by all
psychotherapies. In J.E. Harvey and M.M. Parks
(eds), *Psychotherapy Research and Behavior
Change*. APA.

1983   Nuclear arms and prenuclear leaders. *Political
Psychology*, 4, 393–408.

1984   Nuclear death: An unprecedented challenge to
psychiatry and religion. *American Journal of
Psychiatry*, 141, 1343–8.

Further reading

Bergin, A.E. and Garfield, S.L. (eds) (1994)
Handbook of Psychotherapy and Behavior Change,
4th edn. Wiley.

Patterson, C.H. (1986) *Theories of Counseling and
Psychotherapy*. HarperCollins.

Frank contributed to research on two topics
investigated by Kurt **Lewin**, with whom he
studied for two years: level of aspiration and
determinants of personal influence. Both of
these influenced his perspective on psychotherapy, which became the focus of his research
interest after he became a psychiatrist. His first
area of research in this field was group psychotherapy, but the choice of this subject was
unrelated to his work with Lewin, being determined rather by an opportunity to join a research
project conducted by a psychoanalyst, Florence
Powdermaker. His principle contribution to the
field of psychotherapy has been the hypothesis
that all its forms share features that counteract
the demoralization that is a major reason for

patients seeking psychotherapy, whatever their
specific symptoms or disabilities, and that
therefore many of the benefits of all psychotherapies result from the ability of their shared
features to overcome demoralization. He
attempted to support the hypothesis by empirical
research conducted by an interdisciplinary team
under his direction over about a quarter of a
century, as well as by theoretical articles. Interest in psychotherapy led to some attention to
related fields such as holistic medicine and the
nature of belief systems. Stimulated initially by
having been in the Philippines when the atom
bombs were dropped on Hiroshima and
Nagasaki, he attempted to contribute through
numerous publications to an understanding of
the psychosocial components of the nuclear
arms race.

Frankenhaeuser, Marianne

Born: 1925, Helsinki, Finland **Nat:** Swedish
Ints: Health psychology, gender research,
psychoendocrinology,   psychopharmacology,
psychophysiology, stress, work psychology
Educ: Dip University of Oxford, 1947; BA
University of Helsinki, 1950; MA University of
Stockholm 1954; PhD University of Uppsala,
1959 **Appts & awards:** Chair, Scientific
Council, Swedish Psychological Association,
1970–3; President, European Brain and Behav-
ior Society, 1975–6; Professor of Psychology,
Karolinska Institute, Stockholm, 1980– ; Royal
Award, King of Sweden's Medal of the 8th
Dimension with the Ribbon of the Seraphimer
Order, 1985; International Women's Forum
Award: Women of Achievement, 1989; Hon. Dr
of Political Science, University of Turku,
Finland, 1990; Selected 1994 and 1995 Woman
of the Year, American Biographical Institute,
1995

Principal publications

1959   *Estimation of Time: Experimental Studies of
the Speed of Perception*. Almqvist and Wiksell.

1971   Behavior and circulating catecholamines.
Brain Research, 31, 241–62.

1975   Experimental approaches to the study of
catecholamines and emotion. In L. Levi (ed.),
Emotions: Their Parameters and Measurement.
Raven Press.

1979   Psychoneuroendocrine approaches to the study
of emotion as related and coping. In H.E. Howe and
R.A. Dienstbier (eds), *Nebraska Symposium on
Motivation 1978*. University of Nebraska Press.

1988   To err is human: Nuclear war by mistake? In

A. Gromyko and M. Hellman (eds), *Breakthrough: Emerging New Thinking*. Walker.

1989   Stress on and off the job as related to sex and occupational status in white-collar workers. *Journal of Organizational Behavior*, 10, 321–46 (with U. Lundberg, M. Fredrikson, B. Melin, M. Tuomisto, A.L. Myrsten, M. Hedman, B. Bergman-Losman and L. Wallin).

1991   *Women, Work and Health: Stress and Opportunities*. Plenum (ed. with U. Lundberg and M. Chesney).

1993   *Kvinnlight, Manligt, Stressigt (Stress and Gender)*. Bra Böker.

1996   On the psychology of working life. In O. Svane and C. Johansen (eds), *Work and Health: Keynote Lectures from the First International Conference on the Scientific Basis for Progress in the Work Environment, Copenhagen*. European Commission.

Further reading

Öhman, A. (1992) The history of biological psychology in Sweden: The human side. In B. Everitt, H. Ursin, P. Venables and L. Weiskrantz (eds), *Two Faces of Swedish Psychology, vol. 2. Frontiers in Biological Psychology. An Evaluation of Swedish Research in Biological Psychology*. Ord and Form.

Born into an intellectual family within the Swedish subculture of Finland, Marianne Frankenhaeuser has been one of the foremost Scandinavian psychologists in a career spanning over three decades. After enduring the Finnish–Soviet war as a teenager, she went to study psychology at Oxford under Oliver **Zangwill**, whose clinical approach to memory made a lasting impression. She then acquired a good grounding in physiology, animal experimental psychology, psychophysics and psychopharmacology at the Karolinska Institute in Stockholm and at University College, London. This training placed her in good stead for scientific career as a psychophysiologist with a primary interest in psychoendocrinology.

Frankenhaeuser's research has been broad in scope but methodologically precise. She has focused on human stress and coping as related to health, in particular, by developing psychological approaches to stress in relation to (1) the organization of work; (2) applications of new technology; (3) psychosocial factors in working life; and (4) gender differences. Her approach has been to use laboratory methods to generate basic findings that are then adapted and extended through studies of daily activities in

real-world settings, e.g. by evaluating and then developing intervention strategies for the amelioration and prevention of stress in working environments. These real-world studies then feed back into further laboratory studies, and so on.

Marianne Frankenhaeuser is one of a very small number of psychologists to have contributed actively to the quest for peace and nuclear disarmament. Shifting over time from an optimistic to a pessimistic view about such matters, she has argued that 'To err is human' and discussed the frightening possibility of nuclear war by mistake. This proposition forms part of her concern that the growing gap between our adaptive capabilities and technological advancement could lead to the demise of human civilization as we know it. While it can only be hoped that this grim prospect is unfulfilled, Frankenhaeuser's research has aimed at a picture of human existence on a grand, ecologically relevant scale.

DAVID F. MARKS

Freud, Anna
Born: 1895, Vienna, Austria **Died:** 1982, London, England **Nat:** Austrian **Ints:** Psychoanalysis and developmental psychology **Educ:** Cottage Lyceum, Vienna **Appts & awards:** Chairperson, Vienna Psychoanalytic Society, 1925–38; Hon. LLD, Clarke University, 1950, Sheffield University, 1966; Director, Hampstead Child Therapy Course and Clinic, 1952; Hon. ScD, Jefferson Medical College, Philadelphia, 1964, Chicago, 1966, Yale, 1968; CBE, 1967; Fellow, Royal Society of Medicine, 1978; Hon. PhD, J.W. Goethe University of Frankfurt, 1981; Hon. Fellow, Royal College of Psychiatrists

Principal publications

1937   *The Ego and the Mechanisms of Defence.* Hogarth Press.

1949   Introduction to the technique of child analysis. Nervous and mental diseases: Notes on aggression. *Bulletin, Menninger Clinic*, 13, 143–51.

1949   Nursery school education: Its uses and dangers. *Child Study*, 26, 35–7.

1949   Clinical studies in psychoanalysis: Research project of the Hampstead Child Therapy Clinic. *Psychoanalytic Study of the Child*, 14, 122–31.

1951   Clinical observations on the treatment of manifest male homosexuality. *Psychoanalytic Quarterly*, 20, 337–8.

1952   The role of bodily illness in the mental life of

children. *Psychoanalytic Study of the Child*, 7, 69–81.

1954 Psychoanalysis and education. *Psychoanalytic Study of the Child*, 9–15.

1958 Adolescence. *Psychoanalytic Study of the Child*, 13, 225–78.

1959 The role of the teacher. *Harvard Education Review*, 22, 229–34.

1966 *Normality and Pathology in Childhood*. Hogarth Press.

1969 *Indicators for Child Analysis and Other Papers*. Hogarth Press.

1975 *Studies in Child Psychoanalysis: Pure and Applied*. Yale University Press.

1982 *Psychoanalytic Psychology of Normal Development*. Hogarth Press.

Further reading

Kragh, V. and Smith, G.S. (1970) *Percept Genetic Analysis*. Lund, Gleerups.

Anna, Sigmund **Freud**'s youngest daughter, received no formal university education. However, she became in her own right a notable psychoanalyst, whose principal achievement was to extend the psychoanalytic method so that it could be used with children, a great advantage given the considerable developmental emphasis in psychoanalytic theory.

Just after World War I, Anna Freud began to take over more and more of Freud's secretarial work, a necessity made more pressing by the fact that Freud disliked the telephone, and came to be his assistant. By the time she was 30, Anna had become a teaching analyst and was working with children. By 1935, Anna was secretary, nurse, aide and the obvious successor to her father as leader of the psychoanalytic movement, since by that time her psychoanalytic practice and writing were held in high regard.

In the late 1930s she became involved in helping Jewish psychoanalysts to leave Germany to escape the Nazis, and in 1939 she and her father escaped to Hampstead, where she continued her practice as an analyst and her work with children. This work was of especial interest because it represented the classical tradition of psychoanalysis applied to children, and is to be contrasted with that of another refugee – Melanie **Klein** – whose object relations theory became highly influential in British psychoanalysis.

There can be no doubt that Anna's greatest contribution to psychoanalysis lay in her work with children. This extended well beyond formal psychoanalysis and influenced both psychiatry and child psychology. Such work requires a considerable sensitivity to human beings which the somewhat formal rules of classical psychoanalysis, especially the importance of not breaking the transference, often seem to offset. This is well illustrated by an account of an analysis by Anna Freud, given to me by one of her patients. At the time of his analysis, his wife was having a baby, but suffering some complications. He told Anna Freud of their difficulties; she made no comment but continued her knitting, as was her wont during sessions. When finally the child was born, at the end of the session, Anna handed him a knitted cot cover.

Her other, more theoretical contribution was her work on the defence mechanisms. Of all the psychoanalytic concepts, these may prove the most durable in a scientific account of human behaviour. There is considerable recent European work supporting defence mechanisms and demonstrating their utility in understanding motivation. Much of this work set out avowedly from the base of Anna Freud's work, although not surprisingly it extends it considerably.

Finally, it should be noted that without the devoted care of Anna Freud for her father, it is highly likely that he would have died earlier from cancer and that his later works, even had he survived, would not have been written. Certainly, without her, his flight to England and his brief stay in Hampstead would have been impossible. For this alone, the psychoanalytic movement owes much to Anna Freud.

PAUL KLINE

Freud, Sigmund

Born: 1856, Freiber, Moravia *Died:* 1939, London, England *Nat:* Austrian *Ints:* Psychoanalysis, therapy *Educ:* MD University of Vienna, 1881 *Appts & awards:* Docent, University of Vienna, 1885; Professor in Neurology, University of Vienna, 1902–38; Hon. LLD, Clarke University, 1909; Foreign Member, Royal Society; Founder, Vienna Psychoanalytic Society; Editor, *International Journal of Psychoanalysis*, *Imago*

Principal publications

1896 The Aetiology of Hysteria, 3, 187–221.

1900 The Interpretation of Dreams.

1901 The Psychotherapy of Everyday Life.

1905 Three Essays on Sexuality, 7, 135–243.

1909 Analysis of a phobia in a 5 year old boy, 10, 3–149.

1911   Psychoanalytic notes on an autobiographical account of a case of paranoia (Dementia Paranoides).
1913   Totem and Taboo.
1923   The Ego and the Id, 3–66.
1925   Some physical consequences of the anatomical distinction between the sexes, 19, 243–58.
1927   The future of an illusion, 21, 3–56.
1931   Female sexuality, 21, 221–43.
1933   Femininity, 22, 112–35.
1933   New Introductory Lectures on Psychoanalysis.
1939   Moses and Monotheism.
1966   *The Standard Edition of the Complete Psychological Works of Sigmund Freud*. Hogarth Press and the Institute of Psychoanalysis.

Further reading

Grünbaum, A. (1984) *The Foundations of Psychoanalysis: A Philosophical Critique*. University of California Press.
Kline, P. (1981) *Fact and Fantasy in Freudian Theory*. Routledge.

Sigmund Freud was trained as a physician in Vienna in the 1880s. He published in the field of neurology and aphasia but was unable to obtain an academic appointment on account of the prevailing anti-Semitism. This led him into the field of psychiatry, to studies with **Charcot** in Paris, and to the development, first with Breuer, of psychoanalysis.

From 1890 until his death in England in 1939, Freud was responsible for the evolution of both the ideas of psychoanalysis and its institutions, although as the subject expanded, other collaborators played important parts.

It must be realized that psychoanalysis is both a set of ideas and a therapeutic method, supposedly based upon them. In this entry, I shall concentrate mainly upon the ideas. When Freud first reported the findings of his psychoanalytic method, the talking cure, in which patients were required to free associate to the analyst as they lay on the famous couch, he was greeted with ridicule, scepticism and hostility. The notion of childhood sexuality, that sexual drives were the important dynamics of human behaviour, the universality of the Oedipus complex, and the fact that human beings were not ruled by reason but by unconscious drives offended the European Victorian *Zeitgeist*. This offence was interpreted by Freud as resistance – to the painful truth of the ideas.

Freud claimed to have discovered these truths, previously hidden from psychologists and psychiatrists, by his psychoanalytic method, in which patients were required to free associate, and from dream analysis. These were the database of his theories and as such they are currently seen as problems in the scientific acceptability of psychoanalysis.

In the twenties and thirties psychoanalytic therapy began to be seen as a powerful means of treating psychological disorders, and gradually Freudian ideas became acceptable, especially among the literati. Freud's fame became so great that the Nazis were afraid to destroy his practice and allowed him to emigrate to England after Freud had fully recommended them, an irony which fortunately escaped them. He was also awarded a Fellowship of the Royal Society and, at the time of his death, was seen as one of the major scientific thinkers of his age and perhaps to be held alongside **Darwin** and Einstein.

Psychoanalytic theory embraces every aspect of the human mind. It seeks literally to explain everything. This is its attraction, particularly to those who are untrained in science and who want explanations for the complexities of human behaviour and experience. This is also its weakness from the viewpoint of Popperian scientific method. It is difficult to falsify because it cannot make predictions, only *post hoc* explanations. As a result of this claimed defect, psychoanalysis has been banished by the scientific discipline of psychology to the realms of theories only of historic interest. **Eysenck** has been one of its most vociferous critics on grounds of both scientific methodology and the inefficacy of psychoanalytic therapy.

Yet despite these objections, publications about Freudian theory and therapy continue unabated, and in the United States and France psychoanalytic therapy, albeit in modern guise, continues to be practised. This is because, despite the problems which have been mentioned, psychoanalytic ideas seem to be in accord with human experience, and to account for the real world in ways which modern psychological theories framed in the laboratory and close to data are singularly unable to do.

Freud's output was enormous, but the main ideas can be briefly stated with some clarity. The distinctively Freudian view is that unconscious drives and wishes have a considerable influence on our lives, and that unless these are understood – which is possible only through psychoanalytic therapy – change is impossible. In the healthy individual there is a dynamic balance between the forces of the ego, concerned with reality and largely conscious, the superego, dealing with morality, and the id, the entirely unconscious repository of drives and unacceptable repressed wishes. Neurotics are ruled by their superegos, psychotics by their id, their ego defences having been penetrated. Indeed the aim of therapy is to replace id activity by that of the ego. This notion of unconscious ego defences is one of the most critical in understanding human behaviour. For example, racism can be seen as the projection onto others of unacceptable traits, and the violence of animal rights defenders indicates that their feelings for animals are indications of displacement of Oedipal resentment. The fact of defences means that simple interviews and questionnaires, beloved of social psychology, are bound to fail. It is to be noted that there is some experimental evidence in favour of defences, and the concept is now widely used in personality psychology in an extended form.

Freud is well known for his claims about infantile sexuality passing through oral, anal and phallic stages until, after the latency period, full genital sexuality emerges. This is part of his developmental theories, which culminate in what Freud saw as his major discovery – the Oedipus complex, which he regarded as universal. The male child wishes to kill his father and sleep with his mother, feelings which have to be repressed through fear of talion revenge by the father – the castration complex. This fear of castration leads the male to identify with the father, and thus the superego is formed. The child adopts the values and morals of the parent. Hence the importance in psychoanalytic theory of the family and the perils of one-parent and broken homes. In the female, development is similar. Here the important issue is not fear of castration, but penis envy, the female child believing that she has been castrated. The way this Oedipus complex is dealt with profoundly affects our emotional lives and is considered to be the kernel of neurosis.

This aspect of Freudian theory is now, at the end of the twentieth century, notorious. Modern women find it offensive that they are considered to be driven by penis envy and inferior to men. Freud regarded superego development and hence morality as weaker in women than men because the latter were driven by fear of castration. In addition, the claim that children desire sexual relationships is regarded as repellent in the light of the assertions of sexual abuse that are now fashionable in many types of psychiatry. This is particularly the case because Freud originally also believed that his patients had been sexually abused, but retracted this view and postulated the fantasy. In other words, modern psychiatry of this type has regressed a hundred years, as if psychoanalysis had never occurred. In Freudian terms this is a supreme example of resistance, which, Freud believed, his theories would always have to face.

Freud early on in psychoanalysis developed a theory of dreaming which was central to psychoanalysis and the basis of its data in therapy. Dreams were described as the royal road to the unconscious because the actual dream, the manifest content, was regarded as a disguised version of the latent content, which always expressed a repressed wish. This disguise, the dream work, exemplified the workings of the unconscious, primary processes which were normally hidden. Thus analysis of dreams revealed the unconscious of the patients.

As has been mentioned, one of the attractions of Freudian theory is its enormous scope. With the relatively few concepts already discussed, Freud was able to explain every aspect of human behaviour. A few examples will clarify this explanatory power. Humour and wit are seen as the expression of forbidden wishes. Joke work is akin to dream work. The fact of a joke allows aggressive and sexual statements, which would otherwise be impossible. In Freudian theory there is no such thing as a joke. In jokes, like wine, lies the truth.

Similarly there is no such thing as an accident. The slip of the tongue, the drop from the hand, both express repressed desires. For Freud everything, no matter how trivial, has a meaning. Whose letter was not posted, whose address forgotten, whose crockery broken and whose clothes defiled by tomato sauce? These are the questions which need to be asked and answered, and are so in Freudian theory. Finally, anthropology and religion: the Oedipus complex was used to explain totemism and the taboo on eating the totem animal. It was invoked further to explain the belief in God. God the father is a psychological trust.

In conclusion, it can be said with confidence that Freudian theory is one of the most influential scientific theories in any field in the twentieth century. Recently, critics have attacked its scientific standing and its utility as a basis of therapy. Some psychologists, such as Eysenck, regard it as a baleful influence on psychological science. Yet despite such criticisms it continues to be developed in both America and Europe. As a way of thinking about human beings it is still hugely influential, especially among intelligent non-psychologists. Indeed it seems that what is required for a modern psychology is neither a complete rejection, nor a complete acceptance, as is found in classical psychoanalysis. Freud believed that psychoanalysis was a preliminary step to a scientific psychology – preliminary until a powerful biochemistry was developed. Now, with modern research in genetics and biochemistry, it may be possible to blend psychoanalysis into a truly scientific account of human psychology.

PAUL KLINE

Fromm, Erich Pinchas

Born: 1900, Frankfurt, Germany **Died:** 1980, Locarno, Switzerland **Nat:** German **Ints:** Personality and social, philosophical and theoretical, psychoanalysis, psychotherapy and humanistic **Educ:** DPhil University of Heidelberg, 1922; Diploma of a Professional Psychologist, 1952 **Appts & Awards:** Berlin Psychoanalytic Institute, 1930– ; Institute für Sozialforschung, Frankfurt and New York, 1930–8; New York Academy of Science, 1940– ; Fellow, Washington School of Psychiatry, 1940– ; Adjunct Professor of Psychology, New York University, 1962–76; Fellow, AAAS, 1977– ; Hon. Citizen, Muralto, Switzerland, 1979; Nelly Sachs Prize of Dortmund, 1979; Goethe Medaille of Frankfurt, 1981; Editor, Mexican National Academy of Medicine; Washington Psychoanalytical Society; *Revista di Psicoanalisis, Psiquiatria y Psicologia*; Co-editor, *Contemporary Psychoanalysis* (New York) and many journals in psychoanalysis

Principal publications

1930 Die Entwicklung des Christusdogmas. In *Imago*. Wien.
1932 Über Method und Aufgabe einer analytischen Sozialpsychologie. *Zeitschrift für Sozialforschung*, 1, 28–54.
1932 Die psychoanalytische Charakterologie und ihre Bedeutung für Sozialpsychologie. *Zeitschrift fur Sozialforschung*, 1, 253–77.
1934 Die sozialpsychologische Bedeutung der Mutterrechtstheorie. *Zeitschrift für Sozialforschung*, 3, 196–227.
1936 *Sozialpsychologischer Teil. In Studien über Autorität und Familie*. Horkheimer.
1941 *Escape from Freedom*. Farrar and Rinehart.
1943 Sex and character. *Psychiatry*, 6, 21–31.
1946 Psychoanalytic characterology and its application to the understanding of culture. In S.S. Sargent and M.W. Smith (eds), *Culture and Personality*.
1947 *Man for Himself*. Rinehart.
1955 *The Sane Society*. Rinehart and Winston.
1955/6 The present human condition. *American Scholar*, 25, 29–35.
1956 *The Art of Loving*. Harper and Row.
1957 Man is not a thing. *Saturday Review*, 40, 9–11.
1960 Psychoanalysis and Zen Buddhism. In D.T. Suzuki, E. Fromm and R. de Martino (eds), *Zen Buddhism and Psychoanalysis*.
1968 Marx's contribution to the knowledge of man. *Social Science Information*, 7, 7–17.
1970 The crisis of psychoanalysis. In E. Fromm (ed.), *The Crisis of Psychoanalysis and other Essays on Freud, Marx and Social Psychology*.
1978 *The Anatomy of Human Destructiveness*. Holt, Rinehart and Winston.

Further reading

Alexander, F., Eisenstein, S. and Grotjahn, M. (eds) (1995) *Psychoanalytic Pioneers*. Transaction.
Burston, D. (1991) *The Legacy of Erich Fromm*. Harvard University Press.

First educated by Jewish teachers and Talmudists, Fromm studied sociology with Alfred Weber at Heidelberg. He was trained in psychoanalysis and became a psychoanalyst at the end of the twenties. As a member of the Frankfurt School he developed his own method and a theory of analytic social psychology which can be seen as an attempt to combine psychoanalysis and Marxist sociology. Fromm's special interest was never the individual as such but the individual participating in the social process. Using **Freud**'s concept of character he developed a social characterology giving insight into the unconscious psychic structure of the human being as an 'ensemble of society'. Fromm recognized the dynamic function of stabilizing the prevalent social forces and of making people accept their role as members of a given society and economic system. He validated his insights in field research in the thirties in Germany and in the sixties in Mexico. His attempts to understand social processes by studying the social unconscious stimulated him to reformulate psychoanalytic theory. Humans' strivings are not the outcome of special instincts but answers to special psychic needs, which society teaches through the family, the agent of society. The Frommian psychoanalytic theory is a theory of primary human interrelatedness, as Harry **Stack**

Sullivan put it. Its main contribution and concern are the development of a new method and theory of social psychology and social characterology. Of special importance are Fromm's conceptualization of the authoritarian social character (in the thirties), the Marketing character (in the forties) and the necrophilic character (in the sixties). His main concern was for a new 'science of man'; a humanistic approach seeing people not as things but as open systems of life determined as much by the unconscious as by society.

RAINIER FUNK

G

Gagné, Robert Mills

Born: 1916, North Andover, Massachusetts, USA **Nat:** American **Ints:** Educational psychology, evaluation, measurement and statistics, experimental psychology, general psychology, industrial and organizational psychology, military psychology, school psychology **Educ:** BA Yale University, 1937; PhD Brown University, 1940; **Appts & awards:** Aviation psychologist; Technical Director of two USAF laboratories; Professor of Psychology, Princeton University, 1958–62; President APA Division 19, 1960–1; Director, American Institute for Research, 1962–5; President APA Division 15, 1967–8; President, AERA, 1970–1; AERA-PDK Award, Distinguished Educational Research, 1972; E.L. Thorndike Award for Educational Psychology, 1974; John Smith Memorial Award for the Applications of Psychology, APA, 1982; Professor of Educational Psychology, University of California Berkeley; Professor of Educational Research, Florida State University

Principal publications

1962 (ed.) *Psychological Principles in System Development*. Holt, Rinehart and Winston.
1967 (ed.) *Learning and Individual Differences*. C.E. Merrill.
1979 *Principles of Instructional Design*, 2nd edn. Holt, Rinehart and Winston (with R.A. Reiser).
1983 *Selecting Media for Instruction*. Educational Technology Publications (with R.A. Reiser).
1985 *The Conditions of Learning*, 4th edn. Holt, Rinehart and Winston.
1988 *Essentials of Learning for Instruction*. Prentice-Hall.

Further reading

Ausubel, D.P. and Robinson, F.G. (1969) *School Learning: An Introduction to Educational Psychology*. Holt, Rinehart and Winston.
Davies, I.K. (1971) *The Management of Learning*. McGraw-Hill.
De Cecco, J.P. (1968) *The Psychology of Learning and Instruction—Educational Psychology*. Prentice-Hall.

Good, T.L. and Brophy, J.E. (1980) *Educational Psychology—a Realistic Approach*. Holt, Rinehart and Winston.
Resnick, L.B. and Ford, W.F. (1984) *The Psychology of Mathematics for Instruction*. Erlbaum.
Rowntree, D. (1981) *Developing Courses for Students*. McGraw-Hill.
Stones, E. and Anderson, D. (1972) *Educational Objectives and the Teaching of Educational Psychology*. Methuen.
Taber, J.L., Glaser, R. and Schaefer, H.H. (1965) *Learning and Programmed Instruction*. Addison Wesley.
Travers, J.F., Elliott, S.N. and Kratochwill, T.R (1993) *Educational Psychology, Effective Teaching, Effective Learning*. Brown and Benchmark.

Based on the assumption that no single model accounts for all types of learning, Gagné's theory, which was originally Behaviourist in derivation, developed to become eclectic, amounting largely to a coherent synthesis of Behaviourist and Gestalt theories, but also reaching into early cognitive psychology, systems theory and social learning theory. It is however essentially practical in its orientation, striving to advance the application of psychology to designing instructional systems and environments.

Learning, for Gagné, refers to acquired and enduring changes in the individual's capability. Beginning with work in the military context, his constant search has been to identify and relate the conditions (both internal and external) of learning with its various types (in terms of content) and its outcomes. The essential characteristic of instruction (from the level of lesson planning to that of curriculum design) is that it be a planned sequence of steps that will lead, with greatest efficiency, to achieving intended outcomes. These outcomes in turn are seen as retained dispositions of the learner which Gagné refers to as capabilities. An essential feature of learning, on the other hand, is its hierarchical nature, the more complex always building on the simpler forms.

There are five main types of outcome or capability: attitudes, motor skills, verbal information, cognitive strategies, and intellectual skills. The combination of these in sequence, across the affective, motor and cognitive domains, from lower to higher levels, comprises a learning hierarchy, each member in this sequence being seen either as a supportive or an essential prerequisite internal condition of learning its successor in the sequence.

Beginning therefore by identifying target skills to be learned (e.g. the definite article in the German language), the teacher will work backwards, asking, 'What simpler skills would a learner find necessary or helpful in order to learn this one?' Essential prerequisite skills will be components of the target one (e.g. the capability to identify gender, number and case, in order to supply the correct form of the definite article in German); supportive prerequisites, on the other hand, will be those previously learned capabilities that will be helpful but not essential (e.g. having a generally favourable attitude towards the subject in question).

Gagné identifies eight types of learning which comprise a taxonomy (somewhat similar to those of Bloom and Krathwohl), in that the relationships among the elements are hierarchical, the higher subsuming and depending on those lower down, except for the relationships between types 1 and 2. Moving from the simplest to the most complex, these types or levels are as follows:

(1) Signal learning: classical conditioning in which the learner responds to a signal (e.g. salivation in Pavlov's theory);
(2) Stimulus-response (S-R) learning: operant or instrumental conditioning as described by **Skinner** in which the learner forms S-R bonds from trial-and-error learning; these are reinforced by their outcomes;
(3) Chaining: acquiring chains of two or more S-R bonds which will facilitate the performance of more complex behaviours;
(4) Verbal association: forming S-R connections between words and objects or between words themselves (e.g. naming objects and rote learning);
(5) Discrimination learning: learning to differentiate (the shape, size, colour, texture etc.) of objects whose characteristics were initially not differentiated
(6) Concrete concept learning: discrimination learning underpins the capability to learn a

group of stimulus objects as a class (concrete concepts, or concepts by observation);
(7) Learning defined concepts and rules: concepts and rules play a major organizing role in intellectual functioning; abstract concepts are learned, not by observation, but by definition;
(8) Problem solving: the learner applies concepts and rules to solving a problem, thus developing new capabilities and strategies by adducing a 'higher order' principle.

While this theory has been criticized for treating problem solving univocally, as though solving a crossword puzzle and composing an opera were essentially of the same order, Gagné does acknowledge that 'it does not seem possible at present to specify all the conditions necessary to attain the highest and most complex varieties of human performance such as those displayed in invention or esthetic creativity' (*The Conditions of Learning*, 2nd edn, p. 25). However, it will be clear from the foregoing that, for effective learning to occur, the learner must have mastered and must recall the specific skills, knowledge, concepts or principles that are prerequisite to what is now to be learned.

Gagné's attempt to specify the external and internal conditions of learning included analysing the act of learning into eight steps or phases. Their sequence is as follows:

(1) Motivation: intrinsic motivation is preferable;
(2) Apprehending: capturing and maintaining the learner's attention is essential;
(3) Acquisition: The material is coded into the learner's own 'language' thus enabling it to be stored in short-term memory;
(4) Retention: movement of material from short-term to long-term memory; this can be facilitated by various devices for transforming perceptual into conceptual learning;
(5) Recall: retrieval of the information when needed is one indication that learning has occurred;
(6) Generalization: the realization of the wider significance of what has been learned, beyond its initial context: this amounts to the transfer of learning;
(7) Performance: change in the learner's capability which raises performance to a new level is the best proof that learning has occurred;
(8) Feedback: provision of feedback to the

learner, giving reassurance and reinforcement of the learning achieved.

This framework was seen by Gagné as providing a basis for understanding the interaction of external and internal events, sufficient to plan instructional systems applicable to a variety of settings.

Gagné's major achievement was to bridge the gulf that had developed between learning theory – then largely identified with Behaviourist psychology – and instructional practice. Classical learning theory claimed to have much to say about the process of learning, but nothing about its content. This was no longer acceptable in a context of serious questioning of the effectiveness of both school curricula (in the post-Sputnik era) and of teachers' instructional methods.

Gagné in particular facilitated the analysis of knowledge in such a way as to make it possible to distinguish between content and method of learning, the former to be derived from objectives, the latter from applied psychology of learning. At a time of growing concern about how to cater for individual differences among learners, especially the needs of the very weak and the very strong Gagné's concept of knowledge as cumulative and hierarchically structured, offered one kind of solution for matching the level of difficulty of the material with the level of ability of the child.

Gagné's is not theory for its own sake, but theory to help the practitioner: provided it is not interpreted in a mechanistic or deterministic manner, but rather in a reflexive and probabilistic way, his model can be considered of value to teachers, educational psychologists and other professionals involved in designing instruction.

DES SWAN

Gal'perin, Pyotr Yakovlyevich

Born: 1902, Russia **Died:** 1988, Moscow, Russia **Nat:** Russian **Ints:** Developmental psychology, methodological problems in psychology, psychology, psychology of learning **Educ:** Dr Pedagogical Sciences (Psychology), Moscow State University, 1965 **Appts & awards:** Docent, Faculty of Philosophy, Moscow State University, 1943–65; Professor, Department of Psychology, Moscow State University, 1965–71; Chair of Child Psychology, Faculty of Psychology, Moscow State University, 1971–88; Honoured Science Worker of the Russian Federation

Principal publications
1966   Development of investigations on the formation of mental operations. In *Psychological Research in the USSR*, vol. 1. Progress Publishers.
1966   The psychology of thinking and the doctrine of stage-by-stage formation of mental operations. In *Study of Thinking in Soviet Psychology*. Nauka Publishers (in Russian).
1969   Stages in the development of mental acts. In M. Cole and I. Maltzman (eds), *A Handbook of Contemporary Soviet Psychology*. Basic Books.

Further reading
Gal'perin, P.Y. (1976) *Introduction to Psychology*. Moscow University Press (in Russian).
Gal'perin, P.Y. (1987) On the possibility of building an objective psychology. *Psychology Bulletin of Moscow University*, 6 (in Russian).

Pyotr Yakovlyevich Gal'perin was born 2 October 1902. After graduation from the Medical Institute he worked as a psycho-neurologist and then a psychologist in medical and pedagogical institutions of the Ukraine. In the early 1930s Gal'perin joined **Leont'ev** and Zaporozhetz at Kharkov in their attempts to develop a new approach to psychology – an activity theory – which originated from the cultural-historical approach of the remarkable Soviet psychologist **Vygotsky** (Galperin had always seen himself as Vygotsky's natural successor). During World War II he worked in a hospital and then moved to the Moscow University (Department of Philosophy), where he obtained his second scientific degree and worked until the end.

Gal'perin was known for his original theory of learning and education, which he himself dubbed 'a theory of stage-by-stage formation of mental operations'. This theory had been developed within the more general context of the activity theory whose interpretation by Gal'perin was different from that of its main authors, Leont'ev and **Rubinstein**. Their doctrine dominated Soviet psychology from the 1960s to the 1980s. Gal'perin believed that only one aspect of activity, namely orienting, can really serve as a subject of psychological investigation (actually this was a new, original definition of the subject of psychology, of which there have been few in the long history of psychology – soul, consciousness, behaviour, activity, and now orienting activity). Then, he assumed that all variety in mental activity is a result of interiorization of the external forms of exploratory (orienting) activity. However, the process of interiorization was not understood as a mechanical converting of external activity into its internal form. Gal'perin believed this process to pass through a series of stages.

At each stage an orienting activity is carried out in a new form. All these forms of internal activities were specified in terms of a few parameters, such as (1) the level of interiorization; (2) the extent of generalization; (3) the completeness of the operations accomplished; and (4) the degree of mastery. The first parameter was supposed to be the most important. The four levels of interiorization of an act were postulated when it is based: (1) on material objects, or their material representations (such as signs); (2) on audible speech without direct support from objects; (3) on external speech to oneself; and (4) on internal speech only. Gal'perin and his collaborators (Nechaev, Podol'skii and others) developed an original system of external control of the process of interiorization on which a new system of training was based. The 'trade mark' of this new system of training is a formation of mental acts with a guaranteed level of mastery and generalization. Gal'perin's theory of stage-by-stage formation of mental operations was extensively used as a theoretical and methodological basis for developing a system of programmed learning by his student N.F. Talysina at Moscow University.

Gal'perin was a brilliant lecturer. His lectures on the history of psychology, delivered for more than twenty years at Moscow University, were attended by students from many departments. In a sense, thanks to him, a few generations of Soviet students during the Cold War period became acquainted, not only with psychology based on Marxism, but also with the main trends in Western psychology this century.

T. SOKOLSKAYA AND A. LOGVINENKO

Galton, Francis

Born: 1822, Birmingham, England **Died:** 1911, Haslemere, Surrey, England **Nat:** British **Ints:** Developmental psychology, experimental psychology, evaluation and measurement, Society for the Psychological Study of Social Issues **Educ:** BA University of Cambridge, 1844 **Appts & awards:** Royal Geographical Society Gold Medal, 1853; Fellow, Royal Society, 1856; Hon. Secretary, Royal Geographical Society, 1857–63; Hon. General Secretary, British Association, 1863–7; President, British Association Geography Section, 1872, Anthropology Section, 1885; Royal Society Gold Medal, 1886; Hon. DCL University of

Oxford, 1894; Hon. ScD University of Cambridge, 1895; Royal Society Darwin Medal, 1902; Anthropological Institute Huxley Medal, 1902; Linnean Society Darwin–Wallace Medal, 1908; Knighted, 1909; Royal Society Copley Medal, 1910

Principal publications

1865 Hereditary talent and character. *Macmillan's Magazine*, 12, 157–66, 318–27.
1869 *Hereditary Genius*. Macmillan.
1874 *English Men of Sciences: Their Nature and Nurture*. Macmillan.
1877 Typical laws of heredity. *Proceedings of the Royal Institution*, 8, 282–301.
1883 *Inquiries into Human Faculty and its Development*.
1886 Regression towards mediocrity in hereditary stature. *Journal of the Anthropological Institute*, 15, 246–63.
1888 Co-relations and their measurement, chiefly from anthropometric data. *Proceedings of the Royal Society*, 45, 125–45.
1889 *Natural Inheritance*. Macmillan.
1892 *Fingerprints*. Macmillan.
1901 Biometry. *Biometrika*, 1, 7–10.
1908 *Memories of my Life*. Methuen.

Further reading

Fancher, R.E. (1985) *The Intelligence Men*. Norton.
Forrest, D.W. (1974) *Francis Galton: The Life and Work of a Victorian Genius*. Elek.
Pearson, K. (1914–30) *The Life, Letters and Labours of Francis Galton* (3 vols). Cambridge.

Francis Galton was born into a Quaker family with considerable wealth acquired first from trade as gun manufacturers and more recently from banking. Yet a passion for science permeated both paternal and maternal sides of Galton's family, for his father and grandfather were accomplished amateurs, the latter elected a Fellow of the Royal Society, while his mother was a daughter of Erasmus Darwin, grandfather of Charles Darwin and a notable scientist in his own right.

Despite his early promise as an infant prodigy, Galton's formal educational record at school and university was undistinguished. Following the wishes of his parents, and especially his mother, he began medical training in 1838, apparently without much enthusiasm. After two years, spent initially as an 'indoor pupil' in Birmingham General Hospital and then at King's College London, Galton secured his father's agreement to a break in his studies in order to read mathematics at Cambridge. In his final year there, however, he suffered a nervous breakdown and left with only a pass degree. His medical education, resumed in a somewhat desultory fashion after Cambridge, was abandoned with alacrity a few months later when the death of his father in 1844 brought a large inheritance and thus removed any need for a career or paid employment.

Galton was now free to do as he wished. First came a lengthy tour of the Middle East, followed by four aimless years of country pursuits in Scotland. The next scheme was a two-year expedition to South West Africa which received the blessing of the Royal Geographical Society, but for which Galton himself paid. As well as gaining popular recognition from the accounts of his travels, Galton's achievements as a map maker (during the African expedition), together with meteorological work undertaken in an honorary capacity at Kew Observatory, earned him many distinctions, including election as a Fellow of the Royal Society.

By the early 1860s, however, anthropological interests acquired during his travels; an increasingly strong conviction of the necessity of social reform; and, especially, *The Origin of Species*, recently published by his cousin Charles **Darwin**, had conspired to set Galton off in yet another direction. Henceforth, his main concern would be with enquiries into the inheritance of mental and physical characteristics and their role in determining individual differences.

As a geographer, meteorologist and inveterate counter and measurer of anything and everything, Galton was acquainted with the work of the Belgian astronomer and pioneer statistician, Quetelet. Armed with Quetelet's demonstration that the 'law of errors' (the normal curve) governed variability, not just in astronomical observations but in a variety of phenomena including human physical measurements, Galton could now argue that so general a law should apply equally well to mental abilities. It was with these basic tools that he embarked on a scientific study of heredity.

His first foray was a statistical analysis of eminent men who had earned places in various biographical dictionaries, from which he concluded that ability must be inherited, since a far larger proportion of these distinguished men than might be expected by chance were blood relatives. The implications of such a finding for bringing about social reform were quite clear to Galton: the necessary improvement to the intellectual level of society could be achieved by what amounted to selective breeding. Reports of this new line of enquiry and his notion of 'eugenics' (as he was later to call it) appeared in 1865 as a two-part article in *Macmillan's Magazine*, entitled 'Hereditary talent and character', which was subsequently expanded into a book, *Hereditary Genius* (1869).

Over more than three decades Galton vigorously pursued his studies of the differences among individuals in their physical and mental abilities, and of the hereditary basis of such variation, collecting data from many sources. The most ambitious of these was the anthropometric laboratory that he set up initially at the International Health Exhibition of 1884–5 in London and at which more than 9000 visitors paid threepence apiece to have various anthropometric measurements taken and the strength, sensory acuity and reaction times assessed. (It is worth noting here that Galton regarded sensory acuity, as well as physiological measures such as reaction times, as indicators of mental ability, or intelligence.) The laboratory, housed elsewhere in London after the exhibition closed, continued to provide Galton with mass data on human characteristics for many more years; indeed, it was fingerprint data collected in the laboratory that led to his pioneering scheme for classifying fingerprints, which is still essentially the basis of modern fingerprint identification systems.

Galton's other data-gathering activities included sending out questionnaires (something of a novelty in 1874) to Fellows of the Royal Society, inviting the general public to respond to a questionnaire by offering prizes for the best 'record of family faculties', and making a special study of almost 800 brothers, as well as experimenting with sweet peas, rabbits and moths. In the course of these enquiries, however, he was also investigating certain mental processes, including the association of ideas (for which he acted as both experimenter and subject) and visual imagery. These latter psychological studies are described in *Inquiries into Human Faculty and its Development*.

But hand in hand with all Galton's empirical investigations was the development of a statistical methodology; statistics, he insisted, were 'the only tools by which an opening can be cut through the formidable thicket of difficulties that bar the path of those who pursue the science of man'. The notion of 'reversion' (first mentioned in 1877 and later changed to the now familiar term 'regression') had arisen from his observation that, for instance, the offspring of large, or small, parents (whether sweet pea seeds or humans) tended to be closer in size to the average for the population than to their parents; in other words, they reverted or regressed to 'mediocrity'. It was Galton's attempts to quantify the degree of resemblance between the characteristics of parent and offspring that led to the creation of a regression line, whose slope provides the measure of resemblance. Although realizing that the regression line could present the relationship between any two variables, Galton was well aware that, because its slope depended on both the scale and unit of measurement, it was an imperfect instrument. However, it was not until several years later in 1888 that Galton hit upon the idea of re-expressing the measures in standardized form; thus, the regression slope became a coefficient of correlation, a unit-free measure of association.

The following year, Galton published what has been described by some commentators as his most scientifically influential, if flawed, book, *Natural Inheritance*, which brought together the results of his empirical and statistical work, although before he had the chance to incorporate his latest discovery about correlation. Fortunately for Galton, the book still proved to be enough of a catalyst for others more mathematically able to join in and take over the task of elaborating the correlational methodology. Most notable of these converts to the new school of 'biometry' was Karl **Pearson**, then Professor of Applied Mathematics at University College London. In fact, it was with Galton's financial assistance that biometry flourished at University College. He underwrote the journal *Biometrika*, funded the Galton Laboratory for National Eugenics with Pearson as Director, and finally, with a bequest on his death, endowed the Galton Professorship in Eugenics with Pearson as its first incumbent.

To modern eyes, the evidence for Galton's insistence that ability was a result of heredity rather than of environmental influences seems unconvincing, while his psychological investigations and theorizing might be viewed more as a curiosity than as a fundamental contribution. Perhaps his greatest legacy to psychology derives from his relentless pursuit of the scientific basis for the study of individual differences.

PATRICIA LOVIE AND A.D. LOVIE

Garcia, John
Born: 1917, Santa Rosa, California, USA **Nat:** American **Ints:** Comparative and physiological

psychology **Educ:** AB University of California at Berkeley, 1948; MA University of California at Berkeley, 1949; PhD University of California at Berkeley, 1965 **Appts & awards:** Professor of Psychology and Psychiatry and Biobehavioural Sciences, University of California at Los Angeles; Psychonomic Society, Society of Experimental Psychologists, 1978; H. Crosby Warren Medal for Outstanding Research in Psychology, Society of Experimental Psychologists, 1978– ; AAAS, APA Distinguished Scientific Contribution Award, 1979; National Academy of Sciences, 1983; Consulting Editor, *Journal of Comparative Psychology*

Principal publications

1951 Subcultural variation in authoritarian personality. *Journal of Abnormal and Social Psychology*, 46, 457–69 (with R. Christie).
1955 Conditioned aversion to saccharin resulting from exposure to gamma radiation. *Science*, 122, 157–8 (with D.J. Kimeldorf and R.A. Koelling).
1964 Adaptive responses to ionizing radiations. *Boletin de Instituto de Estudios Medicos y Biologicos*, 22, 101–13 (with N.A. Buchwald, C.D. Hull and R.A. Keolling).
1968 Gustatory-visceral and telereceptor-cutaneous conditioning: Adaptation in the internal and external millieus. *Communications in Behavioral Biology*, part A, 1, 389–415 (with F.R. Ervin).
1969 The use of ionizing radiation as a motivating stimulus. *Psychological Review*, 68, 383–95 (with D.J. Kimeldorf and E.L. Hunt).
1969 X-ray as an olfactory stimulus. In C. Pfaffman (ed.), *Taste and Olfaction III*. Rockefeller University Press (with K.F. Green and B.K. McGowan).
1970 Learned associations over long delays. In G. Bower (ed.), *The Psychology of Learning and Motivation: Advances in Research and Theory*. Academic Press (with S. Revusky).
1970 The use of ionizing rays as a mammalian olfactory stimulus. In L.M. Beidler (ed.), *The Handbook of Sensory Physiology*. Springer-Verlag (with R.A. Koelling).
1975 The futility of comparative IQ research. In N.A. Buchwald and M.A.B. Brazier (eds), *Brain Mechanisms in Mental Retardation*. Academic Press.
1981 The logic and limits of mental aptitude testing. *American Psychologist*, 36, 1172–80.
1984 Alcohol ingestive habits: The role of flavour and effect. In M. Galanter (ed.), *Recent Developments in Alcoholism*. Plenum Press (with J.E. Sherman and K.W. Rusiniak).
1985 X-rays and learned taste aversions: Historical

and psychological ramifications. In T.G. Burish, S.M. Levy and B.E. Meyerowitz (eds), *Cancer, Nutrition and Eating Behavior: A Biobehavioral Perspective*. Erlbaum (with R. Garcia and Y. Robertson).

Further reading
Gross, R.D. (1990) *Key Studies in Psychology*. Hodder and Stoughton.

John Garcia was the second of six sons. His parents had moved to Sonoma County, north of San Francisco Bay, during World War I. He was a mechanic and then a soldier. After World War II the GI Bill provided a means to a college education, and Garcia enrolled as a student first at Santa Rosa Junior College and then at the University of California at Berkeley. His early interests reflect the influences of Frenkel-Brunswick, **Sanford** and Robert **Tryon** and his first publication, with Richard Christie, was a study of ethnocentrism. Garcia left Berkeley without a PhD in 1951 and joined the Radiological Defense Laboratory, San Francisco. The laboratory was investigating the effects of ionizing radiation on biological systems and developing hazard-reduction methods.

The significance of behavioural analysis of ionizing radiation was not clear at this time. This form of radiation was considered imperceptible to human senses. However, Garcia's *Science* article (1955) showed that a single low dose of ionizing radiation could act as an unconditioned stimulus. With Kimeldorf and Hunt (1961) he offered an explanation for the effect in terms of a gastric dysfunction delayed at least four minutes after the onset of radiation, and as such it was more readily associated with taste stimuli than with environmental ones. He completed his PhD at Berkeley in 1965 and then moved to the Harvard Medical School.

Initially Garcia's research findings were greeted with considerable scepticism; they had little impact on learning theory and research. However, further research led to the development of a double dissociation research paradigm which he used to clarify the role of ionization as an olfactory conditioned stimulus (CS) and an aversive unconditioned stimulus (UCS). Taste–illness combinations produced rapid learning but taste–pain did not. Conversely, audio-visual–pain combinations produced rapid learning but audio-visual–illness did not. Moreover, an illness UCS delayed up to thirty minutes after presentation of a taste CS produced strong aversion. These findings imposed important limitations on two general principles of association. First, reinforcers were shown to be selective, rather than general, in their action, and second, contiguity was not necessary for learning.

Gardner, Beatrice
Born: 1933, Vienna, Austria *Nat:* Austrian *Ints:* Developmental, experimental, general, physiological and comparative *Educ:* BA Radcliffe College, 1954; MSc Brown University, 1956; DPhil Oxford University, 1959 *Appts & awards:* Professor of Psychology, University of Nevada Reno NIMH Research Scientist Development Award, 1967–77; Sigma Xi National Lecturer, 1978–80; Foundation Professor, 1985–8; Fellow, Center for Advanced Study, College of Arts and Science, University of Nevada, 1985

Principal publications
1969   Teaching sign language to a chimpanzee. *Science*, 165, 664–872 (with R.A. Gardner).
1971   Two-way communication with an infant chimpanzee. In A. Schrier and F. Stollnitz (eds), *Behavior of Nonhuman Primates*. Academic Press (with R.A. Gardner).
1973   Teaching sign language to the chimpanzee, Washoe [16 mm sound film]. Psychological Cinema Register (with R.A. Gardner).
1974   Comparing the early utterances of child and chimpanzee. In A. Pick (ed.), *Minnesota Symposium on Child Psychology* (with R.A. Gardner).
1975   Evidence for sentence constituents in the early utterances of child and chimpanzee. *Journal of Experimental Psychology: General*, 104, 244–67 (with R.A. Gardner).
1978   Comparative psychology and language acquisition. In K. Salzinser and F. Denmark (eds), *Psychology: The State of the Art*. Annals of the New York Academy of Sciences (with R.A. Gardner).
1984   A vocabulary test for chimpanzees. *Journal of Comparative Psychology*, 98, 381–404 (with R.A. Gardner).
1985   Signs of intelligence in cross-fostered chimpanzees. *Philosophical Transactions of the Royal Society*, B, 308, 159–76 (with R.A. Gardner).

Further reading
Canland, D.K. (1993) *Feral Children and Clever Animals: Reflections on Human Nature*. Oxford University Press.
Gardner, R.A., Gardner, B.T. and Van Cantfort, T.E.

(eds) (1989) *Teaching Sign Language to Chimpanzees*. State University of New York Press.

By rearing young chimpanzees as human children are reared, and studying their growing intelligence as it is studied in children, Beatrice and **R. Allen Gardner** could examine the continuity between animal and human intelligence, and the relation between social and intellectual development and its expression in language. The critical role of early experience in the behaviour of organisms is well known and well documented. Many animals have to learn to identify with their own species, and even such habits as migration or overwintering in the same place are profoundly influenced by species-typical rearing conditions. For obvious ethical reasons it is unlikely that we shall see any experimental account of a human child reared by non-human foster parents. But, in the twentieth century, the Kelloggs and the Hayeses pioneered a form of cross-fostering in which the subjects are chimpanzees and the foster parents are human beings. The human foster parents in these experiments spoke to their adopted chimpanzees as parents speak to hearing children. In sharp contrast to the overlap with young children in every other aspect of development, the chimpanzees acquired hardly any speech.

The innovation of the Gardners' Project Washoe was to replace speech with American Sign Language (ASL), the manual language of the deaf in North America. Washoe learned ASL from her human companions and used signs in a childish and rudimentary way that resembled the early acquisition of speech and sign by human children. Because there are human children who learn ASL as a first language, Washoe's stage-by-stage acquisition of ASL could be compared with that of speech and sign by human children. Of greater significance to the objectives of cross-fostering, two-way communication in ASL made Washoe's social and intellectual environment much more like that of human children. Unlike the case in other research in this field, sign language in their laboratory was a means rather than an end in itself, a means by which the chimpanzees could express their intelligence in ways that would permit comparison with human beings. The laboratory procedures assumed that all aspects of intellectual growth are intimately related. For young chimpanzees no less than for human children, familiarity with simple tools such as keys, devices such as lights, and articles of clothing such as shoes are intimately involved in learning signs or words for keys, lights, shoes, opening, entering and so on. In their laboratory the chimps had supervised access to such objects. While no more free than human children to go outdoors without permission, they were free of mechanical restraints both indoors and out. They not only learned to eat human-style food, they learned to use cups and spoons and to clear the table and wash the dishes after a meal. Project Washoe was followed by a second project that included certain improvements. Washoe arrived in Reno when she was about 10 months old. Moja, Pili, Tatu and Dar each arrived within a few days of birth. Their human companions had a higher level of expertise in ASL; many were deaf or the hearing offspring of deaf parents, or had other extensive experience with ASL. Some were veterans of Project Washoe and all had studied its procedures and results. Washoe, of course, was the only chimpanzee in her day, while the chimpanzees of the second project had each other as frequent companions.

Gardner, Howard Earl

Born: 1943, Scranton, Pennsylvania, USA *Nat:* American *Ints:* Cognitive psychology, developmental psychology, educational psychology, neuropsychology *Educ:* BA summa cum laude (Social Relations) Harvard College, 1965; PhD Harvard University, 1971 *Appts & awards:* Harvard project Zero, Research Associate 1971–3, Co-director, 1972–95, Chairman of Steering Committee, 1995– ; Boston University School of Medicine, Research Associate in Neurology, 1972–5, Assistant Professor of Neurology, 1975–9, Associate Professor, 1979–84, Professor, 1984–7, Adjunct Research Professor, 1987– ; Harvard Graduate School of Education, Lecturer in Education, 1974, Senior Research Associate, 1977–86, Professor, 1986– ; Claude Bernard Journalism Award, 1975; MacArthur Prize Fellowship ('genius prize'), 1981; American Psychological Foundation Award for best book in psychology, 1984; William James Award, 1987; Educational Press of America distinguished achievement award, 1989, 1994; Best Friend of Children's Museums, American Association of Youth Museums, 1992; Hon. Dr, Curry College, 1992, New England Conservatory of Music, 1993, Indiana University, 1995; Governor's (Pennsylvania) Award for Excellence in the Humanities, 1994; Teachers College Medal for Distinguished Service to Education, Teachers College,

Columbia University, 1994; Center for Advanced Study in the Behavioral Sciences Fellow, Stanford University, 1994–5

Principal publications

1975   *The Shattered Mind.* Knopf.

1982   *Art, Mind, and Brain: A Cognitive Approach to Creativity.* Basic Books.

1983   *Frames of Mind: The Theory of Multiple Intelligences.* Basic Books.

1985   *The Mind's New Science: A History of the Cognitive Revolution.* Basic Books.

1991   *The Unschooled Mind: How Children Think and How Schools should Teach.* Basic Books.

1993   *Multiple Intelligences: The Theory into Practice.* Basic Books.

1993   *Creating Minds: An Anatomy of Creativity Seen Through the Lives of Freud, Einstein, Picasso, Stravinsky, Eliot, Graham, and Gandhi.* Basic Books.

1995   *Leading Minds: An Anatomy of Leadership.* Basic Books (with E. Laskin).

Further reading

Gursky, D. (1991) The unschooled mind. *Teacher Magazine*, December , 38–44.

Knox, R. (1995) Brainchild. *Boston Globe Magazine*, 5 November 22–3, 38–42, 45–8.

Weinreich-Haste, H. (1985) The varieties of intelligence: an interview with Howard Gardener. *New Ideas in Psychology*, 3, 47–65.

Howard Gardner grew up in Scranton, Pennsylvania, in the 1940s and 1950s. As a child he became an accomplished pianist and considered a career as a musician. As it was, he did become a piano teacher from 1958 to 1969. His interest in the arts and in teaching remained with him during his undergraduate and graduate education at Harvard University, where he studied with Erik **Erikson** and Jerome **Bruner**. Through his study of cognitive psychology, he became aware that little work had been done on development of abilities in the arts. Gardner was able to link his interests in cognitive development and the arts through his involvement as a research associate with the philosopher Nelson Goodman, on a newly formed project (Project Zero) in the area of the arts as knowing. Project Zero continues in operation, and Gardner is currently Chairman of its Steering Committee.

   In 1971, after completion of his doctorate, Gardner was a postdoctoral fellow at the Harvard Medical School and the Boston University Aphasia Research Center. During that postdoctoral period, he began a series of studies investigating language problems in people suffering brain damage. Gardner's groundbreaking research and theory on the nature of human intelligence and educational processes resulted from the linkage of his interests in cognition and the arts with his knowledge of brain functions.

   Gardner's extensive writings (over twenty books and 400 research articles) have altered the ways in which psychologists and educators view human intelligence and creativity. In 1983 he published *Frames of Mind: The Theory of Multiple Intelligences.* In that book, Gardner put forward the view that intelligence is multifaceted rather than the function of a global cognitive structure, or a general ability factor. Artistic intelligence, for example, is a different facility from the intelligence used in scientific reasoning. His 1985 book *The Mind's New Science* presented Gardner's view that the interdisciplinary field of cognitive science holds promise for an integration of the various perspectives and disciplines essential for understanding creativity. In subsequent works, *The Unschooled Mind* and *Multiple Intelligences: The Theory in Practice*, he laid out the educational implications of his perspective on intelligence and creativity. His work has been highly influential (a number of his books have been translated into ten foreign languages), and he has been formally recognized by educational and psychological organizations. Among his many awards are a MacArthur Prize Fellowship, and the APA's William James Award.

L.P. NUCCI

Gardner, R. Allen

Born: 1930, New York City, USA ***Nat:*** American ***Ints:*** Developmental, general, experimental, physiological and comparative ***Educ:*** BA New York University, 1950; MA Columbia University, 1951; PhD Northwestern University, 1954 ***Appts & awards:*** Professor of Psychology, University of Nevada, APA Fellow, Division 1, Division 3, AAAS Fellow, Sigmax National Lecturer, 1978–80; Fellow, Center for Advanced Study, College of Arts and Science, University of Nevada

For fifteen years, Gardner and his colleagues devoted most of their time to active work in their live-in cross-fostering laboratory. In addition to the raw data of several formal experiments, they have catalogued and edited 35,000 handwritten pages of diary notes, and 25 hours of 16mm motion picture film. (See entry on **Beatrice Gardner** for further details.)

Garfield, Sol Louis

Born: 1918, Chicago, Illinois, USA *Nat:* American *Ints:* Clinical, psychotherapy, community psychology *Educ:* BS Northwestern University, 1938; MA Northwestern University, 1939; PhD Northwestern University *Appts & awards:* Professor, Department of Psychology, Washington University, 1942; Section of the Development of Clinical Psychology as an Experimental-Behavioral Science, APA Division 12, APA Council of Representatives, 1960–3, 1964–6, 1972–5; President, APA Division 12, 1964–5; APA Division 12, Distinguished Contribution to Clinical Psychology Award, 1976; President, Society for Psychotherapy Research, 1976–7; APA Distinguished Contribution to Knowledge Award, 1979, Distinguished Scientist Award, 1981; Editor, *Journal of Consulting and Clinical Psychology*, 1979–84; Consulting Editor, *American Journal of Mental Deficiency*, 1964–6, *Journal of Abnormal Psychology*, 1964–70, 1973–4, *Journal of Consulting and Clinical Psychology*, 1964–72, 1973–7, 1985– ; *Professional Psychology*, 1977– , *Clinical Psychology Review*, 1981– ; Editorial Board, *Cognitive Therapy and Research*, 1978–82

Principal publications

1957 *Introductory Clinical Psychology*. Macmillan.

1963 Expectations regarding psychotherapy. *Journal of Nervous and Mental Disease*, 137, 353–62 (with M. Wolpin).

1966 Clinical psychology and the search for identity. *American Psychologist*, 21, 353–62.

1971 Therapeutic conditions and outcome. *Journal of Abnormal Psychology*, 77, 108–14 (with A.E. Bergin).

1971 *Handbook of Psychotherapy and Behavior Change*. Wiley (ed. with A.E. Bergin).

1971 Evaluation of outcome in psychotherapy. *Journal of Consulting and Clinical Psychology*, 37, 307–13 (with R. Prager and A.E. Bergin).

1974 *Clinical Psychology: The Study of Personality and Behavior*. Aldine.

1976 Clinical psychologists in the 1970s. *American Psychologist*, 31, 1–9 (with R. Kurtz).

1978 Research problems in clinical diagnosis. *Journal of Consulting and Clinical Psychology*, 46, 596–607.

1980 *Psychotherapy: An Eclectic Approach*. Wiley.

1981 Evaluating the psychotherapies. *Behavior Therapy*, 12, 295–307.

1981 Psychotherapy: A 40–year appraisal. *American Psychologist*, 36, 174–83.

1982 Eclecticism and integration in psychotherapy. *Behavior Therapy*, 13, 610–23.

1983 The effectiveness of psychotherapy: The perennial controversy. *Professional Psychology*, 14, 35–43.

Further reading

Corsini, R.J. (1991) *Five Therapists and One Client*. F.E. Peacock.

Freedheim, D.K. *et al.* (eds) (1992) *History of Psychotherapy: A Century of Change*. American Psycholgical Association.

For most of his career, Garfield worked in the broad area of clinical psychology. However, towards the end of his career he devoted most of his teaching, research and practice to psychotherapy, particularly psychotherapy research. While working as a clinical psychologist in mental installations he was involved with diagnostic appraisal, psychopathology, psychiatric and psychological treatments, professional roles, issues and the like. A belief that he carried throughout his career was the need to evaluate empirically and to validate clinical procedures. This was also an emphasis he believed clinical psychologists could contribute to the mental health field. However, he felt that although clinical psychologists have followed traditional procedures in appraising assessment instruments, they have not done so in the area of psychotherapy. His later recent interests were in the evaluation of outcome in psychotherapy, in trying to evaluate the variables that produce change in psychotherapy and the possible integration among diverse therapeutic orientations.

Garner, Wendell Richard

Born: 1921, Buffalo, New York, USA *Nat:* American *Ints:* Experimental, philosophical and theoretical *Educ:* BA Franklin and Marshall College, 1942; AM Harvard University, 1943; PhD Harvard University, 1946 *Appts & awards:* James Rowland Angell Professor of Psychology, Yale University; Chairman, Society of Experimental Psychologists, 1959, 1975; APA, Distinguished Scientific Contribution Award, 1964; National Academy of Sciences, 1965– ; AAAS, Vice-President for Psychology, 1967; President, APA Division 3, 1974; Warren

Medal, Society of Experimental Psychologists, 1976; Hon. DSc Franklin and Marshall College, 1979; Hon. DHL Johns Hopkins University, 1983; Editorial board, *Perception and Psychophysics*, *Journal of Experimental Psychology: Human Perception and Performance*

Principal publications

1947 Auditory thresholds of short tones as a function of repetition rates. *Journal of the Acoustical Society of America*, 19, 600–8.

1949 *Applied Experimental Psychology*. Wiley (with A. Chapanis and C.T. Morgan).

1956 Operationism and the concept of perception. *Psychological Review*, 63, 149–59 (with H.W. Hake and C.W. Eriksen).

1962 *Uncertainty and Structure as Psychological Concepts*. Wiley.

1963 Goodness of pattern and pattern uncertainty. *Journal of Verbal Learning and Verbal Behavior*, 2, 446–52 (with D.E. Clement).

1969 Perceptual independence: Definitions, models and experimental paradigms. *Psychological Bulletin*, 72, 233–59 (with J. Morton).

1970 The stimulus in information processing. *American Psychologist*, 25, 350–8.

1970 Integrality of stimulus dimensions in various types of information processing. *Cognitive Pscyhology*, 1, 225–41 (with G.L. Felfoldy).

1974 *The Processing of Information and Structure*. Erlbaum.

1976 Interaction of stimulus dimensions in concept and choice processes. *Cognitive Psychology*, 8, 98–123.

1978 Aspects of a stimulus: Features, dimensions and configurations. In E.H. Rosch and B.L. Lloyd (eds), *Cognition and Categorization*. Erlbaum.

1978 Selective attention to attributes and to stimuli. *Journal of Experimental Psychology: General*, 107, 287–308.

1982 *Ability Testing*. National Academy Press (ed. with A.K. Wigdor).

1983 Asymmetric interactions of stimulus dimensions in perceptual information processing. In T. Tighe and B. Shepp (eds), *Perception, Cognition and Development: Interactional Analyses*. Erlbaum.

Further reading

Lockhead, G.R. and Pomerantz, J.R. (eds) (1991) *The Perception of Structure: Essays in Honor of Wendell R. Garner*. American Psychological Association.

The research career of Wendell Garner started during World War II, when he carried out research on the visual masking of radar signals,

disguising of auditory radar signals, and shipboard communications. This work, especially that on auditory radar signals, led to over ten years of both applied and basic research on auditory sensory problems, work which showed several kinds of relation between time and intensity for short or interrupted signals. During this period he became involved in the application of information theory to psychology, which led to the book *Uncertainty and Structure as Psychological Concepts*.

His interests had shifted to vision, because he was interested in the perception of structure, and the shift represented a possibly erroneous feeling that there were more problems of structure in vision than in audition. One aspect of this work showed that the figural goodness of dot patterns could be predicted on the basis of number of equivalent patterns. He also worked on auditory patterns, and in this reverted to the use of audition, and showed that pattern goodness was related to the number of perceived pattern alternatives in an ongoing sequence.

Another major line of research concerned interactions of visual dimensions, in which he showed that previous distinctions between integral and separable dimensions based primarily on similarity judgments could be useful with reaction time performance measures, and that both effects of redundancy and selective attention to dimensions had consistent interrelations. His more recent research is primarily concerned with extensions of this work with emphasis on asymmetric relations between dimensions.

Garth, Thomas Russell

Born: 1872, Paducah, Kentucky, USA **Died:** 1939, Denver, Colorado, USA **Nat:** American **Ints:** Race differences, race psychology **Educ:** MA University of Denver, 1910; PhD Columbia University, 1917 **Appts & awards:** Head of Department of Education, State Normal School, Canyon, Texas, 1917–19; Adjunct Professor of Psychology, University of Texas, 1919–22; University of Denver, Professor of Education, 1922–8, Professor of Educational Psychology, 1928–32, Professor of Experimental Psychology, 1928–39

Principal publications

1922 The problem of racial psychology. *Journal of Abnormal and Social Psychology*, 17, 215–19.

1925 A review of racial psychology. *Psychological Bulletin*, 22, 343–64.

1926 Mental fatigue of Indians of nomadic and

sedentary tribes. *Journal of Applied Psychology*, 10, 437–52.
1930   A review of race psychology. *Psychological Bulletin*, 27, 329–56.
1931   *Race Psychology*. Whittlesey.
1931   *The Incidence of Color Blindness Among Indians*. Report to National Research Council and University of Denver.
1934   The problem of race psychology: A general statement. *Journal of Negro Education*, 3, 319–27.
1937   The hypothesis of racial difference. *Journal of Social Philosophy*, 2, 224–31.
1937   *Educational Psychology*. Prentice-Hall.

Further reading
Richards, G. (in press) Thomas Russell Garth (1872–9): The race psychologist who changed his mind. *Journal of the History of the Behavioral Sciences*.

A late entrant to academic life, following an unexceptional earlier career as a country schoolmaster, Garth did not become a professional psychologists until his mid-forties. Though classified as an 'educational psychologist' he was led, under R.S. **Woodworth**'s influence, to the study of race differences, but was always reluctant to use Afro-American subjects because he felt that his southern origins might have rendered him biased. Most of his work was undertaken on American Indians and Mexicans. An experimentalist rather than a psychometrician, he studied phenomena such as fatigue, colour preferences and temperament as well as intelligence. He published more on the topic than any other single psychologist (over fifty sole or joint publications) and was the only one to devote his research energies almost exclusively to the topic. His 1930 *Psychological Bulletin* overview paper and his book *Race Differences* are crucial texts in the history of the topic since, taken jointly, they show Garth effectively abandoning his belief in innate race differences. Three central factors in this shift may be noted: first, he had come to feel that the methodological criteria for demonstrating differences could not be met; second, he had come to suspect that racial levels of performance were not fixed, a phenomenon he called 'racial mobility'; and third, he was increasingly identifying with the cultures and plights of his subject groups, especially the Indians. During the 1930s the thrust of his work was to refute race-difference doctrines and address practical problems faced by Indian and Mexican groups. He also undertook a research programme on differences in incidence of colour blindness – which proved minimal, though marginally lower among Indians. By the end of the 1930s he had abandoned even the residually hereditarian 'racial mobility' notion, arguing that all differences were environmentally determined and that the concept of 'race' was itself essentially meaningless. If not a particularly original theorist, Garth gained wide respect for his thorough and painstaking research and was indifferent to speculative theorizing of the Nordicist kind which went beyond empirical facts.

While Garth's recantation and later research were frequently cited by contemporary psychologists opposing race-difference theories (such as Otto **Klineberg**), his work was almost completely overlooked in the 'Race and IQ' controversy which re-erupted after the late 1960s. This would appear to be primarily because his subjects were not Afro-American, and second because intelligence *per se* did not dominate his work. As the leading race psychologist of his time, his loss of belief in innate race differences had considerable impact, and signified a genuine, hard-won change of heart. Neglect of his central role in the history of the pre-World War II US psychological treatment of race has created a somewhat inaccurate historiographic image of the period, one which focuses almost exclusively on C.C. Brigham's interpretation of the US Army Alpha results and the early 1920s immigration control episode, with their clear eugenic agendas. Moreover, as that rare thing, a scientist who becomes convinced that the central thesis on which he has built this career has been disproved, Garth in any case deserves a place in the discipline's historical annals.

GRAHAM RICHARDS

Gazzaniga, Michael S.

Born: 1939, Los Angeles, USA **Nat:** American **Ints:** Physiological and comparative, neuropsychology **Educ:** AB Darthmouth College, 1961; PhD Cal Tech, 1964 **Appts & awards:** John Simon Guggenheim Memorial Fellowship, 1982–3; Fellow, AAAS, Society of Experimental Psychologists, APA, American Neurological Association; Professor of Neuropsychology in Neurology, Cornell Medica College

Principal publications
1965   Observations on visual perception after disconnections of the cerebral hemispheres in

man. *Brain*, 88, 221 (with J.E. Bogen and R.W. Sperry).

1966   Visuomotor integration in split-brain monkeys with other cerebral lesions. *Experimental Neurology*, 16, 289–98.

1970   *The Bisected Brain*. Appleton-Century-Crofts.

1972   One brain – two minds? *American Scientist*, 60, 311–17.

1977   Manipulo-spatial aspects of cerebral lateralization: Clues to the origin of lateralization. *Neuropsychologia*, 15, 743–50.

1978   *The Integrated Mind*. Plenum (with J.E. LeDoux).

1979   Plasticity in speech organization following commissurotomy. *Brain*, 102, 805–15 (with J.E. LeDoux, C.S. Smylie and B.T. Volpe).

1984   *Handbook of Cognitive Neuroscience*. Plenum.

1984   Dissociation of language and cognition: A psychological profile of two disconnected right hemispheres. *Brain*, 107, 145–53 (with C.S. Smylie).

1985   *The Social Brain*. Basic Books.

1985   MRI assessment of human callosal surgery with neuropsychological correlates. *Neurology*, 35, 1763–6 (with J.D. Holtzman, M.D.F. Deck and B.C.P. Lee).

Further reading

Hock, R.R. (1995) *Forty Studies that Changed Psychology*. Prentice-Hall.

Levy, J. (1985) Right brain, left brain: Fact and fiction. *Psychology Today*, May, 42–4.

Research in the functions of the two halves of the brain was pioneered by Roger **Sperry**. Gazzaniga was concerned to understand the extent to which the two halves of the brain function independently, and whether they have separate and unique abilities. Experimental studies of the two halves of the brain is possible if the communication link between the two, the corpus callosum, is severed. This leaves the person with a 'split brain'. At the time Gazzaniga started his work in this topic, ten people had undergone surgery which produced a split brain. (The procedure was used as a last resort to control seizures in patients with rare and severe forms of epilepsy.) Gazzaniga developed special apparatus which ensured that when a patient looked at an object only the left or the right half of the brain would see it. Using a combination of visual and tactile tasks, Gazzaniga demonstrated that there are 'two brains' inside a person's head. The left half of the brain is better at speaking, writing, math-

ematics and reading and is the primary centre for language. The right half of the brain is superior for recognizing faces and for visual-spatial tasks.

Gazzaniga and Sperry's work made fundamental advances in our understanding of the architecture of the brain. Criticisms of the work relate less to the technical elements and have more to do with the way the notion of 'left-brainers' and 'right-brainers' has seeped into popular culture and myth. There is no activity that uses just one side of the brain, but this part of the message in Gazzaniga's work has been (temporarily) lost.

Gemelli, Agostino

Born: 1878, Milan, Italy *Died:* 1959, Italy *Nat:* Italian *Ints:* Criminology, developmental psychology, experimental psychology, general psychology, military psychology, religious issues *Educ:* MD University of Pavia, 1902; Libera Docenza Psichiatria, 1912 *Appts & Awards:* Founder and President of Editorial Board Vita e Pensiero, 1919–59; Rector Magnificus and Founder, Catholic University Sacred Hearth, 1922–59; Professore straordinario di Psicologia, 1926; Full Professor of Psychology, 1929; Director, Archivio di Psicologia, Neurologia e Psicologia, 1940–59

Principal publications

1906   Contributo alla conoscenza dell'ipofisi: Osservazioni sulla sua fisiologia. *Memorie Pontificia Accademia*, XXIV, 167–88.

1907   Del valore dell'esperimento. *Psicologia*, XI, April, 365–83, June, 585–99; XII, July, 31–42, August, 179–94.

1932   La percezione dello spostamento del corpo umano nella selezione degli aviatori. *Atti Societa Ital. per il Progresso delle Scienze*, II, 194.

1934   *L'analisi elettroacustica del linguaggio*. Vita e Pensiero (with G. Pastori).

1934   Exercice et apprentissage. *Archivio Ital. Psicologia*, XII, 295–330.

1940   L'orientazione prossima nel volo. *Rivista Medicina Aeronautica*, III, 1–48.

1941   Lo studio del reato come mezzo di indagine nella valutazione del delinquente. *Contributi Laboratorio di Psicologia*, IX, 377–416.

1944   Un metodo per l'analisi statistica dell'intensitá sonora del linguaggio. *Contributi Laboratorio di Psicologia*, XII, 11–43 (with G. Sacerdote).

1945   *L'operaio nell'industria moderna*. Vita e Pensiero.

1945 *La Psicologia dell'eta evolutiva.* Giuffré (with
Agata Sidlauskajte).

1946 *La personalita del delinquente nei suoi
fondamenti biologici e psicologici.* Giuffré.

1946 Lo psicologo di fronte ai problemi della
psichiatria. *Recenti Progressi in Medicina,* VIII,
100–26.

1947 *Introduzione alla Psicologia.* Vita e Pensiero
(with Giorgio Zunini).

1951 Percezione e personalitá. *Archivio di
Psicologia, Neurologia e Psichiatria,* XII, 477–91.

1958 La percezione visiva dei movimenti. *Archivio
di Psicologia, Neurologia e Psichiatria,* XIX,
3–12.

Gemelli's scientific contributions, on both the
experimental and the theoretical levels, were
characterized by a continuous, eager endeavour
to approach what is peculiar to human psychic
life. He began work on the histology of the
cerebral nervous system as a pupil of the Nobel
prize winner Camillo Golgi, in Pavia. Following
the line of Koelliker and Waldayer, he enlarged
his perspective in accordance with the thought
of **Sherrington**, **Jackson** and Goldstein, looking at the progressive integration of cerebral
functioning. At this point Gemelli left neurophysiology, as being too narrow for his interests
in human life, and entered the field of psychology. Here he dealt with general and physiological facts, in the **Wundt**ian version, then with
Gestalt psychology, according to the model of
Külpe and the Würzburg School, and eventually
with the psychology of personality, which he
considered from a developmental and clinical
point of view. In all this research he kept faith
with the scientific methodology of his scientific
origins as a student of the cerebral nervous
system; but he endeavoured to integrate the
experimental data in a metapsychological frame
of reference, which he dared to recognize as
referring to an Aristotelian, neo-scholastic point
of view. In fact, in a country as strongly oriented to the introduction of philosophy into
science as Italy is, Gemelli fought against both
the materialistic/positivistic reduction of psychology to physiology, and the idealistic/
historical absorption of it into theories independent from empirical facts.

Within this frame of reference, Gemelli was
able to deal with a very wide field of research,
ranging from perception, emotion, memory and
cognition, and from EEGs, retinograms and
language electro-acoustics, to the personality
dynamics, normal and abnormal, of workmen
and of delinquents, and to life-situations as

represented by university students, soldiers, and
religious and political people. The central point
of Gemelli's thought was that psychology should
be conceptualized as an interdisciplinary science, in which the several methodological
approaches and levels are unified in the ego
function, as far as this is an object of experimentation and of clinical conscious experience.
Psychology stands out in this way as the science
of humanity, a living matter in which subjectivity is relevant; and therefore as a science open to
any endeavour that is able to explain this strange
complexity, and closed to any interpretation
denying it.

LEONARDO ANCONA

Gerbner, George

Born: Budapest, Hungary, 1919 **Nat:** Hungarian
Ints: Research in mass communications,
research on television **Educ:** BA University of
California at Berkeley, 1942; MS University of
Southern California, 1951; PhD University of
Southern California, 1955 **Appts & awards:**
Professor of Communications, Annenberg
School of Communications, University of
Pennsylvania; Fellow, International Communi-
cation Association, 1979; Hon. Dr Humane
Letters, LaSalle College, Philadelphia, 1980;
Media Achievement Award of Excellence,
Philadelphia Bar Association, 1981; Communi-
cator of the Year Award, B'nai B'rith
Communications Lodge, 1981; Broadcast Pre-
ceptor Award, Broadcast Communications Arts
Department, San Francisco State University,
1982. Editor, *Journal of Communication;* Edi-
torial Board, *Communication Quarterly,
Critical Studies in Mass Communications,
Communication Abstracts, International
Journal of Intercultural Relations;* Series Co-
editor, Oxford Communication Books, Longman Communication Books

Principal publications

1956 Toward a general model of communication.
Audio-Visual Communication Review, 4, 171–99.

1969 *The Analysis of Communications Content:
Developments in Scientific Theories and Computer
Techniques.* Wiley (with O.R. Holsti, K.
Krippendorff, W.J. Paisley and P. Stone).

1973 *Communications Technology and Social
Policy.* Wiley (with L.P. Gross and W.H. Melody).

1973 Cultural indicators: The third voice. In G.
Gerbner, L. Gross and W.H. Melody (eds),
Communications Technology and Social Policy.
Wiley

1977   *Mass Media Policies in Changing Cultures.*
Wiley Interscience.

1977   The many worlds of the world's press. *Journal
of Communication*, 27, 52–65 (with G. Marvanyi).

1981   *Communications in the Twenty First Century.*
Wiley (with R.W. Haigh and R.B. Byrne).

1982   Charting the mainstream: Television's
contributions to political orientations. *Journal of
Communication*, 100–27 (with L. Gross, M.
Morgan and N. Signorielli).

1984   *World Communications: A Handbook.*
Annenberg/Longman Communication Books (with
M. Siefert).

1985   Mass media discourse: Message system
analysis as a component of cultural indicators. In
T.A. van Dijk (ed.), *Discourse an Communication.*
De Gruyter.

1986   Living with television: The dynamics of the
cultivation process. In J. Bryant and D. Zillman
(eds), *Perspectives and Behavior.* Erlbaum (with
L. Gross, M. Morgan and N. Signorielli).

Further reading

McQuail, D. and Windahl, S. (1993) *Communication
Models.* Longman

Morgan, M. and Signorielli, N. (1990) *Cultivation
Analysis.* Sage.

Gerbner attempted to develop theories of communication and mass media as social institutions. Beginning with his thesis in 1951 on 'Television and education' and his PhD in 1955, 'Toward a general theory of communication', he conducted studies on press, film and television designed to contribute to understanding their functions in life and society. With colleagues and co-authors, he advanced theories of 'message system analysis', 'institutional policy analysis' and 'cultivation analysis' and applied them to such issues as violence, science, religion, ageing, the representation of women and minorities, and the images of reality about these and other issues held by audiences. His theoretical position can be summarized in his model of communication, which identifies ten key elements: (1) someone, (2) perceives an event, (3) and reacts, (4) in a situation, (5) through some means, (6) to make available materials, (7) in some form, (8) and context, (9) conveying content, (10) with some consequences. The flexible character of the model has led to its use at different levels, including the investigation of interpersonal and intercultural communication. Its strength resides in the manner in which it directs the user to attend to a large number of elements and the interactions between them. For example, it has been influential in promoting an understanding of the cultivation process of the media. The central idea is that the media, specifically television, lead to the adoption of beliefs about the nature of the social world, beliefs which conform to the selective view of reality as portrayed in television fiction and news. Television provides people with a consistent and near-total symbolic environment, in which audiences are supplied with norms for belief and conduct for a wide range of real-life situations.

Gesell, Arnold Lucius

Born: 1880, Alma, Wisconsin, USA **Died:** 1961, New Haven, Connecticut, USA **Nat:** American **Ints:** Child, developmental psychology, mental retardation, youth and family services **Educ:** BPh University of Wisconsin, 1903; PhD Clark University, 1906; MD Yale University, 1915 **Appts & awards:** Director, Yale Clinic of Child Development, 1911–48; Hon. DSc, Clark University, 1930, University of Wisconsin, 1953; Fellow, National Academy of Sciences, AAAS, American Academy of Pediatrics; President, American Academy for Cerebral Palsy, 1952–3; Vice-President, Association Internationale pour la Protection de l'Enfance; Member, Connecticut Commission on Child Welfare, 1919–21, National Research Council, 1937–40, Executive Committee, Connecticut Society for Mental Hygiene, White House Conference on Child Health and Protection, White House Conference on Childhood in a Democracy; National Lectureship, Society of Sigma Xi, 1949; Recipient, Laureate, Kappa Delta Phi, 1958

Principal publications

1929   Learning and growth in identical infant twins:
An experimental study by the method of co-twin
control. *Genetic Psychology Monographs*, 6,
1–124 (with H. Thompson).

1929   Maturation and infant behaviour patterns.
Psychological Review, 36, 307–19.

1938   Scientific approaches to the study of the
human mind. *Science*, 88, 225–30.

1939   Reciprocal interweaving in neuromotor
development. *Journal of Comparative Neurology*,
70, 161–80.

1940   *The First Five Years of Life.* Harper (with C.
Amatruda, L. Ames, B. Castner, H. Halverson, F.
Ilg and H. Thompson).

1941   *Developmental Diagnosis.* Hoeber (with C.
Amatruda).

1943 *Infant and Child in the Culture of Today.*
Harper (with F. Ilg).

1945 *The Embryology of Behavior.* Harper (with C. Amatruda).

1946 *The Child from Five to Ten.* Harper (with F. Ilg.)

1946 The ontogenesis of infant behavior. In L. Carmichael (ed.), *Manual of Child Psychology.* Wiley.

Further reading

Ames, L.B. (1989) *Arnold Gesell: Themes of his Work.* Human Sciences Press.

Arnold Gesell was born and educated in Wisconsin, and obtained teaching experience as well as a BPh prior to undertaking doctoral studies at Clark. Clark was clearly a formative experience for Gesell, especially in the person of G. Stanley **Hall**. Gesell admired Hall's commitment to evolutionary explanation as a unifying conceptual framework. For Hall, evolutionary theory made it possible to understand developmental change of all kinds, animal and human, normal and abnormal. Maturational processes were taken to dominate developmental change, overriding any environmental or cultural influence. Although infinitely more careful a researcher than Hall, Gesell was to remain faithful to these basic tenets. If the evolutionary approach may be thought of as having been something of a paradigm shift in psychology, then Gesell's own work may be said to exemplify 'normal science': the highly disciplined and technically rigorous pursuit of a clearly defined research programme, within a paradigm.

After receiving his PhD, Gesell undertook various teaching posts, followed by a period as professor of psychology in the Los Angeles State Normal School. This post involved collaboration with Lewis **Terman**, a Clark colleague. The association with Terman, and subsequently with Goddard, indicates Gesell's sympathy with a genetic and psychometric approach to mental retardation and to developmental change in general. Gesell's research aspirations, however, went beyond the application of available test instruments. He intended to carry out a much more thorough, normative study of early development, and in order to do so, he decided that medical training was essential. This took him back to Wisconsin and subsequently to Yale. There, medical studies (completed in 1915) took place alongside a post in education. In 1911, the Yale Clinic of Child Develop-

ment was first established; it was to become the focus of Gesell's research activity. He also continued to undertake professional work such as that involved in his post as school psychologist for the State Board of Education of Connecticut.

At Yale, Gesell and his colleagues commenced a meticulous study of early development. He was an enthusiastic employer of photography in this project. Cine film was used from 1924 onwards, both for documentation and for research. In Gesell's words, cine film rendered children's action patterns 'almost as tangible as tissue'. Many of these photographic data were obtained by the use of a specially designed photographic dome, a device that now appears excessively technological. More naturalistic settings were, however, also employed, for example in the filmed records of a baby's typical day. The normative and naturalistic information was gathered together in the *Atlas of Infant Behavior* of 1934.

Gesell's research at Yale increasingly extended through childhood and into adolescence. It attained enormous influence within pediatrics and child welfare as well as psychology. The most concrete manifestation of this influence was the employment of Gesell's texts and tests. The clear message of both was a normative one: behavioural change develops in accordance with fixed patterns. Direct evidence for this came from the method of 'co-twin control' by which the trained performance of one twin was compared to that of the other twin. Gesell's finding was that the untrained twin caught up very rapidly with the trained one. Experimental intervention was not, however, granted much status in Gesell's work. Overwhelmingly the approach was to describe and analyse that which was held to be naturally emerging. Test situations were devised in order to reveal most clearly the significant emerging patterns. Gesell held fast to this maturationist approach despite a changing climate in psychology. Neither the environmentalism of learning theory, nor the environmentalism or other aspects of the psychoanalytic theory of development, made much impact on his programme. Gesell's single-mindedness enabled him to pursue one approach to development with enormous thoroughness. This approach is now considered to be limited, but these limitations would not have become so clear without Gesell's tenacity. The contemporary concern with social and cultural effects in childhood, including infancy, meets very little sympathy in

Gesell. From the point of view of theory or methodology, his work is much closer to the psychology of the early twentieth century than that of the present.

JOHN MORSS

Gibson, Eleanor J.

Born: Eleanor Jack, 1910, Peoria, Illinois, USA **Nat:** American **Ints:** Developmental psychology, experimental psychology, physiological and comparative psychology **Educ:** PhD Yale University, 1938 **Appts & awards:** Assistant Instructor to Assistant Professor, Smith College, 1931–49; Research Associate, Cornell University, 1949–66; Professor, Cornell University, 1966–72; Susan Linn Sage Professor of Psychology, 1972– ; APA, Distinguished Scientist Award, 1968; G. Stanley Hall, Award 1970; Hon. DSc: Smith College, 1972, Rutgers University, 1973, Trinity College, 1982, Bates College, 1985, University of South Carolina, 1987, Emory University, 1990; Guggenheim Fellow, 1972–3; Wilbur Cross Medal, Yale University, 1973; Howard Crosby Warren Medal, 1977; Hon. LHD State University of New York, Albany, 1984, Miami University, 1989; Gold Medal Award, 1986; William James Fellow, American Psychological Society, 1989; Fellow, AAAS, APA; Medal for Distinguished Service, Teachers College, Columbia University, 1983

Principal publications

1940 A systematic application of the concepts of generalization and differentiation to verbal learning. *Psychological Review*, 47, 196–229.

1955 Perceptual learning: Differentiation or enrichment? *Psychological Review*, 62, 32–41 (with J.J. Gibson).

1956 The effect of prolonged exposure to visually presented patterns on learning to discriminate them. *Journal of Comparative and Physiological Psychology*, 49, 239–42 (with R.D. Walk).

1957 Continuous perspective transformations and the perception of rigid motion. *Journal of Experimental Psychology*, 54, 129–38 (with J.J. Gibson).

1960 The 'visual cliff'. *Scientific American*, 202, 64–71 (with R.D. Walk).

1963 Perceptual learning. *Annual Review of Psychology*, 14, 29–56.

1969 *Principles of Perceptual Learning and Development*. Appleton-Century-Crofts.

1975 *The Psychology of Reading*. MIT Press (with H. Levin).

1978 Perception of invariants by five-month-old infants: Differentiation of two types of motion. *Developmental Psychology*, 14, 407–15.

1984 Perceptual development from the ecological approach. *Advances in Developmental Psychology*, 3, 243–86.

1988 Exploratory behavior in the development of perceiving, acting, and the acquiring of knowledge. *Annual Review of Psychology*, 39, 1–41.

1991 *An Odyssey in Learning and Perception*. MIT Press.

Further reading

Neisser, U. (ed.) (1993) *The Perceived Self: Ecological and Interpersonal Sources of Self-knowledge*. Cambridge University Press.

Pick, H.L. Jr. van den Broek, P.W. and Knill, D.C. (eds) (1992) *Cognition: Conceptual and Methodological Issues*. American Psychological Association.

Eleanor Jack was born into a well-established Presbyterian family in Peoria, Illinois. At her high school scholarly brilliance was thought unfeminine, and she took care not to shine too obviously – it was a pleasant surprise, when she went to Smith College, to find that women were encouraged academically, and to take up scientific subjects. After two years at Smith, Eleanor became interested in psychology. It was a very opportune moment. For at that time some remarkable refugees from Europe settled there, notably Kurt **Koffka** and Fritz **Heider**, and her future husband **James Gibson** came to teach at Smith. So the opportunities for a student psychologist were unusual for a small liberal arts college, and Eleanor made full use of them. She had already discovered her leaning towards science, and preferred a careful experimental approach to that of the more phenomenological Koffka. She took James Gibson's course in experimental psychology, and the following year, now as a graduate student reading for a master's degree, one he gave on William **James**. In September of that year they got married, and she became his assistant in a course on social psychology.

A year later, attracted to the 'hard' psychology she had found in James Gibson, but not in Koffka, she went to Yale. Yale at that time did not welcome women, and it was a struggle to establish herself as a research student. Her approach to Robert **Yerkes**, head of the primate laboratory, met with a chilling rebuff. But she eventually got what she came for at Yale, and ended up writing a thesis under the more courteous Clark **Hull**. He insisted on rigorous experimentation, which suited her well, and the construction of a miniature hypothetico-deductive system, which she was happy to go along with. She applied Hullian principles to verbal learning and forgetting, with the help of her own version of the **Pavlov**ian concepts òf differentiation and generalization. She completed her requirements for a PhD, apart from the thesis write-up, in the prodigiously short time of one year.

After Yale, she returned to Smith as a full-time member of the teaching staff, and between that and her growing family she had little opportunity for research. In 1942 James Gibson went to Fort Worth, and later to Santa Ana, California, and Eleanor joined him in these places mainly as wife and mother. This was a fallow period for her intellectually, though the boredom she eventually felt with enforced domesticity and the social round of an air force base sharpened her resolution to return to psychology. After the war the Gibsons went back to Smith, and she again had no time for research.

In 1949 James Gibson went to Cornell, and Eleanor went with him as unpaid Research Associate. She worked for a time on the goats and sheep at Howard Lidell's Behavior Farm, where he used to show visitors his well-publicized demonstrations of experimental neurosis. She was sceptical of the neurosis, and disenchanted by the sloppy scientific standards she found there, but developed an interesting two-factor theory of avoidance learning, based on work with children. A large air force grant enabled her to begin her pioneering work on perceptual learning, starting with distance judgements using traditional pychophysical methods, but in the open air rather than the laboratory. To explain her results she returned to the concepts of generalization and differentiation, and thrashed out a theory of perceptual learning with her husband, which appeared in 1955. They seldom published together, but two years later they did so again, on invariants under transformation. These were key papers in the development of James Gibson's ecological theory, and such rare moments of public collaboration were crucial in the development of both thinkers. Eleanor brought to them her long interest in the importance of differentiation as the basic process in perceptual learning, while James was beginning to make clear how information is contained in transformations of the optic array, rather than in static forms on the retina.

During the mid-fifties she worked with Richard Walk on some of her best-known experiments on perceptual development. In one they found that rats reared in the presence of cut-out shapes did better on discriminations involving these shapes than rats reared in the presence of other shapes. This demonstration of passive perceptual learning has proved difficult to replicate, and is at odds with the more active concept of differentiation she has since developed. More lasting has been the celebrated and very elegant visual cliff experiment, in which animals, as soon as they could walk or crawl, were found to prefer an ordinary surface to a simulated cliff created by a piece of glass suspended above the floor.

Evaluation of her contribution to psychology is complicated by the closeness of her work to that of her husband, who was also her most inspiring teacher at college. He maintained that the division of labour in the unfolding of ecological psychology was equal but different, with her specializing in the question of perceptual development, a modern discipline she effectively founded. Her own early interest in generalizaton and differentiation itself generalized to her later pioneering work on the experimental study of perceptual development, and is perhaps the key to understanding her contribution to ecological psychology. Her concept of differentiation is central to the theory, and links the Gibsons' work to a tradition going back to William James. But while James Gibson became more uncompromising in his rejection of information-processing approaches during the 1960s and 1970s, Eleanor was willing to give them a try. In 1975 she was able to set up her own infant laboratory, and since then, and after her husband's death in 1979, she has become more thoroughly single-minded in her committment to the principles of ecological psychology. She has continued her work on perceptual development, but now gives prominence to the concept of affordance; and she plays a leading role in the activities of the International Society for Ecological Psychology.

ARTHUR STILL

Gibson, James Jerome
Born: 1904, McConnelsville, Ohio, USA **Died:** 1979, Ithaca, New York, USA **Nat:** American **Ints:** Experimental psychology **Educ:** BA Princeton University, 1925; PhD Princeton University, 1928 **Appts & awards:** Head of Unit

for Testing Personnel and Selection, US Army Air Force, Aviation Psychology Program

Principal publications

1929 The reproduction of visually perceived forms. *Journal of Experimental Psychology*, 12, 1–39.

1933 Adaptation, after-effect and contrast in the perception of curved lines. *Journal of Experimental Psychology*, 16, 1–31.

1935 (ed.) Studies in psychology from Smith College. *Psychological Monographs*, 46, 6, whole no. 210.

1938 Determinants of the perceived vertical and horizontal. *Psychological Review*, 45, 300–23 (with O.H. Mowrer).

1941 Perception. *Psychological Bulletin*, 38, 432–68.

1950 *The Perception of the Visual World*. Houghton Mifflin.

1951 What is a form? *Psychological Review*, 58, 403–12.

1955 Perceptual learning: Differentiation or enrichment? *Psychological Review*, 62, 32–41 (with E.J. Gibson).

1959 Perception as a function of stimulation. In S. Koch (ed.), *Psychology: A Study of a Science*. McGraw-Hill.

1960 The concept of the stimulus in psychology. *American Psychologist*, 16, 694–703.

1961 Ecological optics. *Vision Research*, 1, 253–62.

1966 *The Senses Considered as Perceptual Systems*. Houghton Mifflin.

Further reading

Gordon, I.E. (1989) *Theories of Visual Perception*. Wiley.

MacLeod, R.B. and Pick, H.L. Jr (1974) *Perception: Essays in Honor of James J. Gibson*. Cornell University Press.

Marr, D. (1982). *Vision*. Freeman.

Ullman, S. (1980). Against direct perception. *Behavioral and Brain Sciences*, 3, whole issue.

J.J. Gibson was born and raised in the midwest and began his undergraduate studies at Northwestern University. After a year he transferred to Princeton, where he was influenced by E.B. Holt and behaviourism generally. His dissertation was on memory for forms and focused on the role of learning. In 1928 he went to Smith College to take up his first academic appointment, and while he was there he encountered Kurt **Koffka**, whose *Principles of Gestalt Psychology* greatly influenced his thinking and work. During World War II he directed a psy-

chological research unit for the Army Air Forces Aviation Psychology Program. His unit implemented a new way of constructing tests for pilot selection; they used motion pictures to present the test materials. While working on these tests, Gibson began to develop the idea that there is more information available in moving than in static pictures. Following the war he returned to Smith College, but moved on to Cornell, where he remained for the rest of his career.

Gibson's closest and most influential colleague was his wife, Eleanor Jack **Gibson**. She formulated a theory of development which was complementary to his theory of Perception. About their working together he wrote 'We have collaborated on occasion, but not as a regular thing. And when we did we were not a husband-and-wife team, God knows, for we argued endlessly'. He concluded, 'When it is assumed that whatever one Gibson says, the other will agree, we are annoyed, for it isn't so'. In 1950 he published his *Perception of the Visual World*, in which he presented his 'ground theory' of space perception. This suggested that gradients of texture on the ground correspond to retinal gradients and that these are the sensory basis for perceiving depth or space. He became dissatisfied with this theory and began to think that theories of perception which are derived from an analysis of light are formulated at an inappropriate level. A new discipline, which he called ecological optics, was needed. Ecological optics is concerned with the study of optical information at the level appropriate for vision. This means that an adequate theory of visual perception must incorporate an analysis of how organisms look around and move around their environment. It should be about ambient or ambulatory vision. His new theory of visual perception and his formulation of the new discipline of ecological optics were presented in his next book, *The Senses Considered as Perceptual Systems*. This is often referred to as the theory of direct perception.

In order to understand what is special about Gibson's theory of direct perception it is useful to summarize the principal claims of theories of indirect perception as espoused, for example, by **Helmholtz** and by Gestalt psychologists. Theories of indirect perception claim that human beings are not directly aware of the physical world around them. Human visual perception takes the form of sequential samples over time. Unified perceptions are achieved through integration of the sensory input over time. Because sensory inputs are not sufficiently rich to mediate perception, the human brain must add to them. The elaboration of sensations involves processes of memory, habit and so on. Evolutionary pressure for the survival of the species has led to the emergence of inferential processes that deliver 'correct' (i.e. adaptive) solutions most of the time. However, illusions illustrate that sometimes the brain goes beyond the sensory evidence in ways that are not warranted by the limited data. Thus, illusions also confirm the constructional nature of perceiving.

Gibson might point out that many textbooks on perception include diagrams in which the light reflected from an object travels in a straight line to the retina of an observer, but this is a gross oversimplification. Ecological optics is an attempt to represent what happens in the real world. There are numerous light sources and many millions of rays striking the retina. The visual world comprises surfaces under illumination and light arriving at the eye is highly structured containing a large amount of information (Gordon, 1989).

The concept of invariants is essential to Gibson's theory. Gibson considered perception to be an activity – a dynamic process. A perceptual invariant is a higher-order property of patterns of stimulation which remain constant during changes associated with the observer, the environment or both. For example, when you approach an object the pattern of stimulation on your retina changes, but not randomly. There are patterns of flow and this flow is lawful or invariant. Followers of Gibson's theory distinguish between two kinds of invariant: transformational and structural. The former are patterns of change that can reveal what is happening to an object. For instance, when a car moves away from us at a constant speed its apparent size reduces. The decrease in area is proportional to the square of the distance. Wherever this relationship obtains, it means that the distance between us and the object is changing in a regular manner. Where the relationship does not obtain, it must mean either that the object is accelerating or decelerating, or it is changing its size. Structural invariants are higher patterns of relationship that remain constant despite changes in visual stimulation. For example, two cars of an identical make are parked at different distances. It is easy for us to tell that they are the same size. They will usually be viewed against a scene containing a visible horizon, and it can be shown that the ratio of an object's height to the distance between its base and the horizon is invariant across all distances from the viewer.

Another essential and novel part of Gibson's theory is the concept of affordances. This defines a relationship between a perceiving organism and its environment. Affordances are the meanings an environment has for an organism; they guide behaviour. Gibson claimed that affordances can be perceived directly, without prior synthesis or analysis. This means, for instance, that the properties of objects which reveal that they can be grasped can be directly perceived from the pattern of stimulation arising from them.

Several criticisms have been made of Gibson's theory. First, it has been argued (Ullman, 1980) that the theory does not specify what is meant by 'direct perception'. It is possible to build simple models which can be seen to have two distinct motions even though the stimulus array does not change physically. With these models the perception of orientation precedes that of motion, which suggest that perception of the motion of the object is not 'direct' but can be decomposed into stages. Second, Gibson argues that there are invariant properties in physical events which afford the perception of those events. However, Marr (1982) and others have attempted to create computational models of vision and build machines that see. Marr points out that the task is enormously more complex than Gibson supposed. This does not mean that Gibson is wrong, but it suggests that something that he considered to be relatively straightforward turns out to be extremely problematic, and this indicates that part of his theory is underelaborated. Third, Gibson considered affordances to be the most subtle forms of invariance. However, it is extremely difficult to define affordance and to predict a relationship with behaviour. For instance, if certain objects in the world 'afford' eating, what is it in the nature of the optic array that makes explicit this affordance? Related to this is the difficulty of finding invariants and affordances. Gibson's theory gives little guidance on how this difficulty might be overcome.

Despite these limitations and criticisms, Gibson's theory made some important advances in the psychology of perception. First, it placed the environment in the centre of perception research and encouraged the development of a line of research that used ecologically plausible stimuli rather than laboratory-created ones. Second, Gibson's concept of 'ecological optics' stimulated interest in perception in other species and thereby raised general questions about perceptual processes.

Golden, Charles Joshua

Born: 1949, Los Angeles, California, USA *Ints:* Clinical psychology, neuropsychology, rehabilitation psychology, Health psychology *Educ:* BA Pomona College, California, 1971; MA University of Hawaii, 1973; PhD University of Hawaii, 1975 *Appts & awards:* Professor of Medical Psychology Nebraska Psychiatric Institute, University of Nebraska Medical Center, National Academy of Neuropsychologists: Outstanding and Unusual Contributions to the Science and Profession of Neuropsychology, 1981; National Academy of Neuropsychologists, Distinguished Leadership in Neuropsychology, 1982; Editor, *International Journal of Clinical Neuropsychology*, 1981– ; Editorial Board, *Computers in Human Behavior*, 1984– ; *Journal of Consulting and Clinical Psychology*, 1984– ; *Journal of Psychoeducational Assessment*, 1983–

Principal publications

1976   The identification of brain damage by an abbreviated form of the Halstead-Reitan Neuropsychological Battery. *Journal of Clinical Psychology*, 32, 821–6.

1978   Diagnostic validity of a standardized neuropsychological battery derived from Luria's neuropsychological tests. *Journal of Clinical Psychology*, 46, 1258–65 (with T.A. Hammeke and A.D. Purisch).

1978   *Diagnosis and Rehabilitation in Clinical Neuropsychology*. C.C. Thomas.

1979   Localization of cerebral dysfunction with a standardized version of Luria's Neuropsychological Battery. *Journal of Consulting and Clinical Psychology*, 47, 1001–19 (with G. Lewis, J.A. Moses Jr., D.C. Osmon, A.D. Purisch and T.A. Hammeke).

1979   *Clinical Interpretation of Objective Psychological Tests*. Grune and Stratton.

1980   *Interpretation of the Halstead-Reitan Neuropsychological Battery: A Casebook Approach*. Grune and Stratton (with D. Osman, J.A. Moses Jr. and R.A. Berg).

1980   Cerebral ventricular size and neuropsychological impairment in young chronic schizophrenics. *Archives of General Psychiatry*, 37, 619–23 (with J.A. Moses Jr., R. Zelazowski, B. Graber, L.M. Zatz, T.B. Horvath and P.A. Berger).

1981   Hemispheric asymmetries in schizophrenia. *Biological Psychiatry*, 1981, 16, 561–81 (with D. Newlin and B. Carpenter).

1981   The Luria-Nebraska Neurpsychological Battery: Theory and research. In P. McReynolds

(ed.), *Advances in Psychological Assessment*. Science and Behavior Books.

1983   *Clinical Neuropsychology: Interface with Neurologic and Psychiatric Disorders*. Grune and Stratton (with J.A. Moses Jr., J.A. Coffman, W.R. Miller and F.D. Strider).

1983   Regional cerebral blood flow in schizophrenia with the 133–xexon inhalation method. *Archives of General Psychiatry*, 1983, 40, 258–63. (with R.N. Ariel, R.A. Berg, M.A. Quaife, J.W. Dirksen, T. Forsell, J. Wilson and B. Graber).

1984   *Foundations of Clinical Neuropsychology*. Plenum (with P. Vicente).

Further reading

Anderson, R.M. Jr (1994) *Practitioner's Guide to Clinical Neuropsychology*. Plenum.

Goldstein, G. and Hersen, M. (eds) (1990) *Handbook of Psychological Assessment* (2nd edn). Pergamon.

Golden's involvement in psychological assessment and neuropsychology was motivated by an interest in individual differences. At an early stage in his career he saw the need to develop a test procedure which would have good statistical and empirical usefulness but at the same time offer a detailed analysis of the exact nature of a patient's problem to a degree usually possible in day-long, or longer evaluations. This led to the development of the Luria-Nebraska Neuropsychological Battery. This battery consisted of scales covering a wide range of problems. However, unlike other tests, items within each area were varied so as to test variations of a skill rather than one specific ability. It was found that such a procedure could yield reliable and useful statistical scores overall, while the item data itself could be used for fine comparisons as to the nature of the individual's problems. The battery attracted considerable interest and was widely adopted. In subsequent work Golden has been involved in improving the Battery and with developing the Nebraska Neuropsychological Battery. This battery has a wider range of item areas and item difficulty. It is structured so that it is possible to administer only some of the items according to a patient's pattern of strengths and weaknesses as empirically determined. This battery allows for a more detailed evaluation of neuropsychological problems while insuring that other areas are intact. More recent work has focused on the development of instruments designed to improve analysis of individual differences and the ways in which such analysis can be used to predict prognosis or to design intervention, as well as more work into the possible neuropsychological origin of disorders like chronic schizophrenia.

Goldston, Stephen E.

Born: 1931, New York, USA **Nat:** American **Ints:** Prevention of mental and emotional disorders, Society for Community Research and Action **Appts & awards:** NIMH, 1962–85, Special Assistant to the Director for Prevention Programs, 1967–71, Coordinator for Primary Prevention Programs, 1972–80, Chief, Primary Prevention Service Programs, Division of Mental Health Services, 1980–1, Director, Office of Prevention, 1981–5; Special Contribution Award, Division of Community Psychology, APA, 1983; Distinguished Professional Contributions to Public Service Award, APA, 1984; Outstanding Contribution to Prevention in Mental Health Award, National Council of Community Mental Health Centers, 1985; Founder and Associate Director, UCLA Preventive Psychiatry Center, University of California, Los Angeles, School of Medicine, 1985–9; Mental Health Consultant, 1985–

Principal publications

1977 *Primary Prevention: An Idea Whose Time Has Come.* DHEW Publication (ADM), 77–447. US Government Printing Office (ed. with D. Klein).

1986 Primary prevention: Historical perspectives and a blueprint for action. *American Psychologist,* 41, 453–60.

1990 *Preventing Mental Health Disturbances in Childhood.* American Psychiatric Association (ed. with J. Yager, C.M. Heinicke and R.S. Pynoos).

1991 A survey of prevention activities in state mental health authorities. *Professional Psychology: Research and Practice,* 22, 315–21.

1992 *The Present and Future of Prevention: In Honor of George W. Albee* (ed. with M. Kessler, and J.M. Joffe).

Further reading

Albee, G.W. *et al.* (eds) (1988) *Prevention, Powerlessness, and Politics: Readings on Social Change.* Sage.

Kessler, M. and Goldston, S.E. (eds) (1986) *A Decade of Progress in Primary Prevention.* University Press of New England.

Stephen Goldston was born in New York City on 19 April, 1931, and grew up in Mount Vernon, a nearby suburb. He was educated at University College, New York University, where he received his BA in 1952. He completed the graduate programme in public health, leading to the MSPH from Columbia University in 1953. After a two-year tour in the US Army, he returned to Columbia, where he completed an individually tailored doctoral programme in education and psychology. His career included positions in public mental health at the county, municipal and federal government levels. As a member of the New York City Mental Health Board from 1960 to 1962, he served as one of the few consultation and education specialists available to inform the design and implementation of the newly emerging community mental health movement.

Beginning in 1962 and for more than two decades thereafter, Goldston contributed to the USA's response to its mental health needs as a member of the federal government. During his nearly twenty-four years of federal service, he served in multiple positions within the National Institute of Mental Health, including those of Director of the Office of Prevention, Coordinator for Primary Prevention Programs, and Chief, Primary Prevention Service Programs. He participated in planning the national community mental health centres programme as staff associate to President Kennedy's Interagency Committee on Mental Health. Building on his experiences at the county and municipal levels, Goldston was a significant contributor to early understandings of the concepts of consultation and education, and of their significance for the prevention of mental health problems and for the promotion of healthy emotional and behavioural functioning. This work also contributed to understanding the advantages for the mental health professions of moving from the treatment room to the community.

As Special Assistant to the NIMH Director for Prevention Programs, Goldston made his most significant and lasting contribution to mental health. For more than two decades, his consistent advocacy of the incorporation of prevention and health promotion into mental health services was a primary factor in their ultimate acceptance by health and mental health policy makers and their growing acceptance by the mental health sciences. In 1981, as Director of the newly formed Office of Prevention, Goldston was a central contributor to conceptualizing and implementing the national US programme to establish a network of Preventive Intervention Research Centers. From the outset, these Centers were to become the nuclei around which prevention science and service delivery were to develop. They have contributed substantially both to an understanding of the aetiology of mental health disorders and natural processes resulting in emotional and behavioural health, and to successive generations of increasingly sophisticated prevention scientists.

Goldston's lasting contribution to the mental health sciences was his early recognition of the importance for the mental health sciences and professions of adopting the public health principles of disease prevention and health promotion. The challenges confronting him from the outset were the scepticism of policy makers and the lack of a critical mass of mental health scientists committed to validating his belief in the power of prevention. Through planning meetings, state-of-the-art and state-of-the-science conferences, and the nurturing of a series of monographs on prevention theory and practice, Goldston built, brick by brick, the foundation from which has arisen the structure of the USA's current prevention efforts. Through his efforts, like-minded scientists, mental health service providers and mental health policy makers participated in opportunities to meet, share ideas and nurture the genesis of prevention from an idea, to a movement, to an increasingly promising and substantial science.

Beginning with his seminal work with Don Klein, *Primary Prevention: An Idea Whose Time Has Come*, and the foresight reflected in his unfailing support of the annual Vermont Conferences on the Primary Prevention of Psychopathology and the numerous volumes resulting from those conferences, Goldston can justifiably be credited with directly and indirectly contributing to the bulk of the literature summarizing the history of the prevention movement in the USA. That body of work originally informed and continues to inform the continuing emergence and development of prevention science and practice.

RAYMOND P. LORION

Goodglass, Harold

Born: 1920, New York, USA **Nat:** American **Ints:** Clinical neuropsychology **Educ:** BA French City College of New York, 1939; MA New York University, 1948; PhD University of Cincinnati, 1951 **Appts & awards:** Professor of Neurology (Neuropsychology), Boston University School of Medicine; President, International Neuropsychological Society, 1976, APA Division, 1979; ALSHA Distinguished Career Award, 1982; Editorial Board, *Cortex, Brain and Language*

Principal publications

1954 Language laterality in left-handed aphasics. *Brain*, 77, 523–48. (with F.A. Quadfasel).
1963 Disturbance of gesture and pantomime in aphasia. *Brain*, 86, 703–20. (with E. Kaplan).
1964 Phrase length and the type and severity of aphasia. *Cortex*, 1, 133–53 (with F.A. Quadfasel and W.L. Timberlake).
1972 *Assessment of Aphasia and Related Disorder.* Lea and Febiger (with E. Kaplan).
1972 Dichotic ear order effects in Korsakof and normal subjects. *Neuropsychologia*, 10, 21–217 (with E.A. Peck).
1973 *Psycholinguistics and Aphasia.* Johns Hopkins University Press (with S. Blumstein).
1976 Semantic fields, auditory comprehension and naming in aphasia. *Brain and Language*, 3, 359–74.
1977 Parallel processing of verbal and musical materials in right and left hemispheres. *Neuropsychologia*, 45–9 (with M. Calderon).
1980 *Clinical Aspects of Dysphasia.* Springer-Verlag (with M.L. Albert, A. Rubins *et al.*).
1980 Lateralization of linguistic and melodic processing with age. *Neuropsychologia*, 18, 79–83.
1985 Localization of body-parts in brain-injured subjects. *Neuropsychologia*, 23, 161–76 (with C. Semenza).
1985 Is agrammatism a unitary phenomenon? In M.L. Kean (ed.), *Agrammatism.* Academic Press (with L. Menn).
1993 *Understanding Aphasia.* Academic Press.

Further reading

Kirshner, H.S. (ed.) (1995) *Handbook of Neurological Speech and Language Disorders.* Marcel Dekker.
Kohn, S.E. (ed.) (1992) *Conduction Aphasia.* Erlbaum.

Goodglass first encountered patients with aphasia during a hospital internship as a graduate student in clinical psychology. He was immediately drawn to learning more about the paradoxical dissociations among various components of language and memory produced by brain injury. He secured a position as clinical psychologist in a rehabilitation programme for aphasic and other brain-injured veterans of World War II, where his mother was the neurologist Quadfasel, a former student of Kurt Goldstein. His initial collaboration with Quadfasel on aphasia in left-handers encouraged him to pursue independently the psycholinguistic analysis of the various forms of language breakdown.

In 1956, Norman Geschwind joined the group, and the inspiration of his developing views on the anatomy of language was a further strong influence. By 1958, Goodglass was committed to a research career in neuropsychology and aphasia. His first efforts involved the application of psycholinguistic research techniques to the study of selective disorders of syntax, of word retrieval, and of modality-specific and category-specific disorders of word comprehension. At the same time, he attempted to incorporate some of these findings into a clinical examination for aphasia.

The interdisciplinary ambience of the work setting at Boston V.A. Medical Center helped to relate the research to the neural substrate of language, and to make Goodglass sensitive to the clinical problems encountered by speech pathologists. His research programme encompasses experimental studies of cerebral dominance, relating test patterns to clinical syndromes and lesion data, along with the continuing interest in the processes of syntax and word finding.

Goodnow, Jacqueline Jarrett

Born: Toowoomba, Queensland, Australia **Nat:** Australian **Ints:** Adult development and ageing, developmental psychology, family psychology, psychology of women, social and personality psychology **Educ:** BA (Hons) University of Sydney, 1944; PhD Radcliffe (Harvard University), 1951 **Appts & awards:** University Medal, 1944; Wooley Traveling Scholarship, 1948; George Washington University, 1961–72; NIMH Research Career Grant, 1967–72; Macquarie University, 1972–89, Emeritus Professor, 1989–96; Fellow, Center for Advanced Studies in the Behavioral Sciences, Stanford University, 1984–5; Reissue of Bruner, Goodnow and Austin, *A Study of Thinking*, as a Citation Classic, 1986; APA, G. Stanley Hall Award for Distinguished Contributions to Developmental Psychology, 1989; Companion of the Order of Australia, 1992

Principal publications

1956   A *Study of Thinking*. Wiley (reissued 1986, Transaction Books) (with J.S. Bruner and G.A. Austin).

1978   *Children Drawing*. Harvard University Press.

1979   *Children and Families in Australia:*

Contemporary Issues and Problems. Allen and Unwin (with A. Burns).

1985   *Home and School: Child's Eye View*. Allen and Unwin (with A. Burns).

1985   *Women, Social Science, and Public Policy*. Allen and Unwin (with C. Pateman).

1990   *Development According to Parents: The Nature, Sources and Consequences of Parents' Ideas*. Erlbaum (with W.A. Collins).

1992   *Parental Belief Systems*, 2nd edn. Erlbaum (with I. Sigel, and A. McGillicuddy-deLisi).

1994   *Men, Women, and Household Work: A Study of Change*. Oxford University Press (with J.A. Bowes).

1995   *Cultural Practices as Contexts for Development*. Jossey Bass (with P.M. Miller and F. Kessel).

Further reading

Perry, D. (1994) Comments on the Grusec and Goodnow (1994) model of the role of discipline in moral internalization. *Developmental Psychology*, 30, 23–5.

Since the 1960s, Jacqueline Goodnow's work has examined cognition about both the 'physical' and 'social' worlds. During the 1970s this included research on the nature of children's drawing. To all of her research, she has brought an emphasis on the role of the social context on development. In that emphasis, she anticipated much of the theorizing and methodological orientations that were to follow.

Beginning in the 1970s, Goodnow's work began to turn away from analyses of abstract problem solving to investigations into the ways children and adults deal with the problems of everyday life. Her work has included analyses of how parents perceive child development, and how that enters into their approach to child-rearing and discipline. In a series of elegant studies, she looked at how children are assigned and carry out household chores. In that ubiquitous but mundane setting, she uncovered patterns in the ways in which children are brought into the rules of their culture and engaged in a consideration of basic issues of fairness and social hierarchy. By looking at everyday cognition, Goodnow has drawn attention to the ways in which goals and values direct the processes of cognitive development. At a micro-level, this refers to goal setting and directionality in specific problem-solving tasks. On a larger scale, setting goals and sequences can be seen as directing lifelong development. What adults want for their children, and what children perceive as valuable and as options open to them, largely undergird children's cognitive attainments. In the 1980s and 1990s, Goodnow extended this orientation to examine features of lifelong learning, and in her writing on some of the issues facing women.

Goodnow's prolific and influential research and writing have been recognized by awards and honours from professional organizations in the United States and from her native government.

L.P. NUCCI

Gough, Harrison G.

Born: 1921, Buffalo, Minnesota, USA **Nat:** American **Ints:** Clinical, Educational, Personality and Social, Population and Environmental **Educ:** BA University of Minnesota, 1942; MA University of Minnesota, 1947; SSRC Demobilization Fellowship, 1947; PhD University of Minnesota, 1949; Fulbright Research Fellowship, Italy, 1957–8, 1965–6; Guggenheim Fellowship, 1965–6 **Appts & awards:** Professor and Research Psychologist, Department of Psychology and Institute of Personality Assessment and Research, University of California Berkeley; Chairman and Editorial Board, University of California publications in Psychology, 1951–53; Consulting Editor, *Journal of Consulting and Clinical Psychology*, 1956–84; *Journal of Abnormal Psychology*, 1962–74; *Journal of Personality and Social Psychology*, 1980–84; Population, *Behavioral, Social and Environmental Issues*, 1975–80; *Medical Teacher*, 1979–84; *Cahiers de Anthropologie*, 1979–85; Associate Editor, *Journal of Cross-Cultural Psychology*, 1969–82, Advisory Editor, *Pakistani Journal of Psychology*, 1985– ; Editorial Board, *Current Psychology: Research and Reviews*, 1985–

Principal publications

1946 Diagnostic patterns on the Minnesota Multiphasic Personality Inventory. *Journal of Clinical Psychology*, 2, 23–37.

1948 A sociological theory of psychopathy. *American Journal of Sociology*, 53, 359–66.

1957 *Manual for California Psychological Inventory*. Consulting Psychologists Press.

1961 Psychological tests and measurements. In *Encyclopaedia Britannica*, vol. 18, 16th ed.

1962 Clinical versus statistical prediction. In L.J Postman (ed.), *Psychology in the Making*. Knopf.

1965 *The Adjective Check List Manual*. Consulting Psychologists Press, 1956/1980 (with A.B. Heilbrun Jr).

1965 The conceptual analysis of psychological test scores and other diagnostic variables. *Journal of Abnormal Psychology*, 70, 294–302.

1967 Nonintellectual factors in the selection and evaluation of medical students. *Journal of Medical Education*, 42, 642–50.

1971 Some reflections on the meaning of psychodiagnosis. *American Psychologist*, 26, 160–7.

1976 Personality and personality assessment. In M.D Dunnette (ed.), *Handbook of Industrial and Organizational Psychology*. Rand McNally.

1981 A nontransformational test of intellectual competence. *Journal of Applied Psychology*, 66, 102–10 (with D.S. Weiss).

1982 *Manuel de la liste d' ajectifs – Adjective Check List – (A.C.L.)*. Les Editions du Centre de Psychologie Appliqué (with F. Gendre).

Gough is most frequently cited for the California Psychological Inventory, a self-report inventory scaled for folk concepts theorized to possess universal meaning and relevance. The CPI is widely used in the English-speaking world, and has been translated into more than twenty-five languages. Standardized editions exist in French and Italian, and published versions with manuals are also available in Germany, Japan, Poland and Mexico. The Adjective Check List is also frequently used and cited. It contains 300 words or phrases that can be used to describe self, others, ideals, products, cities, environments, personages and abstract ideas. It too has been used in many places, and there are some twenty translations. In addition to these methodological activities, Gough has been interested in, and published on, topics such as creativity, intellectual functioning, cross-cultural measurement, performance in medical school and practice, choice of medical speciality, social maturity, managerial competence, work orientation, modernity, and population psychology. His current interest is in a major new theoretical formulation of the CPI, which will attempt to make clear its structural dimensions and conceptual properties.

Gray, Jeffrey Alan

Born: 1934, London, England **Nat:** British **Ints:** Clinical, experimental analysis of behaviour, personality and social, physiological and comparative, psychopharmacology **Educ:** BA Oxford University, 1957; BA Oxford University, 1959; Diploma in Psychology London University, 1960; PhD London University, 1964

Appts & awards: Professor of Psychology and Head of Department Institute of Psychiatry, University of London; 1983–7; BPS, Member, Myers Lecturer, 1978, President's Award, 1983; Member, Experimental Psychological Society, European Brain and Behaviour Society, International Scientific Committee of the European Training Programme in Brain and Behavior (European Science Foundation); Editorial Board, *Quarterly Journal of Experimental Psychology*, *Psychological Medicine*, *Experimental Brain Research*, *Cahiers de Psychologie Cognitive*

Principal publications

1964 *Pavlov's Typology*. Pergamon Press.

1967 Strength of the nervous system, introversion–extraversion, conditionalbility and arousal. *Behavior Research and Therapy*, 5, 151–69.

1970 The psychophysical basis of introversion–extraversion. *Behavior Research and Therapy*, 8, 249–66.

1970 Sodium amobarbital, the hippocampal theta rhythm and the partial reinforcement extinction effect. *Psychological Review*, 77, 465–80.

1971 *The Psychology of Fear and Stress.* Weidenfeld and Nicolson (London). McGraw-Hill (New York).

1971 The mind–brain identity theory as a scientific hypothesis. *Philosophical Quarterly*, 21, 247–53.

1972 *The Biological Bases of Individual Behaviour.* Academic Press (with V.D. Nebylitsyn).

1975 *Elements of a Two-process Theory of Learning*. Academic Press.

1975 Effect of minor tranquillisers on hippocampal theta rhythm mimicked by depletion of forebrain noradrenaline. *Nature*, 258, 424–5 (with N. McNaughton, D.T.D. James and P.H. Kelly).

1977 Drug effects on fear and frustration: Possible limbic site of action of minor tranquilisers. In L.L. Iversen, S.D. Iversen and S.H. Snyder (eds), *Handbook of Psychopharmacology*, vol. 17, 201–12. Plenum.

1979 Effects of medial and lateral septal lesions on the partial reinforcement extinction at one trial a day. *Quarterly Journal of Experimental Psychology*, 31, 653–74 (with J. Feldon).

1979 Sodium amylobarbitone and responses to non-reward. *Quarterly Journal of Experimental Psychology*, 31, 653–74 (with J. Feldon).

1982 *The Neuropsychology of Anxiety: An Enquiry into the Functions of the Septo-Hippocampal System*. Oxford University Press.

1982 Acquisition and extinction of continuously and partially reinforced running in rats with lesions of the dorsal noradrenergic bundle. *Behaviour Brain Research*, 5, 11–41.

1983 Septal driving of the hippocampal theta rhythm produces a long-term, proactive and non-associative increase in resistance to extinction. *Quarterly Journal of Experimental Psychology*, 35B, 97–118.

1987 Interactions between drugs and behaviour therapy. In H.J. Eysenck and I. Martin (eds), *Theoretical Foundations of Behavior Therapy*. Plenum Press.

1990 Brain systems that mediate both emotion and cognition. *Cognition and Emotion*, 4, 269–88.

1991 Fear, panic and anxiety: What's in a name? *Psychological Inquiry*, 2, 77–8.

1994 A model of the limbic system and basal ganglia: Applications to anxiety and schizophrenia. In M.S. Gazzaniga (ed.), *The Cognitive Neurosciences*. MIT Press.

Further reading

Noyes, R., Jr, Roth, M. and Burrows, G.D. (eds) (1990) *Handbook of Anxiety*. Elsevier.

Jeffrey Gray's major contribution to date has been the construction of an integrated theory of one emotion (anxiety). The theory postulates a behavioural inhibition system, and activity in this system constitutes anxiety. The theory is both large and complex and only the briefest description can be given here. The principal inputs to this behavioural inhibition system are: stimuli that warn of punishment or non-reward, novel stimuli and innate fear stimuli. The principal outputs are: inhibition of motor behaviour, increased level of arousal and increased level of attention to the environment. Anti-anxiety drugs are effective because they act on this system. The brain structures that make up the behavioural inhibition system include: the septal area, the hippocampus and their interconnections; the papez circuit; neo-cortical inputs to the septo-hippocampal system; ascending noradrenergic and serotonergic inputs to the septo-hippocampal system; dopaminergic ascending input to the pre-frontal cortex; and noradrenergic chlorinergic input to the septo-hippocampal system. Other systems are involved, and these systems participate in other functional systems. In humans, the symptoms of anxiety arise from excessive activity in the behavioural inhibition system. Anti-anxiety drugs reduce activity in the ascending monoaminergic projections. Behaviour therapy is effective because it causes systematic habituation of the septo-hippocampal response to anxiogenic stimuli. The theory predicts that people who are especially suscept-ible to anxiety have highly reactive behavioural inhibition systems. The theory encompasses and is buttressed by data from both animal and human studies, embraces neuronal, cognitive and behavioural aspects of anxiety, deals with both normal and pathological anxiety, and includes individual differences (trait anxiety) as well as the state of anxiety in general.

Gray has also been involved in other, related work, including: relating individual differences in extraversion, neuroticism and trait anxiety to differential reactivity to stimuli associated with reward and punishment; articulating a theory of the interactions between instrumental and classi-cal conditioning in a manner that facilitates study of neurobiological and personality aspects of learning; and introducing Western readers to the work of Soviet neo-**Pavlov**ian personality theorists in a manner that relates this work to Western personality research.

Gregory, Richard L.

Born: 1923, London, England **Nat:** British **Ints:** Artificial intelligence and robotics, compara-tive psychology, experimental psychology, perception, philosophy of psychology, phy-siological psychology **Educ:** MA Canterbury University 1950, DSc Bristol University 1983, **Appts & Awards:** CIBA Foundation Research Prize, 1956; Craik Prize for Physiological Psychology, 1958; Waverly Prize and Gold Medal, 1960; Fellow, Corpus Christi College, Cambridge, 1962–7; University of Edinburgh, Professor of Bionics, 1967–70, Emeritus, 1970–88; Professor of Neuropsychology and Head of Brain and Perception Laboratory, University of Bristol, 1970– ; Manager, Royal Institution, 1971–4; Chairman, R.I. Humphrey Davy Committee, 1974; President, British Society for Advancement of Science, Section J, 1975; President, EPS, 1981–2; *Perception*, Founder Editor, 1970, Editor in Chief, 1972– ; Editorial Board, *Leonardo*, 1970, *Spatial Perception*, 1985

Principal publications

1961   The brain as an engineering problem. In W.H. Thorpe and O.L Zangwill (eds), *Current Problems in Animal Behaviour*. Cambridge University Press.

1963   Distortion of visual space as inappropriate constancy scaling. *Nature*, 199, 678.

1963   The origin of the autokinetic effect. *Quarterly Journal of Experimental Psychology*, 15, 252 (with O. Zangwill).

1964   The curious eye of Copelia. *Nature*, 201, 1166 (with H.E. Ross and N. Moray).

1966   *Eye and Brain*. Weidenfeld. (4th edn, 1990.)

1968   Visual illusions. *Scientific American*, 219, 66–76.

1970   *The Intelligent Eye*. Duckworth.

1972   Cognitive contours. *Nature*, 238, 51–2.

1973   *Illusion in Nature and Art*. Duckworth (ed. with Sir E. Gombrich).

1974   (ed.) *Concepts and Mechanisms of Perception*. Duckworth.

1975   Drawing and tracing in three dimensions: Stereoscribe. *Perception*, 4, 221–8.

1975   Illusion destruction by appropriate scaling. *Perception*, 4, 203–20 (with J.P. Harris).

1979   Border locking and the Café Wall illusion. *Perception*, 8, 365–80 (with P. Heard).

1981   *Mind in Science*. Weidenfeld. (Penguin, 1983).

1984   Is consciousness sensational inference? *Perception*, 13, 641–6.

1986   *Odd Perceptions*. Meuthen. (Routledge, 1988).

1986   (ed.) *Oxford Companion to the Mind*. Oxford University Press.

1986   Public perception of science. *Perception*, 15, 423–8.

1989   Light on black boxes. *Perception*, 18, 281–4.

1990   What is caught in neural nets? *Perception*, 19, 561–8.

1991   Putting illusions in their place. *Perception*, 20, 1–4.

1992   How can perceptual science help the handicapped? *Perception*, 21, 1–6.

1994   *Sensation and Perception*. Routledge. (Longman, 1995) (ed. with A. Colman).

1995   Seeing backwards in time. *Nature*, 373, 21–2.

Further reading

Gordon, I.E. (1989) *Theories of Visual Perception*. Wiley.

Barlow, H., Blakemore, C. and Weston-Smith, M. (eds) (1990) *Images and Understanding*. Cambridge University Press.

Following service with the RAF in World War II, Richard L. Gregory read moral sciences (philosophy and experimental psychology) at Cambridge. He subsequently spent two years conducting research, on escape from sub-marines, for the Medical Research Council. He then received a lectureship at Cambridge and a fellowship at Corpus Christi College. It was at Cambridge he started the Special Sense Labora-tory. He worked on a variety of projects, including: recovery of sight after blindness from infancy (with Jean Waller); a cognitive account of visual distortion illusions; the Inappropriate Constancy-Scaling theory; perceptual problems of moon landing and docking in space, for the USAF; and the scanning single-channel eye of a Copepod, Copelia Quadrata. In addition, he invented a number of instruments: a telescopic camera to minimize the effects of atmospheric turbulence for planetary and lunar landing photographs; an optical depth scanning microscope; and a three-dimensional drawing machine.

In 1967 Gregory left Cambridge to start, with Donald Michie and Christopher Longuet-Higgins, the Department of Machine Intelligence and Perception at the University of Edinburgh. There he built one of the first intelligent robots, Freddie. Freddie could recognize objects using a television camera eye and could also handle and manipulate them. Largely due to the failure of government funding for artificial intelligence (AI), Gregory left Edinburgh and moved to Bristol.

There he established the Brain and Perception Laboratory to investigate processes in vision and hearing, with clinical applications. He is Founder and Scientific Director of the Bristol Exploratory Science and Technology Centre. He also served on Ministry of Defence committees on aviation and radar. In 1970 he founded the influential journal *Perception*, of which he is still editor. He later published a selection of essays that began as *Perception* editorials in a book, *Odd Perceptions*.

Gregory's approach to perception is constructivist, and he has likened perception to science 'generating rich predictive hypotheses from barely adequate data'. He suggests that perceptions are constructed from sensations and open to considerable top-down cognitive influences. In his terms, perception is a creative process. His ideas are a development of **Helmholtz**'s (1866) hypothesis that perception is a process involving unconscious influence.

He has had a lifelong interest in anomalies of perception such as illusions and after-effects, and the lessons to be learned from studying these phenomena: 'In visual perception it is easy to create false ghosts and all manner of distortions of size and distance. By looking at 'ambiguous' pictures and objects, we learn that there are rival hypotheses waiting to take over centre stage.'

He has written on a wide range of phenomena including autokinetic movement, the Pulfrich Effect, the **Müller**-Lyer illusion, the Ponzo illusion, and the Moon illusion. He has explained a considerable number of illusions in terms of a general perspective-constancy hypothesis. In certain contexts, portions of illusory figures are perceived as two-dimensional projections of three-dimensional shapes in depth. Due to the operation of a size constancy mechanism, the parts of the figure that are farther away are perceived as larger.

Gregory has also carried out considerable investigations in the area of motion perception. He identified and described two interdependent systems involved in the perception of motion: the image–retina movement system and the eye–head movement system. In the image–retina system, successive stimuli of adjacent retinal loci effectively signal movement. Information from the eye–head system is used to disambiguate that from the image–retina system. Thus observers can differentiate between movements of the retinal image caused by eye movements, and movement of the retinal image caused by physical movement of objects in relation to their background.

Gregory's ideas have been extremely influential in visual perception. He was one of the earliest pioneers in AI, applying perceptual research to machine vision. His approach to perception was very much a top-down one: he considered that the observer constructed hypotheses about his or her sensory input on the basis of his or her knowledge, experience and expectations. Although there was considerable emphasis in the early 1980s on bottom-up accounts of visual perception (e.g. **Marr**), many consider that the pendulum began then to swing back in the direction of top-down accounts. Gregory considers that the growth and sophistication of AI will cause science to emphasize top-down accounts still further. Influential though his work is, it is very accessible. He has written and edited a wide selection of introductory and general interest books on perception, and indeed has written widely about the role of science in general.

MORIA MAGUIRE

Guilford, Joy P.

Born: 1897, Marquette, USA ***Died:*** 1987, Los Angeles, California, USA ***Nat:*** American ***Ints:*** Evaluation and measurement, psychology of the arts and educational psychology, teaching of psychology ***Educ:*** BA University of Nebraska, 1922; PhD Cornell University, 1926; LLD University of Nebraska, 1952; ScD University

of Southern California, 1962 **Appts & awards:**
Emeritus Professor of Psychology, University of
Southern California, Los Angeles; President,
Psychometric Society, 1939, Midwestern PA,
1940, Western PA, 1948, APA 1950, Inter-
national Intelligence in Education, 1977;
Member, National Academy of Sciences, 1954;
Distinguished Scientific Award, APA, 1964;
Richardson Creativity Award, APA, 1966;
Founder's Medal, Creative Educational Founda-
tion, 1970; E.L. Thorndike Award, APA, 1975;
Gold Medal Award, APF, 1982; Editorial
Board, *American Journal of Psychology*, *Psy-
chometrika*, *Educational and Psychological
Measures*

Principal publications

1927 Fluctuations of attention with weak visual
stimuli. *American Journal of Psychology*, 38,
534–83.

1936 *Psychometric Methods*. McGraw-Hill.
(reprinted 1954).

1940 Human abilities. *Psychological Review*, 47,
367–94.

1942 *Fundamental Statistics in Psychology and
Education*. McGraw-Hill. (reprinted 1950, 1956,
1965; ANO, 1973, 1978).

1950 Creativity. *American Psychologist*, 5, 444–54.

1959 *Personality*. McGraw-Hill.

1959 A system of color preferences. *American
Journal of Psychology*, 72, 487–502 (with P.C.
Smith).

1959 Three faces of intellect. *American
Psychologist*, 14, 469–79.

1967 *The Nature of Human Intelligence*. McGraw-
Hill.

1972 Executive functions and a model of behavior.
Journal of General Psychology, 90, 88–100.

1977 *Way Beyond the IQ: Guide to Improving
Intelligence and Creativity*. Creative Education
Foundation.

1980 Cognitive styles: What are they? *Educational
and Psychological Measurement*, 40, 715–35.

1981 Higher-order structure-of-intellect abilities.
Multivariate Behavioural Research, 411–35.

1982 Cognitive psychology's ambiguities: Some
suggested remedies. *Psychological Review*, 89,
48–59.

Further reading

Hunt, J.M. (1992) Joy Paul Guilford, 1897–1987.
American Journal of Psychology, 105, 115–18.

As a child Guilford was struck by the substantial
differences in abilities and interests among
members of his own family, and this influenced

his later interests in differential psychology. In
high school, a course on how to teach pointed
him towards psychology in general. Early in
college he became fascinated with chemistry,
particularly with its periodic table and the
orthogonal thinking involved. Later, as an
undergraduate, he was an assistant in psychology, and this introduced him to student-aptitude
tests. During his first two years in graduate
school he was Director of the University's
Psychological Clinic, which involved testing
individually the intelligence of children. This
experience supported his view that intelligence
is not just one comprehensive ability and that
within the sampling of abilities within intelligence scales there were no assessments of
creative-thinking talents. In further graduate
work, a course on psychophysics revealed the
precision with which psychological measurements could be made. **Spearman**'s book
Abilities of Man appeared, suggesting a way by
which different abilities could be demonstrated
by factor analysis. **Thurstone**'s book *Vectors of
Mind*, which followed shortly, revealed a better
way of isolating human abilities.

During World War II Guilford was Director
of Aviation Psychology Research Units, with
responsibility for developing tests for classifying cadets for training. After the war he initiated
the Aptitudes Research Project at the University
of Southern California. This informed the
development of a model of intellect, a systematic arrangement of abilities in a three-
dimensional matrix, with five mental operations, five kinds of informational substance or
content, and six kinds of informational form or
product. Like the chemists' periodic table, the
model has served as a valuable heuristic device
and a map for improving intellectual abilities
through exercises. There are two sections for
creative talents; other sections account for
problem solving. Guilford argued that the model
was a much-needed framework for an
operational-informational psychology.

Guion, Robert M.

Born: 1924, Indianapolis, Indiana, USA **Nat:**
American **Ints:** Evaluation and measurement,
industrial and organizational **Educ:** BA State
University of Iowa, 1984; MS Purdue Univer-
sity, 1950; PhD Purdue University, 1952 **Appts
& awards:** Emeritus Professor of Psychology,
Bowling Green State University, Fellow, APA,
Division 5, Division 14; James McKeen Cattell
Award for excellence in research design, 1965,

1981; President, APA Division 14, 1972–3, Division 4, 1982–3; Chair, APA Board of Scientific Affairs, 1979–81; Editor, *Journal of Applied Psychology*, 1983–8

Principal publications

1958 Industrial morale: A symposium. I. The problem of terminology. *Personnel Psychology*, 11, 59–64.

1961 Criterion measurement and personnel judgments. *Personnel Psychology*, 14, 141–9.

1965 *Personnel Psychology*. McGraw-Hill.

1965 Industrial psychology as an academic discipline. *American Psychologist*, 20, 815–21.

1965 Synthetic validity in small company: A demonstration. *Personnel Psychology*, 18, 49–63.

1966 Employment tests and discriminatory hiring. *Industrial Relations*, 5, 20–37.

1972 The meaning of work and motivation to work. *Organizational Behavior and Human Performance*, 7, 308–39 (with F.J. Landy).

1973 A note on organizational climate. *Organizational Behavior and Human Performance*, 9, 120–5.

1977 Content validity: the source of my discontent. *Applied Psychological Measurement*, 1, 1–10.

1980 On trinitarian doctrines of validity. *Professional Psychology*, 11, 385–98.

1982 Adverse impact from psychometric perspectives. *Journal of Applied Psychology*, 67, 419–32 (with G.H. Ironson and M. Ostrander).

1988 Personnel Selection and Placement. *Annual Review of Psychology*, vol. 39, Annual Reviews Inc.

1991 Personnel assessment, selection and placement. In M.D. Dunnette and L.M. Hough (eds), *Handbook of Industrial and Organizational Psychology*, vol. 2, Consulting Psychologists Press Inc.

Further reading

Berk, R.A. (ed.) (1986) *Performance Assessment. Methods and Applications*, John Hopkins University Press.

Hackett, R.D. (1989) Work attitudes and employee absenteeism: A synthesis of the literature. *Journal of Occupational Psychology*, 62, 235–48.

Smith, M. and Robertson, I.T. (eds) (1989) *Advances in Selection and Assessment*. Wiley.

When Guion first began teaching personnel selection he used two textbooks. One of them was too difficult for some of students, so he began writing simplified 'translations'. In time some of these papers became the foundation of his own book on personnel testing, a book

which combined some aspects of each of the others yet was, by the time it came out more than a decade later, different from either of them. That book, arising more from classroom need than from central interest in the topic, is probably, in his own opinion, his best-known contribution. It was published in the same year as the US Civil Rights Act became effective, and since he was involved in developing them, federal regulations governing selection testing incorporated practices advocated in this book. Unlike the enforcement agencies, he tried to learn and develop new ideas; he continued to make further contributions to psychometric knowledge and to be known primarily in the field of psychological measurement. Psychometric interest plus interest in human judgement led into work on job evaluation procedures.

Gulliksen, Harold Oliver

Born: 1903, Washington, D.C., USA ***Nat:*** American ***Ints:*** Educational psychology, evaluation and measurement, experimental psychology ***Educ:*** BA University of Washington, Seattle, 1926; MA University of Washington, Seattle, 1927 , PhD University of Chicago, 1931 ***Appts & awards:*** Emeritus Professor, Princeton University; Emeritus Research Psychologist, Educational Testing Service, Princeton; President, Psychometric Society, 1945, APA Division 5, 1950–1; Truman Certificate of Merit, 1948; APF Gold Medal Award, 1991; Managing Editor, *Psychometrika*, 1942–9

Principal publications

1924 An evaluation of some information questions. *Journal of Applied Psychology*, 8, 206–14. (with W.R. Wilson and G. Welch).

1938 A theory of learning and transfer: I and II. *Psychometrika*, 3, 127–49 and 225–51 (with D.L. Wolfe).

1950 *Theory of Mental Tests*. Wiley.

1956 Measurement of subjective values. *Psychometrika*, 21, 229–44.

1959 Mathematical solutions for psychological problems. *American Scientist*, 47, 178–201.

1960 *Psychological Scaling: Theory and Applications*. Wiley (ed. with S. Messick).

1964 *Contributions to Mathematical Psychology*. Holt, Rinehart and Winston (ed. with N. Frederiksen).

1972 *Attitudes of Different Groups toward Work, Aims, Goals and Activities*. Multivariate Behavioral Research Monograph, 72/73 (with D.P. Gulliksen).

Further reading

Lord, F.M. and Novick, M.R. (1968) *Statistical Theories of Mental Test Scores*. Addison-Wesley.

Magnusson, D. (1966) *Test Theory*. Addison-Wesley.

Gulliksen's contributions have been in various aspects of mathematical psychology, including testing, mathematical learning theory and psychological scaling. He entered the University of Washington in 1922, taking courses in psychology and mathematics and decided to major in psychology because jobs in psychology were plentiful at that time. With Wilson and Welch he developed a test to predict college grades, which was reported in his first paper 'An evaluation of some information questions' (1924). This work led him to think that mathematics could be useful in other areas of psychology and while at Ohio State University his interests turned towards mathematical learning theory. He developed a tachistoscope for presenting visual stimuli and controlling rewards and punishments, and used it for his dissertation, 'Transfer of response in human subjects'. In a talk at Ohio State, Louis Leon **Thurstone** described his work on paired comparisons and the law of comparative judgment. It had previously been considered impossible to quantify attitudes, preferences, aesthetics, ethics and so on but paired comparisons seemed to offer an exciting solution. If the disagreements between paired comparisons obeyed the law of comparative judgment, then precise scale values could be calculated. In 1934 Thurstone offered Gulliksen a job in the University of Chicago Board of Examinations and the following decade his major work was test development and test theory. For most of World War II he was with the College Entrance Examination Board in Princeton, developing tests for Navy schools. This work demonstrated that validity coefficients sometimes indicate defects in criteria. Later at Princeton University and Educational Testing Service, he became dissatisfied with the slow progress in scaling and concentrated in this area. His study in ten countries, *Attitudes of Different Groups toward Work, Aims, Goals and Activities* (1972), found that the factors and scale values were similar in many countries. Gulliksen's texts on the test theory and measurement were highly influential and were standard reference handbooks for almost three decades.

Guthrie, Edwin R.

Born: 1886, Lincoln, Nebraska, USA *Died:* 1959, Seattle, Washington, USA *Nat:* American *Ints:* Clinical, experimental, experimental analysis of behavior, philosophical and theoretical *Educ:* BA University of Nebraska, 1907; MA University of Nebraska, 1910; PhD University of Pennsylvania, 1912 *Appts & Awards:* Hon. LLD, University of Nebraska, 1945; Dean of the Graduate School and Executive Officer in Charge of Academic Personnel, University of Washington; APA President, 1945; American Psychological Foundation, Gold Medal Award, 1958

Principal publications

1930 Conditioning as a principle of learning. *Psychological Review*, 37, 412–28.

1934 Pavlov's theory of conditioning. *Psychological Review*, 41, 199–206.

1934 Reward and punishment. *Psychological Review*, 41, 450–60.

1935 *The Psychology of Learning*. Harper and Row. (Revised 1952.)

1938 *The Psychology of Human Conflict*. Harper and Row.

1939 Effect of outcome on learning. *Psychological Review*, 46, 480–5.

1942 Conditioning: A theory of learning in terms of stimulus, response and association. *Yearbook of National Society of the Study of Education*, 41, part II, 17–60.

1944 Personality in terms of associative learning. In J. McVicker Hunt (ed.), *Personality and the Behavior Disorders*. Ronald.

1945 *Cats in a Puzzle Box*. Holt (with G.D. Horton).

1959 Association by contiguity. In S. Koch (ed.), *Psychology: A Study of a Science*, vol. 2. McGraw-Hill.

Further reading

Lefrancois, G.R. (1995) *Theories of Human Learning*. Brooks/Cole.

Malone, J.C. Jr (1990) *Theories of Learning: A Historical Approach*. Wadsworth.

Guthrie's academic background was in philosophy, his first university appointment was in the philosophy department of the University of Washington, and his earliest publications demonstrated his interest in formal logic. While still a postgraduate student, however, he developed an interest in behaviourism. In 1919 he transferred to the department of psychology and, soon after, published (with Stevenson Smith) a textbook based on the idea of the conditioned reflex as the basic unit of learning. But it was not until 1930 that his paper 'Conditioning as a principle of learning', which included most of the basic ideas which became known as Guthrie's Theory of Learning, was published. During the next decade these ideas were developed in a number of works, including his book *The Psychology of Learning*. The theory reflects his early interest in philosophy and particularly in associationism. Its fundamental assumption is that contiguity in time is the basis of associative learning. Guthrie had little time for hypothetical constructs, particularly mentalistic ones, and his theory is essentially peripheralist: what is actually learnt is glandular and motor responses called 'movements'. Simple S-R connections are learnt in a single trial, though, on a more holistic level, learning involves the generation of S-R chains, which may require several trials.

Motivation may arouse activity and rewards may terminate behaviour, but neither is responsible for association; learning is based on the contiguity of stimuli with the cessation of activity. In his later work Guthrie gathered further evidence in support of his theory (e.g. *Cats in a Puzzle Box*) or attempted to extend its application (e.g. to the explanation of psychopathological states: *Psychology and Human Conflict*).

After 1940 Guthrie's time was mainly occupied with his involvement in the war, as a consultant to military intelligence, and with his administrative duties in the university – both as Dean of the Graduate School and, later, as Executive Officer in Charge of Academic Personnel.

R. PRIESTNALL

H

Haber, Ralph Norman

Born: 1932, Lansing, Michigan, USA *Nat:* American *Ints:* Experimental psychology, teaching of psychology *Educ:* BA University of Michigan 1953; MA Wesleyan University 1954; PhD Stanford University 1957 *Appts & awards:* Professor, Department of Psychology, University of Illinois at Chicago; Fellow, APA Division 3, 1970– , APA Division 2, 1983, AAAS, 1971– ; Outstanding Achievement Award, University of Michigan, 1977; Fellow, New York Academy of Science, 1969– , Institute of the Humanities, University of Illinois, 1984–5; Advisory Editor, *Experimental Psychology Series*, 1969–78, *Handbook of Psychology*, Academic Press, 1973–8; Editorial Board, *Psychologische Forschung*, 1973–80, *Acta Psychologica*, 1973– , *Journal of Mental Imagery*, 1977– , *International Mental Imagery Review*, 1980– , *Journal of Visual/Verbal Languaging*, 1981– , *Developmental Neuropsychology*, 1984– , *Journal of Experimental Psychology, HPSP*, 1985–8

Principal publications

1966 (ed.) *Current Research in Motivation.* Holt, Rinehart and Winston.
1968 (ed.) *Contemporary Theory and Research in Visual Perception.* Holt, Rinehart and Winston.
1969 (ed.) *Information Processing Approaches to Visual Perception.* Holt, Rinehart and Winston.
1973 *The Psychology of Visual Perceptions.* Holt, Rinehart and Winston (with M. Hershenson). (Reprinted 1980).
1975 *An Introduction to Psychology.* Holt, Rinehart and Winston (with A. Fried).

Further reading

Atkinson, R.C., Hernstein, R.J., Lindzey, G. and Luce, R.D. (eds) (1988) *Stevens' Handbook of Experimental Psychology, vol. 1: Perception and Motivation.* Wiley.
Koch, S. and Leary, D.E. (eds) (1992) *A Century of Psychology as Science.* American Psychological Association.

Although Haber was interested in questions of perception, his interest was submerged by David **McClelland** at Wesleyan at the height of his creativity in motivation and personality. Haber took up studies in this area and eventually edited a book of seminal papers in this field. He continued to pursue these topics during his graduate work, at Stanford, because, as he states, 'Stanford had no one involved in perceptual science at that time.' Nor was anyone doing perceptual science at Yale, the venue of his first teaching position. Haber's sources of influence came not from direct contact, but from the seminal leaders in the field, such as **Broadbent**, Sperling, **Neisser**, **Kahneman**, Kolers and **Posner**. These scientists, with Haber and others, moved a traditional behaviouristic experimental psychology to one of information processing and, ultimately, to cognitive science during the last decades. As with these other scientists, he felt that he was on the leading edge of a revolution of thinking and experimentation.

Haber moved to Rochester in the middle 1960s as a member of the Center for Visual Sciences, initiated by Robert Boynton. This move clearly solidified his position in the study of perceptual science. With these colleagues, Haber was able to learn from the best minds in the field, and he exemplified an information-processing approach to the study of visual perception. After a few decades of productive scholarship, Haber, along with other leaders in this field, became disenchanted with this approach, and in particular the study of iconic memory. He views his paper 'The impending demise of the icon', published in *Behavioral and Brain Sciences* in 1983, as one of his single most important works. This is ironic because it is a paper that rejects much of his earlier work in the information-processing framework. He believes that the important aspect of this paper was that it fundamentally changed the nature of stage models to account for cognitive processing. In his view, the icon failed, but my view of Haber's early work is not so pessimistic, and I see his paper recanting this early work as one that was misguided. His work in the early sixties, some of it in collaboration with Maurice Hershenson and Naomi Weisstein, set the stage for a systematic study of the temporal course of visual perception. His research is still highly relevant today, as psychology struggles with the relationship between perceptual reports and underlying psychological processes. He studied the effects of repeated brief exposures on the growth of a precept in which subjects actually reported a precept becoming clearer and clearer as short-duration display was exposed repeatedly, with long intervals between successive repetitions.

What was revolutionary about this work was that there is nothing in the visual system that could account for such a dramatic change in perceptual experience. I am not aware of any neural-network modelling that tries to account for this finding. He and Weisstein also traced the nature of backward masking in vision. They were among the first to uncover in the contemporary literature a U-shaped backward masking function that could not be easily explained by a simple integration of visual information over time. This is a type of research that required something like a brief iconic representation in which a second stimulus would replace a previous one.

In the early 1970s, Haber began a lifelong collaboration with his marriage to Lyn Haber, whose background in linguistics complemented his areas of expertise. Their joint work also began to address real-world problems, including the study of spatial perception. Perhaps one of the most interesting projects was their design of a training programme for low-altitude flying for the Air Force. This research generated many other studies, such as the analysis of optimal strategies for operating railroad freight locomotives to minimize fuel and time on route and ultimately to the development of training programmes to teach engineers to drive trains. They also carried out task analyses of train dispatching and air traffic control and redesigned display equipment so that it meshed with the memory and processing demands of the dispatcher. With this type of expertise, the Habers could not stay out of the courtroom, and they have consulted and testified in a number of court cases involving perceptual and memory accuracy issues of witnesses and even judges. They have also done work with handicapped individuals, such as the development of orientation and mobility training programmes for the blind. This work created devices that were more responsive to the measured orientation and navigational abilities and skills of blind people, and eventually led to applications on the developments of visual memory and orientation requirements for autonomous robotic devices.

The Habers are clearly the experts that people in agencies would want to call on with these types of practical problem, because their roots are in the professional and theoretical knowledge of psychological enquiry, but they are not reluctant to apply these principles to the task at hand. The rewards come not only from solving particular problems; the applications reveal some understanding of the principles of human perception, memory, attention and related cognitive processes. Experimental scientists can always benefit from real-world experience; for example, the Habers' fighter pilots demonstrated to them that they could perform visual tasks while looking at the ground just a hundred feet below them passing by at a thousand feet per second, whereas this seems impossible to do on the basis of visual tasks from laboratory settings. What was the source of the discrepancy? In this case, laboratories use cathode ray tubes, or CRTs, that present the information intermittently, rather than continuously as the real world does. Although the perceiver does not notice this intermittence of information, it clearly degrades performance.

In summary, Haber's early research in visual perception was the prototypical centre of information-processing research, looking at the nature of the effect of a set of perceptions, and the time course of perceptual processing. His more mature work provides a perfect exemplar of the productive interplay between basic and applied research. His life and work offer an ideal model and challenge for each of us.

DOMINIC MASSARO

Hackman, J. Richard

Born: 1940, Joliet, Illinois, USA *Nat:* American *Ints:* Industrial and organizational, personality and social psychology, Society for the Psychological Study of Social Issues *Educ:* BA MacMurray College, 1962 (Mathematics); MA University of Illinois, 1964; PhD University of Illinois, 1966 *Appts & awards:* Professor of Social and Organizational Psychology, Harvard University; 6th Annual AIR Creative Talent Award in the field of Measurement and Evaluation: Individual and Group Behavior; Cattell Award, APA, Division 14, 1972; James McKeen Cattell Fellowship for Sabbatical Study, 1974–5

Principal publications

1968 Effects of tasks characteristics on group products. *Journal of Experimental Social Psychology*, 4, 162–87.

1969 Toward understanding the role of tasks in behavioral research. *Acta Psychologica*, 31, 97–128.

1971 Employee reactions to job characteristics. *Journal of Applied Psychology Monograph*, 55, 259–86 (with E.E. Lawler).

1975 *Behavior in Organizations*. McGraw-Hill (with L.W. Porter and E.E. Lawler).

1975 Developing the Job Diagnostic Survey. *Journal of Applied Psychology*, 60, 159–70 (with G.R. Oldham).

1975 Group tasks, group interaction process, and group performance effectiveness: A review and proposed integration. In L. Berkowitz (ed.), *Advances in Experimental Social Psychology*, vol. 8. Academic Press (with C.G. Morris).

1976 Group influences on individuals in organizations. In M.D. Dunnette (ed.), *Handbook of Industrial and Organizational Psychology*. Rand McNally.

1976 Motivation through the design of work: Test of a theory. *Organizational Behavior and Human Performance*, 16, 250–79 (with G.R. Oldham).

1977 *Improving Life at Work*. Santa Monica, CA: Goodyear (with J.L. Suttle).

1977 *Perspectives on Behavior in Organizations*. McGraw-Hill (with E.E. Lawler and L.W. Porter).

1979 *Managing Behavior in Organizations*. Little, Brown (with D.A. Nadler and E.E. Lawler).

1980 *Work Redesign*. Addison-Wesley (with G.R. Oldham).

1986 The psychology of self-management in organizations. In M.S. Pallack and R.O. Perloff (eds), *Psychology and Work: Productivity, Change, and Employment*. APA.

1986 Leading groups in organizations. In P.S. Goodman (ed.), *Designing Effective Work Groups*. Jossey-Bass (with R.E. Walton).

1987 The design of work teams. In J.W. Lorsch (ed.), *Handbook of Organizational Behavior*. Prentice-Hall.

1990 *Leading Groups in organizations*. Jossey-Bass.

1990 *Groups that Work (and Those that Don't): Creating Conditions for Effective Teamwork*. Jossey-Bass.

1992 Group influences on individuals in organizations. In M.D. Dunnette and L.M. Hough (eds), *Handbook of Industrial and Organizational Psychology*, vol. 8, 2nd edn. Consulting Psychologists Press.

Further reading

Frost, P.J. and Stablein (eds) (1992) *Doing Exemplary Research*. Sage.

Gold, B.A. (ed.) (1994) *Exploring Organizational Behavior: Cases, Readings and Experiences*. Dryden.

Pallone, N.J. (1987) The implicit axiology of Hackman and Helmreich. In D.R. Peterson and D.B. Fishman (eds), *Assessment for Decision*. Rutgers Symposia on Applied Psychology, vol. 1. Rutgers University Press.

Richard Hackman is an influential psychologist in industrial and organizational psychology, where he is well known for his work on job characteristics and group effectiveness. On the basis of earlier work by Turner and Lawrence, Hackman and **Lawler** studied employees' reactions such as motivation, satisfaction, performance, and attendance on job characteristics. Together with Oldham, Hackman formulated the job characteristics model. This motivational perspective on work design assumes that three critical psychological states (experienced meaningfulness of work, experienced responsibility for outcomes of the work, and knowledge of the actual results of the work activities) are affected by five core job dimensions (skill variety, task identity, task significance, autonomy and feedback). It is assumed that an individual's growth-need strength moderates the relationship between these core job dimension and the critical psychological states as well as the relationship between the critical psychological states and outcome variables. For assessing the variables of the job characteristics model, Hackman and Oldham developed the Job Diagnostic Survey. Subsequently, this became a widely used instrument and the job characteristics model – together with its implication of work design – gained much attention in industrial and organizational psychology.

With respect to research on groups a core aim of Hackman's work is to identify the factors that account for group effectiveness. In an article published in 1975 (with Charles G. Morris) the ongoing interaction process (namely member effort, task performance strategies, knowledge and skills of group members) were shown to play a central role in the understanding of group effectiveness. In turn the group interaction process was assumed to be affected by group composition, group norms and group task design. Hackman and Morris theorized that critical task contingencies moderate the relationship between the interaction process and group performance effectiveness. Later, Hackman revised this earlier model into a normative model of group effectiveness and pointed out consequences for group leadership. With respect to group research, Hackman was not only influential in theorizing about group effectiveness but also approached real-world working groups with his concepts.

SABINE SONNENTAG

Haggard, Mark P.

Born: 1942, Scotland **Nat:** British **Ints:** Acoustics, experimental psychology, human factors **Educ:** MA Edinburgh University 1963; PhD Cambridge University 1966 **Appts & awards:** Professor of Psychology and Head of Department, Queen's University of Belfast, 1971–6; Chairman, Board of Scientific Affairs, BPS, 1974–6; Founder Director of the MRC Institute of Hearing Research, Nottingham, 1977; Special Professor in Audiological Sciences, University of Nottingham, 1977– ; Fellow, Institute of Acoustics, 1978–81, Acoustical Society of America, 1982– ; President, Psychology Section of the British Association for the Advancement of Science, 1983; Chairman of Scientific Advisers and Member of the Management Committee for the Hearing and Speech Trust, 1986–9; McRea Medallist and Lecturer, ENT Department, Royal Victoria Hospital, Belfast, 1987; Carr Visiting Professor, Auckland, 1990; Queen Elizabeth Queen Mother Fellow of the Nuffield Provincial Hospitals Trust, 1991–3; Editor, *Quarterly Journal of Experimental Psychology*, 1970; Associate Editor, *Quarterly Journal of Experimental Psychology*, 1971–80, *Neuropsychologia*, 1972– , *Journal of Phonetics*, 1973–88; Editorial Board, *British Journal of Audiology*, 1980– , *International Journal of Pediatric Otorhinolaryngology*, 1992–

Principal publications

1968 A simple program for synthesizing British English. *IEEE Transactions on Audio and Electroacoustics*, AU-16, 95–9 (with I.G. Mattingly).
1974 The perception of speech. In S. Gerber (ed.), *The Physics and Psychology of Hearing*. W.B. Saunders.
1975 Understanding speech understanding. In A. Cohen and S. Nooteboom (eds), *Dynamic Aspects of Speech Perception*. Springer-Verlag.
1979 Speech sounds in relation to speech processing. *Experimental Brain Research*, Supp. II, 324–32.

1980 Speech processing in hearing aid design – some critical reflections. In I. Taylor and A. Markides (eds), *Disorders of Auditory Function III*. Academic Press.
1982 The scientific, economic and administrative context of audiological medicine. *Bulletin of the International Association of Physicians in Audiology*, 3, 4–18.
1986 One generation after 1984: The role of psychology. *Bulletin of the British Psychological Society*, 39, 321–4 (with H. Weinreich-Haste).
1987 Hearing. *British Medical Bulletin*, 43 (4), 775–9 (with E.F. Evans).
1989 The core and corps of audiology. *British Journal of Audiology*, 23, 49–51.
1989 Staffing and structure for paediatric audiology services in hospitals and community units. *British Journal of Audiology*, 23, 99–116 (with C. Pullan).
1990 *Clinical Developments in Cochlear Implants*. Duphar Laboratories (ed. with M. Page).
1990 Hearing screening in children – state of the art(s). *Archives of Disease in Childhood*, 65, 1193–5.
1992 Screening children's hearing. *British Journal of Audiology*, 26, 209–15.
1992 A clinical test battery for obscure auditory test dysfunction (OAD): Development, selection and use of tests. *British Journal of Audiology*, 26, (with G. Saunders and D. Field).

Further reading

Moore, B.C. (ed.) (1995) *Hearing. Handbook of Perception and Cognition,* 2nd edn. Academic Press.

Mark Haggard completed his MA in experimental psychology at Edinburgh University in 1963 and went on to complete his PhD at Cambridge in 1966. Although both his degrees are in psychology, he describes himself first and foremost as a 'speech and hearing researcher'. He is best described as an interdisciplinary medical scientist who has forged links between psychology and medical science.

In 1971 he was appointed Head of Department at Queen's University, Belfast. There he began to apply his knowledge of sensation and perception to problems of speech and hearing. In 1977 he became founder director of the Medical Research Council's Institute of Hearing Research (IHR), which rapidly became the leading organization for hearing research in the UK.

His research involvements include a series of epidemiological studies, documenting the nature, prevalence and causes of hearing impairments as they occur in the population. These provide a rationale for planning service provision and a statistical background to medical practice in audiology and the provision of appropriate hearing aids. This has led to an interest in operational and economic aspects of health services that is relatively rare among researchers. With Dr J.W. Hall, he has worked on the discovery and psychoacoustic exploration of 'comodulation analysis', which contributes to the human ability to attend to a single voice among interfering sounds. This project has inspired research internationally. In recent years his interest in developmental psychology has pervaded much of his work.

Haggard's work has had considerable impact outside institutional psychology. He has chaired and served on a number of MRC boards and has contributed to the professional development of audiology by establishing a postgraduate in-service training scheme for audiological scientists. He is currently involved in a major clinical trial on the effectiveness of surgery in OME (glue ear).

MOIRA MAGUIRE

Hall, Granville Stanley

Born: 1844, Ashfield, Massachusetts, USA
Died: 1924, Worcester, Massachusetts, USA
Educ: PhD, Harvard University, 1878 **Appts & awards:** Professor, Johns Hopkins University, 1882–8; Professor and President, Clark University, 1889–1920; APA President, 1892, 1924

Principal publications

1883   Contents of children's minds. *Princeton Review*, 11, 272–94.
1897   Philosophy in the United States. *Mind*, 4, 89–105.
1904   *Adolescence: Its Psychology and its Relations to Physiology, Anthropology, Sociology, Sex, Crime, Religion and Education*. Appleton.
1923   *Life and Confessions of a Psychologist*. Appleton.

Further reading

Burnham, W.H. (1925) The man, Granville Stanley Hall. *Psychological Review*, 32, 89–102.
Evans, R.B. and Cohen, J.B. (1987) The *American Journal of Psychology*: A retrospective. *American Journal of Psychology*, 100, 322–40.
Stanford, E.C. (1924) Granville Stanley Hall. *American Journal of Psychology*, 35, 313–21.
Watson, R.I. and Evans, R.B. (1991) *The Great Psychologists: A History of Psychological Thought*, 5th edn. HarperCollins.

Hall was born in a small farming town and in 1863 enrolled in Williams College in preparation for the ministry. On graduation (1867) he entered the Union Theological Seminary in New York City, and a small grant ($500 secured in 1868) allowed him to travel to Bonn and Berlin, where he studied theology and philosophy. In 1871 he returned to America – in debt and without a degree – and accepted a teaching position at Antioch College, Ohio, where he read **Wundt**'s *Principles of Physiological Psychology*. He moved to Harvard in 1876, where he became friends with William **James** and completed his PhD – one of the first doctorates in psychology in Harvard and the USA – on the muscular perception of space. Hall returned to Germany and studied first with Wundt and then with **Helmholtz**. He returned to a position at Johns Hopkins and in 1883 established a psychology laboratory in a house close to the campus. This is generally regarded as the first working psychology laboratory in the USA (William James's laboratory, established in 1875, was principally used for teaching). Four years later Hall started publishing the *American Journal of Psychology*, with the help of $500 from an anonymous benefactor; it transpired that the benefactor had confused experimental psychology with psychical research, and cancelled his subscription the following year. As editor Hall used his position to criticize the work of James **McCosh**, who represented Scottish realist faculty psychology, and several others. (By the time he sold the journal to Karl **Dallenbach** in 1920 Hall had pumped about $8000 of his own funds into it.) In 1883 he established the *Pedagogical Seminary*, now the *Journal of Genetic Psychology*. Between 1904 and 1915 he published the *Journal of Religious Psychology*, and in 1904 he established the *Journal of Applied Psychology*. Hall is also credited with introducing psychoanalysis to the USA. To commemorate the twentieth anniversary of the founding of Clark University (1909), he invited **Freud** and **Jung** to lecture there.

Hall is not associated with a major programme of empirical work and did not formulate an important theoretical position. He was, however, a strong supporter of evolutionary theory and advocated recapitulation theory. The theory, now discredited, states that each individual in his or her lifetime re-enacts all evolutionary stages of the human race. His approach was essentially questionnaire-based, and with his students he developed and adminis-

tered nearly 200 questionnaires on topics ranging from anger, to dolls and food.

In 1888 he left Johns Hopkins to become first
president of the newly founded Clark University,
where he also established himself as professor of
psychology. In 1892 he arranged a meeting, on 8
July, for twenty-six of the country's leading
psychologists – James and **Dewey** could not
attend – and the American Psychological
Association was founded. During the 1880s and
1890s Hall and James competed for premier
position, and James's followers established the
Psychological Review to compete with the
American Journal of Psychology. Whereas
James's contribution remained primarily one of
ideas, Hall's was essentially organizational.

Hamilton, Max
Born: 1912, Offenbach, Germany **Died:** 1988,
England **Nat:** German **Ints:** Clinical psychol-
ogy, evaluation and measurement, psychophar-
macology **Educ:** MA University of London
Appts & awards: Nuffield Professor of Psy-
chiatry 1963–77, Professor (Emeritus) of
Psychiatry 1987–88, University of Leeds; South
West Regional Hospital Board Research Prize,
1953; President, British Association of Psy-
chopharmacology; Hon. Professor of Psychiatry,
University of Missouri, Columbia, 1970; Fel-
low, Royal College of Physicians, 1970, Royal
College of Psychiatrists, 1971; Fellow, BPS;
President, BPS 1972–3; Hon. Member, Société
Royale de Médicine Mentale de Belgie; Paul
Hoch Award, American Psychopharmacology
Association, 1981

Principal publications
1950   The personality of dyspeptics, with special
reference to gastric and duodenal ulcer. *British
Journal of Medical Psychology*, 23, 182–98.
1953   Use of succinylcholine in ECT, with particular
reference to the effect of blood pressure. *British
Medical Journal*, 195–7 (with D. Adderley).
1955   *Psychosomatics*. Chapman and Hall.
1957   Nomogram for the tetrachoric correlation coefficient. *Nature*, 160, 73.
1958   Measurement in medicine. *Lancet*, 1f, 977–82.
1959   Clinical syndromes in depressive states.
Journal of Mental Science, 105, 985–98 (with J.M.
White).
1959   The assessment of anxiety states by rating.
British Journal of Medical Psychology, 33, 50–5.
1960   A rating scale for depression. *Journal of
Neurology, Neurosurgery and Psychiatry*, 23,
56–62.

1960   A rating scale for depression. *Journal of
Neurology, Neurosurgery and Psychiatry*, 23,
56–62.
1960   Controlled clinical trial of thiopropazate,
chlorpromazine and occupational therapy in chronic
schizophrenics. *Journal of Mental Science*, 106,
4055 (with A.L.G. Smith, H.E. Lapidus and E.P.
Cadogan).
1961   *Lectures on the Methodology of Clinical
Research*. Churchill-Livingstone.
1965   Computer programs for the medical man: A
solution. *British Medical Journal*, 1048–50.
1967   *Readings in Abnormal Psychology*. Penguin.
1967   Development of a rating scale for primary
depressive illness. *British Journal of Social and
Clinical Psychology*, 6, 278–96.
1974   *Fish's Clinical Psychopathology*. John Wright.
1976   *Fish's Schizophrenia*. John Wright.
1977   A simple discriminant function for hepatic
disease. *Journal of Clinical Pathology*, 30, 454–9.
1978   *Fish's Outline of Psychiatry*. John Wright.

Further reading
Lilienfeld, S.O. (1995) *Seeing both Sides: Classic
Controversies in Abnormal Psychology*.
Brooks/Cole.
Wilkinson, G. (ed.) (1993) *Talking about Psychiatry*.
American Psychiatric Press.

Max Hamilton moved to London with his parents at the beginning of World War I. He was
educated in London and moved to University
College Hospital Medical School, London. Here
he was taught by Sir Cyril Burt. He became a
medical officer during World War II in the RAF
and it was during this time, particularly while
observing flight personnel returning from sor-
ties, that he became interested in Psychiatry.
This led him to study psychological medicine
and he became absorbed in issues relating to
methodology, psychometrics, discussions on the
nature of science and statistics, an interest that
dominated his career from then on. Scientific
method was the yardstick by which he judged
himself and others.

He was one of the first to carry out controlled
double-blind studies for clinical trials and
psychotropic drugs. He later devised observer
rating scales for Anxiety States and Depressive
Illness. His Hamilton Depression Rating Scale is
widely used. He became Nuffield Professor of
psychiatry at Leeds University and remained
there until he retired in 1977. His 1960 paper 'A
rating scale for depression' came top twice in
the international citation index for medical
publications.

Because of his interest in psychology, he became closely linked to the BPS where he was Treasurer for a number of years and then President. He was considered a controversial figure and his remarks sparked such objection that a section of the BPS demanded a retraction.

He was described as 'never suffering fools and irascible to the end' but also that he was a kind and generous man particularly in relation to peers and students who sought his help.

H. HANKS

Harlow, Harry Frederick

Born: 1905, Fairfield, Ohio, USA **Died:** 1981, Tucson, Arizona, USA **Nat:** American **Ints:** Clinical psychology, developmental psychology, experimental analysis of behaviour, physiological and comparative psychology **Educ:** AB University of Stanford, 1927; PhD University of Stanford, 1930 **Appts & awards:** Professor, University of Wisconsin, 1930–74; Howard Crosby Warren Medal from the Society of Experimental Psychologists, 1956; President, APA, 1958; Distinguished Scientific Contribution Award, APA, 1960; National Medal of Science, 1967; G. Stanley Hall Award, 1972; Gold Medal, APA, 1973; International Kittay Scientific Medal Award, 1975;

Principal publications

1932 Social facilitation of feeding in the albino rat. *Pedagogical Seminary* (later *Journal of Genetic Psychology*), 41, 211–21.

1949 The formation of learning sets. *Psychological Review*, 56, 51–65.

1950 Learning motivated by a manipulation drive. *Journal of Experimental Psychology*, 40, 228–34 (with M.K. Harlow and D.R. Meyer).

1953 Mice, monkeys, men and motives. *Psychological Review*, 60, 23–32.

1958 The evolution of learning. In A. Roe and G.G. Simpson (eds), *Behavior and Evolution*. Yale University Press.

1958 The nature of love. *American Psychologist*, 13, 673–85.

1958 *Biological and Biochemical Bases of Behavior*. University of Wisconsin Press.

1959 Affectional responses in the infant monkey. *Science*, 130, 421–32 (with R.R. Zimmerman).

1959 Learning set and error factor theory. In S. Koch (ed.), *Psychology: A Study of a Science*, vol. 2. McGraw-Hill.

1962 The heterosexual affectional system in monkeys. *American Scientist*, 17, 1–9.

1974 A reversal of social deficits produced by isolation rearing in monkeys. *Journal of Human Evolution*, 3, 527–34 (with S.J. Suomi and M.A. Novak).

Further reading

Bowlby, J. (1969) *Attachment and Loss, vol. 1: Attachment*. Hogarth and Institute of Psychoanalysis. (Penguin, 1971).

—— (1973) *Attachment and Loss, vol. 2: Separation: Anxiety and Anger*. Hogarth and Institute of Psychoanalysis. (Penguin, 1975).

Hinde, R.A. (1970) *Animal Behaviour: A Synthesis of Ethology and Comparative Psychology*, 2nd edn. McGraw-Hill.

—— (1974) *Biological Bases of Human Social Behaviour*. McGraw-Hill.

Harlow's contributions to psychology comprise a series of empirical findings in three main areas: the learning of problem solving, curiosity and manipulation, and the development of affectional systems. In all three cases, the research involved rhesus monkeys, and the findings had far-reaching implications. He also studied the behaviour of US servicemen who had been prisoners in the Korean war.

In his earlier research on problem solving, Harlow challenged the conventional behaviourist approach (derived from testing rats on one or two problems) by showing that monkeys would learn, in one trial, new problems of the same general type as those encountered before. Harlow's explanation in terms of 'learning sets' foreshadowed the cognitive approaches to animal learning of the 1970s. A related line of research demonstrated the wide range of problems which monkeys would solve in the absence of conventional reinforcers, thereby challenging the homeostatic model of motivation widely favoured at this time.

Harlow's best-known research began by chance when he was rearing monkeys in an isolated, germ-free environment. Noting the emotional disruption which this rearing brought, he set out to demonstrate experimentally that infantile attachment did not depend on a secondary drive, as had been suggested by both **Freud** and **Hull**. The subsequent experiments on long-term effects of isolation rearing produced the now famous socially withdrawn depressive monkeys. These studies, and their later offshoots concentrating on depression, are those which have made Harlow most widely known. They caught the imagination of clinicians, notably the British psychoanalyst, John

Bowlby, and were influential in his theoretical accounts of attachment and separation. In a different way, they also influenced the eminent British ethologist Robert **Hinde**, who initiated a detailed investigation of more subtle disruptions of mother–infant relationships in rhesus monkeys.

JOHN ARCHER

Harré, Rom

Born: 1927, Apiti, New Zealand *Nat:* New Zealander *Ints:* Adult development and ageing, developmental psychology, personality and social, philosophical and theoretical, school psychology *Educ:* BSc Auckland, 1948; MA Auckland, 1952; BPhil Oxford, 1956; MA Oxford, 1960 *Appts & awards:* Fellow of Linacre College, Oxford; University Lecturer in Philosophy of Science, Professor, Philosophy of Science, Oxford University, Adjunct Professor of the Philosophy of Social and Behavioural Sciences, SUNY Binghampton

Principal publications

1972 *The Explanation of Social Behaviour.* Blackwell (with P.F. Secord).

1979 *Social Being: A Theory for Social Psychology.* Blackwell.

1983 *Personal Being: A Theory for Individual Psychology.* Blackwell.

1991 *Physical Being: A Theory for a Corporeal Psychology.* Blackwell.

1994 *The Discursive Mind.* Sage (with G. Gillett).

Further reading

Robinson, D.N. and Leendert, P.M. (eds) (1990) *Annals of Theoretical Psychology*, vol. 6. Plenum.

Shotter, J. (1993) *Cultural Politics of Everyday Life: Social Constructionism, Rhetoric and Knowing of the Third Kind.* University of Toronto Press.

In the early part of his academic career Harré was mainly concerned with the philosophy of science, but he turned his attention to the field of social psychology during the 1970s, producing a blistering critique of experimental social psychology and developing his own ethogenic paradigm from a non-positivistic standpoint. Although he has written on a wide range of psychological topics (such as emotion or the use of autobiography in psychological research), there are three or four books which may be regarded as forming the heart of Harré's canon: *The Explanation of Social Behaviour*, *Social Being*, *Personal Being* and *Physical Being*. The

impact of Harré's work, especially on British social psychology, was at its peak in the 1970s and declined somewhat by the late 1980s, when discursive psychology began to emerge. By 1994, Harré had modified his original ethogenic position somewhat to a stance which was more consonant with the prevailing discursive psychology of the 1990s.

The critique he developed in the early 1970s of the doctrine of the objective experiment is still pertinent to the experimental psychology of the 1990s. Three important facets of this critique will be mentioned here. First, the way people behave within the confines of the psychology laboratory may tell us little about the way they behave in naturally occurring situations (this is similar to the critique that the ethologists were making of animal experimentation at that time). Second, Harré challenged the logic of deploying the experiment as the major research tool in psychology when it could only address issues concerning causal explanation. This seemed odd to Harré, who pointed out that a very large amount of what people do is ordinarily explained teleologically. Third, the image of the human being which comes with the experimental approach is that of the stimulus–response automaton, and Harré desperately wished to replace this feeble notion of the human being with the more dynamic concept of the human agent: for him, people are the efficient causes of their own actions. Thus they are powerful, they can cause things to happen, and because of that they can be held responsible for what they do. Harré therefore introduced a dimension of moral conduct into social psychology and with that an interest in rules governing social behaviour.

In the new paradigm, questions of meaning replaced the goal of prediction, and so research took on a more hermeneutic cast. Because he wanted to develop psychological methodology along the lines of the advanced (non-positivist) sciences, Harré strongly advocated the use of modelling in psychological theorizing. In particular he embraced the dramaturgical standpoint of Goffman, and was also sympathetic to taking formal episodes such as ceremonies or games as models for the more enigmatic social episodes which make up the bulk of everyday experience.

In *Personal Being*, Harré develops the notion that conversation is the primary human reality. He sees persons as the publicly identifiable locations of speech acts, with selves providing the secondary psychological reality as an organizing concept for perceptions, feelings and beliefs. Drawing on Strawson, he pays close attention to indexicals and pronouns when articulating the person–self duality, which he takes great pains to show is quite different from the mind–body duality. The latter, which is axiomatic to much old-paradigm psychological thinking, should, in his view, be replaced by the former. Returning to his earlier stance on modelling in science, he looks for the source of the self concept *qua* theory, and indicates that it is to be found in the way folk talk about persons in their particular sociolinguistic communities. Thus different sociolinguistic communities will produce different kinds of psychological being. *Personal Being* is a stunning book which brims with exciting ideas. For a book of its class, it may well be one of the most under-read in academic psychology, and certainly it would not appear to have had either the attention or the impact that it deserves. But, in a more general sense, Harré has had an enormous impact on the discipline, and his earlier critiques certainly cleared a lot of ground for the later development of discursive social psychology.

JOHN L. SMITH

Harris, Paul L.

Born: 1946, England **Nat:** British **Ints:** Developmental psychology, experimental psychology, personality and social psychology, ***Educ:*** BA Sussex University, 1968; DPhil Oxford University, 1971 ***Appts & awards:*** Research Fellow, Harvard University, Center for Cognitive Studies, 1971–2; Research Fellow, Oxford University, Department of Experimental Psychology, 1972–3; Lecturer, Lancaster University, Department of Psychology, 1973–6; Reader in Psychology, Free University of Amsterdam, 1976–9; Lecturer, London School of Economics, Department of Social Psychology, 1979–81; University Lecturer, Oxford University, Department of Experimental Psychology; Fellow, St John's College, 1981–96; Fellow, Center for Advanced Study in the Behavioral Sciences, 1992–3

Principal publications

1973 Perseveration errors in search by young infants. *Child Development*, 44, 28–33.
1983 Infant cognition. In J.J. Campos and M.M. Haith (eds), *Handbook of Child Psychology. Vol. II: Infancy and Developmental Psychobiology* (general ed. Paul Mussen). Wiley.
1987 Bringing order to the A-not-B error.

Monographs for the Society for Research in Child Development, 51, 52–61.
1988 *Developing Theories of Mind*. Cambridge University Press (ed. with J.W. Astington and D.R. Olson).
1989 *Children and Emotion: The Development of Psychological Understanding*. Blackwell.
1989 *Children's Understanding of Emotion*. Cambridge University Press (with C. Saarni).
1991 *Perspectives on the Child's Theory of Mind*. Oxford University Press (with G.E. Butterworth, A.M. Leslie and H.M. Wellman).
1995 Children's awareness and lack of awareness of emotion. In D. Cicchetti and S.L. Toth (eds), *Rochester Symposium on Developmental Psychopathology. Volume VI: Emotion, Cognition, Representation*. University of Rochester Press.

Further reading

Lewis, C. and Mitchell, P. (eds) (1994) *Children's Early Understanding of Mind: Origins and Development*. Erlbaum.
Saarni, C. and Harris, P.L. (eds) (1991) *Children's Understanding of Emotion*. Cambridge University Press.

Harris's main areas of research include infant cognition, the child's understanding of emotion, and the development of pretence and imagination. His doctoral thesis altered the way in which developmental psychologists view the emergence of object permanence in infants. Object permanence is assessed by first displaying an object to an infant, then covering it and observing whether or not the infant searches for that object. An infant's search is taken as evidence that the infant is aware that the object, though no longer visible, continues to exist. Harris demonstrated that infant search for objects depends critically on information processing variables, notably delay length, rather than on conceptual insight. This position has been upheld and extended in recent years.

In 1976, Harris moved to the Free University in Amsterdam. This placed him in a context with strong links to the clinical treatment of emotionally disturbed children, and led to a new focus of his research on children's understanding of emotion. A synthesis of that research (*Children and Emotion*) was published in 1989. In the same period, Harris co-edited a volume entitled *Developing Theories of Mind*, which gave important impetus to research on children's theory of mind on a wider front. Notwithstanding its title, Harris never espoused the idea of the child as theoretician. Instead, he argued that young children can imagine themselves in different situations, and thereby 'simulate' the beliefs and desires of other people. This claim triggered a research programme on the development of pretence and imagination, in which Harris is still engaged.

L.P. NUCCI

Hartup, Willard W.

Born: 1927, Fremont, Ohio, USA **Nat:** American **Ints:** Developmental psychology, educational psychology, personality and social psychology **Educ:** BS Ohio State University, 1950; MA Ohio State University, 1951; EdD Harvard University, 1955 **Appts & awards:** Assistant Professor of Psychology, Rhode Island College of Education, 1954–5; Iowa Child Welfare Research Station, State University of Iowa, Assistant Professor, 1955–60, Associate Professor, 1960–3; Institute of Child Development, University of Minnesota, Associate Professor, 1963–4, Professor, 1964–93, Associate Director, 1966–71, Director, 1971–82, Regents' Professor, 1993–6; Fellow, Center for Advanced Study in the Behavioral Sciences, Stanford University, 1978–9; Evelyn House Award for Contributions to the Lives of Young Children, Minnesota Association for the Education of Young Children, 1991; G. Stanley Hall Award for Distinguished Contributions to Developmental Psychology, APA, 1991

Principal publications

1958   Nurturance and nurturance-withdrawal in relation to dependency behavior in preschool children. *Child Development*, 29, 191–201.

1959   Social isolation vs. interaction with adults in relation to aggression in preschool children. *Journal of Abnormal and Social Psychology*, 59, 17–22.

1963   Dependency and independence. In H.W. Stevenson (ed.), *Child Psychology: 62nd Yearbook of the National Society for the Study of Education*. University of Chicago Press.

1967   Imitation of peers as a function of reinforcement from the peer group and rewardingness of the model. *Child Development*, 38, 1003–16.

1970   Peer interaction and social organization. In P. Mussen (ed.), *Carmichael's Manual of Child Psychology*. Wiley.

1974   Aggression in childhood: Developmental perspectives. *American Psychologist*, 29, 336–41.

1976   Peer interaction and the behavioral development of the individual child. In E. Schopler

and R.J. Reichler (eds), *Psychopathology and Child Development*. Plenum.

1979   Peer relations and the growth of social competence. In M.W. Kent and J.E. Rolf (eds), *The Primary Prevention of Psychopathology. Vol. 3: Promoting Social Competence in Children*. University Press of New England.

1980   Toward a psychology of childhood: Trends and issues. In W.A. Collins (ed.), *Minnesota Symposium on Child Psychology*, vol. 13. Erlbaum.

1983   Peer relations. In E.M. Hetherington, *Handbook of Child Psychology. Vol. 4: Socialization, Personality and Social Development*. Wiley.

1986   *Relationships and Development*. Erlbaum (with Z. Rubin).

1989   Social relationships and their developmental significance. *American Psychologist*, 44, 120–6.

1992   Peer relations in early and middle childhood. In V.B. Van Hasselt and M. Hersen (eds), *Handbook of Social Development: A Lifespan Perspective*. Plenum.

1996   The company they keep: Friendships and their developmental significance. *Child Development*, 67, 1–13.

Further reading

Ascione, F. (1975) The effects of continuous nurturance and nurturance withdrawal on children's behavior: A partial replication. *Child Development*, 46, 790–5.

Farver, J.M. and Howes, C. (1988) Cross-cultural differences in social interaction: A comparison of American and Indonesian children. *Journal of Cross-Cultural Psychology*, 19, 203–15.

Willard Hartup began his career initially in the field of education, and taught for one year at the Rhode Island College of Education. However, he found that children's development, and not curricular issues, struck him as the more salient aspect of the educative process. As a result, he shifted his focus towards the study of child development. In particular, he became intrigued with processes by which children establish peer relations. His emphasis on peer interactions ran counter to prevailing emphases in the 1950s on the role of parents in children's social development. Hartup's research demonstrated that child–child relations made a significant independent contribution to children's social growth. In particular, he demonstrated that whether children were able to establish friendships, and the nature of the friends they made, have powerful positive and negative impacts on child outcomes.

His work has had a number of practical implications, including identifying patterns of social acceptance and rejection which are associated with children at risk for development of behavioural or emotional problems. In addition, Hartup's research has provided evidence supportive of the efficacy of cross-age peer tutoring in some educational contexts. Finally, his work has helped to establish ways in which peer relations, particularly friendships, can be used in clinical settings to help troubled children improve their social relations and skills.

Hartup has held a number of editorships with the most distinguished journals in the field including Child development, and Developmental Psychology. He served as President of the International Society for the Study of Behavioral Development from 1979 to 1983, and President of the Society for Research in Child Development from 1993 to 1995. He is presently Regents Professor at the Institute of Child Development, University of Minnesota.

L.P. NUCCI

Havighurst, Robert J.
Born: 1900, DePere, Wisconsin **Died:** 1991 **Nat:** American **Ints:** Adult development and ageing, developmental psychology, educational psychology **Educ:** BA Ohio Wesleyan University, 1921; PhD (Chemistry) Ohio State University, 1924 **Appts & awards:** National Research Council in Physics, Harvard University, 1924–6; Chemistry Department, Miami University, 1927–8; Experimental College, University of Wisconsin, 1928–32; Science Education, Ohio State University, 1932–4; Assistant Director for General Education, Rockefeller Foundation, 1934–41; University of Chicago, Professor of Education and Human Development, 1941–65, Emeritus Professor, 1965–91; Kleemeier Award for Research in Gerontology, Gerontological Society, 1967; Thorndike Award for Research, Division of Educational Psychology, American Educational Research Association, 1969; Brookdale Award in Behavioral and Social Science Research, Gerontological Society, 1979

Principal publications
1948/1960/1972 *Developmental Tasks and Education.* University of Chicago Press.
1949 *Adolescent Character and Personality.* Wiley (with H. Taba, A.W. Brown *et al.*).
1955 *American Indian and White Children: A Sociopsychological Investigation.* University of Chicago Press (with Bernice L. Neugarten).

1960 *American Higher Education in the 1960s.* Ohio State University Press.
1962 *Growing Up in River City.* Wiley.
1965 *Society and Education in Brazil.* University of Pittsburgh Press (with J.R. Moreira).
1966 *Education in Metropolitan Areas.* Allyn and Bacon.
1968 *Comparative Perspectives on Education.* Little, Brown.
1970 *Adjustment to Retirement: A Cross-National Study.* Van Gorcum.
1971 *400 Losers.* Jossey-Bass (with Winton M. Ahlstrom).
1972 *To Live On This Earth: American Indian Education.* Doubleday (with E. Fuchs).
1977 *The Future of Big-City Schools: Desegregation Policies and Magnet Alternatives.* McCutchan (with D.U. Levine).

Further reading
Merriam, S. and Millins, L. (1981) Havighurst's adult developmental tasks: A study of their importance relative to income, age, and sex. *Adult Education,* 31, 123–41.
Neugarten, B.L. (1993) Robert Havighurst. *American Psychologist,* 148, 1290–1.
Stewart, R.A. (1973) Adolescence in New Zealand: Problems and prospects. In K.W. Thomson and A.D. Trlin (eds), *Contemporary New Zealand.* Hicks, Smith and Sons.
Thornburg, H. (1970) Adolescence: A reinterpretation. *Adolescence,* 5, 463–84.

After postdoctoral work in physics at Harvard, Havighurst taught science for a few years at the secondary and college levels, but his growing interest in the problems of adolescents and in experimental education led to a major career shift. In 1934 he moved to the General Education Board of the Rockefeller Foundation as assistant director for its programmes in science education. At Rockefeller, under the guidance of Lawrence Frank, he became involved with programmes in child study. By 1937, Havighurst was director of the General Education Board, and in that role became the instrumental figure in supporting research programmes in child development at major universities and research centres throughout the United States. He was also instrumental in providing funds to help refugee scholars from Europe resettle in the United States. Among them were Bruno Bettelheim, Peter Blos, Erik **Erikson** and Fritz Redl.

In 1941, Havighurst was appointed professor of education at the University of Chicago and executive secretary of the university's Committee on Human Development. Collaborating with colleagues in anthropology, sociology and education, Havighurst began a series of cross-sectional and longitudinal studies of personality and moral development in children and adolescents. In 1948 and 1949 he published his highly influential works on human development (*Developmental Tasks and Education* and *Adolescent Character and Personality*), in which he set out his conception of developmental stages as a series of age-related cultural tasks. Havighurst also began in those first years at Chicago a line of cross-cultural research by collaborating with anthropologist W. Lloyd Warner and others in a large-scale study of emotional, social and moral development of children in six Native American groups. Later he would pursue his cross-cultural interests in numerous studies of children and youth in other countries.

His work on human development extended into research and writing on education, and in the next three decades he produced works concerning the education of Native Americans, educational approaches in Latin America, and educational issues within large cities in the United States. Havighurst was prominent as a civil rights activist throughout his adult life. His commitment to social change resulted in works focusing on the education of minority youth, and on the relations between poverty, race and the development minority children. His survey of the Chicago public schools, published in 1964, drew national attention for its far-sighted but controversial plan for school and community desegregation. Havighurst received a number of awards for his work on human development and education, including the American Educational Research Association's Thorndike Award in 1969 for research in educational psychology.

The life-span approach he took towards understanding development led him to studies on the sociology and psychology of ageing. In the 1950s and 1960s, Havighurst directed a ten-year investigation of middle age and old age, known as the Kansas City Studies of Adult Life. Findings from those studies and subsequent research altered conventional wisdom about the ageing process. In 1970, at age 69, he published, *Adjustment to Retirement: A Cross-National Study*. He was recognized in 1979 by the Gerontological Society for his contributions to research on the psychology of ageing with the Brookdale Award in Behavioral and Social Science Research.

Havighurst maintained an active line of research and writing well into his eighties when his health began to fail. He died in 1991 at age 90.

L.P. NUCCI

Hebb, Donald Olding

Born: 1904 **Died:** 1985, Nova Scotia, Canada **Nat:** Canadian **Ints:** Developmental psychology, educational psychology, experimental psychology, personality and social psychology, physiological and comparative psychology **Educ:** PhD Harvard University, 1936 **Appts & awards:** Instructor, Harvard University, 1936–7; Research Fellow, Montreal Neurological Institute, 1937–9; Lecturer, then Assistant Professor, Queen's University, 1939–42; Research Associate, Yerkes Laboratories of Primate Biology, 1942–7; McGill University, Professor of Psychology, 1947–74, Professor Emeritus, 1974; President, Canadian Psychological Association, 1952; Fellow, Royal Society of Canada, 1959; President, APA, 1960; Fellow, Royal Society, 1966; Hon. DSc, University of Chicago, 1961, Waterloo, 1963, York, 1966, McMaster, 1967, St Lawrence, 1972, McGill, 1975, Memorial, 1977; Hon. DHL, Northeastern, 1963; Hon. LLD, Dalhousie, 1965, Queen's, 1967, Western Ontario, 1968, Concordia, 1975, Victoria, BC, 1976, Trent, 1976; Hon. DCL, Bishop's, 1977; Royal Society Visiting Professor, University College London, 1974

Principal publications

1937   The innate organization of visual activity: I Perception of figures by rats reared in total darkness. *Journal of Genetic Psychology*, 51, 101–26.

1937   The innate organization of visual activity: II Transfer of response in the discrimination of brightness by rats reared in total darkness. *Journal of Comparative Psychology*, 24, 277–99.

1939   Intelligence in man after large removals of cerebral tissue: Report of four left frontal lobe cases. *Journal of General Psychology*, 21: 73–87.

1942   The effect of early and late brain injury upon test scores, and the nature of normal adult intelligence. *Proceedings of the American Philosophical Society*, 85, 275–92.

1945   Man's frontal lobes: A critical review. *Archives of Neurology and Psychiatry*, 54, 10–24.

1946   Emotion in man and animal: An analysis of the intuitive processes of recognition. *Psychological Review*, 53, 88–106.

1946   On the nature of fear. *Psychological Review*,
53, 259–76.

1946   A method of rating animal intelligence.
Journal of General Psychology, 34, 59–65 (with
K. Williams).

1949   *The Organization of Behavior*. Wiley.

1958   *A Textbook of Psychology*. Saunders.

1968   The social significance of animal studies. In D.
Lindzey (ed.), *Handbook of Social Psychology, 2*.
Addison-Wesley.

1968   Concerning imagery. *Psychological Review*,
75, 466–77.

1976   Physiological learning theory. *Journal of
Abnormal Child Psychology*, 4, 309–14.

1980   *Essay on Mind*. Erlbaum.

Further reading

Hergenhahn, B.R. and Olson, M.H. (1993) *An
Introduction to Theories of Learning*. Prentice-Hall.

Kelin, R.M. and Doane, B.K. (eds) (1994)
*Psychological Concepts and Dissociative
Disorders*. Erlbaum.

Valentine, E.R. (1989) Neural nets: From Hartley and
Hebb to Hinton. *Journal of Mathematical
Psychology*, 33, 348–57.

Donald Hebb committed himself to psychology
late, at the age of 30. After graduating from
Dalhousie University without special distinction, except in maths and physics, he became a
high school teacher in his home village. He
hoped to become a novelist, but after a year he
took farming and labouring jobs, and started to
read **Freud**. He was sceptical, but interested
enough to approach the McGill psychology
department, where he was told to read **James**'s
Principles of Psychology, and **Ladd** and **Woodworth**'s *Physiological Psychology*. After a
qualifying year, he was accepted as a part-time
graduate student in 1929. At the same time he
took a job teaching in an elementary school. He
enjoyed teaching, and took the opportunity to
make radical changes in the school where he
was principal. He had some success in this, and
might have become an educator, but his studies
in psychology were already moving towards a
lifelong preoccupation with the opposition
between learned and innate factors in behaviour.
He completed a theoretical MA thesis in 1932
designed to establish an extreme environmentalist position – that skeletal reflexes are the result
of prenatal learning. His external examiner was
Boris Babkin, who had been a student of
Pavlov. He passed the thesis but recommended
Hebb to gain laboratory experience, and introduced him to Leonid Andreyev, who had come

to McGill from Pavlov's laboratory. Hebb
became as sceptical of Pavlov's methods as of
Freud's; both being overconfident and dogmatic
in their inferences from observation.

After a difficult year following the death of
his wife in a car accident, he left McGill in 1934.
He had not yet completed his PhD, but after
finishing an extended essay on objective psychology and scientific method, he had finally
decided on a career in psychology. **Yerkes**
offered him an assistantship at Yale, but on
Babkin's recommendation he went instead to
work with Karl **Lashley** in Chicago. After a
year Lashley went to Harvard and Hebb followed him there.

His choice of the unsystematic but brilliant
physiological psychologist was crucial. Increasingly research in psychology was devoted to
testing theories because they were there to be
tested, rather than because of any interest in the
phenomena themselves. By 1934, **Tolman**'s
curiosity about the world of rats had given way
to a fierce and narrow battle between rival
learning theories, and the mechanistic stimulus-
response theory of **Hull** and his students at Yale
was beginning to set the agenda. If Hebb had
gone to Yale he would have found it hard to
avoid getting drawn into that agenda. The
nearest he got to it was meeting Tolman's student Krechevsky in Chicago, and he found little
of interest in the abstract preoccupations of
learning theory. He wanted to discover
something interesting, not to impress with
clever experiments whose importance is para-
sitic on the theories they are designed to test.

Lashley encouraged him to bypass current
theory altogether and go straight to the big,
traditional questions, such as whether perception
is innate or acquired. So he set up experiments
to compare the perceptual abilities of normal
and dark-reared rats. What he thought he found
was no clear differences in transfer tests once
the discrimination is learned, and concluded that
perception does not require experience. Much
later, after publishing the experiments, he realized what he had failed to notice at the time,
that the dark-reared rats took longer to learn the
original discrimination than normal. He began to
realize that there is a subtle interplay between
learning and innate factors, and to work on a
theory that would allow for this.

Meanwhile he was picking up the intellectual
skills he would need to articulate the theory. At
Chicago he learned neurology from C.J.
Herrick, saw salamanders with transplanted
limbs in Paul Weiss's laboratory, and took

physiology with Nathaniel Gleitman. Harvard was still dominated by the legacy of psychophysics, the measurement of mind rather than its biology. So Hebb felt isolated, which increased his dependence on Lashley at this stage of his intellectual development. After completing his PhD at Harvard in 1936, he continued to attend Lashley's seminars, while earning enough to live on as a teaching assistant, and gaining the knowledge of brain anatomy that was to play an important play in his mature theorizing.

In 1937 he returned to Montreal to work with Wilder **Penfield**, who wanted him to use psychological tests to evaluate the effects of brain surgery. Hebb discovered that large lesions in the frontal lobe could have little or no effect on performance in intelligence tests and began to ponder upon this. Characteristically this led to reflection on the nature of intelligence itself and to his classic paper of 1942 on the effect of early and late brain injury upon test scores, where he argued that intelligence is in important respects a product of experience, a conclusion counter to received opinion at the time.

In 1942 Lashley became director of the Yerkes Laboratories of Primate Biology in Florida, and invited Hebb to join him. Lashley's plan was to study the function of the brain in learning by testing chimpanzees on a battery of tasks before and after operation. But this was held up by the difficulty in teaching chimpanzees simple discriminations, and Hebb took time to observe the chimpanzees, and to develop his theories of thought and emotion. Best known is his discovery of the 'horror' (Hebb's word for it) shown by chimpanzees at the sight of a clay model of a chimp's head. On investigating further he found that any isolated part of the body had the same effect, and this became an essential support for his theory of cell assemblies.

The theory was gradually coming together at this time, and Hebb was alert to any phenomena relevant to it. Senden's data on people born blind who recovered their sight, and Riesen's work on pattern perception of dark-reared chimpanzees, confirmed his belief in the importance of experience in perception. Yet Lashley, his teacher, was not much interested. Lashley did not encourage system building or speculative theories, and his importance to Hebb at this time was as a critic who demanded that theories really did conform to the data in all their complexity, and not to an oversimplified selection. Throughout his career Lashley made clear what a serious theory of brain organization must

explain, but would offer no theory himself. He revelled in paradox. On the one hand the brain acts as a whole, on the other there is plenty of evidence for some localization of function. Stimuli impinging on different parts of the retina can be equivalent even though they stimulate different cells. The nervous system seems designed to respond to isolated stimuli through neural connectivity, yet *Gestalt* phenomena in perception were well established by this time. Hebb's own findings that dark-reared rats are unimpaired in discrimination transfer tests, yet take longer to learn; that massive lesions in humans can have little effect; and that familiar percepts with a part missing can have dramatic effects probably helped to confirm Lashley's pessimism about theory. But Hebb was preparing to go further than his teacher, and show that these apparent puzzles can be resolved.

While at Florida in 1944 he came across the work of the brain anatomist Lorente de Nó, showing the prevalence of closed circuits in the organization of the brain, and that more than one neuron may be necessary to excite a second neurone at a synapse. This allows the possibility of *and* and *or* gates, a principle already made use of by McCulloch and Pitts a year earlier, in their mathematical theory of neural nets. It was to become the basis of Hebb's theory in *The Organization of Behavior*, but he did not abstract these principles mathematically. Instead he stuck to what he was familiar with, the language of neurophysiology and anatomy. He used de Nó's findings as the basis of a theory which reconciled the opposition between the brain as a set of straight-through sensory-motor connections, and the brain as a mass action device. If there are closed circuits they may be organized to form what he called cell assemblies, which act as a unit, yet may be distributed throughout the brain. Cell assemblies are the neural correlates of concepts, and their running off as phase sequences forms the basis of experience. When spelt out in full, his theory showed at least the feasibility that the holistic phenomena emphasized by Lashley can after all be explained with a network of neural connections.

The Organization of Behavior had an impact that makes it one of the major achievements in psychology in the twentieth century. Psychology was becoming increasingly specialized, but here was a serious work that brought together the latest research from a range of disciplines from within and outside psychology. Some of the implications of the theory stimulated important research, especially at McGill, on perceptual learning, sensory deprivation and the effects of brain stimulation. But the book was also significant as a rallying point. As an approach to theory in psychology, it provided an interdisciplinary focus around which psychologists, ethologists, neurologists and brain physiologists gathered to find ways of bringing their disciplines together. His brief *Textbook of Psychology* of 1958 carried his way of thinking to a wider audience. Much had to be left out, and Hebb was happy to leave a core that represents an attractively trim psychology defined by the interests of *The Organization of Behavior*.

Nearly fifty years after its publication, neuropsychology has become a prominent part of experimental psychology, and connectionism or parallel distributed processing a familiar source of theory. Both these owe a debt to Hebb, but it is general rather than specific to the details of his theory. He was not a founder like Freud or **Skinner**, but he enlarged our ideas about psychological explanation and set people thinking in a way that has made these modern developments possible.

ARTHUR STILL

Heider, Fritz

Born: 1896, Vienna, Austria **Died:** 1988, Kansas, USA **Nat:** Austrian **Ints:** Personality and social history **Educ:** PhD Karl-Franzens-Universität, Graz, 1920 **Appts & awards:** Professor Emeritus, Department of Psychology, University of Kansas; Hon, D, Karl-Franzens-Universität, Graz, 1981; Guggenheim Fellow, 1947–8, 1951–2; Fulbright Fellow (Oslo), 1960–1; University of Kansas, Byron Caldwell Smith Award, 1963; University Distinguished Professorship, 1963; APA Distinguished Scientific Contribution Award, 1965; University of Kansas, Fellow, AAA&S, 1981

Principal publications

1926   Ding und Medium. *Symposium der Philosophischen Academie*, 1, 109–57.
1939   Environmental determinants in psychological theories. *Psychological Review*, 46, 383–410.
1940   Studies in the psychology of the deaf. *Psychological Monographs*, 52, 53, (with G.M. Heider).
1944   Social perception and phenomenal causality. *Psychological Review*, 51, 358–74.
1946   Attitudes and comparative organization. *Journal of Psychology*, 21, 107–12.

1958   *The Psychology of Interpersonal Relations.* Wiley. (Reprinted, Erlbaum, 1982.)
1959   On Perception and Event Structure and the Psychological Environment. *Psychological Issues.*
1959   On Lewin's Methods and Theory. *Journal of Social Issues, Supplemental Series*, No. 13, 3–13.
1970   *Gestalt* theory: Early history and reminiscences. *Journal of History of the Behavioural Sciences*, 6, 131–9.
1979   On balance and attribution. In P.W. Holland and S. Leinhardt (eds), *Perspectives on Social Network Research.* Academic Press.

Further reading

Heider, Fritz (1983) *The Life of a Psychologist – An Autobiography.* University Press of Kansas.

After completing his PhD (on the role of environmental factors on the perception of distant objects) Heider commenced a period of study at the Psychological Institute, Berlin where he was tutored by **Köhler**, **Wertheimer** and **Lewin**. Some years later Köhler invited him to America and he joined the Research Department of Clarke College for the Deaf and Smith College. In 1947 Roger **Braker** invited him to Kansas University where he remained for the rest of his career.

Heider traced much of the direction of his work as a psychologist to his early years. A sharp realization of self-awareness went back to an incident from his childhood, and a preoccupation with ideas about relations between people intensified during the hard years of World War I (in Austria), and gave the urgent need to reach a clearer understanding that led years later to the book *The Psychology of Interpersonal Relations*. Related to this was an early interest in geography. He loved maps and always wanted to find out how parts of a new region lay in relation to each other. He believed that this played a real part in the need to understand relations among ideas and concepts, and to place results of experimental papers that he read on what he thought of as the map of psychology. Later contact with Kurt Lewin and the philosopher Cassirer, with their emphasis on the importance of theory, strengthened the approach that his fascination with maps had already brought into his psychological thinking.

A familiarity with painting and sketching from early school days certainly influenced his later studies of perception. And as he learned to read and write he began making notes about events and thoughts, a habit that contributed to the book and that continued to fill notebooks that are now being edited for library use. Next came a struggle to find the systematic concepts that he needed to deal with everyday events of life and literature. In the end Spinoza's *Ethics* and Max Wertheimer's work on unit-forming factors started Heider on a track that led to his book, with its ideas on balance and attribution that have resulted in a considerable body of experimental and theoretical work.

von Helmholtz, Hermann Ludwig Ferdinand

Born: 1821, Potsdam, Germany **Died:** 1894, Charlottenburg, Germany **Nat:** German **Ints:** Experimental, general, philosophical and theoretical, physiological and comparative **Appts & awards:** House Surgeon, Charite Hospital Berlin, 1842; Army-Surgeon, Potsdam 1843–8; Lecturer, Academy of Arts, 1848–9; Assistant, Anatomical Museum, Berlin, 1848–9; Professor of Physiology, University of Königsberg, 1849–55; Professor of Physiology and Anatomy, University of Bonn, 1855–8; Order of the Lion of Netherland, 1858; Professor of Physiology, Heidelberg University, 1858–71; Hon. Dr, University of Berlin, 1860; Professor of Physics, Berlin University, 1871–88; Graefe Medal, Heidelberg University, 1880; Faraday Lecture, Royal Institute London, 1881; Vice-Chancellor, Heidelberg University, 1886; Order, Pour la Merite, Heidelberg University, 1886; President of the Imperial Physico-Technical Institute, Charlottenburg, 1888–94; Geheimrat ('His Excellency'), German Emperor, 1891; Golden Doctorate-Jubilee, 1891; Helmholtz Statue, 1899

Principal publications

1847   Über die Erhaltung der Kraft. (On the conservation of energy). *Wissenschaftliche Abhandlungen*, 1, 12–75.
1850   Rate of transmission of the excitatory process in nerves. *Berliner Monatsbericht, Comptes Rendus*, XXX, XXXIII.
1856   *Handbuch der physiologischen Optik.* (*Handbook of Physiological Optics*). Voss.
1860   *Handbuch der physiologischen Optik, Part II.* Voss.
1863   *Die Lehre von den Tonempfindungen als physioloogische Grundlage für die Theorie der Musik.* (*The Theory of Tonal Sensations as the Physiological Basis of Music Theory*). Dover. (Reprinted 1954.)
1867   *Handbuch der physiologischen Optik, Part III.* Voss. (trans J.P.C. Southall, Optical Society of America, 1924).

Further reading

Elbert, H. (1949) Hermann von Helmholtz. *Wissenschaftliche Verlagsgellschaft.*
Hurvich, L.M. and Jameson, D. (1979) Helmholtz's vision looking backward. *Contemporary Psychology*, 5, 901–4.
Koenigsberger, L. (1902) *Hermann von Helmholtz.* (Reprinted, Dover, 1965.)

Von Helmholtz is considered by many as being one of the greatest scientists of the nineteenth century. In his youth he was drawn to the study of physics and mathematics, but for financial reasons he studied medicine at the Royal Military Institute in Berlin, where he received a stipend. While still being a military surgeon in the Prussian Army, he continued to work in theoretical physics and was able to present his treatise on the law of conservation of energy at the age of 26. In the following decades he presented other epoch-making discoveries in the areas of thermodynamics, physiology, metabolism, optics, magnetism, electrodynamics and geology. His diverse experimental and theoretical discoveries resulted in over 200 publications. His research was much facilitated by the various professorships he held in surgery, anatomy, physiology and physics, and also by his invention and construction of an electromagnetic motor, the myograph, the tangent galvanometer and the opthalmoscope.

Although Helmholtz never held a post in psychology proper, his work in physics and physiology resulted in discoveries which were fundamental to psychology in general and to experimental psychology in particular. His discovery of the speed of the neural current in 1852 was a scientific breakthrough. Before this discovery it was believed that neural impulses travel with an 'infinite' speed, because it was also believed that human thoughts have a divine and non-material basis. Helmholtz's work on the conservation of energy lead him to his theory of animal heat in 1847, when he demonstrated that the body's, like a machine's, total energy output is equal to its energy input and that there is no *perpetuum mobile*, either in humans or in machines. Helmholtz was a physicist, and he believed that physics would ultimately explain biology and both would eventually lead to an understanding of cognitive processes. All of his theories and experiments helped to establish psychology as a psychological science, leading it away from spiritualism, metaphysics and theology.

Besides giving psychology a mechanistic

direction, Helmholtz's detailed work on the anatomy and function of the eye and the inner ear contributed much to the understanding of sensory functions. In the area of vision he presented experimental as well as theoretical data on accommodation, after-images, binocular vision, colour vision (Young–Helmholtz theory), contrast, depth perception, eye movements and illusions. His work relating to the anatomy and the optics of the eye and their role in sensing and perceiving was first summarized in the *Handbuch der physiologischen Optik* in 1856. It included Helmholtz's own work as well as that of other investigators. Helmholtz undertook the enormous task of replicating every experiment done by others whose results he discussed in his handbook. In a number of instances these re-examinations lead to new discoveries as, for instance, Helmholtz's invention of the tele-stereoscope. Helmholtz kept on improving his research in optics, publishing a revised edition in 1860, and a third volume in 1866. All three volumes were published in a compendium in 1867. It contains close to 8,000 references and is still one of the standard texts in optics, having been reprinted in 1924 and again in 1964.

Just as impressive as his work in optics is Helmholtz's research in audition, which he summarized in *Die Lehre von den Tonempfindungen als physiologische Grundlage für die Theorie der Musik*. He combined his anatomical knowledge with his research on sound waves to form his 'resonance theory of hearing', which proposed that the outer hair cells in the organ of Corti act as tonal analysers and respond selectively to different tonal frequencies. This enables the ear to discern single or combination tones from the myriad of waves impinging on it. Helmholtz was also the first physicist to investigate timbre and explained that the same note sounds different when played on different types of instruments intensify different arrays of overtones. In contrast to his mentor Johannes Müller, who had formulated the law of specific energies of nerves, Helmholtz postulated the law of specific energies of fibres. Both his theory of colour vision and his resonance theory of hearing required that individual fibres within each nerve carry specific messages to the brain.

Not all of Helmholtz's theories were unanimously accepted, especially in Germany, where his mechanistic views met much opposition in the climate of Kantian nativism. In England, however, his philosophical orientation was more readily accepted, since Locke and Mill had laid the groundwork for empiricism. In the Kantian tradition, most German psychologists believed that certain thought processes and perceptual categories were *a priori* or innately given. In contrast, Helmholtz taught that perceptions must be learned. In depth perception, for example, the body must learn to correlate certain muscular tensions of the ocular muscles with the experienced distances. Helmholtz defined sensations as momentary sensory input, and perception as an input from the past. Perception modifies sensation by adding or detracting from it – a process which Helmholtz termed 'unconscious inference'. This inference is an influence of which individuals are unaware, which is immediate, and which cannot be resisted.

To strengthen empiricism, Helmholtz formed the Mechanist Club with his contemporaries Emil du Bois-Raymond, Ernst Brücke and Carl Ludwig. In opposition to vitalism their dictum stated 'no other forces than common physical ones are active within the organism'. Brücke became **Freud**'s teacher who also held a mechanistic view. In psychology Helmholtz worked with **Fechner**, **Wundt** and Donders, and in physics with Farraday, Tyndall and Lord Kelvin. Perhaps no other individual has had as much direct and indirect influence in establishing psychology as a science as did Hermann von Helmholtz.

FRANK WESLEY

Helson, Harold

Born: 1898, Chelsea, Massachusetts, USA *Died:* 1977, Berkeley, California, USA *Nat:* American *Ints:* Engineering psychology, evaluation and measurement, experimental psychology, philosophical and theoretical psychology *Educ:* BA Bowdoin College, 1921; PhD Harvard University, 1924 *Appts & awards:* Instructor in Psychology, Cornell University, 1924–5; Instructor in Psychology, University of Illinois, 1925–6; Assistant Professor of Psychology, University of Kansas, 1926–8; Associate Professor of Psychology, 1928–33, Professor, 1933–49; Director of the Psychological Laboratory, 1928–49; Bryn Mawr College, Professor of Psychology, Brooklyn College, 1949–51; Professor of Psychology, University of Texas, 1951–61; Howard Crosby Warren Medal, 1953; Distinguished Professor, Kansas State University, 1961–7; APA Distinguished Scientific Contribution Award, 1962; Distinguished Professor, York University, Canada, 1967–8; Professor of Psychology, University of

Massachusetts, 1968–71; Fellow, APA, Society of Experimental Psychologists, AAAS

Principal publications

1925 The psychology of *Gestalt. American Journal of Psychology*, 36, 342–70, 494–526; 37, 25–62, 189–223.

1933 The fundamental propositions of *Gestalt* psychology. *Psychological Review*, 40, 13–32.

1936 Size constancy of the projected after-image. *American Journal of Psychology*, 48, 638–42.

1938 Fundamental problems in color vision. 1. The principle governing changes in hue, lightness and saturation of non-selective samples in chromatic illumination. *Journal of Experimental Psychology*, 23, 459–76.

1940 Fundamental problems in color vision. 2. Hue, lightness and saturation of selective samples in chromatic illuminants. *Journal of Experimental Psychology*, 26, 1–27 (with V.B. Jeffer).

1949 Design of equipment and optimal human operation. *American Journal of Psychology*, 62, 473–97.

1951 *Theoretical Foundations of Psychology*. Van Nostrand.

1959 Adaptation-level theory. In S. Koch (ed.), *Psychology: A Study of a Science*, vol. 1. McGraw-Hill.

1964 *Adaptation-Level Theory: An Experimental and Systematic Approach to Behavior*. Harper and Row.

1967 *Contemporary Approaches to Psychology*. Van Nostrand (edited with W. Bevan).

Further reading

Helson H. (1967) Harry Helson. In E.G. Boring and G. Lindzey (eds), *A History of Psychology in Autobiography*, vol. 5. Appleton-Century-Croft.

Helson's first and most enduring attachment was to *Gestalt* psychology. Although something of the power and promise of this approach had been communicated to American psychology by **Köhler** in an expository paper as early as 1922, it was articles from Helson's PhD thesis published in 1925 and 1926 which made *Gestalt* theory immediately accessible. Indeed, so effective was the account that Koffka, a leading figure in the *Gestalt* movement, wanted to use it in his teaching. This affinity also helps to explain why Helson early devoted himself to basic perceptual research in fields such as colour vision since it was here that *Gestalt* psychology had originated and achieved its first successes.

However, Helson increasingly viewed the movement through American-oriented eyes, which meant more rigorously controlled experimentation, and above all the ruthless quest for quantitative laws. This eventually led him to the mathematical notion of adaptation level (or AL), a dynamically operating concept which he claimed was a legitimate extension of *Gestalt* theory. Helson argued that since the task of perception is to present an ordered world to the perceiver in spite of its ever-changing appearance, so AL provides a neutral or indifference point for achieving this order. Although the most extensive coverage of the theory appeared as late as 1964, the beginnings of AL clearly date from experimental work on colour adaptation undertaken by Helson well before World War II.

Predictably, such a simplistic and quasi-Platonic view of the world was not without its critics, particularly as Helson seemed unwilling to limit AL's field of application. Nevertheless, Helson persisted with his claim that AL offered a quantitative extension to *Gestalt* theory and made sense of a great many otherwise inexplicable sensory data.

Although little reference is usually made to Helson's work for the National Defense Research Committee during World War II, this research is actually of considerable historical significance. Thus, from research intended to answer rather mundane questions about the design of hand-operated controls for anti-aircraft guns, Helson extracted general principles for achieving a more effective relationship between people and equipment. This also offers a neat illustration of his pragmatic personal philosophy and the data-driven nature of much of his theoretical work.

A.D. LOVIE AND PATRICIA LOVIE

Henle, Mary

Born: 1913, Cleveland, Ohio, USA *Nat:* American *Ints:* Experimental, history, philosophical and theoretical *Educ:* AB Smith College, 1934; AM Smith College, 1935; PhD Bryn Mawr College, 1939 *Appts & awards:* Professor Emeritus, Graduate Faculty, New School for Social Research; Fellow, John Simon Guggenheim Memorial Foundation, 1951–2, 1960–1; Board of Advisors, Archives of the History of American Psychology, 1969– ; President, APA Division 26, 1971–2, APA Division 24, 1974–5; Board of Directors, Eastern Psychological Association, 1976–79, 1980–3; President, Eastern Psychological Association,

1981–2; Hon. LHD, New School for Social Research, 1983; Associate Editor, *Behavioral and Brain Sciences;* Editorial Board, *Annals of Theoretical Psychology*, *Behaviorism*

Principal publications

1957   Some problems of eclecticism. *Psychological Review*, 64, 296–305.

1961   (ed.) *Documents of Gestalt Psychology.* University of California Press.

1962   On the relation between logic and thinking. *Psychological Review*, 69, 366–78.

1971   (ed.) *Selected Papers of Wolfgang Köhler.* Liveright.

1971   Of the Scholler of nature. *Social Research*, 38, 93–107.

1973   *Historical Conceptions of Psychology.* Springer-Verlag (ed. with J. Jaynes and J.J. Sullivan).

1975   Fishing for ideas. *American Psychologist*, 30, 795–9.

1976   (ed.) *Vision and Artifact.* Springer-Verlag.

1977   The influence of *Gestalt* psychology in America. *Annals of the New York Academy of Sciences*, 291, 3–12.

1978   *Gestalt* psychology and *Gestalt* therapy. *Journal of the History of the Behavioral Sciences*, 14, 23–32.

1978   Kurt Lewin as metatheorist. *Journal of the History of the Behavioral Sciences*, 14, 233–7.

1978   One man against the Nazis – Wolfgang Köhler. *American Psychologist*, 33, 939–44.

1984   Freud's secret cognitive theories. *Annals of Theoretical Psychology*, 1, 111–34.

1985   Rediscovering *Gestalt* psychology. In S. Koch and D. Leary (eds), *A Century of Psychology*. McGraw-Hill.

1986   1879 and all that. In *Essays in the Theory and History of Psychology*. Columbia University Press.

Further reading

O'Connell, A.N. and Russo, N.F. (eds) (1990) *Women in Psychology: A Bio-bibliographic Sourcebook.* Greenwood.

Mary Henle's brother was a professor of philosophy, her twin sister worked in classical archaeology and her sister was a professor of psychology. Her father emigrated to the United States in 1880 at the age of fifteen from Stuttgart. Mary Henle enrolled at Smith College in Northampton, Massachusetts, and majored in French although she took some courses in psychology. She was so stimulated by the faculty of the Department of Psychology that she decided to pursue a master's degree in psychology.

Among the members of the psychology faculty at Smith at that time were **James** and **Eleanor Gibson**.

As an undergraduate student Henle described her 'good fortune' in being exposed to *Gestalt* psychology, as taught by Kurt **Koffka**, and later the 'privilege' of working with Wolfgang **Köhler**. *Gestalt* psychology provided the foundation for her own thinking. Like most young psychologists of her day, she started out as an experimentalist. Her doctoral dissertation combined the methods of Kurt **Lewin** with hypotheses derived from *Gestalt* psychology. With MacKinnon she published what was probably the first laboratory manual in human motivation and personality, *Experimental Studies in Psychodynamics* (1948). Other experimental work was in perception, memory and finally thinking. In the last area, she became interested in the relation of logic to thinking, among other problems. She found that if one really understands the premises of subjects, the way they understand their task, and other aspects of the experimental situation, it is hard to find a logical fallacy in the thinking of adults untrained in logic. Later, comparable results were obtained with children. The investigations were modest and the conclusions about human rationality were correspondingly cautious; but this research led to renewed interest in the problem and to a good deal of controversy.

Very early in her career, while she still considered herself to be mainly an experimentalist, she was drawn, it seemed inevitably, to theoretical, then to historical issues. She wrote numerous articles on the history of *Gestalt* psychology, as well as others which tried to correct the many current misunderstandings of this approach. She examined ways in which contemporary investigations are exploring *Gestalt* problems (perhaps without knowing their origins), comparing their assumptions to those of *Gestalt* psychology. In connection with other approaches, she examined analytically theories of **Lewin**, **Freud**, **Gibson**, **Titchener**, and others.

Hering, Ewald

Born: 1834, Altgersdorf, Germany ***Died:*** 1918, Leipzig, Germany ***Nat:*** German ***Ints:*** Experimental, philosophical and theoretical, physiological and comparative ***Educ:*** MD University of Leipzig, 1858 ***Appts & awards:*** Physiological Research Unit, University of Leipzig, 1862–5; Josephs-Akademie, 1865–70;

Head, Department of Physiology, University of Prague, 1870–95; University of Leipzig, 1895–1918; Graefe Medal German Opthalmological Society, 1906

Principal publications

1861–4 *Beiträge zur Physiologie: Zur Lehre vom Ortsinne der Netzhaut. (Contributors to Philosophy: Retinal Visual Space Perception.)* Engelmann.

1868 *Über des Gedächtnis als eine allgemeine Funktion der organisierten Materie. (Memory as a Function of Organization of Matter.)* Five speeches published 1921. Englemann.

1868 *Zur Lehre vom Lichtsinne.* (*The Visual Sense*). Gerold and Sohn.

1884 Über die spezifischen Energieen des Nervensystems. *Jahrbuch der Naturwissenschaften,* 5, 113–26.

1896 *Handbuch der physiologischen Optik,* 2nd edn. Voss.

1905–29 *Grundzüge der Lehre vom Lichsinn.* 4 parts. (trans L.M. Hurvich and D. Jameson) (Harvard Press, 1964).

Further reading

Garten, S. (1918) Ewald Hering zum Gedächtnis. (In memory of Ewald Hering). *Archiv der gesammten Physiologie,* 170, 501–22.

Hoffman, B.F. (1918) Ewald Hering zum Gedächtnis. *Mäncher medizinische Wochenschrift,* 65, 539–42.

Hurvich, L.M. (1969) Hering and the scientific establishment. *American Psychologist,* 24, 497–514.

Hering began to study medicine and physiology at the University of Leipzig at the age of 19. After being in private practice for several years he worked exclusively in physiological research in Leipzig and Vienna. Due to his physiological discoveries, he was called to the chair of physiology at the University of Prague to succeed Purkinje in 1870. He succeeded another great physiologist, Carl Ludwig, in 1895 when he was called to chair the physiology department at Leipzig.

Though his life's work was in physiology, Hering's theories and experiments on perception of space and colour have had a great influence on experimental psychology. He postulated that there are only three basic retinal colour receptor substances, which account for the perception of the three 'colour' pairs, red–green, yellow–blue and black–white. Since red and green, for example, cannot be sensed simultaneously,

Hering postulated that there is only one receptor for each complementary pair, where a catabolic stimulation for, say, the red–green pair yields the sensation of red and an anabolic one the sensation of green.

Hering's theory, which become known as the 'three-substance, six-colour theory', existed for several decades as an effective alternative to the Young–**Helmholtz** theory. A century later, however, Hering's theory gained dominance when Hurvich and Jameson demonstrated that opponent processes are involved in the perception of colors.

Hering's idea on the perception of temperature was analogous to his colour theory. He proposed one receptor for both warmth and cold, which he termed *Gegenempfindungen* (opponent sensations), being activated by temperature fluctuations from a certain 'zero' of reference point.

He invented several experimental procedures in laboratory instruments for standardizing colours and for examining colour vision. Well known are his coloured papers, his grey scale, the Hering 'illusion', his colour mixer apparatus, and his colour-blindness tester.

Because certain parts of Hering's procedure required introspective reports, and because his theory was opposed to that of the empiricist Helmholtz, he has often been portrayed as a nativist and perhaps as a forerunner of phenomenology and *Gestalt* psychology. However, his painstaking experimental work in physiology and his view that memory and learning are based on changes in cellular physiology made him one of the foremost empiricists

FRANK WESLEY

Hermann, Imre

Born: 1889, Budapest, Hungary **Died:** 1984, Budapest, Hungary **Nat:** Hungarian **Ints:** History of psychology, psychoanalysis **Educ:** Dr Medical Sciences Budapest University, 1913

Principal publications

1921 Über formale Wahltendenzen. *Zeitschrift für Psychologie,* 345–63.

1923 Die Randbevorzugung als Primärvorgang. *IZPsa,* IX, 137–67.

1929 *Das Ich und das Denken.* Psychoanal. Verlag. (Reprinted 1979.)

1933 Zum Trieben der Primaten. Bemerkungen zu S. Zuckerman (The social life of monkeys and apes). *Imago,* XIX, 113–25.

1936 Sich-Anklammern – Auf-Suche-Gehen. Über

ein in der Psychoanalyse bisher vernachlassigtes Triebgegensatzpaar und sein Verhältnis zum Sadismus-Masochismus. *IPZsa*, XXIII, 349–70.

1940   Studien zur Denkpsychologie. Abhängigkeiten des Denkens. Loslösungstheorie. *Acta Psychologica*, V, 22–102.

1941   Die sexuelle Latenzperiode des menschlichen Kindes. *Zeitschrift für Kinderpsychiatrie*, VIII, 97–110.

1972   *L'instinct filial*. Denoël.

1976   Clinging – going in search. A contrasting pair of instincts and their relation to sadism and masochism. *Psychoanal. Quarterly*, XLV, 5836.

1981   Principaux problèmes de la pathographie de Janos Bolyai àparir des manuscripts originaux concernant sa biographie. *Perspectives Psychiatriques*, 19, 311–27.

Further reading

Deri, S. (1990) Great representatives of Hungarian psychiatry: Balint, Ferenczi, Hermann and Szondi. *Psychoanalytic Review*, 77, 491–501.

Jones, C. (1989) Problems of separation and clinging in masochism. In J.D. Montgomery and A.C. Grief, *Masochism: The Treatment of Self-inflicting Suffering*. International Universities Press.

Nemes, L. (1990) Die klinische Bedeutung der Anklammerungstheorie von Imre Hermann (The clinical significance of Imre Hermann's theory of clinging). *Zeitschrift für psychoanalytische Theorie und Praxis*, 5, 112–21.

Imre Hermann's place among the outstanding representatives of psychoanalysis was assured by his theory on the contrasting instinct pair of clinging–going in search. This theory was outlined in 1936 in German and further elaborated in 1972 in French and 1976 in English. He showed how this instinct pair survive as a phylogenetic, archaic inheritance in infants, how it is fed by the desire for the mother–child dual union, how it is embodied in the libidinal organization, and its relation to orality, to the castration complex, to striving for detachment, and to pathological and normal narcissism. The theory, based on results from ethology, ethnology, anthropology, mythology, psychiatry and social psychology, has received support from several later investigations such as **Harlow**'s rhesus experiments or Lawick Goodall's observations on chimpanzees.

The other field of Hermann's main contributions to psychoanalysis is the psychology of thinking. His most famous work here is his study on the edge-preference in choice behaviour. He applied experimental methods in this study as well, and interpreted the results in a primary process framework. He dealt too with the psychology of giftedness and performed psychoanalytic studies on such great thinkers as Hume, J.S. Mill, **Fechner**, **Darwin**, J. Bolyai, etc. After the death of Ferenczi, he became the informal leader of the Budapest School of Psychoanalysis.

Hersen, Michel

Born: 1940, Brussels, Belgium **Nat:** Belgian **Ints:** Clinical, experimental analysis of behaviour **Educ:** BA Queens College, New York, 1961; MA Hofstra University, 1963; PhD State University of New York, 1966 **Appts & awards:** Professor of Psychiatry and Psychology, University of Pittsburgh School of Medicine; President, Association for Advancement of Behavior Therapy, 1979–80; Editor, *Behavior Modification, Journal of Family Violence, Clinical Psychology Review, Progress in Behavior Modification*; Associate Editor, *Addictive Behaviors*; Senior Series Editor, Applied Clinical Psychology, Plenum; Editorial Board, *Behavior Therapy, Journal of Behavior Assessment, Journal of Consulting and Clinical Psychology, Journal of Behavior Therapy and Experimental Psychiatry, Behavior Change*

Principal publications

1972   A token reinforcement ward for young psychiatric patients. *American Journal of Psychiatry*, 129, 228–33 (with R.M. Eisler, B.S. Smith and W.S. Agras).

1973   Single-case experimental designs: Uses in applied clinical research. *Archives of General Psychiatry*, 29, 319–25 (with D.H. Barlow).

1973   Effects of practice, instructions and modeling on components of assertive behavior. *Behaviour Research and Therapy*, 11, 443–51 (with R.M. Eisler, P.M. Miller, M.B. Johnson and S.G. Pinkston).

1976   Social skills training for chronic psychiatric patients: Rationale, research findings and future directions. *Comprehensive Psychiatry*, 17, 559–80 (with A.S. Bellack).

1976   A multiple-baseline analysis of social-skills training in chronic schizophrenics. *Journal of Applied Behavior Analysis*, 9, 239–46 (with A.S. Bellack).

1979   Limitations and problems in the application of behavioral techniques in psychiatric settings. *Behavior Therapy*, 19, 65–80.

1981   Complex problems require complex solutions. *Behavior Therapy*, 12, 15–29.

1982 *International Handbook of Behavior Modification and Therapy.* Plenum (with A.S. Bellack and A.E. Kazdin).

1983 *Behavioral Assessment: A Practical Handbook,* 2nd edn. Pergamon (with A.S. Bellack).

1983 *The Clinical Psychology Handbook.* Pergamon (ed. with A.E. Kazdin and A.S. Bellack).

1983 A comparison of social skills training, pharmacotherapy, and psychotherapy for depression. *Behaviour Research and Therapy,* 21, 101–8 (with A.S. Bellack and J.M. Himmelhoch).

1984 *Handbook of Psychological Assessment.* Pergamon (ed. with G.R. Goldstein).

1984 *Single-Case Experimental Design: Strategies for Studying Behavior Change.* Pergamon (with D.H. Barlow).

1984 Effects of social skills training, amitriptyline, and psychotherapy in unipolar depressed women. *Behavior Therapy,* 15, 21–40 (with A.S. Bellack, J.M. Himmelhoch and M.E. Thase).

1986 A behavioral-analytic model for assessing social skills in blind adolescents. *Behaviour Research and Therapy,* (with V.B. Van Hasselt, A.E. Kazdin, J. Simon and A.K. Mastantuono).

1995 Parameters of marriage in older adults: A review of the literature. *Clinical Psychology Review,* 15, 891–904 (with M.A. Melton and D.T. Van Sickle).

Further reading

Van Hasselt, V.B. and Hersen, M. (eds) (1996) *Sourcebook of Psychological Treatment Manuals for Adult Disorders.* Plenum.

Van Hasselt, V.B. and Hersen, M. (eds) (1993) *Handbook of Behavior Therapy and Pharmacotherapy for Children: A Comparative Analysis.* Allyn and Bacon.

Although Hersen had a strong research background as a graduate student, he began his career in clinical psychology working in private practice with a psychiatrist for three years. In that time he saw an average of thirty different patients a week, of all ages and diagnoses. These years highlighted a variety of clinical and diagnostic issues that he subsequently tackled with colleagues and students in clinical-research studies. Undoubtedly, the experience also contributed to a keen interest in the single-case approach to research. Also, and probably most important, working intensively with patients in this manner convinced him that clinical psychologists who teach others need to maintain active contact throughout their careers with the day-to-day problems in assessing and treating difficult patients. Otherwise, both their clinical training and research is sterile and remote. In the 1980s, together with colleagues, he contributed a number of scholarly texts and edited books on a variety of clinical issues in the hope of categorizing the field at the time, but also with an eye to the future. Their task was made extremely difficult by the burgeoning literatures encountered along the way, reflecting the increased sophistication and methodology in the field in general. They documented the way clinical psychology, as a discipline, is paying heed to the contributions of scholars from other disciplines, including medicine, biology, genetics and physiology, and were impressed with the vast reservoir of knowledge that has been addressed by colleagues in this exciting discipline.

Hess, Walter Rudolf

Born: 1881, Frauenfeld, Thurgau, Switzerland *Died:* 1973, Locarno, Ticino, Switzerland *Nat:* Swiss *Ints:* Neuropsychology, physiological and comparative *Educ:* MD University of Zurich, 1906 *Appts & awards:* Assistant, Department of Surgery and Opthalmology, University of Freiburg, 1905–8; Medical Practitioner, Specialist in Opthalmology, 1908–12; Assistant and Lecturer in Physiology, Zurich and Bonn, 1913–17; Professor of Physiology and Director of the Physiological Department, University of Zurich, 1917–51; Hon. DPhil, University of Berne, 1933; Marcel Benoist Prize, 1933; Ludwigmedaille der deutschen Gesellschaft fur Kreislaufforschung, 1938; Hon. MD, University of Geneva, 1944; Nobel Prize in Medicine and Physiology (shared with Antonio Egas Moniz), 1949; Hon. DSc, McGill University, Montreal, 1953; Johannes Muller Medal, 1971

Principal publications

1931 Le sommeil. *Comptes Rendues de la Societé de Biologie,* 107, 1333–60.

1932 *Beiträge zur Physiologie des Hirnstammes. Vol. 1: Die Methodik der Lokalisierten Reizung und Ausschaltung subkortikaler Hirnabschnitte.* Thieme.

1936 Hypothalamus und die Zentren des autonomen Nervensystems. *Physiologie. Arch. Psychiat. Nervenkr.,* 104, 548–57.

1944 Hypothalamus Adynamie. *Helv. Physiol. Acta,* 2, 137–47.

1948 *Vegetative Funktionen und Zwischenhirn.* Benno Schwabe.

1949   *Das Zwischenhirn: Syndrome, Lokalisationen, Funktionen.* Benno Schwabe.

1949   Le sommeil comme fonction physiologique. *Journal Physio. Path. Gen.*, 41, 61A-3A.

1951   Head-turning and eye deviation evoked by cortical excitation in the freely moving cat. *Fed. Proc.*, 10, 63 (with D.A. McDonald and R.B. Livingstone).

1952   Functions of the orbital gyri of cats. *Brain*, 75, 244–58.

1954   *Diencephalon: Autonomic and Extrapyrimidal Functions.* Grune and Stratton.

1954   The diencephalic sleep centre. In J.F. Delafresnaye (ed.), *Brain Mechanisms and Consciousness.* Thomas.

1955   Experimental data on role of hypothalamus in mechanism of emotional behaviour. *Arch. Neurol. Psychiat.*, 73, 127–9 (with K. Akert).

1956   Beziehungen zwischen psychisen Vorganen und Organisation des Gehirns. *Studium Gen.*, 9, 467–79.

1957   Beziehungen zwischen psychisen. Part II. *Studium Gen.*, 10, 6, 327–39.

1964   *The Biology of the Mind.* University of Chicago Press.

Further reading

Janig, W. (1988) The function of the automatic system as interface between body and environment. Old and new concepts: W.B. Cannon and W.R. Hess revisited. In D.H. Hellhammer, I. Florin and H. Weiner (eds), *Neurobiological Approaches to Human Disease.* Hans Hauber.

Jasper, H.H., Riggio, S. and Goldman-Rakic, P.S. (eds) (1995) Epilepsy and the functional anatomy of the frontal lobe. *Advances in Neurology*, vol. 66. Raven.

Walter Rudolf Hess was qualified in medicine in Zurich in 1906 and originally specialized in opthalmology. In 1912, however, although he was by then in his early thirties and married with a family, he gave up his successful practice and turned to the study of physiology. In 1917 he became Professor of Physiology and Director of the Physiological Department at the University of Zurich, and he held this position until his retirement in 1951 at the age of 70. On a visit to England after World War I he came under the influence of Langley, the great pioneer in the study of the autonomic nervous system, and also of **Sherrington**. Hess's research was at first directed to the study of blood pressure, then to the regulation of breathing, and finally to the central control of the internal organs through the autonomic nervous system. The impact of his work was, however, delayed because his findings were not published in English for some years and were not in fact widely available until after his retirement. Hess was a pioneer in the study of effects of electrical stimulation of the brain on behaviour, and, using cats as subjects, he demonstrated that electrical brain stimulation in the general region of the hypothalamus could elicit a variety of emotional or motivated behaviours ranging from eating and sleeping to hissing, biting and full-blown rage. This 'affective defence reaction' was integrated and involved direct attack. For this body of work Hess shared the 1949 Nobel Prize for medicine and physiology with Antonio Egas Moniz. Prior to this there had been no comparable detailed studies of localization of functions, but Hess had been able to show that actions and behaviour sequences were controlled by discrete, identifiable neural circuits, with different classes of behaviour having overlapped circuits.

CLARE FULLERTON

Hilgard, Ernest Ropiequet
Born: 1904, Belleville, Illinois, USA *Nat:* American *Ints:* Conditioning, consciousness, general psychology, history of psychology, hypnosis, learning *Educ:* BS University of Illinois, 1924; PhD Yale University, 1930 *Appts & awards:* Instructor in Psychology, Yale University, 1929–33; Stanford University, Assistant Professor, Associate Professor, Professor of Psychology, 1933–69, Chairman, Department of Psychology, 1942–51, Dean of Graduate Division, 1951–5, Director, Laboratory of Hypnosis Research, 1957–79, Emeritus Professor of Psychology and Education, 1969– ; Warren Medal in Experimental Psychology, 1940; Wilbur Cross Medal, 1940; President, Society for the Psychological Study of Social Issues, 1944, APA, 1949; Fellow, Center, Advanced Study of the Behavioral Sciences, 1956–7; Hon. DSc, Kenyon College, 1964; Distinguished Scientific Contribution Award, APA, 1969; President, Division 30 (Psychological Hypnosis), APA, 1970; Yale Graduate School, 1972; Chairman, Society of Experimental Psychologists, 1972; President, International Society of Hypnosis, 1973–6; Hon. LLD, Centre College, 1974; Gold Medal Award, American Psychological Foundation, 1978; Franklin Gold Medal, International Society of Hypnosis, 1980; National Academy of Sciences Award for Scientific Reviewing,

1984; Hon. DSc, Colgate University, 1987; Hon. DSc, Northwestern University, 1987; Member, International Brain Research Organization, 1988; William James Fellow, American Psychological Society, 1989; APA Division 30 Award for Distinguished Contributions to Scientific Hypnosis, 1993; APA Certificate for Distinguished Lifetime Contributions to Psychology, 1994; Hon. PhD, University of Oslo, 1994; Hon. Fellow, BPS; Hon. Member, International Association for the Study of Pain; President, APA Division 26 (History of Psychology), 1981, Society for Clinical and Experimental Hypnosis, 1979–81; APA Divisions 2, 3, 9, 15, 26, 30, 31

Principal publications

1931 Conditioned eyelid reactions to a light stimulus based on the reflex wink to sound. *Psychological Monographs*, 41, whole no. 184.

1940 *Conditioning and Learning*. Appleton Century (with D.G. Marquis). (2nd edn, 1961.)

1948 *Theories of Learning*. Appleton-Century-Crofts. (Subsequent edns, latest 5th, with G.H. Bower, Prentice-Hall.)

1949 Human motives and the concept of self. *American Psychologist*, 4, 374–82.

1953 *Introduction to Psychology*. Harcourt Brace Jovanovich, (Subsequent edns: 10th edn with R.L. Atkinson, R.C. Atkinson, E.E. Smith and D.J. Bem, Harcourt Brace Jovanovich, 1990; 11th, 1993; 12th, 1995; edns by authors other than Hilgard; also in Chinese, French, German, Hebrew, Italian, Portuguese and Spanish edns.)

1961 Hypnosis and experimental psychodynamics. In H. Brosin (ed.), *Lectures on Experimental Psychodynamics*. Pittsburgh University Press.

1965 *Hypnotic Susceptibility*. Harcourt Brace Jovanovich.

1968 *The Experience of Hypnosis*. Harcourt Brace Jovanovich.

1969 Pain as a puzzle for psychology and physiology. *American Psychologist*, 24, 103–13.

1970 Issues bearing on recommendations from the behavioural and social sciences survey committee. *American Psychologist*, 25, 456–68.

1973 The domain of hypnosis: With some comments on alternative paradigms. *American Psychologist*, 28, 972–82.

1975 Hypnosis. *Annual Review of Psychology*, 26, 19–45.

1975 *Hypnosis in the Relief of Pain*. Willam Kaufmann. (2nd edn, 1986; rev. edn, Brunner/Mazel, 1994; with J.R. Hilgard.)

1977 *Divided Consciousness: Multiple Controls in Human Thought and Action*. Wiley/Interscience. (Enlarged edn, 1986).

1978 *American Psychology in Historical Perspective*. APA.

1980 Consciousness in contemporary psychology. *Annual Review of Psychology*, 31, 1–27.

1987 *Psychology in America: A Historical Survey*. Harcourt Brace Jovanovich.

1994 Neodissociation Theory. In S.J. Lynn and J.W. Rhue (eds), *Dissociation: Clinical and Theoretical Perspectives*. Guilford Press.

Further reading

Hilgard, E.R. (1967) *American Psychologist*, 22, 1130–5.
—— (1974) Autobiography. In G. Lindzey (ed.), *A History of Psychology in Autobiography*. vol. 6, 129–60. Prentice-Hall.
Kirsch, I. and Lynn, S.J. (1995) The altered state of hypnosis. *American Psychologist*, 50, 846–58.
Sears, R.R. (1979) Hilgard, Ernest R. In *International Encyclopedia of the Social Sciences*, Biographical Supplement, 18, 303–5.

Ernest Ropiequet Hilgard was born in 1904 in Belleville, Illinois, into a medical family. Early thoughts of a medical career were fatefully changed when his father died on medical service in France in 1918. 'Jack' Hilgard chose chemical engineering as his undergraduate major at the University of Illinois because he liked and had done well at science in high school. However, somewhat undecided about his future after graduation, the 21-year-old Hilgard spent a 'moratorium' year as a YMCA counsellor to enable him to make up his mind about his career. He then obtained a fellowship enabling him to enrol in the Yale Divinity School, where he studied philosophy, Greek, biblical criticism and some social ethics. That summer he also gained valuable industrial experience at a Ford plant near Detroit, sharing first prize for an essay concerned with Henry Ford's methods for preventing unionization of his factories.

The young Hilgard's internal struggle between scientific and humanitarian concerns led him to psychology. Hilgard re-enrolled in 1926 at Yale, where Dodge, **Gesell** and **Yerkes** were on the staff. Three years later he assisted in the organization of the International Congress of Psychology in New Haven and came into contact with **Pavlov**, **Claparède**, Pieron, **Spearman**, **Michotte**, **Piaget**, **Rubin**, **Köhler** and **Lewin** from abroad, and **Boring**, **Lashley**, **Cattell**, **Ladd-Franklin**, **McDougall**, **Thorndike**, **Woodworth** and others from the USA.

Hilgard completed his doctoral dissertation on eyelid conditioning in 1930 under the supervision of Raymond Dodge. This investigation of the differences between reflexes, conditioned reflexes and voluntary action presaged a deep interest in consciousness and the differentiation of involuntary and voluntary action following suggestion and hypnosis. Hilgard remained at Yale for three years and worked with Donald **Marquis** on occipitally decorticated dogs. Hilgard and Marquis's *Conditioning and Learning* set the stage for this primary area of teaching and research during the 1940s and 1950s.

In 1933 Hilgard moved to Stanford, where he spent the remainder of his long and productive working life. For the first seven years he continued to study learning and conditioning while developing an interest in education. Promotion came fairly rapidly and Hilgard was made full professor in 1938 and, following **Terman** and McNemar, accepted a joint appointment in psychology and education. In the early 1940s, new influences led Hilgard to change his orientation. In 1940–1 he and his wife, Dr **Josephine Hilgard**, spent a year's sabbatical at the University of Chicago. Hilgard worked with Daniel Prescott and acquired expertise in testing the abilities of children and interacted with **Thurstone**, Kornhauser, **Gulliksen**, Stouffer, **Tyler** and Wolfe. Josephine Hilgard undertook training at the Chicago Psychoanalytic Institute, bringing her husband into contact with the psychoanalytical orientation for the first time. Then, after Pearl Harbor, Hilgard went to Washington in 1942 to serve in a programme of national opinion surveys with **Likert**, Gallup, Lazarsfeld, Benedict, Gorer, Doob and Peak. While in Washington, Hilgard actively participated in a discussion group with Rensis Likert, Margaret Mead and others. This wartime experience in applied social psychology widened his horizons and completed his conversion from 'conditioned reflexer' to generalist.

Hilgard was made head of department at Stanford in absentia in 1942. After returning there, he developed its laboratories and programmes in developmental and clinical psychology, and wrote *Theories of Learning* and *Introduction to Psychology*, the latter the most influential psychology textbook of all time, selling in various editions over two million copies. In 1951 Hilgard was appointed Dean of the Graduate Division. He brought in Robert **Sears** from Harvard to the headship of psychology, secured large grants from the Ford Foundation to develop the social sciences, and

helped the establishment of the Center for Advanced Study in the Behavioral Sciences on the Stanford campus. However, this period was marred by McCarthyist claims which questioned his loyalty to the United States. Hilgard's liberal views about minority groups, the folly of war, and freedom of speech had been viewed with suspicion as being possibly Communist inspired; this meant that he was not permitted to review classified research projects and so he foreshortened his deanship after four years.

Shortly after returning to the professor's role, Hilgard visited Europe, where he had been invited by Jerome **Bruner** to attend a small conference on cognitive processes at St John's College, Cambridge, where he met **Broadbent**, Mackworth, Oldfield, **Magdalen Vernon**, **Zangwill**, Nuttin, **Brown**, **Miller**, **Pribram** and **Werner**. He also met Lord Adrian, John **Bowlby** and then Anna **Freud** in Maresfield Gardens, Hampstead, where he saw **Sigmund Freud**'s study in what is now the Freud Museum. He attended the International Congress of Psychoanalysis in Geneva where he met Ernest **Jones** and Melanie **Klein**.

In addition to his scholarly and teaching activities, Hilgard enjoyed and gave freely of his time to a wide range of professional and community activities. He was a prime mover in keeping the APA together at a time when there were serious rifts between academic and applied psychologists, during the early 1940s. He served on national policy advisory bodies, as president of Annual Reviews Inc., and in a wide range of regional and local community organizations, schools, and societies.

In 1955 Hilgard was successful in securing $500,000 from the Ford Foundation for a Laboratory of Human Development to be managed by the Sears and the Hilgards. This was followed shortly thereafter by two life-changing decision: (1) to start research on hypnosis and, (2) to throw away all his old lecture notes and, apart from his introductory course, to teach only courses he had not taught before. So Hilgard began to teach abnormal psychology, dynamic psychology and motivation, which he found exhilarating. This new wave of intellectual interest carried him into his emeritus years from 1969 on, and there has been little abatement of intellectual activity ever since. Perhaps there is a lesson here in his autobiography for all of us: 'If I had it all to do again would I do the same? That is a rhetorical question; if I wish to be different now, it is up to me, for there are still some years ahead.'

Modestly, Hilgard himself does not place great value on his own scientific achievements, even expressing disappointment at what he sees as their limitations. He views his research on hypnosis as having most coherence, although the thousands of psychologists who were trained using one or more of his textbooks on learning might well wish to argue that his treatment of conditioning and learning was also of considerable importance in conceptualizing and shaping the field.

Hilgard regarded the core theme of his researches to be 'a concern for aspects of human motivation bearing on planning and choice. However, in reflecting upon his work in late 1970 he believed that it, particularly its eclectic spirit, lacked profundity and that his intellectual style matched that of Woodworth and Boring rather than **Hull**, Lewin, Piaget or **Tolman**.

As I write this biographical entry from a distant and external perspective a quarter-century after Hilgard's original self-evaluation, his contribution is judged to outstrip easily that of Hull, Lewin and Tolman. His neo-dissociation theory was only just beginning to emerge in 1970, and was published in *Psychological Review* in 1973 and in book form in 1977. This theory provides the most systematic theoretical framework for the understanding of volition and consciousness yet produced by any psychologist. It is the standard reference point for all current discussions of hypnosis and is seen generally as an advance in consciousness research. Dissociation is defined as a division of consciousness in which attentive effort, planning and monitoring are conducted without awareness. Neo-dissociation theory contains three main assumptions: (1) a central control system or 'executive ego' that performs planning and monitoring functions; (2) relatively autonomous subordinate cognitive-behavioural systems; (3) a hierarchical arrangement of subsystems of control. The perceived involuntariness of action under hypnosis occurs because the action is controlled by a subsystem which is separated from conscious awareness as a result of an artificially induced communications barrier. A similar explanation is available for the many instances of dissociation that occur routinely in daily life (e.g. distraction, dichotic listening, divided attention, imagining, daydreaming). Thus neo-dissociation theory provides a single account of many mundane phenomena of conscious experience and the more extreme forms of dissociation available in hypnosis.

Ernest Ropiequet Hilgard's contribution to theories and systems of psychology is second to none. His penchant for 'psychologizing' is without equal since William **James**. There has not been a more eclectic, productive and yet deep thinker in twentieth-century psychology than he. Some rivers run wide, some rivers run deep; a few rivers run wide and deep.

DAVID F. MARKS

Hilgard, Josephine Rohrs

Born: 1906, Napoleon, Ohio, USA *Died:* 1989, California, USA *Nat:* American *Ints:* Child psychology; personality; pain; hypnosis *Educ:* BSc Smith College, 1928; MA Yale University, 1930; PhD Yale University, 1933; MD Stanford Medical School, 1940 *Appts & awards:* Elected to medical honors society Alpha Omega Alpha, 1940; Certificate in Psychoanalysis, Washington-Baltimore Psychoanalytic Institute, 1946; Stanford Medical School, Associate Clinical Professor, Clinical Professor, 1947–81, Clinical Professor Emerita, 1971–89; Franklin Gold Medal, International Society of Hypnosis, 1985

Principal publications

1932   Learning and maturation in preschool children. *Journal of Genetic Psychology*, 41, 36–56.

1933   The effects of early and delayed practice on memory and motor performances studied by the method of co-twin control. *Genetic Psychology Monographs*, 14, 493–565.

1975   *Hypnosis in the Relief of Pain*. William Kaufmann   (with E.R. Hilgard) (2nd edn, 1986; rev. edn, Brunner/Mazel, 1994.)

1979   *Personality and Hypnosis,* 2nd edn. University of Chicago Press.

1984   *Hypnotherapy of Pain in Children with Cancer*. William Kaufmann (with S. LeBaron).

1989   The anniversary syndrome as related to late-appearing mental illness in hospitalized patients. In A.L.S. Silver (ed.), *Psychoanalysis and Psychosis*. International Universities Press.

Further reading

My life as a professional, a wife, and a mother (1991). In F.M. Carp (ed.), *Lives of Career Women: Approaches to Work, Marriage, Children*. Plenum/ Insight.

The only child of a physician and a surgeon, Josephine Rohrs Hilgard was born and raised through her high school years in Ohio.

Josephine Rohr's mother took a great interest in her education and tried to steer the young woman towards a career in music. However, after a lack of success with the piano, violin or singing, her mother permitted her to take up the banjo, providing a hobby for the rest of her life. Succeeding with good grades in high school, she spent two years at Radcliffe College studying experimental psychology with **Boring** and social psychology with **McDougall**, followed by two years at Smith College where she majored in child psychology under the direction of Margaret Wooster Curti. Of particular interest was the observational study of children in nursery school which formed part of the course. Josephine Rohrs then went to Yale University to take graduate courses with Arnold **Gesell**. It was at Yale that Josephine Rohrs met her future husband, **Ernest R. 'Jack' Hilgard**, whom she married in 1931. In 1933, she was awarded her PhD and elected to full membership in Sigma Xi, the scientific honor society.

There were difficulties relating to the war, the historical setting, and the move to Stanford. In the 1930s universities were heavily dominated by males, and the anti-nepotism rule at Stanford made it difficult for spouses to work in the same department. Also, private practice was not viable at that time. This led Josephine Hilgard to develop a career in medicine so as to avoid the 'two psychologists' problem. She quickly completed the requirements for acceptance into Stanford Medical School and successfully completed her medical training in 1940, having also started a family, the Hilgards' son Henry having been born in 1936.

Hilgard complemented her MD by studying psychoanalysis in Chicago and Washington-Baltimore, becoming certificated as a psychoanalyst in 1946. While in Rockville, Maryland, she worked with psychotic patients under the guidance of Harry **Stack Sullivan** and Frieda Fromm-Reichmann. Before leaving Washington to return to Stanford the Hilgards adopted a baby daughter, Elizabeth (or 'Lisby'). In 1947 Hilgard began what turned out to be long service with the Department of Psychiatry at Stanford Medical School. Here she became associate clinical professor until she became clinical professor emerita in 1971. Hilgard undertook research in the area of sibling rivalry and 'social heredity', a transgenerational form of sibling rivalry. She reported an extensive series of studies of the so-called 'anniversary reactions' and worked on affiliative therapy, in which well-adjusted and disturbed adolescents interacted under supervision.

Towards the end of her career, Hilgard joined her husband in researching some of the clinical and social aspects of hypnosis. This led to seminal work on individual differences in hypnotic susceptibility in both adults and children. Josephine Hilgard led a full, successful and inspirational life, making a considerable contribution to knowledge concerning child psychology, hypnotherapy and pain, and hypnotic susceptibility. Through her work as a psychotherapist, she helped hundreds of children and parents to live more fulfilling, happier lives.

DAVID F. MARKS

Himmelweit, Hilde Therese

Born: 1918, Berlin, Germany **Nat:** German **Ints:** Cognitive, educational, personality and social, political psychology and decision making, social, study of the media and their impact **Educ:** BA Cambridge, 1940; MA Cambridge, 1942; PhD London 1942 **Appts & awards:** Professor Emeritus of Social Psychology, University of London, 1945; Hon. Doc., Open University, 1976; BPS, Fellow, 1952, Social Psychology Section, Chairman, 1953; Founder Member, European Association of Experimental Social Psychology, 1953; Chairman, Academic Advisory Committee of the Open University, 1969–74; Trustee, International Institute of Communications, 1973–9, Centre for Contemporary Studies, 1980– ; Member, Committee on Television and Social Behavior, United States Social Science Research Council, 1973–9, Annan Committee on the Future of Broadcasting in Britain, 1974–7; Vice-President, International Society of Political Psychology, 1978–81; Nevitt Sanford Award, International Society of Political Psychology, 1981; Editorial Board, *Journal of Social and Clinical Psychology, Journal of Communication, International Journal of Communication Research, Interdisciplinary Science Review, Applied Social Psychology Annual, Media, Culture and Society*

Principal publications

1946 Speed and accuracy of work as related to temperament. *British Journal of Psychology*, 36, 132.

1947 A comparative study of the level of aspiration of normal and neurotic persons. *British Journal of Psychology*, 37, 11.

1951 The measurement of personality in children. *British Journal of Educational Psychology*, 21, 9.

1958 *Television and the Child*. Oxfriord University
Press (with A.N. Oppenheim and P. Vince).

1963 A social psychologist's view of the school
psychological service of the future. *Bulletin of the
British Psychological Society*.

1969 A model for the understanding of school as a
socialization agent. In P. Mussen, J. Langer and M.
Covington (eds), *Trends and Issues in
Developmental Psychology*. Holt, Rinehart and
Winston.

1971 Adolescent and adult authoritarianism
examined: Organisation and stability over time.
Journal of European Social Psychology, 3 (1).

1975 Studies of societal influences: Problems and
implications. In M. Deutsch and H. Hornstein
(eds), *Applying Social Psychology: Implications
for Research, Practice and Training*. Erlbaum.

1976 Continuities and discontinuities in media
usage and taste: A longitudinal study of adolescents
re-examined at ages 25 and 33. *Journal of Social
Issues*, 32 (4).

1979 The audience as critic: An approach to the
study of entertainment. In P. Tannenbaum (ed.),
The Entertainment Functions of Television.
Erlbaum (with B. Swift and M. Jaeger).

1981 *How Voters Decide*. Academic Press (with P.
Humphreys, M. Jaeger and M. Katz).

1982 Social psychological antecedents of
depression: A longitudinal study from adolescence
to early adulthood of a non-clinical population. In
P.B. Balthes and O.G. Brimm (eds), *Life-Span
Development and Behavior*, vol. 4. Academic Press
(with C.F. Turner).

1985 *How Voters Decide*, rev. and updated edn.
Open University Press (with P. Humphreys and M.
Jaeger).

1990 *Societal Psychology*. Sage (with G. Gaskell).

Further reading

Fraser, C. and Gaskell, G. (1990) *The Social
Psychological Study of Widespread Beliefs*.
Clarendon Press/Oxford University Press.

Himmelweit worked first with **Bartlett** and
then as a clinical research psychologist with
children, and in the Army Neurosis Centre
during World War II. The war and its aftermath
left a desire to use social psychology to study
people's adaptability to change. The opportunity arose when she was asked to develop social
psychology at the London School of Economics, first within the sociology department,
and later in an independent department of social
psychology. It provided a unique opportunity to
bring together the traditions of the different
disciplines.

Her interests lay in the interplay of
individuals and institutions within the political
and cultural climate of a society. This approach
required her, when studying an ongoing social
issue, to develop a conceptual framework or a
model that traced the pathways of influences
and processes, specifying the conditions affecting their relative strength. Such a model, to be
of value, had to be dynamic, building on
change. Sometimes the problem studied was
commissioned, e.g. the impact of television on
the young; at other times she sought to elucidate
some theoretical propositions, e.g. that of
sociologists concerning the relative role of
social background and school as socializing
agents, or that of political scientists' theories
concerning voters' decision making.

Her earlier work on personality tests made her
interested in using them in broader studies, but
also aware that the role of individuals' predispositions varies with time and depends on the
social context. In the case of television, it was
possible to do an experimental field study using
controls; in others, she had to draw on existing
variations in institutions and socializing experiences, requiring some novel approaches to
measurement and analysis. Three different
models have been developed which have stood
the test of time: one concerning the displacement and stimulation effects of television, one
of the relative impact of home and school on the
young, and finally a cognitive model of
individuals' voting decisions. In every case, a
longitudinal element was introduced into the
study to trace change over time (in the case of
television, one year and fifteen years; in the
case of voting, over twenty years). The research
also threw light on basic psychological processes by placing them within a social context,
and so examined variations in the role they play
in people's cognitions and behaviour.

Hinde, Robert Aubrey

Born: 1923, Norwich, England *Nat:* British
Ints: Comparative and physiological psychol-
ogy, developmental psychology, ethology,
personality and social psychology *Educ:* BA
Cambridge; BSc London, 1948; DPhil Oxford,
1950; ScD Cambridge, 1958 *Appts & awards:*
Zoological Society Medal, 1961; Research
Professor and Fellow, Royal Society, 1963–89;
Hon. Director, MRC Unit on Development and
Integration of Behaviour at Madingley,
1970–89; Royal Society Fellowship, 1974;
Hon. Fellow, American Ornithologists Union,

1976; Member, US Academy of Arts and Science, 1974, National Academy of Sciences, 1978; Leonard Cammer Award, New York Psychiatric Institute, 1980; Hon. Member BPS, 1981; Commander of the British Empire, 1988

Principal publications

1966, 1970   *Animal Behaviour: A Synthesis of Ethology and Comparative Psychology*. McGraw-Hill.

1970   *Short-Term Changes in Neural Activity and Behaviour*. Cambridge University Press (ed. with G. Horn).

1973   *Constraints on Learning*. Academic Press (ed. with J. Stevenson-Hinde).

1974   *Biological Bases of Human Social Behaviour*. McGraw-Hill.

1976   *Growing Points in Ethology*. Cambridge University Press (ed. with P.P.G. Bateson).

1979   *Toward Understanding Relationships*. Academic Press.

1982   *Ethology: Its Nature and Relations with Other Sciences*. Oxford University Press.

1983   (ed.) *Primate Social Relationships: An Integrated Approach*. Blackwell.

1987   *Individuals, Relationships and Culture*. Cambridge University Press.

1988   *Relationships with Families*. Clarendon Press (ed. with J. Stevenson-Hinde).

1991   *Cooperation and Prosocial Behaviour*. Cambridge University Press (ed. with J. Groebel).

1991   (ed.) *The Institution of War*. Macmillan.

Further reading

Bateson, P. (1991) *The Development and Integration of Behavior: Essays in Honour of Robert Hinde*. Cambridge University Press.

Dewsbury, D.A. (1985) *Leaders in the Study of Animal Behavior*. Bucknell University Press.

Thorpe, W.H. (1979) *The Origins and Rise of Ethology*. Praeger.

Robert Hinde has been a pivotal figure in the integration of ethology with other disciplines, with well over 300 publications related to ecology, comparative psychology, behavioural neuroendocrinology, primatology, developmental psychology, and human behavioural biology. With characteristic modesty, Hinde has described himself as a not-very-outstanding student whose hard work, perseverance and luck paid off. Born the last of four children to a family doctor and nurse, his early education was primarily at Oundle, an English boarding school with a fortunate emphasis on natural history. He spent World War II flying between Scotland and the Maldive Islands, doing his part 'without having to kill anyone'. Following the war he obtained his BA at St John's College, Cambridge, followed by a PhD at Oxford under the influence of David Lack, a renowned ecologist, and the newly arrived Niko **Tinbergen**.

Hinde immediately became curator at William Thorpe's ornithological field station at Madingley, Cambridge, where he has remained to the present. The 1950s were a time of remarkable growth in ethology as well as intense conceptual conflict with American comparative psychologists. Hinde helped meliorate antagonisms with his analytic approach and personability, but his major contribution was his masterful animal behaviour book, summarizing and integrating research from both disciplines. He also contributed to synthesis as an editor of *Advances in the Study of Behavior* from 1965 to 1980.

Hinde is often credited with driving the study of motivation out of ethology with his trenchant critique of **Lorenz**'s general 'hydraulic' model. The credit is ironical in that Hinde did some of the finest research on the interaction of structure and function in motivation, clearly establishing the existence of multiple regulatory processes underlying mobbing in chaffinches and the neuroendocrine and stimulus control of nesting behaviour in canaries. As he indicated in his book *Ethology*, his work can be viewed as a call for a more complex understanding of motivation rather than as an invalidation of the concept.

During the 1950s Hinde first became interested in primate and human development, primarily through participating in a markedly interdisciplinary continuing seminar organized by the psychoanalyst John **Bowlby**. With monetary assistance through Bowlby and the critical collaboration of Thelma Rowell and later Yvette Spencer-Booth, he began to study the effects of separation between mother and infant rhesus monkeys as a function of their pre-separation relationship. Because of his experience with ethology and primates, Hinde subsequently supervised Jane Goodall's thesis on chimpanzee social behavior in Gombe, which led to his role as mentor and facilitator of a wide variety of field research projects on tropical primates and large mammals.

In the 1980s Hinde and his second wife, Joan Stevenson-Hinde, began to delve into the family and school relations of pre-school children and their role in the development of personality. With typical energy and thoroughness he mastered the vast research literature on human development and social interaction. Although troubled by the paucity of good answers, Hinde refused to retreat to the safer stance of a pure natural scientist. Instead he and Stevenson-Hinde combined techniques of ethological observation with more traditional interviews, questionnaires and tests to clarify the development of personality. After retiring as head of the MRC unit at Madingley in 1989, he served as Master of St John's college until 1994, while continuing unabated his most recent work on social relations and war. By squeezing so many careers into one lifetime, Hinde's contribution to any one subject ultimately may have been lessened. But his penetrating understanding of research and his ability to forge ahead at full speed has benefited science and his students immeasurably, as together they translated classical ethology into modern multidisciplinary research.

WILLIAM TIMBERLAKE

Hirsch, Jerry

Born: 1922, New York, USA **Nat:** American **Ints:** Behaviour genetics, comparative psychology, conditioning and learning experimental psychology, **Educ:** BA, University of California at Berkeley, 1952; PhD University of California at Berkeley, 1955 **Appts & awards:** Professor of Psychology and of Ecology, Ethology, and Evolution, University of Illinois at Urbana-Champaign; NIH Fellow, Center for Advanced Study in Behavioral Science, 1960–1; SSRC Auxiliary Research Award, 1962; Animal Behavior Society, Representative-at-Large, 1967; Executive Committee, 1967–76, President, 1975, Representative to AAAS, 1975–90; Chairman, Member Nominating Committee, 1976–9, British Science Council Visiting Research Scholar, 1968; Member, US Delegation to International Ethological Conference Committee, 1975–81; Member, US National Committee to International Union of Biological Sciences of NRC, 1976–82; Member, Executive Committee, APA Division 6, 1983–6; Robert Choate Tryon Memorial Lecturer, University of California at Berkeley 1987; Hon. Dr, Université de René Descartes, Paris, 1987; American Editor, *Animal Behavior*, 1968–72; Editorial Advisory Board, *Behavior Genetics*, 1971– ; Editor, *Journal of Comparative Psychology*, 1982–8

Principal publications

1956   Mass Screening and reliable individual measurement in the experimental behavior genetics of lower organisms. *Psychological Bulletin*, 53, 402–10 (with R.C. Tryon).

1963   Behavior genetics and individuality understood: Behaviorism's counterfactual dogma blinded the behavioral sciences to the significance of meiosis. *Science*, 142, 1436–42.

1967   (ed.) *Behavior-Genetic Analysis*. McGraw-Hill.

1967   Behavior-genetic, or 'experimental', analysis: The challenge of science versus the lure of technology. *American Psychologist*, 22, 118–30.

1975   Jensenism: The bankruptcy of 'science' without scholarship. *Educational Theory*, 25, 3–27, 102.

1977   Behavior-genetic analysis of *Phormia regina*: Conditioning, reliable individual differences, and selection. *Proceedings of the National Academy of Sciences USA*, 74, 5193–7 (with T.R. McGuire).

1981   To 'unfrock the charlatans'. *SAGE Race Relations Abstracts*, 6, 2, 1–65.

1982   *Behavior-Genetic Analysis*. Hutchinson Ross (ed. with T.R. McGuire).

1985   Evolution of an instinct under long-term divergent selection for geotaxis in domesticated populations of *Drosophila melanogaster. Journal of Comparative Psychology*, 99, 380–90 (with J. Ricker).

1986   Behavior-genetic analysis. In J. Medioni and G. Vaysse (eds), *Readings from the 19th International Ethological Conference: Genetic Approaches to Behavior*.

1986   Excitatory conditioning of individual *Drosophila melanogaster. Journal of Experimental Psychology: Animal Behavior Processes*, 12, 131–42 (with M. Holliday).

1986   Que savons nous des rapports entre l'intelligence et l'heredité. *Psychologie Française*, 31, 258–60.

Jerry Hirsch's contributions have been conceptual, methodological and substantive. They have revolutionized our understanding of individual differences to the study of relations between heredity and behaviour (now called behaviour-genetic analysis or, more precisely, behaviour-genetic component analysis) and of racism. They have achieved this through an articulation of the nature of these so-called problems and the possibilities for, or limitations on, their study in bisexual, cross-fertilizing, diploid, metazoan species, by clarifying that relations between heredity and behaviour can be characterized as neither isomorphic (the strong biological determinism required to justify human racism) nor independent (the strong environmental determinism required to justify radical behaviourism). The facts of individuality (individual genotypic uniqueness), norm of reaction (same genotype developing different phenotypes in different environments) and genotype–environment interaction (same environment supporting different development in different genotypes) defeat extremists at both ends of the heredity–environment spectrum. Social **Darwin**ist eugenists cannot breed their ideal type, and egalitarians cannot create conditions that will be equally favourable for, or satisfactory to, all individuals. The development of the method of mass screening and its physical realization in the multiple unit discrimination apparatuses (for geotaxis or phototaxis) have made possible the simultaneous study – the Behaviour Genetic Analysis – in *Drosophila* populations not only of reliably measured phenotypic individual differences in behaviour-trait expression, but of their geneotypic correlates, and of significant evolutionary changes in divergent subpopulations subjected to long-term (thirty years') intermittent artificial selection pressure. The development of the automatic stimulus presentation apparatus has permitted measurement of the excitatory conditioning and extinction of the proboscis-extension feeding reflex in individual *Drosophila*. Thus it is now feasible experimentally to study simultaneously the influence of heredity (the *Drosophila* genetic system) and experience (the conditioning history) in the same replicable individuals – literally an animal model for the experimental analysis of heredity–experience interactions.

Hochberg, Julian

Born: 1923, New York, USA **Nat:** American **Ints:** Engineering psychology, experimental, history of psychology, psychology and the arts **Educ:** BS (Physics) CCNY, 1945; MA University of California at Berkeley, 1947; PhD University of California at Berkeley, 1949 **Appts & awards:** Centennial Professor of Psychology and Chairman of the Department of Psychology, Columbia University; National Academy of Sciences; Society of Experimental Psychologists; Guggenheim Fellowship, APA Division 10, 1968; Past President, EPA, 1977, APA Division 3, 1983; Distinguished Scientific Contribution Award, APA, 1978; Editorial Board, *Journal of Experimental Psychology: Human Perception and Performance*, *Journal of Experimental Psychology: General Contemporary Psychology*, *Psychological Review*, *Perceptual Motor Skills*

Principal publications

1951   Colour adaptation under conditions of homogenous stimulation. (Ganzfeld), *Journal of Experimental Psychology*, 41, 153–9 (with W.A. Triebel and G. Seaman).

1954   *Methods in Psychology*. ONR.

1960   The psychophysics of form: Reversible perspective drawings of spatial objects. *American Journal of Psychology*, 73, 332–4 (with V. Brooks).

1962   Pictorial recognition as an unlearned ability: A study of one child's performance. *American Journal of Psychology*, 75, 624–8 (with V. Brooks).

1964   *Perception*. Prentice-Hall. (2nd, edn. 1978).

1968   In the mind's eye. In R. Haber (ed.), *Contemporary Theory and Research in Visual Perception*. Holt, Rinehart and Winston.

1971   *Art, Perception and Reality*. Johns Hopkins University Press (with E. Gombrich and M. Black).

1978   Film cutting and visual momentum. In Senders (ed.), *Eye Movements and the Higher Psychological Functions*. Erlbaum (with V.Brooks).

1981   Levels of perceptual organisation. In M. Kubovy and J. Pomerantz (eds), *Perceptual Organisation*. Erlbaum.

1983   Visual perception in architecture. *Via*, 26–45.

1984   Form perception: Experience and explanations. In P.C. Dodwell and T. Caelli (eds), *Figural synthesis*. Erlbaum.

1986   Representation of motion and space in video and cinematic displays. In K. Boff *et al.* (eds), *Handbook of Perception and Human Performance*. Wiley.

1986   Visual perception of real and represented objects and events. In N. Smelser and D. Gerstein (eds), *Behaviour and Social Science: Fifty Years of Discovery*. National Academy Press.

1991   Geometrical illusions in solid objects under ordinary viewing conditions. *Perception and Psychophysics*, 50, 547–54 (with P.R. DeLucia).

Further reading

Atkinson, R.C., Hernstein, R.J., Lindzey, G. and Luce, R.D. (1988) *Stevens' Handbook of Experimental Psychology*, vol. 1: *Perception and Motivation*. Wiley.

Ballesteros, S. (ed.) *Cognitive Approaches to Human Perception*. Erlbaum.

Between 1949 and 1962, Hochberg considered that perceptual organization could be captured by a 'simplicity principle': of two possible physical structures that could generate a given stimulus pattern, we perceive the simpler, according to some quantitative measure (in moving objects this can reduce to a rigidity principle). Although that approach survives, in 1962 he was convinced that it was incompatible with the fact that the world is sampled by elective attentional actions, and that the schemata which integrate those glances are subject not to the consistency constraints of the physical world, but to rules yet to be explored systematically. The problem of how humans perceive objects and events has, more recently, become central in cognitive psychology; it is also theoretically important for computer vision, in so far as that discipline seeks to emulate human perception. Both disciplines still tend to overlook the characteristic differences between perceived and physical world, frequently assuming, for example, that we perceive according to a 'rigidity principle' and that illusions are rare enough to be ignored.

Illusions are common in humans, and one would not want them incorporated in 'perceiving machines'; however, machines that communicate pictorially with humans must be designed with explicit knowledge about human perceptual characteristics in mind, i.e. the illusions of static and moving viewing, and the factors that restrict how information is constrained across successive glances. Hochberg looked to the perception of pictures and architecture for the former, and to motion pictures and video cutting for the latter. In more recent work he has pursued **Helmholtz**'s argument that mental structures, opaque to the processes of early vision, intervene between sensory input and our reportable knowledge of the visual world. He points out that the attributes of colour and motion, because they can be defined locally within the retinal image, have appeared easier to explain without drawing on deeply post-retinal or cognitive processes. However he suggests that even the perception of lightness and simple motions may involve mental structures that transform and possibly obscure the contribution of early vision.

Hollander, Edwin Paul

Born: 1927, Rochester, New York, USA **Nat:** American **Ints:** Evaluation and measurement, general, industrial and organizational, personality and social, Society for the Psychological Study of Social Issues **Educ:** BS Western Reserve University, 1948; MA Columbia University, 1950; PhD Columbia University, 1952 **Appts & awards:** Professor of Psychology, Bernard M. Baruch College and University Graduate Center, City University of New York; Professor of Psychol-

ogy, State University of New York at Buffalo; Fulbright Teaching Award, Turkey, 1957–8; NIMH Senior Postdoctoral Award, 1966–7; Fellow, APA; APA Division 1, Council Representative, 1965–6, 1968–70, 1979–81, 1983–6, President, 1980–1; SPSSI, Fellow, Member of Council, 1968–70; AAAS, Fellow, Secretary, Section on Psychology, 1974–8; International Association of Applied Psychology, Executive Committee, 1975–86; EPA, Board of Directors, 1982–5; Psi Chi, Sigma Xi, Distinguished Achievement Award; Psychological Association of Western New York, 1983; Editorial Board, *Journal of Abnormal and Social Psychology*, 1962–4; *British Journal of Social and Clinical Psychology*, 1965–7; *Sociometry*, 1969–72; Advisory Editor, *Transaction*, 1963–70; Associate Editor, *Sociometry*, 1971–2; Editor and Contributor, Special Issue, *Administrative Science Quarterly*, 'Organisational Leadership', March 1971; Associate Editor, *International Review of Applied Psychology*, 1975–9;

Principal publications

1955 Leadership, fellowship and friendship: An analysis of peer nominations. *Journal of Abnormal and Social Psychology*, 50, 163–7 (with W.B. Webb).

1957 The California F Scale in psychological Research: 1950–1955. *Psychological Bulletin*, 54, 47–64 (with H.E. Titus).

1958 Conformity, status and idiosyncrasy credit. *Psychological Review*, 65, 117–27.

1960 Competence and conformity in the acceptance of influence. *Journal of Abnormal and Social Psychology*, 61, 365–9.

1963 *Current Perspectives in Social Psychology.* Oxford University Press (ed. with R.G. Hunt).

1964 *Leaders, Groups and Influence.* Oxford University Press.

1965 Conformity process and prior group support. *Journal of Personality and Social Psychology*, 2, 852–8 (with J.W. Julian and G.A. Haaland).

1965 The validity of peer nominations in predicting a distant performance criterion. *Journal of Applied Psychology*, 49, 434–8.

1967 *Principles and Methods of Social Psychology.* Oxford University Press.

1969 Contemporary trends in the analysis of leadership processes. *Psychological Bulletin*, 71, 387–97 (with J.W. Julian).

1972 *Classic Contributions to Social Psychology.* Oxford University Press (ed. with R.G. Hunt).

1975 Independence, conformity and civil liberties: Some implications from social psychological research. *Journal of Social Issues*, 31, 55–67.

1978   *Leadership Dynamics.* Free Press.
1980   Leadership and social exchange processes. In
K.J. Gergen, M.S. Greenberg and R.H. Willis
(eds), *Social Exchange: Advances in Theory and
Research.* Plenum.
1985   Leadership and power. In G. Lindzey and
E. Aronson (eds), *The Handbook of Social
Psychology,* 3rd edn. Random House.
1990   Relational features of organizational
leadership and followership. In K.E. Clark and
M.B. Cook (eds), *Measures of Leadership.*
Leadership Library of America Inc. (with L.R.
Offermann).
1992   The essential interdependence of leadership
and followership. *Current Directions in
Psychological Science,* 1, 71–5.

Further reading
Chemers, M.M. and Ayman, R. (eds) (1993).
*Leadership Theory and Research: Perspectives and
Direction.* Academic Press.
Rosenbach, W.E. and Taylor, R.L. (eds) (1993)
Contemporary Issues in Leadership (3rd ed).
Westview.

Hollander's interests have primarily involved
work on two major social approaches – leadership and independence – that occur in groups
and organizations. Essentially, leadership is a
directive activity that requires co-operative
efforts. In the transactional approach, presented
in *Leadership Dynamics*, its success depends
upon the followers' responsiveness to the leader's source of authority, competence, motivation
and other personal characteristics such as
gender. Hollander's research with others has
investigated these variables and how they affect
the process and outcome of leadership events.

The basis of the transactional approach to
leadership incorporates the notion that leadership
and followership are mutual activities of influence and counter-influence. The approach goes
beyond the notion that leadership is the cause of
subordinate performance. The argument is that in
any given situation both leaders and followers
give and receive benefits. The relationship is
maintained by this social exchange and the
mutual influence. Hollander proposes that
leaders have validators of their position, who can
support legitimacy or withdraw it. He suggests
that they may uphold the leaders' right to office
in the face of poor performance, because they are
reluctant to admit errors in their own investment
in the leader, and because of a sense of responsibility. This, he argues, may be particularly the
case when the term of office is fixed.

Whilst legitimacy may be awarded by higher
officials, its effectiveness will still depend on the
acceptance of subordinates. In 1958 Hollander
introduced the idea of 'idiosyncratic credit'. This
is the notion that by demonstrating competence
within the group, an individual builds a bank of
credit that makes subsequent ideas more likely to
be accepted. Credit also has the effect of allowing
the leader to demonstrate nonconforming behaviour that would not be acceptable from someone
with less credit, such as a newcomer to the group.

Hollander argues that effective leadership
depends on receiving, processing, retaining and
transmitting information, much of it through
talking with others. It is this foundation that has
resulted in his study of the processes and interactions between leaders and subordinates from
an interactive 'transactional' perspective.

JONATHAN G. HARVEY

Hollingworth, Leta Stetter
Born: 1886, Near Chadron, Nebraska, USA ***Died:***
1939, New York ***Nat:*** American ***Ints:*** Clinical
psychology, developmental psychology, psychology of women ***Educ:*** AB University of Nebraska,
1906; AM Teachers College, Columbia University, New York, 1913; PhD Teachers College,
Columbia University, New York, 1916 ***Appts &
awards:*** Professor of Education, Teachers
College, Columbia University, New York

Principal publications
1914   *Functional Periodicity.* Contributions to
Education, No. 69. Columbia University Press.
1914   Variability as related to sex differences in
achievement. *American Journal of Sociology,* 19,
510–30.
1916   Social devices for impelling women to bear
and rear children. *American Journal of Psychology,*
22, 19–29.
1920   *The Psychology of Subnormal Children.*
Macmillan.
1923   *Special Talents and Defects: Their
Significance for Education.* Macmillan.
1926   *Gifted Children.* Macmillan.
1927   The new woman in the making. *Current
History,* 27, 15–20.
1928   *The Psychology of the Adolescent.* Appleton.
1940   *Public Address.* Science Press.
1942   *Children Above 180 IQ.* World Books.

Further reading
Benjamin, L.T., Jr (1975) The pioneering work of
Leta Stetter Hollingworth in the psychology of
women. *Nebraska History,* 56, 493–505.

Shields, S.A. and Mallory, M.E. (1987) Leta Stetter Hollingworth speaks on 'Columbia's Legacy'. *Psychology of Women Quarterly*, 11, 285–300.

Leta Hollingworth lived her early years under the frontier conditions of midwest America. She entered the University of Nebraska at the age of 16 and after graduation taught in a Nebraska high school. She resigned that position after two years and moved to New York City with her husband, H.L. Hollingworth, who had a post as an assistant in the Department of Psychology at Columbia University. When she began her graduate studies at Teachers College, women were still uncommon and ineligible for any of the full fellowships available. In fact Hollingworth never secured any funding for any of her substantial research projects.

Hollingworth made important contributions to developmental psychology and to the psychology of women. A common theme running through both these areas is the importance of individual and group differences. This emphasis has its origins in Hollingworth's PhD thesis, which was supervised by E.L. **Thorndike**, whose thinking had been strongly influenced by James McKeen **Cattell**. Her early association with the feminist movement led her to laboratory investigations of some supposed sex differences. Thus, she studied sex differences due to periodicity in women and sex differences in variability, the latter involving an elaborate series of measurements of male and female neonates.

In 1914 Hollingworth was appointed to the New York City Civil Service, which involved her in clinical work in hospitals, schools and the courts service. Her work between 1914 and 1920 is presented in *The Psychology of Subnormal Children* and *Special Talents and Defects*. During this period she noted that poor psychological adjustment is not due to low intelligence alone and that emotional and attitudinal factors are crucial. Her discovery that highly intelligent children could suffer severe psychological disturbance rekindled an early interest in gifted children. Forty-five of her seventy-five publications concern the psychology of the gifted child. In 1917 she attended the annual meeting of the APA and with others attempted to form an independent professional organization, the American Association of Child Psychology. That was seen as a highly controversial proposal, since it amounted to the establishment of a new association of professional psychology. Feelings ran high, action was postponed for a year, and the APA established a committee to consider certification of consulting psychologists and to establish a section of clinical psychology.

About 1920 Hollingworth used her influence within the City Civil Service for the segregation of a group of gifted children of 10 years or younger. These children were studied intensively and through their development into adulthood for a period of twenty years. One of her most important discoveries was that intellectual superiority does not predict levels of psychological adjustment through the life-span. An experimental school, established by the New York City Board of Education in 1936, was a development of this work. The school was known as PS 500 or the Speyer School, and Hollingworth was appointed Director. Hollingworth died before the first five-year plan was completed.

Horney, Karen Clementine Danielson

Born: 1885, Hamburg, Germany ***Died:*** 1952, New York, USA ***Nat:*** German ***Ints:*** Clinical psychology, personality and social psychology psychoanalysis, psychology of women ***Educ:*** Doctor of Medicine University of Berlin, 1911 ***Appts & awards:*** Instructor, Director of Curriculum and Training, The Psychoanalytic Institute of the Berlin Society, Berlin, 1918–32; Chicago Institute for Psychoanalysis, 1934; New School for Social Research, New York; New York Psychoanalytic Institute

Principal publications

1916   The flight from womanhood. *International Journal of Psychoanalysis*, 7, 324–39.
1924   On the genesis of the castration complex in women. *International Journal of Psychoanalysis*, 5: 50–65.
1928   The problem of the monogamous ideal. *International Journal of Psychoanalysis*, 9: 318–31.
1933   Maternal conflicts. *American Journal of Orthopsychiatry*, 3, 455–63.
1934   The overevaluation of love: A study of a common present-day feminine type. *Psychoanalytic Quarterly*, 3, 605–38.
1935   The problem of feminine masochism. *Psychoanalytic Review*, 22, 214–33.
1937   *The Neurotic Personality of Our Time*. Norton.
1939   *New Ways in Psychoanalysis*. Norton.
1942   *Self-Analysis*. Norton.
1945   *Our Inner Conflicts*. Norton.
1950   *Neurosis and Human Growth*. Norton.

1968   The technique of psychoanalytic therapy.
    American Journal of Psychoanalysis, 28, 3–12.

Further reading
O'Connell, A. (1980) Karen Horney: Theorist in
    psychoanalysis and feminine psychology.
    Psychology of Women Quarterly, 5, 81–91.
Paris, B.J., (1994) *Karen Horney: A Psychoanalyst's
    Search for Self-Understanding*. Yale University
    Press.

Karen Horney was born in a suburb of
Hamburg, Germany, the second of two children.
Horney's older brother was an attractive, gre-
garious child, and the parents' favorite. Horney
admired both her parents and had a pleasant
relationship with her mother. Her father, however, was often derogatory towards her,
particularly about her looks. Thus, she focused
on academic scholarship and achievement, in
spite of her father's disapproval of education for
women. He did allow her to attend the Realgymnasium for girls in order to prepare for the study
of medicine. After graduation, she entered
medical school at the University of Freiburg,
excelling both academically and socially. She
met and married Oskar Horney, and soon
began her dual role of scholar and mother; the
strain she experienced led her to write about
the social role of women in a patriarchal
society. Horney completed her dissertation, 'A
Casuistic [Clinical] Contribution to the Question of Traumatic Psychoses', and obtained her
medical degree from the University of Berlin in
1911.
    After graduation, Horney gained professional
experience working in a number of psychiatric
hospitals. As a member of the Berlin Psychoanalytic Society, she developed her first formal
psychoanalytic paper in 1917, one in which she
proposed the potential for lifelong growth, a
position that was diametrically opposed to that
of **Freud**, who saw the individual as moving
towards destruction. Horney believed in the
limitless ability for people to develop their
potential throughout life. In *New Ways in Psychoanalysis*, she criticized the notion of the
repetition compulsion. She felt that analysis
should be seen in terms of the whole person; an
individual's character is a consequence of
development, and thus therapy should not focus
exclusively on details of the childhood experience. Horney realized that while sexual
difficulties were often important in the clinical
picture, they were not necessarily the dynamic
centre of the neurosis. When she began to

become bolder in her challenges to Freud, he
often contradicted or denigrated her work.
Horney began to focus on feminine psychology,
writing her most significant papers between
1922 and 1939. She believed psychology was
androcentric, and that it was important to
conceptualize specifically female trends and
attitudes in life. Horney's work in feminine
psychology was formulated while in Germany,
and was concluded in America, where she also
developed her own theory of personality. She
saw America as a place of release from the
dogmatic beliefs of psychoanalytic theory.
Horney characterized the neurotic personality as
one stemming from a marked lack of warmth
and security in parent–child relationships. She
maintained that in order to gain security and
combat anxiety, the child adopts coping strategies. These may take the form of moving
towards others, moving against others, or moving away from others. Horney believed that
neurotics rigidly use one solution exclusively,
regardless of the situation in which they find
themselves. Then, attempts to become an idealized self take precedence, and the individual is
caught by the 'tyranny of the should.' In addition, defence mechanisms such as externaliz-
ation, compartmentalization and blind spots
develop.
    Horney's contribution to psychology is far
reaching. Many of her ideas, such as those on
defence mechanisms, are widely adopted, yet
are not credited to her. That Karen Horney is the
only women whose theory is generally detailed
in personality textbooks is testament to her
contribution in psychology. **Maslow** and **Rogers**
owe her some credit for their ideas on self-
actualization and the fully functioning self.
Both Rogers and Perls adopted Horney's
emphasis on self-awareness in their therapies,
and there are parallels between 'mustabatory'
thought in the approach of Albert **Ellis**, and the
'tyranny of the should' of Horney. The content
of Horney's work is not the only way in which
she has influenced psychology. Also influential
were her responsiveness to the world and her
appreciation of the fact that humans are
dynamic individuals who respond and break
down. Her work showed constant reflection,
and her teaching never suggested that she had
the final answers. For example, her lectures on
psychoanalysis stated that exact techniques
would not be taught, but that viewpoints would
be presented as tools to help students develop
their own way of conducting an analysis. The
perceptive nature of her mind allowed her to

free herself from the conceptions of an earlier period, something rare in the scientific community.

                    V. STAUDT-SEXTON AND J.D. HOGAN

Horowitz, Frances Degen

Born: 1932, Bronx, New York, USA *Nat:* American *Ints:* Developmental psychology *Educ:* BA Antioch College, 1954; Med Goucher College, 1954; PhD University of Iowa, 1959 *Appts & awards:* University of Kansas, Associate Professor, Department of Psychology, Acting Chairman, Department of Human Development and Family Life, 1964–7, Professor, Department of Psychology, Department of Human Development and Family Life, 1969–75, Women's Hall of Fame, 1974, Associate Dean, College of Liberal Arts and Sciences, 1975–8, Vice Chancellor for Research, Graduate Studies and Public Service, Dean, Graduate School, 1978–91; Outstanding Educator of America Award, 1973; National Academy of Sciences' Committee on Scholarly Exchange with the People's Republic of China to lecture at Institute of Psychology, 1982; President, Graduate School and University Center of the City University of New York, 1991– ; Centennial Award, Sustained Contribution to Science Directorate, APA, 1992; Editorial Board, *Developmental Psychology*, 1969–75; Editor, Monographs of the Society for Research in Child Development, 1976–82, Special Issue of *American Psychologist* on Children, 1989, Special Issue of *Merrill-Palmer Quarterly* on Infancy, 1990

Principal publications

1962   The relationship of anxiety, self-concept, and sociometric status among fourth, fifth and sixth grade children. *Journal of Abnormal and Social Psychology*, 65, 212–14.

1963   Effects of social reinforcement on children's behavior. *Journal of Nursery Education*, 18, 276–84.

1973   The effects of environmental intervention programs. In B. Caldwell and H. Ricciuti (eds), *Review of Child Development Research*, vol. III. University of Chicago Press (with L.Y. Paden).

1974   Infant attention and discrimination: Methodological and substantive issues. In F.D. Horowitz (ed.), *Visual Attention, Auditory Stimulation, and Language Discrimination in Young Infants*. Monographs of the Society for Research in Child Development, 39, 1–15.

1976   Current issues in early child development and some implications for teacher training. In H.R.

Spicker, N.J. Anastasiow and W.J. Hodges (eds), *Children With Special Needs: Early Development and Education*. Leadership Training Institute Special Education, University of Minnesota.

1982   Methods of assessment for at-risk and handicapped infants. In C. Ramey and P. Trohanis (eds), *Finding and Educating High-Risk and Handicapped Infants*. University Park Press.

1986   The development of gifted and talented children: Status of knowledge and future directions for research. *American Psychologist*, 41, 1147–52 (with M. O'Brien).

1992   A developmental view on the early identification of the gifted. In P.S. Klein and A.J. Tannenbaum (eds), *To Be Young and Gifted*. Ablex.

Further reading

Horowitz, F.D. (1988) A Jewish woman in academic America. In S. Brehm (ed.), *Seeing Female: Reflections by Women Scholars*. Greenwood Press.

Frances Degen Horowitz was born and grew up in the Bronx, New York, during the Great Depression, the daughter of a garment worker. She lived with her parents and sister, as well as an aunt and her grandmother, and her earliest childhood was spent in the shadows of tenements on Eastburn Avenue just off the Grand Concourse. The experience of growing up Jewish was especially important to Horowitz's development as a person and as a scholar. Though her parents were not well educated, the emphasis in Judaism on the importance of educating children fostered her educational ambitions. Her experience as a Jew in American academia, particularly in the midwest (at the University of Kansas), was also characterized by a sense of social isolation. The gender roles in her home as a child were somewhat nontraditional in that the females, particularly her mother, were stronger and more opinionated than the males, and this fostered a good degree of ambition in Horowitz as a young woman. Though she describes encountering the same negative attitudes about female scholars experienced by many women in academia, she feels fortunate to have entered on the heels of the women's liberation movement, and the subsequent 'opening of the gates'.

Through the years Horowitz has been successful in academia as both a scholar and an administrator. Her primary research interests have included the development of intellectual competence in children from early infancy, and the study of gifted children. She has advocated the concept of affordance, as opposed to **Piaget**'s concept of representation, to account for 'knowing' in infancy. She has also argued for a behavioural analysis of a learned association of stimulus cues with behaviour patterns as a more parsimonious and scientifically useful approach to the development of knowing in infancy. Horowitz has advocated a research emphasis on the developmental course of giftedness and the manner in which it is nurtured, so that policy makers may generate more informed ways of serving such children. Her work with the gifted has focused on understanding the intellectual, social and personality processes in the gifted over the life-span and on developing appropriate educational programmes. Finally, Horowitz has assailed the often simplistic discussion of nature and nurture in developmental psychology. She has offered a conceptualization of a new environmentalism for the study of child development, one which accounts for complex interactions among genetic, biological and environmental variables as they contribute to behavioural development.

J.D. HOGAN AND W. IACCINO

Hovland, Carl Ivor

Born: 1912, Chicago, Illinois, USA **Died:** 1961, New Haven, Connecticut, USA **Nat:** American **Ints:** Experimental, experimental analysis of behaviour, industrial and organizational, military, personality and social **Educ:** BA Northwestern University, 1932; MA Northwestern University, 1933; PhD Yale, 1936 **Appts & awards:** Sterling Professor of Psychology, Yale University, New Haven; USA Director of Experimental Studies and Chief Psychologist, Research Bureau, Information and Education Division, Office Chief of Staff, War Department, Washington, 1942–5; APA Distinguished Scientific Contribution Award, 1957; APA Representative to the Social Science Research Council, USA APA Board of Directors American Academy of Arts and Sciences American Philosophical Society National Academy of Sciences Warren Medal, Society of Experimental Psychologists

Principal publications

1938   Experimental studies in rote-learning theory: II. Reminiscence with varying speeds of syllable presentation. *Journal of Experimental Psychology*, 22, 338–53.

1939   Experimental studies in rote-learning theory: IV. Comparison of reminiscence in serial- and paired-associate learning. *Journal of Experimental Psychology*, 24, 466–84.

1949   *Experiments on Mass Communication.* Princeton University Press, (with A.A. Lumsdaine and F.D. Sheffield).

1951   Human learning and retention. In S.S. Stevens (ed.), *Handbook of Experimental Psychology.* Wiley.

1952   An experimental comparison of conclusion drawing by the communicator and by the audience. *Journal of Abnormal and Social Psychology*, 47, 581–8 (with W. Mandell).

1952   Judgemental phenomena and scales of attitude measurement: Item displacement in Thurstone scales. *Journal of Abnormal and Social Psychology*, 47, 822–32 (with M. Sherif).

1952   The influence of source credibility on communication effectiveness. *Public Opinion Quarterly*, 15, 635–50 (with W. Weiss).

1953   *Communication and Persuasion.* Yale University Press (with I.L. Janis and H. Kelley).

1954   Effects of the mass media of communication. In G. Lindzey (ed.), *Handbook of Social Psychology.* Addison-Wesley.

1957   Extent of opinion change as a function of amount of change advocated. *Journal of Abnormal and Social Psychology*, 54, 257–62 (with H.A. Pritzker).

1957   Assimilation and contrast effects in communication and attitude change. *Journal of Abnormal and Social Psychology*, 55, 242–52 (with O.J. Harvey and M. Sherif).

1957   (ed.) *The Order of Presentation in Persuasion.* Yale University Press.

1959   *Persuasion and Persuasibility.* Yale University Press (ed. with I.L. Janis).

1959   Reconciling conflicting results derived from experimental and survey studies of attitude change. *American Psychologist*, 14, 8–17.

1960   *Attitude Organization and Change.* Yale University Press (with M.J. Rosenberg, W.J. McGuire, R.P. Abelson and J.W. Brehm).

1961   *Social Judgement: Assimilation and Contrast Effects in Communication and Attitude Change.* Yale University Press (with M. Sherif).

Further reading

Miles, W.R. (1962) Carl Ivor Hovland. *American Philosophical Society Year Book 1961.*

Sears, R.R. (1961) Carl Ivor Hovland. *American Journal of Psychology*, 74, 637–9.

In his high school and college days Hovland appeared destined for a musical career, such was his intense interest in music. At Northwestern University, however, he became absorbed in the application of experimental methods to the study of behaviour and was soon a committed behavioural researcher. When he moved to Yale for his doctorate he became greatly involved with Clark **Hull**'s endeavours to establish a rigorous theory of learning, and made original contributions in the fields of retention and rote-learning. He also became involved in John **Dollard**'s work on conflict and aggression and was a contributor to Dollard's classic volume on *Frustration and Aggression.*

At about this time his interest switched to social behaviour, and it is his classic study on persuasive communication and attitude change that has singled him out as an outstanding social scientist. During World War II he became Director of Information and Education in the Office of the Chief of Staff of the War Office at Washington and was assigned to study military morale. In this capacity he reviewed studies on the effects of propaganda films on servicemen during wartime. He also had the opportunity of conducting both experimental and field studies on communication source credibility, opinion change advocacy, order of presentation of message items, and a host of other communication variables relating to the characteristics of the communicator and audience as well as to the form of the communication content.

After the war Hovland returned to Yale and continued research on the conditions under which attitudes can be modified; he also worked as scientific consultant to a number of industrial organizations and government departments. In his final years Hovland shifted his main focus of interest to applying mathematical theory of communication to problems of concept learning, and in the late 1950s before his untimely death, he was in the forefront of the movement to bring information technology into psychology.

H.C. FOOT

Hull, Clark L.
Born: 1884, nr Akron, New York State, USA
Died: 1952, New Haven Connecticut, USA
Nat: American *Ints:* Clinical psychology, experimental psychology, personality and social psychology, philosophical and theoretical psychology, physiological and comparative psychology *Educ:* BA University of Michigan, 1913; PhD University of Wisconsin, 1918 *Appts & awards:* University of Wisconsin, University of Psychology, 1916–27, Assistant Professor, 1920–2, Associate Professor, 1922–5, Professor, 1925–9; Professor of Psychology, Yale

University Institute of Human Relations, 1929–47; President, APA, 1936; Sterling Professor of Psychology, Yale University, 1947–52; Fellow, AAAS

Principal publications
1920 Quantitative aspects of the evolution of concepts: An experimental study. *Psychological Monographs*, 28, No. 123.
1924 The influence of tobacco smoking on mental and motor efficiency. *Psychological Monographs*, 33, No. 150.
1928 *Aptitude Testing*. World Book Co.
1929 A functional interpretation of the conditioned reflex. *Psychological Review*, 26, 498–511.
1929 A mechanical parallel to the conditioned reflex. *Science*, 70, 14–15.
1930 Knowledge and purpose as habit mechanisms. *Psychological Review*, 37, 511–25.
1931 Goal attraction and directing ideas conceived as habit phenomena. *Psychological Review*, 38, 487–506.
1933 *Hypnosis and Suggestibility*. Appleton-Century-Crofts.
1935 The conflicting psychologies of learning – a way out. *Psychological Review*, 42, 491–516.
1937 Mind, mechanism, and adaptive behavior. *Psychological Review*, 44, 1–32.
1940 *Mathematico-Deductive Theory of Rote Learning*. Yale University Press (with C.I. Hovland, R.T. Ross, M. Hall, D.T. Perkins and F.B. Fitch).
1943 *Principles of Behavior*. Appleton-Century.
1951 *Essentials of Behavior*. Yale University Press.
1952 *A Behavior System*. Yale University Press.

Further reading
Koch, S. (1954) Clark L. Hull. In W.K. Estes *et al.* (eds), *Modern Learning Theory*. Appleton-Century-Crofts.
Smith, L.D. (1986) *Behaviorism and Logical Positivism: A Reassessment of the Alliance*. Stanford University Press.

Clark Hull was born into a rural community in New York State, and his early education was sporadic, but he became a teacher at his village school at the age of 17. Later he attended high school, and then the academy of Alma College, where he discovered geometry, and the power of thought itself to generate new connections. He graduated as a mining engineer, but soon after taking up a new job he was left lame by polio, and had to find a less active career. After reading William **James**'s *Principles of Psychology*, he chose psychology with its blend of theory, apparatus and opportunity, and after two years teaching at his old school, he entered the University of Michigan to complete his undergraduate training. There for the first time he became interested in learning and thinking. He took a course in logic and built a logic machine which could display the implications of traditional syllogisms and fallacies. After graduating and a further year school-teaching, he became a teaching assistant at the University of Wisconsin, where he researched for his PhD on concept formation, using Chinese ideographs given nonsense names to be learned. After this he was commissioned to carry out research on the effects of tobacco smoking on efficiency. He also taught a course on aptitude testing, and designed a machine for calculating the correlations involved in developing and using tests. He took over a psychology course given to pre-medical students, which included hypnosis as one of its topics, and this stimulated research published as *Hypnosis and Suggestibility*.

He also took an interest in wider theoretical developments. He liked behaviourism's rejection of introspection in favour of objective, experimental data, but resisted the philosophical extremes of the movement. In his later theorizing he had no objection in principle to terms like 'consciousness', provided they could be shown to play a necessary role in the system. At Wisconsin he discussed *Gestalt* psychology with Joseph Gengerelli, then a graduate student, and managed to bring Kurt **Koffka** over as visiting professor for a year. He studied **Pavlov**'s *Conditioned Reflexes* when it appeared in translation in 1927, and he built a device for simulating the conditioned reflex. This seems to have been the first of many mechanical analogues of learning which were built before being superseded by computer simulation as the preferred medium of model building in experimental psychology.

By 1929 the 45-year-old Hull had established himself as an energetic and eclectic experimental psychologist, a man who could take any problem and make a book out of it. He was called to Yale as Professor of Psychology. Now for the first time he could follow his own interests, with no interference from teaching commitments, and became the intellectual leader of the multidisciplinary Institute of Human Relations. His weekly seminars on behaviour theory are legendary, and attracted audiences of up to seventy. They were attended by a variety of psychologists, psychoanalysts, anthropologists, philosophers, his own students, including Kenneth **Spence** and Neil **Miller**, and

the bearded prophet of neural nets and latter-day connectionism, Warren McCulloch.

Hull began to develop ingenious stimulus–response models, but now on paper rather than actual machines. They described chains of responses with the potential of running off implicitly in detachment from the initially controlling stimuli. This enabled him to explain mechanistically the seemingly non-mechanical aspects of behaviour and learning, such as goal-directedness and persistence, which **Tolman** had claimed as marks of purposiveness. The cross-fertilization with psychoanalysis led to the incorporation of anxiety, drive and drive reduction into the behaviour theories of Hull and his many students. At first he used a learning principle similar to Pavlov's stimulus substitution, but after reviewing **Thorndike**'s *Fundamentals of Learning* in 1935, he relied on the law of effect, with drive reduction as a necessary condition for strengthening stimulus–response bonds.

In 1930 Hull read Newton's *Principia*, and began enthusiastically to steer his psychology towards the hypothetic-deductive form favoured by the physicist, whose theory had held the stage for so long, and had proved truly scientific by allowing itself to be falsified. He attracted mathematicians and logicians to his project, and worked towards a theory that would go beyond rats in mazes to embrace all animal and human behaviour. The fullest and most confident statement of his system was published as *Principles of Behavior* in 1943. He continued to develop the theory until his death in 1952, and though his writing remained distinctive for its egregious use of symbols and apparent precision of quantification, the content had became more piecemeal and cautious in approach.

From about 1935 until well into the 1950s learning theory was dominant in psychology, and Hull was pre-eminent in learning theory. Analysis of citations at the time bears this out triumphantly, but the grandiose hopes for a comprehensive behaviour system based on stimulus–response connections seems quite remote now. His one time rivals Tolman and **Skinner** live more vividly than Hull in the minds of modern students of psychology. Yet much of what he started has continued and been developed under other names. The theorizing about drive led to experiments which have expanded into physiological studies of motivation, pioneered by Hull's student Miller. Cognitive theories based on computer models took over from stimulus–response theory from the late 1950s. But there is a clear continuity here. Hull pioneered the use of mechanistic theories in psychology, and even when he was trying to follow Newton he recognized that the same thing could be done by a machine; and that 'future machines might do the job much more effectively than any he could conceive'. The mathematical leaning theories of the 1950s and 1960s were partly based on Hull's theory, and sixty years on his 'future machines' have arrived. Modern connectionism or parallel distributed processing is nowadays the most visible form of the mechanistic theorizing in psychology which Hull set in motion.

ARTHUR STILL

Hunt, Earl B.

Born: 1933, San Francisco, California, USA **Nat:** American **Ints:** Artificial intelligence, cognition, mathematical psychology and psychometrics **Educ:** BA Stanford University, 1954; PhD Yale University, 1960 **Appts & awards:** Professor of psychology, University of Washington; Fellow, APA, AAAS; Editor, *Cognitive Psychology*, 1974–87; Editorial Board, *Journal of Multivariate Behavioral Research*, 1980–90, *Intelligence*, 1982– , *Journal of Mathematical Psychology*, 1983–9,

Principal publications

1962   *Concept Learning*. Wiley.
1966   *Experiments in Induction*. Academic Press.
1971   What kind of computer is man? *Cognitive Psychology*, 2, 57–98.
1972   How good can memory be? In A. Melton and E. Martin (eds), *Coding Processes in Human Memory*. Winston.
1973   Individual differences in cognition. In G. Bower (ed.), *Advances in Learning and Motivation*, vol. 7. Academic Press (with N. Frost and C. Lunneborg).
1974   Quote the raven? Never more. In L. Gregg (ed.), *Knowledge-Cognition*. Erlbaum.
1974   The mechanics of thought. In B. Kantowitz (ed.), *Human Information Processing: Tutorials in Performance and Cognition*. Erlbaum (with S. Poltrock).
1975   *Artificial Intelligence*. Academic Press.
1975   What does it mean to be high verbal? *Cognitive Psychology*, 1, 194–227 (with J. Lewis and C. Lunneborg).
1978   Individual differences in the verification of sentence–picture relationships. *Journal of Verbal Learning and Verbal Behavior*, 17, 493–507 (with C. MacLeod and N. Mathews).

1981   Individual differences in long-term memory access. *Memory and Cognition*, 9, 599–608 (with J. Davidson and M. Lansman).
1980   Intelligence as an information processing concept. *British Journal of Psychology*, 71, 449–74.
1983   On the nature of intelligence. *Science*, 219, 141–6.
1988   *Indigenous Cognition: Functioning in Cultural Context*. Nijhoff (with J.W. Berry and S.H. Irvine).
1994   *Encyclopedia of Human Intelligence*. Macmillan (ed. with R.J. Sternberg, S.J. Ceci, J. Horn, J.D. Matarazzo and S. Scarr).
1995   *Will We Be Smart Enough? Cognitive Capabilities of the Coming Workforce*. Russell Sage Foundation.
1996   *Thoughts on Thought: A Discussion of Ideas in Cognitive Psychology*. Erlbaum.

Further reading

Komatsu, L.K. (ed.) (1994) *Experimenting with the Mind: Readings in Cognitive Psychology*. Brooks/Cole.
Solso, R.L. and Massaro, D. (eds) (1995) *The Science of the Mind: 2001 and Beyond*. Oxford University Press.
Sternberg, R.J. (ed.) (1994) *Thinking and Problem Solving. Handbook of Perception and Cognition*, 2nd edn. Academic Press.

Earl B. Hunt's scientific interests have centred on cognition in humans and machines. He has also done some research on the physiological basis of memory in animals. His work on machine cognition dealt with the development of programs for recognizing complex non-linear patterns in data. Further studies were conducted on computer systems capable of solving deductive logic problems and, more importantly, of improving their performance with practice. His interest in human cognition has centred on individual differences in the information-processing capacities of people who have high or low scores on tests of general intelligence. This research has contributed to a better understanding of how people differ in their cognitive competencies. More recently it has been extended to individual differences in the ability to solve problems under severe time pressures. This work is at the interface between studies of attention and studies of problem solving and logical thinking. Theoretical models of the distribution of attention in problem solving have been constructed using computer simulation techniques.

Hunt, Joseph McVicker

Born: 1906, Scottsbluff, Nebraska, USA **Died:** 1991, Urbana, Illinois, USA **Nat:** American **Ints:** Developmental, experimental, personality and social, physiological and comparative, Society for the Psychological Study of Social Issues **Educ:** BA University of Nebraska, 1929; MA University of Nebraska, 1930; PhD Cornell University, 1933 **Appts & awards:** Instructor to Associate Professor, Brown University, 1936–46; Institute of Welfare Research of the Community Service Society of New York, Research Consultant, 1944–6, Director, 1946–51; Member, APA Board of Directors, 1949–54, 1970–3; Editor, *Journal of Abnormal and Social Psychology*, 1949–55; President, APA, 1951–2; Professor of Psychology, University of Illinois, 1951–74; Research Career Award, National Institutes of Mental Health, 1962–74; Member, APA Council of Representatives, 1967–70; Gold Medal Award, American Psychological Foundation, 1970; Distinguished Scholar Award, Hofstra College, 1973; Distinguished Contribution Award, Clinical Division, APA, 1973; Professor Emeritus, University of Illinois, 1974–91; G. Stanley Hall Award, Developmental Division, APA, 1976

Principal publications

1938   An instance of the social origin of conflict resulting in psychosis. *American Journal of Orthopsychiatry*, 8, 159–64.

1941   The effects of infant feeding frustration upon adult hoarding in the albino rat. *Journal of Abnormal and Social Psychology*, 36, 338–60.

1944   *Personality and the Behavior Disorders.* Ronald Press. (Rev. edn, 1984, with N.S. Endler, Wiley.)

1958   Situational cues distinguishing anger, fear and sorrow. *American Journal of Psychology*, 71, 136–51 (with M.L.W. Cole and E.E.S. Reis).

1961   *Intelligence and Experience.* Ronald Press.

1963   Motivation inherent in information processing and action. In O.J. Harvey (ed.), *Motivation and Social Interaction: The Cognitive Determinants.* Ronald Press.

1969   *The Challenge of Incompetence and Poverty.* University of Illinois Press.

1972   *Human Intelligence.* Transaction Books.

1975   *Assessment in Infancy: Ordinal Scales of Psychological Development.* University of Illinois Press (with I.C. Uzgiris).

1976   The psychological development of orphanage-reared infants: Interventions with outcomes. *Genetic Psychology Monographs*, 94, 177–226 (with K. Mohandessi, M. Ghodssi and M. Akiyama).

1979   Developmental psychology: Early experience. *Annual Review of Psychology*, 30, 103–43.

1987   *Infant Performance and Experience: New Findings with the Ordinal Scales.* University of Illinois Press.

Further reading

Harris, P. (1983) Infant cognition. In P. Mussen (ed.), *Handbook of Child Psychology*, vol. II. Wiley.

Minton, H.L. and Schneider, F.W. (1980) *Differential Psychology.* Brooks/Cole.

J. McVicker Hunt was born in Scottsbluff, Nebraska, on 19 March 1906. During his undergraduate years at the University of Nebraska, he took courses from a variety of fields including biology, philosophy, economics and sociology. He went on to Cornell University, where he studied under Madison Bentley. Hunt's interest in psychopathology began to take shape through two postdoctoral fellowships, one at the New York Psychiatric Institute and Columbia University (1933–4), and a second at the Worcester State Hospital and Clark University (1934–6). While at Clark, Hunt met and befriended the behaviorist Walter S. Hunter. When Hunter left Clark in 1936 to chair the department at Brown, he took Hunt with him. During his years at Brown, Hunt edited his two-volume work *Personality and the Behavior Disorders*, which was widely used as a graduate text for many years.

Also during his years at Brown, another major interest began to emerge, namely, the study of the long-term effects of early experience. In his research during this period, the influence of Hunter can be seen in Hunt's use of rigorous experimental design and the incorporation of animal models. He was impressed by **Freud**'s arguments regarding the importance of early experience, and the result was a famous series of feeding-frustration studies using rat pups. In this research, infant rats were placed on a food deprivation scale after which they were reared normally to adulthood. When they were again placed on a food deprivation scale, adult rats that had been deprived in infancy hoarded food, demonstrating a conditioned emotionality phenomenon.

As Director of the Institute of Welfare Research of the Community Service Society of New York, Hunt shifted his focus to the effects of social case work. While at the Institute, he developed an anchored judgement scale which more than halved the random variations in case worker ratings of client change. But he came to feel that, despite dramatic examples of improvements in individual cases, 'talking therapy' seemed inadequate for coping with the problems seen in patients. Improvements in the understanding of child rearing seemed to hold more promise.

Hunt's final academic post was at the University of Illinois, where he joined the faculty as Professor of Psychology in 1951, remaining until his retirement in 1974. Here he continued exploring the effects of early experience on long-term development. In 1961 he published *Intelligence and Experience*, a landmark argument against the traditional concept of fixed intelligence. The book was an important factor in persuading the Kennedy and Johnson administrations to make the Head Start Program a part of the War on Poverty in the US. The idea of plasticity in development provided programs like Head Start with the rationale they needed to develop interventions designed to maximize children's potential.

This was followed by an invitation to chair a White House Task Force on the government's role in early childhood education, resulting in extensions of Project Head Start to older children. Eventually, however, Hunt became increasingly dissatisfied with the norm-referenced approach to assessing intelligence and, specifically, infant and child development. Later, Hunt and Ina Uzgiris used **Piaget**ian accounts of sensory motor development to construct scales for assessing infant psychological development. In a well-known series of longitudinal studies in orphanages in Tehran, Hunt used these scales to demonstrate that appropriate attention from care givers can enable foundlings to attain developmental growth than can not only be considered normal, but may even be slightly ahead of home-reared offspring of middle-class parents in the West.

Hunt's enduring influence has been on developmental psychology, especially on the effects of early experience on later performance. But he had a significant influence on other areas as well, including psychological assessment, psychological treatment, and evaluation. He was a model scientist-practitioner and led others to understand that it is possible to pursue joint professional and research careers. He is also one of only a few psychologists who influenced the direction of both the science and the clinical practice of psychology.

D. THOMPSON

I

Insko, Chester A.

Born: 1935, Augusta, Kentucky, USA **Nat:**
American **Ints:** Social psychology **Educ:** AB
University of California, 1957; MA Boston
University, 1958; PhD University of California,
1963 **Appts & awards:** Professor of Psychology,
University of North Carolina; Fellow, APA
Division 8; Associate Editor, *Journal of Experi-
mental Social Psychology*, 1965–70; Editorial
Consultant, *Journal of Personality and Social
Psychology*, 1981–

Principal publications

1964 Primacy versus recency in persuasion as a
function of the timing of arguments and measures.
Journal of Abnormal and Social Psychology, 69,
381–91.

1966 Awareness and the 'conditioning' of attitudes.
Journal of Personality and Social Psychology, 4,
487–96 (with W.F. Oakes).

1967 Triadic consistency: A statement of
affective–cognitive–conative consistency.
Psychological Review, 74, 361–76 (with J.
Schopler).

1967 *Theories of Attitude Change*. Appleton-
Century-Crofts.

1969 A test of three interpretations of attitudinal
verbal reinforcement. *Journal of Personality and
Social Psychology*, 12, 333–41 (with R.B.
Cialdini).

1972 *Experimental Social Psychology: Text with
Illustrative Readings*. Academic Press (with J.
Schopler).

1974 Anticipated interaction and the
similarity–attraction effect. *Sociometry*, 37,
149–62 (with B. Layton).

1975 A balance theory interpretation of dissonance.
Psychological Review, 82, 169–83 (with S.
Worchel, R. Folyer and A. Kutkus).

1979 Interpersonal attraction and the polarity of
similar attitudes: A test of three balance models.
Journal of Personality and Social Psychology, 37,
2262–77 (with A. Tashakkori).

1981 Balance theory and phenomenology. In R.
Petty, T. Ostrom and T. Brock (eds), *Cognitive
Responses to Persuasion*. Erlbaum.

1983 Sampling of similar and dissimilar comparison

persons and objects as a function of the generality
of attribution goal. *Journal of Personality and
Social Psychology*, 46, 763–78 (with M. Alicke).

1991 Rational selective exploitation among
Americans and Chinese: General similarity, with
one surprise. *Journal of Applied Social Psychology*,
21, 1169–206 (with Y. Lin and C.E. Rusbult).

Further reading

Grant, P.R. (1993) Reactions to intergroup similarity:
Examination of the similarity-differentiation and
the similarity-attraction hypotheses. *Canadian
Journal of Behavioral Science*, 25, 28–44.

Henrick, C. (ed.) (1987) *Group Processes*. Sage.

A major school of thought on attitude change
and persuasion was developed by Carl **Hovland**, at Yale University, during and after World
War II. The Yale approach was founded on the
idea that attitudes are learned behaviours and
that persuasion is successful to the degree to
which people attend to, understand and remember the persuasive message. This approach
focuses on four factors that determine persuasion: communication variables, message
variables, channel variables and audience variables. This is sometimes summarized in the
question: *who* says *what* by *what means* to
whom? Chester Insko conducted important
studies of the persuasion processes and its implications for attitude change. In the tradition of
the Yale approach, he conducted experimental
investigations in which the four factors were
varied and controlled systematically. For
instance, in one study he examined the interaction between a communicator's credibility and
the extent of disagreement with the audience in
determining the persuasiveness of the message.
Thus, he considered the effect of one variable
(disagreement between the message and audience beliefs) on another (speaker credibility). In
this study he found that too much agreement
with an audience will backfire, producing less
persuasion. However, the point at which the
'backfire' occurs is higher for high-credibility
communicators, who can be persuasive at higher
levels of disagreement with the audience.

Working within a learning tradition, Insko has examine the effects of selective reinforcement on attitude change. For example, in one telphone study he examined the importance of verbal reinforcement in attitude change by getting the interviewer to respond 'Good' to half the respondents who expressed a negative attitude on a particular issue, and to half of the respondents who expressed a positive attitude. A week later the respondents completed a questionnaire on the same issue, and Insko found that those who had been verbally reinforced for positive attitudes expressed significantly more favourable views than those who had been verbally reinforced for negative attitudes.

Insko's work has been important in demonstrating the usefulness of learning theory for understanding attitude change. However, it has certain limitations. First, most of the empirical studies demonstrate accentuation of attitudes through reinforcement, rather than a reversal in attitudes. Second, in many studies the attitudes which have been considered are relatively unimportant. Third, it is not clear how verbal reinforcement induces attitude change. It could be that verbal responses such as 'Good' lead people to believe that conformity to their current attitude will attract further reinforcements in the future. Or it may be that this kind of reinforcement induces demand characteristics – people exaggerate their current attitude because they believe they are expected to. Insko has demonstrated that contingency awareness is important for attitude change, but it is not clear whether people must understand that a deliberate persuasive attempt is being made.

Iritani, Toshio

Born: 1932, Setagaya-ku, Tokyo, Japan **Nat:** Japanese **Ints:** Humanistic psychology, personality and social psychology, philosophical and theoretical psychology, population and environmental psychology, psychological study of social issues **Educ:** BE Tokyo University of Education, 1955; MA Tokyo University of Education, 1957; PhD Clark University, 1962 **Appts & awards:** Senior Professor of Psychology Department of Mass Communication, Tokai University; Chairperson, Organizing Committee, 24th Convention of Japanese Social Psychology, 1983; Professor of Social Psychology, Tokai University Board of Directors, Japanese Association of Social Psychology, 1984– ; Co-Editor, *Guide-Book of Psychology* (*Kawade-shobo*), 1964; Editorial Board, *Inter-*

national Journal of Psycholinguistics, 1971–9; Editorial Consultant, *English Abstracts, Japanese Journal of Psychology*, 1974–9, *Journal of Psychology (Saiensu-sha)*, 1982– ; Book Series Co-Editor, *Environmental Psychology (Seishin-shobo)*, 1974–5

Principal publications

1963   Piaget's viewpoint of *Gestalt* psychology. *Psychologia*, 6, 46–52.

1969   Dimensions of phonetic symbolism. *International Journal of Psychology*, 4, 9–19.

1969   *New Social Psychology*. Tokai University Press.

1972   Psychology founded on Japanese wisdom. *Contemporary Psychology*, 17, 397–9.

1974   *A Way of Environmental Psychology*. Japanese Broadcasting Corporation (NHK).

1979   *The Value of Children: A Cross-National Study*. East–West Center Press.

1981   An inquiry into the organization of dialogues under the condition of given situations. *International Journal of Psycholinguistics*, 8, 5–16.

1981   *Discourse: Its Mechanism and Deployment*. Chuo-koronsha.

1983   *An Invitation to Psycholinguistics*. Taishukan.

1991   *Group Psychology of the Japanese in Wartime*. Kegan Paul.

Further reading

Braun, J. (1995) The psychology of war: A study in antirelationships. In J. Braun (ed.) *Social Pathology in Comparative Perspective: The Nature and Psychology of Civil Society*. Praeger.

Kess, J.F. and Miyamoto, T. (1994) *Japanese Psycholinguistics*. John Benjamins.

Iritani's professional interest in psychology began with his work on visual depth perception. This was influenced by the work of his father (who was also a psychologist) and figured in both his bachelor's and master's theses. In studying abroad from 1957 to 1962, mainly at Clark University, later at Harvard, MIT and the University of Geneva, his research interest turned to the psychology of language, social psychology and developmental psychology, reflecting the influence of his teachers: Heinz **Werner**, Roger **Brown** and Jean **Piaget**. His work in the first decade after his return to Japan (1962–71) was mainly focused on the introduction of American/European-based psychological studies of psycholinguistics, social and developmental psychology, and he wrote numerous influential textbooks as well as articles intended to be accessible to the lay reader. His work in the second decade (1972–81) became more interdisciplinary, and centred on investigations of social development, population and environmental psychology, in collaboration with social scientists in Japan and abroad. The third and fourth decades (1982–) have seen a focus on the psychological solution of global problems, especially of the maintenance of peace and the prevention of nuclear war. After a period of study in Poland (1976–7) as a visiting professor at the Polish Academy of Sciences and at the University of Warsaw, he became more interested in the social psychology of war and peace, and this led to publications (mostly in Japanese) of the psychology of people during World War II, collecting and using materials from the war period, especially from 1937 to 1945.

J

Jackson, Douglas Northrop

Born: 1929, Merrick, New York, USA **Nat:** American **Ints:** Evaluation and measurement, industrial and organizational psychology, personality and social psychology **Educ:** BSc Cornell University, 1951; MSc Purdue University, 1952; PhD Purdue University, 1955 **Appts & awards:** Assistant to Associate Professor of Psychology, Pennsylvania State University, 1956–63; NIMH Research Fellow, Stanford University, 1962–3; Senior Professor of Psychology, University of Western Ontario, 1964–95; President, Society of Multivariate Experimental Psychology, 1975–6; Citation, Canadian Psychological Association, 1986; President, APA Division of Measurement, Evaluation and Statistics Division, 1989–90; President, Sigma Assessment Systems Inc., 1995

Principal publications

1958 Content and style in personality assessment. *Psychological Bulletin*, 55, 243–52. (with S. Messick)

1969 Multimethod factor analysis in the evaluation of convergent and discriminant validity. *Psychological Bulletin*, 72, 30–49

1971 The dynamics of structured personality tests: 1971. *Psychological Review*, 78, 229–48.

1975 Multimethod factor analysis: A reformulation. *Multivariate Behavioral Research*, 10, 259–76.

1980 Maximum likelihood estimation in confirmatory factor analysis: A cautionary note. *Psychological Bulletin*, 88, 502–8 (with D.W. Chan).

1980 Personality structure and assessment. *Annual Review of Psychology*, 31, 503–51 (with S.V. Paunonen).

1984 *Personality Research Form Manual.* Research Psychologists Press.

1985 Construct validity and the predictability of behavior. *Journal of Personality and Social Psychology*, 49, 554–70 (with S.V. Paunonen).

1991 Dimensions of personality pathology. *Canadian Journal of Psychiatry*, 36, 557–62 (with W.J. Lively and M.L. Schroeder).

Further reading

Kreitler, S. Kreitler, H. (1990) *The Cognitive Foundations of Personality Traits.* Plenum.

Rosen, J.C. and McReynolds, P. (1992) *Advances in Psychological Assessment*, vol. 8. Plenum.

Following a first degree in industrial and labour relations, Douglas Jackson's two postgraduate qualifications were in clinical psychology at Purdue, where he came under the influence of Gardner **Murphy**, for whom he worked as a research assistant from 1952 to 1953. Much of Jackson's later work followed directly from these early interests, with the bulk of his 200-plus publications being in the area of personality psychology, psychometrics and occupational psychology.

Douglas Jackson appreciated the importance of understanding personality processes at a time when most research was into personality structure. For example, his early work (often published jointly with Samuel Messick) examines the processes involved in answering personality test items and concludes that rather than being measurement artefacts, stylistic measures may be useful indicators of personality traits – in much the same way **Raymond Cattell** drew a distinction between Q-data and Q'-data. Jackson also made insightful contributions to many other important areas of debate – for example, revealing some flaws in **Mischel** and Peake's situationalist explanation of personality. Psychometrically he was an enthusiastic exponent of **Campbell** and Fiske's multitrait multimethod, and appreciated the need to eliminate method variance when assessing the validity of test scores. 'Personality structure and assessment' raises some important shortcomings of other scales, such as those ostensibly measuring locus of control and sex roles, the continued use of which is difficult to defend on rational grounds. Douglas Jackson has developed and validated an impressive range of psychological tests, with special emphasis on personality. These include various incarnations of the Personality Research Form (PRF), the Jackson

Personality Inventory, the Jackson Vocational Interest Survey, the Basic Personality Inventory, the Career Directions Inventory and the Multidimensional Aptitude Battery. These tests are distinctive in that they were developed according to specific theoretical models rather than through blind, atheoretical procedures that are currently popular. Indeed, Jackson wrote in 1971 that 'personality measures will have broad import and substantial construct validity to the extent, and only to the extent, that they are derived from an explicitly formulated, theoretically based definition of a trait'. Thus the PRF is based on Murray's theory of needs and presses, and the aptitude battery is based on David Weschler's model of ability.

Apart from his extensive professional and editorial work, Jackson's main contributions to psychology have been through his work into personality processes, and his insistence on psychometric rigour when constructing and validating psychological scales. Given this background it is unsurprising that his tests are widely used and cited. For all of these reasons, Douglas Jackson has made a very substantial contribution to the psychology of individual differences.

COLIN COOPER

Jackson, James S.

Born: 1944, Detroit, Michigan, USA **Nat:** American **Ints:** Adult development and ageing, developmental, evaluation and measurement, personality and social, psychological study of social issues **Educ:** BS Michigan State University, 1966; MA University of Toledo, 1970; PhD Wayne State University, 1972 **Appts & awards:** National Chairman, Association of Black Psychologists, 1972–3; NIMH, Psychology Education Panel, 1974–9; Chairman, Board of Trustees, Association for the Advancement of Psychology, 1978–80; NRC, NAS Committee on Aging, 1978–82; Board of Directors, Public Committee on Mental Health, 1978–84; APA Policy and Planning Board, 1981–5; Behavioral Science Cluster Group, NIMH, 1982–3; Associate Professor of Psychology, University of Michigan, APA, Distinguished Early Career Contribution to Psychology in the Public Interest Award, 1983; APA, Finance Committee, 1984– ; Research, Education and Practice Committee, Gerontology Society of America, 1984–5; Committee on the Status of Black Americans, NRC, NAS, 1985– ; Editorial Board, *Applied Social Psychology Annual*,

1983– , *Journal of Gerontology*, 1985– , Co-editor, *Association of Black Psychologists Newsletter*, 1973–4; Consulting Editor, *Psychology and Aging*, 1985–

Principal publications

1972 Long and short term determinants of social reinforcement effectiveness. *Journal of Personality and Social Psychology*, 24, 122–31 (with R. Baron and B. Fish).

1974 External validity: A survey experiment approach. *Personality and Social Psychology Bulletin*, 1, 4–6 (with M.S. Flynn).

1977 Life satisfaction among black urban elderly. *International Journal of Aging and Human Development*, 8, 169–79 (with J.D. Bacon and J. Peterson).

1979 The aversive effects of non-reciprocated benefits. *Social Psychology Quarterly*, 42, 148–58 (with S. Shumaker).

1981 Group identity development within black families. In H. McAdoo (ed.), *Black Families*. Sage.

1985 Work and retirement among black elderly. In Z. Blau (ed.), *Work, Leisure, Retirement and Social Policy*. JIA (with R. Gibson).

1985 Intergenerational research: Methodological considerations. In N. Datan, A.L. Green and H.W. Reese (eds), *Intergenerational Networks: Families in Context*. Erlbaum.

1989 The influence of racial factors on psychiatric diagnosis: A review and suggestions for research. *Community Mental Health Journal*, 25, 301–11.

1991 *Life in Black America*. Sage.

1993 *Aging in Black America*. Sage (ed. with L.M. Chatters and R.J. Taylor).

Further reading

Jones, R.L. (ed.) (1989) *Black Adult Development and Aging*. Cobb and Henry.

Padgett, D.K. (ed.) (1995) *Handbook of Ethnicity, Aging, and Mental Health*. Greenwood.

During the course of his career James Jackson's interests have encompassed work on social reinforcement processes, reciprocity, mental health and well-being, political behaviour, and life-course change and continuity. Through all these diverse subjects his general concern has been with social psychological processes, particularly among minority group members, and how society and the environment influence, and are influenced by, the individual and primary group.

His early work on social reinforcement sought to understand how social approval served as a reinforcer for subsequent behaviour. The work on reciprocity and helping behaviour was a direct outgrowth of his belief that these processes were implicated in the effaciousness of social approval. It was his concern with the longitudinal study of adaptation in high school students that exposed him to some of the fundamentals of survey research. This interest resulted in a continuing, strong methodological focus in his work. His research on adult development and ageing has been based on the assumption that if social psychological theories are to have any merit they must take into consideration changes in human functioning that are influenced by ageing, period and cohort factors. Theories of human behaviour need to include conceptions of social and psychological functioning that are responsive to continuity and development across the life course. His work on social psychological processes within the North American black population has led to the conclusion that more research is needed on the social psychological realities of life for minority group members within this society. He argues that this approach can enhance our understanding of the processes that are more broadly applicable as general frameworks for the social sciences.

Jackson, John Hughlings

Born: 1835, Green Hammerton, Yorkshire, England **Died:** 1911, London, England **Nat:** British **Ints:** Clinical neurology **Educ:** MD St. Andrews University, 1860; MRCP London, 1861, FRCP London 1868 **Appts & awards:** Member, Royal College of Surgeons, and Licentiate, Royal Society of Apothecaries, 1856; House Physician, York Dispensary, 1856–9; Lecturer in Pathology, Morbid Anatomy and Histology, London Hospital Medical College, 1859; Assistant Physician to the Metropolitan Free Hospital and to the Islington Dispensary, 1859; MD, St Andrews University, 1860; MRCP, London, 1861; Clinical Assistant, Moorfield's Eye Hospital, 1861; Physician to National Hospital, Queen Square, 1862–1906; Lecturer in Physiology, London Hospital, 1863–94; FRCP, London, 1868; Fellow, Royal Society, 1878; President, Pathology and Bacteriology Section, BMA, 1882; First President, Neurological Society, 1885; President, Opthalmological Society, 1890; Moxon Gold Medal, Royal College of Physicians, 1903; LLD, Universities of Glasgow and Edinburgh; DSc, University of Leeds; DM, University of Bologna; Hon. FRCP, Ireland; Corresponding Member, Royal Academy of Medicine, Belgium, 1903

Principal publications

1925 *Neurological Fragments.* Oxford University Press.

1932 *Selected Writings of John Hughlings Jackson.* Hodder & Stoughton.

Further reading

Clarke, E. (1973) John Hughlings Jackson. *Dictionary of Scientific Biography*, 7, 46–50. Charles Scribner's Sons.

Head, H. (1915) Hughlings Jackson on aphasia and kindred affections of speech *Brain*, 38, 1–190.

Stengel, E. (1963) Hughlings Jackson's influence in psychiatry. *British Journal of Psychiatry*, 109, 348–55.

Swash, M. (1986) John Hughlings Jackson: A sesquicentennial tribute. *Journal of Neurology, Neurosurgery and Psychiatry*, 49, 981–5.

Taylor, J. (1925) Biographical memoir. In J.H. Jackson, *Neurological Fragments*. Oxford University Press.

John Hughlings Jackson was born in rural Yorkshire, the son of a Yorkshire yeoman and a Welsh mother. The youngest of several brothers, he lost his mother and then father early in life. He was educated in village schools; his lack of university education he saw as an advantage, giving him greater intellectual freedom. At the age of 15 he was apprenticed to a physician in York, where he spent five years, before coming to London in 1855 to study for a short time with Sir James Paget at St Bartholomew's Hospital. Following this, he worked for three years in York, where he was introduced to the study of mental disease by Daniel Tuke and Thomas Laycock, before returning to London in 1859. He met Jonathan Hutchinson, a fellow Yorkshireman; together they contributed medical reports to the *Medical Time and Gazette*. Hutchinson persuaded Jackson to pursue a medical (rather than literary) career, helping him to achieve his critical appointment to the National Hospital Queen Square in 1862, where he remained, subsequently coming under the influence of Charles Brown-Séquard. The marriage to his epileptic cousin ended with her death after eleven years.

Jackson was the first to use the ophthalmoscope in the study of nervous disorders, recognizing its value in diagnosis. He used observations of behavioural disturbance to draw inferences about localization of function. He correctly identified the critical sites of motor action, sensation and language (confirming Broca's work). He was the first to appreciate that the sequence of involuntary movements which characterize focal epilepsy indicates the spatial layout of excitable foci in the motor cortex. Focal epilepsy, first described by Bravais in 1827, named uncinate seizures and first reported on by Jackson in 1870, was finally named after him by **Charcot**. Jackson observed, seeing the significance of unilateral convulsions, that right-sided epileptiform seizures were associated with mental and speech disorders; and suggested that visual and spatial disabilities might bear a similar relation to the right hemisphere, thus introducing the idea of cerebral asymmetry of function, now widely accepted. His hypothesized motor centres were confirmed shortly afterwards by the experimental work of Fritsch and Hitzig (1870) and Ferrier (1873). He suggested that the cerebellum was the centre for continuous movement (modern tonic theory) and the cerebrum for changing movement. He observed and appreciated the significance of the phenomenon of motor apraxia (1866), thirty-four years before Liepmann's classic case study. He was responsible for the classic study of aphasia, showing that this was often due to left hemisphere lesions, stressing that it was a disorder of language rather than merely speech: an intellectual deficit marked by inability to formulate propositions rather than failure to recall individual words. He was the first to describe perceptual illusions and other dream-like states of consciousness evoked by focal epileptic discharges in the temporal lobes, subsequently studied more fully by **Penfield**.

The ideas of evolution and hierarchical organization of the nervous system he took from Herbert Spencer. In these, development is in the direction of increased complexity, integration and specialization, from automatic centres in the spinal cord and brain stem at the lowest level to the highest level in the prefrontal cerebral cortex. Neurological disease is characterized by dissolution, the most recently developed functions being lost first according to Jackson (1898). Though not always true, this was an important first step in the development of theories of nervous function and dysfunction.

Jackson's theory of the evolution and dissolution of the nervous system notably influenced **Freud**. The discussion of aphasia introduced the concepts of projection, representation, overdetermination and regression which became central to psychoanalysis. His general account of nervous disease speaks of normal energy, resistance and functional regression, and comes very close to postulating a dynamic unconscious. Jackson's interest in positive symptoms indirectly influenced **Bleuler**'s symptomatology of schizophrenia. His recognition of the dual function (practical and scientific) of classifications of mental disorder is still relevant to modern psychiatry.

Widely regarded as the 'father of British neurology', Jackson was a pioneer and pivotal figure in the development of clinical neuroscience. He was clearly ahead of his time, showing an extraordinary sagacity (he was nicknamed 'the sage' by his students), originality, intellectual honesty, modesty and trustworthiness. His success was due to combining acute, accurate observation and great attention to detail with remarkable powers of analysis and inference, enabling him to reach principles of wide generality. He was in the habit of sitting quietly at the end of the day, notebook in hand, to allow the implications of what he had observed to develop in his mind.

He conducted no experiments and wrote no books but produced over 300 articles on a wide range of topics, including syphilis, vertigo (from which he subsequently suffered himself), chorea, tobacco smoking and the psychology of joking (1887 which he subjected to hierarchical analysis: puns, wit, humour). He was retiring by nature; his ideas were slow to be recognized but eventually proved to be enormously influential. The co-founder of *Brain* (1878), he delivered the first Hughlings-Jackson lecture, inaugurated in his honour, to the Neurological Society in 1889.

E.R. VALENTINE

Jahoda, Gustav

Born: 1920, Vienna, Austria *Nat:* Austrian *Ints:* Cross-cultural psychology, developmental, experimental and health psychology, social *Educ:* BSc University of London, 1946; MSc University of London, 1948; PhD University of London, 1952 *Appts & awards:* Professor Emeritus of Psychology, University of Strathclyde; FBPS President and Honorary Fellow, International Association for Cross-Cultural Psychology; Member, European Association of Experimental Social Psychology; Biesheuvel Medal for contributions towards 'the study of man in Africa'; Editor, *European Journal of Social Psychology*, Editorial Board, *British Journal of Social Psychology*, *Journal of Cross-Cultural Psychology*, *International Journal of Psychology*; Guest Editor, Special Issue, *International Journal of Behavioral Development* on 'Cross-cultural studies of child development' (with P.R. Dasen)

Principal publications

1961 *White Man*. Oxford University Press.
(Reprinted 1983.)

1966 On the scope and methods of cross-cultural research. *International Journal of Psychology*, 1, 109–27 (with N. Firjda).

1968 Scientific training and the persistence of traditional beliefs among West African university students. *Nature*, 220, 1356.

1969 *The Psychology of Superstition*. Allen Lane.

1972 *Children and Alcohol*. HMSO.

1975 Belfast children: Some effects of a conflict environment. *Irish Journal of Psychology*, 3, 1–19 (with S. Harrison).

1979 The construction of economic reality by some Glaswegian children. *European Journal of Social Psychology*, 9, 115–27.

1979 A cross-cultural perspective on experimental social psychology. *Personality and Social Psychology Bulletin*, 5, 142–8.

1980 Theoretical and systematic approaches in cross-cultural psychology. In C. Triandis and W. Brislin (eds), *Handbook of Cross-Cultural Psychology, vol. 5: Social Psychology*. Allyn and Bacon.

1982 *Psychology and Anthropology*. Academic Press.

1983 European 'lag' in the development of an economic concept: A study in Zimbabwe. *British Journal of Developmental Psychology*, 1, 113–20.

1983 The cross-cultural emperor's conceptual clothes: The emic-tic revisited. In J.B. Deregowski, S. Dziurawiec and R.C. Annis (eds), *Expiscations in Cross-Cultural Psychology*. Zwets and Zeitlinger.

1984 The development of thinking about socio-economic systems. In H. Tajfel (ed.), *The Social Dimension*. Cambridge University Press.

1992 *Crossroads between Culture and Mind: Continuities and Change in Theories of Human Nature*. Harvard University Press.

Further reading

Bond, M.H. (ed.) (1988) *The Cross-cultural Challenge to Social Psychology*. Cross-cultural research and methodology series, vol. 11. Sage.

Rule Goldberger, N. and Bennet Veroff, J. (eds) (1995) *The Culture and Psychology Reader*. New York University Press.

Jahoda began as a conventional social psychologist, but contact with anthropologists at the University of Manchester persuaded him to take up a post in West Africa. This experience transformed his outlook on psychology and led into pioneering cross-cultural research during the early 1950s, when such work was still regarded as highly eccentric. At the outset the many exciting problems resulting from rapid social change were the main focus of research. After returning to the UK, he made repeated field trips over a period of more than twenty years, dealing more with developmental aspects of perception and cognition. One key problem of both theoretical and practical importance was the difficulty experienced by many Africans with certain specific spatial-perceptual skills. More recently he studied other spheres of functioning where Africans excel Euramericans. Over the years he helped to gain some measure of academic respectability for cross-cultural psychology, though it is not yet widely taught.

Jahoda, Maria

Born: 1907, Vienna, Austria **Nat:** Austrian **Ints:** General, industrial and organizational, personality and social, Psychoanalysis Society for the Psychological Study of Social Issues **Educ:** University of Vienna, 1926–33; Teaching Diploma, 1928; DPhil University of Sussex, 1933; **Appts & awards:** APA Fellow. 1955; Hon. DLit., University of Sussex, 1973; University of Leicester, 1973; University of Bremen; CBE 1975; Hon. Fellow, 1980 BPS; Kurt Lewin Memorial Award, 1980; APA Award for Contributions to Psychology in the Public Interest, 1981; Visiting Fellow Professor Emeritus, Social Psychology Science Policy Research Unit, University of Sussex; 1984

Principal publications

1933 *Die Arbeitslosen von Marienthal*. Hirzl (with P.F. Lazarfeld and H. Zeisl). (English edn, Tavistock.)

1949 *Anti-Semitism and Emotional Disorder*. Harper (with N.W. Ackerman).

1958 *Positive Mental Health*. Basic Books.

1968 The migration of psychoanalysis: Its impact on American psychology. *Perspectives in American History*, II.

1977 *Freud and the Dilemmas of Psychology*. Hogarth.

1979 Toward a participatory society. *New University Quarterly*.

1980 One model of man or many? In A.J. Chapman and D.M. Jones (eds), *Models of Man*. BPS Publishing.

1982 *Employment and Unemployment: A Social-Psychological Analysis*. Cambridge University Press.

1984 Unemployment – curse or liberation. In P.K. Marstrand (ed.), *New Technology and the Future of Work and Skills.* Frances Pinter.

Further reading
O'Connel, A.N. and Russo, N.F. (1990) *Women in Psychology: A Bio-bibliographical Sourcebook.* Greenwood.

Maria Jahoda was born of Jewish parents in Vienna. The background of anti-Semitic discrimination of the period and Austrian fascism of the mid 1930s became significant factors in her early life. After completing Realgymnasium in 1926, she entered both the Pedagogical Academy of Vienna and the doctoral program at the University of Vienna. The leading faculty members in psychology at the University of Vienna were **Karl** and **Charlotte Buhler**. She married Paul Lazarsfeld in 1927 and their daughter Lotte Bailyn, born in 1930, is Professor of Organizational Psychology and Management, Sloan School of Management, at the Massachusetts Institute of Technology. In the 1930s her marriage ended and her husband left for America. She replaced him as Director of the Wirtschaftspsychologische Forschungsstelle.

In November 1936 Jahoda was arrested and imprisoned for her activities in the underground movement. She was subjected to nightly interrogations by the Austrian State Police. Foreign intervention led to her release and expulsion from Austria in July 1937. She was invited to England by Alexander Farquharson, general secretary of the British Institute of Sociology. As the war neared its end, Jahoda's main concern became the reunion with her daughter, who had spent the war years in the United States.

Jahoda's first position in the United States was in the Research Department of the American Jewish Committee. After three years she moved to the Bureau of Applied Social Research at Columbia University where she remained for a year. In 1953, only eight years after she came to America she was elected president of the Society for the Psychological Study of Social Issues. In 1958 Jahoda married Ausen H. Albu, engineer and prominent Labour party member of the British Parliament. Shortly after her arrival in England she was appointed Research Fellow at Brunel College in London. In 1965 the University of Sussex invited her to develop and chair a Department of Social Psychology, the first such department in the United Kingdom.

In dealing with a variety of topics, the major effort of Maria Jahoda has been to engage in a limited, non-reductionist social psychology, giving equal weight to each of its constituent fields. Geographical mobility has made her familiar with three different cultures, and she tried to identify in each some dominant issues that could possibly be illuminated by social psychological research and that made visible connections which remain invisible to the naked eye. In Austria the major issue was unemployment; in the USA it was prejudice, mental health and McCarthyism; in England, both before World War II and more recently, it was employment and unemployment, now linked with the impact of new technology. She argues that theories should be considered as an essential tool for acquiring substantive knowledge about people and the social world, not as the ultimate goal of social psychology.

James, William

Born: 1842, New York, USA ***Died:*** 1910, Chocorua, New Hampshire, USA ***Nat:*** American ***Ints:*** Philosophical and theoretical psychology, religious issues ***Educ:*** MD Harvard University, 1868 ***Appts & awards:*** Instructor (later Lecturer) in Anatomy and Physiology, Harvard, 1872–80; Professor of Philosophy, Harvard, 1880–1910; President, APA, 1894, 1904

Principal publications

1890 *Principles of Psychology,* 2 vols. Holt.
1897 *The Will to Believe.* Longmans Green.
1902 *The Varieties of Religious Experience.* Longmans Green.
1907 *Pragmatism.* Longmans Green.
1909 *The Meaning of Truth.* Longmans Green.
1909 *A Pluralistic Universe.* Longmans Green.

Further reading
Myers, G.E. (1986) *William James: His Life and Thought.* Yale University Press.
Wilshire, B.W. (1984) *William James: The Essential Writings.* SUNY Press.

William James's grandfather, another William James, made a fortune from land speculation at the beginning of the nineteenth century. His father (Henry James Sr, d. 1882) spent it, leading a life of cultured ease while establishing a reputation as an eccentric theologian. William James himself, his brother Henry (the novelist) and three younger siblings benefited from an upbringing in which regular visits to Europe, knowledge of French and German and an interest in every kind of intellectual and artistic activity were taken for granted. But all the male children had to provide for themselves financially; William, in particular, was noted for his obsessive concern with money and was likely to enquire of any new acquaintance what his income was. His was a complex personality, since he inherited the family susceptibility to physical disorders of psychological origin. (This appears to have been a general characteristic of the American middle and upper classes of his time – there is no mystery about the reason for **Freud**'s immediate success when he visited the USA in 1909.) In many ways James resembled Dr Johnson in being a man who would have been remembered as remarkable even if he had achieved nothing at all. It has been said of Johnson that we praise him as a critic while dissenting from every one of his critical opinions. James achieved comparable moral stature: he was hailed as the greatest living American (a distinction not commonly bestowed on philosophers) but it is not easy to determine which, if any, of his achievements posterity should value highly.

James's first impulse was to become a painter but he was persuaded by his father that this offered no secure financial prospect. He then studied medicine at Harvard, and qualified (1868) but never practised. He was offered an appointment teaching anatomy and physiology, which he took up (1872), but his interests shifted in the direction of psychology and philosophy. He taught the first psychology course at Harvard in 1875 and began teaching philosophy in 1879, becoming assistant professor in 1880 and full professor in 1885. He had established a psychological laboratory in the mid-1870s (before **Wundt**, in Leipzig in 1879) in which reaction times to light and sound stimuli were measured and two-point tactile thresholds were established for different parts of the human body. (These topics still figured in my own first-year studies in the 1950s.) James contracted to write his *Principles of Psychology* in 1878. The book was published in 1890, but by that time he had lost interest in experimental psychology, and in 1897 he published *The Will to Believe and Other Essays in Popular Philosophy*. In 1901–2 he delivered the Gifford Lectures in the University of Edinburgh, and in 1902 published *The Varieties of Religious Experience*. In 1907 he published *Pragmatism* and in 1909 *A Pluralistic Universe* (the Hibbert Lectures given at the University of Oxford). He died in 1910 at home in Chocorua, New Hampshire. Since before 1890 his interests in psychology had been limited to the 'subliminal', abnormal psychological states, hypnosis and parapsychology.

James's *Principles of Psychology* is probably his best-known work. It was twelve years in the writing and drew on a variety of sources. He opposed German structuralism and advocated a version of what is now called functionalism. In a reply (1892) to an unfavourable review he insisted that psychology was concerned not with 'soul' or 'mind-stuff' or the 'transcendental ego' but with 'conscious events whose causes lie in large part in the physical world'. A note in his copy of J.S. Mill's *System of Logic* reads 'Mill treats [inductive methods] as if they were mainly methods of discovering causes. Nine times out of ten they are used merely for testing causes hypothetically conceived.' It is for this relatively sophisticated attitude to psychology as a science that modern psychologists owe their greatest debt to James (as we shall see, it did not satisfy James himself). He accepted an implicit dualism in which the old associationist principles of similarity and contiguity could be allowed to operate at an unconscious level as in lower animal species. In human beings consciousness supervened as a 'fighter for ends' to select those aspects of the situation required for reasoning in the service of survival. This 'dissociative' capacity of consciousness was regarded by James as more likely to be given *a priori* (following Kant) than learned (as was held by Herbert Spencer), since the latter view implies Lamarckian inheritance of acquired characters. But (following **Darwin**) James did allow that experience could be 'front door' (learned by the individual) or 'back door' (made possible by brain and body structures evolved in accordance with Darwinian principles). James held that objects in space were given directly in perception, contrary to the empiricist view current in his time (and now) that the eye can give access only to coloured shapes in two dimensions and has to be supplemented by the products of tactile experience in order to achieve perception in depth.

Not much is now remembered of the content of James's psychology. The James–Lange theory of emotion (Lange was a Swedish physiologist who advanced the theory independently of James) held that 'everyday bodily movements said to be expressions of emotion are, to the contrary, either the causes of the emotion or the actual stuff of which the emotion consists'. We are frightened because we run away, not vice versa. What is excluded is the possibility that emotion (a conscious mental state) can 'cause' bodily behaviour. This (the lay view) was too crudely dualist for James, who held that since there was no introspective warrant for distinguishing 'consciousness' from 'conscious contents', the latter could not be allowed independent causal efficacy. There are good empirical grounds for rejecting the James–Lange theory, although modern alternatives still tend to be implicitly dualist. James adopted the term 'specious present' to describe the element of time-sampling that characterizes our everyday perceptual experience. We are at all times aware of what has just happened and of what we think is about to happen – not just of an instantaneous event occurring at the limit separating what is past from what is to come. Most experimental work in perception has employed the strict present (often made stricter by brief presentation times), but James's concept seems to correspond more closely to ordinary experience. James characterized the experience of the new-born as 'one great blooming, buzzing confusion', but it as well to remember that the context makes it clear that he refers to a confused awareness of what is actually present in the baby's immediate environment – he would probably have subscribed to a differentiation theory of perceptual learning, not to an enrichment theory. He employed 'stream of consciousness' as a form of words intended to emphasize the continuity of the succession of images, etc., that characterizes consciousness, against the structuralist view that tended to emphasize the importance of individual 'states' of consciousness. But James's own view is scarcely more acceptable today. For him, normal human consciousness was only 'a narrow extract from a great sea of possible human consciousness of whose limits we know nothing'. Having come to the conclusion that the idea of 'nonconscious' mental contents was self-contradictory, but being obliged to allow 'unconscious' mental events, he was prepared to consider the possibility that such events might be in the consciousness of a secondary personality inhabiting the same body – cases of multiple personality had been observed.

The depth of James's disillusionment with psychology may be perceived from the final sentence of his *Principles*: 'The more sincerely one seeks to trace the actual course of psychogenesis, the steps by which as a race we have come by the mental attributes we possess, the more clearly one perceives "the slowly gathering twilight close in utter night".' He regarded himself as both natural scientist and humanist, and his humanism obliged him to emphasize over and over again the dangers of what he called the 'psychologist's fallacy', the fallacy of conceiving a person's cognitive state as identical with what the psychologist knows about that state – it is always far more than that. For the last twenty years of his life James tried to advance our understanding of human nature through studies involving hypnosis, parapsychology and abnormal mental states. His second main work, *The Varieties of Religious Experience*, is notable for having taken no account at all of what Santayana called 'religious health' – the state of the believer for whom religious belief is an unquestioned part of his life. In 1904 James completed a questionnaire on the subject of religious belief. To the question whether he believed in God because of some argument he replied 'Emphatically no!' Asked whether he believed because he had experienced God's presence, he replied 'No, but rather because I need it so that it "must" be true.' James's undoubted moral stature arises out of his attempts to resolve the conflict between what he took to be full humanity and what could be established as fact by rational methods. He always maintained that where rational methods do not permit us to come to a conclusion we may (indeed must) choose between alternative hypotheses on the basis of subjective preference. The book is concerned almost wholly with twice-born phenomena – for him the ideal human state was 'not the absence of vice but vice there and virtue holding her by the throat'. Not the least remarkable thing about it is perhaps that (according to Bertrand Russell) it almost persuaded Wittgenstein to enter a monastery.

William James's philosophy is not well articulated. Many contemporary philosophers maintain that the best source for it is in fact his *Principles of Psychology*, since his later philosophical works are all directed in part at a popular audience and lack precision. He may be said to have initiated the pragmatist movement. (He professed a debt to C.S. **Peirce**, but it now appears that he exaggerated the degree of his indebtedness.) In pragmatism the meaning and truth of propositions are taken to be derivable from the practical consequences that follow on accepting them. The theory was influential, particularly in the USA in the hands of one of his successors, John **Dewey**. James went on to develop an extreme metaphysical position, 'radical empiricism', which is a monism not of sensations or perceptions but of 'experiences'. Minds and physical objects are simply different arrangements of pure experiences. One bit of experience has to be supposed capable of being both a physical and a mental thing and of participating in two or more minds at the same time. Myers specifies the steps by which James arrived at this position but does not pretend to be able to make it plausible – particularly as, throughout his life, James made remarks that seem to be consistent only with interactive dualism, insisting on the reality of world outside us and on the efficacy of consciousness.

American phenomenologists have adopted James as a precursor, principally because Husserl spoke with guarded approval of his *Principles of Psychology*. But the case is not easy to make, and James is probably best remembered as *sui generis* in every respect.

N.E. WETHERICK

Janet, Pierre Marie Félix

Born: 1859, Paris, France *Died:* 1947, Paris, France *Nat:* French *Ints:* Clinical psychology, psychiatry, psychopathology *Educ:* Licensier en lettres, Ecole Normale Supérieure, 1879–82; Agrégé de Philosophie, 1882; University of the Sorbonne, Dr of Letters, 1889, Dr of Medicine, 1893; *Appts & awards:* Professor, Lycée de Chateauroux, 1882–3, Lycée du Havre, 1883–9; Professor of Psychology, Collège de France, 1902–35

Principal publications

1889 *L'automatisme psychologique*. Félix Alcan.
1892 *L'Etat mental des hystériques*, vol. II. Félix Alcan. (2nd edn, 1911.)
1895 J.M. Charcot et son oeuvre psychologique. *Revue Philosophie*, 39, 569–604.
1898 *Névroses et idées fixes*. Nouv. Ed.
1907 *The Major Symptoms of Hysteria*. Macmillan. (2nd edn, 1920.)
1909 *Les névroses*. Ernest Flammarion.
1919 *Les médications psychologiques*, vol. 2. Félix Alcan.
1923 *La médicine psychologique*. Ernest Flammarion.
1926 *De l'angoisse à l'extase*. Félix Alcan.
1930 Psychological analysis. In C. Murchison (ed.), *Psychologies of 1930*. Clark University Press.

Further reading

Ellenberger, H.F. (1970) *The Discovery of the Unconscious*. Basic Books.

Ey, H. (1968) 'Pierre Janet: The man and the work. In B.B. Wolman, *Historical Roots of Contemporary Psychology*. Harper and Row.
Mayo, E. (1948) *Some Notes on the Psychology of Pierre Janet*. MIT Press.
Schwartz, L. (1950) *Die Neurosen und die dynamische Psychologie von Pierre Janet*. Schwabe.

Pierre Janet was born into an upper middle-class family of scholars, lawyers and engineers. In entering the Ecole Normale Supérieure to study philosophy, he followed in the footsteps of his uncle Paul Janet, a philosopher of some renown. Among his peers were Bergson, Goblot and Durckheim. After graduating, he taught at Chateauroux, moving quickly on to Le Havre, where he taught philosophy and worked voluntarily in the local hospital under the supervision of Drs Gilbert and Powlewicz.

Returning to Paris in 1889, he completed the oral defence of his doctoral thesis, *L'automatisme psychologique*, on the case studies of Léonie, Rose and Lucie; this was the foundation for his dissociation system of psychopathology. Janet followed **Charcot**, his mentor, in the belief that hysteria was caused by 'désagrégations psychologiques' or, translated into English, 'psychological dissociation'. Janet's studies with Léonie had already drawn national and international attention because they appeared to some, but not necessarily to Janet himself, to demonstrate suggestion by telepathy. In Janet's view, the patients' past histories gave them more sophistication with hypnotic procedures than many researchers were willing to allow.

Although he had done the job intermittently since 1985, in 1902 Janet was appointed as **Ribot**'s successor as professor of psychology at the Collège de France in competition against Alfred **Binet**, a post he held until 1934. In 1904, with George Dumas, he founded the *Journal de Psychologie Normale et Pathologique*, and remained as editor until 1937. In 1913, at the International Congress of Medicine in London, Janet criticized **Freud**'s psychoanalysis on the grounds that he, Janet, had priority in discovering the cathartic cure of neuroses and that psychoanalysis was nothing more than a metaphysical system. Arguably, Janet was partially justified on both counts, notwithstanding that Freud and he were both strongly influenced by Charcot, to whom catharsis would have been no stranger.

Janet's psychological system was a combination of analysis and synthesis, all ideas, feelings or sensations tending towards acts. As expounded in *L'automatisme psychologique* in 1889, a dynamic interplay between psychic force and weakness may cause autonomously acting, split-off parts of consciousness creating states of dissociation or hysteria. Forgotten or subconscious traumatic events from early life were responsible for the splits and a cure resulted from their discovery and dissolution. Janet believed that hysteria and neuroses are caused by a depression or exhaustion of the encephalon. These conditions are associated with a narrowing of consciousness and heightened powers of suggestion.

After his death, his 5,000 meticulously handwritten patient files were burnt according to his will for ethical reasons. Others, including Freud, were less careful. Like some other significant philosophers and psychologists (e.g. Leibnitz, Bergson, William **James** and **Hilgard**), Janet saw his vocation as a compromise and potential reconciliation between science and religion. Yet he manifested a critical attitude which, according to Dessoir, 'contained an acid which would dissolve the platinum of facts. But he always remained courteous in his manners'. Could these be the makings of greatness?

DAVID F. MARKS

Janis, Irving Lester

Born: 1918, Buffalo, New York, USA *Died:* 1990, Santa Rosa, California, USA *Nat:* American *Ints:* Social and health *Educ:* BS University of Chicago, 1939; PhD University of Columbia, 1948 *Appts & awards:* Adjunct Professor, University of Berkeley at California; Professor Emeritus, Yale University; APA Distinguished Scientific Contributions Award; Fulbright Award, University of Oslo, 1957–8; Hofheimer Prize, American Psychiatric Association, 1959; AAAS Socio-Psychological Prize, 1967; Fellow, Centre for Advanced Study in the Behavioural Sciences, 1973–4; Guggenheim Fellow, 1973–4; AAAS Fellow, 1974; Senior Fellowship, Netherlands Institute for Advanced Study in the Social Services and Humanities, 1981–2; Kurt Lewin Memorial Award for Research in Social Psychology, APA Division 9, 1985; Editorial Board, *Journal of Experimental Social Psychology*, 1966–70; *American Scientist*, 1969–80, Chairman, Editorial Board, *Journal of Conflict Resolution*, 1972– ; Overseas Editorial Board, *British Journal of Social Psychology*, 1975– ; Associate Editor, *Journal of Behavioural Medicine*, 1980–

Principal publications

1953   Effects of fear arousing communications. *Journal of Abnormal and Social Psychology*, 48, 78–92 (with S. Feshbach).

1959   Motivational factors in the resolution of decisional conflicts. In M.R. Jones (ed.), *Nebraska Symposium on Motivation*. University of Nebraska Press.

1965   Effects of education and persuasion on national and international images. In H. Kelman (ed.), *International Behaviour*. Holt.

1965   Effectiveness of emotional role playing in modifying smoking habits and attitudes. *Journal of Experimental Research in Personality*, 1, 84–90.

1967   Effects of fear arousal on attitude change: Recent developments in theory and experimental research. In L. Berkowitz (ed.), *Advances in Experimental Social Psychology*, vol. 3. Academic Press.

1968   Attitude change via role playing. In R.P. Abelson, E.A. Aronson, W.J. McGuire, T.M. Newcomb, M.J. Rosenberg and P.H. Tannenbaum (eds), *Theories of Cognitive Consistency: A Sourcebook*. Rand-McNally.

1970   Facilitating effects of daily contact between partners who decide to cut down on smoking. *Journal of Personality and Social Psychology*, 17, 25–35 (with D. Hoffman).

1971   *Stress and Frustration*. Harcourt Brace Jovanovich.

1977   *Decision Making: A Psychological Analysis of Conflict, Choice and Commitment*. Free Press (with L. Mann).

1979   Attribution, control, and decision making: Social psychology and health care. In G.C. Stone, F. Cohen and N.E. Adler (eds), *Health Psychology*. Jossey-Bass (with J. Rodin).

1982   *Counselling on Personal Decisions: Theory and Research on Short-term Helping Relationships*. Yale University Press (with D. Quinlan *et al.*).

1982   *Groupthink: Psychological Studies of Policy Decisions and Fiascos*. Houghton Mifflin.

1982   *Stress, Attitudes and Decisions: Selected Papers*, Psychology Centennial Series. Praeger.

1984   The patient as decision maker. In D. Gentry (ed.), *Handbook of Behavioural Medicine*. Guilford Press.

1985   International crisis management in the nuclear age. In S. Oskamp (ed.), *Applied Psychology Annual*, vol. 6. Sage.

Further reading

Aldag, R.J. and Fuller, S.R. (1993) Beyond fiasco: A reappraisal of the groupthink phenomenon and a new model of group decision processes. *Psychological Bulletin*, 113, 533–52.

During his early years at Yale, Janis worked closely with Carl I. **Hovland**, who headed an influential research project on communication and attitude change until his untimely death in 1962. Janis's research included pioneering work on the effects of fear-arousing appeals and facilitating effects of role playing on internalization. His major work, *Psychological Stress*, presents systematic data and case study observations on reactions of surgical patients. In that book he introduced new theoretical concepts – 'the work of worrying' and 'emotional inoculation' (or 'stress inoculation') – which help to explain how maladaptive behaviour can be prevented by appropriate preparatory communications. Late in the 1950s his research began to focus on real-life personal health decisions, such as giving up smoking or going on a low-calorie diet. His book (written in collaboration with Leon Mann) *Decision Making* presents a descriptive theory of how choices are made under stress together with an integrative analysis of pertinent research findings from the behavioural sciences. In the 1980s his research centred on the social influence of counsellors on adherence to stressful decisions. This involved testing hypotheses derived from the theory of self-esteem enhancement induced by a supportive relationship with a nurturant, norm-setting communicator.

In collaboration with colleagues at Yale, he published *Counselling on Personal Decisions*. This book presents the theory and reports twenty-three controlled field experiments that help to explain when, how and why people succeed in adhering to difficult decisions, such as going on a diet, as a consequence of verbal interchanges with a counsellor. Janis also contributed to the study of group dynamics in relation to decision making. His book on *Groupthink* presents detailed case studies of ill-conceived foreign policy decisions. The book delineates a pattern of concurrence seeking that fosters over-optimism, lack of vigilance, and sloganistic thinking in cohesive executive groups.

Jasper, Herbert Henri

Born: 1906, La Grande, Oregon, USA **Nat:** American **Ints:** Neuropsychology, physiological psychology **Educ:** BA Reed College, 1927; MA University of Oregon, 1929; PhD University of Iowa, 1931; DSc University of Paris, 1935 **Appts & awards:** Professor Emeritus, University of Montreal; Hon. Dr, Université de Bourdeaux,

1949, Université de Aix-Marseille, 1960, McGill University, 1971, University of Western Ontario, 1977; Founding President, International Federation of Electroencephalography and Clinical Neurophysiology, International Brain Organization, American EEG Society; William G. Lennox Award for research in epilepsy; Karl Lashley Prize, American Philosophical Society; McLaughlin Medal, Royal Society of Canada; Prix de l'Association des Médecins de la Langue Française; Ralph W. Gerard Prize in Neuroscience; Founding Editor, *Journal of Electroencephalography and Clinical Neurophysiology*

Principal publications

1941 Electroencephalographic classification of the epilepsies. *Archives of Neurological Psychiatry*, 45, 903–43 (with J. Kersham).
1949 Diffuse projection systems: The integrative action of the thalamic reticular system. *EEG Clinical Neurophysiology*, 1, 405–20.
1954 *Epilepsy and the Functional Anatomy of the Human Brain*. Little, Brown (with W. Penfield).
1956 Habituation of the arousal reaction. *Brain*, 79, 655–80 (with S. Sharpless).
1961 The thalamic reticular system. In D.E. Sheer (ed.), *Electrical Stimulation of the Brain: An Interdisciplinary Survey of Neurobehavioural Systems*. University of Texas Press.
1963 *Progress in Brain Research*. vol. 1: *Brain Mechanisms*. Elsevier (ed. with G. Morruzzi and A. Fessard).
1968 Neurophysiological mechanisms in learning. In E. Stellar and J.M. Sprague (eds), *Progress in Physiological Psychology*. Academic Press (with B. Doane).
1975 Structural and systems approach to central representation of motor functions: Importance of state dependent reactions. *Canadian Journal of Neurological Sciences*, 2, 315–22.

Further reading

Jasper, H.H. *et al.* (eds) (1995) *Epilepsy and the Functional Anatomy of the Frontal Lobe*. Raven.
Worden, F.G., Swazey, J.P. and Adelman, G. (eds) (1992) *The Neurosciences: Paths of Dicovery*. Birkhauser.

Jasper's major contribution lies in the early development of studies of the brain, not only in relation to the use of electroencephalography in the understanding and diagnosis of neurological diseases of the brain but also, and perhaps principally, in understanding the mechanisms of normal brain function, with particular reference to perceptual awareness, states of consciousness, and learning or conditioning. With the opportunities provided at the Montreal Neurological Institute it was possible for Jasper to record electrical activity from the exposed human brain during neurosurgical operations for focal epilepsy carried out by Wilder **Penfield**. This made possible the correlation of changes in electrical activity with functional localization in the cerebral cortex in relation to clinical signs of epilepsy; that is, sensation or motor disturbances as well as states of consciousness. Jasper was one of the first to appreciate that the electroencephalogram had its great limitations, because of the difficulty and complexity of interpreting the gross electrical waves recorded from the surface of the cortex; so he developed microelectrode techniques to record from individual cells. His development of such techniques for use in conscious animals, particularly in monkeys, which were used to study unit discharge from various parts of the brain during conditioning or learned motor behaviour, was taken up in many laboratories throughout the world.

Jasper argued that it was necessary to advance beyond an analysis of the electrical activity of the brain and believed that chemical changes must be considered together with electrical ones. He began by showing that the liberation of acetylcholine (ACh) from the cortical surface was closely related to the pattern of the electroencephalogram and to the responsiveness of animals. In other words, when animals were acutely aroused there was a marked increase in the liberation of ACh, and when they were asleep there was a very marked decrease. The one exception was that in paradoxical sleep there was also an increase in ACh liberation. He went on to study liberation of other chemical substances, including all of the amino acids and later the monoamines, in relation to electrical activity and behaviour. This has led to a revolution in understanding of the organization of the brain in relation to chemical mediator and modulator substances, of which there are now very many, including the peptides. In the course of these neurochemical studies Jasper demonstrated with his colleagues the inhibitory properties of gamma aminobutyric acid (GABA) and the excitatory properties of glutamic acid and aspartic acid. These two observations have been of considerable importance, since GABA has been shown to be the principal inhibitory substance of the brain and glutamate and aspartate have been shown to be important excitatory substances.

Jaspers, Karl Theodore

Born: 1883, Oldenburg, Germany **Died:** 1969, Basle, Switzerland **Nat:** German **Ints:** Clinical psychology, philosophical and theoretical psychology **Appts & awards:** University of Heidelburg, Privatdozent in Psychology, 1913–20, Professor of Philosophy, 1921–37, 1945–48; University of Basle, Professor of Philosophy, 1949–69

Principal publications

1913   *General Psychopathology*, trans. J. Hoenig and M.W. Hamilton. Manchester University Press. (1962, from the 7th German edn, 1959.)

1919   *Psychologie der Weltanschauungen*. Springer-Verlag. (4th edn. 1954.)

1932   *Philosophy* (3 vols), trans. E.R Ashton. Chicago University Press. (1969–71, from the 3rd German edn, 1956.)

1935   *Reason and Existence*, trans. W. Earle. Noonday Press (1955, from the 3rd German edn, 1949.)

1948   *The Perennial Scope of Philosophy*, trans. R. Mannheim. Routledge Kegan Paul. (1949; 4th German edn, 1955.)

Further reading

Schilpp, P.A. (1957) *The Philosophy of Karl Jaspers.* Tudor Publishing.

Karl Jaspers was born in 1883 into a prosperous north German family. From childhood he suffered a heart condition which ruled out physical exertion. He nevertheless survived to the age of 86 by exercising the most rigid control over his activities, social and professional. He was unable to take up any full-time medical appointment or engage in any public political activity; he did, however, manage to write more than thirty books and innumerable articles on psychology, philosophy, cultural history and contemporary social and political issues. He held very strong anti-nationalist political views. On the outbreak of World War I he tried to persuade the European universities to oppose the war jointly, in the name of universally held cultural values – in fact they all followed their own nationalist line. After World War II he tried to persuade the American occupying force to govern Germany as a virtual colony for twenty years, on the grounds that the only Germans then capable of participating in democratic government were minor ex-Nazis or people who had already shown their incapacity in the pre-Nazi period. Needless to say such views did not recommend him to the authorities. He was deprived by the Nazis of his university chair in 1937 and forbidden to publish after 1938. His wife was Jewish – all in all their survival was little short of miraculous. He was restored to his chair in 1945, but in 1949 he moved to Basle in Switzerland after nearly half a century at Heidelburg.

He had initially studied law but switched to medicine, in particular to psychiatry. In 1913 he published the first edition of a textbook (*General Psychopathology*) which established his reputation on the Continent and was sufficiently highly regarded, fifty years later, to persuade the University of Manchester to sponsor an English translation of the seventh edition. He was, however, physically unable to contemplate a career in medicine and his interests shifted to psychology and philosophy. The successive editions of his textbook were based on published research reports, since he did no clinical work himself after 1915. He was concerned solely with the comprehension of meaningful psychological relationships that demonstrated an 'inner causality' as opposed to the 'outer (genuine) causality' that it was the business of physical and biological science to discover. This objective obliged him to consider all theoretical approaches, since any of them might succeed in finding an example of the 'inner causality' he was interested in. He denied the possibility of arriving at one all-embracing theory of human nature – human beings were, in his view, too complex. Of **Freud** he wrote 'Freud sees with great acuteness whàt are the results of repressed sexuality, but he never once asks what happens when mind and spirit are repressed.' These latter questions could not, in Jaspers's view, be avoided and ruled out any theory that pretended to be all-embracing. Freud had simply vulgarized the insights of Kierkegaard and Nietzsche, and the vulgarization accounted for the popularity of his ideas.

Later Jaspers wrote 'Where I had, scientifically, something to say, I wrote objectively on the matter: when I philosophised, I wrote from the standpoint of the Encompassing.' In his textbook he had had something to say, scientifically, and the book is an empirical study in the wide sense of that term. His subsequent philosophical work was concerned with what he called the 'Encompassing' – with 'what is neither object nor act-of-thinking (subject) but contains both within itself'. His philosophical writing is for that reason extremely difficult to understand. It is widely accepted in British and American philosophy that any attempt to be 'encompassing' will necessarily sacrifice clarity. One has in effect to choose between clarity and adequacy to the complexities of the subject matter. Jaspers (and many other continental philosophers) chose to attempt adequacy. He never acquired a popular following and had nothing like the influence of Freud on contemporary ideas. Continental existentialist philosophy, though it too harked back to Kierkegaard and Nietszche, took its origins from Heidegger and Sartre, not from him. He was nevertheless a remarkable man whose time may be yet to come.

N.E. WETHERICK

Jaynes, Julian
Born: n.d. **Nat:** American **Ints:** Philosophical and theoretical psychology **Educ:** Harvard University; Yale University **Appts & awards:** Attached to the Department of Psychology, Princeton University, 1965–

Principal publications
1970 The problem of animate motion in the 17th century. *Journal of the History of Ideas*, 31, 219–34.

1974 In the shadow of the enlightenment. *Journal of the History of the Behavioral Sciences*, 10, 3–15, 144–59 (with W. Woodward).

1976 The evolution of language in the late pleistocene. In S. Harnad (ed.), *The Origins and Evolution of Language*. Annals of the New York Academy of Sciences, no. 280.

1977 *The Origin of Consciousness in the Breakdown of Bicameral Mind*. Houghton Mifflin. (Pelican paperback, 1982; new edn, 1990, with afterword; Penguin, 1993.)

Further reading
Dennett, D. (1986) Julian Jaynes' software archaeology. *Canadian Psychology*, 27, 149–54.

Julian Jaynes was educated at Harvard and Yale and has been teaching at Princeton since 1965. He has achieved a major reputation outside psychology but is frequently dismissed with contempt inside because he has had the temerity to try to answer questions that are not susceptible to direct 'scientific' investigation. (His own 'scientific' credentials are impeccable, since he contributed to the revolutionary work on animal learning of the late 1960s and 1970s.) It is a fact of common observation that individuals (and indeed societies) differ in the extent to which they see themselves as units participating in an organic whole in which each has a function to perform of greater or lesser significance, or as 'individuals' in the full sense, originators of their own behaviour who are prepared to co-operate in society only on the basis of consent freely given. The latter view is the basis of democratic society, and Jaynes's suggestion that it is not universal in the human species and was unknown till about 3,000 years ago is sufficient grounds for some relatively sophisticated psychologists to dismiss it as 'politically unacceptable' (for the rest, the fact that it is not 'scientific' is enough).

Jaynes writes 'Man and his early civilisation had a profoundly different mentality from our own ... men and women were not conscious as we are, were not responsible for their actions ... instead each person had a part of his nervous system ... by which he was ordered about like any slave, a (hallucinated) voice or voices which was what we call volition ... and was related to the hallucinated voices of others in a carefully established hierarchy.' He argues that the first effect of the evolution of language was to enhance greatly the efficiency of social groups in which a hierarchy had been established (originally by violence). An alpha-male baboon can make another member of his group do what he wants in his presence, here and now. But in a human group, a verbal instruction can be carried in the head of the recipient and obeyed in another time and place. There is much evidence that the earliest civilizations (e.g. Sumeria) worked on this basis. A voice was literally 'heard' in the head, instructing the individual what to do, and this voice was interpreted as the voice of the individual's 'god'. In the earliest Greek poetry (e.g. the *Iliad*) what an individual does is the responsibility of the god, whose instructions must be obeyed. Only later (e.g. in the *Odyssey*) do individuals take responsibility for their own actions. In the oldest books of the Old Testament, those who hear the voice of God are honoured as prophets; in the last books, to claim to have heard the voice of God is a capital offence. What had happened was that social pressures (possibly the result of population increase) had disrupted societies so that the 'voices' no longer spoke in a 'carefully established hierarchy'. To maintain cohesion it was necessary to adopt draconian penal codes, but even these could not succeed in the long term, as the internal voices came to be interpreted as the volitions of the individual and not as instructions that had to be obeyed. The only possible ground of social cohesion was then consent freely given, which the Greeks adopted shortly after.

Jaynes refers to this change as the 'breakdown of the bicameral mind'; the mind became unicameral in many individuals but 'the vestiges of the bicameral mind ... live at the very heart of a culture or subculture, moving out and filling up the unspoken and the unrationalised'. Evidence of their continued presence may be found in the 'voices' that sometimes instruct a schizophrenic man to kill his wife -- which he believes he cannot disobey; in hypnosis; in the phenomena of political consent, where the view expressed in the old English prayer 'God bless the squire and his relations / and keep us in our proper stations' is still powerful in many societies.

Jaynes's theory is the most successful attempt I know of to account for the evolution of specifically human society on the basis of historical evidence. To understand his argument one must, however, realize that 'consciousness' for him means 'consciousness involving awareness of self, not just 'perceptual awareness of the world outside us' as possessed by lower organisms. Jaynes's sense was at one time the most common sense of the term; he is not suggesting that until 3,000 years ago we lacked perceptual awareness of our environment. One must also remember that his theory, though it takes for granted a neurological base, does not stand or fall by the state of our knowledge of the functions of the left and right hemispheres of the brain at the time he developed the theory (the mid-1970s). A further volume on the 'effects of consciousness' is promised for future publication.

N.E. WETHERICK

Jensen, Arthur Robert

Born: 1923, San Diego, California, USA *Nat:* American *Ints:* Developmental psychology, educational psychology, evaluation and measurement, experimental psychology, personality and social psychology, physiological and comparative *Educ:* BA University of California at Berkeley, 1945; MA San Diego State University, 1952; PhD Teachers College, Columbia University, 1956 *Appts & awards:* NIMH Research Fellow, 1956–8; Guggenheim Fellow, 1964–5; Professor of Educational Psychology, University of California at Berkeley Vice-President, American Educational Research Association, 1971

Principal publications

1969   How much can we boost scholastic achievement? *Harvard Educational Review*, 39, 1–123.

1972 *Genetics of Education*. Harper and Row.
1973 *Educability and Group Differences*. Harper and Row.
1980 *Bias in Mental Tests*. Free Press.
1982 Reaction time and psychometric *g*. In H.J. Eysenck (ed.), *A Model for Intelligence*. Springer-Verlag.
1985 The nature of the black-white difference on various psychometric tests: Spearman's hypothesis. *Behavioral and Brain Sciences*, 8, 193–219.
1987 Process differences and individual differences in some cognitive tasks. *Intelligence*, 11, 107–36.
1989 Raising IQ without increasing *g*? Review of the Milwaukee Project: Preventing mental retardation in children at risk. *Developmental Review*, 9, 234–58.
1993 Physical correlates of human intelligence. In P.A. Vernon (ed.), *Biological Approaches to the Study of Human Intelligence*. Ablex. (with S.N. Sinha)

Further reading

Mogdil, S. and Mogdil, C. (1987). *Arthur Jensen: Consensus and Controversy*. Falmer.

After obtaining his PhD from Columbia, the first decade of Arthur Jensen's life was spent applying **Hull**ian theory to verbal learning. When this theory entered its death throes, Jensen moved fields to the psychology of individual differences, where he concentrated on the field of general intelligence and scholastic performance. His particular interest lay in the highly controversial field of individual, cultural, social-class and racial differences in scholastic performance, and his 1969 paper attempted to understand why members of certain minority groups appeared to perform less well in school than members of the white majority. One source of such differences might be the inappropriateness of certain psychological testing procedures for members of minority groups, and Jensen's (1980) book is a masterly psychometric treatise on the nature, origins and empirical evidence for bias in tests of general ability. He also developed an information-processing theory of intelligence and succeeded where **Galton** failed in showing a relationship between general intelligence and measures derived from choice reaction-time tasks. He has subsequently studied several physical and neurological correlates of general intelligence.

Few psychologists have a term of abuse named after them, but 'Jensenism' entered the language as part of the outcry against his 1969 paper. The work that generated such opprobrium suggested that, in addition to studying the way in which environmental and cultural factors affected intelligence, it might also be necessary to consider the possibility that different racial groups may differ in their mean levels of general intelligence, and that such differences may be genetically determined through a process of natural selection. These suggestions were politically highly sensitive because of their implications for the likely efficacy of remedial educational programmes, and because they questioned the egalitarian basis of American society. Jensen's suggestions were seized by the political right (and opposed on principal by the political left, which included many in the psychological community), the debate being fuelled more by rhetoric than by hard data.

The subsequent rise in prominence of human behaviour genetics, and the general acceptance that many aspects of individual differences are to some extent under genetic control, have led to a change in climate: John Loehlin's carefully worded article in the journal *Intelligence* recently suggested that it may be scientifically legitimate to perform research into racial differences in ability under certain circumstances. Empirical evidence has also suggested that the social 'explanations' offered by Jensen's critics are themselves unable to explain fully the observed group differences in ability. The controversy generated by this 1969 paper has, unfortunately, largely overshadowed Jensen's other very substantial and utterly uncontroversial contributions to the psychometry of ability, chronometric studies of intelligence and correlates of ability.

COLIN COOPER

Jing, Qicheng (C.C. Ching)

Born: 1926, Beijing, China **Nat:** Chinese **Ints:** Development, experimental psychology, general psychology, history of psychology, industrial and organizational psychology, perception **Educ:** BEd Fu Jen University, 1947; MA Fu Jen University, 1950 **Appts & Awards:** Professor of Psychology and Deputy Director, Institute of Psychology, Chinese Academy of Sciences; Visiting Scholar, University of Michigan, 1979–80; Chairman, Sub-Committee of Colour: Technical Committee on Ergonomics Standardisation, Bureau of National Standards, 1980– ; Deputy Chairman, Department of Psychology, Beijing University, 1980–3; Deputy Chairman, Academic Committee, Institute of Psychology, Chinese Academy of Sciences, 1981– ; Deputy

Director, Academic Committee, Institute of Psychology, Chinese Academy of Sciences, 1981– ; Advisory Council International Association for the Study of Attention and Performance, 1981– ; Chairman, Committee on International Academic Exchanges, Chinese Psychological Society, 1981– ; Academic Committee, Beijing University, 1981–3; Deputy Director, Child Development Centre of China, 1983; Executive Committee, International Union of Psychological Science, 1984; President, Chinese Psychological Society, 1984– ; Education Panel, State Council Degree Commission, 1985– ; Editorial Board, *Acta Psychologica Sinica*, 1960, *International Journal of Psychology*, 1984; Foreign Editor, *Encyclopaedia of Psychology* (Wiley), 1984

Principal publications

1958   *Theoretical Foundation of Structuralism of W. Wundt and E. Titchener*. Science Publishers.

1962   Natural science and psychological theory. *New Construction*, 12, 31–46.

1963   Perception; Attention. In J.C. Cao (ed.), *General Psychology*. People's Education Press.

1965   Kinetic depth effect caused by vergence of the eyes. *Acta Psychologica Sinica*, 4, 323–32.

1979   *Colorimetry*. Science Publishers (with S. Jiao, B. Yu and W. Hu).

1980   Visual performance of young Chinese observers. *Lighting Research and Technology*, 12, 59–63 (with B. Yu, S. Jiao, L. Kuan and K. Chao).

1981   Sensory and perceptual skills in the People's Republic of China. *Psychologia*, 24, 133–45 (with S. Jiao).

1982   The one-child family in China: The need for psychosocial research. *Studies in Family Planning*, 13, 208–12.

1983   *The Human Intellect*. Shanghai Science and Technology Publishers (with S. Pan, F. Liu and L. Xu).

1983   Color vision; Space perception. In B.Y. He, S.Y. Chen and H.C. Zhang (eds), *Experimental Psychology*. Beijing University Press.

1984   Psychology in China. In R.J. Corsini (ed.), *Encyclopaedia of Psychology*. Wiley.

1984   Psychophysics of binocular vision. In *Issues in Cognition: Proceedings of a Joint Conference in Psychology*. NAS/CAS. NAS and APA.

1985   *General Psychology*, (collection of entries from *Chinese Encyclopaedia*). Chinese Encyclopaedia Publishers.

1989   Recent development of psychology in China. *Japanese Journal of Psychology*, 60, 117–21.

1994   Development of psychology in China. The

origins and development of psychology: Some national and regional perspectives. *International Journal of Psychology*, 29, 667–75.

Further reading

Jing, Q. (1989) Recent development of psychology in China. *Japanese Journal of Psychology*, 60, 117–21.

Jing, Q. (1994) Development of psychology in China. The origins and development of psychology: Some national and regional perspectives. *International Journal of Psychology*, 29, 667–75.

Professor Jing has published extensively in the fields of visual function, perception of size and distance and colour measurement. His book *Colorimetry* was the first book published in Chinese on colour science, and is considered as a standard reference in his country. Jing has wide interests in the general field of psychology. He has published on systems and schools of psychology and on problems of the philosophy of science in psychology. He also has interests in child development and has published articles on the single-child family in China.

Jing is active in Chinese psychology. He was the first psychologist from mainland China to visit the West since the founding of the People's Republic of China in 1949. Since 1978 he has represented the Chinese Psychological Society at various annual conferences throughout the world, including those of the Australian Psychological Society, the APA, and the International Congress of Psychology. Jing has initiated a number of exchanges in psychology between China and other countries.

MORIA MAGUIRE

Johnson-Laird, Philip Nicholas

Born: 1936, Rothwell, Yorkshire, England **Nat:** English **Ints:** Experimental psychology, philosophical and theoretical psychology, psychology and the arts **Educ:** BA University College London, 1964; PhD University of London, 1967 **Appts & awards:** Department of Psychology, Princeton University; Rosa Morison Memorial Medal, University College London, 1964; James Sully Scholarship, 1964–6; Spearman Medal, BPS, 1974; Hon. Dr, Gothenburg University, 1983; President's Award, BPS, 1985; Stuart Professor of Psychology, Princeton University, 1989; Editorial Board, *Quarterly Journal of Experimental Psychology*, 1970–2, *Cognitive Psychology*, 1975– , *Cognition*, 1975– , *Cognitive Sci-*

ence, 1977– , *Cognition and Brain Theory*, 1980–5, *Journal of Semantics*, 1982– , *Cognitive Development Abstracts*, 1983– , *Language and Cognitive Processes*, 1985– ; Editorial Consultant, *Behavioral and Brain Sciences*

Principal publications

1968   *Thinking and Reasoning*. Pelican (ed. with P.C. Wason).

1970   A theoretical analysis of insight into a reasoning task. *Cognitive Psychology*, 1, 134–48 (with P.C. Wason).

1970   Memory for syntax. *Nature*, 227, 412 (with R. Stevenson).

1972   *Psychology of Reasoning*. Batsford and Harvard University Press (with P.C. Wason).

1974   Experimental psycholinguistics. *Annual Review of Psychology*, 25, 135–60.

1976   *Language and Perception*. Cambridge University Press and Harvard University Press (with G.A. Miller).

1977   *Thinking*. Cambridge University Press (ed. with P.C. Wason).

1977   Procedural semantics. *Cognition*, 5, 189–214.

1978   The psychology of syllogisms. *Cognitive Psychology*, 10, 64–99 (with M. Steedman).

1980   Mental models in cognitive science. *Cognitive Science*, 4, 71–115.

1982   Thinking as a skill. *Quarterly Journal of Experimental Psychology*, 34a, 1–29.

1983   *Mental Models*. Cambridge University Press and Harvard University Press.

1983   A computational analysis of consciousness. *Cognition and Brain Theory*, 6, 499–508.

1984   Syllogistic inference. *Cognition*, 16, 1–61.

1984   Only connections: A critique of semantic networks. *Psychological Bulletin*, 96, 292–315 (with D.J. Herrmann and R. Chaffin).

1987   The mental representation of the meaning of words. *Cognition*, 25, 189–211.

1990   The development of reasoning. In G. Butterworth and P. Bryant (eds), *Causes of Development: Interdisciplinary Perspectives*. Harvester Wheatsheaf.

1993   *Human and Machine Thinking*. Erlbaum.

1994   *The Computer and the Mind*. Fontana, 2nd edn. (1st edn, 1988.)

Further reading

Johnson-Laird, P.N. and Byrne, R.M. (1993) Precis of deduction. *Behavioral and Brain Sciences*, 16, 323–80.

Klauer, K.C. and Oberauer, K. (1995) Testing the mental model theory of propositional reasoning. *Quarterly Journal of Experimental Psychology:*

Human Experimental Psychology, 48A, 671–87.

Reisenzein, R. (1995) On Oatley and Johnson-Laird's theory of emotion and hierarchical structures in the affective lexicon. *Cognition and Emotion*, 9, 383–416.

Johnson-Laird's work can be structured around five topics: the psychology of reasoning, psycholinguistics, creativity, emotions and consciousness. The work on reasoning has led to the theory that people make deductive inferences, not following internalized formal rules of inference (as suggested by **Piaget**, Brain and many others), but using internal models of the premises. They use their understanding of the premises to construct a model, or image, of them; they formulate an informative conclusion based on this model; and then, if they are prudent, they search for an alternative model of the premises that serves as a counter-example to this conclusion. If there is no such model, the conclusion is logically valid. This theory emphazises the role of meaning in making inferences. Johnson-Laird modelled it in computer programs and has shown that it gives a good account of many experimental results. His work on psycholinguistics has concerned the process of syntactic parsing, lexical semantics and the interpretation of sentences. Its central thesis is that the major psychological theories of meaning have failed to take reference into account, and that the proper way in which to remedy this omission is to treat the interpretation of discourse as a process that leads to the construction of mental models of the world based on discourse. His research continues in these two areas, but in addition he has developed computational models of creativity, emotionality and consciousness. He proposed a theory of musical improvisation, which has been modelled in programs that construct chord sequences and improvise melodies to them.

Jones, Edward, E.

Born: 1926, Buffalo, New York, USA **Nat:** American **Ints:** Abnormal psychology, personality and social psychology **Educ:** AB Harvard College, 1949; PhD Harvard University, 1953 **Appts & Awards:** Fellow, APA, 1963– ; AAA&S 1982– , APA Publications Board, Member, 1964–70, Chairman, 1967–69; APA Ad Hoc Communication Committee, 1968–70; APA Council of Representatives, 1969–72; APA Board of Scientific Affairs, 1975–6; APA Committee on Scientific Awards, Member,

1981–4, Chairman, 1982–4; SSRC Board of Directors, 1975–6; Editorial Board, *Journal of Experimental Social Psychology*, 1965– , *Contemporary Psychology*, 1966–82, Executive Committee, Society of Experimental Social Psychology, Member, 1976–81, Chairman, 1979–80; APA Distinguished Scientific Contribution Award, 1977; Stuart Professor of Psychology, Princeton University, 1977–89; *Social Cognition*, 1980– , *British Journal of Social Psychology*, 1981– ; Editorial Committee, *Annual Review of Psychology*, 1975–76

Principal publications

1954   Authoritarianism as a determinant of first-impression formation. *Journal of Personality*, 23, 107–27.

1962   Some determinants of reactions to being approved or disapproved as a person. *Psychological Monographs*, 76, no. 521 (with K.G. Gergen and K.E. Davis).

1963   Some conditions affecting the evaluation of a conformist. *Journal of Personality*, 31, 270–88 (with R.G. Jones and K.J. Gergen).

1967   *Foundations of Social Psychology*. Wiley (with H.B. Gerard).

1971   *Order Effects in Impression Formation: Attribution Context and the Nature of the Entity*. General Learning Press (with G. Goethals).

1971   *The Actor and the Observer: Divergent Perceptions of the Causes of Behavior*. General Learning Press (with R. Nisbett).

1971   The bogus pipeline: A new paradigm for measuring affect and attitude. *Psychological Bulletin*, 76, 349–64 (with H. Sigall).

1972   Attitude similarity, expectancy violation, and attraction. *Journal of Experimental Social Psychology*, 8, 222–35 (with G.A. Wein).

1973   Delay of consequences and riskiness of decisions. *Journal of Personality*, 41, 613–37 (with C. Anderson Johnson).

1973   *Ingratiation: An Attributional Approach*. General Learning Press (with C. Wortman).

1984   *Social Stigma: The Psychology of Marked Relationships*. Freeman (with A. Farina, A. Hastorf, H. Markus, D. Miller and R. Scott).

1976   The self-monitor looks at the ingratiator. *Journal of Personality*, 44, 654–74 (with R. Baumeister).

1979   The rocky road from acts to dispositions. *American Psychologist*, 34, 107–17.

1982   Toward a general theory of strategic self-presentation. In J. Suls (ed.), *Psychological Perspectives on the Self*, vol. 1. Erlbaum (with T. Pittman).

1982   Choice and attitude attributions: The influence of constraint information on attributions across levels of generality. *Social Cognition*, 1, 1–20 (with N. Cantor and T. Pittman).

1990   *Interpersonal Perception*. Freeman.

Further reading
Brown, R. (1986). *Social Psychology – The Second Edition*. Free Press.

The empirical and conceptual writing of Jones has typically questioned assumptions, scrutinized methods or analysed concepts. When an early interest in personality encountered the attractive rigour of psychometrics, he spent years examining the problems of studying personality. He enquired as to whether they were due to individual variability over time, to inhomogeneity of subjects, to the perspective of the observer, to diversity in the processes by which subjects decide on their responses, or to the multiple meanings of given words. Identifying one source of the difficulties after another, he finally decided that the source was our vague attributive concepts, for no one of which has a comprehensive set of measuring procedures been developed.

With David Campbell he introduced a simple approach to convergent and discriminant validation, and then went on to examine method factors as a pervasive source of unwanted variance generating high specificity for each method. He suggests that the more complex and sophisticated our methods, the stronger are method effects. Looking beyond personality and related areas in psychology, he realized that many other parts of social science share these difficulties and methodological problems. The implications of that view were dominant in his later work.

Thus, the main theme of his work has been the diagnosis of problems in doing social/behavioural research and the identification of potential therapy for these problems. He has also been involved in personnel selection and assessment and in the evaluation of psychotherapy. He worked with Starkey Duncan on the structure and strategies in face-to-face interactions, and on how actions at one moment are linked to both preceding and subsequent actions of the actor or others. His ideas and conclusions are presented in *Interpersonal Perception*.

Jung, Carl Gustav
Born: 1875, Kesswil Constance, Switzerland
Died: 1961, Küsnacht, Zurich, Switzerland **Nat:** Swiss **Ints:** Religious issues, personality and

social, philosophical and theoretical, psychoanalysis, psychology and the arts **Educ:** Licence (Medicine) Basel, 1900; MD Basel, 1902 **Appts & awards:** Hon. LLD, Clarke University, 1909, Fordham University, 1920, Calcutta University, 1938; Founding Editor, *Image*, 1912, *International Journal of Psychoanalysis*, 1913; Hon DSc, Harvard University, 1936, Allahabad, 1938, Oxford University, 1938; FRS Med., London, 1939; Professor of Medical Psychology, University of Basel, 1944–61

Principal publications

1907   Psychological investigations with the galvonometer and phenomograph in normal and insane individuals. *Brain*, 30, 153–218.

1920   *Collected Papers on Analytical Psychology.* Balliere, Twidale and Cox.

1933   *Psychological Types.* Kegan Paul. (French edn, Trubner.)

1958   *The Undiscovered Self.* Routledge and Kegan Paul.

1959   *Flying Saucers: Modern Myth of Things Seen in the Skies.* Routledge and Kegan Paul.

1960   *Collected Works, 1902–60* (18 vols). Routledge and Kegan Paul.

Further reading

Douglas, W. (1961) Carl Gustav Jung. *American Journal of Psychology*, 74, 639–41.

Harms, E. (1962) Carl Gustav Jung. *American Journal of Psychiatry*, 118, 728–32.

C.G. Jung was a significant figure in the history of the psychoanalytic movement, and it might be said that it was due to his contribution that the theories of **Freud** extended beyond the confines of middle-class Viennese society. Together with Ferenczi he founded the *International Journal of Psychoanalysis* and produced a *Year Book of the Proceedings of the International Psychoanalytical Society* regularly, up to the outbreak of World War I. It could be fairly argued that it was Jung who perceived certain psychogenic aspects of schizophrenia that had been ignored by previous research into mental diseases. His early experimental work with word association demonstrated the affective component of cognitive functioning, which he went on to study in clinical settings.

After breaking with Freud in 1913, Jung spent the next twenty years travelling, writing and in psychotherapeutic work. In his late fifties he returned to academic teaching and continued lecturing with therapeutic activities until his death in 1961. Jung always regarded himself as an empiricist seeking to investigate in detail certain aspects of human behaviour and value systems that were of personal interest. In particular he was intrigued by the nature of religious experience, dreams, and the common belief in certain myths that seemed to pervade human society regardless of culture, race or creed. Unfortunately he attracted the label of being a mystic, being deeply involved in parapsychology through the middle years of his life. The orthodox psychoanalytic movement was partially responsible (see **Jones**), and it was not until Jung's later years that serious interest was taken in his writings and he was once again regularly invited to teach in traditional university settings. The break with Freud came about over the nature of human motivation and culminated in a final separation when Jung published 'The psychology of the unconscious' (included in *Collected Works* as 'Symbols of transformation') in 1912. The details of their break has been described by many authors and involved a deal of personal acrimony, but it is now apparent that their theoretical standpoints were irreconcilable, and Freud was not a man to compromise. Jung founded the Society for Analytical Psychology, which reflected his science-based approach to the study of human cognitions and emotions. His text *Psychological Types* (1933) might be regarded as his most significant work; in it he revealed the nature of his approach: 'my field of work is not the determination of external characteristics, but the investigation and classification of psychic data which can be inferred from them ... it is a descriptive study of the psyche which enables us to formulate certain theories about its structure. From the empirical application of these theories there is finally developed a conception of psychological types.'

ALAN DABBS

K

Kagan, Jerome

Born: 1929, Newark, New Jersey, USA **Nat:** American **Ints:** Developmental psychology, personality and social psychology, physiological and comparative psychology **Educ:** BS Rutgers University, 1950; MA Harvard University, 1954; PhD Yale University, 1954 **Appts & awards:** Professor of Human Development, Harvard University; President, APA Division 7; Hofheimer Prize, American Psychiatric Association, 1962; Wilbur Lucius Cross Medal, Yale University, 1982; Member, Program Committee, AAAS, 1993–4; G. Stanley Hall Award, Division 7, APA 1994; Editorial Board, *Child Development*, *Developmental Psychology*

Principal publications

1962 *Birth to Maturity.* Wiley (with H.A. Moss).
1964 Information processing in the child. *Psychological Monographs*, no. 78.
1967 On the need for relativism. *American Psychologist*, 22, 131–42.
1971 *Change and Continuity in Infancy.* Wiley.
1972 Do children think? *Scientific American*, 226, 74–82.
1973 Cross-cultural perspectives on early development. *American Psychologist*, 28, 947–61 (with R.E. Klein).
1973 Memory and meaning in two cultures. *Child Development*, 44, 221–3.
1976 Emergent themes in human development. *American Scientist*, 64, 186–96.
1978 *Infancy.* Harvard University Press (with R. Kearsley and P. Zelazo).
1978 Infant antecedents of cognitive functioning. *Child Development*, 49, 1005–23.
1979 *A Cross-Cultural Study of Cognitive Development.* Monographs of the Society for Research in Child Development, 44, no. 5 (with R.E. Klein, G.E. Finley, B. Rogoff and E. Nolan).
1981 *The Second Year.* Harvard University Press.
1984 *The Nature of the Child.* Basic Books.
1984 Behavioral inhibition to the unfamiliar. *Child Development*, 55, 2212–25.
1984 Behavioral inhibition in young children. *Child Development*, 55, 1005–19 (with C.C. Garcia and J.S. Reznick).
1988 The physiology and psychology of behavioral inhibition in children. *Annual Progress in Child Psychiatry and Child Development*, 102–27 (with J.S. Reznick and N. Snidman).
1994 On the nature of emotion. *Monographs of the Society for Research in Child Development*, 59, 7–24, and 250–83.

Further reading

Ekman, P. and Davidson, R.J. (eds) (1994) *The Nature of Emotion: Fundamental Questions.* Oxford University Press.
March, J.S. (ed.) (1995) *Anxiety Disorders in Children and Adolescents.* Guilford.

Jerome Kagan began his career with an interest in the degree of preservation of individual characteristics from infancy and early childhood through adolescence and adulthood. This work was guided by a strong environmentalist premise that minimized the role of maturation and temperamental differences among children. After failing to find commanding support for preservation of behaviour from infancy to childhood, and following a year of fieldwork in a small Indian village in northwest Guatemala, he turned to the study of biological factors in development. For twelve years he studied the biological contributions to the emergence of developmental competences and to the differences among young children, with a special interest in vulnerability to fearfulness and apprehension. He argues that enhancement of memory, symbolism, a moral sense and self-consciousness emerge in a regular order in the first two years of life in all children exposed to reasonably normal environments. His later work has addressed the temperamental qualities referred to as inhibited and uninhibited behaviour to the unfamiliar. This led him to propose that children, like other animals, are born with differential excitability of the stress circuit that involves the hypothalamus, pituitary, adrenal, and the sympathetic arm of the autonomic nervous system. It is hypothesized that children with high levels of excitability in this circuit tend to be shy, timid and vigilant; those with low levels of excitability show the opposite profile. Most of the latter group retain their behavioural characteristics for many years, while about half of the inhibited shy children retain their behavioral style. He continues to investigate the long-term consequences of these two temperamental qualities and also the aetiology of these dispositions. He regards children as highly adaptive and guided by strong evolutionary pressure to sustain a positive developmental progression even when faced with relatively hostile environments.

Kahneman, Daniel

Born: 1934, Tel Aviv, Israel ***Nat:*** Israeli ***Ints:*** Experimental and social psychology ***Educ:*** BA Hebrew University, Jerusalem, 1954; PhD University of California, 1961 ***Appts & awards:*** Professor of Psychology, University of California at Berkeley; Katz–Newcomb Lecturer in Social Psychology, 1979– ; Fellow, Centre for Advanced Studies in the Behavioral Sciences, 1977–78; Fellow, APA, Canadian Psychological Association; APA Distinguished Scientific Contribution Award, 1982

Principal publications

1968   Methods, findings and theory in studies of visual masking. *Psychological Bulletin*, 70, 404–25.
1971   Belief in the law of small numbers. *Psychological Bulletin*, 76, 105–10 (with A. Tversky).
1973   *Attention and Effort.* Prentice-Hall.
1973   On the psychology of prediction. *Psychological Review*, 80, 237–51 (with A. Tversky).
1973   Availability: A heuristic for judging frequency and probability. *Cognitive Psychology*, 5, 207–32 (with A. Tversky).
1981   The framing of decisions and the psychology of choice. *Science*, 211, 453–8 (with A. Tversky).
1982   *Judgment under Uncertainty: Heuristics and Biases.* Cambridge University Press (ed. with P. Slovic and A. Tversky).
1982   On the study of statistical intuitions. *Cognition*, 11, 123–41 (with A. Tversky).
1982   Variants of uncertainty. *Cognition*, 11, 143–57 (with A. Tversky).
1983   Extensional vs. intuitive reasoning: The conjunction fallacy in probability judgment.

Psychological Review, 293–315 (with A. Tversky).
1984   Choices, values and frames. *American Psychologist*, 39, 341–50 (with A. Tversky).
1986   Norm theory: Comparing reality to its alternatives. *Psychological Review* (with D.T. Miller)).
1992   The reviewing of object files: Object-specific integration of information. *Cognitive Psychology*, 24, 175–219 (with A. Treisman and B.J. Gibbs).

Further reading

Brady, M.E. and Lee, H.B. (1991) Theoretical comparison of the decision theories of J.M. Keynes, Kahneman-Tversky and Einhorn-Hogarth. *Psychological Reports.* 69, 243–51.
Moser, P.K. (ed.) (1990) *Rationality in Action: Contemporary Approaches.* Cambridge University Press.
Roese, N.J. and Olson, J.M. (eds) (1995) *What Might Have Been: The Social Psychology of Counterfactual thinking.* Erlbaum.

Kahneman spent his childhood in France and returned to Israel in 1946. He graduated from high school in 1951 and studied psychology and mathematics at Hebrew University. In 1955 he joined a military unit responsible for the classification and selection of recruits. He constructed and validated a semi-structured interview schedule for personality assessment. When training interviewers he noted that they were often poor judges of the quality of their work. They only made valid predictions of a recruit's military adjustment when forced to think in concrete terms of his civilian past. However, they were often most confident when attempting to predict the future on the basis of vague impressions. After his discharge, Kahneman returned to the Hebrew University, taking courses in logic and philosophy of science. The university offered him support for graduate study abroad and he chose to go to Berkeley.

His collaboration with Amos **Tversky** started in 1969 when Kahneman invited Tversky to lecture on probability assessment at the Hebrew University. Their first paper concerned the law of small numbers. Their continued collaboration led to fundamental advances in our understanding of heuristics and biases. In most of their work they focused on heuristics concerning probabilistic thinking, and specifically three heuristics: availability, representativeness, and anchoring and adjustment. The availability heuristic refers to people's tendency to estimate the likelihood of an event on the basis of the ease with which instances of that event come to mind. They demonstrated that people generally overestimate the probability of an event if concrete instances of it readily come to mind. The representativeness heuristic refers to the tendency to assess the probability that a stimulus belongs to a certain class by judging the degree to which that event corresponds to an appropriate mental model. For example, in a classic study subjects were provided with prief personality sketches, supposedly of engineers and lawyers. They were invited to assess the likelihood that each sketch described a member of one profession or the other. Half the subjects were told the population from which the sketches were drawn consisted of thirty engineers and seventy lawyers and the other half were told that there were seventy engineers and thirty lawyers. Subjects ignored information about prior probabilities and estimated the probability of the class membership by assessing how similar each personality sketch was to their mental model of an engineer or model. Finally, anchoring and adjustment refers to a general judgement process in which an initially given or generated response acts as an anchor, and supplementary information is insufficiently used to adjust that response.

Kahneman and Tversky's analysis of the cognitive and situational factors that cause these errors and biases has provided important insight into the psychological processes that govern human judgements and decision making and has informed the development of new ways of improving the quality of our thinking.

Kazdin, Alan Edward

Born: 1945, Cincinnati, Ohio, USA **Nat:** American **Ints:** Clinical, experimental analysis of behavior, evaluation, psychotherapy **Educ:** BA San Jose State University, 1967; MA Northwestern University, 1968; PhD Northwestern University, 1970 **Appts & awards:** Professor of Psychiatry and Psychology, Western Psychiatric Institute and Clinic, University of Pittsburgh School of Medicine; Fellow, APA, 1975– , Center for Advanced Study in the Behavioral Sciences, 1976–7; President, Association for the Advancement of Behavior Therapy, 1977–8; Editor, *Behavior Therapy*, 1979–83, *Journal of Consulting and Clinical Psychology*, 1985–90, Associate Editor, *Journal of Applied Behavior Analysis*, 1975–6; *Behavior Therapy*, 1975–9; Series Editor,

Developmental Child Psychiatry and Clinical Psychology (Sage), 1983– ; Editorial Board, *Journal of Applied Behavior Analysis*, 1974–5, 1978–80, 1982–3, 1985–6, *Behavior Therapy*, 1974–5, 1984– , *Journal of Behavior Therapy and Experimental Psychiatry*, 1976– , *Behavior Modification*, 1977– , *Cognitive Therapy and Research*, 1977–9, *Journal of Consulting and Clinical Psychology*, 1977–84, *Journal of Behavioral Assessment*, 1978– , *Child Behavior Therapy*, 1978–81, *Behavioral Counseling Quarterly*, 1979–84, *Behavioral Assessment*, 1979–86, *Applied Research in Mental Retardation*, 1980– , *Clinical Psychology Reviews*, 1980– , *Topics in Early Childhood Special Education*, 1980– ; *Psicologia e Scuola*, 1980– , *Education and Treatment of Children*, 1981– , *Behavioral and Brain Sciences*, 1981– , *Child and Family Behavior Therapy*, 1982– , *Journal of Abnormal Child Psychology*, 1984– , *Professional School Psychology*, 1986– , *Family Violence and Pathology*, 1986–

Principal publications

1975 *Behavior Modification in Applied Settings.* Dorsey.

1978 *History of Behavior Modification.* University Park.

1980 *Research Design in Clinical Psychology.* Harper and Row.

1982 *Single-Case Research Designs.* Oxford University Press.

1982 Symptom substitution, generalization, and response covariation. *Psychological Bulletin*, 91, 349–65.

1982 The token economy: A decade later. *Journal of Applied Behavior Analysis*, 15, 431–45.

1983 Psychiatric diagnosis, dimensions of dysfunction and child behavior therapy. *Behavior Therapy*, 14, 73–99.

1983 Hopelessness, depression and suicidal intent among psychiatrically disturbed inpatient children. *Journal of Consulting and Clinical Psychology*, 51, 504–10 (with N. French, A. Unis, K. Dawson and R. Sherick).

1984 Acceptability of aversive procedures and medications: Treatment alternatives for deviant child behavior. *Journal of Abnormal Child Psychology*, 12, 289–302.

1984 Statistical analyses for single-case experimental designs. In D. Barlow and M. Hersen (eds), *Single-Case Experimental Designs*. 2nd edn Pergamon.

1985 *Treatment of Antisocial Behavior.* Dorsey.

1993 Psychotherapy for children and adolescents:

Current progress and future research directions. *American Psychologist*, 48, 644–57.

Further reading

Eron, L.D. *et al.* (eds) (1994) *Reason to Hope: A Psychosocial Perspective on Violence and Youth.* American Psychological Association.

Kazdin, A.E. (1995) *Conduct Disorders in Childhood and Adolescence* (2nd edn). Sage.

Verhulst, F.C. and Koot, H.M. (eds) (1995) *The Epidemiology of Child and Adolescent Psychopathology.* Oxford University Press.

Kazdin's initial research began in the early 1970s with an exclusive focus on topics within behaviour therapy and behaviour modification. This included investigations of the process and outcome dimensions of the token economy, vicarious reinforcement, covert conditioning therapies and applied behaviour analysis. These treatments were investigated in the context of outpatient work with socially withdrawn adults or with children with various behavioural problems in school. He has also published influential texts on research design in applied settings. His interests then shifted to clinical work with children, particularly the treatment of antisocial behaviour in children and the assessment of childhood depression. A shift in setting from an academic psychology department to a psychiatric institute reinforced this change in direction of his research towards more problem-oriented topics, such as depression, suicidal ideation, child abuse and firesetting.

Keele, Steven W.

Born: 1940, Bremerton, WA, USA **Nat:** American **Ints:** Experimental **Educ:** BS University of Oregon, 1962; MS University of Wisconsin, 1965; PhD University of Wisconsin, 1966 **Appts & awards:** Professor of Psychology, University of Oregon; Editorial Board, *Journal of Motor Behavior*; Consulting Editor, *Journal of Experimental Psychology*: HP&P

Principal publications

1973   *Attention and Human Performance.* Goodyear.

1978   Mechanisms of attention. In E. Carterette and M. Friedman (eds), *Handbook of Attention*, vol. IX, Academic Press (with T. Neill).

1981   Behavioral analysis of movement. In V.B. Brooks (ed.), *Handbook of Physiology: The Nervous System: Motor Control*, American Physiological Society.

1985   Do perception and motor production share common timing mechanisms: A correlational analysis. *Acta Psychologica*, 60, 173–91 (with R. Pokorny, D.M. Corcos and R. Ivry).

1986   Motor control. In L. Kaufman, J. Thomas and K. Boff (eds), *Handbook of Perception and Performance*. Wiley.

1987   Sequencing and timing in skilled perception and action: An overview. In A. Allport, D. MacKay, W. Prinz and E. Scheerer (eds), *Language Perception and Production*. Academic Press.

1989   Timing functions of the cerebellum. *Cognitive Neurosciences*, 1, 136–52.

1990   Motor programs: Concepts and Issues. In M. Jeannerod (ed.), *Attention and Performance*, vol. XIII. Erlbaum.

1991   A computational model of attentional requirements in sequence learning. *Proceedings of the Cognitive Science Society* (with P.J. Jennings).

1992   Attention in the representation of sequence: Experiment and Theory. *Journal of Human Movement Science*, 11, 125–38 (with P.J. Jennings).

1993   *Handbook of Motor Control.* (German edition). Hogrefe: Berlin. (To be published by Academic Press in English.)

Further reading

Mayer, D.E. and Kornblum, S. (eds) (1993) *Attention and Performance 14: Synergies in Experimental Psychology, Artifical Intelligence, and Cognitive Neuroscience*. MIT Press.

Early in his career Keele spent two postdoctoral years working with one of the world's most prominent cognitive psychologists, Dr Michael **Posner**. At his suggestion he wrote a review, 'Movement Control in Skilled Motor Performance' which was published in the *Psychological Bulletin*. The time was perfect for such a review, and it was widely cited, then and now, primarily for its introduction of the concept of motor programs. Motor control has remained a dominant interest for Keele.

Another interest concerns attention in which he carried out research and summarized earlier views in a small but influential text, *Attention and Human Performance*. Later those ideas were updated and expressed in a review written jointly with T. Neill for the *Handbook of Perception*. In more recent research he continues to investigate both topics. In the motor domain he has been interested in whether a central clock in the brain coordinates both diverse muscular systems and perception of time as well. Some studies have examined whether the clock is an interval timer or a pacemaker and other studies have examined neurological patients that seem to have timing problems in an attempt to work out brain mechanisms involved. In the attentional domain, he has been inquiring into just how an attentional system operates to combine features analysed by different parts of the brain into a single percept.

Kelley, Harold H.

Born: 1921, Boise, Idaho, USA **Nat:** American **Ints:** Social psychology **Educ:** AB University of California at Berkeley, 1942; MA University of California at Berkeley, 1943; PhD Massachusetts Institute of Technology, 1948 **Appts & awards:** Professor, Department of Psychology, University of California at Los Angeles; President, APA Division 8, 1965–6, Western Psychological Association, 1969–70; APA Distinguished Scientific Contribution Award, 1971; Katz–Newcomb Lecture in Social Psychology, University of Michigan, AAAS, 1976; Member, National Academy of Sciences, 1978; John M. MacEachern Memorial Lectures, University of Alberta, 1978; Walker-Ames Professor, University of Washington, 1981; Distinguished Scientific Award (with John W. Thibaut), Society of Experimental Social Psychology, 1981

Principal publications

1953 *Communication and Persuasion*. Yale University Press (with C.I. Hovland and I.L. Janis).
1959 *The Social Psychology of Groups*. Wiley (with J.W. Thibaut).
1967 Attribution theory in social psychology. In D. Levine (ed.), *Nebraska Symposium on Motivation*. University of Nebraska Press.
1968 Interpersonal accommodation. *American Psychologist*, 23, 399–410.
1970 The social interaction basis of cooperators' and competitors' beliefs about others. *Journal of Personality and Social Psychology*, 16, 66–91 (with A.J. Stahelski).
1972 *Attribution: Perceiving the Causes of Behavior*. General Learning Press (with E.E. Jones, D.E. Kanouse, R.E. Nisbett, S. Valins and B. Weiner).
1972 Causal schemata and the attribution process. In E.E. Jones, D.E. Kanouse, H.H. Kelley, R.E. Nisbett, S. Valins and B. Weiner (eds), *Attribution: Perceiving the Causes of Behavior*. General Learning Press.
1976 Attributional conflict in young couples. In J.H.

Harvey, W.J. Ickes and R.F. Kidd (eds), *New Directions in Attribution Research*, vol. 1. Erlbaum (with B.R. Orvis and D. Butler).
1978 *Interpersonal Relations: A Theory of Interdependence*. Wiley (with J.W. Thibaut).
1979 *Personal Relationships: Their Structures and Processes*. Erlbaum.
1980 The causes of behavior: Their perception and regulation. In L. Festinger (ed.), *Retrospections on Social Psychology*. Oxford University Press.
1983 The situational origins of human tendencies: A further reason for the formal analysis of structures. *Personality and Social Psychology Bulletin*, 9, 8–30.
1984 The theoretical description of interdependence by means of transition lists. *Journal of Personality and Social Psychology*, 47, 956–82.

Further reading
Brown, R. (1986) *Social Psychology – The Second Edition*. Free Press.
Forterling, F. (1989) Models of covariation and attribution: How do they relate to the analogy of analysis of variance? *Journal of Personality and Social Psychology*, 57, 615–25.
Peterson, R.L. *et al.* (1992) *The Core Curriculum in Professional Psychology*. American Psychological Association.
Pryzwansky, W.B. and Wendt, R.N. (1987) *Psychology as a Profession: Foundations of Practice*. Pergamon.

Kelley is probably best known for his work on attribution processes. Kelley (like Fritz **Heider**, the 'father' of attribution theory) assumes that when we are forming an attribution we gather information that will help us form a judgement. Kelley argues that the information we use consists of how a person's behaviour covaries across time, place, different actors and different targets of the behaviour. Kelley draws attention to three particular types of information: consensus, distinctiveness and consistency. Consensus information refers to the extent to which other people behave in the same way towards the same stimulus as the actor (i.e. the person we are watching) does. Distinctiveness information refers to the extent to which one particular actor behaves in the same way towards different stimuli. Consistency information concerns the extent to which the behaviour between one actor and one stimulus is the same across time and circumstances. According to Kelley's theory these three sources of information combine into one of two patterns. People are most likely to make an internal attribution (deciding that the behaviour was something to do with the actor) when the consensus and distinctiveness of the act are low but its consistency is high. People are more likely to make an external attribution (deciding that the behaviour has something to do with the other person, not the actor) if consensus, distinctiveness and consistency information are all high. A special kind of external attribution (called a situational attribution) is made when consistency information is low and a clear internal or external attribution cannot be made.

Kelley's theory contrasts with that of **Jones** and **Davis** – referred to as the correspondent inference theory – which contends that we make internal attributions about a person when there are few non-common effects of his or her behaviour and the behaviour is unexpected. Whereas Jones focused on the information people use to make a dispositional or internal attribution, Kelley focused on the first step in the process of social perception – how people decide whether to make an internal or external attribution. Kelley's covariation theory, like Jones and Davis's correspondent inference theory, take the view that causal attributions proceed on a rational basis. While there is a good deal of empirical support for both theories, the assumption that people make attributions on a rational basis has often been challenged.

Kelley's work has consistently focused on the interpersonal level of analysis, which he regards as standing between the psychological and the sociological. Much of his work has focused on close analysis of dyadic relationships, this being motivated by an attempt to be as systematic as possible and to have the analysis controlled by its own logic rather than by intuitions. The key concept in his work has been that of interdependence, adopted from Kurt **Lewin**. For many years, **Thibaut** (his close co-worker) and Kelley used the pay-off matrix, from game theory, as the conceptual tool for dissecting interdependence. He expanded this analytic tool in a simple yet powerful way using the notion of the 'transition list', which describes not merely control over each person's outcomes (as does the pay-off matrix) but also control over the movement ('transition') from one matrix to another. These tools are used for characterizing the 'situation' that interdependent people face – in all its variations and with its various properties, systematically defined. The domain of systematically defined 'situations' is then examined for what it is that people should, by functional or evolutionary reasoning, possess

in the way of higher-level adaptive tendencies (e.g. concern about justice, joint welfare, dominance–submission, etc.). Then these higher-order 'personal' tendencies, as they affect behaviour in various situations, become the basis for predicting and understanding various recurrent patterns of social interaction. This method of analysis has been useful in trying to sort out 'person'–'situation' distinctions as they occur throughout social science and in attributional and moral evaluational phenomena.

Kelley, Noble Henry

Born: 1901, Thamesville, Ontario, Canada **Nat:** American **Ints:** Clinical, consulting, psychotherapy, state psychological association affairs **Educ:** PhD State University of Iowa, 1936 **Appts & awards:** Professor Emeritus, Southern Illinois University; President, Conference of State Psychological Association, Kentucky, 1949; Trustee, 1950–74, Executive Officer, Secretary and Treasurer, 1951–70, American Board of Professional Psychology (ABPP); President, APA Division 13, 1966–7; APA Division 12 Award for Distinguished Contribution to Science and the Profession of Clinical Psychology, 1969; ABPP Citation of Achievement, 1972; APA Distinguished Contribution Award, 1974; Distinguished Contribution to Psychology Award, Florida Psychological Association, 1977

Principal publications

1937 Historical aspects of bone conduction. *Laryngoscope*, 1937, 47, 19–37.
1937 The effect of binaural occlusion of the external auditory meati on the sensitivity of the normal ear for bone conducted sound. *Journal of Experimental Psychology*, 21, 211–17.
1937 A comparative study of the responses of normal and pathological ears to speech sounds. *Journal of Experimental Psychology*, 21, 342–52.
1939 Study in presbycusis: Auditory loss with increasing age and its effects on the perception of music and speech. *Archives of Otolaryngology*, 29, 506–13.
1940 *Workbook in General Psychology – With Laboratory Studies*. Burgess.
1942 *A Manual for General Psychology*. Hobson.
1959 The role of the Master's degree in doctoral training. *American Psychologist*, 14, 501–3.
1961 The American Board of Examiners in professional psychology: In retrospect and now. *American Psychologist*, 16, 132–41 (with F.H. Stanford and K.E. Clark).

1976   American Board of Professional Psychology. In B.B. Wolman (ed.), *International Encyclopedia of Psychiatry, Psychology, Psychoanalysis and Neurology*. Van Nostrand Reinhold.

Noble Kelley was instrumental in the organizational and professional development of psychology in North America. When he began studying psychology, in 1930, APA membership was around 1,100 and professional psychology was little more than a gleam in the eyes of a few pioneers. It was the dislocations of World War II that created new needs for psychological knowledge, skills and service. The first bid came from the USA Veteran Administration which estimated a need for 4,700 professional psychologists. Beginning with its reorganization in 1945, the APA took on the additional responsibility of developing a new profession. His interests shifted to this new enterprise and his energies for the next thirty years were directed toward the development of a discipline and a profession with high standards of education, achievement and ethical conduct. His service included Division 13 presidency and also presidency of two state psychological associations.

During his term as the Kentucky President, the first legislation in the USA to license psychologists, not by speciality, was enacted. Further service included membership on the APA Education and Training Board and two elected terms on the APA Council of Representatives. His most consistent and dedicated efforts went to the American Board of Professional Psychology, Inc., where he served as a trustee for twenty-four years and as its Executive Officer for nineteen years. Interested in the field of mental health, he was a member and once President of the Midwestern Association of College Psychiatrists and Clinical Psychologists. In the 1940s one of the early psychological services centred on a university campus was established under his direction. Under appointment by the Governor of the State of Illinois, he served eight years as a member of the Illinois Psychiatric Training and Research Authority.

Kelly, George Alexander

Born: 1905, Perth, Kansas, USA **Died:** 1967, Columbus, Ohio, USA **Nat:** American **Ints:** Clinical psychology, feneral psychology, personality and social psychology, philosophical and theoretical psychology, psychotherapy

Educ: BA Park College, Kansas, 1926; MA University of Kansas, 1928; BEd University of Edinburgh, 1930; PhD University of Iowa, 1931 **Appts & awards:** Professor and Director of Clinical Psychology, State University of Ohio, 1946–65; President, APA Divisions 12 and 13; Distinguished Professorship, Brandeis University, Boston, 1965

Principal publications

1955   *The Psychology of Personal Constructs*, vols 1 and 2. Norton.

1958   The theory and technique of assessment. *Annual Review of Psychology*, 9, 323–52.

1961   Suicide: The personal construct point of view. In N.L. Farberow and E.S. Schneidman (eds), *The Cry for Help*. McGraw-Hill.

1962   Europe's matrix of decision. In M.R. Jones (ed.), *Nebraska Symposium on Motivation*, University of Nebraska Press.

1963   Nonparametric factor analysis of personality theories. *Journal of Individual Psychology*, 19, 115–47.

1964   The language of hypothesis: Man's psychological instrument. *Journal of Individual Psychology*, 20, 137–52.

1965   The strategy of psychological research. *Bulletin of the BPS*, 18, 1–15.

1969   *Clinical Psychology and Personality: Selected Papers of George Kelly*, ed. B.A. Maher (published posthumously). Wiley.

1970   A brief introduction to personal construct theory. In D. Bannister (ed.), *Perspectives in Personal Construct Theory* (published posthumously). Academic Press.

1970   Behavior is an experiment. In D. Bannister (ed.), *Perspectives in Personal Construct Theory* (published posthumously). Academic Press.

1977   The psychology of the unknown. In D. Bannister (ed.), *New Perspectives in Personal Construct Theory* (published posthumously). Academic Press.

Further reading

Fransella, F. (1980) Man-as-scientist. In A.J. Chapman and D.M. Jones (eds), *Models of Man*. British Psychological Society.

—— and Thomas, L. (eds) (1988) *Experimenting with Personal Construct Psychology*. Routledge and Kegan Paul.

Sechrest, L. (1977) Personal constructs theory. In R.J. Corsini (ed.), *Current Personality Theories*. Peacock.

George Kelly grew up in Kansas and obtained his undergraduate education at Friends University and at Park College, Missouri. In the 1930s, in Kansas, he founded and directed a unique travelling psychological clinic for teachers, parents and children, at a time when the majority of American psychologists saw little future in this direction. He also spent some time as a Navy aviation psychologist. His early clinical experiences were in the public schools of Kansas, where he observed that teachers would refer pupils with complaints that appeared to reflect something about the teachers themselves. This led Kelly to the view that there is no objective, absolute truth and that phenomena are meaningful only in relation to the ways in which they are interpreted by individuals, a view referred to as constructive alternativism.

Kelly argued for a perspective from which people are regarded as 'scientists' in the sense that all of us have ways of interpreting our world (our construct systems), act purposefully in terms of these interpretations (behaviour is an experiment), and modify (sometimes verbally and sometimes non-verbally) our construing systems, in terms of experienced outcome. Kelly's theory is radical in being reflexive (accounting for its own construction) and in dispensing with the traditional distinction between emotion and cognition. Most notably, in the 1950s, when positivism and behaviourist psychologies dominated the field, he proposed an extensive and systematic intellectual alternative in the form of personal construct theory. As a technique related to his theory, he devised the repertory grid method, whereby the links between a person's constructs can be brought to light by examining the statistical relationships between a person's judgements. He also experimented with forms of self-characterization and with psychotherapeutic methods such as fixed role therapy.

While Kelly rejected attempts to label his approach, his emphasis on the ways in which people attend to and interpret information meant that his ideas were increasingly associated with emergent information-processing approaches (see **Broadbent**). An association with cognitive psychology was reinforced through Kelly's use of the 'person as scientist' metaphor. Kelly's contributions have been criticized for a number of reasons: (1) his theory has had relatively little to offer on the issues of growth and development; (2) it is not specific about the motivational basis for many people's decisions (i.e. the connections between construct systems and motivational forces are obscure); and (3) in dispensing with the distinction between cognition and emotion

his theory underemphasizes the role played by emotional and affective factors. Kelly was particularly concerned to reject the last criticism and to point out that any apparent neglect of affective issues was never translated into clinical practice. His ideas enjoy greater popularity in Britain than elsewhere. It is sometimes suggested that this neglect is partly due to Kelly's tendency to avoid forging links with the ideas of others, and that this was reciprocated and accounts for a diminution of his contribution.

Kelman, Herbert Chanoch

Born: 1927, Vienna, Austria *Nat:* Austrian *Ints:* Ethics of social research, international conflict and conflict resolution, personality and social, psychological study of social issues, political psychology *Educ:* BA Brooklyn College, 1947; BHL Seminary College of Jewish Studies, 1947; MS Yale University, 1949; PhD Yale University, 1951 *Appts & awards:* Richard Clarke Cabot Professor of Social Ethics, Harvard University; Fellow, Center for Advanced Study in the Behavioral Sciences, 1954–5, 1967; AAAS Socio-Psychological Prize, 1956; USPHS Special Fellow, Oslo Institute for Social Research, 1960–1; Fellow, Western Science Behavioral Institute, 1964, Battelle Seattle Research Center, 1972–3, Bellagio Study and Conference Center, 1977, 1985, Woodrow Wilson International Center for Scholars, 1980–1; President, APA Division 9, 1964–5, Division 8, 1970–1; Hon. AM, Harvard University, 1969; Kurt Lewin Memorial Award, Society for the Psychological Study of Social Issues, 1973; Fourth Annual Award, International Society for Educational, Cultural and Scientific Interchanges, 1977; Chair, ASA Section on Social Psychology, 1977–8; Guggenheim Fellow, 1980–1; APA Award for Distinguished Contributions to Psychology in the Public Interest, 1981; Hon. LHD, Brooklyn College, City University of New York, 1981, Hofstra University, 1983; New York Academy of Science Award, 1982; Intra-American Psychology Award, 1983; Sanford Award, International Society of Political Psychology, 1983; Career Contribution Award, Massachusetts Psychological Association, 1983; Member, APA Council on Foreign Relations, 1983; President, International Society of Political Psychology, 1985–6; Editorial Board Consultant, *Journal of Conflict Resolution*, 1957, *Sociometry*, 1959–62, *Journal of Social Issues*, 1959–65, *Journal of Abnormal and Social*

Psychology, 1962–4, *Human Relations*, 1964–90, *Journal of Personality and Social Psychology*, 1965–7, *Journal of Applied Behavioral Science*, 1965–70, *Psychiatry*, 1969–85, *International Studies Quarterly*, 1970–80, *Ethos*, 1973– , *Journal of Law and Human Behavior*, 1975–82, *Bulletin of the Research Exchange on the Prevention of War*, 1984–6

Principal publications

1958 Compliance, identification, and internalization: Three processes of attitude change. *Journal of Conflict Resolution*, 2, 51–60.

1961 Processes of opinion change. *Public Opinion Quarterly*, 25, 57–78.

1965 (ed.) *International Behavior: A Social-Psychological Analysis*. Holt.

1967 Human use of human subjects: The problem of deception in social psychological experiments. *Psychological Bulletin*, 67, 1–11.

1968 *A Time to Speak: On Human Values and Social Research*. Jossey-Bass.

1969 Patterns of personal involvement in the national system: A social-psychological analysis of political legitimacy. In J.N. Rosenau (ed.), *International Politics and Foreign Policy*, Free Press.

1970 *Cross-National Encounters: The Personal Impact of an Exchange Program for Broadcasters*. Jossey-Bass (with R.S. Ezeikel and R.B. Kelman).

1972 The rights of the subject in social research: An analysis in terms of power and legitimacy. *American Psychologist*, 27, 989–1016.

1973 Violence without moral restraint: Reflections on the dehumanization of victims and victimizers. *Journal of Social Issues*, 29, 25–61.

1978 *Ethics of Social Intervention*. Hemisphere (ed. with G. Bermant and D. Warwick).

1980 The role of action in attitude change. In H.E. Howe Jr. and M.M. Page (eds), *Nebraska Symposium on Motivation 1979: Attitudes, Values and Beliefs*. University of Nebraska Press.

1982 Creating the conditions for Israeli–Palestinian negotiations. *Journal of Conflict Resolution*, 26, 39–75.

1985 Overcoming the psychological barrier: An analysis of the Egyptian–Israeli peace process. *Harvard Negotiation Journal*, 1, 213–34.

1989 *Crimes of Obedience: Toward a Social Psychology of Authority and Responsibility*. Yale University Press.

Further reading

Crelinsten, R.D. and Schmid, A.P. (eds) (1995) *The Politics of Pain: Torturers and their Masters*. Westview.

Worchel, S. and Simpson, J.A. (eds) (1993) *Conflict Between People and Groups: Causes, Processes, and Resolutions*. Nelson-Hall.

Kelman is associated with the development of a social psychology cognizant of the wider cultural and social context – one that considers behaviour in its social and political context, addressing major social issues, and reflects on its own role in society. His work has focused on social influence, power and attitude change. Starting with research on persuasive communication, he proposed a distinction among three processes of influence, reflecting different types of linkage between the individual and society. In the political realm, the processes correspond to different political orientations. These in turn have been related to conceptions of legitimate authority and personal responsibility for actions under orders, particularly 'crimes of obedience'. He has also investigated the role of action in attitude change, and explored influence processes in applied settings, including psychotherapy, international educational exchanges, and problem-solving workshops in international conflict resolution. He was actively involved in founding the 'peace research' movement, including the *Journal of Conflict Resolution*, during the 1950s; and in the University of Michigan's Research Center on Conflict Resolution during the 1960s. He edited *International Behavior*, widely accepted as a seminal integration of social-psychological contributions to international relations. He has been involved in developing what he terms interactive problem solving, a third-party approach to resolving international conflicts. He has applied this approach to the Arab–Israeli conflict, notably in an action research programme based at the Harvard Center for International Affairs. His work on the ethics of social science – including issues in human experimentation and social intervention – has been important in sustaining awareness among psychologists of the ethical implications of the procedures and uses of social research.

Kiesler, Charles, A.
Born: 1934, St Louis, Missouri, USA ***Nat:*** American ***Ints:*** Personality and social, society for the psychological study of social sciences, health psychology, history of psychology, community psychology, population and environmental psychology, psychology and the law ***Educ:*** BA Michigan State University, 1958;

MA Michigan State University, 1960; PhD Stanford University, 1963 **Appts & awards:** Provost, Vanderbilt University, Nashville; NIMH Postdoctoral Fellow, 1960–3; APA Fellow, Society of Experimental Social Psychology, Executive Committee, 1973–6, Chair, 1974–5; APF Secretary, 1975; AAAS Fellow, Executive Committee 1975–9; BSERP (APA), 1983–6, Chair, 1985–6; Chair, Committee on Policy Implementation, 1984–7; Series Editor, *Topics in Social Psychology*, Addison-Wesley, 1969–71; Associate Editor, *Journal of Personality and Social Psychology*, 1971–3; Editorial Board, *Sociometry*, 1970–2, *European Journal of Social Psychology*, 1977–81, *Review of Personality and Social Psychology*, 1979–86, *Health Psychology*, 1982–4; *American Psychologist*, Editor, 1975–81; Associate Editor, 1985

Principal publications

1966   A test of a model for commitment. *Journal of Personality and Social Psychology*, 3, 349–53 (with J. Sakamura).

1968   Interaction of commitment and dissonance. *Journal of Personality and Social Psychology*, 8, 331–8 (with M.S. Pallak and D.D. Kanouse).

1969   On inferring one's belief from one's behavior. *Journal of Personality and Social Psychology*, 11, 321–7 (with R.E. Nisbett and M.P. Zanna).

1969   *Attitude Change: A Critical Analysis of Theoretical Approaches*. Wiley (with B.E. Collins and N. Miller).

1969   *Conformity*. Addison-Wesley (with S.B. Kiesler).

1971   *The Psychology of Commitment*. Academic Press.

1975   Minority influence: The effect of majority reactionaries and defectors, and minority and majority compromisers upon majority opinion and attraction. *European Journal of Social Psychology*, 5, 237–56 (with M.S. Pallak).

1976   The arousal properties of dissonance manipulations. *Psychology Bulletin*, 83, 1014–25 (with M.S. Pallak).

1979   *Psychology and National Health Insurance: A Sourcebook*. APA (ed. with N. Cummings and G. Vanderbos).

1980   Mental health policy as a field of inquiry for psychology. *American Psychologist*, 35, 15.

1982   Mental hospitals and alternative care: Non-institutionalization as potential public policy for mental patients. *American Psychologist*, 37, 349–60.

1982   Public and professional myths about mental hospitalization: An empirical reassessment of policy-related beliefs. *American Psychologist*, 37, 1323–39.

1983   Psychology and mental health policy. In M. Hersen, A.E. Kazdin and A.S. Bellak (eds), *The Clinical Psychology Handbook*. Pergamon.

1984   Episodic rate of mental hospitalization: Stable or increasing? *American Journal of Psychiatry*, 141, 44–8 (with A.E. Silbulkin).

1986   Hospitalization for mental disorders in general hospitals. *American Behavioral Scientist*, 30, 231–45 (with A.E. Sibulkin and M.S. Pallak).

1987   *Mental Hospitalization: Myths and Facts about a National Crisis*. Sage (with A.E. Sibulkin).

1989   Not up to evaluation standards. *Contemporary Psychology*, 34, 693 (with T.L. Morton).

1991   Handbook of mental health policy: Needed but narrow. *American Psychologist*, 46 (11) 1245–52.

1993   *The Unnoticed Majority in Inpatient Psychiatric Care*. Plenum.

Further reading

Kessler, M., Goldtson, S.E. and Joffe, J.M. (eds) (1992) *The Present and Future of Prevention: In Honor of George W. Albee*. Sage.

Kiesler, C.A. *et al.* (eds) (1979) *Psychology and National Health Insurance: A Sourcebook*. American Psychological Association.

Kiesler trained as an experimental social psychologist with Leon **Festinger** at Stanford. His early research interests focused on theoretical issues regarding how people process and respond to information transmitted or represented by others and how one's behaviour – particularly behaviour consistent with one's beliefs – affects one's thoughts and feelings regarding subsequent events. From 1975 to 1979 he was Executive Officer of the APA, during which time he was responsible for reviewing, assessing and affecting public policy and national legislation. That interest in public policy, reflected in more recent publications, has continued and he is currently carrying out research oriented toward mental health policy and mental hospitalization.

Kimura, Doreen
Born: 1993, Winnipeg Manitoba, Canada **Nat:** Canadian **Ints:** Clinical neuropsychology, physiological and comparative **Educ:** BA McGill University, 1956; MA McGill University, 1957; PhD McGill University, 1961 **Appts & awards:** Professor, Department of Psychology, University of Western Ontario;

Fellow, APA and CPA; Ontario Mental Health Foundation Research Associate, 1973–81; John Dewan Award, Ontario Mental Health Foundation, 1992; Editorial Board, *Human Neurobiology*, 1982–7, *Journal of Human Movement*, 1983–6

Principal publications

1973   Manual activity during speaking. I Right-handers. *Neuropsychologia*, 11, 45–50.

1973   Manual activity during speaking. II Left-handers. *Neuropsychologia*, 11, 51–5.

1974   Normal studies on the function of the right hemisphere in vision. In S.J. Dimond and J.G. Beaumont (eds), *Hemisphere Function in the Human Brain*. Paul Elek (with M. Durnford).

1979   Neuromotor mechanisms in the evolution of human communication. In H.D. Steklis and M.J. Raleigh (eds), *Neurobiology of Social Communication in Primates: An Evolutionary Perspective*. Academic Press.

1981   Neural mechanisms in manual signing. *Sign Language Studies*, 33, 291–312.

1982   Left-hemisphere control of oral and brachial movements and their relation to communication. *Philosophical Transactions of the Royal Society*, B298, 135–49.

1983   Sex differences in cerebral organization for speech and praxic functions. *Canadian Journal of Psychology*, 37, 19–35.

1984   *Neuropsychology Test Procedures*. DK Consultants.

1989   *Speech and Language: Readings from the Encyclopaedia of Neuroscience*. Birkhauser.

1989   Right-hand superiority for throwing but not for intercepting. *Neuropsychologia*, 27, 1399–1414 (with N. Watson).

1993   *Neuromotor Mechanisms in Human Communication*. Oxford University Press.

1993   Sex differences in route-learning. *Personality and Individual Differences*, 14, 53–65 (with L.A.M. Galea).

1994   Dermatoglyphic asymmetry and sexual orientation in males. *Behavioral Neuroscience*, 108, 1–4.

Further reading

Houk, J.C., Davis, J.L. and Beiser, D.G. (eds) (1995) *Models of Information Processing in the Basal Ganglia*. MIT Press.

Doreen Kimura attended primary and high school in Saskatchewan, then completed undergraduate and doctoral studies in physiological psychology at McGill University in Montreal. She was a postdoctoral fellow for two years at the Montreal Neurological Institute, spent a year at the Montreal Neurological Institute and a year at the Otologic Research Institute at the UCLA Medical Center, then moved to the Neurological Clinic at the Kantonsspital Zürich, Switzerland. She subsequently spent three years in Hamilton, Ontario, appointed to the Medical School but working as a Research Associate in St Joseph's Hospital. In 1967 she went to the University of Western Ontario (UWO) Department of Psychology in London, Ontario, where she has remained ever since. She is a Professor in Psychology and has an Honorary Lectureship in Clinical Neurological Sciences. She is also the co-ordinator of the Clinical Neuropsychology Programme.

Kimura is associated with the neurobiology of human abilities, particularly on the brain and hormonal mechanisms of human problem-solving functions. Her studies on patients with neurological damage to one half of the brain have elucidated the functions of the left and right cerebral hemispheres. She has found evidence, from studying patients with speech disorders after left-hemisphere pathology, that the left hemisphere's contribution to communication is an outgrowth of its important role in complex motor control. In contrast, the right hemisphere is critical for a variety of basic visuo-perceptual abilities, such as fusing the images from the two eyes to yield information about depth, and the capacity to recognize an object when spatially rotated. The tests she devised for neurological patients have become widely used in the field of neuropsychology.

Studies in people without brain damage have supplemented her research with clinical groups in further uncovering left and right hemisphere functions. Presentation of lateralized stimuli to the two ears or two visual fields, or observing which hand is used during various tasks, have led to new information pertinent to functional brain asymmetry. For example, the finding that speech sounds are reported more accurately from the right ear (opposite to the left hemisphere) has enabled us to ask questions about the details of how speech is processed in the two hemispheres. These normal techniques are also very widely employed by neuropsychologists throughout the world.

In the course of studying both neurologically damaged patients and normal persons, it became clear that there were individual distinguishing factors which influenced the pattern of brain organization, and of intellectual function, from person to person. Two of these factors are the person's hand preference and the person's sex. Consequently, more recent studies have focused on such individual differences, and the hormonal influences which presumably organize some of them. Kimura has shown that variations in level of the male hormone, testosterone, are associated with variations in spatial and mathematical ability. This is true for both men and women, though the pattern is not the same in each sex. Moreover, natural fluctuations in sex hormones such as oestrogen and testosterone, seen across the menstrual cycle in women or across the seasons in men, are accompanied by changes in cognitive ability pattern. In order to study such relationships in normal young people, hormones are measured in saliva, and an assay lab was established at UWO for this purpose by Kimura and her co-workers in 1991.

Much of the research in this area of individual differences suggests that the brain is organized for certain cognitive functions early in foetal life, by sex hormones or by other factors such as asymmetric growth rate. Kimura's very latest studies indicate that directional asymmetry of the body is influenced by the sex and the sexual orientation of an individual; and that such asymmetry can be a marker for particular cognitive patterns, and perhaps even for overall intellectual level.

Kinsbourne, Marcel

Born: n.d., Vienna, Austria **Nat:** Austrian **Ints:** Clinical neuropsychology, developmental, psychopharmacology **Educ:** BA Oxford University, 1952; BM, BCh Oxford University, 1955; MA Oxford University, 1956; DM Oxford University, 1963 **Appts & awards:** Director, Department of Behavioral Neurology, Shriver Centre; Honorary Life Member, Association Costaricense de Pédiatria; Advisory Board, Association of Educational Therapists; Executive Committee, Experimental Psychology Society, 1963–5; International Neuropsychological Society, Membership Chairman, 1972–5, Executive Committee 1976–80, Program Committee, 1977, President, 1977–8; Advisory Council, International Association for the Study of Performance, 1976–84; International Academy of Research of Learning Disabilities, Development Committee, 1978–80, Membership Chairman, 1978–80; Editorial Duties, *Acta Psychologica, Behavioral and Brain Sciences, Biological Psychiatry, Brain and Cognition, Developmental Psychol-*

ogy, *Journal of Communication Disorders, Journal of Psycholinguistic Research, Remedial and Special Education, Semiotic Injury, Applied Psycholinguistic, Brain and Language, Human Development, Journal of Clinical Neuropsychology, Journal of Motor Behavior, Reading Research Quarterly, Topics in Learning and Learning Disabilities*

Principal publications

1990   Hemispheric control of spatial attention. *Brain and Cognition*, 12, 240–66 (with P.A. Reuter-Lorenz and M. Moscovitch).

1995   The intralaminar thalamic nuclei: Subjectivity pumps or attention–action coordinators? *Consciousness and Cognition: An International Journal*, 4, 167–71.

Further reading

Dennett, D.C. and Kinsbourne, M. (1992) Time and the observer: The where and when of consciousness in the brain. *Behavioral and Brain Sciences*, 15, 183–247.

Zaidel, D.W. (ed.) (1994) *Neuropsychology Handbook of Perception and Cognition*, 2nd edn. Academic Press.

Marcel Kinsbourne has been concerned to identify mental operations that contribute to human mental function. He argues that this cannot be accomplished solely by the study of the intact mature human. Additionally, methods of experimental psychology may be applied to the analysis of selective cognitive impairments in focally handicapped and selectively developed mentally delayed individuals, after a qualitative analysis of the disordered behaviour, putting it on an objective and quantitative basis. The models he entertains attempt to take account not only of deficit but also of bias (between opponent processes), variability (of unstable opponent systems) and compensatory function (by undamaged brain).

In accordance with these principles he has worked with intact young, mature and elderly subjects and with neuropsychological and psychopathological cases, adults and children. Some of the methods used are derived from contemporary information-processing and laterality research. Others he devised for special purposes including the qualitative detection of neuropsychological deficit (finger sense test, finger stick test, simple tests sensitive to neglect of space), the quantification of academic readiness (visual, auditory and associate degree in readiness tests) and a demonstration of the organizational characteristics of the cerebral hemispheres (concurrent task methodologies, hemispheric priming, lateral gaze methodology, induced lateral orientation), as well as information-processing paradigms (visual masking by pattern, semantic memory procedures) and a novel paradigm for evaluating state-dependent learning. In psychopharmacology, he initiated and refined the acute controlled medication trial by use of which both stimulant effects on cognitive function and the nature of the varieties of attention deficit in children can more readily be uncovered.

In collaboration with **Dennett** he has published a critical analysis of the Cartesian Theater model (CTM) and the Multiple Drafts Model (MDM) of consciousness. According to the CTM, there is a place in the brain where discriminations in all modalities are registered and available for subjective judgement. The timing of events is thought to determine subjective order. According to the MDM, discriminations are distributed in space and time in the brain. These events are thought to have temporal properties, but those properties do not determine subjective order because there is no single stream of consciousness, only a parallel stream of conflicting and continuously revised contents. Kinsbourne suggests that the contents of consciousness are contributed by a subset of cell assemblies – intralaminar nuclei (ILN) – that is in control of response processes at any given time. ILN differ from other thalamic nuclei in projecting not to a specific cortical area, but diffusely. ILN, when adequately activated, co-ordinate attention and action. Thus, our sense of subjectivity is an emergent property of certain neuronal circuits, when they are in certain functional states.

Kintsch, Walter

Born: 1932, Temeschwar, Romania **Nat:** Romanian **Ints:** Environmental psychology, learning and memory, psychology of language **Educ:** MA University of Kansas, 1957; PhD University of Kansas, 1960 **Appts & awards:** Professor of Psychology and Director of Institute of Cognitive Science, University of Colorado, 1960; Member, NIMH Small Grants Study Section, 1970–4; Editor, *Journal of Verbal Learning and Verbal Behaviour*, 1977–80; Governing Board, Cognitive Science Society, 1978–85; NSF Study Section, Memory and Cognition, 1979–82; Governing Board, Psychonomic Society, 1981–84; NIMH Research Planning Committee, 1987–8; Chair, Cognitive Science Society, 1987–90, Psychonomic Society, 1987–90; Member, National Academy of Education, Society of Experimental Psychologists; Fellow, APA; Distinguished Research Award of the American Psychological Association, 1992

Principal publications

1970 *Learning, Memory and Conceptual Processes.* Wiley.

1974 *The Representation of Meaning in Memory.* Erlbaum.

1978 Towards a model of discourse comprehension and production. *Psychological Review*, 85, 363–94 (with T.A. van Dijk).

1982 *Discourse Processing.* North-Holland (ed. with A. Flammer).

1983 *Strategies of Discourse Comprehension.* Academic Press (with T.A. van Dijk).

1984 *Method and Tactics in Cognitive Science.* Erlbaum (ed. with P.F. Polson and J.R. Miller).

1985 Understanding and solving word arithmetic problems. *Psychological Review*, 92, 109–29 (with J.G. Greeno).

1985 Context effects in word recognition. *Journal of Memory and Language*, 27, 336–49 (with E.F. Moss).

1985 Automatic and strategic effects of knowledge retrieval. *Cognitive Science*, 9, 261–83 (with W.H. Walker).

1988 The role of knowledge in discourse comprehension: Construction-integration model. *Psychological Review*, 95, 163–82.

1992 A theory of word algebra problem comprehension and its implications for the design of learning environments. *Cognition and Instruction*, 9, 329–89 (with M.J. Nathan and E. Young).

1992 A cognitive architecture from comprehension. In H.L. Pick Jr, P. Ban den Broek and D.C. Knill (eds), *Cognition: Conceptual and Methodological Issues* APA.

1992 How readers construct situation models for stories: The role of syntactic cues and causal inferences. In A.F. Healy, S.M. Kossly and R.M. Shifrin (eds), *From Learning Processes to Cognitive Processes: Essays in Honor of William K. Estes*, vol. 2. Erlbaum.

1994 The psychology of discourse processing. In M. Gernsbacher (ed.), *Handbook of Psycholinguistics*. Academic Press.

1994 Discourse processing. In G. d'Ydewalle, P. Edlen and P. Bertelson (eds), *International Perspectives on Psychological Science, vol. 2: The State of the Art*. Erlbaum.

1994   Text comprehension, memory and learning. *American Psychologist*, 49, 294–303.

1995   Long term working memory. *Psychological Review*, 102, 211–45 (with K.A. Ericsson).

Further reading

Britton, B.K. and Gulgoz, S. (1991) Using Kintsch's computational model to improve instructional text: Effects of repairing inference calls on recall and cognitive structures. *Journal of Educational Psychology*, 83, 329–45.

Mills, C.B., Diehl, V.A. *et al.* (1993) Procedure text: Predictions of importance ratings and recall by models of reading comprehension. *Discourse Processes*, 16, 279–315.

Rodenhausen, H. (1992) Mathematical aspects of Kintsch's model of discourse comprehension. *Psychological Review*, 99, 547–9.

Walter Kintsch came to the US in 1955, from four years teaching at elementary school in Austria. He entered the University of Kansas as a graduate psychology student and received his PhD in 1960. He worked with Ed Wike on a dissertation which compared the merits of **Hull**ian and **Spence**an concepts of interaction in incentive and habit strength.

An interest in the possibility of a scientific, quantitative model of human behaviour (e.g. as it was embodied, then, in Hull's *Principles of Behaviour*) had been the driving force behind Kintsch's decision to pursue psychology as a career. His first enthusiasm was for mathematical modelling, and from Kansas he proceeded to Indiana University to take a postdoctoral position working with William **Estes**, who assisted Kintsch to begin a research programme exploring memory and the techniques of mathematical learning theory. The research was developed while he was at the Universities of Missouri in Columbia and California at Riverside. Summers during the 1960s were spent in Ventura Hall at Stanford in the company of Estes, **Suppes**, **Atkinson** and **Bower**, and he participated in the 1960s effort involving complex Markov models of learning. When this approach proved to be too limiting, he and many others of that group moved into the memory area.

Kintsch spent a year as a visiting professor at Stanford and in 1968 went to the University of Colorado in Boulder. The role of organization became the focus of his work. He realized that in order to comprehend organizational effects fully, it would be more advantageous to work with naturally organized material. So he abandoned the traditional word lists or nonsense materials that were almost universally employed then and rediscovered semantics for himself. For Kintsch semantics, or meaning in the context of meaningful tasks, was an indispensable tool for studying how people process language, as was the propositional analysis of texts which he developed in due course (in *The Representation of Meaning in Memory*). It transpired that this would be one of the factors that made possible the upsurge in the psychological study of language processing. He began a study of text comprehension and memory, which has remained his pervading concern.

The year 1974 saw the beginning of a ten-year collaboration with the Dutch linguist Teur van Dijk, from the University of Amsterdam. In 1978 they published a joint article in *Psychological Review* outlining what was regarded as the first psychological processing model of discourse comprehension, which, in its explicitness and testability, represented a certain advance in the field. However, Kintsch regarded it as an initial model, as yet failing to deal explicitly with the role of knowledge in text comprehension. In 1983 Kintsch and van Dijk published *Strategies of Discourse Comprehension*, in which they outlined a comprehension-processing model of language comprehension, based on the notion of strategies or heuristics rather than rules.

The model outlines how knowledge is incorporated into the discourse strategies used to form multilevel representations involved in discourse comprehension and memory. The underlying theory posits that verbal input is decoded into a list of primary propositions which are organized into larger units on the basis of some knowledge structure to form a coherent text base. From that a macrostructure is constructed, which represents the most essential information in the text base. The comprehender's knowledge, beliefs and goals play a crucial role in this process. In parallel with this, a situational model integrates the comprehender's existing knowledge with the information derived from the text that is being processed. The end product of comprehension is a multilevel processing record, which includes memory traces of the actual linguistic imput of the meaning of the text at both a local and a global level, and of the effect the text had on the comprehender's world knowledge. The work marked a shift away from matters of text alone to a more encompassing field, involving both the situation described by the text and the knowledge necessary to construct situation models. In 1985,

Kintsch and J.G. Greeno published 'Understanding and solving word arithmetic problems' in *Psychological Review*. They showed that the model could be made complete and explicit in certain cases, in this instance with word-arithmetic problems, and complete computer simulations followed.

Kintsch's most recent work has been concentrated on a model of text comprehension, the construction-integration model. This combines the constructive process of the text base (from linguistic input) with the comprehender's knowledge base and an integration phase, where the text base is integrated into a coherent whole. The model combines symbolic production systems generating approximate mental representations and connectionist techniques, to refine the representations and their pertinence to context. It is as a cognitive architecture for comprehension that the model has proved most useful for modelling the results of priming experiments in discourse, recognition and recall of texts, summarization, understanding arithmetic word problems or UNIX commands, and planning routine actions. The model has been practically applied in various research projects, to computer-based tutoring of word-algebra problems, modelling programmers' usage of a UNIX operating system, and information retrieval.

Kintsch's seminal research in the analysis of text memory is regarded as instrumental in developing the field of verbal learning and memory to deal with complex questions of text comprehension and memory.

CATE COX

Klein, Melanie

Born: 1882, Vienna **Died:** 1960, London **Nat:** Austrian **Ints:** Psychoanalysis and training, child analysis **Appts & awards:** Berlin Psychoanalytic Society, 1923; British Psycho-Analytical Society, 1927; Melanie Klein Trust founded 1955; Special issue of *International Journal of Psychoanalysis* for Klein's 70th birthday

Principal publications

1932   *The Psycho-Analysis of Children*. Hogarth Press.

1935   Contribution to the psychogenesis of manic-depressive states. *International Journal of Psychoanalysis*, 16, 145–7.

1937   *Love, Hate and Reparation*. Hogarth (with J. Riviere).

1940   Mourning and its relation to manic-depressive states. *International Journal of Psychoanalysis*, 21, 125–53.

1946   Notes on some schizoid mechanisms. *International Journal of Psychoanalysis*, 27, 99–110.

1948   On the theory of anxiety and guilt. *International Journal of Psychoanalysis*, 29, 114–23.

1950   On the criteria for the termination of a psychoanalysis. *International Journal of Psychoanalysis*, 31, 78–80.

1952   The origins of transference. *International Journal of Psychoanalysis*, 33, 433–8.

1952   The mutual influences in the development of ego and id. *The Psychoanalytical Study of the Child*, 7, 51–53.

1955   *New Directions in Psychoanalysis*. Tavistock (with Heimann and Money-Kyrle).

1957   *Envy and Gratitude*. Tavistock.

1958   On the development of mental functioning. *International Journal of Psychoanalysis*, 34, 84–90.

1959   Our adult world and its roots in infancy. *Human Relations*, 12, 291–363.

1960   A note on depression in the schizophrenic. *International Journal of Psychoanalysis*, 41, 509–11.

1961   *Narrative of a Child Analysis*. Hogarth.

1963   Some reflections on the oresteia and on the sense of loneliness. In *Our Adult World and Other Essays*, ed. E. Jaques and B. Joseph. Basic Books published posthumously.

Further reading

Bott Spillius, E. (1988) *Melanie Klein Today: Developments in Theory and Practice, vol. 1: Mainly Theory*. Tavistock/Routledge.

Grosskurth, P. (1985) *Melanie Klein: Her World and Her Work*. Hodder and Stoughton.

Sayers, J. (1991) *Mothering Psychoanalysis*. Penguin Books.

Melanie Klein was one of the most influential and controversial psychoanalysts in Britain, one of the current analytic schools being named after her. She trained originally as a nursery-school teacher. She was analysed by Sandor Ferenczi in Budapest in 1914, then by K. Abraham in Berlin during 1924. In 1925 she was invited to lecture in London by Ernest Jones, where she settled the following year.

Her work extended that of **Freud** to whose ideas she remained loyal. She concentrated particularly on early (pre-Oedipal) experiences and introduced the concept of 'positions' in development rather than stages (as in Freud) Klein developed a new technique of analysis for children based on the interpretation of play rather than words alone. Therapy was otherwise conducted in the classical manner. By 1927 an overt split was demonstrated between the methods advocated by Klein and those of Anna **Freud**, leading to the development of two factions and acrimonious argument.

One of her most controversial ideas was to date the Oedipus complex to an earlier period of life than proposed by Freud. She traced anxiety and guilt to the child's early relationship with the mother (and breast). Fantasies from this period led to the development of the distortions characteristic of schizophrenia and the manic-depressive psychoses (until then thought to be unamenable to psychoanalysis). She emphasized destructive aggression as the manifestation of the death instinct. In the first year of life the infant experiences at different times love for and hate or envy of the mother's breast (the paranoid-schizoid position). When object constancy is attained the baby realizes that these feelings are directed to the same object (the depressive position): then guilt and a desire for reparation result.

Klein was known as an intuitive therapist, but in retrospect is felt by critics to have overvalued the contribution of fantasy as opposed to practical aspects of care giving and the quality of the mother–child relationship. Her theoretical contribution and research into the first two years of life have been of major importance in the field of psychoanalysis. In spite of her belief in instincts, Klein's work is classified as an object relations theory, influencing for example W.R.D. Fairbairn and D.W. Winnicot.

H. HANKS AND P. STRATTON

Kline, Paul

Born: 1937, London, England **Nat:** British **Ints:** Evaluation and measurement, industrial and organizational psychology, personality and social psychology, psychoanalysis, educational psychology **Educ:** BA Reading University, 1958; MEd Aberdeen University, 1963; PhD Manchester University, 1968 **Appts & awards:** Lecturer/Reader/Professor of Psychometrics, Department of Psychology, University of Exeter, 1969–95; DSc Manchester University, 1981

Principal publications

1972   *Fact and Fantasy in Freudian Theory.* Wiley.

1977   *Scientific Analysis of Personality and Motivation*, Academic Press (with R.B. Cattell).

1979   *Psychometrics and Psychology.* Academic Press.

1983   The factors in personality questionnaires among normal subjects. *Advances in Behaviour Research and Therapy*, 5, 141–202 (with P. Barrett).

1988   *Psychology Exposed, or the Emperor's New Clothes.* Routledge.

1993   *Handbook of Psychological Testing.* Routledge.

Further reading

Fredenborg, J. (1991) *Paul Kline: A Bibliography.* Universitetsbiblioteket i Oslo.

Gale, A. and Eysenck, M.W. (eds) (1992) *Handbook of Individual Differences: Biological Perspectives.* Wiley.

Hampson, S.E. and Colman, A.M. (eds) (1995) *Individual Differences and Personality.* Longman.

Until his retirement in 1995 Paul Kline was Britain's only professor of psychometrics. Following the experience of teaching classics at a school in Wales, he trained as an educational psychologist and later read for his PhD at Manchester under the supervision of Frank Warburton. Although his own thesis topic was the nature and aetiology of the **Freud**ian anal character, Warburton's advocacy of the methods of **Cattell** and of the importance of factor analysis for revealing the fundamental structure of human abilities and temperament were a strong influence. From Manchester Kline moved to the University of Exeter, first to its School of Education and then to the Department of Psychology, where Raymond Cattell and Richard Lynn had previously established a tradition of individual differences research.

Kline's work followed two basic strands: the scientific evaluation of aspects of Freudian theory (in which his 1972 text is a standard work), and applied psychometric studies on the structure of personality and ability and its underlying processes. However, his many books deal with several other areas, including the use of tests for vocational guidance, factor analysis and the principles of test construction, as well as the mainstream of the psychometric (generally Cattelian) approach to intelligence and personality. His metatheoretical book *Psychology Exposed* is undoubtedly his most controversial work. This critically examines the relevance of several branches of psychological theory to human life. It argues that many branches of the discipline are of solely hermeneutic interest, or else contain so many conceptual and methodological flaws that they are of dubious scientific value, whilst conventional experimental psychology is unable to come to grips with what is essentially human.

Kline's insistence on psychometric rigour has been coupled with an interest in unconventional approaches to the assessment of individual differences (e.g. performance tests, projective tests, measures of unconscious mental processes) – an unusual combination of interests born from the belief that self-report questionnaires alone are unlikely to reveal the whole richness of human personality. 'Fifty years of personality questionnaires,' he once said, 'and all we can do is ask people if they enjoy parties.' An incisive, knowledgeable and controversial speaker, he has enjoyed challenging cosy assumptions not rigorously supported by experimental data – and supporting controversial theories that *do* appear to have empirical support. Such an approach has not always endeared him to the psychological establishment.

His many books are widely cited, and have performed a valuable service in introducing psychometrics and differential psychology to several generations of undergraduates, graduate students and professionals. More importantly, his work shows that psychometric and experimental rigour may sometimes be able to render even aspects of psychoanalytic theory susceptible to empirical investigation.

COLIN COOPER

Klineberg, Otto

Born: 1899, Quebec City, Canada **Died:** 1992, Columbia, USA **Nat:** Canadian/American (1938–) **Ints:** Personality and social psychology, Society for the Psychological Study of Social Issues **Educ:** BA McGill University, 1919; MA Harvard University, 1920; MD McGill University, 1925; PhD Columbia University, 1927 **Appts & awards:** National Research Council Fellowship, 1928; Research, Associate, Anthropology Department, Columbia State University, 1929; Department of Psychology, Columbia University, 1931– ; Vice-President, American Orthopsychiatry Association Guggenheim Fellowship (to China), 1935–6; Butler Medal, Columbia University, 1950; Kurt Lewin Memorial Award, 1956; Hon. PhD University of Brazil, Rio de Janeiro, 1958; Hon. PhD Howard University, Washington,

DC, 1961; Annual Award, New York Society of Clinical Psychologists, 1961; Professor Emeritus of Social Psychology, Columbia University, 1962; Vice-President, Federation Internationale des Ecoles des Parents, 1964; President, World Federation for Mental Health, 1966–7, Hon. President, 1970– ; Hon. President, European League for Mental Health, 1971–4; Hon. PhD Drew University, Madison, 1972; Medal, University of Liège, Belgium, 1974; Annual Award, International Society for Educational, Cultural and Scientific Interchanges, 1978; APA Distinguished Award for Contributions of Psychology in the Public Interest, 1979; Award from Brazil, Contribution to Development of Psychology in Brazil, 1979; Columbia University Graduate School (part-time member), CUNY, 1982; Hon. Life Member, New York Academy of Science, 1983; Social Psychology Award, New York State Psychological Association, 1984; APF Gold Medal Award, Lifetime Contribution by a Psychologist in the Public Interest, 1985; APA Award for Distinguished Contributions to the International Advancement of Psychology, 1991; President, IUPsS, Eastern Psychological Association, APA; President, Division 9, Inter-America Society of Psychology; President, Psychological Society of São Paulo

Principal publications

1935 *Negro Intelligence and Selective Migration.* Columbia University Press.

1940 *Social Psychology*, 2nd edn 1954. Holt, Rinehart and Winston.

1950 Race differences: The present position on the problem. *International Social Science Bulletin*, 2, 460–7.

1958 Culture and personality. In G.S. Seward and J.P. Seward (eds), *Current Psychological Issues*. Holt.

1964 *The Human Dimension in International Relations*. Holt, Rinehart and Winston.

1971 Back and White in international perspective. *American Psychologist*, 26, 119–28.

1979 Cross-cultural psychology in historical perspective. In H. Triandis (ed.), *Handbook of Cross-cultural Psychology*, vol. 1. Allyn and Bacon.

Further reading

Hollander, E.P. (1993) Otto Klineberg (1899–92). *American Psychologist*, 48, 909–10.

Klineberg, O. (1974) Autobiography. In G. Lindzey (ed.), *A History of Psychology in Autobiography*, vol. 6. Prentice-Hall.

Otto Klineberg was raised in the multicultural and multilingual society of Montreal and it is possible to trace his intellectual evolution from this source. He was one of eight children whose parents had come from the Austro-Hungarian Empire in childhood. He might easily have pursued a career in medicine but his enthusiasm for psychology lead to a PhD at Columbia University where he studied under Robert **Woodworth**, A.T. Poffenberger and Gardner **Murphy** and attended E.L. **Thorndike**'s lectures at Teachers College. Under Woodworth he completed his PhD on performance test speed from children of different races. During World War II he was a colonel with the US Strategic Bombing Survey and conducted research on the effects of the air war on Germany. Later he was instrumental in establishing the World Federation for Mental Health, organized research in UNESCO and fostered the work of the IUPsS.

Klineberg made distinctive contributions to social psychology in four areas: cross-cultural differences, racial differences, international affairs and the social psychology of mental health. In cross-cultural psychology he found that pupils migrating from the less affluent southern states of America to integrated schools in the north improved their IQ scores to a level matching their northern-born Black peers. This led to the controversial and important 'Negro Intelligence and Selective Migration'. He played an important role in helping to win the 1954 Supreme Court school desegregation case of Brown v. Board of Education. In 1940 he published a landmark textbook in social psychology which influenced numerous students of social psychology for many years. His emphasis on cross-cultural factors and on applications of psychology to race and international relations were distinctive features of this text and influenced the development of research in these areas. His work on the psychology of international affairs, published in the 1950s and 1960s, remains applicable to contemporary affairs.

Klüver, Heinrich

Born: 1897, Schleswig-Holstein, Germany
Died: 1979, Oak Lawn, Illinois, USA **Nat:** German-American **Ints:** Experimental psychology, physiological and comparative psychology, psychopharmacology, clinical neuropsychology **Educ:** PhD Stanford University, 1924 **Appts & awards:** Professor of Experimental Psychology, University of Chicago, 1938–57; Sewell L. Avery Distinguished Service Professor of Bio-

logical Psychology, University of Chicago, 1957–79; Karl Spencer Lashley Award in Neurobiology, American Philosophical Society, 1960; Samuel W. Hamilton Award, American Psychopathological Association, 1963; APF Gold Medal Award, 1965; Hon. MD University of Basle, 1965; Hon. PhD University of Hamburg, 1969; Hon. MD University of Kiel, 1971

Principal publications

1928 Studies on the eidetic type and on eidetic imagery. *Psychological Bulletin*, 25, 69–104.
1928 *Mescal: The Divine Plant and its Psychological Effects*. Kegan Paul.
1931 Do personality types exist? *American Journal of Psychiatry*, 10, 781–8.
1933 *Behavior Mechanisms in Monkeys*. University of Chicago Press.
1936 An analysis of the effects of the removal of the occipital lobes in monkeys. *Journal of Psychology*, 2, 49–61.
1937 Re-examination of implement-using behavior in a Cebus monkey after an interval of three years. *Acta Psychologica*, 2, 347–97.
1938 An analysis of certain effects of bilateral temporal lobectomy in the rhesus monkey, with special reference to 'Psychic blindness'. *Journal of Psychology*, 5, 33–54 (with P.C. Bucy).
1939 Preliminary analysis of functions of the temporal lobe in monkeys, *Archives of Neurology and Psychiatry*, 42, 979–1000 (with P.C. Bucy).
1942 Functional significance of the geniculo-striate system. *Biological Symposia*, 7, 253–99.

Further reading

Aggleton, J.P. (ed.) (1992) *The Amygdala: Neurobiological Aspects of Emotion, Memory, and Mental Dysfunction*. Wiley-Liss.

After serving as an infantry soldier in the First World War Heinrich Klüver went to the University of Hamburg for three years, followed by a year at Berlin. At Hamburg he studied under William Stern, who had set up the department and laboratory there, was a pioneer of child psychology, and well known for his 'personalistic' psychology of experience. He also studied with the neo-Kantian philosopher Ernst Cassirer and both Stern and Cassirer had a subtle appreciation of the relationship between philosophy and empirical investigation which Klüver carried with him when he went to the States in 1923. After his PhD from Stanford in 1924 he went to Minnesota for two years, where he first met Karl **Lashley**, who introduced him to animal psychology. For the next two years he was at Columbia, and became friendly with Selig Hecht, the authority on physiological optics, then worked with Lashley in Chicago, at the Institute for Juvenile Research. He joined the University of Chicago in 1933 and remained there till his death in 1979.

By 1933 he had carried out and published important work on eidetic imagery and on the effects of mescal (with himself as subject), and also *Behavior Mechanisms in Monkeys*, in which the full range of his philosophical and experimental background converges in sharp focus. The title is too modest. It is indeed a fine monograph on the behaviour of monkeys in discrimination tasks, but it also contains, as a theme running through the book, a discussion of the nature of perception and discrimination. It is a subtle and thorough dismantling of the empiricist tradition in which phenomenal similarity is explained by objective similarity due to common elements. There are hints of Stern's personalism, Cassirer's perception of invariants, *Gestalt* Psychology, and years of discussion with Karl Lashley, but Klüver assimilated what they had to offer, and produced an original masterpiece.

After 1933 Klüver began the work for which he is most famous. In 1936 he found that blindness to form was produced following bilateral removal of the occipital lobes of monkeys, and while not the whole story, it was the starting point for future research on this matter. He also investigated the visual functions of the temporal lobes, and described the psychic blindness, hypersexuality and aggressiveness that follow temporal lobectomy, a package of changes known as the Klüver–Bucy syndrome. Following the accidental discovery of free porphyrin compounds in the brain, he developed the copper phthalocyanin stain, widely used in histology. After Stephan Polyak's death in 1955, Klüver spent two years on the very important but self-effacing task of putting together and editing the former's monumental *The Vertebrate Visual System*.

ARTHUR STILL

Koffka, Kurt

Born: 1886, Berlin, Germany *Died:* 1941, Massachusetts, USA *Nat:* German-American *Ints:* Developmental, experimental psychology, philosophical and theoretical psychology and general *Educ:* PhD University of Berlin, 1909 *Appts & awards:* Professor, University of Gies-

sen, 1911–27; Co-founder and Editor, *Psychologische Forschung*, 1921–35; Visiting Professor, Cornell University, 1924–5; Research Professor, Smith College, 1927–32; Research Fellow, USSR Government, 1932; Professor, Smith College 1932–41

Principal publications

1912 *Zur Analyse der Vorstellungen und ihrer Gesetze. Eine experimentelle Untersuchung.* (An analysis of perceptions and their laws. An experimental investigation). Quelle and Meyer.

1915 Zur Grundlegung der Wahrnehmungspsychologie. Eine Auseinandersetzung mit V. Benussi. (On the basis of perception. A discourse with V. Benussi.) *Zeitschrift für Psychologie*, 73, 11–90.

1922 Perception: An introduction to the *Gestalt* Theory. *Psychological Bulletin*, 19, 531–85.

1924 *Growth of the Human Mind.* (Reprinted by Transaction Books, 1980.)

1935 *Principles of Gestalt Psychology*. Harcourt, Brace.

Further reading

Eisen, W. (1943) Kurt Koffka: 1886–1941. *British Journal of Psychology*, 33, 69–76.

Harrower-Erickson, M.R. (1942) Kurt Koffka. *American Journal of Psychology*, 55, 278–81.

Köhler, W. (1942) Kurt Koffka: 1886–1941. *Psychological Review*, 42 (2), 97–101.

Kurt Koffka studied philosophy at the University of Berlin. He also spent one study-year in Edinburgh which made him proficient in English and influenced him to pursue the more 'realistic' field of psychology. He wrote his dissertation under **Stumpf** on the perception of musical rhythm. Stumpf's interests in phenomenology and tonal sensations prepared Koffka to accept Wertheimer's ideas on *Gestalt* psychology when he met him later in Frankfurt. Koffka had also been influenced by Ehrenfels who had formed the concept of 'Gestaltqualität' to describe that a melody sounds different than its isolated tones and that a single tone does not possess form-quality by itself, but derives it from the other tones – the melody. Furthermore, Koffka's own protanopic weakness motivated him to investigate colour-vision, after-images and figure-ground phenomena. Since he could only differentiate between red and green under specific brightness and background conditions he became interested in the investigation of the effect of molar fields rather than in single stimuli.

Koffka's formal involvement with *Gestalt* Psychology began when he met **Köhler** in Frankfurt in 1911 and when both men served as subjects in **Wertheimer**'s experiment demonstrating apparent motion – the 'Phi Phenomenon'. With great fervour Wertheimer, Köhler and Koffka founded *Gestalt* Psychology to save psychology from elementarism, sensationism and associationism. Of the three men Koffka was the most vocal protagonist. From his post in Giessen he wrote the 'Beiträge zur *Gestalt* Psychologie' (Contributions to *Gestalt* Psychology), reporting on a total of eighteen experiments in visual perception conducted by him and his students. These contributions were published intermittently in the *Zeitschrift für Psychologie* (1913–21). During the First World War Koffka worked with aphasic patients in Giessen to assess hearing losses and sound localization. In 1921 Koffka became co-founder and editor for the *Psychologische Forschung*, a journal founded explicitly for the dissemination of experimental data and theory pertaining to *Gestalt* psychology.

Koffka was largely responsible for the introduction of *Gestalt* psychology to the US. His fluency in English and his clear writing style facilitated his 1922 article in the *Psychological Bulletin*. He maintained that *Gestalt* Theory is more than just a theory of perception, but rather a new comprehensive way to understand psychology – if not all human endeavours. Koffka introduced Wertheimer's 'bundle hypothesis' to discuss sensation in relation to the 'degree of consciousness'. He also related sensation to imagery differentiating between momentary impressions and the 'residuum' – the sensations left behind to form part of our memory. Koffka also succeeded in integrating *Gestalt* concepts into developmental psychology. His book *Die Grundlagen der psychischen Entwicklung: Eine Einführung der Kinderpsychologie* was first published in German in 1921 and later in English under the title, *Growth of the Human Mind*. It had much popular appeal and was translated into French, Spanish, Russian, Chinese and Japanese. The book brought educational psychology and child rearing within the scope of *Gestalt* psychology by emphasizing trial and error learning. In general, Koffka stressed the interaction between innate capacities and environmental conditions, favouring Stern's 'theory of covergence'. The text contains many practical examples while discussing children's physical development, their motor- and ideational learning, their thought processes and memory. In several chapters divergent views are criticized, especially **Watson**'s behaviourism, **Thorndike**'s connectionism and Karl **Bühler**'s developmental stages. It is suggested that associations do not exist, but only 'configurations'.

In 1932 Koffka was invited by the USSR to undertake ethno-psychological research in Uzbekistan. He fell ill with a relapsing fever, unable to finish his work. Back in the US and still not well he began his major work *Principles of Gestalt Psychology*. It is a most thorough attempt to design a complete theoretical system of human behavior. It discusses a multitude of perceptual phenomena, categorizing them into 24 different 'Laws', such as the Law of Closure, Success, Fittingness, Good Continuation, Prägnanz, Proximity, Simplest Path, Transposition, etc. Some of these laws are used as frameworks in the discussion of reflexes, the Ego emotion, society and personality. Koffka's *Principles* has 15 chapters and over 700 pages, and has become a classic in psychology.

FRANK WESLEY

Kohlberg, Lawrence

Born: 1927, Bronxville, New York **Died:** 1987, Boston, Massachusetts, USA **Nat:** American **Ints:** Developmental psychology **Educ:** BA University of Chicago, 1949; PhD University of Chicago, 1958 **Appts & awards:** Veterans Administration Trainee, 1953–4; Research Associate, University of Chicago, 1955–6; Child Medical Center, Boston, 1958–9; Associate Professor of Psychology, Yale University, 1959–61; Fellow, Center for Advanced Study in the Behavioral Sciences, 1961–2; Department of Psychology, University of Chicago, 1962–8; Graduate School of Education, Harvard University, 1968–87

Principal publications

1963 The development of children's orientations toward moral order, Part 1: Sequence in the development of moral thought. *Vita Humana*, 6, 11–33.

1966 A cognitive-developmental analysis of children's sex-role concepts and attitudes. In E.E. Maccoby (ed.), *The Development of Sex Differences*. Stanford University Press.

1969 Stage and sequence: The cognitive-developmental approach to socialization. In A. Goslin (ed.), *Handbook of Socialization Theory and Research*. Rand-McNally.

1976 Moral stages and moralization: The cognitive developmental approach. In T. Lickona (ed.), *Moral Development and Behavior*. Holt, Rinehart and Winston.

1981 *The Philosophy of Moral Development*. Harper and Row.

1981 *Essays on Moral Development, vol. 1: The Philosophy of Moral Development*. Harper.

1981 *The Meaning and Measurement of Moral Development*. Clark University Press.

Further reading

Gilligan, C. (1982) *In a Different Voice*. Harvard University Press.

Hock, R.R. (1995) *Forty Studies that Changed Psychology*. Prentice-Hall.

Modgil, S. and Modgil, C. (eds) (1986) *Lawrence Kohlberg*. Falmer.

Lawrence Kohlberg was the son of a wealthy businessman. He went to prestigious schools but instead of continuing on the path of privilege he joined the Merchant Marines after leaving high school. He was to join a ship smuggling Jewish refugees from Europe into Palestine through the British blockade. The moral dilemma posed by such actions – to justify disobeying the law – was to figure in almost all of his psychological research. Kohlberg entered the University of Chicago at a time when it was possible to get credit for a course by passing the final examination. He took sufficient exams to get his BA in one year. His 1958 doctoral dissertation on moral judgement was an unusual topic for investigation at that time, and it prefigured the next thirty years of his work.

According to **Piaget**, young children regard rules as obligatory prescriptions which cannot be questioned or changed. He linked the staged development of moral reasoning to cognitive growth. Kohlberg refined and extended Piaget's theory by asking 10-, 13- and 16-year-old boys to resolve a series of moral dilemmas. The dilemmas were presented as vignettes in which the boy was to choose between obeying the law or authority figure and acting in an antagonistic fashion while serving a human need. Kohlberg was less interested in the actual decision than in the underlying structure of the child's reasoning. Analysis of children's responses to different dilemmas led him to conclude that moral development follows an invariant sequence of three moral levels, each comprising two distinct moral stages. Each stage represents a particular method of thinking rather than a particular type of moral decision. The defining characteristics

of Kohlberg's three moral stages and six levels are as follows:

Level 1: Preconventional morality – the child conforms to rules imposed by authority figures to avoid punishment or obtain personal rewards. Stage 1: Punishment and obedience orientation – the goodness or badness of an act depends on its consequences. Stage 2: Naive hedonism – a person at this second stage of moral development conforms to rules in order to gain reward or satisfy personal objectives.

Level 2: Conventional morality – the individual now strives to obey rules and social norms in order to win others' approval or to maintain social order. Praise and blame-avoidance replace tangible rewards and punishments as motivators of ethical conduct. Stage 3: 'Good boy' or 'Good girl' orientation – moral behaviour is that which pleases, helps or is approved of by others. Stage 4: Social-order-maintaining morality – the child considers the perspectives of the generalized other, i.e. the will of the community or society as reflected in law. What is 'right' is what conforms to the rules of legitimate authority.

Level 3: Post-conventional (or principled) morality – right and wrong are defined in terms of broad principles of justice that could conflict with written laws or with the dictates of authority figures. Stage 5: Morality of contract, individual rights, and democratically accepted law. At this social contract stage, the individual is aware that the purpose of just laws is to express the will of the majority and to further human values. Laws that accomplish these ends and are impartially applied are viewed as social contracts that one has an obligation to follow, whereas imposed laws that compromise human rights or dignity are considered unjust and worthy of challenge. Stage 6: Morality of individual principles of conscience. At this 'highest' moral stage, the individual defines right and wrong on the basis of the self-chosen ethical principles of his or her own conscience. These principles are abstract moral guidelines or principles of universal justice (and respect for individual rights) that transcend any law or social contract that may conflict with them.

Although Kohlberg believed that his stages form an invariant and universal sequence of moral growth that is closely tied to cognitive development, he also claimed that cognitive growth, of itself, is insufficient to guarantee moral development. In order to move beyond the pre-conventional level of moral reasoning, children must be exposed to people or situations that introduce cognitive disequilibria – conflicts between existing moral concepts and new ideas that will force them to re-evaluate their viewpoints. So, like Piaget, Kohlberg believed that both cognitive development and relevant social experiences underlie the growth of moral reasoning.

Criticisms of Kohlberg's account of moral development can be grouped around six issues. First, are Kohlberg's stages an invariant sequence? Not surprisingly, it took some time for a corpus of empirical literature to emerge, and the general conclusion to be drawn from experimental and longitudinal studies suggest that Kohlberg's moral stages do seem to represent an invariant sequence.

Second, Kohlberg posits a fundamental relationship between the development of thinking and that of moral reasoning. In general, the evidence suggests that this relationship does exist. Proficiency at role taking and adopting the perspective of others appears to be necessary for the onset of conventional morality, and formal operations appear to be necessary for post-conventional or principled morality. However, Kohlberg emphasized that intellectual growth does not guarantee moral development. A person who has reached the highest stages of intellect may continue to reason at the pre-conventional level about moral issues. Both intellectual growth and relevant social experiences are necessary before children can progress from pre-conventional morality to Kohlberg's highest stages.

Third, in the early 1960s Kohlberg's account of personality and social development challenged the major assumptions of socialization – the idea that people are shaped primarily by social and cultural forces. He emphasized that from a young age children actively interpret and give meaning to their social experiences, and that cognitive development is a key to understanding social and moral development. Kohlberg's position has sometimes been wrongly characterized as a purely cognitive account of moral judgement, but his 'social experience' hypothesis indicates that his is better considered a cognitive-social account. The literature supports the proposition that social experience contributes to moral growth.

Fourth, Kohlberg's theory has been criticized for claiming that moral reasoning predicts moral behaviour. There is a good deal of research to show that the moral judgements of young children do not predict their actual behaviour in situations in which they are induced to cheat or violate other normal norms.

Fifth, psychologists have asked whether there is consistency to moral reasoning, as the theory suggests. Children and adolescents have been found to be fairly consistent in the type (or stage) of reasoning that they use to resolve different moral issues. However, it could be that this coherence simply reflects the fact that all of Kohlberg's dilemmas are abstract and hypothetical and that inconsistent reasoning would emerge on more tangible dilemmas. Most of the empirical evidence indicates that there is an underlying consistency to moral reasoning – a coherence that is attributable not solely to the abstract and hypothetical nature of Kohlberg's moral dilemmas.

Sixth, it has been claimed that Kohlberg's theory is biased against women. Gilligan has argued that Kohlberg's stages were based on interviews with males and that, in some studies, women seemed to be cast as the moral inferiors of men, typically reasoning at stage 3 while men usually reasoned at stage 4. She argued that females develop a different moral orientation to males, one that is not adequately represented in Kohlberg's theory, and that these different moral orientations are a product of sex typing. Although Gilligan's ideas about sex differences in moral reasoning have not been generally supported, she forcefully demonstrated that there is much more to morality than a concern with rules, rights and justice, and that reasoning based on compassionate concerns can be just as principled and mature as the 'justice' orientation favoured by Kohlberg.

Kohlberg's ideas are at the heart of debates on the psychology of moral judgement. In addition to formulating a robust cognitive-social account of moral development, he developed a set of developmental markers for identifying a person's stage of moral thinking, and published this as a scoring system and manual that have guided thousands of subsequent studies.

In 1973 Kohlberg contracted a disease while visiting Central America that was to ruin his health for the next thirteen years. He was reported missing on 17 January 1987, and his body was later found in marshland near Logan Airport, Boston. He had taken his own life by drowning.

Köhler, Wolfgang

Born: 1887, Reval, Estonia **Died:** 1967, New Hampshire, USA **Nat:** German **Ints:** General, experimental psychology, physiological and comparative, philosophical and theoretical psychology **Educ:** PhD University of Berlin, 1909 **Appts & awards:** Anthropoid Research Station, Canary Island, 1913–20; Psychological Laboratory, University of Berlin, 1920; Professor, University of Göttingen, 1921; Head, Department of Psychology, University of Berlin, 1922–35; William James Lecture, Harvard, 1934; Swarthmore College, Professor, 1935–58, Research Professor, 1946; APA, Distinguished Scientific Contribution Award, 1957, President, 1958; Gifford Lectures, University of Edinburgh, 1958; Honorary Citizen, City of Berlin, 1965; Hon. President, Deutsche Gesellschaft für Psychologie, 1967; Hon. Doctoral Degrees from Pennsylvania, Chicago, Freiburg, Münster, Tübingen, Uppsala Universities, and from Swarthmore and Kenyon Colleges; Member, American Academy of Arts and Sciences; Member, American Philosophical Society; Member, National Academy of Science

Principal publications

1913 Über unbemerkte Empfindungen und Urteilstäuschungen (Unnoticed feelings and misjudgements). *Zeitschrift für Psychologie*, 66, 51–80.

1917 *Intelligenzprüfung an Menschenaffen*. (The mentality of apes, English translation, Harcourt Brace, 1925.)

1929 *Gestalt Psychology*. Liveright (rev. edn, 1947).

1938 *The Place of Value in a World of Facts*. Liveright.

1958 The present situation in brain physiology. *American Psychologist*, 13, 150–4.

1965 Unsolved problems in the field of figural after-effects. *Psychological Record*, 15, 63–83.

1969 *The Task of Gestalt Psychology*. Princeton University Press (posthumous).

Further reading

Asch, S.E. (1968) Wolfgang Köhler: 1887–1967. *American Journal of Psychology*, 81, 110–19.

Henle, M. (1978) One man against the Nazis – Wolfgang Köhler. *American Psychologist*, 33, 939–44.

Wolfgang Köhler was one of the founders of *Gestalt* Psychology. His experiment with the ape 'Sultan' is known to every psychology student. This experiment included a task requiring the ape to fit two poles together in order to reach a banana. It forms the basis for Köhler's idea of 'insight learning' – a sudden realization

of a pertinent relationship. Working with apes and chickens Köhler showed also that animals are capable of perceiving relationships by responding to the larger or the brighter of two stimuli, even overriding the very stimulus on which they were trained. The *Gestalt* psychologists called this phenomenon the 'Law of Transposition' and use it to criticize behaviourism for putting too much emphasis on the effect of a single stimulus while neglecting the molar aspects of stimulating situations.

In 1917 Köhler published *Intelligenzprüfungen an Menschenaffen* (*The Mentality of Apes*). This book translated into English and French was received with great interest by the education public. It described Köhler's animal experiments in the theoretical framework of the *Gestalt*ists, emphasizing the formation of sudden relationships in reasoning and thought processes – the 'Aha! Phenomenon' – where learning plays only a minimal role and where the perceptual nature of problem solving is emphasized.

As a student Köhler was influenced by Max Planck and in his thinking he remained a physicist throughout his life. He believed that physics will ultimately explain biological events, and that in turn, biology will provide the answers for psychology. Investigating acoustic and visual sensations and illusions Köhler discovered certain regularities and therefore he postulated neural brain fields to account for various perceptual phenomena. He refined **Wertheimer**'s concept of 'psychophysical isomorphism' by postulating macroscopic field processes where neural impulses exciting one point in the brain spread to distal parts. These psycho-chemical properties of the nerve tissue form the organic correlates of such *Gestalt* concepts of Grouping, Segregation, Prägnanz and Closure. Grouping (sometimes referred to as Proximity) describes the perception of objects close together in the visual field which are perceived as a group of objects instead of a number of unrelated objects. Prägnanz is another *Gestalt* principle that holds that percepts take the most recognizable form possible in the given circumstances. 'Closure' describes the tendency to perceive an incomplete figure as complete, as e.g., an open circle as a closed one.

While Köhler disseminated *Gestalt* Psychology to the public via his writings he was also very influential among academics. He was a co-founder and co-editor of the *Psychologische Forschung*. His book, *Gestalt Psychology*, published in 1929 and revised in 1947, is considered the most important exposition of the *Gestalt* movement. Köhler was a clear writer and an impressive speaker. Endangering his own life, he resisted the Nazis for several years when they threatened to take over his Psychological Institute at the University of Berlin. He emigrated to the USA in 1935 at the age of 48, where he was successful as a teacher and humanist for three more decades.

FRANK WESLEY

Korchin, Sheldon Jerome

Born: 1921, New York, USA *Died:* 1989, Berkeley, California, USA *Nat:* American *Ints:* Clinical, community psychology, personality and social, psychological study of social issues, psychotherapy *Educ:* BA Brooklyn College, 1942; MA Clark University, 1943; MA Harvard University, 1944; PhD Harvard University, 1946 *Appts & awards:* University of California at Berkeley, Professor; Department of Psychology, Director, Psychology Clinic, Chair, Graduate Program in Clinical Psychology; Member, Diplomate American Board Professional Psychology, 1955; NIMH Visiting Scientist, 1959–60; Fulbright Professorship, 1960–1; APA: Education and Training Board, 1964–8, Committee on Post-doctoral Training, 1968–9, Award for Distinguished Contribution to the Science and Practice of Clinical Psychology (Committee to make awards), 1979–81, Board of Social and Ethical Responsibility for Psychology 1979–81 (Chair 1982), Task Force on Psychology and the Handicapped, 1979–82, Task Force on Psychology and Public Policy, 1979–82, Public Interest Award, 1984–5 (Chair 1985), Division of Clinical Psychology NIMH Senior Research Fellowship, 1969–70; Fulbright Research Award, 1976–7; APA Division 12, Distinguished Contribution Award, 1978; California State Psychological Association, Distinguished Contribution Award, 1979; President, IAAP Division of Clinical and Community Psychology, 1982–6; Member, National Academy of Practice, 1983; Editorial Board, *Psychiatry: Journal of Interpersonal Relations*, 1965– , *Journal of Clinical and Consulting Psychology*, 1967–72, *Journal of Abnormal Psychology*, 1969–74, *Psicologia Clinica*, 1981–

Principal publications

1955 *Anxiety and Stress.* McGraw Hill (with H. Basowitz, H. Persky and R.R. Grinker).

1956 The judgment of ambiguous stimuli as an index of cognitive functioning in aging. *Journal of Personality*, 25, 81–95.

1960 The differential effects of 'shame' and 'disintegrative' threats on emotional and adrenocortical functioning. *Archives of General Psychiatry*, 2, 640–51 (with M. Herz).

1964 Anxiety and cognition. In C. Scheerer (ed.), *Cognition: Theory, Research, Promise.* Harper & Row.

1965 Some psychological determinants of stress behavior. In S. Klausner (ed.), *The Quest for Self-Control.* Free Press.

1965 Personality characteristics of the Mercury astronauts. In G.H. Grosser, H. Wechsler and M. Greenblatt (eds), *The Threat of Impending Disaster.* MIT Press (with G.E. Ruff).

1976 *Anxiety and Stress.* McGraw-Hill (with H. Basowitz, H. Persky and R.R. Grinker). Modern Clinical Psychology. Basic Books.

1980 Clinical psychology and minority problems. *American Psychologist*, 35, 262–9.

1981 The future of clinical assessment. *American Psychologist*, 36, 1147–58 (with D. Schuldberg).

1982 Ethical perspectives in clinical research. In P.C. Kendall and J.N. Butcher (eds), *Handbook of Research in Clinical Psychology.* Wiley (with P.A. Cowan).

1983 *Minority Mental Health.* Praeger (ed. with E.E. Jones).

1983 Principles common to all psychotherapies. In C.E. Walker (ed.), *Handbook of Clinical Psychology.* Dow Jones-Irwin (with S.H. Sands).

1983 The history of clinical psychology: A personal view. In M. Hersen, A. Kazdin and A.S. Bellak (eds), *The Clinical Psychology Handbook.* Wiley.

Further reading

Cowan, P.A. (1990) Sheldon J. Korchin (1921–1989): Obituary. *American Psychologist*, 45, 1267.

Routh, D.K. (1994) *Clinical Psychology since 1917: Science, Practice, and Organization.* Plenum.

Korchin is best known for contributions in three areas: (1) personology and clinical psychology, in a theoretical and historical context; (2) social psychology and social problems; and (3) stress, anxiety and coping, in people of unusual competence and in people of disadvantaged status (disabled and minorities), as well as more average and more neurotic groups. Although one or another of these themes was more salient at a particular time in his career, all existed from student days. Moreover, these themes are represented equally in his teaching and administrative as well as scholarly activities. He was a strong advocate of the need to understand psychological phenomena in their theoretical and historical contexts rather than simply as empirical events, and to study them as they occur naturally rather than in laboratory settings. In this regard his thinking was influenced by two of his teachers – Robert White and **Gordon Allport**. Within clinical psychology and personality theory, his writings contributed principally through their synthesis of major issues, through which one can see 'the big picture', rather than through the creation of specific concepts, findings or techniques. Within social psychology – considered in its social context – he was been responsible for the emergence (from the late 1960s) of a major emphasis on training of minority students and research on minority issues in the graduate programme at Berkeley.

Kosslyn, Stephen Michael

Born: 1948, Santa Monica, California **Nat:** American **Ints:** Neural substrates and computational models of visual mental imagery, neuropsychology **Educ:** BA University of California, Los Angeles (UCLA), 1970; PhD Stanford University, 1974 **Appts & awards:** Professor, Department of Psychology, Harvard University, Research Psychologist, McLean Hospital; Assistant Professor of Psychology, The Johns Hopkins University, 1974–7; Associate Professor of Psychology, Harvard University, 1977–81; Boyd McCandless Young Scientist Award, 1978 (Developmental Psychology); Associate Professor of Psychology, Brandeis University, 1981–2; National Academy of Sciences, Initiatives in Research Award, 1983; Full Professor of Psychology, Harvard University, 1983– ; Fellow of American Psychological Association (Division 3), 1984; Fellow, American Association for the Advancement of Science, 1987; Associate Psychologist in Neurology, Massachusetts General Hospital, 1990– ; Consultant, John D. and Catherine T. MacArthur Foundation, 1992– ; Research Psychologist, McLean Hospital, 1993– ; elected to Academia Rodinensis pro Remediatione, Switzerland, 1993

Principal publications

1973   Scanning visual images: Some structural implications. *Perception and Psychophysics*, 14, 90–4.

1975   Information representation in visual images. *Cognitive Psychology*, 7, 341–70.

1976   Can imagery be distinguished from other forms of internal representation? Evidence from studies of information retrieval times. *Memory and Cognition*, 4, 291–7.

1977   A simulation of visual imagery. *Cognitive Science*, 1, 265–95 (with S. P. Schwartz).

1978   Measuring the visual angle of the mind's eye. *Cognitive Psychology*, 10, 356–389.

1978   Visual images preserve metric spatial information: Evidence from studies of image scanning. *Journal of Experimental Psychology: Human Perception and Performance*, 4, 47–60 (with T.M. Ball and B.J. Reiser).

1979   On the demystification of mental imagery. *Behavioural and Brain Sciences*, 2, 535–48 (with S. Pinker, G.E. Smith and S.P. Schwartz).

1980   *Image and Mind*. Harvard University Press.

1981   The medium and the message in mental imagery: A theory. *Psychological Review*, 88, 46–66.

1983   *Ghosts in the Mind's Machine*. Norton.

1987   Seeing and imagining in the cerebral hemispheres: A computational approach. *Psychological Review*, 94, 148–175.

1990   *An Invitation to Cognitive Science: Visual Cognition and Action*, vol. 2. Cambridge, MA: MIT Press (ed. with D. Osherson and J. Hollerbach).

1990   When is imagery used in daily life? A diary study. *Journal of Mental Imagery*, 14, 131–52 (with C. Segar, J. Pani and L.A. Hillger).

1991   A cognitive neuroscience of visual cognition: Further development. In R. Logie and M. Denis (eds), *Mental Images in Human Cognition*. North-Holland.

1992   *Wet Mind: The New Cognitive Neuroscience*. Free Press (with O. Koenig).

1993   Visual information processing: A twenty-five year retrospective (with M.H. van Kleeck). In D. Meyer and S. Kornblum (eds), *Attention and Performance*, XXV. Erlbaum.

1993   Visual mental imagery activates topographically organised visual cortex: PET investigation. *Journal of Cognitive Neuroscience*, 5, 263–87 (with N.M. Alpert, W.I. Thompson, V. Maljkovic, S.B. Weise, C.F. Chabris, S.E. Hamilton, S.L. Raunch and F.S. Buonnano).

1994   *Image and Brain: The Resolution of the Imagery Debate*. MIT Press.

1994   Mental imagery and ageing. *Psychology and Ageing*, 9, 90–102 (with I.E. Dror).

1994   Encoding shape and spatial relations: The role of receptive field size in coordinating complementary representations. *Cognitive Science*, 18, 361–86 (with R.A. Jacobs).

1995   Role of imagery in perception: Or, there is no such thing as immaculate perception (with A.L Sussman). In M.S. Gazzaniga (ed.), *The Cognitive Neurosciences*. MIT Press.

Further reading

Annett, J. (1995) Imagery and motor processes. *British Journal of Psychology*, 86, 161–7.

Driskell, J.E., Copper, C., and Moran, A. (1994) Does mental practice enhance performance? *Journal of Applied Psychology*, 79, 481–92.

Jeannerod, M. (1994) The representing brain: Neural correlates of motor intention and imagery. *Behavioural and Brain Sciences*, 17, 187–245.

McNamara, T.P. (1994) Knowledge representation. In R.J. Sternberg (ed.), *Thinking and Problem Solving*. Academic Press.

Stephen Kosslyn is a cognitive scientist whose research speciality concerns the exploration of neural substrates of visual 'mental imagery' or the capacity to represent experiences of things (including people, objects and sensations) which are not physically present. In his theory images are regarded primarily as 'analogical' representations because, like a map or a diagram, they correspond in a non-arbitrary, isomorphic way with the objects that they depict. Put simply, a visual mental image corresponds to a view of an object. Although they are experienced as visuo-spatial representations, images are believed to be generated from stored propositional knowledge in long-term memory (LTM). For example, before the image of an object (e.g. a car) can be generated, propositional information is required to describe its parts and the nature of their inter-relationships. Kosslyn's analogical theory of imagery is supported by both experimental and neurological findings. For example, people usually take longer to scan the distance between two points which are far apart on a map than to scan the distance between imagined landmarks which are relatively closer to each other (Kosslyn *et al.*, 1978). Also, Kosslyn and Sussman (1995) have identified common neural pathways shared between imagery and perceptual processes. For example, Kosslyn *et al.* (1993) used positron emission tomography to show that imagery activates topographically organized parts of the visual cortex. Likewise, Kosslyn *et al.* (1993) discovered that regional cerebral blood flow (rCBF) patterns evoked during visual imagery resemble those detected during visual perception. On the basis of such research evidence, Kosslyn proposed that visual imagery is 'functionally equivalent' to visual perception.

In his computational model (Kosslyn and Koening, 1992), Kosslyn suggested that images are represented in a two-dimensional internal array. The image is generated as a pattern of activation in the cells of this array. This pattern, which may be formed from visual processing or from memory, can be moved, scanned or rotated. The spatial medium in which images are generated allows the relative distance between actual features of the object to be preserved analogically in the image. This preservation is apparent from 'scanning' studies which show that there is a direct relationship between the speed with which people can visually inspect images for certain information and the actual distance between the targets in question. The information from which images are generated comprises 'image files' (which contain 'literal' encodings or information about the imaged object's appearance) and 'propositional files' (which contain factual information about the names and sizes of the constituent parts of the object) in LTM. The image files contain the co-ordinates of the object to be represented whereas the propositional files contain descriptions of its key features. Image generation is believed to involve the action of a number of specific modules or sub-routines designated by the task they perform on the stored LTM information (e.g. 'PICTURE', 'PUT' and 'FIND'). Unfortunately, although persuasive, Kosslyn's evidence is not conclusive. For example, expectancy effects may hamper accurate interpretation of experimental research on imagery (see **Pylyshyn**, 1981). Thus in image scanning tasks, participants might adjust their scanning speeds to comply with their expectations that longer distances between imaged locations should require longer scanning time than relatively shorter distances. Overall, Kosslyn's research on imagery is significant for at least four reasons (McNamara, 1994). First, his studies highlight the methodological importance of using converging operations to explore human cognitive processes. In particular, experimental evidence derived from mental scanning studies is neatly supplemented by neuroscientific data on specific brain sites that are activated during imagery experiences. Secondly, using experimental research and case studies of people with brain-damage, Kosslyn has postulated theories concerning the possible neural implementation analogical representations. Thirdly, Kosslyn has stimulated debate on the relationship between mental imagery and perception. Finally, by arguing that imagery is a bridge between perception and motor control (Kosslyn and Sussman, 1995), Kosslyn has renewed interest in such topics as 'mental practice' (see review by Driskell *et al.*, 1994). Unfortunately, because

Kosslyn has been concerned almost exclusively with visual mental imagery, important non-visual properties of this construct (e.g. kinaesthetic or 'feeling-oriented' qualities) of images have been ignored. This oversight has prevented progress in understanding imagery usage by skilled performers such as athletes (see Annett, 1995; Jeannerod, 1994).

AIDAN MORAN

Krasner, Leonard

Born: 1924, Brooklyn, New York, USA **Nat:** American **Ints:** Clinical psychology, community psychology, experimental analysis of behaviour, health psychology, population and environmental psychology **Educ:** BS City College of New York, 1946; MA Columbia University, 1948; PhD Columbia University, 1950 **Appts & awards:** Professor, State University of New York, Stony Brook; Phi Beta Kappa, 1946; Sigma Xi, 1950; Co-Editor, Psychology Series (Pergamon Press), 1968– ; Chairman, APA Board of Professional Affairs, 1970–1; Member, APA Board of Directors, 1972–5

Principal publications

1965 *Case Studies in Behavior Modification.* Holt, Rinehart and Winston (ed. with L.P. Ullmann).
1965 *Research in Behavior Modification.* Holt, Rinehart and Winston (ed. with L.P. Ullmann).
1965 The behavior scientist and social responsibility: No place to hide. *Journal of Social Issues*, 21, 9–30.
1967 Verbal operant conditioning and awareness. In E. Salzinger (ed.), *Research in Verbal Behavior and Some Neurophysiological Implications.* Academic Press.
1969 *A Psychological Approach to Abnormal Behavior.* Prentice-Hall (with L.P. Ullmann).
1969 Behavior modification: Values and training. In C.M. Franks (ed.), *Assessment and Status of the Behavior Therapies.* McGraw-Hill.
1971 Behavior therapy. In P.H. Mussen and M.R. Rosenzweig (eds), *Annual Review of Psychology*, vol. 22. Annual Reviews.
1973 *Behavior Influence and Personality.* Holt, Rinehart and Winston (with L.P. Ullmann).
1976 On the death of behavior modification: Some notes from a mourner. *American Psychologist*, 31, 387–9.
1978 The future and the past in the behaviorism–humanism dialogue. *American Psychologist*, 33, 799–804.
1980 (ed.) *Environmental Design and Human Behavior.* Pergamon Press.

1982 Behavior modification and social control: Issues and myths. In J.P. Gibbs (ed.), *The Future of Social Control.* Sage.
1984 A study of the 'value' systems of behavioral scientists. *American Psychologist*, 39, 840–50 (with A. Houts).

Further reading

O'Donohue, W.T. and Krasner, L. (eds) (1995) *Theories of Behavior Therapy: Exploring Behavior Change.* American Psychological Association.

Since receiving his doctorate Krasner has been involved in most aspects of clinical psychology as a science and as a profession. He initiated the graduate training programme at the State University of New York at Stony Brook, in the mid-1960s, the first behaviourally oriented clinical programme in the USA and a model for many others. His research interests have developed from the perspective of the clinical psychologist as scientist-practitioner and as an agent of social change. His early research work considered the use of verbal conditioning as an analogue of psychotherapy and as a prototype of interpersonal social influence in hypnosis, placebo effects, behaviour therapy and the token economy. His research interests and his interests in social issues have resulted in a series of papers and books which have focused on the historical origin, development, ethical implications and social consequences of behaviour modification as a treatment procedure, as a theoretical conception of human behaviour, and as a revolutionary scientific paradigm. Concern with the issues of values and science has been an integral part of his research efforts in the field of behaviour modification. He has emphasized and documented the way in which the techniques, philosophy and methodology of what was initially a small group of scientists has been extended to many social institutions. In the late 1970s he initiated a systematic investigation of the relationship between the 'value systems' of scientists and the influence of these systems on their research and on the broader society in which they function.

Krech, David

Born: 1909, Svenchanka, Belorussia **Died:** 1977 Berkeley, CA, USA **Nat:** Russian/American **Ints:** Physiological and comparative, personality and social, general psychology, teaching **Educ:** BS New York University, 1930; MA New York University, 1931; PhD University of California,

1933 *Appts & awards:* APA, Distinguished Scientific Contribution award, 1970; Hon. Dr, University of Oslo, 1976;

Principal publications

1932   'Hypotheses' in rats. *Psychological Review*, 6, 516–32.

1938   A study of the continuity of the problem-solving process. *Psychological Review*, 45, 107–33.

1948   *Theory and Problems of Social Psychology.* McGraw-Hill (with R.S. Crutchfield).

1950   Dynamic systems, psychological fields and hypothetical constructs. *Psychological Review*, 57, 283–90.

1951   The problem of personality and its theory. *Journal of Personality*, 21, 118–68 (with G.S. Klein).

1958   *Elements of Psychology.* Knopf (with R.S. Crutchfield).

1959   Acetycholine metabolism and behavior of rats. *Science*, 129, 62–4 (with M.R. Rosenzweig and E.L. Bennett).

1960   A search for relations between brain chemistry and behavior. *Psychological Bulletin*, 57, 476–92 (with M.R. Rosenzweig and E.L. Bennett).

1962   *Individual in Society.* McGraw-Hill (with R.S. Crutchfield and E.L. Ballachey).

1962   Variation in environmental complexity and brain measures. *Journal of Comparative and Psychological Psychology*, 55, 1092–5 (with M.R. Rosenzweig, E.L. Bennett and J.F. Zolman).

1964   Chemical and anatomical plasticity of brain. *Science*, 146, 610–19 (with E.L. Bennett, M.C. Diamond and M.R. Rosenzweig).

1969   *Elements of Psychology*, 2nd edn. Knopf (with R.S. Crutchfield, N. Livson, A.R. Rollin and W.A. Wilson).

1970   *Elements of Psychology: Briefer Course.* Knopf (with R.S. Crutchfield, N. Livson, A.R. Rollin and W.A. Wilson).

1970   Brain research: Some recent developments and some speculations for the future. In C.S. Wallia (ed.), *Toward Century 21*. Basic Books.

1986   Modifying brain chemistry and anatomy by enrichment or impoverishment of experience (with M.R. Rosenzweig, E.L. Bennett and M.C. Diamond). In G. Newton and S. Levine (eds), *Early Experience and Behavior*. Charles C. Thomas.

Further reading

Bornstein, R.F. (1992) The dependent personality: Developmental, social, and clinical perspectives. *Psychological Bulletin*, 112, 3–23.

Forsyth, D.R. (ed.) (1987) *Social Psychology*. Brook/Cole.

David Krech initially developed his interest in animal learning during his student career at NYU. This interest was pursued in his PhD with E.C. **Tolman** at Berkeley and also in his post-doctoral fellowship with K.S. **Lashley** at Chicago, the latter resulting in the publication of the non-continuity hypothesis of problem solving (1938).

Krech was dismissed from his first teaching post at Colorado in 1939 for holding questionable political opinions, following which he worked as editor for a neo-marxist political organization. During World War II he became fascinated by attitudes and social psychology and it was in this context that he returned to Berkeley where he began a long term friendship and collaboration with Richard **Crutchfield** culminating in the innovative text *Theory and Problems of Social Psychology*. In 1948 he became involved in launching the 'New Look' in psychology, originated by **Bruner** and Postman, which emphasized social psychological factors in perception. In 1949 Krech travelled to Norway to expand interest in social psychology. His period as a visiting professor was extremely successful and he was subsequently awarded an honorary doctorate by Oslo University.

On his return to Berkeley, Krech reverted to his original interest in animal studies but with a new orientation. He established an interdisciplinary team to explore the relationship between learning and neurochemistry. This team produced some sixty papers describing evidence of a direct effect of differential experience, in the form of learning or sensory stimulation, on brain chemistry and brain anatomy. In addition to being an innovative researcher, Krech dedicated much of his time to teaching, one result of which was the publication of the widely used textbook *Elements of Psychology*.

Unfortunately, a serious heart attack and subsequent health problems led Krech to retire at the age of 62, but during his last six years he collaborated on a new textbook, revised earlier texts, travelled and lectured.

MICHELLE MORGAN

Külpe, Oswald

Born: 1862, Candau, Latvia *Died:* 1915, Munich, Germany *Nat:* German *Ints:* Experimental psychology, psychology and the arts, philosophical and theoretical psychology *Educ:* Dr Medicine, University of Giessen, 1907; PhD University of Leipzig, 1887 *Appts & awards:*

Head, Department of Psychology, University of Würzburg, 1894–1909; Director, Psychological laboratory, University of Bonn, 1909–13

Principal publications

1887   Zur Theorie der sinnlichen Gefühle (Theory of Sensory Feelings), *Vierteljahresschrift der wissenschaftlichen Philosophie*, 11, 424–82.

1893   *Grundriss der Psychologie (Foundations of Psychology)*. Englemann.

1895   *Einleitung in die Philosophie (Introduction to Philosophy)*. Englemann.

1902   Über die Objektivierung and Subjektivierung von Sinneseindrucken (The objectification and subjectification of sensory impressions). *Philosophische Studien*, 19, 508–56.

1903   Ein Beitrag zur experimentellen Aesthetik (A contribution to experimental Aesthetic). *American Journal of Psychology*, 14, 479–95.

Further reading

Lindenfeld, D. (1978) Oswald Külpe and the Würzburg School. *Journal of the History of the Behavioural Sciences*, 14, 132–41.

Ogden, R.M. (1951) Oswald Külpe and the Würzburg School. *The American Journal of Psychology*, 64, 4–9.

Kulpe studied history and philosophy in Riga and Leipzig before he became interested in psychology. He began his psychological studies in Berlin and later in Göttingen under G.E. **Müller** before returning to Leipzig where he took his PhD under **Wundt** in 1887. He remained in Wundt's laboratory until 1894, investigating mental processes by examining their conscious attributes such as sensations and images.

Though Külpe followed Wundt's method of introspection, he did not obtain the expected results. Some of his subjects, for instance, were unable to form an image of the colour red when asked to close their eyes. Yet, they were able to talk and think about red. Külpe named this phenomenon 'imageless thought'.

When Külpe established his laboratory at the University of Würzburg in 1894 he and some of his students, notably Max **Wertheimer**, Narziss Ach, Henry Watt and Kurt **Koffka**, continued to examine the role of imageless thought in relation to problem solving. During a task of naming opposites (for example, night–day) they found that the answer 'day' is given immediately and automatically after hearing 'night' without intervening images. Part of the correct solution for such problems stems from the task or the 'Aufgabe'; Külpe emphasized the 'mental set' which predisposes one to respond in a given manner.

Though Külpe is not known as the founder of the *Gestalt* School he inspired it through his Würzburg School and his students. He was an amiable person, an outstanding pianist and much respected teacher. His texts became popular among academics and the education public. His *Introduction to Philosophy* reached its 7th edition. He was also a much wanted lecturer: in the decade before his death he received 'calls' from almost all of the German universities.

FRANK WESLEY

L

Ladd, George Trumball

Born: 1842, Painesville, Ohio, USA **Died:** 1921
Nat: American **Ints:** General psychology,
history of psychology **Educ:** AB Andover
Theological Seminary, 1864 **Appts & awards:**
Southworth Lecturer on Congregationalism,
Andover Theological Seminary, 1876; Professor
of Philosophy, Bowdoin College, 1879;
Professor of Mental and Moral Philosophy,
Yale, 1881–1901; Co-Founder, APA, 1892;
Second President, APA, 1893; Japanese Order
of the Rising Sun, 3rd Class, 1899, 2nd Class,
1907; University Professor, Yale, 1901–5; Gold
Medal of the Imperial Educational Society of
Japan

Principal publications

1878   The Unknown God of Herbert and the Promise
and Potency of Professor Tyndall. Hauser.
1887   Elements of Physiological Psychology.
Scribner's (rev. R.S. Woodworth, 1911).
1890   Introduction to Philosophy: An Inquiry after a
Rational System of Scientific Principles in their
Relation to Ultimate Reality. Scribner's.
1891   Outlines of Physiological Psychology.
(abbreviation of Elements, 1887).
1892   Psychology as so-called 'natural science'.
Philosophical Review, 1, 24–53.
1894   Psychology, Descriptive and Explanatory.
Scribner's.
1894   Primer of Psychology. Scribner's.
1894   Primer of Descriptive Psychology. Scribner's.
1895   Philosophy of Mind: An Essay in the
Metaphysics of Psychology. Scribner's.
1897   Philosophy of Knowledge: An Inquiry into the
Nature, Limits and Validity of Human Cognitive
Faculty. Scribner's.
1898   Outlines of Descriptive Psychology: A Text-
Book of Mental Science for Colleges and Normal
Schools. Longmans Green (abbreviation of
Psychology, Descriptive and Explanatory, 1894).
1905   The Philosophy of Religion (2 vols). Scribner's.
1905   The child's capacity for religion. In T.
Stephens (ed.), The Child and Religion: Eleven
Essays. G.P. Putnam's.
1909   The confusion of pragmatism. Hibbert
Journal, 7(4), 784–801.
1909   Knowledge, Life and Reality. Longmans
Green.
1917   Why Women Cannot Compose Music. Yale
Publishing Association.
1918   The Secret of Personality. Longmans Green.

Further reading

Boring, E.G. (1950) A History of Experimental
Psychology, 2nd edn. Appleton-Century-Crofts.
Mills, E.S. (1969) George Trumball Ladd: Pioneer
American Psychologist. Press of the Case Western
Reserve University.
O'Donnell, J.M. (1985) The Origins of Behaviorism:
American Psychology 1870–1920. New York
University Press.

While generally identified as one of the 'new
psychologists' who converted psychology into
an institutionalized academic scientific discipline in the US during the 1880s and 1890s, Ladd
retained many of the concerns of the older 'mental
and moral philosophy' tradition. Although not
unique in this, his affiliations with the earlier
approaches of the German H. Lotze (whose
lectures, along with several other works, he
translated) and of his patron Noah **Porter** were
especially marked. In particular, as a qualified
Congregationalist minister, he shared Porter's
concern with bridging the widening gap between
psychology and religion, and it was at Porter's
behest that he moved to Yale in 1881 to take
over the mental and moral philosophy course.

As devout cleric who was already deeply
concerned about theological issues, it was from
this direction that Ladd began his investigations
of contemporary 'mental science' on entering
academia in 1879. Any religiously centred
philosophy must, he believed, take into account
the new scientific psychology then beginning to
emerge, particularly W. **Wundt**'s experimental
'physiological psychology'. It was in this context, rather than with the intent of overthrowing
the previous tradition, that Ladd wrote his
Elements of Physiological Psychology, thereby
providing the first systematic English-language
account of developments in Germany – and it
was this text above all which earned him his

place among the founders of the 'new psychology'. Initially he maintained a high profile as a representative of this movement, founding a laboratory at Yale, being a co-founder of the APA and its second president, and continuing to write extensively on psychology, producing a clutch of further textbooks. But notwithstanding his role in stimulating experimental psychology, Ladd himself conducted relatively little experimental research and strains soon began to show. By the mid-1890s he was engaged in controversy with William **James**, whom he viewed as a materialist, and in 1895 *Philosophy of Mind*, intended as a general statement of his theoretical position and concept of psychology, met with scant success. Meanwhile his relations with younger members of his Yale department, notably E.W. Scripture (who had taken over the laboratory) and C.H. Judd were becoming fraught. This was partly due to his autocratic temperament but was exacerbated by differences in understanding of the nature and goals of psychology. As the situation deteriorated Ladd's position within the university became increasingly difficult. In 1901 he was demoted to 'university professor' and while Scripture was fired in 1903, Ladd himself was sensationally forced to retire two years early in 1905. None of this inhibited his literary productivity, which ranged across psychology, philosophy, theology, education and his Asian travels. In 1892 and 1899 he had visited Japan, his 1899 trip being extended to Korea and India, where he gave invited lectures at numerous universities. He remained active following his retirement, making a third visit to Japan in 1907. Nor was he backward in writing magazine articles concerning contemporary social and political issues, generally from a conservative Republican standpoint (he opposed the establishment of the League of Nations, for example). His later writings, of little psychological importance, were mostly of a popular moralistic kind, although his attack on pragmatism is of some significance and the 1917 monograph on *Why Women Cannot Compose Music* has enduring curiosity value.

Throughout his career Ladd saw psychology as ultimately subservient to philosophy, and a reading of his works on philosophy and religion reveals the extent to which a revised version of Porter's framework continued to dominate his thought, although he viewed consciousness as a more active principle than did Porter, for whom it was basically reflective. Like Porter he also insisted that the scientific quest for 'final

causes' was a valid one. Theoretically he is generally cast as a pioneer 'functionalist', in that he espoused the existence of an active purposive self. Physiological level events must therefore be understood as serving this self in an adaptive purposive fashion. Ladd's interests lay primarily in the theoretical and philosophical aspects of this, and he never pursued the relevance of functionalism to practical and applied issues in the way his immediate 'functionalist' successors did. His version of functionalism was, unlike theirs, part and parcel of his philosophical-cum-religious commitment to final causes. Theirs by contrast was rooted in the prevailing evolutionary orientation of late nineteenth-century science. It should, however, be additionally noted that Ladd's Japanese connections were especially influential in establishing psychology as a discipline in Japan, his ex-student Matataro Matsumoto becoming a leading figure and several of his textbooks being translated into Japanese.

In many respects Ladd's established historiographic niche as a founder of American psychology is due to the timely appearance of his *Elements of Physiological Psychology*, which came at an opportune moment to be adopted as a textbook by advocates of the new approach. His own position was far from that of revolutionary proponent of the 'new psychology'; rather he saw psychology as a continuation of mental and moral philosophy by other means. While traditional histories of psychology tended to present the 'new psychology' as a unified movement, glossing over its internal heterogeneity, Ladd's case reveals quite how divided it was regarding fundamental issues. Mills's biography portrays a deeply pious, lonely, emotionally repressed and patriarchal man for whom the scholar's life was in the nature of spiritual vocation. Such a temperament had little appeal to the rising generation of modernist US psychologists, such as J.B. **Watson**, for whom psychology was an applicable hard scientific and secular discipline.

GRAHAM RICHARDS

Ladd-Franklin, Christine

Born: 1847, Windsor, Connecticut, USA **Died:** 1930, New York, USA **Nat:** American **Ints:** Experimental psychology **Educ:** PhD Johns Hopkins University, 1926 **Appts & awards:** Columbia University, Hon. LLD, Vassar College, 1887; With Georg Müller in Göttingen, 1891–2 and Helmholtz in Berlin, 1904–9;

Lecturer in Logic and Psychology, Johns Hopkins University, 1910–30

Principal publications

1887   The experimental determination of the Horopter. *American Journal of Psychology*, 1, 99–111.
1929   *Colour and Colour Theories*.

Further reading

Furomoto, L. (1988) Shared knowledge: The experimentalists, 1904–9. In J.G. Morawski (ed.), *The Rise of Experimentation in American Psychology*. Yale University Press.
—— (1992) Joining separate spheres – Christine Ladd-Franklin, woman–scientist (1847–1930). *American Psychologist*, 47, 175–82.

Christine Ladd-Franklin is noted principally for her early work on colour vision. Her career is also of interest because it illustrates the gender-linked societal forces that operated to exclude women from a career in psychology. In responding to a request for information for James McKeen **Cattell**'s *American Men of Science* (1906), Ladd-Franklin described her father's occupation as 'Gentleman Farmer and Merchant in New York'. Ladd-Franklin's mother died when she was just 12 years old. Family correspondence indicates that her mother and her sister, who was later to provide the money for Ladd-Franklin to attend college, were staunch supporters of women's rights.

She enrolled in Vassar College in 1866 and spent just two years there (1866–7 and 1868–9). After graduating she supported herself by teaching in high schools for about ten years. In 1878 she moved to Baltimore, where she began to study mathematics and logic at the newly established Johns Hopkins University. Although she was able to attend certain classes, the policy of the university was not to admit women as students except by special permission. Completing her work for a PhD in mathematics and logic in 1882 was important in allowing her to describe herself as a scientist, even though Johns Hopkins would not award her the degree because she was a woman. By 1887 she had begun to publish on the topic of vision, particularly colour vision, and her work was well received. She developed **Hering**'s hypothesis that the red–green visual substance was a later evolutionary development of the blue–yellow substance. She suggested that monochromal, black–white vision is the most primitive form of vision. White became

differentiated into blue–yellow vision and later still yellow differentiated into red–green.

In 1894 she travelled to Berlin where she worked with Arthur König, a physicist with an interest in colour vision. Her research was severely handicapped by the lack of an institutional base for her experimental work. The situation improved somewhat in 1904 when she was appointed a lecturer on symbolic logic at Johns Hopkins. As part of its 50th Anniversary Celebration in 1926, Johns Hopkins finally awarded the PhD she had earned in 1882.

Laing, Ronald David

Born: 1927, Glasgow, Scotland **Died:** 1992 **Nat:** British **Ints:** Family psychology, humanistic psychology, psychoanalysis, psychotherapy **Educ:** MB, ChB Glasgow University, 1951; DPM University of London, 1955 **Appts & awards:** Professor, Tavistock Clinic and Tavistock Institute of Human Relations; Director, Langham Clinic for Psychotherapy; Fellow, Royal Society of Medicine; Chairman, Philadelphia Association, 1964–82; Editor, Studies in Existentialism and Phenomenology (Tavistock); Editorial Board, *Review of Existential Psychology and Psychiatry*; *Existential Psychiatry*; Advisory Board, Longman

Principal publications

1958   An examination of Tillich's theory of anxiety and neurosis. *British Journal of Medical Psychology*, 30, 117.
1958   The collusion function of pairing in analytic groups. *British Journal of Medical Psychology*, 31 (with A. Esterson).
1960   *The Divided Self: A Study of Sanity and Madness*. Quadrangle Books.
1961   *The Self and Others: Further Studies in Sanity and Madness*. Tavistock.
1964   *Reason and Violence: A Decade of Sartre's Philosophy 1950–60*. Tavistock (with D. Cooper).
1964   Is schizophrenia a disease? *International Journal of Social Psychology*, X(3).
1965   *Sanity, Madness and the Family, vol. 1: Families of Schizophrenics*. Tavistock (with A. Esterson).
1966   *Interpersonal Perception: A Theory and a Method of Research*. Tavistock (with H. Phillipson and R.A. Lee).
1967   *The Politics of Experience*. Ballantine.
1971   *The Politics of the Family*. Pantheon.
1976   *The Politics of Experience and the Bird of Paradise*. Penguin.
1978   *Conversation with Children*. Allen Lane.

1982   *The Voice of Experience.* Penguin.
1985   *Wisdom, Madness and Folly.* Macmillan/
   McGraw-Hill.

Further reading

Crown, S. and Freeman, H.L. (eds) (1994) *The Book
   of Psychiatric Books.* Jason Aronson.
Mullen, B. (1995) *Mad to be Normal: Conversations
   with R.D. Laing.* Free Association Books.
Oakley, C. (1993) Dangerous liaisons: The rivalrous
   resemblance of David Cooper and R.D. Laing. *Free
   Associations*, 4, 277–93.

Ronald Laing began his career at the Central
Army Psychiatric Unit, Military Hospital
Netley, and after a period of two years moved to
the Psychiatric Unit, Military Hospital Catter-
ick. He then joined the Tavistock Clinic and
Institute. Laing was an existential psychiatrist
who offered a radical critique of abnormal
behaviour and social and medical models for its
treatment. He was critical of the extent to which
psychoanalytic concepts may conceal or distort
human experience, and of the tendency to label
the patient 'sick' as opposed to looking at
'sickness' in the patient's family or in society.
For example, he argued that schizophrenia is not
an illness but a label for another kind of problematic experience and behaviour. The behaviour
we call schizophrenic is in fact a special sort of
strategy that a person invents in order to live in
an unliveable situation. Thus, schizophrenia is a
creative, adaptive response to extremely difficult personal circumstances. Rather than trying
to remove the patient's symptoms, Laing argued
that we should accept his or her experience as
valid, understandable and potentially meaningful and beneficial. He claimed that the families
of schizophrenics frequently engage in double-
bind communication in which the listener is
placed in a 'no-win' situation. For example, the
mother of a schizophrenic patient might say
something like: 'You don't really love me;
you're only pretending you do.' This statement
requests an expression of love while simultaneously rendering such a display impossible. It
is hardly surprising, Laing argues, that a person
would come to think and behave in a bizarre
fashion when faced with this kind of dialogue.

Laing's ideas have been particularly popular
among those who object to the hypocrisies of
society in its treatment of those considered to be
abnormal. Those who experience the suffering
associated with schizophrenia may also take
comfort in the belief that they are going through
a positive growth process. However, there is
little evidence that experiencing a mental illness
such as schizophrenia can generally make one a
'better person'. For example, when released
from the hospital most schizophrenics live a
marginal existence, isolated from social relationships. Laing's argument – that mental illness
is better thought of as a disease of society rather
than localized in a small number of individuals
– reminds us that abnormality is in the eye of
the beholder and says more about the perspective of the beholder than it does about those
individuals considered to be mad.

Lamb, Michael E.

Born: 1953, Lusaka, Zambia **Nat:** American
Ints: Clinical psychology, cross-cultural psy-
chology, development psychology, personality
development **Educ:** BA University of Natal,
Durban, 1972; MA Johns Hopkins University,
1974; MA, 1975, MPhil, 1975 and PhD 1976,
Yale University **Appts & awards:** Assistant
Professor, University of Wisconsin, 1976–8,
University of Michigan, 1978–80; Professor of
Psychology, Psychiatry and Pediatrics, Univer-
sity of Utah, 1980–7; Senior Research Scientist
and Chief, Section on Social and Emotional
Development, National Institute of Child Health
and Human Development, 1987–

Principal publications

1974   A defense of the concept of attachment.
   Human Development, 17, 376–85.
1976   (ed.) *The Role of Father in Child
   Development.* Wiley. (Rev. edn, 1984).
1976   Infant approach behavior as related to
   attachment. *Child Development*, 47, 571–8 (with
   R.T. Tracy and M.D.S. Ainsworth).
1978   (ed.) *Social and Personality Development.*
   Holt, Rinehart and Winston.
1979   Toward a general theory of infantile
   attachment: A comparative review of aspects of the
   social bond. *Behavioral and Brain Sciences*, 1,
   417–64 (with D.W. Rajecki and P. Obmascher).
1979   Paternal effects and the father's role: A
   personal perspective. *American Psychologist*, 34,
   938–43.
1982   *Socialization and Personality Development.*
   Oxford University Press (with E.F. Zigler and I.L.
   Child).
1982   *Nontraditional Families: Parenting and Child
   Development.* Erlbaum.
1986   Characteristics of married and unmarried
   adolescent mothers and their parents. *Journal of
   Youth and Adolescence*, 15, 487–96 (with A.B.
   Elster, L.J. Kahn and J. Traver).

1990   Do we really know how day care affects children? *Journal of Applied Developmental Psychology*, 11, 351–79 (with K.J. Sternberg).

1994   The investigation of child sexual abuse: An interdisciplinary consensus statement. *Child Abuse and Neglect*, 18, 1021–8.

Michael Lamb grew up in Zambia and spent his adolescent years in South Africa. The sharp contrast in the racial tolerance of the two countries left a lasting mark on his professional development. He had acquired an abiding research interest in early behavioural development as a student of Mary **Ainsworth** at Johns Hopkins University, yet, from the start, he was also most concerned with the infant's larger social world as the determinant of specific attitudes and directions in personality development. His doctoral dissertation at Yale dealt with the relationships of infants with both their mothers and fathers. The synthesis of ethological and dynamic psychological concepts offered by the **Bowlby**/Ainsworth theory of early attachment thus served as a springboard for Lamb's progressively broadening interest in the complex determinants of early development and their consequences for later effective functioning.

In the late 1970s and early 1980s, Lamb and colleagues were concentrating mainly on the conceptual and empirical foundations of attachment theory. Their influential comparative review of the various interpretations of early attachment was praised for its thoroughness, and for pointing out that early experience is not the sole or necessarily the crucial determinant of long-term behavioural outcomes. But it was also chastised for misapplication of some concepts from evolutionary biology, and for undue generalization from behaviours of lower organisms to humans. Lamb continued to insist that research on early human development must take into account a host of intervening experiences and extraneous events that may 'ameliorate, accentuate, or maintain the effects of early experience and initial formation of mother–infant bond'.

Lamb's career has continued to unfold, with a broadening track of interests and a transition from laboratory studies of simple cause–effect relationships in early attachment to research on pressing social issues relating to the early behavioural development of children and adolescents. By the early 1990s his investigations ranged from the influence of parental values and role modelling in early child development to problems associated with adolescent mothering.

He has conducted extensive studies of child abuse, domestic violence, day care and other non-parental child-care systems, and the reliability of children as court witnesses. All in all, Lamb's career and research represent a highly successful interface between basic behavioural studies and applied social science research. He has been an effective builder of the much-needed bridge between basic research on specific determinants of behavioural development in children and the real world of growing up in North America.

JOSEPH K. KOVACH

Lambert, Nadine M.

Born: 1926, Utah, USA **Nat:** American **Ints:** Developmental psychology, educational psychology, evaluation and measurement, school psychology **Educ:** BA University of California at Los Angeles, 1948; MA Los Angeles State University, 1955; PhD University of Southern California, 1965 **Appts & awards:** Professor, School of Education, University of California at Berkeley; APA, Membership Committee, Committee on Professional Standards, Board of Professional Affairs, Council of Representatives, Board of Directors; President, California Association of School Psychologists; Elected to National Academy of Practice; Distinguished Service Award, Division of School Psychology, APA; Sandra Goff Award for Outstanding Contribution to School Psychology in California; Editorial Board, *American Journal of Orthopsychiatry*, *Journal of Applied Developmental Psychology*; Consulting Editor, *American Psychologist*, *Journal of School Psychology*

Principal publications

1965   *Protection and Promotion of Mental Health of Children*. USPHS.

1974   *The Educationally Retarded Child*. Grune and Stratton.

1977   Conceptual model for non-intellectual behavior and its relationship to early achievement. *Journal of Educational Psychology*, 69, 481–90.

1978   Prevalence of hyperactivity in elementary school children as a function of social system definers. *American Journal of Orthopsychiatry*, 48, 446–63.

1979   Prevalence of treatment regimens for children considered hyperactive. *American Journal of Orthopsychiatry*, 47, 482–90.

1980   *Moral Development and Socialization*. Allyn and Bacon.

1980   The prevalence of learning disabilities in a sample of children considered hyperactive. *Journal of Abnormal Child Psychology*, 8, 33–50.

1980   Behavioral profiles of children with different levels of achievement. *Journal of School Psychology*, 18, 58–66.

1981   *A Process for Assessment of Effective Student Functioning.* CTB/McGraw-Hill Publishers Test Service.

1981   Psychological evidence in *Larry P v. Wilson Riles* – an evaluation by a witness for the defense. *American Psychologist*, 36, 950–2.

1981   Development of a simplified diagnostic scoring method for the school version of the Adaptive Behavior Scale. *American Journal of Mental Deficiency*, 86, 138–47.

1984   The contribution of a predispositional factors to diagnosis of hyperactivity. *American Journal of Orthopsychiatry*, 55, 190–221.

Further reading

Gutkin, T. and Reynolds, C. (eds) (1990) *The Handbook of School Psychology*. Wiley.

The career of Nadine Lambert has centred on studies of individual differences among children and youth that are associated with the risk of educational failure and mental health disorders. These research efforts have provided the foundation for her school psychology programme. This was begun in 1965 at the University of California at Berkeley, and aims to prepare scientists/professional school psychologists who can intervene on behalf of children and adolescents by collaborating with education professionals to promote the schooling of all pupils. This view of school psychology requires one to select, from among theories and empirical evidence in psychology, those elements that are applicable to measuring the psychological and educational needs of children, and in turn to design educational and psychological interventions. In order to be effective in such endeavours, the school psychologist must develop skills in consultation and collaboration with teachers and other education professionals, so that they can translate the psychological information that is shared during consultation into their own accommodation in the pupil's educational programme.

One example of Lambert's research that has promise for a better understanding of children and schooling is her work on the life histories of hyperactive children, and specifically on how various intervening factors mediate a predisposition to develop the presenting symptoms of inattention, impulsivity and a high activity level as well as associated conduct disorders. Her earlier work on the development of classroom measures of school adaptation and adjustment has provided useful methods for monitoring the nature of these attributes over time, and for assessing the probability of students' success in school roles, as well as for identifying behaviours to target for interventions. Lambert has also been involved in developing her graduate training experiences and research programmes into models for a school psychological service; its aim is to achieve her goal of the effective translation of psychological knowledge into the educational process for all children.

Lambert, Wallace Earl

Born: 1922, Amherst, Nova Scotia, Canada *Nat:* Canadian *Ints:* Experimental psychology, multicultural studies, psycholinguistics, social psychology *Educ:* BA Brown University, 1947; MA Colgate University, 1950; PhD University of North Carolina, 1953 *Appts & awards:* Assistant, Associate and Full Professor, McGill University, 1954– ; Visiting Professor, Cornell University, 1958, 1981, Columbia University, 1963, 1977, Stanford University, 1969, 1970, 1971, University of Michigan, 1967, 1973, Philippine Normal College, Manila, 1968, Université de Paris, 1971, Indiana University, 1975, Adelphi University, 1979, University of Massachusetts, 1982, Brigham Young University, 1984, American University in Cairo, 1987; Fellow, Center for Advanced Studies in the Behavioral Sciences, 1964–5; Hon. Dr, Carleton University, 1968, York University, 1973, Laurentian University, 1974, University of Western Ontario, 1982; President, Canadian Psychological Association, 1969–70; Elected to National Academy of Education, 1976; Queen's Jubilee Medal of Distinction, 1978; Honorary President, Canadian Psychological Association, 1982–3

Principal publications

1956   Ethnic cleavage among young children. *Journal of Abnormal and Social Psychology*, 53, 380–3 (with Y. Taguchi).

1959   Attitudes toward immigrants in a Canadian community. *Public Opinion Quarterly*, 23, 537–46 (with F.E. Jones).

1962   The relation of bilingualism to intelligence. *Psychological Monographs*, 76 (27, no. 546) (with E. Peal).

1967   Social psychology and bilingualism. *Journal of Social Issues*, 23, 91–109.

1970   What are they like these Canadians? A social psychological analysis. *Canadian Psychologist*, 11, 303–33.

1972   *Language, Psychology and Culture. Essays by W.E. Lambert. Selected and Introduced by S. Anwar*. Stanford University Press.

1981   Bilingualism and language acquisition. In H. Winitz (ed.), *Native Language and Foreign Language Acquisition*. Academy of Sciences Press.

1987   The fate of old country values in a new land: A cross-national study of child rearing. *Canadian Psychology*, 28, 9–20.

1990   *Coping with Cultural and Racial Diversity in Urban America*. Praeger (with Donald M. Taylor).

Further reading

Reynolds, A.G. (1991) *Bilingualism, Multiculturalism, and Second Language Learning: The McGill Conference in Honour of Wallace E. Lambert*. Erlbaum.

Wallace E. Lambert was born in Amherst, Nova Scotia, but spent much of his childhood and early adult years in Massachusetts. Having served three years in the European theatre of operations during World War II, he completed his studies with a BA degree from Brown University in 1947, an MA from Colgate University in 1950, and a PhD from the University of North Carolina. He moved back to Canada in 1954 and has taught at McGill University in Montreal ever since. As happened to so many talented young men and women of his generation who experienced the Great Depression and World War II, he was drawn into higher education by an inner call to improve the human condition. The polarized world of Montreal and Quebec became his laboratory for both social science research and social action.

Lambert became interested in the 'one-way bilingualism' and generally lower social status of the francophone natives, and in the then still widely held anglophone attribution of negative or demeaning implications to bilingualism. For examining the origins of the related stereotypical opinions in a controlled setting, Lambert asked perfectly bilingual speakers to read the same short passage in French and again in English translation. Uninformed of the matched guise, bilingual listeners were then asked in separate sessions to rate the speakers' personalities by their verbal expressions and intonations from tape recordings of the passage listened to in their native tongue and again in their second language. To Lambert's considerable surprise, the French as well as the English Canadian students judged the unknown speakers' personality more favourably when the passage was read in English. The stereotype of anglophone superiority appeared to be shared by both English- and French-speaking Canadians of Quebec. Lambert set out to examine the legitimacy for the related claims of negative cognitive effects from bilingualism. Contrary to the prevalent claims, he found bilingual children actually performing better than monolingual children on various cognitive tests, and doing so on the average by nearly one standard deviation. Confirmed by others in several countries, the study set the stage for a large research effort on bilingualism, ethnicity, the roots of prejudices and stereotyped presumptions, and multiculturalism.

Lambert demonstrated that a second language can be acquired quickly and perfectly by 'immersion' into entirely monolingual cross-education (education entirely in French for children from English-speaking families, and vice versa for children from French-speaking families, in his experiments). Such education was found to result in perfect functional bilingualism and enrichment of content learning that was expressed equally well in both the immersion and the native tongues of the children. It also reliably improved the cross-cultural and cross-ethnic attitudes of children. His immersion technique has become a highly acclaimed method for establishing not only bilingual but also bicultural identities.

JOSEPH K. KOVACH

Langer, Ellen J.

Born: 1947, New York City, USA *Nat:* American *Ints:* Adult development and ageing, personality and social, health, psychological study of social issues, psychology of women *Educ:* BA New York University, 1970; PhD Yale University, 1974 *Appts & awards:* Professor of Psychology, Chair, Social Psychology Program, Harvard University; 1982; Fellow, APA; Executive Committee, SESP; Guggenheim Fellow; Sloan Foundation Fellow; Editorial Board, *Contemporary Psychology, Journal of Abnormal Psychology, Journal of Personality and Social Psychology, Personality and Social Psychology Bulletin, Review of Personality and Social Psychology, Sex Roles, Journal of Social and Clinical Psychology*

Principal publications

1974   A patient by any other name … : Clinician group differences in labelling bias. *Journal of Consulting and Clinical Psychology*, 42, 4–9 (with R. Abelson).

1975   Reduction of psychological stress in surgical patients. *Journal of Experimental Social Psychology*, 11, 155–65 (with I. Janis and J. Wolfer).

1975   The illusion of control. *Journal of Personality and Social Psychology*, 32, 311–28.

1976   The effects of enhanced personal responsibility for the aged: A field experiment in an institutional setting. *Journal of Personality and Social Psychology*, 34, 191–8 (with J. Rodin).

1978   Self-induced dependence. *Journal of Personality and Social Psychology*, 36, 886–93 (with A. Benevento).

1978   Rethinking the role of thought in social interaction. In J. Harvey, W. Ickes and R. Kidd (eds), *New Directions in Attribution Research*. Erlbaum.

1979   When practice makes imperfect: The debilitating effects of overlearning. *Journal of Personality and Social Psychology*, 37, 2014–25 (with L. Imber).

1981   Premature cognitive commitment. *Journal of Personality and Social Psychology*, 41, 1051–63.

1982   Old age: An artifact? In S. Kiesler and J. McGaugh (eds), *Aging: Biology and Behavior*. Academic Press.

1983   *Psychology of Control*. Sage.

1986   *Human Growth Beyond Formal Operations*. Oxford University Press (ed. with C. Alexander and R. Oetzel).

1987   Prevention of mindlessness. *Journal of Personality and Social Psychology*, 53, 280–7 (with P. Piper).

1989   *Mindfulness*. Addison-Wesley. (trans. into Japanese, French, Swedish, German, Spanish, Italian, Finnish and Dutch).

1990   *Higher Stages of Human Development: Perspectives on Adult Growth*. Oxford University Press.

1996   *Beliefs, Reasoning and Decision-Making: Psycho-Logic in Honor of Robert Abelson*. Erlbaum (with R. Schank).

Further reading

Hock, R.R. (1995) *Forty Studies that Changed Psychology*. Prentice-Hall.

Characteristics of Langer's work include a persistent clinical orientation and a concomitant interest in trying to extend human potential. First this manifested itself in research focused on finding ways to encourage people to reach currently accepted limits. The clinical concerns led to experimental studies of the importance of perceived control in hospital and the nursing-home settings at a time when it was not yet an accepted practice. After witnessing the dramatic changes that occurred after subtle interventions with the elderly, Langer began to investigate just how far one could move beyond these limits by social psychological means. Her research on the mindlessness/mindfulness distinction suggested that many psychological and physiological end points that are believed to be wired into the nervous system are instead premature cognitive commitments. For example, longevity may be far greater than the predicted eighty-five years, vision may be better than 20/20, and old age may be a period of growth and not inevitable decline. As such, it suggests that the illusion of control may not be an illusion after all.

Lashley, Karl Spencer

Born: 1890, Davis, USA ***Died:*** 1958, Poitiers, France ***Nat:*** American ***Ints:*** Experimental analysis of behaviour, physiological and comparative, clinical neuropsychology ***Educ:*** BA University of West Virginia, 1901; MS University of Pittsburgh, 1911; PhD Johns Hopkins University, 1914 ***Appts & awards:*** Research Professor in Neuropsychology, Harvard University; President, APA, 1929; Hon. DSc, University of Pittsburgh, 1936, University of Chicago, 1941, Western Reserve University, 1951, University of Pennsylvania; Warren Medal in Psychology, 1937; President, Eastern Psychological Association, 1938; Hon. MA, Harvard University, 1942; Elliot Medal in Zoology, 1943; Baly Medal in Physiology, 1953; Hon LLD, Johns Hopkins University, 1953

Principal publications

1921   Studies of cerebral function in learning: III. The motor areas. *Brain*, 44, 255–86.

1929   *Brain Mechanism and Intelligence: A Quantitative Study of Injuries to the Brain*. University of Chicago Press.

1930   Basic neural mechanism in behavior. *Psychological Review*, 1–24.

1934   The mechanism of vision: VIII. The projection of the retina upon the cerebral cortex of the rat. *Journal of Comparative Neurology*, 60, 57–79.

1941   Thalamo-cortical connections of the rat's brain. *Journal of Comparative Neurology*, 75, 67–121.

1942 The problem of cerebral organisation in vision. *Biological Symposia*, 7, 301–22.

1946 The cytoarchitecture of the cerebral cortex of Ateles: A critical examination of architechtonic studies. *Journal of Comparative Neurology*, 85, 233–302.

1958 Cerebral organisation and behavior. In *The Brain and Human Behavior: Proceedings of the Association for Research in Nervous and Mental Disease*. Williams and Wilkin.

Further reading

Dewsbury, D.A. (1993) Contributions to the history of psychology: XCIV. The boys of summer at the end of summer: The Watson–Lashley correspondence of the 1950s. *Psychological Reports*, 72, 263–69.

Furchtgott, E. (1995) A tribute to Lashley. *American Psychologist*, 50, 178–9.

Weidman, N. (1994) Mental testing and machine intelligence: The Lashley–Hull debate. *Journal of the History of the Behavioral Sciences*, 30, 162–80.

Lashley's major work was in the area of brain function and learning, using learning and discrimination tasks to study the effects of ablation at sites in the rat's brain. His academic training was originally in zoology, but he became interested in psychology while researching for his doctorate. He worked with J.B. **Watson** and was strongly influenced by the behavouristic approach. During his postdoctoral period he started to work with S.I. Franz at St Elizabeth's Hospital, Washington DC. He studied some neurological cases there, including patients who had received spinal injuries resulting in limb differentiation. His paper on these is still well cited by researchers in motor behaviour, and he is credited with formulating the concept of the motor programme. At this time he also acquired the necessary techniques for performing ablation studies with rats, which allowed him to look for the neural basis of the connectionism of behaviouristic theory. He attempted to find localized sites in the brain specific to various visual discriminations involved in maze learning and these results suggested field theory. It has been said that the discriminations required in his tasks involved cues in modalities other than vision, which would lead to cautious acceptance of this conclusion.

He proposed two influential principles. The first, mass action, is the mediation of certain learning tasks by the cortex as a whole. Greater localization than he suggested has subsequently been found, but mass action events have been found within localized areas. The second is equipotentiality or the ability of certain parts of a sensory system to assume the functions of the other parts. This has subsequently been supported.

Lashley also made a major contribution to neuroanatomy by tracing the connections from the retina to the lateral geniculate nucleus and then to the cortex, and by demonstrating the point-to-point projections later confirmed with more sophisticated techniques.

ANN COLLEY

Latané, Bibb

Born: 1937, New York, USA **Nat:** American **Ints:** Experimental, personality and social, physiological and comparative, psychological study of social issues **Educ:** BA Yale University, 1958; PhD University of Minnesota, 1963 **Appts & awards:** Professor of Psychology and Director, Institute for Research in Social Science, University of North Carolina; AAAS Socio-Psychological Prize, 1968, 1980; Richard M. Elliott Award, 1970; President, APA Executive Committee, 1970–80, Division 8, 1978; APA Council, 1971–5; Guggenheim Fellowship, 1974; Midwestern Psychological Association, Council, 1976–9, President, 1983; Cattell Fellowship, 1981; Editor, *Social Science Newsletter*, 1983– ; Associate Editor, *Sociometry*, 1972–5; Editorial Board, *Journal of Applied Social Psychology*, 1970– ; Overseas Editorial Board, *British Journal of Social Psychology*, 1979–

Principal publications

1964 Crime, cognition and the autonomic nervous system. In M.R. Jones (ed.), *Nebraska Symposium on Motivation 1964*. University of Nebraska Press (with S. Schachter).

1966 Emotionality and reactions to disaster. *Journal of Experimental Social Psychology*, 2, Supplement 1, 95–102 (with L. Wheeler).

1970 *The Unresponsive Bystander: Why Doesn't He Help?* Appleton-Century-Crofts (with J.M. Darley).

1972 Social attraction in animals. In P.C. Dochwell (ed.), *New Horizons in Psychology II*. Penguin (with D. Hotersall).

1976 Politicians on TV: The image is the message. *Journal of Social Issues*, 32, 116–32 (with J. Keating).

1978 The regulation of social contact in rats: Time, not distance. *Journal of Personality and Social Psychology*, 36, 1128–37 (with C. Werner).

1979   Many hands make light the work: Cases and consequences of social loafing. *Journal of Personality and Social Psychology*, 37, 822–32 (with K. Williams and S. Harkins).

1981   All alone in front of all those people: Stage fright as a function of number and type of co-performers and audience. *Journal of Personality and Social Psychology*, 70, 73–85 (with J. Jackson).

1981   Ten years of research on group size and helping. *Psychological Bulletin*, 89, 308–24 (with S. Nida).

1981   The social impact of majorities and minorities. *Psychological Review*, 88, 738–53 (with S. Wolf).

1981   The psychology of social impact. *American Psychologist*, 36, 373.

Further reading

Hock, R.R. (1995) *Forty Studies that Changed Psychology*. Prentice-Hall.

Latané, B. (1987) From student to colleague: Retracing a decade. In N.E. Grunberg, R.E. Nisbett, J. Rodin and J.E. Singer (eds), *A Distinctive Approach to Psychological Research: The Influence of Stanley Schachter*. Erlbaum.

Bibb Latané, with his colleague John Darley, conducted fundamental research into the reasons why bystanders do not intervene to assist others. The basis for his research concerned an attack on Kitty Genovese (in New York City, 1964). The attack lasted thirty-five minutes and was witnessed by thirty-eight people, although only one telephoned the police and none came to her assistance. Latané and Darley hypothesized that the reason no one took steps to help Genovese was a 'diffusion of responsibility'. That is, the greater the number of bystanders the greater the likelihood that each will believe that 'someone else will help, so I don't need to'. Latané and Darley conducted ingenious naturalistic studies to test their hypothesis, for which they found substantial empirical support.

Bibb Latané is the author or co-author of more than a hundred articles and chapters. His book (with Darley) describes his research on social determinants of bystander intervention in emergencies, social attraction in animals, social impact theory and group influence, and the causes and consequences of 'social loafing' or the reduction of productivity in groups. In addition, he was influential in the founding of the *Personality and Social Psychology Bulletin* and the *Review of Personality and Social Psychology*. These are now major publication outlets covering both brief empirical and longer integrative manuscripts in personality and social psychology. He also founded the *Social Science Newsletter*, an interdisciplinary quarterly, and the Nags Head Conference Center, a major focal point for immediate in-depth interchange of social scientific information.

Lawler, Edward E. III

Born: 1938, Washington DC, USA **Nat:** American **Ints:** Industrial and organizational psychology, personality and social **Educ:** BA Brown University, Rhode Island, 1956; PhD University of California at Berkeley, 1964 **Appts & awards:** Professor of Organizational Behavior, University of Southern California, Los Angeles; McKinsey Foundation Award, 1968; Fellow, APA, 1970, Academy of Management; Distinguished Scientific Award, American Compensation Association, 1972; Book of the Year Award, American College of Hospital Administrators, 1972; APA Council of Representatives, 1973–6; Board of Directors, American Centre for Quality of Working Life, 1973–7; Editorial Board, *Organizational Behavior and Human Performance*, *Journal of Applied Psychology*, 1970–82, *Accounting Organizations and Society*, 1975–93 *Journal of Organizational Behavior*, 1980, *New Management* 1982–88, *Human Resources Management*, 1983–90

Principal publications

1971   *Pay and Organizational Effectiveness: A Psychological View*. McGraw-Hill.

1973   *Motivation in Work Organizations*. Brooks/Cole.

1973   Effects of job redesign: A field experiment. *Journal of Applied Social Psychology*, 3, 49–62 (with J.R. Hackman and S. Kaufman).

1974   For a more effective organization – match the job to the man. *Organizational Dynamics*, 3, 19–29.

1974   Organizational climate: Relationship to organizational structure, process and performance. *Organizational Behavior and Human Performance*, 11, 139–55 (with D.T. Hall and G.R. Oldham).

1976   New approaches to pay: Innovations that work. *Personnel*, 53, 11–23.

1977   Developing a motivating work climate. *Management Review*, 66, 25–38.

1977   Adaptive experiments: An approach to organizational behavior research. *Academy of Management Review*, 2, 576–85.

1977   *Perspectives on Behavior in Organizations*. McGraw-Hill (ed. with J.R. Hackman and L.W. Porter).

1978   Methods of peer assessment. *Psychological Bulletin*, 85, 555–86 (with J. Kane).
1980   Motivation: Closing the gap between theory and practice. In K.D. Duncan, M.M. Grunberg and D. Wallis (eds), *Changes in Working Life*. Wiley.
1981   *Pay and Organization Development*. Addison-Wesley.
1982   Strategies for improving the quality of work life. *American Psychologist*, 37, 486–93.
1983   *Managing Creation: The Challenge of Building a New Organization*. Wiley (with D. Perkins and R. Nieva).
1984   Performance appraisal revisited. *Organizational Dynamics*, 13, 20–35 (with A.M. Mohrman and S.M. Resnick).
1994   From job-based to competency-based organizations. *Journal of Organizational Behavior*, 15, 3–15.
1994   Effective reward systems: Strategy, diagnosis, and design. In A. Howard (ed.), *Diagnosis for Organizational Change: Methods and Models*. Guilford Press.

Further reading
Kelly, J.E. (1992) Does job re-design theory explain job re-design outcomes? *Human Relations*, 45, 743–74.
Mathieu, J.E., Hofmann, D.A. and Farr, J.L. (1993). Job perception–job satisfaction relations: An empirical comparison of three competing theories. *Organizational Behavior and Human Decision Processes*, 56, 370–87.

Lawler graduated in psychology from Brown University, Providence, Rhode Island (1960), and received his PhD in psychology from the University of California at Berkeley in 1964. He was Assistant Professor of Industrial Adminis-trated Psychology at Yale University (1964–7) and then Associate Professor of Administrative Sciences and Psychology (1967–72). He then moved to the University of Michigan, where he was Chair of the Organizational Psychology Program and Professor of Psychology and Pro-gram Director, Institute for Social Research. At the University of Southern California he founded (1978) and became Director of the Center for Effective Organizations, recognized by both academic and commercial institutes as one of the world's leading management research organiz-ations. He is consultant to many corporations and governments and the majority of the Fortune 100 companies. Lawlor's publications include twenty-two books and more than two hundred articles.

Lawler's early interest in motivation led to the development of extensive research on job design

and reward systems. His principal contributions are in (1) the development of expectancy theory, (2) seminal research on pay and job design, (3) the development of labor–management co-operation, and (4) performance evaluation based on both participant-involvement strategies and (5) high-involvment managerial systems. His paper with Hackman and Kaufman on job design is his most frequently cited article in the field of organizational psychology. He has challenged the efficacy of designing organiz-ations around job structures, an approach that has dominated the fields of organizational behaviour and human resource management for decades. However, in the global competitive environment which large, complex organiz-ations face, a competency-based approach and the capabilities that individuals need to acquire and develop should be the major focus. He argues that reward systems, career tracks, selec-tion systems and the structure of organizations all need to change to focus on competencies.

Lazarus, Arnold Allan
Born: 1932, Johannesburg, Transvaal, South Africa ***Nat:*** South African ***Ints:*** Clinical pathology, counselling, experimental analysis of behaviour, Psychologists in Independent Prac-tice, psychotherapy ***Educ:*** BA University of Witwatersrand, 1956; MA University of Witwa-tersrand, 1957; PhD University of Witwaters-rand, 1960 ***Appts & awards:*** Professor Graduate School of Applied and Professional Psychology, Rutgers University; Vice-President, Transvaal Workers Educational Association, 1960–3; President, South African Society for Clinical and Experimental Hypnosis (Southern Division), 1963–4; President, Association for Advance-ment of Behavior Therapy, 1968–9; Fellow, APA, 1972– ; Chairman, New Jersey Psy-chological Association for Professional Standards, Review Committee, 1974–5; Meri-torious Achievement Award, Arizona State Psychological Association, 1980; Hon. Presi-dent, Latin American Society of New Behavioral Sciences 1980– ; Distinguished Service Award, American Board of Professional Psychology, 1982; Steering Committee, Psychologists for Social Responsibility, 1982– ; Distinguished Psychologist Award, Division of Psychotherapy, APA, 1992; Editorial Board, *Journal of Individ-ual Psychology*, 1976– , *Current Psychological Research and Reviews*, 1984– , *Current Psy-chological Research*, 1980–2, *Current Psychological Reviews*, 1980–2, *Group Psycho-*

therapy, Psychodrama, and Sociometry, 1981, *Psychotherapy in Private Practice*, 1982, *Journal of Psychotherapy and the Family*, 1984

Principal publications

1961   Group therapy of phobic disorders by systematic desensitization. *Journal of Abnormal and Social Psychology*, 63, 505–10.

1965   Towards the understanding and effective treatment of alcoholism. *South African Medical Journal*, 3, 736–41.

1968   Learning theory and the treatment of depression. *Behaviour Research and Therapy*, 6, 83–9.

1971   *Behavior Therapy and Beyond*. McGraw-Hill.

1973   Multimodal behavior therapy: Treating the BASIC ID. *Journal of Nervous and Mental Disease*, 156, 404–11.

1976   *Multimodal Behavior Therapy*. Springer-Verlag.

1977   Has behavior therapy outlived its usefulness? *American Psychologist*, 32, 550–4.

1981   *The Practice of Multimodal Therapy*. McGraw-Hill.

1982   Resistance or rationalization? A cognitive-behavioral perspective. In P.L. Wachtel (ed.), *Resistance: Psychodynamic and Behavioral Approaches*. Plenum (with A. Fay).

1984   Multimodal therapy. In R.J. Corsini (ed.), *Current Psychotherapies*, 3rd edn. Peacock.

1984   *In the Mind's Eye*, Guilford Press.

1985   (ed.) *Casebook of Multimodal Therapy*. Guilford Press.

1986   On sterile paradigms and the realities of clinical practice: Critical comments on Eysenck's contribution to behaviour therapy. In S. Mogdil and C. Mogdil (eds), *Hans Eysenck: Consensus and Controversy*. Falmer Press.

1989   *The Practice of Multimodal Therapy*. Johns Hopkins University Press.

1993   *Don't Believe it For A Minute!* Impact Publishers (with C.N. Lazarus and A. Fay).

Further reading

Dryden, W. (ed.) (1991) *The Essential Arnold Lazarus*. Whurr Publishers.

—— (ed.) (1991) *A Dialogue with Arnold Lazarus: It Depends*. Oxford University Press.

The terms 'behaviour therapy' and 'behaviour therapist' first appeared in the scientific literature in 1958 when Lazarus published an article in the *South African Medical Journal* on new methods of psychotherapy. He then added a few additional 'firsts' to the list: the first application of systematic desensitization in a group; the first application of emotive imagery to children (with Arnold Abramovitz); the first use of broad-spectrum behaviour in a group; and one of the first applications of learning theory to the treatment of depression.

Early in his career, he became aware that the narrow stimulus–response theories that characterized behaviour therapy in the 1960s and early 1970s were inadequate, and he argued for a broader conceptualization. His book *Behavior Therapy and Beyond* was the forerunner to what came to be called 'cognitive-behaviour therapy'. But even this was insufficient. Careful follow-ups revealed a disappointingly high relapse rate, especially in people who had been treated for depression, anxiety and panic disorders, obsessions and compulsions, and marital and family disturbances. Gradually, he evolved the multimodal orientation which emphasized the need to assess and treat seven interactive dimensions or modalities – behaviour, affect, sensation, imagery, cognition, interpersonal relationships and biological considerations. Here we find a truly comprehensive psychotherapy, one that takes cognizance of individual differences and becomes custom-made for each client. He has treated in excess of 2000 clients, some of whom were seen individually, as a couple, in family therapy, and in groups.

Lazarus, Richard S.

Born: 1922, New York City, USA **Nat:** American **Ints:** Emotion theory and research, health psychology or behavioural medicine, personality and social psychology, research clinical psychology, stress and coping theory **Educ:** PhD University of Pittsburgh, 1948 **Appts & awards:** Professor of Psychology, University of California at Berkeley; Member, Center for Social Science Theory, University of California at Berkeley, 1960–2, Chairman, 1961–2; Special Fellow, USPHS Waseda University, Tokyo, 1963–4; Guggenheim Fellow, 1969–70; Miller Professor, University of California at Berkeley, 1970–1; Award for Distinguished Scientific Achievement in Psychology, California State Psychological Association, 1984; Reviewer for many journals and for NSF and NIMH

Principal publications

1951   Autonomic discrimination without awareness: A study of subception. *Psychological Review*, 58, 113–22 (with R.A. McCleary).

1952   *Fundamental Concepts in Clinical Psychology*. McGraw-Hill (with G.W. Shaffer).

1952   The effects of psychological stress upon performance. *Psychological Bulletin*, 49, 293–317 (with J. Deese and S.F. Osler).

1964   A laboratory approach to the dynamics of psychological stress. *American Psychologist*, 19, 400–11.

1966   *Psychological Stress and the Coping Process.* McGraw-Hill.

1967   Cognitive and personality factors underlying threat and coping. In M.H. Appley and R. Trumbull (eds), *Psychological Stress: Issues and Research.* Appleton-Century-Crofts.

1970   Toward a cognitive theory of emotions. In M. Arnold (ed.), *Feelings and Emotions.* Academic Press (with J.R. Averill and E.M. Opton Jr).

1978   Stress-related transactions between person and environment. In L.A. Pervin and M. Lewis (eds), *Perspectives in Interactional Psychology.* Plenum.

1980   An analysis of coping in a middle-aged community sample. *Journal of Health and Social Behavior*, 21, 219–39 (with S. Folkman).

1983   The costs and benefits of denial. In S. Breznitz (ed.), *The Denial of Stress.* International Universities Press.

1984   *Stress, Appraisal and Coping.* Springer-Verlag (with S. Folkman).

1984   Puzzles in the study of daily hassles. *Journal of Behavioral Medicine*, 7, 375–89.

1985   *Stress and Coping: An Anthology.* Columbia University Press (ed. with A. Monat).

Further reading

Ekman, P. and Davidson, R.J. (eds) (1994) *The Nature of Emotion: Fundamental Questions.* Oxford University Press.

Goldberger, L. and Breznitz, S. (eds) (1993) *Handbook of Stress: Theoretical and Clinical Aspects* (2nd edn). Free Press.

Steptoe, A. and Wardle, J. (eds) (1994) *Psychosocial Processes and Health: A Reader.* Cambridge University Press.

The central theme of Richard Lazarus's work has been the psychodynamics of stress and emotion and its place in human adaptation. He takes the view that emotions tell us about what is important to people and how they think they are faring in their daily encounters. In the 1950s he was concerned mainly with how personality factors shape perception, thought and defence, a theme sometimes referred to as the New Look Movement. In the 1960s, in search of more naturalistic, laboratory-based methods for studying stress, he introduced the use of stressful motion picture films and the simultaneous measurement of psychophysiological reactions

to these films. Systematic efforts were made to influence how subjects appraised or construed what was happening in the film. The findings highlighted the power of cognitive appraisal processes – that is, how people evaluate what is happening – to raise or lower the levels of stress response.

In the 1970s he shifted from laboratory to field studies, centring on appraisal processes and coping. In this research with colleagues he developed the Daily Hassles and Uplifts Scale and Ways of Coping Checklist, which he and many others have used to study the role of stress and coping in morale, social functioning and physical health. His later research interests have centred on factors within the person that contribute to patterns of vulnerability to stress and the likelihood of reacting with distress in certain situations. Some daily hassles engage central problems in the person's psychological make-up, whereas others are only peripheral. The former appear to be more important to health outcomes than the latter. He considers the goal of understanding the psychodynamics of emotion as the creation of better ways to prevent or ameliorate psychological and physical dysfunction.

Lefcourt, Herbert Michael

Born: 1936, Brooklyn, New York, USA *Nat:* American *Ints:* Health psychology, personality and social, psychological study of social issues *Educ:* BA Antioch College, 1958; MA Ohio State University, 1960; PhD Ohio State University, 1963 *Appts & awards:* Professor, Department of Psychology, University of Waterloo; Fellow, APA, Canadian Psychological Association, Society for Personality and Social Psychology, Society for Psychological Study of Social Issues, American Psychological Society; Member, NIMH Cognition and Personality Study Section, 1975–9; Rockefeller Foundation Scholar in Residence, Bellagio, 1985; Editorial Boards, *Journal of Personality*, 1973–82, *Journal of Consulting and Clinical Psychology*, 1977–8, *Journal of Personality and Social Psychology*, 1983– , *Journal of Social and Clinical Psychology*, 1983– ; Associate Editor, *Personality and Social Psychology Bulletin*, 1984

Principal publications

1976   *Locus of Control: Current Trends in Theory and Research.* Erlbaum.

1979   The multidimensional–multiattributional causality scale: The development of a goal specific locus of control scale. *Canadian Journal of Behavioral Science*, 11, 286–304 (with C. VonBaeyer, E.E. Ware and D. Cox).

1981   Locus of control as a modifier of the relationship between stress and moods. *Journal of Personality and Social Psychology*, 41, 357–69 (with R. Miller, E. Ware and D. Sherk).

1981   Coping with stress: A model for clinical psychology. *Academic Psychology Bulletin*, 3, 355–64.

1982   *Locus of Control*, 2nd edn. Erlbaum.

1983   The stress buffering function of social intimacy. *American Journal of Community Psychology*, 11, 127–39 (with R. Miller).

1983   The sense of humor as a moderator of the relationship between stressors and moods. *Journal of Personality and Social Psychology*, 45, 1313–24 (with R. Martin).

1983   The construction and development of the Miller Marital Locus of Control Scale. *Canadian Journal of Behavioral Science*, 15, 266–79 (with P. Miller and E. Ware).

1984   Locus of control and social support: Interactive moderators of stress. *Journal of Personality and Social Psychology*, 47, 378–89 (with R.A. Martin and W. Saleh).

1984   The situational humor response questionnaire: A quantitative measure of the sense of humor. *Journal of Personality and Social Psychology*, 47, 145–55 (with R. Martin).

1984   Locus of control, causal attributions, and affects in achievement-related contexts. *Canadian Journal of Behavioral Science*, 16, 57–64.

1985   Locus of control for affiliation and behavior in social interactions. *Journal of Personality and Social Psychology*, 48, 755–9 (with R.A. Martin, C. Fick and W. Saleh).

1986   *Humor and Stress: Antidote to Adversity*. Springer-Verlag.

Further reading

Lefcourt, H.M. (ed.) (1981–4) *Research with the Locus of Control Construct*, 3 vols. Academic Press.

The continuous interest of Lefcourt has been in examining personality characteristics that help to account for persistence in the face of potential failures and apathy despite the possibility of attaining valued goals. During this research activity he has focused largely upon the locus of control construct. One of his major contributions has been to help flesh out the network in which the locus of 'nomological' control construct is embedded. More recently the thrust has been to construct devices for predicting control-related behaviour in specific areas of concern. This

interest led to the editing of a series of books in which he presented all of the research that he could find in which investigators had developed area- or goal-specific locus-of-control measures. It is through this development of area-specific measures that the control literature will probably continue to grow. In addition he has conducted a number of investigations in which he has been testing the efficacy of various characteristics as moderators of stress. He explored certain effects of intimacy, social support, most recently humour and investigativeness as personal characteristics that may serve to reduce the effects of stressors. While the focus of his research has varied, the underlying theme has remained the same. This is most evident in a recent investigation which looked at the characteristics of marriage partners, especially their beliefs about their effectiveness in determining marital experiences, that serve to make stressful marriage experiences less onerous. He has been looking at the personality characteristics of individuals that in turn affect the availability of social resources (the social support and intimacy in marriage) which have served as stress moderators. With his social learning orientation, his concern has long been upon effective or instrumental behaviour and the personality and situational variables related to it.

Lenneberg, Eric Heinz

Born: 1921, Dusseldorf, Germany ***Died:*** 1975, White Plains, New York, USA ***Nat:*** German ***Ints:*** Clinical neuropsychology, developmental, general, mental retardation, physiological and comparative ***Educ:*** MA (Linguistics) University of Chicago, 1951; PhD Harvard University, 1958 ***Appts & awards:*** Editor, *Journal of Psycholinguistic Research*

Principal publications

1960   Language, evolution and purposive behaviour. In S.J. Dimond (ed.), *Culture in History: Essays in Honour of Paul Radin*. Columbia University Press.

1962   The relationship of language to the formation of concepts. *Synthese*, 8, 103–9.

1962   Understanding language without ability to speak: A case report. *Journal of Abnormal and Social Psychology*, 65, 419–25.

1964   The capacity for language acquisition. In J.A. Fodor and J.J. Katz (eds), *The Structure of Language: Readings in the Philosophy of Language*. Prentice-Hall.

1964   (ed.) *New Directions in the Study of Language*. MIT Press.

1965   The vocalization of infants born to deaf and
hearing parents. *Human Development*, 8, 23–37
(with F.G. Rebelsky and I.A. Nichols).

1966   Verbal communication and colour memory in
the deaf and hearing. *Child Development*, 37,
765–79 (with D. Lantz).

1967   *Biological Foundations of Language*. Wiley.

1969   On explaining language. *Science*, 164,
635–43.

1970   The neurobiology of language: Practical
applications. *Bulletin of the Orton Society*, 20,
7–13.

1971   Of language knowledge, apes and brains.
Journal of Psycholinguistic Research, 1, 1–29.

1975   *Foundations of Language Development: A
Multidisciplinary Approach*. Academic Press (ed.
with E. Lenneberg).

1976   Problems in the comparative study of
language. In R.B. Masterson, W. Hodos and H.
Jerison (eds), *Evolution, Brain and Behaviour:
Persistent Problems*. Erlbaum.

Further reading

Rieber, R.W. (1976) *The Neuropsychology of
Language: Essays in Honor of Eric Lenneberg*.
Plenum.

Lenneberg initiated a distinct, interdisciplinary
field of study, 'the biology of language'. It has led
to the collection of data from psychology, linguistics, anthropology, neurology, physiology and
genetics, bearing on the extent to which language
has biological foundations, and is a cause and
effect of human evolution. This synthesizing
approach places him in the European tradition of
Goldstein and **Hughlings Jackson**, adopting a
more holistic and organic view of the brain than
their American counterparts. It is also an approach
which, when first formulated in the 1950s, contrasted markedly with the prevalent behaviourist
explanation of language, which, though also
postulating an evolutionary continuity, did so in
terms only of general learning mechanisms.
Lenneberg's approach to language was additionally characterized by an interest in pathologies
such as mongolism, aphasia and deafness, both
for their theoretical implications and in seeking
improved methods of diagnosis and treatment.

He carried out studies of language acquisition
in normal and pathological cases which indicated an innate developmental schedule, and
extended to language acquisition the biological
concept of 'critical periods' in development.
Early collaboration with R. **Brown** in experimental work on the role of language in cognition
led to a sustained interest in the place of langu-

age in concept formation, again in both normal
and pathological development.

CAROL SHERRARD

Leont'ev, Aleksei Nikolaevich

Born: 1903, Moscow, Russia ***Died:*** 1979,
Moscow, Russia ***Nat:*** Russian ***Ints:*** Cognitive
psychology, experimental psychology, general
psychology, methodological problems in psy-
chology, philosophical roots of psychology
Educ Moscow University, 1924; Dr Pedagogi-
cal   Sciences   (Psychology),   Leningrad
Pedagogical Institute, 1940 ***Appts & awards:***
Professor, 1941, Chair, 1945, Dean, 1966–79,
Faculty of Psychology, Moscow State Univer-
sity;   Member,   Academy   of   Pedagogical
Sciences of Russian Federation, 1950; Vice-
President, International Union of Psychological
Sciences, 1957–76; Honored Member, La
societa italiana di psicologia scientifica, 1963;
Laureate of Lenin's, 1963, and Lomonosov's,
1977, Prizes; Hon. Dr, Université de Paris,
Sorbonne, 1968, University of Budapest, 1973,
Hungarian Academy of Sciences, 1973, La
sociedad espanola de psicologia, 1974

Principal publications

1931   *The Development of Memory*. (in Russian).

1959   *Problems in Development of the Mind*. Press
of the Academy of Pedagogical Sciences (in
Russian).

1960   *Rehabilitation of Hand Functions*. Pergamon
Press (with A.V. Zaporozhets).

1975   *Action, Consciousness, Personality*. Politizdat
Publishers (in Russian).

Further reading

Leont'ev, A.N. (1957) The nature and formation of
human psychic properties. In B. Simon (ed.),
Psychology in the Soviet Union. Routledge and
Kegan Paul.

—— (1969) On biological and social aspects of
human development: The training of auditory
ability. In M. Cole and I. Maltzman (eds), *A
Handbook of Contemporary Soviet Psychology*.
Basic Books.

Leont'ev was a recognized leader of Soviet
psychology in the 1950s–70s. He was best
known for his work on genesis of mind, for
which he was granted Lenin's prize (the highest
scientific award in the former Soviet Union).
Leont'ev was born on 5 February 1903 in Moscow. He graduated from Moscow University in
1924. He began his scientific career at the Mos-

cow Institute of Psychology (founded in 1912). His supervisor was the Founder and Head (until 1923) of the Institute, the famous Russian psychologist and philosopher, Professor G.I. Chelpanov. Before long Leont'ev deserted the idealistic psychological doctrine developed by Chelpanov and joined **Vygotsky** in his attempt to build a new psychology based on Marxist philosophy – he devoted all his scientific life to this cause. After a few years of fruitful collaboration with Vygotsky and his other followers (**Luria** and Zaporozhetz) on the so-called 'cultural-historical theory of mind' at Moscow, he moved to Kharkov (Ukraine) in the early 1930s. There he started to develop a new approach that was known in Russia as an 'activity theory'. It was his attempt to pilot the ship of new Soviet psychology between the Scylla of mentalism and the Charybdis of behaviourism. The activity theory has much in common with the ecological approach developed later by J.J. **Gibson**. The main emphasis is placed on the mutuality of an organism and its environment. The theory claims that the internal structure of the mind reflects the structure of overt behaviour, a primacy of activity being stressed.

Leont'ev put forward a hypothesis of the genesis of the mind according to which the mind evolved through four main stages: sensitivity, perception, intelligence and consciousness. He hypothesized that sensitivity emerged due to the transition from the homogeneous environment to the object environment.

During World War II Leont'ev and colleagues worked on the rehabilitation of motor skills for wounded soldiers in hospital. After the war he returned to fundamental problems of general psychology and activity theory. He organized a section of child psychology in the Moscow Institute of Psychology and tried to apply general principles of the activity theory to child development. He developed a doctrine of leading activity, according to which each period of childhood is characterized by a specific leading activity that plays a crucial role in the mental and physical development of a child. This principle was further developed by D.B. Elkonin in his theory of childhood. Leont'ev was a distinguished organizer of science. He made great efforts to restructure Soviet psychology as a science after it was nearly crushed at the end of Stalin's rule. He organized the first faculty of psychology in the country at Moscow University, and was its first Dean for successive terms from 1966 to 1979.

T. SOKOLSKAYA AND A. LOGVINENKO

Levy-Leboyer, Claude

Born: Claude Gugenheim, 1928, Paris, France **Nat:** French **Ints:** Environmental psychology, health psychology, occupational psychology **Educ:** D. Lettres et Sciences Humaines, Paris, Sorbonne, 1970 **Appts & awards:** Professor and Vice-President, Université René Descartes, Laboratoire de Psychologie de l'Environnement, Centre Henri Pieron; NATO Grants, 1968, 1972; Ordre national du mérite (checlion), 1980; Fellow, British Psychological Association, 1982; Friancqui Prize, Ghent, Belgium, 1984; Palmes academique (officer) 1985; Hon. Dr, University of Surrey, 1992; President, International Association of Applied Psychology; Editor, *Psychologie Française*, 1971–4, *Revue Internationale de Psychologie Appliquée*, 1974–82, *Handbook of work psychology* (PUF); Editorial Board, *Revue Européenne de Psychologie Appliquée*, *Revue Internationale de Psychologie Sociale*, *Work and Stress*, *Journal of Environmental Psychology*, *Journal de Psychologie Sociale*, *Journal of Personality and Social Behavior*, *Social Behaviour*, *Leadership Quarterly*, *European Review of Work and Organisational Psychology*, *Applied Psychology: An International Review*

Principal publications

1972   *L'ambition professionale et la mobilité sociale*. PUF.

1974   *La psychologie des organisations*. PUF.

1980   *Psychologie et environment*. PUF. (English trans., 1982.)

1984   *Vandalism, Behaviour, and Motivation*. North-Holland.

1984   *La crise des motivations*. PUF.

1987   *Traité de psychologie du travail*. PUF (with J. Cl. Spérandio).

1990   Representation des activités de travail et des activités hors travail chez de jeunes cadres. (Work and nonwork activities: Representation among young managers). *Revue Internationale de Psychologie Sociale*, 3, 357–82 (with M. Gosse, P. Lidvan and D. Martin).

1991   Neighbourhood noise annoyance. *Journal of Environmental Psychology*, 11, 75–86 (with V. Naturel).

1995   Leadership performance: Towards a more complex model. *Applied Psychology: An International Review*, 44, 43–4.

Further reading

Smith, M. and Robertson, I.T. (eds) (1989) *Advances in Selection and Assessment*. Wiley.

Claude Levy-Leboyer's first line of research consisted of a series of experimental investigations of the effects of fatigue on a motor task. Her interests shifted rapidly towards social psychology and her PhD examined the relationship between leaderless groups and individual personality traits. A visit to the US on a NATO grant (1968) introduced her to leading-edge research in organizational psychology, a discipline not well developed in France at that time. Since then she has sustained a strong line of research in the social dimensions of occupations, in the psychology of motivation and work motivation, in the devaluation of work and in the various meanings and status of work in different cultures. In 1972 she secured a large grant to stimulate research on the effects of noise and this led to the development of significant contributions to environmental psychology. *Psychologie et environment* was the first book of its kind published in France and stimulated the expansion of research in this area. Her own work has demonstrated that the only components of the living environment that influence the degree of satisfaction with living space are those linked to the immediate environment of the home: the amount of greenery in the district, appropriable and accessible green spaces situated near the dwellings, social relationships with the neighbours, and the presence and quality of these contacts. This contrasts with earlier studies and suggests that a shift from functional to more complex quality-of-life needs has taken place.

Lewin, Kurt

Born: Prussia 1890, Mogilno, **Died:** 1947, Newtonville, Massachusetts, USA **Nat:** German **Educ:** PhD University of Berlin, 1947 **Appts & awards:** University of Berlin, 1922–32; Stanford University, 1932; Cornell University, 1933–5; Child Welfare Research Station, University of Iowa, 1935–43; Director, Research Center for Group Dynamics, MIT, 1944–7

Principal publications

1935　*A Dynamic Theory of Personality*. McGraw-Hill.

1936　*Principles of Topological Psychology*. McGraw-Hill.

1939　Patterns of aggressive behavior in experimentally created social climates. *Journal of Social Psychology*, 10, 271–99 (with R. Lippit and R. White).

1943　Defining the 'field at a given time'. *Psychological Review*, 50, 292–310.

1948　*Resolving Social Conflicts: Selected Papers on Group Dynamics*. Harper and Row (ed. with G.W. Lewin).

1951　*Field Theory in Social Science: Selected Theoretical Papers*. Harper and Brothers (ed. D. Cartwright).

Further reading

Heider, F. (1959) On Lewin's methods and theory. *Journal of Social Issues*, Supplemental Series, 13, 3–13.

Henle, M. (1978) Kurt Lewin as metatheorist. *Journal of the History of the Behavioral Sciences*, 14, 233–7.

Watson, R.I. and Evans, R.B. (1991) *The Great Psychologists: A History of Psychological Thought*, 5th edn. HarperCollins.

Kurt Lewin was the second of four children. When he was 15 his family moved to Berlin. After completing secondary school Lewin entered the University of Berlin, where he received his PhD under the supervision of Karl Stump. After several years of military service, for which he was awarded Germany's Iron Cross, he returned to Berlin and worked with Max **Wertheimer**, **Koffka** and **Köhler** until 1932. While on a visiting professorship at Stanford University he decided to settle, and brought his wife, Gertrud Weiss, and their four children to the USA in 1932.

The starting point for Lewin's work is a distinction he draws between the Aristotelian and Galilean view of nature. For Aristotle, various objects fell into categories according to their essence. Individual differences are distortions caused by external forces interfering with an object's or organism's natural growth tendencies. For Galileo, the behaviour of an object or organism is determined by the total forces acting on it. Individual differences could be understood in terms of the dynamic forces acting on individual organisms or objects. Lewin argued that much of psychology was stuck in an Aristotelian view of science. Moving to a Galilean perspective would require psychologists to abandon a commitment to concepts of instinct, type and average (which implies the existence of distinct categories) and to emphasize the complex, dynamic forces acting on an individual.

The most important concept in Lewin's approach is that of life space. A person's life space comprises all influences acting on him or her at a given time. These influences, which Lewin called psychological facts, included internal events, such as hunger and fatigue, external events, such as a social situations, and recollections of prior experiences. In order to explain what he meant by life space Lewin used concepts from topology. Topology represents the spatial relationships among objects. Thus, a person's life space can be represented as an ellipse and each psychological fact as a region within the ellipse. Each region can be assigned a valence according to whether it acts in a beneficial (+ sign) or non-beneficial (− sign) way on the person. The force fields resulting for the various positive and negative influences in a person's life space he called hodological space. The nature of this space at any given moment determined the direction and rate of behaviour. Lewin referred to events outside the personal space as the foreign hull. Because of the dynamic nature of the forces acting on the person, events in the foreign hull could become part of the life space and events within the life space could become part of the foreign hull. One of Lewin's best known equations, $B = f(P, E)$ (or $B = f(L)$) summarizes his argument that behaviour is a function of both person and environment, or of the life space.

Like other *Gestalt* psychologists of the time Lewin argued that people sought to maintain a cognitive balance in response to pressure from psychological needs. Motivation has its origins in the tensions induced by psychological needs (which Lewin called quasi-needs) causing people to move through the life space. While Bluma **Zeigarnik** was completing her doctorate under Lewin's supervision she tested Lewin's hypothesis that needs cause tensions that persist until the needs are satisfied. She found that people tend to remember uncompleted tasks better than completed ones (the Zeigarnik effect), and she explained that this was because the stress caused by the intention to complete the task had not been alleviated and these tasks remained parts of the person's life space.

The concept of conflict figures prominently in Lewin's theory, and he investigated three types. Approach–approach conflict occurs when a person is attracted to two goals simultaneously. Avoidance–avoidance conflict occurs when a person is repelled by two unattractive goals at the same time. Approach–avoidance conflict involves one goal about which the person has mixed feelings. It is often the most difficult conflict to resolve.

In his later work Lewin extended his ideas to the analysis of group dynamics. He suggested that a group could be regarded as a physical system just like a brain. The nature and configuration a group can have a profound impact on its elements or members. His studies of group dynamics were to pave the way for research into encounter groups (T-groups), sensitivity training and leadership institutes. To test parts of his theory he devised ingenious experiments in naturalistic settings. For example, in one study (with Lippit and White, 1939), boys were placed into one of three groups: democratic (the leader encouraged group discussion and participation), authoritarian (the leader made the decision and told others what to do), or laissez-faire (the boys did whatever they wanted). The democratic group was productive and friendly, the authoritarian group was aggressive and the laissez-faire group was generally unproductive. Lewin concluded that group leadership influenced the group *Gestalt*, which impacted on the behaviour of its members. His ingenuity and success as an experimentalist have sometimes earned Lewin the title of 'father of experimental social psychology'; that may be disputed, but there is no doubting his formidable influence on the first generation of experimental social psychologists in North America.

Several criticisms have been made of Lewin's field theory. First, his life space diagrams are always historical – they describe what has happened and have little predictive power. Second, the theory does not properly specify the relation of the life space to the external environment. Third, developmental and learning theorists have argued that field theory does not pay sufficient attention to the formative and motivational influences of early experiences. Lewin felt that this criticism was totally unjustified and pointed to the fact that he always considered historical information to be essential for an understanding of the current state of affairs in the life space. Despite these criticisms his theory remains an enduring influence in social psychology. It certainly lacks formal completeness but it remains a cogent account of a person's psychological environment.

Although Lewin's name is strongly linked with the Research Center for Group Dynamics at MIT, he was its Director for just three years. Following his untimely death the Center moved to the University of Michigan, where it prospered along the lines Lewin had envisaged.

Lewis, Michael

Born: 1937, Brooklyn, NY, USA ***Nat:*** American ***Ints:*** Developmental psychology, personality and social psychology, physiological and comparative psychology ***Educ:*** BA 1958 University of Pennsylvania, PhD 1962 University of Pennsylvania ***Appts & awards:*** Professor of Psychology, Rutgers University, 1979– ; Adjunct Professor, Department of Pediatrics, Rutgers Medical School, 1980–2; University Distinguished Professor, Department of Pediatrics and Psychiatry, University of Medicine and Dentistry of New Jersey, Robert Wood Johnson Medical School, 1993– ; Fellow, APA, American Association for the Advancement of Science, New York Academy of Sciences; Series Editor, Genesis of Behavior (Plenum), Perspectives in Developmental Psychology (Plenum); Consulting Editor for Human Development, *Journal of Sex Roles, Psychological Inquiry, Infant Behavior and Development*

Principal publications

1965 The psychological effect of effort. *Psychological Bulletin*, 64, 183–90.

1969 Infants' responses to facial stimuli during the first year of life. *Developmental Psychology*, 1, 75–86.

1971 Individual differences in the measurement of early cognitive growth. In J. Hellmuth (ed.), *Exceptional Infant, 2*. Brunner/Mazel.

1976 Infants' response to strangers: Midget, adult and child. *Child Development*, 47, 323–32.

1978 The child's social world. In R.M. Lerner and J.D. Spanier (eds), *Child Influences on Marital and Family Interaction: A Life-Span Perspective*. Academic Press.

1979 *Social Cognition and the Acquisition of Self*. Plenum (with J. Brooks-Gunn).

1982 Discovering the competent handicapped infant: A process approach to assessment and intervention. *Topics in Early Childhood Special Education*, 2, 1–16 (with R. Brinker).

1983 *Children's Emotions and Moods: Developmental Theory and Measurement*. Plenum (with L. Michalson).

1983 Screening and diagnosing handicapped infants. *Topics in Early Childhood Special Education*, 3, 14–28 (with J. Brooks-Gunn).

1986 The role of emotion in development. *Journal of Children in Contemporary Society*, 7, 7–22.

1988 Young children's social networks as a function of age and dysfunction. *Infant Mental Health Journal*, 9, 142–57 (with C. Feiring and J. Brooks-Gunn).

1989 Commentary: Continuity, developmental and discontinuity analyzed. *Human Development*, 32, 216–22.

1989 Infant, mother and mother–infant interaction behavior and subsequent attachment. *Child Development*, 60, 831–7 (with C. Feiring).

1991 *Language Interaction Intervention Program*. Communication Skill Builders (with L. Weistuch).

1992 *Shame, The Exposed Self*. Free Press.

1993 The development of deception. In M. Lewis and C. Saarni (eds), *Lying and Deception in Everyday Life*. Guilford Press.

1993 *Handbook of Emotions*. Guilford Press (ed. with C. Saarni).

Further reading

Horowitz, F.D. and Colombo, J. (eds) (1990) *Infancy Research: A Summative Evaluation and a Look to the Future*. Wayne State University Press.

Lewis, M. and Haviland, J.M. (eds) (1993) *Handbook of Emotions*. Guilford. Taylor Parker, S. Mitchell, R.W. and Broccia, M.L. (eds) (1994) *Self-awareness in Animals and Humans: Developmental Perspectives*. Cambridge University Press.

Michael Lewis attended the University of Pennsylvania, where he earned a BA degree with honors in sociology in 1958. The following year, he turned to psychology for graduate training at the same institution, earning his PhD in 1962. The primary focus of his research has been the normal development of intellectual abilities during the earliest years of life. His focus on normal development has enabled him to formulate a theory of the sequence of intellectual development in the child and relate this to changes which occur in the organization of central nervous system functioning. An important advancement introduced by Lewis is a set of techniques used to measure central nervous system functioning. This measurement system has become the standard in predicting normal or dysfunctional development. More importantly, these measurement instruments have led to the development of computer-based techniques for enhancing intellectual ability in children with a variety of developmental disorders, such as Down's syndrome and cerebral palsy.

Lewis has also produced influential work on the course of emotional development, particularly the normal course of emotional growth. His book *Children's Emotions and Moods* was one of the first volumes devoted to normal emotional development. His more recent book, *Shame, The Exposed Self*, turns toward the study of deviant as well as normal development.

In recent years Lewis has also directed his efforts towards the study of giftedness in the very young. Of particular interest to him has been the detection of early indications of giftedness in children of low socioeconomic status. This interest has led him to develop the Gifted Inner City Project in the city of Newark, NJ. This project has attempted to identify gifted inner-city children and to develop an educational programme for them, the ultimate goal of which is to cultivate the next generation of leaders in the city of Newark.

Lewis has been a prolific writer and researcher, publishing more than three hundred articles and chapters in professional journals and scholarly texts. He is also an active participant on many committees, such as the American Foundation of Maternal and Child Health, International Association for Infant Mental Health, William T. Grant Foundation National Consortium on Infant Stress, and New Jersey Governor's Council on the Prevention of Mental Retardation and Developmental Disabilities.

J.D. HOGAN AND W. IACCINO

Locke, Edwin A.

Born: 1938, New York, USA **Nat:** American **Ints:** Industrial and organizational, philosophical and theoretical psychology, psychotherapy **Educ:** BA Harvard University, 1960; MA Cornell University, 1962; PhD Cornell University, 1964 **Appts & awards:** Professor of Business and Management and of Psychology, University of Maryland; Fellow, APA, 1972, Academy of Management; Editorial Board, *Journal of Applied Psychology*, *Organizational Behavior*, *Human Decision Processes*

Principal publications

1968   Toward a theory of task motivation and incentives. *Organizational Behavior and Human Performance*, 3, 157–89.

1968   The motivational effects of knowledge of results: A goal setting phenomenon? *Psychological Bulletin*, 70, 474–85 (with N. Cartledge and J. Koeppel).

1975   *A Guide to Effective Study.* Springer-Verlag.

1976   The nature and causes of job satisfaction. In M.D. Dunnette (ed.), *Handbook of Industrial and Organizational Behavior.* Rand-McNally.

1977   The myths of behavior mood in organizations. *Academy of Management Review*, 2, 543–53.

1979   Participation in decision making: One more

look. In B.M. Shaw (ed.), *Research in Organisational Behavior.* JAI (with D.M. Schweiger)

1981   Goal setting and task performance: 1969–80. *Psychological Bulletin*, 90, 125–52 (with K.N. Shaw, L.M. Saari and G.P. Latham).

1983   Performance appraisal under capitalism, socialism and the mixed economy. In F. Landy, S. Zedeck and J. Cleveland (eds), *Performance Measurement and Theory.* Erlbaum.

1984   *Goal Setting for Individuals, Groups and Organizations.* Science Research Associates (with G.P. Lathan and A. Gosselin).

1984   The effects of self efficacy, goals and task strategies on task performance. *Journal of Applied Psychology*, 69, 241–51. (with E. Frederick, C. Lee and P. Bobko).

1984   Job satisfaction. In M.M. Gruneberg and T. Wall (eds), *Social Psychology and Organisational Behavior.* Wiley.

1986   *Generalizing from Laboratory to Field Settings.* Lexington Books.

1990   *A Theory of Goal Setting and Task Performance.* Prentice-Hall.

1991   *The Essence of Leadership.* Lexington-Macmillan.

1993   Effect of dysfunctional thought processes on subjective well-being and job satisfaction. *Journal of Applied Psychology*, 78, 475–90.

Further reading

Earley, P.C. and Lituchy, T.R. (1991) Delineating goal and efficacy effects: A test of three models. *Journal of Applied Psychology*, 76, 81–98.

White, P.H. *et al.*, (1995) Testing the contribution of self-evaluation to goal-setting effects. *Journal of Personality and Social Psychology*, 69, 69–79.

Edwin Locke and Gary Latham, in collaboration, have concentrated their research and writings in the areas of work motivation and morale with an additional interest in the philosophy of science. In the area of motivation they have investigated the relationship between goal setting and task performance. Goal-setting theory is now generally considered to be the most valid in the field of work motivation. Locke has also developed a theoretical model to explain job satisfaction and has contributed many articles in this area.

With Dave Schweiger, he has focused on important summary and integrative work on the topic of participation in decision making. Their conclusions in this area have come as a surprise to many.

Locke has published extensively: his writings

on the philosophy of psychology have been concerned with the fundamental fallacy of behaviorism. He has shown that it is wrong in theory and, if taken literally, cannot be applied in practice.

Loevinger, Jane

Born: 1918, St Paul, MN, USA **Nat:** American **Ints:** Developmental, evaluation and measurement, personality and social, philosophical and theoretical, psychoanalysis **Educ:** BA University of Minnesota, 1937; MS University of Minnesota 1938; PhD University of California at Berkeley, 1944 **Appts & awards:** Professor of Psychology and Stuckenberg Professor of Human Values and Moral Development, Washington University, 1955–6; MM Justin Fellow, AAUW, 1962–3; President, Division of Philosophical and Theoretical Psychology, APA, 1970–4, Division of Evaluation and Measurement, APA, 1982–3; Personality and Cognition Research Review Committee, Member NIMH, UPSPHS; Consulting Editor, *Psychological Review*, 1983, *Journal of Personality and Social Psychology*, 1984–

Principal publications

1943 On the proportional contributions of differences in nature and in nurture to differences in intelligence. *Psychological Bulletin*, 40, 725–56.

1947 A systematic approach to the construction and evaluation of tests of ability. *Psychological Monographs*, 61 (no. 285).

1953 Maximizing the discriminating power of a multiple-score test. *Psychometrika*, 18, 309–17 (with G.C. Gleser and P.H. DuBois).

1954 The attenuation paradox in test theory. *Psychological Bulletin*, 51, 493–504.

1957 Objective tests as instruments of psychological theory. *Psychological Reports*, 3, 635–94.

1962 Measuring personality patterns of women. *Genetic Psychology Monographs*, 65, 53–136 (with B. Sweet, A.G. Ossorio and K. LaPerriere).

1965 Person and population as psychometric concepts. *Psychological Review*, 72, 143–55.

1966 Three principles for a psychoanalytic psychology. *Journal of Abnormal Psychology*, 71, 432–43.

1970 *Measuring Ego Development 1. Construction and Use of a Sentence Completion Test.* Jossey-Bass (with R. Wessler).

1970 *Measuring Ego Development 2. Scoring Manual for Women and Girls.* Jossey-Bass (with R. Wessler and C. Redmore).

1976 *Ego Development: Conceptions and Theories.* Jossey-Bass.

1978 *Scientific Ways in the Study of Ego Development.* Clark University Press.

1979 Construct validity of the sentence completion test of ego development. *Applied Psychological Measurement*, 3, 281–311.

1984 On the self and predicting behavior. In R.A. Zucker, J. Aronoff and A.I. Rabin (eds), *Personality and the Prediction of Behavior.* Academic Press.

Further Reading

Novy, D.M., Frankiewicz, R.G. *et al*. An investigation of the structural validity of Loevinger's model and measure of ego development. *Journal of Personality*, 62, 87–118.

O'Connell, A.N. and Russo, N.F. (eds) (1988) *Models of Achievement: Reflections of Eminent Women in Psychology*, vol. 2. Erlbaum.

Jane Loevinger was originally drawn to psychology by an interest in **Spearman**'s work on mental organization. This interest led first to a masters degree in psychometrics with D.G. Paterson. Later, an inability to find a non-circular definition of reliability led to her doctoral thesis on fundamental considerations on measuring ability. A seminar with E. **Erikson** began a lifelong interest in the logic of psychoanalysis. Other professors at Berkeley who influenced her were E.C. **Tolman**, E. Brunswick, E. Frenkel-Brunswik and J. Neyman in statistics.

Turning to personality measurement, she constructed the Family Problems Scale, concerning attitudes of mothers and others to problems of child rearing (with Blanch Sweet Usdansky, Kitty LaPerriere, Abel Ossorio and others). They found that careful psychometric techniques did not yield the scales expected, and especially that some hypotheses ostensibly derived from the theory of psychosexual stages were not borne out. Their use of the concept of ego development came out of this work. With Elizabeth Nettles and Virginia Ives Word, Loevinger used a sentence completion test (SCT) to validate the ego development interpretation of the Family Problems Scale. The SCT required a scoring manual, a task that occupied their interest for many years. This work was not purely technological but also a way to clarify the order and structure of ego stages and to add many previously unsuspected details. The interplay of theory and data in that work has been a theme of Loevinger's writing, and has involved a running debate with

Kohlberg, who advocated classical moral stages defined by necessary and sufficient conditions, whereas she defended ego stages as fuzzy sets or prototypes. A by-product of test construction work has been further work on psychometrics, especially construct validity.

Loftus, Elizabeth F.

Born: 1944, Los Angeles, USA *Nat:* American *Ints:* Cognition, law, learning, memory, psychological statistics *Educ:* BA University of California at Los Angeles, 1966; MA Stanford University, 1967; PhD Stanford University, 1970 *Appts & awards:* Fellow, APA Divisions 3, 35 and 41, Phi Beta Kappa, 1965, Pi Mu Epsilon, 1965; Assistant, Associate, then Full Professor of Psychology, 1973– , Adjunct Professor of Law, 1984– , University of Washington; Fellow, Centre for Advanced Study in the Behavioural Sciences, 1978–9; Hon. DSc, Miami University, 1982; President, Western Psychological Association, 1984; President, APA Division 41, 1985, APA Division 3, 1988; Hon. Dr Leiden University, 1990; Hon. Fellow, BPS, 1991; Doctor of Laws, John Jay College of Criminal Justice, 1994; Fellow, American Psychological Society

Principal publications

1975   Leading questions and the eyewitness report. *Cognitive Psychology*, 7, 560–72.
1975   A spreading activation theory of semantic processing. *Psychological Review*, 82, 407–28 (with A.M. Collins).
1976   *Human Memory: The Processing of Information.* Erlbaum (Japanese edn, University of Tokyo Press) (with G.R. Loftus).
1978   Semantic integration of verbal information into a visual memory. *Journal of Experimental Psychology: Human Learning and Memory*, 4 19–31 (with D.G. Miller and H.J. Burns).
1979   Effective interrogation of the eyewitness. *International Journal of Clinical and Experimental Hypnosis*, 27, 342–57 (with E.R. Hilgard).
1979   *Eyewitness Testimony.* Harvard University Press (Japanese edn, Seishin Shobo).
1980   *Memory.* Addison-Wesley (reprint, Ardsley Press; Swedish edn, Liber Forlag; Hebrew edn, Or Am; French edn, Le Jour, Editeur; Spanish edn, Compania Editorial Continental; Danish edn, Hernon Publishers).
1981   *Psychology.* Random House (with C.B. Wortman).
1983   Silence is not golden. *American Psychologist*, 38, 564–72.

1985   Questioning witnesses. In S. Kassin and L. Wrightman (eds), *The Psychology of Evidence and Courtroom Procedure.* Sage (with J. Goodman).
1988   *Statistics.* Random House (with G.R. Loftus).
1990   Ten cases of eyewitness identification: Logical problems and procedural problems. *Journal of Criminal Justice*, 18, 291–319 (with W.A. Wagenaar).
1993   The reality of repressed memories. *American Psychologist*, 48, 518–37.
1994   *The Myth of Repressed Memory.* St Martin's Press (with K. Ketcham).

Further reading

Davies, G.M. and Logie, R.H. (eds) (1993) *Memory in Everyday Life.* North-Holland/Elsevier.
Kennedy, T.D. and Haygood, R.C. (1992) The discrediting effect in eyewitness testimony. *Journal of Applied Social Psychology*, 22, 70–82.
Ney. T. (ed.) (1995) *True and False Allegations of Child Sexual Abuse: Assessment and Case Management.* Brunner/Mazel.

Elizabeth Loftus began her career in psychology in the verbal learning field. 'Beth' Loftus initially focused upon the coding and retrieval of words within semantic networks using the construct of 'spreading activation'. Through the publication of over two dozen papers during the late 1960s and early 1970s, she quickly established her reputation as a hard-nosed experimental psychologist. In the early 1970s Loftus's interests expanded to include remembering and misremembering of episodes following interactions between different kinds of information, e.g. linguistic, memorial and visual. This work now has legendary status, and is among the most heavily cited research ever conducted in experimental psychology.

Loftus's eyewitness paradigm presents the eyewitness with photographic slides depicting an incident, e.g. an automobile accident, and asks a series of questions about it, some of which may be misleading. Loftus observed that the typical eyewitness tends to blend the verbal information of the questions with the visual information of the slides. This 'blending' appears to be irreversible, like the cooked mixture of ingredients in a cake. Loftus's research suggests that such memory blends result not in the false recollection of merely minor details, but in dramatic and potentially crucial mistakes both in and out of the courtroom. Eyewitness memory appears to be malleable and easily (mis)led, and innocent people may be falsely identified, crime scenes misrecalled and innocent defendants unfairly convicted as a consequence.

A second applied area for Loftus's research has been the memory of traumatic events, including allegedly 'repressed' memories from childhood of physical, psychological or sexual abuse. Such recollections are often 'enhanced' using hypnosis, imagination exercises, sexualized dream interpretation, guided visualization, sodium amytal or other 'truth serums', and are reported in courtrooms across the world to convict the alleged perpetrators, often middle-aged or elderly parents, who have little means of defence. Loftus believes that the malleability of such memories lends such poor reliability to the evidence as to render it of questionable value, and therefore inadmissible in a court of law. Loftus's contributions to psychology and law are without parallel and there is every likelihood of many more to follow.

DAVID F. MARKS

Lorenz, Konrad Z.

Born: 1903, Vienna, Austria **Died:** 1989, Altenberg, Austria **Nat:** Austrian **Ints:** Clinical psychology, comparative psychology, ethology, medicine, personality and social psychology, zoology **Educ:** MD Vienna, 1928; PhD Vienna, 1932 **Appts & awards:** Recipient of many awards and honorary degrees; Professor of Comparative Psychology, Königsberg, 1940; Professor of Experimental Biology, Max Planck Institute at Seewiesen, 1947–73; Nobel Prize for Physiology and Medicine, 1973

Principal publications

1952   *King Solomon's Ring*. Crowell.
1963   *On Aggression*. Harcourt, Brace, and World.
1965   *The Evolution and Modification of Behavior*. University of Chicago Press.
1970–1   *Studies in Animal and Human Behavior*, 2 vols. Harvard University Press.
1977   *Behind the Mirror: A Search for a Natural History of Human Knowledge*. Harcourt, Brace, Jovanovich.
1981   *The Foundations of Ethology*. Springer-Verlag.
1987   *The Waning of Humaneness*. Little-Brown.

Further reading

Dewsbury, D.A. (1985) *Leaders in the Study of Animal Behavior*. Bucknell University Press.
Krebs, J.R. and Sjolander, S. (1992) Konrad Lorenz. *Biographical Memoirs of Fellows of the Royal Society*, 38, 211–28.
Nisbett, A. (1976) *Konrad Lorenz*. Dent and Sons.

Konrad Lorenz was a powerful, charismatic personality who emphasized the inborn nature of behaviour patterns in all species, patterns that could be specified objectively and studied analytically. As a child on his family's estate in Altenberg, he roamed the waterways and forests near the Danube and kept an impressive menagerie of birds, fish, amphibians, reptiles and invertebrates. He was a talented observer (discovering imprinting in geese) as well as a good student, but he displeased his father with his lack of interest in medicine and his attention to Gretel Gebhardt, a gardener's daughter. Konrad eventually fulfilled his father's wish and obtained an MD degree in Vienna in 1928, but he also married Gretel and did not become a practising physician.

For the next twelve years Lorenz worked with his animals on the family estate, supported at first by an assistantship at the Anatomical Institute that allowed further training in comparative anatomy and psychology, and then by his wife, who worked at night at an obstetrical hospital. He completed a remarkable series of papers outlining the philosophy, theory and observations of his approach. After discovering a kindred spirit in Niko **Tinbergen** in 1936, Lorenz invited the latter to Altenberg for two months in the spring of 1937, where they hatched the new science of ethology. Together they conceptualized the innate releasing mechanism and performed a convincing series of experiments illustrating it. Tinbergen was able to fit unintrusive experiments to Lorenz's intuitions and models, providing ethology with both an observational and an experimental base.

In 1940, aged 37, Lorenz obtained his first full-time academic position, the Chair of Comparative Psychology at Königsberg in Germany. But the very next year he was drafted by the German military, finally serving as a doctor on the Russian front. In 1944 he was captured and spent more than four years in prison camps as the camp doctor, confessor and self-professed clown. When he returned to Austria in 1949, he was able, with the assistance of many people, to resume his work. Within a short time he was awarded a prestigious position with support for his students at the new Max Planck Institute of Experimental Physiology at Seewiesen. Evenings at his house and dinner table formed a critical part of the education received by students and faculty who worked with him. After he retired from Seewiesen in 1973, the Austrian government helped him establish an institute for research on evolution and cognition, located eventually in Altenberg.

From an early age Lorenz held beliefs that came to be identified with National Socialism, including that the science of eugenics could be used to improve the human race. He was initially sympathetic to the Nazis, but was later horrified by their brutality and genocide of Jews and deeply regretted his failure to foresee these events. Some have criticized his early sympathy harshly, but ethology survived as an international movement on the basis of warm personal relations that continued in spite of the war.

Among early ethologists, Lorenz was the most philosophically and historically sophisticated, and the most interested in establishing an evolutionary and philosophical basis for a science of human behaviour (an evolutionary epistemology). His early writings were somewhat contentious, sharply contrasting his ethological approach with deficits in both purposive and behaviourist psychology. This aroused the ire of American comparative psychologists, who rejected his concept of instinct and combined with other scientists to drub his motivational models and hydraulic view of aggression. Although his replies were generally adept, he left these battles to focus increasingly on the whole of the human condition. Lorenz was an intuitive observer of behaviour who avoided both classic subjectivism and reductionist empiricism. His penchant for dogmatic statements was balanced by his enthusiasm and personal charm. He tried in a unique way to come to grips with the biological nature of human behaviour, thereby providing an important backdrop for continuing evolutionary analyses.

WILLIAM TIMBERLAKE

Lubbock, Sir John (Lord Avebury after 1900)
Born: 1834, London, England *Died:* 1913 *Ints:* Anthropology, physiological and comparative psychology, social psychology *Appts & awards:* Vice-Chancellor, London University, 1872–80; Chairman, Society for the Extension of University Teaching, 1894–1902; Principal, Working Men's College, Great Ormond Street, 1883–8; President at one time or another, twenty-five learned societies; Council Member, Royal Society Privy Councillor, MP

Principal publications

1865 *Prehistoric Times.* Williams and Norgate.
1868 The early condition of man. *Anthropological Review*, 6, 1–21.
1870 *The Origin of Civilization and Primitive Condition of Man.* Longmans Green.
1872 The development of relationships. *Journal of the Royal Anthropological Society*, 1, 1–29.
1882 On the sense of colour among some lower animals. *Nature*, 25, 422–4; 27, 618.
1882 *Ants, Bees and Wasps.* Routledge, Trench and Trubner.
1883 On the sense of colour among some lower animals I and II. *Journal of the Linnaean Society*, 16, 121–7; 1884, 17, 205–14.
1911 *Marriage, Totemism and Religion.* Longmans Green.

Lubbock's contribution to psychology lay in two main areas. First, he is remembered for his pioneer studies of animal behaviour, particularly on ants and bees, the results of which are reported in the 1882 and 1888 publications. These extended to an apparently successful attempt at teaching his dog 'Van' to read single words! His experimental methods were particularly rigorous and he eschewed anthropomorphism. Lubbock was a lifelong **Darwin**ian (having been a close companion of Darwin since childhood). His research on ants and bees resulted in a number of basic discoveries regarding their sensory capacities, social behaviour and lifespan. Second, he played a crucial, though largely forgotten role in establishing the evolutionary perspective on human behaviour in his *Origin of Civilization* (1870). His influence here was arguably greater than Sir Charles Lyell's since he did not, like Lyell, prevaricate on the issue and was, in any case, a primary source for much of Lyell's material. He is referenced more than anyone else in Darwin's *Descent of Man*, and knew **Galton** (who built him some of his ant research equipment). It is reasonable to see his early advocacy as a factor in the establishment of an evolutionary/functional approach to psychology in the UK. There is a third sense in which Lubbock was probably influential, although this is as yet largely unresearched; his persistent promotion of higher education and the spread of scientific knowledge in particular. (He is among those cited as supporting the establishment of a psychology laboratory at University College, London, in 1897, for example.) Certainly his extraordinary extended network of political, financial, academic and scientific contracts was a powerful resource for all those concerned in advancing British science during the latter part of the nineteenth century. As well as animal behaviour and anthropology, Lubbock was involved in archaeology, botany and geology, whilst enjoying successful parallel careers in politics and banking.

GRAHAM RICHARDS

Luce, Robert Duncan

Born: 1925, Scranton, Pennsylvania, USA **Nat:** American **Ints:** Evaluation and measurement, experimental **Educ:** BS MIT, 1945; PhD MIT, 1950 **Appts & awards:** Victor S. Thomas Professor of Psychology, Department of Psychology and Social Relations, Harvard University; Member, Society of Experimental Psychologists, 1963– ; Member, AAA&S, 1966– ; APA Distinguished Scientific Contributions Award, 1970; Member, NAS, 1972– ; Hon. MS, Harvard University, 1976; President, Psychometric Society, 1976–7; President, Society for Mathematical Psychology, 1979; Chairman, Assembly of Behavioral and Social Sciences, NRC, 1978–9; Editorial Board, *Journal of Mathematical Psychology*, 1964–

Principal publications

1957 *Games and Decisions*. Wiley (with H. Raiffa).
1959 *Individual Choice Behavior*. Wiley (ed. with R.R. Bush and E. Galanter).
1959 On the possible psychophysical laws. *Psychological Review*, 66, 81–95.
1963 *Handbook of Mathematical Psychology, vols 1, 2 and 3*. Wiley (with D.H. Krantz, P.S. Suppes and A. Tversky).
1971 *Foundations of Measurement*. Academic Press.
1972 A neural timing theory for response times and the psychophysics of intensity. *Psychological Review*, 79, 14–57 (with D.M. Green).
1973 Speed–accuracy tradeoff in auditory detection. In S. Kornblum (ed.), *Attention and Performance*, vol. 4. Academic Press (with D.M. Green).
1976 Attention bands in absolute identification. *Perception and Psychophysics*, 20, 49–54 (with D.M. Green and D.L. Weber).
1976 The algebra of measurement. *Journal of Pure and Applied Algebra*, 8, 197–233 (with L. Narens).
1977 Sequential effects in judgements of loudness. *Journal of Experimental Psychology: Human Perception and Performance*, 3, 92–104 (with W. Jesteadt and D.M. Green).
1978 Dimensionally invariant laws correspond to meaningful qualitative relations. *Philosophy of Science*, 45, 1–16.
1982 Evidence from auditory simple reaction times for change and level detectors. *Perception and Psychophysics*, 32, 117–33 (with S.L. Burbeck).

1985 Classification of concatenation structures according to scale type. *Journal of Mathematical Psychology*, 29 1–72 (with L. Narens).
1986 *Response Times*. Oxford University Press.
1988 *The Behavioral and Social Sciences: Achievements and Opportunities*. National Academy Press (with D. Gerstein, N.J. Smelser and S. Sperlich).
1989 *Foundations of Measurement, vol. II*. Academic Press (vol. III, 1990) (with D.H. Krantx, P. Suppes and A. Tversey).
1993 *Sound and Hearing*. Erlbaum.

Further reading

Bockenholt, U. (1992) Multivariate models of preference and choice. In F.G. Ashby (ed.), *Multidimensional Models of Perception and Cognition*. Erlbaum.
Bundesen, C. (1993) The relationship between independent race models and Luce's choice axiom. *Journal of Mathematical Psychology*, 37, 446–71.

After early work on group interaction (networks and *n*-person game theory) Luce's work turned to several related topics. One was probability models of choice, with the high points being the choice axiom of 1959, several resulting choice models, and a reanalysis (with W. Edwards) of the **Weber–Fechner** problem and clarification of its relation to **Thurstone**ian models. Although these models rarely account fully for any data, often they are part of the story and have led to interesting generalizations (e.g. Amos **Tversky**'s elimination by aspects).

Out of this Luce developed a concern about the bridges between local and global psychophysics, which led to studies of response variability and sequential effects in absolute identification and magnitude estimation (with D.M. Green and others). Together with Green he proposed a variant on Thurstone's model that identified sensory attention with the size of the sample on which decisions are based, and led to two extreme decision strategies called timing and counting. A number of experiments resulted that were explicable in these terms and difficult to understand otherwise; however, the data make clear that more is involved. Another major approach has been axiomatic measurement, which he regards as being his best theoretical work. Included were: an axiomatization of thresholds (semi-orders) related to Fechnerian scaling; additive conjoint measurement (with J.W. Tukey), application to conditional expected utility (with D.H. Krantz), and non-additive generalizations (with M.A. Cohen and L.

Narens); improvements of extensive measurement (with A.A.J. Marley and F.S. Roberts), including a new version of utility; the melding of extensive and conjoint concepts to axiomatize dimensional analysis, and a demonstration that dimensional invariance, like invariance in geometry is a special case of meaningfulness; and the study of scale types (with L. Narens), resulting in very surprising limitations on measurement structures.

Luria, Aleksandr Romanovich

Born: 1902, Kazan, Russia **Died:** 1977, Moscow, Russia **Nat:** Russian **Ints:** Clinical neuropsychology, clinical psychology, experimental psychology, physiological and comparative psychology **Educ:** Dr Pedagogical Sciences (Psychology) Moscow University, 1936; Dr Medical Sciences Moscow University, 1943 **Appts & awards:** Head, Department of Neuropsychology, Moscow State University, 1945–77; Hon. Doc., University of Leicester, 1968, University of Nijmegen, 1969, University of Lublin, 1973, Brussels University, 1975, University of Tampere, 1975; Vice-President, International Union of Psychological Sciences, 1969–72; Editorial Board, *Voprosy Psikhologie*, *Neuropsychology*, *Cortex*, *Cognition*

Principal publications

1958 Brain disorder and language analysis. *Language and Speech*, 1, 14–34.
1961 *The Role of Speech in the Regulation of Normal and Abnormal Behaviour*. Pergamon.
1963 *Restoration of Function After Brain Injury*. Macmillan.
1963 Disturbance in the regulative role of speech. In S.M. Warren and K. Akert (eds), *The Frontal Granular Cortex and Behavior*. McGraw-Hill (with E. Homskaya).
1965 Two kinds of motor preservation in massive injury of the frontal lobes. *Brain*, 88, 1–10.
1966 *Higher Cortical Function in Man*. Basic Books.
1968 *The Mind of a Mnemonist*. Basic Books.
1969 Frontal lobe syndromes. In P.S. Vinken and G.W. Bruyn (eds), *Handbook of Clinical Neurology*, vol. 2. North-Holland.
1970 *Traumatic Aphasia*. Mouton.
1970 The functional organization of the brain. *Scientific American*, 222, 66–78.
1971 Memory disturbances in local brain lesions. *Neuropsychologia*, 9, 367–76.
1972 Aphasia reconsidered. *Cortex*, 8, 34–40.
1972 *The Man with a Shattered World*. Basic Books.

1973 *The Working Brain*. Penguin.
1973 Towards the mechanisms of naming disturbances. *Neuropsychologia*, 11, 417–21.
1977 A modern assessment of the basic forms of aphasia. *Brain and Language*, 129–51 (with J.T. Hutton).

Further reading

Cole, M. and Cole, S. (eds) (1979) *The Making of Mind*. Harvard University Press.

Luria was born in Kazan of Jewish extraction and entered Kazan University in 1918, where he studied social science. When he graduated in 1921 he was urged by his father to enter medical school, but his primary ambition was to become a psychologist. He compromised by pursuing the two careers together – at that time it was possible to enter more than one faculty. He began by taking medical classes and for his training in psychology spent time at the Pedagogical Institute and the Kazan Psychiatric Hospital. He interrupted his medical studies two years later in order to take a position as a laboratory assistant at the Kazan Institute for the Scientific Organization of Work, where he investigated the effects of hard work on mental activity. This took him to Moscow, where, in 1923, he was appointed to a junior post at the Moscow Institute of Psychology, working under the direction of N.K. Kornalov. There he pursued a research programme concerned with the effects of emotional stress on human motor reactions. This work owed something to **Pavlov**'s research on experimental neuroses in dogs, although Luria never accepted Pavlov's position that complex human behaviour could be satisfactorily explained in terms of reflexes and conditioned reflexes.

In 1924 Luria made the acquaintance of L.S. **Vygotsky**, whose interest in the effects of nervous disease on intellectual functioning was probably partly responsible for directing Luria towards neuropsychology and continuing his medical studies. Work with Vygotsky on the evolution of psychological processes lead to a jointly authored work, *Studies in the History of Behaviour* (1930). After passing his medical examinations in 1937 he approached N.N. Bourdenko, head of the Neurosurgical Institute (Moscow), in order to obtain an internship. In his autobiography he described the following two years as 'the most productive of my life. I had no staff and scientific responsibilities except routine medical work ... I began to devise my own approach to the neuropsychology of local brain injury.' In 1939 he moved to the Neurological Clinic of the Institute of Experimental Medicine (Moscow), where he became Head of the Laboratory of Experimental Psychology.

At the outbreak of war in 1941 he became a medical officer with responsibilities for the assessment and rehabilitation of brain-injured servicemen. His work was later transferred to the Institute of Neurosurgery in Moscow, where he continued to work until 1950. In that year he was summarily dismissed, apparently on ideological grounds – he was less then enthusiastic about the methods and ideas of Pavlov – and moved his research base to the Institute of Defectology founded by Vygotsky many years earlier. He was later restored to his post in Moscow, where he continued his work virtually until his death.

During his undergraduate years and for a period of time after graduation, Luria was an ardent supported of psychoanalysis and was strongly influenced by **Freud**, **Adler** and **Jung**. He founded a psychoanalytic circle in Kazan, which he brought to the attention of Freud. Later he repudiated psychoanalysis in favour of a more rigorous, experimental approach. Luria is credited with the first serious experimental investigations of conflict. Drawing on his early interests in psychoanalysis, he exploited the properties of Jung's word-association technique by requiring subjects to give part of a response to a generic stimulus (e.g. 'house–room') and then introduced an 'impossible' stimulus (e.g. 'moon–?'). The extent of conflict was inferred from changes in reaction time. More generally he developed the 'Luria technique', in which both voluntary and involuntary motor responses, as well as verbal responses, are measured. He distinguished three types of conflict arising from: (1) the prevention of excitation from

extending into action, (2) lack of readiness for reacting, and (3) the diversion of suppressed activity into central processes.

Luria's innovative methods for restoring brain functioning were developed during his period as a medical officer in World War II, and are based on his view of the brain as a complex functional system rather than a single entity. His position is summarized in his three 'basic laws' of higher cortical functioning: that of the hierarchical structure of cortical zones; that of diminishing specificity; and that of progressive lateralization. Luria also made a substantial contribution to the development and refinement of clinical tests for brain damage, which correlated with surgical and pathological reports.

The strength in Luria's approach lies in three features: (1) it is based on an explicit theoretical formulation of cerebral organization, although it should be noted that parts of the model have been contradicted by empirical evidence; (2) it emphasises the qualitative aspects of performance – *how* something is done, not only the absolute level of performance; and (3) it is flexible in its approach to the diagnosis of deficits, and in this respect is thought to result in greater accuracy and more fine-grained description of a patient's problems. As against these considerations, his system depends largely on the clinical acumen of individual neuropsychologists. Thus, a gifted clinician such as Luria can use these to good effect, as illustrated in his ground-breaking case studies. However, there have been no rigorous evaluations of Luria's procedures, with the result that the psychometric properties of his 'clinical-analytical' approach are often treated with suspicion, and generally it has not fared well outside Europe. Although Luria published extensively over a fifty-year period, many of his publications in Russian are unobtainable.

M

McClelland, David Clarence

Born: 1917, Mount Vernon, New York, USA
Nat: American **Ints:** Experimental, personality
and social, philosophical and theoretical, Social
Issues **Educ:** AB Wesleyan University, 1938;
AM University of Missouri, 1939; PhD Yale
University, 1941 **Appts & awards:** Professor of
Psychology, Department of Psychology and
Social Relations, Harvard University; Fellow,
APA, 1948, AAS, 1957; APA Education and
Training Board, 1951–2; NRC Advisory Com-
mittee (Fellowship Selection), 1951–5; APA
Representative to NRC, 1951–6; Board of
Directors, Psychological Committee, Connec-
ticut State Hospital at Middletown, 1952–6;
Fulbright Advisory Panel on Psychology,
1953–6, Chair, 1956; Hon. MA, Harvard
University, 1956; NIMH Training Grants Com-
mittee for Clinical Psychology, 1956–61; Hon.
ScD, Wesleyan University, 1957; Hon. DPhil,
Mainz University, 1958; Hon. LLD, MacMur-
ray University, 1963; Hon. DLitt, Albion
College, 1970; APA Committee on Psychology
in National and International Affairs, 1965–8;
APA Committee on Scientific Awards, 1968–9;
Past President, Connecticut Valley Association
of Psychologists, Connecticut State Psychologi-
cal Society; Consulting Editor, *Journal of
Abnormal and Social Psychology*, *Journal of
Cross-Cultural Society*, *Journal of Personality*

Principal publications

1951 *Personality*. Sloane.
1955 *Studies in Motivation*. Appleton-Century-
Crofts.
1961 *The Achieving Society*. Van Nostrand.
1963 *The Roots of Consciousness*. Van Nostrand.
1975 *Power: The Inner-Experience*. Halstead-
Wiley.

Further reading

Sorrentino, R.M. and Higgins, E.T. (eds) (1986)
*Handbook of Motivation and Cognition:
Foundations of Social Behavior*. Guilford.

David McClelland is the founder and chairman
of the Board of McBer and Co. and Professor of
Psychology at Harvard University. His forty
years of research have resulted in an internationally recognized theory of human motivation. He
has also initiated projects to apply his theory and
research findings in the areas of management,
small business, post-secondary education,
mental health, behavioural medicine, economic
development and modernization of developing
countries. He has written numerous books and
articles on human motivation and related topics
and holds honorary doctorates in science,
philosophy, law and literature.

Maccoby, Eleanor Emmons

Born: 1917, Tacoma, Washington, USA **Nat:**
American **Ints:** Developmental psychology,
personality and social psychology, psychology of
women **Educ:** BA University of Washington,
Seattle, 1939; MA University of Michigan, 1949;
PhD University of Michigan, 1950 **Appts &
awards:** Lecturer, Harvard University, 1950–7;
Professor of Psychology, Stanford University,
1958– ; Professor Emeritus, Stanford Univer-
sity; Barbara Kimball Browning Professorship,
Stanford University; President, Western Psy-
chological Association, 1974–5, Society for
Research in Child Development, 1981–3; Vice-
Chair, Committee on Child Development and
Public Policy of the National Research Council,
1977–83; Walter J. Gores Award for Excellence
in Teaching, 1981; American Educational
Research Association Award for Distinguished
Contributions in Educational Research, 1984;
APA Distinguished Scientific Contributions
Award, 1988

Principal publications

1954 Why children watch television. *Public
Opinion Quarterly*, 18, 239–44.
1957 *Patterns of Child Rearing*. Row-Peterson
(with R.R. Sears and H. Levin).
1957 Identification and observational learning from
films. *Journal of Abnormal and Social Psychology*,
55, 76–87 (with W.C. Wilson).
1958 *Readings in Social Psychology*. Henry Holt
(ed. with T.R. Newcomb and E. Hartley).

1958 Community integration and the social control
of juvenile delinquency. *Journal of Personality*, 14,
38–51 (with J.P. Johnson and R.M. Church).

1966 Parents' differential reactions to sons and
daughters. *Journal of Personality and Social
Psychology*, 4, 237–43.

1970 *Experiments in Primary Education*. Harcourt
Brace Jovanovich (with M. Zellner).

1974 *The Psychology of Sex Differences*. Stanford
University Press (with C.N. Jacklin).

1980 *Social Development: Psychological Growth
and the Parent–Child Relationship*. Harcourt Brace
Jovanovich.

1984 Socialization and developmental change.
Child Development, 55: 317–28.

1984 Children's dispositions and mother–child
interaction at 12 and 18 months: A short-term
longitudinal study. *Developmental Psychology*, 20:
459–72 (with M.E. Snow and C.N. Jacklin).

1987 Gender segregation in childhood. In H. Reese
(ed.), *Advances in Child Behavior and
Development, vol. 20*. Academic Press (with C.N.
Jacklin).

1992 The role of parents in the socialization of
children: An historical overview. *Developmental
Psychology*, 28, 1006–17.

Further reading

Lindzey, G. (ed.) (1989) *A History of Psychology in
Autobiography, vol. 8*. Stanford University Press.

Stevens, G. and Gardner, S. (1982) *The Women of
Psychology, vol. 2: Expansion and Refinement*.
Schenkman.

Eleanor Emmons was born in Tacoma, Washington, in 1917, the second of four daughters. Her father owned a small business, and her mother was a musician and singer. During her childhood her parents became members of the Theosophical Society, which emphasized Eastern religions. She grew up sharing her family's theosophical interests in spiritualism and extrasensory perception and their strong inclination to act on their principles (though she later became dissatisfied with some of the doctrines espoused by the society, which included spiritualism and extrasensory perception, and, in reaction, became a staunch empiricist).

In 1934, Eleanor Emmons entered Reed College in Portland, Oregon. Her first psychology course was taught by William Griffith, a behaviourist and former student of Edwin **Guthrie**. Attracted to the behaviouristic perspective offered by Griffith, she went to the University of Washington in Seattle for her junior and senior years to study with Guthrie. In September

1938 (her senior year) she married Nathan Maccoby, a graduate student in social psychology, whom she had met the year before. In 1940, Eleanor Maccoby moved to Washington, DC, when her husband took a job with the US Civil Service Commission. She first took a job at the State Technical Advisory Service of the Social Security Board where she wrote test items. Then she joined the staff of Rensis Likert's Division of Program Surveys of the Department of Agriculture, and worked with such distinguished psychologists as Jerome **Bruner** and Ernest **Hilgard**, among others.

In 1947, Likert moved his organization to the University of Michigan, and Maccoby and her husband moved to Michigan to continue working with him. There Maccoby earned her MA degree in 1947 and PhD in 1950, with a dissertation on conditioning in pigeons. In the same year she joined Robert **Sears** at Harvard to supervise fieldwork for interviews of mothers as part of an ambitious study on child-rearing practices. This work culminated in the 1957 publication of *Patterns of Child Rearing*, with Sears and Harry Levin. Also while at Harvard, Maccoby performed some of the earliest studies on the impact of television viewing on children and families. Though she was a productive researcher, gender discrimination prevented her from advancing beyond the level of lecturer at Harvard. In 1958 she went to Stanford at the invitation of Sears, entering at the level of associate professor.

During the 1960s, Maccoby came under the influence of John **Flavell**, and her intellectual interests shifted from the more constrictive stimulus–response theoretical framework in which she was trained to a cognitive-developmental framework. Her interest in gender differentiation in childhood was stimulated by the emergence of sex differences in many studies in which they had not been anticipated. She later became a member of a Social Sciences Research Council Committee on Socialization, and, as part of her duties, was asked to edit a book on sex differences. This led eventually to the publication, with Carol Jacklin, of her most influential book, *The Psychology of Sex Differences*. This monumental work contained a literature review of some 1600 studies of gender differences. Maccoby and Jacklin concluded that there were four differences between the sexes: verbal ability is superior in females, visuospatial ability is superior in males, males have more mathematical ability, and males are more aggressive than females. Since its publication this book has generated controversy. However, it has become one of the most influential works on gender studies.

Maccoby's more recent work focused on children's socialization and the development of sex differences. Findings from a longitudinal study of children up to age 6 reinforced her interactionist perspective, emphasizing the mutuality of influence between parent and child. Her interest in social policy issues led to a collaboration with Robert Mnookin, a Stanford law professor, on a longitudinal study concerned with the causes of gender differentiation and the impact it has on family functioning over a three-year post-divorce period. The overarching theme of her work has been an attempt to integrate socialization processes and the individual differences they generate with developmental timetables for change.

J.D. HOGAN AND W. IACCINO

McCosh, James (sometimes M'Cosh)

Born: 1811, Ayrshire, Scotland **Died:** 1895, Princeton, New Jersey, USA **Nat:** British **Ints:** History of psychology, philosophical psychology **Appts & awards:** Professor of Logic and Metaphysics, Queen's College, Belfast, 1852–68; President, College of New Jersey (later Princeton University), 1868–88; Emeritus Professor, 1889–95

Principal publications*

1856 *Typical Forms and Special Ends in Creation.* Thomas Constable (with George Dickie).

1860 *The Intuitions of the Mind Inductively Investigated.* John Murray.

1862 *The Supernatural in Relation to the Supernatural.* Macmillan.

1866 *An Examination of Mr J.S. Mill's Philosophy.* Macmillan.

1870 *The Laws of Discursive Thought: Being a Text-book of Formal Logic.* Macmillan Carter.

1874 *The Scottish Philosophy.* Carter.

1880 *The Emotions.* Macmillan (reissued 1887 with an additional chapter as *Psychology: The Motive Powers*, Scribner's).

1883 *Development: What It Can and Cannot Do.* Scribner's.

1883 *Energy: Efficient and Final Cause.* Clark, Scribner's.

1886 *Psychology: The Cognitive Powers.* Macmillan. (Revised edn, 1894.)

1890 *The Religious Aspect of Evolution.* Nisbet. Putnam's.

* Many of these were republished both in the US and Britain with various publishers.

Further reading

Fay, J.W. (1939) *American Psychology before William James.* Rutgers University Press.

Hoeveler, David J., Jr (1981) *James McCosh and the Scottish Intellectual Tradition from Glasgow to Princeton.* Princeton University Press.

O'Donnell, J.M. (1985) *The Origins of Behaviorism: American Psychology 1870–1920.* New York University Press.

Richards, G. (1995) 'To know our fellow men to do them good': American psychology's enduring moral project. *History of the Human Sciences*, 8, 1–24.

Sloane, W.M. (ed.) (1896) *The Life of James McCosh. A Record Chiefly Autobiographical.* Clark.

Wozniak, Robert H. (1982) Metaphysics and science, reason and reality: The intellectual origins of genetic epistemology. In John M. Broughton and D. John Freeman-Noir (eds), *The Cognitive-Developmental Psychology of James Mark Baldwin: Current Theory and Research in Genetic Epistemology.* Ablex.

McCosh, like Noah **Porter**, has generally been considered a mental and moral philosopher of little enduring significance. In recent years it has become increasingly evident that he played a major role in facilitating the emergence of the 'New Psychology' in the US, even though his allegiance to the Scottish Realism approach never wavered. Prior to his 1868 emigration to the United States, to become President of the College of New Jersey (later Princeton University), he had already established a reputation as an opponent of John Stuart Mill's associationism with his *The Intuitions of the Mind* and *An Examination of Mr J.S. Mill's Philosophy.* His massive *The Scottish Philosophy* played a major historiographical role in defining what is now known as the 'Scottish School'. Notwithstanding his philosophical and evangelical Christian commitments, McCosh maintained a keen interest in contemporary scientific developments and eventually accepted a pious version of evolutionary theory, expounded most fully in *The Religious Aspect of Evolution.* Two later works of special significance are *The Emotions* and *Psychology: The Cognitive Powers.* The first contains passages of an almost **James**ian kind while the latter took full cognizance of contemporary work such as Wilhelm Preyer's (especially in the revised edition), as well as reporting an attempted replication of **Galton**'s imagery research. In the 1880s McCosh was instrumental in encouraging James Mark

Baldwin's ambitions, writing the preface to Baldwin's translation of T. **Ribot**'s *Contemporary German Psychology* and obtaining for him his first academic post. Wozniak has shown how deeply Baldwin's initial theoretical framework was rooted in McCosh's thought. Another of his protégés was the now less well known physiological psychologist Moses Allan Starr, who went on to study under **Charcot** and **Helmholtz**. From the early 1880s McCosh was drawing students' attention to the work of **Wundt** and stressing the importance of understanding 'physiological psychology' (as then conceived). As a college president he earned a high reputation for innovation and presided over a major expansion of Princeton's faculty and student numbers. His pastoral concern for students also became legendary. Along with Noah Porter, McCosh was instrumental in establishing the academic foundations for the New Psychology of the late 1880s and 1890s, while his innovatory approach at the institutional level and greater willingness to stay abreast of current developments in the field contrast with Porter's temperamental conservatism in all things.

GRAHAM RICHARDS

McDougall, William

Born: 1871, Chadderton, Lancashire, England **Died:** 1938, Durham, North Carolina, USA **Nat:** British **Ints:** Clinical psychology, cross-cultural psychology, experimental psychology, general psychology, parapsychology, peace psychology, personality and social psychology, psychoanalysis, psychology, psychological hypnosis, psychological study of social issues, physiological and comparative, theoretical and philosophical psychology **Educ:** Bsc, MSc (Science) Victoria University, 1890; BA (Science) Cambridge University, 1894; MB, ChB, MA Cambridge University, 1897; MA Oxford University **Appts & awards:** Fellow, St John's College, Cambridge University, 1898–1903; Physician, Cambridge Anthropological Expedition to Torres Straits, 1899–1900; 1st class in the Natural Science Tripos at Cambridge, Pt. I in 1892, Pt. II in 1894; Grainger Prize, Cambridge, 1898; Co-founder, BPS, 1901; Reader in Experimental Psychology, University College, London, 1901–7; Wilde Reader in Mental Philosophy, Oxford University, 1903–20; Fellow, Royal Society of London, 1912, Corpus Christi College, Oxford, 1912; Vice-President, Psychiatric Section, Royal Society of Medicine, 1914–18, President, 1918–20; Major, Royal Army Medical Corps, 1915–19; Hon. DSc, Victoria University of Manchester, 1919; President, British Society for Psychical Research, 1920–1; William James Chair of Psychology, Harvard University, 1920–7; Chair of Psychology, Duke University, 1927– ; Hon. Fellow, St John's College, Cambridge, 1938

Principal publications

1901   On the seat of the psycho-physical processes. *Brain*, 24, 577–630.
1901   New observations in support of Thomas Young's theory of light- and colour-vision, I–III, *Mind*, 10, 52–97, 210–45, 347–82.
1902–6   The physiological factors of the attention process, I–IV. *Mind*, 11, 316–51; 12, 289–302, 473–88; 15, 329–59.
1903   Hearing, smell, taste, cutaneous sensations, etc. In A.C. Haddon, (ed.), *Reports of the Cambridge Anthropological Expedition to the Torres Straits, Pt. 2, Vol. 2.* Cambridge University Press (with C.S. Myers).
1905   *Physiological Psychology.* Dent.
1908   *An Introduction to Social Psychology.* Methuen.
1911   *Body and Mind: A History and Defense of Animism.* Methuen.
1912   *Psychology: The Study of Behavior.* Holt.
1912   *The Pagan Tribes of Borneo.* Macmillan (with C. Hose).
1920   *The Group Mind.* Cambridge University Press.
1923   *An Outline of Psychology.* Methuen.
1926   *Outline of Abnormal Psychology.* Scribner's.
1927   Psychical research as a university study. In C. Murchison (ed.), *The Case For and Against Psychical Belief.* Clark University Press.
1927   *Janus, The Conquest of War: A Psychological Inquiry.* Dutton.
1929   *The Battle of Behaviorism.* Norton (with J.B. Watson).
1929   *Modern Materialism and Emergent Evolution.* Methuen.
1931   *World Chaos: The Responsibility of Science.* Kegan Paul.
1932   *The Energies of Men: A Study of the Fundamentals of Dynamic Psychology.* Methuen.
1934   *The Frontiers of Psychology.* Methuen.
1936   *Psycho-Analysis and Social Psychology.* Methuen.

Further reading

Boden, M.A. (1972) *Purposive Explanation in Psychology.* Harvard University Press.
Burt, C. (1955) The permanent contributions of McDougall to psychology. *British Journal of Educational Psychology*, 25, 10–22.

Hearnshaw, L.S. (1964) *A Short History of British Psychology, 1840–1940*. Methuen.

Heidbreder, E. (1973) William McDougall and social psychology. In M. Henle, J. Jaynes and J. Sullivan, (eds), *Historical Conceptions of Psychology*. Springer-Verlag.

Spearman, C. (1938) The life and work of William McDougall. *Character and Personality*, 7, 175–83.

William McDougall's educational preparation for a career in psychology was extraordinary. His formal education included secondary schooling in England and Germany, and numerous earned university degrees, including medicine. In addition, he did research in neurophysiology with C.S. **Sherrington** at St Thomas Hospital, in anthropology with A.C. Haddon and W.H. Rivers during their expedition to New Guinea, and in experimental psychology with G.E. **Muller** at Göttingen in Germany. He worked with Francis **Galton** on mental testing and influenced the early development of factor analysis by Charles **Spearman** and Cyril **Burt**. McDougall's plans for psychoanalysis with Karl **Jung** were disrupted by World War I. This broad educational background allowed him to participate in most areas of psychology and to appreciate fully the contributions to psychology from related disciplines. McDougall's research career and writings were remarkably diverse, including a continuous programme of research in psychophysics and brain science, the development of social psychological theory, several very successful textbooks, clinical practice, critical commentaries on behaviourism, dynamic psychology and *Gestalt* psychology, research on psychic phenomena and Lamarkian theory, and numerous books on such contemporary social issues as eugenics, international peace, religion and moral order.

For McDougall, the supreme goal of psychology was to understand human nature in all of its complexity, and the most powerful method of psychology was experimentation. He argued that psychology should not be isolated from other disciplines and should not be narrowed to a set of orthodox topics; hence, his involvement with psychic research, his experiments on Lamarkian theories, and his discomfort with 'schools' of psychology. McDougall's determination and daring in psychology were perhaps influenced by his early struggles in England to introduce experimental psychology to the university and hypnosis to clinical practice. But McDougall also strove for theoretic synthesis and unification. In early work in psychophysics and brain physiology, he revived Young's theory of vision and proposed a mind–body solution with features of field theory, cell assemblies and cybernetics. In his *Introduction to Social Psychology*, he tried to relate species psychology to individual psychology, and later, in *Group Mind*, to relate individual psychology to cultural or national collective psychological configurations.

McDougall's major achievement was a comprehensive theory of instincts, emotions and purposiveness, which he called hormic psychology. On the basis of this, he became the foremost critic of behaviourism for its lack of teleology, and was pleased late in his career to hear behaviourists speaking of 'drives'. His medical work during World War I treating 'shell-shock' demonstrated that **Freud**ian theory was too narrowly focused on sexual and childhood causes of neurosis. Though his ideas were often critical and antagonistic, his books were very widely read in Europe and the US and did much to popularize psychology and promote its study in universities.

McDougall claimed that he was intellectually indebted to William **James** and very much inspired by him. A 1908 visit by James was one of McDougall's most treasured memories. Indeed, the careers of McDougall and James were remarkably similar: both had elite secondary schooling in Europe, both trained in medicine, both joined expeditions to tropical hinterlands, both had encyclopaedic knowledge of psychology, both were early experimentalists who moved towards theory and social commentary, both were well-reputed writers, both boldly engaged unorthodox topics, both held top academic positions. But William James is still seen as a major figure in psychology and is still cited; whereas William McDougall is now only a footnote to early social psychology as the author of the first textbook on the topic, an attribution which in fact is not true. McDougall himself realized that he was not having a lasting impact on psychology and attributed this to an aloof temperament and an intellectual arrogance. However, his gradual isolation probably had more to do with his mid-career move to the United States, where his Britishness and his criticisms of behaviourism were not welcomed.

F.W. RUDMIN

McGaugh, James Lafayette

Born: 1931, Long Beach, California, USA *Nat:* American *Ints:* Experimental psychology, physiological and comparative psychology, psychopharmacology *Educ:* BA San Jose State University, 1953; PhD University of California at Berkeley, 1959 *Appts & awards:* Professor of Psychobiology; Director, Center for the Neurobiology of Learning and Memory, University of California; USA NAS–NRC Senior Post-Doctoral Fellowship, 1961; Council Member, Society for Neuroscience, 1974–8; Executive Committee, APA Division 6, 1980–3; APA Distinguished Scientific Contribution Award, 1981; Distinguished Alumnus Award, San Jose State University, 1982; Extraordinarious Award, University of California, Irvine, 1982; Editor, *Behavioral and Neural Biology*, 1972; Editorial Advisory Board, Oxford Psychology Series, 1979; Series Co-editor, Behavioral Biology (Academic Press)

Principal publications

1959 The effect of strychnine sulphate on maze-learning. *American Journal of Psychology*, 72, 99–102 (with L. Petrinovich).

1965 Effects of drugs on learning and memory. *International Review of Neurobiology*, 8, 139–96 (with L. Petrinovich).

1966 Time-dependent processes in memory storage. *Science*, 153, 1351–8.

1971 Modification of memory storage processes. *Behavioral Science*, 16, 45–63 (with R.G. Dawson).

1972 *Memory Consolidation*. Albion (with M. Herz).

1974 Conceptual and neurobiological issues in studies of treatments affecting memory storage. In G.A. Bower (ed.), *The Psychology of Learning and Motivation, vol. 8*. Academic Press (with P.E. Gold).

1975 A single-trace two-process view of memory storage processes. In D. Deutsch and J.A. Deutsch (eds), *Short-Term Memory*. Academic Press (with P.E. Gold).

1976 Cognition and consolidation. In L. Petrinovich and J.L. McGaugh (eds), *Knowing, Thinking and Believing*. Plenum.

1980 *Behavioral Neuroscience*. Academic Press (with C. Cotman).

1983 Preserving the presence of the past: Hormonal influences on memory storage. *American Psychologist*, 38, 161–74.

1984 *Neurobiology of Learning and Memory*. Guilford Press (ed. with G. Lynch and N.M. Weinberger).

1984 Hormonal influences on memory. *Annual Review of Psychology*, 34, 297–323.

1990 Significance and remembrance: The role of neuromodulatory systems. *Psychological Science*, 1, 15–25.

1995 Differential effects of pretraining inactivation of the right of left amygdala on retention of inhibitory avoidance training. *Behavioral Neuroscience*, 109, 642–7 (with M. Coleman).

Further reading

McGaugh, J.L., Bermudez-Rattoni, F. and Prado-Alcala, R.A. (eds) (1995) *Plasticity in the Central Nervous System: Learning and Memory*. Erlbaum.

Squire, L.R. and Butters, N. (eds) (1992) *Neuropsychology of Memory*, 2nd edn. Guilford Press.

McGaugh is known primarily for his work on time-dependent processes in memory storage in animals. This has involved investigations of the effects on memory of drugs, electrical stimulation of the brain, and the administration of hormones. His experimental work has demonstrated that retention can be enhanced as well as impaired by such treatments if the treatments are administered shortly after training. He has interpreted these findings as indicating that the treatments affect memory by modulating the neurobiological processes underlying the storage of recently acquired information. McGaugh has been particularly interested in the implications of these findings for understanding the endogenous processes involved in memory modulation. He suggests that hormones released during or shortly following experiences modulate memory-storage processes, and he attaches particular significance to the role of adrenergic catecholamines (epinephrine and norepinephrine) as well as opioid peptide hormones. However, there is a substantial corpus of evidence which suggests that a variety of hormones and transmitter systems is involved in memory modulation. His later research is focused on the brain systems through which hormones work to influence memory storage. The goal of this work is to increase our understanding of the systemic basis of disorders of learning and memory in ways that can influence the development of rational therapy for memory disorders.

McGuire, William J.

Born: 1925, New York, USA *Nat:* American *Ints:* Experimental psychology, health psychology, history of psychology, personality and social psychology, philosophical and theoretical psychology, psychological study of social issues *Educ:* BA Fordham College, 1949; MA Fordham University, 1950; PhD Yale University, 1954 *Appts & awards:* Fulbright Scholar, University of Louvain, 1950–1; SSRC, Postdoctoral Fellow, University of Minnesota, 1954–55; AAAS Annual Socio-Psychology Award, 1963; Hovland Memorial Award, Yale University, 1963; NSF Advisory Panel, 1963–5; Fellow, Center for the Advanced Study in the Behavioral Sciences, 1965–6; Member, NIMH Advisory Panel, 1968–72; Professor, Department of Psychology, Yale University, 1970; London School of Economics, Guggenheim Fellow, NIMH Senior Postdoctoral Fellowship, 1970–1; NIMH Senior Postdoctoral Fellowship, London School of Economics, 1970–1; APA Division 8, President, 1972–3; Consulting Editor, *Journal of Abnormal and Social Psychology*, 1962–4, *Psychological Bulletin*, 1964–7, *Journal of Experimental Social Psychology*, 1966–7, *Public Opinion Quarterly*, 1975–84, *Journal of Cognitive Therapy and Research*, 1976–80, *European Journal of Social Psychology*, 1978– ; *Basic and Applied Social Psychology*, 1984– ; Editor, *Journal of Personality and Social Psychology*, 1964–7; Associate Editor, *Current Contents: Social and Behavioral Science*, 1968–72, *Journal of Social Issues*, 1969–74; *British Journal of Social Psychology*, 1979–84, *Journal of Consumer Research*, 1982–5,

Principal publications

1957   (*et al.*) *The Order of Presentation in Persuasion*. Yale University Press.

1960   (*et al.*) *Attitude Organization and Change*. Yale University Press.

1960   A syllogistic analysis of cognitive relationships. In C.I. Hovland *et al.* (eds), *Attitude Organization and Change*. Yale University Press.

1961   Inducing resistance to persuasion: Some contemporary approaches. In L. Berkowitz (ed.), *Advances in Experimental Social Psychology, vol. 1*. Academic Press.

1968   Personality and susceptibility to social influence. In E.F. Borgatta and W.W. Lambert (eds), *Handbook of Personality Theory and Research*. Rand-McNally.

1968   (*et al.*, eds) *Theory of Cognitive Consistency*. Rand-McNally.

1969   Attitude and attitude-change. In G. Lindzey and E. Aronson (eds), *Handbook of Social Psychology, vol. 3*, 2nd edn. Addison-Wesley.

1973   The yin and yang of progress in social psychology: Seven koan. *Journal of Personality and Social Psychology*, 26, 446–56.

1976   Historical comparisons: Testing psychological hypotheses with cross-era data. *International Journal of Psychology*, 11, 161–83.

1979   Effects of household sex composition on the salience of one's gender in the spontaneous self-concept. *Journal of Experimental Social Psychology*, 15, 77–90 (with C.V. McGuire and W. Winton).

1981   The probabilogical model of cognitive structure and attitude change. In R. Petty, T. Ostrom and T. Brock (eds), *Cognitive Responses in Persuasion*. Erlbaum, 1981.

1983   A contextualist theory of knowledge: Its implications for innovation and reform in psychological research. In L. Berkowitz (ed.), *Advances in Experimental Social Psychology, vol. 16*. Academic Press.

1984   Search for the self: Going beyond self-esteem and the receptive self. In R.A. Zucker, J. Aronoff and A.I. Rabin (eds), *Personality and the Prediction of Behavior*. Academic Press.

1986   The self in society: Effects of social contexts on the sense of self. *British Journal of Social Psychology*, 25, 259–70 (with J. McGuire, C.V. McGuire and J. Cheever).

1989   Who's afraid of the big bad media? In A.A. Berger (ed.), *Mass Media and American Society*. Longman.

1990   Dynamic operations of thought systems. *American Psychologist*, 45, 504–12.

1993   *Explorations in Political Psychology*. Duke University Press (ed. with S. Iyengar and W.J. McGuire).

1994   Use of historical data in psychology: Comments on Münsterberg (1899). *Psychological Review*, 101, 243–7.

Further reading

Gergen, K.J. and McGuire, W.J. (1992) Social psychology. In S. Koch and D.E. Leary (eds), *A Century of Psychology as Science*. APA.

Iyengar, S. and McGuire, W.J. (eds) (1993) *Explorations in Political Psychology*. Duke University Press.

Wyer, R.S., Jr and Srull, T.K. (eds) (1991) *The Content, Structure, and Operation of Thought Systems. Advances in Social Cognition*, vol. 4. Erlbaum.

Although William McGuire is usually considered a social psychologist, his early work as a graduate student in the 1950s at Fordham, Louvain and Yale focused on cognitive processes; a series of studies on mass audio-visual instruction included the earliest research on vicarious learning from witnessing the reinforcement of an actor's good performance. His research on how belief systems operate by the laws of probability theory and logic (plus some alogical functioning principles such as wishful thinking and temporal inertia) was completed during graduate years at Yale and a postdoctoral year at the University of Minnesota. This work began the active responding approach to social cognition. It showed that attitude change spreads gradually to unmentioned related issues and can be induced by the Socratic method and other modes of manipulating the salience of information already possessed by the believer, as well as by the usual procedure of providing new information from an outside source.

Subsequent attitude research, done at Yale University, the University of Illinois, Columbia University and the University of California at San Diego, investigated inducing resistance to persuasion, relationships between personality variables and persuadability, and anticipatory attitude change. More recently, McGuire has investigated how distinctiveness determines what is salient in one's sense of self and how the types of verb used in free self-descriptions reveal the processes involved in thinking about the self and others. He has also investigated the cognitive structure and functioning implications of seemingly arbitrary word-order regularities. While carrying out this empirical research McGuire has written a number of theoretical and review articles, developed a perspectivist theory of knowledge, edited journals, served on research review panels, and consulted widely on applied problems in the mass media and public health areas.

McGurk, Harry

Born: 1936, Glasgow, Scotland **Nat:** British **Ints:** Developmental psychology **Educ:** BA University of Strathclyde, 1968; PhD University of Strathclyde, 1972 **Appts & awards:** Professor Emeritus, Developmental Psychology, Thomas Coram Research Unit, Institute of Education, University of London, 1994; BPS, Member, 1971–80, Fellow, 1980– , Council, 1981–4, Chairman, Developmental Psychology Section, 1982–4, Member, Executive Committee, Developmental Psychology Section, 1988–90; Secretary, International Society for the Study of Behavioural Development, 1975–81; Member, Executive Committee, International Society for the Study of Behavioural Development, 1983–90; President Elect, International Society for the Study of Behavioural Development, 1994– ; Member, Royal Society of Medicine, 1994– ; Editor, *International Journal of Behavioural Development*, 1984–90; University of Surrey Press, Chairman, Editorial Board, 1986–90, Board of Directors, 1988–90; Member, Editorial Board for Developmental Psychology (Erlbaum), 1988–

Principal publications

1972 The salience of orientation in young children's perception of form. *Child Development*, 43, 1047–52.

1972 The evaluation of infant intelligence. *Science*, 178, 1174–7 (with M. Lewis).

1974 Pictorial depth perception: A developmental study. *British Journal of Psychology*, 65, 367–76 (with G. Jahoda).

1974 Space perception in early infancy: Perception within common auditory-visual space? *Science*, 186, 649–59 (with M. Lewis).

1974 The development of pictorial depth perception: Cross-cultural replications. *Child Development*, 45, 1042–7 (with G. Jahoda).

1975 *Growing and Changing*. Methuen.

1976 (ed.) *Ecological Factors in Human Development*. North-Holland.

1976 Hearing lips and seeing voices. *Nature*, 264, 746–8 (with J. MacDonald).

1977 Auditory visual co-ordination in neonates. *Child Development*, 48, 138–43 (with C. Turnure and S. Creighton).

1978 *Issues in Childhood Social Development*. Methuen.

1978 Auditory-visual coordination during the first year of life. *International Journal of Behavioural Development*, 1, 229–39 (with J. MacDonald).

1978 Visual influences on speech perception processes. *Perception and Psychophysics*, 24, 253–7 (with J. MacDonald).

1982 *Brain and Behavioral Development*. University of Surrey Press (with J. Dickerson).

1983 Effective motivation and the development of communicative competence in blind and sighted children. In A.E. Mills (ed.), *Language Acquisition in the Blind Child*. Croom Helm.

1988 Children's conversations with adults. *Children and Society*, 2, 20–34 (with M. Glachen).

1993 Cerebral palsied children's interactions with siblings. I. Influence of severity of disability, age and birth order. *Journal of Child Psychology and Psychiatry*, 347, 57, 621–47 (with E. Dallas and J. Stevenson).

1993 Cerebral palsied children's interactions with siblings. II. Interactional structure. *Journal of Child Psychology and Psychiatry*, 347, 57, 649–73 (with E. Dallas and J. Stevenson).

Further reading

Dekle, D.J. *et al.* (1992) Audiovisual integration in perception of real words. *Perception and Psychophysics*, 51, 355–62.

Green, K.P. and Gerdman, A. (1995) Cross-modal discrepancies in coarticulation and the integration of speech information: The McGurk effect with mismatched vowels. *Journal of Experimental Psychology: Human Perception and Performance*, 21, 1409–26.

McGurk, H. (ed) (1992) *Childhood Social Development: Contemporary Perspectives*. Erlbaum.

Harry McGurk is a developmental psychologist. His initial research was concerned with basic perception-cognitive processes: infant ability to discriminate between different rotations and orientations of the same form while preserving form identity, and young children's ability to discriminate depth relations in pictures. Work in both areas was methodologically innovative, and many of the procedures presently used to study infant concept acquisition and categorical discrimination can be traced to the variations on the basic habituation paradigm which he introduced during the early 1970s. Methods used to study pictorial depth perception, developed with Gustav **Jahoda**, were much more sensitive than any previously employed, and they have been used to demonstrate the basic similarity of the processes invested in such perception among children from African, Asian and European cultures.

Later McGuire became interested in the development of bi-modal perception and especially in the development of co-ordination between vision and hearing. This work led to the discovery of the so-called 'McGurk Effect' – the illusions of speech experienced by normally hearing children and adults when viewing dubbed film. For example /ba/ voice dubbed onto /ga/ lips is heard as /da/ by normally hearing listeners as young as 18 months of age.

More recently he has investigated the development of basic perceptual and other skills in social context. This includes work on parents' concepts of their children, how these influence the interpretation of and attribution of social significance to early behaviour, and how, in turn, this facilitates or impedes the development of personal and social competence during infancy and early childhood.

McKellar, Thomas Peter Huntly

Born: 1921, Dunedin, New Zealand **Nat:** New Zealander **Ints:** Abnormal psychology, general psychology, history of ideas, imagination, perception, thinking **Educ:** BA University of New Zealand, 1941; MA University of New Zealand, 1942; PhD University of London, 1949 **Appts & awards:** University of Otago, New Zealand, Professor of Psychology, 1968–86, Emeritus Professor, 1986– ; Visiting Professor, Middlesex University, 1992– ; Fellow, BPS; Honorary Fellow, New Zealand Psychological Society

Principal publications

1954   Between wakefulness and sleep: Hypnagogic imagery. *British Journal of Psychology*, 45, 266–327 (with L. Simpson).

1956   Types of synaesthesia. *Journal of Mental Science*, 100, 141–7 (with L. Simpson).

1957   *Imagination and Thinking: A Psychological Analysis*. Cohen and West/Basic Books.

1963   The method of introspection. In J.M. Scher (ed.), *Theories of Mind*. Free Press.

1967   Negative hallucination, dissociation, and the 'Five Stamps' experiment. *British Journal of Social Psychiatry*, 1, 260–76 (with H. Tonn).

1968   *Experience and Behavior*. Penguin.

1977   Autonomy, imagery and dissociation. *Journal of Mental Imagery*, 1, 93–108.

1979   *Mindsplit: The Psychology of Multiple Personality and the Dissociated Self*. Dent.

1982   The nature and function of eidetic imagery. *Journal of Mental Imagery*, 6, 1–124 (with D.F. Marks).

1986   Imagery and the unconscious. In D.F. Marks (ed.), *Theories of Image Formation*. Brandon House.

1989   *Abnormal Psychology: Its Experience and Behaviour*. Routledge.

1995   Creative imagination: Hypnagogia and surrealism. *Journal of Mental Imagery*, 19, 33–42.

Further reading

Horn, D.L. (1991) The normalizing of abnormal behavior. *Contemporary Psychology*, 36, 894–5.

Schacter, D.L. (1976) The hypnagogic state: A critical review of the literature. *Psychological Bulletin*, 83, 452–81.

After taking his first degrees in New Zealand and doing personnel selection work for the RNZAF, Peter McKellar departed in 1945 for PhD study at London University. Following his move to Aberdeen University, he conducted experimental studies on hallucinogens with his co-worker, Lorna Simpson. McKellar became interested in phenomena like synaesthesia and hypnagogic imagery. The resemblance between mescaline-induced and hypnagogic imagery was examined.

His return to New Zealand was in 1968 to the headship of the Department of Psychology at Otago University, the world's southernmost university. In the tradition of William **James**, Peter McKellar's work reveals a sustained interest in subjective experience, particularly in 'hidden differences between people'. In 1954 David Bakan reconsidered introspection and argued that psychologists too often have failed to 'look into any minds – least of all their own.' He added: 'and their work shows it!' McKellar agrees. He believes that 'mind' is a word of everyday speech, not science, but finds it curious that 'the most relevant branch of science – human psychology – had from 1920 until 1960 placed a peculiarly strong taboo on its use'. In this and other robust defences of introspective inquiry McKellar engaged in what he calls 'psychological natural history', the description and classification of subjective phenomena of nature.

A long-standing interest in the history of science, philosophy and literature helped McKellar to side-step the obvious and merely fashionable and indeed sometimes to anticipate and help to create the *Zeitgeist*. Thus McKellar's *Imagination and Thinking* helped rehabilitate the scientific study of mental imagery before the so-called 'cognitive revolution' of 1960. In 1977, McKellar anticipated the theoretical reinvestigation of hypnotically induced dissociation, successfully replicating some of **McDougall**'s research with the addition of positive as well as negative hypnotic hallucinations. In this period Ernest **Hilgard** was also conducting his 'hidden observer' experiments. With these, and Hilgard's 'neo-dissociation' theory, now dissociation – like imagery before it – has returned to mainstream psychology.

McKellar travelled widely in Asia, Europe, America and Oceania, retaining an understandable interest in cross-cultural psychology. A favourite place is the American Southwest, where he learned about Pueblo and Navajo cultures and the abnormal psychology of indigenous Americans.

Horn's review in *Contemporary Psychology* of McKellar's *Abnormal Psychology* notes how McKellar's approach carefully avoids being a mere elaboration of 'major diagnostic subgroups' but instead 'is organized primarily around complex psychological phenomena'. Horn also notes that the book's 'seven basic principles of psychology, the "William James", "**Koffka**", "Hobbes" and other basic potential "laws of psychology"', offer guides to psychol-

ogy's future. Peter McKellar's contribution has been the recognition that a scientific study of experience and behaviour is predicated upon a proper description and classification of human subjective experience. His investigation of the human imagination provides a foundation stone.

DAVID F. MARKS

MacKinnon, Donald Wallace

Born: 1903, Augusta, Maine, USA **Died:** 1987, Stockton, California, USA **Nat:** American **Ints:** Creativity, personality theory and assessment **Educ:** BA Bowdoin College, 1924; MA Harvard University, 1926; PhD Harvard University, 1933 **Appts & awards:** Sheldon Traveling Fellow of Harvard, 1930–31; Bryn Mawr, 1933–47; US Office of Strategic Services, 1944–6; University of California at Berkeley, 1947–71; Director, Institute of Personality Assessment and Research, University of California at Berkeley, 1949–70; President, APA Division 8 (Personality and Social Psychology), 1952; Member, Psychology Panel, US Armed Forces, 1953–6; Member, Board of Directors, APA, 1956; Member, Standing Committee on Research, Educational Testing Service, 1957–64; Member, Psychology Sub-Committee of National Institutes of Health, 1961–5; Member, Advisory Research Board, National Merit Scholarship Corporation 1962–4; Member, Board of Directors, California State Psychological Association, 1962–5; Richardson Foundation Creativity Award, APA, 1967; Professor Emeritus, University of California at Berkeley, 1971–87; Visiting Fellow, Center for Creative Leadership, 1973–4; Founders Medal, Creative Education Foundation, 1978; Henry A. Murray Award, APA Division 8, 1981; Member, Board of Trustees, Creative Education Foundation 1984–7

Principal publications

1944 The structure of personality. In J. McV. Hunt (ed.), *Personality and the Behavior Disorders*. Ronald Press.

1951 Personality. *Annual Review of Psychology*, 2, 113–6.

1952 Fact and fancy in personality research. *American Psychologist*, 8, 138–46.

1962 The nature and nurture of creative talent. *American Psychologist*, 17, 484–95.

1962 The personality correlates of creativity: A study of American architects. In G.S. Nielsen (ed.), *Proceedings of XIV International Congress of Applied Psychology*. Munksgaard.

1978   *In Search of Human Effectiveness:
Identifying and Developing Creativity.* Creative
Education Foundation, Creative Synergetic
Associates.

Further reading

Craik, K.H., Gough, H.G., Hall, W.B. and Helson, R.
(1989) Donald W. MacKinnon (1903–1987).
American Psychologist, 44, 731–2.
OSS Assessment Staff (1948) *Assessment of Men:
Selection of Personnel for the Office of Strategic
Services.* Rinehart.

Impressed, as most of us are, by creative
achievements, D.W. MacKinnon studied effective, creative persons – artists, architects,
inventors – and the settings in which they work.
He relied at first on psychodynamic explanations, primarily those of **Rank**, **Jung** and
Freud, as well as on the ideas and methods of
his mentor, Henry **Murray**. Throughout his
career, he continued to emphasize the importance of intrapsychic dynamics; but the influence
of Murray and many other American psychologists led him to acknowledge the crucial role of
individual differences in ability and motivation,
and of circumstances conducive to creative
endeavour. He was intrigued by the question:
What are the characteristics of a fertile intellectual environment? Why were **Lewin**'s
research groups at Berlin and the University of
Iowa, and Murray's at Harvard (in which
MacKinnon had participated as a graduate
student), for example, so much more productive
of ideas and research output than other, comparable groups?

A skilful administrator and co-ordinator,
MacKinnon made his biggest contributions to
psychology by establishing research centres. He
served for two years at Field Station S in the
assessment programme of the US Office of
Strategic Services (OSS, the predecessor of
today's Central Intelligence Agency) and then,
for twenty-one years, as Director of the University of California's Institute of Personality
Assessment and Research (IPAR, since
renamed the Institute of Personality and Social
Research). His career can be seen as a sustained
effort to identify and recruit effective
individuals and to assemble them into effective
groups.

Although half of *Assessment of Men* is
devoted to the methods and results of an intensive selection procedure applied to 2371
candidates at Station S, there are few specifics
about who did what. However, MacKinnon's

role as Acting Director of the Harvard Psychological Clinic during the 1920s and as a
leader in the OSS assessment programme in the
1940s documents his commitment and influence
as an early champion of multimethod assessment and multivariate analysis. He was one of
the five principal authors of *Assessment of Men*.

Shortly after he accepted a faculty position at
Berkeley, IPAR was founded and he was named
Director. MacKinnon made IPAR into a highly
effective research facility; under his leadership it
soon earned international renown. Work at IPAR
maintained the OSS selection programme's
emphasis on intensive multimethod assessment,
but was much broader in terms of populations
studied and research designs used. In general, it
went beyond the OSS approach by extending the
study of individual differences to include outcome variables. In particular, it placed heavy
emphasis on predictive validity, and examined
short- and long-term development sequences.

MacKinnon played a large role in the success
of IPAR. He was able to obtain funds (from the
University of California, the Carnegie Corporation of New York, and the Rockefeller
Foundation) and work space, to attract and keep
capable investigators, to foster independence
and collaboration, and to hold the focus of IPAR
research programmes for several years on creativity and the psychology of effectively
functioning individuals. He possessed notable
skills in working with social scientists, stimulating them to concerted effort by providing them
with near-optimal circumstances for creative
activity. In retrospect then, his professional life
can be seen as a realization of the applied
psychologist's dream, where one's academic
interests blend into real-world accomplishment.

R.N. WOLFE

Mackintosh, Nicholas John

Born: 1935, London, England *Nat:* British *Ints:*
Experimental, evaluation and measurement,
physiological and comparative *Educ:* BA Uni-
versity of Oxford, 1960; MA, DPhil University
of Oxford, 1963 *Appts & awards:* Member,
Experimental Psychology Society, 1963– ;
Fellow, Royal Society Experimental Psychology
Committee, 1976–84; Professor and Head of
Department of Experimental Psychology, Uni-
versity of Cambridge, 1981– ; Fellow, King's
College; Member, BPS, 1982– ; President's
Award, 1986; Editorial Board, *Journal of Com-
parative and Physiological Psychology*,
1969–73, *Journal of Experimental Psychology:*

Animal Behavior Processes, 1975– , Oxford Psychology Series (Oxford University Press), 1979– , Weidenfeld Psychology Series (Weidenfeld and Nicolson), 1981– ; Editor, *Quarterly Journal of Experimental Psychology*, 1977–80, *Quarterly Journal of Experimental Psychology, Section B: Comparative and Physiological Psychology*, 1981–4

Principal publications

1965 Selective attention in animal discrimination learning. *Psychological Bulletin*, 64, 124–50.

1965 Discrimination learning in the octopus. *Animal Behaviour Supplement*, 1, 129–34.

1969 *Fundamental Issues in Associative Learning*. Dalhousie University Press.

1969 *Mechanisms of Animal Discrimination Learning*. Academic Press (with W.K. Honig).

1969 Further analysis of the overtraining reversal effect. *Journal of Comparative and Physiological Psychology Monograph*, 67, pt. 2, 1–18.

1969 Comparative psychology of serial reversal and probability learning: Rats, birds and fish. In R. Gilbert and N.S. Sutherland (eds), *Animal Discrimination Learning*. Academic Press.

1971 Blocking as a function of novelty of CS and predictability of UCS. *Quarterly Journal of Experimental Psychology*, 23, 359–66 (with C. Turner).

1974 *The Psychology of Animal Learning*. Academic Press (with N.S. Sutherland).

1975 A theory of attention: Variations in the associability of stimuli with reinforcement. *Psychological Review*, 82, 276–98.

1977 Locus of the effect of a surprising reinforcer in the attenuation of blocking. *Quarterly Journal of Experimental Psychology*, 29, 327–36 (with D.J. Bygrave and B.M.B. Picton).

1979 Reinforcer specificity in the enhancement of conditioning by post-trial surprise. *Journal of Experimental Psychology: Animal Behaviour Processes*, 5, 162–77 (with A. Dickinson).

1979 Instrumental (type II) conditioning. In A. Dickinson and R.A. Boakes (eds), *Mechanisms of Learning and Motivation*. Erlbaum (with A. Dickinson).

1983 *Conditioning and Associative Learning*. Oxford University Press.

1985 The IQ question. In *Report of a Committee of Inquiry into the Education of Children from Ethnic Minorities*. HMSO.

1994 The evolution of intelligence. In J. Khalfa (ed.), *Intelligence*. Cambridge University Press.

1994 (ed.) *Handbook of Perception and Cognition, vol. 9: Animal Learning and Cognition*. Academic Press.

Further reading

Khalfa, J. (ed) (1994) *What is Intelligence?* Cambridge University Press.

Mackintosh, N.J. and Colman, A.M. (eds) (1995) *Learning Skills*. Longman.

Professor Mackintosh describes his interest in animal psychology as originating from his reading of **Köhler**'s *Mentality of Apes* and **Tinbergen**'s *Study of Instinct* before he ever started to read psychology. From the first, therefore, he had little sympathy for the theories of learning advanced by **Hull**, **Spence** and others, and his research was always directed towards emphasizing alternative views. Initially, there were ideas about discrimination learning, acquired from Stuart Sutherland, based on the perceptual notion that animals must learn to categorize stimuli as well as associate them with their consequences. But in due course, as it rather surprisingly became evident that the effects of selective attention observed in discrimination learning could also be observed in **Pavlov**ian conditioning, he began to study simple conditioning, and the theories of attention which such a study suggested had rather little in common with the position from which he had started.

Kohler and Tinbergen also provided an interest in animals other than rats and pigeons, and from the first he dabbled in research on octopus, fish, doves, chickens and crows. The octopus turned out to behave very much like a rat in these experiments, but other animals did not always do so. One challenge of comparative psychology, then, is to understand the difference in process or mechanism underlying an apparent difference in behaviour (there are of course others, such as whether differences in behaviour are correlated with differences in ecology). The notion that we are looking for differences in 'intelligence' is not a particularly helpful one – we are looking for detailed differences in subprocesses. But this thought naturally leads one to wonder whether the notion of intelligence is any more useful when applied to people, and that leads to another side interest for Mackintosh in intelligence testing.

Magnusson, David N.

Born: 1925, Nassjo, Sweden ***Nat:*** Swedish ***Ints:*** Development, personality, social ***Educ:*** BA University of Stockholm, 1955; Filosofie licentiate, University of Stockholm, 1957; PhD University of Stockholm, 1959 ***Appts & awards:***

Chairman, Swedish Psychological Association, 1961–2, Swedish Association for University Professors, 1970–8; Professor of Psychology and Chairman, Department of Psychology, University of Stockholm, 1969–92, Emeritus, 1993– ; Member, Royal Academy of Letters, History and Antiquities, 1977– ; Vice-Chairman, Swedish Research Council for Social Sciences and Humanities, 1977–83; Royal Academy of Sciences, Member, 1979, Executive Committee, 1986– , Vice-President, 1991– , Chairman, Economics and Social Science Section, 1991; Hon. Dr, University of Jyvaskyla, Finland, 1984; Swedish Representative, Executive Council of European Science Foundation, 1984– ; Editor, *Multivariate Behavioral Research, Applied Psychological Measurement, German Journal of Psychology, Annual Review of Social Psychology, Journal of Theoretical Psychology, Zeitschrift für Psychologie, Journal of Child Psychology and Psychiatry, Anxiety Research, European Journal of Personality, European Journal of Psychology of Education, Personality and Individual Differences, Development and Psychopathology*

Principal publications

1967   *Test Theory.* Addison-Wesley

1975   *Adjustment: A Longitudinal Study* (with A. Duner and G. Zetterblom).

1977   *Personality at the Crossroads* (with N.S. Endler).

1980   Personality in an interactional paradigm of research. *Zeitschrift für Differentielle und Diagnostische Psychologie*, 1, 17–34.

1981   *Toward a Psychology of Situations: An Interactional Perspective.* Academic Press.

1981   Stability of cross-situational patterns of behavior. *Journal of Research in Personality*, 15, 488–96.

1983   *Human Development: An Interactional Perspective.* Academic Press (with V. Allen).

1985   Implications of an interactional paradigm of research on human development. *International Journal of Behavior and Development*, 8, 115–37.

1990   *Data Quality in Longitudinal Research.* Cambridge University Press (with L.R. Bergman).

1991   Coping, control and experience of anxiety: An interactional perspective. *Anxiety Research*, 3, 1–16 (with B. Törestad and A. Oláh)

1993   *Longitudinal Research on Individual Development: Presentations and Future Perspectives.* Cambridge University Press.

David Magnusson considers the goal of psychological theory and research to be the under-standing and explanation of why individuals think, feel, react and act as they do in real-life situations. The general frame of reference for Magnusson's work and its contribution to that goal has been an interactional perspective based on two main propositions, which should be taken together: (1) that an individual develops and functions in a dynamic, continuously ongoing and bi-directional interaction with the environment at various levels of generality; and (2) that in this process of interaction, the way an individual functions is determined by a continuously ongoing, reciprocal interaction among internal sub-systems of psychological and biological factors within the individual. The first of these two propositions has been emphasized for many decades and belongs to what may be called classical interactionism, while the second proposition belongs to what may be designated modern interactionism, fostered by the rapid development in endocrinology, pharmacology and neuropsychology. Magnusson's theoretical contributions have, in his own words, 'concentrated on making explicit the theoretical, methodological and research strategical consequences of an interactional perspective and on emphasizing the necessity of taking them seriously'.

Empirically he has presented studies using an interactional perspective for investigating why individuals think, feel, react and act as they do. These studies have been concerned with individual functioning in a contemporaneous perspective, particularly with individuals' cross-situational patterns of relevant variables. For the study of the individual functioning developmentally he initiated and conducted a longitudinal research programme in which two representative cohorts, comprising 1000–1100 boys and girls each, have been followed from school age to adulthood, using data for psychological and biological factors on the individual side and social and physical factors on the environmental side.

Mailloux, Noel

Born: 1909, Napierville, Quebec, Canada *Nat:* Canadian *Ints:* Clinical, psychoanalysis, psychology and religion, theoretical and philosophical *Educ:* BA University of Montreal, 1930; PhD St Thomas University of Rome, 1934; SThL, St Thomas University of Rome, 1938 *Appts & awards:* Research Fellowship, Department of Psychology, University of Cincinnati, 1939; Professor of Experimental Psychology,

Faculty of Philosophy and Theology of the Dominica Order, Ottawa, Ontario, 1939–42; Charter Member, Board of Directors, École Normale Secondaire, Montreal, 1941–66; Head, Department of Psychology, University of Montreal, 1942–57, 1969–73; Director of Scientific and Professional Services, Residential Treatment Center for Children, Montreal, 1943–74; President, Quebec Psychological Association, 1945–6; Diplomate in clinical psychology from the American Board of Examiners in Professional Psychology 1948; Director, Research Center on Human Relations, Montreal, 1950–75; President, Canadian Psychological Association, 1954–5; Career Research Award, Canadian Mental Health Association, 1959; President, Quebec Corrections Association 1960–2; Vice-Dean, Faculty of Philosophy, University of Montreal, 1960–9; President, Canadian Corrections Association, 1962–5; Fellow, Royal Society of Canada, 1963; Member, Council of the Society for the Scientific Study of Religion, 1964–6; Service Medal, Officer of the Order of Canada, 1967; Life Member, Canadian Social Welfare Council, 1968; Professor Emeritus, University of Montreal, 1975– ; Hermann Mannheim Award of the International Center for Criminology, 1978; Leon-Gerin Prize for Contribution to the Cultural Development of Quebec, 1979; Thérèse Casgrain Award for Advancement of Social Causes, 1988; Certificate of Recognition, Canadian Federation of Social Sciences, 1990; Editorial Board, *Contributions à l'Étude des Sciences de l'Homme, Canadian Journal of Psychology, Canadian Journal of Criminology, Excerpta Criminologica, Catholic Psychological Record, Psychologia, Acta Criminologica*

Principal publications

1940   The work curve of psychotic individuals. *Journal of Abnormal and Social Psychology*, 36, 110–14.

1942   The problem of perception. *Thomist*, 4, 266–85.

1943   L'enfant et la formation de son caractère. *L'Enseignement Secondaire au Canada*, 23, 8–25.

1948   Research planning in clinical psychology. *Canadian Journal of Psychology*, 2, 19–22.

1953   Psychic determinism, freedom and personality development. *Canadian Journal of Psychology*, 9, 131–43.

1959   Sanctity and the problem of neurosis. *Pastoral Psychology*, 10, 37–43.

1960   A clinical study of religious attitudes and a new approach to psychopathology. In H.P. David

and J.C. Brengelman (eds), *New Perspectives in Personality Research*. Springer-Verlag (with L. Ancona).

1964   Scrupulosity in pastoral work. In W.C. Bier (ed.), *Personality and Sexual Problems in Pastoral Work*. Fordham University Press.

1965   Functioning of the superego in delinquents. In D.E. Cameron (ed.), *Forensic Psychiatry and Child Psychiatry*. Little, Brown.

1967   La communication pastorale avec les groups d'adolescents antisociaux. *La Revue Canadienne de Criminologie*, 9, 60–97.

1977   Re-education and rehabilitation of the criminal. In S. Landau and L. Sebba (eds), *Criminology in Perspective: Essays in honor of Israel Drapkin*. Heath.

Further reading

Landau, S. and Sebba, L. (eds) (1977) *Criminology in Perspective*. Heath.

Noel Mailloux received a baccalaureate degree at the University of Montreal and two advanced degrees at St Thomas University in Rome. He became a Dominican priest in 1937, and spent his life as a practitioner (psychotherapist and priest, sometimes separate, sometimes combined) and institutionalizing agent for applied psychology in Montreal. His commitments were to Roman Catholicism and psychodynamic theory; he believed they could be reconciled and combined to form a viable basis for the helping professions.

For half a century, Father Mailloux was an effective social activist on behalf of clinical psychology in Canada. Although he wrote extensively, the average reader will have difficulty appreciating his *oeuvre*; it consists mainly of short essays in comparatively obscure journals in several languages. To obtain a complete set of his papers, one would need access to the 'Catholic underground' as well as the resources of a mainstream library; to read all, one would have to be literate in French, English, German, Spanish and Italian. His writings in English do not convey a flavour of the activism which was his chief contribution to psychology.

Mailloux's journal articles span an impressive range of years (1936–84) and topics (educational psychology, child development, criminology and delinquency, the interface of psychology and theology, methods of diagnosis and treatment, practitioners' ethics, research agendas for clinical psychology in Canada, the philosophy of personal values and morality), as well as languages. They number well over a hundred. He was also active as a contributor to edited collections, and as a member of the editorial board of several journals.

Father Mailloux's continuing influence is embodied in the institutions he helped to establish. The best known of these are the Canadian Psychological Association and its journals, and the Psychology Department of the University of Montreal. Mailloux was active in the Canadian Psychological Association at its inception, serving on its membership and research planning committees. He was nominated to the Board of Directors for 1947–8, by which time the Association had grown to 500 members, and later served as its president.

In founding and leading the University of Montreal's Psychology Department, and as Vice-Dean of the Faculty of Philosophy, Mailloux was a purposeful administrator. He obtained resources, space, facilities; he recruited capable instructors and research psychologists. His pioneering efforts soon bore fruit. As the University of Montreal developed into a multiversity, the Psychology Department grew rapidly; it now consists of fifty-one faculty members and offers programmes leading to advanced degrees in all psychological specialities.

Mailloux's organizational initiatives cast him in other roles as well. He was instrumental in forming the Quebec Psychological Association during the 1930s and served as its president in 1945–6. He founded a residential treatment facility for problem children and was its director for thirty years. He was one of the founders of Montreal's Ecole Normale Secondaire, and helped to oversee its operations for fifteen years. He established the University's Research Centre on Human Relations, serving as its first Director.

An energetic social engineer, Father Mailloux created psychological institutions of various kinds. Many of them have already turned out to be highly consequential, exerting important effects on his home university, on social programmes in Montreal, and on twentieth-century psychology in Quebec and throughout Canada.

R.N. WOLFE

Mandler, George

Born: 1924, Vienna, Austria **Nat:** Austrian **Ints:** Cognitive science, experimental psychology, general psychology, history of psychology, personality and social psychology **Educ:** BA New York University, 1949; MS New York University, 1950; PhD Yale University, 1953 **Appts & awards:** Professor of Psychology and Director, Center for Human Information Processing, University of California at San Diego; APA, Council of Representatives, 1970–3, 1979–82, 1986–8; Guggenheim Fellow, 1971; Society of Experimental Psychologists Board of Advisors, Archives of the History of Psychology, 1974–82; Board of Trustees, Association for the Advancement of Psychology, 1974–82; USA President, Division of Experimental Psychology, 1978; President, APA, Division of General Psychology, 1982; President, Federation of Behavioral, Psychological and Cognitive Societies, 1981; Chairman, Governing Board, Psychonomic Society, 1983; Editorial Board, *Psychological Monographs*, 1963–6, *Journal of Verbal Learning and Verbal Behavior*, 1968–84, *Contemporary Psychology*, 1976, *Motivation and Emotion*, 1977– , *Cognitive Psychology*, 1978– , *Social Cognition*, 1980– , *Journal of Memory and Language*, 1984–; Series Co-editor, Perspectives in Psychology (Wiley), 1964–76; Advisory Editor, Wiley, 1965–82, Erlbaum, 1974– ; Editor, *Psychological Review*, 1970–6

Principal publications

1952 A study of anxiety and learning. *Journal of Abnormal and Social Psychology*, 47, 166–73 (with S.B. Sarason).

1954 Response factors in human learning. *Psychological Review*, 61, 243–4.

1958 Autonomic feedback: The perception of autonomic activity. *Journal of Abnormal and Social Psychology*, 56, 367–73 (with J.M. Mandler and E.T. Uviller).

1959 *The Language of Psychology*. Wiley (with W. Kessen).

1962 From association to structure. *Psychological Review*, 69, 415–27.

1964 *Thinking: From Association to Gestalt*. Wiley (with J.M. Mandler).

1964 The interruption of behavior. In D. Levine (ed.), *Nebraska Symposium on Motivation*. University of Nebraska Press.

1967 Organization and memory. In K.W. Spence and J.T. Spence (eds), *The Psychology of Learning and Motivation*. Academic Press.

1975 *Mind and Emotion*. Wiley.

1975 Consciousness: Respectable, useful and probably necessary. In R. Solso (ed.), *Information Processing and Cognition: The Loyola Symposium*. Erlbaum.

1980 Recognizing: The judgment of previous occurrence. *Psychological Review*, 87, 252–71.

1982 Simulating amnesic symptoms in normals. *Science*, 218, 1243–4.
1984 Cohabitation in the cognitive sciences. In W. Kintsch, J.R. Miller and P.G. Polson (eds), *Method and Tactics in Cognitive Science*. Erlbaum.
1984 *Mind and Body*. Norton.
1985 *Cognitive Psychology: An Essay in Cognitive Science*. Erlbaum.

Further reading
Kessen, W., Ortony, A. and Craik, F. (eds) (1991) *Memories, Thoughts, and Emotions: Essays in Honor of George Mandler*. Erlbaum.

George Mandler's introduction to psychology was delayed by the advent of German fascism; first, as a refugee (in England) and later, when he served in the US Army. The combined experience left a lasting interest in the social conditions of the human mind (and of psychology).

When he started graduate studies, his initial interest was in clinical psychology. However, that direction was soon displaced by a concern with theoretical and experimental work – to a large extent due to the influence of Carl I. **Hovland** at Yale. In the end he completed a clinical degree, but an experimental thesis. That dual interest continued in the following years as he worked in parallel on problems of anxiety and emotion and on human memory and thinking. He became part of the changing scene in American psychology and in particular of the disengagement from behaviourism, working on structural and organizational factors in memory, as well as on the psychological (cognitive) conditions of emotional experience. These interests led naturally to an analysis of consciousness and its functional utility in human thought and action. When he had the opportunity in 1965 to start a new department, as well as the Center for Human Information Processing, at the University of California at San Diego, his involvement with the 'new' psychology was complete.

Within ten years his interests in emotion and thinking coalesced into his first effort at a cognitive psychology of emotion. At the same time he continued his problem-solving proclivities with the experimental study of memory. His concern with the social context of psychology continued, as reflected in his analysis of the context of the new cognitive psychology. He remains primarily concerned with the problem of the social conditions of the human mind within the framework of a responsible cognitive psychology.

Marr, David Courtney
Born: 1945, Rugby, England **Died:** 1980, Boston, Massachusetts, USA **Nat:** British **Ints:** Cognitive science, experimental psychology, physiological and comparative psychology, theoretical and philosophical psychology **Appts & awards:** Senior Fellowship, Kings College Cambridge, 1972; Research Scientist, MIT, 1976–80

Principal publications
1976 Cooperation computation of stereo disparity. *Science*, 194, 283–7.
1979 A computational theory of human stereo vision. *Proceedings of the Royal Society of London*, B 204, 301–28 (with T. Poggio).
1980 Theory of edge detection. *Proceedings of the Royal Society of London*, B 207, 187–217.
1982 *Vision*. W.H. Freeman (posthumous).

Further reading
Gordon, I.E. (1989) *Theories of Visual Perception*. Wiley.
Morgan, M.J. (1984) Computational theories of vision. *Quarterly Journal of Experimental Psychology*, 36A, 157–65.

While holding a research fellowship at Cambridge David Marr used his knowledge of mathematics to construct a model of the workings of the cerebellum. Aware of the limitations in the model and technical difficulties associated with its implementation in software he visited the Artificial Intelligence Laboratory at MIT in 1973. He returned in 1975 and decided to remain there. He had an extraordinarily productive five years at MIT. He suffered with leukaemia for three of those five years and died at the age of 35 at the height of his career and just three weeks after his marriage. He finished his highly influential book *Vision* (published posthumously in 1982) just before his death.

David Marr made fundamental contributions to the development of a computational approach to visual perception. He developed and tested theories of how the brain carries out intelligent tasks, such as seeing, by casting them in the form of computer programs. His approach makes an important distinction between representation and description: 'A representation is a formal system for making explicit certain entities or types of information, together with a representation of how the system does this.... The result of using a representation to describe a given entity (is) a description of the entity in that representation.' He introduced three levels of explanation which he argued must be kept separate in thinking about an informational process, such as vision. The three levels are: the computational theory, the algorithm and the hardware implementation. At the level of computational theory we are concerned with determining the goal of the computation, its appropriateness and the strategy for carrying it out. At the level of algorithm we are concerned with the implementation of the computational theory in software. At the level of hardware implementation we are concerned with building a machine that implements the computational theory. For example, when considering the perception of contour one must begin by asking why it is useful to extract contour information from the visual image and how might this information be represented in the brain? When these kinds of questions have been answered we can proceed to the development of an algorithm that can detect contours in a visual image and produce a symbolic representation of what is seen. Finally, we can attempt to specify a machine that can actually detect and represent contour information according to the theory and using the algorithm.

Marr's theory of vision is modular: it is an information-processing system organised in stages. He distinguishes four stages: the image, the primal sketch, the 2-and-a-half-D sketch and the 3-D model representation. The image can be thought of as a spatial distribution of intensity values across the retina and is the starting point of seeing. The primal sketch involves producing an organized representation of the intensity values with regard to their spatial and geometrical distribution. The 2-and-a-half-D sketch involves producing a representation of the orientation and general depth of visible surfaces. The 3-D model produces a representation of the visual scene in an object-centred framework, independent of particular positions and orientation on the retina.

Marr's computational approach to visual perception made fundamental changes to the way psychologists and vision scientists have developed and tested their theories. The idea of different levels of explanation has been particularly powerful. The requirements for formal rigour when specifying and implementing a computational theory have forced psychologists and vision scientists to make explicit assumptions which had been taken for granted or gone unnoticed. Aspects of Marr's work have attracted considerable criticism, principally on technical details and in his application of his approach to particular problems in vision, such as stereopsis. However, as he noted in the preface to *Vision*, he recognized that some of the ideas in the book were premature and not fully worked through but time was against him, and it was better to get the book finished in that form than to never publish it at all. The enduring impact of his work has shown this to have been a wise and a brave decision.

Maslow, Abraham H.

Born: 1908, New York City, USA *Died:* 1970, Menlo Park, California, USA *Nat:* American *Ints:* Abnormal psychology, human motivation, personality *Educ:* BA, 1930, MA, 1931, PhD, 1934 University of Wisconsin, Madison *Appts & awards:* Department of Psychology: Columbia Teachers College, 1935–7, Brooklyn College, 1937–51, Brandeis University, 1951–69; Carnegie Teaching Fellowship, 1935–7; President, Massachusetts Psychological Association, 1960–2; President, New England Psychological Association, 1962–3; President, APA, 1967; Humanist of the Year Award, American Humanist Association, 1967; Laughlin Foundation Fellowship, 1969–70; Hon. Dr, Xavier University, Cincinnati; Founded, *Eupsychian Management: A Journal*

Principal publications

1937   Chapter on cross-cultural psychology. Ross Stagner (ed), In *The Psychology of Personality*.
1941   *Principles of Abnormal Psychology*. Harper and Row (with B. Mittelman). (Rev. edn, 1951.)
1942   *The Social Personality Inventory: A Test for Self Esteem in Women*. Consulting Psychologists Press.
1943   A theory of human motivation. *Psychological Review*, 50, 370–96.
1943   The dynamics of personality organization I and II. *Psychological Review*, 50, 541–58.
1951   Volunteer-error in the Kinsey study, co-authored with J. Sakoda. *Journal of Abnormal and Social Psychology*, 47, 259–62.
1954   *Motivation and Personality*. Harper and Row. (Rev. edn, 1970.)
1959   *New Knowledge in Human Values*. Harper and Row.
1962   *Toward a Psychology of Being*. Van Nostrand. (2nd edn, 1968.)
1964   *Religion, Values and Peak Experiences (Lectures)*. Ohio State University Press.
1965   *Eupsychian Management: A Journal*. Irwin.
1966   *The Psychology of Science: A Reconnaissance*. Harper and Row.

1971   *The Farther Reaches of Human Nature.*
Viking.

Further reading

Goble, F. (1970) *The Third Force: The Psychology of Abraham Maslow.* Grossman.

Hoffman, E. (1988) *The Right to be Human: A Biography of Abraham Maslow.* St Martin's.

Lowry, R.J. (ed.) (1973) *Dominance, Self-Esteem and Self-Actualization: Germinal Papers of A.H. Maslow.* Brooks/Cole.

—— (ed.) (1979) *The Journals of A.H. Maslow*, 2 vols. Brooks/Cole.

Undergraduate coursework at the City College of New York and Cornell University stimulated Maslow's interest in psychology. In 1928, he transferred to the University of Wisconsin, majoring in psychology and completing degrees at Madison campus. The professors who most influenced him were behaviourists: Clark **Hull**, Norman Cameron, William Sheldon and Harry **Harlow**. His dissertation research, on dominance and sexuality in monkeys, was supervised by Harlow.

After a two-year appointment as assistant to E.L. **Thorndike** at Columbia Teaching College, Maslow took a teaching position at Brooklyn College and remained there until 1951. Throughout the Columbia and Brooklyn College years, he interacted with many scholars in the New York City area, particularly those affiliated with Columbia University and the New School for Social Research. Maslow became acquainted with **Fromm**, **Koffka**, **Wertheimer**, **Horney**, Sullivan, Benedict, Linton, **Mead**, Horkheimer, Kardiner, **Adler**, Goldstein and Ansbacher and was influenced by their ideas. During the late 1930s he conducted anthropological fieldwork on the Blackfoot Indian Reservation near Gleichen, Alberta, and wrote a chapter on cross-cultural psychology for Ross Stagner's *The Psychology of Personality* (1937).

In the mid-1940s, Maslow was contacted by Alfred Kinsey, the noted sexologist, who knew of his doctoral research at Wisconsin and who planned to interview a sample of Brooklyn College women regarding their sexual behaviour. Potential collaboration between the two was thwarted, however, when Maslow challenged the sampling procedures used in Kinsey's survey of women. In his 1951 report co-authored with J. Sakoda, Maslow documented his claim that Kinsey's sample was biased, hence not representative of the population.

Maslow presented his main contribution to psychological thought in his two 1943 *Psychological Review* articles, and elaborated on them in his 1954 book *Motivation and Personality*. His theory focuses on distinctions between lower (deficiency) and higher (growth) needs. It postulates a nested hierarchy – physiological, safety, belongingness and love, esteem, self-actualization – with the lower needs being prepotent: in most cases, they have to be satisfied in order for the higher needs to come into play. Satisfaction of needs is essential for normal development. Confronted with a choice between satisfying a lower or a higher need, people will usually opt to satisfy the lower. Satisfaction of lower needs is of course necessary for survival and physical health, but maximum psychological health and growth arise only from attempts to satisfy higher needs.

Many of the theory's basic propositions concern higher needs, as contrasted with lower needs, for example:

(1) they are later phyletic or evolutionary developments;
(2) they are later ontogenetic developments;
(3) they are less vital to survival – they can be postponed longer;
(4) if unfulfilled, they are more likely to disappear completely;
(5) though they are less subjectively urgent, their satisfaction leads to 'more profound happiness, serenity and richness of the inner life' as well as to 'desirable civic and social consequences';
(6) their emergence and satisfaction entail more preconditions and require a more favourable environment.

Maslow was much concerned with higher needs. He conjectured that other needs might lie beyond self-actualization – the needs to know and understand, perhaps, self-transcendence needs, aesthetic needs – and sought to characterize those whose lives seemed to be lived mostly at the level of higher needs (e.g. Schweitzer, Einstein).

Maslow elucidated the relation between needs and values, describing the dynamics of how values change as needs are fulfilled (or not). Needs, he said, influence values in several ways: we tend to overestimate the importance of those things which can satisfy the most powerful of our ungratified needs; we tend to underestimate the importance of the satisfiers of the less powerful of our ungratified needs, and the strength of these needs; we tend to underestimate and devalue the importance of satisfiers of needs already gratified, and to underestimate the strength of those needs. Our values, in turn, tend to determine our cognitive activities: attention, perception, learning, remembering, forgetting and thinking.

Emphasizing as it does personal growth and 'becoming', and the subjective aspect of motives and values, Maslow's theory represents a fulfilment model of personality. As such, it is classified in textbooks together with the views of other theorists variously labelled as Third Force psychologists, phenomenological psychologists, existentialists, humanists and organismic psychologists. Partly for this reason, partly because it is simple and plausible, and partly because they are likely to have seen it before (most psychology textbooks now devote some pages to Maslow, as do many texts in communication, education and business management), it is appealing to college students.

Equivocal connections between motives and action make it an easy matter for critics to assail any theory of human motivation. Maslow's nested hierarchy of motivational systems is particularly susceptible in this regard, and has received its fair share of attacks. Wahba and Bridwell's review (in the April 1976 issue of *Organizational Behavior and Human Performance*) is illustrative, damning the theory as so inexplicit as to be untestable.

Other psychologists have concluded that the theory presents a good framework for the investigation of individual differences (e.g. Williams and Page's research in the June 1989 issue of *Journal of Research in Personality*). In a sample of university students, Williams and Page's Maslowian Assessment Survey shows respectable psychometric properties as a measure of four aspects (gratification, importance, salience, and role in self-concept) of the safety, belongingness and esteem needs. Student samples yield no consistent patterns of individual differences in self-actualization needs. These authors' findings indicate, first, that the safety, belongingness and esteem needs are well worth studying in university populations, whereas physiological and self-actualization needs are probably not; and, second, that the supposed prepotency is not borne out. Thus, although Maslow's theory has little empirical support with respect to the order of priority of needs, it may be useful as a descriptive model of personality.

Without citing Maslow, socioanalytic theory (presented in Hogan's chapter from the Nebraska Symposium on Motivation, 1982)

resembles the stripped-down version of Maslow's hierarchy. Given adequate food, shelter, etc., humans crave predictability (read safety) in their world. Next, they need to be accepted as a member of a group (belongingness), then to gain status within it, through achievement and/or reputation (the two basic sources of self-esteem, according to Maslow). Socioanalytic theory presumes that belongingness is often attained through mere compliance and conformity ('getting along') and that to achieve status one must adopt other forms of self-presentation (persuasion or intimidation, for example, 'getting ahead') as well as competence in performing tasks valued by the group. Because the self-presentations instrumental to getting along are to some extent incompatible with those that enable one to get ahead, it is difficult to satisfy the two needs simultaneously; and sometimes one gets ahead only at the expense of alienating former friends or comrades. Having got ahead of one's peers, for example, one may have to go back and shore up relations with them. Thus social life is forever problematic; even well-adjusted, effective people, our leaders and those we admire, continually seek to balance the gratification of their needs for belongingness and esteem.

Although Maslow did not notice this incompatibility – most of the self-presentation literature and all of the writing on socioanalytic theory appeared after his death – he was well aware of how difficult it was to find self-actualizing people: his 1970 list contained only nine living and nine 'historical'.

R.N. WOLFE

Matarazzo, Joseph

Born: 1925, Caiazzo, Italy **Nat:** American **Ints:** Assessment, evaluation, health psychology, intelligence **Educ:** BA Brown University, 1946; MS Northwestern University, 1950; PhD Northwestern University, 1952 **Appts & awards:** Professor and Chairman, Oregon Health Sciences, University of Oregon, 1957– ; Fellow, APA Divisions 2, 3, 12, 19, 20, 26, 38 and 40; Hofheimer Prize, Annual Research Award of the American Psychiatric Association, 1962; Annual Distinguished Service to the Profession of Psychology Award of the American Board of Professional Psychology, 1986; President, APA, 1989–90; APA Distinguished Professional Contributions to Knowledge Award, 1991; President, American Psychological Foundation, 1992–6; President Elect, International Congress of Applied Psychology, San Francisco, 1998

Principal publications

1954   An experimental study of aggression in the hypertensive patient. *Journal of Personality*, 22, 423–47.

1958   Psychological test and organismic correlates of interview interaction patterns. *Journal of Abnormal and Social Psychology*, 56, 329–38 (with R.G. Matarazzo, G. Saslow and J.S. Phillips).

1965   A postdoctoral residency program in clinical psychology. *American Psychologist*, 20, 432–9.

1972   *Wechsler's Measurement and Appraisal of Adult Intelligence*, 5th edn. Oxford University Press.

1980   Behavioral health and behavioral medicine: Frontiers for a new health psychology. *American Psychologist*, 35: 807–17.

1982   Behavioral health's challenge to academic, scientific, and professional psychology. *American Psychologist*, 37(1), 1–14.

1982   Changing smoking behavior: A critique. In R.J. Gatchel, A. Baum and J.E. Singer (eds), *Behavioral Medicine and Clinical Psychology: Overlapping Disciplines*. Erlbaum (with W.A. Hunt).

1984   *Behavioral Health: A Handbook of Health Enhancement and Disease Prevention*. Wiley (with S.H. Weiss, J.A. Herd, N.E. Miller and S.M. Weiss).

1990   Psychological assessment versus psychological testing: Validation from Binet to the school, clinic and court-room. *American Psychologist*, 45, 999–1071.

1992   Psychological testing and assessment in the 21st century. *American Psychologist*, 47, 1007–18.

Further reading

Matarazzo, J.D. (1994) Psychology in a medical school: A personal account of a department's 35-year history. *Journal of Clinical Psychology*, 50, 7–36.

Giuseppe (Joseph) D. Matarazzo was born as the tenth of eleven children in Caiazzo, near Naples, Italy, to parents who were US citizens. The Matarazzo family sailed to and settled in a poor, inner-city area of Schenectady, New York, where 'Joe' underwent the first twelve years of his education. He enlisted in the US Navy at age 17. Aboard ship he became intrigued by stories of interesting cases told by a young Navy physician and consequently entered Brown University to study psychology, not realizing that Brown did not provide the clinical training he was set on obtaining.

Matarazzo worked as assistant to Carl Pfaffman and took courses from Hunter, **Schlosberg**, Riggs and Kimble. In 1948 he transferred to Northwestern University for his clinical training, where mentor William A. Hunt forced him to complete considerable amounts of further coursework in statistics and general/experimental psychology. Matarazzo believes these were of more help in his subsequent clinical practice than the courses he took in applied psychology. He married Dr Ruth G. Matarazzo, also a clinical psychologist, in 1949. He completed his PhD while on internship at Washington University School of Medicine, St Louis, where, in 1951, he began teaching psychology to first-year medical students. In 1957, after a sojourn at Harvard Medical School, Matarazzo was invited by Dean David W. Baird at the Oregon Health Sciences University to establish the first autonomous Department of Medical Psychology in the USA. He has chaired it ever since. Dean Baird's own clinical experience had convinced him that the majority of patients who consult their family physician have a psychological basis for their symptoms, a view shared by the Matarazzos.

Joseph Matarazzo has been a prolific researcher, teacher, clinician and administrator. He has regarded psychology as both a career and a hobby. His 200-plus research publications span three areas: (1) intellectual and neuropsychological functions; (2) non-verbal indices of empathy and related psychological processes; (3) health psychology, especially the role of lifestyle risk factors in health and illness. Matarazzo has always advocated the scientist-practitioner model: 'I have repeatedly perceived that science is the backbone of the practice of psychology.' As a 'founding father' of health psychology, Matarazzo gave this significant new field its name, definition and *raison d'être*.

DAVID F. MARKS

Maudsley, Henry

Born: 1835, near Settle, Yorkshire, England
Died: 1918, Bushey Heath, Hertfordshire, England **Nat:** British **Ints:** Clinical psychology, general psychology, philosophical and theoretical psychology, psychiatry **Educ:** MD, University College, London, 1857 **Appts & awards:** Medical Superintendent, Cheadle Royal, 1856; Medical Superintendent,

Manchester Royal Lunatic Hospital, 1859–62; Joint Editor, *Journal of Mental Science*, 1863–78; Physician, West London Hospital, 1864–74; Lecturer on Insanity, St Mary's Hospital, 1868–9; Professor of Medical Jurisprudence, University College London, 1869–79; President, Medico-Psychological Association, 1870

Principal publications

1867   *The Physiology and Pathology of Mind*. Macmillan.

1870   *Body and Mind: An Enquiry into their Connection and Mutual Influence*. Macmillan.

1886   *Natural Causes and Supernatural Seemings*. Kegan.

1908   *Heredity, Variation and Genius, with an Essay on Shakespeare and Address on Medicine*. Bale, Sons and Danilsson.

1916   *Organic to Human – Psychological and Sociological*. Macmillan.

1918   *Religion and Realities*. Bale, Sons and Danilsson.

Further reading

Lewis, A. (1951) Henry Maudsley: His work and influence. *Journal of Mental Science*, 97, 259–77.

Turner, T. (1988) Henry Maudsley – psychiatrist, philosopher and entrepreneur. *Psychological Medicine*, 18, 551–74.

Maudsley is often regarded as a 'shadowy figure' (a reputation partly due to the destruction of most of his private papers) in British psychiatry, a name known through the hospital, completed in 1915, that bears his name. His text *Physiology and Pathology of the Mind*, and revisions (*Physiology of the Mind*, 1876, and *Pathology of the Mind*, 1879) were influential in the foundation of British medical psychology. He also made important contributions to criminology – he staunchly opposed arguments for the hanging of lunatics – and to medical education generally. He was a leading figure in the Medico-Psychological Association (MPA) and had considerable editorial influence on the *Journal of Mental Science* (*JMS*). His personal qualities often brought him into conflict with peers and his hypercritical commentaries on others' work tended to border on rudeness; many of his obituarists referred to his cynical nature and degenerationist philosophy. Partly as a consequence of his personal attributes, his own works tended to attract disproportionately harsh and unfair criticism. The year 1878

marked a watershed in his career: he resigned from the editorship of the *JMS*, following a period of sustained criticisms of his editorial policy. He did not attend the 1879 Annual Meeting and attended just three further annual meetings (1880, 1881 and 1887) before resigning from the MPA. Thereafter he became increasingly isolated from his professional colleagues and perhaps increasingly disillusioned with the manifest ineffectiveness of the therapeutics of the day. He devoted increasing amounts of time to philosophy, in which he was an ardent positivist in the tradition of Auguste Comte, though much of his writings convey a deep sense of pessimism concerning the future for the human condition.

Mead, George Herbert

Born: 1863, South Hadley, Massachusetts, USA **Died:** 1931, Chicago, Illinois, USA **Nat:** American **Educ:** AB Oberlin College, 1883; Harvard University, 1887–8; AB Harvard University, 1888; studied psychology and philosophy in Europe, 1888–91; University of Michigan, 1891; University of Chicago, 1894–

Principal publications

1934   *Mind, Self and Society* (ed. C.W. Morris). University of Chicago Press.

1977   *On Social Psychology: Selected Papers*. University of Chicago Press.

Further reading

Aboulafia, M (ed.) (1991) *Philosophy, Social Theory, and the Thought of George Herbert Mead*. State University of New York Press.

Sampson, E.E. (1993) *Celebrating the Other: A Dialogic Account of Human Nature*. Westview.

Mead's contributions are in three main areas: systematic pragmatism, the history of ideas, and social psychology and social philosophy. Although he published extensively in social psychology, Mead never systematized his position. However, *Mind, Self and Society* contains an arrangement of teaching and research papers that attempt such a systematization. Mead's contribution to psychology is primarily in his analysis of the origins of self. According to Mead, the self has its origins in social interaction, and language has a central role here. The child at first lacks self-consciousness, but through social interaction, communication and language the child develops self-awareness and learns to play the role of other people, and thereby experiences social feedback. As a result the child comes to consider its behaviour objectively – the self is experienced as a social object, and others are experienced as acting towards the child's self as an object. Thus, the idea of self arises in a social setting, and since there are many social settings there are possibilities for developing multiple selves.

Mead had considerable influence on many eminent psychologists, notably **Sullivan** (they were at Chicago at the same time) and **Dewey** who went from Michigan to Chicago at the same time as Mead.

Meehl, Paul Everett

Born: 1920, Minneapolis, Minnesota, USA **Nat:** American **Ints:** Clinical, evaluation and measurement, philosophical and theoretical psychology, psychotherapy **Educ:** BA University of Minnesota, 1941; PhD University of Minnesota, 1945 **Appts & awards:** University of Minnesota, Regent's Professor of Psychology, Professor of Psychiatry, Professor of Philosophy; Hon. DSc, Adelphi University; President, Midwestern Psychological Association, 1954, APA, 1962; APA Distinguished Scientific Contribution Award, 1958; Member, American Academy of Arts and Sciences, 1965; APA Division 12, Distinguished Contribution Award, 1967; Bruno Klopfer Distinguished Contribution Award, 1979; APA Division 12, Distinguished Scientist Award, 1976; APA Award for Distinguished Professional Contributions, 1994

Principal publications

1945 The dynamics of structured personality tests. *Journal of Clinical Psychology*, 1, 296–303.

1946 The K factor as a supressor variable in the Minnesota Multiphasis Personality Inventory. *Journal of Applied Psychology*, 30, 254–64 (with S.R. Hathaway).

1948 On a distinction between hypothetical constructs and intervening variables. *Psychological Review*, 55, 95–107 (with K. MacCorquodale).

1951 *Atlas for Clinical use of MMPI*. University of Minnesota Press (with S.R. Hathaway).

1954 *Clinical versus Statistical Prediction*. University of Minnesota Press.

1954 *Modern Learning Theory*. Appleton-Century-Crofts (with W.K. Estes and S. Koch).

1955 Antecedent probability and the efficiency of psychometric signs, patterns or cutting scores. *Psychological Bulletin*, 52, 194–216 (with A. Rosen).

1955 Construct validity in psychological tests. *Psychological Bulletin*, 52, 281–302 (with L.J. Cronbach).

1956 Wanted – a good cookbook. *American Psychologist*, 11, 263–72.

1962 Schizotaxia, schizotypy, schizophrenia. *American Psychologist*, 17, 827–38.

1973 *Psychodiagnosis: Selected Papers*. University of Minnesota Press.

1975 Hedonic capacity: Some conjectures. *Bulletin of the Menninger Clinic*, 39, 295–307.

1978 Theoretical risks and tabular asterisks: Sir Karl, Sir Ronald, and the slow progress of soft psychology. *Journal of Consulting and Clinical Psychology*, 46, 806–34.

1982 Taxometric methods. In P. Kendall and J. Butcher (eds), *Handbook of Research Methods in Clinical Psychology*. Wiley (with R. Golden).

1990 Toward an integrated theory of schizotaxia, schizotypy, and schizophrenia. *Journal of Personality Disorders*, 4, 1–99.

1995 Bootstraps taxometrics. *American Psychologist*, 50, 266–75.

Further reading

Cicchetti, D. and Grove, W.M. (eds) (1991) *Thinking Clearly about Psychology: Essays in Honor of Paul E. Meehl*, vol. 1: *Matters of Public Interest*; vol. 2: *Personality and Psychopathology*. University of Minnesota Press.

Paul Meehl came to psychology when a teenager through reading **Freud**, but his training at Minnesota was quantitative, behaviouristic and strongly empiricist. Hence his best-known work on clinical versus statistical prediction reflected this interest/schooling conflict. Early research (with MacCorquodale) on animal learning stopped when C.L. **Hull**'s theory became indefensible. The philosophical side of Meehl's interests was stimulated by the positivist Feigl, who was at Minnesota when Meehl was a senior. The 'open concepts' problem fascinated him, as shown by the 1955 article with **Cronbach** on construct validity and by his later interest in taxometrics. Although he is often considered a rigorous empiricist (e.g. MMPI scale development, clinical interviewing and animal learning), he was a philosophical, speculative psychologist rather than a data-driven researcher. His enduring contributions have been theoretical and methodological, as reflected in his later work on classification problems in psychopathology. For Meehl, classification in psychopathology is a problem in applied mathematics, and that perspective partly reflects critical assessment of the lack of significant progress in psychology and commitment to multidisciplinary perspectives on psychology. For example, he argues that there is evidence for the existence of real taxa in psychopathology, and he contends that psychology has not used appropriate methods to identify them. Outside of research, his professional activities continued in the shape of a small private practice of psychotherapy in which he used a mix of psychoanalytic and rational-emotive methods.

Mehrabian, Albert

Born: 1939, Tabriz, Iran *Nat:* Iranian *Ints:* environmental psychology, measurement, personality *Educ:* BSc MIT, 1961; PhD Clark University, 1964 *Appts & awards:* Professor, Department of Psychology, University of California at Los Angeles; Fellow, APA; Editorial Board, *Journal of Non Verbal Behavior*, *Journal of Psycholinguistic Research*

Principal publications

1967 Inference of attitudes from nonverbal communication in two channels. *Journal of Consulting Psychology*, 31, 248–52 (with S.R. Ferris).

1970 *Tactics of Social Influence*. Prentice-Hall.

1971 Piagetian measures of cognitive development for children up to age two. *Journal of Psycholinguistic Research*, 1, 113–26 (with M. Williams).

1971 Verbal and nonverbal interaction of strangers in a waiting situation. *Journal of Experimental Research in Personality*, 5, 127–38.

1972 *Non-Verbal Communication*. Aldine-Atherton.

1976 *Public Places and Private Spaces*. Basic Books.

1977 Evidence for a three-factor theory of emotions. *Journal of Research in Personality*, 11, 273–94 (with J.A. Russell).

1977 A questionnaire measure of individual differences in stimulus screening and associated differences in arousability. *Environmental Psychology and Nonverbal Behavior*, 1, 89–103.

1978 Measures of language skills for two- to seven-year-old children. *Genetic Psychology Monographs*, 98, 3–49 (with C. Moynihan).

1978 Environmental effects on parent–infant interaction. *Genetic Psychology Monographs*, 97, 3–41 (with C.A. Fallender).

1978 A questionnaire measure of individual

differences in achieving tendency. *Educational and Psychological Measurement*, 38, 475–8 (with L. Bank).

1980 *Basic Dimensions for a General Psychological Theory*. Delgeschlagen, Gumm and Hain.

1980 Analysis of personality measures in terms of basic dimensions of temperament. *Journal of Personality and Social Psychology*, 38, 492–503 (with E. O'Reilly).

1981 *Silent Messages*. Wadsworth.

1985 Temperament characteristics of suicide attempters. *Journal of Consulting and Clinical Psychology* (with L. Weinstein).

1995 Relationships among three general approaches to personality description. *Journal of Psychology*, 129, 565–81.

Further reading

Strelau, J. and Angleitner (eds) (1991) *Explorations in Temperament: International Perspectives on Theory and Measurement*. Plenum.

When Albert Mehrabian began studying non-verbal communication, he was struck by the diversity of bodily and vocal cues, each of which could have a particular significance, and possibly a different significance in different contexts. Typical studies during the 1960s tended to focus on a very few of these cues and attempted to detail the significance of each cue in terms of arbitrarily selected concepts that suited the particular investigator. Thus, integration of the available findings within a coherent framework was extremely difficult. Having entered psychology with an engineering background, Mehrabian tended to conceptualize psychological phenomena in terms of variables and their interrelationships. He also appreciated the importance of concise and systematic description as the foundation of any scientific activity. Factor analyses of some of the data from the studies in which numerous non-verbal behavioural variables had been scored, and from other studies that had identified relationships between groups of cues and referents, were innovative and useful.

Mehrabian argues that non-verbal communication essentially has a limited set of referent dimensions dealing with expression and communication of feelings and attitudes. Thus, instead of focusing on the numerous behavioural cues, he analysed the referents of non-verbal communication to try to achieve a system of organization. Emotions were analysed in terms of three basic and independent dimensions: pleasure–displeasure, arousal–non-arousal, and dominance–submissiveness (although those were labelled differently in earlier studies). Attitudes (e.g. like–dislike, preference, approach–avoidance) were in turn analysed in terms of emotions – these relationships were clarified in studies published from the mid- to late 1970s. Once this framework for conceptualizing referents of non-verbal communication was in place, he set about summarizing the existing literature and generating studies that would explore systematically important phenomena in the field (e.g. status communication, deceit, fidgeting, persuasion) that had been neglected or studied only minimally. Work in the area of non-verbal communication led to a recognition of the importance of emotions as mediating factors in understanding human behaviour.

He successfully applied the three-dimensional theory and measures of emotions to the study of social interactions, to the description of environments, and to the description of persons in terms of temperament. With colleagues he used the three basic dimensions of emotional response as independent factors in studies to explore amount of food consumption, alcohol consumption, or sexual desire and sexual dysfunction as a function of emotional states (i.e. temperament dimensions of trait pleasure–displeasure, trait arousability, and trait dominance–submissiveness). This has resulted in a powerful and general system of personality description and measurement. Mehrabian and his colleagues have shown experimentally how a large number of personality measures in common use can be described in terms of the three-dimensional temperament framework. They have also shown that the latter framework can be used in a variety of applied contexts. For instance, they pinpointed an extremely common, and heretofore neglected, characteristic of suicide attempters – contrary to traditional clinical beliefs, such individuals are arousable (i.e. emotional and volatile).

Meichenbaum, Donald

Born: 1940, New York, USA **Nat:** American **Ints:** Clinical psychology, developmental psychology, personality and social psychology **Educ:** BA City College of New York, 1962; MA University of Illinois, 1965; PhD University of Illinois, 1966 **Appts & awards:** Professor of Psychology, University of Waterloo; Fellow, APA, CPA; Associate Editor, Cognitive Therapy and Research Series; Editor, Stress and Coping (Plenum); Editorial Boards, *Biofeedback and Self-Regulation, Journal of Abnormal Child Psychology, Canadian Journal of Behavioral Sciences, Behavior Therapy, Journal of Clinical Neuropsychology*

Principal publications

1969 The effects of instructions and reinforcement on thinking and language behaviors of schizophrenia. *Behavior, Research and Therapy*, 7, 101–14.

1971 Group insight vs. group desensitization in treating speech anxiety. *Journal of Clinical and Consulting Psychology*, 36, 410–21 (with J. Gilmore and A. Fedoravicius).

1971 Training impulsive children to talk to themselves: A means of developing self-control. *Journal of Abnormal Psychology*, 77, 115–26 (with J. Goodman).

1971 An examination of model characteristics in reducing avoidance behavior. *Journal of Personality and Social Psychology*, 17, 298–307.

1972 Cognitive modification of test-anxious college students. *Journal of Consulting and Clinical Psychology*, 35, 370–80.

1973 Training schizophrenics to talk to themselves: A means of developing attentional control. *Behavior Therapy*, 4, 515–34 (with R. Cameron).

1975 Theoretical and treatment implications of developmental research on verbal control of behavior. *Canadian Psychologist*, 16, 22–7.

1976 Cognitive factors in biofeedback therapy. *Biofeedback and Self-Regulation*, 1, 201–16.

1977 *Cognitive Behavior Modification.* Plenum.

1979 The application of biofeedback for the regulation of pain: A critical review. *Psychological Bulletin*, 86, 1322–38 (with D. Turk and W. Berman).

1980 A cognitive-behavioral perspective on intelligence. *Intelligence*, 4, 271–84.

1983 *Pain and Behavioral Medicine.* Guilford Press (with D. Turk and M. Genest).

1984 *Coping with Stress.* Wiley.

1984 *Stress Reduction and Prevention.* Plenum (with M. Jaremko).

1984 *The Unconscious Reconsidered.* Wiley (with K. Bowers).

1989 *Exploring Choices: The Psychology of Adjustment.* Scott, Foresman (with R. Price, E. Phares, N. McCormick and J. Hyde).

1994 *A Clinical Handbook/Practical Therapist Manual for Assessing and Treating Adults with Post Traumatic Stress Disorder.* Institute Press.

1996 *Achievement, Mastery and Teaching: Fostering Independence in School.* Brookline Books.

Further reading

Freedy, J.R. and Hobfoll, S.E. (1994) Stress
inoculation for reduction of burnout: A
conservation of resources approach. *Anxiety, Stress
and Coping*, 6, 311–25.

Goldsamt, L.A., Goldfried, M.R., Hayes, A.M. and
Kerr, S. (1992) Beck, Meichenbaum, and Strupp:
A comparison of three therapies on the dimension
of therapist feedback. *Psychotherapy*, 29, 167–76.

Mahoney, M.J. (ed.) (1995) *Cognitive and
Constructive Psychotherapies: Theory, Research,
and Practice*. Springer-Verlag.

As a graduate student, Donald Meichenbaum
carried out research on schizophrenic thought
disorder, and he has remained fascinated with
the role thinking plays in psychotherapy ever
since. This´ interest led to theoretical and
empirical studies of thinking in a wide array
of populations including impulsive children,
'neurotics', pain patients and stressed
individuals. The question of how thoughts,
feelings, behaviour and their resultant consequences interact has been his major research
concern. He has been concerned with developing assessment techniques to tap individuals'
automatic thoughts (internal dialogue or cognitive events) and cognitive processes such as
metacognitions and cognitive structures or
schemas. One research strategy he and his
colleagues have followed has been to use intervention studies as a means of explicating the
nature of the relationship between thoughts,
feelings and behaviour. These studies with both
children and adults have contributed to an interest in such issues as treatment generalization,
client resistance, treatment non-adherence and
patient non-compliance. This has led to the
development of an influential cognitive behavioural approach to behaviour modification,
designed to integrate the clinical concerns of
psychodynamic and semantic therapists with the
technology of behaviour therapy. He has demonstrated successful applications of this approach
in his work on post-traumatic stress disorder and
cognate disorders.

Melzack, Ronald

Born: 1929, Montreal, Quebec, Canada *Nat:*
Canadian *Ints:* Clinical neuropsychology,
physiological and comparative psychology
Educ: BSc McGill University, 1950; MSc
McGill University, 1951; PhD McGill Univer-
sity, 1954 *Appts & awards:* Emeritus Professor
of Psychology, McGill University; Board of
Directors, Canadian Psychological Association,
1970–3; Jacob Bronowski Memorial Lecture,
University of Toronto, 1981; Fellow, Royal
Society of Canada (FRSC), 1982; J.J. Bonica
Award of the Eastern Pain Society, 1983; Presi-
dent, International Association for the Study of
Pain, 1984–7; Editorial Board, *Experimental
Neurology, Pain, Journal of Behavioral Medi-
cine, American Journal of Chinese Medicine*

Principal publications

1965   Pain mechanisms: A new theory. *Science*,
150, 971–9 (with P.D. Wall).

1971   Phantom limb pain: Implications for the
treatment of pathological pain. *Anesthesiology*, 35,
409–20.

1973   *The Puzzle of Pain*. Penguin.

1975   The McGill Pain Questionnaire: Major
properties and scoring methods. *Pain*, 1, 277–99.

1977   Pain signalling systems in the dorsal and
ventral spinal cord. *Pain*, 4, 94–132 (with S.G.
Dennis).

1982   Stimulation-produced analgesia: Evidence for
somatotopic organization in the midbrain. *Brain
Research*, 51, 301–11 (with W.Y. Soper).

1982   *The Challenge of Pain*. Penguin (with P.D.
Wall).

1983   (ed.) *Pain Measurement and Assessment*.
Raven Press.

1984   *Textbook of Pain*. Churchill Livingstone (ed.
with P.D. Wall).

1984   The myth of painless childbirth (the John
Bonica Lecture). *Pain*, 19, 321–37.

1989   Measurement of nausea. *Journal of Pain and
Symptom Management*, 4, 157–60.

1992   *Handbook of Pain Assessment*. Guildford (ed.
with D.C. Turk).

Further reading

Larbig, W. (1991) Gate control theory of pain
perception: Current status. In J.G. Carlson and A.R.
Seifert (eds), *International Perspectives on Self-
regulation and Health*. Plenum.

Melzack has made important contributions to
our understanding of the neural mechanisms that
subserve pain, as well as that of a variety of
clinical problems such as labour pain and the
relative contributions of different psychological
factors to pain perception. His original interest
in the effects of early experience on adult
behaviour led to the important discovery, in
D.O. **Hebb**'s laboratory in the early 1950s, that
dogs reared in isolation (in a modified kennel
cage) did not respond normally to injurious
stimulation. Unlike their normally reared litter-

mates, these dogs frequently ignored flaming matches and pin-pricks. The results indicated very clearly that the sensory input evoked by injury is somehow modulated by the brain. Research on ascending and descending pain-signalling pathways (with W.K. Livingston) led to the conclusion that the central midbrain area exerts a descending control over pain signals at the earliest synaptic level. Melzack and Livingston also found that pain signals are transmitted to the brain by multiple ascending pathways that have different conduction rates and destinations in the brain.

Melzack was appointed to MIT, where he met Patrick D. Wall, with whom he collaborated closely. In 1965, they proposed the gate control theory of pain, a major breakthrough in the field of pain research and therapy. The theory proposes that the sensory input is gated (or modulated) in the dorsal horns of the spinal cord and that the output of dorsal-horn cells is influenced by psychological as well as physiological factors. An extension of the theory with Kenneth L. Casey proposed that pain is a multidimensional sensory, affective and evaluative experience. Research with Warren Torgerson on the language of pain was the basis of the McGill Pain Questionnaire (MPQ), a new tool for the measurement of subjective pain experience, published in 1975. The MPQ consists of twenty sets of verbal descriptors which have numerical values that yield indices of the sensory, affective and evaluative dimensions of pain experience. The MPQ has been shown to provide a reliable, valid way of measuring pain, and is now one of the most widely used methods of pain measurement in clinical settings.

Merei, Ferenc

Born: 1909, Budapest, Hungary **Died:** 1986, Budapest, Hungary **Ints:** Developmental psychology, personality and social psychology, psychotherapy **Educ:** Diplome de Licencié des Lettres, Sobonne, Paris, 1933; Dr Psychological Sciences, Hungarian Academy of Sciences, 1979 **Appts & awards:** Director, Hungarian Institute for Pedagogy, 1949, Institute for Psychology of Metropolitan Budapest, 1954–8, Laboratory for Clinical Psychology of the Hungarian Institute for Neurology and Psychiatry, 1964–76

Principal publications

1945 Zum problem von konstitution und process in der schizophrenie auf grund des Rorschach-versuches. *Schweizer Archiv für Neurologie und Psychiatrie*, 45, 127–40 (with G. Boszormenyi).

1947 *Az Egyuttes Elmeny* (*Group Leadership and Institutionalization*). Officina.

1971 *Kozossegek Rejtett Halozata* (*Hidden Networks in Groups*). Kozgazdasagi es Jogi Kiado.

1985 *Lelektani Naplo* (*Psychological Diary*). Muvelodeskuato Intezet.

Further reading

Kardos, L., Pleh, C. and Popper, P. (eds) (1987) *Studies in Clinical Psychodiagnostics and Psychotherapy*. Akademiai Kiado.

Virag, T. (1988) An analysis of the Psychological Diary of Merei Ferenc: Reasoning processes and the interpretation of manifest dream text. *Magyar Pszichologiai Szemle*, 44, 56–82.

Ferenc Merei was as a student of the French psychologist Henri Wallon, and in the early part of his career focused on studies of cognitive development. He became involved in clinical psychology after joining Lipot Szondi's laboratory in 1938, where his research focused on the genesis of schizophrenia and on the demand characteristics of **Rorschach** pictures. After World War II he was principally concerned with understanding and controlling the psychological processes which lead to people to go to war and to engage in its ferocities and atrocities. This led him to a programme of research in which he showed that the power of the group and the common experience that a group can accumulate, as well as the group tradition, can overcome an individual leader's power within the group. He argued that the power of leadership can prevail only if it is perceived to conform to the group traditions. He was particularly interested in the experiential language of groups and its role in preserving the sensory and emotional charge in groups memories of their experiences. He considered this function of language to be crucial for the emotionally charged recall of the original experience.

Merleau-Ponty, Maurice

Born: 1908, Rochefort-sur-mer, France **Died:** 1961, France **Nat:** French **Ints:** Philosophy **Educ:** Ecole Normale Supérieur, 1926–30; Agregation, 1931 **Appts & awards:** Professor, Lyon, Sorbonne, Collège de France; Teacher before the World War II; French Army during the war; Co-Editor with Sartre and de Beauvoir of *Les Temps Modernes*

Principal publications

1942 *La Structure du comportement*. PUF.
1945 *Phénomenologie de la perception*. NRF Gallimard.
1947 *Humanisme et terreur*. Gallimard.
1948 *Sens et non-sens*. Nagel.
1953 *Eloge de la philosophie*. NRF Gallimard.
1955 *Les Aventures de la dialectique*. Gallimard.
1960 *Signes*. NRF Gallimard.

Further reading

Dillon, M.C. (1988) *Merleau-Ponty's Ontology*. Indiana University Press.
Edie, J.M. (1987) *Merleau-Ponty's Philosophy of Language*. University Press of America.
Madison, G.B. (1973) *La Phénomenologie de Merleau-Ponty*. Klincksieck.
Robinet, A. (1970) *Merleau-Ponty*. PUF.
Spiegelberg, H. (1969) *The Phenomenological Movement, vol. II*, 2nd edn. Martinus Nojhoff.
Tilliette, X. (1970) *Merleau-Ponty*. Seghers.

Merleau-Ponty has been presented both as a phenomenologist and as an existentialist, but a study of his thought reveals the limited utility of general labels of this kind. Whilst he was the first French thinker to use the term 'phenomenology' in the title of a major work and to identify philosophy with phenomenology, he did not rely greatly on the methods of Husserl; and equally, although he shared many of the concerns of his friend Sartre, Merleau-Ponty disagreed with the latter on such fundamental issues as the extent of human freedom. He argued that experience is shot through with pre-existent meanings, largely derived from language and experienced in perception.

Merleau-Ponty arrived at these views gradually, beginning from a prolonged and extensive study of the psychology of perception. His first significant work, *La Structure du comportement*, is essentially a critique of the major psychological theories of perception of the time, notably behaviourism and *Gestalt* theory (as put forward by **Köhler**). Merleau-Ponty denied that there is a causal relationship between the physical and the mental and he therefore found the behaviourist account of perception, entirely in terms of causation, unacceptable. *Gestalt* theory he found not false but not developed sufficiently to do justice to the facts of perception. His general conclusion was that a new approach was needed if perception was to be understood properly.

This new approach was his version of phenomenology, and its application to perception is the subject of his second and most important work, *Phénomenologie de la perception*. The fundamental premise of this work is that of the primacy of perception: our perceptual relation to the world is *sui generis*, and logically prior to the subject–object distinction. Theories of perception which deny this are rejected in the opening chapters of the work; for example, all sense-data theories are dismissed, since they attempt to reconstruct experience by using artificial abstractions which presuppose the subject–object dichotomy. By contrast Merleau-Ponty goes on to explore the phenomenal field by using a much expanded notion of *Gestalt*. It is argued that the elements of *Gestalt*s are both inherently meaningful and open or indeterminate.

One of the most original features of this phenomenology is his theory of the role of the body in the world as perceived (*le monde perçu*), an area of thought he develops at much greater length than does Sartre. Merleau-Ponty contends that a number of the most fundamental features of perception are a result of our physical incarnation: our perception of space is conditioned by our bodily mode of existence; or again, we regard perceived things as constant because our body remains constant. Further, Merleau-Ponty contends that perception is a committed (*engagé*) act, not one in which we are merely passive. We discover meanings in the worlds, and commit ourselves without complete logical justification, to believing in its future.

The concluding section of the work draws out some important consequences of these views, firstly concerning Cartesianism. As with Husserl, Merleau-Ponty's thought to some extent defines itself by reference to that of Descartes. Merleau-Ponty is logically bound to deny that Cartesianism is acceptable, and this he does. The Cartesian presupposition of a distinction between meditating ego and transcendent cogitata is incompatible with the thesis of the primacy of perception, and thus Merleau-Ponty classifies the cogito of the second *Meditation* as a merely 'verbal cogito'. He replaces it with a 'true cogito' of the form 'there is a phenomenon: something shows itself'. Put in metaphysical terms, the fundamental category revealed by Merleau-Ponty's philosophy is what he terms 'being-in-the-world' (*être-au-monde*). The subjective and the objective are facets of this prior, embracing structure.

This thesis conditions his analysis of time, in which he argues that the notions of time and subjectivity are mutually constitutive. Time is not a feature of the objective world, but is a dimension of subjectivity: past and future appear in our present and can only occur in a temporal being. Time is more than the form of the inner life, and more intimately related to subjectivity than is suggested by regarding it as an attribute or property of the self. To analyse time, Merleau-Ponty contends, is to gain access to the complete structure of subjectivity.

In the final pages of the *Phenomenology of Perception* Merleau-Ponty discusses the nature and limits of human freedom, a theme developed further in the political works, *Humanisme et terreur* and *Les Aventures de la dialectique*. He rejects the Sartrean doctrine that we are condemned to be (absolutely) free, replacing it with his own view that we are condemned to meaning. Experience comes ready furnished with meanings and so, although we are free to make choices, the field of freedom is accordingly circumscribed. These meanings are conveyed by a number of social institutions, but above all by language. As he puts it in his discussion of the cogito, 'Descartes, and *a fortiori* his reader, begin their meditation in what is already a universe of discourse.' Unsurprisingly, it was to be a consideration of the role of language as a vehicle for intersubjectivity to which Merleau-Ponty turned in his final years, but he did not live to work out a complete theory.

Merleau-Ponty also developed an interest in aesthetics, especially of the visual arts. This follows from his theory of the primacy of perception: he found in painting a fuller appreciation of our special perceptual relation with the world than in science or in philosophies, which analyse perception in terms of the primacy of the subject–object distinction.

R. WILKINSON

Meschieri, Luigi

Born: 1919, Bologna, Italy **Nat:** Italian **Ints:** Educational psychology, evaluation and measurement, health psychology, psychology and law **Appts & awards:** Professor of Psychology, Università La Sapienza Laurea, University of Rome, 1941; Specializzazione University of Rome, 1944; Libera Docenza, 1950; Fellow, UNO, Social Services, Geneva and Paris, 1950; Visiting Fulbright-Hays Professor, USA, 1955; President, Società Italiana di Psicologia (SIPS), 1973–5, 1979–81, 1985–8; Editorial Board, *Rivista di Psicologia*, 1960–78, *Psicologia contemporanea*, 1974– , *Psicologia Italiana*, 1979–

Principal publications

1951   Contributo metodologico allo studio dell'antisocialita nell'individuo normale. *Giustizia Penale*, 56, 385–408.

1951   Fattori psicologici e validita della stima del livello intellettuale di individui fotografati. *Zacchia*, 26, 1–27.

1954   *Corso di Psicologia differenziale e applicata.* La Goliardica.

1956   *Corso di Psicologia per Assistenti Sociali.* La Goliardica.

1957   Associazione, evocazione, riconoscimento in rapporto all'atteggiamento affettivo. *Rivista di Psicologia*, 51, 283–307.

1957   Contributo sperimentale allo studio degli stereotipi regionali in Italia. *Supplemento a La Ricerca Scientifica*, 27, 1–67.

1960   *Caratteristiche, problemi e risultati dell'Orientamento Professionale.* Atena.

1964   Mental and physical efficiency after wine and ethanol solutions ingested on an empty and on a full stomach. *Quarterly Journal of Studies on Alcohol*, 25, 535–40 (with G. Lolli).

1979   Importanza della rilevazione di atteggiamenti e comportamenti durante le degenza ospedaliera. In M. Cesa-Bianchi (ed.), *Psicologia e ospedale generale.* F. Angeli.

1980   Il questionario: Un supporto al Colloquio e all'Intervista. In G. Trentini (ed.), *Manuale del Colloquio e dell'Intervista.* Mondadori (with P. Pirani).

Meschieri's attention was first attracted to psychology while studying medicine at the University of Rome. He was struck by the combination of biological and social sciences which he had assumed to be diametrically opposed. Fascism inhibited the development of the social sciences at the time, and perhaps as a consequence, there was a 'social flavour' in the teaching on many science subjects, including endocrinology, genetics and neuropsychiatry. He learned statistical and quantitative methods through contacts with economists and criminologists. He was probably the only Italian student of medicine before World War II who had followed a course in methodological statistics involving demography and what was later called biometrics.

At the outbreak of war, while still a student and after brief training, he served on the medical-psychological selection board for naval specialists, a service started at the Consiglio Nazionale delle Ricerche (CNR) by Agostino **Gemelli**, following the trend he had pioneered for aviation pilots in 1914. This allowed him an opportunity to collect data for two theses: for graduation in medicine ('The learning of visual-motor skills') and for a specialization in industrial medicine ('A new accident-proneness test'). His career in the CNR in Rome progressed from Research Assistant up to Director of the Institute of Psychology, thirty years later.

In the challenging climate of post-war reconstruction, his work at the CNR entailed meeting the widely varying requests of public, private, military and civil bodies, for advice in researching and applying psychology. Since there were no qualified psychologists from the universities, he worked with his colleagues at the CNR to develop the theoretical and practical training of suitable personnel from these bodies, afterwards checking their work and finally proceeding to a systematic follow-up. In the late 1960s the climate of the Institute gradually changed, due to Maoist ideology, bureaucracy and trade union pressures, and this affected his attitude to research as a public service. He devoted himself almost entirely to university teaching, especially of differential, social and educational psychology, in courses leading to both degrees and specialization, mainly for students of various professions (e.g. teachers and physicians). From the early 1950s he spent increasing amounts of time building up the Società Italiana di Psicologia regionally and nationally.

Michotte, (Van den Berck) (Baron) Albert Edward

Born: 1881, Brussels, Belgium **Died:** 1965, Louvain, Belgium **Nat:** Belgian **Educ:** Licence University of Louvain, 1899; PhD University of Louvain, 1900 **Appts & awards:** University of Louvain, 1905–56; University of Utrecht, 1914–18 (University of Louvain was burned down); President, 15th International Congress of Psychology, 1957

Principal publications

1904 *Contributions to the histology of the nerve cell.*

1905 *Les signes régionaux: Nouvelles recherches expérimentales sur la répartition de la sensibilitétactile dans les états d'attention.*

1910 Etude expéimentale sur la choix volontaire et ses antécédents immédiats. *Arch. de psychol.*, 10, 113–320.

1912 Description et functionnement d'un nouveau tachistoscope de comparaison. *Arch. de psychol.*, 12, 1–13.

1929 Quelques aspects de la psychologie de la

perception négligés dans les recherches expérimentales. *Proc. IXth International Congress of Psychology*, 307.

1946 *La perception de la causalité* (English trans., *The Perception of Causality*, 1969).

1962 *Causalité, permanence et réalité phénoménales: Etudes de psychologie expérimentale.*

1964 Les compléments amodaux des structures perceptives. *Studia Psychologica.*

Further reading

Michotte, A., Thiners, G. and Butterworth, G. (eds) (1991) *Michotte's Experimental Phenomenology of Perception.* Erlbaum.

Under the direction of Professor Armand Thiéry, who had been the Director of the Laboratory of Experimental Psychology at Louvain since 1894, Michotte began research on tactual sensation, which resulted in the publication in 1905 of his first experimental work. From 1905 to 1908, Michotte worked for one semester of each year in Germany – first with **Wundt** at Leipzig, then with **Külpe** at Würzburg. His first work (1906–14), before World War I, concentrated on logical memory and voluntary choice. It employed principally the method of 'systematic experimental introspection', as influenced by Külpe. Back in Belgium after the war, Michotte resumed his teaching and research at Louvain. In 1944 he organized an Institut de Psychologie, which could grant the degree of 'docteur en psychologie'.

The main theme of Michotte's research is perception. His first experimental work in 1905 dealt with the problem of the tactual perception of space. It was under the influence of **Binet** and Külpe, and also due in part to his training in philosophy, that Michotte's interest led him to the experimental study of the 'higher mental process'. For one thing, he studied the role of thought in logical memory and in association. He undertook research on voluntary choice, a study which was widely acclaimed in the period preceding 1914. These various investigations employed Külpe's 'systematic experimental introspection', but Michotte's positive turn of mind led him to make various objective measurements which often turned out to be quite important in interpreting the data.

In respect of Michotte's research on logical memory, a point of theoretical importance, the revival of a part of the 'whole', then leads to the direct reproduction of the other part. It sets up a process of active search for the missing part, which leads to the reconstruction of the integral 'whole'. This conception, which clearly involved a *Gestalt* way of seeing the process, was worked out in 1908, although it was not published until 1912. That is considered to be the year of the birth of *Gestalt* psychology in the field of perception, but Michotte had already elaborated a *Gestalt* conception in the field of memory.

In respect of Michotte's research on voluntary choice, the important fact that he affirms is the existence, for who is choosing, of an immediate experience of his own activity, which may be called 'consciousness of action'. This work contributed greatly to freeing European experimental psychology from its static and elementistic character by stressing the motivational factor involved and the consciousness of action in 'mental' life. This work on voluntary choice drew Michotte's attention to the dynamical aspect of psychic functions and to action rather than static content.

After World War I and the resulting four years absence from his laboratory, Michotte lost his confidence in the introspective method of the Würzburg school. His research then took a new direction. Nevertheless, he continued to be inspired by the two major ideas that were born in the first period of his professional thinking. On the one hand, there was the idea of an activity of integration which constructs structure of wholeness, and, on the other, the idea that action is always central in the study of psychic functions.

The most important research accomplished at Michotte's laboratory in the period between the two wars was that showing the formation of *Gestalt*s, the motor and temporal structures formed in motor training. During this same period, Michotte's other principal idea was slowly maturing, the idea that came to inspire his entire work, namely that it is within the frame of action that we must study such other processes as perception and emotion. Systematic experimental research on this subject was not begun by Michotte until 1939. It was in this field of the perception of action and the related problems that Michotte carried out a great variety of experiments in the course of the last twenty-five years of his life.

This research lead Michotte to investigate various other aspects of perception; for instance, the study of animal movements including the 'intentional' character of certain movements and their affective or emotional value (as in flight or attack) in relation to projection of phenomenal characters into the perceived object; also the phenomenal permanence of objects which are partially or even totally hidden with respect to the 'amodal' complement of perceptual structures, and the impression of phenomenal reality with respect to perspective in drawing or as applied to cinematography.

Milgram, Stanley

Born: 1933, New York, USA **Died:** 1984, New York, USA **Nat:** American **Ints:** Personality and social, society for the psychological study of social issues **Educ:** BA Queens College, New York, 1954; PhD Harvard University 1960 **Appts & awards:** Annual Socio-psychological Prize, AAAS, 1965; Executive Director, Comparative International Program, Department of Social Relations, Harvard, 1966–7; Fellow, APA, 1970–84, AAAS, 1971–84; Guggenheim Fellow, 1972–3; Distinguished Professor of Psychology, Graduate Center, City University of New York, 1980–4; Fellow, AAAS, 1983–4

Principal publications

1961   Nationality and conformity. *Scientific American*, 205, 45–51.
1963   Behavioral study of obedience. *Journal of Abnormal and Social Psychology*, 67, 371–8.
1965   Some conditions of obedience and disobedience to authority. *Human Relations*, 18, 57–76.
1967   The small world problem. *Psychology Today*, 1, 60–7.
1967   Obedience to criminal orders: The compulsion to do evil. *Patterns of Prejudice*, 1, 3–7.
1969   Collective behavior: Crowds and Social Movements. In G. Lindzey and E. Aronson (eds), *Revised Handbook of Social Psychology*. Addison-Wesley (with H. Toch).
1969   The lost letter technique. *Psychology Today*, 3, 30–3, 66, 68.
1970   The experience of living in cities. *Science*, 167, 1461–8.
1973   *Television and Antisocial Behavior*. Academic Press (with L. Shortland).
1974   *Obedience to Authority*. Harper and Row.
1975   The image freezing machine. *ASMP Journal of Photography in Communications*.
1977   *The Individual in a Social World*. Addison-Wesley.

Further reading

Baumrind, D. (1964) Some thoughts on ethics of research: After reading Milgram's 'Behavioral study of obedience'. *American Psychologist*, 19, 421–3.

Cialdini, R.B. (1993) *Influence: Science and Practice*. HarperCollins.

Hock, R.R. (1995) *Forty Studies that Changed Psychology*. Prentice-Hall.

Turner, J.C. (1991) *Social Influence*. Brooks/Cole.

Stanley Milgram believed that many important human problems can be illuminated by applying scientific and specifically experimental methods to their exploration. While working for his doctorate at Harvard University he used experimental methods to determine if Norwegians or Frenchmen conformed more to group pressure. His conclusions were that pressures for conformity were greater in the relatively small, homogeneous society of Norway than in France, with its tradition of intellectual dissent. While teaching at Yale University, he turned to the study of obedience to authority. These experiments examine the degree to which ordinary people will comply with the orders of authority when those orders go against conscience. Milgram created a laboratory situation that turned out to offer a very powerful way of investigating obedience. Essentially, someone taking orders from a scientist can be persuaded to deliver what they believe to be an extremely dangerous electric shock (450 volts) to someone whom they understand to be an innocent victim with a heart condition. In a set of twenty-one experiments Milgram found that about two-thirds of subjects were willing to administer a life-threatening electric shock to the victim. The study has been replicated in dozens of countries, and while there is some variation in the percentage of subjects prepared to administer this level of shock, a fair summary is to state that about two-thirds were obedient. In 1965, this work was awarded the annual socio-psychological prize of the American Association for the Advancement of Science. It is no accident perhaps, that when translations of this work appeared, they appeared first in Hebrew and in German. The interpretations that can be placed on Milgram's findings, together with the ethical issues they raise, are still debated today. They are often explained in terms of the presence of: (1) normative pressures (the experimenter placed considerable pressure on subjects to do what they were told – unlike the less pressured procedures adopted by Solomon **Asch**); (2) informational influence (the tendency to allow others to reach a decision on what to do when faced with an ambiguous or crisis situation); and (3) conflicting social norms (once the first shock had been administered, participants

placed additional pressures on themselves to continue to obey).

In the late 1960s Milgram's interest in other forms of social influence led him to consider crowd behaviour. His laboratory looked out onto 42nd street, New York. He arranged for various numbers of pedestrians (all of them confederates – students or colleagues) to stop and gaze up at a sixth-floor window. Behind the window Milgram filmed the crowd. He systematically varied the number of confederates and measured the size of the crowd that would gather. With one confederate gazing about 45 per cent of pedestrians stopped to look up, but with fifteen confederates about 85 per cent of the passers-by stopped. This is a different type of social force – contagion rather than obedience – but it is a powerful demonstration that, as the number of sources of influence increase, the intensity of their social impact seems also to increase. This work informed a generation of experimental investigations of social impact (e.g. see **Latané**).

After spending three years at Yale University, Milgram returned to Harvard for four years of teaching and research, serving also as executive director of the Comparative International Program, in the Department of Social Relations. He carried out research on a set of original experimental techniques, notably the lost letter technique and the small world problem. Milgram is still widely regarded as one of the most gifted experimental social psychologists in the history of the discipline.

Miller, George Armitage

Born: 1920, Charleston, West Virginia, USA **Nat:** American **Ints:** cognitive science, experimental psychology **Educ:** BA University of Alabama, 1940; MA University of Alabama, 1941; AM Harvard University, 1944; PhD Harvard University, 1946 **Appts & awards:** Member, Institute for Advanced Study, Princeton, 1950, 1970–2; Member, Society of Experimental Psychologists, 1952– ; Member, AAA&S, 1957– ; Co-Director, Center for Advanced Study in the Behavioral Sciences, 1958–9; Co-Director, Center for Cognitive Studies, Harvard University, 1960–7; President, Eastern Psychological Association, 1962; Member, NAS, 1962– ; APA Distinguished Scientific Contribution Award, 1963; Fulbright Research Professor, Oxford University, 1963–4; President, APA, 1969; President, American Philosophical Society, 1971– ;

Warren Medal of Society of Experimental Psychologists, 1972; Visitor, Institute for Advanced Study, Princeton, 1972–6, 1982–3; Hon. D, Université Catholique de Louvain, 1976; Distinguished Service Award, American Speech and Hearing Association, 1976; Hon. DSc, Yale University, 1979, Columbia University, 1980, University of Sussex, 1984; Sesquicentennial Professor, University of Alabama, 1981; Chairman, AAAS Section J (Psychology), 1981; Editor, *Psychological Bulletin*, 1981–82; New York Academy of Science Award in Behavioral Sciences, 1982; James S. McDonnell Distinguished University Professor of Psychology, Princeton University, 1982–

Principal publications

1947   The masking of speech. *Psychological Bulletin*, 44, 104–9.

1948   The perception of repeated bursts of noise. *Journal of the Acoustical Society of America*, 20, 160–70.

1949   Statistical behavioristics and sequence of responses. *Psychological Review*, 56, 311–24.

1951   Speech and language. In S.S. Stevens (ed.), *Handbook of Experimental Psychology*. Wiley.

1951   *Language and Communication*. McGraw-Hill.

1952   Finite Markov processes in psychology. *Psychometrika*, 17, 149–67.

1953   What is information measurement? *American Psychologist*, 8, 3–11.

1954   Communication. *Annual Review of Psychology*, 5, 401–20.

1956   The magical number seven, plus or minus two: Some limits on our capacity for processing information. *Psychological Review*, 63, 81–97.

1960   *Plans and the Structure of Behavior*. Holt (with E. Galanter and K.H. Pribram).

1962   *Psychology: The Science of Mental Life*. Harper and Row.

1963   Finite models of language users. In D. Luce, R. Bush and E. Galanter (eds), *Handbook of Mathematical Psychology, vol 2*. Wiley.

1969   *The Psychology of Communication: Seven Essays*. Basic Books.

1976   *Language and Perception*. Harvard University Press (with P.N. Johnson-Laird).

Further reading

Posner, M.I. (ed.) (1989) *Foundations of Cognitive Science*. Bradford.

Simon, H.A. (1974) How big is a chunk? *Science*, 183, 482–8.

George Miller grew up in Charleston, West Virginia, until 1937, when he entered George Washington University. In 1938 he transferred to the University of Alabama, where he completed his BA. In 1941 he was appointed Instructor in Psychology at Alabama University, and two years later enrolled in Harvard as a graduate student. He joined the Psycho-Acoustical Laboratory and conducted evaluation studies on radio-telephone systems for the army. He used this as an opportunity to examine the masking of speech, and this was the topic of his PhD thesis. In 1948 he secured a position as assistant professor at Harvard and began teaching an advanced course on the psychology of speech and communication. These lectures formed the core of his *Language and Communication*. He became interested in the mathematical theory of communication and studied mathematics as a Visiting Fellow at the Institute for Advanced Study at Princeton (1950). The following year he moved to the MIT Lincoln Laboratory. In 1955 he was appointed Associate Professor of Psychology at Harvard and promoted to full professor three years later. During 1958–9 he was at the Center for Advanced Study in the Behavioral Sciences, where he collaborated with Galanter and **Pribram** on *Plans and the Structure of Behavior*.

Miller is best known as an advocate of the information-processing view of memory and specifically for his work on human memory and thinking. He is associated with the concept of 'chunking' as a means to overcome the limitations of short-term memory. He argued that people can work round the limited-capacity short-term memory system by grouping items and using a symbol to represent the group. For instance, a number sequence such as: 7 1 4 1 2 1 9 9 7 can be difficult to remember, but it is much easier if it is chunked and organized thus: week (7 days), fortnight (14 days), months (12), year (1997). An important claim in Miller's theory is that the number of chunks a person can repeat back is limited to seven, plus or minus two. This represents a limit on short-term information processing. This claim was challenged by **Simon** with the following demonstration. Try memorizing the following words: Lincoln, milky, criminal, differential, address, way, lawyer, calculus, Gettysburg. It is quite difficult, but much easier if the words are rearranged thus: Milky Way, Gettysburg Address, criminal lawyer, differential calculus. The ability to create chunks such as these is strongly dependent on prior learning. This suggests that short-term memory cannot precede long-term memory in a simple sequential fashion. Either long-term memory is used to guide short-term memory or new relations are constructed on the basis of existing knowledge. Simon modified Miller's claim and suggested that the capacity of short-term memory is about five chunks. There is evidence to suggest that while the number of chunks a person can remember is relatively constant through the life-span, as Miller suggested, the amount of information per chunk increases as knowledge increases.

Miller, Neal Elgar

Born: 1909, Milwaukee, USA **Nat:** American **Ints:** Behavioural medicine, health psychology, physiological psychology, learning, experimental psychology **Educ:** BS University of Washington, 1931; MS Stanford University, 1932; PhD Yale University, 1935 **Appts and Awards:** Professor Emeritus and Head, Laboratory of Physiological Psychology, Rockefeller University; Member, National Academy of Science, 1958; President, APA, 1960–1; Member, AAAS, 1961; Hon. DSc, University of Michigan, 1965, University of Pennsylvania, 1968, St Lawrence University, 1973, La Salle College, 1979, Rutgers University, 1985; President, Society for Neuroscience, 1971–2; APA Gold Medal Award, 1971; Hon. PhD, University of Uppsala, 1977; McAlpin Medal, Mental Health Association, 1978; President, APA Division 38, 1980–1; APA Distinguished Contributions to Knowledge Award, 1983; President, Biofeedback Society of American, 1984–5; APA Outstanding Lifetime Achievement Award, 1991; Editor, numerous journals and member of editorial boards

Principal publications

1939 *Frustration and Aggression.* Yale University Press (with J. Dollard, L.W. Doob, O.H. Mowrer and R.R. Sears).

1941 *Social Learning and Imitation.* Yale University Press (with J. Dollard).

1947 *Psychological Research on Pilot Training.* US Government Printing Office.

1948 Studies of fear as an acquirable drive: I. Fear as motivation and fear reduction as reinforcement in the learning of new responses. *Journal of Experimental Psychology*, 38, 89–101.

1948 Theory and experiment relating psychoanalytic displacement to stimulus–response generalization. *Journal of Abnormal and Social Psychology*, 43, 155–78.

1950 *Personality and Psychotherapy.* McGraw-Hill (with J. Dollard).

1959 Liberalization of basic S-R concepts: Extensions to conflict behavior, motivation and social learning. In S. Koch (ed.), *Psychology: A Study of a Science, study I, vol. 2.* McGraw-Hill.

1961 Learning and performance motivated by direct stimulation of the brain. In D.E. Sheer (ed.), *Electrical Stimulation of the Brain.* University of Texas Press.

1963 Animal experiments on emotionally induced ulcers. *Proceedings of III World Congress of Psychiatry, 1961*, 3, 213–19.

1965 Chemical coding of behavior in the brain. *Science*, 148, 328–33.

1979 A learned visceral response apparently independent of skeletal ones in patients paralyzed by spinal lesions. In N. Birbaumer and H.D. Kimmel (eds), *Biofeedback and Self-Regulation.* Erlbaum (with B.S. Brucker).

1981 Learning in the homeostatic regulation of visceral responses. In G. Adam, I. Mescaros and E.I. Banyai (eds), *Advances in Physiological Science, vol. 17.* Akademiai Kiado.

1983 Behavioral medicine: Symbiosis between laboratory and clinic. *Annual Review of Psychology*, 34, 1–31.

1984 *Behavioral Health: A Handbook of Health Enhancement and Disease Prevention.* Wiley-Interscience (with J.D. Matarazzo, S.M. Weiss and J.A. Herd).

1985 Effects of emotional stress on the immune system. *Pavlovian Journal of Biological Science*, 20, 47–52.

1987 *Health Psychology: A Discipline and a Profession.* University of Chicago Press (ed. with G.C. Stone *et al.*).

Further reading

Hergenhahn, B.R. (1990) *An Introduction to Theories of Personality,* 3rd edn. Prentice-Hall.

Monte, C.F. (1995) *Beneath the Mask: An Introduction to Theories of Personality,* 5th edn. Harcourt Brace.

The work of Neal Miller integrated knowledge from laboratory experiments, clinical observations and social and anthropological data in books on frustration and aggression, on social learning and imitation, and on personality and psychotherapy. The last book demonstrated in detail how neuroses can be learned and how therapy is a process of learning more adaptive social and personal habits. This removed psychotherapy from the exclusive domain of medicine and provided a rational foundation for psychotherapy based on principles of learning and social behaviour. After that, he and his students performed experiments combining behavioural, physiological and pharmacological techniques in the study of motivation. These resulted in the first demonstration of instrumental learning motivated by direct electrical stimulation of the brain proof that eating and drinking elicited in this way have the motivational characteristics of a normally elicited drive. Next, he and his students demonstrated that eating could be elicited by adrenergic chemostimulation of the brain, that such eating had all the characteristics of normal hunger, and that an adrenergic neurotransmitter in the brain is involved in normal hunger. Another series of studies demonstrated that instrumental learning could modify visceral responses. Work on patients with high spinal lesions, in collaboration with Bernard Brucker, provided strong evidence that they could learn to elicit large increases in blood pressure directly without any involvement of skeletal muscles. The learning by these spinal patients corrected a serious homeostatic defect, orthostatic hypotension; this result raised the theoretical possibility that visceral learning may play a role in normal homeostasis that hitherto has been neglected.

Minami, Hiroshi

Born: 1914, Tokyo, Japan *Nat:* Japanese *Ints:* Counselling psychology, personality and social psychology, philosophical and theoretical psychology, psychotherapy *Educ:* BA Kyoto University, 1940; PhD Cornell University, 1943; DLitt Kyoto University, 1962 *Appts & awards:* Director, Japan Psychology Center, Tokyo; President, Japan Society of Image Arts and Sciences; Japan Society of the Traditional Performing Arts; Best Book of the Year Prize for *Social Psychology*, 1952; Editor, *Nihonjin No Ningenkanei Jiten* (*Studies of Human Relations in Japan*); Editorial Board, *German Journal of Psychology*; Editor, Studies on Japanese Modernism; *People's History in Modern Japan*

Principal publications

1946 The effect of activity upon learning and retention in the cockroach. *American Journal of Psychology*, 59, 1–58 (with K.M. Dallenbach).
1953 *Nihonjin No Shinri*. Iwanami. (Reprinted as

The Psychology of the Japanese People, University of Tokyo Press, 1971).
1954 Human relations in the Japanese society. *Annals of the Hitotsubashi Academy*, 3, 148–62.
1957 On some characteristics of mass entertainment in contemporary Japan. *Annals of the Hitotsubashi Academy*, 7, 133–43.
1958 On the system of social behavior. *Annals of the Hitotsubashi Academy*, 9, 68–75.
1976 *Kodorironshi*. Iwanami.
1978 *Taikei Shakai Shinrigaku*. Kobunsha.
1980 *Ningen Kodogaku*. Iwanami.
1983 *Nihonteki Jiga*. Iwanami.

Further reading

Gielen, U.P. *et al.* (1992) *Psychology in International Perspective: 50 Years of the International Council of Psychologists*. Swets & Zeitlinger.
Murofushi, K. Historical bases and current status of comparative psychology in Japan. In E. Tobach (ed.) *Historical Perspectives and the International Status of Comparative Psychology*. Erlbaum.

After graduating from Kyoto University, Minami spent three years at Cornell completing a PhD under the supervision of Karl M. **Dallenbach**. He returned to Japan and is credited with the first systematic presentation of social psychology there. His work stimulated wider interest in the study of the Japanese national character, and this served as the impetus for the publication of *The Psychology of the Japanese People*, which was translated into English in 1971. His involvement with the Japanese traditional performing arts reflects his broader, personal interests in his country's culture. His interest in the psychological analysis of changes in Japanese psyche from the 1950s to the 1980s – a period of rapid industrialization in that country – led to the publication in 1983 of *The Japanese Ego Structure*. Another of his books, *The Science of Human Behavior* (1980) offered a broad review of biological, physiological and social aspects of human behaviour and was highly influential in the Japanese psychology curriculum of the 1980s. Minami's interest in industrialization processes and the effects of American influences on the Japanese people in the pre-war period was the motivation for a comprehensive study of Japanese modernism before World War II. His psychological analyses of the history and culture of Japan led to a role as editor for an influential book series entitled Studies on Japanese Modernism, and a ten-volume, primary-source *People's History in Modern Japan*.

Minsky, Marvin Lee

Born: 1927, New York City, USA *Nat:* American *Ints:* Artificial intelligence, cognitive science *Educ:* BA Harvard University, 1950; PhD Princeton University, 1954 *Appts & awards:* Lincoln Laboratory, MIT, 1957–8; MIT, Assistant Professor of Mathematics, 1958–61, Associate Professor of Electrical Engineering, 1961–4; Professor and Co-Founder, MIT's Artificial Intelligence Laboratory, 1961; Founder, LOGO Computer Systems, Inc.; Director, MIT Artificial Intelligence Laboratory, 1964–74; Turing Award, Association for Computing Machinery, 1970; Donner Professor of Science, MIT, 1974–89; Doubleday Lecturer, Smithsonian Institute, 1978; Messenger Lecturer, Cornell University, 1979; President, American Association for Artificial Intelligence, 1981–2; Hon. Dr, Free University of Brussels, 1986, Pine Manor College, 1987; Killian Award, MIT, 1989; Japan Prize Laureate, Government of Japan, 1990; IJCAI Research Excellence Award, 1991; Toshiba Professor of Media Arts and Sciences, MIT, 1990–

Principal publications

1956 Some universal elements for finite state automata. In C.E. Shannon and J. McCarthy (eds), *Automata Studies: Annals of Mathematics Studies*, no. 34. Princeton University Press.

1959 Some methods of heuristic programming and artificial intelligence. In D.V. Blake and A.M. Uttley (eds), *Proceedings on Symposium on Mechanization of Thought Processes*. HMSO.

1961 Learning in random nets. In C. Cherry (ed), *Proceedings of Fourth London Symposium on Information Theory*. Butterworth (with O. Selfridge).

1961 Steps toward artificial intelligence. *Proceedings IRE*, 49(1), January.

1962 Progress in artificial intelligence. *Discovery*, 23(10), 33–7.

1966 Artificial intelligence. *Scientific American*, 215(3), 247–60.

1967 *Computation: Finite and Infinite Machines.* Prentice-Hall.

1968 *Semantic Information Processing.* MIT Press.

1969 *Perceptrons.* MIT Press (with Seymour Papert). (Rev. edn, 1987.)

1974 *Artificial Intelligence.* MIT Press (with Seymour Papert).

1975 A framework for representing knowledge. In P.H. Winston (ed), *The Psychology of Computer Vision.* McGraw-Hill.

1980 Computer science and the representation of knowledge. In M. Dertouzos and J. Moses (eds), *The Computer Age: A Twenty-Year View.* MIT Press.

1980 K-lines: A theory of memory. *Cognitive Science*, 4, 117–33.

1985 *Robotics.* Doubleday.

1986 *The Society of Mind.* Simon & Schuster.

1988 Preface: Connectionist models and their prospects. In D. Waltz, J.A. Feldman and S. Papert (eds), *Connectionist Models and their Implications.* Ablex.

1991 A response to four reviews of *The Society of Mind. Artificial Intelligence*, 48, 371–96.

1992 *The Turing Option.* Warner Books (with Harry Harrison).

1994 On the problem of conscious machines. *Proceedings, National Research Council of Canada's 75th Anniversary Symposium on Science and Technology.* National Research Council of Canada.

1994 Negative expertise. *International Journal of Expert Systems*, 7, 13–19.

Further reading

Gazzaniga, M.S. (ed) (1995) *The Cognitive Neurosciences.* MIT Press.

Shapiro, S.C., Eckroth, D. and Vallasi, G.A. (1987) *Encyclopaedia of Artificial Intelligence,* 2 vols. Wiley.

Smoliar, S.W. (1991) Review of *The Society of Mind. Artificial Intelligence*, 48, 349–70.

Marvin Lee Minsky is famous in cognitive science not only as a pioneer in the fields of artificial intelligence, robotics and knowledge representation (e.g. he devised the construct of 'frames') but also as an inventor of note, having helped to develop computer languages (e.g. LISP) and mechanical computational devices (e.g. the first LOGO 'turtle', in conjunction with Seymour Papert). Indeed, while a post-doctoral fellow at Harvard in the 1950s, Minsky designed a revolutionary optical instrument called the 'confocal scanning microscope', which enabled the viewer to observe successively deeper layers in a specimen without having to undertake the arduous task of cutting the specimen into sections.

Minsky was one of the first computer scientists to develop a theoretical model (called 'frame theory') of the knowledge structures that underlie performance of everyday cognitive tasks. Influenced by **Bartlett**'s ideas on 'schemas', Minsky proposed that our knowledge is encoded in packets called 'frames' (borrowing a photographic metaphor), which facilitate our understanding of many aspects of everyday phenomena. In some ways, a frame resembles a form which is 'filled out' by the mind in an effort to interpret and make predictions from recurrent everyday situations. Using frames, people can rapidly gain access to stored knowledge and expectations about commonly encountered experiences. For example, if one opened the door of one's house one evening, one would be shocked to discover that on the other side lay a sleeping tiger! Perceptual recognition of this unexpected stimulus would be delayed because it violates the interpretation yielded by one's standard 'room frame'. Support for this theory is provided by research which shows that drawings of objects are easier to identify when presented in their usual contexts than when presented in anomalous situations. Computationally, frames are sufficiently large as units of knowledge to be useful to people in imposing structure on new situations, while still being independent enough to serve as modules in our flexible mental database.

Within our minds, 'framed' knowledge is alleged to be stored at different levels of abstraction. At the top, or most abstract, level, invariant features of the situation are represented. These features usually reflect things that are almost always true about the event in question (e.g. the fact that people usually bring presents to a child's party). Conversely, lower levels of the frame (called 'terminals' or 'slots') contain information which is more variable (e.g. a birthday present for a child should be something which she or he would like to receive). Frames are also believed to possess 'default' values which are characteristics of objects that can be taken for granted unless there is evidence to the contrary. By this theory, an important function of memory is to find the appropriate frames required to deal with a given situation. Therefore, a 'scenario' is a sequence of frames that describe how we expect things to occur. Like many other semantic network theorists, Minsky believed that frames are organized in an 'inheritance' hierarchy.

Throughout his career, Minsky has been intrigued by the commonsense knowledge which underlies everyday intelligence. The size and complexity of such knowledge has proved to be a barrier to simulation attempts in artificial intelligence. For example, despite receiving no formal instruction in the laws of gravity, a 3-year-old child typically stacks blocks from the bottom up, whereas a computer may attempt this task by dropping the blocks from the top down.

Also, whereas we take for granted the fact that chairs painted in different colours remain the same, computers have to be programmed meticulously to achieve similar insights. This 'commonsense problem' may help to explain why thinking is easy for people but exceedingly difficult for computers.

In 1986, Minsky produced a remarkable book, *The Society of Mind*, which proposed that 'intelligence' is not a monolithic construct but emerges from interactions among a 'society' of cognitive 'agents'. Speculations about the identity and interaction of these processes are presented in 270 self-contained, one-page vignettes in this book. Suggesting that the brain performs its great diversity of functions by exploiting the advantages of many different kinds of knowledge representation, Minsky argues that cognitive diversity provides the greatest challenge to artificial intelligence researchers. Although ambitious in scope and provocative in design, *The Society of Mind* has been criticized (e.g. Smoliar, 1991) for its inclusion of fragmented and unsupported assertions. Nevertheless, its metaphor of a 'society' of cognitive processes anticipates current neuroscientific research (e.g. see Gazzaniga, 1995) on the modularity of mind. For this reason, and also for his development of 'frame theory', Minsky is rightly regarded as an inspirational thinker in cognitive science.

AIDAN MORAN

Mischel, Walter

Born: 1930, Vienna, Austria **Nat:** American **Ints:** Personality assessment (APA Division 8), personality and social developmental psychology **Educ:** BA New York University, 1951; MA College of City University of New York, 1953; PhD Ohio State University, 1956 **Appts & awards:** Niven Professor of Humane Letters, Columbia University, 1944– ; University of Colorado, 1956–8; Harvard University, 1958–62; Stanford University, 1962–83; Columbia University, 1983– ; Clinical and Personality Sciences Fellowship Review Committee, NIMH, 1970–3; President, Division of Clinical Psychology, Section III (Development of Clinical Psychology as an Experimental Behavioral Science), APA, 1971; National Science Foundation Distinguished Visiting Scientist, 1971, 1973; Committee on Scientific Awards, APA, 1975–7; Fellow, Center for Advanced Study in the Behavioral Sciences, 1976–7; Chairman, Personality and Cognition

Research Review Committee, NIMH, 1976–80; Distinguished Scientist Award, APA, Division of Clinical Psychology, 1978; Advisory Council, Princeton University Department of Psychology, 1978–83; Scientific Advisory Board, Max Planck Gesellschaft, Berlin 1981–90; Distinguished Scientific Contribution Award, APA, 1982; Trustee, Association for the Advancement of Psychology, 1982–6; President, APA Division 8, 1985; Merit Award, NIMH, 1989–95; Publication Board, APA 1989–95; William James Fellow, APA, 1990– ; Fellow, American Academy of Arts and Sciences, 1991–

Principal publications

1968   *Personality and Assessment*. Wiley.
1969   Continuity and change in personality. *American Psychologist*, 24, 1013–18.
1973   Toward a cognitive social learning reconceptualization of personality. *Psychological Review*, 80, 252–83.
1977   On the future of personality measurement. *American Psychologist*, 32, 246–54.
1982   Beyond déjà vu in the search for cross-situational consistency. *Psychological Review*, 34, 730–55 (with P. Peake).
1983   Alternatives in the pursuit of the predictability and consistency of persons: Stable data that yield unstable interpretations. *Journal of Personality*, 51, 578–604.
1988   Conditional hedges and the intuitive psychology of traits. *Journal of Personality and Social Psychology*, 55, 454–69 (with J.C. Wright).
1989   Intuitive interactionism in person perception: Effects of situation–behavior relations on dispositional judgments. *Journal of Personality and Social Psychology*, 56, 41–53 (with Y. Shoda and J.C. Wright).
1989   Delay of gratification in children. *Science*, 244, 933–8 (with Y. Shoda and M.L. Rodriguez).
1990   Personality dispositions revisited and revised: A view after three decades. In L.A. Pervin (ed.), *Handbook of Personality: Theory and Research*. Guilford Press.
1993   The role of situational demands and cognitive competencies in behavior organization and personality coherence. *Journal of Personality and Social Psychology*, 65, 1023–35 (with Y. Shoda and J.C. Wright).
1995   A cognitive-affective system theory of personality: Reconceptualizing situations, dispositions, dynamics and invariance in personality structure. *Psychological Review*, 102, 246–68 (with Y. Shoda).

Further reading

Buss, A.H. (1989) Personality as traits. *American Psychologist*, 44, 1378–88.
Danziger, K. (1990) *Constructing the Subject*. Oxford University Press.
Epstein, S. and O'Brien, E.J. (1985) The person–situation debate in historical and current perspective. *Psychological Bulletin*, 98, 513–37.
Hogan, R. and Jones, W.H. (1985) Preface. In R. Hogan and W.H. Jones (eds), *Perspectives in Personality: A Research Annual, vol. 1*. JAI Press.
Kenrick, D.T. and Funder, D.C. (1988) Profiting from controversy: Lessons from the person–situation debate. *American Psychologist*, 43, 23–34.

George **Kelly** and Julian **Rotter** figure prominently in Mischel's background. He studied under both, became familiar with their theories and methods, and adapted some of their explanatory constructs for inclusion in his cognitive social-learning theory. Mischel devoted most of his career to developing and testing this theory, but is also well known for his role in the person–situation debate.

Mischel's *Personality and Assessment* contained a penetrating critique of trait theory, which prompted a fruitful exchange of views. His case rested on an extensive empirical base consisting of **Pearson** *r*s between global trait measures and observations of trait-relevant behaviour. Cognitive abilities excepted, these *r*s were nearly always low; individual differences in personality characteristics accounted for small portions (usually 5 per cent or less, seldom as much as 10 per cent) of variance in people's actions. Whereas intelligence-related behaviours displayed appreciable consistency across situations, personality-related behaviours clearly did not.

Investigators responded to the critique in various ways. Some undertook to study situational determinants in conjunction with traits, some focused on cross-situational variability *per se*, some explained away the low *r*s as due to error in specifying or measuring traits and/or trait-relevant behaviours. Noting the particular limitations of each of these responses as well as the inadequacy they share – a tendency to disregard or treat too superficially the psychological processes involved – Mischel then identified the real challenge confronting personality theorists as that of reconceptualizing dispositions in enough detail to take into account the perceived situation together with the individual's feelings, values, goals and plans.

Mischel's research career represents a sustained effort to explicate the psychological processes so often ignored at the hands of trait theorists. In his 1995 Psychological Review article with Shoda, he presented a framework for examining conjectures about meditational sequences within the person.

Mischel's theory postulates five classes of dispositional variable. When assessed and considered together in various situations, these comprise a set of mediating units which may enable the psychologist to discern 'a stable network of relations that characterize an individual'. Each disposition is describable in terms of a cognitive and an affective component:

(1) encodings: categories for construing situations, events, others and oneself (similar to Kelly's personal constructs);
(2) expectancies and beliefs: concerning self-efficacy, the social world and if–then sequences in particular situations (similar to Rotter's expectancy);
(3) affects: feelings, emotions and affective responses;
(4) goals and values: how expected if–then sequences in particular situations will influence affective states; how compatible they will be with one's goals and values; their likely impact upon life projects (similar in part to Rotter's values);
(5) competencies and self-regulatory plans: knowledge of one's behavioural abilities and limitations *vis-à-vis* alternatives for action in particular situations and likely outcomes.

These five kinds of variables overlap, and interact in a sequence that determines behaviour. Each is a product of the individual's development and social learning. Each has a structural and a functional aspect.

To test the theory, objective and subjective descriptions of situations are needed. Mischel's processing model starts with features of situations; one's encoding of a situation is prior to everything else in that it activates distinctive patterns of cognition, affect and behaviour. Situation features supposedly engage processing structures, which generate certain processing dynamics; these produce characteristic behaviours for the person × situation combination.

For the past forty Years, Mischel has been a highly productive investigator. His studies are guided by the theory; their data are for the most part highly compatible with it and often flesh it out in an interesting way. The more widely cited experiments elucidate crucial theoretical points, e.g. the self-regulatory mechanisms that enable us to delay gratification, the fact that real-life situations can be reliably described in terms of their demand profiles, the importance of match vs. mismatch between person variables and features of the situation, the extent to which we make allowance for social context in our perceptions of others, our reliance on probabilistic and situational hedges in trait ascription, why it is that we tend to be rather inaccurate reporters of our own cross-situational consistency, etc.

Mischel seems to have overstated his case in *Personality and Assessment*, inadvertently perhaps, or for polemic effect. Whatever the reason, it is clear that the book outraged a good many trait theorists. It drew critical fire when it first appeared, and was still a viable target for trait theorists' attacks seventeen years later: 'the notion that there is no stable core to personality is inherently self-refuting, e.g., Walter Mischel is the same clever, hard-working, provocative man today that he was in 1968' (Hogan and Jones, 1985).

Although Mischel may have started out as an opponent of the trait approach, it is clear that he does not now deny the existence of consistent patterns of individual differences among children, or adolescents, or adults; in fact, he specifies five kinds of individual difference information that are necessary if the psychologist is to arrive at a full understanding of anyone. What he objects to most is personologists' readiness to rely on global traits. To be satisfied with results expressed in terms of broad traits is, in his view, to stop short of knowledge of the basic workings of personality. Another way psychologists are apt to limit their understanding is to remain content with describing the actions of groups of people, not even attempting to predict what particular individuals will do when confronted with particular objective situations.

A potential difficulty is posed by the fact that Mischel's approach takes individual differences as a point of departure but seeks ultimately to describe each person's more or less unique phenomenology. These are arguably two separate endeavours, and it is questionable whether a theory can do justice to both at the same time: 'If the subject is an individual consciousness, we get a very different kind of psychology than if the subject is a population of organisms' (Danziger, 1990). Thus far, Mischel has been able to integrate and balance the two approaches quite persuasively. Whether he and his associates will continue to reconcile them so successfully remains to be seen.

Mischel ranks among today's most influential psychologists. Practically all recent undergraduate and graduate textbooks in personality devote a chapter, or at least half a chapter, to his theory and research. He has written a personality text himself (now in its fifth edition), and has contributed to all the major journals, symposia, handbooks and other forums in American psychology. He is an active participant in the institutional machinery of psychological associations and research funding. His views have been studied by several generations of students; it is likely that they will be perpetuated, extended and refined well into the twenty-first century, by Mischel himself, by his closest associates (e.g. Yuichi Shoda, Jack Wright, Nancy Cantor, Philip Peake) and by other scholars throughout the world.

R.N. WOLFE

Montessori, Maria

Born: 1870, Chiaravalle, Italy **Died:** 1952, Noordwijk aan Zee, Holland **Nat:** Italian **Ints:** Developmental psychology, educational psychology, personality psychology, new pedagogy **Educ:** MD (first woman to receive this) University of Rome, 1896 **Appts & awards:** Assistant Physician, Psychiatric Clinic, University of Rome, 1884–99; Directress, State Orthophrenic Institute, Rome, 1898–1900; Lecturer, Anthropology and Hygiene, Royal Feminine Teacher Training College, Rome, 1900–4; Lecturer, Pedagogical Anthropology, Royal University of Rome, 1904–16; Founder, Casa dei Bambini (Montessori School), Rome, 1907, United States, 1911, London, 1913, Spain, 1913; Founder, international training course, London, 1919, Amsterdam, 1924; Hon. LLD, University of Durham, 1923; Founder, Montessori Society India, 1926, Montessori Society, Argentina, 1927, Association Montessori Internationale (AMI), 1929, Montessori Society of Ireland, 1934, Montessori in India, 1939–46, Montessori Association Pakistan, 1949; Hon. Fellow, Educational Institute of Scotland, 1946; Honoured by the Italian Parliament, 1947; Cross of the Legion of Honour, France, 1949; Delegate, UNESCO General Assembly, Florence, 1950; Hon. Dr, University of Amsterdam, 1950; Professor, University of Perugia, 1950; Nominated for Nobel Peace Prize, 1950

Principal publications

1909 *The Montessori Method.* (Reprint, intro. J.McV. Hunt. Schocken, 1964.)

1916 *The Advanced Montessori Method,* 2 vols. (Reprint, Kalakshetra Publications, 1965.)

1932 *Peace in Education.* Montessori Society.

1936 *The Child in the Family.* (Reprint, Henry Regney.)

1936 *The Secret of Childhood.* (Reprint, Schocken, 1966.)

1946 *Education for a New World.* Kalakshetra.

1948 *To Educate the Human Potential, Discovery of the Child, What You Should Know about Your Child* (All Kalakshetra).

1949 *The Absorbent Mind.* Theosophical Publishing House.

1950 *The Formation of Man.* Kalakshetra.

Further reading

Elkind, D. (1967) Piaget and Montessori. *Harvard Educational Review,* 37, 4, 535–45.

Gebhart-Seele, P. (1985) *The Computer and the Child: A Montessori Approach.* Computer Science Press.

Gross, M.J. (1978) *Montessori's Concept of Personality.* University Press of America.

Hainstock, E.G. (1978) *The Essential Montessori.* New American Library.

Hornberger, M.A. (1984) The developmental psychology of Maria Montessori (unpublished doctoral dissertation). Teachers College, Columbia University, 1982. Dissertation Abstracts International, 44 (11), 33206A–33207A.

Hunt, J.McV. (1964) Introduction. In M. Montessori, *The Montessori Method.* Schocken.

—— (1975) Children learn in different ways. In *Proceedings of the American Montessori Society Seminar.* American Montessori Society.

Kohlberg, L. (1968) Montessori with the culturally disadvantaged: A cognitive developmental interpretation and some research findings. In R. Hess and R.M. Baer (eds), *Early Education.* Aldine.

Kramer, D. (1976) *Maria Montessori – A Biography.* Putnam's Sons.

Lillard, P.P. (1972) *Montessori – A Modern Approach.* Schocken.

Montessori, M.M., Jr (1976) *Education for Human Development: Understanding Montessori.* Schocken.

Phillips, S. (1977) Maria Montessori and contemporary cognitive psychology. *British Journal of Teacher Education,* 3, 1, 55–68.

Piaget, J. (1970) *Science of Education and the Psychology of the Child.* Longman.

Swan, D. (1987) Foreword. In David Gettman, *Basic Montessori Learning Activities for Under-Fives.* Helm.

—— (1989) Maria Montessori: Prophetic psychologist – teacher extraordinary. *AMI Communications*, 2/3, 4–11.

Although Maria Montessori was trained in medicine and anthropology, it was in the area of education, initially in the education of deprived children, that her major theories began to unfold. Standing at the point of coincidence of mass schooling with the emerging discipline of empirical psychology, Montessori was to play a major role in the application of psychological theory to educational practice. Drawing on the theories of Jean Itard and Edward Séguin in particular, she believed that direct observation of the child, not in a laboratory but in the classroom, was the most scientific approach to understanding, and to laying the basis of a sound pedagogy. Unlike others she insisted on the psychophysical unity of the child, and the unity of cognition, development and education, in the formation of the personality. Despite her sometimes mystical and archaic language, she formulated psychological theories that were sometimes in tune, and sometimes very much at variance, with contemporary psychology, while at times showing remarkable anticipation of later major developments in psychology, including aspects of cognitivism and humanistic psychology.

Noting a qualitative difference between the psychic life of the adult and that of the child, she saw the personality evolving, impelled by energy (a vitalistic, late nineteenth-century notion), spontaneity and sensitivity, through a number of transformations, and in response to its encounters with the environment. Key concepts here are the reflex arc, the absorbent mind, sensitive periods and the active intellect. The reflex arc as the pathway of discharge of physical energy was, to her, the physical counterpart of the psychic energy discharged in thinking itself, just as the absorption of knowledge by the mind corresponds to biological assimilation. The first six years of life were marked by the child's capacity to assimilate knowledge, and to co-ordinate and integrate its own mental and physiological development. The mind also developed through a series of sensitive periods, e.g. for language learning, motor adaptation, sensory discrimination and perception, images, morality, socialization, etc. The role of education, in the detailed system devised by her, is to match and stimulate from without these inward processes of growth and self-development through this 'prepared environment'.

Montessori's influence on psychology was more indirect, through her influence on **Piaget** – which he acknowledged (Piaget, 1971) and Elkind (1967) discussed – and again through the *Zeitgeist* of child-centred education and her contribution to the pedagogical revolution of the twentieth century, which are only now beginning to be superseded in some places. Her emphasis on spontaneous activity, on self-development primarily through movement, and on naturalistic observation as a scientific method are all evident also in Piaget's work. Other contemporary psychologists who have shown a serious interest in her work are **Hunt** on the plasticity of intelligence and the 'problem of the match', **Kohlberg** on attention, Phillips on her anticipation of contemporary cognitive psychology, Hornberger on her affinity with contemporary constructivism, and Swan on the analogy between her notion of autonomy in learning and that found in the humanistic psychology of Carl **Rogers**.

DES SWAN

Morgan, Clifford Thomas

Born: 1915, Minnetola, New Jersey, USA *Died:* 1976, Austin, Texas, USA *Nat:* American *Ints:* Experimental psychology, industrial and organizational psychology, physiological and comparative psychology *Educ:* BA Maryville College, Tennessee, 1935; AM Rochester University, 1937; PhD Rochester University, 1939 *Appts & awards:* Chairman of Psychology, Johns Hopkins University, 1943–55; Founder and First President, Psychonomic Society, 1946–8; President, APA Division 6, 1946–8; Chairman, APA Board of Publications, 1960–1; Editor, Psychology Series (McGraw-Hill), 1950–9, *Psychological Abstracts*, 1960–3; Chairman, Psychonomic Society Journal Board, 1964–76

Principal publications

1940   Studies in hunger: I. The effects of insulin upon the rat's rate of eating. *Journal of Genetic Psychology*, 56, 137–47 (with J.D. Morgan).

1940   Studies in hunger: II. The relation of gastric denervation and dietary sugar to the effect of insulin upon food intake in the rat. *Journal of Genetic Psychology*, 57, 153–63 (with J.D. Morgan).

1942 Cortical localization of symbolic process in the rat: I. *Journal of Comparative Psychology*, 34, 107–26 (with E. Stellar and M. Yarosh).

1943 Cortical localization of symbolic process in the rat: II. The effect of cortical lesions on delayed alternation. *Journal of Neurophysiology*, 6, 173–80 (with W.M. Wood).

1943 Cortical localization of symbolic process in the rat: III. Impairment of anticipatory function in prefrontal lobectomy in rats. *Journal of Experimental Psychology*, 32, 453–63 (with M.A. Epstein).

1943 *Physiological Psychology*. McGraw-Hill.

1945 Effects of cortical lesions upon audiogenic seizures. *Journal of Comparative Psychology*, 38, 199–208 (with H.M. Weiner).

1946 Food hoarding in rats as a function of environmental temperature. *Journal of Comparative Psychology*, 39, 371–8 (with R.A. McCleary).

1949 *Applied Experimental Psychology*. Wiley (with A. Chapanis and W.R. Garner).

1950 *Physiological Psychology*. McGraw-Hill (with E. Stellar).

1956 *Introduction to Psychology*. McGraw-Hill.

1965 *Physiological Psychology*. McGraw-Hill.

Further reading

Atkinson, R.C. *et al.* (eds) (1988) Stevens' *Handbook of Experimental Psychology*. Wiley.

Thompson. J.G. (1988) *The Psychobiology of Emotions*. Plenum Press.

Clifford Morgan is associated with the new wave of physiological psychology in the 1930s and 1940s and he published ground-breaking studies of hunger and of symbolic processing in the brain. His leadership culminated in the publication of *Physiological Psychology*, the leading textbook of its time. After World War II, there was further rapid growth in physiological psychology, led in large part by the Department of Psychology at Johns Hopkins, reconstituted, developed and chaired by Morgan, 1946–54. A second major contribution, during World War II, was Morgan's leading role in the development of human engineering, marked by the publication of *Applied Experimental Psychology* (with **Chapanis** and **Garner**) in 1949. A third publication also broke new ground – his *Introduction to Psychology* (1956). The book was planned and edited by Morgan, who recruited a dozen of his colleagues to write the basic chapters in their areas of expertise. It became the leader in the field. After leaving Hopkins in 1959, Morgan became a lecturer in psychology at Wisconsin and at Santa Barbara. During this period, he was heavily involved in reshaping the APA Publications Board, performed a rescue operation on *Psychological Abstracts*, started the Psychonomic Society, and founded the journal *Psychonomic Science* and a series of other journals of the Society. In 1968, he moved to the University of Texas at Austin, where he remained until his death on 12 February 1976. Morgan's career was punctuated by three changes in direction: he had a highly successful research career, but gave it up to chair the Hopkins department; he gave that up to write textbooks; and he gave that up to found a scientific society and its journals.

Morgan, Conwy L.

Born: 1852, London, England **Died:** 1936, Hastings, England **Nat:** British **Ints:** Philosophical and theoretical, physiological and comparative psychology **Educ:** Associateship in Mining and Metallurgy, School of Mines, Royal College of Science, 1871 **Appts & awards:** Lecturer, Clark University and Harvard University, 1878–83; Lecturer, South Africa, 1884–1909; University College Bristol, Professor of Zoology and Geology, Professor of Psychology and Education, 1901; Hon. DSc, Bristol University, 1910; Professor Emeritus, Bristol University, 1910–19; President, Aristotelian Society, 1926

Principal publications

1890 *Animal Life and Intelligence*. Edward Arnold.

1894 *An Introduction to Comparative Psychology*. Scott.

1895 Some definitions of instinct. *Natural Sciences*, 7, 321–9.

1896 *Habit and Instinct*. Edward Arnold.

1896 Animal automatism and consciousness. *Monist*, 7, 1–17.

1900 *Animal Behaviour*. Edward Arnold.

1905 *The Interpretation of Nature*. J.W. Arrowsmith

1923 *Emergent Evolution*. Williams and Norgate.

1929 *Mind at the Crossways*. Williams and Norgate.

1930 *The Animal Mind*. E. Arnold & Co.

1933 *The Emergence of Novelty*. Williams and Norgate.

Further reading

Grindley, G.C. (1936) Obituary notice: Professor Conwy Lloyd Morgan. *British Journal of Psychology*, 27, 1–13.

Lloyd Morgan was one of the European pioneers of the study of animal behaviour. In a series of books published around the turn of the century, he introduced and developed many of the areas of comparative psychology that have occupied researchers up to the present. He is probably best known for his 'canon', which applied the law of parsimony to animal behaviour: 'In no case may we interpret an action as the outcome of the exercise of a higher psychical faculty, if it can be interpreted as the exercise of the outcome of one which stands lower in the psychological scale.'

Morgan justified this in terms of natural selection: if a lower-level process makes possible a suitably adaptive behaviour there will be no selection pressure for further evolution. A major theme in Morgan's writing is the relationship between mind and body. In *Animal Life and Intelligence* he rejected the dualistic approach of predecessors such as Romanes, and espoused a monist philosophy. He distinguished between the subjective, introspective approach of the mainstream human psychology of the time and comparative psychology, which, he argued, starts from objective observations of behaviour. A great deal of Morgan's research was into animal learning and through his studies, mainly of trial and error learning, he arrived at the principle which was to be labelled by **Thorndike** some years later as 'the law of effect'.

Towards the end of his career Morgan's interests shifted to philosophy and metaphysics and in one of his last books (*Emergent Evolution*) he applied his own views on the emergence of novelty of behaviour. Morgan spent most of his working life at University College Bristol, later to become Bristol University, where he was the first Vice-Chancellor.

R. PRIESTNALL

Morris, Robert Lyle

Born: 1942, Canonsburg, Pennsylvania, USA **Nat:** American **Ints:** Experimental, humanistic, industrial and organization, philosophical and theoretical, physiological and comparative **Educ:** BS University of Pittsburgh, 1963; PhD Duke University, 1969 **Appts & awards:** Koestler Professor of Parapsychology, Department of Psychology, University of Edinburgh; AAAS Council, 1971–3; Parapsychological Association, AAAS Representative, 1971–7, President, 1974, 1985, Treasurer, 1975, Vice-President, 1976, Secretary, 1977; Mid S. Weiss Award for Psychical Research, 1973; American Society for Psychical Research, Board of Trustees, 1979–83, Secretary, 1980–2; Vice-President, Society for Scientific Exploration, 1985; Associate Editor, *Proceedings of the Parapsychological Association/Research in Parapsychology*, 1970–7, 1981– , *Journal of the Society for Scientific Exploration*, 1983– ; Publications Committee, *Journal of the American Society for Psychical Research*, 1976– ; Consulting Editor, *Zetetic Scholar*, 1980–

Principal publications

1970   Psi and animal behavior: A survey. *Journal of American Society for Psychical Research*, 64, 242–60.

1971   Factors affecting the maintenance of the pair bond in the Blond Ring Dove. *Animal Behavior*, 19, 398–406 (with C. Erickson).

1972   An exact method for evaluating preferentially matched free response material. *Journal of American Society for Psychical Research*, 66, 401–7.

1977   Parapsychology: A biological perspective. In B. Wolman (ed.), *Handbook of Parapsychology*. Van Nostrand Reinhold.

1978   A survey of methods and issues in ESP research. In S. Krippner (ed.), *Advances in Parapsychological Research, 2: Extrasensory Perception*. Plenum.

1978   Studies of communication during out-of-body experiences. *Journal of American Society for Psychical Research*, 72, 1–24.

1982   A comparison of two popularly advocated visual imagery strategies in a psychokeinesis task. *Journal of Parapsychology*, 46, 1–16 (with M. Nanko and D. Phillips).

1982   Mainstream science, experts and anomaly: A review of Science and the Paranormal: Probing the Existence of the Supernatural, G.O. Abell and B. Singer (eds). *Journal of American Society for Psychical Research*, 76, 257–81.

1982   Comparison of striving and nonstriving instructional sets in a PK study. *Journal of Parapsychology*, 46, 297–312 (with J. Debes).

1982   Assessing experimental support for precognition. *Journal of Parapsychology*, 46, 321–36.

1986   *Foundations of Parapsychology*. Routledge and Kegan Paul (with H. Edge, J. Palmer and J. Rush).

1990   Volition and psychokinesis. *Journal of Parapsychology*, 54, 331–70 (with L.R. Gissurarson).

1991   A review of apparently successful methods for the enhancement of anomalous phenomena. *Journal of the Society for Psychical Research*, 58, 1–9.

1994   A study of free response ESP performance and mental training techniques. In *Research in Parapsychology 1991*. Scarecrow.

Further reading

Flew, A. (ed.) (1987) *Readings in the Philosophical Problems of Parapsychology*. Prometheus.
Shapin, B. and Coly, L. (eds) (1992) *Parapsychology*. Parapsychology Foundation.

As a teenager, Morris became interested in exploring aspects of human experience that were apparently being ignored by the scientific community as a whole. After completing a BS in psychology at the University of Pittsburgh, he entered graduate school at Duke University, Durham, North Carolina, in biological psychology. He completed a doctorate with a study of avian social behaviour, animal behaviour being an area of equal interest. At the same time, he began formal parapsychological training and research at the Institute for Parapsychology near Duke. He sought to understand the strengths and weaknesses of the approaches that had been tried in the past. More specific research areas involved restricted-choice work with animals and discrete-outcome psychokinesis work with humans.

After completing two years of postdoctoral research at Duke in avian social behaviour, he joined the staff of the Psychical Research Foundation in Durham and began exploring internal states associated with unusually strong performances in restricted choice ESP experiments, and with out-of-body experiences. He taught various parapsychology and psychology courses for six years at University of California campuses at Santa Barbara and Irvine. During this time he became interested in the techniques whereby we can be misled by ourselves and others to think that something 'psychic' has happened. The research turned towards exploring the popularly available techniques reputed to improve psychic performance, including strategies for use in psychokinesis research. He continued this research at the School of Computer and Information Science at Syracuse University, and developed protocols for the use of computers in parapsychological research before moving to the University of Edinburgh, where he has continued with research.

Morton, John

Born: 1933, Nelson, Lancashire, England **Nat:** British **Ints:** Clinical neuropsychology, developmental, general, experimental psychology,

philosophical and theoretical **Educ:** MA University of Cambridge, 1957; PhD University of Reading, 1960 **Appts & Awards:** BPS Member, Standing Press Committee, 1972–84, Chairman, 1984–8; Member, EPS Committee, 1973–4; BPS Member, Conference Committee, 1975–9; Professor and Director, Medical Research Council Cognitive Development Unit, 1982– ; BPS Council Member, 1984; Editorial Board, *Cognitive Psychology*, 1976; Associate Editor, *Cognition*, 1979–

Principal publications

1969   Interaction of information in word recognition. *Psychological Review*, 76, 165–78.
1969   Precategorical acoustic storage (PAS). *Perception and Psychophysics*, 5, 365–73 (with R.G. Crowder).
1970   A functional model for memory. In D.A. Norman (eds), *Models of Human Memory*. Academic Press.
1971   (ed.) *Biological and Social Factors in Psycholinguistics*. Logos Press.
1976   Perceptual centres (P-centers). *Psychological Review*, 83, 405–8 (with S. Marcus and C. Frankish).
1976   On recursive reference. *Cognition*, 4, 309.
1977   *Psycholinguistics Series I*. Elek Press (ed. with J.C. Marshall).
1979   *Psycholinguistics Series II*. Elek Press (ed. with J.C. Marshall).
1979   Interacting with the computer: A framework. In P.J. Boutmy and A. Danthine (eds), *Teleinformatics 79, IFIP*. North-Holland (with P.J. Barnard, N. Hammond and J.B. Long).
1980   The logogen model and orthographic structure. In U. Frith (ed.), *Cognitive Processes in Spelling*. Academic Press.
1981   The acoustic correlates of 'speech-like': A use of the suffix effect. *Journal of Experimental Psychology; General*, 110, 568–93 (with S. Marcus and P. Ottley).
1984   On reducing language to biology. *Cognitive Neuropsychology*, 1, 83–116 (with J. Mehler and P.W. Jusczyk).
1985   Headed records: A model for memory and its failures. *Cognition*, 20, 1–23 (with D.A. Bekerian and R.H. Hamersley).
1989   An information-processing account of reading acquisition. In D.A. Galaburda (ed.), *From Neurons to Reading*. MIT Press.
1991   *Biology and Cognitive Development: The Case of Face Recognition*. Blackwell (with M.H. Johnson).
1992   The organization of the lexicon in Japanese: Single and compound kanji. *British Journal of*

Psychology, 83, 517–31 (with S. Sasanuma, K. Patterson and N. Sakuma).

1994 Memory. In S. Guttenplan (ed.), *A Companion to the Philosophy of Mind*. Blackwell.

Further reading

de Boysson-Bardies, B. *et al.* (eds) (1993) *Developmental Neurocognition: Speech and Face Processing in the First Year of Life*. Kluwer.

Galaburda, A.M. (ed.) (1989) *From Reading to Neurons*. MIT Press.

Glaser, W.R. (1992) Picture naming. Special Issue: Lexical access in speech production. *Cognition*, 42, 61–105.

Morton has worked to bridge the gap between theory and application in cognitive psychology, believing that experiment is only a tool and serves no purpose independently. The work he is best known for is the logogen model, which first appeared in print in 1964, and has been evolving ever since. Originally it was one of the first attempts at an information-processing model for any degree of complexity. More recently the model has provided the basis for a new way of looking at acquired dyslexia and has thus played a role in establishing the field of cognitive neuropsychology. He has also worked with speech therapists, using the model as a framework to structure the design of new therapeutic procedures. He has tended to go for breadth rather than depth of coverage. Thinking about memory in the context of the logogen model led him to predict the suffix effect and PAS; a lot of the subsequent work using the suffix effect was actually about speech perception and not memory (which the reviewers found difficult to understand). Work still coming from those Cambridge days includes a large collaborative project on human–computer interaction and the design of usable systems. This work led to a belief in the need for multiple models of cognitive activity to be used simultaneously, rather than looking for a single grand synthesis. He also published a series of publications on a new memory model called headed records. This was triggered by the need for a theory within which everyday memory and its failures could be discussed. The work on memory is a bridge to a new position as a developmentalist.

Mowrer, Orval Hobart

Born: 1907, Missouri, USA **Died:** 1982, Champaign, Illinois, USA **Nat:** American **Ints:** Clinical psychology, consulting psychology, experimental psychology, personality and social, philosophical and theoretical psychology **Educ:** BA University of Missouri, 1931; PhD Johns Hopkins University, 1932 **Appts & awards:** Sterling Fellow, Yale University, 1934–6; Instructor in Psychology, Institute of Human Relations, Yale, 1936–40; Harvard University, Assistant Professor of Education, 1940–3, Associate Professor, 1943–8; University of Illinois at Urbana, Research Professor of Psychology, 1948–75, Professor Emeritus, 1975–82; President, APA, 1954; Certificate of Merit, University of Missouri, 1956

Principal publications

1938 Determinants of the perceived vertical and horizontal. *Psychological Review*, 45, 300–21 (with J.J. Gibson).

1938 Enuresis – a method for its study and treatment. *American Journal of Orthopsychiatry*, 8, 436–59 (with W.M. Mowrer).

1939 A stimulus–response analysis of anxiety and its role as a reinforcing agent. 46, 553–65.

1950 *Learning Theory and Personality Dynamics*. Wiley.

1960 *Learning Theory and Behavior*. Wiley.

1960 *Learning Theory and the Symbolic Processes*. Wiley.

1964 *The New Group Therapy*. Van Nostrand.

1980 *Psychology of Language and Learning*. Plenum.

Further reading

Rescorla, R.A. and Solomon, R.L. (1967) Two-process learning theory: Relationships between Pavlovian conditioning and instrumental learning. *Psychological Review*, 71, 151–82.

Mowrer led what he called a 'double life'. He was a bright student and a successful psychologist, but suffered a 'tortured' private life. The clever student went to the University of Missouri in 1925, did well for a time, but then left as a result of a public scandal following the distribution of a sex questionnaire as a student project. He had to wait until 1931 to receive his degree. By then he was at Johns Hopkins, and had almost completed his PhD on spatial orientation under Knight Dunlap. From 1932 to 1936 he continued this research with fellowships at Northwestern, Princeton and Yale. Psychology at Yale was dominated by the Institute of Human Relations. This was dedicated to inter-disciplinary research, and several different disciplines were brought together in the seminars and research of Clark **Hull**. The result was a conceptual mix of conditioning, drive, anxiety and symbolic processes to which Mowrer was an active contributor from 1936, when he began to develop his two-factor theory of learning, in which learned anxiety acts as a secondary drive. There was an active input from psychoanalysts as well as learning theorists at the Yale Institute, and Mowrer himself went into intensive psychoanalysis during a bout of severe depression. The depression lifted, but later returned, a pattern repeated several times. While at Yale he and his wife published a widely used treatment for enuresis.

In 1940 he obtained a teaching job at Harvard School of Education. His closest affinities at Harvard were with the Psychological Clinic, and the group that eventually formed the Department of Human Relations under Talcott Parsons. In 1944 he spent a year with the Office of Strategic Services in Washington, where he took a seminar with Harry Stack **Sullivan**. Sullivan had developed an interpersonal view of psychopathology and therapy, which drew on G.H. **Mead**. Mowrer's contact with Sullivan and the failure of psychoanalysis to effect a permanent cure of his depression led to his own theory and practice of therapy through interaction with significant others. He came to believe that much pathology is the result of guilty secrets, often about sex and stemming from adolescence, and that it is not sufficient to unburden with a therapist. A change in social lifestyle is required and confession to significant others or in a therapy group is a crucial start to this. He built on these ideas in the development and theory of integrative groups. His depressive bouts became less frequent but did not disappear, and he killed himself at the age of 75.

Mowrer's reputation as a pioneer of two-factor learning theory is well established. It may still have value as a way of incorporating emotion in the cognitive learning theories and therapies that are now popular. His contribution to the theory and practice of groups is less clear. The importance of self-disclosure is now accepted, but was by no means exclusive to Mowrer.

ARTHUR STILL

Müller, Georg Elias

Born: 1850, Grimma, Saxony *Died:* 1934, Göttingen, Germany *Nat:* German *Ints:* Experimental psychology *Educ:* PhD University of Göttingen, 1873 *Appts & awards:* University of Göttingen, 1876–9; University of Czernowitz, 1880; University of Göttingen, 1881–1921

Principal publications

1873   Zur Theories der sinnlichen Aufmerksamkeit (dissertation).
1876   *Habilitationschrift.*
1878   *Zur Grundlegung der Psychophysik.*
1882   *Revision der Hauptpunkte der Psychophysik.*
1889   *Zur Analyse der Unterschiedsempfindlichkeit* (with F. Schumann).
1896   *Zur Psychophysik der Gesichtsempfindungen* (with W.G. Smith).
1903   *Gesichtspunkte und Tatsachen der psychophysischen Methodik.*
1921   *Zur Analyse der Gedächtnistätigkeit und des Vorstellungsverlaufes.*
1930   *Über die Farbenempfindung: psychophysische Untersuchungen.*

Further reading

Boring, E.G. (1935) Georg Elias Müller. *American Journal of Psychology*, 47, 344–8.
Katz, D. (1935) Georg Elias Müller. *Psychological Bulletin*, 32, 377–80.
Kroh, O. (1935) Georg Elias Müller, ein Nachruf. *Zeitschrift für Psychologie*, 134, 15–190.

At the University of Göttingen Müller was a pupil of Lotze, who in turn had been a pupil of Herbart at the same institution. At **Fechner**'s death, Müller became the leading psychophysicist of the day and his laboratory (founded at Göttingen, 1881) attracted numerous distinguished students including E. Jaensch (eidetic imagery), E. Rubin (figure–ground distinction) and C.E. **Spearman**.

Müller's doctoral dissertation ('Zur Theories der Sinnlichen Aufmerksamkeit') was the first empirical study of attention and it had considerable influence on subsequent investigations, particularly through the work of E.B. **Titchener**. His principal contributions were in three fields: psychophysics, visual sensation and memory. In psychophysics he developed the method of constant stimuli (with L. Martin), and used the Müller–Urban Weights (as they were known) to define the ogive that best fits the data obtained by the method of constant stimuli, and from which the difference threshold is determined. Fechner's procedures involved comparisons between two stimuli, whereas Müller's modification allowed the simultaneous comparison of several stimuli against one standard stimulus, thereby permitting a more accurate estimation of subjective judgements.

In vision, Müller enlarged on Fechner's approach to psychophysics by including an analysis of physiological factors. His research on colour vision incorporated aspects of **Hering**'s theory of colour vision. According to this theory the three colour pairs (white–black, yellow–blue and red–green) depend on reversible photochemical substances. He also assumed the existence of a constant grey ('cortical grey'), produced by the molecular action of the cortex, from which all colour sensations differ.

Müller's most important work lies in the field of memory, where he made significant additions to the work of **Ebbinghaus**. He improved Ebbinghaus's technique by developing instruments (with F. Schumann) that controlled the speed of presentation of the stimulus material to be learned and by introducing certain rules concerning the choice of stimulus material (syllables). The 'method of hits' (*Treffermethode*) was a particularly useful innovation: a stimulus is presented to the subject, who has then to recall the one that had originally followed it. The technique allowed the measurement of both the number of items recalled and the speed of recall of each item, which (with Pilzecker) he showed to be a significant indication of the strength of association. Müller also made extensive use of the 'method of paired associates' devised by Mary **Calkins**. Important findings from Müller's work include the following: the attitude of the learner has an important influence on learning (preparatory set or *Anlage*); intention to learn influences quick learning; mere repetition without an intention to learn is largely ineffectual; the initial and final numbers in a sequence are learnt more quickly than those in the middle of the series (with W.G. Smith). He also found that when two associations are of equal strength but unequal age, a repetition strengthens the older more than the younger (Jost's law, with A. Jost) and that, in general, it is more effective to learn in 'wholes' than in 'parts'. These achievements led to the formal expression of the 'laws of association' that had been debated for centuries. Before retiring from his chair (1921) Müller summarized and systematized his work on memory in three volumes (*Zur Analyse der Gedächtnistätigkeit und des Vorstellungsverlaufes*). After his retirement he became involved in an intensive debate with Wolfgang **Köhler** in which he questioned the novelty of *Gestalt* psychology and argued that the work of his students (e.g. Jaensch and Rubin) anticipated most of its fundamental concepts. Müller argued that sensory and emotional experiences are united into groups by acts of attention (i.e. he leaned towards empiricism), whereas *Gestalt*

theorists adopted a more nativistic interpretation of sensation. At a time when psychology was becoming established as an experimental science and finding an intellectual home in universities, Müller exercised almost as significant an influence as did **Wundt**.

Münsterberg, Hugo

Born: 1863, Danzig, East Prussia **Died:** 1916, Danzig, East Prussia **Nat:** Prussian **Ints:** Experimental, industrial and organizational, philosophical and theoretical, psychology and the arts, psychology and the law, psychotherapy **Educ:** PhD University of Leipzig, 1885; MD University of Heidelberg, 1887 **Appts & awards:** Professor, University of Freiburg, 1887–92; President, APA, 1898; Hon. AM, Harvard University, 1901; Hon. LLD, Washington University, St Louis, 1904; International Congress of Arts and Sciences at St Louis, 1904; Hon. LittD, Lafayette College, 1907; President, American Philosophical Association, 1908; Exchange Professor, University of Berlin, 1910; President, AAAS; Vice-President, Washington Academy of Sciences; Vice-President, International Philosophical Congress at Heidelberg; Editor, *Harvard Psychological Studies*

Principal publications

1894 Studies from the Harvard psychological laboratory: I. Memory, attention and psychophysics. *Psychological Review*, 1, 34–60.
1894 The motor power of ideas. *Psychological Review*, 1, 441–53.
1894 The localisation of sound. *Psychological Review*, 1, 461–76.
1899 Psychology and history. *Psychological Review*, 6, 1–31.
1900 Psychological atomism. *Psychological Review*, 7, 1–17.
1903 The position of psychology in the system of knowledge. *Psychological Monographs*, 4, 17, 641–54.
1904 *The Americans*. McClure Philips.
1908 *On the Witness Stand*. Doubleday.
1909 *The Eternal Values*. Houghton Mifflin.
1915 *Psychology General and Applied*. Appleton.
1917 *Business Psychology*. Extension University.

Further reading

Landy, F.J. (1993) Early influences on the development of industrial/organizational psychology. In T.K. Fagan and G.R. Vandenbos (eds), *Exploring Applied Psychology: Origins and Critical Analyses*. APA.

Spillman, J. and Spillman, L. (1993) The rise and fall of Hugo Münsterberg. *Journal of the History of the Behavioral Sciences*, 29, 322–38.

Stagner, R. (1988) *A History of Psychological Theories*. Macmillan.

At best Münsterberg is American psychology's enigma: at worst its skeleton in the cupboard. He was a medically qualified doctor who, whilst 'head hunted' as an experimentalist to develop Harvard Psychology Department, had philosophy as his first love and founded and shaped applied psychology. While having a world reputation he declined offers from London, Koeningsburg and Berlin because of his love for America – an America which, nevertheless, he always held in lower esteem than his fatherland, and an America which eventually rejected him because of his apologistic attitude in the run-up to World War I. Political rejection, however, should not cloud his professional contribution.

Anastasi refers to Münsterberg as the 'first all round applied psychologist in America'. Despite being brought from Germany by William **James** for his early experimental expertise, he was inexorably drawn to the application of psychological knowledge to practical affairs. He it was who, between the years of 1905 and 1916, in a veritable explosion of popularist books and articles, roused academic psychology from its abstract cogitations in the ivory-tower laboratory and drafted the blue-print for applied psychology, a main trunk of present-day psychology whose time may only now be fully at hand. Because he was a great publicist he became a 'storm centre, the object of both vehement attacks and unstinted praise'. None the less, despite his contribution being essentially popularist and armchair, Münsterberg in that period did more than anyone before or since to found, define and extend the field of applied psychology. He was an investigator of penetrating sharpness. No one working in the field of forensic, industrial, clinical or, to a lesser extent, educational psychology or art appreciation can fail to have benefited from his proselytizing. While his own endeavours and achievements in these specific fields must be accepted as uneven, history must evaluate his contribution not in terms of what he found but rather in terms of what he sought. He was a founding father of applied psychology ('psychotechnics') in the truest sense.

B.R. CLIFFORD

Murchison, Carl Allanmore

Born: 1887 Hickory, North Carolina, USA **Died:** 1961, Provincetown, MA **Nat:** American **Ints:** Criminology, social psychology **Educ:** AB Wake Forest College, 1909; PhD Johns Hopkins University, 1923; ScD Wake Forest College, 1930 **Appts & awards:** University of Miami, Assistant Professor of Psychology, 1916–17, Associate Professor of Psychology, 1919–22; Johnston Scholar, Johns Hopkins University, 1922–3; Clark University, Professor of Psychology, 1923–36, Chairman, 1924–36; Founder, Journal Press, 1936; Hon. Dr, University of Athens, 1937

Principal publications

1924   American white criminal intelligence. *Journal of Criminal Law and Criminology*, 15, 239–316, 135–95.

1925–6   Eighteen papers, many co-authored, on foreign and 'Negro' criminals. *Pedagogical Seminary*, 31–3.

1926   *Criminal Intelligence*. Clark University Press.

1926   (ed.) *Psychologies of 1925*. Clark University Press.

1927   (ed.) *The Case For and Against Psychical Belief*. Clark University Press.

1929   *Social Psychology*. Clark University Press.

1929   (ed.) *The Foundations of Experimental Psychology*. Clark University Press.

1929, 1932   (ed.) *The Psychological Register, vols 2 & 3*. Clark University Press. (Volume 1, written in 1928 and intended to cover deceased psychologists, was never published.)

1930   (ed.) *Psychologies of 1930*. Clark University Press.

1930, 1932, 1936   (ed.) *History of Psychology in Autobiography, vols 1–3*. Clark University Press.

1931   (ed.) *A Handbook of Child Psychology*. Clark University Press.

1934   (ed.) *A Handbook of General Experimental Psychology*. Clark University Press.

1935   (ed.) *A Handbook of Social Psychology*. Clark University Press.

1935–6   The experimental measurement of a social hierarchy in *Gallus domesticus*. *Journal of Genetic Psychology*, 46, 76–102; *Journal of Social Psychology*, 6, 3–30; *Journal of General Psychology*, 12, 3–39, 296–312; 13, 227–48 (five reports).

Further reading

Nafe, J.P. (1961) Clyde Murchison 1887–1961. *American Journal of Psychology*, 74, 641–2.

Following extensive military involvement as a psychological instructor and examiner during World War I, Murchison received his PhD in his mid-thirties (under Knight Dunlap). The dozen years or so during which Murchison's psychological career subsequently lasted were remarkably productive, but this productivity lay less in his own research than in his role as a book and journal editor and publisher. His early studies of 'criminal intelligence' were relatively atheoretical and yielded a large quantity of heterogeneous data in which clear-cut patterns were hard to discern. Many of the papers concerned 'Negro' criminals, but there is little in the way of explicit racialist interpretation of the African-American data. In his *Social Psychology*, he in any case dismissed the very existence of human groups 'in any objective sense' as an illusion. This latter work itself is subtitled *The Psychology of Political Domination* and presents a semi-philosophical overview of the topic rather than empirical research. It was hardly representative of the new US social psychology already emerging in the late 1920s, which came of age with his own 1935 *Handbook*. The theme was, however, continued in a rather different way in his 1935–6 research on social hierarchy formation in chickens, his most successful original work.

In the event Murchison's talents lay primarily in a different direction, and were deployed in such a way that he must be considered to have been perhaps the single most important 'organization man' in pre-World War II US psychology. Initially this was done under the aegis of the Clark University Press, Murchison founding, editing, managing and financing *Genetic Psychology Monographs* (1925), *Journal of General Psychology* (1927), *Journal of Social Psychology* (1929), *Journal of Psychology* (1935) and *Social Psychology Monographs*, as well as renaming *Pedagogical Seminary* as *Journal of Genetic Psychology* (1924). After 1936, as an independent publisher, he took over the continued publication of these journals. These labours were augmented by his penchant for editing: his three *Handbooks* helped integrate and further develop their respective fields (The *Handbook of Social Psychology* being perhaps the most influential in this respect), and *Psychological Register* became a primary reference book. His most original project (suggested initially by E.G. **Boring**) was undoubtedly the History of Psychology in Autobiography series, which possesses enduring value for the light it sheds

(and not infrequently fails to shed!) on both the contributors themselves and the nature of the discipline in its formative years. *Psychologies of 1925* and *Psychologies of 1930*, for their part, presented balanced, semi-popular overviews of the state of the discipline, which a generation of young psychologists took as their point of departure.

Murchison's historical role was virtually unique and of crucial importance, although in some respects remains difficult to assess clearly. In particular, one is bound to ask how far his editing and publishing activities were guided by more personal agendas regarding the direction he wished to see the discipline taking and his own theoretical preferences. It is perhaps ironic that he never contributed an entry of his own to the History of Psychology in Autobiography.

GRAHAM RICHARDS

Murphy, Gardner

Born: 1895, Ohio, USA **Died:** 1979, Washington DC, USA **Nat:** American **Ints:** Experimental, general, personality and social, philosophical psychology, psychological study of social issues **Educ:** BA Yale University, 1916; MA Harvard University, 1917; PhD Columbia University, 1922 **Appts & awards:** Hon. DSc, City University of New York, 1975; Hon. PhD, University of Hamburg, 1976; Butler Medal, Columbia University; Richard Hodgson Fellow in Psychical Research, Harvard University; John Dewey Society Lecturer; Festschrift for Gardner Murphy APA Gold Medal; Chairman, APA Division 9; President, Eastern Psychological Association; APA President; President, Research Society for Psychical Research; American Society for Psychical Research; General Editor, Harper Psychology Series; Editor, *Journal of Parapsychology*, 1939–41, *Sociometry, An Outline of Abnormal Psychology*, Modern Library, 1929, *William James and Psychical Research*, 1968 (with R.O. Ballou)

Principal publications

1929 *Historical Introduction to Modern Psychology*. Harcourt, Brace and World. (Rev. edn, 1972.)
1931 *Experimental Social Psychology*. Harper and Row (with L.B. Murphy). (Rev. edn, 1937.)
1932 *Approaches to Personality*. Harper and Row (with F. Jensen).
1933 *General Psychology*. Harper and Row.

1938   *Public Opinion and the Individual.* Harper and Row (with R. Likert).
1945   *Human Nature and Enduring Peace.* Houghton Mifflin.
1945   Three papers on the survival problem. *Journal of the American Society for Psychical Research.*
1947   *Personality: A Bisocial Approach to Origins and Structure.* Harper and Row.
1953   *In the Minds of Men: A UNESCO Study of Social Tensions in India.* Basic Books.
1956   Affect and perceptual learning. *Psychological Review,* 63, 1–15.
1958   *Human Potentialities.* Basic Books.
1960   Organism and quantity. In B. Kaplan and S. Wapner (eds), *Perspectives in Psychological Theory.* International University Press.
1960   *Development of the Perceptual World.* Basic Books (with C.M. Solley).
1961   *Challenge of Psychical Research: A Primer of Parapsychology.* Harper and Row.
1961   *Freeing Intelligence through Teaching.* Harper and Row.

Further reading

Frick, W.B. (1989) *Humanistic Psychology: Conversations with Abraham Maslow, Gardner Murphy and Carl Rogers..* Wyndham Hall.
Stagner, R. (1988) *A History of Psychological Theories.* Macmillan.

In a poll of psychologists, Gardner Murphy was voted second only to **Freud** in his influence on their thinking. His ground-breaking books both organized the knowledge within a field and cross-fertilized it with material from what had been considered separate areas, providing new insights and directions for research.

The special quality of his work was the introduction of new ideas and his integration of them with the old, thus modifying and enriching prior thinking. An example is a series of collaborative experiments, combining psychophysics with personalizations of how perception varies with needs and attitudes. The thrust of his thinking was that each individual, though constrained by biological limitations and motivated by biological drives, will modulate responses according to past experience, self-image and the particular situation. Hunger, for example, motivates some to increased effort, others only to self-pity, others in still other ways, and there is potentiality for change.

His life encompassed two careers: psychology and parapsychology. He entered psychology because of its relevance to psychical research, and his involvement with parapsychology con-

tinued steadily, resulting in three books and 110 articles on psychical research. Here also he opened new, promising lines of investigation and used his sophistication to advance methodology. He especially urged replication to ensure findings were solid, and advocated a field theory like his psychological theorizing, which embraced biological functions, needs and attitudes and especially interpersonal relations.

Murphy was an outstanding teacher. His lectures, with their wide-ranging knowledge, speculation and integrations, broadened the horizons of even the most learned. He encouraged and stimulated his students as he criticized them. He devoted himself to finding opportunities by which students and colleagues could advance their careers. His concern with furthering creative potential permeated his life as well as his writings.

Murray, Henry, Alexander

Born: 1893, New York City, USA **Died:** 1988, Cambridge, Massachusetts, USA **Nat:** American **Ints:** Clinical, interaction of dispositional and situational determinants of behaviour, motivation, personality, personnel selection, projective tests **Educ:** BA Harvard University, 1915; MD Columbia University, 1919; MA Columbia University, 1920; PhD Cambridge University, 1927 **Appts & awards:** Internship in Surgery, Presbyterian Hospital, New York City, 1924–6; Rockefeller Institute for Medical Research, 1926–7; Harvard University, 1927–62; Member, American Academy of Arts and Sciences, 1935, Legion of Merit, 1946; Distinguished Scientific Contribution Award, APA, 1961; Hon. Degrees, Lawrence College, 1964, University of Louvain, 1966, University of Oslo, 1969, Kent State University, 1971, Adelphi University, 1973; Distinguished Contribution Award, Society for Personality Assessment, 1967; Gold Medal Award, American Psychological Foundation, 1969

Principal publications

1938   (*et al.*) *Explorations in personality.* Oxford.
1940   What should psychologists do about psychoanalysis? *Journal of Abnormal and Social Psychology,* 35, 150–75.
1943   (*et al.*) *Thematic Apperception Test.* Harvard University Press.
1945   A clinical study of sentiments. *Genetic Psychology Monographs,* 32, 3–311 (with C. Morgan).
1948   (*et al.*) *Assessment of Men.* Rinehart.

1951 Some basic psychological assumptions and conceptions. *Dialectica*, 5, 266–92.

1951 Toward a classification of interaction. In T. Parsons and E.A. Shils (eds), *Toward a General Theory of Action*. Harvard University Press.

1953 Outline of a conception of personality. In C. Kluckhohn, H.A. Murray and D. Schneider (eds), *Personality in Nature, Society and Culture*, 2nd edn. Knopf (with C. Kluckhohn).

1959 Preparations for the scaffold of a comprehensive system. In S. Koch (ed.), *Psychology: A Study of Science, vol. 3*. McGraw-Hill.

Further reading

Anderson, J.W. (1988) Henry A. Murray's early career. *Journal of Personality*, 56, 139–71.

Entwisle, D.R. (1972) To dispel fantasies about fantasy-based measures of achievement motivation. *Psychological Bulletin*, 77, 377–91.

Epstein, S. (1979) Explorations in personality today and tomorrow: A tribute to Henry A. Murray. *American Psychologist*, 34, 649–53.

Haydn, H. (1969) Henry A. Murray. *American Scholar*, 39, 123–36.

McClelland, D.C., Atkinson, J.W., Clark, R.A. and Lowell, E.L. (1953) *The Achievement Motive*. Appleton.

Maddi, S.R. and Costa, P.T. (1972) *Humanism in Personology: Allport, Maslow and Murray*. Aldine/Atherton.

Rorer, L.G. (1990) Personality assessment. In L.A. Pervin (ed.), *Handbook of Personality Theory and Research*. Guilford Press.

Shneidman, E.S. (ed.) (1981) *Endeavours in Psychology: Selections from the Personology of Henry A. Murray*. New York: Harper and Row.

Smith, M.B. and Anderson, J.W. (1989) Obituary. *American Psychologist*, 44, 1153–4.

During the 1920s, Henry Murray's interests shifted from medicine, physiology and embryology to personality. 'Depth psychology was obviously my meat … Several weeks with Dr **Jung** at different times, three years with Dr Morton Prince, an orthodox **Freud**ian psychoanalysis, and a period of training with Dr Franz **Alexander** and Dr Hanns Sachs, ten years of therapeutic practice – these experiences were hugely influential in shaping my personality and my thought.' Other powerful influences he acknowledged include Freud's theory of unconscious motivation, Whitehead's world-view and entity theory, **Lewin**'s psychodynamic concepts – particularly the principles of topology, hodology and contemporaneity – and **McDougall**'s theory of instincts. Murray was familiar with

cultural anthropology, mythology, history, sociology and American literature, most notably the writings of Melville; he interwove content from these disciplines with psychological principles and evolutionary theory to develop, during the 1930s, his own comprehensive theory of personality.

Due to its complexity and breadth in terms of purported applicability, the theory resists brief description. The twenty-five 'primary propositions' listed at the beginning of *Explorations in Personality* are definitions for, and presumed relationships between, many of his constructs. Therefore his theory is far more amenable to testing, more susceptible to empirical refutation, than earlier theories of human motivation. His taxonomic schemes for needs, press and themas were embodied in a scoring manual for the Thematic Apperception Test, and have been reiterated in most general psychology texts, as well as most texts in the areas of personality and/or human motivation, for the past half-century.

Murray was a perspicacious, innovative investigator. He was one of the first American psychologists to provide deliberately theory-laden procedures for operational definition of constructs, one of the first to insist on multi-method assessment, one of the first to offer an explanation of human behaviour in which person and environment variables receive more or less equal weight, and one of the first to design research focusing simultaneously on dispositional and situational determinants of people's actions.

Many capable colleagues and students were drawn to Murray's research programmes at the Harvard Psychological Clinic in the 1930s and the Office of Strategic Services assessment programme during World War II. The heuristic impact of his theory and methods of assessment was very strong, but his personal charisma came into the picture too. Individual differences in various psychogenic needs – particularly achievement, affiliation and dominance – stimulated a great deal of research, the notions of press and thema comparatively little. Several of his followers devoted large portions of their careers to pursuing one or another element of his theory: the study of need for achievement carried out by D.C. **McClelland** and his associates, E.H. **Erikson**'s developmental theory, R.W. White's writings on competence and development, and D.W. Fiske's advocacy of multi-method measurement are cases in point. Some widely used omnibus personality inventories, such as **Jackson**'s Personality Research Form, **Gough** and Heilbrun's Adjective Check List, and Edwards's Personal Preference Schedule, yield scores on Murray's needs.

An immensely influential theorist and persuasive writer, Murray had few rivals during his lifetime. The research tradition he established is being carried on vigorously now by his numerous intellectual descendants and promises to be a force in the twenty-first century, not only because of these descendants but also through the recently founded Henry A. Murray Research Center of Radcliffe College: A Center for the Study of Lives. The Center provides scholars with access to archival materials of several kinds – most notably some two hundred data sets – & awards small grants for worthy projects.

Although Murray ranks among the foremost contributors to the psychology of personality, responses to his contributions include one important demurrer. As he said, he was known in some circles as an 'imprecision instrument maker' because of his role in devising and promoting the Thematic Apperception Test. This test has been very widely used for fifty years and doubtless has many defenders, but a persuasive case has been made that it is inadequate or worse as a scientific instrument. Its defects have been noted by D.R. Entwisle, and those of projective techniques in general by L.G. Rorer among others. As T.S. Szasz points out, such devices are more useful for ceremonial than technical purposes.

R.N. WOLFE

Murrell, Kenneth F.H.

Born: 1908, Barry, Mid-Glamorgan, Wales **Died:** 1984, Barry, Mid-Glamorgan, Wales **Nat:** British **Ints:** Engineering psychology, experimental analysis of behaviour, industrial psychology, military psychology, teaching of psychology **Educ:** MA Chemistry Oxford University, 1930 **Appts & Awards:** Professor Emeritus, University of Wales; Council Member, BPS; Chairman, Division of Occupational Psychology; Ergonomics Society, Founder Member, Hon. Secretary and Treasurer, Hon. Member for Life; Member, Council, International Ergonomics Society; Distinguished Foreign Colleagues Award, Human Factors Society, 1972; Fellow, Royal Photographic Society, for Remarkable Pioneering Photographs of Subterranean Regions of the Mendip Hills; Member, Scientific Advisory Committee to the Trade Unions Congress, UK

Principal publications

1954 Equipment layout. In W.F. Floyd and A.T. Welford (eds), *Human Factors in Equipment Design*. Lewis.

1958 *Fitting the Job to the Worker: A Study of American and European Research into Working Conditions in Industry*. Organization for European Economic Corporation (EPA).

1959 Major problems of industrial gerontology. *Journal of Gerontology*, 14, 216.

1960 A comparison of three dial shapes for check reading instrument panels. *Ergonomics*, 3, 231.

1962 Industrial aspects of ageing. *Ergonomics*, 5, 147.

1962 Operator variability and its industrial consequences. *International Journal of Production Research*, 1, 3, 39–55.

1962 A study of pillar-drilling in relation to age. *Occupational Psychology*, 36, 45 (with A.F. Powesland and B. Forsaith).

1965 *Ergonomics*. Chapman and Hall.

1976 *Men and Machines*. Methuen.

1977 *Motivation at Work*. Methuen.

Further reading

Department of Scientific and Industrial Research (1961) *Proceedings of the Conference on Ergonomics in Industry, 1960*. HMSO.

Oborne, D.J. (ed.) (1995) *Ergonomics and Human Factors*, vol. 1. Edward Elgar.

A full catalogue of Murrell's achievements would be too long for inclusion here. His capacity for productive effort remained undiminished, yielding an output of over a hundred scientific papers and reports, and three books. As a wartime member of the Royal Navy Scientific Service, he pioneered a series of human engineering projects dealing with issues like the design of multiple-dial information panels and display of operational action information. Some of these have passed into literature as classics in their field. By the time he left the Service in 1952 his unit was virtually an applied experimental psychology research group.

Later, his Nuffield-founded research unit at Bristol was acclaimed for its laboratory and industrial studies of how ageing affects workers. Murrell widened the scope of this unit to examine human performance more generally among people in industrial occupations. His concept of the 'actile period' was just one of the theoretical insights emerging from this work.

Perhaps the most significant of his achievements was his role in founding the Ergonomics Research Society in 1950. It was Murrell who coined the term 'ergonomics' to designate a multidisciplinary application of psychology, anatomy and physiology to optimize the efficiency and well-being of people at work. It is a lasting memorial to his vision and determination that not only has the Society established itself as the undisputed scientific and professional 'voice' of ergonomics in Britain, but similar learned societies have subsequently been set up in many other countries. It is also fitting that the first definitive text in the field, still widely read and cited, was Murrell's *Ergonomics: Man in his Working Environment*, published in 1965.

DONALD WALLIS AND OONAGH HARTNETT

Mussen, Paul Henry

Born: 1922, Paterson, New Jersey, USA *Nat:* American *Ints:* Developmental, educational, personality and social *Educ:* AB Stanford University, 1942; MA Stanford University, 1943; PhD Yale University, 1949 *Appts and Awards:* Professor of Psychology and Research Psychologist, Institute of Human Development, University of California at Berkeley; Fellow, Fund for the Advancement of Education, University of California at Berkeley, 1955–6, Center for Advanced Behavioral Sciences, Stanford, 1968–9; Fulbright Award, Florence, Italy, 1960–1; Executive Committee, International Organization for the Study of Human Development, 1970–3; President, Western Psychological Association, 1973–4; President, APA Division 7, 1976–7; Problems and Planning Committee, SSRC, 1976–9; Consulting Editor, *Child Development, Journal of Child Psychology and Psychiatry, Journal of Consulting Psychology, Journal of Educational Psychology, Merrill-Palmer Quarterly, Psychology of Women Quarterly*; Editor, *Annual Review of Psychology*, 1968–74; Advisory Editor, *Journal of Genetic Psychology, Genetic Psychology Monographs*

Principal publications

1950   Some personality and social factors related to changes in children's attitudes toward Negroes. *Journal of Abnormal and Social Psychology*, 45, 423–41.

1957   Self-conceptions, motivations and interpersonal attitudes of late- and early-maturing boys. *Child Development*, 28, 243–56 (with M.C. Jones).

1959   Masculinity, identification, and father–son relationships. *Journal of Abnormal and Social Psychology*, 23, 521–4 (with L. Distler).

1961   Some antecedents and consequents of masculine sex-typing in adolescent boys. *Psychological Monographs*, 75, 1–24.

1967   Early socialization: Learning and identification. In *New Direction in Psychology, III.* Holt, Rinehart & Winston.

1968   Generosity in nursery school boys. *Child Development*, 39, 755–65 (with E. Rutherford).

1969   Early sex-role development. In D.A. Goslin (ed.), *Handbook of Socialization Theory and Research*. Rand-McNally.

1976   Some cognitive, behavioral, and personality correlates of maturity of moral judgment. *Journal of Genetic Psychology*, 128, 123–35 (with S. Harris and E. Rutherford).

1977   *Roots of Caring, Sharing and Helping: The Development of Prosocial Behavior in Children.* Freeman (with N. Eisenberg-Berg).

1978   Empathy and moral development in adolescence. *Developmental Psychology*, 14, 185–6 (with N. Eisenberg-Berg).

1980   Personality correlates of sociopolitical liberalism and conservatism in adolescents. *Journal of Genetic Psychology*, 137, 165–77 (with N. Eisenberg-Berg).

1981   *Present and Past in Middle Life.* Academic Press (ed. with D.H. Eichorn, M.P. Honzik, N. Haan and J.A. Clausen).

1981   A longitudinal study of patterns of personality and political ideologies. In D. Eichorn *et al.* (eds), *Present and Past in Middle Life.* Academic Press.

1983   (ed.) *Handbook of Child Psychology.* Wiley.

1984   *Child Development and Personality.* Harper and Row (with J.J. Conger, J. Kagan and A. Huston).

Further reading

Parke, R.D. *et al.* (eds) (1994) *A Century of Developmental Psychology.* APA.

Throughout his professional career Mussen tried to address research issues that are socially relevant. Most of his research hypotheses have in fact been derived from one or another of the so-called 'great theories' – social learning theory, psychoanalytic theory, cognitive developmental theory – but the research problems themselves have dealt with such concepts as identification, positive social behavior, sex-typing, and the effects of individual differences in rate of maturing on psychological development.

Mussen argues that psychology as a discipline must justify itself in terms of contributions to human welfare and improved social and political relationships. Research questions should therefore be designed to provide answers of potential social utility. Theory is most useful in specifying variables to be investigated, but the basic questions should be derived from sensible analyses of social needs. Most of his research has been 'naturalistic' – he attempted to observe and study real children in the real world, encountering real (rather than contrived) situations. Discussions in his published articles stress the implications of research findings for interventions or change that may be beneficial to individuals or to society. For example, his empirical research in prosocial behaviour has as its goal the understanding of factors that contribute to raising the levels of such behaviour in children. All of the books he has written or edited emphasize the usefulness of empirical findings in the promotion and betterment of the human condition and the quality of life.

N

Nathan, Peter E.

Born: 1935, Saint Louis, Missouri, USA **Nat:** American **Ints:** Clinical psychology **Educ:** AB Harvard College 1957; PhD Washington University 1962 **Appts & awards:** Director, Center of Alcohol Studies, 1970–87; NIAAA Research Review Committee, 1974–6; Secretary-Treasurer, Council of University Directors of Clinical Psychology, 1975–8; APA Council, 1976–9, 1981–4; Chair, NJ State Mental Health Board, 1977–84; President, APA Division 12, Section 3, 1978; Board, Research Society in Alcoholism, 1983– ; Rutgers University, Henry and Anna Starr Professor of Psychology, Department of Clinical Psychology, Graduate School of Applied and Professional Psychology, 1983–9; President, APA Division 12, 1984; Chair, NIAAA Centers Grant Program Review Committee, 1985; Professor, Provost University of Iowa, 1992– ; Editorial Boards: *Journal of Consulting and Clinical Psychology*, 1973– , *Addictive Behaviours*, 1975– , *Psychotherapy*, 1978– , *Professional Psychology*, 1979– , *Alcoholism*, 1983– , Associate Editor: *Journal of Clinical Psychology*, 1975– , *American Psychologist*, 1977–85; Executive Editor, *Journal of Studies on Alcohol*, 1983–9

Principal publications

1967 *Cues, Decision and Diagnosis*. Academic Press.

1970 Behavioral analysis of chronic alcoholism. *Archives of General Psychiatry*, 22, 419–30 (with N.A. Titler, L.M. Lowenstein, P. Solomon and A.M. Rossi).

1971 An experimental analysis of the behavior of alcoholics and nonalcoholics during prolonged experimental drinking. *Behavior Therapy*, 2, 455–76 (with J.S. O'Brien).

1975 *Psychopathology and Society*. McGraw-Hill (with S.L. Harris) (reprinted 1980).

1978 Blood alcohol level discrimination: Pre-training monitoring accuracy of alcoholics and non alcoholics. *Addictive Behaviors*, 3, 209–14 (with D. Lansky, S.M. Ersner-Hershfield and T.R. Lipscomb).

1978 *Behavioral Approaches to Alcoholism*. RCAS (with G.A. Marlatt).

1978 *Alcoholism*. Plenum (with T. Loberg and G.A. Marlatt).

1980 Effect of family history of alcoholism, drinking pattern and tolerance on blood ethanol level discrimination. *Archives of General Psychiatry*, 37, 571–6 (with T.R. Lipscomb).

1983 *Clinical Case Studies in the Behavioral Treatment of Alcoholism*. Plenum (with W. Hay).

1983 Failures in prevention. *American Psychologist*, 38, 459–67.

1990 Integration of biological and psychosocial research on alcoholism. *Alcoholism: Clinical and Experimental Research*, 14, 368–74.

Further reading

Loberg, T., Miller, W.R. *et al.* (eds) (1989) *Addictive Behaviors: Prevention and Early Intervention*. Swets and Zeitlinger.

Nathan's interests might appear to be broad, in that he has carried out research on a variety of issues both within and beyond alcoholism, his principal research interest over the last twenty years. He has consistently utilized behavioural methodologies and philosophy, always tried to investigate matters which others have not studied, and has always tried to study, from a basic science perspective, issues with clear clinical relevance. His principal contributions are in the demonstration that worthwhile and important studies of basic phenomena associated with alcoholism, from the behavioural perspective, can be studied in naturalistic laboratory settings. He has also provided evidence that it is appropriate to give alcohol to alcoholics under controlled laboratory settings (since what differentiates alcoholics from non-alcoholics, is, above all, their behaviour when they are drinking and the consequences of their drinking). More generally he has shown that psychologists have important contributions to make in the study of alcoholic behaviour.

Neisser, Ulric

Born: 1928, Kiel, Germany **Nat:** German **Ints:** Experimental, social issues, theoretical **Educ:** BA Harvard University, 1950; MA Swarthmore College, 1952; PhD Harvard University, 1956 **Appts & awards:** Robert W. Woodruff Professor of Psychology, Emory University, Atlanta, Georgia; Fellow, APA Fellow, Center for Advanced Study in the Behavioral Sciences, 1973–4; Society of Experimental Psychologists; Editorial Board, *American Journal of Psychology*, *Applied Cognitive Psychology*, *Philosophical Psychology*

Principal publications

1960   Pattern recognition by machine. *Scientific American*, 203, 60–8 (with O.G. Selfridge).

1963   Searching for ten targets simultaneously. *Perceptual and Motor Skills*, 17, 955–61 (with R. Novick and R. Lazar).

1967   *Cognitive Psychology*. Appleton-Century-Crofts.

1975   Selective looking: Attending to visually specified events. *Cognitive Psychology*, 7, 480–94.

1976   *Cognition and Reality*. Freeman.

1976   General, academic and artificial intelligence. In L. Resnick (ed.), *The Nature of Intelligence*. Erlbaum.

1976   Skills of divided attention. *Cognition*, 4, 215–30 (with E. Spelke and W. Hirst).

1978   Memory: What are the important questions? In M.M. Gruneberg, P.E. Morris and R.N. Sykes (eds), *Practical Aspects of Memory*, Academic Press.

1981   John Dean's memory. *Cognition*, 9, 1–22.

1982   *Memory Observed: Remembering in Natural Contexts*. Freeman.

1983   Point of view in personal memories. *Cognitive Psychology*, 15, 467–82 (with G. Nigro).

1986   *The School Achievement of Minority Children: New Perspectives*. Erlbaum.

1988   *Remembering Reconsidered: Ecological and Intellectual Factors in Categorization*. Cambridge University Press (with E. Winograd).

1993   *The Perceived Self: Ecological and Interpersonal Sources of Self-Knowledge*. Cambridge University Press.

1994   *The Remembering Self: Construction and Accuracy in the Self-Narrative*. Cambridge University Press (with R. Fivush).

Further reading

Junger, J. (1986) Psychological or communicative adequacy: On the problem of the characterization of the speaker in functional grammar. *Communication and Cognition*, 19, 59–84.

Neisser, U. and Fivush, R. (1994) *The Remembering Self: Construction and Accuracy in the Self-narrative*. Cambridge University Press.

Slife, B. and Rubinstein, J. (eds) (1992) *Taking Sides: Clashing Views on Controversial Psychological Issues* (7th edn). Dushkin.

Neisser is best known for his 1967 book *Cognitive Psychology*, which gave that field its name as well as an overall conceptual framework. At that time he believed that cognition could best be studied by modelling the flow of information through various mental stages. He coined such terms as 'iconic memory', 'echoic memory', 'preattentive processes' and 'figural synthesis' to identify some of those stages, and devised such methods as visual search and selective looking to explore them.

Later – partly as a result of conversations with a colleague, J.J. **Gibson**, and partly just by observing the development of the field – he became convinced that the formulation of information-processing models is not as effective a research strategy as he first considered. It underestimates the available stimulus information, relies too much on results obtained in artificial settings, and can divert attention from understanding how cognition really occurs in the natural information-rich environment. He articulated this conviction in *Cognition and Reality* (1976), and supported it with experiments (especially on selective and divided attention); in 1982 he applied it specifically to the study of memory in his book *Memory Observed*. Partly as a result of these efforts, the ecological approach has become a viable alternative to the information-processing approach in many areas of cognitive psychology. He has also been consistently concerned with the claims made for 'artificial intelligence', and with the problem of intelligence more generally. Most of his recent empirical research has been in the area of memory, imagery and skill learning.

Nesselroade, John Richard

Born: 1936, Silverton, West Virginia, USA **Nat:** American **Ints:** Adult development and ageing, developmental psychology, evaluation, measurement and statistics **Educ:** BSc Marietta College, Ohio, 1961; MA University of Illinois at Champaign, 1965; PhD University of Illinois at Champaign, 1967 **Appts & awards:** Associate Professor of Psychology, West Virginia University, 1970–2; Cattell Award for Multivariate Research, Society of Multivariate Experimental

Psychology, 1972; Secretary-Treasurer, Society of Multivariate Experimental Psychology, 1972–6; Pennsylvania State University: Associate Professor of Human Development, 1972–5, Professor of Human Development, 1975–83, Research Professor of Human Development, 1983–90, Distinguished Professor of Human Development, 1990–1; President, American Psychological Association Division 20, 1982–3; Hamilton Professor of Psychology, University of Virginia, Charlottesville, 1991–

Principal publications

1972 Note on the longitudinal factor analysis model. *Psychometrika*, 37, 187–91.

1973 *Life-Span Developmental Psychology: Methodological Issues*. Academic Press (with H.W. Reese).

1974 'Sometimes it's okay to factor difference scores': The separation of trait and state anxiety. *Multivariate Behavioral Research*, 9, 273–82 (with D.G. Cable).

1976 The discovery of the anxiety state pattern in Q-data, and its distinction, in the LM model, from depression, effort stress, and fatigue. *Multivariate Behavioral Research*, 11, 27–46 (with R.B. Cattell).

1977 *Life-Span Developmental Psychology: Introduction to Research Methods*. Brooks/Cole (with P.B. Baltes and H.W. Reese).

1979 *Longitudinal Research in the Study of Behavior and Development*. Academic Press (ed. with P.B. Baltes).

1980 Regression toward the mean and the study of change. *Psychological Bulletin*, 88, 622–37 (with S.M. Stigler and P.B. Baltes).

1983 Temporal selection and factor invariance in the study of development and change. In P.B. Baltes and O.G. Brim Jr. (eds), *Life-Span Development and Behavior*, vol. 5. Academic Press.

1984 Paradigm loss and paradigm regained: Critique of Dennefer's portrayal of life-span developmental psychology. *American Sociological Review*, 49, 841–7.

1988 Sampling and generalizability: Adult development and aging research issues examined within the general methodological framework of selection. In K.W. Shaie, R.T. Campbell, W. Meredith and S.C. Rawlings (eds), *Methodological Issues in Aging Research*, Springer-Verlag.

1992 Types of change: Application of configural frequency analysis in repeated measurement designs. *Experimental Aging Research*, 18, 169–83 (with A. von Eye).

1994 Using multivariate data to structure developmental change. In S.H. Cohen and H.W. Reese (eds), *Life-Span Developmental Psychology: Methodological Contributions*. Erlbaum (with J. McArdle).

Further reading

Heatherton, T.F. and Weinberger, J.L. (eds) (1994) *Can Personality Change?* American Psychological Association.

Magnusson, D., Bergman, L., Rudinger, G. and Torestad, B. (eds) (1994) *Problems and Methods in Longitudinal Research: Stability and Change*. Cambridge University Press.

Nesselroade earned his bachelor's degree in 1961 from Marietta College, Ohio. From there he moved on to the University of Illinois at Champaign, earning his MA and PhD degrees in 1965 and 1967 respectively. His early training and interests led him to an analytical and quantitative study of human behaviour. His graduate and postgraduate work centred on personality, broadly defined, as well as multivariate methodology. In the early 1970s, Nesselroade allied himself with several developmental psychologists who were articulating a life-span perspective for the study of human development. His earlier interest in the study of temperament, abilities and other individual difference dimensions, coupled with his new interest in the life-span perspective, led him to formulate some new research methods for studying development and change.

Nesselroade articulated the basic assumptions of a multivariate approach to the study of behavioural phenomena, and related these assumptions to the study of development. These assumptions are that any consequent is likely to be a function of multiple determinants, that any determinant is likely to have multiple consequents, and that the examination of multiple systems of antecedent–consequent relationships is a useful way to study complex systems. Nesselroade's methodology offered developmental psychologists a way to deal with multiple dependent variables in the life-span perspective.

Another important contribution of Nesselroade's is his effort to specify further the nature of processes in antecedent–process–consequent approaches to studying development. His incorporation of multivariate research approaches into life-span developmental psychology has stimulated empirical studies of both short-term and long-term changes and methodological improvements for use in such studies. Also of interest to Nesselroade has been the identification of ways to fuse idiographic and nomothetic orientations to the study of behavioural development and change, as well as the roles of time and change concepts in specifying and organizing phenomena of interest to researchers in developmental psychology. He continues to seek dynamic models which may represent the relationships among variables relevant to life-span developmental psychology, such as his recent applications of linear structural equation modelling and configural frequency analysis.

J.D. HOGAN AND W. IACCINO

Neugarten, Bernice Levin

Born: 1916, Norfolk, Nebraska **Nat:** American **Ints:** Adult development and ageing, developmental psychology **Educ:** BA University of Chicago 1936; MA University of Chicago 1937; PhD University of Chicago 1943–5 **Appts & awards:** University of Chicago, Associate Professor of Human Development, 1960–4, Full Professor, 1964–9; Chair of Human Development, 1969–80; President, Gerontological Society of America, 1969; Kleemeier Award for Research on Aging, 1971; Series Advisory Editor, Lifespan Development and Behavior, 1977–85; Illinois Psychological Association Distinguished Psychologist Award, 1979; APA, Distinguished Scientific Contribution Award from the Division on Adult Development and Aging, 1980; Professor of Human Development and Social Policy, North-western University, 1980–8; Deputy Chair, White House Conference on Aging, 1981; Sandoz International Prize for Research in Gerontology, 1987; Rothschild Distinguished Scholar, Center on Aging, Health, and Society, University of Chicago, 1988– ; Associate Editor, *Journal of Gerontology*, 1958–1, *Human Development*, 1962–8; Advisory Editor, *Journal of Genetic Psychology*, 1959–65, *Human Development*, 1969–82, *Social Service Review*, 1972–81

Principal publications

1957 Age–sex roles and personality in middle age: A thematic apperception study. *Psychological Monographs*, 72, whole no. 470 (with D.L. Gutmann).
1964 *Personality in Middle and Late Life*. Atherton Press.
1968 (ed.) *Middle Age and Aging*. University of Chicago Press.

1969 Continuities and discontinuities of psychological issues into adult life. *Human Development*, 12, 121–30.
1970 Adaptation and the life cycle. *Journal of Geriatric Psychiatry*, 4, 71–87.
1973 Sociological perspectives on the life cycle. In P.B. Baltes and K.W. Schaie (eds). *Life-span Developmental Psychology: Personalities and Socialization*. Academic Press (with N. Datan).
1976 *The Psychology of Aging: An Overview. Master Lectures on Developmental Psychology*. American Psychological Association.
1982 (ed.) *Age or Need? Public Policies for Older People*. Sage.
1986 The changing meaning of age in the aging society. In A. Pifer and L. Bronte (eds), *Our Aging Society: Paradox and Promise*. Norton (with D.A. Neugarten).

Further reading

Riley, M.W. (ed.) (1988) *Sociological Lives: Social Change and the Life Course*, vol. 2. Sage.
Stevens, G. and Gardner, S. (1982) *The Women of Psychology*, vol. 2: *Expansion and Refinement*. Schenkman.

Bernice Levin was born in a small town in Nebraska in 1916, the elder of two children. Her father had come to the United States from Lithuania in his early twenties. While her parents, David and Sadie Levin, did not have much formal education, they valued it highly and encouraged their gifted daughter. She skipped grades frequently and graduated from high school at age 15. In 1933 her parents sent her to attend the University of Chicago. She arrived in Chicago aged 17 and has lived in the Hyde Park area ever since her second year there. Bernice supported herself with scholarships and part-time work. She earned her BA degree in English and French literature in 1936, and the following year, at age 21, she completed an MA degree in educational psychology. With W. Lloyd Warner and Robert **Havighurst**, she participated in a community study of a small town in Illinois, and gathered data for her dissertation on the influence of social class on the friendship patterns of children and adolescents. She met Fritz Neugarten on campus, when he came to Chicago from Paris, and they married in 1940. She received her PhD in Human Development in 1943, the first such degree given by the University of Chicago. She then took several years off to raise her two children.

Her life experiences had an influence on her later theoretical work on adult development. The ages at which she completed her BA and MA degrees were relatively early, and the age when she first took a faculty position was relatively advanced (35 years). The deconstruction of societal norms regarding the appropriate age to engage in certain activities became a hallmark of Neugarten's later work. In 1951 she joined the faculty at the University of Chicago and, in 1960 was offered a tenure-track position. By 1964 she had become a full professor, and in 1969 she became chair of the Committee on Human Development. In 1980 she left the University of Chicago to start a new doctoral programme in Human Development and Social Policy at Northwestern University. She returned in 1988 as Rothschild Distinguished Scholar at the Center on Aging, Health and Society at the University of Chicago.

Neugarten's work has been substantially influenced by the fields of sociology and anthropology. In fact, her graduate training at the University of Chicago was in the multidisciplinary Human Development programme of the Division of the Social Sciences, which included anthropologists and sociologists as well as psychologists. Neugarten has suggested that the group of scholars who made up this faculty can be said to have played the leading role in creating the academic field of adult development and ageing. Her interest in sociological issues is evident from her dissertation research, which dealt with social class as a predictor of the friendship patterns of children and adolescents. She has described her decision to focus on adult development as involving a large factor of chance. Early in her career she was asked to teach a new course called 'Maturity and old age', and to join a research team that was beginning a study on middle-aged and ageing people in the Kansas City area. Neugarten proceeded to study all that she could find on personality change in adulthood, mostly **Erikson**, in order to teach the course. She renamed the course 'Adult development and ageing', and soon began to make her mark in the field.

Neugarten's major influence on adult development theory is her emphasis on a life-span perspective and her de-emphasis on age as a predictor. She concluded that the life-span is fluid and that age is a poor predictor of where a person fits into society physically, socially and intellectually. She rejected a simple stage theory of adult development, pointing out that adult development is characterized by a high degree of variability and individual differences. She emphasized the fact that people grow old in very different ways, and the range of individual differences becomes greater with the passage of time. Neugarten's position regarding the use of chronological age as a criterion for the distribution of public benefits has placed her in conflict with advocacy groups for the elderly. However, she has undeniably been an advocate for the legions of vigorous older individuals in American society, those whom she has labelled the 'young old'.

J.D. HOGAN AND W. IACCINO

Nisbett, Richard E.

Born: 1941, Littlefield, Texas, USA *Nat:* American *Ints:* Cognitive psychology, experimental psychology, social psychology *Educ:* AB Tufts University, 1962; PhD Columbia University, 1966 *Appts & awards:* NSF Fellowship for Research and Writing, 1969; Morse Junior Faculty Fellowship for Research and Writing, Yale, 1969; Research Scientist, Research Center for Group Dynamics, 1978– ; Langfeld Lecturer, Princeton University, 1980; Fellow, Center for Advanced Studies in the Behavioral Sciences, 1981; APA Donald D. Campbell Award for Distinguished Research in Social Psychology, 1982; Donald Taylor Memorial Lecturer, Yale University, 1984; APA Award for Distinguished Scientific Contributions, 1992; University of Michigan, Professor, Department of Psychology, 1992– ; Editorial Boards: *Journal of Personality and Social Psychology*, 1969–71, 1973–7, 1979– , *Journal of Experimental Social Psychology*, 1973–8; *Cognitive Psychology*, 1977– , *Journal for the Theory of Social Behavior*, 1979–83, *European Journal of Social Psychology*, 1982– , *Psychological Review*, 1982–

Principal publications

1966 Cognitive manipulation of pain. *Journal of Experimental Social Psychology*, 2, 227–36 (with S. Schachter).

1971 *The Actor and the Observer: Divergent Perceptions of the Causes of Behavior*. General Learning Press (with E.E. Jones).

1972 Hunger, obesity and the ventromedical hypothalamus. *Psychological Review*, 79, 433–53.

1972 *Attribution: Perceiving the Causes of Behavior*. General Learning Press (with E.E. Jones).

1974 *Social Psychology: Explorations in Understanding*. CRM (with K. Gergen).

1974   *Thought and Feeling: Cognitive Alteration of Feeling States.* Aldine-Atherton (with H.S. London).

1975   Attribution and the psychology of prediction. *Journal of Personality and Social Psychology*, 32, 932–43 (with E. Borgida).

1977   Telling more than we can know: Verbal reports on mental processes. *Psychological Review*, 84, 231–59 (with T.D. Wilson).

1980   *Human Inference: Strategies and Shortcomings of Social Judgment.* Prentice Hall.

1981   The dilution effect: Nondiagnostic information weakens the implications of diagnostic information. *Cognitive Psychology*, 13, 248–77 (with H. Zukier and R. Lemley).

1983   Statistical heuristics in everyday reasoning. *Psychological Review*, 90, 339–63 (with D. Krantz, D. Jepson and Z. Kunda).

1986   *Induction: Processes of Inference, Learning and Discovery.* MIT Press (with J.H. Holland, K.J. Holyoak and P. Thagard).

1991   *The Person and the Situation: Perspectives of Social Psychology.* McGraw-Hill.

1992   *Rules for Reasoning.* Erlbaum.

Further reading

Howe, R.B. (1991) Introspection: A reassessment. *New Ideas in Psychology*, 9, 25–44.

Sperber, D., Premack, D. and Premack, A.J. (eds) (1995) *Causal Cognition: A Multidisciplinary Debate.* Clarendon Press/Oxford University Press.

Initially Nisbett was interested in emotion and feeding behaviour. These topics were 'inherited' from his advisor, Stanley **Schachter**, but were nevertheless his own. His chief contribution to the study of emotion was to demonstrate (1966) the importance of arousal symptom attribution. When arousal is (wrongly) attributed to a non-emotional source, little emotion is experienced. His major contribution to the study of obesity was to show that a great many of the behavioural peculiarities of the obese may be attributed to hunger, due to their attempts to hold weight below its set point. His next major interest was in the attribution of causality for social behaviour. He showed (with Jones, 1971) that actors tend to attribute their behaviour to situational factors, while observers tend to attribute the behaviour of actors to their individual dispositions, i.e. personality traits. He next studied people's accuracy about the causes of their behaviour. He showed that they are often inaccurate, and that beliefs about causality owe more to prior theories about human behaviour than to observation of the workings of one's mind (with Wilson, 1977). He then studied human inductive inference about everyday life events and demonstrated (1980) that people make many errors of a statistical nature. He also showed that these errors are correctable by formal training in statistics.

O

O'Leary, K. Daniel

Born: 1940, USA **Nat:** American **Ints:** Clinical, developmental, experimental analysis of behavior, family psychology, psychotherapy **Educ:** BA Pennsylvania State University, 1962; MA University of Illinois, 1965; PhD University of Illinois, 1967 **Appts & awards:** Professor of Psychology, State University of New York at Stony Brook; Professor of Psychiatry and Psychology, University of Pennsylvania, 1967–; First Prize for Research, American Personnel and Guidance Association, New Orleans, 1974; Fellow, APA Divisions 7, 12, 25; President, APA Division 12, Experimental-Clinical Section, 1978; President, Association for Advancement of Behavior Therapy, 1982–3; APA Division 12, Section 3, Distinguished Scientist Award, 1985; Editorial Boards: *Journal of Applied Behavior Analysis*, 1970–1, 1980– , *Journal of Consulting and Clinical Child Psychology*, 1973–84, *Behavior Therapy*, 1973–6; *Behavior Assessment*, 1981– ; *Journal of Interpersonal Violence*; Associate Editor: *Journal of Applied Behavior Analysis*, 1971–3, *Journal of Abnormal Child Psychology*, 1972– ; Editor, *Journal of Applied Behavior Analysis*, 1977–80

Principal publications

1967 Behavior modification of an adjustment class: A token reinforcement program. *Exceptional Children*, 33, 637–42 (with W.C. Becker).

1968 Anticipatory socialization for psychotherapy: Method and rationale. *American Journal of Psychiatry*, 124, 1202–12 (with P.H. Wender).

1971 Token reinforcement program in the classroom: A review. *Psychological Bulletin*, 75, 379–398 (with R. Drabman).

1975 *Behavior Therapy: Application and Outcome*. Prentice Hall (with G.T. Wilson).

1975 Shaping data collection congruent with experimental hypotheses. *Journal of Applied Behavior Analysis*, 8, 43–51 (with R.N. Kent and J. Kanowitz).

1976 A controlled evaluation of behavior modification with conduct problem children.

Journal of Consulting and Clinical Psychology, 44, 586–96 (with R.N. Kent).

1977 *Classroom Management: The Successful Use of Behavior Modification* (rev. with new readings and commentaries). Pergamon (with S.G. O'Leary).

1977 Treatment of conduct problem children: BA and/or PhD therapists. *Behavior Therapy*, 8, 653–8 (with R.N. Kent).

1980 *Principles of Behavior Therapy*. Prentice-Hall (with G.T. Wilson).

1980 Pills or skills for hyperactive children. *Journal of Applied Behavior Analysis*, 13, 191–204.

1981 Marital violence: Characteristics of abusive couples. *Journal of Consulting and Clinical Psychology*, 49, 63–71 (with A. Rosenbaum).

1981 A comparative outcome study of behavioral marital therapy and communication therapy. *Journal of Marital and Family Therapy*, 159–69 (with H. Turkewitz).

1984 *Mommy I Can't Sit Still: Coping with the Aggressive and Hyperactive Child*. Horizon.

1984 The image of behavior therapy. *Behavior Therapy*, 15, 219–33.

1986 (ed.) *Assessment of Marital Discord*. Erlbaum.

1993 Men and women's attributions of blame for domestic violence. *Journal of Family Violence*, 8, 289–302 (with A.L. Cantos and P. Neidig).

Further reading

Fincham, F.D. and Bradbury, T.N. (eds) (1990) *The Psychology of Marriage: Basic Issues and Applications*. Guilford.

Jacobson, N.S. and Gurman, A.S. (eds) (1995) *Clinical Handbook of Couple Therapy*. Guilford.

As a graduate student, O'Leary worked with Wesley Becker at the University of Illinois, where he was making the transition from analytic research on the circumplex model to research on behavioural interventions with school children. They initiated token reinforcement programmes with classes for emotionally disturbed children and found very dramatic reductions in disruptive behaviour and increases in productivity. That work with Becker, Modsen and associates, along with related research on the effects of praise, soft reprimands and classroom rules, had a lasting impact on approaches to school discipline. Later with Ron Kent he completed methodological research on observational technology on consultation models with parents and teachers of aggressive children, and it became clear that these children could be influenced significantly via a consultation approach. It also became apparent, however, that family problems such as marital discord could moderate this success and the ability to maintain good behaviour.

In 1975 he began marital treatment research with Hillary Turkewitz and has been involved in marital research since then. Basically, Turkewitz and O'Leary showed that communication approaches and a combined behavioural approach with a communication component were equally effective in increasing marital satisfaction, and the treated groups showed greater changes than the control groups. They found that violence in the family of origin, poor communication, general aggressive response patterns, impulsivity, poor self-esteem, and lack of positive feelings towards one's mate are correlates of physical abuse in marriage. They followed 400 couples from pre-marriage to 30 months post-marriage. Approximately 40 per cent of women and 35 per cent of men prior to marriage indicated that they had engaged in some form of physical aggression against their partner. Further, these rates were approximately the same 18 months after marriage. More recent research focuses on the meaning of physical aggression to partners, reasons for disagreements between spouses in their reports of interpartner aggression, stability of interpartner aggression and theoretical models of spouse abuse.

Olds, James

Born: 1922, Chicago, Illinois, USA **Died:** 1976, Laguna Beach, California, USA **Nat:** American **Ints:** Experimental, physiological and comparative, psychopharmacology **Educ:** BA Amherst College, Massachusetts, 1947; MA Harvard University, 1951; PhD Harvard University 1952 **Appts & awards:** Professor, California Institute of Technology; Newcome–Cleveland Prize, AAAS (with N.E. Miller), 1956; Hoffheimer Prize, American Psychiatric Association, 1958; Warren Medal, Society of Experimental Psychologists, 1962; APA Distinguished Scientific Contribution Award, 1967; Kittay International Award, Kittay Scientific Foundation, 1976

Principal publications

1954   Positive reinforcement produced by electrical stimulation of the septal area and other regions of the rat brain. *Journal of Comparative and Physiological Psychology*, 47, 419–28 (with P. Milner).

1956   *The Growth and Structure of Motives*. Free Press.

1958   Effects of hunger and male sex hormone on self-stimulation of the brain. *Journal of Comparative and Physiological Psychology*, 51, 320–4.

1958   Satiation effects in self-stimulation of the brain. *Journal of Comparative and Physiological Psychology*, 51, 675–8.

1961   Emotions and associative mechanisms in rat brain. *Journal of Comparative and Physiological Psychology*, 54, 120–6 (with M.E. Olds).

1961 Hypothalamic substrates of reward. *Physiological Reviews*, 42, 554–604.

1962   Identical 'feeding and rewarding' systems in the lateral hypothalamus of rats. *Science*, 135, 374–5 (with D.L. Margules).

1964   Subcortical lesions and maze retention in the rat. *Experimental Neurology*, 10, 296–304 (with M.E. Olds and D. Hogberg).

1966   The limbic system and behavioral reinforcement. In *Progress in Brain Research*, vol. 27. Elsevier.

1972   Learning centers of rat brain mapped by measuring latencies of conditioned unit responses. *Journal of Neurophysiology*, 35, 202–19 (with J.F. Disterhoft, M. Segal, C.L. Kornblith and R. Hirsch).

1972   Mapping the mind onto the brain. In F.G. Worden, J.P. Swazey and G. Adelman (eds), *The Neurosciences: Path of Discovery*. MIT Press.

Further reading

Thompson, R.F. (1979) James Olds. *American Journal of Psychology*, 92, 151–2.

James Olds, who is probably best known for his seminal studies of brain recording and brain stimulation in freely moving animals, has often been described as one of the most significant neuroscientists of this century. His early education convinced him that the way forward in psychology was through a more complete understanding of the nervous system, and his move to **Hebb**'s laboratory at McGill University in 1953 allowed him to develop the techniques necessary to carry out research in this area. His discovery with P.M. Milner that stimulation of the brain in certain areas (mainly in the limbic system) is pleasurable and has equivalent effects to natural reinforcement is often described as accidental, though R.F. Thompson, in his obituary to Olds, has argued that while there may have been an element of luck in the early positioning of the electrodes, Olds would have eventually found the reinforcement centres anyway, since that is what he was looking for. The discovery, first published in 1954, in the same year as **Delago** reported his findings on aversive centres in the brain, marked a turning point in motivational theory. It provided support for the traditional hedonistic approach to motivation and posed some serious questions for the then predominant drive-reduction theories. It also stimulated a vast amount of research into the detailed anatomy and pharmacology of the reinforcement system, much of this by Olds himself and his co-workers. In all, Olds published around a hundred papers, most of them on stimulation (electrical and chemical) and microelectrode recording from the brains, usually of rats, in instrumental learning situations. He also published one book, *The Growth and Structure of Motives* (1956), fairly early in his career.

R. PRIESTNALL

Orne, Martin Theodore

Born: 1927, Vienna, Austria **Nat:** American/ Austrian **Ints:** Clinical psychology, forensic psychology, hypnosis, memory, methodology, law, psychiatry **Educ:** AB (cum laude) Harvard College, 1948; AM Harvard University, 1951; MD Tufts University Medical School, 1955; Residency in Psychiatry, Massachusetts Mental Health Center, 1957–60; PhD Harvard University, 1958 **Appts & awards:** Professor of Psychiatry and Director, University of Pennsylvania Medical School, 1967– ; Member APA Divisions 1, 6, 8 and 30 (Fellow status in 6, 8 and 30); Benjamin Franklin Gold Medal, International Society of Hypnosis, 1982; APA Distinguished Scientific Award for the Applications of Psychology, 1986; American Academy of Psychiatry and the Law, Seymour Pollack Award, 1991; American Psychological Society, James McKeen Cattell Fellow Award in Applied Psychology, 1992

Principal publications

1959   The nature of hypnosis: Artifact and essence. *Journal of Abnormal and Social Psychology*, 58, 277–99.

1962   On the social psychology of the psychological experiment: With particular reference to demand characteristics and their implications. *American Psychologist*, 17, 776–83.

1968   Anticipatory socialization for psychotherapy: Method and rationale. *American Journal of Psychiatry*, 124, 1202–12 (with P.H. Wender).

1969   Demand characteristics and the concept of quasi-controls. In R. Rosenthal and R. Rosnow (eds), *Artifact in Behavioral Research*, Academic Press.

1971   The simulation of hypnosis: Why, how and what it means. *International Journal of Clinical and Experimental Hypnosis*, 19, 277–96.

1974   Hypnosis. *Encyclopaedia Britannica*, Helen Hemingway Benton (with A.G. Hammer).

1979   The use and misuse of hypnosis in court. *International Journal of Clinical and Experimental Hypnosis*, 27, 311–41.

1984   On the differential diagnosis of multiple personality in the forensic context. *International Journal of Clinical and Experimental Hypnosis*, 32, 118–69 (with D.F. Dinges and E.C. Orne).

1988   Reconstructing memory through hypnosis: Forensic and clinical implications. In H.M. Pettinati (ed.), *Hypnosis and Memory*, Guilford Press (with D.F. Dinges, E.C. Orne and W.G. Whitehouse).

1988   Hypnotic hyperamnesia: Enhanced memory accessibility or report bias? *Journal of Abnormal Psychology*, 97, 289–95 (with D.F. Dinges, E.C. Orne and W.G. Whitehouse).

1989   Hypnosis. In H.I. Kaplan, and B.J. Sadock (eds), *Comprehensive Textbook of Psychiatry: V*. Williams & Wilkins (with D.F. Dinges).

1991   Disorders of self: Myths, metaphors, and the demand characteristics of treatment. In G. Goethals and J. Strauss (eds), *The Self: An Interdisciplinary Approach*. Springer-Verlag.

1996   'Memories' of anomalous and traumatic autobiographical experiences: Validation and consolidation of fantasy through hypnosis. *Psychological Inquiry* (with D.F. Dinges, E.C. Orne and W.G. Whitehouse).

Further reading

(1987) *American Psychologist*, 42, 4, 289–94.

Gross, R.D. (1990) *Key Studies in Psychology*. Hodder & Stoughton.

Over four decades, Orne's research has been concerned with some fundamental processes and questions which lie at the core of, or on the interfaces between psychology, psychiatry and law: demand characteristics, memory, amnesia, confabulation, lie detection, multiple personality, dissociation, trance, and hypnosis. The social context of experimental and clinical situations has been of central importance to

Orne's approach. He articulated and demonstrated the importance of the 'demand characteristics' construct in a much cited and reprinted paper published in 1962. This paper and others changed the way many experimentalists evaluated the reactions of their research participants and how clinicians viewed the responses of their clients/patients to hypnosis and other psychological therapies and interventions.

Controlled investigation of behavioural, cognitive, emotional and experiential changes accompanying hypnosis has been a central theme of Orne's experimental research. Methodological innovation for the study of the 'artifact and essence' of hypnosis in the form of simulator controls enabled Orne to argue that hypnotic experience was qualitatively different from that expected and enacted by role-playing controls. On the other hand, claims of enhanced memory under hypnosis were disputed by Orne, whose studies suggested that increased confidence and a lower criterion for the reporting of pseudo-memories as memories, rather than increased sensitivity, were the underlying basis for the results obtained. However, he did not dispute the emotional validity of 'recollected trauma' to the patient, noting the relief to symptoms which sometimes follows hypnotically induced recollections.

Orne fruitfully applied a similar analysis to the study of multiple personality disorder (MPD). In the light of this, the recent MPD epidemic in the USA (notably absent elsewhere) appears to be entirely iatrogenic, an artefact of a complex mixture of motivational factors, suggestion and expectancy, a theory with which others independently concur. Orne's contribution to psychology, psychiatry and the criminal justice system has been made possible by his methodological ingenuity in investigating socially significant issues through scientifically rigorous experimentation.

DAVID F. MARKS

Osgood, Charles Egerton

Born: 1916, Sommerville, Massachusetts, USA
Died: 1991, Champaign, Illinois, USA **Nat:** American **Ints:** Experimental psychology and international relations, personality and social psychology, population and environmental psychology, psychological study of social issues **Educ:** BA Dartmouth College, 1939; PhD Yale University, 1945 **Appts & awards:** Emeritus Professor, University of Illinois, 1949; APA Award for Distinguished Contributions to the Science of Psychology, 1960; President, APA, 1963; APA Division 9, Kurt Lewin Award for Contribution to the Solution of Social Issues, 1971; NAS, 1972– ; Hon. Life Member, New York Academy of Sciences, 1977–

Principal publications

1952   The nature and measurement of meaning. *Psychological Bulletin*, 49, 197–237.
1953   *Method and Theory in Experimental Psychology*. Oxford University Press.
1960   The cross-cultural generality of visual–verbal synesthetic tendencies. *Behavioral Science*, 5, 146–69.
1963   On understanding and creating sentences. *American Psychologist*, 18, 735–51.
1964   Semantic differential technique in the comparative study of cultures. In A.K. Romney and R.G. D'Andrade (eds), *American Anthropologist*, 66 (no. 3, pt 2). Special publication.
1966   Dimensionality of the semantic space for communication via facial expression. *Scandinavian Journal of Psychology*, 7, 1–30.
1966   *An Alternative to War or Surrender*. University of Illinois Press.
1966   *Perspective in Foreign Policy*. Pacific.
1967   On the strategy of cross-national research into subjective culture. *Social Sciences Information*, 6, 5–37.
1970   Speculation on the structure of interpersonal intentions. *Behavioral Science*, 15, 237–54.
1971   Exploration in semantic space: A personal diary. *Journal of Social Issues*, 27, 5–64.
1974   Probing subjective culture. Part 1. Cross-linguistic tool-making. *Journal of Communication*, 24, 31–4. Part 2: Cross-cultural tool using. *Journal of Communication*, 24, 82–100.
1979   *Lectures on Language Performance*. Springer-Verlag.
1979   From Yang and Yin to 'and' or 'but' in cross-cultural perspective. *International Journal of Psychology*, 14, 1–35.

Further reading

Osgood, C.E. (1980) Charles E. Osgood. In G. Lindzey (ed.), *A History of Psychology in Autobiography*, vol. 7. Freeman.
—— (1992) The tale of an eager then lonely then contented dinosaur. *Studies in the Linguistic Sciences*, 22, 42–58.
Rieber, R.W. and Voyat, G. (1983) Charles Osgood's views on the psychology of language and thought. In R.W. Rieber and G. Voyat (eds), *Dialogues on the Psychology of Language and Thought*. Plenum.

Charles Osgood's father was the business manager of the Jordan Marsh department store in
Boston. His parents divorced when he was 6 and
he had a relatively unhappy childhood. He
enrolled at Dartmouth College, intending to earn
a living as a newspaper writer, and was attracted
to psychology while studying there. A year after
receiving his BA he married Cynthia Luella
Thornton. He spent an extra year at Dartmouth
and then enrolled for graduate studies at Yale.
At Yale he was Robert **Sears**'s research assistant
and worked with Arnold **Gesell** and Irvin Child.
He describes (1980) Clark **Hull** as the major
influence on his thinking, but successfully
avoided falling under Hull's authoritarian control. He completed his thesis under the nominal
direction of Donald Marquis, who was taken up
with war duties for most of the time. After
graduating he spent part of 1945 at Smoky Hill
Army Air Force Base, Salina, Kansas, and
the New London Submarine Base. He was
offered a post at the University of Connecticut,
where he remained until 1949, when he moved
to the University of Illinois at Urbana-
Champaign. Osgood's contributions can be
grouped under five themes: behaviourism
versus cognitivism, psycholinguistics, theory of
meaning, cross-cultural research and peace
studies.

Behaviourism versus cognitivism: Osgood
regarded himself as a behaviourist who argued
that simple stimulus–response theories of the
kind expounded by B.F. **Skinner** were incapable
of explaining most of human behaviour,
especially more complex behaviour such as
language and thinking. He suggested that it was
necessary to postulate unobservable 'meaning
responses' to account for complex behaviours, a
position which contradicted that formulated by
radical behaviourists. Nevertheless, Osgood
continued to regard his work as essentially
behaviourist because the core semantic features
were always derived from actual behaviour
towards stimuli in the environment.

Psycholinguistics: Osgood's contributions
were organizational and scientific. The former
relate to his involvement as an organizer and
participant in numerous seminars, conferences
and summer schools mostly in the 1950s.
Osgood's work in psycholinguistics was formulated from a behaviourist standpoint and, like
Skinner's position, attracted little attention
following **Chomsky**'s incisive critique of the
limitations of that approach. Thus, his work on
the importance of semantics over syntax was
largely ignored.

Theory of meaning: Osgood adopted a
Hullian framework when formultating his
mediational theory of meaning. He suggested
that words represent things because they produce an abbreviated replica of actual behaviour
towards those things. With Suci and Tannenbaum he developed the semantic differential as
an objective measure of meaning. The technique
involves asking a respondent to rate a given
concept on a series of seven-point, bi-polar
rating scales. Analysis of variability in
responses revealed three underlying dimensions:
evaluation (good–bad), potency (strong–weak)
and activity (active–passive). Osgood also
investigated how people maintain consistency or
congruity in their evaluations of issues and
people. Unlike other approaches which are
based on *Gestalt* psychology, Osgood argued
that people learn to make cognitive respresenta-
tions of issues and people, and that these
representations are associated with hedonic
evaluations. The result of two incongruous
representations is a compromise that achieves
congruity. The Congruity Principle states that
evaluative changes to restore congruity will
occur inversely to the intensity of evaluation.
This means that a person who is held in high
esteem will be less likely to have his or her
evaluations lowered as a function of espousing a
position which an audience evaluates negatively
but with less strength. The semantic differential
is still widely used although it is now regarded
as measuring emotional responses to words (i.e.
affective meaning) rather than lexical meaning
per se.

Cross-cultural psychology: Osgood took a
minor in anthropology while he was at Dartmouth, and his early interest in cultural issues
was rekindled when he spent a year (1958–9)
at the Center for Advanced Study in the
Behavioral Sciences. He was particularly interested in whether the findings he had reported
with the semantic differential technique were
specific to the English language and the American culture. He conducted a huge cross-cultural
study involving 30 language/culture groups and
620 concepts. He found fairly strong support for
the universality of the evaluation–potency–
activity structure.

Peace studies: Osgood felt that psychologists
could and should become actively involved
in averting war, especially nuclear war. His
major contribution was his GRIT strategy
(Graduated and Reciprocated Initiatives in
Tension-Reduction). The purpose of GRIT is to
induce trust and co-operative responses among

protagonists. At its simplest the strategy proceeds as follows: Nation A devises small steps, well within its limits of security, designed to reduce tensions and induce reciprocating steps from Nation B. If these unilateral initiatives are applied persistently, and are reciprocated, then the margin for risk taking is widened and somewhat larger steps of the same kind can be taken. In this way both parties begin backing down the escalation ladder.

Osipow, Samuel H.

Born: 1934, Allentown, Pennsylvania, USA *Nat:* American *Ints:* Consulting psychology, counselling, health, industrial and organizational, psychology of women *Educ:* BA Lafayette College, 1954; MA Columbia University, 1955; PhD Syracuse University, 1959 *Appts & awards:* Chairperson and Professor of Psychology, Department of Psychology, Ohio State University; Board of Directors, APA; Chair, Board of Directors, Council for the National Register of Health Service Providers in Psychology; President, APA Division 17, 1977–8; Editor: *Journal of Vocational Behavior*, 1970–5, *Journal of Counseling Psychology*, 1975–81; Advisory Editor, Vocational Psychology Series (Erlbaum); Editorial Board: *Contemporary Psychology*, *Journal of Vocational Behavior*

Principal publications

1968 *Theories of Career Development*. Prentice Hall. (2nd edn, 1973, 3rd edn, 1983, 4th edn, 1995).

1970 *Strategies in Counseling for Behavior Change*. Prentice Hall.

1971 The effects of manipulated success ratios on task preferences. *Journal of Vocational Behavior*, 1, 93–8 (with A.B. Scheid).

1975 *Emerging Woman: Career Analysis and Outlooks*. Charles E. Merrill.

1976 A scale of educational-vocational undecidedness: a typological approach. *Journal of Vocational Behavior*, 9, 233–43 (with C.G. Carney and A. Barak).

1979 Career choices: Learning about interests and intervening in their development. In A. Mitchell, J.D. Krumboltz and B. Jones (eds), *Social Learning Theory of Career Decision Making*. Carroll.

1979 Occupational mental health: another role for counseling psychologists. *Counseling Psychologist*, 8, 39–41.

1980 *A Survey of Counseling Methods*. Dorsey (with W. Walsh and D. Tosi).

1982 Counseling psychology in business and industry: Applications in the world of work. *Counseling Psychologist*, 10, 19–25.

1982 Research in career counseling. *Counseling Psychologist*, 10, 27–34.

1983 *The Handbook of Vocational Psychology*, Vol. 1, *Foundations*; vol. 2, *Applications*. Erlbaum.

1984 Measuring occupational stress, strain and coping. *Applied Social Psychology Annual*. Sage (with A.R. Spokane)

1985 Occupational stress, strain and coping across the lifespan. *Journal of Vocational Behavior*, 27, 98–108 (with R. Doty and A.R. Spokane).

1986 Career issues through the lifespan. In B. Hammond, *Master Lectures in the Psychology of Work*. APA.

1986 An occupational analysis of counseling psychology: How special is the speciality? *American Psychology*, 41 (with L. Fizgerald).

Further reading

Abeles, N. (1981) Review of Osopow, S., Walsh, W. and Tosi, D.: A survey of counselling methods. *Contemporary Psychology*, 26, 280–1.

Samuel Osipow's work focuses on drawing together the aspects of theory and application in the area of vocational guidance and career counselling. Perhaps his principal contribution in a plethora of publications since the 1960s is his *Theories of Career Development* 1968, now in its fourth edition. Osipow identifies and explains the theoretical foundations of the field, describing major research findings and the relative strengths and weaknesses of the positions discussed. Finally he seeks to draw out principles for the practice of vocational guidance and career counselling by commenting on utility. It is this approach, which bridges the gap between theory and practice in a wide-ranging and varied field, that makes the work of Samuel Osipow so valuable to students and practitioners alike.

JONATHAN G. HARVEY

P

Paivio, Allan Urho

Born: 1925, Thunder Bay, Ontario, Canada **Nat:** Canadian **Ints:** Cognition, imagery, language, memory **Educ:** BSc McGill University, 1949; MSc McGill University, 1957; PhD McGill University, 1959 **Appts & Awards:** University of Western Ontario: Assistant Professor, 1962–3, Associate Professor, 1963–7, Professor of Psychology, 1967–92, Professor Emeritus, 1992– , Hon. Professor Emeritus (Kinesiology), 1992– ; APA, Division 3 (Fellow); President, Canadian Psychological Association, 1974–5; Queen's Silver Jubilee Medal, 1977; Fellow of Royal Society of Canada, 1978; Canadian Psychological Association Award for Distinguished Contributions to Psychology as a Science, 1982; Killam Research Fellowship, 1990, 1991–2; Hon. LLD, University of Western Ontario, 1993

Principal publications

1965 Abstractness, imagery, and meaningfulness in paired associate learning. *Journal of Verbal Learning and Verbal Behavior*, 4, 32–8.

1968 Concreteness, imagery, and meaningfulness values for 925 nouns. *Journal of Experimental Psychology*, 78 (1, pt 2) (with J.C. Yuille and S.A. Madigan).

1969 Mental imagery in associative learning and memory. *Psychological Review*, 76, 241–63.

1971 *Imagery and Verbal Processes.* Holt, Rinehart & Winston.

1973 Picture superiority in free recall: Imagery or dual coding? *Cognitive Psychology*, 5, 176–206 (with K. Csapo).

1975 Neomentalism. *Canadian Journal of Psychology*, 29, 263–91.

1975 Perceptual comparisons through the mind's eye. *Memory and Cognition*, 3, 635–47.

1975 Coding distinctions and repetition effects in memory. In G.H. Bower (ed.), *The Psychology of Learning and Motivation*, vol. 9. Academic Press.

1978 Comparisons of mental clocks. *Journal of Experimental Psychology: Human Perception and Performance*, 4, 61–71.

1980 A dual-coding approach to bilingual memory. *Canadian Journal of Psychology*, 34, 390–401 (with A. Desrochers).

1981 *The Psychology of Language.* Prentice Hall (with I. Begg).

1982 Imagery, memory, and the brain. *Canadian Journal of Psychology*, 36, 243–72 (with J. te Linde).

1983 The mind's eye in arts and science. *Poetics*, 12, 1–18.

1983 Factor analysis of a questionnaire on imagery and verbal habits and skills. *Canadian Journal of Psychology*, 37, 461–83 (with R.A. Harshman).

1986 *Mental Representations: A Dual-Coding Approach.* Oxford University Press.

1989 Referential processing: Correlates of naming pictures and imaging to words. *Memory and Cognition*, 17, 163–74 (with J.M. Clark, N. Digdon and T. Bons).

1989 Observational and theoretical terms in psychology: A cognitive perspective on scientific language. *American Psychologist*, 44, 500–12 (with J.M. Clark).

1991 Dual coding theory: Retrospect and current status. *Canadian Journal of Psychology*, 45, 255–87.

1994 Memory for pictures and sounds: Independence of auditory and visual codes. *Canadian Journal of Experimental Psychology*, 48, 380–98 (with V. Thompson).

1994 Concreteness and memory: When and why? *Journal of Experimental Psychology: Learning, Memory and Cognition*, 20, 1196–204 (with M. Walsh and T. Bons).

Further reading

Denis, M. (1991) *Image and Cognition.* Harvester Wheatsheaf.

Lockhart, R.S. (1987) Code dueling. Review of mental representations: A dual coding approach. *Canadian Journal of Psychology*, 41, 387–9.

Tippett, L.J. (1992) The generation of visual images: A review of neuropsychological research and theory. *Psychological Bulletin*, 112, 415–32.

Yuille, J.C. (ed.) (1983) *Imagery, Memory and Cognition: Essays in Honor of Allan Paivio.* Erlbaum.

Allan Urho Paivio's secondary education in the late 1930s and early 1940s was targeted towards a career in mining engineering or geology. However, with a passion for sports (especially track and field, gymnastics, weight-lifting and, more lately, snooker) and having had positive experiences as a part-time YMCA instructor in his final years of secondary school, 'Al' Paivio's interests turned towards physical education. Following service in the Navy, he married Kathleen Austin, moved to Montreal, started a family, earned a BSc in physical education at McGill University, and started his first career by opening a health and fitness centre. Inspired by a professor who had taught him an introductory psychology course as an undergraduate and also by some courses he took on public speaking and human relations, Paivio's interest was kindled in the psychology of language, communication and memory, and he started his second career by entering the graduate programme at McGill. While completing his PhD, Paivio moved to Cornell University, where he worked for sixteen months as a research psychologist in the area of child development and family relations. Then, in 1962, after three years as assistant professor at the University of New Brunswick, Paivio joined the University of Western Ontario where he has remained ever since.

Paivio's research on memory, imagery and language took its initial inspiration from the 'conceptual-peg' experience: a universal ability to associate new stimulus items with a structured set of existing items stored in memory by the use of compound mental images. The process is analogous to hanging coats onto a series of uniquely marked pegs, enabling the later identification and safe return of each coat to its owner. Paivio witnessed an application of the conceptual-peg experience as a mnemonic technique at a public-speaking course in 1950. Employed by orators since classical times, this method has been a core feature of memory systems down the ages, with twentieth-century versions presented by Dale Carnegie, Harry Lorayne and others. Paivio's happenstance experience with mnemonic imagery techniques stimulated him to construct the dual-coding theory, one of the most influential theories of cognition this century. Paivio has worked systematically on different aspects of dual-coding theory over four decades, and that work continues.

Beginning with a study of noun–adjective associative memory with Wallace **Lambert** at McGill in the mid-1950s, the first phases of dual-coding research aimed to identify the effective variables of the conceptual-peg experience, focusing upon the the attributes of the words that serve as conceptual pegs and then on the cognitive processes responsible for connecting the new stimuli with the pegs themselves. The concreteness or imagery value of the word-peg items was found to be particularly important as a predictor of accurate retrieval when other potential mediators were controlled (e.g. meaningfulness, familiarity). This contradicted verbal learning theory, which assumed that verbal associative meaningfulness was the most important mediator of paired-associate recall. The role of imagery as the effective mediator of associative learning was corroborated by self-reports provided by research participants and by studies that manipulated the instructions, which found that imagery instructions produce better performance than non-imagery instructions in the learning and recall of word pairs.

Successful empirical investigations of the conceptual-peg hypothesis led Paivio to develop a general theory of cognition, which was intended to provide a descriptive and explanatory account of memory in the form of two different but complementary modes of representation: verbal and imagistic. The verbal system is assumed to be specialized for sequential information processing while the imagery system is specialized for synchronous, integrative information processing. Paivio suggested that the two forms of coding are 'independent but interconnected' in such a way that they supplement each other in additive fashion for the retrieval of items from memory, an assumption that is well supported by empirical evidence. The theory was later extended to accommodate observations on biligualism, by making the assumption that the bilingual has two verbal systems but a single imagery system which mediates between them. Further extensions of the independent coding hypothesis allow for the possibility of several sensorimotor codes corresponding to different kinds of information (visual, auditory, haptic, taste, smell, emotion), available in verbally or non-verbally encoded stimuli or memories. These extensions of the theory are supported by performance data from memory and other cognitive tasks as well as by neuropsychological evidence of regional cortical specialization in sensorimotor processing.

Paivio's dual-coding theory has not escaped criticism; it has been argued by some that it is difficult, if not impossible, to refute. However, Paivio argues that all of the assumptions and hypotheses that make up the theory are testable. For example, in the tests of independence and additivity of imaginal and verbal codes, the results could have disconfirmed the predictions. World-pair concreteness and relatedness could have interacted as Marschark and Hunt's theory predicts, rather than turning out to be independent and additive, as predicted from dual-coding theory. The imagery value of nouns could have been displaced early on as an explanation of concreteness effects by some other correlate of concreteness, but this has not yet happened, although thirty or so alternatives have been investigated. In fact some data have been troublesome for the theory. For example, symbolic comparisons involving colour attributes did not yield a picture superiority effect, contrary to what was expected from the theory. That inconsistency with findings for other symbolic attributes is yet to be resolved.

There are many possible theories of representation, including single-code, dual-code, multiple-code, hierarchical and hybrid-code theories, and it is a complex task trying to operationalize these different theories in ways which make unambiguous, crucial tests feasible. Cognitive processes may be too complicated, invisible and intractable to be captured by a theory as simple as dual-coding theory. None the less, the latter's many structural and processing assumptions are complex enough to require more careful consideration than has been given to them by some critics and proponents of alternative theories.

Another possible limitation has been a reluctance to give credibility to self-reports of conscious experience as a source of usable data. In studying mental imagery this can be self-defeating, because the phenomena of interest are a salient part of conscious experience and, in certain cases, can be easily reportable. The conceptual-peg experience upon which Paivio based his research programme is a good example. Paivio's use of self-reports of strategy usage was an exception to his general principle of mistrusting self-reports. However, these are general issues about the investigation of conscious experience, which cognitive science has yet to solve, and such solutions are unlikely to be found quickly. One of Allan Paivio's contributions has been to pursue the theoretical 'holy grail' doggedly by empirical investigation, and, in this respect, he is without peer.

Paivio's research gained impact from and contributed to the *Zeitgeist* of the so-called 'cognitive revolution' *c.* 1960. Mental imagery became the *cause célèbre* of the new cognitivist era, and Paivio's research was responsible for establishing it as an explanatory construct in the science of psychology. It is impossible to overestimate the resistance in academic psychology's behaviourist and post-behaviourist phases to mental imagery as a theoretical construct until Paivio's systematic research programme could establish its credentials once and for all. The findings of other imagery researchers, for example Roger **Shepard** and Stephen **Kosslyn**, were much more readily acceptable by the research community only as a consequence of the major breakthroughs which Paivio and his group had already made in the core area of the cognitive psychology of the 1960s, that of verbal learning and memory.

One of the most highly cited authors at the peak of his productivity during the 1970s, Allan Paivio was among only seven authors (with A. **Bandura**, L. **Festinger**, D. **Hebb**, G. **Miller**, C. **Osgood** and P. Samuelson) to appear in both the 100 most-cited articles and the 100 most-cited books. In 1975, he was ranked twentieth among living psychologists in the Social Science Citation Index, the highest ranked among living Canadians. Allan Paivio has been an inspiration and mentor to many graduate students, and the chief PhD supervisor to thirty people who have contributed collaboratively and independently to the scientific understanding of imagery and cognition. His personal warmth, integrity and good humour have endeared him to the many students and researchers who have come into contact with him.

Reflecting on the difficulties and uncertainties of existence, Paivio cites four factors which he believes are conducive to high achievement: (1) preservation and expansion of knowledge and skills through continued study, sustained rehearsal and regular practice ('use it or lose it'); (2) the use of imagery for memory improvement and enhancing motivation; (3) fun and enjoyment each day and within one's chosen career; (4) the encouragement and support of his wife Kathleen and family in his career development. That family now consists of five adult children (the oldest, Sandra, is a clinical psychologist) and eight grandchildren. Al Paivio lives his own philosophy, continuing to enjoy psychological research, and life, to the fullest possible extent.

DAVID F. MARKS

Parke, Ross D.

Born: 1938, Huntsville, Ontario, Canada **Nat:** Canadian/American **Ints:** Child, youth and family services, developmental psychology, personality and social psychology **Educ:** BA University of Toronto 1962, Msc University of Toronto 1963, PhD University of Waterloo 1965 **Appts & awards:** Professor, Department of Psychology, University of Wisconsin at Madison, 1970–1; Fels Clinical Professor of Research Pediatrics, University of Cincinnati College of Medicine, 1971–5; Professor of Psychology, University of Illinois at Urbana-Champaign, 1975–90; Clinical Professor, School of Clinical Medicine, University of Illinois at Urbana-Champaign, 1979–90; Belding Scholar of the Foundation for Child Development, New York, 1980; University of Illinois, Department of Psychology Graduate Student Organization Award for Excellence in Advising and Teaching at the Graduate Level, 1989; Elected Chair, Council of Editors, APA, 1989–90; Fellow, American Psychological Society, 1990; Presidential Chair in Psychology, University of California, Riverside, 1990–92; Professor of Psychology, University of California, Riverside, 1990– ; Director, Center for Family Studies, University of California, Riverside, 1992– ; Sabbatical Award, James McKeen Cattell Foundation, 1994; Associate Editor, *Child Development*, 1973–7; Editor, *Developmental Psychology*, 1987–92

Principal publications

1967 Nurturance, nurturance withdrawal, and resistance to deviation. *Child Development*, 38, 1101–10.

1969 Some effects of punishment on children's behavior. *Young Children*, 23, 225–40.

1972 Mother–father–newborn interaction: Effects of maternal medication, labor, and sex of infant. *APA Proceedings*, 85–6 (with S. O'Leary and S. West).

1974 Father–infant interaction. In M.H. Klaus, T. Leger and M.A. Trause (eds), *Maternal Attachment and Mothering Disorders*. Johnson & Johnson.

1975 *Child Psychology: A Contemporary Viewpoint*. McGraw-Hill (with E.M. Hetherington). (4th edn, 1993).

1976 The father's role in infancy: A reevaluation. *Family Coordinator*, 25, 365–71.

1977 Punishment: Effects, side effects, and alternative strategies. In H. Hom and P. Robison (eds), *Psychological Processes in Early Education*. Academic Press.

1979 Interactional designs. In R.B. Cairns (ed.), *The Analysis of Social Interactions: Methods, Issues, and Illustrations*. Erlbaum.

1981 *Fathers*. Harvard University Press.

1984 Historical and contemporary perspectives on fathering. In K.A. McCluskey and H.W. Reese (eds), *Life-Span Developmental Psychology: Historical and Generational Effects in Life-Span Human Development*. Academic Press (with B.R. Tinsley).

1987 Fathers as agents and recipients of support in the postnatal period. In Z. Boukydis (ed.), *Support for Parents in the Postnatal Period*. Ablex (with B.R. Tinsley).

1992 Epilogue: Remaining issues and future trends in the study of family–peer relationships. In R.D. Parke and G. Ladd (eds), *Family–Peer Relationships: Modes of Linkage*. Erlbaum.

1994 Progress, paradigms and unresolved problems: A commentary on recent advances in our understanding of children's emotions. *Merrill-Palmer Quarterly*, 40, 157–69.

Further reading

Parke, R.D. and Ladd, G.W. (eds) (1992). *Family–peer Relationships: Modes of Linkage*. Erlbaum.

Shapiro, J.L., Diamond, M.J. and Greenberg, M. (eds) (1995) *Becoming a Father: Contemporary, Social, Developmental, and Clinical Perspectives*. Springer-Verlag.

Ross Parke was born in the town of Huntsville, Ontario, Canada. He received his undergraduate training at the University of Toronto, earning a BA degree in 1962, and his Master's degree at the same institution in 1963. Parke moved on to the University of Waterloo in Canada, where he earned his PhD in 1965. Soon after graduation he obtained a position as assistant professor in the psychology department at the University of Wisconsin at Madison. Five years later, in 1970, he was appointed to a full professorship at Wisconsin.

Parke's early research interests were in the area of modelling and aggression in young children. Of particular concern to him were the determinants of self-control with respect to aggressive impulses. His most significant work has been in the area of parent–infant interaction, with a particular emphasis on the role that fathers play in infancy and early childhood. Until Parke's research, study of the attachment behaviour of the newborn was almost exclusively limited to the mother–infant dyad. From **Freud** to **Bowlby**, psychology had historically ignored the significance of fathers in its theories of parenthood. Parke asserted that it was a mistake to conclude that fathers are less competent caregivers simply because societal norms historically demanded that mothers be the primary ones. Two reasons may be proposed for the emergence of Parke's tripartite model: the change in societal norms regarding sex roles, and **Harlow**'s finding that 'contact comfort', as opposed to food, has primary reinforcing qualities for infant monkeys. This latter finding made it theoretically possible for fathers to be as reinforcing as mothers.

The hallmark of Parke's research in this area is his use of the observational method. This distinguishes his work from that of earlier research on child-rearing practices, which used a 'reconstruction through retrospection' methodology. Parke's research on fatherhood has highlighted the role of the father in child-rearing, and he has proposed the development of training and support systems, based on his research, to encourage optimal fathering. Among his findings is the observation that there are few parental sex differences on measures of interaction with newborns. While mothers tend to spend more time than fathers in feeding and caretaking activities, fathers and mothers have not been found to differ in their caretaking competence, as measured by sensitivity to infant cues in the feeding situation. In addition to his research activity on parental interaction and its effects on child development, Parke has studied the evaluation of abused children. He is currently involved in a long-term project on family–peer linkage in middle childhood.

J.D. HOGAN AND W. IACCINO

Patterson, Gerald R.

Born: 1926, Lisbon, North Dakota, USA **Nat:** American **Ints:** Antisocial behaviour, behaviour modification, delinquency, marital conflict, social interaction, social learning theory **Educ:** BS University of Oregon, 1949; MA University of Oregon, 1951; PhD University of Minnesota, 1956 **Appts & awards:** Fellow in Psychology, Wilder Clinic, St Paul Minnesota, 1953–5; Instructor in Medical Psychology, Psychiatric Institute, University of Nebraska Medical School, 1955–7; Professor, Department of Psychology, University of Oregon, Eugene, 1957–66; Research Professor, School of Education, University of Oregon, Eugene, 1967–8; NIMH Career Development Award, 1967–72; Research Scientist, Oregon Research Institute, Eugene, 1967–77; Research Scientist, Oregon

Social Learning Center, 1977– ; Distinguished Scientist Award, Division of Clinical Psychology of the APA, 1982; Distinguished Scientific Award for the Applications of Psychology of the APA, 1984; Distinguished Professional Contribution Award, Section on Clinical Child Psychology of the APA, 1986; Founders Award for Distinguished Contributions to the Profession of Psychology, Pacific University Department of Psychology, Forest Grove, Oregon, 1993

Principal publications

1960   A nonverbal technique for the assessment of aggression in children. *Child Development*, 31, 643–53.

1964   An empirical approach to the classification of children. *Journal of Clinical Psychology*, 20, 326–37.

1967   Assertive behavior in children: A step toward a theory of aggression. *Monographs of the Society for Research in Child Development*, 32 (no. 113) (with R.A. Littman and W. Bricker).

1968   *Living with Children: New Methods for Parents and Teachers*. Research Press (with M.E. Gullion).

1971   *Families: Applications of Social Learning to Family Life*. Research Press.

1975   *A Social Learning Approach to Family Intervention*, vol. 1, *Families with Aggressive Children*. Castalia (with J.B. Reid, R.R. Jones and R.E. Conger).

1978   The observation system: Methodological issues and psychometric properties. In J.B. Reid (ed.), *A Social Learning Approach to Family Intervention*, vol. 2, *Observations in Home Setting*. Castalia (with J.B. Reid and S.L. Maerov).

1980   Mothers: The unacknowledged victims. *Monographs of the Society for Research in Child Development*, 45.

1982   *A Social Learning Approach to Family Intervention*, vol. 3, *Coercive Family Processes*. Castalia.

1983   Stress: A change agent for family process. In N. Garmezy and M. Rutter (eds), *Stress, Coping and Development in Children*. McGraw-Hill.

1984   Family interaction: A process model of deviancy training. *Aggressive Behavior*, 10, 253–67 (with T.J. Dishion and L. Bank).

1986   Performance models for antisocial boys. *American Psychologist*, 41, 432–44.

1987   *Parents and Adolescents: Living Together*. Castalia (with M.S. Forgatch).

1989   A developmental perspective on antisocial behavior. *American Psychologist*, 44, 329–35 (with B.D. deBaryshe and E. Ramsey).

1990   *Depression and Aggression in Family Interaction.* Erlbaum.

1992   *A Social Learning Approach to Family Intervention*, vol. 4, *Antisocial Boys.* Castalia (with J.B. Reid and T.J. Dishion).

1995   The development and ecology of antisocial behavior. In D. Cicchetti and D. Cohen (eds), *Manual of Developmental Psychopathology.* Cambridge University Press (with T.J. Dishion and D. French).

Further reading

Morris, E.R. and Braukmann, C.J. (1987) *Behavioral Approaches to Crime and Delinquency.* Plenum.

Rutter, R. and Garmezy, N. (1983) Developmental psychopathology. In P. Mussen (ed.), *Handbook of Child Psychology*, vol. 4, Wiley.

Gerald Patterson was born in Lisbon, North Dakota, and raised in Ely, Minnesota. His long-standing interest in the out-of-doors began early, when he first considered a career as a guide in the Quetico wilderness. These plans were interrupted by World War II, where he served in the combat infantry in Okinawa. After the war, with the availability of the GI Bill, Patterson decided to go to college. A Veteran Administration clinical psychologist adminis-tered a series of career counselling measures, and suggested he become a psychologist, and preferably a psychotherapist. He pursued this advice at the University of Oregon, where he studied individual differences with Leona **Tyler** and **Hull**ian learning theory with Richard Littman. It was also during this time that Patter-son first became interested in delinquency. While working as a probation officer, he became convinced that current psychological theory had limited application in this area.

After earning both his BS and MA degrees at Oregon, he entered the University of Minnesota, where he became caught up in the enthusiastic empiricism of Paul **Meehl**, Donald Paterson, John **Anderson** and the others on the faculty at the time. Here the open-mindedness of the psychology department was particularly attrac-tive to him. As he saw it, any question was legitimate and no particular theory dictated the questions which could be pursued empirically. But while the atmosphere of the department stimulated Patterson to pursue new directions for the problems of delinquency and related questions, he also came to appreciate the demands of high-quality scientific work.

During his last two years of graduate study, Patterson worked as a Fellow in Psychology at the Wilder Clinic in St Paul, Minnesota. Armed with the psychoanalytic theory predominant at that time, he again saw that the best theory and the most competent staff had only limited impact on antisocial and hyperactive children. Even more troubling was the realization that these cases made up the bulk of the case load of child guidance clinics.

For his dissertation, Patterson attempted to build a taxonomic system based on behaviour observed in the clinic and parental reports of the children's symptoms. He then went on to work at the Psychiatric Institute in Omaha, where he came into contact with the therapeutic skills appropriate for working with extremely disturbed children. About this time he also developed a non-verbal technique for assess-ment of aggression in children, publishing this in 1960.

As a Professor of Psychology at the Univer-sity of Oregon, Patterson developed himself along the lines of a research clinician, offering a rather unusual mix of psychoanalysis based on the work of Harry Stack **Sullivan**, Carl **Rogers**, Meehl and Starke R. Hathaway. As time went on the department brought in others who gradually began to represent a more behavioural approach to psychological intervention. In 1967, Patterson joined the Oregon Research Institute, focusing his attention on measurement method-ology, personality and cognitive processes. The group has generated new methods of measure-ment as well as developing behavioural approaches to treating conflict in families.

With his colleague John Reid, he founded the Oregon Social Learning Center in 1977. While the original focus of his work there was on problems of parent training for families of antisocial, abused and delinquent children, research interests grew to include long-term prediction of delinquency, treatment of child abuse and analysis of resistance to treatment. In 1992, Patterson published *A Social Learning Approach: to Family Intervention*, vol. 4, *Anti-social Boys*, the fourth in a four-volume series focusing on family therapy, parent training, coercive family processes and antisocial behav-iour. The first of this series, *Families with Aggressive Children* was published in 1975, and offered a detailed description of treatment procedures for families with antisocial children. The second, co-authored with his long-term colleague Reid in 1978, offered an in-depth examination of the Family Interaction Coding System, a method for measuring interaction processes in the home setting. The third,

Coercive Family Processes, published in 1982, investigated how different types of family interaction lead to different constellations of child problems. The fourth volume focuses on the development of an early or late onset model of delinquency. This model is designed to test the assumption that antisocial behaviour can be prevented.

Gerald Patterson is highly regarded for his innovative and inventive research on family intervention processes and aggressive adolescents, as well as for a well-respected parental training programme. His work appears in virtually all reviews of deviant family interaction, childhood aggression, and their treatment.

D. THOMPSON

Paul, Gordon L.

Born: 1935, Marshalltown, Iowa, USA **Nat:** American **Ints:** Clinical, consulting, experimental, evaluation of measurement, personality and social **Educ:** BA University of Iowa, 1960; MA University of Illinois at Urbana-Champaign, 1962; PhD University of Illinois at Urbana-Champaign, 1964 **Appts & awards:** Cullen Distinguished Professor, University of Houston; Phi Beta Kappa, 1960– , Chi Gamma Iota, 1961– ; Creative Talent Award, American Institute for Research, 1964; NIMH, Blue-Ribbon Advisory Committee, 1971, Executive Committee, APA Division 12, 1972–3; Fellow, APA, 1973; Executive Council, APA Division 12, 1974–7; APA Division 12 Distinguished Scientist Award 1977; Research Award, Mental Health Association of Houston and Harris County, 1985; Editorial Board: *Journal of Behavior Therapy and Experimental Psychiatry*, 1969, *Behavior Therapy*, 1969–75, *Schizophrenia Bulletin*, 1971–85 (Advisory Board, 1985), *Journal of Abnormal Psychology*, 1972–6, *Journal of Behavioral Assessment*, 1979–85, *Journal of Behavioral Residential Treatment*, 1983– , *Journal of Psychopathology and Behavioral Assessment*, 1985– ; Consulting Editor: *Journal of Applied Behavior Analysis*, 1966–77, 1981– , *Psychological Bulletin*, 1967, *Journal of Abnormal Psychology*, 1970–2, 1976, *Psychomatic Medicine*, 1971–7, *Psychophysiology*, 1971–7, *Journal of Consulting and Clinical Psychology*, 1972, *Archives of General Psychiatry*, 1973–4, *Behavior Therapy*, 1976, *Professional Psychology*, 1977– , *Behavioral Assessment*, 1979–83, *Hospital and Community Psychiatry*, 1980, *Biobehavioral Reviews*, 1980–4, *Journal of Community Psychology*, 1983– , *American Psychologist*, 1983– , *Schizophrenia Bulletin*, 1985– , *British Journal of Clinical Psychology*, 1985–

Principal publications

1966   *Insight vs. Desensitization in Psychotherapy*. Stanford University Press.

1967   The strategy of outcome research in psychotherapy. *Journal of Consulting Psychology*, 31, 109–18.

1968   Two year follow up of systematic densitization in therapy groups. *Journal of Abnormal Psychology*, 73, 119–30.

1969   Behavior modification research: Design and tactics. In C.M. Franks (ed.), *Behavior Therapy: Appraisal and Status*. McGraw-Hill.

1969   Outcome of systematic desensitization I: Background, procedures and uncontrolled reports of individual treatment. In C.M. Franks (ed.), *Behavior Therapy: Appraisal and Status*. McGraw-Hill.

1969   Outcome of systematic desensitization II: Controlled investigations of individual treatment, technique variations, and current status. In C.M. Franks (ed.), *Behavior Therapy: Appraisal and Status*. McGraw-Hill.

1972   Maintenance psychotopic drugs in the presence of active treatment programs: A 'triple-blind' withdrawal study with long-term mental patients. *Archives of General Psychiatry*, 27, 106–15.

1973   *Anxiety and Clinical Problems: Treatment by Systematic Desensitization and Related Techniques*. General Learning Press (with D.A. Bernstein).

1977   *Psychosocial Treatment of Chronic Mental Patients: Milieu vs. Social Learning Programs*. Harvard University Press (with R.L. Lentz).

1980   Comprehensive psychosocial treatment: Beyond traditional psychotherapy. In J.S. Straus, M. Bowers, T.W. Downey, S. Fleck, S. Jackson and I. Levine (eds), *Psychotherapy of Schizophrenia*. Plenum.

1981   Social competence and the institutionalized mental patient. In J.D. Wine and M.D. Smye (eds), *Social Competence*. Guilford Press.

1985   The impact of public policy and decision making on the dissemination of science-based practices in mental institutions: Playing poker with everything wild. In R.A. Kasschau, L. Rehm and L.P. Ullman (eds), *Psychological Research, Public Policy and Practice: Toward a Productive Partnership*. Praeger.

1986   *Principles and Methods to Support Cost Effective Quality Operations: Assessment in*

Residential Treatment Settings, Part I. Research Press.

1986 Rational operations in residential treatment settings through ongoing assessment of client and staff functioning. In D.R. Peterson and D.B. Fishman (eds), *Assessment for Decision.* Rutgers University Press.

1987 *Observational Assessment Instrumentation for Service and Research. The Time-Sample Behavior Checklist: Assessment in residential treatment settings, Part 2.* Research Press.

1989 Involuntary commitments to public mental institutions: Critical issues in the assessment of relevant functioning and the overrepresentation of blacks. *Psychological Bulletin*, 106, 171–83 (with K.P. Lindsey).

1991 Outcome research. *Hospital and Community Psychiatry*, 42, 1172.

Further reading

Patterson, D.R. and Fishman, D.B. (eds) (1987) *Assessment for Decision. Rutgers Symposia on Applied Psychology*, vol. 1. Rutgers University Press.

Gordon Paul describes the overall goals of his research programme as being identical to the mission statement of the Mental Health Association: to promote mental health, prevent mental illness, and improve the care and treatment of the mentally ill. More specifically, the programme is directed to theoretical and empirical analyses of the nature of: (1) positive aspects of human functioning associated with mental health; (2) negative aspects of human functioning associated with mental illness; and (3) the best contexts, techniques and procedures that can be employed for assessment and intervention or treatment to ameliorate the negative aspects of functioning, and to enhance and maintain the positive aspects, in a practical and cost-effective way.

Paul argues that although the problems and populations toward which scientific efforts are focused have varied over time, his research programme has been ground in a broad interactive-systems view of development, functioning and change. From this perspective the unique complexities and interrelationships of peoples' problems and of interventions in the mental health field can best be understood by attending to intrapersonal factors and physical-social settings and contexts of both clients' life environments and treatment environments as well. His writings reflect an approach to clinical problems and treatment based on the ongoing assessment/hypothesis-testing strategies and concepts of experimental-behavioural science in which the basic units of analysis consist of functional relationships among variables and events rather than diagnostic categorizations of people.

Pavlov, Ivan Petrovich

Born: 1849, Ryazan, Russia *Died:* 1936, Leningrad, Russia *Nat:* Russian *Ints:* Animal behaviour, behaviour analysis, behaviour modification, clinical psychology, educational psychology, general psychology, personality, philosophy, physiological psychology, psychiatry, psychology of learning, psychophysiology, theoretical psychology *Educ:* First Degree, University of St Petersburg, 1875; Doctorate, Imperial Medical and Surgical Academy, St Petersburg, 1879; Postdoctoral, Universities of Breslau (Wroclaw) and Leipzig, 1884–6 *Appts & awards:* Military Medical Academy Gold Medal, 1879; Professor of Pharmacology, 1890–5, Professor of Physiology, 1890–1939, Military Medical Academy, St Petersburg; Nobel prize for work on digestion, 1904; Member, Imperial Academy of Russia, 1907; Foreign Member, Royal Society, 1907; Member, USSR Academy of Sciences, 1917; Decree of Lenin provided new laboratory and support, 1921; Head, Institute of Physiology of Higher Nervous Activity, Koltushi Biological Station, 1929–36

Principal publications

1874 The effect of the laryngeal nerve on blood circulation: The afferent accelerators of tachycardia. *Abstract in Transactions of the St Petersburg Society of Naturalists*, 5, 66–7 (in Russian).

1878 The nerve supply of the pancreas. *Pflueger's Archive fuer die gesamte. Physiologie des Menschen und der Tiere*, 17, 173–89.

1883 Efferent nerves of the heart. *Clinical Archive for Internal Diseases*, 8, 645–719 (in Russian).

1897/1955 Lectures on the work of the principal digestive glands. In *Collected Works*. Foreign Languages Publishing House.

1903–23/1928 *Nervous Activity (Behavior) of Animals*. International Publishers.

1927/1960 *Conditioned Reflexes: An Investigation of the Physiological Activity of the Cerebral Cortex*. Dover.

1934 *Complete Works* (5 vols). USSR Academy of Sciences.

1940–9 The conditioned reflex. In *Great Medical Encyclopaedia*.

1955 *Selected Works*, ed. K.S. Koshtoyants. Foreign Languages Publishing House.

Further reading

Asratyan, E.A. (1953) *I.P. Pavlov: His Life and Work*. Foreign Languages Publishing House. (trans. of 1949 Russian edn, USSR Academy of Sciences Publishing House).

Gray, J.A. (1979) *Pavlov*. Fontana.

Kaplan, M. (ed.) (1966) *Essential Works of Pavlov*. Bantam.

Ivan Petrovich Pavlov was born in Ryazan, approximately 200 km southeast of Moscow, on 14 September 1849. He was the son of a modest village priest, the eldest of eleven children. Although able to read by the age of 7, Pavlov was seriously injured as the result of a fall, and the start of his school career was delayed until he was 11. He then attended the Ryazan church school, and after graduating progressed to the Ryazan Ecclesiastical Seminary, expecting to follow his father and become a priest. However, it was at the seminary where he studied and first became interested in natural science, having read **Darwin** and Sechenovs's *Reflexes of the Brain*.

Pavlov did not complete his studies at the seminary, but entered St Petersburg University in 1870, where he continued to study natural science and decided to make his career as a physiologist. After graduating in 1875 he went to the Military Medical Academy to pursue research, and to study for the MD degree in order to equip himself for a career in physiology. At the Academy he served for two years as the assistant to the professor (Ustimovich) and worked on the cirulatory system for his MD dissertation. After completing his doctorate there he went to Germany (1884–6), where he studied in Leipzig with Carl Ludwig and in the Heidenhain laboratories in Breslau. Heidenhain was studying digestion in the dog, using an exteriorized section of the stomach. However, Pavlov perfected the technique by overcoming the problem of maintaining the external nerve supply. The exteriorized section became known as the Heidenhain–Pavlov pouch.

In 1890 Pavlov was appointed professor in the department of pharmacology in the Military Medical Academy. One year later he was invited to organize the department of physiology in the newly formed Institute of Experimental Medicine, and in 1895 was appointed to the chair. In about 1879 he began his work on the physiology

of digestion, for which received the Nobel prize in 1904. The first report of his research on the area, 'Lektsii o rabotie glavnych pishchevaritel'nykh zhelez' (The work of the digestive glands), was published in 1897, and was translated into English in 1902. Pavlov remained professor of physiology until he resigned in protest against the expulsion of sons of priests from the Academy (he was himself a son of a priest but would not have been expelled).

From 1921 until his death, Pavlov held laboratory meetings known as the 'Wednesday meetings' where he spoke bluntly on many topics, including his views on psychology. It was widely held that he was opposed to psychology and penalized the use of psychological terms amongst his staff. However, it was significant that he was teaching the objectivization of the processes of adaptive animal behaviour. He was opposed to the mixture of the subjective with the objective in his research. The research into the conditioned reflex had begun in a period when the explanation of the adaptive phenomena of the digestive reflex was still based on the acceptance of the 'psychic' factor as the regulator of bodily phenomena.

Pavlov's research into conditioning grew from his prize-winning work on digestion. In much of this work he used dogs with oesophageal and stomach fistulae. He investigated the nervous mechanisms controlling the secretions of the various digestive glands, and how these nervous mechanisms were stimulated by food. He exposed the structures of interest surgically, and worked on them in a healthy animal. It was crucial to his success that he was also a brilliant surgeon, as similar experiments had been attempted in the laboratory in Breslau that he had visited in the mid-1880s, but had failed because the experimenters lacked Pavlov's surgical skill. On the exposed part of the gut he could directly insert food or chemicals, and observe the effects on the activity of the digestive glands. He also developed the method of 'sham feeding', where a slit is made in the animal's throat so that food entering through the mouth falls out through the neck before reaching the stomach. The animal can be fed through a second opening made into the stomach. By sham feeding, Pavlov observed the effect of food in the mouth on the secretion of digestive juices elsewhere in the gut; he found that the taste of food in the mouth causes the release of gastric juices in the stomach. A smaller quantity of juice is released if food is put directly into the stomach. (Sham feeding was used and developed extensively by later scientists.)

Pavlov hypothesized a complex neurophysiological system of cortical excitation and inhibition in support of the outward evidence of the conditioned reflex. He believed that the two 'fundamental' processes of excitation and inhibition of the nervous system formed the basis of all behavioural reaction, whether normal or pathological. The proper harmonious behaviour of the organism depended on the balance achieved by the mutual limitation of the fundamental processes. His study of experimental neuroses was founded on the basis of the relationship and conflict between excitation and inhibition during the forming of the mechanisms of higher nervous activity. He developed a series of three fundamental dimensions in brain activity: (1) the absolute strengths of excitation and inhibition; (2) the balance between the two processes; and (3) their lability in a particular nervous system. He also classified the types of higher nervous activity, relating his neurological dimensions to Hippocrates' four classes of temperament: melancholic (weak in both excitatory and inhibitory processes); choleric (dominant excitatory processes); phlegmatic (a state of equilibrium); and sanguine (balanced, with lively external behaviour).

Work on conditioned reflexes led him into the psychology of learning, where, as a careful experimenter, he laid the foundation of modern learning theory. His theory of conditioning in which novel stimuli come to elicit reflex reactions, although based entirely on experiments with animals, provided a solid base for the understanding of how organisms, including humans, can be ready for events in present and future environments even though they evolved and developed in the environments of the distant and immediate past. The mechanisms of biological systems adapting to changing environments in accordance with the theory of natural selection, and the emphasis on the importance of reflexes by Sechenov, were elaborated further by Pavlov, and only needed the extra variation of operant conditioning, offered later by **Skinner** and other American experimental psychologists, for psychology to have a powerful theory of learning. Pavlov's theorizing was objective, determinist and behaviourist, and such Russian physiology is thought to have inspired John B. **Watson**'s behaviourist revolution.

Technically, Pavlov provided most of the terms and laws of the experimental psychology of learning, e.g. conditioning, conditioned reflex, unconditioned reflex, reinforcement, extinction, spontaneous recovery, discrimination, generalization, differentiation, inhibition, disinhibition and higher-order conditioning. He also provided a model for experimentation ignored in the West until the operant laboratories adopted similar methods in the 1950s. The approach was to experiment at length on the same single subject until the data obtained showed a steady and prolonged effect. Also, Pavlov required no statistical methods to determine whether he had a significant result; repeated measures ensured that each result was replicated many times before he concluded that a finding was secure.

Throughout his working life Pavlov was outspokenly opposed to the Bolsheviks. His international reputation prevented reprisal, and despite his candid remarks the Bolsheviks supported his research, realizing the possible implications in mass retraining. In 1921 he asked Lenin's permission to transfer his research abroad, but was refused – Lenin wanted prestigious scientists. However, the People's Commissars directed that his working conditions be improved. From 1925 until 1936 he worked mainly in three laboratories, the Institute of Physiology of the Soviet Academy of Sciences, the Institute of Experimental Medicine, and the biological laboratory at Koltushy (now Pavlovo) near Leningrad. In the years approaching his death, Pavlov continued to work on conditioned reflexes and extended his work to include behaviour and problem solving in anthropoid apes. When Hitler came to power in Germany, Pavlov eventually made his peace with the Soviet government. In 1935, he was proclaimed the foremost physiologist in the world at the fifteenth International Physiological Congress. Pavlov died of pneumonia on 27 February 1936, at the age of 87. In his honour the Soviet government renamed the First Leningrad Medical Institute 'The Pavlov Institute'. He was buried on 1 March 1936 in the Volkov cemetery.

Pavlov started work on the cardiovascular and digestive systems of rabbits and dogs, yet he provided by his objective and functional analysis of the behaviour of the nervous system the foundation of modern brain research and, as his recognition of the importance of verbal conditioning in understanding language shows, perhaps our future knowledge of how the human brain confers consciousness on its possessor given the social and physical environment.

Pavlov left biology, physiology, medicine, psychiatry and psychology changed forever.

LEO BAKER AND CATE COX

Pearson, Karl

Born: 1857, London, England *Died:* 1936, Coldharbour, Surrey, England *Nat:* British *Ints:* Evaluation and measurement *Educ* BA 1879, LLB 1881, MA 1882, University of Cambridge *Appts & awards:* University College London, Goldsmid Professor of Applied Mathematics and Mechanics, 1884–1911, Emeritus Professor, Professor of Geometry, Gresham College, 1891–4; Director, Biometric Laboratory, 1903–33, The Francis Galton Laboratory for National Eugenics, 1907–33; Galton Professor of Eugenics, 1911–33; Fellow, Royal Society, 1896; Royal Society Darwin Medal, 1898; Royal Anthropological Institute Huxley Medal, 1903; Hon. LLD, University of St Andrews; Hon. DSc, University of London; Hon. Fellow, King's College Cambridge, 1903, Royal Society of Edinburgh, University College, London

Principal publications

1892 *The Grammar of Science*. Walter Scott.
1894–1916 Nineteen papers in the series 'Mathematical Contributions to the Theory of Evolution' (mainly in *Philosophical Transactions of the Royal Society of London* and *Drapers' Company Research Memoirs*).
1901 On lines and planes of closest fit to systems of points in space. *Philosophical Magazine*, 2 (6th series), 559–72.
1914–30 *The Life, Letters and Labours of Francis Galton* (3 vols). Cambridge University Press.

Further reading

Morant, G. (ed.) (1939) *A Bibliography of the Statistical and Other Writings of Karl Pearson*. Cambridge University Press.
Pearson, E.S. (1938) *Karl Pearson*. Cambridge University Press.
Yule, G.U. and Filon, L.N.G. (1936–8) Karl Pearson 1857–1936. *Obituary Notices of Fellows of the Royal Society*, 2, 72–104.

Karl Pearson was the son of a lawyer and studied mathematics at Cambridge University. He spent most of his career applying statistics to biology, and is regarded as one of the fathers of modern statistics. In his early thirties he acquired an interest in heredity, eugenics and biological questions in general and in the application of statistics to those problems. His interests were shaped by Charles **Darwin**'s theory of evolution, which he sought to test by various means. Pearson shared with philosophers such as Hume and Mach a view of causality as concomitant variation ('correlation'). Encouraged by Sir Francis **Galton** and Walter Weldon, he developed the mathematical formulation of the idea of correlation that Galton had conceived. The result was the widely used Pearson Product-Moment Correlation Coefficient. Pearson also developed the non-parametric chi square. Both statistics have been used extensively in psychological research, and have been essential to the development of multivariate statistical techniques and to the development of a tradition of quantitative inquiry within the discipline. Pearson's ideas on correlation and chi square were first published in a series of eighteen papers (between 1893 and 1912) under the title 'Mathematical Contributions to the Theory of Evolution'.

Pearson became involved in an important debate with William Bateson on the nature of evolution and its measurement. Pearson advocated a biometric approach by emphasizing the importance of continuous variation as the basic material of natural selection. Bateson worked within the tradition of the Czech plant geneticist Mendel (whose works had been rediscovered in 1900) and attached greater importance to discontinuous variation and to breeding studies as the best way to understand the mechanism of evolution. After Weldon's death (1906), Pearson spent less time arguing the biometricians' case and devoted his energies to the development of statistics as a distinct science.

With Galton and Weldon he founded the influential journal *Biometrika*, which he edited until his death. Under his editorship the journal gained a reputation for its blatant partisanship, rejecting outright or amending without consultation manuscripts which its editor considered controversial. His views on the philosophy of science presented in his early lectures are to be found in *The Grammar of Science*.

Peirce, Charles, S.

Born: 1839, Cambridge, Massachusetts, USA *Died:* 1914, Milford, Pennsylvania, USA *Nat:* American *Ints:* Experimental psychology, general psychology, philosophical and theoretical psychology *Educ:* AB Harvard University, 1859; MA Harvard University, 1862; BSc (Chemistry) Harvard University, 1863 *Appts & awards:* Physicist and mathematician, United

States Coast Survey, 1859–91; National Academy of Sciences, 1877; Occasional Lecturer, Harvard University, Johns Hopkins and several other universities, 1879–1884

Principal publications

1867   On a new list of categories. *Proceedings of the American Academy of Arts and Sciences*, 7, 287–98.

1868   Questions concerning faculties claimed for man. *Journal of Speculative Philosophy*, 2, 103–14.

1877   Note on the sensation of color. *American Journal of Science*, 13, 247–51.

1883   (ed.) *Studies in Logic, by Members of the Johns Hopkins University.* Little, Brown.

1884   On small differences of sensation. *Memoirs of the National Academy of Sciences*, 3, 73–83 (with J. Jastrow).

1887   Logical machines. *American Journal of Psychology*, 1, 165–70.

1892   The law of mind. *Monist*, 2, 533–59.

Peirce published 84 papers, 55 'notes', 236 book reviews and 66 book notices.

1931–5   *Collected Papers*, vols 1–6, ed. C. Hartshorne and P. Weiss. Harvard University Press.

1958   *Collected Papers*, vols 7–8, ed. A.W. Bucks. Harvard University Press.

Further reading

Cadwallader, T.C. (1974) Charles S. Peirce (1839–1914): The first American experimental psychologist. *Journal of the History of the Behavioral Sciences*, 10, 291–8.

—— (1975) Peirce as an experimental psychologist. *Transactions of the Charles S. Peirce Society*, 11 (3), 167–86.

Fisch, M.H. and Cope, J.I. (1952) Pierce at the Johns Hopkins University. In P.P. Wiener and F.H. Young (eds), *Studies in the Philosophy of Charles Sanders Peirce.* Harvard University Press.

Weiss, P. (1934) Biography of Charles S. Peirce. In *Dictionary of American Biography*, 14, 398–403.

Charles Sanders Peirce worked principally for the US Coast Survey as a mathematician, astronomer and physicist. In 1887 he moved to Milford, Pennsylvania, to write up the results of his Coast Survey research for publication, which was submitted in 1889 to the Superintendent of the Coast and Geodetic Survey. The report was too advanced for its time and was not well received, prompting Peirce to resign from 31 December 1891. He was able to secure some income from professional fees as a consulting engineer, although most of his limited income came from his writings. These included significant contributions to the *Century Dictionary* of 1889–91 and to *Baldwin's Dictionary of Philosophy and Psychology* of 1901–5. His intellect was universally recognized, but he was considered a difficult man to deal with and too abstract to be a good teacher. Despite his numerous academic contacts (**Dewey, Royce**, J.M. **Cattell**) he was unable to secure a university post. He died penniless on his farm, Arisbe.

Charles Peirce is the founding father of pragmatism, although it was William **James** who developed and popularized the philosophy. Peirce argued that the best way to make ideas clear was to consider their practical consequences. The usefulness and practicality of ideas and their implications for policy and practice are the criteria of their merit. Since the practical consequences of a concept can only be experienced through the senses, Peirce's pragmatism can be considered a further development of empiricism (derived from Kant and the British empiricists). Peirce defined James's conception of pragmatism as implying that 'the end of man is action', whereas his own philosophy was intended as a theory of logical analysis. For Peirce, pragmatism was concerned with investigating proper methods of procedure in the natural sciences and equating the meaning of theoretical concepts and terms with their impact on experience. To distinguish his position from that of James, he called his own approach 'pragmaticism'. The more practical aspects of pragmatism were pursued principally by John **Dewey** in his philosophy and theory of education.

Peirce's interest in psychology can be dated to his boyhood writings. The first entry in his notebook of 1853 states: 'Everyone's mind has a certain base which can't be decreased or enlarged. This can be filled, covered with mind or with memory. And everyone can take their choice and cover their Foundation with MIND or MEMORY; or PASSION or GENIUS. But here I mean mind in contradistinction to memory. Ought mind to be used in contradistinction to memory?' While he did not have a formal training in psychology, he was familiar with the ideas and methods of **Wundt**, **Fechner** and others. His experimental investigations included studies of colour vision and the psychophysics of small differences of sensation (with Jastrow, and reported in Jastrow's autobiography as the first psychological experiment at Johns Hopkins University). Peirce is primarily regarded as a philosopher rather than an experimental psychologist, but it was not always so. For example, in November 1875 William James wrote a letter to the President of Johns Hopkins University recommending Peirce for the 'Chair or Chairs of Logic and Mental Science', and he wrote again four years later stating that 'In the psychological line proper the only workers I know of are Peirce and (G.S.) Hall'. Peirce's article on 'Logical machines' in the first issue of the *American Journal of Psychology* anticipated core debates in artificial intelligence and cognitive science some eighty years later.

Penfield, Wilder Graves

Born: 1891, Spokane, WA, USA **Died:** 1976, Montreal, PQ, Canada **Nat:** American/Canadian **Ints:** Neurosurgery; Clinical neurophysiology; Clinical neuropsychology **Educ:** B. Litt Princeton University, 1913; Rhodes Scholarship 1914, 1918–20; BA Oxford University, 1917; MD Johns Hopkins University, 1918; Beit Memorial Research Fellow, 1920; BSc Oxford University, 1920; MA Oxford University 1920; DSc Oxford University 1935; DSc Princeton University, 1939; **Appts & awards:** Associate Professor of Surgery, Columbia University, 1920; Junior Attending Surgeon, Presbyterian Hospital, New York City, 1921–8; Assistant Professor of Surgery, Columbia University, 1924–8; Assistant Neurologist, Vanderbilt Clinic, 1924–8; Assistant Surgeon, New York Neurological Institute, 1925–8; Neurosurgeon, Royal Victoria and Montreal General Hospitals, 1928–60; Associate Professor of Neurosurgery, McGill University, 1928–34; Professor of Neurology and Neurosurgery, McGill University, 1934–54; Director, Montreal Neurological Institute, 1934–60; President, Association for Research in Nervous and Mental Diseases, Royal College of Physicians and Surgeons of Canada, 1939–44; Fellow: Royal Society, 1943, Royal Society of Canada, 1943; Companion of St Michael and St George, 1943; Fellow, Royal Society of Medicine London, 1947; United States Medal of Freedom with Silver Palm, 1948; Legion of Honour, 1950; President, American Neurological Association, 1951; Hon. DCL Oxford University, 1953; British Order of Merit, 1953; Chevalier Legion d'Honneur, 1953; Jacoby Award of the American Neurological Association, 1953; Médaille Lannelongue of the Académie de Chirurgie of France, 1958; Lister Medal, Royal College of Surgeons, 1961; President Vanier Institute of

the Family, 1965–8; Companion of the Order of Canada, 1967; Gold Medal, Royal Society of Medicine, 1967; Triennial Gold Medal of the Royal Society of Medicine, 1968; twenty-five honorary degrees, and fifteen medals, honours and awards

Principal publications

1941   *Epilepsy and Cerebral Localisation.* Springfield. Ill.: C.C. Thomas (with T.C. Erickson).

1950   *The Cerebral Cortex of Man.* New York: Macmillan (with T.B. Rassmussen).

1951   *Epileptic Seizure Patterns.* Springfield, Ill.: C.C. Thomas (with K. Kristiansen).

1954   *Epilepsy and the Functional Anatomy of the Human Brain.* London: Churchill (with H. Jasper).

1958   *The Excitable Cortex in Conscious Man.* Springfield, Ill.: C.C. Thomas.

1959   *Speech and Brain Mechanisms.* Princeton, NJ: Princeton University Press (with L. Roberts).

1975   *The Mystery of the Mind.* Princeton, NJ: Princeton University Press.

Further reading

Penfield, W.G. (1977) *No Man Alone: A Neurosurgeon's Life.* Boston: Little, Brown.

Born in Spokane, Washington, the son of a physician and a Bible teacher, Penfield was educated at Princeton, where he attended Edward Conklin's biology lectures, and Oxford, where he held two Rhodes scholarships and studied under Sir William Osler. He served in military hospitals in France, 1915–17. He took his medical degree at Johns Hopkins University, Baltimore, with an Internship under Harvey Cushing in Boston. When Penfield returned to Oxford to study neurophysiology, Sir Charles **Sherrington** influenced his decision to become a neurosurgeon. Penfield studied neurology and pathology with Godwin Greenfield and Gordon Holmes at the National Hospital for Nervous Diseases at Queen Square, London.

On his return to America in 1921, he specialized in neurosurgery, studying with Ramon y Cahal in Madrid and Oetfried Foerster in Breslau, before moving to Montreal in 1928. Here he established the Montreal Neurological Institute, with help from the Rockefeller Institution (1934), remaining its director until 1960. In addition to numerous scientific publications, he wrote historical novels, biography, autobiography and essays.

Penfield worked as a neurologist and neurosurgeon, specializing in the scientific understanding and clinical treatment of epilepsy. From the 1930s he made increasing use of the technique of exposing the cortex in conscious human patients, with the aim of localizing the epileptic focus prior to surgery while sparing the speech area. To this end, a cortical EEG was taken and the cortical surface explored by electrical stimulation. Penfield (with Erickson) described the work in 1941 and neither his findings nor his interpretation changed greatly thereafter.

Penfield identified two effects of electrical stimulation: interference and activation. Interference referred to the prevention of movements other than reflex acts, or of speech other than uncontrolled vocalization. Activation was not directly demonstrated, but Penfield assumed there must be a system (which he and Jasper termed the 'centrecephalic system' or *ces*), in the region of the third ventricle, that integrated projections from the sensory cortex with 'volitional impulses' to the precentral gyri, leading to willed acts. This system represented, he thought, the highest level of cortical integration. He noted, as had others, that lesions in these areas could produce loss of consciousness. Penfield described consciousness as akin to a continuum of brightness, from alertness and awareness of one's own purposes through to dream state and coma, but appearing to the patient as more completely light or dark because post-ictal confusional states were generally forgotten. He distinguished between the continuum of responsiveness and that of consciousness, which could occur in the presence of paralysis.

Stimulation of the temporal cortex provided some of Penfield's most notable observations of 'psychical discharges', or reports of complex experiences. These were also of two types: experiential hallucinations, first observed by him in a patient in 1933, and interpretative illusions. The former were supposedly veridical flashbacks in which 'reactivation of a strip of the record of the stream of consciousness' had, he thought, taken place, allowing access to all (and only) those events to which the patient attended at the time. Interpretative illusions were misinterpretations of current experience, for example the *déjà vu* experience and perceptual distortions. Penfield inferred that the ganglionic records of experience were not near the surface of the temporal lobes as he had at first supposed, but in the hippocampi and their links with the *ces*. He regarded the reactivated record as identical with the original neuronal

activity, but postulated further a record of temporal succession. Such a record would presumably enable the patient to distinguish and, hence, to recognize a reactivated record as having occurred before the present, and to distinguish it from contemporaneous conscious experience.

Penfield carefully collected and discussed his clinical observations of epileptic patients over a long period. Given the delicacy of the technique and the strain involved for the patients, there have been few who have attempted to replicate or extend the psychological aspects of his findings. He was well aware of the artificiality of the stimulus, as well as of Sherrington's observations of such effects of repeated stimulation as facilitation and reversal, and also of the possibly confounding effect of exploring epileptic cortex. He nevertheless thought that, given appropriate caution and experimental safeguards, including checking subjects' responses for reliability, stimulation was a guide not only to sources of epileptic foci but also to localization. As he admitted, however, more complex and categorically distinct response modes than naming and counting – reading and writing, for example – could have been more fully explored, despite the limitations of the technique. The thoroughness of Penfield's clinical observation is unlikely to be matched, but it is to be regretted that he failed to record in standardized and numerical terms the number and types of observations made on each patient, the consistency of intra-subject responses, or the inter-subject constancy of location of functional areas. With respect to his postulate of a *ces*, while the origin of some temporal lobe epilepsy is thought to be subcortical, it has not been established that this area is the origin of executive function, much evidence strongly implicating the frontal lobes. In addition, his concept of consciousness as a continuum, including dreams, dependent on the *ces*, deserved modification in the light of animal work in the 1950s, since the control of states of sleep and alertness was shown to depend in part on several zones in the brain stem having complex relations with each other as well as with the forebrain. Penfield's view of memory implies a partial and variably accessible but unadulterated record, a view not subjected to experimental verification and at variance with much experimental data (as well as with common observation) on the many factors, including mood, leading to distortions of memory, and also having little room for integration with psychological theories of differing types of memory system.

Penfield's stature and achievements rest securely on his comprehensive and widely recognized contributions to neuroscience, with particular reference to epilepsy. Future advances in the explanation of the psychological phenomena he elicited may depend on the use of modern imaging techniques as well as on the precise distinctions made possible by double dissociation methodology, but his observational data have a unique importance and must be taken into account by any theory attempting to relate brain function to experience and behaviour. His description of the effects of temporal lobe stimulation may have relevance for, for example, theories of the neuropsychology of schizophrenia and of near-death experiences.

E. R. VALENTINE AND MARY J. PICKERSGILL

Peterson, Donald R.

Born: 1923, Pillager, Minnesota, USA **Nat:** American **Ints:** Clinical psychology **Educ:** BA University of Minnesota, 1948; MA University of Minnesota, 1950; PhD University of Minnesota, 1952 **Appts & awards:** Dean, Graduate School of Applied and Professional Psychology, Rutgers University; Member, APA Publication Board, 1975; Chairman, APA Committee on Accreditation; President, National Council of Schools of Professional Psychology; APA Fellow, Division 12; APA Award for Distinguished Contributions to Professional Psychology, 1983; Editor: *Journal of Abnormal Psychology, Rutgers Professional Psychology Review*

Principal publications

1959   Personality structure in 4–5 year olds in terms of objective tests. *Journal of Clinical Psychology*, 4, 355–69 (with R.B. Cattell).

1961   Behavior problems of middle children. *Journal of Consulting Psychology*, 25, 205–9.

1965   Scope and generality of verbally defined personality factors. *Psychological Review*, 72, 48–58.

1965   A role for cognition in the behavioral treatment of child's eliminative disturbance. In L.P. Ullman and L. Krasner (eds), *Case Studies in Behavior Modification*. Holt (with P. London).

1967   Pancultural factors of parental behavior in Sicily and the United states. *Child Development*, 38, 967–91 (with G. Migliorino).

1968   *The Clinical Study of Social Behavior*. Appleton-Century Crofts.

1976   Is psychology a profession? *American Psychologist*, 31, 572–81.

1979   *The Behavior Problem Checklist*. Authors (with H.C. Quay).

1979   *Manual for the Behavior Problem Checklist*. Authors (with H.C. Quay).

1979   Assessing interpersonal relationships by means of interaction records. *Behavioral Assessment*, 1, 221–336.

1982   Functional analysis of interpersonal behavior. In J.C. Anchin and D.J. Kiesler (eds), *Handbook of Interpersonal Psychotherapy*. Pergamon.

1982   Career experiences of doctors of psychology. *Professional Psychology*, 13, 268–77 (with M.M. Eaton, A.R. Levine and F.P. Snepp).

1983   *The Revised Behavior Problem Checklist*. Franklin Press (with H.C. Quay).

1984   The case for the PsyD. In G. Sumprer and S. Walfish (eds), *Clinical, Counselling and Community Psychology*. Irvington.

1991   Connection and disconnection of research and practice in the education of professional psychologists. *American Psychologist*, 46, 422–9.

1992   Interpersonal relationships as a link between person and environment. In W.B. Walsh, K.H. Craik and R.H. Price (eds) *Person-Environment Psychology: Models and Perspectives*. Erlbaum.

Further Reading

Bourg, E.F., Bent, R.J., Callan, J.E., *et al.* (eds) (1987) *Standards and Evaluation in the Education and Training of Professional Psychologists: Knowledge, Attitudes, and Skills*. Transcript Press.

Dana, R.H. and May, W.T. (eds) (1987) *Internship Training in Professional Psychology*. Hemisphere.

Donald R. Peterson was an early advocate of quality professional education and training for students in psychology. His writings of professional approaches to clinical psychology training have earned him widespread recognition. He founded the first Doctor of Psychology training programme in the USA and was the Dean of the first university-based graduate school of professional psychology. In reviewing (1991) the history of education for psychological practice he distinguished three phases: preprofessional phase, a scientist-professional phase, and a professional phase. He points out that each phase is ground in its own assumptions about relations between research and practice. Peterson argues that educators must be alert to the fact that the scope of psychological practice extends beyond individual testing and psychotherapy to the systematic study and planned improvement of groups and organizations.

Disciplined inquiry, linked with the change from the individual to organizational levels, forms the core of contemporary psychological practice. Since conceptually guided, empirically informed and technically skilled assessment is the central function of professional psychologists, then education for practice must emphasize training in the strategies of inquiry on which effective practice depends. The strategies of inquiry appropriate for scientific research are not the same as those required for professional service and this too should be reflected in approaches to professional training.

Pheterson, Gail Isra

Born: 1948, Rochester, New York, USA **Nat:** American **Ints:** Community psychology, personality and social, psychology of women, Society for the Psychological Study of Gay and Lesbian Issues, Society for the Psychological Study of Social Issues **Educ:** PhD University of California, 1974 **Appts & awards:** Professor, Department of Psychology, University of Paris VII; National Defense Education Act Fellowship, 1970–2; NIMH Training Fellowship, 1972–3; Citation Classic Award for 'Evaluation of women' (1971), Institute for Scientific Information, 1983

Principal publications

1971   Evaluation of women as a function of their sex, achievement and personal history. *Journal of Personality and Social Psychology*, 19, 114–18 (with S. Kiesler and P. Goldberg). (Reprinted in J. Brigham and L. Wrightsman (eds), *Contemporary Issues in Social Psychology* (2nd and 3rd edns), Brooks/Cole, 1973, 1976; also in R. Unger and F. Denmark (eds), *Women: Independent or Dependent Variable*, Psychological Dimensions, 1974.)

1981   Love in freedom. *Journal of Humanistic Psychology*, 21, 3.

1982   Bondgenootschap tussen vrouwen: Een theoreties en empiriese analyse van onderukking en bevrijding. *Psychologie en Maatschappij (Psychology and Society)*, 20.

1990   The category 'prostitute' in scientific inquiry. Special issue: II. Feminist perspectives on sexuality. *Journal of Sex Research*, 27, 397–407.

1995   *Trends and Issues in Theoretical Psychology* (ed. with I. Lubek, R. van Hezewijk and C.W. Tolman). Springer-Verlag.

(forthcoming)   *The Whore Stigma: Female Dishonour and Male Unworthiness*. Dutch Ministry of Social Affairs and Employment.

(forthcoming)   Alliance between women: Psychological processes against racism, anti-semitism and heterosexism. *Signs: Journal of Women in Culture and Society*.

Further reading

Adelman, J. and Enguidanos, G.M. (eds) (1995) *Racism in the Lives of Women: Testimony, Theory, and Guides to Antiracist Practice*. Haworth

Gail Pheterson's first independent research was an experimental investigation of women's attitudes towards other women. That study demonstrated that female prejudice against women dissipates when the women being judged are socially legitimized by official acclaim. This theme has continued throught her professional career, and she has made important contributions to understanding the contribution of race, class, sexuality, appearance, history of abuse and ethnicity as determinants of prejudice. For several years, she conducted 'Alliance Groups' of black and white, Jewish and Gentile, lesbian and heterosexual, and disabled and able-bodied women as well as groups of men and women. The purpose was to study the effects of social status upon female personality, upon relationships between women, and upon the women's liberation movement. In 1982, she initiated alliance groups for prostitute, ex-prostitute and non-prostitute women in both the US and the Netherlands. From this research she learned that the stigmatization of women as 'whores' is a central mechanism underlying divisions between women. Furthermore there is increasing evidence that the 'whore' label functions to justify and perpetuate violence against women and girls. More generally, Pheterson argues that social science research, and sex research in particular, is characterized by prejudices against women branded as prostitutes. Thus, the category 'prostitution' is based more on symbolic and legal representations of the bad woman or whore than on a set of characteristics within a population of persons. In adhering to this category, it is claimed, researchers are locked into misguided investigations, and important questions about the relation of sexual-economic exchange to erotic behavior, social life, and physical survival of diverse groups remain unanswered.

Piaget, Jean

Born: 1896, Neuchatel, Switzerland **Died:**

1980, Geneva, Switzerland **Nat:** Swiss **Ints:** Cognitive science (genetic epistemology), developmental, educational, experimental, society of personality and social, theoretical **Appts & awards:** Research Director, Institut Jean-Jacques Rousseau, Geneva, 1921–5; Professor of Psychology, Sociology and the Philosophy of Science, University of Neuchâtel, 1925–9; Professor of the History of Scientific Thought, University of Geneva, 1929–39, Director, International Bureau of Education, Geneva, 1929–67; Director, Institute of Educational Sciences, University of Geneva, 1932–71; Professor of Experimental Psychology and Sociology, University of Lausanne, 1938–51; Professor of Sociology, University of Geneva, 1939–51, Professor of Experimental Psychology, University of Geneva, 1940–71, Professor of Genetic Psychology, Sorbonne, Paris, 1952–63; Director, International Centre for Genetic Epistemology, Geneva, 1955–80; Emeritus Professor, University of Geneva, 1971–80; President: Swiss Commission UNESCO, Swiss Society of Psychology, French Language Association of Scientific Psychology, International Union of Scientific Psychology; Co-Director, Department of Education UNESCO; Member, Executive Council UNESCO and twenty academic societies; Honorary doctorates at Harvard University, 1936, Manchester University, 1959, Cambridge University, 1962, Bristol University, 1970, CNAA, 1975, and twenty-six other universities; Erasmus prize (1972) and ten other prizes; Co-Editor, *Archives de Psychologie* and seven other journals

Principal publications

1918 *Recherche.* La Concorde.
1928 *Judgment and Reasoning in the Child.* Routledge and Kegan Paul. (1st pub. 1924).
1949 *Traité de logique.* Colin.
1950 *Introduction à l'épistémologie génétique* (3 vols). Presses Universitaires de France.
1951 *Play, Dreams and Imitation in Childhood.* Heinemann. (1st pub. 1945).
1952 *Child's Conception of Number.* Routledge and Kegan Paul (with A. Szeminska) (1st pub. 1941).
1953 *Origins of Intelligence in the Child.* Routledge and Kegan Paul. (1st pub. 1936).
1954 *Construction of Reality in the Child.* Routledge and Kegan Paul. (1st pub. 1937).
1958 *Growth of Logical Thinking.* Routledge and Kegan Paul. (with B. Inhelder). (1st pub. 1955).
1967 *Logique et connaissance scientifique.* Gallimard.

1971 *Biology and Knowledge.* Edinburgh University Press. (1st pub. 1967).
1973 *Main Trends in Psychology.* George Allen & Unwin. (1st pub. 1970).
1977 *Recherches sur l'abstraction réfléchissante* (2 vols). Presses Universitaires de France.
1981 *Intelligence and Affectivity.* Annual Reviews. (1st pub. 1954).
1983 Piaget's theory. In P. Mussen (ed.), *Handbook of Child Psychology*, vol. 1. Wiley. (1st pub. 1970).
1985 *Equilibration of Cognitive Structures.* University of Chicago Press. (1st pub. 1975)
1986 Essay on necessity. *Human Development*, 29, 301–13. (1st pub. 1977).
1987 *Possibility and Necessity* (2 vols). University of Minnesota Press. (1st pub. 1981, then 1983).
1989 *Psychogenesis and the History of Science.* Columbia University Press (with R. Garcia). (1st pub. 1983).
1991 *Towards a Logic of Meanings.* Erlbaum (with R. Garcia). (1st pub. 1987).
1992 *Morphisms and Categories.* Erlbaum (with G. Henriques and E. Ascher). (1st pub. 1990).
1995 *Sociological Studies.* Routledge. (1st pub. 1977).
1995 Commentary on Vygotsky's criticisms. *New Ideas in Psychology*, 13, 325–40. (1st pub. 1962).
Piaget published more than 50 books and 500 papers as well as 37 volumes in the series Etudes d'Epistémologie Génétique. All of these publications are listed in *The Jean Piaget Bibliography* (1989), Jean Piaget Archives Foundation, Geneva.

Further reading

Beilin, H. (1992) Piaget's enduring contribution to developmental psychology. *Developmental Psychology*, 28, 191–204.
Chapman, M. (1988) *Constructive Evolution: Origins and Development of Piaget's Thought.* Cambridge University Press.
Gruber, H. and Vonèche, J. (1995). *The essential Piaget. 100th Anniversary edition.* Aronson.
Kitchener, R. (1986) *Piaget's Theory of Knowledge.* Yale University Press.
Smith, L. (1992) *Jean Piaget: Critical Assessments* (4 vols). Routledge.
—— (1993) *Necessary Knowledge: Piagetian Perspectives on Constructivism.* Erlbaum.
—— (1996) *Critical Readings on Piaget.* Routledge.
Vidal, F. (1994) *Piaget before Piaget.* Harvard University Press.
Vonèche, J.J. (1985) Genetic epistemology: Piaget's theory. In *International Encyclopedia of Education*, vol. 4. Pergamon.

(Auto)biographies

Bringuier, J.C. (1980). *Conversation with Jean Piaget*. University of Chicago Press.

Evans, R. (1973) *Jean Piaget, the Man and his Ideas*. Dutton.

Piaget, J. (1952) Autobiography. In E. Boring (ed.), *History of Psychology in Autobiography*, vol. 4. Clark University Press.

—— (1976) Autobiographie. *Revue Européenne des Sciences Sociales*, 14, 38–9, 41–43.

Jean Piaget displayed an exceptional interdisciplinary expertise in the elaboration of a research programme which is already a major contribution to human knowledge. His pre-eminence in psychology is evident in three ways. First, Piaget's work has commanded massive international attention for most of the century: 'the most criticised author in the history of psychology, and … I came through alive', as he put it. Second, his work offers a brilliant demonstration of how to translate philosophical questions, such as 'What is knowledge?', into empirical questions for psychology, namely 'How does knowledge develop?'. Third, his answers constitute a scientific paradigm which continues to set the standard today for the evaluation of alternative accounts of intellectual development.

He was born in 1896 in Neuchatel, gaining in 1917 his *licence* in natural sciences and then in 1918 a doctorate in biology from his local university. He displayed an early interest in the living world. Piaget's first publication was in 1910, and he had published more than thirty papers in biology by 1918, when he made a 'psychological turn'. He studied in Zurich under **Bleuler** and worked with Simon in Paris. **Freud** sat in the audience when Piaget gave his first paper in psychology. In 1921 Piaget was offered the post of Research Director by **Claparède** in Geneva, later gaining his first chair in Neuchatel in 1925. He moved in 1929 to the first of three chairs in Geneva, where he remained until his retirement and an emeritus award in 1971. His concurrent appointments included chairs at Lausanne and the Sorbonne. He was also Director of the International Bureau of Education and of the International Centre for Genetic Epistemology. Piaget was admitted as a member of sixteen learned societies, received twelve international prizes and was awarded thirty-one honorary doctorates. He died in Geneva in 1980, with posthumous publications continuing to appear.

Although Piaget is internationally known for his work in child psychology, he regarded his work as a contribution to genetic epistemology, i.e. the theory of knowledge directed upon the development (genesis) of knowledge. His research programme was outlined in his first book (1918), with elaborations during the next sixty years. A key insight concerns 'universal knowledge' This notion has two distinct meanings, one about the transfer of knowledge and the other about knowledge of a universal. Transfer is a standard problem in psychology, concerning generalization across contexts and domains. Piaget's problem is instead about access, namely how a knowing subject attains a specified level of knowledge of a universal along an endless series in the growth of rational knowledge.

The philosophical question 'Do universals exist?' has two classic answers in realism and nominalism. Realism in mathematics is the view that each number exists independently of its instances in the actual world, processing necessary properties. Five is that unique number which is independent of the five continents or the five English vowels and which is necessarily prime. This view secures the objectivity and intersubjectivity of mathematics by generating an ontological slum. Nominalism is the view that number-words are simply convenient ways of making reference to numbers which do not themselves exist. This view secures the cultural variability of numerals but leads to relativism by putting numbers on a par with fictions such as the planet Vulcan.

Piaget met this problem head-on in his early work in biology as to the reality of species, siding with nominalism. His advance in *Recherche (Search)* was to outline an epistemological 'tertium quid' (third alternative) to realism and nominalism. This answer is constructivism, which sets out to reconcile the objectivity of knowledge and its socio-cultural variability.

An analogy is useful: regard a universal as a mountain to be climbed. There are many routes on a mountain, a grassy track on one slope, a steep rock-face on another. But the contours are the same: the 2000 contour is the same height, whatever the route, ground or company. There are levels or stages (contours) in the development of knowledge which are invariant to domains and socio-cultural contexts. Even if development is ascent to a higher level, this does not mean there is one route up the mountain. Nor does it mean that we are always climbing upwards; paths lead from the track to the rock-face with as many routes up, along or down contours as you will. Child development and mountain walks are endlessly varied. Note that the analogy breaks down because any mountain has a unique summit, whereas the growth of novel knowledge is never complete.

Quite simply, universals are rational constructions of the mind, comprehending variable socio-cultural contexts and domains. Piaget's central argument is that if rational knowledge is a fact, its development must be at least partly rational during child development and the history of science. Piaget's research programme characterizes the sequences and mechanisms by which rational knowledge develops. This leaves open psychologically interesting but non-rational aspects of intellectual development.

It might be wondered whether universals need to be known since children acquire knowledge of their own world *hic et nunc*. Actual objects exemplify properties open to observation and learning; will this not do for psychology? But this is simply to postpone the problem. Can anything at all be observed, such as an object which is both red and green all over? In virtue of what are all equilaterals equiangular? What is it about reality which makes the former false and the latter true? There is more to reality than the actual world. Piaget's epistemology addresses the question of the further requirements such that knowledge is not only compatible with an intellectual norm but is also due to that norm. Rational knowledge requires access through the use of intellectual structures. The task for psychology is 'to find out whether structures do exist and to analyse them'. Piaget has used formal models based on group theory, category theory and entailment logic to characterize intellectual structures. Four standard features of these accounts concern conservation (invariance), novelty, necessity and construction.

Conservation is the consistent use of defining criteria of a concept. In a seminal study (1952) of number conservation, the task is contextualized as laying out a table with six bottles placed in line. A child is shown a tray with a dozen glasses and requested to select enough glasses so that the glasses and bottles are the same. Then the child is invited to lengthen or shorten either line whilst keeping the number of bottles and glasses constant. This task has several striking features. It makes sense to children by matching their experience in laying a table. It requires the child's own activities which reveal underlying numerical abilities. It shows that children who can count correctly may still display non-conserving responses: 'there are six glasses and six bottles but more bottles since this line is longer'. Such findings are awesomely replicable. Piaget's interpretation is that some degree of 'logical space' – comparable to space in working memory – provides the organization which is generative of true judgement based on reasoning. This organization is constructed over time through successive levels. These levels are stages which are characteristic of the *thinking* displayed on the task, not of the thinker as such. And yet this interpretation has been repeatedly challenged.

The challenge is that thinking is not stage-like, since other factors, such as language, memory or social experience, influence numerical development. Now of course they do, as Piaget noticed. First, the challenge runs together distinct positions as to whether logical organization is the sole factor or one essential factor. The challenge is only decisive if Piaget is committed to the former; yet the latter is his position. There is no available research to fault this position. Second, conservation is only one aspect of intellectual development. Necessity and novelty are also implicated. Piaget's argument is that a good organization combines conservation (available knowledge is preserved) and novelty (better knowledge develops) through necessity (knowledge is connected into necessary systems). There is insufficient research on the other factors to show how conservation is combined with novel construction marked by necessity.

Novel knowledge is a welcome fact of life. In Piaget's (1950) account, any knowledge occurs as a term in an endless sequence, linked to its more primitive antecedents and its better successors. Numerical understanding based on conservation requires the prior understanding that each glass is an object with a capacity to exist independently of observation. This is object-permanence (conservation). This realization is no easy matter. Very young infants do not search for unobserved objects at all: young infants search selectively, making the A-not-B (stage IV) error; older infants can make exhaustive searches. Some developmentalists using sensory tracking or duration of observation doubt whether actual objects require construction. But this is to miss the point: independence is independence of observations based on tracking and duration of observation.

Numbers have properties which can themselves be conserved through operations on operations. A paradigm example is proportionality or the numerical equality of equivalent ratios.

Children's experience in using balances with weights and distance as variables provides a context for this type of conservation. Piaget's advance is the characterization of the organisation (structure) which underpins this familiar experience and which is more advanced than that used in number conservation. This is evident in companion studies which show that proportional understanding is facilitated by analogical understanding based on the ability to make selective comparisons (morphisms). This ability is evident in early childhood. Numbers are also generative of novel knowledge, evident as reasoning through recurrence. Children's knowledge, that adding one object to each of two equal collections preserves their numerical equality, is generalized to the conservation of the equality of any two numbers at all under equal addition.

Conservation requires *necessity*, or that which could not be otherwise. Mathematical properties are in all cases necessary properties. It is not necessary for there to be twelve months in a year – things could have been otherwise. But it is necessary that $7 + 5 = 12$, since that could not be otherwise. Modal knowledge about possibility and necessity is required to draw this distinction. Shown an object whose five visible sides are white, one 5-year-old inferred that 'the box is all white and so the back can't be another colour'. There is a clear example of pseudo-necessity but, for all that, it shows that young children have some inkling of necessary knowledge. Necessity appears in number conversation: there is 'always the same – there can't be more in one line than in the other'. It is also evident in combinatorial search. Similarly, all valid deductions are necessities which could not be otherwise, and this is so irrespective of the domain-specificity of the content. Modal knowledge is the basis of valid deduction which is truth-preserving but not truth-producing.

Equilibration is an essential, but never the sole, factor in *construction*. Any living individual is an organization which is itself in action in the causal nexus which includes biological and socio-cultural interactions. The individual acquires knowledge in virtue of the organization embedded in its own actions. This organization undergoes development since there are different levels in the logic of action. Piaget's argument is in two steps.

One step concerns the formation of knowledge. Factors in nature and nurture are necessary but not sufficient. The activities of living beings always include a biological element. But how could an innate, biological mechanism generate true knowledge? How could a contingency generate necessity? Again, socio-cultural transmission is always necessary in the formation of human knowledge. But why is culture so pervasive and yet differential in its effects from the amoeba to Einstein? How does cultural transmission turn into intellectual advance? An interaction between nature and nurture is not the same as organization. So there is a further factor as well. This is equilibration. Equilibration is necessary, but never by itself sufficient, in virtue of its co-ordination of other necessary factors.

The second step concerns the growth of knowledge in that better knowledge develops from available knowledge. Any individual is the centre of a stream of ideas, images, feelings and values arising from within the mind or through socio-cultural transmission. But novel knowledge requires mental transformation: 'each individual is called upon to think and to rethink the system of collection notions'. This immediately creates the problem of intellectual coherence in that one and the same idea should be conserved by each individual who is party to a psycho-social exchange. Conservation is a precondition of rational disagreement rather than dogmatic consensus. Equilibration is the optimizing search for coherence. This search is unsuccessful in virtue of the ineliminable occurrence of blindspots and pseudo-understanding at every developmental level. This search is successful in virtue of reasoning based on the norms of reason, which are accessed at some appropriate level. Good reasons provide the connecting link between conserved ideas and some novel successor in one and the same train of thought. Thus intellectual search is not Cartesian certainty but rather Piagetian coherence in the endless but always incomplete progression towards rationality.

In short, there are several principles in Piaget's constructivism: (1) knowledge always occurs in systems which are marked by some degree (level, stage) of organization; (2) new knowledge is generated from available knowledge in virtue of the construction of a better organization, and thus the unit of analysis is the transition-sequence between different levels; (3) any developmental sequence is endlessly progressive and regressive over time; (4) logical models with their own formal criteria characterize the several levels of development – age is a convenient indicator, and never a criterion, of any developmental level; (5) equilibration is a principal mechanism of development. The growth of new knowledge is as much a human marvel as it is a mystery.

LESLIE SMITH

Piotrowski, Zygmunt Antoni

Born: 1904, Poznań, Poland **Nat:** Polish **Ints:** Personality structure, perceptanalysis, psychopathology, schizophrenia vs. psychoneurosis, sleep and dreams **Educ:** PhD University of Poznań, Poland, 1927 **Appts & awards:** Visiting Professor, Hahnemann Medical College and Graduate School, Philadelphia, 1957–70; Hon. DSc, Hahnemann Medical College, Philadelphia, 1980

Principal publications

1937   A comparison of congenitally defective children with schizophrenic children with regard to personality structure and intelligence type. *Proceedings of the American Association on Mental Deficiency*, 42, 78–90.

1937   The Rorschach inkblot method in organic disturbances of the central nervous system. *Journal of Nervous and Mental Disease*, 86, 525–37.

1938   The prognostic possibilities of the Rorschach method in insulin treatment. *Psychiatric Quarterly*, 12, 679–89.

1939   Rorschach manifestations of improvement in insulin treated schizophrenics. *Psychosomatic Medicine*, 1, 508–26.

1950   A new evaluation of the Thematic Apperception Test. *Psychoanalytic Review*, 37, 101–27.

1954   Clinical diagnosis of manic depressive psychosis. In P. Hoch and J. Zubin (eds), *Depression*. Grune & Stratton (with N.D.C. Lewis).

1957   *Perceptanalysis: A Fundamentally Reworked, Expanded and Systematized Rorschach Method*. Macmillan.

1962   *The Hand Test*. Thomas (with B. Bricklin and E.E. Wagner).

1963   *The Perceptanalytic Executive Scale: A Tool for the Selection of Top Managers*. Grune & Stratton (with M. Rock).

1969   Delia: A relatively well-functioning young woman and her bizarre Rorschach record. In J.E. Exnez (ed.), *The Rorschach Systems*. Grune & Stratton.

1970   Test differentiation between effected and attempted suicides. In K. Wolff (ed.), *Patterns of Self-Destruction*. Thomas.

1977   The Movement Responses [Rorschach]. In Maria Rickens (ed.), *Rorschach's Psychology*. R.E. Kruger.

1980   CPR: The psychological X-ray in mental disorders (computerized Rorschach). In J.B. Sidowski, J.H. Johnson and T.A. Williams (eds), *Technology in Mental Health Care Delivery Systems*. Ablex.

1986   *Dreams PDS: A Key to Self-Awareness*. Erlbaum.

Further Reading

DeCato, C.M. (1993) On the Rorschach M response and monotheism. *Journal of Personality Assessment*, 60, 362–78.

Teahan, J.E. (1982). The disease model is alive and well in Zygmunt Piotrowski. *American Psychologist*, 37, 1409–10.

Having discovered in more than fifty very different individual cases that the **Rorschach** was a valuable available instrument of personality investigation, Piotrowski used the Rorschach experimental method consistently as part of a standard psychological examination. He considered that no other technique samples so many enduring, diverse and relevant mental forces determining an individual's internal psychodynamics and overt psycho-social behaviour as does the Rorschach when properly handled. He felt that changes should be made in the Rorschach: the definitions of the meanings of the concepts employed had to be tightened, and the specification of concepts' empirical referents or correlates required even greater attention. He undertook both tasks, taking care that the descriptions of the empirical referents did not overlap; that is, each concept had to mean something specific, and consequently their empirical referents had to differ from one another. He considered the ambiguous inkblots as objects on which to concentrate attention. The subjects – having no ready answers to the unfamiliar forms, which could be interpreted in several different ways with equal plausibility – had to rely on their habitual reaction modes, enhancing validity. Standardized verbal language is neither understood nor spoken during the first, most impressionable period of life, but visumotor cues help the child to orient itself in the world during the initial period. He argued that the importance of spontaneously responding with images is so great that visumotor elements in subjects' responses that are not related to existing graphic details in the inkblots are less reliable, and dynamically of lesser importance, than are such elements that are meaningful interpretations of visually perceptible graphic details of inkblots.

Pisoni, David B.

Born: 1945, New York, USA *Nat:* American *Ints:* Artificial intelligence, cognition, developmental processes in speech, hearing impairment, human factors, memory, psycholinguistics, speech perception, speech synthesis *Educ:* BA City University of New York, 1968; PhD University of Michigan, 1971 *Appts & awards:* Indiana University: Professor of Psychology and Cognitive Science, 1971– , Director, Speech Research Laboratory, 1973– , Adjunct Professor of Linguistics, 1990– , Adjunct Professor of Otolaryngology–Head and Neck Surgery, School of Medicine, 1993– ; Member, Study Section, NIMH Personality and Cognition Research Review Committee, 1974–8; Research Associate, Speech Communications Group, MIT, 1975–6, 1978–9, 1985–6; Editorial Board, *Cognitive Psychology*, 1974–6, *Speech Perception*, 1981– , *Computer Speech and Language*, 1986– ; Consulting Editor, *Perception and Psychophysics*, 1975–8; Associate Editor, *Perception and Psychophysics*, 1978–5

Principal publications

1975 *Cognitive Theory*, vol. 1. Erlbaum (co-edited with F. Restle, R. Castellan and N. Lindman).

1977 *Cognitive Theory*, vol. 2. Erlbaum. (co-edited with N. Castellan and G. Potts).

1977 Evidence for a special speech perception subsystem in the human. In T. Bullock (ed.) *Recognition of Complex Acoustic Signals*. Dahlem Konferenzen (with A. Lieberman).

1978 Speech perception. In W.K. Estes (ed.) *Handbook of Learning and Cognitive Processes*, vol. 6. Erlbaum.

1980 Some developmental processes in speech perception. In G. Yeni-Komshian, J. Kavanagh and C. Ferguson (eds), *Child Phonology: Perception and Production*. Academic Press (with R. Aslin).

1981 Some current theoretical issues in speech perception. *Cognition* 10, 249–59.

1982 Perception of speech: The human listener as a cognitive interface. *Speech Technology*, 1(2), 10–23.

1985 Some constraints on the perception of synthetic speech generated by rule. *Behaviour Research Methods, Instruments and Computers*, 17, 1581–4 (with H. Nusbaum).

1986 Effects of alcohol on the acoustic phonetic properties of speech. In *Alcohol, Accidents and Injuries*. Society of Automotive Engineers (with M. Yuchtman and S. Hathaway).

1988 Testing the performance of isolated utterance speech recognition devices. *Computer Speech and Language*, 2, 87–108 (with H. Nusbaum).

1989 Speech perception: Analysis of biologically significant signals. In R.J. Dooling and S.H. Hulse (ed.), *The Comparative Psychology of Complex Acoustical Perception*. Erlbaum (with J. Mullennix).

1992 Some comments on talker normality in speech perception. Some effects of training Japanese listeners to identify English (r) and (l). Both in Y. Tohkura, E. Vatikiotis-Bateson and Y. Sagisaka (eds), *Speech Perception: Production and Linguistic Structure*. Ohmsha.

1992 Comprehension of synthetic speech produced by rule: A review and theoretical interpretation. *Language and Speech*, 35(4), 351–89 (with S. Duffy).

1993 Effects of age on serial recall of natural and synthetic speech. *Journal of Speech and Hearing Research*, 36(3), 634–9 (with L. Humes, K. Nelson and S. Lively).

1993 Training Japanese listeners to identify English (r) and (l): II The role of phonetic environment and talker variability in learning new perceptual categories. *Journal of the Acoustical Society of America*, 94(3), 1242–55 (with S. Lively and J. Logan).

1994 Speech perception as a talker-contingent process. *Psychological Science*, 5(1), 42–6 (with L. Nygaard and M. Sommers).

1994 Training Japanese listeners to identify English (r) and (l): III Long term retention of new phonetic categories. *Journal of the Acoustical Society of America*, 96 (4), 2076–87 (with S. Lively, R. Yamanda, Y. Tohkura and T. Yamanda).

1995 Comprehension of synthetic speech produced by rule. In R. Bennet, A. Syrdal, and S. Greenspan (eds), *Behavioural Aspects of Speech Technology: Theory and Applications*. Elsevier (with J. Ralston and J. Mullennix).

Further reading

Gernsbacher, M.A. (ed.) (1994) *Handbook of Psycholinguistics*. Academic Press.

Miller, J.L. and Eimas, P.D. (eds) (1995) *Speech, Language, and Communication. Handbook of Perception and Cognition* (2nd edn), vol. 11. Academic Press.

Winitz, H. (ed.) (1987) *Human Communication and its Disorders*, vol. 1. Ablex.

Professor Pisoni's interest in speech perception has spanned his entire career. Before completing his first degree he began working as a research assistant on the Verbal Behaviour Project at the New York State Department of Mental Hygiene.

While working on his PhD he was employed as a Visiting Research Fellow at Haskins Laboratories and as a Teaching Fellow at the University of Michigan. After completing his PhD he was appointed Professor of Psychology and Cognitive Science at Indiana University , a position he has remained in to this day. He holds a number of other research and teaching positions throughout the US. His research interests are wide ranging and he is a member of eight professional bodies, including the AAAS, the Human Factors Society and the Linguistic Society of America. He has conducted research on many aspects of speech and linguistics: developmental processes, word recognition and lexical access, speech analysis and recognition, spoken language understanding, human memory, speech production and synthesis, voice technology, artificial intelligence, hearing impairment and cochlear implants. He has collaborated with a wide variety of researchers in various fields in the course of this research, and has forged important links between psychology and other areas of science. To date he has been the recipient of twenty-five research grants, and work is currently in progress on eight of these projects. Professor Pisoni serves as a consultant to many corporate bodies including Texas Instruments, Bell Laboratories, Digital Equipment Corp. and General Motors Research Labs.

MORIA MAGUIRE

Polanyi, Michael

Born: 1891, Budapest, Hungary **Died:** 1976, Oxford, England **Nat:** Hungarian **Ints:** Philosophical and theoretical psychology, religious issues, Society for the Psychological Study of Social Issues **Appts & Awards:** Privatdozent, Berlin University, 1923; University of Manchester: Professor of Physical Chemistry, 1933–48, Professor of Social Studies, 1948–58; FRS, 1944; Gifford Lecturer, Aberdeen, 1951–2; Senior Research Fellow, Merton College, Oxford, 1958–61; Numerous honorary doctorates and special lectureships

Principal publications

1951   *The Logic of Liberty*. Routledge
1958   *Personal Knowledge*. Routledge.
1964   *Science, Faith and Society* (2nd edn). Chicago University Press.
1966   *The Tacit Dimension*. Routledge.
1968   Logic and Psychology. *American Psychologist*, 23, 27–43.

1969   *Knowing and Being*. Routledge.
1975   *Meaning*. Chicago University Press (with H. Prosch).
Publications in physical science are not listed.

Further reading

Ignotus, P. (1961) *The Logic of Personal Knowledge: Essays Presented to Michael Polanyi on his 70th Birthday*. Routledge.
Wigner, E.P. and Hodgkin, R.A. (1977) Michael Polanyi 1891–1976. *Biographical Memoirs of Fellows of the Royal Society*, vol. 23.

Michael Polanyi was born in Budapest in 1891 and studied medicine at Budapest University. He served as a medical officer in the Austro-Hungarian Army in World War I, but his interests had already moved away from medicine to physical science – his first publication (1910) was on the chemistry of the hydrocephalic fluid. After the war he studied and carried out research in Berlin, but antipathy to Nazism led him to accept the Chair of Physical Chemistry at Manchester in 1933, and he stayed in Great Britain for the rest of his life. Almost all his publications after 1933 are in English. In the 1930s and 1940s he was already publishing widely on philosophical, economic and political issues, and in 1948 he moved to a Chair in Social Studies. In 1958 he retired to a Fellowship at Merton College, Oxford, and he died there in 1976; unfortunately in his last years he had lost his memory almost completely.

His work in physical chemistry was widely recognized and he published several hundred papers. In 1914–16 he developed a theory of the adsorption of gases onto the surface of solids which was the subject of much controversy. In 1932, the Nobel Prize for Chemistry was awarded to the originator of the main competing theory, but within five years it was clear that Polanyi had been correct. His reputation suffered a temporary eclipse, which he discussed in a paper published in *Science* in 1964 (reprinted in *Knowing and Being*). This event was of great significance for Polanyi, and a recurring theme of his later work is opposition to any kind of political control of science or, for that matter, the arts. These views were reinforced by a visit to the Soviet Union in the 1930s, where he was lectured by Bukharin on the virtues of 'socialist' mathematics.

The central, recurring theme of Polanyi's thought is the conflict between, on the one hand, the fact that all knowledge is personal knowledge and, on the other, the fact that the only basis on which to decide what science (or what artistic activity) is 'good' and worthy of public support is consensus among interested, qualified persons. This can lead to the suppression of work that later turns out to have been of value and the encouragement of work that later appears valueless, but there is no escape from the predicament. Political control is worst of all, because the consensus imposed is likely to be that of less qualified persons, but the consensus of qualified persons (e.g. in academies of science, arts, etc.) may also be wrong in retrospect and be the cause of great harm to individual dissenters.

To hold that a theory in science is true or that a work of art is of real aesthetic value is always, in Polanyi's view, to make an assertion to which the asserter commits himself or herself. 'Commitment' is a central concept, because it is never possible to show beyond question that a view to which one is committed is correct – however strong may be the commitment. Deductive demonstration depends on shared premises, and premises may not be shared; empirical demonstration depends on agreed samples of observations, and samples may not be agreed. Always there will be those who insist that they have arrived at premises or observation-samples that ought to be accepted by every right-thinking person, and that consequently the conclusions they have drawn and to which they are personally committed are true and binding on all such persons and may legitimately be imposed on the rest. Polanyi's recognition that this is never the case carries the implication that we must all be resigned to perpetual struggle. It does not become true that wrapping public buildings in sheets of coloured plastic produces a result that has aesthetic significance simply because the man who does the wrapping is committed to the view that it does. Nor is the view necessarily false simply because no one had ever thought so before.

Polanyi lays great emphasis on what he calls 'the structure of tacit knowing'. The beginning student of biology who looks down a microscope for the first time, at a blood sample, sees very little. It takes practice to 'see' the different cells in the sample, but it is difficult to say exactly what has been learned that enables the student to detect different kinds of cell in what was previously an undifferentiated, multi-coloured mass. In Polanyi's view, what has occurred is 'tacit learning' that permits explicit recognition of the cell structures, and moreover,

this is no more than a paradigm case of all learning. 'All thought contains components of which we are subsidiarily aware in the focal context of our thinking.' Thinking is not only intentional, as Brentano and the phenomenologists believe, it is 'fraught with the roots that it embodies'.

It is not difficult to see that Polanyi's view implies a major role for psychology in determining the detail of the structures he posits. He made considerable use of the psychological data available in his time. In his view, however, all beliefs, whether in science, the arts or religion, rely on commitment. Science is at an advantage because there is a reality to which we must submit, which will ultimately eliminate false scientific beliefs. But belief in God and belief in atoms both require commitment. Polanyi's is the only modern scientific metaphysic that allows a place for religious beliefs. Polanyi insisted that it must do so, even though he did not include himself among those 'who can through religion sublimate our dissatisfaction with our own moral shortcomings or those of our societies'. As a consequence, Polanyi has been taken up enthusiastically by religious thinkers and dropped, as some kind of mystic, by the rest. He is a good man fallen among theologians; his importance as a scientific thinker deserves greater emphasis than it receives at present. He has a great deal to offer psychology in particular, amongst the other sciences.

N.E. WETHERICK

Porter, Noah

Born: 1811, Farmington, CT, USA ***Died:*** 1894 ***Nat:*** American ***Ints:*** History of psychology, philosophical psychology ***Appts & awards:*** Clark Professor of Moral Philosophy and Metaphysics, Yale, 1846–71; President, Yale, 1871–86; Hon. DD, University of Edinburgh, 1886

Principal publications

1868   *The Human Intellect*. Scribner's.

1870   *Books and Reading: Or What Books Shall I Read and How Shall I Read Them?*. Scribner's.

1871   *The Sciences of Nature versus the Science of Man*. Dodd & Mead.

1871   *The Elements of Intellectual Science*. Scribner's (an abridgement of *Human Intellect*).

1882   *Science and Sentiment: Papers Chiefly Philosophical*. Scribner's.

1885   *Elements of Moral Science*. Scribner's.

Further reading

Fay, J.W. (1939) *American Psychology before William James*, Rutgers University Press.

O'Donnell, J.M. (1985) *The Origins of Behaviorism: American Psychology 1870–1920*. New York University Press

Richards, G. (1995) 'To know our fellow men to do them good': American Psychology's enduring moral project. *History of the Human Sciences*, 8(3), 1–24.

Starr, H.E. (1935) Noah Porter. In *American Dictionary of Biography*, vol. 15.

At first glance Porter was an archetypal US mental and moral philosopher of the kind to which the 'New Psychologists' of the 1880s and 1890s (and most disciplinary historians prior to the 1980s) expressed so much antipathy. Closer examination of such works as *Human Intellect* and *The Science of Man versus the Science of Nature*, however, reveals that he was fully cognizant of the contemporary European work of figures such as **Wundt**, **Fechner** and **Bain**. Far from rejecting the German introspective experimental school, Porter, and other mental and moral philosophers of the period, actually saw it as an ally, since they read its message as a defence of the autonomy of psychology against the reductionist and physiological orientation of the evolution-influenced British school. *Human Intellect* is a complex and, in places, sophisticated work in which such issues as the nature of psychological language, the requirements of scientific introspection and the goals of the discipline are all treated. Porter's opposition to evolutionary and physiological trends was no mere blinkered dogmatism but argued in considerable depth. He argues quite subtly (especially in *The Sciences of Nature versus the Science of Man*) that, given the foundational position of the human intellect in the generation of scientific knowledge, its own operations cannot themselves be understood within the terms of concepts drawn from specific fields of scientific endeavour. His image of the 'Intellect' is of an ascending hierarchy of 'powers' from sensation up to reason, but to this fairly orthodox sequence he added a differentiation between 'natural consciousness', shared by all, and 'reflective' or 'philosophical' consciousness, the prerogative of but a few and attainable only by special dedication and discipline. A crude 'energy-distribution' model is invoked to explain this. Belief in God and the validity of seeking final causes are, he argues, conclusions which the rational, reflectively conscious person must eventually draw despite the pitfalls and temptations of scepticism. His system thus remained subordinated to a broader moral and religious agenda.

As President of Yale, Porter earned a reputation for adamant conservatism, resisting all measures for university reform. He also earned a regular place in the footnotes of works on the history of evolutionary theory for banning William G. Sumner from using Herbert Spencer's *Sociology* as a textbook. His best-known cultural role was as editor of successive editions of *Webster's Dictionary*. As far as psychology is concerned, however, the validity of the stereotyped image is further undermined by the fact that, following the establishment of friendly informal relations, he invited G.T. **Ladd** to Yale to take over his courses in 1881. Ladd's own theoretical position, moreover, bore many affinities to Porter's.

Human Intellect and its abridgement for long remained the most important mental and moral philosophy course textbooks in US colleges and universities. Along with that of James **McCosh**, Porter's case should, if nothing else, alert us to the risk of a too facile condemnation of the pre-'New Psychology' US tradition, and a too easy acceptance of the notion that the 1880s saw a radical break with this. Furthermore, Porter showed himself conscious of certain theoretical problems related to the reflexive nature of the discipline and the nature of psychological language which are only now resurfacing, even if his religious convictions prevented him from exploring and resolving these in a manner which would be acceptable today.

GRAHAM RICHARDS

Porteus, Stanley David

Born: 1883, Box Hill, Victoria, Australia *Died:* 1972, Hawaii, USA *Nat:* Australian *Ints:* Clinical psychology, psychological testing, race psychology *Appts & awards:* Superintendent of Special Schools, State Education Department, 1913–18; Co-Director, University of Melbourne Laboratory of Educational Anthropology, 1916–17; Lecturer in Experimental Education and Director of Research, Psychological Laboratory, Vineland Training School, New Jersey, 1919–25; Professor of Clinical Psychology and Director of the Psychological and Psychopathic Clinic, University of Hawai, 1922–48; APA Division of Clinical Psychology Distinguished Contributor Award, 1962

Principal publications

1919   Porteus tests: The Vineland revision. *Training School Research Publications*, no. 6.

1922   Studies in mental deviations. *Training School Research Publications*, no. 24.

1925   Guide to the Porteus Maze Test. *Training School Research Bulletin*, no. 25.

1924   *The Maze Test and Mental Differences.* Smith (repr. 1933).

1926   *Temperament and Race.* Badger (with M.E. Babcock).

1928   *The Matrix of the Mind.* University Press Association (with F. Wood Jones).

1930   Race and social differences in performance tests. *Genet. Psy. Monog.* VIII (2) (with D. Dewey).

1931   *The Psychology of a Primitive People: A Study of the Australian Aborigine.* Longmans Green.

1937   *Primitive Intelligence and Environment.* Macmillan.

1941   *The Practice of Clinical Psychology.* American Book Co.

1944   *Mental Changes after Bilateral Prefrontal Lobotomy* Journal Press (with R.D. Kepner).

1948   *The Maze Test: Validation and Psychosurgery* Journal Press (with H. Peters).

1950   *The Porteus Maze Test and Intelligence.* Pacific Books.

1955   *The Maze Test: Recent Advances.* Pacific Books.

1959   *The Maze Test and Clinical Psychology.* Pacific Books.

1965   *Porteus Maze Tests: 50 Years of Application.* Pacific Books.

1969   *A Psychologist of Sorts.* Pacific Books.

Further reading

Turtle, A.M. (1991) Peron, Porteus, and the Pacific Islands regiment: The beginnings of cross-cultural psychology in Australia. *Journal of the History of the Behavioral Sciences*, 27, 7–20.

Australia's first professional psychologist, Porteus is remembered primarily for the widely used Porteus Maze Test (the first version predating his emigration to the US as H.H. Goddard's successor at Vineland Training School in 1919). Before World War II much of his research energy was devoted to the study of 'race differences' (often deploying the Maze Test, which he considered remarkably culture-fair). Early work with Aboriginal children and the 'feeble minded' in Australia, and subsequent years at Vineland, led him to accept a broadly eugenic viewpoint. However, departing from Goddard, he denied the ability of intelligence tests to predict successful social adjustment, preferring a broader measure of 'social efficiency', for which he developed a battery of tests, including the Maze Test. In addition to intelligence these purportedly measured such traits as self-control, tact, prudence and planning, which, Porteus claimed, served the purpose far better.

Moving to Hawai in 1922, while remaining associated with Vineland until 1925, his attention turned to race differences, Hawaii ostensibly providing an ideal opportunity for controlling for environmental factors. Since, excepting the indigenous Hawaiians, the major 'racial groups' (Japanese, Chinese, Filipino, Porto Rican and Portuguese) had all started as plantation labourers, any current differences must, he asserted, arise from their innate abilities. He first explored this in *Temperament and Race*, in which he applied his 'social efficiency' notion, using ratings of the various 'races' provided by a variety of white respondents familiar with them. This work, for all its pose of open-mindedness, was essentially a 'scientific racist' treatise. The resultant top ranking of the Japanese led to what must, by any standards, be considered an extremely paranoid discussion of the insidious threat Japanese immigrants posed to North America and Australia, which are European 'by right of peaceful conquest'. His 1930 monograph, which included investigations of 'racially mixed' children, showed a slight moderation in his position, but his conclusions remained much as before. Carnegie Foundation funding subsequently enabled him to study the abilities of the Aborigines in Australia, his methodology later attracting the derision of anthropologists such as C.G. Seligman.

Primitive Intelligence and Environment, his last major work on this topic, followed a final field expedition to study the so-called 'Bushmen' of the Kalahari. By then, however, his approach was being overshadowed by that of the rising environmentalist 'culture and personality' school, and appeared naive by comparison. Nevertheless he continued to publish papers on the Aborigines throughout the post-war years (often in the right-wing *Mankind Quarterly*), and was a keen, if paternalistic, advocate of their interests, denying their traditional status as the 'lowest' of the 'races' (although not challenging this ranking practice itself). During the 1940s he became more involved in clinical psychology and diagnostic uses of the Maze Test, the value of which he continued to promote in a succession of post-war publications. In his 1969 autobiography, Porteus somewhat disingenuously described his early interests as being in 'the effect of environment on mental and cultural evolution' (a phrase lifted, unreferenced, by L. Zusne in his 1984 *Biographical Dictionary of Psychology* entry).

Porteus was an important and original pioneer in mental testing. His prolific race differences research has been largely forgotten, primarily because he disputed the value of intelligence tests in this context and did not study African-Americans.

GRAHAM RICHARDS

Posner, Michael I.

Born: 1936, Cincinnati, Ohio, USA **Nat:** American **Ints:** Experimental psychology **Educ:** BS University of Washington, Seattle, 1957; MS University of Washington, Seattle, 1959; PhD University of Michigan, Ann Arbor, 1962 **Appts & awards:** Fellow, APA Division 3, AAAS, 1976; Paul M. Fitts Award, Human Factors Society; Guggenheim Fellow, 1979–80; APA Distinguished Scientific Contribution Award, 1980; Member, National Academy of Science, 1981; Professor, Washington University School of Medicine, 1985; Editor, *Journal of Experimental Psychology: Human Perception and Performance*, 1974–9

Principal publications

1964 Information reduction in the analysis of sequential tasks. *Psychological Review*, 71, 491–504.

1965 Memory and thought in human intellectual performance. *British Journal of Psychology*, 56, 197–215.

1967 Chronometric analysis of classification. *Psychological Review*, 74, 392–409 (with R.F. Mitchell).

1967 *Human Performance*. Brooks/Cole (with P.M. Fitts).

1969 Reduced attention and the performance of 'automated movements'. *Journal of Motor Behavior*, 1, 245–58.

1975 Psychobiology of attention. In M. Gazzaniga and C. Blakemore (eds), *Handbook of Psychobiology*. Academic Press.

1976 Visual dominance: An information processing account of its origins and significance. *Psychological Review*, 83, 157–71 (with M.J. Nissen and R. Klein).

1978 *Chronometric Explorations of Mind*. Erlbaum.

1980 Orienting of attention. The 7th Sir F.C. Bartlett Lecture. *Quarterly Journal of Experimental Psychology*, 32, 3–25.

1981 Cognition and personality. In N. Cantor and J. Kihlstrom (eds), *Personality, Cognition and Social Interaction*. Erlbaum.

1982 Information processing models: In search of elementary operations. *Annual Review of Psychology*, 33, 477–514 (with P. McLeod).

1984 Effects of parietal lobe injury on covert orienting of visual attention. *Journal of Neuroscience*, 4, 1863–74 (with J.A. Walker, F.J. Friedrich and R. Rafal).

1985 *Attention and Performance*, vol. 11, *Mechanics of Attention*. Erlbaum (ed. with O.S.M. Marin).

Further reading

Posner, M.I. (ed.) (1989) *Foundations of Cognitive Science*. Bradford.

Michael Posner was born in Cincinnati, Ohio, but his family moved to California two months after he was born. This was the time of the Great Depression. The family moved on and finally settled in Seattle, where he went to high school and enrolled at the University of Washington. Posner was attracted to teaching as a career, and at Washington he majored in physics and minored in philosophy. His first course in psychology was taken by correspondence while he was undergoing a six-month training period at Fort McClellan, Alabama. After leaving McClellan he obtained a position in human engineering at Boeing, which paid for his masters research at the University of Washington. The thesis tested ideas related to F.C. **Bartlett**'s book *Thinking*. Posner then moved to the University of Michigan, Ann Arbor, and commenced work with Paul **Fitts**. His PhD thesis examined the use of information theory to study thinking. This included investigations of speeded judgements of identity to determine the codes on which pattern recognition is based. His doctoral work was interrupted for almost a year due to the Berlin Crisis (1961). Posner went from the army to a new position at the University of Wisconsin. He stayed at Wisconsin for three years and then moved to the University of Oregon because of his interest in Fred Attneave's work.

Posner's contributions lie chiefly in his analysis of internal mental operations that underlie ordinary skills. In studies in which subjects matched letters and letter strings, he was able to trace the separate time course of the visual representation of a letter and its phonetic recording. He developed techniques which allowed him to manipulate the time course of the visual and phonetic codes experimentally. This work was useful in understanding routine tasks such as reading and listening. Later work benefited from a period at the Applied Psychology Unit, Cambridge, where he conducted studies of event-related cortical potentials. This led to an analysis of the potential links between information-processing analysis and neuropsychology. These are presented in his *Chronometric Explorations of Mind* (1978).

Poulton, Eustace Christopher

Born: 1918, Woldingham, Surrey, England **Nat:** British **Ints:** Engineering, evaluation and measurement, experimental, industrial and organizational **Educ:** BA University of Cambridge, 1940; MB, BChir University of Cambridge, 1942; MA University of Cambridge, 1943; Hon. ScD University of Cambridge, 1976 **Appts & awards:** MRCS, 1942; LRCP, 1942; Retired Assistant Director, Medical Research Council, Applied Psychology Unit; Research Fellow, Harvard University, Psychological Laboratory, 1953–4; BPS Myers Laboratory, 1976; Silver Jubilee Medal, 1977; Editorial Board, *Journal of Motor Behavior*, 1969–

Principal publications

1953   Two-channel listening. *Journal of Experimental Psychology*, 46, 91–6.

1957   Previous knowledge and memory. *British Journal of Psychology*, 48, 259–70.

1966   Engineering psychology. *Annual Review of Psychology*, 17, 177–200.

1966   Unwanted asymmetrial transfer effects with balanced experimental designs. *Psychological Bulletin*, 66, 1–18 (with P.R. Freeman).

1967   Tracking a variable rate of movement. *Journal of Experimental Psychology*, 73, 135–44.

1968   The new psychophysics: Six models for magnitude estimation. *Psychological Bulletin*, 69, 1–19.

1970   *Environment and Human Efficiency*. Thomas.

1974   *Tracking Skill and Manual Control*. Academic Press.

1975   Range effects in experiments on people. *American Journal of Psychology*, 88, 3–32.

1976   Arousing environmental stresses can improve performance, whatever people say. *Aviation Space and Environmental Medicine*, 47, 1193–204.

1979   *The Environment at Work*. Thomas.

1979   Models for biases in judging sensory magnitude. *Psychological Bulletin*, 86, 777–802.

1981   Human manual control. In V.B. Brooks (ed.), *Handbook of Physiology. The Nervous System III*. American Physiology Society.

1989   *Bias in Quantifying Judgments*. Erlbaum.

Further reading

Baker, M.A. and Holding, D.H. (1993) The effects of noise and speech on cognitive task performance. *Journal of General Psychology*, 120, 339–55.

Ferraro, F.R., Kellas, G. and Simpson, G.B. (1993) Failure to maintain equivalence of groups in cognitive research: Evidence from dual-task methodology. *Bulletin of the Psychonomic Society*, 31, 301–3.

The breadth and depth of Poulton's contributions to ergonomics, human factors and engineering psychology can be structured into six areas. (1) Tracking and motor skills: in 1948 he stumbled on the advantages of true motion displays over relative motion displays. In 1961 he discovered that low-order control systems are always easier for people to use than higher-order control systems, with both true-motion and relative-motion displays. This eventually led to the redesign of a number of British Army control systems for manually operated missiles. (2) Channel listening: Poulton was one of the first to work on listening to messages from two loudspeakers simultaneously. As soon as a quiet loudspeaker starts presenting a message, he found that the listener switches his attention to it, and so is likely to miss information presented at the same time through the loudspeaker he or she is supposed to be listening to. (3) Reading: printing and comprehension: in experiments on reading for comprehension, he found that people remember best what they know before they start. Thus, in training people to read faster, the best results are obtained by using passages on familiar topics. The rate of comprehension remains approximately constant over a range of reading speeds. (4) Bias in quantifying judgements: while working under S.S. **Stevens** at Harvard in 1953–4, he conducted fundamental investigations of major biases that influence observers when they attempt to quantify their judgements. (5) Environmental stresses: Poulton carried out experiments demonstrating the detrimental effects of more environmental stresses on performance than anyone else anywhere. These included noise, vibration and ship motion, wind, cold, heat, compression, hypoxia, breathing pure oxygen, the effect of 1mg Hyoscine, and loss of sleep. (6) Within-subjects designs: Poulton was concerned about the dangers of using within-subjects experimental design, especially because many psychologists did not always consider the inevitable bias from asymmetric transfer that these designs produce.

Premack, David

Born: 1926, Aberdeen, USA **Nat:** American **Ints:** Developmental psychology, experimental psychology, philosophical and theoretical psychology, physiological and comparative psychology **Educ:** BA University of Minnesota, 1949; MA University of Minnesota, 1951; PhD University of Minnesota, 1955 **Appts & awards:** Professor of Psychology, University of Pennsylvania; Ford Foundation Fellow, 1953–4; Artist in Residence, Yaddo Inc., 1955; USPHS Postdoctoral Fellow, 1956–9; Fellow, Center for Advanced Study in the Behavioral Sciences, 1973–4; Visiting Scientist, Japan, 1979; Guggenheim Fellow, 1978–9; Van Leer Jerusalem Foundation Fellow, 1980; Fellow, Wissenschaftskollege, Berlin, 1985–6; Fellow, AAAS, Society of Experimental Psychologists; Associate Editor, *Learning and Motivation*, 1970–4; Board of Editors, *Journal of Applied Behavioral Analysis*, 1972–5; Consulting Editor: *Journal of Experimental Psychology: Animal Behavior Proceedings*, 1974–83; *Journal of Human Evolution Cognition*, 1978; Associate Editor, *Behavior and Brain Sciences*, 1977–82

Principal publications

1959   Toward empirical behavior laws: Positive reinforcement. *Psychological Review*, 66, 219–33.
1965   Reinforcement theory. In D. Levine (ed.), *Nebraska Motivation Symposium*. University of Nebraska Press.
1970   A functional analysis of language. *Journal for the Experimental Analysis of Behavior*, 14, 107–25.
1971   Catching up with common sense or two sides of a generalization: Reinforcement and punishment. In R. Glaser (ed.), *On the Nature of Reinforcement*. Academic Press.
1971   Mechanisms of self-control. In W. Hunt (ed.), *Learning Mechanisms in Smoking*. Aldine Press.
1971   Language in chimpanzee? *Science*, 172, 808–22.
1972   Concordant preferences as a precondition for affective but not for symbolic communication. *Cognition*, 1, 251–64.
1972   *Teaching Language to an Ape*. Scientific American (with A.J. Premack).

1976   *Intelligence in Ape and Man*. Erlbaum.
1976   On the abstractness of human concepts: Why it would be difficult to talk to a pigeon. In R. Bolles, S. Hulse and W.K. Honig (eds), *Cognitive Factors in Animal Learning*.
1978   Does the chimpanzee have a theory of mind? *Behavioral and Brain Sciences*, 4, 515–26 (with G. Woodruff).
1982   Pedagogy and aesthetics as sources of culture. In M. Gazzaniga (ed.), *Handbook of Cognitive Neuroscience*.
1983   *The Mind of an Ape*. Norton Press (with A.J. Premack).
1985   *Gavagai! Or the Future History of the Animal Language Controversy*. MIT Press.

Further reading

Premack, D. (1982) The codes of man and beasts. *Behavioral and Brain Sciences*, 6, 125–67.

David Premack attended the University of Minnesota at a time when philosophy formed an integral part of the psychology curriculum, and his work on learning, language and cognition has been influenced by that background. For instance, in reinforcement theory, he was concerned with whether behavioural phenomena could be explained on the behavioural level, without recourse to other levels. Premack is probably best known through the pinciple that bears his name. In learning theory it can be difficult to determine what will be a good reinforcer. For example, praise may be most effective with one person and money with another. The Premack Principle states that any frequent ('prepotent') response can be used to reinforce an infrequent response. For example, using this principle it has been shown that playing computer games (the prepotent response) can be used to manage the behaviour of children who often play these games.

In his work on language, he started from the position that when philosophy of mind contrasts the human and animal mind, language is assigned a special status. But what is language? Premack queried whether it is possible to account for language acquisition within a strict behaviourist framework, and if not, why not. Early failures to teach chimps to use language were followed by successes on the Washo Project (see R. A. **Gardner** and B.T. **Gardner**) and by Premack's chimp pupil Sarah. He taught Sarah to use 130 'words' consisting of plastic chips arranged on a magnetic board (this was the symbolic language used to communicate with Sarah). One of her outstanding achievements was the use of sentences involving conditional relationships: 'If Sarah take apple, then Mary give Sarah candy.'

Intention, he pointed out, is no less a pivotal concept in philosophy than language – from which it is only a small step to ask whether the chimpanzee has a theory of mind. Premack argues that people attribute intention and belief to one another, but whether or not they are correct in doing so it is irrelevant to the question of whether other species make similar attributions. Indeed, if the ape were no less misguided than humans are in making such attributions, it would be of great interest to find that two species make the same error. (An identical argument applies to causal inference: since we are not warranted in making this inference, it is all the more interesting to find the inference in other species.) Devising methods that would answer these questions in species that do not speak adds to the interest, and leads to an ultimately more rewarding question: Are there limits on what we can know of a mind when we cannot interrogate that mind? This is the topic of his book *Gavagai!* (1985).

Pribram, Karl Harry

Born: 1919, Vienna, Austria *Nat:* Austrian/ American *Ints:* Experimental, physiological and comparative, philosophical and theoretical, neuropsychology, psychoanalysis *Educ:* BS University of Chicago, 1939; MD University of Chicago, 1941 *Appts & awards:* Diplomate, American Board of Neurological Surgery, 1948; Fellow, Center for Advanced Study in the Behavioral Sciences, 1958; Professor, Departments of Psychology, Psychiatry and Behavioral Sciences, Stanford University, 1962– ; NIH Lifetime Career Research Award, 1962; Fellow, AAA&S, AAAS; President, APA Division 6, 1967–8; Central Council, International Brain Research Organization; Founding President, International Neuropsychological Society, 1967–9; Chairman, Committee on International Relations in Psychology, 1973; Paul Hoch Award, American Psychopathological Association, 1975; President, APA Division 24, 1979–80; Society for Experimental Psychologists; Fellow, New York Academy of Sciences; President, Professors for World Peace, 1982– ; Editorships and Consulting Boards, *Neuropsychologia, Journal of Mathematical Biology, Advances in Behavioral Biology, Human Motivation, International Journal of Neuroscience, Journal of Neurosci-*

ence Research, Behavioral and Brain Sciences, Journal of Mental Imagery, Journal of Autism and Developmental Disorders, Imagination, Cognition and Personality, Journal of Human Movement Studies, Journal of Social and Biological Structures, ReVision, SISTM Quarterly, Indian Journal of Psychophysiology, Interamerican Journal of Psychology, International Journal of Psychophysiology, Gestalt Theory Cognition and Brain Theory, Biology and Cognition

Principal publications

1960   *Plans and the Structure of Behaviour.* Holt (with G.A. Miller and E. Galanter).

1960   (ed.) *Brain and Behaviour,* vols 1–4. Penguin.

1960   On the neurology of thinking. *Behavioral Science,* 4, 265–87.

1960   A review of theory in physiological psychology. *Annual Reviews in Psychology,* 11, 1–40.

1964   An experimental analysis of the behavioral disturbance produced by a left frontal arachnoid endothelioma (meningioma). *Neuropsychologia,* 4, 257–80.

1969   The effects of radical disconnection of occipital and temporal cortex on visual behaviour of monkeys. *Brain,* 92, 301–12 (with D.N. Spinelli and S.C. Reitz).

1971   *Languages of the Brain: Experimental Paradoxes and Principles in Neuropsychology.* Prentice Hall. (Brooks/Cole, 1977; Brandon House, 1982).

1973   *Psychophysiology of the Frontal Lobes.* Academic Press (ed. with A.R. Luria).

1975   Arousal, activation and effort in the control of attention. *Psychological Review,* 82, 116–49 (with D. McGuinness).

1975   *The Hippocampus,* vols 1 and 2. Plenum.

1979   The effect of inferotemporal or foveal prestriate oblation on social reversal learning in monkeys. *Neuropsychologia,* 17, 1–10 (with C.A. Christensen).

1980   Mind, brain and consciousness: The organisation of competence. In J.M. Davidson and R.J. Davidson (eds), *Psychobiology of Consciousness.* Plenum.

1981   Emotions. In S.B. Filskov and T.J. Boll (eds), *Handbook of Clinical Neuropsychology.* Wiley.

1982   Perception and memory of facial affect following brain injury. *Perceptual and Motor Skills,* 54, 859–69 (with G.P. Prigatano).

1982   Localization and distribution of function in the brain. In J. Orbach (ed.), *Neuropsychology after Lashley.* Erlbaum.

1985   *The Hippocampus*, vols 3 and 4. Plenum.
1987   The subdivisions of the frontal cortex
    revisited. In E. Perecman (ed.) *The Frontal Lobes
    Revisited*. IRBN Press.
1991   *Brain and Perception: Holonomy and
    Structure in Figural Processing*. Erlbaum.
1995   (ed.) *Scale in Conscious Experience: Is the
    Brain too Important to be Left to Specialists to
    Study?*. Erlbaum (with J. King).

Further reading
Donchin, E. and Coles, M.G. (1991) While an
    undergraduate waits. Special Issue in Honor of Karl
    H. Pribram: Localization and distribution of
    cognitive function. *Neuropsychologia*, 29, 557–69.

Pribram received a BS in anatomy in 1939 at the
University of Chicago and an MD from the
same institution in 1941. He was associated with
the **Yerkes** Laboratories of Primate Biology for
a decade, and succeeded **Lashley** as director. He
relinquished the directorship when ownership of
Yerkes was transferred from Yale to Emory
University. During this period he had an
appointment as Lecturer and Assistant Professor
of Research in physiology and psychology at
Yale University School of Medicine, and was
invited to become a member of the Harvey
Cushing Society. He also served as Director of
Research at the Institute of Living. In 1958, he
received a Fulbright Fellowship and was invited
to the Center for Advanced Study in the
Behavioral Sciences at Stanford University.
He accepted the invitation in order to pursue
collaborative work with George **Miller** and
Eugene Gallanter. Since that time he has
authored numerous theoretical and empirical
articles, completed the influential *Languages of
the Brain*, and collaborated with M. Gill on
Freud's Project Reassessed (1976). He was
invited to stay on at Stanford University,
receiving a Lifetime Career Research Award in
Neuroscience in 1962 from the National
Institutes of Health. Pribram is probably best
known for his work on plans (with Miller and
Galanter).

This work is structured around two key
concepts: the plan and the image. A plan is any
hierarchical process in an organism that can
control the order in which a sequence of operations is to be performed. (This conception of
plan is similar to F.C. **Bartlett's** concept of
schema and is often preferred because it
emphasizes the structured use of experience
without specifying the form in which experience
is used.) An image is the accumulated, organ-

ized knowledge an organism has about itself and
the its environment. Human action is represented by components called TOTE units (Test-
Operate-Test-Exit). For example, in hammering
a nail the nail is first Tested (does it stand up),
then Operated on (hammered), then Tested (is
the nail driven home) and then the process is
Exited. TOTEs can be built on one another in a
hierarchical fashion with increasingly general
TOTE units near the top of the hierarchy. Thinking of the structure of human action in terms of
TOTES does not mean that behaviour is so
organized, but it demonstrated for the first time
that the feedback and mechanism approach to
human actions could have considerable explanatory power, sufficient to challenge the
prevailing behaviourist ideas.

Proshansky, Harold Milton
Born: 1920, New York City, USA **Died:** 1990,
New York **Nat:** American **Ints:** Personality and
social psychology, population and environmental psychology, Society for the Psychological
Studies of Social Issues **Educ:** BA City College
of New York, 1941; MA Columbia University
1942; PhD New York University, 1952 **Appts &
awards:** President, Graduate School and University Center, CUNY, New York City; NIH
Research Fellowship, 1958–9; Fellow, APA,
1961; Senior NIH Research Fellowship,
1969–70, Honorary Research Fellowship,
University College, University of London,
1969–70; American Association for the
Advancement of Science, 1975; President,
Division 9, APA; Member of Council of Division 9, APA; Representative to Council of
Division 9, APA; Elected Member, Association
for Advancement of Psychology; Life Member,
New York Academy of Sciences, 1984; Co-
Editor, *Journal of Social Issues*, 1963; Co-
Editor, Basic Studies in Social Psychology
(Holt, Rinehart & Winston), 1965; Consulting
editor, Holt, Rinehart & Winston, 1965–72;
Editorial Board, *Journal of Social Issues*,
1970–8, *International Journal of Group Ten-
sions*; Editorial Advisory Board, *Environment
and Behavior*, 1970–8, Member, Editorial
Advisory Board, *Social Ecology*; Member of the
Hon. Editorial Advisory Board, *Habitat,
Journal of Human Settlements*, 1978–82

Principal publications
1942   The effects of reward and punishment on
    perception. *Journal of Psychology*, 13, 295–305.
1943   A projective method for the study of attitudes.

Journal of Abnormal-Social Psychology, 38, 302–5.

1965   *Basic Studies in Social Psychology*. Holt, Rinehart & Winston

1968   The development of Negro self-identity. In M. Deutsch, A. Jensen and I. Katz (eds), *Race and Social Class in Psychological Development*. Holt, Rinehart & Winston.

1969   Ethnic tension and prejudice. (rev.). In G. Lindzey and E. Aronson (eds), *Handbook of Social Psychology*. Addison-Wesley.

1970   *Environmental Psychology: Man and His Physical Setting*. Holt, Rinehart & Winston. (rev. edn, 1976).

1970   Bedroom size and social interaction of the psychiatric ward. *Environment and Behavior*, 2, 255–70.

1972   For what are we training our graduate students? *American Psychologist*, 27, 205–12.

1973   The environmental crisis in human dignity. *Journal of Social Issues*, 29, 1–19.

1975   *Introduction to Environmental Psychology*. Holt, Rinehart & Winston.

1976   *Genetic Destiny: Scientific Controversy and Social Conflict*. Holt, Rinehart & Winston.

1976   Environmental psychology and the real world. *American Psychologist*, 4, 303–10.

1979   The role of physical settings in life crisis experiences. In I.G. Sarason and C.D. Spielberger (eds), *Stress and Anxiety*. Halstead Press.

Further reading

Altman, I. and Christensen, K (eds) (1990) *Environment and Behavior Studies: Emergence of Intellectual Traditions*. Plenum.

Rivlin, L.G. and Denmark, F.L. (1995) Harold M. Proshansky (1920–1990). *American Psychologist*, 50, 538.

At one time Proshansky considered himself to be an experimental social psychologist with social problem interests that went beyond the laboratory, e.g. intergroup prejudice and social conflict. The most useful approach was the experimental paradigm, seeking to achieve a small number of universal principles that would in time explain human social behaviour in all its complexities. Some fifteen years later he decided that the approach was neither useful nor appropriate. He left social psychology with a determination to study complex social problems in the real world. He turned in particular to the physical environment for two reasons: it was a seriously neglected area of concern; and, having had an earlier interest in art and the design of space, he found the problems of intrinsic inter-

est. His text *Environmental Psychology* (1970) has had a formative influence on the generation of psychologists that follows him.

As interest in the environment (built and natural) increased, so did his conviction that the behavioural sciences, including environmental psychology, can only lead to an understanding of complex human problems if we are guided by the following seven assumptions. (1) In the task of understanding and resolving complex human social problems, the distinction between basic and applied science has no meaning. (2) The subject of study must be actual human problems as they exist in the real world, and the integrity of these problems must be maintained – that is, they cannot and should not be redefined in the attempts to emulate the methodology of the physical and natural sciences. (3) Complex social problems can and should be defined at varying levels of social organizations, such that different disciplines focus on different aspects of these problems. However, any single discipline must continually carry out its particular level of analysis in an interdisciplinary framework. If it does not then the integrity of the problem itself is lost or distorted. (4) Data and method have fundamental roles in every science, but their exact nature and use must be determined by the problem and state of our knowledge about that problem. (5) All sciences are value laden, involving values that extend from ethical contributions to epistemic choices. The recognition and appropriate expression of these values in doing research is critical in the growth of a science of human behaviour. (6) In a social problem-oriented science, the search for knowledge cannot and should not be the search for general principles, but rather its focus must be the immediate setting analysed in times of the past (historical context) and future. (7) No behavioural science can be worth much unless its analytical and theoretical orientations include the process of social change in relation to the dimensions of place and time. The understanding of complex human problems will, at its root, require conceptualization of stability and change as they relate to the experience of individuals in social groups.

Pylyshyn, Zenon Walter

Born: 1937, Montreal, Quebec, Canada ***Nat:*** Canadian ***Ints:*** Cognitive science, experimental psychology, philosophical and theoretical psychology ***Educ:*** BEng (Engineering-Physics) McGill University, 1959; MSc (Control

Systems) University of Saskatchewan, 1961; PhD (Experimental Psychology) University of Saskatchewan, 1963 **Appts & awards:** Professor, Psychology and Computer Science, University of Western Ontario, 1963–93; Donald O. Hebb Award, Canadian Psychological Association, 1990; Director, Centre for Cognitive Science; Board of Governors' Professor of Cognitive Science and Director, Centre for Cognitive Science, Rutgers University, 1993– ; Killam Fellowship, Institute for Mathematical Studies in the Social Sciences and the Centre for Cognitive Sciences, MIT; Fellow, Canadian Institute for Advanced Research (CIAR), National Director, CIAR Programme in Artificial Intelligence and Robotics; President: Cognitive Science Society, Society for Philosophy and Psychology; Fellow: Canadian Psychological Association, American Association for Artificial Intelligence; Editorial Board: *Cognitive Science, Cognitive Psychology, Cognition, Computational Intelligence, Medical Expert Systems, Minds and Machines, Mind and Language, Artificial Intelligence*

Principal publications

1973 What the mind's eye tells the mind's brain: A critique of mental imagery. *Psychological Bulletin*, 80, 1–24.

1978 Computational models and empirical constraints. *Behavioural and Brain Sciences*, 1, 93–127.

1978 Imagery and artificial intelligence. In C.W. Savage (ed.), *Minnesota Studies in the Philosophy of Science*, vol. 9. *Perception and Cognition Issues in the Foundations of Psychology*. University of Minnesota Press.

1979 Validating computational models: A critique of Anderson's indeterminacy of representation claim. *Psychological Review*, 86, 383–94.

1980 Computation and cognition: Issues in the foundation of cognitive science. *Behavioural and Brain Sciences*, 3, 111–69.

1981 The imagery debate: Analogue media versus tacit knowledge. *Psychological Review*, 88, 16–45.

1981 How direct is visual perception? Some reflections on Gibson's 'ecological approach'. *Cognition*, 9, 139–96.

1984 *Computation and Cognition: Toward a Foundation for Cognitive Science*. MIT Press.

1988 Connectionism and cognitive architecture: A critical analysis. *Cognition*, 28, 3–71 (with J. Fodor).

1989 The role of location indexes in spatial perception: A sketch of the FINST spatial-index model. *Cognition*, 32, 65–97.

1991 The role of cognitive architecture in theories of cognition. In K. VanLehn (ed.), *Architectures for Intelligence: The Twenty-Second Carnegie Mellon Symposium on Cognition*. Erlbaum.

1993 What enumeration studies can show us about spatial attention: Evidence for limited capacity preattentive processing. *Journal of Experimental Psychology: Human Perception and Performance*, 19, 331–51 (with L.M. Trick).

1994 Some primitive mechanisms of spatial attention. *Cognition*, 50, 363–84.

1994 Multiple parallel access in visual attention. *Canadian Journal of Experimental Psychology*, 48, 260–83.

Further reading

Boden, M.A. (1988) *Computer Models of Mind*. Cambridge University Press.

Hampson, P.J. and Morris, P.E. (1996) *Understanding Cognition*. Blackwell.

McClelland, J.L., Rumelhart, D.E. and PDP Research Group (1986) *Parallel Distributed Processing*, vol. 2. *Psychological and Biological Models*. MIT Press.

Paivio, A. (1971) *Imagery and Verbal Processes*. Holt, Rinehart & Winston.

Reilly, R. (1989). On the relationship between connectionism and cognitive science. *Irish Journal of Psychology*, 10, 162–87.

Suppes, P., Pavel, and Falmagne, J.Cl. (1994) Representations and models in psychology. *Annual Review of Psychology*, 45, 517–44.

Zenon Pylyshyn is one of the foremost theorists in the field of computational models in cognitive science. His research has spanned such topics as operator performance in control systems, the computer analysis of texts, machine vision, spatial attention and the role of diagrams in helping people to reason about geometry. Perhaps his most famous studies, however, are those which concern two important theoretical critiques: that of the 'picture metaphor' underlying analogical models of mental imagery and that of the connectionist paradigm in cognitive science.

In the early 1970s, Pylyshyn published a seminal paper entitled 'What the mind's eye tells the mind's brain: A critique of mental imagery'. This questioned the validity of the theory (adopted by **Paivio**, 1971) that images were analogous to 'internal' pictures in the sense that they were isomorphic with visual arrays. Briefly, Pylyshyn attacked this 'pictures in the head' approach on both conceptual and empirical grounds. For example, he argued that the logical consequence of this approach was the postulation of a 'homunculus' in an effort to explain who or what was 'looking' at these 'pictures' in the 'mind's eye'. In addition, empirical evidence revealed significant differences between the processing of mental images and that of perceptual displays. For example, whereas it is easy to re-examine a real photograph visually, an image cannot be reinterpreted to attempt to locate a hidden object that was not noticed originally. Similarly, mental images of ambiguous visual stimuli cannot be reinterpreted readily, although people can easily transform a visual stimulus perceptually. Combining these arguments, Pylyshyn proposed that images were 'epiphenomenal' constructs, reflecting merely the symptoms or incidental by-products of more fundamental cognitive activity (presumably, manipulation of propositional knowledge). Later, Pylyshyn buttressed his critique of analogical theory by suggesting that many imagery findings can be explained by the possibility that people are using their cognitive abilities and prior knowledge to simulate perceptual processes. In other words, he denied **Kosslyn**'s claims that images can be 'scanned' or 'rotated' – what happens is merely the result of people's manipulation of their propositional knowledge. Thus Pylyshyn proposed that the 'mental scanning' studies were methodologically flawed as a result of contamination by participants' knowledge and beliefs, and the linear relationship between mental scanning times and scanned distances could have been caused by participants' prior knowledge about physics (especially, distance–speed relationships). In other words, 'scanning' studies may be more important for highlighting the role of 'tacit knowledge' in cognitive performance than for corroborating the analogical nature of imagery as a mental representation.

Pylyshyn's criticisms of analogical theory were attacked subsequently by **Kosslyn**, who argued that if an image is an incidental by-product of propositional coding of information, the size of the image should not matter to the meaning it conveys. But results show that the speed of making decisions about imagined features is proportional directly to the size of the image involved. For example, subjects 'zoomed in' more quickly on features of an imaginary rabbit when it was compared with an image of a fly than when it was compared with a mental image of an elephant. In response to the criticisms, Pylyshyn postulated that it would be

uneconomical of the mind to maintain a store of separate images for different parts of its stored knowledge. More plausible by far, he argued, was the possibility that the mind stores abstract descriptions (called 'propositions') rather than concrete depictions of things.

As an empirical test of his ideas, Pylyshyn conducted an interesting variation on **Kosslyn**'s 'mental scanning' paradigm. One condition of the study involved asking subjects to imagine a spot moving between a lighthouse and a bridge on a map. In another condition, he asked them to imagine themselves walking between these locations. Results indicated that, as Kosslyn had shown, the time taken to reach the designated destination varied directly with the distance involved. But Pylyshyn also found that if subjects imagined shifting their gaze as fast as possible between the lighthouse and the bridge, the latency of response was *not* proportional to the distance 'travelled'. Furthermore, if subjects were asked to 'run' between these locations, they responded faster than when asked to 'walk' between them. According to Pylyshyn, this result was due to people's prior knowledge about speed–distance relationships. For example, people know that running is faster than walking and that the time required to shift one's gaze between two locations is always faster than that needed to 'walk' that same distance. In one experimental condition of this study, he asked people to scan a distance between two points on an imaged map. As usual, the time taken to perform this task was proportional to the relative distance between the points. But this typical 'scanning effect' disappeared in another experimental condition, where the group had to imagine shifting their gaze rapidly between one point and another. This finding indicated that the latter group did not appear to be scanning the image in a consistent manner. Using such evidence, Pylyshyn concluded that imagery depends on stored knowledge (e.g. descriptions of objects) which is 'propositional' (i.e. abstract), rather than analogical, in character. Indeed, he proposed that if imagery involves description, then it should be a 'cognitively penetrable' phenomenon or one which is modifiable by the person's knowledge or beliefs. In other words, if imagery is regarded as part of the functional architecture of the mind, then it should not be 'penetrable' by one's beliefs or wishes, which are propositional in nature. But Pylyshyn had shown that imagery can be influenced by tacit knowledge or expectations. Therefore, he concluded that imagery is cognitively penetrable and based on propositional representations.

Propositional representations are abstract mental sentences which describe conceptual relations between specified predicates or objects. They involve relations and arguments. For example, the sentence 'The cat sat on the mat' could be represented by the proposition SAT (CAT, MAT) where 'sat' is the relation and 'cat' and 'mat' are the 'arguments'. According to Pylyshyn, propositions are the main way in which the mind stores information. However, critics such as **Johnson-Laird** point out that propositional representations are inadequate for the task of explaining language because they do not contain information about referents.

In the late 1980s, Pylyshyn provided a valuable critique of the emerging paradigm of 'connectionism' (or parallel distributed processing – PDP; McClelland *et al.*, 1986) in cognitive science. Briefly, this approach seeks to explain cognitive activity through the product of the combined action of large-scale neural networks rather than as the outcome of central, symbolic representational structures. Reviewing the theoretical adequacy of this approach, **Fodor** and Pylyshyn pointed out that, unlike the classical (or 'symbolic') information-processing paradigm, connectionist models fail to address the logical and semantic relationships which exist between associated nodes. Therefore, in the opinion of these authors, such models were not 'structure sensitive' and could not, in principle, account for the generativity of our thinking. However, as Hampson and Morris (1996) explain, symbol-processing accounts of cognition also encounter difficulties when attempting to explain the role of inference and intentionality in cognition. Furthermore, connectionist models have been developed to take account of some of the temporal and logical relationships which are assumed to characterize mental processes (e.g. see Reilly, 1989). Overall, therefore, it seems symbolic and connectionist approaches may be complementary rather than antagonistic, because they address different levels of cognitive activity. To explain, high-level (cognitively penetrable) processes may be implemented neurally as low-level (cognitively impenetrable) distributed representations.

Perhaps the best summary of Pylyshyn's influence on cognitive science comes from the citation accompanying his nomination for the Donald **Hebb** Award by the Canadian Psychological Association in 1990. Here, his friend and colleague, Jerry Fodor, stated that Pylyshyn is 'one of the very few cognitive psychologists who has combined a wide-ranging program of experimental psychology with highly distinguished contributions to the literature on theoretical and foundational issues'.

AIDAN MORAN

Q

Quay, Herbert C.

Born: 1927, Portland, Maine, USA **Nat:** American **Ints:** Clinical and developmental **Educ:** BS Florida State University, 1951; MS Florida State University, 1952; PhD University of Illinois, 1958 **Appts & awards:** Distinguished Contribution Award, American Association of Correctional Psychologists, 1974; Professor, University of Miami, 1984–92, Emeritus, 1992– ; President, APA Division of Clinical Psychology, 1985; Distinguished Professional Contribution Award, Section on Clinical Child Psychology, Division of Clinical Psychology, APA 1991; Editor, *Journal of Abnormal Child Psychology*, 1972; Editorial Board, *Clinical Psychology Review*

Principal publications

1963 *Research in Psychopathology*. Van Nostrand.

1964 Personality dimensions in delinquent males as inferred from the factor analysis of behavior ratings. *Journal of Research in Crime and Delinquency*, 1, 33–7.

1964 Dimensions of personality in delinquent boys as inferred from the factor analysis of case history data. *Child Development*, 35, 479–84.

1965 Psychopathic personality as pathological stimulation seekings. *American Journal of Psychiatry*, 122, 180–3.

1967 Conditioning visual orientation of conduct problem children in the classroom. *Journal of Experimental Child Psychology*, 5, 512–17 (with R.L. Sprague, J.S. Werry and M.M. McQueen).

1968 *Children's Behavior Disorders: Selected Readings*. Van Nostrand.

1977 Psychopathic behavior: Reflections on its nature, origins and treatment. In I.C. Uzgiris and F. Weizman (eds), *The Structuring of Experience*. Plenum.

1979 *Psychopathological Disorders of Childhood*. Wiley (with J.S. Werry).

1983 Psychological theories of crime causation. In S.H. Kadish (ed.), *Encyclopedia of Crime and Justice*. Free Press.

1983 A dimensional approach to children's behavior disorders: The Revised Behavior Problem Checklist. *School Psychology Review*, 12, 244–9.

1984 *Managing Adult Inmates*. American Correctional Association.

1984 Behavioral disorders of children. In N.S. Endler and J.McV. Hunt (eds), *Personality and the Behavioral Disorders* (2nd edn). Wiley (with A.M. LaGreca).

1986 A critical analysis of DSM-III as a taxonomy of psychopathology in childhood and adolescence. In T. Millon and G. Klerman (eds), *Contemporary issues in psychopathology*. Guilford Press.

1987 Institutional treatment. In H.C. Quay (ed.), *Handbook of Juvenile Delinquency*. Wiley.

1988 Attention deficit disorder and the behavioral inhibition system: The relevance of the neuropsychological theory of Jeffrey A. Gray. In L.M. Bloomingdale and J.A. Sergeant (eds), *DSM-IV Source Book*. American Psychiatric Association.

1993 The psychobiology of undersocialized aggressive conduct disorder: A theoretical perspective. *Development and Psychopathology*, 5, 165–80.

Further reading

Routh, D.K. (ed.) (1994) *Disruptive Behavior Disorders in Childhood*. Plenum.

Quay's major interest and contribution has been in the classification, aetiology and treatment of childhood and adolescent psychopathology with particular emphasis on conduct disorder. He was involved in early factor-analytic inquiries into the structure of deviant behaviour in children. Later this was to inform the development of a revised version of the Behavior Problem Checklist, the earlier version and later versions both developed in collaboration with Donald R. **Peterson**. Quay also worked on the genesis of psychopathy (antisocial personality). In 1965 he formulated the stimulation-seeking theory of this disorder, which gave rise to a number of studies confirming that, in both children and adolescents, severe aggressive behaviour was related to psychophysiological underarousal and stimulation-seeking. Later he used Jeffrey A. **Gray**'s theory in formulating hypotheses about underlying mechanisms in attention deficit disorder, conduct disorder, and anxiety withdrawal disorder.

Quillian, M. Ross

Born: 1931 **Nat:** American **Ints:** Cognitive science **Educ:** MA University of Chicago, 1961; PhD Carnegie Institute of Technology (Carnegie-Mellon University), 1967 **Appts & awards:** Graduate Student, Research Assistant, University of Chicago, 1955–60; Instructor in Sociology, Presbyterian-St Luke's Medical Centre, Chicago, 1959–60; MIT, Research Laboratory for Electronics, 1961–2; Graduate Student, Carnegie Institute of Technology, 1965–71; Research Consultant, Bolt Beranek and Newman, Inc., 1971; University of California, Irvine, Associate Professor of Political Science, School of Social Sciences, 1995, Associate Professor Emeritus, 1995–

Principal publications

1966   Semantic memory. Unpublished PhD dissertation, Carnegie Institute of Technology, Pittsburgh, Pennsylvania.
1967   A revised design for an understanding machine. *Mechanical Translation*, 7.
1967   Word concepts: A theory and simulation of some basic semantic capabilities. *Behavioural Science*, 12, 410–30.
1968   Semantic memory. In M. Minsky (ed), *Semantic Information Processing*. MIT Press.
1969   The teachable language comprehender: A simulation program and theory of language. *Communications of the Association for Computing Machinery*, 12, 459–76.
1969   Retrieval time from semantic memory'. *Journal of Verbal Learning and Verbal Behaviour*, 8, 240–7 (with A.M. Collins).
1972   Experiments on semantic memory and language comprehension. In L.W. Gregg (ed.), *Cognition in Learning and Memory*. Wiley.
1972   How to make a language user. In E. Tulving and W. Donaldson (eds), *Organisation and Memory*. Academic Press.

Further reading

Collins, A.M. and Loftus, E.F. (1975) A spreading activation theory of semantic processing. *Psychological Review*, 82, 407–28.
Conrad, C. (1972) Cognitive economy in semantic memory. *Journal of Experimental Psychology*, 92, 149–54.
McClelland, J.L. and Rumelhart, D.E. (1986) A distributed model of human learning and memory. In J.L. McClelland and D.E. Rumelhart (eds),

Parallel Distributed Processing: Explorations in the Microstructure of Cognition, vol. 2, Psychological and Biological Models. MIT Press.
Ripps, L.J., Shoben, E.J. and Smith, E.E. (1973) Semantic distance and the verification of semantic relations. *Journal of Verbal Learning and Verbal Behaviour*, 12, 1–20.
Rosch, E. (1973) Natural categories. *Cognitive Psychology*, 4, 328–49.
Shapiro, S.C., Eckroth, D. and Vallasi, G.A. (1987) *Encyclopaedia of Artificial Intelligence* (2 vols). Wiley.

M. Ross Quillian is famous for his development, in the 1960s, of an influential model of 'semantic memory', or our mental store of general conceptual knowledge (e.g. the meanings of words and concepts). The earliest version of this model emerged from the doctoral research which he conducted in Carnegie-Mellon University.

Quillian conducted some of the earliest research in the field of 'semantic memory' or our mental store of conceptual knowledge. His doctoral research on text comprehension is significant in the history of cognitive science because it offered perhaps the first computational model of the way in which the mind represents and retrieves semantic information (e.g. word meanings). This 'network' model of semantic memory was called the Teachable Language Comprehender or (TLC) and was tested empirically in collaboration with Allan M. Collins, a psychologist.

Following his move to the University of California, Irvine, in 1971, Quillian shifted his attention to the problem of 'societal organisation'. At present, he is engaged in elaborating this 'forumarchic' model of society through his teaching and writing.

The TLC model was designed to explore how semantic information could be represented computationally or to 'permit the "meanings" of words to be stored'. Influenced by Aristotle's ideas about mental taxonomies, Quillian postulated that conceptual knowledge is organized as a hierarchical network of associated characteristics. For example, the concept of 'robin' was considered to be subordinate to that of 'bird', which itself was deemed to be subordinate to the concept of 'animal'. Symbolically, each concept was represented as a point or 'node' and the relationships between concepts were represented as links or 'pointers'.

An important assumption (entitled 'cognitive economy') made by Collins and Quillian (1969) was that the properties of any concept in the semantic network are stored at the highest or most inclusive level in the hierarchy. In this way, hypothetical 'storage space' is saved because features of subordinate concepts can be 'inherited' or *inferred* rather than listed explicitly. To illustrate, information which is true of 'birds' in general (e.g. the fact that they have feathers) does not have to be specified at the nodes corresponding to each type of bird (e.g. robins, eagles). To test the veracity of this assumption, Collins and Quillian gave subjects the 'sentence verification' task, in which they were requested to verify or negate simple statements (e.g. 'A canary is a bird') as rapidly as possible. The statements included both true and false sentences. The authors predicted that if semantic networks display cognitive economy, then sentences which require longer chains of inheritance should take longer to verify than sentences which have shorter links between subject and predicate. In other words, the speed of mental search was assumed to reflect the number of semantic levels traversed in the conceptual hierarchy (i.e. the 'semantic distance' between the subjects and predicate in the sentence). Therefore, verification time for a sentence like 'A canary is an animal' should exceed that for 'A canary is a bird' because more associative levels have to be traversed in the former case. In general, this hypothesis was corroborated, giving rise to the 'category size' effect (or the finding that larger conceptual categories require longer sentence verification times than do smaller ones).

Unfortunately, despite its ingenuity, the TLC model was challenged by subsequent researchers on several grounds. Firstly, many concepts (e.g. natural categories such as 'furniture'; **Rosch**, 1973) do not have a clear set of defining features and hence are not easily represented in a hierarchical fashion. Similarly, the allegedly hierarchical relationships between other types of concept proved difficult to replicate. For example, results showed that sentences involving immediate superordinates sometimes took longer to confirm than those involving more distant superordinates. Thus people took longer to verify 'A collie is a mammal' than 'A collie is an animal', even though the concept 'collie' is closer hierarchically to 'mammal' than it is to 'animal' (Rips *et al.*, 1973). Secondly, Conrad (1972) questioned the 'cognitive economy' principle by showing that the speed of sentence verification was determined more by the familiarity of the properties than by their location in the semantic hierarchy. Thirdly, 'typicality' effects occurred in which people took longer to verify sentences involving atypical examples of a concept than typical ones. For example, it takes longer to verify that an 'emu' is a bird than that a 'robin' is. In spite of these reservations, the legacy of the Collins and Quillian model is substantial. For example, the 'spread of activation' assumption influenced modern connectionist models of memory (e.g. McClelland and Rumelhart, 1986). In addition, the TLC model represented the first major attempt to produce a computer program that could simulate the flexibility of inferential reasoning, which is a key characteristic of human semantic memory.

AIDAN MORAN

R

Rank, Otto

Born: 1884, Vienna, Austria *Died:* 1939, New York City, USA *Nat:* Austrian *Ints:* Humanistic, philosophical and theoretical, psychoanalysis, psychology and the arts, psychotherapy *Educ:* PhD University of Vienna, 1912 *Appts & awards:* Secretary, Vienna Psychoanalytic Society, 1906–18; Co-Editor, *Imago*, 1912–26, *Internationale Zeitschrift Für Psychoanalyse*, *c*.1912–25; Managing Director, Internationaler Psychoanalytischer Verlag, 1919–*c*.26.

Principal publications

1914 *The Myth of the Birth of the Hero.* Journal of Nervous and Mental Disease Publishing Co.
1929 *The Trauma of Birth.* Routledge.
1932 *Art and Artist.* Knopf.
1936 *Will Therapy, and Truth and Reality.* Knopf.
1975 *The Don Juan Legend.* Trans. and ed. with intro. by David G. Winter. Princeton University Press.

Further reading

Atwood, G.E. and Stolorow, R.D. (1993) *Faces in a Cloud: Inter-Subjectivity in Personality Theory.* Jason Aronson.
Lieberman, E.J. (1985) *Acts of Will: The Life and Work of Otto Rank.* Free Press.
MacKinnon, D.W. (1965) Personality and the realization of creative potential. *American Psychologist*, 20, 273–81.
Menaker, E. (1982) *Otto Rank: A Rediscovered Legacy.* Columbia University Press.
Rudnytsky, P.L. (1991) *The Psychoanalytic Vocation: Rank, Winnicott and the Legacy of Freud.* Yale University Press.

Largely self-educated, young Rank so impressed **Freud** whey they met in 1905 that the latter encouraged and supported Rank's formal studies. Freud welcomed him to the weekly meetings of his Viennese inner circle, and eventually made Rank secretary. For many years Rank pursued explorations of myth and literature from the point of view of psychoanalysis, while working steadily with the material and concepts of psychoanalysis in reporting the weekly meetings and through other frequent interactions with Freud and Freud's other associates, and eventually as co-editor of two psychoanalytic journals and director of the movement's publishing house.

Rank's early psychoanalytic interpretations of what it means to be an artist, and of recurrent themes in myth and literature, were later supplemented by discussions of psychoanalytic issues in therapy. Rank eventually became a lay analyst.

A major change in Rank's position among analysts came with his publication in 1929 of *The Trauma Of Birth*. The great emphasis here on people's relation to their mother might seem a threat to Freudian emphasis on the importance of the father. Freud did not at first view it in this way, but in time followed other analysts in being severely critical. But the aspect of it that Rank emphasized in his later writing seems clearly valid – the aspect that follows from giving birth a metaphorical meaning. Life means a constant conflict between the pleasurably exciting yet threatening move forward to new possibilities and the relaxing yet stultifying comfort of what is old and familiar.

Feeling rejected, but also seeking forward movement such as he was symbolizing by birth, Rank left Vienna and his central position in the psychoanalytic movement there, visiting Paris and the United States, conducting therapy, writing and lecturing. Major publications presented new ideas on the psychology of the artist, on techniques and theory of therapy, and on education; much was clearly predictive of major later developments in psychodynamic theory and practice. Rank's psychology of the artist received striking validation in the research of **MacKinnon** (1965) on creativity in architects. Psychologist David Winter reports much agreement with the results of his own independent research on the power motive. Rank's emphases on the value of brief therapy, on the importance of a clearly defined end of therapy, on narcissism, on analysis of the ego, on childhood relation to social objects of crucial importance, and on the organized individual as a source of action are all among those seen variously by Menaker (1982), Lieberman (1985) and Rudnytsky (1991) as 'rediscovered legacies' of Rank's career. The appearance of some of these emphases is, in psychologist Carl **Rogers** and sociologist Ernest Becker, clearly related to influence from Rank; in Erik **Erikson** and much of modern psychoanalysis it may primarily involve later recognition of what Rank was able to see early.

IRVIN L. CHILD

Rapoport, Anatol

Born: 1911, Lozovaya, Russia **Nat:** Russian **Ints:** Experimental psychology, personality and social psychology, psychological study of social issues **Educ:** SB University of Chicago, 1938; SM University of Chicago, 1940; PhD University of Chicago, 1941 **Appts & awards:** Fellow, Center for Advanced Study in the Behavioral Sciences, 1954–5; Fellow AAA&S, 1960; President, Society for General Systems Research, 1965–6, Hon. D, University of Western Michigan, 1971; President, Canadian Peace Research and Education Association, 1972–5; Lenz International Peace Research Prize, 1975; Society for General Systems Research, Comprehensive Achievement Award, 1983; Professor of Peace Studies, University of Toronto, 1984– ; Editor, *General Systems*, 1956–77; Associate Editor: *Journal of Conflict Resolution*, 1956– , *Behavioral Science*, 1956– ; *Bulletin of Mathematical Biology*, 1970– ; Editorial Boards: *International Journal of Game Theory*, *Theory and Decision*, *Instructional Science*, *Communication*

Principal publications

1960 *Fights, Games, and Debates*. University of Michigan Press.
1961 An essay on mind. In J.M. Scher (ed.), *Toward a Definition of Mind*. Free Press.
1962 The use and misuse of game theory. *Scientific American*, 207, 108–18.
1963 Mathematical models of social interaction. In R.D. Luce, R.R. Bush and E. Galanter (eds), *Handbook of Mathematical Psychology*, vol. 2. Wiley.
1964 *Strategy and Conscience*. Harper and Row.
1965 *Prisoner's Dilemma*. University of Michigan Press (with A.M. Chammah).
1966 A taxonomy of 2 × 2 games. *General Systems*, 11, 11–26 (with M. Guyer).
1967 Exploiter, leader, hero, martyr: The four archetypes of the 2 × 2 game. *Behavioral Science*, 12, 81–4.
1967 Games as tools of psychological research. *Systematics*, 5, 114–34.
1974 *Conflict in Man-Made Environment*. Penguin.
1976 Directions in mathematical psychology, I. *American Mathematical Monthly*, 83, 85–106; II. 153–72.
1980 Decision pressures in 2 × 2 games. *Behavioral Science*, 25, 107–19 (with K.W. Lendenmann).
1984 *Mathematical Models in the Social and Behavioral Sciences*. Wiley
1986 *General System Theory*. Abacus.
1989 *The Origins of Violence*. Paragon.
1992 *Decision Theory and Decision Behavior*. Kluwer.
1993 *Peace, an Idea Whose Time has Come*. University of Michigan.
1994 *Gewissheiten und Zweifel*. Verlag Darmstädter Blätter.

Further reading

Ford, K.M., Glymour, C.N. and Hayes, P.J. (eds) (1995) *Android Epistemology*. MIT Press.
Glad, B. (ed.) (1990) *Psychological Dimensions of War*. Sage.

The early work of Anatol Rapoport dealt with formal mathematical models of diffusion phenomena, which could be interpreted in terms of either the spread of excitation in a neural net or the spread of a behaviour pattern, a disease or a mood by personal contacts. In the course of reading on these topics, he was particularly struck by the work of Lewis F. Richardson on mathematical models of arms races and of war moods. Being also concerned with the threats posed by the Cold War and the incipient arms race, he became increasingly involved in what is loosely called 'peace research' from the point of view that identifies war, figuratively speaking, as a disease of humanity. Of the various approaches to this theme, he dismissed the psychological study of aggression as of questionable relevance. War, he argues, is no longer a matter of 'fighting' but rather one of organizing a vast cultural and economic enterprise, with inputs from the most advanced sectors of science and technology. He considers two approaches to the study of war to be particularly fruitful, one through system theory and the other through analysis of strategic thinking. The latter led to investigations of the theory of games. He was able to show that by the use of experimental games, the seductive power of the zero-sum game paradigm makes it exceedingly difficult for parties in conflict to escape from 'social traps'; that is, mutually disadvantageous 'in-conflict' outcomes in situations where mutually advantageous outcomes could be achieved. His name is linked particularly with the debate on the Prisoner's Dilemma game and similar paradoxes stemming from a sharp divergence of individual and collective rationality.

Ratliff, Floyd

Born: 1919, La Junta, Colorado, USA **Nat:** American **Ints:** Clinical and neuropsychology, experimental psychology, history of psychology, physiological and comparative psychology, psychology and the arts **Educ:** BA Colorado College, 1947; MA Brown University, 1949; PhD Brown University, 1950 **Appts & awards:** Member, Society of Experimental Psychologists, 1957– ; Member, NAS, 1966– ; Howard Crosby Warren Medal, Society of Experimental Psychologists, 1966; Fellow, AAA&S, 1968; Member, American Philosophical Society, 1972; Professor of Biophysics and Physiological Psychology, Rockefeller University, 1974; Hon. DSc, Colorado College, 1975; Edgar D. Tillyer Award, Optical Society of America, 1976; Medal for Distinguished Service, Brown University, 1980; Distinguished Scholar, US– China Exchange Program, 1981–2; Pisart Vision Award, The Lighthouse, New York Association for the Blind, 1983; APA Distinguished Scientific Contribution Award, 1984; President, H.F. Guggenheim Foundation, 1985– ; Associate Editor, *Biological Abstracts*, 1958–61; Editorial Board, *Journal of General Physiology*, 1969–

Principal publications

1952 The role of physiological nystagmus in monocular acuity. *Journal of Experimental Psychology*, 43, 163–72.

1954 *Behavioral Studies of Visual Processes in the Pigeon*. Harvard University (with D.S. Blough).

1957 Inhibitory interaction of receptor units in the eye of Limulus. *Journal of General Psychology*, 40, 357–76 (with H.K. Hartline).

1959 The responses of Limulus optic nerve fibres to patterns of illumination on the receptor mosaic. *Journal of General Physiology*, 42, 1241–55 (with H.K. Hartline).

1963 Spatial and temporal aspects of retinal inhibitory interaction. *Journal of the Optical Society of America*, 53, 110–20 (with H.K. Hartline and W.H. Miller).

1965 *Mach Bands: Quantitative Studies of Neural Networks in the Retina*. Holden-Day.

1971 The logic of the retina. *Journal of Philosophy*, 68, 591–7.

1972 Inhibitory interaction in the retina of Limulus. In M.G.F. Fuortes (ed.), *Handbook of Sensory Physiology* vol. VII/2, *Physiology of Photoreceptor Organs*. Springer-Verlag (with H.K. Hartline).

1974 (ed.) *Studies of Excitation and Inhibition in the Retina: A Collection of Papers from the Laboratories of H.K. Hartline*. Rockefeller University Press.

1978 Equivalence classes of visual stimuli. *Vision Research*, 18, 845–51 (with L. Sirovich).

1978 The spatiotemporal transfer function of the Limulus lateral eye. *Journal of General Physiology*, 72, 167–202 (with S.E. Brodie and B.W. Knight).

1982 Some new methods for the analysis of lateral interactions that influence the visual evoked potential. *Annals of the New York Academy of Sciences*, 388, 113–24 (with V. Zemon).

1984 Intermodulation components of the visual evoked potential: Responses to lateral and superimposed stimuli. *Biological Cybernetics*, 50, 401–8 (with V. Zemon).

Further reading

Anderson, J.A. and Rosenfeld, E. (eds) (1988) *Neurocomputing: Foundations of Research*. MIT Press.

Bridgeman, B. (1977) A correlational model applied to metacontrast: Reply to Weisstein, Ozog, and Szoc. *Bulletin of the Psychonomic Society*, 10, 85–8.

Floyd Ratcliff was the son of a blacksmith and rancher. He attended public elementary and high schools in Cheraw, Manzanola, and Pueblo, Colorado. During the Great Depression he twice dropped out from high school, and his undergraduate education was interrupted by World War II. During the war he served as an artilleryman in Europe. After the war Ratliff returned to Colorado College and shifted his interests away from biology to psychology. At Brown University he completed his PhD – a thesis on nystagmus, minuscule involuntary eye movements – under the supervision of Lorrin Riggs. Later he and Riggs developed an optical system which stopped these motions, thereby stabilizing the image on the retina. They showed that stabilized images quickly disappear.

Ratliff focused on the integrative neural mechanisms underlying visual perception of contour and contrast, specifically lateral inhibitory interactions in the visual pathways. After his PhD he joined H. Keffer Hartline at the Laboratory of Biophysics, Johns Hopkins University. After a brief period at Harvard he returned to Hartline's laboratory (then at the Rockefeller Institute) in 1954. There he examined how inhibitory influences generated at two or more different points in the retina combine when they act together at another point. This led to two significant findings. The first was the discovery of disinhibition: the release of one point in the retina by a second such point when the second is itself inhibited by a third. Disinhibition has subsequently been found to be an important regulator of neural activity in the nervous system. This work led to the formulation of the Hartline–Ratliff equations, which describe inhibitory interactions in the retina. This work was the first comprehensive mathematical account of the integrative activity of a real neural network. The second finding was the demonstration of how lateral inhibition 'tunes' neural networks to transmit certain spatial and temporal frequencies of stimulation and even to the amplification of responses at some frequencies. This was unexpected, because it was thought that the usual effect of inhibition was to suppress responses. In his later work (with Scott, Brodie and Knight), he extended the Hartline–Ratliff equations and formulated a general mathematical model that could predict responses of the retina to any arbitrary stimulus varying over large ranges in space and time.

Floyd Ratliff is credited with uniquely combining psychology with physiology, physics and mathematics in objective explorations of visual perception. His principal contributions have been in extending our understanding of the role of eye movements in visibility, in explaining the dynamics of excitation and inhibition in retinal networks, and in developing the application of evoked potential techniques to the assessment of visual disorders.

Reich, Wilhelm

Born: 1897, Dobvcynica, Galicia, Austria **Died:** 1957, Maine, USA **Nat:** Austrian **Ints:** Personality and social psychology, psychoanalysis, psychotherapy **Educ:** MD University of Vienna, 1922

Principal publications

1927 *Der Funkton des Orgasmus*. Internationaler Psychoanalytischer Verlag. (trans. *The Function of the Orgasm*, Farrar, Straus and Giroux, 1961).

1933 *Charakter-Analyse*. Sexpol Verlag. (trans. *Character Analysis*, Farrar, Straus and Giroux, 1961).
1960 *Selected Writings*. Farrar, Straus and Giroux.
1969 *The Sexual Revolution*. Farrar, Straus and Giroux.

Further reading

Alexander, F., Eisenstein, S. and Grotjahn, M. (eds) (1995) *Psychoanalytic Pioneers*. Transaction.
Marcus, S. (1989) Psychoanalytic biography and its problems: The case of Wilhelm Reich. In A.M. Cooper *et al*. (eds), *Psychoanalysis: Toward the Second Century*. Yale University Press.

The importance of Reich's contributions to the development of psychotherapeutic theory and practice has been obscured somewhat by his own powerful and abrasive personality, by the unhappy story of his last days in America, where he died in prison, and by some unfortunate beliefs that he held about the value of his own work. Released from these beliefs, dissected out from the irrelevancies of his own biography, and freed from the hostile reactions of the many contemporary critics who merely found his work distasteful, Reich's stature can be appreciated.

Before his break with **Freud**, and his expulsion from the International Psychoanalytic Association in 1934, Reich, as director of the Seminar for Psychoanalytic Therapy from 1924 to 1930, did much to transform psychoanalysis from enthusiastic amateurism to professional competence and a body of systematic theory. Later, especially in *Character Analysis*, Reich made major contributions to the theory and practice of therapy. His insight that both psychological traits of character and also physical habits of posture or reaction are motivated by and reflect people's need to defend themselves against threatening thoughts or feelings released psychoanalysis from its narrower definitions of neurosis and its preoccupation with purely verbal methods of therapy. His 'vegetable therapy', working directly with the body, made possible the subsequent therapeutic advances of Frederick Perls (in Gestalt therapy) and Alexander Lowen (in bioenergetics).

Reich did his own insights a disservice by insisting on presenting them in quasi-scientific language, by seeking for physical instantiations of psychological entities (most notably the widely ridiculed 'orgone energy'), and by presenting 'proofs' that travestied the scientific method. Had he not so persistently followed

Freud down this mistaken path, he would have avoided much of the criticism that eventually lead to the decline of his own life and sanity.

Rescorla, Robert Arthur

Born: 1940, Pittsburgh, Pennsylvania, USA **Nat:** American **Ints:** Experimental analysis of behaviour, experimental psychology **Educ:** BA Swarthmore College, 1962; PhD University of Pennsylvania, 1966 **Appts & awards:** APA Division 3, Executive Committee, 1980–3, President, 1985; Psychonomic Society, Governing Board, 1980–5, Publication Board, 1982–7, Chairman, 1985–7; Eastern Psychological Association, Board of Directors, 1983–6; Guggenheim Fellow, 1984–5; AAAS Member of Nominating Committee (Psychology), 1985–7; Chairman of Section J 1988–9; Society of Experimental Psychologists, 1985– ; Professor, Chairman, Department of Psychology, University of Pennsylvania, 1986– ; Consultant Editor: *Journal of Experimental Psychology: Animal Behavior Processes*, 1976– , *Psychological Review*, 1982–

Principal publications

1967 Pavlovian conditioning and its proper control procedures. *Psychological Review*, 74, 71–80.
1967 Two-process learning theory: Relationships between Pavlovian conditioning and instrumental learning. *Psychological Review*, 74, 151–72 (with R.L. Solomon).
1968 Probability of shock in the absence of CS in fear conditioning. *Journal of Comparative and Physiological Psychology*, 66, 1–5.
1969 Pavlovian controlled inhibition. *Psychological Bulletin*, 72, 77–94.
1972 A theory of Pavlovian conditioning: Variations in the effectiveness of reinforcement and nonreinforcement. In A. Black and W.F. Prokasy (eds), *Classical Conditioning II*. Appleton-Century-Crofts (with A.R. Wagner).
1976 Behavioral approaches to the study of learning. In E. Bennett and M.R. Rosenzweig (eds), *Neural Mechanisms of Learning and Memory*. MIT Press (with P.C. Holland).
1978 Some implications of a cognitive perspective on Pavlovian conditioning. In H. Fowler, W.K. Honig and S. Hulse (eds), *Cognitive Aspects of Animal Behavior*. Erlbaum.
1980 *Pavlovian Second-Order Conditioning: Studies in Associative Learning*. Erlbaum.
1981 Simultaneous associations. In P. Harzem and

M. Zeiler (eds), *Advances in the Analysis of Behavior*, vol. 2. Wiley.
1985 Contextual learning in Pavlovian conditioning. In P.D. Balsam and A. Tomie (eds), *Context and Learning*. Erlbaum (with P.J. Durlach and J.W. Grau).
1985 Conditioned inhibition and facilitation. In R.R. Miller and N.S. Spear (eds), *Conditioned Inhibition*. Erlbaum.
1990 Associative learning in animals: Asch's influence. In I. Rock (ed.), *Cognition and Social Psychology: Essays in Honor of Solomon E. Asch*. Erlbaum.
1994 A note on depression of instrumental responding after one trial of outcome devaluation. *Quarterly Journal of Experimental Psychology*, 47B, 27–37.

Further reading

Kop, P.F.M. and De Klerk, L.F.W. (1994) Influential mathematical models in the psychology of learning. In M.A. Croon and F.J.R. Van de Vijver (eds), *Viability of Mathematical Models in the Social and Behavioral Sciences*. Swets & Zeitlinger.
Mackintosh, N. (ed.) (1994) *Animal Learning and Cognition*. Academic Press.

Rescorla's contributions to psychology have centred on the study of elementary learning processes in non-human organisms. Most of his efforts have gone into understanding associative processes as exemplified by **Pavlov**ian conditioning. One can identify three major concerns in his work. The first is with the conditions which produce associative learning. This led to the development of the contingency theory of conditioning and to its molecular analysis in terms of the Rescorla–Wagner model of Pavlovian conditioning. The second concern has been with the contents of learning, with what actually gets associated. This interest led him to the study of second-order conditioning and to the development of analytic techniques for dissecting how events are encoded as part of an association. It also led to studies with colleagues on the learning which goes on within an event. The third interest is with how learning evidences itself in behaviour. This led to the development of various procedures for detecting underlying associations, including observational procedures. He has approached these three problems most extensively in the study of elementary associations in which the organism learns the Pavlovian relation among two events. He has also conducted similar studies of the

Pavlovian relations among multiple events as well as the learning of instrumental, goal-directed behaviour.

Reuchlin, Maurice Gaston Jean

Born: 1920, Marseille, Bouches-du-Rhone, France *Nat:* French *Ints:* Counselling, evaluation and measurement, history, philosophical and theoretical, personality and social *Educ:* Doctorat d'Etat, Université de Paris (Sorbonne), 1962 *Appts & awards:* Professor of Differential Psychology, Université René Descartes; Société Française de Psychologie: Treasurer, 1959, Executive Secretary, 1960–1, Deputy Chairman, 1964–5, Chairman, 1965–6, Council Member, 1967–71; Société de Biotypologie: Executive Secretary, 1956–66, Chairman, 1966–74; Hon. Member, Spanish Society of Psychology, 1975– ; Hon. doctorates, University of Louvain, 1979, University of Geneva, 1985; Associate, Académie Royale des Sciences, des Lettres et des Beaux-Arts de Belgique, 1984– ; Co-Editor, *Le Travail Humain*, 1959– ; Editor, *L'Orientation Scolaire et Professionnelle*, 1972–84; Editorial Board, *L'Orientation Scolaire et Professionnelle*, *Enfance*, *L'Année Psychologique*, *Journal de Psychologie Normale et Pathologique*, *Biométrie Humaine*, *Monographies Françaises de Psychologie*, *Revue Française de Pédagogie*

Principal publications

1957 *Histoire de la Psychologie*. Presses Universitaires de France (reprinted, 1984).

1962 *Les Methodes Quantitatives en Psychologie*. Presses Universitaires de France (reprinted, 1975).

1969 *La Psychologie Différentielle*. Presses Universitaires de France (reprinted, 1985).

1973 Formalisation et réalisation dans la pensée naturelle: une hypothèse. *Journal de Psychologie*, 70, 389–408.

1976 *Précis de Statistique*. Presses Universitaires de France (reprinted, 1982).

1977 *Psychologie*. Presses Universitaires de France (reprinted, 1984).

1977 Epreuves d'hypothèse nulle et inférence fiduciaire en psychologie. *Journal de Psychologie*, 74, 277–92.

1978 Processus vicariants et différences individuelles. *Journal de Psychologie*, 75, 133–45.

1978 Un essai d'analyse de la distinction 'psychologie en laboratoire' – 'psychologie sur le terrain'. *Le Travail Humain*, 41, 319–24.

1980 Théories en psychologie, explication et interprétation psychologiques. In M. Richelle and X. Séron (eds), *L'Explication en Psychologie*. Presses Universitaires de France.

1981 Options fondamentales et options superficielles. *Revue de Psychologie Appliquée*, 31, 97–115.

1981 Apports de la psychologie différentielle à la psychologie générale. *Journal de Psychologie*, 78, 377–95.

1981 Aspects scientifiques et aspects sociaux de la diversité humaine. *Bulletin de Psychologie*, 35, 285–90.

1982 Croisées de chemins. In P. Fraisse (ed.), *La Psychologie de Demain*. Presses Universitaires de France.

1984 Psychologie differentielle et psychologie sociale experimentale. *L'Année Psychologique*, 84, 267–95, 411–32.

Further reading

Saklofske, D.H. and Zeidner, M. (eds) (1995) *International Handbook of Personality and Intelligence: Perspectives on Individual Differences*. Plenum.

Reuchlin's first encounter with psychology took place while training to become a professional guidance counsellor. Professor H. Pieron encouraged him to pursue an interest in psychology and offered an opportunity to conduct research in counselling. This led Reuchlin to develop tests designed to be specific to counselling psychology and their study by methods of factor analysis. While a great deal of his career has been concerned with teaching and researching in counselling psychology, he always felt the need to place issues related to counselling within the larger framework of the action of the educational system as a whole. His interests turned to psycho-socio-pedagogical surveys covering large numbers of subjects and variables. At the same time, theoretical interests began to occupy a greater and eventually dominant part of his professional activity. Differential psychology became his academic specialization.

Reuchlin proposed that the study of individual differences could serve as a means of investigating the general processes underlying their occurrence, and he used this idea in his studies of **Piaget**'s theories. He founded the Laboratory of Differential Psychology at the CNRS, where a number of researchers have pursued this goal. He also made important contributions to methodology, developing a critical examination of the notions underlying quantitative methods (including statistics) in psychology. He tried to clarify the concept of levels of measurement by describing systematically the connections between mathematicians' formalisms and the information psychologists describe or analyse using the same formalisms. On a more general level, he is the author of several historical and epistemological works.

Rhine, Joseph Banks

Born: 1895, Pennsylvania, USA **Died:** 1980, North Carolina, USA **Nat:** American **Ints:** Experimental, philosophical **Educ:** BA University of Chicago, 1922; MS University of Chicago, 1923; PhD University of Chicago, 1925 **Appts & awards:** Instructor, University of West Virginia and Thompson Institute; Duke University: Hon. Postdoctoral Fellow, Professor; Director, Foundation for Research on the Nature of Man; President, Society for Psychical Research; Editor: *Journal of Parapsychology*, *Parapsychology Today*, 1968; Co-Editor: *Citadel, Progress in Parapsychology*, 1971

Principal publications

1934   *Extra-Sensory Perception.* Boston Society for Physical Research.
1937   *New Frontiers of the Mind.* Farrar & Rinehart.
1940   *Extra-Sensory Perception after 60 Years.* Bruce Humphries (with J.G. Pratt, B.M. Smith, C.E. Stuart and J.A. Greenwood).
1942   A confirmatory study of salience in precognition tests. *Journal of Parapsychology*, 6, 190–219 (with B. Humphrey).
1943   The psychokinetic effect: I. The first experiment. *Journal of Parapsychology*, 7, 20–43 (with L.E. Rhine).
1945   Telepathy and clairvoyance reconsidered. *Journal of Parapsychology*, 9, 176–93.
1951   Telepathy and human personality. *Journal of Parapsychology*, 15, 6–39.
1953   *New World of the Mind.* William Sloane.
1956   Research on spirit survival re-examined. *Journal of Parapsychology*, 20, 121–31.
1957   *Parapsychology.* Thomas (with J.G. Pratt)
1960   On parapsychology and the nature of man. In S. Hook (ed.), *Dimensions of Mind.* New York University Press.
1969   Psi-missing re-examined. *Journal of Parapsychology*, 33, 136–57.
1975   Psi methods re-examined. *Journal of Parapsychology*, 39, 38–58.
1977   History of experimental studies. In B.B. Wolman (ed.), *Handbook of Parapsychology.* Van Nostrand Reinhold.

1978   A search for the nature of mind. In T.S. Krawiec (ed.), *The Psychologists,* vol. 3. Clinical Publishing (with L.E. Rhine).

Further reading

Beloff, J. (1989) The Rhine legacy. Philosophical Psychology, 2, 231–9.
Berger, A.S. (1988) *Lives and Letters in American Parapsychology: A Biographical History,* 1850–1987. McFarland.

J.B. Rhine, searching for scientific evidence on the distinctive quality of life, turned from botany to psychical research – a field where, in the 1920s, case reports were impressive but experimental evidence was sparse. He thereafter devoted himself to experimentation in psychical research, which he renamed parapsychology. His experiments used statistics to evaluate responses to concealed, randomized 'targets'. Responses identified targets at levels not explicable by perception, inference or chance. He coined the term 'extrasensory perception' (ESP) to designate such extra-chance correspondences, including (1) targets known to one (clairvoyance), (2) targets known to someone (either clairvoyance or telepathy) and (3) targets selected after responses (precognition).

In ESP an individual receives information paranormally. Rhine next investigated the converse, where an individual imposes a change paranormally on something external. He named this psychokinesis (PK), direct influence upon external objects or events without muscular or other body intervention. His initial example was influencing the fall of dice.

When critics suggested methodological loopholes, Rhine's invariable response was to tighten the methods and eliminate the loopholes. He and his co-workers found extra-chance success, under tightly controlled conditions, for clairvoyance, precognition and PK. Rhine argued that all evidence for telepathy or spirited survival could be reduced to these three processes. He considered psi (ESP and PK) non-physical because neither distance nor any physical variable investigated, like electromagnetic shielding, influenced the results (except as subjects felt challenged or discouraged). He emphasized psychological factors in psi success, such as a pleasant, challenging interpersonal atmosphere, and lack of boredom.

Rhine gave many parapsychologists their initial training. His popular lectures and books were persuasive, but his claims remained controversial among scientists who read the popular but not the technical reports.

GERTRUDE R. SCHMEIDLER

Ribot, Théodule-Armand

Born: 1839, Guingamp, France **Died:** 1916, Paris, France **Nat:** French **Ints:** Pathology, physiological and evolutionary psychology **Educ:** Ecole normale, Paris, 1862–65, Teacher's Licence Salpêtrière Hospital, Paris **Appts & awards:** Chair of Experimental Psychology, Collège de France, Paris, 1888; Founder and First Editor, *Revue Philosophique*, 1876; Editorial Board, *L'Année Psychologique*, 1894

Principal publications

1873   *L'Hérédité Psychologique.*
1875   *La Psychologie Anglaise Contemporaine.*
1879   *La Psychologie Allemande Contemporaine.*
1881   *Maladies de la Mémoire.* Baillière.
1883   *Maladies de la Volonté.* Alcan.
1885   *Maladies de la Personnalité.* Alcan.

Further reading

Centenaire de Th. Ribot, 1839–9: Jubilé de la Psychologie Scientifique Française. Alcan.
Hearnshaw, L. (1987) *The Shaping of Modern Psychology.* Routledge.
Janet, P. (1901) L'Oeuvre psychologique de Th. Ribot. *Journal de Psychologie Normale et Pathologique*, 12, 268–82.

Ribot, who is usually described as the founder of scientific psychology in France, was born in the small town of Guingamp in Brittany in 1839. Between the years 1862 and 1865 he studied at the Ecole Normale in Paris, where his training as a philosopher qualified him to teach philosophy in a French lycée. He became an avid reader and admirer of Herbert Spencer, and also became acquainted with the work of other evolutionary thinkers such as Lamarck, Charles **Darwin** and Haeckel. His reading also included the work of Lewes, **Maudsley**, Tuke, **Bain** and **Galton**, and he was an admirer of the French psychological historian Hippolyte Taine. His school teaching career was relatively short, for he left the provinces in 1872, and went back to Paris. He held no post until 1885, but devoted himself to writing, and over a period of three or four years he followed courses in histology and physiology. In addition, at the Salpêtrière hospital in Paris he attended the famous lessons of the neurologist Jean-Martin **Charcot**, where he became acquainted with Charcot's studies of hysteria and learned the method of clinical analysis. In 1885 he was made director of a course in experimental psychology at the Faculty of Letters, and in 1888 he was appointed to the Chair of Experimental Psychology at the Collège de France. A laboratory was set up in the new Sorbonne building, but as Ribot had little interest in practising experiments himself he appointed Beaunis as director.

Ribot's main aim was to establish psychology as an independent science, to separate it from ethics and philosophy, make it objective, and bring it closer to the biological sciences. His general stance was therefore anti-metaphysical, and he subscribed to a general positivist philosophy of science. According to this philosophy, only observations and experiments could provide scientific status to psychology. One of Ribot's early works, *L'Hérédité Psychologique* (his doctoral thesis), embodies several aspects of his thinking that became elaborated in later works. For example, he insisted upon the biological basis of psychology, and extended the range of phenomena that could be explained by heredity to include psychological aspects, thereby introducing a relatively new domain into psychology itself. He also took a broad evolutionary perspective of behaviour and development of societies. His frequent references to Darwin and Spencer confirm his support for evolutionary ideas. Specifically, Ribot was responsible for the introduction in France of Spencer's theory of 'dissolution', the inverse process of evolution. Ribot used this to furnish explanations of the disorders of personality, of attention, of the will and of memory. In connection with the last, 'dissolution' became known as 'la loi de Ribot' (Ribot's law). In his strong interest in the pathological, Ribot was both following and leading in this direction in French psychology, influenced by the psychiatric tradition established by Pinel and Esquirol. It was argued by Ribot that the study of the pathological threw light on the 'normal' states. *L'Hérédité Psychologique*, like many of his publications, became popular among academic and lay alike, and it was mainly with the latter in mind that Ribot wrote. His reviews of current psychological thought in England and Germany were published as *La Psychologie Anglaise Contemporaine* and *La Psychologie Allemande Contemporaine*. Thus he was a great synthesizer and disseminator of scientific knowledge, not only in France, but in the countries into whose languages his works were translated. He can be seen as a major figure in nineteenth-century

French psychology by virtue of his own work, the status which he brought to French psychology, and the patronage that he bestowed on aspiring psychologists.

DIANA FABER

Rivers, William Halse Rivers

Born: 1864, Chatham, England **Died:** 1922, Cambridge, England **Nat:** British **Ints:** Clinical psychology, cross-cultural psychology, physiological psychology **Educ:** MB St Bartholemew's Hospital, University of London 1886; MD London, Fellow of Royal College of Physicians, 1888 **Appts & awards:** Clinical Assistant, Bethlem Royal Hospital, 1892; Lecturer on Experimental Psychology, University College, London, 1892; Assistant Lecturer on Mental Disease, Guys Hospital, 1893; Lecturer on physiology of sense organs, Cambridge University, 1893; Hon. MA, Lecturer in Physiological and Experimental Psychology, Cambridge University, 1897; Fellow, St John's College, Cambridge, 1902; FRS, 1908; Physician, Maghull Military Hospital, 1915; Captain, RAMC, Senior Psychiatrist, Craiglockhart Hospital for Officers, 1916; Psychologist to the Royal Flying Corp, Central Hospital, Hampstead, 1917; Praelector of Natural Science Studies, St John's College, Cambridge, 1919

Principal publications

1901   Introduction. Vision. Both in A.C. Haddon (ed.), *Reports of the Cambridge Anthropological Expedition to Torres Straits*, vol. 2, pt 1. Cambridge University Press.

1906   *The Todas*. Macmillan.

1908   *The Influence of Alcohol and other Drugs on Fatigue*. E. Arnold.

1908   A human experiment in nerve division. *Brain*, 31, 323–450 (with Henry Head).

1914   *Kinship and Social Organization*. Constable.

1914   *The History of Melanesian Society* (Percy Sladen Trust Expedition to Melanesia, 2 vols). Cambridge University Press

1918   *Dreams and Primitive Culture*. Manchester University Press/Longmans Green.

1920   *Instinct and the Unconscious*. Cambridge University Press.

1923   *Conflict and Dream*. Kegan Paul, Trench & Trübner.

1923   *Psychology and Politics*. Kegan Paul, Trench & Trübner.

1924   *Medicine, Magic, and Religion* (Fitzpatrick Lectures before the Royal College of Physicians in London, 1915, 1916). Kegan Paul, Trench & Trübner.

1926   *Psychology and Ethnology*. Kegan Paul, Trench & Trübner.

Further reading

Haddon, A.C., Bartlett, F.C. and Fegan, E.S. Obituary. William Halse Rivers Rivers, M.D., F.R.S., President of the Royal Anthropological Institute, born 1864, died June 4th, 1922. *Man*, 22, 97–104.

Langham, I. (1981) *The Building of British Social Anthropology. W.H.R. Rivers and his Cambridge Disciples in the Development of Kinship Studies, 1898–1931*. D. Reidel

Slobodin, R. (1978) *W.H.R. Rivers*. Columbia University Press

Rivers's relatively early death, and the rise to dominance of US psychology, for many years obscured the significance of his work and role in the discipline's development. Following early medical training under Hughlings **Jackson** (whose influence on his work was profound) and a short spell in Jena under T. Ziehen, Rivers directed both James **Sully**'s new psychological laboratory at University College, London, and the newly founded laboratory at Cambridge University, where he had been earlier appointed to teach sensory perception by Michael Foster. His psychological work falls into three broad categories. Physiological psychology, which ranged from perception to psychoneurology and the effects of alcohol and other substances on fatigue, was Rivers's first area of research and one which he pursued for many years. He was influenced by both Ewald **Hering**'s work and Hughlings Jackson's neurological theories. The latter led him to differentiate between 'protopathic' and 'epicritic' levels of neural organization, the first of these being characterized by 'all or nothing' responses, the latter by continuous quantitative change. The most famous research concerning this was that conducted with Henry Head on the regeneration of sensation in the experimentally severed nerves of Head's left forearm, begun in 1903. The protopathic level is seen as more fundamental, while the higher processes are epicritic in character. Secondly, Rivers's interest in perception enabled him to undertake the first cross-cultural experimental research on perceptual phenomena during the 1898 Torres Strait Expedition, work which largely challenged notions of 'primitive superiority' in such functioning (derived ultimately from Herbert

Spencer), although it also raised questions about apparent deficiency in perception of blue hues among his respondents. During the expedition he also oversaw the research by his students C.S. Myers and W. **McDougall** on other psychophysical phenomena. He continued his cross-cultural studies of psychophysical performance, notably among the Todas in southern India. Thirdly, his physiological work continued prior to World War I in research on fatigue, and his reputation in this area facilitated his appointments to treat shell-shock victims, first at Maghull Military Hospital, Lancashire, as a civilian and then as a captain in the Royal Army Medical Corps at Craiglockhart Hospital for Officers near Edinburgh (where he treated the poet and writer Siegfried Sassoon). This psychiatric work brought psychoanalytic ideas to Rivers's attention. While departing from **Freud** and **Jung** on such issues as the universality of symbolism and the necessarily sexual character of dreams, he acknowledged the importance of the unconscious and recognized the operation of the main Freudian defence mechanisms and dream processes, which he expounded in the influential *Instinct and the Unconscious*. This work did much to ensure psychoanalysis a sympathetic hearing in inter-war Britain, coming as it did from such a, by then, authoritative figure. He also strongly rejected the notion of 'primitive mind' and, while rarely addressing the topic directly, was clearly unsympathetic to racialist doctrines. (The fatigue studies themselves also initiated the further pioneering work in industrial and applied psychology undertaken by C.S. Myers during World War I, under the auspices of the Industrial Fatigue Research Board, and ultimately led to the establishment of the National Institute of Industrial Psychology.)

Even this omits his anthropological work, which played a central part in the creation of modern British (and indeed US) anthropology. The Torres Strait Expedition awakened an interest in the topic which only deepened during the remainder of his life, and resulted in numerous subsequent travels and expeditions, notably to southern India, Melanesia and Egypt. He continued to undertake cross-cultural psychological research, but his main contribution was his development of a methodology for studying kinship and social organization, abandoning the previously prevalent 'evolutionary' orientation of British anthropology for a 'historical' and proto-functionalist approach. This lies beyond the purview of the present work, but it should be noted that in this capacity

he profoundly influenced figures such as A. Radcliffe Brown and other doyens of the post-Great War 'functionalist' schools. Under the influence of his friend, the Australian anatomist and palaeontologist G. Elliot Smith, Rivers's later accepted the now discredited 'diffusionist' position. (Some controversy surrounds this, since Elliot Smith is suspected by some of biased editing of the posthumously published works.)

For Rivers the human sciences were a unity, and he always sought to interrelate the physiological, psychological and social levels in his own work; but his efforts to maintain this unity proved in vain as the new 'structuralist-functionalist' anthropologists – notably B. Malinowski, Radcliffe Brown (whom Rivers taught) and E.E. Evans Pritchard – sought to create an autonomous disciplinary territory of their own. His pupil F.C. **Bartlett**'s first work, *Psychology and Primitive Culture* (1923), must be viewed as being written very much with this concern in mind. As a co-founder of the BPS, teacher and colleague of Myers and McDougall, and popular central figure in both the discipline and wider academic circles, Rivers exerted enormous background influence over psychology's early years in Britain, maintaining a breadth of vision and undogmatic flexibility which counterbalanced more narrowly focused or dogmatic trends. Areas as varied as cross-cultural studies, applied psychology (via his fatigure work) and psychotherapy owe much to his efforts, both in Britain and abroad.

By the end of his life Rivers had ideologically moved towards the left, and had agreed to stand as a Labour candidate for London University in the 1922 General Election, but this was pre-empted by his somewhat premature and unexpected death. (H.G. Wells stood instead and was roundly defeated.)

GRAHAM RICHARDS

Rizzolatti, Giacomo
Born: 1937, Kiev, USSR **Nat:** Russian **Ints:** Experimental psychology, neuropsychology, physiological and comparative psychology **Educ:** MB University of Padua, 1961; PhD University of Padua, 1964 **Appts & awards:** Professor of Human Physiology, Instituto di Fisiologia Umana, Universita di Parma; Award, Italian Neurophysiological Society, 1965; Italy Libera Docenza, University of Rome, 1969; IBRO-UNESCO Fellowship, 1970; Fulbright Scholarship, 1980; Golgi Award for Studies in

Neurophysiology, Academia Nazionale dei Lincei, Rome, 1982; President, Italian Neuropsychological Society, 1982–5; President, European Brain Behaviour Society, 1984–6; Editorial Board, *Behavioral Brain Research*, *Neuropsychologia*, *Experimental Brain Research*

Principal publications

1967 Microelectrode analysis of transfer of visual information by the corpus callosum. *Archives Italiennes de Biologie*, 105, 583–96 (with G. Berlucchi and M.S. Gazzaniga).

1971 Simple reaction times of ipsilateral and contralateral hand to lateralized visual stimuli. *Brain*, 94, 419–30 (with G. Berlucchi, W. Heron, R. Hyman and C. Umilta).

1971 Opposite superiorities of the right and left cerebral hemispheres in discriminative reaction time to physiognomical and alphabetical material. *Brain*, 94, 431–42 (with G. Berlucchi and C. Umilta).

1974 Inhibitory effect of remote visual stimuli on the visual responses of the cat superior colliculus: spatial and temporal factors. *Journal of Neurophysiology*, 37, 1262–75 (with R. Camarda, L.A. Grupp and M. Pisa).

1977 Spatial compatability and anatomical factors in simple and choice reaction time. *Neuropsychologia*, 15, 195–302 (with G.P. Anzola, G. Bertoloni and H.A. Buchtel).

1979 Interference of concomitant motor and verbal tasks on simple reaction time: a hemispheric difference. *Neuropsychologia*, 17, 323–30 (with G. Bertoloni and H.A. Buchtel).

1981 Afferent properties of periarcuate neurons in Macaque monkeys. II. Visual responses. *Behavioural Brain Research*, 2, 147–63 (with C. Scandolara, M. Matelli and M. Gentilucci).

1983 Deficits in attention and movement following the removal of postarcuate (area 6) and prearcuate (area 8) cortex in Macaque monkeys. *Brain*, 106, 655–73 (with M. Matelli and G. Pavesi).

1985 Evidence of interhemispheric transmission in laterality effects. *Neuropsychologia*, 23, 203–14 (with C. Umilta, G.P. Anzola, G. Luppino and C. Porro).

Further reading

Boller, F. *et al.* (eds) (1988) *Handbook of Neuropsychology, Vol. 1.* Elsevier Science.

Robertson, I.H. and Marshall, J.C. (eds) (1933) *Unilateral Neglect: Clinical and Experimental Studies.* Erlbaum.

Umilta, C. and Moscovitch, M. (eds) (1994) *Attention and Performance 15: Conscious and Nonconscious Information Processing.* MIT Press.

There are three fields all belonging to neuropsychology to which Rizzolatti has contributed. The first is hemispheric specialization. In 1967 **Berlucchi**, **Gazzaniga** and Rizzolatti discovered that in the cat, visual cortical areas of the two hemispheres are connected one with another exclusively along the vertical meridian. Visual information outside this strip has to reach the association areas in order to cross the corpus callosum. Since these areas are differently specialized in the right and left hemisphere of man, Rizzolatti thought (Rizzolatti, Berlucchi and Umilta, 1971) that by using tachistoscopically presented lateralized stimuli he could study hemispheric differences in normal human subjects. With Berlucchi and Umilta he showed a right hemisphere superiority for faces and a left hemisphere superiority for letters. After this paper, he was involved in several studies aiming to measure the time necessary for sensory information to cross the corpus callosum, to assess the importance of anatomical and cognitive factors in reaction times and in testing models of hemispheric specialization.

The second field in which he is interested is space perception. His main contribution here was that the space around the body, peripersonal space, is coded differently from far space. He reached this conclusion first on the basis of single neuron recordings from the frontal lobe and afterwards on the basis of lesion experiments. In the monkey an ablation of the inferior area-6 produces deficits in the peripersonal space but not in the far space, whereas a lesion of the frontal eye fields impairs predominantly the perception of far space (Rizzolatti, Matelli and Pavesi, 1983).

Finally, since his student years with Moruzzi, he has been interested in attention. In this field his contributions concern the role of superior colliculus and of the premotor areas in spatial attention. He summarized his work in this field by proposing that spatial attention is a distributed system mediated by several circuits to a large extent independent of one another and that this type of attention is strictly linked with the organization of movements in space.

Roback, Abraham Aaron

Born: 1890, Poland **Died:** 1965, Cambridge, Massachusetts, USA **Nat:** Polish **Ints:** History of psychology, personality and social psychology **Educ:** BA McGill University, 1912; AM Harvard University, 1913; PhD Harvard University, 1917 **Appts & awards:** Instructor,

University of Pittsburgh, 1917; Professor, Northeastern University, 1918–20; Special Lecturer, Clark University, 1920; Instructor, Harvard University, 1920–3; Fellow, National Research Council, 1923–5; Instructor, MIT, 1926; Lecturer, Commonwealth of Massachusetts, University Extension Division, 1926–48, 1959–65; Professor and Head of Psychology Department, Emerson College, 1949–59; Fellow: APA, AAAS; Hon. Fellow and Governor, Jewish Academy of Arts and Sciences; First Editor, *Canadian Jewish Chronicle*; Editorial Advisory Board, *Aufbau*

Principal publications

1917   Psychology as applied to the natural sciences. *Journal of Applied Psychology*, 1, 144–60.
1918   The interference of will-impulses. *Psychological Monographs*, no. 25.
1919   The Freudian doctrine of lapses and its failings. *American Journal of Psychology*, 30, 274–90.
1920   The applied psychology of names. *Journal of Applied Psychology*, 4, 348–60.
1921   Subjective tests vs. objective tests. *Journal of Educational Psychology*, 12, 439–44.
1922   Intelligence and behavior. *Psychological Review*, 29, 54–62.
1923   *Psychology*. Sci-Art.
1923   *Behaviorism and Psychology*. Sci-Art.
1927   *The Psychology of Character*. Harcourt Brace.
1929   *Jewish Influence in Modern Thought*. Sci-Art.
1934   Personalysis: A study in method. *Journal of Personality*, 3, 144–56.
1936–7   Fifty years of the dissociation school. *Journal of Abnormal and Social Psychology*, 32, 131–7.
1952   *A History of American Psychology*. Library Publishers.

Further reading

Allport, C.W. (1965) Aaron Abraham Roback. *American Journal of Psychology*, 78, 689–90.

Roback's contributions are principally in two fields: psychology and the Yiddish language. Many of his writings in the latter field centre on ethnopsychological issues. He wrote thirty books, and twenty-two of these were on psychological topics. His orientation was broadly humanistic, with an emphasis on character analysis. In this regard *The Psychology of Character* (1927) is his book of most enduring value, and was the first such book published in English. It both presents a history of characterology and states a theory of character. Roback's

second interest was history of psychology. His *A History of American Psychology* (1952), also a 'first', remains a valuable contribution, especially because it rescues from oblivion early American contributors to the development of psychology. Roback was the principal collaborator or consultant and contributor to seven dictionaries and encyclopedias. His books have been translated into half a dozen languages. His enormous output of publications in the periodicals literature, some two thousand items, consisted mainly of English, Yiddish and German articles on the Yiddish language and Jewish literature and folklore.

Rodin, Judith

Born: 1944, Philadelphia, USA *Nat:* American *Ints:* Adult development and ageing, health, personality and social, Society for the Psychological Study of Social Issues *Educ:* AB University of Pennsylvania, 1966; PhD Columbia University 1970; Irvine NSF Postdoctoral Fellow, Neurobiology for Scientists *Appts & awards:* Woodrow Wilson Fellow, 1966–7; Columbia University Distinguished Faculty Fellow, 1967–70; AIR Creative Talents Dissertation Award, 1970; Yale University Junior Faculty Fellow, 1974–5; APA, Distinguished Scientific Award, 1977, Outstanding Health Psychology Contribution Award, 1980; Stanford Medical School, McCormick Distinguished Lectureship, 1982; EPA, President, 1982–3; APA Division 38, President, 1982–3; Scientific Advisor for the Health Program and Chairman, John D. and Catherine T. McArthur Research Network, Health Behavior, 1984– ; Katz–Newcomb Lecture, 1984; President, Professor of Psychology, Professor of Medicine and Psychiatry, University of Pennsylvania 1994–; Associate Editor: *Personality and Social Psychology Bulletin*, 1976–9, *Environmental Psychology and Nonverbal Behavior*, 1977–9, *International Journal of Obesity*, 1977– , *Journal of Personality and Social Psychology*, 1978–9, *Journal of Social Issues*, 1978–80, *Behavioral Medicine*, 1978–84, *Cognitive Theory and Research*, 1979–80, *Health Psychology*, 1981– ; Chief Editor, *Appetite*, 1979

Principal publications

1974   *Obese Humans and Rats*. Erlbaum/Halsted (with S. Schachter).
1976   Externality in the nonobese: The effects of environmental responsiveness on weight. *Journal*

of Personal and Social Psychology, 33, 338–44 (with J. Slochower).

1976 The effects of choice and enhanced personal responsibility for the aged: A field experiment in an institutional setting. *Journal of Personality and Social Psychology*, 34, 191–8 (with E. Langer).

1977 Long-term effects of a control-relevant intervention with the institutionalized aged. *Journal of Personality and Social Psychology*, 35, 897–902 (with E. Langer).

1981 The current status of the internal external obesity hypothesis: What went wrong. *American Psychologist*, 36, 361–72.

1982 *Exploding the Weight Myths*. London Century Press.

1982 *Health Behavior and Aging*. National Academy Press (with D.L. Parron and F. Solomon).

1982 Smoking and its effects on body weight and the system of calorie regulation. *Journal of Clinical Nutrition*, 35, 366–80 (with J. Wack).

1985 Insulin levels, hunger and food intake: An example of feedback loops in body weight regulation. *Health Psychology*, 4, 1–18.

1985 Women and weight: A normative dis-content. In *Nebraska Symposium on Motivation* (with L. Silberstein and R. Striegel-Moore).

1987 *A Distinctive Approach to Psychological Research: The Influence of Stanley Schachter*. Erlbaum (with G. Stone, S. Weiss, J. Matarazzo, and N. Miller).

1990 *Self-Directedness through the Life Course*. Erlbaum (with C. Schooler and W. Schaie).

1991 *Women and New Reproductive Technologies: Medical, Psychological, Legal and Ethical Dilemmas*. Erlbaum (with A. Collins).

1992 *Body Traps*. William Morrow.

Further reading

Brownell, K.D. and Fairburn, C.G. (eds) (1995) *Eating Disorders and Obesity: A Comprehensive Handbook*, Guilford.

Steptoe, A. and Wardle, J. (eds) (1994) *Psychosocial Processes and Health: A Reader*. Cambridge University Press.

Judith Rodin's first major contribution has been to suggest that a psycho-social biological approach can be used effectively to understand numerous aspects of human behaviour. The most obvious application is health psychology, and much of her theoretical work is cited there. However, there is no doubt that many affective and behavioural responses can be best understood by considering the interaction between social-cultural variables, individual difference

factors, and physiological status, and her influence is not confined to the psychology of health behaviours.

A second major contribution has been to add theory-driven intervention research to several areas in gerontology and health, based on the construct of competence or self-determination. Especially significant has been her work with **Langer**, showing the ability to increase feelings of control in infirm, aged people in nursing homes, with substantial improvements in morbidity and mortality. Her interests have remained relatively stable over the years, although the particular substantive domain in which they have been expressed has changed: she continues to be concerned about the interaction between mind and body as it affects human behaviour.

Roe, Anne

Born: 1904, Denver, Colorado, USA ***Died:*** 1991, Tucson, Arizona, USA ***Nat:*** American ***Ints:*** Clinical, counselling, evaluation and measurement, personality and social ***Educ:*** BA University of Denver, 1923; MA University of Denver, 1925 ***Appts & awards:*** ABPP, Diplomate, Clinical Psychology, Board of Trustees, 1953–9; APA, Fellow, Divisions 2, 8, 12, 17, Board of Directors, 1962–5; President: APA Division 12, 1957–8, New England PA, 1962–5; Hon. MA, Harvard University, 1963; Hon. LHD, Lesley College; Hon. ScD, Kenyon College; Fellow, APGA, NVGA; American Academy of Arts and Sciences; numerous committee assignments. Richardson Creativity Award, APA, 1968; APA Division 12 Award for Distinguished Contributions to Psychology, 1972; Medal for Distinguished Service, Teachers College, Columbia University, 1977; Establishment of Anne Roe Award; Harvard Graduate School of Education, 1980; Leona E. Tyler Award, APA Division 17, 1984; Editorial Board, *Journal Applied Psychology*

Principal publications

1936 *Adult Intelligence*. Commonwealth Fund (with T. Weisenburg and K.E. McBride).

1939 *Quantitative Zoology*. McGraw-Hill (with G.C. Simpson).

1942 Intelligence in mental disorder. *Annals of the New York Academy of Sciences*, 42, 361–490 (with D. Shakow).

1944 Adult adjustment of children of alcoholic parents raised in foster homes. *Quarterly Journal of Studies on Alcohol*, 4, 517–22.

1953 *The Making of a Scientist.* Dodd Mead.

1956 *The Psychology of Occupations.* Wiley.

1957 Early determinants of vocational choice. *Journal of Counseling Psychology*, 4, 212–17.

1958 *Behavior and Evolution.* Yale University Press. (ed. with C.G. Simpson).

1964 *The Origin of Interests.* APGA Inquiry Studies no. 1 (with M. Siegelman).

1966 Psychology and the evolution of man. *Harvard Educational Review*, 36, 139–54.

1972 Perspectives on vocational development. In J.M. Whiteley and R.A. Resnikoff (eds), *Perspectives on Vocational Development.* APGA.

1972 Woman power: How is it different? In I. Berg (ed.), *Human Resources and Economic Welfare.* Columbia University Press.

Further reading

Brown, D. and Brooks, L. (1990) *Career Choice and Development: Applying Contemporary Theories to Practice* (2nd edn). Jossey-Bass.

Wrenn, R.L. (1992) Anne Roe (1904–1991). *American Psychologist*, 47, 1052–3.

After an intensive psychometric study of a group of adults for comparison with aphasics and hemiplegics without aphasia, with D. Shakow, Anne Roe completed a detailed study of intelligence in mental disorder, a pioneer examination of types among different varieties of mental disease. The clinical studies of men of superior performance were unique at the the time and had a major influence on later studies of creativity. She worked first with leading painters, then with leading research scientists (biologists, anthropologists, psychologists and physicists). These studies included long interviews covering early history, choice of career, developments of particular lines of work, intelligence and personality tests. With the scientists there was also a follow-up some fifteen years later, giving further details on their work and an extensive analysis of productivity over the years.

Her next important research venture was to examine the whole field of occupations from the perspective of a psychologist. This required the development of a classification of occupations which made psychological sense, and which has had a considerable impact, as well as an interpretation of choices and satisfactions in terms of personality theory and external circumstances. This resulted in a textbook on the psychology of occupations and later in a number of studies, including a theoretical statement of early determinants of occupational choice. Although only

parts of the theory have held up (not all have been studied), it stimulated new approaches. In studies with M. Siegelman she found it necessary to develop a parent–child relations questionnaire, which has been used in a number of studies. She developed a general formula covering major factors determining vocational or other choices. In an autobiographical piece she cites two other important contributions, both with C.G. Simpson, linking psychology with paleontology. The first was *Quantitative Zoology* (1939), a first text in the application of statistical methods to biological data which was comprehensible to non-mathematicians. The second was the convening of two conferences including biologists, anthropologists and psychologists, resulting in the book *Behavior and Evolution* (1958).

Rogers, Carl Ransom

Born: 1902, Oak Park, Illinois, USA *Nat:* American *Ints:* Educational psychology, humanistic psychology, psychotherapy, personality and social psychology, philosophical and theoretical psychology *Educ:* BA University of Wisconsin, 1924; MA Teachers College, Columbia University, 1928; PhD Teachers College, Columbia University, 1931 *Appts & awards:* Resident Fellow, Center for Studies of the Person; Vice-President, American Orthopsychiatric Association, 1941–2; President: American Association for Applied Psychology, 1944–45, APA 1946–7, American Academy of Psychotherapists, 1956–8; Nicholas Murray Butler Medal (Silver), Columbia University, 1955; APA Distinguished Scientific Contribution Award, 1956; Hon. DHL: Lawrence College, 1956, University of Santa Clara, 1971, Union for Experimenting Colleges and Universities, Cincinnati, 1984; Hon. D, Gonzaga University, 1968; Fellow, AAA&S, 1961– , Center for Advanced Study in the Behavioral Sciences, 1962–3; Humanist of the Year, American Humanist Association, 1964; Distinguished Contribution Award, American Pastoral Counselors Association, 1967; Award of Professional Achievement, American Board of Professional Psychology, 1968; APA Division 29, Distinguished Professional Psychologist Award, 1972; APA First Distinguished Professional Contribution Award, 1972; Hon. DSc: University of Cincinnati, 1974, Northwestern University, 1978; Hon. PhD, University of Hamburg, 1975; Hon. DSocSci, University of Leiden, 1975;

Principal publications

1951   *Client-Centred Therapy*. Houghton Mifflin.

1954   (ed.) *Psychotherapy and Personality Change*. University of Chicago Press (with R.F. Dymond).

1956   Some issues concerning the control of human behavior. (Symposium with B.F. Skinner.) *Science*, 124, 1057–66.

1957   The necessary and sufficient conditions of therapeutic personality change. *Journal of Consulting Psychology*, 21, 95–103.

1957   A note on the nature of man. *Journal of Counseling Psychology*, 4, 199–203.

1958   A process conception of psychotherapy. *American Psychologist*, 13, 142–9.

1959   A theory of therapy, personality and interpersonal relationships as developed in the client-centered framework. In S. Koch (ed.), *Psychology: A Study of a Science*, vol. 3, *Formulations of the Person and the Social Context*. McGraw-Hill.

1959   Persons or science (parts 1 and 2). *Pastoral Psychology*, 10, no. 92, no. 93.

1959   Toward a theory of creativity. In H. Anderson (ed.), *Creativity and Cultivation*. Harper & Brothers.

1961   *On Becoming a Person*. Houghton Mifflin.

1964   Toward a modern approach to values: The valuing process in the mature person. *Journal of Abnormal and Social Psychology*, 68, 160–7.

1980   *A Way of Being*. Houghton Mifflin.

1981   Building person-centered communities: The implications for the future. In A. Villoldo and K. Dychtwald (eds), *Millennium: Glimpses into the 21st Century*. Tarcher.

1983   *Freedom to Learn for the 80's*. Charles Merrill.

1984   One alternative to nuclear planetary suicide. In R. Levant and J. Shlien (eds), *Client-Centered Therapy and the Person-Centered Approach: New Directions in Theory, Research and Practice*. Praeger.

Further reading

Rogers, C.R. (1967) Autobiography. In E.G. Boring and G. Lindzey (eds), *A History of Psychology in Autobiography*, vol. 5. Appleton-Century-Crofts.

Smith, M.B. (1950) The phenomenological approach in personality theory: Some critical remarks. *Journal of Abnormal and Social Psychology*, 45, 516–22.

Carl Rogers was the middle child in a large, close-knit, religious family. His early interests in the natural sciences led him first to the study of agriculture at the University of Wisconsin. After two years he decided to enter the ministry.

Following a trip to China and the Philippines with the World Student Christian Federation, Rogers attended Union Theological Seminary, New York City, and later transferred to Teachers College, Columbia University, where he obtained a degree in clinical and educational psychology. As an intern at the Institute for Child Guidance, Rogers was impressed by the emphasis on eclectic psychoanalytic techniques and ideas, and much of his later work demonstrates this strong commitment to eclecticism. For example, he used a variety of research therapeutic techniques including projective tests (Rorschach and Thematic Apperception Test), personality inventories (such as the MMPI), rating scales and Q-technique. In 1928 he joined the staff of what was later to become the Rochester Guidance Center, and following a period of nine years as its director, he accepted a professorial position at Ohio State University (1940). In 1945 he accepted a professorship at the University of Chicago; there he directed the Counsel Center, where he elaborated his client-centred method of psychotherapy. In 1957 he moved to the University of Wisconsin, where he held positions in the departments of psychology and psychiatry. While at Wisconsin he used his approach and techniques with people with schizophrenia, but without the same level of success he had achieved with student populations while at Chicago. In 1964 he moved to La Jolla, California, where he joined the staff of the Western Behavioral Sciences Institute and later helped to found the Center for Studies of the Person.

Rogers is best known for the development of a method of psychotherapy called non-directive or person-centred, and for his pioneering research on the therapy process. As a theoretician Rogers is primarily concerned with the development and growth of the person, and consequently his theory of personality is not as structurally explicit as many others. Two concepts are fundamental to his theory: the organism and the self. The organism is the physical creature that actually experiences the world. The totality of experiences constitute the organism's phenomenal field. It is impossible to know another's phenomenal field except through empathic inference. Rogers argues that behaviour is a function not of external reality or of surrounding stimuli but of the phenomenal field. Within a phenomenological framework, it is necessary to determine how people can separate fact from fiction and construct a correct representation of reality. For Rogers, the only way to test reality is to check the correctness of the information on which one's hypothesis about the world is based against other sources of information. In other words the person uses sensory information to supplement information stored up from previous experiences. Through experience a part of the phenomenal field becomes differentiated – this is the self. The self is defined as the 'organized, consistent conceptual *Gestalt* composed of perceptions of the characteristics of the "I" or "me" and the perception of the relationship between the "I" or "me" to others and to various aspects of life, together with the values attached to these perceptions'. Rogers distinguishes between the self as it is (the self-structure) and the ideal self (what the person would like to be). The degree of congruence between the self and the organism determines maturity and psychological well-being. When the person's perceptions and interpretations reasonably reflect reality as perceived by others, the self and the organism are said to be congruent. When there is a significant discrepancy, people feel threatened and anxious and tend to think and behave in stereotypical or constricted ways. The organism is thought to have a single motivating force, the drive to self-actualization. Two important needs that are linked with the organism's drive to maintain and enhance itself are that for the positive regard of others and that for self-regard. In regarding the person as oriented towards growth, self-actualization and fulfilment, Rogers is similar to **Jung**, **Adler**, **Maslow** and **Horney**.

Rogers's chief concern is with understanding how incongruence develops and how self and organism can be made more congruent. In his person-centred psychotherapy, the therapist enters into an interpersonal relationship with the client rather than adopting a role of doctor (as in the doctor–patient model) or scientist (as in the scientist–subject model). Therapists are expected not to hide behind a professional facade but to let the client known their own thoughts and feelings. Accepting the thoughts and feelings of the client unconditionally allows the client to explore increasingly strange and novel feelings in themselves. Feeling safe is essential for the therapeutic process to work. Rogers came to the view that the therapeutic process is a model of all interpersonal relationships. He formulated a general theory of interpersonal relationships, which he summarized as follows. The theory assumes that if: (1) two people are minimally willing to be in contact, (2) each is able and minimally willing to communicate, and (3) contact continues over

time, then the greater the degree of congruence of experience and communication in one person the stronger the tendency towards reciprocal communication and mutual understanding. His client-centred (later called person-centred) therapy is distinctive in three ways. First, it is founded on a belief in the capacity and potential of the client. Second, the therapeutic relationship is seen as pivotal - everything follows from the quality of the person–therapist relationship. Third, there is a belief that the progress of therapy follows a predictable pattern based on the interpersonal characteristics of the person–therapist relationship: when certain conditions exist a certain process will occur.

Rogers was a pioneer in the scientific investigation of the therapeutic process. The confidentiality of therapy sessions had acted as a barrier to research and fostered the growth of a mystique about counselling and psychotherapy. Rogers introduced the practice of recording therapy sessions with the client's permission and demonstrated that this neither interfered with nor jeopardized the process or outcome. Having a permanent record of a therapy session made possible the systematic analysis of therapist–client dialogue and opened up ways of identifying complex relationships that could not be detected in a session itself or from therapy. Rogers applied content analysis procedures to classify and count a client's statements in order to explore hypotheses about a client's personality, self-concept and growth through the therapeutic process. This approach was to inform the development of widely used rating scales for the measurement of process and change during psychotherapy.

When Rogers began to publish and lecture on his person-centred approach, he was surprised at the level of controversy his ideas generated. Much of the early criticism was directed against his efforts to redefine the role of the 'patient', the perceived threat to the integrity of the therapy session by the use of recording devices, his relative neglect of the unconscious, and his efforts to demystify the psychotherapeutic process. Enduring criticisms concern the somewhat naive phenomenology underlying his theory of the person (Smith, 1950).

Rogers's numerous contributions can be summarized as follows. (1) He developed a mode of psychotherapy which is built around a growth model, rather than a medical one. This model is based on the hypothesis that the individual has within himself or herself the capacity for self-understanding and self-direction; it demonstrates that these capacities are released in a relationship with certain definable qualities; and it incorporates the view that the human organism is basically constructive and trustworthy. (2) He formulated a theory of the necessary and sufficient conditions which initiate a definable process in a therapeutic relationship and the changes in personality and behaviour which occur as a result of this process. (3) He developed an approach to therapy which is characterized by the terms 'non-directive', 'client-centred' and 'person-centred'. (4) He lifted the veil of mystery from psychotherapy, and opened it to scrutiny and study, by recording therapeutic interviews. (5) He completed a number of important studies on the process and outcome of therapy, and the connection between the qualities in the relationship and the changes which occur. (6) He encouraged the application of the dynamic principles learned in therapy to a wide variety of fields: teaching and learning; marriage relationships; family life; intensive groups; administration and management; resolution of conflict; community development.

Rokeach, (Mendel) Milton

Born: Poland 1918, Hrubieszow, **Died:** 1988, Los Angeles, California, USA **Nat:** American **Ints:** Social psychology **Educ:** BA Brooklyn College, 1941; MA University of California at Berkeley, 1941; PhD University of California at Berkeley, 1947 **Appts & awards:** APA Fellow; AAAS Fellow; APA Council, 1958–9; APA Division 9, Executive Council, 1958–68; Fellow, Center for Advanced Study in the Behavioral Sciences, 1961–2; President, APA Division 9, 1966–7; Professor of Sociology and Psychology, 1972–88; Director, Unit on Human Values, Social Research Center, Washington State University, 1976–88; Vice-President, International Society for Political Psychology, 1981–2; Research Excellence Award, Washington State University, 1983; Distinguished Psychologist Award, Washington State Psychological Association, 1983; Kurt Lewin Memorial Award, 1984; Hon. Doctorate University of Paris, 1984

Principal publications

1948   Generalized mental rigidity as a factor in ethnocentrism. *Journal of Abnormal and Social Psychology*, 43, 259–78.
1951   'Narrow-mindedness' and personality. *Journal of Personality*, 20, 234–51.

1954   The nature and meaning of dogmatism. *Psychological Review*, 61, 194–204.
1960   *The Open and Closed Mind: Investigations into the Nature of Belief Systems and Personality Systems*. Basic Books.
1964   *The Three Christs of Ypsilanti: A Psychological Study*. Knopf/Columbia University Press.
1965   The principle of belief congruence and the congruity principle as models of cognitive interaction. *Psychological Review*, 72, 128–42 (with G. Rothman).
1966   Attitude change and behavioral change. *Public Opinion Quarterly*, 30, 529–50.
1968   A theory of organization and change within value-attitude systems. *Journal of Social Issues*, 24, 13–33.
1968   *Beliefs, Attitudes and Values: A Theory of Organization and Change*. Jossey-Bass.
1972   Behavior as a function of attitude-toward-object and attitude-toward-situation. *Journal of Personality and Social Psychology*, 22, 194–201 (with P. Kleijunas).
1973   *The Nature of Human Values*. Free Press/Macmillan.
1974   Change and stability of American value systems, 1968–71. *Public Opinion Quarterly*, 38, 222–38.
1979   The two-value model of political ideology and British politics. *British Journal of Social and Clinical Psychology*, 18, 169–72.
1980   Some unresolved issues in theories of beliefs, attitudes, and values. In H.E. Howe and M. Page (eds), *Nebraska Symposium on Motivation, 1979*. University of Nebraska Press.

Further reading

Eysenck, H.J. (1954) *The Psychology of Politics*. Routledge and Kegan Paul.
Lesko, W.A. (1994) *Readings in Social Psychology: General, Classic, and Contemporary Selections* (2nd edn). Allyn & Vacon.
Schwarts, S.H. (1990) Individualism–collectivism: Critique and proposed refinements. *Journal of Cross Cultural Psychology*, 21, 139–57.

Milton Rokeach's parents were orthodox Hassidim; his father was a rabbi. His family moved to Brooklyn, New York, in the mid-1920s. After graduating from Brooklyn, Rokeach went to Berkeley, where his graduate work was interrupted by World War II. He enlisted in the Air Force Psychology Testing Program. After the war he returned to Berkeley where he, Donald T. **Campbell** and Murray Jarvik were employed as research staff on a study of prejudice in children. His PhD was on individual differences in ethnocentrism and problem-solving rigidity among college students.

While Rokeach was at Berkeley, Else Frenkel-Brunswik was working on the concept of intolerance of ambiguity. People who are intolerant of ambiguity are relatively 'closed' to new information. Rokeach suggested that closed-mindedness is a general personality trait which is related to the ability to form new cognitive systems – perceptual, conceptual and aesthetic. In order to measure this variable he developed the Dogmatism Scale, which is usually considered a measure of general authoritarianism. Closed-mindedness is characterized by a high level of rejection of opposing beliefs and a relatively low level of connectedness between belief systems. Open-mindedness is associated with greater analytic ability, a willingness to entertain novel and strange problems, and a capacity to synthesize new beliefs into a new cognitive system. Rokeach argued that dogmatism is not specific to any particular political, religious or social group but is present in some individuals in all groups, but directed against different targets. He believed that dogmatism, like authoritarianism, is linked with early family socialization experiences. He predicted that dogmatic people of disparate political and religious persuasion would manifest the same glorification of their parents and other symptoms of repressed anxiety and hostility. Rokeach argues that people strive to maintain cognitive consistency – internal consistency between what they say, think, believe and do – within a hierarchically structured system that places values at the top of the hierarchy. This contrasts with Leon **Festinger**'s approach, for example, which offers a motivational analysis of the consequences of inconsistency.

Rokeach's theory of dogmatism has its historical roots in *Gestalt* psychology and specifically in Kurt **Lewin**'s ideas concerning conflict. Although Rokeach's concept of dogmatism is closely linked to the concept of prejudice, his ideas attracted less attention than the earlier work of Adorno and others on the authoritarian personality. It is also somewhat similar to Hans **Eysenck**'s psychology of politics, in that both propose that there are strong psychological similarities in those of opposing political persuasion. His theory of dogmatism, like that of authoritarianism, was criticized for failing to pay sufficient attention to the role of socio-cultural and situational determinants of intolerance.

Rorschach, Hermann

Born: 1884, Zurich, Switzerland ***Died:*** 1922, Herisau, Switzerland ***Nat:*** Swiss ***Ints:*** History of Swiss deviant religious sects, psychoanalytic diagnosis, visual projective test methodology ***Educ:*** Dr Med. Zurich, 1912 ***Appts & awards:*** Resident physician/psychiatrist in various mental asylums, at the last of which, in Herisau, he was Associate Director at his untimely death; Vice-President, Swiss Psychoanalytic Society, 1919–22

Principal publications

1921 Psychodiagnostik. In W. Morgenthaler (ed.), *Arbeiten zur angewandten Psychiatrie*, vol. 2. Bircher.

1927 (posth.) Zwei schweizerische Sektenstifter (Binggeli und Unternährer) (Two Swiss founders of sects). *Imago*, 13, 395–441.

Further reading

Ellenberger, H. (1954) The life and work of Hermann Rorschach (1884–1922). *Bulletin Menninger Clinic*, 18, 173–219.

Rorschach's stature has been obscured by the development and partial eclipse of the projective test that bears his name. The only firm links between the two are the reduced set of ten inkblots, accepted by the publisher from the fifteen he had carefully selected, and his theoretic stance, giving precedence to the phenomenology of card responses, especially those compounding other sense modalities, rather than their objective referents. Rorschach was still revising his ideas during the protracted publishing difficulties of the test, and after publication considered it already obsolete. Months later, depressed by publication failure and adverse criticism, his death by inoperable peritonitis ended his ambitious plans to unify the history of religion, sociology and psychopathology, and, in **Bleuler**'s words, 'the hope of an entire generation of Swiss Psychiatry'.

His mother died when he was 12 and his father, an artist school teacher, when he was 18. His teenage nickname, signifying his painting skill, was 'Klex' ('Klecksen' is German for daubing, but 'Klecks' also means inkblot). However, his intensive clinical experiments with inkblots lay many years ahead. Undergraduate studies brought him under the direct influence of Bleuler and **Jung** at Zurich University, the Burghölzli, where their use of Jung's Word Association Test in applying **Freud**'s new psychoanalytic concepts to psychotic patients created Europe-wide interest. Intending to emigrate, he took a low-paid residential post, married a Russian colleague, and enjoyed four years of happiness and productivity. He emigrated to Russia but soon returned, disappointed with his poor research prospects. He then had to accept a low-paid resident's post. He abandoned tentative inkblot experiments to give priority to psychoanalysis and a new interest – deviant religious sects. This interest grew out of interviews with a former asylum inmate (Binggeli) who, as the founder of such a sect, had been committed for ritual sexual practices including incest. Rorschach now believed that this study was to be his life's work. Through interviews with Binggeli and other sect members, and recourse to historical records, he constructed genealogies and found that not only had one of Binggeli's ancestors been head of a precursor sect also preaching the holiness of incest, but nine others had been involved with such sects. Similar sects were mentioned in records dating from the twelfth century. Two papers were published, but the full text of his intended book had to await posthumous publication, because – for pre-emptive reasons – he suddenly reverted to his inkblot studies. These were driven by his intense curiosity over the phenomena of synaesthesia, the interaction of different sense modalities, with which he was personally familiar, but were conceived as only a component of his aims. Within three years he had reduced his inkblot set to fifteen and had prepared the supporting text for the ill-fated 'Psychodiagnostik'.

It is timely to re-evaluate Rorschach, in the twilight of the psychological theories that dominated his times. Had he remained in Russia, the history of psychology there might have been very different. Had he published his work on religious sects, perhaps Freud's influence in suppressing awareness of child sexual abuse might not have been so effective. Had he been able to develop his integrated theories, his very different concept of introversion and extroversion (as complementary functions – 'creative introversion' and 'extratension', the balance being a person's *Erlebnistypus*) might have supplanted Jung's. We might have been spared the use of the inkblot test to attempt validation of preconceived personality and psychopathological constructs employing inappropriate statistical techniques. The period of arid behaviourism then being initiated by his contemporary J.B. **Watson** might have been stillborn, supplanted by a phenomenological

psychology backed by the philosophy of Husserl and Heidegger. Rorschach's biography is a salutary reminder that orderly evolution in psychological theory is illusory.

H. GORDON BEVANS

Rosch (Heider), Eleanor
Born: 1938 *Nat:* American *Ints:* Cognition, concept formation, cross-cultural psychology, Eastern psychologies, psychologies of religion *Educ:* BA Reed College, Oregon, 1963; PhD Harvard University, 1969 *Appts & awards:* University of California at Berkeley, Professor of Psychology, Co-Founder, Berkeley Cognitive Science Program, 1971; Research Associate, Department of Psychology, Brown University; Member, US Social Science Research Council Committee on Cognitive Research, 1972–6; Creative Talent Award for seminal research on natural categories

Principal publications
1972   The structure of the colour space in naming and memory for two languages. *Cognitive Psychology*, 3, 337–54.
1972   Probabilities, sampling and ethnographic method: The case of Dani colour names. *Man*, 7, 448–66.
1972   Universals in colour naming and memory. *Journal of Experimental Psychology*, 93, 10–20.
1973   On the internal structure of perceptual and semantic categories. In T.E. Moore (ed.), *Cognitive Development and the Acquisition of Language*. Academic Press.
1973   Natural categories. *Cognitive Psychology*, 4, 328–50.
1974   Linguistic relativity. In A. Silverstein (ed.), *Human Communication: Theoretical Perspectives*. Halsted.
1975   Cognitive representations of semantic categories. *Journal of Experimental Psychology: General*, 104, 192–233.
1975   Cognitive reference points. *Cognitive Psychology*, 7, 532–47.
1975   Family resemblances: Studies in the internal structure of categories. *Cognitive Psychology*, 7, 573–605 (with C.B. Mervis).
1975   The nature of mental codes for colour categories. *Journal of Experimental Psychology: Human Perception and Performance*, 104, 303–22.
1976   Basic objects in natural categories. *Cognitive Psychology*, 8, 382–439 (with C.B. Mervis, W.D. Gray, D.M. Johnson and P. Boyes-Braehm).
1976   Structural bases of typicality effects. *Journal of Experimental Psychology: Human Perception*

and Performance, 2, 491–502 (with C. Simpson and R.S. Miller).

1978   Principles of categorisation. In E. Rosch and B.B. Lloyd (eds), *Cognition and Categorisation*. Erlbaum.

1981   Categorisation of natural objects. *Annual Review of Psychology*, 32, 89–115.

1987   Linguistic relativity. *Etc.*, 44, 254–79.

1987   Wittgenstein and categorisation research in cognitive psychology. In M. Chapman and R. Dixon (eds), *Meaning and Growth of Understanding: Wittgenstein's Significance for Developmental Psychology*. Erlbaum.

1988   Coherence and categorisation: A historical review. In F.S. Kessel (ed.), *The Development of Language and Language Researchers: Essays in Honour of Roger Brown*. Erlbaum.

1988   What does the tiny vajra refute? Causality and event structure in Buddhist logic and folk psychology. *Berkeley Cognitive Science Report*, no. 54.

1991   *The Embodied Mind: Cognitive Science and Human Experience*. MIT Press (with F.J. Varela and E. Thompson).

Further reading

MacLaury, R.E. (1991) Prototypes revisited. *Annual Review of Anthropology*, 20, 55–74.

Margolis, E. (1994) A reassessment of the shift from the classical theory of concepts to prototype theory. *Cognition*, 51, 73–89.

Medin, D.L. (1989) Concepts and conceptual structure. *American Psychologist*, 12, 1469–81.

Ross, B.H. and Spalding, T.L. (1994) Concepts and categories. In R.J. Sternberg (ed.), *Thinking and Problem Solving*. Academic Press.

Eleanor Rosch Heider has been an influential figure in cognitive psychology for over twenty-five years. In the earlier part of her career, she conducted a series of seminal empirical studies on the question of how everyday 'concepts', or cognitive categories, are represented in the mind. The influence of these studies has extended beyond cognitive psychology to anthropology. More recently, however, she has addressed more theoretical issues such as the insights of Buddhist psychology on the experience of 'self'.

Rosch's empirical research is significant because it challenges the traditional, Aristotelian theory that concepts are stored in the mind as logical lists of sufficient and necessary conditions defining membership of a given category. Rejecting this idea, Rosch argued that most everyday concepts have a graded internal structure that is characterized by a 'prototype' (described as a reference point or 'best example') at the centre and 'fuzzy boundaries' (or loose lines of demarcation between positive and negative examples) at the periphery. Just as Wittgenstein had proposed that although a rope comprises many strands, no single strand runs its entire length, Rosch suggested that defining attributes do not need to be shared by all examples of a given concept. Instead, all members of a mental category may be shown to have a 'family resemblance' to each other. This resemblance may be recognized perceptually rather than defined logically. For example, not all 'cups' have handles or are used for drinking purposes. Thus handle-less receptacles are found in Chinese restaurants, and trophies called 'cups' are awarded for success in sport. In general, Rosch concluded that the meaning of many everyday concepts (or 'natural categories') is derived not from their defining features but rather from the characteristics that describe their most typical member.

A prototype is the member of a category which shares a maximum of attributes with other members and a minimum of attributes with members of different categories. People are thought to decide whether or not an object or item belongs to a specific category by comparing the item with the prototype of that category. In other words, something is deemed to be an example (instance) of a natural concept if it is more similar to the prototype of that category than it is to that of another category. Rosch believed that an item will be classified as an example (instance) of a category if it is 'similar' to the prototypical member of that category. But how is similarity assessed? Rosch's theory is somewhat vague on this issue. Accordingly, some researchers claim that we use several 'exemplars', rather than a single prototype, to establish similarity. For example, in deciding whether something is a bird or not, we may consider mental examples of songbirds, birds of prey (e.g. hawks) or sea birds (e.g. terns). One of the great contributions of Rosch's prototype theory is that it helps to explain how people can form concepts of groups that contain rather loosely structured items. However, an unresolved issue concerns the degree to which our conceptual structures are culture-bound. For example, different cultures may identify different prototypes for the same category. Interestingly, one of the earliest sources of evidence in favour of the 'prototype' theory of concept formation came from Rosch's famous cross-cultural study of colour naming among Americans and members of the Dani tribe of Indonesian New Guinea. Despite the fact that the languages used by these two samples differed substantially in the number of terms available to describe these colours, both groups displayed superior recognition for certain colours, which were deemed to be 'focal' or 'prototypical' examples of their categories.

Rosch's interest in Eastern religions has led her to suggest that cognitive science can benefit significantly from certain insights yielded by the Buddhist meditative tradition. Thus in *The Embodied Mind* (1991) she and her colleagues argue that one of our most cherished representations – our experience of self – is illusory: 'No tradition has ever claimed to discover an independent, fixed, or unitary self within the world of experience.' In contrast to the empirical cognitive perspective, Buddhist psychology proposes that cognition should be regarded as a form of 'embodied action'. According to Rosch, this interpretation highlights the role of bodily experience in the generation of thought. However, the theoretical implications of this alternative approach to the mind have not yet been evaluated adequately.

AIDAN MORAN

Rosenthal, Robert

Born: 1933, Giessen, Germany **Nat:** German **Ints:** Clinical psychology, evaluation and measurement, educational psychology, personality and social psychology **Educ:** BA University of California at Los Angeles, 1953; PhD University of California at Los Angeles, 1956 **Appts & awards:** AAAS Socio-Psychology Prize (with K. Fode), 1960; Professor of Social Psychology, Harvard University, 1967– ; Fellow, APA Divisions 8, 12; Fellow, AAAS; President, North Dakota Psychological Association; Treasurer, Society for Projective Techniques; Member, Society of Experimental Social Psychology; Diplomate in Clinical Psychology, ABEPP; APA Division 13, Cattell Fund Award (first prize, with L. Jacobson), 1967; Senior Fulbright Scholar, Australian-American Educational Foundation, 1972; Guggenheim Fellow, 1973–4; Distinguished Career Contribution Award, Massachusetts Psychological Association, 1979; Wiener Award, University of Manitoba, 1979; Chair, Dept of Psychology 1992–; Editorial Boards: *Current Psychological Research*, *Current Psychological Reviews*, *Current Psychology: Research and Reviews*, *Journal of Consulting and Clinical Psychology*, *Journal of Educational Psychology*, *Journal of Educational Psychological Research*, *Journal of Experimental Social Psychology*, *Journal of Nonverbal Behavior*, *Journal of Personality*, *Replications in Social Psychology*

Principal publications

1961 Teachers' expectations: Determinants of pupils' IQ gains. *Psychological Reports*, 19, 115–18.

1963 On the social psychology of the psychological experiment: The experimenter's hypothesis as unintended determinant of experimental results. *American Scientist*, 51, 268–83.

1966 *Experimenter Effects in Behavioral Research*. Appleton-Century-Crofts. (Irvington, 1976).

1967 Covert communication in the psychological experiment. *Psychological Bulletin*, 74, 356–67.

1968 *Pygmalion in the Classroom: Teacher Expectation and Pupils' Intellectual Development*. Holt, Rinehart & Winston (with L. Jacobson).

1968 Experimenter expectancy and the reassuring nature of the null hypothesis decision procedure. *Psychological Bulletin Monograph Supplement*, 70, 30–47.

1975 *The Volunteer Subject*. Wiley (with R.R. Rosnow).

1978 Combining results of independent studies. *Psychological Bulletin*, 85, 185–93.

1979 The file drawer problem and tolerance for null results. *Psychological Bulletin*, 86, 638–41.

1979 *Sensitivity to Nonverbal Communication: The PONS Test*. Johns Hopkins University Press (with J.A. Hall, M.R. DiMatteo, P.L. Rogers and D. Archer).

1981 Pavlov's mice, Pfungst's horse and Pygmalion's PONS: Some models for the study of interpersonal expectancy effects. In T.A. Sebeok and R. Rosenthal (eds), *The Clever Hans Phenomenon: Communication with Horses, Whales, Apes and People. Annals of the New York Academy of Sciences*, 364, 182–98.

1982 Conducting judgment studies. In K.R. Scherer and P. Ekman (eds), *Handbook of Methods in Nonverbal Behavior Research*. Cambridge University Press.

1983 Assessing the statistical and social importance of the effects of psychotherapy. *Journal of Consulting and Clinical Psychology*, 51, 4–13.

1984 *Meta-Analytic Procedures for Social Research*. Sage.

Further reading

Hock, R.R. (1995) *Forty Studies that Changed Psychology*. Prentice Hall.

Pfungst, O. (1911) *Clever Hans (the Horse of Mr von Osten): A Contribution to Experimental, Animal and Human Psychology.* Holt, Rinehart & Winston.

Rosenthal, R. and Rubin, D.B. (1978) Interpersonal expectancy effects: The first 345 studies. *Behavioral and Brain Sciences,* 3, 377–86.

Rosenthal taught at the University of North Dakota between 1957 and 1962, where he was Director of the PhD programme in clinical psychology. Since 1967 he has been Professor of Social Psychology at Harvard University. His research has centred on the role of the self-fulfilling prophecy in everyday life and in laboratory situations. His studies include the effects of teachers' expectations on students' academic and physical performance, the effects of experimenters' expectations on the results of their research, and the effects of healers' expectations on their patients' mental and physical health.

The importance of self-fulfilling prophecy in scientific research was first brought to the attention of psychologists in the case of 'Clever Hans', a horse owned by Mr von Osten that was famous for its ability to read, spell and solve math problems. It was shown (by Otto Pfungst, 1911) that Hans was responding to unintentional non-verbal signals from his questioners. Rosenthal demonstrated similar effects in a range of psychological experiments. For example, in one study a group of students were told they would be working with rats bred for high intelligence and another were told they would be working with rats that were slow to learn. Although the groups of students were in reality assigned a sample of rats randomly, the group with the 'intelligent' rats reported superior maze learning, to the one with the 'dull' rats. Rosenthal termed this the 'Pygmalion effect' (in Greek mythology, Pygmalion fell in love with his sculpture of a woman). Rosenthal considered that similar effects may be at work in education and that teachers' expectations may unintentionally influence students' behaviour in the classroom. With Lenore Jacobson he demonstrated that effects do occur: 'When teachers expected that certain children would show greater intellectual development, those children did show greater intellectual development.'

Subtle non-verbal communication can have an important function in producing these effects. Rosenthal has also published important studies of its role in: (1) the mediation of interpersonal expectancy effects (which led to the development of a widely used measure of sensitivity to non-verbal communication – the PONS test); and (2) the relationship between female and male members of small work groups and small social groups. He has also made important contributions to the study of sources of artefact in behavioural research and in various quantitative procedures. In the realm of data analysis, his special interests are in analysis of variance, contrast analysis and meta-analysis. His more recent books and articles are about these areas of data analysis and about the nature of non-verbal communication in teacher–student, doctor–patient, manager–employee and psychotherapist–client interaction.

Rotter, Julian B.

Born: 1916, Brooklyn, New York, USA ***Nat:*** American ***Ints:*** Clinical psychology, health psychology, personality and social psychology ***Educ:*** BA (Chemistry) Brooklyn College, 1937; MA State University of Iowa, 1938; PhD Indiana University, 1941 ***Appts & awards:*** Professor of Psychology, University of Connecticut; Distinguished Contribution to the Science and Profession of Clinical Psychology Award, APA Division of Clinical and Abnormal Psychology, 1968; NIMH Senior Research Fellowship, 1968–9; President, APA Division of Personality and Social Psychology, 1969; President, APA Division of Clinical Psychology, 1970; APA Council, 1974–7; President, EPA, 1976–7; Consulting Editor: *Journal of Applied Psychology, Journal of Abnormal and Social Psychology, Psychological Bulletin*

Principal publications

1954   *Social Learning and Clinical Psychology.* Prentice Hall. (Johnson, 1973).

1960   Some implications for a social learning theory for the prediction of goal directed behaviour from test procedures. *Psychological Review,* 67, 301–16.

1961   The growth and extinction of expectancies in chance controlled and skilled tasks. *Journal of Psychology,* 52, 161–77.

1964   *Clinical Psychology.* Prentice Hall.

1966   Generalized expectancies for internal versus external control of reinforcement. *Psychological Monographs,* 80, 1–28.

1967   A new scale for the measurement of interpersonal trust. *Journal of Personality,* 35, 651–65.

1971   Generalized expectancies for interpersonal trust. *American Psychologist,* 26, 443–552.

1975   *Personality.* Scott, Foresman (with D. Hochreich).

1975   Some problems and misconceptions related to the construct of internal versus external control of reinforcement. *Journal of Consulting and Clinical Psychology*, 43, 56–67.
1980   Trust, trustworthiness and gullibility. *American Psychologist*, 35, 1–7.
1982   *The Development and Applications of Social Learning Theory: Selected Papers*. Praeger.

Further reading
Hock, R.R. (1995) *Forty Studies that Changed Psychology*. Prentice Hall.
Lefcourt, H.M. (ed.) (1981–4) *Research with the Locus of Control Construct* (3 vols). Academic Press.

Julian Rotter majored in chemistry, but his interests in psychology led to an MA and PhD at Iowa and Illinois respectively. After serving as a military psychologist in World War II, he joined George **Kelly** at Ohio State University; he stayed there until 1963, when he moved to the University of Connecticut.

Rotter is a social learning theorist who argues that there are important individual differences in where people place the responsibility for what happened to them. He introduced the concept of expectancy – a person's belief or subjective judgement that in a particular psychological situation behaving in a certain way will lead to reinforcement. At one extreme are people who believe they can influence the reinforcements they receive – they have an internal locus of control. At the other are people who believe that reinforcements are a matter of luck or fate – they have an external locus of control. Rotter developed the widely used Internal–External Locus of Control Scale to measure individual differences in locus of control. People with high external locus of control tend to have a greater sense of powerlessness and lower achievement motivation and to be more conformist. The dimension of internal–external locus of control has been generally accepted as a relatively stable aspect of human personality. However, the assumption that people high in external locus of control are generally less well adjusted has been challenged.

Rotter's work has been particularly important in advancing social learning theory. He has demonstrated that verbalized expectancies, increments and decrements in expectancies, and the generalization of expectancies behave in a lawful and predictive fashion, as do reinforcement values and their changes. Specific expectancies determine increasing variance, and generalized expectancies deter-

mine decreasing variance as experience with a task or psychological situation increases. It is in the area of personality measurement that social learning theory has made its most substantial and systematic contributions. Rotter argues that although new statistical techniques for analysis of test responses have flourished, it is still impossible to devise a useful test without an adequate theory of the nature of the characteristic that is being measured and an analysis of the determinants of test-taking behaviour. The same is true of validation procedures. Rotter argues that what a test can and cannot predict should be determined according to some laws, not be merely a matter of luck or trial and error. Personality tests developed by him include: the Rotter Level of Aspiration Board, the Rotter Incomplete Sentences Blank, the Rotter Internal–External Control Scale, and the Interpersonal Trust Scale.

Royce, Joseph R.

Born: 1921, New York City, USA *Nat:* American *Ints:* Behaviour genetics, emotionality, factor analysis, personality theory, theoretical/philosophical psychology *Educ:* BA Dennison University, 1941; PhD University of Chicago, 1951 *Appts & awards:* Doctoral Research Fellow, Jackson Laboratory, 1948–50; Faculty Fellow, Interdisciplinary Program of Graduate Studies, 1955–60; NRC Experimental Psychology Committee, 1961–5; APA Division of Theoretical Philosophy Psychology, Council of Representatives, 1963, President 1969; Distinguished Visiting Scholar, University of Hawaii, 1964; Education Testing Service, 1965; Australian National University 1965; Canadian Council SR, RES Fellow, 1965–6; Distinguished Contribution to Psychology Award, Psychological Association of Alberta, 1983; Editorial Boards: *Multi-Variate Behavior Research*, 1965–75, *Applied Psychology Measurement*, 1967–78, *Multi Disciplinary Perspective*, 1969–78, *Journal of Psycholinguistics*, 1970– , *German Journal of Psychology*, 1977– ; Founder, *Newsletter, Division of Theoretical/Philosophical Psychology, APA*, Editor, 1965–9; Founder, *Annals of Theoretical Psychology*, Co-Editor, 1984–8

Principal publications
1963   Factors as theoretical constructs. *American Psychologist*, 18, 522–8. (reprinted in D.N. Jackson and S. Messick (eds), *Problems in Human Assessment*, McGraw-Hill, 1967).

1964   *The Encapsulated Man.* Van Nostrand.
1966   Concepts generated from comparative and hysiological observations. In R.B. Cattell (ed.), *Handbook of Multivariate Experimental Psychology.* Rand McNally.
1970   *Toward Unification in Psychology.* University of Toronto Press.
1970   The present situation in theoretical psychology. In J.R. Joyce (ed.), *Toward Unification in Psychology.* University of Toronto Press. (Reprinted in B.B. Wolman, *Handbook of General Psychology*, Prentice Hall, 1973).
1973   *Multivariate Analysis and Psychological Theory.* Academic Press.
1973   Behavior genetic analysis of mouse emotionality: I Factor Analysis. *Journal of Comparative and Physiological Psychology*, 83, 36–47 (with W. Poley and L.T. Yeudall).
1973   Behavior genetic analysis of mouse emotionality: II Stability of factors across genotypes. *Animal Learning of Behavior*, 1, 116–20 (with D. Poley).
1975   Behavior genetic analysis of mouse emotionality: III The diallel analysis. *Behavior Genetics*, 5, 351–72 (with T.M. Holmes and W. Poley).
1976   Psychology is multi: Methodological, variate, epistemic, world-view, systemic, paradigmatic, theoretical and disciplinary. In W.J. Arnold (ed.), *Nebraska Symposium on the Conceptual Foundations of Theory and Method in Psychology.* University of Nebraska Press.
1978   Factor analytic studies of human brain damage: I First and second order factors and their brain correlates. *Multivariate Behavioral Research*, 4, 381–418 (with L.T. Yeudall and C. Bock).
1978   How we can best advance the construction of theory in psychology. *Canadian Psychological Review*, 19, 259–76.
1978   The life-style of a theory oriented generalist in a time of empirical specialists. In T.S. Krawiec (ed.), *The Psychologists*, vol. III. Clinical Psychology.
1979   *Theoretical Advances in Behaviour Genetics.* Sitjhoff & Norduff (with L.D. Mos).
1983   *Theory of Personality and Individual Differences: Factors, Systems and Processes.* Prentice Hall (with A.D. Powell).

Further reading

Eysenck, H.J. (1984) Much ado about personality. *Contemporary Psychology*, 29, 206–7.

van Gigch, J.P. (1990) Systems science, the discipline of epistemological domains, contributes to the design of the intelligent global web. *Behavioral Science*, 35, 122–37.

Joseph Royce is a theoretical experimental psychologist with special interest in factor analysis, behaviour genetics (in which he was a pioneer), emotion and individual differences. The first half of his professional life was focused on experimental research, primarily on the genetic basis of factors of mouse emotionality (this research was pursued over twenty years). He also investigated avoidance conditioning in inbred mouse strains and autokinesis in humans, and developed a psycho-epistemological inventory. The second half of his career has focused on theory and metatheory. During this period he completed a twenty-year programme of work on a general theory of individual differences (leading to the book with Powell in 1983). During this period he was also heavily involved in administrating the Department of Psychology and in founding and administering the Center for Advanced Study in Theoretical Psychology, Alberta, and his metatheoretical interests were concentrated on exploring the conceptual foundations of psychology. Throughout his career Royce's work has characteristically been interdisciplinary. For example, during the first half of his career he was concerned with mathematics as it relates to factor analysis, and with biology, especially genetics and neurology, as it relates to behaviour genetics and neuropsychology. During the second half these interest became increasingly theoretical and philosophical, as exemplified by his *Encapsulated Man* (1964).

Rubin, Zick

Born: 1944, New York, USA ***Nat:*** American ***Ints:*** Adult development, developmental, personality and social, psychology and social issues, psychology and the law ***Educ:*** BA Yale University, 1965; PhD University of Michigan, 1969 ***Appts & awards:*** Louis and Frances Salvage Professor of Social Psychology, Brandeis University; Socio-psychological Prize, AAAS, 1969; National Media Award (books category), American Psychological Foundation, 1980; National Media Award (magazine articles category), American Psychological Foundation, 1980; Editorial Boards: *Behavioral Science*, 1969–75, *American Journal of Sociology*, 1974–6, *Social Psychology Quarterly*, 1977–9,

Qualitative Sociology, 1982– ; Contributing Editor, Spectrum Books, Patterns of Social Behavior Series (Prentice Hall)

Principal publications

1968   Do American women marry up? *American Sociological Review*, 33, 750–60.

1970   Measurement of romantic love. *Journal of Personality and Social Psychology*, 16, 265–73.

1973   *Liking and Loving: An Invitation to Social Psychology*. Holt, Rinehart & Winston.

1974   Lovers and other strangers: The development of intimacy in encounters and relationships. *American Scientist*, 62, 182–90.

1974   *Doing unto Others*. Spectrum Books. (Prentice Hall).

1975   Who believes in a just world? *Journal of Social Issues*, 31(3), 65–89 (with L.A. Peplau).

1976   Couples research as couples counseling. *American Psychologist*, 31, 17–25 (with C. Mitchell).

1976   Breakups before marriage: The end of 231 affairs. *Journal of Social Issues*, 32, 147–68 (with C.T. Hill and L.A. Peplau).

1980   *Children's Friendships*. Harvard University Press.

1980   Self-disclosure in dating couples: Sex roles and the ethic of openness. *Journal of Marriage and the Family*, 42, 305–17 (with C.T. Hill, L.A. Peplau and C. Dunkel-Schetter).

1981   Loving and leaving: Sex differences in romantic attachments. *Sex Roles*, 7, 821–35 (with L.A. Peplau and C.T. Hill).

1984   How parents influence their children's friendships. In M. Lewis (ed.), *Beyond the Dyad*. Plenum (with J. Sloman).

1985   *Psychology: Being Human* (4th edn). Harper & Row.

Further reading

Hendrick, S.S. and Hendrick, C. (1992) *Liking, Loving and Relating*. Brooks/Cole.

Sternberg, R.J. (1987) Liking versus loving: A comparative evaluation of theories. *Psychological Bulletin*, 102, 331–45.

—— and Barnes, M.L. (eds) (1988) *The Psychology of Love*. Yale University Press.

Much of the work of Zick Rubin has concerned the psychology of close relationships. His work began in the Doctoral Program in Social Psychology (run jointly by the Department of Psychology and Sociology) at the University of Michigan. Theodore Newcomb had carried out ground-breaking research on the social psychology of interpersonal attraction, and Rubin

followed the path that Newcomb had cleared, but changed from 'liking' to 'loving'. Using existing work on liking, Rubin developed two scales, one on liking and another on love. He employed both instruments in a number of studies and found, for example, that loving scores are more highly correlated with people's estimates of their likelihood to marry than were liking scores. In the early 1970s his research continued, and he directed a longitudinal study of the development of relationships among a large sample of college student dating couples. He found that over a six-month period, degree of love measured at Time 1 partially predicted relationship progress at Time 2, but only for couples in which both partners were highly romantic. At the same time he conducted a series of experimental studies of self-disclosure between strangers. Some of the links between these two lines of research are discussed in 'Lovers and other strangers' (1974). According to Rubin love consists of attachment (encompassing a passionate, possessive component of love), caring (incorporating a giving component of live) – both individually oriented constructs – and intimacy, a dyadically oriented construct. In 1977, with the arrival of his first child, his attention turned to children's friendships, especially in the pre-school years. Subsequently, as the father of two boys, he turned his attention to father–son relationships, and he has published influential texts on the development of children's friendships.

Rubinstein, Sergei Leonidovich

Born: 1889, Odessa, Russia ***Died:*** 1960, Moscow, Russia ***Nat:*** Russian ***Ints:*** General psychology, methodological problems in psychology, problem solving ***Educ:*** PhD Marburg University, 1914 ***Appts & awards:*** Head, Department of Psychology, Leningrad Pedagogical Institute, 1930–42; Laureate of Stalin's Prize, 1941; Director, Institute of Psychology, Academy of Pedagogical Sciences of Russian Federation, 1942–5; Head, Department of Psychology, Moscow State University, 1942–50; Corresponding Member, USSR Academy of Science, 1943; Head, Sector of Psychology, Institute of Philosophy, USSR Academy of Sciences 1945–60; Member, Academy of Pedagogical Sciences of Russian Federation, 1950

Principal publications

1935   *Foundation of Psychology* (in Russian).

1940   *Foundation of General Psychology* (in Russian).

1957   *Existence and Consciousness* (in Russian).

1958   *Principles and Ways of Development of Psychology* (in Russian).

1958   *On Thinking and the Ways to Study It* (in Russian).

1973   *The Problems of General Psychology.* Pedagogika (in Russian).

Further reading

Rubinstein, S.L. (1914) *Eine Studie zum Problem der Methode.*

—— (1934) Problems of psychology in Karl Marx's works. *Soviet Psychotechnique*, 7 (1) (in Russian).

—— (1946) *Foundation of General Psychology* (2nd edn) (in Russian).

Sergei Leonidovich Rubinstein was born on 18 June 1889 in Odessa. He was educated in Germany, where he studied philosophy, sociology, psychology, physics and mathematics. His first scientific work was devoted to the problem of the method common to the natural and social sciences, which he tried to derive from Hegel's philosophical system. It determined his main theme: the philosophical roots of psychology and the problem of an objective method in psychology.

At the beginning of the 1920s he had the Chair of Psychology at Odessa University. During this period he had been working on the problem of the subject, which he approached from the position of Hegel's and then Marx's philosophy. Rubinstein was a convinced Marxist, arriving at Marxist philosophy on his own long before it became an official ideology of the Soviet Union. However, it was not always safe to be a thoughtful Marxist in the former Soviet Union, and he was forced to leave the university and take up a job in the Odessa Science library.

He then moved to Leningrad, where he had been offered a chair of psychology at the Pedagogical Institute. There he developed a methodological approach to psychological problems on the basis of dialectictical materialism, the key principle of which was the unity of activity and consciousness. Along with this theoretical work, many interesting experimental studies in various fields of psychology (perception, memory, thinking) were undertaken under his guidance at the Institute in the 1930s. He summarized his view of contemporary psychology in his fundamental book *Foundation of General Psychology* (1940). It still remains unsurpassed among textbooks of psychology written in Russian.

In 1942 Rubinstein was transferred to Moscow to head the Institute of Psychology. Before long he established a chair of psychology at Moscow University and invited a galaxy of Soviet psychologists – **Leont'ev**, **Luria**, **Galperin**, **Zeigarnik**. At the same time he instituted a sector of psychology at the Institute of Philosophy of the USSR Academy of Science. In the 1950s Rubinstein published a few books devoted to the methodological problems of psychology, the principle of determinism in psychology, and thinking, which showed him to be one of the leading figures of Soviet psychology at the time.

A. LOGVINENKO AND T. SOKOLOSKAYA

Rutter, Michael Llewellyn

Born: 1933, Brummanna, Lebanon ***Nat:*** Lebanese ***Ints:*** Child development, psychiatry ***Educ:*** MB ChB University of Birmingham Medical School, 1950–5; Academic DPM University of London, 1962 ***Appts & awards:*** Nuffield Medical Travelling Fellowship, 1961–2; Belding Travelling Scholar, 1963; FRSPsych, Royal College of Psychiatrists, 1971; FRCP Royal College of Physicians, London, 1972; Goulstonian Lecturer, Royal College of Physicians, London, 1973; American Association on Mental Deficiency Research Award, 1975; Hon. Fellow, BPS, 1978; Rock Carling Fellow of the Nuffield Provincial Hospitals Trust, 1979; Salmon Lecturer, New York, 1979; Fellow, Centre for Advanced Study in the Behavioral Sciences, California, 1979–80; Hon. Director, MRC Child Psychiatry Unit, Institute of Psychology, London, 1984; Hon. D, Leiden, 1985; CBE, 1985; FRS, 1987; European Editor, *Journal of Autism and Developmental Disorders*; Editorial Boards: *Child Development*, *Journal of Child Psychology and Psychiatry*, *Psychological Medicine*, *Journal of Special Education*, *Child Psychiatry and Human Development*, *Journal of Abnormal Child Psychology*, *Journal of the American Academy of Child Psychiatry*, *Applied Psycholinguistics*, *Journal of Anxiety Disorders*, *La Revista Psiquiatrica Peruana 'Hermilio Valdizan'*; Corresponding Associate Commentator, *Behavioral and Brain Sciences*; Consulting Editor, *Journal of Clinical Neuropsychology*; Associate Editor, *Applied Research in Mental Retardation*; Advising Editor, Life Span Development and Behavior Sciences Series; Advisory Board, Emotional Development (Cambridge University Press)

Principal publications

1981   *Maternal Deprivation Reassessed* (2nd edn). Penguin.

1983   *Stress, Coping and Development*. McGraw-Hill (ed. with N. Garmezy).

1983   *Juvenile Delinquency: Trends and Perspectives*. Penguin (with H. Giller).

1984   Psychopathology and development: (1) Childhood antecedents of adult psychiatric disorder; (2) Childhood experiences and personality development. *Australian and New Zealand Journal of Psychiatry*, 18, 225–34, 314–27.

1984   Parental psychiatric disorder: Effects on children. *Psychological Medicine*, 14, 853–80.

1984   Continuities and discontinuities in socio-emotional development: Empirical and conceptual perspectives. In R. Emde and R. Harmon (eds), *Continuities and Discontinuities in Development*. Plenum.

1985   (ed.) *Child and Adolescent Psychiatry: Modern Approaches* (2nd edn). Blackwell Scientific (with L. Hersove).

1985   Parenting behaviour of mothers raised 'in care'. In A.R. Nicol (ed.), *Longitudinal Studies in Child Psychology and Psychiatry: Practical Lessons from Research Experience*. Wiley (with D. Quinton).

1985   The treatment of autistic children. *Journal of Child Psychology and Psychiatry*, 26, 193–214.

1985   Family and school influences on behavioural development. *Journal of Child Psychology and Psychiatry*, 26, 349–68.

1985   Black pupils' progress in secondary school. I. Reading attainment between 10 and 14. *British Journal of Developmental Psychology*, 3, 113–21 (with B. Maughan and G. Dunn).

1985   Effects of lead on children's behaviour and cognitive performance: A critical review. In K.R. Mahaffey (ed.), *Dietary and Environmental Lead: Human Health Effects*. Elsevier (with W. Yule).

1985   Family and school influences on cognitive development. *Journal of Child Psychology and Psychiatry*, 26, 683–704.

1985   Resilience in the face of adversity: Protective factors and resistance to psychiatry disorder. *British Journal of Psychiatry*, 147, 598–611.

1986   *Depression in Young People: Developmental and Clinical Perspectives*. Guilford Press (with C. Izard and P. Read).

1988   *Parenting Breakdown: The Making and Breaking of Intergenerational Links*. Avebury (with D. Quinton).

1991   *Biological Risk Factors for Psychosocial Disorders*. Cambridge University Press (with P. Casaer).

1993   *Developing Minds: Challenge and Continuity Across the Lifespan*. Penguin (with M. Rutter).

1994   *Stress, Risk and Resilience in Children and Adolescents: Processes, Mechanisms and Interventions*. Cambridge University Press (with R.J. Haggerty, L.R. Sherrod and N. Garmezy).

Further reading

King, R.A. and Noshpitz, J.D. (1991) *Pathways of Growth. Essentials of Child Psychiatry*, vol. 2, *Psychopathology*. Wiley.

Lewis, M. and Miller, S.M. (eds) (1990) *Handbook of Developmental Psychopathology*. Plenum.

Quay, H.C. and Werry, J.S. (1986) *Psychopathological Disorders of Childhood*. Wiley.

Sir Michael Rutter was educated at Moorestown Friends School, USA, Wolverhampton Grammar School, England, and Bootham School, York, England. He completed his basic medical education at the University of Birmingham, England, qualifying in 1955. After taking residencies in internal medicine, neurology and pediatrics, he proceeded to the **Maudsley** Hospital, London, for training in general psychiatry and then child psychiatry. He spent the year 1961/2 on a research fellowship studying child development at the Department of Pediatrics, Albert Einstein College of Medicine, New York, returning then to work in the Medical Research Council Social Psychiatry Research Unit. In 1965 he took an academic position at the University of London's Institute of Psychiatry, where he has remained ever since, becoming professor and head of the Department of Child and Adolescent Psychiatry in 1973.

His research activities include stress resistance in children, developmental links between childhood and adult life, schools as social institutions, reading difficulties, interviewing skills, neuropsychiatry, infantile autism and psychiatric epidemiology. Rutter argues that psychologists often assume that the biological norm comprises an accumulation of skills and capacities, leading eventually to an increasing stabilization of individual differences. According to this view, changes and discontinuities are of central importance. Rutter challenges that position and argues that people have a capacity to seek social niches that provide for continuity in environmental influences, and that life stresses often serve to accentuate, rather than change, pre-existing characteristics. In his approach to understanding development he also challenges the assumption that development ends at adolescence. Instead he argues that internal maturational effects and environmental influences continue to shape psychological functioning well into adult life. He emphasizes the need to study turning points in life trajectories during childhood and adulthood. Thus, although his primary contributions are in developmental child psychopathology, his view of development is closer to that of Erik **Erikson** and the broader tradition of life-span developmental psychology than to that of **Piaget** or **Vygotsky**, for example. Rutter considers the psychological effects of turning points as deriving from the specifics of their impact in different parts of the general population. The concept of resilience is central to much of his research and clinical work: some subsections of the population are particularly resilient when confronted with harsh maturational and environmental challenges. Rutter does not regard turning points as related to age transitions, universal social experiences or life stressors. Rather they tend to apply to internal and external changes that create a force in a different direction from the developmental course before their operation. Our sense of developmental 'carrying forward' arises because (1) the new experience closes off or opens up opportunities, or (2) because it involves an enduring change in the environment, or (3) because it brings about an enduring effect on a person's self-concept. Rutter advocates experimental work directed at uncovering where the turning point influences come from, and their impact on psychological development.

S

Sahakian, William

Born: 1921, Boston, Massachusetts, USA *Nat:* American *Ints:* Consulting psychology, history of psychology, philosophical and theoretical, psychotherapy *Educ:* BS Northeastern University, 1944; PhD Boston University, 1951 *Appts & awards:* Professor of Psychology and Philosophy, Suffolk University, Boston; Hon. DSc, Curry College, Milton, MA, 1956; Forum for Logotherapy Editorial Board, 1979; Ontoanalytic Association Certificate, 1970; Outstanding Educators of America Award, 1971; Meritorious Achievement in Psychology Award, Institute of Logotherapy Diplomate, 1983

Principal publications

1975   *History and Systems of Psychology.* Wiley.
1977   *Psychology of Personality* (3rd edn). Houghton Mifflin.
1980   Philosophical psychotherapy. In R. Herink (ed.), *The Psychotherapy Handbook.* New American Library.
1982   *History and Systems of Social Psychology* (2nd edn). McGraw-Hill.
1984   *Introduction to the Psychology of Learning* (2nd edn). Peacock.
1994   Infection theory. In R. Corsini (ed.), *The Encyclopedia of Psychology* (2nd edn). Wiley.

William Sahakian lived and worked in the Boston area of the USA throughout his career. He has written widely used textbooks on a range of topics in psychology as well as popular introductions to various topics in philosophy. He is, however, best known for two original theoretical contributions to psychology. 'Philosophical psychotherapy' is a variant of Viktor Frankl's logotherapy and is perhaps unique in using the term philosophy in its everyday non-technical sense in which one may talk of 'taking a philosophical attitude to something'. Sahakian points out that with neurotic as with physical symptoms, the ideal result is to get rid of the symptom. However, where a physical symptom is beyond cure, it is sometimes possible for the person affected to regulate his or her life so as to approximate to normality, despite the symptom.

Why should this not be possible with neurotic symptoms as well? His recommendation is 'Stop worrying ... there is nothing in heaven or earth worth losing your composure.' He claims that the therapy is often successful with clients who have tried other forms of psychotherapy without success. The client learns to stop worrying about failure to eliminate the symptom, and this leads him or her to stop worrying about the symptom. Few details are given about symptoms or about the other therapies that were tried and failed (about 250 varieties are listed in Herink's handbook). The best examples are, in Sahakian's view, cases of sudden religious conversion; the object of his therapy is to foster emotional control by changing the client's personal 'philosophy'.

'Infection theory' is a theory of the social psychology of psychology itself. Sahakian points out that theories in psychology tend to cluster round fundamental concepts associated with one person (he cites **Lewin** and **Skinner** as examples). They are advanced by that person's students and associates. This leads to 'an inbreeding of ideas', and other important topics may be neglected (Sahakian cites, in personality theory, love, faith, hope, aesthetic feeling, etc.). It is hardly possible to deny that this kind of thing may occur, in psychology as in the other sciences. If the influence radiated by the one person genuinely contributes to the advancement of the science there can be no objection, but opinions may, of course, differ on that. It is not easy to see how else a scientific discipline might be organized. For good or ill, some scientific researchers become more fashionable (attracting students and associates) than others.

N.E. WETHERICK

Sanford, Nevitt

Born: 1909 *Nat:* American *Ints:* Personality and social, educational *Educ:* AB University of Richmond, 1924; MA Columbia University, 1930; PhD Harvard University, 1934 *Appts & awards:* President, APA, Division 8, 1955, Division 9, 1957; Hon. ScD, University of

Richmond, 1962; Hon. LLD, University of Notre Dame, 1967; Centennial Award for Education, New York State University College of Fredonia, 1967; Hon. LHD, University of Nevada, Colgate University, 1968; Research Scientist Award, NIMH, 1969–74; Kurt Lewin Memorial Award, Society for the Psychological Study of Social Issues, 1969; Award for Distinguished Contribution in Clinical Psychology, 1970; President, Western Psychological Association, 1971; Award for Distinguished Professional Achievement, American Board of Psychology, 1978; N. Sanford Award, International Society of Political Psychology, 1979; H.A. Murray Award, Division 9, 1980; Book Series Co-Editor, Behavioral Science (Jossey-Bass); Editorial Consultant: *Journal of Consulting Psychology*, 1946–64, *Journal of Abnormal and Social Psychology*, 1952–60, *Transaction*, 1963– , *Journal of Applied Behavioral Sciences*, 1963– , *Community Mental Health Journal*, 1965– , *Suicide and Life-Threatening Behavior*, 1972

Principal publications

1943   Some personality correlates of morale. *Journal of Abnormal and Social Psychology*, 38, 8–20 (with H.S. Conrad).

1944   Some specific war attitudes of the college students. *Journal of Psychology*, 17, 153–85 (with H.S. Conrad).

1944   A scale for the measurement of anti-semitism. *Journal of Psychology*, 17, 339–70.

1945   Some personality factors in anti-semitism. *Journal of Psychology*, 20, 271–91 (with E. Frenkel-Brunswick).

1950   *The Authoritarian Personality*. Harper (with T.W. Adorno, E. Frenkel-Brunswick and D. Levinson).

1955   A new instrument for studying authoritarianism in personality. *Journal of Psychology*, 40, 73–84 (with M. Freedman and H. Webster).

1956   Personality development during the college years. *Journal of Social Issues*, 12, 1–71.

1956   Surface and depth in the individual personality. *Psychological Review*, 63, 349–59.

1968   Education for individual development. *American Journal of Orthopsychiatry*, 38, 858–68.

1970   *Issues in Personality*. Jossey-Bass.

1970   Whatever happened to action research? *Journal of Social Issues*, 26, 3–23.

1971   *Sanctions for Evil: Sources of Social Destructiveness*. Jossey-Bass (with C. Comstock).

1971   Science and social development. *Education*, 92, 1–18.

1979   *College and Character*. Montaigne (with J. Axelrod).

1980   *Learning After College*. Montaigne (with C. Comstock).

Further reading

Sanford, Nevitt (1990) What have we learned about personality? In S. Koch and D.E. Leary (eds), *A Century of Psychology as Science*. APA.

Clinical psychology did not represent a significant presence in American universities until after World War II. The exception was the Harvard Psychological Clinic, established by Morton Prince in 1927 and directed by Henry A. **Murray** from the 1930s. The clinic was an importance source of research on personality variables and produced a generation of influential clinical psychologists, including D.W. **Mackinnon**, S. Rosenzweig and R. Nevitt Sanford.

Sanford is best known for his contributions in three areas: (1) personality theory and human problems; (2) authoritarian personality and social destructiveness; and (3) higher education and adult development. In his investigations in each of these areas he has been concerned primarily to identify underlying patterns. So, in understanding authoritarianism he asks whether the explanation is to be found mostly in the 'culture', or in 'personality', or in both.

He argues that the only way to answer this and similar questions is through the intensive study of individuals. During the 1950s he was at the forefront of attempts at increased recognition of the importance of social factors in understanding personality. For example, he argued that the self-concept could be altered by social factors in the present or very recent past. He was responsible for alerting personality theorists to the importance of learning through such concepts as role dispositions, interpersonal reaction systems and social values.

One of the important, but sometimes unrecognized, contributions of his work lies in the manner in which he works with both social variables and intrapsychic variables: he argues for the importance of both the dynamic unconscious and social and environmental forces. The importance he attaches to social influences is also apparent in his work on adult development and higher education. In this his work was strongly influenced by the ideas of Erik **Erikson**. He considers education – broadly conceived as social influence – to have the potential to alter almost any aspect of the person. The significance he attaches to the social is also apparent in his views on the nature of research. He considers psychological research to be an essentially social activity which influences researchers and their subjects. Working from that position, he has advocated the pursuit of psychological investigations through 'action research', in which research is considered as a form of social action and action as a form of research.

Sarbin, Theodore Roy

Born: 1911, Cleveland, Ohio, USA **Nat:** American **Ints:** Personality and social, philosophical and theoretical, psychological hypnosis, psychological study of social issues, psychology and law **Educ:** AB Ohio State University, 1936; MA Western Reserve University, 1937; PhD Ohio State University, 1941 **Appts & awards:** Professor Emeritus of Psychology and Criminology, University of California, Santa Cruz; Fulbright Fellow, 1962; Guggenheim Fellow, 1965–6; Fellow, Center for Advanced Studies, Wesleyan University, 1968–9; Clement Staff Essay Award, Psychoanalytic Review, 1971; President, APA Division 30, 1977–8; Morton Prince Award, Society of Clinical and Experimental Hypnosis, 1978; Society of Clinical and Experimental Hypnosis Award, best theoretical paper published in 1979, 1980; Golden Pendulum Award, International Society of Professional Hypnosis, 1984; Consulting Editor: *Sociometry*, 1958–63, *Behaviorism*, 1972–84; Series Editor, The Person in Psychology (Holt, Rinehart & Winston), 1965–73; Board of Editors: *Psychological Record*, 1972– ; Board of Consulting Editors: *Journal of Abnormal Psychology*, 1975–80, *American Journal of Community Psychology*, 1977–82

Principal publications

1944   The logic of prediction in psychology. *Psychological Review*, 51, 210–28.
1960   *Clinical Inference and Cognitive Theory*. Holt, Rinehart & Winston (with R. Taft and D. Bailey).
1967   The concept of hallucination. *Journal of Personality*, 35, 359–80.
1967   On the futility of the proposition that some people be labelled 'mentally ill'. *Journal of Consulting Psychology*, 31, 447–53.
1968   Ontology recapitulates philology: The mythic nature of anxiety. *American Psychologist*, 23, 411–18.
1969   Schizophrenic thinking: A role theory interpretation. *Journal of Personality*, 37, 190–206.

1972   *Hypnosis: The Social Psychology of Influence Communication*. Holt, Rinehart & Winston (with W.C. Coe).
1977   Contextualism: A world view for modern psychology. In A. Landfield (ed.), *Nebraska Symposium on Motivation*. University of Nebraska Press.
1979   Hypnosis and psychopathology: On replacing old myths with fresh metaphors. *Journal of Abnormal Psychology*, 88, 506–26 (with W.C. Coe).
1980   *Schizophrenia: Medical Diagnosis or Moral Verdict*. Pergamon (with J.C. Mancuso).
1981   On self-deception. In T.A. Sbeok and R. Rosenthal (eds), *The Clever Hans Phenomenon: Communication in Horses, Whales, Apes, and People. Annals of the New York Academy of Sciences*, 364, 220–35.
1982   The Quixotic principle: A belletristic approach to the psychology of imagining. In V.L. Allen and K.E. Scheibe (eds), *The Social Context of Conduct: Psychological Writings of Theodore Sarbin*. Praeger.
1983   *Studies in Social Identity*. Praeger (ed. with K.E. Scheibe).
1983   Role transition as social drama. In V.L. Allen and E. Van de Vliert (eds), *Role Transitions*. Plenum.
1986   (ed.) *Narrative Psychology: The Storied Nature of Human Conduct*. Praeger.
1989   Emotions as situated actions. In L. Cirillo, B. Kaplan and S. Wapner (eds), *Emotions in Ideal Human Development*. Erlbaum.
1995   A narrative approach to 'repressed memories'. *Journal of Narrative and Life History*, 5, 51–66.

Further reading

Lee, D.J. (ed.) (1994) *Life and Story: Autobiographies for a Narrative Psychology*. Praeger.
Vitz, P.C. (1990) The use of stories in moral development: New psychological reasons for an old education method. *American Psychologist*, 45, 709–20.

Work in the late 1930s and early 1940s on prediction convinced Sarbin that actuarial methods were to be preferred over case-study ones, since the former had the virtue of assigning a probability to a prediction. His early work on prediction received a good deal of notice. It was not until later that he realized that probabilistic predictions were silent where a single case was involved. At the same time, an interest in hypnosis crystallized, and he carried out a research programme that led him to conceptualize the conduct of the hypnotized person as the enactment of a specialized social role. A more developed treatment of role, together with other dramaturgic concepts, became the cornerstone of a social psychological theory.

Sarbin has treated a number of psychological concepts from the standpoint of role theory: that is, that human beings engage in strategic conduct in order to meet their practical and symbolic obligations. This theory competed with the prevailing mechanistic ones, which had no place for the actor as agent, as initiator of action, or as author of personal scripts. From the standpoint of a contextualist along with students and collaborators, he published discussions to demonstrate how psychological constructs, initially coined as metaphors, became reified, hypostatized and mythologized. Hallucination, imagination, hypnosis, superstition, the criminal type, mental illness, schizophrenia and anxiety are among the concepts he studied to reveal the mischief that follows upon metaphor-to-myth transformations. He also extended the dramaturgic network into hermeneutics and became involved in demonstrating the utility of looking upon human action as narrative.

Scarr, Sandra Wood

Born: 1936, Washington, DC, USA **Nat:** American **Ints:** Child, youth and family services, developmental psychology, evaluation, measurement and statistics, Society for the Psychological Study of Social Issues **Educ:** AB 1958 Vassar College; AM 1963 Harvard University; PhD 1965 Harvard University **Appts & awards:** Associate Professor, Graduate School of Education, University of Pennsylvania, 1970–1; Professor of Child Psychology, University of Minnesota, 1973–7; Professor of Psychology, Yale University, 1977–83; Commonwealth Professor of Psychology, University of Virginia, 1983– ; Distinguished Contributions to Research in Public Policy, APA, 1988; Founding Member, American Psychological Society, 1988; Fellow, American Academy of Arts and Sciences, 1989; James McKeen Cattell Award for Distinguished Contributions to Applied Research, American Psychological Society, 1993; President, American Psychological Society, 1996–7; Associate Editor, *American Psychologist*, 1976–80; Editor, *Developmental Psychology*, 1980–6; Co-Editor, *Current Directions in Psychological Science*, 1991–5

Principal publications

1968   Environmental bias in twin studies. *Eugenics Quarterly*, 15, 34–40.

1971   Race, social class and IQ. *Science*, 174, 1285–95.

1971   Heredity and behavior development. In *Encyclopedia of Education*. Macmillan.

1973   The effects of early stimulation on low birth weight infants. *Child Development*, 44, 94–101.

1974   *Socialization*. Merrill (with P. Salapatek).

1976   IQ test performance of black children adopted by white families. *American Psychologist*, 31, 726–39 (with R.A. Weinberg).

1976   Blood group, behavioral, and morphological differences among dizygotic twins. *Social Biology*, 22, 372–4.

1980   Perceived and actual similarities in biological and adoptive families: Does perceived similarity bias genetic influence? *Behavior Genetics*, 10, 445–8 (with E. Scarf and R.A. Weinberg).

1980   Heritability and educational policy: Genetic and environmental effects on IQ, aptitude, and achievement. *Educational Psychologist*, 15, 1–22 (with D. Yee).

1981   Testing for children: Implications for assessment and intervention strategies. *American Psychologist*, 36: 1159–66.

1982   Genetic differences in intelligence. In R.J. Sternberg (ed.), *Handbook of Intelligence*. Cambridge University Press (with L. Carter-Saltzman).

1983   The Minnesota adoption studies: Genetic differences and malleability. *Child Development*, 54, 260–7 (with R.A. Weinberg).

1983   How people make their own environments: A theory of genotype–environmental effects. *Child Development*, 54, 424–35 (with K. McCartney).

1984   *Mother Care/Other Care*. Basic Books.

1986   The early childhood enterprise: Care and education of the young. *American Psychologist*, 41, 1140–6 (with R.A. Weinberg).

1987   Three cheers for behavior genetics. *Behavior Genetics*, 17, 219–28.

1989   Working mothers and their families. *American Psychologist*, 44, 1402–9 (with D. Phillips and K. McCartney).

1990   Facts, fantasies, and the future of child care in the United States. *Psychological Science*, 1, 26–35 (with D. Phillips and K. McCartney).

1992   Developmental theories for the 1990s: Development and individual differences. *Child Development*, 63, 1–19.

1993   IQ correlations in transracial adoptive families: An eleven year follow-up. *Intelligence*, 17, 541–55 (with R.A. Weinberg and I.D. Waldman).

1993   Child care research: Issues, perspectives, and results. *Annual Review of Psychology*, 44, 613–44 (with N. Eisenberg).

1993 Biological and cultural diversity: The legacy
of Darwin for development. *Child Development*,
64, 1333–53.

Further reading
Stevens, G. and Gardner, S. (1982) *The Women of
Psychology*, Vol. 2, *Expansion and Refinement*.
Schenkman.

Sandra Scarr was born in Washington, DC, in
1936, the oldest of two daughters of Jane Powell
and John Ruxton Wood, MD. She attended
Vassar College as an undergraduate and
received the AB degree, in sociology, in 1958.
After graduation, Scarr spent a year in a 'family
and child service' agency, working primarily
with members of ethnic minority groups
and with people from low socioeconomic
back-grounds. She became dissatisfied with
the traditional way in which such individuals
were treated, concluding that they were in
need more of assistance in economic areas
than of psychotherapy. Scarr then spent a year
as a research assistant in the Laboratory of
Socio-Environmental Studies at the National
Institute of Mental Health. These early professional experiences were to guide Scarr in
her future academic and professional career,
and they reflect her dedication to developing
new ways of treating members of ethnic
minority groups and low socioeconomic groups,
as well as her commitment to empirical
research.

In 1960 Scarr entered Harvard University in
the Department of Social Relations. After
receiving her MA degree in 1963, she moved
first to Washington, DC, then to Pennsylvania,
to be with her husband, Harry Alan Scarr, as he
pursued his academic career. While in Washington, she took a part-time position as assistant
professor at the University of Maryland's Institute for Child Study. It was here that she
finished writing her dissertation, an important
twin study under the direction of Irving Gottes-
man. While in Pennsylvania, Scarr advanced
from the level of visiting assistant professor of
psychology in 1966 to associate professor in
1970 at the Graduate School of Education.
During her stint at the University of Pennsylvania, Scarr performed much of her most noted
research on race and test performance. It was
also here that she met her second husband,
Philip Salapatek, while conducting research
with him on infant distress. She collaborated for
several years with Salapatek on studies of
infancy, until their divorce in 1976. In 1977 she

accepted a position as professor of psychology
at Yale University.

Scarr moved to the University of Virginia in
1983. Her research in the areas of child development, intelligence, and genetics has resulted in
the publication of more than two hundred articles and four books. Her application of
behavioural genetics to developmental psychology has been an important contribution to the
field. She has rejected the traditional nature/
nurture dichotomy and has instead combined the
two, and incorporated her background in sociology and anthropology into her research
designs. Recently, she has been studying parental discipline, in particular looking at individual
differences in how parents structure their
discipline.

In June 1995, she took leave from the University of Virginia to become CEO and Chairman
of the Board of Directors of Kinder Care Learning Centers, Inc. She is also on the Steering
Committee on Prevention Research for the
NIMH, and has consulted with dozens of
organizations to improve early education, child
care and family relations. Her firm commitment
to empirical research is evidenced by her role as
a founding member of the American Psychological Society (APS), and her resignation,
in 1990, from the APA, which has been seen by
some to underemphasize psychology's scientific
basis. Scarr was elected president of the APS for
1996 and, as part of her goals, has promised to
make research on child care a major part of that
organization's agenda.

J.D. HOGAN AND W. IACCINO

Schachter, Seymour
Born: 1922, New York City, USA *Nat:* American *Ints:* Personality and social psychology
Educ: BS Yale University, 1942; MA Yale
University, 1944; PhD University of Michigan,
1950 *Appts and Awards:* Fulbright Fellowship,
1952; General Electric Foundation Award,
1959–62; AAAS Socio-Psychological Prize,
1959; Robert Johnston Nivens Professor of
Social Psychology, Department of Psychology,
Columbia University, 1961; Fellow,
Guggenheim Foundation, 1967; APA Distinguished Scientific Contributions Award,
1968

Principal publications
1951 Deviation, rejection, and communication.
Journal of Abnormal and Social Psychology, 46,
190–207.

1959   *The Psychology of Affiliation.* Stanford
University Press.
1962   Cognitive, social, and physiological
determinants of emotional states. *Psychological
Review*, 69, 379–99.
1964   The interaction of cognitive and physiological
determinants of emotional state. In L. Berkowitz
(ed.), *Advances in Experimental Social
Psychology*, vol. 1. Academic Press.
1965   A cognitive-physiological view of emotion. In
O. Klineberg and R. Christie (eds), *Perspectives in
Social Psychology*. Holt, Rinehart & Winston.
1966   Cognitive manipulations of pain. *Journal of
Experimental Social Psychology*, 2, 227–36 (with
R.E. Nisbett).
1977   Nicotine regulation in heavy and light
smokers. *Journal of Experimental Psychology:
General*, 106, 5–12.

Further reading

Grunberg, N.E., Nisbett, R.E., Rodin, J. and Singer,
J.E. (eds) (1987) *A Distinctive Approach to
Psychological Research: The Influence of Stanley
Schachter*. Erlbaum.
Marshall, G.D. and Zimbardo, P.G. (1979) Affective
consequence of inadequately explained
physiological arousal. *Journal of Personality and
Social Psychology*, 37, 970–88.
Schachter, S. (1989) Autobiography. In G. Lindzey
(ed.), *A History of Psychology in Autobiography*,
vol. 8. Stanford University Press.

After completing his MA, Stanley Schachter
was a sergeant in the US Air Force, working on
visual problems in the Biophysics Division
of the Aero-Medical Laboratory at Wright
Field. At the end of the war he continued his
graduate training at MIT, where he worked
(1946–8) with Leon **Festinger** in the Research
Center for Group Dynamics. When its Director,
Kurt **Lewin**, died, the Center moved to the
University of Michigan, and Schachter moved
with it. In 1949 he went to the University
of Minnesota as an assistant professor, becoming associate professor in 1954 and full
professor in 1958. During this period he also
served as research director of the Organization
for Comparative Social Research, and visiting
professor at the University of Amsterdam an
Stanford. He moved to Columbia University in
1965.

Stanley Schachter formulated a theory of
emotional experience – the two-factor theory of
emotion – which emphasizes the importance of
cognitive factors. William **James**'s theory of
emotion was a precursor of Schachter's theoreti-

cal stance, which formed the basis of subsequent
research on attribution and misattribution.
Schachter accepted the Jamesian notion that
emotional experience depends on the perception
of one's own bodily changes, but he differed
from James in assuming that physiological
reactions do not inform the individual of
hedonic quality. Schachter's theory attempted to
integrate two conflicting theories of emotion
and stated that any emotional state requires two
conditions: physiological arousal and situational
cues. With his colleague Jerome E. **Singer** he
argued that the labels people attach to feelings
of arousal are determined primarily by external
factors. In general, people interpret arousal as
one emotion or another depending on the situation. In other words, people's emotions are
more arbitrary than people commonly suppose
and depend on what the most plausible explanation for their arousal happens to be. People
perceive themselves as experiencing the emotion
that external cues suggest they should be feeling. For example, arousal experienced in the
presence of a person perceived to be attractive
might be interpreted or labelled 'attraction' or
'sexual excitement'. Some people can make
faulty interpretations of situations and of the
causes of their arousal, and this can lead to
misattribution.

To test the theory Schachter and Singer conducted an ingenious experiment in which
subjects were told that they wished to examine
the effects of a vitamin compound. One group
of subjects were injected with epinephrine (a
drug producing heightened physiological
arousal) and given accurate information about
the effects of the drug. Another group were not
given this information about the effects of the
drug. Subjects in both groups found themselves
in a room with an accomplice who behaved
either euphorically or angrily. Schachter and
Singer predicted that subjects who were
informed of the effects of the drug would attribute their arousal to its effects whereas others
would attribute their feelings to either the
euphoria or the anger of the accomplice. Results
supported both predictions. This means that
people are prone to misattributions of arousal –
they attribute their arousal to the wrong source,
resulting in a mistaken or exaggerated emotion.
A modified version of Schachter's theory
assumes that internal arousal can provide information concerning both the intensity and the
evaluative quality of affective experience and
that such internal arousal can precede
misattribution.

The two-factor theory of emotion has some limitations. First, it tends to overlook other parts of emotion, such as the role of facial expression. Second, its developmental basis is somewhat limited. For example, how can a young child, who lacks the cognitive structures required to learn and apply labels to emotions, be said to have an emotion? Despite these limitations, Schachter demonstrated a role for cognition in emotion and showed how it is more than physiological arousal.

Schafer, Roy

Born: 1922, New York, USA **Nat:** American **Ints:** Psychoanalysis, psychotherapy **Educ:** BS City College of New York, 1943; MA University of Kansas, 1947; PhD Clark University, 1950 **Appts & awards:** Private Practice, Training and Supervising Analyst, Columbia University Center for Psychoanalytic Training and Research; Adjunct Professor, Department of Psychiatry, Cornell University Medical College; President, Western New England Psychoanalytic Society, 1965–7; First Freud Memorial Professor, University College London, 1975–6; Annual Award, Society for Personality Assessment, 1978; APA Award for Contributions to Professional Knowledge, 1982; American Board of Professional Psychology Award for Professional Contributions, 1983; Division of Psychoanalysis of APA Award for Contributions to Psychoanalysis, 1984–; Editorial Boards: *Journal of the American Psychoanalytic Association*, *Psychoanalytic Psychology*, *Psychological Issues*, *Psychoanalysis and Contemporary Thought*

Principal publications

1954   *Psychoanalytic Interpretations in Rorschach Testing.* Grune & Stratton.
1960   The loving and beloved superego in Freud's structural theory. *Psychoanalytic Study of the Child*, 15, 163–88.
1964   The clinical analysis of affects. *Journal of the American Psychoanalytic Association*, 12, 275–99.
1967   Ideals, the ego ideal and the ideal self. *Psychological Issues*, 5, 129–74.
1968   *Aspects of Internalization.* International Universities Press.
1968   The mechanisms of defence. *International Journal of Psychoanalysis*, 49, 49–62.
1973   The termination of brief psychoanalytic psychotherapy. *International Journal of Psychoanalytic Psychotherapy*, 2, 135–48.
1974   Problems in Freud's psychology of women.

Journal of the American Psychoanalytic Association, 22, 459–85.
1976   *A New Language for Psychoanalysis.* Yale University Press.
1978   *Language and Insight.* Yale University Press.
1981   Narrative action in psychoanalysis. Heinz Werner Memorial Lectures.
1983   *The Analytic Attitude.* Basic Books.
1984   The pursuit of failure and the idealization of unhappiness. *American Psychologist*, 39, 398–405.
1985   The interpretation of psychic reality, developmental influences and unconscious communication. *Journal of the American Psychoanalytic Association*, 33, 537–54.
1985   Wild analysis. *Journal of the American Psychoanalytic Association*, 33, 275–99.
1992   *Retelling a Life: Narration and Dialogue in Psychoanalysis.* Basic Books.

Further reading

Feldman, L. (1988) *The Anatomy of Psychotherapy.* Analytic Press.
Mitchell, S.A. and Black, M.J. (1995) *Freud and Beyond: A History of Modern Psychoanalytic Thought.* Basic.
Strenger, C. (1991) *Between Hermeneutics and Science: An Essay on the Epistemology of Psychoanalysis.* International Universities Press.

The first phase of Schafer's career is characterized by a concentration on diagnostic psychological testing, particularly on the application of psychoanalytic principles to test interpretation, from which issued several books and many articles. Around 1959, he moved to psychoanalysis proper after first completing analytic training. Then for about ten years he concentrated on expanding, extending and refining **Freud**ian metapsychology. From 1970 he worked on learning what he described as 'two new languages' for psychoanalysis, specifically 'action language', in an effort to replace nineteenth-century mechanistic concepts and world views with modern, philosophically more acceptable concepts. This work extended into narrative theory in that hermeneutic, historically narrative aspects of analytic work, together with concepts derived from literary theory, have been emphasized in place of the obsolete and inappropriate natural science perspective that controlled Freud's 'metapsychology'. Theorists in other humanistic disciplines and some in psychoanalysis have been working along similar lines. In Schafer's work the main psychological themes and technical principles of psychoanalysis have been not so much changed as seen in a new light.

Schaffer, Heinz Rudolph

Born: 1926, Berlin, Germany **Nat:** German **Ints:** Child, youth and family services, developmental **Educ:** BA Birkbeck College, University of London, 1950; PhD Glasgow University, 1962 **Appts & awards:** BPS Fellow, 1968; Social Sciences Research Council, Member, Psychology Committee, 1972–8, Council Member, 1976–8, Chairman, Psychology Committee, 1976–8; Preschool Education Working Group, Member, 1977–80; Young People in Society Working Group, Chairman, 1977–82; Children in Care Panel, Chairman, 1978–82; British Association for the Advancement of Science, President, Section J (Psychology), 1984–5; ACPP, Chairman-Elect, 1985–6; Professor of Psychology, Emeritus, University of Strathclyde, 1991– ; Co-Editor, *British Journal of Psychology*, 1968–76; Consultant, *Child Development*, 1968–74; Editorial Boards: *Journal of Child Psychology and Psychiatry*, 1974– , *Infancia y Aprendizaje*, 1980– , *Current Psychological Research*, 1980–8, *Current Psychological Reviews*, 1980–8, *Enfance*, 1982– , *Journal of Reproductive and Infant Psychology*, 1983– ; General Editor, Behavioral Development – a monograph series (Academic Press), 1979–84

Principal publications

1964 The development of social attachment in infancy. *Monographs of the Society for Research in Child Development*, 29 (3), whole no. 94 (with P.E. Emerson).

1966 The onset of fear of strangers and the incongruity hypothesis. *Journal of Child Psychology and Psychiatry*, 7, 95–106.

1971 *The Growth of Sociability*. Penguin.

1971 (ed.) *The Origins of Human Social Relations*. Academic Press.

1972 The onset of wariness. *Child Development*, 43, 165–75 (with A. Greenwood and M.H. Parry).

1974 Cognitive components of the infant's response to strangers. In M. Lewis and L.A. Rosenblum (eds), *The Origins of Fear*. Wiley.

1977 *Mothering*. Open Books/Fontana; Harvard University Press.

1977 (ed.) *Studies in Mother–Infant Interaction*. Academic Press.

1978 The development of interpersonal behavior. In H. Tajfel and C. Fraser (eds), *Introduction to Social Psychology*. Penguin.

1979 Acquiring the concept of dialogue. In M. Bornstein and W. Kessen (eds), *Psychological Development from Infancy: Image and Intention*. Erlbaum.

1979 Maternal control techniques in a directed play situation. *Child Development*, 50, 989–98 (with C.K. Crook).

1980 Child compliance and maternal control techniques. *Developmental Psychology*, 16, 54–61 (with C.K. Crook).

1983 Verbal and nonverbal aspects of mother's directives. *Journal of Child Language*, 10, 337–55.

1984 *The Child's Entry into a Social World*. Academic Press.

1984 Adult–child interaction under dyadic and polyadic conditions. *British Journal of Developmental Psychology*, 2, 33–42 (with C. Liddell).

1990 *Making Decisions About Children: Psychological Questions and Answers*. Blackwell.

Further reading

Lewis, M. and Feinman, S. (eds) (1991) *Social Influences and Socialization in Infancy*, Plenum.

Heinz Schaffer has been concerned with understanding the nature of early human development. He argues that such understanding can only come about by examining the child in its social context. His contributions therefore involve various aspects of that child–context relationship. Some of his earlier research focused on young children's reactions to their removal from home and family. This pointed to the powerful role of early social attachments, and much of his subsequent work was devoted to investigating how attachments are formed, with special reference to age when first manifested and the kinds of individual on whom they are focused. This led in turn to two lines of investigation: first, experimental studies of the behaviour of infants to gradations in novelty and familiarity and the way in which different response systems reflect the development of recognition and recall memories; second, the microanalysis of parent–child interactive sequences. The latter was particularly concerned with the manner in which adult and child come to establish joint topics for their interaction, and also the study of parental control techniques – an area that reflected his personal dissatisfaction with prevailing socialization theories and the belief that basic mutuality, not conflict, underlies adult's socializing of children: hence the stress on social preadaptedness, parental sensitivity and child compliance. Later he widened the focus of this research from the dyad to the polyad in order to do justice to the child's multi-person world. This lead to involvement (e.g. his 1990 book) in disseminating the quite substantial body of knowledge about early social development to those professions that are concerned with making decisions about children.

Schaie, K. Warner

Born: 1928, Stettin, Germany **Nat:** American **Ints:** Adult development and ageing, developmental psychology **Educ:** AA City College of San Francisco, 1951; BA University of California at Berkeley, 1952; MS University of Washington, Seattle, 1953; PhD University of Washington, Seattle, 1956 **Appts & awards:** Assistant Professor of Psychology, University of Nebraska, 1957–64; Associate Professor of Psychology, West Virginia University, 1964–73; Director of Human Resources Research Institute, West Virginia University, 1965–8; Associate Director of Gerontology Research Institute, Andrus Gerontology Center, University of Southern California, 1973–81; Professor of Psychology, University of Southern California, 1973–82; Professor of Human Development and Psychology, Department of Individual and Family Studies, Pennsylvania State University, 1981– ; Distinguished Contribution Award, APA, Division 20, 1982; Director, Pennsylvania State University Gerontology Center, 1985– ; Fellow, Center for Advanced Study in the Behavioral Sciences, 1990–1; Distinguished Scientific Contributions Award, APA, 1992; Affiliate Professor of Psychiatry and Behavioral Science, University of Washington, 1992–

Principal publications

1955   A test of behavioral rigidity. *Journal of Abnormal and Social Psychology*, 51: 604–10.
1958   Rigidity–flexibility and intelligence: A cross-sectional study of the adult life-span from 20–70. *Psychological Monographs*, 72(462), whole no. 9.
1965   A general model for the study of developmental problems. *Psychological Bulletin*, 64, 91–107.
1968   The cross-sequential study of age changes in cognitive behavior. *Psychological Bulletin*, 70, 671–80 (with C.R. Strother).
1977   Quasi-experimental designs in the psychology of aging. In J.E. Birren and K.W. Schaie (eds), *Handbook of the Psychology of Aging*. Van Nostrand Reinhold.

1983   The Seattle Longitudinal Study: A 21-year exploration of psychometric intelligence in adulthood. In K.W. Schaie (ed.), *Longitudinal Studies of Adult Psychological Development*. Guilford Press.
1983   Fourteen-year cohort-sequential studies of adult intelligence. *Developmental Psychology*, 9, 531–43 (with C. Hertzog).
1989   Perceptual speed in adulthood: Cross sectional and longitudinal studies. *Psychology and Aging*, 4, 443–53.
1990   *Handbook of the Psychology of Aging* (3rd edn). Academic Press (with J.E. Birren).
1991   *Adult Development and Aging* (3rd edn). HarperCollins (with S.L. Willis).
1994   The course of adult intellectual development. *American Psychologist*, 49, 304–13.

Further reading

Pierce, R.A. and Black, M.A. (eds) (1993) *Life-Span Development: A Diversity Reader*. Kendall/Hunt.
Sonderegger, T.B. (ed.) (1992) *Nebraska Symposium on Motivation 1991: Psychology and Aging*. University of Nebraska Press.

K. Warner Schaie was born in 1928 in Stettin, Germany, a town which on modern maps is part of Poland. Before the advent of World War II he fled with his family to Shanghai, China, and worked as a printer's apprentice during the Japanese occupation. In 1947 he moved to California and worked his way through college as a printer. He obtained an Associate's degree from the City College of San Francisco, and in 1952 earned a BA degree in psychology from the University of California at Berkeley. While an undergraduate, Schaie developed an interest in the cognitive functioning of the elderly.

During his years of graduate study at the University of Washington, Schaie began to exhibit the research and theoretical interests which were to propel him to prominence in the field. His master's thesis involved the development of the 'Test of Behavioral Rigidity', and his doctoral dissertation investigated the relationship between primary mental abilities and rigidity–flexibility. Subjects for this study were the initial cohort of the Seattle Longitudinal Study.

During his first academic appointment, at the University of Nebraska, Schaie taught courses in intellectual and personality assessment. It was not until his final year at Nebraska that he was able to obtain grant support to extend the findings of his dissertation research. With Charles Strother, Schaie analysed the longitudinal and cross-sectional data from this study. These analyses served to explicate Schaie's general developmental model, as well as to demonstrate his use of sequential methods of analysis for developmental data.

In 1964, Schaie moved to the University of West Virginia, where he developed an APA-accredited doctoral programme in clinical psychology. He later initiated the formation of a life-span developmental psychology programme. In 1973, Schaie joined James Birren, a pioneering figure in the psychology of ageing, at the Andrus Gerontology Center of the University of Southern California. Here Schaie set out to develop, among other things, ecologically valid measures of intellectual functioning, and to work on the assessment of perceived competence.

In 1981 Schaie moved to Pennsylvania State University. As head of the Gerontology Center, and with his wife Sherry Willis, he researched the efficacy of cognitive training paradigms in the reversal of age-related intellectual decline. He has also worked with behavioural geneticist Robert Plomin on an exploration of adult family similarity in cognitive development.

Schaie's impact on the psychology of adult development and ageing has been far-reaching. When honouring him for a Distinguished Scientific Contributions Award in 1992, the APA cited Schaie's ground-breaking formulation of cohort-sequential longitudinal designs to examine the dynamic interactions between ontogenetic development and cultural change. Also, his longitudinal research programme on adult intelligence has had a major impact on the field, providing data which have challenged earlier models of cognitive ageing to account for latent cognitive potential in old age.

J.D. HOGAN AND W. IACCINO

Schank, Roger

Born: 1946, New York, USA **Nat:** American **Ints:** Artificial intelligence, explanation, memory, natural language processing **Educ:** BS Mathematics Carnegie Institute of Technology, 1966; MA University of Texas at Austin, 1967; PhD 1969; MA Yale University, 1976 **Appts & awards:** Professor of Computer Science and Psychology; Editor, *Cognitive Science Journal*; Board of Editors: *Information Systems*, *Pragmatics Discourse Processing*, *Brain and Behavioral Science*, *Experimental Psychology*, *Human Learning and Memory*; Program Chairman, IICAI Vancouver, 1981

Principal publications

1975 *Conceptual Information Processing*. North-Holland.

1975 The structure of episodes in memory. In Bobrow and Collins (eds), *Representation and Understanding: Studies in Cognitive Science*. Academic Press.

1977 *Scripts, Plans, Goals and Understanding: An Inquiry into Human Knowledge Structures*. Erlbaum (with R. Abelson).

1977 Scripts, plans and knowledge. In P.N. Johson-Laird and P.C. Wason (eds), *Thinking Reading in Cognitive Science*. Cambridge University Press.

1978 A goal directed production system for story understanding. In D.A. Waterman and F. Hayes-Roth, *Pattern Directed Inference Systems*. Academic Press.

1978 Computer understanding of stories. In F. Klix and V.E.B. Deutscher, *Human and Artificial Intelligence*. Verlag der Wissenschaften (with W. Lehnert).

1979 Interestingness: Controlling inferences. *Artificial Intelligence*, 12, 273–97.

1980 How much intelligence is there in artificial intelligence. *Intelligence*, 4, 1–14.

1980 An integrated understander. *American Journal of Computational Linguistics*, 6, 1, 13–30 (with M. Lebowitz and L. Birnbaum).

1980 Language and memory. *Cognitive Science*, 4(3), 243–84.

1981 *Reading and Understanding: Teaching from An Artificial Intelligence Perspective*. Erlbaum.

1982 *Dynamic Memory: A Theory of Learning in Computers and People*. Cambridge University Press.

1982 What's the point? *Cognitive Science*, 6, 31, 255–75 (with G. Collins, E. Davis, P. Johnson, S. Lytinen and B. Reiser).

1984 *The Cognitive Computer: On Language, Learning and Artificial Intelligence*. Addison-Wesley (with P. Childers).

Further reading

Posner, M.I. (ed.) (1989) *Foundations of Cognitive Science*. Bradford.

Roger Schank's principal contributions have been in the formulation of script theory (with Abelson) and its later modification, dynamic memory theory. The concept of schema was first proposed by F.C. **Bartlett**, who defined it as a knowledge framework built up through experience that guides the interpretation of new information and guides future actions. The concept is somewhat woolly, but Schank and Abelson refined and developed it. They suggest that people acquire schemata, or scripts as they called them, for commonly experienced structured events. Their classic example involves lunch at a restaurant. This setting involves expectations about what will happen when we enter the restaurant, how we will be treated and how we will leave. Scripts are sequences of actions we follow when engaged in stereotypical situations. Schank and Abelson offered considerable empirical support for the existence of schemata or script-like knowledge structures. However, the early formulation of the theory was limited by the inflexibility of script structure. For example, it could neither account for ordered behaviour in novel or unexpected situations, nor explain how people could understand goal-directed behaviour in situations for which they had not learned a script (e.g. a medical operation or a bank robbery). To take account of these limitations Schank modified script theory and presented his dynamic memory theory.

This introduces the notion of memory organization packets (MOPs). MOPs are generalized clusters of events called scenes. Scenes are collections of the high-level components of scripts. MOPs organize sets of scenes and add specific contextual information. The addition of MOPs and scenes adds flexibility to the theory because scenes can be combined and recombined in any required organization. Above MOPs is a higher level of organization, called thematic organisation points (TOPs). TOPs are less tied to a particular set of situations and apply generally to the themes of whole sequences of episodes. TOPs play an important part in reminding a person what to do.

Schank's theory has a number of problems associated with the fact that it is somewhat unprincipled. This means that it is usually fairly easy to create a schema or script for just about any pattern of behaviour observed. In other words, the theory is good at accounting for behaviour in an *ad hoc* and *post hoc* fashion but has limited predictive use.

Schein, Edgar H.

Born: 1928, Zurich, Switzerland **Nat:** Swiss **Ints:** Consulting psychology, industrial and organizational psychology, personality and social psychology, psychological study of social issues **Educ:** BA University of Chicago, 1947; BA, MA Stanford University, 1948; PhD Harvard University, 1952 **Appts & awards:** Sloan Fellows Professor of Management, MIT;

Editorial Advisory Board, *Sloan Management Review*; Co-Editor, MIT Series on Organizational Development, 1968–

Principal publications

1961 *Coercive Persuasion*. Norton.
1969 *Process Consultation*. Addison-Wesley.
1978 *Career Dynamics*. Addison-Wesley.
1980 *Organizational Psychology* (3rd edn). Prentice Hall.
1985 *Organizational Culture and Leadership*. Jossey-Bass.

Further reading

Frost, P.J. *et al.* (eds) (1991) *Reframing Organizational Culture*. Sage.
Montross, D.H. and Shinkman, C.J. (eds) (1992) *Career Development: Theory and Practice*. Charles C. Thomas.

Throughout his career Schein has been concerned to clarify the relationship between the individual and the organization. His early work has its origins in his observations of Chinese Communists' methods of indoctrination in the Korean War. He then turned to organizations and showed how socialization methods used in management development could be likened to indoctrination.

Schein wrote one of the first textbooks on organizational psychology and helped to clarify the concept of process consultation in the field of organization development. Career development research came next, and led to the concept of career anchors that has been studied by following a panel of forty-four MIT alumni. His later work has focused on organizational culture – what it is, how to measure it, how it evolves, and whether or not it can be managed. The role that leadership plays in this process is now his main interest.

In his book *Organizational Psychology* Schein gives an excellent overview of the field, outlining the development of ideas and conceptualizations of the organization and discussing perspectives on the organization, such as those of the complex open system and the dynamic developing system. Whilst highlighting the complexity of organizations, he argues that if we are not to be the victims of them we must seek to understand the phenomena at work. We must seek sufficient understanding to be able to influence them. He suggests that the concepts around the notion of the complex open system are rather static and global and argues for a more dynamic concept of organization and development. This is one in which the organization is seen as an 'open, complex system in dynamic interaction with multiple environments, attempting to fulfil goals and perform tasks at many levels and in varying degrees of complexity, evolving, and developing as the interaction with the environment forces new internal adaptations'. It is within this context that Schein has turned his attention to the issue of leadership, its impact and role within organizations.

JONATHAN G. HARVEY

Schlosberg, Harold
Born: 1904, Brooklyn, New York **Died:** 1964, Providence, Rhode Island **Nat:** American **Ints:** Evaluation and measurement, experimental analysis of behaviour, experimental psychology **Educ:** AB Princeton University, 1925; MA Princeton University, 1926; PhD Princeton University, 1928 **Appts & awards:** Chairman, Department of Psychology, Brown University; President APA, Division 3, 1952; Vice-President and Chairman AAAS Section 1 (Psychology), 1952; Fellow, AAAS; President, Eastern Psychological Association, 1953–4; Chairman, Panel of Consultants in Psychophysiology to the Surgeon General, US Army, 1964; Editorial board, *Annual Review of Psychology*, *Psychological Review*

Principal publications
1928   A study of the conditioned patellar reflex. *Journal of Experimental Psychology*, 11, 468–94.
1937   The relationship between success and the laws of conditioning. *Psychological Review*, 44, 379–94.
1952   The description of facial expression in terms of two dimensions. *Journal of Experimental Psychology*, 44, 229–37.
1954   *Experimental Psychology*. Holt (with R.S. Woodworth).
1954   Three dimensions of emotion. *Psychological Review*, 61, 81–8.
1960   The secondary reward value of inaccessible food for hungry and satiated rats. *Journal of Comparative Physiological Psychology*, 53, 385–7 (with C.H. Pratt).
1965   Time relations in serial visual perception. *Canadian Psychology*, 1965, 6a, 161–72.

Schlosberg is probably best known as a communicator of psychology. He collaborated in the revision of R.S. **Woodworth**'s *Experimental Psychology* (originally published in 1938) to produce the 'bible' – the Woodworth and Schlosberg 1954 edition of the book – which was to dominate the teaching of experimental psychology for about two decades. The seventy or so research papers written by Schlosberg, on topics such as motivation, emotion, learning and perception, reflect his wide interests within experimental psychology. His contributions can be grouped into three career phases. His earliest research was in the field of learning and conditioning and he published several articles in which he argued for a functional distinction between the processes of learning demonstrated by the models of **Thorndike** and **Pavlov**. Later work reflects a shift in emphasis: he became interested in the psychophysical scaling of the facial expression of emotion and argued that it could be described in terms of two and later three dimensions. His last research was in the field of visual perception, particularly in the phenomena associated with the timing of stimuli such as background masking. Schlosberg was noted for his ingenuity in producing measuring devices for the variables in which he was interested, and for his ability to clearly explain his methodology and results.

Schneider, Benjamin
Born: 1938, New York, USA **Nat:** American **Ints:** Industrial and organizational **Educ:** BA Alfred University, 1960; MBA Baruch College (CUNY), 1962; PhD University of Maryland, 1967 **Appts & awards:** Professor of Psychology and Business Management, Department of Psychology, University of Maryland, 1971–9, 1982– ; APA, Fellow, 1976, Division 14, President, 1984–5; Charter Fellow, American Psychological Society, 1975; Member at Large, Society for Industrial and Organizational Psychology, 1977–80; Organizational Behavior Division, Academy of Management, President, 1981–2, Fellow, 1992; James McKeen Cattell Award, Society for Industrial and Organizational Psychology (with C.J. Bartlett), 1966–7; Editorial Boards: *Academy of Management Journal*, 1971–84, *Administrative Science Quarterly*, 1977–83; Series Co-Editor, Organization and Management Series (Lexington), 1984–

Principal publications
1973   Organizational climates and careers: The work lives of priests (with D.T. Hall).
1975   Organizational climates: An essay. *Personnel Psychology*, 28, 447–79.

1976   *Staffing Organizations.* Goodyear (with N.
       Schmitt). (2nd edn, Scott-Foresmam, 1986).
1980   The service organization: Climate is crucial.
       Organizational Dynamics, Autumn, 52–65.
1980   Employee and customer perceptions of service
       in banks. *Administrative Science Quarterly*, 25,
       252–67 (with J.P. Parkington and V.M. Buxton).
1983   Interactional psychology and organizational
       behavior. In L.L. Cummings and B. Staw (eds),
       Research in Organizational Behavior. JAI Press.
1983   An interactionist perspective on organizational
       effectiveness. In K. Cameron and D. Whetten
       (eds), *Organizational Effectiveness: A Comparison
       of Multiple Models.* Academic Press.
1983   On the etiology of climates. *Personnel
       Psychology*, 36, 19–39 (with A. Reichers).
1984   Industrial-organizational psychology
       perspective. In A.P. Brief (ed.), *Research on
       Productivity.* Praeger.
1985   Organizational behavior. *Annual Review of
       Psychology*, 36, 573–611.
1988   *Facilitating Work Effectiveness.* Lexington.
1990   *Organizational Climate and Culture.* Jossey-
       Bass.
1991   Service quality and profits: Can you have your
       cake and eat it too? *Human Resource Planning*, 14,
       151–7.
1992   A passion for service: Using content analysis
       to explicate service climate themes. *Journal of
       Applied Psychology*, 77, 705–16.
1994   Do customer perceptions generalize: The case
       of student and chair ratings of faculty effectiveness.
       Journal of Applied Psychology, 79, 685–90.
1995   *Winning the Service Game.* Harvard Business
       School Press.

Further reading

Bowen, D.E. *et al.* (1990) *Service Management
   Effectiveness: Balancing Strategy, Organization
   and Human Resources, Operations, and Marketing.*
   Jossey-Bass.
Frost, P.J. *et al.* (eds) (1991) *Reframing
   Organizational Culture.* Sage.
Harris, D.H. (ed.) (1994) *Organizational Linkages:
   Understanding the Productivity Paradox.* National
   Academy Press.

Schneider's research interests developed under
C.J. Bartlett in his course on personnel selection.
In that course he wondered about the necessity
to revalidate tests as they were moved from
setting to setting, and reasoned that perhaps the
climate of the setting influenced test validity.
This thought led to a subsequent interest in the
conceptualization and assessment of organizational climate. This interest was greatly

enhanced during his first position (at Yale
University), where he was influenced by Chris
Argyris, Douglas T. (Tim) Hall and Edward E.
Lawler. This influence took the form of pushing
Schneider towards an organizational behaviour
perspective on the workings of organizations
and the people in them. This early graduate
immersion in personnel psychology, with subsequent thorough exposure to organizational
behaviour, contributed to many of his current
concerns about the nature of person–situation
interactions in the workplace.

His more recent framework for understanding how organizations come to look the way
they do is that a cycle of attraction, selection
and attrition yields particular kinds of people in
particular organizations and that it is this type
of person that defines the style and culture of
the place. This framework implies that it is
people, not structure, technology, size and so
on, that cause organizations to look and feel the
way they do. More recent work on trying to
understand what it is in organizations that
facilitates effectiveness can be traced also to
early concerns for the interaction of persons
and settings. Schneider's work on conceptualization of services and the nature of service
organizations (banks, insurance companies)
also has this person–situation flavour. Perhaps
the most interesting outcome of this latter work
is the finding that employees and customers of
service organizations tend to agree on the
quality of the service offered and received. This
finding has many implications, among which
are the following: consumer behaviour and
organizational behaviour are not so distinct as
may have been imagined; if services and the
people who produce them are different from
goods and the persons who manufacture them,
then the models of management developed in
the manufacturing sector may not be appropriate for managing service organizations and
the people in them. At a more general level, his
work has been influenced by the observation
that workers would much rather do a good job
than a bad one and that they surmount enormous obstacles in their attempts to be effective.
This has influenced his more recent work, in
which he is attempting to understand more
precisely what it means to facilitate work
effectiveness.

Scott, John Paul

Born: 1909, Kansas City, USA ***Nat:*** American
Ints: Physiological and comparative psychology

Educ: BA University of Wyoming, 1930; BA Oxford University, 1932; PhD University of Chicago, 1935 **Appts & awards:** Jordan Prize, Indiana Academy of Science, 1947; Fellow, APA, 1948; Maine Psychological Association, 1953–4; Member, AAAS; Chairman, Animal Behavior Society, 1957–8; Vice-President, Eugenics Society, 1963; New York Zoological Society; Center for Advanced Study in the Behavioral Sciences, 1963–4; President, International Society for Developmental Psychobiology, 1972–3; International Society for Research on Aggression, 1973–4, Council, 1975; Behavior Genetics Association, 1975–6; Regents Professor of Psychology (Emeritus), Bowling Green State University, 1980– ; Editorial Boards: *Aggressive Behavior*, *Journal of Applied Ethology*

Principal publications

1942 Genetic differences in the social behavior of inbred strains of mice. *Journal of Heredity*, 33, 11–15.

1943 Effects of single genes on the behavior of Drosophila. *American Naturalist*, 77, 184–90.

1945 Social behavior, organization and leadership in a small flock of domestic sheep. *Comparative Psychology Monographs*, 18, 1–29.

1950 The social behavior of dogs and wolves: An illustration of sociobiological systematics. *Annals of the New York Academy of Science*, 51, 1009–21.

1956 Hereditary differences in the development of dominance in litters of puppies. *Journal of Comparative and Physiological Psychology*, 49, 353–8 (with A. Pawlowski).

1956 The analysis of social organization in animals. *Ecology*, 37, 213–21.

1958 *Animal Behavior*. University of Chicago Press. (reprinted 1972).

1958 *Aggression*. University of Chicago Press. (reprinted 1972).

1965 *Genetics and the Social Behavior of the Day*. University of Chicago Press (with J.L. Fuller).

1968 Differential human handling and the development of agonistic behavior in basenji and Shetland sheepdogs. *Developmental Psychobiology*, 1, 133–40 (with F.H. Bronson and A. Trattner).

1971 *Social Control and Social Change*. University of Chicago Press (with F. Scott).

1977 Social genetics. *Behavior Genetics*, 7, 327–66.

1977 Agnostic behavior: Function and dysfunction in social conflict. *Journal of Social Issues*, 33, 9–21.

1978 *Critical Periods*. Dowden, Hutchinson & Ross.

1982 Biology and political behavior: A systems analysis. *American Behavioral Scientist*, 25, 243–72.

Further reading

Clynes, M. and Panksepp, J. (eds) (1988) *Emotions and Psychopathology*. Plenum.

Davis, H. and Balfour, D.A. (eds) (1992) *The Inevitable Bond: Examining Scientist-Animal Interactions*. Cambridge University Press.

An inspection of Scott's publications shows that he has been strongly motivated by observing the destructive effects of warfare and the malfunctioning of political-economic systems. He started with the problem of the effects of genetics on social behaviour, and by way of preparation studied zoology at Oxford (tutored by E.B. Ford) and took a PhD in Developmental Genetics under Sewall Wright.

His first publication in the field, a study of the effects of single genes on the phototropic behaviour of fruit flies, came a few years later, but he felt a need to concentrate on studying species more closely related to *Homo sapiens* in order to discover anything of human significance, and followed with a study showing differences in fighting behaviour in inbred strains of mice. Later he came to regard genetics as only one of many factors that influence aggression. During his first post as a lecturer at Wabash College he developed a comprehensive theoretical system for the analogous of social behaviour, and this system guided most of his further research. The first result was the publication of a study on social behaviour and social organizations in sheep, which he used as a model for studies in sociobiology.

In 1945 he studied genetics and the social behaviour of dogs, a twenty-year study in collaboration with John L. Fuller, in which they combined the technique of behavioural development and social interaction with genetics. This resulted in a book that helped to establish the field of behavior genetics. As a result of the sheep and dog studies, Scott became impressed with the phenomenon of critical periods, and followed this with publications that established a theoretical basis for it. It now stands as a technique with numerous applied uses in organizational development at any level. Scott is also interested in the phenomena of attachment and separation, and contributions in this field have direct application to the genesis of certain kinds of maladaptive behaviour.

In later years, Scott was concerned with the concept of systems as a generally integrative theory uniting and explaining the phenomena of biological and behavioural science.

Searle, John Rogers

Born: 1932, Denver, USA *Nat:* American *Ints:* Philosophical and theoretical psychology *Educ:* 1955 BA; 1959 MA University of Oxford; 1959 DPhil University of Oxford *Appts & awards:* Rhodes Scholar, Oxford, 1952–5; Lecturer in Philosophy, Christ Church, Oxford, 1956–9; Professor, University of California at Berkeley, 1959– ; Guggenheim Fellow 1975–6; Member, American Academy of Arts and Sciences, 1977– ; Reith Lecturer, BBC, 1984

Principal publications

1969 *Speech Acts: An Essay in the Philosophy of Language*. Cambridge University Press.
1980 Minds, brains and programs. *Behavioral and Brain Sciences*, 3, 417–58.
1983 *Intentionality: An Essay in the Philosophy of Mind*. Cambridge University Press.
1985 *Minds, Brains and Science*. Harvard University Press.
1992 *The Rediscovery of Mind*. MIT Press.
1995 *The Construction of Social Reality*. Allen Lane.

Further reading

Lepore, E. and Van Gulick, R (1991) *John Searle and His Critics*. Blackwell.

John Searle was educated at the University of Wisconsin and at Oxford, where he graduated in 1955. In 1959, he returned to the USA, to the University of California at Berkeley, and has remained there. Early in his career he developed the theory of speech acts, originated by J.L. Austin at Oxford, in which a distinction is drawn between the propositional content of an utterance (its 'meaning') and its 'illocutionary force' (which defines the object of the speaker in conveying that meaning on that occasion – as an assertion, a promise, a request, etc.). Searle proposed a taxonomy of speech acts which is still the subject of lively controversy among philosophers of language. More recently, he has extended the argument from language to intentional states generally. He continues to draw a distinction between the propositional content of a state and its mode of psychological existence. He argues that an intentional state can only exist against a background of non-intentional mental phenomena (skills, abilities, etc.). Unlike most philosophers, Searle treats intentionality as primarily a form of perception or action, rather than of belief or desire. Mental phenomena are, for Searle, first-person phenomena. He rejects the third-person approach associated with, for example, **Dennett** but, like Dennett, denies the need for any intermediate level of theorizing between intentional and pre-intentional mental phenomena and neurophysiology.

Searle believes that the mind/body problem arises only because the distinction between mental and physical has been taken for granted. He advocates a kind of common-sense view, that mental processes (e.g. consciousness) are caused by 'objective' micro-processes in the brain but are at the same time 'subjective' macro-level features of the brain. Macro-level events in the brain are caused by micro-level events in the same unmysterious sense that the liquidity of water is caused by some of the properties of its component molecules. There is not one ontological category ('mind' or 'body') or two ('mind and body'), but an indefinitely large number 'from quarks…to balance of payments problems'. Searle's view on this subject may well be the only genuinely rational view, but the distinction between mental and physical is so deeply embedded in our customary modes of thinking that, common-sense or not, it has not been widely accepted – the argument continues as before.

Searle introduced the famous (among psychologists) 'Chinese Room' argument. He imagined a room containing baskets of Chinese symbols and a book of instructions (in English) specifying that any input message consisting of given Chinese symbols should receive a reply consisting of other specified symbols. An operator speaking only English was thus able to offer what appeared to be rational responses to questions posed in Chinese, without knowing any Chinese or having any idea what the dialogue was about. In Searle's view this argument shows that computers can model thought processes but cannot actually think – they have the syntax but lack the semantics necessary for genuine thinking. Nobody supposes that a computer model of the digestive processes could actually digest anything. Proponents of strong AI (artificial intelligence) find Searle's argument unconvincing, since they assume that semantics will ultimately be brought within the sphere of syntax: though it is not at present clear how this will be done (if indeed it can be done). Searle expresses surprise that his argument has been found unacceptable by anybody. For him (and for many philosophers) the nature of intentionality – how it is that 'horse' (the word) can mean horse (the animal) – is a central and unresolved issue, whereas computer scientists and psychologists tend to assume that more and better symbolling will necessarily do the trick, since nothing else is available as far as they are aware at present.

N.E. WETHERICK

Sears, Robert Richardson

Born: 1908, Palo Alto, California, USA **Nat:** American **Ints:** Adult development and ageing, developmental, history of psychology, personality, psychology and the arts **Educ:** BA Stanford University, 1929; PhD Yale University, 1932 **Appts & awards:** Hon. MA, Harvard University, 1950; APA President, 1951; APA Division 7, G. Stanley Award; President, Western Psychological Association, 1963; President, SRCD, 1970; Distinguished Scientific Contribution Award, APA, 1975; Distinguished Scientific Contribution Award, SRCD, 1983; Gold Medal Award, American Psychological Foundation (with Pauline F. Sears), 1980; Member, American Academy of Arts and Sciences; David Starr Jordan Professor of Social Sciences in Psychology (Emeritus), Stanford University; Editor, Monographs of Society for Research in Child Development 1970–5

Principal publications

1936 Functional abnormalities of memory with special reference to amnesia. *Psychological Bulletin*, 31, 229–74.
1939 *Frustration and Aggression*. Yale University Press (with J. Dollard, L.W. Doob, N.E. Miller and O.H. Mowrer).
1941 Success and failure: A study of motility. In Q. McNemar and M.M. James (eds), *Studies in Personality*. McGraw-Hill.
1943 *Survey of Objective Studies of Psychoanalytic Concepts*. SSRC.
1946 Effect of father separation on preschool children's doll play aggression. *Child Development*, 17, 219–43 (with M.H. Pintler and P.S. Sears).
1950 Relation of cup-feeding in infancy to thumb-sucking and oral drive. *American Journal of Orthopsychiatry*, 20, 123–38 (with G.W. Wise).
1951 A theoretical framework for personality and social behavior. *American Psychologist*, 6, 476–83.

1953 Some child-rearing antecedents of aggression and dependency in young children. *Genetic Psychology Monographs*, 47, 135–234.
1957 *Patterns of Child Rearing*. Row Peterson (with E.E. Maccoby and H. Levin).
1965 *Identification and Child Rearing*. Stanford University Press (with L. Rau and R. Alpert).
1973 (ed.) *The Seven Ages of Man*. Kaufman (with S.S. Feldman).
1975 Your ancients revisited: A history of child development. In M. Hetherington (ed.), *Review of Child Development Research. Volume 5*. University of Chicago Press.
1977 Sources of life satisfaction of the Terman gifted men. *American Psychologist*, 32, 119–28.
1981 The role of expectancy in adaptation to aging. In S.B. Keisler, J.N. Morgan and V.K. Oppenheimer (eds), *Aging: Social Change*. Academic Press.
1982 Mark Twain's exhibitionism. *Biography*, 5, 95–117 (with R. Weissbourd).

Further reading

Grusec, J.E. (1992) Social learning theory and developmental psychology: The legacies of Robert Sears and Albert Bandura. *Developmental Psychology*, 28, 776–86.
Sears, R.R. (1992) Psychoanalysis and behavior theory: 1907–1965. In S. Koch and D.E. Leary (eds), *A Century of Psychology as Science*. American Psychological Association.

Sears' graduate training was in neuropsychology and conditioned reflexes. His first teaching position called for courses in personality and abnormal psychology, however, and he found these fields more related to his interest in human motivation. His wife, Pauline Sears, herself a clinical psychologist, suggested psychoanalysis as a framework when he was faced with the task of learning enough personality psychology to be able to teach it. He did not like the mentalistic approach but was much taken with the motivational theory and psychodynamics. This led into several years of research and theory-building concerned with converting **Freud**ian theory to behaviour theory, especially in respect of concepts of projection, repression, frustration, aggression and dependency.

Quite abruptly (in 1941) he became a child psychologist by being appointed Director of the Iowa Child Welfare Research Station. His interests at once shifted from action theory of psychodynamics and social behaviour to a learning-theory approach to child rearing and personality development. Most of this work was collaborative, much of it with Pauline and students, and other colleagues with whom he co-authored many publications. In 1953, after a four-year period at Harvard, he moved to Stanford, where he continued this developmental work until 1961, when he became Dean of the School of Humanities and Sciences. A decade of purely administrative work left him close to retirement. Since **Terman**'s death in 1956, Sears had been his scientific executor for the longitudinal study of gifted children, so, in 1973, with both Sears and Pauline retiring, they shifted their research to ageing. The gifted 'children', now aged 60, provided an ideal vehicle. Retirement also left freedom to do a little historical writing and to make a serious effort to understand Mark Twain's psychological life history.

Seashore, Carl Emil

Born: 1866, Melinda, Sweden **Died:** 1949, Iowa City, USA **Nat:** American **Ints:** Audition, educational, experimental, psychology of music and art, vision **Educ:** Graduate, Gustavus Adolphus College, St Peter, Minnesota, 1890; PhD Yale University, 1895 **Appts & awards:** Dean, Graduate School University of Iowa, 1890; Director, Psychological laboratory, University of Iowa, 1897; President, APA, 1947

Principal publications

1919 *Seashore Measures of Musical Talent.* Columbia Gramophone.
1919 *The Psychology of Musical Talent.* Silver-Burdett.
1938 *The Psychology of Music.* McGraw-Hill.
1939 Revision of the Shore Measures of Musical Talents. *University of Iowa Studies: Aims and Progress in Research*, 65, 1–66 (with J.C. Saetveit and D. Lewis).
1949 *In Search of Beauty in Music.* Ronald Press.

Further reading

Murchison, C. (ed.) (1961) *History of Psychology in Autobiography. Vol. 1.* Russell and Russell.

Carl Emil Seashore was born in Melinda, Sweden, 28 January 1866. His parents were farmers. In his youth the family emigrated to the United States. At the time, Seashore was proficient in both Swedish and English, and he graduated from Gustavus Adolphus College in St Peter, Minnesota. From there he went to the graduate school at Yale University receiving his

PhD in 1895. There, he studied with the pioneering psychologists, G.T. **Ladd** and S.T. Scripture. He learned their brass instrument experimental psychology and the predominant structural psychology of E.B. **Titchener**. This predominant systematic position dominated his experimental work and theoretical thinking.

While in college he developed a strong interest in music, a passion which would dominate the rest of his psychological experimentation. He sang in the college choir and participated in other musical and instrumental activities. In graduate school he learned what was then known about psychological statistics and measurement.

As one of the earliest pioneers in the psychology of music he developed the first standardized test, the Seashore Measures of Musical Talent. His theory in musical measurement was called a 'theory of specifics': he believed there was no general musical 'talent' but that musical aptitude consisted of a number of specific, unrelated talents, which were inborn and not subject to environmental change. Everyone had these musical talents in various degrees, and these innate abilities existed as degrees of discrimination: the more acute the discriminations the greater the talent. The original set of six tests was recorded on 78 r.p.m. phonograph records. Using the psychophysical method of constant stimuli, the subject heard a tone (or click) as the standard and then a second one, which differed from it in various degrees (loudness, pitch, etc.). These were related to perceptual aspects of the sound wave. The original six tests consisted of pitch (frequency), loudness (amplitude), time (duration), consonance and dissonance, rhythm (patterning) and, finally, tonal memory. He maintained that there might be other factors contributing to musical talent, but these were six that he could measure and the potentially talented person must do well on all tests. If parents had their child given these tests and it did poorly, there was no need to spend amounts of money on music lessons, since the child had little or no talent and would not develop any. During the 1920s and 1930s these tests were very popular in identifying 'talented' children.

In the late 1930s Seashore revised his tests in keeping with more sophisticated recording techniques. The test of consonance and dissonance was abandoned, as it seemed (despite the theories of **Stumpf** and **Helmholtz**) there were no real standards as to what constituted consonant and dissonant intervals. In the revision he substituted a test of timbre, in which the third and fourth overtones were altered or stayed the same. Later studies using external criteria for validation found the tests of pitch, rhythm and tonal memory to be useful; the others seemed not very useful predictors.

Seashore was also interested in musical performance, studying various aspects of the piano, violin and voice. His last book, *In Search of Beauty in Music*, stresses the importance of music's ability to arouse emotions and feelings in the listener in order to be considered beautiful. After developing his music tests, Seashore (always interested in the psychology of vision) collaborated with Norman C. **Meier** in developing a test of artistic appreciation, known as the Meier–Seashore Art Appreciation Test. In this test the subject viewed two art objects (usually pictures) and was asked to tell which one was better. One was the original just as the artist had painted it, the second had an alteration making it less attractive, aesthetically. The subjects with good artistic appreciation would pick the original as created by the artist.

There were those who objected to Seashore's strict natavistic and specific nature of musical talents. Among his most trenchant critics was James **Murcell**, who, in a series of articles in the *Journal of Music Education*, took Seashore to task, maintaining that musical talent was more generalized and not just made up of a series of specific talents.

ROBERT W. LUNDIN

Secord, Paul F.

Born: 1917, Chicago, USA **Nat:** American **Ints:** Personality and social, philosophical and theoretical **Educ:** BA Ripon College, 1942; MA Stanford University, 1948; PhD Stanford University, 1950 **Appts & awards:** Nevada State Board of Psychological Examiners, President, 1963–8; APA, Member, Council of Representatives, 1966–9, 1970–3, Education and Training Board, 1968–73; APA Division 8, Secretary-Treasurer, 1970–3, President, 1974–5; Society for Experimental Social Psychology, Chairman, Executive Committee, 1971–3; Society for Philosophy and Psychology, President, 1977–8; Professor of Psychology of Education, Adjunct Professor of Sociology, University of Houston, Texas, 1978; ASA Distinguished Contribution to Scholarship Award, 1984; Fellow, APA, ASA; Associate Editor, *Sociometry*, 1969–72; Editorial Board, *Journal of Social Issues*, 1969–73; Editor, *Journal for the Theory of Social Behavior*, 1970–84

Principal publications

1956   Personalities in faces: VI. Interaction efforts in the perception of faces. *Journal of Personality*, 24, 270–84 (with T.M. Stritch).

1961   An interpersonal approach to stability and change in individual behavior. *Psychological Review*, 68, 21–32 (with C.W. Backman).

1963   Stereotyping and the generality of implicit personality theory. *Journal of Personality*, 31, 65–78 (with S. Berscheid).

1964   *Social Psychology*. McGraw-Hill (with C.W. Backman) (reprinted 1974).

1964   Interpersonal congruency, perceived similarity and friendship. *Sociometry*, 27, 115–27 (with C.W. Backman).

1966   *Problems in Social Psychology*. McGraw-Hill (with C.W. Backman).

1968   *A Social Psychological View of Education*. Harcourt Brace (with C.W. Backman).

1972   *The Explanation of Social Behavior*. Blackwell (with R. Harré).

1974   The development and attribution of person concepts. In T. Mischel (ed.), *Understanding Other Persons*. Blackwell (with B.H. Peevers).

1977   Making oneself behave. In T. Mischel (ed.), *The Self: Psychological and Philosophical Issues*. Blackwell.

1977   Social psychology in search of a paradigm. *Personality and Social Psychology Bulletin*, 3, 41–50.

1982   *Consciousness, Human Action and Social Structure*. Sage.

1982   The origin and maintenance of social roles: The case of sex roles. In W. Ickes and E.W. Knowles (eds), *Personality Roles and Social Behavior*. Springer-Verlag.

1983   Implications for psychology of the new philosophy of science. *American Psychologist*, 38, 399–413 (with P.T. Manicas).

1984   Determinism, free will and self-intervention: A psychological perspective. *New Ideas in Psychology*, 2, 25–33.

Further reading

Robinson, D.N. and Mos, L.P. (eds) (1990) *Annals of Theoretical Psychology, Vol. 6*. Plenum.

The central focus of the professional life of Paul Secord has been interdisciplinary, embracing psychology and sociology at first, and later philosophy. This orientation grew from a conviction that social behaviour can only be explained fully by taking into account factors ranging from biological to societal. The narrow disciplinary boundaries that characterize conventional fields thus result in impoverished explanations of social behaviour. This perspective is reflected in research and writing conducted jointly with sociologists and philosophers, as well as in active membership in interdisciplinary professional organizations. Secord's university appointments have reflected this move, as he has worked in interdisciplinary departments.

He chose social psychology as a field because it seemed to be broader in scope than many of the psychological specialities, and from the start he considered contributions from both psychology and sociology to the understanding of social behaviour. During fifteen years at the University of Nevada, he took a leadership role in developing an interdisciplinary social psychology programme leading to the BA, MA and PhD degrees, a programme still in place. At the same time his research and writing included collaboration with sociologists, and he later expanded this interdisciplinary work to include the philosophy of mind and the philosophy of social science.

He has been active in the two most important social psychology organizations in the USA, the Division of Personality and Social Psychology of the APA and the Society for Experimental Social Psychology, and he has served as chairman for these organizations. He was an active member of the group that founded the Society for Philosophy and Psychology, of which he later became president. He cites his most notable effort as the foundation and editing of the interdisciplinary *Journal for the Theory of Social Behavior*, carried out jointly with Rom **Harré**.

Seligman, Martin E.P.

Born: 1942, Albany, New York, USA *Nat:* American *Ints:* Adult development and ageing, clinical psychology, developmental psychology, experimental psychology, personality and social psychology *Educ:* AB Princeton University, 1964; PhD University of Pennsylvania, 1967 *Appts & awards:* Fellow, AAAS; Guggenheim Fellow, 1974–5; Fellow, APA; APA Distinguished Scientific Contribution Award, 1976; 1976– , Professor of Psychology and Director of Clinical Training, University of Pennsylvania; NIMH Subcommittee on Child Development; Co-Chairman, Senior Advisory Board on Longitudinal Studies of Puberty, SSRC Committee on Lifespan Development, 1979– ; Editorial Boards: *Journal of Experimental Psychology: Animal Behavior Processes*, *Behavior Modification, Cognition and Clinical*

Science; Advisory Board, *Clinical Behavior Therapy Review*

Principal publications

1967 Failure to escape traumatic shock. *Journal of Experimental Psychology*, 74, 1–9 (with S.F. Maier).

1970 Consequences of unpredictable and uncontrollable trauma. In F.R. Brush (ed.), *Aversive Conditioning and Learning*. Academic Press (with S.F. Maier and R.L. Solomon).

1970 On the generality of the laws of learning. *Psychological Review*, 77, 406–18.

1971 Preparedness and phobias. *Behavior Therapy*, 2, 307–20.

1972 *Biological Boundaries of Learning*. Appleton-Century-Crofts (ed. with J. Hager).

1974 Depression and learned helplessness. In R.J. Friedman and M.M. Katz (eds), *The Psychology of Depression: Contemporary Theory and Research*. Winston-Wiley.

1975 *Helplessness: On Depression, Development and Death*. Freeman (ed. with J. Maser). (2nd edn, 1991).

1977 *Psychopathology: Experimental Models*. Freeman (with J. Maser).

1980 *Human Helplessness: Theory and Application*. Academic Press (ed. with J. Garber).

1984 *Abnormal Psychology*. Norton (with D.R. Rosenhan). (2nd edn, 1989; 3rd edn, in press).

1984 Causal explanations as a risk factor for depression: Theory and evidence. *Psychological Review*, 91, 347–74 (with C. Peterson).

1991 *Learned Optimism*. Knopf.

1993 *What You Can Change and What You Can't*. Knopf.

Further reading

Hunsley, J. (1989) Vulnerability to depressive mood: An examination of the temporal consistency of the reformulated learned helplessness model. *Cognitive Therapy and Research*, 13, 599–608.

Maier, S.F. (1993) Learned helplessness: Relationships with fear and anxiety. In S.C. Stanford and P. Salmon (eds), *Stress: From Synapse to Syndrome*. Academic Press.

Mikulincer, M. (1994) *Human Learned Helplessness: A Coping Perspective*. Plenum.

Martin Seligman become a general psychologist, not from conviction about the domain of psychology, but because he tried to pursue one phenomenon – learned helplessness – to its end. In the service of this, he worked on learned helplessness in dogs and rats, quite in the mould of animal learning theory. When he tried to extend this to human laboratory helplessness, he found himself in need of social psychology and attribution theory in particular. Work on helplessness and depression made him a clinical psychologist, and work on helplessness and illness brought him into contact with behavioural medicine and physiological psychology. Study of the way helplessness changed over the life-span forced him toward life-span developmental psychology. More recently, working within the same theoretical framework, he has considered how people learn to be optimistic.

Several other problems attracted his attention. First, the evolutionary constraints on what can and cannot be learned: he argues that only a minute fraction of what we perceive gets stored and can be used, and that evolutionary constraints and intentional learning are the major filters. The rest is irrevocably lost. Second, he has examined the structure and function of dreaming. He argues that a dream consists of three components: periodic visual hallucinations unrelated in content to one another, emotional episodes only weakly related to the first, and the attempt to make sense of the first two by weaving them into a coherent plot. Finally, he has turned his attention to the prediction of the future, suggesting that the actions of groups and individuals might be predictable from a content analysis of their style of construing causes.

Shakow, David

Born: 1901, New York, USA **Died:** 1981, Bethesda, Maryland, USA **Nat:** American **Ints:** Clinical, experimental, psychoanalysis **Educ:** PhD Harvard University; DSc University of Rochester, 1976 **Appts & awards:** Chief, Laboratory of Psychology, Intramural Research Program, NIMH, 1954–66; Distinguished Scientific Contribution Award, APA; President, APA Division 12; Distinguished Contribution Award, APA Division 12; Stanley Dean Award; Award for Notable Contribution to Psychopathology, APA Division 12; Salmon Medal for Distinguished Service in Psychiatry

Principal publications

1946   *The Nature of Deterioration in Schizophrenic Conditions.*
1961   Reaction time in schizophrenia and normal subjects as a function of preparatory and intertrial intervals. *Journal of Nervous and Mental Disease*, 133, 283–7 (with T.P. Zahn and D. Rosenthal).
1962   Segmental set. *Archives of General Psychiatry*, 6, 1–17.
1963   Psychological deficit in schizophrenia. *Behavioral Science*, 8, 275–305.
1963   Effects of irregular preparatory intervals on reaction time in schizophrenia. *Journal of Abnormal and Social Psychology*, 67, 44–52 (with T.P. Zahn and D. Rosenthal).
1967   Some psychophysiological aspects of schizophrenia. *Excerpta Medica Congress*, series no. 151, *The Origins of Schizophrenia*. Proceedings of the First Rochester International Conference.
1969   On doing research on schizophrenia. *Archives of General Psychiatry*, 20, 618–42.
1977   *Schizophrenia: Selected Papers.*
1979   *Adaptation in Schizophrenia: The Theory of Segmental Set.*

Further reading

Reisman, J.M. (1991) *A History of Clinical Psychology*. 2nd edn. Hemisphere.
Salzinger, K. (1973) *Schizophrenia: Behavioral Aspects*. Wiley.

Shakow was a major figure of twentieth-century American psychology, one of only a few persons honoured by the APA with two of its most prestigious awards. The award for scientific activity was given for basic contributions that enlarged the understanding of processes underlying the psychological deficit manifested by schizophrenic patients. These studies began in 1932 and concluded fifty years later, when Shakow's final publication on this subject appeared a year after his death. He brought into focus the issue of attentional dysfunction in schizophrenia, with his concept of 'segmental set'. His work permitted a distinction to be made between deterioration (an irreversible performance decrement) and deficit. Shakow and his colleagues showed that deficits were to be found not at a reflexive level but at higher levels of cognitive and perceptual behaviour. The award for professional achievement recognized his role as the father of contemporary clinical psychology. Shakow, by precept and example, provided leadership for training clinical psychologists in espousing the view that the clinical psychologist's role is that of both scientist and practitioner in the mental health field.

Shallice, Timothy

Born: 1940 **Nat:** British **Ints:** Experimental psychology, neuropsychology **Educ:** BA Cambridge University, 1962; PhD London

University, 1965 **Appts and Awards:** Baylis
Major Scholar in Mathematics, St John's Col-
lege, Cambridge, 1957; Lecturer, Psychology
Department, University College London,
1966–72; Senior Research Fellow in Neuro-
psychology, Institute of Neurology, London,
1972–7; Research Psychologist (Principal
Grade), National Hospital for Nervous Dis-
eases, London, 1977–8; Scientist (Senior
Grade) Medical Research Council, Applied
Psychology Unit, Cambridge, 1978–86;
Honorary Attached Research Worker, National
Hospital for Neurology, London, 1978– ;
Scientist (Special Appointment – Professorial
Grade) Medical Research Council, Applied
Psychology Unit, Cambridge, 1986–90; Profes-
sor, Psychology Department, University College
London, 1990– ; Hon. D, Université Libre de
Bruxelles, 1992; Professor, Scuola Internazion-
ale Superiore di Studi Avanzati, Trieste,
1994–

Principal publications

1969   The selective impairment of auditory verbal
short-term memory. *Brain*, 92, 885–96 (with E.K.
Warrington).
1970   Independent functioning of verbal memory
stores: A neuropsychological study. *Quarterly
Journal of Experimental Psychology*, 22, 261–73
(with E.K. Warrington).
1977   The possible role of selective attention in
acquired dyslexic patients. *Neuropsychologia*, 15,
31–41 (with E.K. Warrington).
1977   Auditory verbal short-term memory
impairment and conduction aphasia. *Brain and
Language*, 4, 479–91 (with E.K. Warrington).
1979   Case study approach in neuropsychological
research. *Journal of Clinical Neuropsychology*, 1,
183–211.
1981   Phonological agraphia and the lexical route in
writing. *Brain*, 104, 413–29.
1982   Specific impairments of planning.
*Philosophical Transactions of the Royal Society,
London B*, 298, 199–209.
1984   Category specific semantic memory
impairment. *Brain*, 107, 829–54 (with E.K.
Warrington).
1986   Attention to action: Willed and automatic
control of behaviour. In R.J. Davidson, G.E.
Schwartz and D. Shapiro (eds), *Consciousness and
Self Regulation: Advances in Research*, vol. 4.
Plenum (with D.A. Norman).
1986   Lexical processing in the absence of explicit
word identification: Evidence from a letter-by-letter
reader. *Cognitive Neuropsychology*, 3, 429–58
(with E. Saffran).

1988   *From Neuropsychology to Mental Structure.*
Cambridge University Press.
1991   Lesioning an 'attractor' network:
Investigations of acquired dyslexia. *Psychological
Review*, 98, 74–95 (with G. Hinton).
1991   Deficits in strategy application following
frontal lobe damage in men. *Brain*, 114, 727–41
(with P.W. Burgess)
1993   Deep dyslexia: A case study of connectionist
neuropsychology. *Cognitive Neuropsychology*, 10,
377–500 (with D.C. Plaut).
1994   Brain regions associated with the acquisition
and retrieval of verbal episodic memory. *Nature*,
386, 633–5 (with P. Fletcher, C.D. Frith, P.
Grasby, R.S. Frackowiak and R.J. Dolan).

Further reading

Plaut, D.C. (1995) Double dissociation without
modularity: Evidence for connectionist
neuropsychology. Special Issue: Modularity and the
brain. *Journal of Clinical and Experimental
Neuropsychology*, 17, 291–321.
Umilta, C. and Moscovitch, M. (eds) (1994) *Attention
and Performance 15: Conscious and Nonconscious
Information Processing*. MIT Press.

Tim Shallice was educated at St John's College,
Cambridge, in mathematics. He obtained his
PhD in 1965 at London University, working
with Elizabeth **Warrington**. It was here that he
combined his background in memory and perception with the clinical interests that have
shaped his career. He has played a leading
role in developing a speciality of British psychology, the close analysis of clinical material
combined with controlled experiments in
neurological patients to elucidate human brain
function. Some of his earliest significant work
involved the clarification of verbal memory
using these techniques, in collaboration with
Warrington.

Shallice's work is characterized by a use of
rigorous experimental techniques to study large
questions such as the nature of the mind and the
basis of human consciousness. He was led to
these larger problems partly by his studies of
memory in neurological patients, where memory
turned out to be one of the keys to consciousness. The first work on this issue was early in
his career and was approached from studies of
attention, at a time when most psychologists still
viewed consciousness with disdain. Disguised as
'deliberate attentional resources', it appeared in
a 1980 pre-print co-authored with Donald
Norman, and attained considerable influence in
that form before being published later. This and

subsequent work outlined a functional theory of consciousness with the idea that such a complex phenomenon as consciousness could not have evolved by accident, and that it must have a function like any other mental capability.

Later studies have emphasized language deficits in neurological patients, part of an effort to elucidate the neurological mechanisms of language production and understanding. Much of this work is summarized in Shallice's 1988 book, *From Neuropsychology to Mental Structure*. The book parallels the scientific contribution of Shallice's career; it begins with a historical introduction to neuropsychology, and then examines memory, language, cognitive processes and consciousness, studied largely with close analysis of patients. The existence of astonishingly specialized deficits, even if rare, establishes that small parts of the brain can manage quite specific mental capabilities. Development of single-patient methods has facilitated this work.

Shallice's most recent work, some of it in collaboration with Geoffrey Hinton, has added neural network modelling to clinical data. By creating a neural network, training to do a specific task, and then disabling part of it, Shallice has been able to simulate the symptoms of several brain damage syndromes. Damage to different designs of simulated networks yields different kinds of deficit, providing another way of evaluating the networks themselves. The work suggests that the connectivity of brain networks is organized in ways similar to that of the artificial neural networks.

Shallice's work is valued particularly for methodological rigour combined with relevance to both applied problems and theoretical models of brain function. The more recent combining of single-case and group clinical data with modern parallel distributed models of brain function is a unique step.

B. BRIDGEMAN

Shepard, Roger N.

Born: 1929, Palo Alto, California, USA *Nat:* American *Ints:* Cognitive, experimental, mathematical, philosophical and theoretical, psychology and the arts *Educ:* BA Stanford University, 1951; MS Yale University, 1952; PhD Yale University, 1955 *Appts & awards:* Professor of Psychology, Stanford University; Fellow, Center for Advanced Study in the Behavioral Sciences, 1971–2; Guggenheim

Fellow, 1971–2; President, Psychometric Society, 1973–4; APA Distinguished Scientific Contribution Award, 1976; National Academy of Sciences, 1977; Member, American Academy of Arts and Sciences, 1980; President, APA Division 3, 1980–1; Howard Crosby Warren Medal of the Society of Experimental Psychologists, 1981; Fowler Hamilton Visiting Research Fellow, Christ Church, Oxford, 1987

Principal publications

1957 Stimulus and response generalization: A stochastic model relating generalization to distance in psychological space. *Psychometrika*, 22, 325–45.

1962 The analysis of proximities: Multidimensional scaling with an unknown distance function I and II. *Psychometrika*, 27, 125–40, 219–46.

1964 Attention and the metric structure of the stimulus space. *Journal of Mathematical Psychology*, 1, 54–87.

1964 Circularity in judgments of relative pitch. *Journal of the Acoustical Society of America*, 36, 2346–53.

1967 Recognition memory for words, sentences and pictures. *Journal of Verbal Learning and Verbal Behavior*, 6, 156–63.

1971 Mental rotation of three-dimensional objects. *Science*, 171, 701–3 (with J. Metzler).

1972 *Multi-dimensional Scaling: Theory and Applications in the Behavioral Sciences* (2 vols). Seminar Press (with A.K. Romney and S.B. Nerlove).

1973 Chronometric studies of the rotation of mental images. In W.G. Chase (ed.), *Visual Information Processing*. Academic Press (with L.A. Cooper).

1979 Quantification of the hierarchy of tonal functions within a diatonic context. *Journal of Experimental Psychology: Human Perception and Performance*, 5, 579–94 (with C.L. Krumhansl).

1981 Psychophysical complementarity. In M. Kubovy and J. Pomerantz (eds), *Perceptual Organization*. Erlbaum.

1982 *Mental Images and their Transformations*. MIT Press/Bradford Books (with L.A. Cooper).

1984 Ecological constraints on internal representation: Resonant kinematics of perceiving, imagining, thinking and dreaming. *Psychological Review*, 91, 417–47.

1990 Psychologically simple motions as geodesic paths: I. Asymmetric objects. *Journal of Mathematical Psychology*, 34, 127–88 (with E.H. Carlton).

1992 Representation of colors in the blind, color-blind, and normally sighted. *Psychological Science*, 3, 97–104 (with L.A. Cooper).

Further reading

Barlow, H., Blakemore, C. and Weston-Smith, M.
(eds) (1992) *Images and Understanding.*
Cambridge University Press.

Finke, R.A. (1989) *Principles of Mental Imagery.*
MIT Press.

Roger Shephard's interests fall into three categories: the physical world with its underlying regularities; the human mind with its rich capacities for experience and creation; and the achievements of that mind, whether by those who have discerned underlying order in the world (e.g. Newton, Einstein) or by those who have seemingly created it (e.g. Bach, Beethoven). Accordingly, he was torn between the desire to pursue physics, psychology and the arts (whether visual or musical). He managed to merge all three. Shephard argues that the mind's powers for discerning and for creating order cannot have sprung, arbitrarily, out of nothing. These powers may represent an evolutionary internationalization of the order long inherent in the world. If so, any regularities behind the apparent diversity of concrete mental events may be as abstract as the physical laws of Newton or Einstein. Thus formulated, mental principles, including those that give rise to the seemingly free creations of art and music, may ultimately reveal their affinity with principles of physics and geometry. Working with colleagues, he began to gather evidence to test these ideas. First, in experiments on real, apparent and imagined motions – both of visual objects in literal three-dimensional space and of auditory objects (viz. melodies or chords) in the metaphorical space of musical pitch – the psychologically preferred motions follow the (helical) paths prescribed by abstract kinematic geometry. Second, data on stimulus generalization, when analysed by multidimensional scaling, reveal a universal (exponential) relation to psychological distance. This relation is entailed by a geometrical connection between any size an individual assumes for the set of stimuli sharing the important consequence of the given stimulus, and the corresponding uncertainty of the location of that set in the abstract psychological space of the stimuli.

Sherif, Muzafer

Born: 1906, Ödmish, Izmir, Turkey **Nat:** Turkish **Ints:** Experimental, general, history, psychology of women, society for the psychological study of social issues. **Educ:** BA International College Turkey, 1926; MA Uni-

versity of Istanbul, 1929; MA Harvard University, 1932; PhD Columbia University, 1935 **Appts & awards:** Rockefeller Foundation Fellow, 1935–6; US State Department Fellow, 1945–7; Executive Committee, Society for the Psychological Study of Social Issues, 1960–2; APA Kurt Lewin Memorial Award, 1966; Guggenheim Fellow, 1967; APA Distinguished Scientific Award, 1968; Distinguished Scientific Award, 1968; Distinguished Senior Social Psychologist Award, 1978; Society of Experimental Social Psychology, 1978; Distinguished Contribution to Social Psychology Award, Social Psychology Section, ASA, 1978; Fellow, APA Divisions 1, 9, 26, 35; Professor of Sociology and Director of Psycho-Social Studies Program (Emeritus), Pennsylvania State University; Associate Editor, *American Journal of Sociology*, 1953–6

Principal publications

1936   *Psychology of Social Norms.* Harper (Octagon Books, 1965; Harper Torchbooks, 1966; Farrar, Straus & Giroux, 1973).

1948   The necessity of considering current issues as part and parcel of persistent major problems. *International Journal of Opinion and Attitude Research*, 2, 63–8.

1952   A study in ego functioning: Elimination of stable anchorages in individual and group situations. *Sociometry*, 15, 272–305 (with O.J. Harvey).

1954   Integrating field work and laboratory in small group research. *American Sociological Review*, 19, 759–71.

1961   Conformity–deviation norms and group relations. In B. Bass and I. Berg (eds), *Conformity and Deviation.* Harper.

1961   *Intergroup Conflict and Cooperation: The Robbers Cave Experiment.* Institute of Group Relations.

1963   Social psychology: Problems and trends in interdisciplinary relations. In S. Koch (ed.), *Psychology, a Study of a Science*, Vol 6. McGraw-Hill.

1964   *Reference Groups: An Exploration into Conformity and Deviation of Adolescents.* Harper & Row.

1965   *Attitude and Attitude Change: The Social Judgment-Involvement Approach.* Saunders (with C.W. Sherif and R. Nebergall).

1965   The individual in his group in its setting: Parts I and II. In M. Sherif and C.W. Sherif (eds), *Problems of Youth: Transition to Adulthood in a Changing World.* Aldine (with C.W. Sherif).

1965   Superordinate goals in the reduction of intergroup conflict: An experimental evaluation. In

M. Schwebel (ed.), *Behavioral Science and Human Survival*. Science and Behavior Books.

1966   *In Common Predicament: Social Psychology of Intergroup Conflict and Co-operation*. Houghton Mifflin.

1966   Theoretical analysis of the individual–group relationship in a social situation. In G. DiRenzo (ed.), *Concepts, Theory and Explanation in the Social Sciences*. Random House.

1968   Self concept. In D.L. Sills, *International Encyclopedia of the Social Sciences*. Free Press.

1968   If the social scientist is to be more than a mere technician. Kurt Lewin Memorial Address. *Journal of Social Issues*, 25, 41–61.

Further reading

Brown, R. (1986) *Social Psychology: The Second Edition*. Free Press.

Muzafer Sherif worked in many areas of social psychology, where he identified the core problem as being the normative functioning of the human species. He consistently argued that in every aspect of life people generate norms, or standards to regulate their thinking, even consciousness, in interaction.

Sherif conducted a highly influential study of intergroup behaviour called the 'Robbers Cave Experiment'. Eleven-year-old boys attending a summer camp were assigned to different cabins. The campers in each group quickly formed attachments with one another – this was the first phase of the study. During the second phase the boys engaged in a competitive tournament with prizes of a trophy and individual awards. Sherif predicted that this conflict would develop into prejudice – and after two weeks this was supported with evidence of intensely negative views of one another and bouts of verbal and physical abuse. In the final phase of the study Sherif and his colleagues were able to reduce the conflict not by increased physical contact (which only made matters worse) but by arranging it so that the groups each had to work to shared superordinate goals, namely repairing the water supply previously sabotaged by the researchers. While the study is often criticized on methodological grounds – it was conducted over a short period of time and under circumstances manipulated by Sherif and his colleagues – it nevertheless demonstrated how intergroup competition can escalate into social conflict.

His books and publications make normative human experience and behaviour focal in all areas of interaction. His *Psychology of Social Norms* (1936) is basic to all of the other books

and publications. Applications of his ideas and findings are presented in 'Social Interaction: Process and Products'. Most of these applications relate to attitude and attitude change; analysis of reference groups and idols which, in a major way, he considered to stem from our basic formulation of normative experience; ingroup and intergroup relations, both co-operation and conflict; and other social, economic and political areas.

Sherrington, Sir Charles Scott

Born: 1857, London, England *Died:* 1952, Eastbourne, England *Nat:* British *Ints:* Experimental psychology, general psychology, physiological and comparative psychology *Educ:* MB University of Cambridge, 1885 *Appts & awards:* Fellow, St Thomas Hospital London, 1887–93; Professor of Pathology, University of London, 1891–5; Professor of Physiology, University of Liverpool, 1895–1913; Wayneflete Professor of Physiology, University of Oxford, 1913–35; President, Royal Society, 1920–5; Knighted, 1922; Nobel Prize in Medicine, 1932; twenty-two Honorary Degrees and numerous other honours including Order of Merit (highest British civilian distinction); Editorial Board, *British Journal of Psychology*, 1904–35

Principal publications

1901   *Text-Book of Physiology*.

1906   *Integrative Action of the Nervous System* (reprinted five times).

1942   *Goethe on Nature and on Science*.

1947   *Preface to The Integrative Action of the Nervous System*.

Numerous publications in learned journals.

Further reading

Creed, R.S. (1953) Sir Charles Scott Sherrington. *British Journal of Psychology*, 44, 1–4.

Fulton, J.F. (1952) Sir Charles Scott Sherrington. *Journal of Neurophysiology*, 15, 167–90.

Sherrington's father, a physician, died when he and his two brothers were children, and they were reared in the home of their stepfather, also a physician. His brothers became successful lawyers while Sherrington was originally attracted to the classics. In 1880 he entered Gonville and Caius College, Cambridge, to study medicine. He was a contemporary of Head, Mott, Richet and **Rivers**, all of whom he knew well. At the end of his pre-clinical training he spent a year with Goltz and Ewald in Strasbourg. He worked with C.S. Roy (the 'father of English physiology') and on a trip to Spain met with Ramon y Cajal. He also visited the laboratories of Virchow and Koch in Berlin (1886–7) and then returned to London to take up an appointment as a lecturer at St Thomas' Hospital. He was elected to the Royal Society in 1893. He was also a poet (his poetry was published in a single volume, *The Assaying of Brabantius*) and philosopher, with a passionate interest in the relationship between mind and body (e.g. *Goethe on Nature and on Science*, 1942).

Synapse/synaptic, proprioceptive, recruitment, occlusion, final common path, fractionation – these are just some of the ordinary terms in neurology and neuropsychology which are due to Sherrington and which give an impression of the extent of his influence. Sherrington is an outstanding figure in the history of physiology. The significance of his work can only be fully appreciated by comparing his published work against conventional textbooks of the time. Among his many achievements are demonstrations that: muscular activity is as important in the maintenance of posture as in the execution of movements; in movements antagonistic muscles are reciprocally innervated; many complex movements can be understood as combinations of simple reflexes in which central excitation and central inhibition are algebraically summated. Much of his later experimental work was directed to understanding spinal rhythmical reflexes, the motor cortex of anthropoid apes, the stretch reflex (with E.G.T. Liddell), the role of central inhibition in the co-ordination of movements, and the spinal ipsilateral flexion reflex (notably with J.C. Eccles). His contributions to the understanding of vision and the emotions attracted much attention from psychologists. He disproved the hypothesis that single vision with two eyes is due to anatomical confluence of the twin paths from corresponding points on the two retinas. On the contrary: 'The cerebral seats of right-eye and left-eye visual images ... are separate. Conduct paths no doubt interconnect them, but are shown to be unnecessary for visual unification of the two images.' He reported important advances in contrast phenomena, eye movements, and the role of proprioceptors in the extrinsic ocular muscles. In his investigations of emotion he was keen to test William **James**'s hypothesis that the feeling of bodily changes as they occur defines the experience of emotion (i.e. visceral sensations are essential for emotion). He demonstrated that this was wrong and that, while visceral and organic sensations and the memories and associations of them contribute to primitive emotions, they reinforce rather than initiate.

Shock, Nathan Wetherill

Born: 1906, Lafayette, Indiana, USA *Died:* 1989, Baltimore, Maryland, USA *Nat:* American *Ints:* Adult development and ageing, physiological and comparative psychology *Educ:* BS Purdue University, 1926; MS Purdue University, 1927; PhD University of Chicago, 1930 *Appts & awards:* Scientist Emeritus, Retired Scientific Director, National Institute on Aging, Francis Scott Key Medical Center; Gerontology Society of America, Secretary, 1951–8, President, 1960; Fellow, APA; President, APA Division 20, 1952–3; Hon. DSc, Purdue University, 1954; Chairman, Society of Experimental Biology and Medicine, Maryland Section, 1956; Chairman, American Association for the Advancement of Science, Medical Sciences Section, 1959; Modern Medicine Achievement Award, 1960; Willard O. Thompson Award, American Geriatrics Society, 1965; First Annual Research Award, Gerontology Society of America, 1965; Distinguished Service Award, American Heart Association, 1965; President, International Association of Gerontology, 1969–71; O.A. Randall Award, National Council on Aging, 1977; Kesten Memorial Award, University of Southern California, 1978; First Brookdale Award for Research in Gerontology, 1979; Hon. D. Hum. Lett., Johns Hopkins University, 1981; Distinguished Achievement Award, American College of Nutrition, 1981; First Award of Distinction, American Federation for Aging Research, 1982; Hon. Member, Sociedad Argentina de Gerontologia y Geriatrie, British Society for Research on Ageing, Gerontologie de Chile; Editor, *Macy Conference on Problems of Aging* (Josiah Macy Foundation), 1949–53; *Gerontology Section, Biological Abstracts*, 1953–82; Editor-in-Chief, *Journal of Gerontology*, 1963–8

Principal publications

1930 Mental performance and the acid base balance of the blood in normal individuals. *Proceedings of the Indiana Academy of Science*, 40, 193–202.

1935 Studies of the acid base balance of the blood. IV. Characterization and interpretation of displacements of the acid base balance. *Journal of*

Biological Chemistry, 112, 239–62 (with A.B. Hastings).

1951   Gerontology (later maturity). *Annual Review of Psychology*. Annual Reviews.

1951   *A Classified Bibliography of Gerontology and Geriatrics*. Stanford University Press. (Supplement I, 1957; Supplement II, 1963).

1951   *Trends in Gerontology*. Stanford University Press.

1961   Physiological aspects of aging in man. *Annual Review of Physiology*. Annual Reviews.

1966   *Perspectives in Experimental Gerontology*. Thomas.

1977   Biological theories of aging. In J.E. Birren and K.W. Schaie (eds), *Handbook of the Psychology of Aging*. Van Nostrand.

1977   Systems of integration. In C.E. Finch and L. Hayflick (eds), *Handbook of the Biology of Aging*. Van Nostrand Reinhold.

Further reading

Aiken, L.R. (1995) *Aging: An Introduction to Gerontology*. Sage.

Vellas, B., Albearede, J.L. and Garry, P.J. (eds) (1994) *Facts and Research in Gerontology 1994: Epidemiology and Aging*. Springer.

Shock's early research, at the University of Chicago (1930–2), was focused on studies of the effect of experimentally changing the acidity of the blood on performance of mental tasks by human subjects. From 1933 to 1941 he was associated with a multidisciplinary study of physiological and psychological changes taking place in children as they passed through adolescence. Repeated observations were made at six-month intervals on fifty girls and fifty boys over the age span of 10 to 18 years. Individual growth rates for a broad spectrum of physiological tests were assessed for each individual child. The most important finding was that growth patterns for many physiological characteristics for individual children often deviated widely from that predicted from averages of observations made on different children at each age point. In 1941 he joined the staff of the National Institute of Health and was given responsibility to develop a multidisciplinary programme in gerontology, the first of its kind in the USA. It grew to become the Intramural Research Program of the National Institute on Aging when it was established in 1975. His research focused on a multidisciplinary approach, in which measurements of physiological, biochemical, clinical and psychological functions were made on approximately 600 males and 400 females at

biannual intervals over a period of more than twenty-five years. His work has shown that ageing is a complex process and there are considerable individual differences in the ageing paths of different functions. Age decrements are more marked in performances of complex than in those of simple tasks. He demonstrated that although there is a general pattern of ageing that is set by genetic processes, variations in the rate of ageing among individuals are determined by differences in lifestyles and environmental factors. Ageing is accelerated by smoking and obesity and can be slowed by maintaining both physical and mental activity. He concluded that most of the decrements in performance that are seen in old people are the results of disease rather than ageing itself.

W. IACCINO AND J.D. HOGAN

Simon, Herbert Alexander

Born: 1916, Milwaukee, Wisconsin, USA ***Ints:*** Artificial intelligence, cognitive science ***Educ:*** BA University of Chicago, 1936; PhD University of Chicago, 1943 ***Appts & awards:*** Richard King Mellon University Professor of Computer Science and Psychology, Department of Psychology, Carnegie-Mellon University; Hon. DSc, Yale University, 1963, Case Institute of Technology, 1963, Marquette University, 1981, Columbia University, 1983, Gustavus Adolphus College, 1984; Hon. LLD, University of Chicago, 1964, McGill University, 1970, University of Michigan, 1978, University of Pittsburgh, 1979; Member, National Academy of Sciences, 1967; Hon. FilD, Lund University, 1968; APA Scientific Contribution Award, 1969; Dr Economic Science Erasmus University, Netherlands, 1973; Association for Computing Machinery, Turing Award, 1975; AEA Distinguished Fellow, 1976; Nobel Prize in economic science, 1978; Docteur, University of Paul Valery, 1984; American Political Science Association, James Madison Award, 1984

Principal publications

1947   *Administrative Behavior*. Macmillan. (3rd edn, Free Press, 1976.)

1956   Rational choice and the structure of the environment. *Psychological Review*, 63, 129–38.

1958   Elements of a theory of human problem solving. *Psychological Review*, 65, 151–66 (with A. Newell and J.C. Shaw).

1961   Computer simulation of human thinking. *Science*, 134, 2011–17 (with A. Newell).

1962   A theory of the serial position effect. *British*

Journal of Psychology, 53, 307–20 (with E.A. Feigenbaum).

1963   Human acquisition of concepts for sequential patterns. *Psychological Review*, 70, 534–46 (with K. Kotovosky).

1967   Motivational and emotional controls of cognition. *Psychological Review*, 74, 29–39.

1969   Information-processing analysis of perceptual processes in problem solving. *Psychological Review*, 76, 473–83 (with M. Barenfeld).

1972   *Human Problem Solving*. Prentice Hall (with A. Newell).

1973   Perception in chess. *Cognitive Psychology*, 4, 55–81 (with W.G. Chase).

1979   *Models of Thought*. Yale University Press.

1981   *The Sciences of the Artificial* (2nd edn). MIT Press.

1984   *Protocol Analysis*. MIT Press (with A. Ericsson).

Further reading

Anderson, J.R. (1985) *Cognitive Psychology and its Implications*. Freeman.

Nisbett, R.E. and Wilson, T.D. (1977) Telling more than we know: Verbal reports on mental processes. *Psychological Review*, 84, 231–59.

Posner, M.I. (ed.) (1989) *Foundations of Cognitive Science*. Bradford.

Sheehy, N.P. and Chapman, A.J. (eds) (1995) *Cognitive Science*, vol. 2. Edward Elgar.

'Herb' Simon's education and career began in political science and economics. Undergraduate work included a study of recreation administration in Milwaukee, and after graduation he continued his research into governmental decision making, first (1936–9) as an assistant to Clarence E. Ridley of the International City Manager's Association, and then (1939–42) as Director of Administrative Measurement Studies in the Bureau of Public Administration, University of California at Berkeley. During this period Simon wrote his doctoral dissertation on organisational decision making, later published as *Administrative Behavior* (1947). From 1942 to 1949 he was a faculty member at the Illinois Institute of Technology and chairman of the Department of Political and Social Science. World War II developments in operations research and cybernetics paralleled Simon's interests in decision-making processes, and he was involved in the development of decision models of management. In 1949 he joined the Graduate School of Industrial Administration at Carnegie Institute of Technology (now Carnegie-Mellon University), where he pursued

empirical investigations of organizational decision making while continuing to work in management science. He became a consultant to the RAND Corporation's Systems Research Laboratory (about 1952), which was to lead to a significant collaboration with Allen Newell.

Research on decision-making processes in organizations led Simon to a concern with problem-solving processes; then, through early contacts with electronic computers, he came to recognize that they could be used to simulate human thinking. With computer simulation and thinking-aloud protocols as their principal research tools, he and Allen Newell launched in 1955 a programme of research that became a part of the information-processing revolution in cognitive psychology. They first achieved a demonstration that computers could be programmed to solve problems by heuristic search. There followed the General Problem Solver, a program explaining many of the phenomena of rote verbal learning by the serial-anticipation and paired-associate methods.

In their studies of human problem solving, Newell and Simon developed several concepts which have had a pervasive influence within cognitive science and more broadly. They proposed that problem solving involves trying to select operators (the means) that can be applied to a particular problem state in order to achieve a goal state (or end). Means–end analysis is thought to proceed within a problem space, comprising the potential states of knowledge and operators that transform one state of knowledge into another. Means–end analysis makes heavy demands on controlled processing: the goal state and relevant intermediate states must be considered jointly. Newell and Simon's implementation of their theory in a computer program has provided a reference model for numerous subsequent efforts to specify formally the information processes that define cognition. Their theory of problem solving performs the process it explains: their computer program thinks rationally but without recourse to a deductive logic.

By the 1960s Simon was working with Barenfeld, Gilmartin and Chase on the knowledge component of skilled performance in tasks like chess playing, and the evocation of expert knowledge by recognition of cues in the task situation. Other research (with Hayes) explored how human subjects understood verbal task instructions. Later research focused upon simulating and explaining the processes of scientific discovery, and analysing learning processes in physics, mathematics and other school subjects. Thus, trying to broaden, step by step, the range of cognitive processes that could be explained within the information-processing paradigm, Simon addressed an ever-widening array of cognitive tasks that people face in school and their professional work.

Simon and Newell's approach emphasizes the relative invariance observable in people's strategies on domain-free problems. They suggest that this similarity reflects the fact that the human information-processing system is not as complex or sophisticated as often supposed: people have a few basic heuristics for dealing with a wide variety of problems. For example, Chase and Simon showed that 50,000 visual configurations are sufficient to describe all of the board positions that could arise in normal chess play. Thus, the ability to detect a particular configuration can be used as a sound basis for planning sequences of moves. Expert chess players learn to recognize common configurations as single perceptual units. When considering a particular position, experts would recall six or seven configurations, each containing from three to five pieces. Six or seven items is within the information-processing range of working memory, and the intellectual skill of chess players could be explained in terms of memory due to perceptual learning.

Powerful though it is, the General Problem Solver has been mainly applied to artificial, puzzle-like problems and much less successfully to 'real-world' problems, which involve a considerably greater amount of more generalized, background knowledge. Nevertheless three aspects of the approach endure: searching a problem space, goal-directed problem solving, and context-free problem-solving methods.

Singer, Jerome L.

Born: 1924, New York City, USA *Nat:* American *Ints:* Clinical psychology, personality and social psychology, psychoanalysis, psychotherapy *Educ:* BA College of the City of New York, 1943; PhD University of Pennsylvania *Appts & awards:* Professor of Psychology and Child Study, 1972– ; Co-Director, Family Television Research and Consultation Centre; Director of Graduate Studies in Psychology, Yale University; APA Divisions 8, 12, 29, 38, 39; President, Eastern Psychological Association, 1973; APA, Division of Personality and Social Psychology, 1983; Chair, Board of Scientific

Affairs, 1987; Townsend Harris Medal for Distinguished Contributions to Science, City College, City University of New York, 1990

Principal publications

1955 Delayed gratification and ego-development: Implications for clinical and experimental research. *Journal of Consulting Psychology*, 19, 259–66.

1964 Eye movements accompanying daydreaming, visual imagery and thought suppression. *Journal of Abnormal and Social Psychology*, 69, 244–52 (with J.S. Antrobus and J. Antrobus).

1966 *Daydreaming*. Random House.

1971 Experimental studies of ocular motility during daydreaming and mental arithmetic. *Transactions of the New York Academy of Science*, Series II, 33, 694–709 (with J.S. Antrobus and S. Greenberg).

1973 *The Child's World of Make-Believe: Experimental Studies of Imaginative Play*. Academic Press (with chapters by J. Freyberg, M. Pulaski, E. Biblow and S. Gottlieb).

1974 *Imagery and Daydream Methods in Psychotherapy and Behavior Modification*. Academic Press (transl. German).

1976 Imaginative play and pretending in early childhood: Some experimental approaches. In *Child Personality and Psychopathology*. Wiley (with D.G. Singer).

1978 *The Power of the Human Imagination*. Plenum (with K.S. Pope).

1978 *The Stream of Consciousness: Scientific Investigations in to the Flow of Human Experience*. Plenum (with K.S. Pope).

1981 *Television, Imagination and Aggression: A Study of Preschoolers*. Erlbaum (with D.G. Singer).

1990 (ed.) *Repression and Dissociation: Implications for Personality Psychopathology and Health*. University of Chicago Press.

1991 Organized knowledge structures in personality: Schemas, self-schemas, prototypes and scripts. A review and research agenda. In M.J. Horowitz (ed.), *Person Schemas and Maladaptive Interpersonal Patterns*. University of Chicago Press (with P. Salovey).

1995 (ed.) *Mind, Brain and Complex Adaptive Systems*. Addison-Wesley (with H. Morowitz).

Further reading

Singer, J.L. (ed.) (1990) *Repression and Dissociation: Implications for Personality Theory, Psychopathology, and Health*. University of Chicago Press.

Zillman, D. *et al.* (eds) (1994) *Media, Children, and the Family: Social Scientific, Psychodynamic, and Clinical Perspectives*. Erlbaum.

Jerome L. Singer was brought up in New York City, entering the City University for his undergraduate studies. Following military service in World War II, he attended the University of Pennsylvania for doctoral training in clinical psychology. His research interests have been concerned with three main topics: (1) the imagination, especially fantasy and day-dreaming, their links to cognition and emotion, and their clinical implications; (2) the psychological effects of television on children and adolescents (working extensively in this area with his wife, Dr Dorothy G. Singer); (3) the study of repression, defence mechanisms and personality.

Singer's studies of day-dreaming, conducted at the City College of the City University of New York with John Antrobus and others, provided objective evidence under controlled laboratory conditions of internal cognitive processes in the form of fantasy and day-dreaming. Eye-movement activity proved to be almost as useful an indicator of waking imagery as REMs are of nocturnal dreams. These studies made a significant contribution and facilitated the return of mental imagery and conscious experience to the mainstream of general and experimental psychology in the 1960s.

The Singers' television research has been equally important and influential. The research programme has investigated the impact of television on the imaginative play of pre-schoolers, the enhancement of children's readiness to learn, adolescent behaviour, social knowledge and co-operative behaviour. This work has led to efforts to influence educators, parents and the television industry.

In his study of repression, Singer adopted a trait approach in defining a 'repressive personality style' which has adaptive functions but also may be a precursor to psychological (e.g. hysterical) and physical (e.g. psychosomatic or neoplastic) disorders. Singer's repression research has been influenced by the ideas of Sidney J. Blatt, Daniel A. Weinberger and Gary E. Schwartz. Singer is impressed by the accumulating evidence from health psychology that repression is associated with physical as well as psychological ill-health. Thus individuals whose self-reports reflect both high defensiveness and low anxiety appear to be at a greater risk for a diagnosis of cancer, or, if diagnosed, for showing a poor course of treatment. Singer's career has been broad in scope and prolific in output. He has made a major contribution.

DAVID F. MARKS

Sinha, Durganand

Born: 1922, Banaili, Purnea, India *Nat:* Indian *Ints:* Cross-cultural, developmental, industrial and organizational, personality and social, psychology and problems of social change and national development *Educ:* BA Patna University, 1943; MA Patna University, 1945; MSc St John's College, Cambridge University, 1949 *Appts & awards:* Director, A.N. Sinha Institute of Social Studies, Patna; Member, Social Psychology Section, Indian Sociological Conference, 1960; Member, Section of Psychology and Educational Sciences, Indian Science Congress, 1966; Member, Executive Committee, International Association of Applied Psychology, 1968– ; Indian Psychological Association, Secretary, 1974–7, President, 1978; President, Indian Academy of Applied Psychology, 1975–6; International Association of Cross-Cultural Psychology, Deputy Secretary General, 1976–8, Vice-President, 1978–80, President, 1980–2; Editor in Chief, *Journal of Social and Economic Studies,* 1984– ; Editorial Boards: *International Journal of Behavioral Development, German Journal of Psychology, Psychological Studies, Journal of Psychological Research, Journal of Indian Psychology, Indian Psychologist, NIMHANS Journal;* Editorial Advisor, Special issue, 'Psychology and the Developing Countries', *International Review of Applied Psychology,* 1973; Co-Editor, Special issue, 'The Impact of Psychology on the Third World Development', *International Journal of Psychology,* 1984

Principal publications

1952 Behavior in a catastrophic situation: A psychological study of reports and rumours. *British Journal of Psychology,* 43, 200–9.

1962 Union attitude and job satisfaction in Indian workers. *Journal of Applied Psychology,* 46, 246–51.

1969 *Indian Villages in Transition: A Motivational Analysis.* Associated Publishing House.

1973 Psychology and problems of developing countries. *International Review of Applied Psychology,* 22, 5–27.

1974 *Motivation and Rural Development.* Minerva.

1974 Topological and Euclidean spatial features noted by children: A cross-cultural study. *International Journal of Psychology,* 19, 159–72 (with G. Jahoda and J.B. Deregowski).

1974 Deprivation and development of skill for pictorial depth perception. *Journal of Cross-cultural Psychology,* 5, 434–50 (with P. Sjukla).

1979 Perceptual style among nomadic and

transitional agriculturist Birhors. In L.H. Eckensberger, W.J. Lonner and Y.H. Poortinga (eds), *Cross-Cultural Contributions to Psychology*. Swets & Zeitlinger.

1980   Socio-cultural factors in the development of perceptual and cognitive skills. In W.W. Hartup (ed.), *Review of Child Development Research*. Academic Press.

1980   Sex differences in psychological differentiation among different cultural groups. *International Journal of Behavioral Development*, 3, 455–66.

1981   *Socialization of the Indian Child*. Concept Publishing.

1982   *Deprivation: Its Social Roots and Psychological Consequences*. Concept Publishing.

1983   Human assessment in the Indian context. In S.H. Irvine and J.W. Berry (eds), *Human Assessment and Cultural Factors*. Plenum.

1984   Psychology in the context of Third World development. *International Journal of Psychology*, 19, 17–29.

1985   *Psychology in a Third World Country: A Case Study of India*. Sage.

1990   Interventions for development out of poverty. In R.W. Brislin (ed.) *Applied Cross-Cultural Psychology*. Sage.

Further reading

Special Issue: In honour of Professor Durganand Sinha. *Psychology and Developing Societies*, 1992, 4, 21–38.

Since starting research, Sinha's interests have changed from time to time. There is, however, a common thread. Whether working on memory or perception, anxiety, job satisfaction, psychological factors in rural development, changes in cognitive structure among tribals due to acculturation, or psychological dimensions of poverty, he has tried to focus on sociocultural factors. His paper on rumours in the *British Journal of Psychology* (1952) formed one of the bases for **Festinger**'s theory of cognitive dissonance. In the paper on factors associated with satisfaction and dissatisfaction in work (1958), he anticipated the bi-polar theory of job satisfaction. Later he was concerned with the social relevance of research in psychology. He focused on human adaptive processes in the context of social change and has been preoccupied with gearing psychological researches to national needs.

In recognition of his work in this direction and that of colleagues in Allahabad University, the University Grants Commission named the department as a centre of excellence for the Psychological Study of Social Change and Development. Sinha has been instrumental in establishing the Division of Psychology and National Development under the aegis of the International Association of Applied Psychology. Being one of the few psychologists to analyse psychological factors in agroeconomic development, he has been concerned with the development of 'rural psychology' as a distinct subdiscipline. Psychological dimensions of poverty, changes in the Indian family as a result of socioeconomic development and their repercussions on child development, and the psychological impact of acculturation among tribals are later research interests. His work emphasizes the importance of macro-variables in psychological researches, without which the discipline would make at best peripheral contributions to larger issues of social change and development.

Skinner, Burrhus Frederick

Born: 1904, Susquehanna, Pennsylvania, USA
Died: 1990, Cambridge, Massachusetts, USA
Nat: American **Ints:** Educational psychology, experimental analysis of behaviour, experimental psychology, general psychology, psychopharmacology **Educ:** BA Hamilton College, New York, 1926; MA Harvard University, 1930; PhD Harvard University, 1931 **Appts & awards:** Junior Fellow, Harvard Society of Fellows, 1933–6; Instructor in Psychology, University of Minnesota, 1936–7; Indiana University, Assistant Professor, 1937–9, Associate Professor, 1939–45, Professor of Psychology, 1945–8; Professor, Harvard University, 1948–57; Edgar Pierce Professor of Psychology, 1958–74; Professor Emeritus, 1975–90; over twenty-five honorary doctorates, including DSc University of Chicago, 1967, University of Exeter, 1969, Indiana University, 1970, McGill University, 1970, Harvard University, 1985, DLitt, Tufts University, 1977, LHD, Johns Hopkins University, 1979; APA citation for Lifetime Contribution to Psychology, 1990

Principal publications

1931   The concept of the reflex in the description of behavior. *Journal of General Psychology*, 5, 427–58.

1938   *Behavior of Organisms*. Appleton-Century-Crofts.

1948   *Walden Two*. Macmillan.

1953   *Science and Human Behavior*. Macmillan.

1957   *Verbal Behavior*. Appleton-Century-Crofts.

1957   *Schedules of Reinforcement.* Appleton-
Century-Crofts (with C.B. Ferster).
1959   *Cumulative Record.* Appleton-Century-Crofts.
1968   *The Technology of Teaching.* Appleton-
Century-Crofts.
1969   *The Contingencies of Reinforcement.*
Appleton-Century-Crofts.
1971   *Beyond Freedom and Dignity.* Knopf.
1974   *About Behaviorism.* Knopf.
1976   *Particulars of my Life.* Knopf.
1978   *Reflections on Behaviorism and Society.*
Prentice Hall.

Further reading

Bjork, D.W. (1993) *B.F. Skinner: A Life.* Basic
Books.
Catania, C.A. and Harnad, S. (eds) (1988) *The
Selection of Behavior: The Operant Behaviorism of
B.F. Skinner: Comments and Consequences.*
Cambridge University Press.
Lattal, K.A. (ed.) (1992) Special issue: Reflections
on B.F. Skinner and psychology. *American
Psychologist*, 47, 1269–1533.
Modgil, S. and Modgil, C. (eds) (1987) *B.F. Skinner:
Consensus and Controversy.* Falmer.
Smith, L.D. (1986) *Behaviorism and Logical
Positivism: A Reassessment of the Alliance.*
Stanford University Press.

For his first twenty-three years, Skinner's life was one of haphazard passions with little overall plan. He built and invented well beyond the ordinary boyish range, from a steam cannon to a device with strings and pulleys to remind him to hang up his pyjamas. At 14 he learnedly championed Bacon as the writer of Shakespeare's plays, and discovered Bacon's philosophy of science, with its prophetic confidence in scientific solutions to practical problems. He played music, including saxophone in a school band. He kept animals – not domestic pets, but turtles, snakes, toads, lizards and chipmunks. At Hamilton College, where he majored in English literature, he organized elaborate practical jokes against the college authorities. He marvelled at the psychology in Joyce and Proust, but also read **Pavlov** and Jacques Loeb, notorious for his mechanistic approach to biology. He wrote poetry and stories, and met Robert Frost, who was impressed by his work and encouraged him to become a writer, which he tried for a year from 1926.

But writing did not give him the sense of direction he sought, and he turned to science as 'the art of the twentieth century'. He encountered behaviourism through reading Bertrand Russell, and was struck by Russell's comparison of the reflex to the concept of force in physics, and the relevance of behaviourism to epistemology. At the end of 1927 he applied to Harvard for graduate study in psychology.

At Harvard in 1928 he followed his new passion, unhampered by previous training in psychology, or by formal supervision. He took a course with Walter Hunter, who had explored the intelligence of animals with experiments on problem solving. He studied reflexes with Hudson Hoagland, and tropisms with Crozier, who had been Loeb's student. These were physiology courses, but both focused on observable responses rather than underlying processes. Crozier gave Skinner space to study rats, and encouraged him without directing him. Remembering a rule learned from Pavlov ('control the environment and you will see order in behaviour') Skinner used his skills as an inventor to search for regularities in the behaviour of the whole organism. He built a succession of devices for eliciting and recording the posture and the eating behaviour of rats. When order began to appear, he brought it into focus by improving or redesigning the apparatus. In this way he invented the Skinner Box and the cumulative recorder, and found that regularities show themselves in frequency patterns rather than individual stimulus–response connections. He discovered that the sound of food being delivered acts as a conditioned reinforcer, and how powerful this could be. Rats first learned to run to food at the sound, and then to press a lever which operated the food magazine, sometimes in one trial. This instantaneous learning has the marks of insight, but Skinner was not tempted to speculate on this, or on whether his rats showed purpose. He had pinned down a regularity, which he consolidated with his discovery that lever-pressing stabilizes under intermittent reinforcement.

This austere and original approach was not the result of his experiments. Some of these took up half of his PhD dissertation, but the other half was on the history of the concept of the reflex, and forms a prolegomena to his science of behaviour. He was guided mainly by Percy Bridgman's *The Logic of Modern Physics* and Ernst Mach's *Science of Mechanics.* From Bridgman's operationalism he learned to focus on what is involved in an experiment on reflexes, rather than on the theories about it. He concluded that the essence of reflexology is not the study of the reflex arc, but the setting up and exploitation of a regularity between stimulus and response. Mach had traced the evolution of physics as a development out of ordinary human interactions with the environment. Force is inherent in everyday activities, and physics studies it by isolating it and bringing it under control. Likewise, Skinner concluded, the study of the reflex is a refinement of a process pervasive in everyday behaviour. But it is a process investigated in isolation from other bodily activities; and what Skinner looked for and found during the 1930s was a different kind of reflex, a controlled regularity involving the whole organism. At first he worked on his own with little reference to other learning theories, except his immediate colleagues, especially Fred Keller. But after his PhD he had lengthy discussions with **Tolman**, **Hull** and other theorists, and came to place his own ideas in relation to theirs.

By putting his emphasis on regularity, rather than the causal link between stimulus and response, Skinner made a significant move away from the prevailing stimulus–response psychology. The regularities he found resided in frequency of responding rather than the response itself. Furthermore the key controlling variable was not the causal antecedent, but the consequence of the response, the reinforcement. To accommodate this change he refined and enlarged the traditional language of behaviourism. During the 1930s he published papers reporting his results and thrashing out precise definitions for his science of behaviour. This work became *Behavior of Organisms* (1938). Terms like 'operant' and 'reinforcement' are defined in functional terms, each in relation to the others. He was describing the behaviour of an organism–environment system rather than causal links between logically independent events. In 'stimulus control', the stimulus does not cause a response like one billiard ball hitting another, but sets the scene for a particular pattern of responding, conditioned by the contingencies of reinforcement. Later he introduced distinctions to accommodate the effects of language and culture, especially that between 'rule-governed' and 'contingency-shaped' behaviour.

After 1938, Skinner's life is best told through his projects rather than his appointments. Each was stimulated, according to his own account, by a chance problem. His interest in language, which culminated in *Verbal Behavior* (1957), was triggered by a challenge from A.N. Whitehead in 1934. For that book he drew on his background in literature and criticism in an

analysis of word usage. In the same spirit he provided 'An operational analysis of psychological terms' (1945), and later wrote on consciousness in *On Behaviorism*. At the start of World War II, the sight of a flock of pigeons, while he was wondering how to help the war effort, led him to his 'Pigeons in a Pelican', where the discriminative pecking of trained pigeons was to be used to guide missiles to their target. It worked, but never saw service. For his second daughter he invented the baby box, a controlled environment for keeping an infant amused and meeting its needs. The thought of returning to competitive pressures after the war led to his interest in the design of cultures, and the writing of his novel *Walden Two* (1948). The widespread interest in that novel, as well as the outrage that greeted it, were repeated when he published *Beyond Freedom and Dignity* in 1971. As a dutiful parent in 1953, Skinner occasionally attended his daughter's classes, and was struck by the gulf between teaching methods and known processes of learning. He spent ten years trying to bridge this gap with the invention of teaching machines and programmed instruction. At that time he was also encouraging the development of behaviour therapy using operant conditioning, based on his operationalist belief that what is essential in **Freud** is the survival of patterns of behaviour from childhood, not that of guilt and aggression.

Throughout, Skinner continued to publish on his basic science, work that culminated in the encyclopaedic *Schedules of Reinforcement* with C.B. Ferster in 1957. The years around 1957 mark a turning point. Mainstream experimental psychology was moving away from dependence on stimulus–response theories like Clark Hull's and into cognitive psychology and a theoretical language based on computer modelling. Noam **Chomsky**'s ferocious onslaught on *Verbal Behavior* probably hastened this process. Whatever its personal target, intellectually it was an attack on stimulus–response theory rather than on Skinner's functional analysis. Hull's approach dropped from sight, but Skinner's flourished with the founding of the *Journal for the Experimental Analysis of Behavior* and *Behaviorism*. His radical behaviourism diverged from mainstream experimental psychology, but established itself as a distinct discipline.

If honours and public interest are the measure of a psychologist, Skinner was the major American psychologist of the twentieth century. As with **Darwin** and Freud, the strength of feeling for and against his views has been extreme. Yet he was not representative. Psychology has become increasingly dependent on hypothesis testing, both statistically and through the development of theory, first stimulus–response theories, more recently cognitive and physiological theories. Skinner was an implacable foe of these goals from the start, and this is consistent with the philosophy of science that he worked out in 1930 and practised throughout his life.

But he was at odds with the mainstream in other ways which throw light on his success, and on the controversy caused within and outside academic psychology. He made up for his aversion to theory with a willingness to speculate about applications of his scientific findings. At the height of his career he was optimistic about the possibilities, but at the end he recognized with despair that he had failed to convince the world, and that our mismanaged technology is moving us towards destruction. Each of his main projects – teaching machines and programmed learning, the design of cultures, and behavior therapy – has had an impact, but they have not been accepted as a behavioural technology that could reverse this fate. Perhaps his most visible success has been in self-management. Unlike most other psychologists, he applied his principles to his own life, taking a problem-solving approach to everything from sleep to old age. In his work patterns he lived the Protestant ethic to the full – but did it painlessly by using the pleasant reinforcers of daily output and success, rather than the demanding ideals of service and salvation.

A final contribution to his success has been a paradoxical one: his concepts have been widely misunderstood, and many critics have relied on second-hand accounts. 'Stimulus control' has been especially vulnerable – 'control' is not a word to use lightly if you seek wide acceptance of your ideas. The perceived crassness has turned people away, and the underlying philosophy has never been adequately challenged. It has instead survived unscathed, and connections with other thought in the twentieth century have yet to be explored fully.

ARTHUR STILL

Slovic, S. Paul

Born: 1938, Chicago, USA **Nat:** American **Ints:** Engineering, environmental, experimental, personality and social, psychological study of social issues **Educ:** BA Stanford University, 1959; MA University of Michigan, 1962; PhD University of Michigan, 1964 **Appts & awards:** Fellow, APA, AAAS; Sigma Xi Phi Kappa Phi; Fulbright Scholar, 1973–4; Research Associate, Decision Research, 1976–86; President, Society for Risk Analysis, 1983–4; Adjunct Professor, Department of Psychology, University of Oregon, 1986– ; Editorial Boards, *Journal of Research in Personality, Journal of Experimental Psychology, Organizational Behavior and Human Performance, Risk Analysis*

Principal publications

1964   Assessment of risk taking behavior. *Psychological Bulletin*, 61, 220–33.

1968   An analysis-of-variance model for the assessment of configural cue utilization in clinical judgment. *Psychological Bulletin*, 69, 338–49 (with P.J. Hoffman and L.G. Rorer).

1968   The relative importance of probabilities and payoffs in risk-taking. *Journal of Experimental Psychology*, 78(3), pt 2 (with S. Lichtenstein).

1969   Reversals of preference between bids and choices in gambling decisions. *Journal of Experimental Psychology*, 89, 46–55 (with S. Lichtenstein).

1971   Comparison of Bayesian and regression approaches to the study of information processing in judgment. *Organizational Behavior and Human Performance*, 6, 649–744 (with S. Lichtenstein).

1974   Who accepts Savage's axiom? *Behavioral Science*, 19, 368–73 (with A.Tversky).

1977   Behavioral decision theory. *Annual Review of Psychology*, 28, 1–39 (with B. Fischhoff and S. Lichtenstein).

1977   Preferences for insuring against probable small losses: Insurance implications. *Journal of Risk and Insurance*, 44, 237–58 (with B. Fischhoff, S. Lichtenstein, B. Corrigan and B. Combs).

1978   Rating the risks. *Environment*, 21, 14–20, 36–9 (with B. Fischhoff and S. Lichtenstein).

1978   *Disaster Insurance Protection: Public Policy Lessons*. Wiley (with H. Kunreuthen).

1981   *Acceptable Risk*. Cambridge University Press (with B. Fischhoff, S. Lichtenstein, S.L. Derby and R. Keeney).

1982   *Judgment Under Uncertainty*. Cambridge University Press (ed. with D. Kahneman and A. Tversky).

1986   Decision making. In R.C. Atkinson, R.J. Herrnstein, G. Lindsey and R.D. Luce (eds), *Handbook of Experimental Psychology* (2nd edn) Wiley (with S. Lichtenstein and B. Fischhoff).

1987   Perception of risk. *Science*, 236, 280–5.

1992   Intuitive toxicology: Expert and lay judgments of chemical risks. *Risk Analysis*, 13, 675–82 (with N. Kraus and T. Malmfors).

Further reading

Bell, D.E., Raiffa, H. and Tversky, A. (eds) (1988) *Decision Making: Descriptive, Normative, and Prescriptive Interactions*. Cambridge University Press.

Gregory, R. and Mendelsohn, S.R. (1993) Perceived risk, dread, and benefits. *Risk Analysis*, 13, 259–64.

Paul Slovic was a passionate basketball player. He attended De Paul University on a basketball scholarship but was too short to make it as a college player. He transferred to Stanford and to psychology. He became interested in the study of decision making when he was a graduate assistant to Clyde **Coombs**, who was conducting experimental tests of expected utility theory. When Professor Coombs went on sabbatical leave, Slovic began to work with Ward Edwards, who was doing pioneering research in what was later to be called 'Behavioral Decision Theory'.

Slovic's early interests were in individual differences in risk-taking behaviour. However, he soon found that situational or task factors seemed to have a much more powerful influence on decision making than did personality factors. On receiving his PhD and moving to the Oregon Research Institute (ORI), Paul Hoffman, Lew Goldberg and others interested him in problems of modelling information processing in human judgement. With Sarah Lichtenstein, he began to apply the information-processing approach to the study of risk-taking decisions. They observed powerful effects of the response mode on the evaluation of simple gambles, enabling them to produce complete reversals of preference as a function of how those preferences were elicited – a finding that has posed a challenge to all major descriptive theories of decision making.

Amos **Tversky** and Daniel **Kahneman** spent a year at ORI and further broadened Slovic's interest in the difficulties that people have when processing information in risk-taking situations. In 1971 he met Gilbert White, a geographer interested in people's behaviour under the threat of natural disasters. At his urging, and with colleagues, Slovic began to examine 'societal risk taking', attempting to understand the cognitive processes that influence the behaviour of individuals and society in the face of risks to health and safety. Slovic and his colleagues attempted to demonstrate that effective policy must be based on an understanding of how people think about risk. Without this under-

standing, well-intended government regulations may be ineffective or even counter-productive. In 1983 he became the first social scientist to be elected president of the Society for Risk Analysis, and in 1991 he received the society's Distinguished Contribution Award. In 1987 he was elected to the National Council on Radiation Protection and Measurements, and in 1992 he was elected to the council's board of directors. He has consulted widely for industry, government and public interest groups. In 1986, Slovic joined the psychology faculty of the University of Oregon in addition to becoming president of Decision Research. At a time of global environmental change, in which human actions are implicated as the primary causal agent, his contributions are both perspicacious and much needed.

Snyder, Mark

Born: 1947, Montreal, Canada **Nat:** Canadian **Ints:** Clinical, developmental, personality and social, society for the Psychological Study of Social Issues, teaching **Educ:** BA McGill University, 1968; PhD Stanford University, 1972 **Appts & awards:** Society of Experimental Social Psychology Dissertation Award, 1973; Professor, Department of Psychology, University of Minnesota, 1978–92, Professor and Chair, 1992– ; Fellow, Center for Advanced Study in the Behavioral Sciences, 1980–1; Fellow, APA Division 8, 1988– ; Editorial Boards: *Journal of Personality*, 1976– , *Journal of Personality and Social Psychology*, 1977–80, *Review of Personality and Social Psychology*, 1979– , *Journal of Experimental Social Psychology*, 1980– , Advisory Board, *Social Cognition*, 1980– ; Advisory Editor, *Contemporary Psychology*, 1985–

Principal publications

1974 Self-monitoring of expressive behavior. *Journal of Personality and Social Psychology*, 30, 526–37.

1977 Social perception and interpersonal behavior: On the self-fullfilling nature of social stereotypes. *Journal of Personality and Social Psychology*, 35, 656–66 (with E. Tanke and E. Berscheid).

1978 Hypothesis-testing processes in social interaction. *Journal of Personality and Social Psychology*, 36, 1202–12 (with W.B. Swann Jr).

1979 Self-monitoring processes. In L. Berkowitz (ed.), *Advances in Experimental Social Psychology*, vol. 12. Academic Press.

1981 On the self-perpetuating nature of social

stereotypes. In D.L. Hamilton (ed.), *Cognitive Processes, Stereotyping and Intergroup Behavior.* Erlbaum.

1981 On the influence of individuals on situations. In N. Cantor and J. Kihlstrom (eds), *Personality, Cognition and Social Interaction.* Erlbaum.

1984 When belief creates reality. In L. Berkowitz (ed.), *Advances in Experimental Social Psychology*, vol. 18. Academic Press.

1985 Personality and social behavior. In G. Lindzey and E. Aronson (eds), *Handbook of Social Psychology* (3rd edn). Random House (with W. Ickes).

1985 To carve nature at its joints: On the existence of discrete classes in personality. *Psychological Review*, 92, 317–49 (with S. Gangestad).

1985 Appeals to image and claims about quality: Understanding the effectiveness of advertising. *Journal of Personality and Social Psychology*, 49, 586–97 (with K.G. DeBono).

1987 *Public Appearances/Private Realities: The Psychology of Self-Monitoring.* Freeman.

1989 The Relationship Closeness Inventory: Assessing the closeness of interpersonal relationships. *Journal of Personality and Social Psychology*, 57, 792–807 (with E. Berscheid and M. Omoto).

1993 Basic research and practical problems: The promise of a 'functional' personality and social psychology. *Personality and Social Psychology Bulletin*, 19, 251–64.

Further reading

Snyder, M. (1995) Self-monitoring: Public appearances versus private realities. In G.G. Brannigan and M.R. Merrens (eds), *The Social Psychologists: Research Adventures.* McGraw-Hill.

From the earliest, Mark Snyder's interests in human nature have focused on the curious links that can and do exist between appearances (how people present themselves to others) and realities (their own true underlying attitudes, values, personalities and conceptions of self). Often there are striking contradictions between superficial appearances and the realities that lurk beneath the surface. He sought to answer the question of where 'personality' and the 'self' reside: in the public face or in the private reality. The concept of self-monitoring – the way people observe, regulate and control the image of themselves that they display in public – figures strongly in his explanation. High self-monitors are especially sensitive to social situations and expectations, whereas low self-monitors tend to be less interested in controlling the impressions they create. High self-monitors take a flexible approach to defining themselves, whereas low self-monitors tend to convey their beliefs and principles regardless of the situation. Snyder found – primarily through theoretical and empirical explorations of the psychological construct of self-monitoring – that for some people (those low in self-monitoring, as assessed by the Self-Monitoring Scale) the public and private person mesh well, while for others (those high in self-monitoring) there is what amounts to a kaleidoscope of changing appearances tailored to meet considerations of situational appropriateness, often bearing little or no relation to underlying attitudes and dispositions. From a long-standing attempt to chart the implications of the generalized interpersonal orientations associated with self-monitoring (implications for how people think, feel and act as individuals and the dynamics of their relationships with their friends and romantic partners) have grown larger theoretical perspectives on the mutual interplay of individuals and their social worlds, theoretical perspectives presented in the chapter in *Handbook of Social Psychology* (1985). Although it is not clear why people develop different self-monitoring styles, Snyder's work has posed an insightful challenge to the idea that each person has a 'true self'.

Sokolov, Evgeny Nikolaevich

Born: 1920, Nizhnii Novgorod, Russia **Nat:** Russian **Ints:** Neurophysiology, psychology, psychophysiology **Educ:** Dr Biological Sciences Moscow State University, 1961 **Appts and Awards:** Professor, Chair, Department of Psychophysiology, Moscow State University, 1971– ; Foreign Member, USA National Academy of Sciences, 1975, American Academy of Arts and Sciences, 1976, Finnish Academy of Sciences and Letters, 1984; Member, USSR Academy of Pedagogical Sciences, 1985; Pavlov's Gold Medal Award, Academy of Sciences of the USSR

Principal publications

1963 *Perception and the Condition Reflex.* Pergamon.

1969 *Mechanisms of Memory.* Moscow University Press (in Russian).

1976 Learning and memory: Habituation as negative learning. In M.R. Rosenzweig and L.L. Bennett (eds), *Neural Mechanisms of Learning and Memory*. MIT Press.

1979   *Psychophysiology*. Moscow University Press (in Russian).

1981   *Neuronal Mechanisms of Memory and Learning*. Nauka.

1984   *Colour Vision*. Moscow University Press (with C.A. Izmailov) (in Russian).

1986   *Theoretical Psychophysiology*. Moscow University Press (in Russian).

1989   *Neurointelligence: From Neuron to Neurocomputer* Nauka (in Russian).

Further reading

Sokolov, E.N. (1957) Higher nervous activity and the problem of perception. In B. Simon (ed.) *Psychology in the Soviet Union*. Routledge & Kegan Paul.

—— (1960) Neuronal models and the orienting response. In M.A.B. Brazier (ed.), *The Central Nervous System and Behavior*. Josia Macey Jr Foundation.

—— (1963) Higher nervous function: The orienting reflex. *Annual Review of Physiology*, 25, 545–80.

—— (1988) SPR Award, 1988. For distinguished contributions to Psychophysiology: Evgeny Nikolaevich Sokolov. *Psychophysiology*, 26, 385–91.

—— and Vaitkavichus, H.H. (1978) Model of the analyser of the intensity of light. *Biophysics*, 21, 544–8.

—— and Vinigradova, O.S. (1975) *Neuronal Mechanisms of the Orienting Reflex*. Erlbaum.

Voronin, L.G., Leont'ev, A.N., Luria, A.R., Sokolov, E.N. and Vinogradova, O.S. (eds) *Orienting Reflex and Exploratory Behavior*. American Institute of Biological Sciences.

Evgeny Nikolaevich Sokolov was born in Nizhnii Novgorod on 23 September 1920. After serving as a military interpreter for four years during the war (1941–5), he entered the Foreign Languages Department of the Moscow Pedagogical Institute. He next became a postgraduate student in the laboratory of the Institute of Philosophy of the USSR Academy of Sciences, headed by the well-known Russian psychophysiologist S.V. Kravkov. It was there that, while studying an effect of auditory stimulation on the facilitation of visual sensitivity, Sokolov found that the initial visual response to an auditory stimulus at the beginning of presentation disappeared after a few repetitions of the auditory stimulus. Moreover, the same was found to happen to the galvanic skin response. In this way Sokolov first encountered the orienting response ('what-is-it' reflex, in **Pavlov's** terms), whose theoretical explanation later brought him international recognition. According to this theory, orienting arises in response to a mismatch between an internal neural model of the external environment and current sensory information about this environment. Sokolov argued that an orienting response, which Pavlov believed to be an experimental artefact to be eliminated in physiological investigations, played an important role on its own in animal and human behaviour. His intensive work on the orienting response in the 1950s was summarized in his book *Perception and the Condition Reflex* (1963), which has been translated and published in the USA, England, Japan and other countries.

Sokolov's work on the orienting response has had a great influence on psychophysiology (acknowledged by an award of the Society for Psychophysiological Research for 'distinguished contributions to psychophysiology' in 1988), because it filled the gap between psychophysiology and cognitive psychology on the one hand and neurophysiology on the other. As a system responding to novelty in stimulation, the orienting response can be considered as a cognitive filter, taking it into the realm of cognitive science. At the same time, Sokolov's theory of orienting includes a neuronal model of stimulation that allows us to treat behavioural reactions in terms of neuronal mechanisms. It is central to Sokolov's approach to psychophysiology to consider it as a science about neuronal mechanisms of behaviour. In the 1960s the same approach was applied to memory, analysed in terms of habituation of the orienting response at the level of single nerve cells.

For the last two decades, Sokolov has been intensively studying neuronal mechanisms of colour vision in collaboration with a group of his students at the Moscow University. Especially fruitful was his collaboration with C.A. Izmailov, which resulted in a new so-called 'spherical' model of human colour vision. They developed a neuronal model of large colour differences as revealed from multidimensional scaling of surface colours. In this work Sokolov's understanding of a general principle of psychophysiological investigation, which he articulates as 'human being–neuron–model', was fully implemented. His extensive work led Sokolov to receive many honors, including his election as a foreign member of Western academies and some prestigious awards.

T. SOKOLSKAYA AND A. LOGVINENKO

Spearman, Charles Edward

Born: 1863, London, England *Died:* 1945, London, England *Nat:* British *Ints:* Evaluation and measurement psychology, experimental psychology, history of psychology, personality and social psychology, philosophical and theoretical psychology *Educ:* PhD University of Leipzig, 1906 *Appts & awards:* University College London, Reader in Experimental Psychology, 1907–11, Grote Professor of Mind and Logic, 1911–28, Professor of Psychology, 1928–31, Emeritus Professor; Fellow, Royal Society, 1924; President, 1923–6, Hon. Member, 1934, BPS; President, Psychology Section, British Association for the Advancement of Science, 1925; Hon. LLD, University of Wittenberg, 1929; also hon. member of several foreign academies of science and psychological societies

Principal publications

1904   The proof and measurement of association between two things. *American Journal of Psychology*, 15, 72–101.

1904   'General intelligence' objectively determined and measured. *American Journal of Psychology*, 15, 202–93.

1923   *The Nature of 'Intelligence' and the Principles of Cognition*. Macmillan.

1927   *The Abilities of Man, their Nature and Measurement*. Macmillan.

1930   *Creative Mind*. Cambridge University Press.

1950   *Human Ability*. Macmillan (with L. Wynn Jones) (published posthumously).

Further reading

Lovie, P. and Lovie, A.D. (1996) Charles Edward Spearman. F.R.S (1863–1945). *Notes and Records of the Royal Society of London*, 50, 1–14.

Spearman, C. (1930) C. Spearman. In C. Murchison (ed.), *A History of Psychology in Autobiography*, vol. 1. Clark University Press.

Thomas, F.C. (1935) *Ability and Knowledge*. Macmillan.

Thomson, G. (1946) Charles Spearman 1863–1945. *Obituary Notices of Fellows of the Royal Society*, 5, 372–85.

As an infantry officer with some fifteen years of active service, mainly in India, Spearman seems an unlikely candidate to become one of the most influential of twentieth-century British psychologists. However, a fascination from boyhood with things philosophical, a small but heavily used personal library of philosophical and psychological classics, and many unanswered questions, led him, aged 34, to resign his commission and start on the academic life.

Spearman's formal training in psychology began in 1897 in **Wundt**'s experimental psychology laboratory at Leipzig, from which he eventually obtained a PhD in 1906. The following year, he secured a part-time post at University College London, where he remained until retiring as Emeritus Professor in 1931. It was essentially due to Spearman's intellectual efforts and reputation that there emerged a distinct 'London School' of psychology – a hard-nosed, statistical and psychometric approach to studying human faculties – and, with it, the first internationally recognised centre of psychological research in Britain.

Spearman first attracted attention in 1904 while still a student, with the espousal of a 'two-factor' theory of intelligence which predicted a common, or general, intellective function underlying every mental ability to some degree, as well as a function specific to the task in hand; later, these were called *g* and *s*. However, Spearman was no mere theorizer: by adapting existing correlational methods to mitigate the effects of unwanted factors and observational errors, and then applying these refined procedures to scores from various mental ability tests on schoolchildren, he demonstrated that the pattern of intercorrelations was consistent with the notion of a common factor with which any mental activity was 'saturated' to a certain, and calculable, degree. Thus were laid the foundations of factor analysis.

For close on three decades, the two-factor theory came under almost constant attack. Some critics challenged the idea that human intelligence could be encapsulated so simply, or even that *g* existed at all; others were unconvinced by Spearman's mathematical arguments. Strengthening its theoretical and statistical foundations to confound the opposition kept Spearman and his many helpers (students and colleagues) well occupied over these years. By the early 1930s, however, the notion of a simple, two-factor structure of intelligence was being gradually eclipsed by the ascendance of multiple-factor theories favoured by Young Turks like **Thurstone**. Even so, this cannot diminish Spearman's achievement as the originator of that most psychological of all statistical methods, factor analysis.

In view of the enormous effort expended on the two-factor theory, it is perhaps surprising to discover that Spearman himself saw his work on mental testing as secondary to the quest for fundamental laws of psychology. His major contribution here, described in detail in *The Nature of 'Intelligence' and the Principles of Cognition* (1923), took the form of an empirical epistemology, termed noëgenesis, whose principles are surprisingly in tune with modern approaches to cognition.

PATRICIA LOVIE AND A.D. LOVIE

Spence, Janet Taylor

Born: 1923, Toledo, Ohio, USA *Nat:* American *Ints:* Clinical, experimental, personality and social, psychology of women *Educ:* AB Oberlin College, 1945; MA, PhD University of Iowa, 1949 *Appts & awards:* Ashbel Smith Professor of Psychology and Educational Psychology, University of Texas at Austin; Gold Medal, Hollins College, 1968; President, Southwestern Psychological Association, 1971; Ford Foundation Fellowship, 1974–5; APA, Board of Directors, 1975–7; President, 1984; Trustee, James McKeen Cattell Foundation, 1978– ; Governor, Center for Creative Leadership, 1984–6; Member, American Academy of Arts and Science, 1984– ; Fellow, Center for Advanced Studies in the Behavioral Sciences, 1978–9; Secretary-Treasurer, Psychonomic Society; Editorial Boards: *Journal of Abnormal and Social Psychology*, 1960–4, *Journal of Experimental Psychology*, 1972–4, *Abnormal Psychology*, 1974–6, *Sex Roles*, 1975–81, *Child Development*, 1975– , *Contemporary Psychology*, 1979–85, *Journal of Personality and Social Psychology*, 1985– , *Journal of Clinical Psychology*, 1985– ; Associate Editor, 1969–74, Editor, 1974–9; *Contemporary Psychology*; Series Co-Editor, Psychology of Learning and Motivation (Academic Press)

Principal publications

1951 The relationship of anxiety to the conditioned eyelid response. *Journal of Experimental Psychology*, 41, 81–92.

1953 A personality scale of manifest anxiety. *Journal of Abnormal and Social Psychology*, 48, 285–90.

1966 Verbal versus nonverbal reinforcement combinations in the discrimination learning of middle- and lower-class children. *Child Development*, 38, 29–38 (with L.L. Segner).

1967 *The Psychology of Learning and Motivation*, Vol. 1. Academic Press (ed. with K.W. Spence).

1971 (ed.) *Essays in Neobehaviorism*. Appleton-Century-Crofts (with H.H. Kendler).

1972 The effects of blank versus non-informative feedback and 'right' and 'wrong' on response repetition in paired-associate learning: A reanalysis and reinterpretation. *Journal of Experimental Psychology*, 94, 1246–8.

1972 Who likes competent women? Competence, sex-role congruence of interest, and subjects' attitudes towards women as determinants of interpersonal attraction. *Journal of Applied Social Psychology*, 2, 197–213 (with R. Helmreich).

1975 Ratings of self and peers on sex-role attributes and their relations to self-esteem and conceptions of masculinity and femininity. *Journal of Personality and Social Psychology*, 32, 29–39 (with R. Helmreich and J. Stapp).

1978 *Masculinity and Femininity: Their Psychological Dimensions, Correlates and Antecedents.* University of Texas Press (with R.L. Helmreich).

1980 Making it in academic psychology: Demographic and personality correlates of attainment. *Journal of Personality and Social Psychology*, 39, 896–908 (with R. Helmreich, W.W Beane, G.W. Lucker and K.A. Matthews).

1982 *Elementary Statistics* (4th edn). Prentice Hall (with J.W. Cotton, B.J. Underwood and C.P. Duncan).

1983 Achievement-related motives and behavior. In J.T. Spence (ed.), *Achievement and Achievement Motives: Psychological and Sociological Approaches*. Freeman.

1983 (ed.) *Achievement and Achievement Motives: Psychological and Sociological Approaches*. Freeman.

1985 Gender identification and its implications for masculinity and femininity. In T.B. Sonderegger (ed.), *Nebraska Symposium On Motivation and Achievement: Psychology and Gender*, vol. 32. University of Nebraska Press.

1986 Achievement and achievement motivation: A cultural perspective. *Proceedings of the 23rd International Congress of Psychology*. North-Holland (with C. Izard).

1992 Workaholism: Definition, measurement, and preliminary results. *Journal of Personality Assessment*, 58, 160–78 (with A.S. Robbins).

1993 Gender-related traits and gender ideology: Evidence for a multifactorial theory. *Journal of Personality and Social Psychology*, 64, 624–35.

Further reading

Koestner, R. and Aube, J. (1995) A multifactorial approach to the study of gender characteristics. Special Issue: Levels and domains in personality. *Journal of Personality*, 63, 681–710.

O'Connell, A.N. and Russo, N.F. (eds) (1990) *Women in Psychology: A Bio-Bibliographic Sourcebook*. Greenwood.

Janet Taylor's Spence's mother and grandmother were both graduates of Vassar College and her mother earned a master's degree in economics at Columbia as well. Her father was active in the Socialist party and became a labour union business manager. Her mother, an activist Republican, developed a career path that moved from the League of Women Voters to the management of several election campaigns to the head of a social service agency concerned with families and dependent children. Janet Taylor and **Kenneth Spence** were married in 1959 and Janet Taylor Spence returned to Iowa City the following fall. The marriage forced Spence to face the nepotism policies that were to constrain her career for the next eight years. Only in 1967, when Kenneth Spence's untimely death made the nepotism issue moot, did Janet Spence move back to the psychology department track that she had left in 1960.

The many contributions of Janet Spence may seem to fall into several disjunctive sets, but underneath there is a common theme: individual differences in personality traits and motives that have important implications for real-life behaviours. Starting with her dissertation research, for which she developed the (Taylor) Manifest Anxiety Scale, her early work was devoted to the investigation of anxiety as a person variable, particularly its motivational properties. The theoretical framework of her research was **Hull–Spence** learning theory, its most novel feature postulating an interaction between motivational (drive) level and task characteristics in determining performance.

Her marriage to K.W. Spence was followed by two rapid changes in locale, first to Iowa and then to Texas, and from an appointment in a Department of Psychology to other kinds of position, due to nepotism rules. These essentially brought this work to an end. However, she continued to bring similar learning principles to bear on schizophrenia, while working in a veteran's hospital, and on aspects of developmental psychologists, while working in a school for the retarded and a Department of Educational Psychology.

An abrupt change in topic came about in 1970, following K.W. Spence's death, when she moved within the University of Texas to the position of Chair of the Department of Psychology, and with the emergence of the women's movement. With colleagues she undertook a series of studies related to attitudes about women's roles and gender-differentiating personality characteristics. These ultimately led to studies of instrumental and expressive personality characteristics and intrinsic achievement motives, and their implications for real-life behaviours. These factors have been found to have important (and similar) ramifications in both sexes for phenomena ranging from marital interactions to job performance, which she continues to explore.

Spence, Kenneth Wartenbee

Born: 1907, Chicago, USA **Died:** 1967, Austin, Texas, USA **Nat:** American **Ints:** Experimental, physiological and comparative **Educ:** BA McGill University, 1929; MA McGill University, 1930; PhD Yale University, 1933 **Appts & awards:** Wales Gold Medal in Mental Sciences, McGill University, 1929; Governor-General's Medal for Research, McGill University, 1930; Head, Department of Psychology, University of Iowa, 1942–64; Howard Warren Crosby Medal of the Society of Experimental Psychologists, 1953; Member, National Academy of Science, 1954; APA Distinguished Scientific Contribution Award, 1956; *Journal of Experimental Psychology*, *The Psychology of Learning and Motivation: Advances in Research and Theory*

Principal publications

1936   The nature of discrimination learning in animals. *Psychological Review*, 43, 427–49.

1937   The differential response in animals to stimuli varying in a single dimension. *Psychological Review*, 44, 430–44.

1938   Gradual versus sudden solution of discrimination problems in chimpanzees. *Journal of Comparative Psychology*, 25, 213–24.

1942   Theoretical interpretations of learning. In Moss (ed.), *Comparative Psychology* (rev. edn). Prentice Hall.

1944   The nature of theory construction in contemporary psychology. *Psychological Review*, 51, 47–68.

1948   The postulates and methods of behaviorism. *Psychological Review*, 55, 67–9.

1951   Anxiety and strength of the UCS as determiners of the amount of eyelid conditioning. *Journal of Experimental Psychology*, 42, 183–8 (with J.A. Taylor (Spence)).

1952   The nature of the response in discrimination learning. *Psychological Review*, 59, 89–93.

1956   *Behavior Theory and Conditioning*. Yale University Press.

1960   *Behavior Theory and Learning*. Prentice Hall.

1966   Cognitive factors in the extinction of the

conditioned eyeblink in human subjects.
Psychological Review, 73, 445–9.
1967   *The Psychology of Learning and Motivation*
(2 vols). Academic Press.

Further reading
Amsel, A. (1995) Kenneth Wartenbee Spence.
Biographical Memoir, National Academy of
Sciences, vol. 66.
Kendler, H.H. (1967) Kenneth Wartenbee Spence.
Psychological Review, 74, 335–41.

Kenneth Spence was a giant among learning
theorists. His name and Clark **Hull**'s are usually
joined to identify the most influential neo-
behaviouristic learning theory of the 1940s and
1950s. His contribution to this theory was explicitly acknowledged by Hull, but it can also be
inferred from the level of correspondence maintained by the two men.

The items here taken from Spence's bibliography were selected to represent the major
facets of his contribution to psychology. They
fall into three major categories: philosophy of
science, learning theory, and the experimental
psychology of learning. (In some of the
philosophy-of-science work, Gustav Bergmann
was a collaborator.) One of Spence's contributions was to to clarify for all of us the role in
psychology of operationism and the nature of
theory construction; and to point up the difficulties that exist in the formulation of psychological theories. One of his insights was that, unlike
physical scientists, psychologists are faced with
the necessity of constructing theories at the
point of trying to establish low-level lawfulness;
they cannot do it simply by empirical means.
Spence's contributions to learning theory, apart
from his collaboration in the Hull–Spence
system, were of two kinds. One was in his
acknowledged skill as a commentator on, and
interpretator of, the characteristics of the
theories and systems of others. The chapter in
the edited volume by Moss (1942) is an
example, as is a later chapter in the **Stevens**
Handbook of Experimental Psychology.
Tolman is reported to have said that he never
really understood his system until he saw
Spence's analysis of it. His other kind of contribution to learning theory was original,
beginning with the famous early papers on
discrimination learning – the theory of discrimination, the analysis of transposition, the
derivation of continuity out of the seemingly
sudden solution of discrimination problems.

Spence's own best summary of his theoretical

contributions is in his Silliman lectures at Yale,
published as *Behavioral Theory and Conditioning* (1956). The earliest experimental contributions were the chimpanzee work at the
Yerkes Laboratory in Orange Park, Florida, and
maze-learning studies. The continuing experimental interests of Kenneth Spence in his own
work, and in the work of his graduate students,
were in instrumental discrimination learning and
human classical eyeblink conditioning. His work
in these areas is still, arguably, the best of its
kind and still frequently cited: in a six-year
period from 1962 until 1967 (the year of his
death), Kenneth Spence was the most cited
psychologist in a survey of fourteen journals
judged to be the most prestigious in the field.
One must not, finally, overlook another facet of
Kenneth Spence's contribution: the seventy-
seven PhD students that came out of his laboratories, a large number of whom have been able
to make significant contributions of their own.

K.W.S. AMSEL

Sperry, Roger Wolcott

Born: 1913, Hartford, USA **Died:** 1994,
Pasadena, USA **Nat:** American **Ints:** Neuro-
psychology **Educ:** AB Oberlin College, 1935;
MA Oberlin College, 1937; PhD University of
Chicago, 1941 **Appts & awards:** Hixon Profes-
sor of Psychobiology, Division of Biology,
California Institute of Technology, 1954; Mem-
ber, National Academy of Sciences, 1960;
Member, American Academy of Arts and Sci-
ences, 1963; Experimental Psychology Study
Section Committee, Member, NIH, 1966–70,
Chairman, 1969–70; H. Crosby Warren Medal,
Society of Experimental Psychologists, 1969;
APA Distinguished Scientific Contribution
Award, 1971; Hon. DSc, Cambridge University,
1972, Kenyon College, 1979, Rockefeller
University, 1980; Nobel prize in medicine/
psychology (shared), 1981; Albert Lasker
Medical Research Award, 1979; and many other
awards

Principal publications

1968   Mental unity following surgical disconnection
of the cerebral hemispheres. In *The Harvey
Lectures*, series 62. Academic Press.
1968   Hemispheric disconnection and unity in
conscious awareness. *American Psychologist*, 23,
723–33.
1968   Plasticity of neural maturation. *Developmental
Biology*, supplement 2, 27th Symposium.
Academic Press.

1969 A modified concept of consciousness.
Psychological Review, 76, 532–6.

1970 Perception in the absence of the neo-cortical
commisures. *Perceptual Disorders*, 48, 123–38.

1970 An objective approach to subjective
experience: Further explanation of a hypothesis.
Psychological Review, 77, 585–90.

1971 How a developing brain gets itself properly
wired for adaptive function. In E. Tobach, E. Shaw
and L.R. Aronson (eds), *The Biopsychology of
Development*. Academic Press.

Further reading
Schmitt, F.O. and Warden, E.G. (eds) (1974) *The
Neurosciences: Third Study Program*. MIT Press.

Roger Sperry spent his childhood in Hartford,
Connecticut, and went to Oberlin College on a
four-year scholarship. After receiving an AB
and MA in psychology, he completed a PhD at
the University of Chicago. On a National
Research Council postdoctral fellowship he
went to Harvard, and during World War II,
while based at the Yerkes Laboratories of
Primate Biology in Orange Park, Nevada, he
participated in a project involving the surgical
repair of nerve injuries. He joined the
University of Chicago faculty in 1946 and
served as a section chief of the National Institute of Neurological Diseases and Blindness
(1952–4) when he became Hixon professor at
Caltech.

Sperry's early work, starting in the late 1930s,
dealt with problems of functional plasticity and
selective growth in brain connections. One of
his major contributions is his work on the
embryogenesis of neuronal nets, in which he
showed that behavioural networks develop and
organize themselves independently from the
function they eventually come to perform.
Sperry showed that growth of central connections follows with an orderly, pre-programmed
precision. His early work went against the
commonly accepted principle that experience
and conditioning could transform an equipoten-
tial mesh of randomly connected neurons into a
structured, purposefully oriented neural network. One of his earliest experiments involved
repositioning the eyeball of amphibians, by
rotating it 180 degrees on its optic axis, while
leaving the optic nerve intact. The animal's
optokinetic responses as well as predatory
reactions were then made in a direction opposite
from normal – a frog would strike at an insect
by jumping to a point diametrically opposite to
the location of the lure. No amount of relearning

could modify those responses (despite the
remarkable capacity of the amphibian nervous
system to regenerate when altered), suggesting
that they were not organized through a learning
process. The chemo-affinity theory Sperry
developed in the early 1940s to account for his
findings linked the functional interconnections
of neuronal elements to developmental principles of differentiation and cytochemistry. The
existence and regulative role of preferential cell-
to-cell affinities which he postulated have been
confirmed by scores of experiments motivated
by this theory.

Another of Sperry's contributions relates to
the callosal section in animals. This work was
completed in the 1950s, and was a precursor to
human split-brain studies. The idea that the right
hemisphere was not an unconscious and minor
part of the brain, subservient to the elaborate
control of the left, was first articulated by
Hughlings **Jackson**. The idea was largely
ignored (except in the work of Brenda Milner,
Russel Brain, Oliver **Zangwill** and some others)
until Sperry demonstrated that the right hemisphere has its own consciousness and that it can
be conscious and intelligent (e.g. in non-verbal
and visual-spatial tasks) in a way different from
the left. His work on human split-brain studies
has stimulated additional research by many of
his prominent collaborators, such as **Gazzaniga**.
He was awarded one half of the Nobel prize
for physiology and medicine for his work on
the functional specialization of the cerebral
hemispheres.

Spielberger, Charles D.
Born: 1927, Atlanta, Georgia, USA **Nat:** American **Ints:** Clinical psychology, emotion, health
psychology, learning, stress, personality **Educ:**
BS (chemistry) GA Institute of Technology,
1949; BA (psychology) University of Iowa,
1951; MA University of Iowa, 1953; PhD,
University of Iowa, 1954 **Appts & awards:**
University of South Florida, Professor,
1967–72, Director, Center for Research in
Behavioral Medicine and Health Psychology,
1977– , Distinguished University Research
Professor, 1985– ; Fellow, APA Divisions 1, 3,
5, 8, 12, 13, 17, 26, 27, 38, 42, 47; President,
Southeastern Psychological Association,
1972–3; President, APA Division 27, 1974–5,
APA Division 12, 1989–90, APA, 1991–2;
President, Psi Chi, the National Honor Society in
Psychology, 1980–3; President, International
Society for Test Anxiety Research, 1984–6;

President, International Council of Psychologists, 1986–7; President, Society for Personality Assessment, 1986–8; Hon. LLD, Pacific Graduate School of Psychology, 1990; Hon. D, Hungarian University of Physical Education, Budapest, 1991; President, International Stress Management Association, 1992– ; APA Centennial Awards for Distinguished Contributions to Knowledge and Professional Practice, and for Distinguished Sustained Contributions to Education in Psychology, 1992; Chairman, National Council of Scientific Society Presidents, 1994; President-Elect, International Association of Applied Psychology, 1994

Principal publications

1962   The role of awareness in verbal conditioning. In C.W. Eriksen (ed.), *Behaviour and Awareness.* Duke University Press (also in *Journal of Personality*, 30, supplement).

1966   *Anxiety and Behavior.* Academic Press.

1970   (ed.) *Community Psychology: Perspectives in Training Research.* Appleton-Century-Crofts (with I. Iscoe).

1972   (ed.) *Anxiety: Current Trends in Theory and Research* (2 vols). Academic Press.

1975–96   (ed.) *Stress and Anxiety*, vols 1–13; *Stress and Emotion: Anxiety, Anger and Curiosity*, vols 14–16. Hemisphere/Wiley (with I.G. Sarason and others).

1979   *Understanding Stress and Anxiety.* Harper & Row (also in Dutch, German, Greek, Italian, Portuguese, Spanish and Swedish editions).

1979–95   *Advances in Personality Assessment*, vols 1–10. LEA (ed. with J.N. Butcher).

1987   Effects of smoking on heart rate, anxiety, and feelings of success during social interaction. *Journal of Behavioral Medicine*, 10, 629–38 (with D.G. Gilbert).

1988   The State–Trait Anxiety Inventory (STAI). In M. Hersen and A.S. Bellack (eds), *Dictionary of Behavioural Assessment Techniques.* Pergamon.

1991   War-related stress: Addressing the stress of war and other traumatic events. *American Psychologist*, 46, 848–55 (with S.E. Hobfoll, S. Breznitz, C. Figley, S. Folkman, B. Lepper-Green, D. Meichenbaum, N.A. Milgram, I. Sandler, I. Sarason and B. van der Kolk).

1995   (ed.) *Test Anxiety: Theory, Assessment, and Treatment.* Hemisphere/Taylor and Francis (with P.R. Vagg).

1996   Personality characteristics of users of smokeless tobacco compared with cigarette smokers and non-users of tobacco products. *Personality and Individual Differences*, (with J.P. Foreyt, G.K. Goodrick and E.C. Reheiser).

Further reading

Butcher, J.N. and Spielberger, C.D. (1995) *Advances in Personality Assessment, Vol. 10.* Erlbaum.

Spielberger, C.D. and Vagg, P.R. (eds) (1995) *Test Anxiety: Theory, Assessment, and Treatment.* Series in Clinical and Community Psychology. Taylor and Francis.

Charles D. Spielberger was born and educated in Georgia. He gave active service to the US Navy Reserve in 1945–6 and remains a Commander to the present day. After working at Iowa, Duke and Vanderbilt Universities, in 1967 Spielberger moved to the University of South Florida at Tampa. He is a prolific publisher, editor and educator who has made major contributions to the scholarly development of psychology and to its professional organization. His main research interests cover a fairly broad range of areas in and around clinical and health psychology, including behavioural medicine. Spielberger's main focus has been the study of emotion, stress and coping. His work in these fields has been of enormous influence and his Stress and Emotion book series is regarded as essential reference material.

One of Spielberger's major contributions has been his State–Trait Anxiety Inventory (STAI) developed in the 1960s. The STAI was derived from analysis of 177 existing scale items on large data-sets collected from college students. The STAI measures the state and trait forms of anxiety with twenty items, each using ratings along four-point scales of frequency for trait and intensity for state. The instrument shows good construct validity and has been a standard measure of anxiety for over two decades. A similar, useful instrument assesses anxiety levels in children.

In addition to his scholarly activities Spielberger has been a leading figure in a number of significant professional and scientific bodies. He served as the 100th President of the APA during 1991–2, has served on the APA's Board of Scientific Affairs, co-chaired the Joint Committee for Revising Test Standards and was President Elect of the International Association of Applied Psychology until 1994. Few psychologists have made such continuous and sustained impact on the field at both the scientific and organizational levels.

DAVID F. MARKS

Sternberg, Robert J.

Born: 1949, Maplewood, New Jersey, USA
Nat: American ***Ints:*** Developmental, edu-

cational, evaluation and measurement, experimental, personality and social *Educ:* BA Yale University, 1972; PhD Stanford University, 1975 *Appts & awards:* Stanford Sidney Siegel Memorial Award, 1975; APA Distinguished Award for Early Career Contribution to Psychology, 1981; APA Division 7, Boyd R. McCandless Young Scientist Award, 1982; Society of Multivariate Experimental Psychology, Cattel Award, 1982; Professor, Department of Psychology, Yale University, 1986; Guggenheim Fellowship, 1985–6; Series Editor, Advances in the Psychology of Human Intelligence (Erlbaum); Associate Editor, *Intelligence*, 1977–82, *Child Development*, 1981–4; Consulting Editor, *Memory and Cognition*, 1979–81, *Journal of Educational Psychology*, 1979–81

Principal publications

1977   *Intelligence, Information Processing and Analogical Reasoning: The Componential Analysis of Human Abilities.* Erlbaum.

1977   Component processes in analogical reasoning. *Psychological Review*, 84, 353–78.

1977   Intelligence, information processing and analogical reasoning. In R.J. Sternberg (ed.), *The Componential Analysis of Human Abilities.* Erlbaum.

1977   The nature of mental abilities. *American Psychologist*, 34, 214–20.

1980   Sketch of a componential theory of human intelligence. *Behavioral and Brain Sciences*, 3, 573–84.

1981   Testing and cognitive psychology. *American Psychologist*, 36, 1181–9.

1982   (ed.) *Handbook of Human Intelligence.* Cambridge University Press.

1985   *Beyond IQ: A Triarchic Theory of Human Intelligence.* Cambridge University Press.

1986   *Intelligence Applied: Understanding and Increasing your Intellectual Skills.* Harcourt.

1986   *The Triangle of Love.* Basic Books.

1987   (ed.) *Teaching Thinking Skills: Theory and Practice.* Freeman (with J.B. Baron).

1988   (ed.) *Advances in the Psychology of Human Intelligence*, vol. 4. Erlbaum.

1991   *Love the Way You Want It.* Bantam.

1993   *The Psychology of Gender.* Guilford Press.

1994   (ed.) *Mind in Context.* Cambridge University Press (with R.K. Wagner).

Further reading

Demetriou, A. and Efklides, A. (eds) (1994) *Intelligence, Mind, and Reasoning: Structure and Development.* North-Holland/Elsevier Science.

Hampson, S.E. and Colman, A.E. (eds) (1995) *Individual Differences and Personality.* Longman.

Tzeng, O.C.S. (1992) *Theories of Love Development, Maintenance, and Dissolution: Octagonal Cycle and Differential Perspectives.* Praeger.

Sternberg's research has developed through three main phases. In the first phase the research was motivated by a 'componential' theory of human intelligence and a 'componential' methodology for testing the theory. Underlying the theory and methodology was the notion that intelligence comprises a set of elementary information processes, or components, that can be combined in various ways to generate performance on a wide variety of intellectual tasks. These components are of three basic kinds: (1) metacomponents, which plan, monitor and evaluate one's problem-solving performance; (2) performance components, which execute the instructions of the metacomponents and provide feedback to them; and (3) knowledge-acquisition components, which learn how to solve the problems in the first place. In the second phase, his conception of intelligence was broadened through a 'triarchic' theory of intelligence, according to which intelligence has three aspects: (1) its relation to the internal world of the individual (components); (2) its relation to the external world of the individual through the functions of adaptation to, selection of and shaping of environments; and (3) its relation to the experience of the individual through the individual's applying the components in the everyday world to novel tasks and situations, and through the automatization of the components. In the third phase, he placed the triarchic theory within a broader context in which intelligence is conceived of as mental self-government: the collection of mechanisms, structures and contents that enables the individual to carry out his or her transactions with the self, others and the environment. Although his main area of research has been on intelligence and its development, he has become interested in the study of love, and has proposed a 'Triangular' theory according to which love in its various aspects and manifestations is understood in terms of emotional, motivational and cognitive elements, as well as their interactions with each other and with the environment.

Stevens, Stanley Smith

Born: 1906, Ogden, Utah, USA *Died:* 1973, Vail, Colorado *Nat:* American *Ints:* Evaluation and measurement, experimental psychology, philosophical and theoretical psychology, physiological and comparative psychology, teaching of psychology **Educ:** BA Stanford University, 1931; PhD Harvard University, 1933 **Appts & awards:** Harvard University, Assistant in Psychology, 1932–5, Instructor in Experimental Psychology, 1936–8, Assistant Professor, 1938, Associate Professor, 1944, Professor of Psychology, 1946, Professor of Psychophysics, 1962; National Research Council Fellowship, 1934–5; Rockefeller Foundation Fellow, 1935–6; Warren Medal, Society of Experimental Psychologists, 1943; Distinguished Scientific Contribution Award, APA, 1960; Beltone Institute Award, 1966; Rayleigh Gold Medal Award, British Acoustical Society, 1972

Principal publications

1934 The relation of saturation to the size of the retinal image. *American Journal of Psychology*, 46, 70–9.

1934 The volume and intensity of tones. *American Journal of Psychology*, 46, 397–498.

1935 The operational basis of psychology. *American Journal of Psychology*, 47, 323–30.

1936 A scale for the measurement of a psychological magnitude: Loudness. *Psychological Review*, 43, 405–16.

1938 *Hearing: Its Psychology and Physiology.* Wiley (with H. Davis).

1939 Psychology and the science of science. *Psychological Bulletin*, 36, 221–63.

1942 *The Varieties of Temperament.* Harper & Row (with W.H. Sheldon).

1946 On the theory of scales of measurement. *Science*, 103, 677–80.

1951 (ed.) *Handbook of Experimental Psychology.* Wiley.

1955 The measurement of loudness. *Journal of the Acoustical Society of America*, 27, 815–29.

1957 On the psychophysical law. *Psychological Review*, 64, 153–81.

1957 Ratio scales and category scales for a dozen perceptual continua. *Journal of Experimental Psychology*, 54, 377–411 (with E.H. Galanter).

1959 Cross-modality validation of subjective scales for loudness, vibration, and electric shock. *Journal of Experimental Psychology*, 57, 201–9.

1961 To honor Fechner and repeal his law. *Science*, 133, 80–6.

1962 The surprising simplicity of sensory metrics. *American Psychologist*, 17, 29–39.

1966 A metric for the social consensus. *Science*, 151, 530–41.

1968 Measurement, statistics, and the schemapiric view. 161, 849–56.

1971 Issues in psychophysical measurement. *Psychological Review*, 78, 426–50.

1975 *Psychophysics: Introduction to its Perceptual, Neural and Social Prospects.* Wiley.

Further reading

Bolles, R.C. (1993) *The Story of Psychology: A Thematic History.* Brooks/Cole.

Michell, J. (1990) *An Introduction to the Logic of Psychological Measurement.* Erlbaum.

Most of S.S. Stevens' intellectual life was devoted to applying mathematics to psychology, not to the twentieth-century novelties of learning and testing, but in the most solidly traditional areas of psychophysics and the problem of measurement. There is little in his early development to foreshadow this dedication, except a debate on education in high school, which sparked an interest in intelligence tests. After finishing school he became a Mormon missionary for three years. He then entered the University of Utah and took a variety of advanced courses, but not mathematics. In his final year he discovered comparative psychology, and began to shock the parent's Sunday school class which he taught with J.B. **Watson**'s environmentalism (and shocked himself perhaps, since later he became a firm advocate of nature over nurture).

After Utah he spent two years at Stanford University, and by the end of that time he had acquired a wide-ranging scientific education. In 1931 he went to Harvard to complete his PhD. He began by belatedly filling in on mathematics by taking advanced statistics with T.L. Kelley. He also studied physiology with W.J. Crozier, a powerful advocate of demonstrable lawfulness in behaviour as the essence of biological science. In Crozier's laboratory he met B.F. **Skinner**, who introduced him to power functions in the 'eating curves' of rats. In this famous encounter Stevens confessed complete ignorance of power curves, and the pioneer of radical behaviourism advised this twentieth-century **Fechner** that: 'The only way to get over an inferiority complex about mathematics is to learn some.'

Stevens began his first published experiment as part of E.G. **Boring**'s course on experimental psychology. Boring suggested that he work on a puzzle about colour mixing; if you mix red and green in a colour wheel it only looks grey if you stand at the right distance. This was an eminently measurable and orderly phenomenon, since Stevens discovered that the right distance varies with the proportions of the two colours. He had not learned much perception at this stage in his career (he failed Boring's course in perception), but he was fascinated by the lawfulness he managed to demonstrate in these experiments, and it sealed his commitment to scientific research. He took a degree in experimental psychology and did so well that Boring offered him an assistantship. He started research on tonal volume, which became the dissertation for his PhD in 1933, and began to work with Hallowell Davis on mapping the frequency response of the guinea-pig's cochlea. By this time his mathematical education was well under way. He audited courses on mathematics and physics and was for a time a Research Fellow in Physics before finally settling on psychology in 1936.

Stevens was never content to be just a sound experimenter. From the start of his research he explored the philosophy of what he was doing, which led him to the logic of measurement. Measurement was a key problem for a scientific psychology. It seemed that a science begins with the possibility of measurement in an area of empirical investigation, a possibility that had been realized so unquestionably in physics. If psychology was to be brought into this scientific fold, a definition of measurement was required broad enough to include the study of mind or behaviour. Einstein had demonstrated that a consideration of the apparently simple measurements of time and length could throw up paradoxes of great theoretical moment, and the physicist Percy Bridgman built on Einstein's success to develop his *operationism*. According to Bridgman, valid measurement depends less on the solidity of the subject matter than on the operations of measurement and the lawfulness they generate. This was welcome news for psychology, still embroiled in controversy over what its subject matter actually is. Like his fellow student Skinner, Stevens seized on operationism as a way out of the impasse, and set out to establish psychology as a true science based on measurement.

During the 1930s Stevens continued his work on the ear with Hallowell Davis, which culminated in their book on hearing in 1938. He began to publish his ideas on operationism, as well as on measurement, and he showed that his interests were in measurement throughout psychology, rather than confined to psychophysics, by collaborating with W.H. Sheldon on research

published as *Varieties of Temperament* (1942). By the end of the decade Stevens was part of a group that met regularly to discuss the philosophy of science. It included Percy Bridgman, the leading logical positivist Rudolf Carnap, and the great mathematician G.D. Birkhoff. Birkhoff taught that science can be viewed as a process of isolating invariants under transformation, and Stevens applied this to classification of scales of measurement. He named four scales, nominal, ordinal, interval and ratio, classified according to the transformations that leave the scale form invariant. The classification is so familiar, as he ruefully pointed out, that nobody bothers to cite its origin.

But more important for Stevens at the time was that it provided a logical starting point for his work on the scaling of sensations, especially sound. There was considerable disagreement about the possibility of measuring subjective events. Can they be analogous to physical events in this respect, or are they fundamentally different and out of reach of the processes of measurement? By defining measurement scales in terms of operations rather than of the nature of what is measured, Stevens had begun to put psychophysics on the same level as physics. All that needed to be shown is that the operations of measurement, which are the methods of psychophysics, give rise to the reliable assignment of numbers. He had already done this convincingly with the sone scale of loudness in 1936, and he continued to extend this to other aspects of sound and to other modalities throughout his career.

In 1940 Stevens became director of the psycho-acoustical laboratory at Harvard. America was not yet in the war, but preparations were being made and the laboratory was started with generous military funding. By the end of the war Stevens headed a unit of fifty research workers, and in 1944 he was promoted to a tenured professorship. This had seemed unlikely earlier, since he made no secret of his dislike of formal teaching with undergraduate classes. But his excellence as a teacher in other ways, through guidance in research and writing, as well as his success in building up the psycho-acoustical laboratory, had been recognized by Harvard.

After the war there was a change in tempo in his career. He was now a senior Harvard professor, much in demand as an adviser to government bodies, and he settled down to edit the *Handbook of Experimental Psychology* (1951), a uniquely detailed book of experimental methods and results in all branches of scientific psychology. His editorial input was very thorough, and it took three years to prepare. It did as much as anything to consolidate the scientific credentials of psychology, yet for him in retrospect this was time 'squandered', and he despaired of getting back to the laboratory and to hands-on research.

When he did manage to do so in 1953 it was to break away from the dogma that had dominated psychophysics since its beginning – that equal intervals in magnitude of sensation are measurable in 'just noticeable differences'. This was a consequence of the **Weber**–Fechner law, and although Stevens and other psychophysicists were well aware of discrepancies with data, it had proved hard to dislodge. Worse still, different psychophysical methods gave rise to different scales, and Stevens hankered to find a simpler invariant underlying this variability. He found it by getting observers to assign numbers directly to subjective impressions, with the constraint that the ratio of numbers should correspond to the ratio of impressions. He discovered that the results were best described not by Fechner's logarithmic law, but by a power law – equal ratios in the stimulus correspond to equal ratios in the subjective judgement. This has been found by Stevens and others to apply consistently over different dimensions and modalities.

This success convinced Stevens of what he had always suspected, that psychophysics was and should remain the central discipline of psychology. Unfortunately psychology's interests were widening and moving away from psychophysics. Psychology, as he saw it, had deserted psychophysics, and in 1962 he displayed his sense of isolation by persuading Harvard to change his title to Professor of Psychophysics.

In an autobiographical sketch, Stevens saw as his main achievement the formulation of two invariants that establish simple order against a background of apparent disorder. The first was his definition of four measurement scales, each defined in terms of possible transformations. Was this a great achievement? Certainly it has become familiar in statistics, perhaps because of Sidney Siegel's use of the scales in his immensely popular *Nonparametric Statistics*. Siegel presented the theory of scales without acknowledgement to Stevens, and as though it were an unquestionable classification of measurement itself, part of the order of things rather than an elegant mathematical structure

imposed on the much messier operations of measurement. As a result it has become a prominent feature of the anonymous landscape with which beginning students of psychology become familiar, rather than as an ingenious construction by Stevens around 1940. Outside psychology, though, in the theory of measurement itself, it is less momentous, an important insight and an elegant oversimplification rather than a turning point. The second invariant was contained in the power law, and there is no doubt that this is a great achievement in the history of psychophysics. Whether it is a great scientific achievement will depend on the eventual status of psychophysics within psychology. That in turn depends on whether Stevens's operationist account of science, which established the scientific potential of subjective experience, remains as convincing as it was to him.

ARTHUR STILL

Stogdill, Ralph M.

Born: 1904, Convoy, Ohio, USA *Died:* 1978, Columbus, Ohio, USA *Nat:* American *Ints:* Consulting, counselling, evaluation and measurement, industrial and organizational, personality and social *Educ:* BA Ohio State University, 1930; MA Ohio State University, 1930; PhD Ohio State University, 1934 *Appts & awards:* Ohio State Leadership Studies, 1946–75: Professor of Business Organization, 1960–68; Professor of Management Sciences & Psychology (retired 1975), Ohio State University, 1968–75; Fellow, APA; Fellow, President, Management History Division, Academy of Management; Outstanding Research Award, APA Division 13, 1970; Outstanding Research Award, Southern Illinois University's Biennial Symposium on Leadership, 1974

Principal publications

1948 Personal factors associated with leadership: A survey of the literature. *Journal of Psychology*, 25, 35–71.
1949 The sociometry of working relationships in formal organizations. *Sociometry*, 12, 276–86.
1950 Leadership, membership and organization. *Psychological Bulletin*, 47, 1–14.
1955 A factorial study of administrative behavior. *Personnel Psychology*, 8, 165–80 (with C.L. Shartle, R.J. Wherry and W.E. Jaynes).
1959 *Individual Behavior and Group Achievement: A Theory*. Oxford University Press.
1962 New leader behavior description subscales.

Journal of Psychology, 54, 259–69 (with O.S. Goode and D.R. Day).

1965 *Managers, Employees, Organizations: A Study of 27 Organizations*. Research Monograph no. 125, Bureau of Business Research. Ohio State University.

1970 *The Process of Model-Building in the Behavioral Sciences*. Ohio State University. (Norton, 1972).

1972 Group Productivity, drive and cohesiveness. *Organizational Behavior and Human Performance*, 8, 26–43.

1974 *Handbook of Leadership: A Survey of Theory and Research*. Free Press. (rev. and updated as B.M. Bass (1981), *Stogdill's Handbook of Leadership: A Survey of Theory and Research*, Free Press).

1974 Historical trends in leadership theory and research. *Journal of Contemporary Business*, 3, 4, 1–17.

1974 Preference for motivator and hygiene factors in a hypothetical interview situation. *Personnel Psychology*, 27, 109–24 (with S. Kerr and A. Harlan).

1974 Toward a contingency theory of leadership based upon the consideration and initiating structure literature. *Organizational Behavior and Human Performance*, 12, 62–82 (with S. Kerr, C.A. Schriesheim and C.J. Murphy).

1975 Differences in factor structure across three versions of Ohio State Leadership Scales. *Personnel Psychology*, 28, 189–206 (with C.A. Schriesheim).

1977 *Leadership Abstracts and Bibliography, 1904–1974*. Monograph AA-10, College of Administrative Science. Ohio State University.

Further reading

Hakel, Milton D. (1980) Ralph M. Stogdill. *American Psychologist*, 35, 101.

Over a period of thirty years from the publication of his influential and widely reprinted 1948 literature review on leadership to the 1977 publication of *Leadership Abstracts and Bibliography, 1904–1974*, Ralph Stogdill exerted intellectual leadership within this field of inquiry. As Hakel pointed out in his obituary, Stogdill's research contribution on leadership consisted of over fifty articles based on original data, sixteen books and monographs, plus many contributed chapters, all of which were marked by superb attention to detail and analytical clarity. The culmination of his life's work was his *Handbook of Leadership* (1974), for which his characteristic thoroughness led him to review and abstract all known empirical work on leadership (which amounted to over 5,000 articles, of which 3,962 were published in *Leadership Abstracts and Bibliography, 1904–1974*). In addition he developed eight different sets of measurement scales (notably the Leadership Behavior Description Questionnaire – LBDQ – in various forms) with manuals, and directed five films on aspects of leadership and leader development.

Up until 1948 leadership studies reflected attempts to establish the traits possessed by leaders (i.e. the 'great man' theory). Stogdill's 1948 review identified five physical traits, four intelligence/ability traits, sixteen personality traits, six task-related characteristics, and nine social characteristics which related to leadership ability. However, he concluded that not all leaders possess all those qualities, and that no guidance was available on the required strength of any given trait; thus the study of traits was not fruitful. He was prominent (along with Shartle) in shifting the focus of leadership research from traits to the behaviour of leaders. This gave birth to Ohio State University (OSU)'s pioneering Leadership Studies programme.

Stogdill made little attempt to distinguish leadership from management, taking the view that this was only a problem 'at the verbal level'. (In his integrative commentary at the 1982 Biennial Symposium on Leadership, Mintzberg echoed this when he criticized the failure of much leadership research to relate to managerial behaviour.) A multidimensional approach, in which the leader is seen as the one who recognizes people's personal desires and does what is needed to help them to be realized, was developed by Stogdill via the constructs of consideration and initiating structure.

Perhaps Stogdill's major contribution is to be seen in his attempts to draw together into integrated wholes some of the fragments of research on social behaviour within organizations. His concern with building theories that were testable both in detail and in total was an essential feature of his approach.

His work had a cumulative quality, growing within the framework and research policy of the OSU Leadership Studies programme. He sought to discover principles that apply to organizations in general as opposed to those applicable only to particular types of organization. This required using the same methods and measuring the same variables from one study to another, which meant that research was both expensive and slow. Stogdill remained convinced that any marked advance in the development of management technology would have its origins in systematic (if slow) organizational research, and to this end he devoted most of his professional life in an exemplary manner.

RICHARD M.S. WILSON

Stokols, Daniel

Born: 1948, Miami, Florida, USA *Nat:* American *Ints:* Environmental, facilities design and planning, social and health psychology *Educ:* BA University of Chicago, 1969; MA University of North Carolina at Chapel Hill, 1971; PhD University of North Carolina at Chapel Hill, 1973 *Appts & awards:* APA Publications Committee Division 9, 1975–7, 1980– ; Executive Committee, APA Division 34, 1977–80; Executive Council, APA Division 9, 1980–2; Executive Board, Environmental Design Research Association, 1980–3; Fellow, APA Divisions 9, 34; President, APA Division 34, 1982–3; Professor of Social Ecology, University of California, Irvine, 1983– ; Member, AAAS; Associate Editor, *Representative Research in Social Psychology*, 1971–82, *Environment and Behavior*, 1980– ; Editor: *Representative Research in Social Psychology*, 1972–3; Guest Editor, *Representative Research in Social Psychology*, 4, 1973, *Non Environment Systems*, 5, 1975, *Environment and Behavior*, 8, 1976, *Journal of Social Issues*, 38, 1982, *Environment and Behavior*, 15, 1983; Editorial Boards: *Environmental Psychology and Nonverbal Behavior*, 1977–9, *Review of Personality and Social Psychology*, 1979– , *Basic and Applied Social Psychology*, 1979–, *Applied Social Psychology Annal*, 1983– ; Book Review Editor, *Journal of Environmental Psychology*, 1980– ; Consulting Editor, Environment and Behavior Series (Cambridge University Press), 1983–

Principal publications

1972 On the distinction between density and crowding: Some implications for future research. *Psychological Review*, 79, 275–7.
1973 Reactions to victims under conditions of situational detachment: The effects of responsibility, severity and expected future interaction. *Journal of Personality and Social Psychology*, 25, 199–209.
1975 Toward a psychological theory of alienation. *Psychological Review*, 82, 26–44.

1976 Social-unit analysis as a framework for research in environmental and social psychology. *Personality and Social Psychology Bulletin*, 2, 350–8.
1977 *Perspectives on Environment and Behavior Theory: Research and Applications*. Plenum.
1978 Environmental psychology. *Annual Review of Psychology*, 29, 253–95.
1978 A typology of crowding experiences. In A. Baum and Y. Epstein (eds), *Human Response to Crowding*. Erlbaum.
1979 A congruence analysis of human stress. In G. Sarason and C.D. Spielberger (eds), *Stress and Anxiety*. Wiley.
1982 The environmental context of behavior and well-being. In D. Perlman and P. Cozby (eds), *Social Psychology: A Social Issues Perspective*. Holt, Rinehart & Winston.
1983 Residential mobility and personal well-being. *Journal of Environmental Psychology*, 3, 5–19 (with S. Shumaker and J. Martinez).
1984 Traditional, present oriented and futuristic modes of group–environment relations. In K. Gergen and M. Gergen (eds), *Historical Social Psychology*. Erlbaum.
1986 *Behavior, Health and Environmental Stress*. Plenum (with S. Cohen, G.W. Evans and D.S. Krant).
1986 *Handbook of Environmental Psychology*. Wiley (with I. Altman).
1990 Instrumental and spiritual views of people-environment relations. *American Psychologist*, 45 641–6.
1995 The paradox of environmental psychology. *American Psychologist*, 50, 821–37.

Further reading

McAndrew, F.T. (1993) *Environmental Psychology*. Brooks/Cole.

Daniel Stokols's contributions to psychology are associated primarily with his research on the effects of physical and social conditions within work environments on employees' health, motivation, performance and morale. His work is essentially multidisciplinary and is focused on a series of experimental studies of office environments at the Department of Social Ecology's Environmental Simulation Laboratory. As part of this research, survey data on employees' health, productivity and quality of work life were gathered at the offices of several Irvine-area corporations and public agencies. Additional areas of Stokols's research include the health and behavioural impacts of environmental stressors such as traffic congestion and overcrowding, aircraft noise and residential relocation; the development of concepts and methods for identifying situational factors that influence people's reactions to environmental stressors; and the application of psychological research on stress to the design and improvement of residential and work environments.

Stone, George Chester

Born: 1924, Los Angeles, USA *Nat:* American *Ints:* Health psychology *Educ:* AB University of California at Berkeley, 1948; MA University of California at Berkeley, 1951; PhD University of California at Berkeley, 1954 *Appts & awards:* Lecturer, Professor, University of California, San Francisco, 1958–90; APA Divisions, 39, 36, 9; First Annual Award for Outstanding Contributions to Health Psychology, Division of Health Psychology, APA, 1980; President, Division of Health Psychology, APA, 1985–6; Editor, *Health Psychology*, 1980–4

Principal publications

1961   Nondiscrimated avoidance behavior in human subjects. *Science*, 133, 641–2.

1976   On the circumspect pooling of reaction times. In L. Petrinovich, and J. McGaugh (eds), *Knowing, Thinking, and Believing*. Plenum.

1979   Patient compliance and the role of the expert. *Journal of Social Issues*, 35, 34–59.

1979   *Health Psychology – A Handbook: Theories, Applications and Challenges of a Psychological Approach to the Health Care System*. Jossey-Bass (with N.E. Adler, F. Cohen, and associates).

1983   Health psychology. In J.L. Ruffini (ed.), *Advances in Social Science and Medicine*. Pergamon (with N.E. Adler).

1987   The scope of health psychology. In G.C. Stone (ed.), *Health Psychology: A Discipline and a Profession*. University of Chicago Press.

1987   (ed.) *Health Psychology: A Discipline and a Profession*. University of Chicago Press.

1990   An international review of the emergence and development of health psychology. *Psychology and Health*, 4, 3–17.

1991   Health psychology. In *Encyclopedia of Human Biology*, vol. 4. Academic Press.

1994   Religious beliefs and health. In J.P. Dauwalder (ed.), *Psychology and the Promotion of Health*. Hofgre & Huber.

Further reading

Stone, G.E. *et al.* (eds) (1987) *Health Psychology: A Discipline and a Profession*. University of Chicago Press.

George Stone's commitment to psychology began during World War II, when he was 19. Stone read *A Brief History of Human Stupidity* by Walter B. Pitkin, detailing many ways in which human societies have devastated lives and environments when knowledge was readily available to establish more favourable conditions. Stone resolved to understand why this was so, and what could be done about it. However, in obtaining his PhD and establishing a family, Stone lost sight of this purpose and was guided by other intellectual, economic and academic considerations for twenty years, during which he did research and teaching in social perception, psychopharmacology, avoidance behaviour and human information processing.

The turmoil of the 1960s and the threat of nuclear annihilation realerted Stone to the urgency of understanding folly and evil. Stone's medical school setting led him to choose health-related behaviour as a domain in which to pursue these concerns (e.g. self-destructive behaviours, failures to adhere to medically prescribed regimes). During two-plus decades Stone's interests evolved from reinforcement theory to the study of 'master belief systems' in a world of meaning and purpose, and how these influence choices and behaviours. The end-point was the recognition that, while the ontological status of such concepts as 'God', 'the purpose of life' and 'Good and Evil' cannot be established by science or reason, scientific psychology can investigate the consequences of these assumptive beliefs.

George Stone's reputation grew as he publicly recognized the great opportunities for applying psychology to the whole arena of the health-care system, rather than merely in that part inhabited by mental health patients. At the University of California Medical Centre, Stone led a small group that began developing an organizational base for health psychologists within the APA. Although work of this kind is not usually subjected to written criticism, it established Stone as one of the 'founding fathers' of health psychology.

George Stone's most influential paper was his 1979 article in the *Journal of Social Issues*, 'Patient compliance and the role of the expert'. The essence of the argument was that 'compliance' should be considered an attribute of the client–expert transaction rather than of the client only. Understanding the essentially social nature of client–expert transactions became a formative principle in the development of the biopsychosocial model of health as an alternative to the medical model. George Stone's scientific insights and organizational leadership have been of key importance in establishing the field of health psychology.

DAVID F. MARKS

Stout, George Frederick

Born: 1860, South Shields, England **Died:** 1944, Sydney, Australia **Nat:** British **Ints:** Philosophical and theoretical psychology **Educ:** MA (Philosophy) Cambridge University, 1885 **Appts & awards:** Lecturer in Philosophy, Cambridge University, 1887–96; Lecturer in Comparative Psychology, University of Aberdeen, 1896–9; Reader in Mental Philosophy, Oxford University, 1899–1903; Professor of Metaphysics and Logic, St Andrews University, 1903–36; FBA, 1903; Gifford Lecturer University of Edinburgh, 1919–21; Hon. Dr, Universities of Aberdeen, Durham, St Andrews; Editor, *Mind*, 1891–1920

Principal publications

1896   *Analytic Psychology* (2 vols). Sonnenschein. (3rd edn, 1909).
1898–9   *Manual of Psychology* (2 vols). University Tutorial Press. (5th edn, with C.A. Mace, 1938).
1930   *Studies in Philosophy and Psychology.* Macmillan.
1931   *Mind and Matter.* Cambridge University Press.
1952   *God and Nature.* Cambridge University Press.

Further reading

Mace, C.A. (1948) Obituary. *Proceedings of the British Academy*, 31
Mace, C.A. (1954) The permanent contribution to psychology of George Frederick, Stout. *British Journal of Educational Psychology*, 24, 64–75.

G.F. Stout was the son of a shipbroker of South Shields. He showed great promise at school and went on to study at Cambridge, where he was the first ever student from South Shields. He had a distinguished undergraduate career in classics and philosophy but, after graduation, came under the influence of James Ward and turned his attention to psychology. In 1884 he was appointed Fellow of St John's and later College Lecturer in Philosophy; his pupils included G.E. Moore and Bertrand Russell. His main interest was, however, still in psychology; in 1888 he published the first of a series of papers in *Mind* on the early nineteenth-century

association theorist, J.F. Herbart. In 1891 he became editor of *Mind*, which at that time (and within living memory) described itself as a journal of philosophy and psychology. Under his editorship it became the most influential of all philosophy journals but, as his interests changed, psychology figured progressively less frequently in its pages. In 1896 he also took up one of the first teaching appointments in psychology to be established in Great Britain, the Anderson Lectureship at Aberdeen. He stayed in Aberdeen only till 1899, but in that time wrote his *Manual of Psychology* (1898–9), which continued in use for half a century. In 1899 he became first holder of the Wilde Readership in Mental Philosophy at Oxford, where he remained till 1903; during that time he published valuable definitions of terms, in Baldwin's *Dictionary of Philosophy and Psychology* (1901). In 1903 he took up the Chair of Logic and Metaphysic at St Andrews. He delivered the Gifford Lectures at Edinburgh in 1919–21, but subsequently modified the views he had expressed very substantially. The lectures were published, in two volumes, but not till 1931 and 1952 (posthumously). Unfortunately for Stout, his former pupils (Moore and Russell) had changed the course of philosophy, and his work was no longer relevant to contemporary concerns. In 1930 he published a collection of papers which includes a magisterial essay on his original mentor in psychology, James Ward. Stout appears to have retained some interest in and sympathy for experimental psychology since, in 1925, he appointed C.A. Mace specifically to teach that subject in his department.

Stout's approach to psychology was at a conceptual level. He defined psychology as a 'positive science of mental process' concerned with what is, not with what ought to be. His objection to association theory was that the associated mental contents would have to be subject to what he called 'noetic synthesis' in order to function. This appeared to him to require the operation of a superordinate 'mind', but he insisted that this must be an 'embodied mind' – he was not a dualist. His dilemma foreshadows that of contemporary cognitive psychology: what exactly is it that manipulates mental contents?

Stout's influence must have been felt very strongly by anyone studying psychology in Great Britain before World War II, but very few were. While the subject was at that time widely studied in the USA, it had taken a different, more empirically oriented turn.

N.E. WETHERICK

Strelau, Jan

Born: 1931, Gdansk, Poland ***Nat:*** Polish ***Ints:*** Personality and social, physiological and comparative, psychology of individual differences ***Educ:*** MA University of Warsaw, 1958; PhD University of Warsaw, 1963; Dr Habil University of Warsaw, 1967 ***Appts & awards:*** Secretary General, Polish Psychological Association, 1964, 1967; President, Committee for Psychological Sciences of the Polish Academy of Sciences 1981– ; Professor of Psychology and Head of Department of Psychology of Individual Differences, University of Warsaw, 1983– ; President, European Association of Personality Psychology, 1983– ; Board of Directors, International Society for the Study of Individual Differences, 1983; Fellow, Netherlands Institute for Advanced Study in Social Sciences and Humanities, 1983–4; Editor in Chief, *Polish Psychological Bulletin*, 1972; Editorial Boards: *Personality and Individual Differences*, *Studia Psychologica*, 1976–

Principal publications

1969 *Temperament i Typ Ukladu Nerwowego.* Panstwowe Wydawnictwo Naukowe (2nd edn, 1974).

1970 Nervous system type and extraversion–introversion. A comparison of Eysenck's theory with Pavlov's typology. *Polish Psychological Bulletin*, 1, 17–24.

1972 A diagnosis of temperament by nonexperimental techniques. *Polish Psychological Bulletin*, 3, 97–105.

1972 The general and partial nervous system types – data and theory. In V.D. Nebylitsyn and J.A. Gray (eds), *Biological Bases of Individual Behavior*. Academic Press.

1974 Temperament as an expression of energy level and temporal features of behavior. *Polish Psychological Bulletin*, 5, 119–27.

1975 Pavlov's typology and current investigations in this area. *Nederlands Tijdschrift voor der Psychologie*, 30, 177–200.

1975 Reactivity and activity style in selected occupations. *Polish Psychological Bulletin*, 6, 199–206.

1982 Biologically determined dimensions of personality or temperament? *Personality and Individual Differences*, 3, 355–60.

1983 *Temperament–Personality–Activity.* Academic Press.

1983 A regulative theory of temperament. *Australian Journal of Psychology*, 35, 305–17.

1984 *Das Temperament in der Psychischen Entwicklung.* Volk & Wissen.

1984 Temperament and personality. In H. Bonarius, G. Van Heck and N. Smid (eds), *Personality Psychology in Europe: Theoretical and Empirical Developments*. Swets & Zeitlinger.

1984 Biological determination of personality dimensions. In V. Sarris and A. Parducci (eds), *Perspectives in Psychological Experimentation: Toward the Year 2000*. Erlbaum.

1985 *Temperamental Bases of Behavior: Warsaw Studies on Individual Differences.* Swets & Zeitlinger.

1985 *The Biological Bases of Personality and Behavior.* Hemisphere (with F.H. Farley and A. Gale).

1987 *Personality Dimensions and Arousal.* Plenum (with H.J. Eysenck).

1992 *Temperament i inteligencja* (*Temperament and Intelligence*). Panstwowe Wydawnictwo Naukowe.

1992 *Badania nad temperamentem: Teoria, diagnoza, zastosowania* (*Studies on Temperament: Theory, Diagnosis and Applications*). Ossolineum.

1992 *Rąznice indywidualne: Mozliwo'sci i preferencje* (*Individual Differences: Capacities and Preferences*). Ossolineum.

Further reading

Bates, J.E. and Wachs, T.D. (eds) (1994) *Temperament: Individual Differences at the Interface of Biology and Behavior*. American Psychological Association.

Spielberger, C.D. *et al.* (eds) (1995) *Stress and Emotion: Anxiety, Anger, and Curiosity*. Taylor and Francis.

Jan Strelau's early research was primarily bound up with **Pavlov**ian typology. Using different kinds of stimulus (conditioned and unconditioned) as well as different indicators (e.g. EEG) he was able to show that the diagnosis of nervous system properties depends on the specificity of stimulus properties (strength of excitation and inhibition, mobility and balance of nervous processes). This led to the Strelau Temperament Inventory (STI), which has been translated from Polish into several languages. On the basis of questionnaire data he found that it was possible to relate the Pavlovian properties of the nervous system to several personality (temperament) dimensions, like extraversion–introversion, neuroticism and anxiety. Drawing on Pavlovian and neo-Pavlovian typology, the theory of action and the concept of optimal level of activation, he developed, with colleagues, a concept of temperament known as the regulative theory of temperament (RTT).

The idea of the RTT is that temperament plays an important role in regulating the inter-relations between people and their environment. Two basic features comprising the energetic characteristic of behaviour, i.e. reactivity and activity, are particularly emphasized in this theory. In studies published since the 1960s Strelau and his colleagues have demonstrated the importance of temperamental features in regulating the stimulative value of the surroundings, and the role of an individual's behaviour in the control of need for stimulation. Evidence has been collected from laboratory studies which shows that temperament plays an important role in everyday human actions, especially in school and professional performance. Taking as a point of departure the understanding of temperament as a product of biological evolution, and personality as a result of sociohistorical conditions, he conducted with colleagues a series of studies which demonstrated interdependencies between both phenomena.

Stumpf, Carl

Born: 1848, Wiesentheid, Lower Franconia **Died:** 1936, Berlin, Germany **Nat:** German **Ints:** Experimental psychology **Educ:** DPhil University of Göttingen, 1868 **Appts & awards:** Privatdozent, University of Göttingen, 1870–3; Professor, University of Würzburg, 1873–8; Professor of Philosophy, University of Halle, 1884–9; Professor of Philosophy, University of Munich, 1889–94; Professor of Philosophy, Director of the Institute of Experimental Psychology, Friedrich-Wilhelm University of Berlin, 1894–1922; Joint President, 3rd International Congress of Psychology, Munich, 1896; Rector, University of Berlin, 1907–8; Hon. D, University of Berlin, 1910; Prussian Order of Merit

Principal publications

1883, 1890 *Tonpsychologie* (2 vols). Hirzel.
1898 *Konsonanz und Dissonanz* (*Theory of Consonance and Dissonance*). Beiträge zur Akustik und Musikwissenschaft.
1907 *Erscheinungen und psychische Funktionen* (*Presentations and Mental States*). Reimer.
1907 *Zur Einteilung der Wissenschaften* (*On the Classification of Scientific Disciplines*). Reimer.

Further reading

DeWitt, L.A. and Crowder, R.G. (1987) Tonal fusion of consonant musical intervals: The oomph in Stumpf. *Perception and Psychophysics*, 41, 73–84.
Langfeld, H.S. (1937) Carl Stumpf: 1848–1936. *American Journal of Psychology*, 49, 316–20.
Lewin, K. (1937) Carl Stumpf. *Psychological Review*, 44, 189–94.
Reisenzein, R. and Schönpflug, W. (1992) Stumpf's cognitive-evaluation theory of emotion. *American Psychologist*, 47, 34–45.
Stumpf, C. (1930) In C. Murchison (ed.), *A History of Psychology in Autobiography I*. Clark University Press.

Carl Stumpf was born in Wiesentheid in Franconia. His father and maternal grandfather were physicians and several other close relatives were scientists or scholars. Both his parents were musical, and Stumpf soon showed himself to be a competent musician. He played six instruments, including violin and cello, and composed a number of pieces, his first at the age of 10. He might well have become a professional musician. The combination of scientific and musical influences at this formative period was obviously significant in his later development. From 1865 to 1867 he studied a variety of subjects, including aesthetics and jurisprudence ('in order to have a profession that would leave him time for music'), at the University of Würzburg, where he came under the influence of Brentano, who taught him the value of a scientific approach to philosophy. On Brentano's advice, he went to Göttingen to study under Lotze, who encouraged his interest in science, and where he took courses in physics and physiology.

Having obtained his PhD with a philosophical dissertation in 1868, he returned to Würzburg, continuing his studies under Brentano, in philosophy and theology, entering the ecclesiastical seminary with the intention of becoming a priest. But Brentano's logical acumen prevented Stumpf from accepting the dogmatic teaching of the Roman Catholic church ('the whole structure … crumbled to dust before his eyes'). In 1870 he obtained an instructorship at Göttingen, redirecting his career towards philosophy and psychology. Here he met **Weber** and **Fechner**: the former demonstrated sensory fields to him, while with the latter he discussed the problem of the unity of consciousness, and served as a subject for an experiment on the golden section.

In 1873 he returned to Würzburg as professor of philosophy, and began work on his *Tonpsychologie* in 1875. In 1874 he visited London, where he studied the works of John Stuart Mill and Herbert Spencer in the British Museum. There followed several further moves to chairs of philosophy, the first at Prague in 1879, where his colleagues included Marty, Mach and **Hering** and where, in 1880, he resumed work on his *Tonpsychologie*, despite the fact that the necessary apparatus was almost entirely lacking. The first edition appeared in 1883 ('finished only after it went to press').

The year 1882 saw a visit from William **James**. In 1884 Stumpf moved to Halle, where Husserl became his first student and later associate. He carried out experiments on tone fusion on the cathedral organ and made his first sortie into primitive music, studying a group of Belakula Indians (amongst others) who visited the town. In 1889 he moved to Munich, where at last apparatus for his studies in acoustics was provided by the faculty. He set up his 'first experimental laboratory': a dismantled tuning-fork piano, 'bought for a song' by an assistant at the Physical Institute, served as a continuous tone series. Stumpf used to take the instruments out of their store into the lecture rooms on Sundays in order to carry out observations and experiments. He was thus enabled to complete the second volume of the *Tonpsychologie*. Finally, in 1894, after initial hesitation, he moved to the prestigious chair of philosophy at Berlin, where his colleagues included **Helmholtz**, **Ebbinghaus** and Dilthey and his experimental assistants Schumann, Rupp and Von Hornborstel. He was involved in the founding of the psychological institute, and saw it expand from three dark rooms to sumptuous apartments in the imperial palace. He was co-founder of the Verein für Kinderpsychologie (whose intention was to encourage teachers and parents to take an interest in the mental development of the child) and the Phonographie Archiv, a collection of over 10,000 records of primitive music gathered by missionaries and travellers. He founded the Beiträge zur Akustik und Musikwissenschaft. He was director of a commission set up by the Ministry of Education to collect recordings of native dialects and songs from prisoners of war, and chaired the committee which undertook the investigation of 'Clever Hans' with the help of Pfungst's ingenious experiments. He retired in 1921 to pursue epistemological problems, and was succeeded by Köhler.

Stumpf's major treatise was the two-volume *Tonpsychologie*, the most important work on the psychology of hearing since Helmholtz's. He was concerned to investigate the phenomena and laws governing the perception of simple and compound tones. He studied the attributes of pitch, loudness, brightness and volume; his work gave insight into the nature of musical appreciation beyond illusions. He discussed attention, fatigue, analysis and comparison, revising basic concepts in psychophysics and stimulating systematic psychology in these areas. He isolated and studied the psychological phenomenon of tonal fusion, which anticipated the *Gestalt* psychological principle that the whole is not the sum of its parts, and put forward a theory of consonance, which first appeared in 1898. Consonance was defined in terms of fusion, for which he postulated three laws: the degree of fusion is a function of the vibration ratio of the components, it reduplicates for notes an octave above, and it is not affected by timbre. The first of these has received empirical confirmation using behavioural methods. DeWitt and Crowder (1987) found that latencies and errors in discriminating a chord as composed of two separate tones were greater when it was less likely that the pitch combinations produced could be interpreted as representing harmonics of a single fundamental. Stumpf made numerous contributions to the psychology of music, investigating such phenomena as beats (which he showed could be avoided by holding the end of one tuning fork to one ear and the end of the other fork to the other ear), difference tones, subjective tones, double hearing (the result of an operation on his ear drum) and stretched octaves (deviations from physically pure pitch). He also extended his investigations to the perception of speech sounds and vowel synthesis, and carried out pioneer cross-cultural studies of primitive music.

Two important papers in 1907 ('Erscheinnungen und psychische Funktionen' and 'Zur Einteilung der Wissenschaften') were based on, but extended, Brentano's theory. Stumpf favoured Brentanian act psychology rather than **Wundt**ian content psychology, distinguishing the act of hearing (function) from the tone heard (content). He claimed that the study of function formed part of psychology, whereas structure was the subject matter of phenomenology, but his own psychology was in fact quite phenomenological.

Brentano's influence is also apparent in Stumpf's theory of emotion. According to him, all mental states are intentional and either intellectual (e.g. beliefs) or affective. Emotions are evaluations, hence intrinsically representational, and necessarily caused by beliefs (which are required to distinguish different emotions). Reisenzein and Schönpflug (1992) argue that

Stumpf produced a clearly formulated, but largely ignored, cognitive theory of emotion which is relevant to the current cognition– emotion debate. They argue that his objections to non-cognitive theories of emotion retain their force against modern versions of these, that his views go beyond them in several ways, constituting a thoroughly interesting alternative, and raise a number of issues given only marginal attention in recent discussion. In addition, his theory is more lucidly formulated, particularly with regard to the issues of the nature of cognitive appraisals and emotions and the relations between these. The lack of clarity about the nature of cognitive appraisals in emotion may have fostered recent criticisms of cognitive theories, and failure to recognize the importance of distinguishing between evaluations and evaluative beliefs has led cognitive theorists to postulate non-appraisal components needlessly. Stumpf held that the central evaluative component of emotion is fundamentally different from a belief. This does not preclude the existence of other non-cognitive affective states (e.g. pleasurable feelings), but these are not emotions.

Stumpf never quite lost his interest in philosophy: he was much concerned with metaphysical and epistemological questions, but those which come closest to psychology e.g. space and colour perception. He cultivated scientific psychology in the interests of philosophy but his empirical work was essentially psychological. Writing did not come easily to him, and he was not manually dextrous. He left experimental details to others, though deeply respectful of rigorously controlled research. He did not attempt to develop a systematic psychology (his *Tonpsychologie* comes closest), or a school, preferring his students to be independent. His most famous students, **Koffka** and **Köhler** (whom Stumpf had recommended for his position at the anthropoid station on Tenerife), became members of the *Gestalt* school. **Wertheimer** was a pupil and close associate of Stumpf's assistant, Schumann. Stumpf was important on account of his highly original empirical work and his theoretical orientation, his chief contributions being to tone perception and music psychology.

E.R. VALENTINE

Sullivan, Harry Stack

Born: 1892, Norwich, New York, USA *Died:* 1949, Paris, France *Nat:* American *Ints:* Clinical, personality and social, psychoanalysis, psychotherapy, Society for the Psychological Study of Social Issues *Educ:* MD Chicago College of Medicine and Surgery, 1917 *Appts & Awards:* Professor in the Washington School of Psychiatry, 1939–47; William Allanson White Memorial Award for distinguished contribution to psychiatry, 1948; Consultant to UNESCO; Member, US Preparatory Commission leading to the foundation of the World Federation for Mental Health; President, William Alanson White Psychiatric Foundation; Co-Editor, *Psychiatry*, 1938–46

Principal publications

1924 Schizophrenia; its conservative and malignant features: a preliminary communication. In H.S. Sullivan (ed.), *Schizophrenia as a Human Process*. Norton.

1924 Socio-psychiatric research: Its implications for the schizophrenia problem and for mental hygiene. In H.S. Sullivan (ed.), *Schizophrenia as a Human Process*. Norton.

1924 The modified psychoanalytic treatment of schizophrenia. In H.S. Sullivan (ed.), *Schizophrenia as a Human Process*. Norton.

1933 Mental disorders. In *Encyclopaedia of the Social Sciences*. Macmillan.

1934 Psychiatry. In *Encyclopaedia of the Social Sciences*. MacMillan.

1936 A note on the implications of psychiatry and the study of interpersonal relations, for investigation in the social sciences. *American Journal of Sociology*, 42, 848–61.

1940 *Conceptions of Modern Psychiatry*. Norton (republished 1953).

1948 The meaning of anxiety in psychiatry and in life. *Psychiatry*, 11, 1–13.

1949 Psychiatry: Introduction to the study of interpersonal relations. In B. Mullahy (ed.), *A Study of Interpersonal Relations*. Hermitage.

1950 The illusion of personal individuality. *Psychiatry*, 13, 317–32.

1950 Tensions interpersonal and international: A psychiatrist's view. In *UNESCO Publication, Tensions that Cause Wars: Common Statement and Individual Papers*. Cantril University of Illinois Press.

1956 *Clinical Studies in Psychiatry*. Norton.

1953 *The Interpersonal Theory of Psychiatry*. Norton.

1954 *The Psychiatric Interview*. Norton.

1964 *The Fusion of Psychiatry and Social Science*. Norton

Further reading

Emch, A.F. (1949) Harry Stack Sullivan. *Psychiatry*, 12, 1.

Hall, G.S. and Lindzey, G. (1957) *Theories of Personality*. Wiley.

Harry Stack Sullivan was a highly observant and original teacher, clinician and thinker, whose work has had an enormous and probably underestimated impact on psychiatry and the social sciences. Colleagues wrote of him as a deeply wise and compassionate man, with huge enthusiasm for his work. Influenced by **Freud**, Robert Park, **Mead** and Mever, he in turn had influence upon numerous writers, including **Festinger**, George **Kelly** and many practising clinicians. Sullivan's productive career spans three interacting areas: clinical, theoretical and social. While working clinically he developed psychodynamic therapy for use with psychotic patients, previously thought to be unsuitable for analysis. He saw psychotic symptoms as resulting from the patient's own interpersonal history, in particular the experience of not being 'interpersonally validated' in childhood. He also worked closely with obsessional patients.

Possibly his main contribution was in the theoretical development of psychiatry as a science of human relations, primarily concerned with interpersonal relationships. As editor of the journal *Psychiatry*, he defined psychiatry as 'all that is known of persons and their interactions' and, according to **Allport**, helped 'to bring about the fusion of psychiatry and social science'. In later life he called himself a social psychologist, and was one of the first to suggest that individuality is in some senses an illusion. While pointing to individual loneliness he also believed that uniqueness was a myth.

The third sphere was the social and political. He wrote on such diverse subjects as the problems of black youth in the southern USA, anti-Semitism in Nazi Germany, and international hostilities. He thought that psychiatry had a crucial role to play in alleviating these problems, as he believed that fear lay at the root of the behaviour of isolated and bewildered people, be they schizophrenic patients, ghetto dwellers or members of nations involved in international conflict.

Sully, James

Born: 1843, Bridgwater, England **Died:** 1923, London, England **Nat:** British **Ints:** Developmental psychology, experimental psychology, general psychology **Educ:** BA London University, 1866; MA London University, 1868 **Appts & awards:** Grote Professor of Mind and Logic, University College, London, 1892–1903; Co-Founder, BPS, 1901.

Principal publications

1874 *Sensation and Intuition*. Kegan Paul.
1877 *Pessimism*. Kegan Paul.
1881 *Illusions: A Psychological Study*. Kegan Paul.
1884 *Outlines of Psychology*. Longmans Green.
1886 *The Teacher's Handbook of Psychology*. Longmans Green.
1892 *The Human Mind, A Text-Book of Psychology* (2 vols). Longmans Green.
1895 *Studies of Childhood*. Longmans Green.
1902 *An Essay on Laughter*. Longmans Green.
1918 *My Life and Friends*. Fisher Unwin.

Further reading

Dawes Hicks, G. (1928) A century of philosophy at University College, London. *Journal of Philosophical Studies*, 3, 468–82.
Hearnshaw, L.S. (1964) *A Short History of British Psychology 1840–1940*. Methuen.

Sully's contribution to the history of psychology can easily be underestimated. In connection with his MA Sully had studied under Lotze (at Göttingen) and **Helmholtz** (at Berlin), which marked him as one of the first British psychologists to be thoroughly acquainted the new psychology emerging in Germany. Unlike his exact contemporary James Ward, who travelled a somewhat similar route, he soon, however, abandoned the philosophical concerns underlying German psychology, turning to evolution-influenced empirical research. During the 1870s and 1880s he lacked an academic base, gaining a livelihood from writing, teaching and a paternal allowance. He was also a member of the George Eliot and G.H. Lewes literary circle, about which he reminisced fondly in his autobiography. While not an original theorist he diligently strove to promote psychology in Britain through his textbooks, of which the *Outlines of Psychology* (1884) and later *The Teacher's Handbook of Psychology* (1886) were especially successful, the former subsequently being enlarged and thoroughly revised as *The Human Mind* (1892). Additionally, in *Illusions* (1881), he made an important early foray into the general field of human psychological fallibility in perception, memory and reasoning. The *Outlines* was especially significant in moving beyond Alexander **Bain**'s by then obsolescent texts and adumbrating the wave of US-authored textbooks of the later 1880s and 1890s. *Studies of Childhood* (1895) was the fullest British-authored exposition of the evolutionary recapitulationist theory of child development (tinged, in his case, with romanticism), and presented original research on e.g. children's drawings. In 1892 he became the Grote Professor of Mind and Logic at University College, London, where, in 1897, he established the first British psychological laboratory (having acquired Hugo **Munsterberg**'s equipment on the latter's emigration to the US). In 1892 he was also Joint Secretary of the 2nd International Congress of Psychology, held in London. Throughout this period he regularly contributed to *Mind*. His most significant achievement in the long term was perhaps his convening of the meeting at University College, London, on 24 October 1901 at which the Psychological Society (British Psychological Society after 1906) was founded, W.H.R. **Rivers**, William **McDougall** and A.F. Shand being among the ten participants. In 1902 he published his unique monograph *An Essay on Laughter*, retiring from the Grote Professorship the following year (to be succeeded by Carveth Read) and producing little further professional work, his 1918 autobiography being his last book. (L. Zusne's *Biographical Dictionary of Psychology* (1984) erroneously gives 1912 as his retirement date.)

If Sully's most productive years fell a little too early for him to have been able to undertake quantitative experimental research of a fully modern kind, he was central in facilitating the disciplinary and institutional emergence of modern psychology in Britain, and was a tireless promoter of its cause. Theoretically he identified strongly with the broad evolutionary orientation of the late nineteenth century, but this was leavened by a sensitivity to philosophical issues acquired in Germany. His prompt retirement at 60 in 1903 may perhaps be construed as a fairly bright move as far as his reputation is concerned, since unlike some, more philosophically inclined, contemporaries (such as Read and G.F. **Stout**) he did not have to endure the experience of becoming marginalized from the mainstream of the discipline and being viewed as an academic fossil. He had achieved the task he had set himself – founding psychology in Britain as an academic discipline – and was content to let others exploit this accomplishment.

GRAHAM RICHARDS

Super, Donald E.
Born: 1910, Honolulu, Hawaii, USA ***Nat:***

American ***Ints:*** Adult development and ageing, counselling, development, evaluation and measurement, industrial and organizational ***Educ:*** BA Oxford University, 1932; MA Oxford University, 1936; PhD Columbia University, 1940 ***Appts & awards:*** Adjunct Professor of Psychology, University of Florida; Fellow, APA, BPS, AAAS; Scholar, Advanced School of Education, Teachers College, Columbia University, 1936–8; President, APA Division 17, 1951–2; President, American Personnel and Guidance Association, 1953–4; Fulbright Lecturer, University of Paris, 1958–9; US State Department Specialist in Japan, 1961; Research Award, American Personnel and Guidance Association, 1961; President, National Vocational Guidance Association, 1968–9; Eminent Career Award, National Vocational Guidance Association, 1972; International Association for Educational and Vocational Guidance, 1975– , Hon. President since 1983; Hon. Fellow, Spanish Psychological Association; APA Division 17 Leona Tyler Award, 1982; APA Distinguished Contributions Award for Applications of Psychology, 1983; Editorial Boards: *National Vocational Guidance Associations Decennial Volume*, 1962– , *International Review of Applied Psychology*, 1964–85, *Journal of Vocational Behavior*, 1972– , *L'Orientation Scolaire et Professionnelle*, 1985– , *British Journal of Guidance and Counselling*, *Contemporary Psychology*, *Journal of Applied Psychology*, *Journal of Educational Psychology*, *British Journal for Occupational Psychology*

Principal publications

1941 Advocations and vocational adjustment. *Character and Personality*, 10, 51–61.

1951 Vocational adjustment: Implementing a self-concept. *Occupations*, 30, 88–92.

1953 A theory of vocational development. *American Psychologist*, 8, 185–90.

1955 Transition: From vocational guidance to counseling psychology. *Journal of Counseling Psychology*, 2, 3–9.

1957 *The Psychology of Careers*. Harper & Row.

1960 *The Vocational Maturity of 9th Grade Boys*. Teachers College Press (with P.L. Overstreet).

1962 *Appraising Vocational Fitness by Means of Psychological Tests*. Harper & Row. (Rev. with J.O. Crites, 1962.)

1964 *La Psychologie des Intérets*. Presses Universitaires de France.

1969 An experimental computer-based, educational and occupational orientation system for counseling.

Personnel and Guidance Journal, 47, 564–9 (with F.J. Minor and R.A. Myers).

1979   Vocational maturity in adulthood. *Journal of Vocational Behavior*, 14, 255–70 (with J.M. Kidd).

1980   A life-span, life-space approach to career development. *Journal of Vocational Behavior*, 13, 382–98.

1982   *Career Development in Britain*. Hobson's Press (with A.G. Watts and J.M. Kidd).

1983   Assessment in career guidance: Developmental counseling. *Personnel and Guidance Journal*, 61, 555–61.

1984   A developmental approach. In D. Brown and L. Brooks (eds), *Theory and Practice of Counseling Psychology*. Jossey-Bass.

1985   Work leisure and career development needs and programs of the future. In D.T. Hall (ed.), *Career Development in Organizations*. Jossey-Bass.

Further reading

Montross, D.H. and Shinkman, C.J. (eds) (1992) *Career Development: Theory and Practice*. Charles C. Thomas.

Zytowski, D.G. (1994) A super contribution to vocational theory: Work values. Special Issue: From vocational guidance to career counseling: Essays to honor Donald E. Super. *Career Development Quarterly*, 43, 25–32.

It was work with unemployed young and middle-aged men at the depth of the Great Depression of the 1930s that aroused Super's interest in vocational psychology and in career development. How did people cope with unemployment? What impact did it have on their careers? This was a situationally based challenge, and although it led to a focus on the individual as decision maker, as to some degree construer of his or her own self, it also involved a focus on the situation and on the person's construction of it. This dual focus is shown in his influential book *Psychology of Careers* (1957), although the chapters on situational determinants of careers are often undervalued. The ideas presented on situational factors were based partly on a study of economic history and economics at Oxford, partly on his work with the unemployed and partly on his reading of Lazarsfeld *et al.* (1933). Graduate study at Teacher's College, Columbia University, confirmed an interest in understanding the dynamics of vocational adjustment and development, and led to a career as a researcher seeking better theoretical foundations for vocational or career counselling and better tools with which to do the work. Two major research programmes, the Career Pattern Study and the Work Importance Study, formed the empirical basis of his substantive contributions to vocational psychology.

Suppes, Patrick

Born: 1922, Tulsa, USA ***Nat:*** American ***Ints:*** Educational, evaluation and measurement, experimental, philosophical and theoretical psychology ***Educ:*** BS University of Chicago, 1943; PhD Columbia University, 1950 ***Appts & awards:*** Professor of Psychology, Stanford University, 1950– ; Distinguished Scientific Contribution Award, American Academy of Sciences; President, APA; Member, American Academy of Arts and Sciences; Hon. D, University of Nijmegen, 1979, University of Paris V, 1982

Principal publications

1969   Stimulus/response theory of finite automata. *Journal of Mathematical Psychology*, 6, 327–55.

1971–90   *Foundations of Measurement* (3 vols). Academic Press (with D.H. Krantz, R.D. Luce and A. Tversky).

1984   *Probabilistic Metaphysics*. Blackwell.

1989   Current directions in mathematical learning theory. In E. Degreef and E.E. Roskam (eds), *Mathematical Psychology in Progress*. Springer-Verlag.

1991   *Language for Humans and Robots*. Blackwell.

1993   *Models and Methods in the Philosophy of Science: Selected Essays* (Synthese Library, vol. 226). Kluwer Academic.

Further reading

Savage, C.W. and Ehrlich, P. (eds) (1992) *Philosophical and Foundational Issues in Measurement Theory*. Erlbaum.

Wright, G. and Ayton, P. (eds) (1994) *Subjective Probability*. Wiley.

Patrick Suppes was born in Tulsa, Oklahoma, in 1922, educated in Chicago and Columbia, and has been at Stanford University since 1950, holding a full professorship since 1959. He has made many substantial contributions to psychology at the philosophical, experimental and applied levels, and was also founder and chief executive of a related commercial organization, the Computer Curriculum Corporation, 1967–90. Suppes's most notable characteristic is a mastery of mathematics and physical science far beyond the reach of most psychologists and philosophers, combined with a detached and objective awareness of how these sciences resemble psychology and how they differ. He is one of the few psychologists to have taken the idea of psychology as a science seriously, not merely as a pious aspiration to be expressed in the early pages of chapter 1 and then forgotten.

Suppes's active life covers the whole period of the birth and development of computers and he has been at the forefront throughout, being particularly concerned with computer applications in teaching and learning at all levels, including arithmetic and second-language learning in children, and learning at university level. His most recent publications summarize his life's work, and references to numerous earlier papers that were influential in their time may be found in them. The most substantial of these (in every sense of the word) is his three-volume *Foundations of Measurement* (1971–90). The argument in these volumes is technical and accessible only to specialists, but its influence has filtered down to some extent to workers at the coal face. His *Probabilistic Metaphysics* (1984) presents the views on science (including psychology) which permeate his writings. His basic premise is that 'randomness and probability are real phenomena, and therefore are not to be accounted for by our ignorance of true causes'. Certainty of knowledge is unachievable. Logic (at the level of complexity at which it covers arithmetic) and mathematics (including arithmetic, geometry and set theory) are incomplete; so, therefore, must be the empirical sciences that depend on logic and mathematics. At the level of quantum theory there are 'no hidden variables'. At the level of behaviour theory, even if we know the initial probability of a response, the parameters that determine how fast behaviour will change under different reinforcement schedules, and which reinforcement schedule was in operation, it remains the case that the response on any given trial is not uniquely determined. The sciences are in fact diverging; there is no bounded, fixed scientific theory towards which they converge. Suppes holds that though mind is absolutely dependent on brain it cannot be reduced to brain, simply because the neural hardware employed may differ from individual to individual. Elsewhere he writes: 'the network of neurons in a human brain may constitute ... a computationally irreducible system. The implications of this conjecture for having theories of learning or performance as detailed as one might ask for are

quite pessimistic'. It follows that, in psychology, prediction may frequently be impossible; but prediction is impossible in many relatively simple physical systems, or works (as in psychology) only under conditions of strict experimental control. Biological systems, of which the system controlling human behaviour is one, are in fact more predictable than many physical systems. Suppes speculates: 'Perhaps in the next century we will come to think of psychology as being a better predictive science than physics.' His chapter 'Current directions in mathematical learning theory' (1989) considers the state of the art, but also develops his own (1969) work on stimulus/response theory which he has on occasion referred to as his most significant achievement.

Suppes has made major contributions to the theory and experimental psychology of language. The meaning of a word, phrase, utterance, etc., is, in his view, a procedure or collection of procedures; it is private and probabilistic for each individual. The public meaning may be thought to correspond to the temperature of a gas, and the private procedures of each individual to the motions of the particles that make up the gas. *Language for Humans and Robots* (1991) is a collection of his articles on the subject from the last twenty years. There are four main themes. (1) He introduces the concept of 'congruence of meaning' (analogous to congruence of geometric shape). Every utterance asserts an inbuilt hierarchy of propositions, but propositions are only identical when the utterances from which they are abstracted are congruent. Suppes is critical of the tendency of philosophers to regard the proposition as a given. (2) He is also critical of the tendency to emphasize grammar and syntax in the study of children's speech, rather than semantics; and of the neglect of propositional attitudes in children. (3) He advocates a model–theoretic semantics without quantifiers or variables, having only constants – giving sets and relations and operations thereon. He shows how such a semantics may be obtained from his 'procedural' semantics. (4) He investigates methods of teaching robots to obey verbal instructions, and criticizes the relative neglect of 'learning' in artificial intelligence and computer science.

Models and Methods in the Philosophy of Science (1993) is a collection of Suppes's contributions to that subject, containing much matter of interest that is not directly relevant to psychology. Having regard to the depth and breadth of his contributions, Suppes is one of the few psychologists who can seriously be compared with major figures in the older-established scientific disciplines. He has achieved very high repute in his profession but not the degree of influence that ought to have been his, perhaps because of the intrinsic difficulty of much of his work.

N.E. WETHERICK

Swets, John A.

Born: 1928, Grand Rapids, USA **Nat:** American **Ints:** Educational, engineering, experimental, evaluation and measurement **Educ:** BA University of Michigan, 1950; MA University of Michigan, 1953; PhD University of Michigan, 1954 **Appts & awards:** Chief Scientist, Information Sciences, BBN Laboratories; AAAS, Fellow, 1965, Council, 1985–8; Acoustical Society of America, Fellow, 1959, Executive Council, 1967–70; APA, Fellow, 1967; Regents Professor, University of California, 1969; Howard Crosby Medal, Society of Experimental Psychologists, 1985; Member, National Academy of Sciences, 1990; APA Award for Distinguished Scientific Contributions, 1990; Editorial Board, *Medical Decision Making*, 1980–5

Principal publications

1954 A decision-making theory of visual detection. *Psychological Review*, 61, 401–9 (with W.P. Tanner Jr).

1961 Is there a sensory threshold? *Science*, 134, 168–77.

1961 Decision processes in perception. *Psychological Review*, 68, 301–40 (with W.P. Tanner Jr and T.G. Birdsall).

1964 *Signal Detection and Recognition by Human Observers*. Wiley.

1965 Computer-aided instruction. *Science*, 572–6 (with W. Feurzeig).

1966 *Signal Detection Theory and Psychophysics*. Wiley (with D.M. Green).

1973 The relative operating characteristic in psychology. *Science*, 182, 990–1000.

1974 *Psychology and the Handicapped Child*. Government Printing Office (with L.L. Elliott).

1979 On the prediction of confusion matrices from similarity judgments. *Perception and Psychophysics*, 26, 1–19 (with D.J. Getty, J.B. Swets and D.M. Green).

1979 Assessment of diagnostic technologies. *Science*, 205, 753–9 (with R.M. Pickett, S.F. Whitehead, D.J. Getty, J.A. Schnur, J.B. Swets and B.A. Freeman).

1982 *Evaluation of Diagnostic Systems: Methods from Signal Detection Theory*. Academic Press (with R.M. Pickett).

1984 Mathematical models of attention. In R. Parasuraman and R. Davies (eds), *Varieties of Attention*. Academic Press.

1985 Foundations of reasoning: vol. 1. In *Odyssey: A Curriculum for Thinking*. Mastery Education (with M.J. Adams, J. Buscaglia and M. de Sanchez).

1986 Indices of discrimination or diagnostic accuracy: Their ROCs and implied models. *Psychological Bulletin*, 99, 100–17.

1986 Form of empirical ROCs in discrimination and diagnostic tasks: Implications for theory and measurement of performance. *Psychological Bulletin*, 99, 181–98.

1991 Normative decision making. In J. Baron and R.V. Brown (eds), *Teaching Decision Making to Adolescents*. Erlbaum.

Further reading

Link, S.W. (1992) *The Wave Theory of Difference and Similarity*. Erlbaum.

MacMillan, N.A. and Creelman, C.D. (1991) *Detection Theory: A User's Guide*.

Swets started out as a student to approach brain processes from both ends and the middle. He would do sensory experiments, infer what he could from language behaviour (*à la* **Lashley**), and model mathematically the integrative aspects. He studied phonetics, phonemics and speech acoustics; attended a course on neuroanalytomy; and elected courses in logic and the foundations of mathematics. In the sensory experiments, he wanted to acknowledge that stimuli feed into an active and organized system, and specifically to quantify the instructive stimulus. In conversations with fellow graduate students Spike Tanner and Ted Birdsall, it was clear that a theory of signal detection based on statistical decision theory contained the key ideas. After a thesis at Michigan, J.C.R. Licklider arranged an assistant professorship at MIT. When he left for the Research Company BBN, six years later, Swets followed. The move was to allow him to continue basic research and to substitute applied research for teaching and other departmental responsibilities. As it turned out, he did only basic research, in the contexts of applied problems.

Signal detection theory as developed by Swets and others is a mathematical, theoretical system which recognizes that the observer is not simply a passive recipient of stimuli, but is actively engaged in a process of deciding whether or not he or she is confident to say of a stimulus 'yes, I detected it'. Though he worked in a few fields without detection theory and its analytical technique, the Receiver Operating Characteristic (ROC) (for example, in applications of BBN's advanced computer facilities), he is principally known for his work on decision processes in perception using that theory. A dominant research focus in his later work is on the analysis and weighted combination of perceptual features that observers make in arriving at decisions about complex stimuli, such as radiograms. More recently, with colleagues, he believes that their assemblage of techniques in this area can improve the radiologist's diagnostic accuracy in a variety of imaging modalities. He continued his research on various projects conducted with associates at the Harvard Medical School.

T

Tajfel, Henri

Born: 1919, Poland **Died:** 1982, Bristol **Nat:** Polish **Ints:** Personality and social, philosophical and theoretical, psychological study of social issues **Educ:** BA Birkbeck College, London University, 1954; PhD Birkbeck College, London University **Appts & awards:** Professor of Social Psychology University of Bristol; Supernumerary Fellow, Linacre College, Oxford; Fellow, Centre for Advanced Studies in the Behavioral Sciences; President, European Association of Experimental Social Psychology, 1969–72; Professor Extraordinarius, University of Leiden; Co-Editor, *European Journal of Social Psychology*; Editor, *European Social Psychology Monographs*; Editorial Board, *European Studies in Social Psychology*

Principal publications

1963 Classification and quantitative judgment. *British Journal of Psychology*, 54, 101–14 (with A.K. Wilkes).

1969 Cognitive aspects of prejudice. *Journal of Social Issues*, 25, 79–97.

1969 Social and cultural factors in perception. In G. Lindzey and E. Aronson (eds), *Handbook of Social Psychology*, vol. 3. Addison-Wesley

1970 Experiments in intergroup discrimination. *Scientific American*, 223, 96–102.

1971 Social categorisation and intergroup behavior. *European Journal of Social Psychology*, 1, 149–177 (with C. Flament, M.G. Billig and R.F. Bundy).

1972 La categorisation sociale. In S. Moscovici (ed.), *Introduction à la Psychologie Sociale*, vol. 1. Larousse.

1972 Experiment in a vacuum. In J. Israel and H. Tajfel (eds), *The Context of Social Psychology*. Academic Press.

1974 Social identity and intergroup behavior. *Social Science Information*, 13, 65–93.

1977 (ed.) *The Context of Social Psychology*. Academic Press (with J. Israel).

1978 (ed.) *Differentiation Between Social Groups: Studies in the Social Psychology of Intergroup Relations*. Academic Press.

1981 Social stereotypes and social groups . In J.C. Turner and H. Giles (eds), *Intergroup Behavior*. Blackwell.

1982 *Human Groups and Social Categories*. Cambridge University Press, Editions de la Maison des Sciences de l'Homme.

1984 *The Social Dimension: European Developments in Social Psychology*, vols 1 and 2. Cambridge University Press, Editions de la Maison des Sciences de l'Homme.

Further reading

Berkowitz, N.H. (1994) Evidence that subject's expectancies confound intergroup bias in Tajfel's minimal group paradigm. *Personality and Social Psychology Bulletin*, 20, 184–95.

Bornstein, G. and Crum, L. (1988) The use and interpretation of the Tajfel matrices in minimal group research: A critical examination. *Representative Research in Social Psychology*, 18, 25–34.

Insko, C.A., Schopler, J., Kennedy, J.F., Dahl, K.R. *et al.* (1992) Individual–group discontinuity from the differing perspectives of Campbell's Realistic Group Conflict Theory and Tajfel and Turner's Social Identity Theory. *Social Psychology Quarterly*, 55, 272–91.

Rabbie, J.M., Schot, J.C. and Visser, L. (1989) Social identity theory: A conceptual and empirical critique from the perspective of a behavioural interaction model. *European Journal of Social Psychology*, 19, 171–202.

Henri Tajfel's career was decisively shaped by the events of World War II, his own internment, the Holocaust (he lost both parents and a brother) and his experience of rehabilitating refugees. He is credited with formulating a genuinely social account of the psychological bases to prejudice, discrimination and intergroup conflict. Psychological investigation, he insisted, is culturally, historically and economically specific and cannot be separated from these forces. Initially he examined how categories (national, religious, large-scale, small-scale) are used for organizing the social world, and how this process led to errors in impressions of others: overaccentuations of intercategory differences and within-category similarities. This work influenced cognitive theories of stereotyping, although Tajfel later argued that the justificatory ideological role of stereotypes was equally crucial.

He is probably better known for his later research work on 'minimal group' experiments, demonstrating that merely being categorized as a group member provides sufficient motive for discriminatory behaviour. Despite the arbitrary nature of group assignment, with no history of group interaction or self-interest involved, people in these 'minimal groups' would tend to maximize the positive value of their own group *vis-à-vis* the 'outgroup'. Empirical evidence led Tajfel to argue that conflict of vested interests can be meaningfully compared with 'social competition' to preserve perceived value differences. This was elaborated in social identity theory, through which Tajfel delineated the strategies minority groups might adopt in relation to dominant majority groups. This prompted a line of research into perceptions of legitimate intergroup comparisons and the motivations for social change. Although social identity theory is not without its critics, it has stimulated research in at least two other areas: speech accommodation theory and intragroup processes.

Taylor, James Garden

Born: 1897, Drumblade, Scotland *Died:* 1973, Bovingdon, England *Nat:* British *Ints:* Experimental psychology, philosophical and theoretical psychology *Educ:* Graduated in philosophy, University of Aberdeen, 1919 *Appts & awards:* Lecturer/Senior Lecturer in Psychology, University of Capetown, 1924–62.

Principal publications

1958   Experimental design: A cloak for intellectual sterility. *British Journal of Psychology*, 49, 106–16.

1962   Mind as a function of neural organisation. In, J. M. Scher (ed.), *Theories of the Mind*. New York: Free Press of Glencoe (with J. Wolpe)

1962   *The Behavioral Basis of Perception*. Yale University Press.

1968   The role of axioms in psychology. *Bulletin of the British Psychological Society*, 21, 221–27.

1971   A system built upon noise. *Bulletin of the British Psychological Society*, 24, 121–25.

1973   A behavioural theory of images. *South African Journal of Psychology*, 3, 1–10.

Further reading

Farrell, B.A (1965) Critical notice of *The Behavioral Basis of Perception* (1962). *Mind*, 74, 259–80.

Kohler, I. (1964) The formation and transformation of the perceptual world. *Psychological Issues*, 3, Monograph no. 12.

James Garden Taylor was born in north east Scotland, the son of a schoolmaster, in 1897. He graduated from the University of Aberdeen in 1919 in philosophy, which at that time could include an element of psychology. Being partially crippled, he was unfit for military service. He then followed some courses in the Aberdeen Medical School and worked for a time for the precursor of the Industrial Psychology Research Unit. In 1924 he took up a lectureship in psychology at the University of Cape Town, where he remained till his retirement in 1962. He subsequently worked for a time in Canada and the USA, returning to Great Britain about 1967.

His publication history is curious. He contributed a paper on colour perception to the British Association meeting in Edinburgh in 1921 and published a book intended for the general reader in 1938, entitled *Popular Psychological Fallacies*. But this has nothing to say about his own work, though he is known to have had research interests at the time. Between 1956 and his death in 1973 he published a series of sophisticated theoretical and experimental papers, mainly in the *British Journal of Psychology* (1956, 1958, 1971, 1972) and the *Bulletin of the British Psychological Society* (1968, 1970, 1971), and the book which is his principal work, the *Behavioral Basis of Perception* (1962). Taylor was strongly influenced by **Hull**ian behaviour theory, but he applied it to the earliest stages of perceptual learning. The problem he set himself was: how does the child learn to perceive objects in the external world as stable, when his or her eyes, head and body move independently, varying the angle and distance between the receptor surfaces and the object and, of course, the aspect of the object; thus generating widely different patterns of retinal stimulation all corresponding to one object? Conceivably, perceptual stability might have been innate, but there is evidence that the human organism at least can learn very quickly to compensate for gross distortions of visual input, achieved by wearing spectacles fitted with reversing or otherwise distorting lenses.

This suggests that the child may be equipped to learn to perceive a stable perceptual world, though at the early age at which this learning is accomplished there is little scope for experimental investigation. Since human adults possess this learning capacity, it is reasonable to suppose that the capacity must have evolved for some purpose beyond enabling them to participate successfully in experiments that would not be undertaken till the end of the nineteenth century.

Taylor proposed that the visual system operated by establishing millions of conditioned links between stimuli impinging on points on the retinal surface and responses of the organism. Ross Ashby's cybernetic theory (particularly his concept of multistability) enabled Taylor to show mathematically how the variable patterns of retinal stimulation could all become linked to the response pattern that defined the object: defining it independently of its aspect, or distance, or the position of the retinal surfaces. He extended the theory to the perception of colour to explain how it is that, in ordinary circumstances, an object appears to be of its colour irrespective of the wavelength composition of the light falling on it (which will usually have been reflected off other coloured surfaces). This is, of course, essential if colour is to be of any use to the organism as a predictive cue.

Taylor insisted that psychology should be concerned solely with the phenomena of consciousness. He defined perceptual consciousness as 'a state of multiple simultaneous readiness for responses to the environment, acquired in the course of the subject's life. What determines those responses is the properties of the environment that are relevant to the subject's life needs and not the intrinsic character of the sensory input.' Taylor appears to have developed his approach to perception and consciousness in relative isolation, during his time in South Africa. He proposes answers to questions about perceptual development that are not asked in other theories, and relies on a form of experimental evidence (the effects of distorted visual input) that is treated with the gravest suspicion by other theorists when it is not ignored altogether. But the evidence is in print and has not been decisively refuted.

N.E. WETHERICK

Taylor, Shelley E.

Born: 1946, Mount Kisco, New York, USA
Nat: American **Ints:** Health psychology, social psychology **Educ:** AB Connecticut College, 1968; PhD Yale University, 1972 **Appts & awards:** Fellow, APA Divisions 8, 9, 38; Co-Director, Health Psychology Programme, 1979– ; Distinguished Scientific Award for an Early Career Contribution to Psychology, American Psychological Association, 1980; Professor of Psychology, University of California, 1981– ; Senior Outstanding Scientific Contribution Award, Division 38, Health Psychology, APA, 1994; Donald Campbell Award for Distinguished Scientific Contribution to the Field of Social Psychology, 1995

Principal publications

1978   Salience, attention, and attribution: Top of the head phenomena. In L. Berkowitz (ed.), *Advances in Experimental Social Psychology*. Academic Press (with S.T. Fiske).

1979   Hospital patient behaviour: Helplessness, reactance or control? *Journal of Social Issues*, 35, 156–81.

1982   Stalking the elusive vividness effect. *Psychological Review*, 89, 155–81 (with S.C. Thompson).

1983   Adjustment to threatening events: A theory of cognitive adaptation. *American Psychologist*, 38, 1161–73.

1984   *Social Cognition*. Random House (with S. T. Fiske). Second edition, 1991, McGraw-Hill.

1986   *Health Psychology* (1st, 2nd and 3rd edns). Random House (also 1991, 1995).

1988   Illusion and well-being: A social psychological perspective on mental health. *Psychological Bulletin*, 103, 193–210 (with S.E. Brown).

1989   Social comparison activity under threat: Downward evaluation and upward contacts. *Psychological Review*, 96, 569–75 (with M. Lobel).

1989   *Positive Illusions: Creative Self-Deception and the Healthy Mind*. Basic Books.

1991   The asymmetrical impact of positive and negative events: The mobilization–minimization hypothesis. *Psychological Bulletin*, 110, 67–85.

1994   'Realistic acceptance' as a predictor of decreased survival time in gay men with AIDS. *Health Psychology*, 13, 299–307 (with G.M. Kemeny, H.-Y.J. Wang and B.R. Visscher).

1995   The effects of mindset on positive illusions. *Journal of Personality and Social Psychology*, 69, 213–26 (with P.M. Gollwitzer).

Further reading

van Goozen, S.H.M. *et al.* (eds) (1994) *Emotions: Essays on Emotion Theory*. Erlbaum.

Kaplan, H.B. (ed) (1966) *Psychosocial Stress: Perspectives on Structure Theory, Life-Course, and Methods*. Academic Press.

As a graduate student at Yale, Shelley Taylor trained in experimental methods and conducted research on social cognition. Moving to Harvard in 1972, Taylor was influenced by the social relations faculty and conducted interview studies of people's reactions to traumatic events. She carried out research on salience with Susan Fiske, arguing that people who are particularly salient are seen as having disproportionate impact on situations in which they participate. Extending this to tokenism, Taylor demonstrated that the salience of a minority-group member enhances the stereotyping of the individual.

In 1979, Taylor joined UCLA, where she helped to establish one of the leading health psychology programmes in United States. Interview studies with cancer patients led to a theory of cognitive adaptation concerning the substantial psychological restorative capacities that most people demonstrate in the face of trauma. In 1988, with Jonathan Brown, she developed a framework for understanding mental health, arguing that mild positive illusions, especially self-aggrandizement, an exaggerated sense of personal control, and unrealistic optimism, facilitate coping. Taylor suggested that positive illusions are typically associated with good mental health, rather than compromising it, as some models of mental health predict.

Taylor's work on coping has been highly influential in social cognition research and health psychology. None the less, the work has been criticized on two grounds. Individual difference researchers have argued that the positive-illusions approach does not offer a tenable model of individual responses to stressful events, and that positive illusions may compromise, rather than enhance, psychological functioning. Taylor's response to these criticisms has been that the positive-illusions framework does not make an individual difference prediction that more illusion is better, but rather that environmental feedback keeps illusions within the range at which they are adaptive.

A second criticism suggested that positive illusions are infrequent in non-Western societies and unassociated with mental health. The ethnocentrism of individualistic Western psychology is a general problem which needs to be addressed if psychological science is to develop universal laws of experience and behaviour successfully. Taylor responded with the idea that positive illusions may centre on the focal beliefs that are the sustaining principles or myths of a society. In collectivist societies, positive illusions, if they exist, may centre on perceptions of the group and not the individual. Taylor's contribution to social and health psychology has stemmed from her theoretical insights into how people sustain a sense of well-being in the face of adversity.

DAVID F. MARKS

Teitelbaum, Phillip

Born: 1928, Brooklyn, New York, USA **Nat:** American **Ints:** Experimental psychology, physiological and comparative psychology, psychopharmacology **Educ:** BSc City University of New York, 1950; MA Johns Hopkins University, 1952; PhD Johns Hopkins University, 1954 **Appts & awards:** Fellow, APA, 1963, APA Division of Physiological Psychology, 1964; National Academy of Sciences, 1974– ; APA Distinguished Scientific Contribution Award, 1978; Distinguished Graduate Research Professor, Department of Psychology and Affiliate Professor of Neurology, University of Florida, 1984; Editorial Board, *Brain Research*, 1973–7; General Editorial Reviewer: *American Journal of Physiology, American Journal of Psychology, American Journal of Psychiatry, American Scientist, Behavioral Neuroscience, Behavioral Biology, Brain Research, Journal of Personality and Social Psychology, Physiology and Behavior, Psychological Review, Science*

Principal publications

1962   The lateral hypothalamic syndrome: Recovery of feeding and drinking after lateral hypothalamic damage. *Psychological Review*, 69, 74–90.

1967   *Fundamental Principles of Physiological Psychology*. Prentice Hall.

1971   The encephalization of hunger. In E. Stellar and J.M. Sprague (eds), *Progress in Physiological Psychology*, vol. 14. Academic Press.

1977   Levels of integration of the operant. In W.K. Honig and J. Staddon (eds). *Handbook of Operant Behavior*. Prentice Hall.

1979   A proposed natural recovery of geometry of recovery from akinesia in the lateral hypothalamic rat. *Brain Research*, 164, 237–67.

1982   Disconnection and antagonistic interaction of movement subsystems in motivated behavior. In A.R. Morrison and P. Strick (eds), *Changing*

Systems of the Nervous System: Proceedings of the First Institute of Neurological Sciences Symposium in Neurobiology. Academic Press.

1982   What is the 'zero condition' for motivated behavior? In B. Hoebel and D. Novin (eds). *The Neural Basis of Feeding and Reward. Proceedings of a Satellite Symposium of the Society for Neuroscience Annual Meeting.* Heer Institute.

1986   The lateral hypothalamic double disconnection syndrome: A reappraisal and a new theory of recovery of function. In S.H. Hulse and B.F. Green Jr. (eds), *G. Stanley Hall: Essays in Honor of 100 Years of Psychological Research in America.* Johns Hopkins University Press.

1989   Seemingly paradoxical jumping in cataleptic haloperidol-treated rats is triggered by postural instability. *Behavioural Brain Research*, 35, 195–207 (with T.K. Morrissey, S.M. Pellis and V.C. Pellis).

1990   Labyrinthine and visual involvement in the dorsal immobility response of adult rats. *Behavioural Brain Research*, 39, 197–204 (with S.M. Pellis and M.E. Meyer).

1991   Air righting without the cervical righting reflex in adult rats. *Behavioural Brain Research*, 45, 185–8 (with S.M. Pellis and V.C. Pellis).

1992   Toward a synthetic physiological psychology. *Psychological Science*, 3, 4–20 (with S.M. Pellis).

1993   Haloperidol exaggerates proprioceptive-tactile support reflexes and diminishes vestibular dominance over them. *Behavioural Brain Research*, 56, 197–201 (with A.J. Cordover and S.M. Pellis).

1994   Compound complementarities in the study of motivated behavior. *Psychological Review*, 101, 312–17 (with E.M. Stricker)

Further reading

Holmes, C.B. (1992) Psychology as an evolving science. *Psychological Science*, 3, 320–1.

Teitelbaum, P. and Satinoff, E. (eds) (1983) *Motivation: Handbook of Behavioral Neurobiology.* Plenum.

Teitelbaum conducted extensive work on the lateral hypothalamic syndrome in terms of stages of recovery, where each stage is equivalent to a level of hierarchical function, successively more encephalized. While this approach had been fruitful, he discarded it after concluding that the same perceptual labelling process that causes us to describe behaviour in terms of discrete, seemingly unrelated, self-contained functional acts had led him to characterize discrete stages of recovery. He takes the view that recovery is a continuous process, operating in behavioural subcomponents that are typically not differentiated in the usual descriptions of behaviour. These subcomponents become evident in dimensions of movement which grow in amplitude day by day, in recovery and in infantile development. The same dimensions of movement also characterize the action of dopaminergic drugs. We normally make sense out of the flow of behavioural movements by highlighting a particular feature of them that seems to be adaptive, e.g. feeding, drinking, fighting, etc. However, in circumstances when behaviour seems purposeless or maladaptive, we may become alerted to the fact that we do not understand it.

His studies indicate that in left hemisphere recovery, in infantile development, and during the course of dopaminergic drug action, a behavioural 'act' should not be considered a discrete entity, but rather a composite aggregate of independent movement subsystems. The composite form is determined by the particular values of the amplitudes of movement that have been differentially developed, recovered, or induced by the drug. A 'stage' is like a 'level of function' is like an 'act'. While he regarded the stages as composite aggregates formed by the differential rate of recovery of eating and drinking, he nevertheless thought in terms of stages. Later he took the view that he was in fact studying the aggregate of the movement subsystems involved in approach to food and their interaction with mouthing. Particular stages of these yield the four stages of recovery. These are not unitary levels of function but should be recognized as the composite aggregate of particular reactivation magnitudes of a few behavioural subcomponents. The emphasis in his thinking shifted to the analysis of behavioural subsystems rather than regulation of the internal environment. The way the internal environment regains control of these subsystems should add up to the behavioural phenomena of the recovery of the regulation of food and water intake. He argued that the subsystems seem to be a part of all exploratory approach and interaction with goal objects, and speculated that they may form intermediate-level building blocks which are relevant to many forms of motivated behaviour.

More generally, he has argued that psychology should be viewed as a hybrid science that is both abstract and experimental. He proposes the development of a synthetic physiological psychology to build psychology apart from medicine, by using physical reduction of the central nervous system of animals and people to abstract laws of pure psychological function. To guarantee their abstractness, these laws could be embodied formally in the thought and behaviour of a robot. He argues that this approach offers the possibility of integrating the diverse subfields of psychology.

Terman, Lewis Madison

Born: 1877, Needham, Indiana, USA **Died:** 1956, Palo Alto, California **Nat:** American **Ints:** Developmental psychology, educational psychology, evaluation and measurement, school psychology **Educ:** BA, MA Indiana University, 1903; PhD Clark University, 1905 **Appts and Awards:** Hon. D, Indiana, Clark, California, South California and Pennsylvania Universities; Head, Psychology Department, Stanford University, 1922; President, American Psychological Society, 1923; Member, American Academy of Arts and Sciences, 1932

Principal publications

1906 Genius and stupidity. *Pedagogical Seminary*, 13, 307–73.
1912 A tentative revision and extension of the Binet–Simon measuring scale of intelligence, Parts 1–3. *Journal of Educational Psychology*, 3, 61–74, 133–43, 198–208, 277–89 (with H.G. Childs).
1914 Teeth and civilization. *Forum*, 51, 418–24.
1914 Precocious children. *Forum*, 52, 893–8.
1916 *The Measurement of Intelligence*. Houghton Mifflin.
1916 Mentality tests: A symposium. *Journal of Educational Psychology*, 7, 348–60 (with others).
1919 *The Intelligence of School Children*. Houghton Mifflin.
1920 The psychology, biology and pedagogy of genius. *Psychological Bulletin*, 17, 397–409 (with J.M. Chase).
1920 *National Intelligence Tests*. World Books (with others).
1924 The mental test as a psychological method. *Psychological Review*, 31, 93–107.
1925–59 *Genetic Studies of Genius*, vols 1–4. Stanford University Press.
1931 The gifted child. In C.A. Murchison (ed.), *Handbook of Child Psychology*.
1937 *Revised Stanford–Binet Scale*. Houghton-Mifflin (with M.A. Merrill).
1938 *Psychological Factors in Marital Happiness*. McGraw-Hill.
1940 Psychological approaches to the biography of genius. *Science*, 92, 293–301.
1960 *Stanford–Binet Intelligence Scale (Third Revision)* (with M.A. Merrill).

Further reading

McNemar, Q. (1942) *The Revision of the Stanford–Binet Scale*. Houghton Mifflin.
Minton, H. and Lewis, M. (1988) *Terman: Pioneer in Psychological Testing*. New York University Press.
Terman, L.M. (1932) Trails to psychology. In C. Murchison (ed.), *A History of Psychology in Autobiography*. Clark University Press.

Lewis Terman was born into a farming family in Indiana, and he took the only avenue of escape from the hard life of farming by attending, between 1892 and 1896, the Central Normal College in Danville, Indiana, which gave him both a high school education and a vocational teacher training. During this period he also had experience in school teaching, and later, in 1898, he became the principal of a township high school in Indiana, where he remained until 1901. He then entered Indiana University where he gained both a Bachelor's and a Master's degree; he extended his readings of psychology to include the work in German of **Ebbinghaus**, **Wundt** and Kraepelin, and that of the French psychologists **Ribot**, Taine and **Binet**. His early interests were in degeneracy, mental deficiency, criminality and 'genius', which he later termed 'giftedness'. In 1903 he entered Clark University, which he found very congenial to his temperament. He was inspired by Stanley **Hall**, President of the Education Department, but as Terman became interested in the technology of testing he devoted his thesis to this area, and published it as 'Genius and stupidity'.

In 1906 Terman was appointed Professor at Los Angeles Normal School, and in 1910 he accepted the post of Assistant Professor in the School of Education at Stanford University. He soon set about constructing a tentative revision of Binet's Scale of Intelligence, the 1908 version, to make it suitable for American children; but the first real revision which incorporated Stern's method of calculating the intelligence quotient (IQ) was published in 1916. The popularity of this scale established Terman's reputation. During World War I he became one of a group of psychologists, which included Bingham, Whipple, Goddard and **Yerkes**, who constructed the famous Army Tests at Vineland. In 1922 Terman was appointed Head of the Psychology Department at Stanford, where he stayed until his retirement.

Soon after the end of the war Terman became involved in the construction of three further tests, the 'National Intelligence Tests', 'Terman's Group Test of Mental Abilities', and the Stanford Achievement Test. In 1919 *The Intelligence of School Children* was published to promote the educational use of the Stanford–Binet test by teachers, for Terman's ambition was that there should be available a test for every child; he also wanted 'gifted' children to benefit from a differentiated school curriculum and mode of teaching. In 1923 he was elected as President of the American Psychological Society, and took advantage of his address to claim for mental testing the status of experimental psychology, which would enhance the reputation of the applied psychology to which he was committed. Terman's advocacy of testing brought him into conflict with the critics of the Army Tests, namely Bagley and Lippmann, and later in 1939 drew him into the nature/nurture debate, in which he opposed the environmental hypothesis supported by colleagues such as Stoddard at Iowa.

One of Terman's enduring interests was in gifted individuals. Having calculated **Galton**'s IQ as a child to be approximately 200, he formed the idea of tracing the life histories and careers of children judged to be gifted or precocious. This longitudinal investigation, which Terman initiated and organized, led to the first volume of *The Genetic Studies of Genius* in 1925. The follow-up studies, by Terman with others, were reported in volumes 2–5 in 1926, 1930, 1947 and 1959. Terman's other research interests were in hygiene, the construction of biographies, sex differences and marital happiness.

Terman is remembered principally for his contribution to the mental testing movement, in which he had been influenced by both Galton and Binet. He admired most of all Galton, and evidence of his influence lies in Terman's studies of genius (cf. Galton, *Hereditary Genius*, 1869) and his near-total rejection of the influence of environment on intelligence. Although Terman admired **Spearman**'s theory of general intelligence, he was not convinced by the latter's method of supporting it. Terman's affinity with Binet lay in their shared interest in the intellectual processes which were involved in intelligence, and the tasks in which intelligence manifested itself. Terman's admiration for Binet's work is testified by the revisions that he made of the scales, in which he sought to retain the principles on which the original had been constructed. His reputation also rested on his studies of genius, in which Terman himself took great pride. Finally, Terman's enthusiasm and work did much to enhance the reputation of the psychology department of University of Stanford, where he spent the greater part of his career.

DIANA FABER

Teuber, Hans Lukas

Born: 1916, Berlin, Germany **Died:** 1977, Virgin Gorda, British Virgin Islands **Nat:** German **Ints:** Clinical psychology, neuropsychology, physiological and comparative psychology **Educ:** BA University of Basel, 1939; PhD Harvard University, 1947 **Appts & awards:** Professor of Psychology, MIT; Karl Spencer Lashley Award, American Philosophical Society, 1966; Apollo Achievement Award, NASA, 1969; Kenneth Craik Award, St Johns College, York University, 1971; Hon. D, Université Calude Bernard, 1975; Hon. D, Université de Genève, 1975; James R. Killian Jr Faculty Achievement Award, MIT, 1977; Editorial Boards: *International Journal of Neuropsychology*, *Journal of Psychiatric Research*, *Experimental Brain Research*, *Neuropsychologia*

Principal publications

1946 Disturbances in the visual perception of space after brain injury. *Transactions of the American Neurological Association*, 71, 159–61 (with M.B. Bender).

1949 Alterations in pattern vision following trauma of occipital lobes in man. *Journal of General Psychology*, 40, 37–57 (with M.B. Bender)

1960 *Visual Field Defects after Penetrating Missile Wounds of the Brain*. Harvard University Press (with W.S. Battersby and M.B. Bender).

1960 *Somatosensory Changes after Penetrating Brain Wounds in Man*. Harvard University Press (with J. Semmes, S. Weinstein and L. Ghent).

1961 Sensory deprivation, sensory suppression and agnosia: Notes for a neurological theory. *Journal of Nervous and Mental Diseases*, 132, 32–40.

1964 The riddle of frontal lobe function in man. In J.M. Warren and K. Akert (eds) *The Frontal Granular Cortex and Behaviour*. McGraw-Hill.

1972 Disorders of memory following penetrating missile wounds of the brain. *Neurology*, 18, 287–8.

1972 Unity and diversity of frontal lobe functions. *Acta Neurobiologica Experimentalis*, 32, 615–56.

1975 Effects of focal brain injury on human

behavior. In D.B. Tower (ed.), *The Nervous System: The Clinical Neurosciences.* Raven Press.

Hans-Lukas Teuber was a pioneer in research into the relationship between brain lesions, brain anatomy and behaviour. His early work with M.B. Bender (1947–8) was responsible for bringing the methods of psychophysics to clinical neurology. This research into perceptual distortions after brain damage not only described the distortions resulting from lesions at particular sites but also applied rigorous psychophysical methodology in defining the conditions which increased these distortions.

While leading a research group at the Bellevue Medical Centre (1946–61) and studying brain lesions in veterans of the Korean War, he started to tackle the problems of functional cerebral localization and laterality. In order to attribute a given deficit with a lesion at a particular site, he developed the principle of double dissociation of symptoms which is now basic to clinical neuropsychology. In his 1960 book with Bender and Battersby he drew three important and influential conclusions from his experimental results: that lesions can have both specific and nonspecific effects, that bilateral lesions can produce effects which are not a simple addition of the effects of two unilateral lesions, and that unilateral lesions can disrupt hemispheric interaction. At MIT (1961–77) Teuber developed the Corollary Discharge Hypothesis which has subsequently influenced researchers in physiological psychology and in motor behaviour. He also constructed a neurological theory of visual distortions from diverse causes.

Teuber's influence extended beyond neuropsychology into the neurosciences in general, with his writings and research on the visual agnosias, cerebral mechanisms for language, memory deficits and amnesia, and the functions of the frontal lobes. His influence on neuropsychology with its own methodology, is distinct from, yet closely related to, the other neurosciences and behavioural sciences.

ANN COLLEY

Thibaut, John Walter

Born: 1917, Marion, Ohio, USA **Nat:** American **Ints:** Personality and social, psychology and the law **Educ:** AB University of North Carolina, 1939; PhD MIT, 1949 **Appts & awards:** Alumni Professor of Psychology Emeritus, University of North Carolina; Fellow, Center for Advanced

Study in the Behavioral Sciences, 1956–7; NSF Panel, Research Grants in the Behavioral Sciences, 1957–60; NIMH Panel, Fellowships, 1961–3; Special USPHS Fellow, Sorbonne, Paris, 1963–4; SSRD Committee on Faculty Research Grants, 1963–6; APA Policy and Planning Board, 1964–7; SSRC Board of Directors, 1966–9; APA Council of Representatives, 1970–1; Fellow, American Academy of Arts and Sciences, 1978– , Society of Experimental Social Psychology Distinguished Senior Scientist Award, 1981; APA Distinguished Scientific Contributions Award, 1983; Founding Editor, *Journal of Experimental Social Psychology*, 1965–70; Editorial Boards: *Sociometry*, *Transaction*, *Journal of Personality*, *Social Forces*, *Journal of Applied Social Psychology*, *International Interactions*, *European Journal of Social Psychology*, *Journal of Experimental Social Psychology*

Principal publications

1950   An experimental study of the cohesiveness of underprivileged groups. *Human Relations*, 3, 251–78.

1955   Some determinants and consequences of the perception of social causality. *Journal of Personality*, 23, 113–33 (with H. Riecken).

1956   Psychological set and social conformity. *Journal of Personality*, 25, 115–29 (with L.H. Strickland).

1958   Interaction goals as bases of inference in interpersonal perception. In R. Tagiuri and L. Petrullo (eds), *Person Perception and Interpersonal Behavior.* Stanford University Press (with E.E. Jones).

1959   *The Psychology of Groups.* Wiley (with H.H. Kelley).

1965   The development of contractual norms in a bargaining situation under two types of stress. *Journal of Experimental Social Psychology*, 1, 89–102 (with C. Faucheux).

1972   Adversary presentation and bias in legal decision-making. *Harvard Law Review*, 86, 86–401 (with W.L. Walker and E.A. Lind).

1975   *Procedural Justice: A Psychology Analysis.* Erlbaum (with W.L. Walker).

1976   *Contemporary Topics in Social Psychology.* General Learning Press (with J.T. Spence and R. Carson).

1978   *Interpersonal Relations: A Theory of Interdependence.* Wiley (with H.H. Kelley).

1978   A theory of procedure. *California Law Review*, 66, 201–26 (with W.L. Walker).

1979   The relation between procedural and distributive justice. *Virginia Law Review*, 65, 1401–20 (with W.L. Walker and E.A. Lind).

1983   Trade versus expropriation in open groups: A comparison of two types of social power. *Journal of Personality and Social Psychology*, 44, 977–99.

Further reading
Brown, R. (1986) *Social Psychology*. Free Press.
Forterling, F. (1989) Models of covariation and attribution: How do they relate to the analogy of analysis of variance? *Journal of Personality and Social Psychology*, 57, 615–25.

From undergraduate and graduate studies in philosophy before World War II, Thibaut carried into his psychological work a continuing interest in some of the socially interdependent situations that exemplify moral problems. (Hegel's analysis of the master–slave relationship illustrates this source of influence.) His characteristic approach was to identify significant situations that can be analysed in theoretical terms (and hence be related conceptually to other situations) and can be evaluated in laboratory experimental formats. Long collaboration with H.H. **Kelley** enabled him to analyse more systematically the critical situations of social interdependence that interest him. His close collaborators C. Faucheaux, C.A. **Insko** and the law professor W.L. Walker all shared a part of his concerns and broadened the practical relevance of much of his work, for example to legal decision making.

Thoresen, Carl Edwin

Born: 1933, San Francisco, USA *Nat:* American *Ints:* Counselling psychology, health psychology *Educ:* BA/BS University of California, Berkeley; MA/MS Stanford University, 1960, PhD Stanford University, 1964 *Appts & awards:* Fellow, APA Divisions 15, 17, 38; Outstanding Research Award, American Personnel and Guidance Association, 1966, 1968; John Simon Guggenheim Fellow, 1973–4; Stanford University, Professor of Education and Psychology, 1975– , Director, Health Psychology Program, 1990– ; President, Counseling Psychology Division, APA, 1977–8; Research and Training Director, Meyer Friedman Institute, Mount Zion Medical Center, University of California, 1985– ; Hon. PhD, Uppsala University, 1986

Principal publications

1964   Effects of behavioral counseling in group and individual settings on information-seeking behavior. *Journal of Counseling Psychology*, 11: 324–33 (with J. Krumboltz).

1968   Similarity of social models and clients in behavioral counseling: Two experimental studies. *Journal of Counseling Psychology*, 15, 393–401 (with J. Krumboltz).

1969   *Behavioral Counseling: Cases and Techniques*. Holt, Rinehart & Winston (with J. Krumboltz).

1972   Covert behavior modification: An experimental analogue. *Journal of Behavior Therapy and Experimental Psychiatry*, 3, 7–14 (with B.G. Danaher and M.J. Mahoney).

1973   *Behavior Modification in Education: National Society for the Study of Education Yearbook*. University of Chicago Press.

1974   *Behavioral Self-Control*. Holt, Rinehart & Winston (with M.J. Mahoney).

1974   Social modeling and systematic desensitization approaches in reducing dentist avoidance. *Journal of Counseling Psychology*, 21, 415–20 (with D.W. Shaw).

1976   *Counseling Methods*. Holt, Rinehart & Winston (with J. Krumboltz).

1977   *How to Sleep Better: A Drug-Free Program for Overcoming Insomnia*. Prentice Hall (with T.J. Coates).

1978   Sleep recordings in the laboratory and the home: A comparative analysis. *Psychophysiology*, 9, 157–62 (with T.J. Coates).

1980   *The Behavior Therapist*, Brooks/Cole (with T.J. Coates).

1982   Feasibility of altering the Type A Behavior Pattern in post-myocardial infarction patients. *Circulation*, 66, 83–92 (with M. Friedman, J.J. Gill *et al.*).

1984   Alteration of Type A Behavior and reductions in cardiac recurrences in post-myocardial infarction patients. *American Heart Journal*, 108, 237–48 (with M. Friedman, J.J. Gill *et al.*).

1985   Counseling for health. *Counseling Psychologist*, 13, 15–87 (with J. Eagleston).

1988   Reducing risk of AIDS in adolescents. *American Psychologist*, 43, 965–70 (with J. Flora).

1995   Anxiety, depression and heart disease in women. *International Journal of Behavioral Medicine*, 1, 305–19 (with Low).

Further reading
Steptoe, A. and Wardle, J. (eds) (1994) *Psychosocial Processes and Health: A Reader*. Cambridge University Press.
Strube, M.J. (ed.) (1991) *Type A Behavior*. Sage.

Thoresen's career in psychology started in graduate school at Stanford with a major focus on cognitive processes accompanying behaviour change in adolescents. Serving as a counsellor and teacher for five years in a middle school had whetted his appetite for learning more effective ways of helping people with their problems. Influenced by the work of three mentors—John Krumboltz's focus on counselling as a teaching/learning-based process, Albert **Bandura**'s exciting use of vicarious learning and social modelling to alter fears and phobias, and Leonard Krasner's operant approach – Thoresen explored ways to use positive reinforcement and social modelling to encourage prosocial behaviour.

Drawing upon insights from **Skinner** and Kanfer, Thoresen hit upon the idea of behavioural humanism and self-control viewed from a cognitive behavioural orientation. He saw the humanists seeking laudable ends while the behaviourists had the means to achieve them; hence behavioural humanism was a synthesis of these two orientations. Concurrently he applied behavioural self-control to a major social problem, and Learning House, a residential home for out-of-control children, emerged in Palo Alto as a place where children could learn self-management skills from specially trained teaching-parents. For several years Thoresen directed an effective programme that helped children and parents gain better control of their emotions and behaviour as well as improve the social and academic skills of children.

In the early 1970s, Meyer Friedman, the cardiologist who described the Type A Behaviour Pattern, invited Thoresen's collaboration in the Recurrent Coronary Prevention Project. Could behavioural self-control help post-coronary patients change their Type A lifestyle (i.e. excessive time urgency, hostility and competitiveness) and would this reduce cardiac morbidity and mortality? The answers proved positive. Thoresen's experiences leading groups of post-coronary and healthy adults triggered a new concern: can we reverse the excessively individualistic, self-absorbed lifestyle of industrialized countries, or what Thoresen calls 'individualism gone berserk'? Thoresen believes that spiritualism offers promise in reducing health risks through the provision of increased meaningfulness and life satisfaction.

DAVID F. MARKS

Thorndike, Edward Lee

Born: 1874, Williamsburg, Massachusetts, USA
Died: 1949, Montrose, New York ***Nat:*** American ***Ints:*** Educational psychology, evaluation and measurement, experimental psychology, school psychology ***Educ:*** BA Wesleyan University, 1895; BA Harvard University, 1896; MA Columbia University 1897; PhD Columbia University, 1898 ***Appts & awards:*** Instructor in Education and Teaching, Western Reserve University, 1898–9; Teachers College, Columbia University, Instructor in Genetic Psychology, 1899–1901, Adjunct Professor of Educational Psychology, 1901–4, Professor, 1904–40, Professor Emeritus, 1941–9; Fellow, National Academy of Sciences, 1917; Fellow, American Association for the Advancement of Science (President, 1934); Hon DSc, Wesleyan University, 1923, Columbia University, 1929, Chicago University, 1932, Athens University, 1937; Hon. LLD, University of Iowa, 1923, Harvard University, 1933, Edinburgh University, 1936; William James Lecturer, Harvard University, 1942–3

Principal publications

1898   Animal intelligence: An experimental study of the associative processes in animals. *Psychological Review Monograph Supplements*, 2, no. 8.
1901   The influence of improvement in one mental function upon the efficiency of other functions. *Psychological Review*, 8, 247–61 (with R.S. Woodworth).
1911   *Animal Intelligence*. Macmillan.
1913   *Educational Psychology*, vol. I: *The Original Nature of Man*. Teachers College.
1913   *Educational Psychology*, vol. II: *The Psychology of Learning*. Teachers College.
1932   *The Fundamentals of Learning*. Teachers College.
1935   *The Psychology of Wants, Interests and Attitudes*. Appleton-Century.
1962   *Psychology and the Science of Education: Selected Writings of Edward L. Thorndike*. Teachers College (ed. G. Joncich)

Further reading

Boakes, R.A. (1984) *From Darwin to Behaviorism: Psychology and the Minds of Animals*. Cambridge University Press.
Joncich, G. (1968) *The Sane Positivist: A Biography of Edward L. Thorndike*. Wesleyan University Press.

Edward Lee Thorndike was the second son of a Methodist minister, who moved his family from place to place as his job demanded. It was an austere household, with a strong sense of propriety and the most earnest of moral codes. Three of the sons became outstanding academics, and they all started at Wesleyan University.

At Wesleyan Thorndike took a course in psychology, which used as text James **Sully**'s *Outlines of Psychology*. He later recalled that his interest remained lukewarm until he read William **James**'s *Principles of Psychology*, but Sully's approach contained much that Thorndike was to make his own. It advocated the 'genetic' approach (which meant the study of mind from an evolutionary and developmental approach), stressed the importance of individual differences, noted the narrow spread of training, and referred to the 'stamping in' of impressions.

With this solid example, and inspired by *Principles of Psychology*, he went to Harvard and took the course on psychology with William James. At first his main graduate study was literature, but he soon changed to psychology, and proposed to carry out research on orphan children. Although supported by James it was unacceptable to the managers of the orphanage, so Thorndike turned to animal research. He started with chickens, which he tested in his lodgings and then in the basement of the James household, since there was no laboratory space at Harvard. In 1897 he transferred to Columbia, which offered more space and financial support, and began his research on trial and error under the distant supervision of James McK. **Cattell**. 'Trial and error' had been used by Lloyd **Morgan** to designate problem solving in animals that was intelligent but not rational, and Thorndike designed a 'puzzle box' to test this on cats and dogs under laboratory conditions. He confirmed that the animals solved the puzzles and could remember the solutions, but he failed to find any learning due to imitation and passive guidance. This conflicted with accepted opinion, and led Thorndike to write up his thesis in a deliberately challenging way, being especially critical of the work of George Romanes, which he dismissed as 'anecdotal'. Instead of Morgan's account of learning through the association of ideas of action and of consequences, he proposed in effect that learning takes place through connection between stimulus and response. The animal has no idea of the consequence, which serves merely to 'stamp in' the connection. This is Thorndike's version of trial and error and the law of effect. Although he continued to refer to connections between felt sense impressions and movements, it is a crucial move away from Morgan's directed trials with accidental success, to the later, mechanical conception of random trial and error.

During the twentieth century Thorndike's 'cats in a puzzle box' has been a towering presence in psychology, comparable in its mythic quality to Galileo's experiment with falling bodies, or even Newton and the apple. It has represented a moment of the triumph of science over prejudice, of controlled experiment over anecdotal evidence, and 'trial and error' has entered the English language. As an experiment it has striking shortcomings, recognized immediately by his critics. Most obvious is that cats pushed into boxes are not at their best, especially when subjected to what Thorndike reported as 'utter hunger'. The connectionism and the Law of Effect used to explain the results were derived from Herbert Spencer, and there is an obvious similarity in structure to **Darwin**'s theory of natural selection. That similarity had already been recognized by **Baldwin** several years before, and many have 'discovered' it again since, but it does not seem to have occurred to Thorndike himself. Yet the impact was analogous. Just as Darwin removed purpose from evolution, so Thorndike showed the way to remove purpose from learning, and to establish it as a mechanical process. Yet he did it by constructing an environment in which the likelihood of intelligent behaviour was low, even though (as recent commentators have noted) he became well aware that there are biological constraints on the learning capacities of different species, and that individuals differ in their ability to form connections.

Having set up his paradigm, Thorndike seemed content, for the rest of his prolific career, to build on it and apply it to education, searching especially for laws to describe how the stamping in of one connection spreads to others. He wrote a massive textbook of educational psychology, and made significant contributions to mental measurement and personnel selection. Although he was one of the world's best-known psychologists for many years, he took surprisingly little part in contemporary debate. So although he worked away at his theory, it grew with little of the sharpening that comes from hostile criticism. Debates about trial and error certainly raged fiercely, especially following *Mentality of Apes*, where **Köhler** opposed trial and error to his own observations of 'insight' in chimpanzees. But the debate was largely with Thorndike's paradigm experiments and his mechanistic theory taken to extremes, rather than with Thorndike himself. He made little effort to accommodate his theory to behaviourism, so it retained throughout the mild mentalism inherited from Spencer.

When *The Fundamentals of Learning* was published in 1932 it was reviewed by Clark **Hull** with an air of surprise, that here before everybody's nose was an alternative to the **Pavlov**ian principles that had made the running so far for theories of learning. It certainly had a big impact then on the development of Hull's theory, yet when critics summed up Thorndike's theory after his death, the judgements were harsh. It is not just that the connectionist theory was stated in old-fashioned terms, but his many experiments did not work for the theory as he supposed, and were too artificial to have any interest in their own right. His version of connectionism is now little known, and even the name has been appropriated by a generation born after Thorndike's death, whose allegiance is to the possibilities of computer simulation. Thorndike had a long and active career, but as a prophet he took early retirement at an unusually early age.

ARTHUR STILL

Thorndike, Robert Ladd

Born: 1910, Montrose, New York, USA **Died:** 1990, Lacey, Washington **Nat:** American **Ints:** Educational, evaluation and measurement, experimental, industrial and organizational **Educ:** BA Wesleyan University, 1931; MA Columbia University, 1932; PhD Columbia University, 1935 **Appts & awards:** Assistant Professor of Psychology, George Washington University, 1934–6; Assistant Professor of Psychology, Teachers College, Columbia University, 1936–9, Associate Professor, 1940–8, Professor of Psychology and Education, 1948–76, Richard March Hoe Professor Emeritus, 1976–90; President, Psychometric Society, 1953; Board of Directors, APA, 1958–61; Educational Testing Service award for distinguished service to measurement, 1972; President, American Educational Research Association, 1974–5; Phi Delta Kappa award for educational research, 1983

Principal publications

1933   The effect on the interval between test and retest on the constancy of the IQ. *Journal of Educational Psychology*, 24, 543–49.
1942   Regression fallacies in the matched groups experiment. *Psychometrika*, 7, 85–102.
1947   The prediction of intelligence at college

entrance from earlier test. *Journal of Educational Psychology*, 38, 129–48.
1948   An evaluation of the adult intellectual intelligence from Terman's gifted children. *Journal of Genetic Psychology*, 72, 17–27.
1949   *Personnel Selection: Test and Measurement Techniques*. Wiley.
1950   The problem of classification of personnel. *Psychometrika*, 15, 215–35.
1951   Community variables as predictors of intelligence and academic achievement. *Journal of Educational Psychology*, 42, 321–38.
1955   *10,000 Careers*. Wiley.
1964   *Concepts of Over- and Under-Achievement*
1971   (ed.) *Educational Measurement*. American Council on Education.
1973   *Reading Comprehension Education in Fifteen Countries*.
1977   *Measurement and Evaluation in Psychology and Education* (4th edn). Wiley (with E.P. Hagen).
1982   *Applied Psychometrics*. Houghton Mifflin.

Further reading

Cronbach, L.J. (1992) Robert L. Thorndike (1910–1990): Obituary. *American Psychologist*. 47, 1237.

Robert's father E.L.**Thorndike** was one of the great psychologists of the twentieth century; creator of the famous paradigm of trial-and-error learning. He was also a pioneer of statistics and educational testing who yet had no formal mathematical training. From an early age Robert seemed set to make sure that he would be better prepared in this respect; one of his early teachers encouraged his spelling practice by rewarding it with an opportunity to do arithmetic, and later his undergraduate major was in mathematics, with a thorough training in statistics. He followed his father into educational psychology, by specializing in psychometrics, after a doctoral thesis on animals. He used factor analysis in order to separate out differing abilities in the learning of rats. These techniques and this focus on specific abilities remained his chief preoccupation, though applied to human skills and personnel selection rather than to rats. The focus on multiple abilities placed Thorndike firmly in the tradition of L.L. **Thurstone**. As an Air Force psychologist during World War II he came into close contact with leading psychometricians, including J.C. **Flanagan**, A.P. Horst and J.P. **Guilford**. His developing expertise in the analysis of multiple abilities enabled him to identify the weaknesses of tests of aircrew performance, and to devise more subtle techniques. The result of this work was published in 1949 as *Personnel Selection*. Later he took the opportunity to carry out a large-scale follow-up study, in which he tracked the civilian careers of ex-Air Force personnel. The differentiation of abilities for the purposes of long-term prediction proved limited, and he began to place more reliance on global abilities.

In 1954 he published with Irving Lorge a group test of mental abilities for use in schools, which eventually became the widely used Cognitive Ability test, which he developed with Elizabeth Hagen. Later he worked on a new version of the Stanford–**Binet**. The aim was to produce a battery of tests, and to generate a profile rather than just an IQ. But it did not work out as simply as that, and in this work too he concluded that general cognitive ability is more important than he and many others had supposed.

Robert Thorndike may not have been a great innovator, but he was brilliant at repair work and restoration, at seeing the faults in a test, and in redesigning it with that limited but very important originality that such activities make possible.

ARTHUR STILL

Thouless, Robert Henry

Born: 1894, Norwich, England *Died:* 1984, Cambridge, England *Nat:* British *Ints:* Educational psychology, experimental psychology, parapsychology, psychology of religion *Educ:* MA University of Cambridge, 1915; PhD University of Cambridge, 1922 *Appts & awards:* Lecturer in Psychology, University of Manchester, 1919–26; Fellow, Corpus Christi College, Cambridge, 1921–4; Lecturer in Psychology, University of Glasgow, 1926–38; President, Psychology Section, British Association, 1937; Lecturer, Department of Education, Cambridge, 1938–61, Reader, 1945, Reader Emeritus, 1961; President, Society for Psychical Research, 1942–4, British Psychological Society, 1949; Hon. DSc, University of Cambridge, 1953; Consultant to National Foundation for Educational Research, 1964–84; Editor, *British Psychological Society Monograph Supplements*, 1955–60

Principal publications

1923   *An Introduction to the Psychology of Religion*. Cambridge University Press (rev. edn, 1971).
1924   *The Lady Julian*. London.

1925   *Social Psychology*. University Tutorial Press (5th edn, 1967).
1927   *The Control of the Mind*. London.
1931/2   Phenomenal regression to the 'real' object, I and II. *British Journal of Psychology*, 21, 339–59; 22, 1–30.
1935   The tendency to certainty in religious belief. *British Journal of Psychology*, 26, 16–32.
1936   *Straight and Crooked Thinking*. Pan Books (rev. edn, 1974).
1936   Test unreliability and function fluctuation. *British Journal of Psychology*, 26, 325–43 (with B. Wiesner).
1947   The psi processes in normal and 'paranormal' psychology. *Proceedings of the Society for Psychical Research*, 48, 177–96.
1954   *Authority and Freedom* (Hulsean Lectures). Cambridge University Press.
1963   *Experimental Psychical Research*. Penguin.
1972   *From Anecdote to Experiment in Psychical Research*. Routledge & Kegan Paul.
1984   Do we survive death? *Proceedings of the Society for Psychical Research*, 57, 1–52.

Further reading

Stokes, D.M. (1993) Mind, matter, and death: Cognitive neuroscience and the problem of survival. *Journal of the American Society for Psychical Research*, 87, 41–84.

Robert Thouless's first degree was in physics, at Corpus Christi College, Cambridge, 1915, but after serving in the Royal Engineers at Salonika during World War I, he returned to Cambridge where he gained a PhD in 1922 on the strength of a thesis which became his *Introduction to the Psychology of Religion*.

Thouless was one of the select few who dominated British psychology during the inter-war years. His interests and range of expertise were exceptionally broad. His career may be understood as having two main sources of inspiration: a deep but undogmatic religious faith and a firm commitment to the empirical approach. Thus he believed in a spiritual order behind the natural order that is open to scientific analysis, while, at the same time, accepting religion as a human phenomenon that may be studied empirically like any other. As an experimental psychologist, his most notable achievement was the work he did on what he called 'regression to the real object'. Thus, a subject who is given an oblique view of a circle will still see it as more circular than the actual ellipse as formed on the retina. However, he also made an important impact on education, on social psychology and on the use of statistics in psychology.

Given his outlook, it is no surprise that he was attracted to psychical research. He was among the first in this country to take up the challenge presented by the work of J.B. **Rhine** at Duke University. Although his own ESP experiments were not notably successful, he made an original contribution to the study of PK (psychokinesis) with dice, using himself as subject. Unlike Rhine, however, he never lost interest in the age-old topic of an afterlife, and it was fitting that his last publication (which came off the press only a few days before he died) dealt with that enigma. He even devised a coded message, which he took with him to the grave, in the hope that he might demonstrate survival by revealing the code posthumously through a medium. No such message, however, has yet been received.

His most enduring legacy to psychical research, however, may have been a philosophical one. In his article of 1947, he provides the clearest formulation of the dualist-interactionist conception that embraces normal and 'psi phenomena' (the term 'psi', now universally used in parapsychology, was his own coinage to embrace both ESP and PK). Thus, whereas in normal perception and action we interact with the environment only via the brain, in paranormal perception or action we are, says Thouless, *pro tem* able to interact directly with the environment.

JOHN BELOFF

Thurstone, Louis Leon
Born: 1887, Chicago, USA **Died:** 1955, Chapel Hill, USA **Nat:** American **Ints:** Methodology, multiple-factor analysis, psychometrics, psychophysics **Educ:** BEng Cornell University, 1912; PhD University of Chicago, 1917 **Appts & awards:** Assistant Professor, then Professor, Carnegie Institute of Technology, 1917–24; Professor of Psychology, University of Chicago, 1924–52; President, APA, 1932, Psychometric Society, 1936; Director, Psychometric Laboratory, University of North Carolina (re-named the L.L. Thurstone Psychometric Laboratory), 1952–5

Principal publications

1925 A method of scaling psychological and educational tests. *Journal of Educational Psychology*, 16, 433–51.
1926 The scoring of individual performance. *Journal of Educational Psychology*, 17, 446–57.

1927 A law of comparative judgment. *Psychological Review*, 34, 273–86. (Reprinted, *Psychological Review* (1994), 101, 266–270.)
1927 Psychophysical analysis. *American Journal of Psychology*, 38, 368–89.
1928 Attitudes can be measured. *American Journal of Sociology*, 33, 529–54.
1930 The learning function. *Journal of General Psychology*, 3, 469–93.
1931 Multiple factor analysis. *Psychological Review*, 38, 406–27.
1934 The vectors of mind. *Psychological Review*, 41, 1–32.
1938 *Primary Mental Abilities*. Psychometric Monograph Series, no. 1.
1944 *A Factorial Study of Perception*. University of Chicago Press.
1945 The prediction of choice. *Psychometrika*, 10, 237–53.
1954 *An Analytical Method for Simple Structure*. University of Chicago Press.
1959 *The Measurement of Values*. University of Chicago Press.

Further reading

Atkins, D.C. (1964) Louis Leon Thurstone: Creative thinker, dedicated psychologist. In N. Frederiksen and H. Gulliksen (eds), *Contribution to Mathematical Psychology*, Holt, Rinehart & Winston.
Dawes, R.M. (1994) Psychological measurement. *Psychological Review*, 101, 278–81.
Luce, R.D. (1994) Thurstone and sensory scaling: Then and now. *Psychological Review*, 101, 271–77.
Thurstone, L.L. (1952) Autobiography. In E.G. Boring and G. Lindzey (eds), *A History of Psychology in Autobiography*, vol. 4. Appleton-Century-Crofts.

Louis Leon Thurstone was from a Swedish family and received elementary education in both the USA and Sweden. Thurstone's early interests were in engineering, physics and mathematics, and two early publications at age 18 and 25 were concerned with a 'green' way of extracting the energy of the Niagara River and a novel method of trisecting angles. Studying electrical engineering, Thurstone invented a method for putting sound on motion-picture film and designed a new motion-picture camera and projector which removed flicker. This system impressed Thomas Edison, who offered Thurstone a position in his laboratory in 1912.

While teaching in the engineering college at the University of Minnesota, he received instruction in psychology from H. Woodrow and J.B. Miner and became interested in the 'learning function'. In 1914, Thurstone began graduate study under Angell at Chicago. In 1917, he was appointed to an assistantship under W. Bingham at the Carnegie Institute of Technology in Pittsburgh where he remained for seven years. However, Thurstone's theoretical contributions came to fruition following his marriage to Thelma Gwinn and a move back to Chicago in 1924.

Critical of extant psychometric theory and of the triviality of most psychophysical research, Thurstone provided theory and methods for scaling psychological continua for which no corresponding physical dimensions necessarily existed (e.g. attitudes towards crime, religion, movies or smoking) using the method of paired comparisons. He argued that the variance or 'dispersion' of a distribution of test scores provided a unit of psychological measurement. The theory, methods and 'law of comparative judgement' based on the 'discriminal dispersion' construct were published in a series of eleven publications between 1927 and 1934. Thurstone, and others, extended this work by developing multidimensional scaling by applying matrix algebra to judgements produced from the method of triads. Although Thurstonian scaling was influential, forming the basis for the theory of signal detectability, the methods are laborious and impractical and rarely used today.

Thurstone's second innovation was his method of multiple-factor analysis. He worked on this from 1929 and presented the principal axes solution in 1932. This was a central feature of his APA Presidential Address that year, published two years later in *Psychological Review*. Thurstone reinterpreted the single *g*-factor approach of **Spearman** as a special case of the matrix solution of his own multiple-factor formulation. He was surprised at the criticism his multiple-factorial approach received, but it was important groundwork for psychometric research in the second half of the twentieth century.

DAVID F. MARKS

Tinbergen, Nikolaas

Born: 1907, The Hague, Netherlands **Died:** 1988, Oxford, England **Nat:** Dutch/British **Ints:** Clinical psychology, comparative psychology, ethology, zoology **Educ:** PhD University of Leiden, 1932 **Appts & awards:** Professor of Experimental Biology, University of Leiden,

1947; Professor of Zoology, University of Oxford, 1966; Nobel prize for physiology and medicine, 1973; Many honors including the Jan Swammerdam Medal, 1973, APA Distinguished Scientific Contribution Award; Member of many honorary scientific organisations, including the Royal Society

Principal publications

1951 *The Study of Instinct*. Oxford University Press.
1953 *The Herring Gull's World*. Collins.
1953 *Social Behavior in Animals*. Methuen.
1958 *Curious Naturalists*. Country Life.
1972–3 *The Animal in its World* (2 vols). Allen & Unwin.
1983 *Autistic Children: New Hope for a Cure*. Allen & Unwin (with E. Tinbergen).

Further reading

Dawkins, M.S, Halliday, T.R. and Dawkins, R. (eds). (1991) *The Tinbergen Legacy*. Chapman & Hall.
Dewsbury, D.A. (1985) *Leaders in the Study of Animal Behavior*. Bucknell University Press.
Hinde, R.A. (1990) Nikolaas Tinbergen. *Biographical Memoirs of Fellows of the Royal Society*, 36, 547–55.

Niko Tinbergen grew up in the Netherlands, about a mile from the sea. Like his four siblings, he was encouraged to follow his own interests – in his case, a fascination with wildlife and nature. In pre-university days Tinbergen was not a distinguished student but an avid amateur naturalist and sports participant. At one point he abandoned zoology because of its focus on classifying and comparing dead animals, but his experience at a newly established bird observatory persuaded him there was a place for a behavioural biology of live animals. Tinbergen's thesis work on digger wasps established an approach to behaviour that combined naturalistic observation and non-intrusive experimentation. On the basis of observations of solitary wasps provisioning their offspring in multiple burrows, Tinbergen wondered how a foraging wasp found its way back to a particular burrow. He used simple experiments to show that the wasps rapidly learned local landmarks around each burrow. Returning to Leiden from a 14-month meterological expedition to wild Greenland with his bride, Elizabeth Rutten, he set up laboratory practicals studying the behaviour of stickleback fish. He also established a permanent field station at Hulshorst to study insects and birds. It is said he wrote 'Study nature and not books' over the library door.

At a meeting in London in 1936 and during a few spring months in Austria in 1937, Tinbergen and Konrad **Lorenz** discovered their common love of animals and their complementary styles of thinking. Tinbergen fitted non-intrusive experiments to Lorenz's intuitions and models, with the result that ethology (as they agreed to call their new science) began with both an observational and an experimental base. Its development was disrupted by World War II, during which Tinbergen taught at Leiden until 1942, when he was sent to a detention camp for protesting the dismissal of Jewish faculty.

Following the war Tinbergen was appointed Professor of Experimental Biology at Leiden, but in 1949, despite the disapproval of his peers and a significant drop in pay and status, he accepted a lectureship at the University of Oxford in England. There, with the enthusiastic help of W.H. Thorpe at Cambridge and many talented students, Tinbergen established ethology as a significant movement in English-speaking science. His energy and enthusiasm were expressed in the diversity of his students' work, in his role in establishing the journal *Behaviour*, and in film-making and popularizing. In 1951 he published his most famous book, *The Study of Instinct*. In it he identified four questions about behaviour, immediate causation, ontogeny, function and evolution, that have served to unify the subsequent study of behaviour. His own research with gulls moved from the study of immediate causation and development towards the analysis of function and evolution.

In the 1960s Tinbergen dealt increasingly with the implications of ethology for human behaviour. He worked for nearly two years to help create a course on human biology at Oxford. His initial lecture was 'War and peace in animals and man'. Relative to Lorenz, he focused more on stimulus mechanisms than motivation, but they both saw the relevance of ethology to the study of humans. Approaching retirement, Tinbergen began to work with his wife on the perceptual world of early childhood autism, while his broader interests encompassed the interaction of humans and the earth's environment. He came to feel that ethology was not so much a separate branch as a phase in the evolution of the behavioural sciences, a phase that should be incorporated into further work. As noted in a memoir by Robert **Hinde**, Tinbergen combined the eye of an artist, the sensitivity of a poet, a stubborn persistence if he thought he was right, and a wonderful flexibility when he was unsure.

WILLIAM TIMBERLAKE

Titchener, Edward Bradford

Born: 1867, Chichester, England **Died:** 1927, Ithaca, New York, USA **Nat:** British **Ints:** Anthropology, experimental, history, numismatics, philosophical and theoretical **Educ:** AB University of Oxford, 1890; PhD University of Leipzig, 1892 **Appts & awards:** Head, Psychology Department, Cornell University, 1892–7; Editor, *Studies from the Department of Psychology of Cornell University*, 1894–1927; American Editor, *Mind*, 1894–c.1917; Co-operating Editor, *American Journal of Psychology*, 1895–1920; Contributing Editor, *Century Dictionary and Cyclopedia (Psychology)*, 1909, 1911; Editor, *American Journal of Psychology*, 1921–5

Principal publications

1899 The postulates of structural psychology. *Philosophical Review*, 8, 290–9.

1901–5 *Experimental Psychology* (4 vols). Macmillan.

1908 *Lectures on the Elementary Psychology of Feeling and Attention*. Macmillan.

1909 *Lectures on the Experimental Psychology of the Thought Processes*. Macmillan.

1910 *A Text Book of Psychology*. Macmillan.

1912 Description versus statement of meaning. *American Journal of Psychology*, 23, 165–82.

1912 Prolegomena to a study of introspection. *American Journal of Psychology*, 23, 427–48.

1912 The schema of introspection. *American Journal of Psychology*, 23, 485–508.

1914 On 'Psychology as the Behaviorist Views It'. *Proceedings of the American Philosophical Society*, 53, 1–17.

1915 Sensation and system. *American Journal of Psychology*, 26, 258–67.

1917 The psychological concept of clearness. *Psychological Review*, 24, 43–61.

1921 Wilhelm Wundt. *American Journal of Psychology*, 32, 161–78.

1925 Experimental psychology: A retrospect. *American Journal of Psychology*, 36, 313–23.

1929 *Systematic Psychology: Prolegomena*. Macmillan.

Further reading

Boring, E.G. (1927) Edward Bradford Titchener. *American Journal of Psychology*, 38, 489–506.

Edward Bradford Titchener, described as the dean of experimental psychology in America during his lifetime, was influential in bringing the 'new psychology', the experimental psychology of Wilhelm **Wundt** and others, to the United States, thus effecting the transition from mental philosophy to psychology as we know it today. His most important contribution is undoubtedly in establishing the scientific status of psychology. To this end, he published his laboratory manuals, the four-volume *Experimental Psychology* (1901–5), long used and much imitated; he developed experimental methods and designed apparatus; and he insisted on the rigorous training of experimental psychologists. His new PhDs were always in demand. Titchener never abandoned the introspective, structuralist position. No longer important in psychology today, this owes its demise to the systematic, careful and clear manner in which Titchener explored it, revealing its limitations. Freeing psychology from structuralism must be counted as one of his important contributions.

All his life, Titchener was the focus of controversy. In this role he was important in the major new developments of his time. Functionalism arose as a reaction to the structural emphasis of Titchener (and Wundt); to the concern with the contents, not the functions, of consciousness; and to the exclusion of adaptation, of individual differences, developmental and animal psychology, and applied psychology. Behaviourism came as a protest against Titchener's exclusive concern with consciousness. Gestalt psychology arose in part as a reaction to the atomism of Titchener's counterparts in Germany. As a stimulus for the crystallization of new points of view in psychology, Titchener occupied a unique position. His influence was world-wide, his books being translated into German, French, Russian, Italian, Spanish, Japanese and Polish.

E.B.T. HENLE

Tizard, Jack

Born: 1919, Stratford, New Zealand **Died:** 1979, England **Nat:** New Zealander **Ints:** Developmental, mental retardation, social issues **Educ:** MA New Zealand, 1940; BLitt University of Oxford, 1948; PhD University of London, 1951 **Appts & awards:** Chairman, Association of Child Psychology and Psychiatry, 1964–65; Kennedy International Scientific Award, 1968; Chairman, Education Research Board, SSRC,

1969–71: Research Award, American Association on Mental Deficiency, 1973; Hon. Member, British Paediatric Association; CBE, 1973; President, BPS, 1975–76;

Principal publications

1952   The occupational adaption of high grade mental defectives. *Lancet*, 2, 6–20 (with N. O'Conner).

1956   *The Social Problem of Mental Deficiency*. Pergamon (with N. O'Conner).

1964   *Community Services for the Mentally Handicapped*. Oxford University Press.

1966   The experimental approach to the treatment and upbringing of handicapped children. *Developmental Medicine and Child Neurology*, 8(4), 310–21.

1969   Prevalence of imbecility and idiocy among children. *British Medical Journal*, 1, 216–19 (with N. Goodman).

1970   *Education, Health and Behaviour*. Longmans (with M.L. Rutter and T.K. Whitemore).

1972   Research into services for the mentally handicapped: Science and policy issues. *British Journal of Mental Subnormality*, 18, 1–12.

1973   Maladjusted children in the child guidance service. *London Educational Review*, Summer issue, 22–37.

1974   Early malnutrition, growth and mental development in man. *British Medical Bulletin*, 30, 169.

1975   Race and IQ: The limits of probability. *New Behaviour*, 24 April, 6–9.

1975   *Varieties of Residential Experience*. Routledge & Kegan Paul (with R.V.G. Clarke and I. Sinclair).

1975   The objectives and organization of educational and day services for young children. *Oxford Review of Education*, 1, 211–21.

1976   Psychology and social policy. *BPS Bulletin*, 29, 225–38.

1982   Collaboration between teachers and parents in assisting children's reading. *British Journal of Educational Psychology*, 52, 1–15.

Further reading
Child Development and Social Policy: The Life and Work of Jack Tizard. British Psychological Society.

Jack Tizard had a passionate belief that psychology should be used to improve the human lot, and that the proper study of practical problems is as likely to advance science as are laboratory experiments. He placed special stress on the importance of setting up and evaluating 'model' services and institutions. Epidemology, his other main interest, he saw as important only for its role in planning services. In his early research with Neil O'Conner he showed that 'institutionalized' mentally retarded adults could be trained to do factory work under normal employment conditions. His concern with the deadening impact of institutionalization persisted. In the famous Brooland experiment, he demonstrated the improvement in language development and behavior that followed the transfer of severely retarded children from a large hospital to a small residential nursery school. He went on to more general studies of the nature of management practices in institutions that lead to 'institutionalization', operationalized using Goffman's concept of the total institution.

In the last seven years of his life, Tizard moved from the area of mental retardation. He was responsible for setting up two model nurseries for 0–5-year-olds, which were to have flexible hours and to combine day care and education, and to be available free, like a primary school, for all under-5s in the immediate neighbourhood, rather than for 'problem' or 'needy' families. He also set up an experiment in primary schools, which showed that almost all parents could be involved effectively in helping their children to read. His special combination of social concern and rigorous methodology was applied to many other policy issues, including the race and IQ issue, the effects of malnutrition on development, and the needs of physically handicapped adolescents and adults. He also wrote with authority about the relationship between social science and social policy, and the essential conditions for successful policy research.

BARBARA TIZARD

Tobach, Ethel

Born: 1921, Russia **Nat:** Russian **Ints:** Experimental psychology, history of psychology, physiological and comparative psychology, psychology of women, psychological study of social issues **Educ:** BA Hunter College, 1949; MA New York University, 1952; PhD New York University, 1957 **Appts & awards:** Curator, American Museum of Natural History, Department of Mammalology, New York; Career Development Award USPHS, 1964–74; Fellow, New York Academy of Science, 1966, Animal Behaviour Society, 1967; Fellow, APA Division 9, 1971, Division 6, 1974. Division 35, 1977; elected to Hunter College Hall of Fame, 1975; Hon. DSc, Southampton College, LIU,

1975: New York Metropolitan Chapter of AWS, Award for Distinguished Work in Science, 1978; AWP Distinguished Career Award, 1979; New York State Board of Psychology, 1979–85; President, APA Division 6, 1984–5; Board of Directors, Eastern Psychological Association, 1984–5; President, International Society of Comparative Psychology, 1984–6; Editorial Board, *Curator*; Editorial Committee, *Biological Psychiatry*; Associate Editor, *Journal of Comparative Psychology*

Principal publications

1962 Eliminative responses in mice and rats and the problem of emotionality. In E.L. Bliss (ed.), *Roots of Behaviour*. Paul Hoeber.

1970 *Development and Evolution in Behaviour: Essays in Memory of T.C. Schneirla*. Academic Press (ed. with L.R. Aronson, J.S. Rosenblatt and D.S. Lehrman).

1971 *The Biopsychology of Development*. Academic Press (ed. with L.R. Aronson and E. Shaw).

1973 *Comparative Psychology at Issue*. New York Academy of Science (ed. with H.E. Adler and L.L. Adler).

1977–83 (ed.) *Genes and Gender*, vols 1–4. Gordian Press (with Betty Rosoff).

1977 Development: Considerations of chemoception. *Annals of the New York Academy of Sciences*, 290, 260–9.

1977 Femaleness, maleness and behaviour disorders in nonhumans. In E.S. Gomberg and V. Franks (eds), *Gender and Disordered Behaviour*. Bruner/Mazel.

1981 Evolutionary aspects of the activity of the organism and its development. In R.M. Lerner and N.A. Busch-Rossnagle (eds), *Individuals as Producers of their Development*. Academic Press.

1982 The synthetic theory of evolution. In G. Tembrock and H.D. Schmidt (eds), *Evolution and Determination of Animal and Human Behaviour*. Vep Deutscher Verlag des Wissenschaften.

1984 *Behavioural Evolution and the Concept of Levels of Integration*. Erlbaum (ed. with G. Greenberg).

Further reading

Greenberg, G. and Tobach, E. (eds) (1990) *Theories of the Evolution of Knowing*. Erlbaum.

Hood, K.E., Greenberg, G. and Tobach, E. (eds) (1995) *Behavioral Development: Concepts of Approach/Withdrawal and Integrative Levels*. Garland.

Martin, L.M.W., Nelson, K. and Tobach, E. (1995) *Sociocultural Psychology: Theory and Practice of Doing and Knowing*. Cambridge University Press.

Ethel Tobach's principal contributions are in the study of the evolution and development of social-emotional behaviour. As a comparative psychologist, she has elucidated the continuities and discontinuities in the evolutionary history of animals in regard to stress responses, aggression and social behaviour. Her approach has been to apply the concept of integrative levels experimentally in field and laboratory studies of animal behaviour, and to human societal behaviour, with the aim of understanding the role of genetic processes in behaviour. First, she studied the fawn-hooded rat: she was instrumental in having this species identified as marked by a storage pool disease, an expression of an inherited dysfunction in blood platelet serotonin, important as a neurotransmitter and in reproduction, activity, emotional behaviour and feeding. She investigated genetic processes in the behavioural development of this stock, which can be viewed as a natural experimental model. Second, in studies of humans she has argued that genetic processes are often misunderstood and that this misunderstanding emerges as genetic determinism used to justify racism and sexism. Two areas of research reflect her integrative-levels approach to behavioural phenomena. First, her emphasis on developmental processes lead to a series of experiments on olfaction in the rat pup. Second, she examined continuities and discontinuities in the sea-hare (*Aplysia*) in respect to its inking behaviour in the context of social-reproductive behaviour. To encourage comparative psychology as a significant subdiscipline in psychology, she was active in the re-establishment of the *Journal of Comparative Psychology* and the founding of the International Society for Comparative Psychology.

Tolman, Edward Chace

Born: 1886, West Newton, Massachusetts, USA **Died:** 1959, Berkeley, California, USA **Nat:** American **Ints:** Experimental psychology, general psychology, personality and social psychology, philosophical and theoretical psychology **Educ:** BSc MIT, 1911; MA Harvard University, 1912; PhD Harvard University, 1915 **Appts & awards:** Instructor in Psychology, Northwestern University, 1915; University of California, Instructor in Psychology, 1918–20, Assistant Professor,1920–2, Associate Professor, 1923–8, Professor, 1928–54, Professor Emeritus, 1954; President, APA, 1937; Chairman, Society for Psychological Study of Social

Issues, 1940; Hon. DSc, Yale University, 1951, McGill University, 1954; Hon. LLD, University of California, 1959

Principal publications

1920   Instinct and purpose. *Psychological Review*, 27, 217–33.
1922   A new formula for behaviorism. *Psychological Review*, 29, 44–53.
1923   A behavioristic account of the emotions. *Psychological Review*, 30, 217–27.
1925   Behaviorism and purpose. *Journal of Philosophy*, 22, 36–41.
1927, 1928   Habit formation and higher mental processes in animals. *Psychological Bulletin*, 24, 1–35; 25, 24–53.
1932   *Purposive Behavior in Animals and Men.* Century.
1935   The organism and the causal texture of the environment. *Psychological Review*, 42, 43–77 (with E. Brunswick).
1942   *Drives towards War.* Appleton-Century.
1948   Cognitive maps in rats and men. *Psychological Review*, 55, 189–208.
1951   A psychological model. In T. Parsons and E.A. Shils (eds), *Toward a General Theory of Action.* Harvard University Press.
1958   *Behavior and Psychological Man: Essays in Motivation and Learning.* University of California Press.

Further reading

Smith, L.D. (1986) *Behaviorism and Logical Positivism: A Reassessment of the Alliance.* Stanford University Press.
Still, A.W. (1987) Tolman's perception. In A.P. Costall and A.W. Still (eds), *Cognitive Psychology in Question.* Harvester.

Edward Chace Tolman was born into a wealthy liberal family of Quakers and pacifists. He learned their values, but like his brother, a distinguished theoretical chemist, he reacted against his father's devotion to business. At MIT Tolman pleased his family by studying electrical engineering, but he read William **James**'s *Principles of Psychology* in his final year, and enrolled at Harvard for philosophy and psychology in 1911. James had died shortly before, but his mixture of philosophy and psychology was carried on by his students, R.B. Perry and E.B. Holt. Behaviourism was in the air, and both Perry and Holt were busy translating their Jamesian functionalism into behavioural terms. **Yerkes** taught comparative psychology, with J.B. **Watson**'s *Behavior* (1914) as textbook by the time Tolman took his course. But **Münsterberg** was still a powerful figure at Harvard, and insisted that introspection was *the* method for psychology. Yet the experiments actually done in his laboratory, including Tolman's own dissertation on the effect of odour on learning and relearning of nonsense syllables, involved purely objective measures. This tension between theory and practice was thoroughly dissipated by Yerkes and Watson, and Tolman was soon on track for the peculiarly Jamesian behaviourism that he made his own. His theories were played out on the behaviour of rats in mazes, but he did not finally commit himself to this until he moved to California in 1918 and taught a new course on comparative psychology, modelled on that given by Yerkes.

Tolman brought to behaviourism a philosophy very different from Watson's stimulus–response (S–R) atomism. William James had argued against an atomistic view of the mind, and also against its complement, mind and perception as a construction by the 'machine shop of the mind'. He held a holistic view in which complex relations are perceived directly, and this was built on by Perry and Holt. Another version, derived from Husserl's phenomenology and the work of **Külpe** at Würzburg, but still traceable back to James, was being developed by Gestalt psychologists in Germany. While at Harvard Tolman took courses by Perry and Holt, and also spent time with the Gestaltist Kurt **Koffka** during a brief stay in Germany to learn the language.

The German language had a singular importance in Tolman's thinking. English stacks the cards in favour of an atomism that treats events in isolation, and it was from the example of German, with its ready neologisms, that Tolman attempted to do justice to the irreducible relatedness that he perceived in the behaviour of rats. Some of his own inventions have become part of the technical vocabulary – terms descriptive of the environment like *manipulanda* and *discriminanda* that are relative to the organism, and of states of the organism like *expectancies*, and the thoroughly Teutonic *means-end-readiness* and *sign-Gestalt-expectation* that are relative to the environment. For Tolman these are the descriptors that make up a non-atomistic behaviour, what Perry called 'behavior *qua* behavior' and what Tolman later referred to as 'molar', to contrast with the more mechanistic 'molecular' approach favoured by atomistic behaviorists like Watson himself.

The 1920s were a fruitful period for Tolman, when he and his students in California began to publish experiments to demonstrate his viewpoint, and anchor his terminology – experiments on latent learning, vicarious trial and error, and hypotheses in rats, which remained a challenge to the S–R theorists who became dominant after 1930. Tolman faced a double problem. He needed to convince fellow behaviourists that his terms were scientific, and also to convince mentalists like **McDougall** that he was able to do justice to the full complexities of behaviour. He tried to define them analytically rather than just ostensively, and this opened the way for Clark **Hull** and his followers to devise mechanistic and hypothetico-deductive equivalents. Tolman's answer was to depend more on intervening variables and on diagrammatic representations of his theory, which retained the holistic relational concepts, but look too uncomfortably like an engineer's block diagrams to fit easily with his earlier theories.

After the 1930s, learning theory was dominated by the S–R theories of Hull and his colleagues. Tolman was now in opposition, and did not have the opportunity to push forward his relational theory of behaviour. During the 1940s he contributed to a revival of interest in latent learning, but the experiments were different in spirit from those of twenty years earlier. They were directed against the ruling S–R theory, rather than celebrations of exciting new insights.

If Tolman continued to develop his relational view of behaviour, it was in a much broader psychological framework. During the 1930s he worked with the contextualist philosopher Stephen Pepper, and continued to be drawn towards German psychology. He collaborated with Egon Brunswick, and his later concepts of 'behaviour-spaces' and 'belief-value matrices' are more global versions of 'sign-Gestalt-expectations' and 'means-end readinesses', which bear the mark of Kurt **Lewin**'s topological thinking. They lend themselves to the broad theorizing of his lengthy chapter for *Toward a General Theory of Action* (1951), a collaborative book from the Harvard Department of Social Relations under Talcott Parsons. His family's radicalism became more apparent in his writings. 'Cognitive maps in rats and men' was not just a statement of the evidence against S–R theory, it was also an impassioned plea to reduce the frustration that leads to the hatred and intolerance engendered by narrow cognitive maps. During the war his bruised pacifism found expression in *Drives towards*

War (1942). He was one of the founders of the Society for the Psychological Study of Social Issues, and in the McCarthy era he led the protest against the University of California loyalty oath.

It is probably a mistake to see the cognitive turn in learning theory that took place after 1960 as a return to Tolman. It is true that recent computer-based theories of the mind use terms like 'expectancy' and 'cognitive maps' which derive from Tolman, but in spirit they are closer to the mechanistic theorizing of Hull than to the relational concepts favoured by Tolman. He was a great psychologist, but was unable to capitalize fully on the insights of his behaviour theory of the 1920s.

ARTHUR STILL

Torrance, Ellis Paul

Born: 1915, Milledgeville, Georgia, USA **Nat:** American **Ints:** Creativity, education of the gifted, educational, future studies, school psychology **Educ:** BA Mercer University, 1940; MS University of Minnesota, 1944; PhD University of Michigan, 1951 **Appts & awards:** Alumni Foundation Distinguished Professor of Educational Psychology (retired), University of Georgia; Trustee, Creative Education Foundation; TAG, CEC, Distinguished Contributions Award, 1973; NAGC Distinguished Scholar, 1974– ; CEF Founder's Medal, 1979; Fellow, National Academy of Physical Education, 1979; NAAE, Award for contributions to art education, 1980; Arthur Lipper Award for contributions to human creativity, 1982; Hall of Fame, National Association of Creative Children and Adults, 1985; Series Editor, Mentors (Bearly); Guest Editor, *Journal of Research and Development in Education*, 4(3), 1971, 12(3), 1979; Editorial Board, *Journal of Creative Behavior, Gifted Child Quarterly, Creative Child and Adult Quarterly, Gifted Children Newsletter, Highlights for Children, Journal of Research and Development in Education, La Educacion Hoy, Education Digest, Journal of Humanistic Education, Journal of Group Psychotherapy; Psychodrama, Sociometry*

Principal publications

1962   *Guiding Creative Talent*. Prentice Hall.
1963   *Education and the Creative Potential*. University of Minnesota Press.
1965   *Constructive Behavior: Stress, Personality and Mental Health*. Wadsworth.

1969   *Search for Satori and Creativity*. Creative Education Foundation.
1972   Can we teach children to think creatively? *Journal of Creative Behavior*, 6, 114–43.
1972   Career patterns and peak creative achievements of creative high school students twelve years later. *Gifted Child Quarterly*, 16, 75–88.
1975   Sociodrama as a creative problem solving approach to studying the future. *Journal of Creative Behavior*, 9, 182–95.
1976   Creativity in mental health. In S. Arieti and Chrzanowski (eds), *New Dimensions in Psychiatry*, vol. 2. Basic Books.
1979   An instructional model for enhancing incubation. *Journal of Creative Behavior*, 13, 23–35.
1981   Predicting the creativity of elementary school children (1958–1980). *Gifted Child Quarterly*, 25, 55–62.
1984   *Mentor Relationships: How they Aid Creative Achievement, Endure, Change and Die*. Bearly.
1984   The role of creativity in the identification of the gifted and talented. *Gifted Child Quarterly*, 28, 153–6.
1986   Teaching creative and gifted learners. In M.C. Wittrock (ed.), *Handbook of Research on Teaching* (3rd edn). Macmillan.

Further reading

Gage, N.L. and Berliner, D.C. (1992) *Educational Psychology*. Houghton Mifflin.
Torrance, E.P. (1984) Some products of twenty five years of creativity research. *Educational Perspectives*, 22, 3–8.

Torrance's early interests were in issues to do with stress and survival, but this work attracted relatively little attention. His greatest impact is associated with his considerable corpus of work on creativity. His primary achievements can be listed as follows. (1) He developed and refined a battery of tests of creative thinking ability which have enjoyed wide use. (2) He discovered that the developmental characteristics of most creative thinking abilities are different from those involved in intelligence tests and logical reasoning tests. (3) He showed that the common 'fourthgrade slump' in creativity could be offset through intelligent use of instructional materials. (4) He showed that the use of intelligence tests to identify gifted students misses about 70 per cent of those who are equally gifted creatively. (5) He found that children identified as creatively gifted, but who fall short of the IQ cutoff for gifted classification (e.g. IQ of 130), tend to out-achieve as adults those who meet the IQ criterion of giftedness and fail to meet creativity criteria of giftedness. (6) Having a mentor is significantly related to adult creative achievement. (7) Having a childhood future career image – 'being in love with something' - and persisting with it is related significantly to adult creative achievement. (8) Having certain teachers in elementary school increases one's chances of adult creative achievement. (9) Creative thinking ability tests appear to have little racial or socioeconomic status bias. (10) Children in emotionally handicapped classes display more creative strengths than national norms. (11) A variety of technologies for training in creative problem solving produces creative growth without interfering with other kinds of educational achievement.

In addition to making these substantive and enduring contributions, Torrance founded the Future Problem Solving Program which has grown into a US national and international programme, and the International Network of Gifted Children and their Teachers. He has also been responsible for the introduction of an instructional model for enhancing incubation and creativity, and for the implementation of the model on a large scale through the Ginn Reading 360 and 720 Programmes.

Treisman, Anne

Born: Anne Taylor, Wakefield, England **Nat:** British **Ints:** Experimental psychology **Educ:** BA University College Cambridge, Modern Languages; BA University College Cambridge, Psychology, 1961; DPh University of Oxford **Appts & awards:** Professor, Department of Psychology, University of California at Berkeley; Spearman Medal, BPS Medical Research Council; Psycholinguistics Research Unit Psychology Department, Bell Telephone Laboratories Lecturer and Fellow, St Anne's College, Oxford University of British Columbia, Canada; Fellow, Royal Society, London, 1989; Howard Crosby Warren Medal, Society for Experimental Psychologists, 1990

Principal publications

1960   Contextual cues in selective listening. *Quarterly Journal of Experimental Psychology*, 12, 242–8.

1964   Selective attention in man. *British Medical Bulletin*, 20, 12–16.

1967   Selective attention: Perception or response. *Journal of Experimental Psychology*, 19, 1–17 (with G. Geffen).

1969   Strategies and models of selective attention. *Psychological Review*, 76, 282–99.

1973   Divided attention to ear and eye. In S. Kornblum (ed.), *Attention and Performance IV*. Academic Press (with A. Davies).

1975   Brief visual storage of shape and movement. In P.M.A. Rabbitt and S. Dornic (eds), *Attention and Performance V*. Academic Press (with R. Russell and J. Green).

1980   A feature integration theory of attention. *Cognitive Psychology*, 12, 97–136 (with G. Gelade).

1982   Illusory conjunctions in the perception of objects. *Cognitive Psychology*, 14, 107–41 (with H. Schmidt).

1982   Perceptual grouping and attention in visual search for features and for objects. *Journal of Experimental Psychology: Human Perception and Performance*, 8, 194–214.

1984   Emergent features, attention and object perception. *Journal of Experimental Psychology: Human Perception and Performance*, 10, 12–21 (with R. Paterson).

1985   Preattentive processing in vision. *Computer Vision, Graphics and Image Processing*, 31, 156–177. (Reprinted in Z. Pylyshyn (ed.), *Computational Processes in Human Vision: An Interdisciplinary Perspective*, Ablex.)

1986   Properties, parts and objects. In K. Boff, L. Kaufman and J. Thomas (eds), *Handbook of Perception and Human Performance*, vol. 2. Wiley.

1988   Features and objects: The fourteenth Bartlett Memorial Lecture. *Quarterly Journal of Experimental Psychology*, 40, 201–37.

1988   Feature analysis in early vision: Evidence from search asymmetries. *Psychological Review*, 95, 15–48 (with S. Gormican).

1990   Form perception and attention: Striate cortex and beyond. In L. Spillman and J. Werner (eds), *Visual Perception: The Neurophysiological Foundations*. Academic Press (with P. Cavanagh, B. Fisher, V. Ramachandran and R. Van der Heydt).

1990   Implicit and explicit memory for visual patterns. *Journal of Experimental Psychology: Learning, Memory and Cognition*, 16, 127–37 (with G. Musen).

1990   Conjunction search revisited. *Journal of Experimental Psychology: Human Perception and Performance*, 16, 459–78.

Further reading

Boff, K.R., Kaufman, L. and Thomas, J.P. (eds) (1986) *Handbook of Perception and Human*

Performance, vol. 2: *Cognitive Processes and Performance*. Wiley.

Bundesen, C. and Shibuya, H. (eds) (1995) *Visual Selective Attention. Visual Cognition*, vol. 2, nos 2 & 3. Erlbaum.

Spillman, L. and Werner, J.S. (eds) (1990) *Visual Perception: the Neurophysiological Foundations*. Academic Press.

Anne Treisman was born in Wakefield, England, the elder daughter of Percy Taylor and his French wife, Suzanne. She lived through the war years in a village near Rochester, Kent, where her father was chief education officer, then moved with her family to Berkshire. She studied modern languages (mostly French literature) at Cambridge University and obtained a first class BA with distinction, which earned her the award of a research scholarship. She used this scholarship to obtain a second BA in psychology in just one year.

In 1957 she commenced studies for a DPh in psychology at Oxford University under the supervision of Carolus Oldfield. At that time, information theory was transforming psychologists' views of the mind from the behaviourist switchboard to an active processor of information. Donald **Broadbent** had introduced a new area of research – selective listening – and Treisman decided to use the two-channel tape recorder she had been allocated for testing aphasics to do research on auditory attention in normal people instead. After three years of research she married Michel Treisman, a fellow graduate, who soon became a lecturer in psychology in the Oxford department. A year later, she completed her thesis on selective attention and speech perception, which gained her degree and later the Spearman Medal from the BPS.

The next four years were spent as a member of the MRC Psycholinguistics Research Unit doing more research in selective listening. In 1966 and 1967 she and her husband Michel were invited as visiting scientists to work in the Psychology Department at Bell Telephone. Treisman's interests began to shift from audition to vision and to how attention modulates perception in these two different sense modalities. In the next few years, back at Oxford, she was appointed a university lecturer in psychology and a Fellow of St Anne's College. Around this time she began to explore the idea that attention is involved in integrating separate features to form perceptual representations of objects. Testing her children one day, she found that search for a red X among red Os

and blue Xs was very slow and laborious, much harder than search for either shape or colour alone. The same proved to be true with adult subjects in the laboratory, and Treisman began a new programme of experiments to explore feature integration, attention, and object perception, which is still a major part of her current research. In 1976, her marriage broke up. She spent the academic year 1977–8 at the Center for Advanced Study in Behavioral Research at Stanford; she married Daniel **Kahneman** at the end of that year, and they moved together to positions at the University of British Columbia, Canada. After Vancouver they moved to the University of California at Berkeley, where they are both professors in the Psychology Department.

Triandis, Harry C.

Born: 1926, Patras, Greece **Nat:** Greek **Ints:** Cross-cultural psychology, industrial and organizational, national development, personality and social, population, study of social issues **Educ:** BEng McGill University, 1951; MCom University of Toronto, 1954; PhD Cornell University, 1958 **Appts & awards:** Professor, Department of Psychology, University of Illinois; Chairman, Society of Experimental Social Psychology, 1972–4; Guggenheim Fellow, 1972–3; Award from the Interamerican Society of Psychology, 1974; President, International Association of Cross-Cultural Psychology, 1974–6; APA Division 9, 1975–6; APA Division 8, 1976–7; Hon. Fellow, International Association of Cross-Cultural Psychology, 1982; Vice-President, IAAP, 1982–90; Fellow, American Psychological Society; Distinguished Fulbright Professor, 1983; Interamerican Society of Psychology, 1985–7; Editorial Boards: *Journal of Abnormal and Social Psychology*, 1963–5, *Journal of Personality and Social Psychology*, 1965–9, *Journal of Applied Psychology*, 1970–9; *Journal of Cross-Cultural Psychology*, 1970– ; *Journal of Applied Social Psychology*, 1971– ; *Journal of Social Psychology*, 1975– ; *International Journal of Intercultural Relations*, 1976– ; *Ethos*, 1979– ; *Applied Social Psychology Annual*, 1979– ; *Review of Personality and Social Psychology*, 1979– ; *Revisita Interamericana de Psicologia*, 1980– ; *American Behavioral Scientist*, 1981–

Principal publications

1965 Some determinants of social distance among Americans, German and Japanese students. *Journal of Personality and Social Psychology*, 2, 540–51 (with E.E. Davis and S.I. Takezawa).

1967   Frequency of contact and stereotyping. *Journal of Personality and Social Psychology*, 7, 316–28 (with V. Vassiliou).

1968   Three cross-cultural studies of subjective culture. *Journal of Personality & Social Psychology Monograph Supplement*, 8, no. 4, 1–42 (with V. Vassiliou and M. Nassiakou).

1971   *Attitude and Attitude Change*. Wiley

1972   *The Analysis of Subjective Culture*. Wiley.

1973   Culture training, cognitive complexity and interpersonal attitudes. In D.S. Hoopes (ed.), *Reading in Intercultural Communication*. Regional Council for International Education.

1976   The future of pluralism. *Journal of Social Issues*, 32, 179–208.

1976   *Variations in Black and White Perceptions of the Social Environment*. University of Illinois Press.

1977   *Interpersonal Behavior*. Brooks/Cole.

1978   Some universals of social behavior. *Personality and Psychology Bulletin*, 4, 1–16.

1980   *Handbook of Cross-Cultural Psychology* (6 vols), (ed.), Allyn & Bacon.

1980   Values, attitudes and interpersonal behavior. In H. Howe and M. Page (eds), *Nebraska Symposium on Motivation, 1979*. University of Nebraska Press.

1983   Dimensions of cultural variations as parameters of organizational theories. *International Studies of Management and Organization*, 12, 139–69.

1983   Etic plus emic versus pseudoetic: A test of a basic assumption of contemporary cross-cultural psychology. *Journal of Cross-Cultural Psychology*, 14, 489–500 (with G. Marin).

1984   A theoretical framework for the more efficient construction of culture assimilators. *International Journal of Intercultural Relations*, 8, 301–30.

1994   *Handbook of Industrial and Organizational Psychology* (2nd edn, vol. 4). Consulting Psychologists Press (with M. Dunnette and L. Hough).

1994   (ed.) *Individualism and Collectivism: Theory, Method and Applications*. Sage. (with U. Kim, C. Kagitcibasi, S. Choi and G. Yoon).

Further reading

Goldberger, N.R. and Veroff, J.B. (eds) (1995) *The Culture and Psychology Reader*. New York University Press.

Kitayama, S. and Markus, H.R. (eds) (1994) *Emotion and Culture: Empirical Studies of Mutual Influence*. American Psychological Association.

Landis, D. and Bhagat, R.S. (eds) (1996) *Handbook of Intercultural Training* (2nd edn). Sage.

The main focus of the work of Harry Triandis has been the analysis of the link between culture and social behaviour. This required the analysis of the culture construct, the development of models linking the theoretical constructs of the analysis of subjective culture to behaviour, and the development of theoretical frameworks accounting for the culture–behaviour link. Numerous methodological and ethical issues in the conduct of such research had to be faced. Primary concerns for him have been intergroup relations, including stereotypes, interpersonal attraction, and social distance across ethnic and cultural barriers. As well, intergroup negotiations, problem solving in culturally heterogenous groups, and group creativity have been investigated. He has also undertaken studies of the meaning of pluralism in modern societies. Within this broad framework he has conducted numerous studies, for example on the effects of culture on emotional perceptions, on semantic structures, on interpersonal relations, on economic development, on cognitive processes, on role differentiation, on role perceptions, on social distance, on cognitive consistency, on person perception, on attitudes, on values, on interpersonal communication, on the meaning of work and leisure, on child-rearing practices, and on specific behavioural patterns.

Applications of his research have ranged from population psychology to organizational and cross-cultural management (as reflected in his more recent publications). Both laboratory work and field work have been undertaken in Greece, Germany, Japan, India and the USA, and with collaborators in other parts of the world. Applications of his work have been specially focused on cross-cultural training. A cognitive approach that trains visitors to make attributions isomorphic to the attributions that hosts make about their own behaviour, called the culture assimilator, has been widely tested in many parts of the world. It has been shown to increase the accuracy of the attributions that the visitors make, and to decrease the tendencies towards stereotyping. When authorities have positive attitudes towards minorities, greater knowledge of minority cultures leads to positive evaluations of the minority ethnic groups.

Tryon, Robert Choate
Born: 1901, Butte, Montana, USA ***Died:*** 1967, Berkeley, California, USA ***Nat:*** American ***Ints:*** Evaluation and measurement, experimental

psychology, physiological and comparative **Educ:** PhD University of California at Berkeley, 1928 *Appts & awards:* Assistant Professor/ Professor, Department of Psychology, University of California at Berkeley, 1931–67

Principal publications

1929 The genetics of learning behavior in rats. *Yearbook of the National Society for Studies in Education*, 39, 111–19.

1939 *Cluster Analysis*. Edwards Bros.

1940 Studies in individual differences in maze ability VII: The specific components of maze ability and a general theory of psychological components. *Journal of Comparative Psychology*, 30, 283–338.

1955 Mass screening and reliable individual measurement in the experimental behavior genetics of lower organisms. *Psychological Bulletin*, 53, 402–10 (with J. Hirsch).

1957 Reliability and behavior domain validity. *Psychological Bulletin*, 54, 229–49.

1970 *Cluster Analysis*. McGraw-Hill (with D.E. Bailey).

1973 Basic unpredictability of individual responses to discrete stimulus presentation. *Multivariate Behavioral Research*, 8, 275–5.

Further reading

Innis, N.K. (1992) Tolman and Tryon. *American Psychologist*, 47, 190–7.

Robert Tryon was not born to a privileged family: none of his seven siblings progressed beyond high school. Nevertheless he entered Berkeley and after graduating in 1924 enrolled as a graduate student there with **Tolman**. Ada **Yerkes** had earlier noted in passing that the behavioural characteristics of selectively bred rats showed some differences from the norm, a finding that Tolman and Tryon were to develop into the discipline of behaviour genetics – a term that was coined by Tryon himself. As well as the obvious issues of environmental control and mate selection, Tryon's statistical interest was clear in his attempts to ensure that the maze-running paradigm showed both reliability and validity. The result of this work was the strains of maze-bright and maze-dull rats that still bear his name. His 1929 paper was painted with a broad brush: 'to what degree are individual differences in mental ability (e.g., the ability due to learn) due to heredity factors, and to what degree environmental factors?' – a question that still entertains many differential psychologists.

The 1930s saw a broadening of Tryon's research interests, possibly reflecting a need to break away from the shadow of Tolman. From individual differences in rats he turned towards individual differences in humans. He took a particular interest in contemporary developments in factor analysis, where the merits of the **Spearman**, **Burt**, Holzinger and **Thurstone** conceptualizations were hotly debated. As anyone who has tried it will attest, performing factor analysis by hand is an excruciatingly time-consuming and error-prone process for even small sets of data; Tryon attempted to develop a conceptually similar alternative that was practically feasible. His 1939 monograph on cluster analysis outlined how the broad principles of factor analysis could be approximated with considerably less computational effort. Following his period of war service Tryon returned to psychometrics, with a number of fundamental papers connected with reliability theory (especially the domain-sampling model) and communality estimation.

To found one area of science (behaviour genetics) and devise a major statistical tool in another (cluster analysis) is a truly outstanding achievement. Tryon's pioneering work in behaviour genetics posed a fundamental question about the role of genetic factors in human ability and personality, albeit one whose 'political correctness' waxes and wanes over time. It also raised important issues about the ecological validity of experimental designs, and suggested the general importance of measuring and statistically controlling for individual differences in all experiments. The careful attention paid to statistical and psychometric issues is in sharp contrast to some other early animal work, foreshadowing Tryon's later contributions to psychometric theory. Cluster analysis remains a popular tool in many branches of psychology, even though it requires many semi-arbitrary decisions about the number and composition of clusters and lacks the solid theoretical basis of factor analysis. In addition, new developments in clustering techniques now require such analyses to be performed by computer, thereby removing at a stroke the principal advantage of the technique. Nevertheless it is widely used, and can be invaluable where the data fail to meet the distributional requirements of factor analysis. Tryon's psychometric papers and his work in developing the basic techniques of cluster analysis – not to mention the Herculean task of programming various generations of BC-TRY using primitive languages – represents a major contribution to psychological methodology.

COLIN COOPER

Tulving, Endel

Born: 1927, Estonia **Nat:** Estonian **Ints:** Cognitive, experimental **Educ:** BA University of Toronto, 1953; MA University of Toronto, 1954; PhD Harvard University, 1957; Hon. DPhil, Umea University **Appts & awards:** Professor, Department of Psychology, University of Toronto; Senior Research Fellow, NRC Canada, 1964–5; Fellow, Center for Advanced Study in Behavioral Sciences, 1972–3; Governing Board, Psychonomic Society, 1974–80; Commonwealth Visiting Professor, Oxford University, 1977–8; Fellow, APA, CPA, Royal Society of Canada, AAAS; APA Distinguished Contributions to Psychology as a Science Award, 1984; Editor, *Journal of Verbal Learning and Verbal Behavior*, 1969–72, *Psychological Research*, 1976–

Principal publications

1972 Organization of Memory. Academic Press (ed. with W. Donaldson).

1973 Encoding specificity and retrieval processes in episodic memory. *Psychological Review*, 80, 352–73 (with D.M. Thomson).

1974 Recall and recognition of semantically encoded words. *Journal of Experimental Psychology*, 102, 778–87.

1975 Structure of memory traces. *Psychological Review*, 82, 261–75 (with M.J. Watkins).

1975 Depth of processing and the retention of words in episodic memory. *Journal of Experimental Psychology: General*, 104, 268–94 (with F.I.M. Craik).

1976 Encoding specificity: Relation between recall superiority and recognition failure. *Journal of Experimental Psychology: Human Learning and Memory*, 2, 349–61.

1977 The measurement of subjective organization in free recall. *Psychological Bulletin*, 84, 539–56 (with R.J. Sternberg).

1978 Retrieval independence in recognition and recall. *Psychological Review*, 85, 153–71 (with A.J. Flexsor).

1980 Exceptions to recognition failure to recallable words. *Journal of Verbal Learning and Verbal Behavior*, 19, 194–209 (with J.M. Gardiner).

1981 Similarity relations in recognition. *Journal of Verbal Learning and Verbal Behavior*, 20, 479–96.

1982 Priming effects in word-fragment completion are independent of recognition memory. *Journal of Experimental Psychology: Learning, Memory and Cognition*, 8, 336–42 (with D.L. Schachter and H.A. Stark).

1983 *Elements of Episodic Memory*. Clarendon Press.

1985 How many memory systems are there? *American Psychologist*, 40, 385–98.

1989 Memory, performance, knowledge and experience. *European Journal of Cognitive Psychology*, 1, 3–26.

1990 Priming and human memory systems. *Science*, 247, 301–16 (with D.L. Schachter).

Further reading

Baddeley, A.D. (1990) *Human Memory: Theory and Practice*. Erlbaum.

Parkin, A.J. (1993) *Memory: Phenomena, Experiment and Theory*. Blackwell.

Tulving is recognized as the psychologist who, more than any other, has directed attention to one of the most important issues in the analysis of memory: the relationship between the encoding and the retrieval of mental events. Tulving and **Craik** have argued that what is encoded into memory depends on the particular conditions pertaining at the time. For example, every time we see a near-miss between a car and a pedestrian we do not encode as part of that memory everything we know about cars, only the specific characteristics of the car in question. In order to recall the details of a particular car, it is necessary for there to be sufficient overlap between the information currently being processed by the cognitive system and the details of the original event encoded in memory. Hence, when we see another near-miss it may re-evoke the memory of an earlier incident in ways that seeing tens of thousands of different cars would not. Tulving's account of memory is sometimes summarized as the encoding-specificity principle: a cue will aid retrieval if it provides information that had been processed during the encoding of the to-be-remembered material. The interaction between the processing of current events and stored memory traces he later termed ecphory. Later work with Flexer led to the development of a mathematical formulation predicting the degree of encoding specificity. However, this formulation has been criticized on several grounds; for example, it does not take into account the considerable priming effects of the recognition task on recall. Specifically, performance on a recall task may be artificially high because on many of the trials subjects have seen the to-be-remembered material when they spontaneously generated it in the recognition phase, which gives them an unfair advantage on some of the trials. Other criticisms have focused on the generality of recognition failure among different types of material. For example, recognition failure tends to be greater when subjects are given pairs of abstract nouns (honour–anxiety) and 'typical' instructions than when they are given 'elaborate' instructions. This suggests that when paired associate terms are abstract or unrelated to one another, they do not provide much context for one another and the effects of encoding specificity are weaker. When the paired-associates are strongly related, either semantically or through a subject's efforts to learn, then the effects of encoding specific will be stronger. Despite these criticisms Tulving's account of the relationship between encoding and retrieval is supported by numerous independent studies.

Tulving has also made important contributions to the analysis of long-term memory, arguing that it involves two sorts of knowledge, procedural and propositional. Procedural knowledge involves knowing *how* to perform skilled actions, such as riding a bicycle or driving a car. Propositional knowledge involves knowing *that* certain things have happened or are true; this is factual knowledge. Propositional knowledge he has further defined as involving episodic and semantic memory. Episodic knowledge involves memories for things that have happened to people – their personal experiences of the world. (Episodic memory has motivated much of the later development of research and theory on autobiographical memory.) Semantic knowledge involves the store of knowledge remembered independently of time and place – generalized information about the world. Tulving has used an 'onion model' to describe the relationships between the three memory systems. Procedural memory is regarded as the most basic subsystem; out of this arises semantic memory; and finally there is episodic memory about the semantic. This theoretical position makes important predictions about the development of memory and the consequences of brain injury which have yet to be properly tested.

Tulving has developed elegant methods for studying the structure of memory traces and has elucidated the concepts of subjective organization, availability versus accessibility, encoding specificity, and episodic versus semantic memory, all of which animate contemporary debate on memory.

Turiel, Elliot

Born: 1938, Rhodes, Greece *Nat:* American *Ints:* Developmental psychology, educational psychology, social and personality psychology *Educ:* BBA City College of New York, 1960; PhD Yale University, 1965 *Appts & awards:* National Institute of Mental Health Pre-Doctoral Fellow, 1961–5; Research Associate, Center for Urban Education and Bank Street College of Education, 1965–7; Assistant Professor of Psychology, Columbia University, 1966–9; Associate Professor of Education and Social Psychology, Harvard University, 1969–75; John Simon Guggenheim Memorial Foundation Fellow, 1972–3; University of California, Santa Cruz, 1975–7, Associate Professor of Psychology, Professor, 1977–80; National Institute of Mental Health Post-Doctoral Fellow, University of California at Berkeley (Department of Sociology), 1978–9; Fellow, Van Leer Jerusalem Foundation, 1979–80; University of California at Berkeley (Division of Educational Psychology), Professor of Education, 1980–96, Chair, Division of Educational Psychology, 1986–92, Associate Dean for Academic Affairs, 1994–96

Principal publications

1966 An experimental test of the sequentiality of developmental stages in the child's moral judgments. *Journal of Personality and Social Psychology*, 3, 611–18.

1969 Developmental processes in the child's moral thinking. In P. Mussen, J. Langer and M. Covington (eds), *Trends and Issues in Developmental Psychology*, Holt, Rinehart & Winston.

1971 Moral development and moral education. In G. Lesser (ed.), *Psychology and Educational Practice*. Scott, Foresman (with L. Kohlberg).

1974 Conflict and transition in adolescent moral development. *Child Development*, 45, 14–29.

1975 The development of social concepts: Mores, customs, and conventions. In J.M. Foley and D.J. DePalma (eds), *Moral Development: Current Theory and Literature*. Erlbaum.

1978 The development of concepts of social structure: Social convention. In J. Glick and A. Clarke-Stewart (eds), *The Development of Social Understanding*. Gardner Press.

1979 Distinct conceptual and developmental domains: Social convention and morality. In C.B. Keasey (ed.), *Social Cognitive Development: Nebraska Symposium on Motivation, 1977, 25*. University of Nebraska Press.

1983 *The Development of Social Knowledge:*

Morality and Convention. Cambridge University Press.

1986   Heterogeneity, inconsistency and asynchrony in the development of cognitive structures. In I. Levin (ed.), *Stage and Structure: Reopenning the Debate.* Ablex (with P. Davidson).

1987   Morality: Its structure, functions and vagaries. In J. Kagan and S. Lamb (eds), *The Emergence of Moral Concepts in Young Children*, University of Chicago Press.

1991   Judging social issues: Difficulties, inconsistencies, and consistencies. *Monographs of the Society for Research in Child Development*, 56(2), serial no. 224 (with E. Hildebrandt and C. Wainryb).

1994   Morality, authoritarianism, and personal agency. In R.J. Sternberg and P. Ruzgis (eds), *Personality and Intelligence.* Cambridge University Press.

1996   Equality and hierarchy: Conflict in values. In E. Reed, E. Turiel and T. Brown (eds), *Values and Knowledge.* Erlbaum.

1997   Moral development. In W. Damon (ed.), *Handbook of Child Psychology* (5th edn), vol. 3, N. Eisenberg (ed.), *Social, Emotional, and Personality Development.* Wiley.

Further reading

Saltzstein, H. (1991) Why are nonprototypical events so difficult, and what are the implications for social developmental psychology? Commentary on Turiel, E., Hildebrandt, E. and Wainryb, C. Judging social issues: Difficulties, inconsistencies, and consistencies. *Monographs of the Society for Research in Child Development*, 56(2), serial no. 224.

Sigel, I.E. (1984) The domains of social knowledge. Review of *The Development of Social Knowledge: Morality and Convention. Contemporary Psychology*, 29, 537–9.

Smetana, J.G. (1995) Morality in context: Abstractions, ambiguities, and applications. In R. Vasta (ed.), *Annals of Child Development*, vol. 10. Jessica Kingsley.

Elliot Turiel was born on the Island of Rhodes. In 1944, when the island was taken by the Germans, his family narrowly escaped capture by the Nazis. They fled to Turkey by means of a rowing boat, and remained in Turkey until the end of the war. The family then moved to New York, where Turiel grew up. He completed graduate studies at Yale University in the 1960s, during a time in which there was a good deal of tension between the behaviouristic tradition of American psychology and the then newly popular cognitive approaches. He was greatly influenced by the writings of Jean **Piaget**, and others pursuing structural approaches to development. He was also influenced by Lawrence **Kohlberg**'s work on the development of morality, particularly his emphasis on relating philosophical analyses of the domain to psychological analyses of learning and development. Turiel's dissertation was an experimental test of the sequentiality of stages of moral development described by Kohlberg, and his early research was often done in collaboration with him. By the mid-1970s, Turiel's research led him to the view that young children construct judgements about the social world which entail distinctions among fundamental aspects of social interactions. On the basis of that work, he proposed that morality and social convention form distinct conceptual systems rather than emerging developmentally within a single framework as had been maintained by Kohlberg, and Piaget before him.

In 1975, Turiel left Harvard to join the faculty at the University of California, Santa Cruz, where he continued to develop his ideas regarding domains of social knowledge. In a series of highly influential book chapters published between 1975 and 1979, he spelled out the basic framework of his account of social development. In 1980, he joined the faculty of the graduate school of education at the University of California at Berkeley, where he is currently a professor and associate dean for academic affairs. In 1983, his book, *The Development of Social Knowledge: Morality and Convention* was published, which summarized research he and his students had conducted that sustained the proposition that issues of morality (justice, fairness rights), form a developmental system distinct from conceptions of social organization and societal convention. In 1987, Turiel and his students extended their analysis of social judgements to account for contextual and cultural variations in the ways in which morality and societal convention interact. In the 1990s this work has incorporated analyses of the ways in which informational assumptions held by individuals affect their moral judgements. More recently, Turiel has shifted his attention to the ways in which hierarchical cultural systems affect the development of individuals' conceptions of authority and personal autonomy. His work has had a significant impact on the discussions regarding the role of culture in children's social development, and has also impacted on research and development of approaches to moral education.

L.P. NUCCI

Tversky, Amos

Born: 1937, Haifa, Israel **Nat:** Israeli **Ints:** Decision making, inductive reasoning, mathematical psychology, measurement theory, similarity **Educ:** BA Hebrew University, 1961; PhD University of Michigan, 1965 **Appts & awards:** Professor, Department of Psychology, Stanford University, 1978– ; Member, AAAS, 1982; APA Distinguished Scientific Contribution Award, 1982; Society of Experimental Psychologists, 1983; MacArthur Prize, 1984; Foreign Associate, NAS, 1985; Editorial Boards: *Journal of Mathematical Psychology, Journal of Economic Behavior and Organization, Synthese*

Principal publications

1967 *Decision Making.* Penguin, (ed. with W. Edwards).

1968 The foundations of multi-dimensional scaling. *Psychological Review*, 75, 127–42 (with R. Beals and D.H. Krantz).

1969 The intransitivity of preferences. *Psychological Review*, 76, 31–48.

1970 *Mathematical Psychology: An Elementary Introduction.* Prentice Hall (with C.H. Coombs and R.M. Davies).

1971–90 *Foundations of Measurement* (3 vols). Academic Press (with D.H. Krantz, R.D. Luce and P. Suppes).

1971 Conjoint measurement analysis of composition rules in psychology. *Psychological Review*, 78, 151–69 (with D.H. Krantz).

1972 Elimination by aspects: A theory of choice. *Psychological Review*, 79, 281–99.

1973 On the psychology of prediction. *Psychological Review*, 80, 237–51 (with D. Kahneman).

1974 Judgment under uncertainty: Heuristics and biases. *Science*, 185, 1124–31 (with D. Kahneman).

1977 Features of similarity. *Psychological Review*, 84, 327–52.

1979 Prospect theory: An analysis of decision under risk. *Econometrica*, 47, 263–91 (with D. Kahneman).

1981 The framing of decisions and the psychology of choice. *Science*, 211, 453–8 (with D. Kahneman).

1982 (ed.) *Judgment Under Uncertainty: Heuristics*

and Biases. Cambridge University Press (with D. Kahneman and P. Slovic).

1984 Choices, values and frames. *American Psychologist*, 39, 341–50 (with D. Kahneman).

1988 *Decision Making: Descriptive, Normative and Prescriptive Interactions.* Cambridge University Press (with D.E. Bell and H. Raiffa).

Amos Tversky's father was a veterinarian and his mother a social worker and later a member of Parliament. After several years of military service, he entered the Hebrew University of Jerusalem and took courses in philosophy and psychology. In 1961, he left Israel for graduate training at the University of Michigan. There he worked with Ward Edwards, and his first elective was a course in mathematical psychology taught by Clyde **Coombs**. He left Michigan in 1965, spent the following year at the Center for Cognitive Studies at Harvard University, and returned to Jerusalem in 1966. He began extensive collaborative work with Daniel **Kahneman** in 1969. They noted that people's choices depart systematically and significantly from the classical rational theory of choice, and that many of the puzzling phenomena of choice can be traced to the interaction between the framing of the options and the psychophysics of value and belief. Tversky's prospect theory incorporates the representation or framing process and the evaluation process, and offers an alternative to the classical theory of choice and risk.

Tversky has contributed to the development of conjoint measurement and its applications to psychology. Specifically, he has dealt with the finite theory of additive measurement, and worked on the development of polynomial conjoint measurement together with David H. Krantz. He has also worked on the descriptive analysis of choice and showed that some assumptions (e.g. transitivity, simple scalability) are too restrictive. He constructed more general models (e.g. the additive-difference model, the elimination-by-aspects model) to accommodate these results, and developed a set-theoretical approach to the study of similarity as an alternative to the classical geometric approach. In collaboration with Kahneman, he investigated the heuristics people use to assess uncertainty and estimate probability, and the biases to which they are prone. He and Kahneman also analysed the cognitive and psychophysical determinants of choice and the manner in which the framing of options affects the choice among them.

Tyler, Leona Elizabeth

Born: 1906, Chetek, Winsconsin, USA **Nat:** American **Ints:** Counselling, developmental, evaluation and measurement, general, theoretical and philosophical **Educ:** BS University of Minnesota, 1925; MS University of Minnesota, 1939; PhD University of Minnesota, 1941 **Appts & awards:** Professor Emeritus, University of Oregon, 1955; President, Oregon Psychological Association, 1956–7, Western Psychological Association, 1957–8; APA, President Division 17, 1959–60, Board of Directors, 1966–8, 1971–4, Policy and Planning Board, 1968–70, President, 1972–3; Hon. DHL, Linfield College, 1979; APP award for distinguished contributions to psychology, 1990; Consulting Editor, *Personnel Guidance Journal*, 1956–62; Associate Editor, *Journal of Counseling Psychology*, 1954–66; Editorial Consultant, *Contemporary Psychology*, 1966–75; Editorial Committee, *Annual Review of Psychology*, 1972–6; Editorial Board, *Intelligence*, 1977–84

Principal publications

1947   *Psychology of Human Differences*. Appleton-Century-Crofts (reprinted in 1956 and 1965).

1953   *Work of the Counselor*. Appleton-Century-Crofts (reprinted in 1961 and 1965).

1955   The development of 'vocational interests'. I. The organization of likes and dislikes in ten-year-old children. *Journal of Genetic Psychology*, 86, 33–44.

1959   Toward a workable psychology of individuality. *American Psychologist*, 14, 75–81.

1961   Research explorations in the realm of choice. *Journal of Counseling Psychology*, 8, 195–201.

1963   *Tests and Measurements*. Prentice Hall (reprinted in 1973 and 1983).

1964   The antecedents of two varieties of interest pattern. *Genetic Psychology Monographs*, 70, 177–227.

1972   Human abilities. *Annual Review of Psychology*, 23, 177–206.

1973   Design for a hopeful psychology. *American Psychologist*, 28, 1021–9.

1978   *Individuality*. Jossey-Bass.

1981   More stately mansions – psychology extends its boundaries. *Annual Review of Psychology*, 32, 1–20.

1983   *Thinking Creatively: A New Approach to Psychology and Individual Lives*. Jossey-Bass.

Further reading

Goldman, L. (1971) *Using Tests in Counseling*. Prentice-Hall.

Leona E. Tyler. (1991) *American Psychologist*, 46, 330–2.

Leona Tyler was the eldest of four children. Her father was an accountant and later a house restoration contractor. Her mother managed their home. The family moved to Mesabi Iron Range, Minnesota, during Leona's childhood. Her first degree was in English, a subject which she taught for twelve years. A meeting with D.G. Paterson, an applied psychologist, opened the possibility of a graduate assistantship at the University of Minnesota. In 1940, before she completed her PhD, she took up an appointment as head of the Personnel Research Bureau at the University of Oregon. After World War II she established a veteran's counselling service (funded by the Veterans Administration) at the university, and later rehabilitation and counselling programmes. Sabbatical trips to the **Maudsley** Hospital (1951–2, to work with Hans **Eysenck**) and a Fulbright to Amsterdam (1962–3) were influential in shaping her scholarship and research. In 1972–3 she was the eighty-first APA president and the fourth woman to occupy that position.

The primary focus of Leona Tyler's research has been individuality. She argues that representing individual personality as a profile of scores or a point in n-dimensional space is not a particularly useful way of understanding or helping individuals. Such an approach misses an opportunity to understand the unique directions in which individuals develop over their lifetime. For a number of years she was engaged in interest measurement research using the Strong Blank and others constructed in the same way. From this she moved on and attempted to identify patterns of choices characterizing individuals. Studying the ways in which choices are organized brought her into contact with ideas on cognitive structure and on projective techniques for studying personality. The theoretical system she developed to hold these ideas together is based on the central thesis that possibilities are always more numerous than actualities and a person can actualize only a fraction of them. Thus to understand an individual it is necessary to examine the way this selection of possibilities to be actualized has occurred, either through external constraints or through voluntary choices.

U

Uttal, William R.

Born: 1931, Mineola, New York, USA **Nat:** American **Ints:** Experimental, philosophical and theoretical, physiological and comparative **Educ:** BS University of Cincinnati, 1951; PhD Ohio State University, 1957 **Appts & awards:** Research Psychologist, Naval Ocean Systems Center, Hawaii Laboratory; Patent Award, IBM Corporation, 1962; Fellow, APA Division 6, 1967, Division 3, 1971; NIMH Special Post-Doctoral Fellowship, 1965–6; NIMH Research Scientist Award, 1971–6; President, National Conference on the Use of On-Line Computers in Psychology, 1973–4; Fellow, AAAS, 1975; James McKeen Cattell Award, 1978–9; Fellow, Collegiate Institute for Values and Science, University of Michigan, 1978; MacEachran Memorial Lecturer, University of Alberta, 1982; Scholar in Residence, Rockefeller Foundation, Bellagio Study Center, 1983; Visiting Scientist (Japan), Japanese Society for the Promotion of Science, 1983; Associate Editor, *Computing – Archives for Electronic Computing*, 1963–75; Board of Editors, *Behavior Research Methods and Instrumentation*, 1968– ; Consulting Editor, *Journal of Experimental Psychology: Human Perception and Performance*, 1976–80

Principal publications

1958 A comparison of neural and psychophysical responses in the somesthetic system. *Journal of Comparative and Physiological Psychology*, 52, 485–90.

1962 On conversational interaction. In J. Coulson (ed.), *Programmed Learning and Computer Based Instructions*. Wiley.

1964 Systematics of the evoked somatosensory cortical potential. *Annals of the New York Academy of Sciences*, 112, 60–81 (with L. Cook).

1967 Evoked brain potentials: Signs or codes? *Perspectives in Biology and Medicine*, 10, 627–39.

1967 On the psychophysical discriminability of somatosensory nerve action potential patterns with irregular intervals. *Perception and Psychophysics*, 2, 341–8 (with P. Smith).

1968 *Real Time Computers: Technique and Applications in the Psychological Sciences*. Harper & Row.

1970 On the physiological basis of masking with dotted visual noise. *Perception and Psychophysics*, 7, 321–7.

1971 The psychobiological silly season, or what happens when neurophysiological data become psychological theories. *Journal of General Psychology*, 84, 151–66.

1973 *The Psychobiology of Sensory Coding*. Harper & Row.

1975 Parameters of tachistoscopic stereopsis. *Vision Research*, 15, 705–12 (with J. Fitzgerald and T.E. Eskin.).

1978 *The Psychobiology of Mind*. Erlbaum.

1981 *A Taxonomy of Visual Processes*. Erlbaum.

1984 *The Detection of Nonplanar Surfaces in 3–D Space*. Erlbaum.

1984 Psychology and biology. In M.H. Bornstein (ed.), *Psychology in Relation to the Allied Disciplines*. Erlbaum.

Further reading

Honson, J.A. (eds) (1988) *State of Brain and Mind*. Birkhauser.

Masin, S.C. (eds) (1993) *Foundations of Perceptual Theory*. North-Holland/Elsevier Science.

William Uttal entered psychology from physics after becoming fascinated with sensory neuro-physiology, following earlier training in the physical sciences and as a electronics officer in the USAF. Following graduate school he joined the IBM Research Center, where he was one of the first psychologists to become involved with digital computers. While there he led the group that developed the 'Coursewriter' language for computer-assisted instruction, and carried out a number of psychobiological research projects. In 1963 he moved to the University of Michigan, where he continued to work on vision and somatosensation and also undertook a synoptic and theoretical review of sensory psychology with particular emphasis on vision. This review emerged as a trilogy of books (*The Psychobiology of Sensory Coding* (1973), *The Psychobiology of Mind* (1978), and *A Taxonomy of Visual*

Processes (1981)), with a fourth on form perception (1984). These books critically examine our understanding of sensory processes in general and vision in particular. During this same period, a second series of books covering his empirical research and theoretical analyses of how forms are perceived was also published. His contributions include pioneering efforts in the computerization of psychological research, his work done on generative, computer-assisted instruction, his elucidation of some of the general principles of visual computation, and the philosophical and conceptual analysis of the field of sensation embodied in the trilogy. During this time there was a gradual shift in his thinking, from that of a radical 'neuro-reductionist' to the conviction that the relevant neural processes underlying even the simplest form of sensation are so complex that it is unlikely that we shall ever be able to explain the magnificent leap from the function of discrete neurons to the processes of cognition.

V

Vernon, Magdalen Dorothea

Born: 1901, Oxford, England *Died:* 1991, Beckenham, England *Nat:* British *Ints:* Perception, reading *Educ:* MA, Newnham College, Cambridge University, 1923; ScD, Cambridge University, 1953 *Appts & awards:* Reading University, Lecturer, 1946–55, Reader, 1955–6, Professor of Psychology, 1956–67, Emeritus Professor, 1967–91; Founder Member, Experimental Psychology Group, 1946 (later renamed Experimental Psychology Society); President, Experimental Psychology Group, 1952–3; President, BPS, 1958–61

Principal publications

1931 *The Experimental Study of Reading.* Cambridge University Press.

1934 The binocular fusion of flicker. *British Journal of Psychology*, 24, 351–74.

1937 *Visual Perception.* Cambridge University Press.

1940 The relation of cognition and phantasy in children. *British Journal of Psychology*, 30, 273–94.

1946 Learning from graphical material. *British Journal of Psychology*, 36, 145–58.

1947 Different types of perceptual ability. *British Journal of Psychology*, 38, 79–89.

1952 *A Further Study of Visual Perception.* Cambridge University Press.

1957 *Backwardness in Reading.* Cambridge University Press.

1962 *The Psychology of Perception.* Penguin.

1966 *Experiments in Visual Perception.* Penguin.

1969 *Human Motivation.* Cambridge University Press.

1970 *Perception Through Experience.* Methuen.

1971 *Reading and its Difficulties.* Cambridge University Press.

Magdalen Vernon was born into an academic family: her father, H.M. Vernon, was a Fellow of Magdalen College, Oxford, and well known for his distinguished work with the Industrial Health Research Board. His interests influenced the career choices not only of his daughter, but also of her younger brother, **Philip Vernon**, who became equally well known in the field of educational psychology. An open scholarship from Oxford High School took 'Maggie' to Newnham College, Cambridge, in 1919, and after graduating she joined the talented group working alongside Professor Frederick **Bartlett** at the Cambridge Psychological Laboratory. There she spent from 1927 to 1946 as a member of the the Medical Research Council's scientific staff. Starting from a study of eye movements in proof-reading, her work expanded into other areas of visual perception. A stream of papers and a book followed and she became an international expert on experimental studies of reading.

In 1937 came the publication of *Visual Perception*, a remarkable work for its time (published a year before the first edition of **Woodworth**'s *Experimental Psychology*), which continued in revised editions as an essential handbook for students over a period of twenty years. No one could expect to get a degree in psychology without having read M.D. Vernon. Her experimental work at Cambridge included a valuable period of collaboration with Kenneth Craik on problems of dark adaptation. She gained and successfully held over a long period an international reputation in the visual perception field.

In 1946 Vernon moved to a lectureship at Reading and ten years later was appointed as professor and head of department. Under Vernon's leadership, the department successfully expanded and moved to larger, refurbished buildings on the main campus of the university at Whiteknights. Although quite small in size, Vernon's department gained a solid reputation as a good department for experimental and general psychology, and a surprisingly large number of eminent psychologists studied there at undergraduate or PhD level. Students remember her for her good-humoured, no-nonsense comments and searching questions at seminars, and the way she had of treating everybody as an equal, whether a first-year student or a Minister of Education. She often told her colleagues that they were wrong and, although they did not much like it, more often than not she was right.

Vernon was deeply interested in theories of perception and entered fully into discussions about fundamental issues. Heavily influenced by Frederick Bartlett's ideas, she was interested in the constructive nature of perception. She believed, and obtained a good deal of supportive evidence, that individual perceivers construct their perceived worlds to maximize as far as possible their stability, endurance and consistency. On the other hand, Vernon was equally interested in the wide individual differences which enter into the perception of even the simplest of material. Like Bartlett before her, Vernon assumed that the perceiver used a large number of complex schemata (internal processes for apprehending and reacting to particular classes of situation), which were constructed over the course of the individual's lifetime. Any new experiences were processed in the light of schemata or chains of schemata by dint of 'effort after meaning' (another term borrowed from Bartlett) until they were understood and reacted to in the most effective manner. As Vernon appreciated, her description of the operation of schemata remained incomplete and awaited further in-depth studies, possibly using developmental methods with large numbers of participants.

DAVID F. MARKS AND ROY DAVIES

Vernon, Philip Ewart

Born: 1905, Oxford, England **Died:** 1987, Alberta, Canada **Nat:** British **Ints:** Cross-cultural psychology, developmental psychology, evaluation and measurement, educational psychology, personality, psychology and the arts, social psychology **Educ:** BA University of Cambridge, 1927; MA University of Cambridge, 1930; PhD University of Cambridge, 1931; DSc University of London, 1952 **Appts & awards:** Emeritus Professor of Educational Psychology, University of Calgary; President, BPS, 1954; President, Industrial, Educational, and Scottish Sections, BPS; Honorary Life Fellow, President, Psychology Section, BAAS; Honorary Life Fellow, Canadian Psychological Association, 1972; Fellow, US National Academy of Education; Hon. LLD, University of Calgary, 1978; Editor, *British Journal of Educational Psychology*, 1956–61; Editorial Advisory Boards: *Canadian Journal of Behavioral Science*, *Journal of Cross-Cultural Psychology*, *Journal of Special Education*

Principal publications

1934   Auditory perception. *British Journal of Psychology*, 25, 123–39, 265–83.

1947   Research on personnel selection in the Royal Navy and the British Army. *American Psychologist*, 2, 35–51.

1950   *The Structure of Human Abilities*. Methuen.

1950   The validation of Civil Service Selection Board procedures. *Occupational Psychology*, 24, 75–95.

1950   An application of factorial analysis to the study of test items. *British Journal of Statistical Psychology*, 3, 1–15.

1954   Practice and coaching effects in intelligence tests. *Forum of Education*, 18, 269–80.

1955   The psychology of intelligence and g. *Quarterly Bulletin of the BPS*, 26, 1–14.

1958   A new look at intelligence testing. *Educational Research*, 1, 1–12.

1964   *Personality Assessment: A Critical Survey*. Methuen.

1965   Environmental handicaps and intellectual development. *British Journal of Educational Psychology*, 35, 9–20, 117–26.

1967   Psychological studies of creativity. *Journal of Child Psychology and Psychiatry*, 8, 153–64.

1972   The validity of divergent thinking tests. *Alberta Journal of Educational Research*, 18, 249–58.

1977   *The Psychology and Education of Gifted Children*. Methuen (with G. Adamson and D. Vernon)

1979   *Intelligence: Heredity and Environment*. Freeman.

1982   *The Abilities and Achievements of Orientals in North America*. Academic Press.

Vernon's earliest publications, and his PhD thesis, were in the area of the psychology of musical appreciation, and auditory perception. He was also interested in Gordon **Allport's** work on personality, and went to work with him at Harvard University (1930–1). Together they produced an important study of expressive movements and the widely used Study of Values test. He returned to this area with books in 1953 and 1964, trying to reconcile the opposition between ideographic (or clinical) and nomothetic (or psychometric) approaches to personality, together with interview and projective techniques vs. questionnaires and objective assessments. However, his most long-standing interests were in mental measurement and individual differences, including: intelligence test construction; factor analysis and item analysis techniques; uses of tests for selection in the

Army and Navy, and for educational selection to advanced schooling; effects of practice and coaching on test performance; developmental studies, and cross-cultural comparisons of abilities; problems of hereditary and environmental influences; gifted and talented children and adults; also retarded and learning disabled.

Though he spent most of his career in universities – mainly Glasgow, London, and the University of Calgary – he worked for two years in a child guidance clinic, and for six years in the Armed Forces personnel departments. Particularly in the 1960s, he carried out lengthy field studies in the West Indies, Tanzania and Uganda, Canada (native Indians and Eskimos), and Latin American and other countries. He always advocated a balanced or middling view on genetic vs. environmental issues, arguing that both sides have made valuable research contributions. Following **Hebb**'s interactionist theory, he held that intelligence is partially dependent on genetic individual differences, but also on the stimulating or adverse effects of home and school upbringing. He suggested that the same may be true of group (e.g. ethnic) differences, though we lack the methodology to prove or disprove this.

Vinogradova, Olga

Born: 1929, Moscow, USSR *Nat:* Russian *Ints:* Neurospychology, physiological psychology *Educ:* Doctor of Biological Sciences, 1983 *Appts & awards:* Head, Laboratory of Systemic Organization of Neurons, Institute of Biological Physics, Academy of Sciences, Moscow; Kenneth Craik Prize, St John's College, Cambridge, 1977; Editorial Board, *Neuropsychologia*, 1978–85

Principal publications

1959   Role of the orienting reaction in the process of conditioning in human subjects. In E.N. Sokolov (ed.), *Orienting Reflex and the Problems of Higher Nervous Activity*. Academy of Educational Sciences (in Russian).

1959   An objective investigation of the dynamics of semantic systems. *British Journal of Psychology*, 50, 89–105 (with A.R. Luria).

1961   *The Orienting Reflex and its Neurophysiological Mechanisms*. Academy of Educational Sciences (in Russian).

1970   Hippocampus and the orienting reflex. In E.N. Sokolov and O.S. Vinogradova (eds), *Neuronal Mechanisms of the Orienting Reflex*. Moscow University Publishing House.

1975   *Hippocampus and Memory*. Nauka (in Russian).

1978   Neuronal aspects of septo-hippocampal relations. In J. Gray and L. Weiskratz (eds), *Functions of the Septo-Hippocampal System*. Elsevier (with E.S. Brazhnik).

1985   Spontaneous and evoked activity of the neurons in the intrabrain allo- and xenografts of the hippocampus and septum. In A. Bjorklund and U. Stenevi (eds), *Transplantation in the Mammalian CNS*. Elsevier.

Vinogradova started her career working with A.R. **Luria** and E.N. **Sokolov** in 1952 on investigations of orienting reactions in humans. She applied methods for the investigation of the orienting response (OR) to the diagnosis of mental retardation and to the objective measurement of auditory and visual sensitivity in young children with defects of hearing and sight. She also applied these methods to investigations of semantic fields and their interactions, using verbal stimuli in normal and mentally retarded people. When the phenomenology of the OR was well understood and theoretically interpreted, she decided to look for its neuronal correlates and possible mechanisms. Thus, in 1962, she started to work with animals using the methods of OR investigation while recording neuronal activity of various brain structures. After finding that the hippocampal (CA3) neuronal effects closely reproduces all of the characteristic features of the OR, she commenced a systematic investigation of the neuoronal activity of all anatomical subdivisions of the hippocampus and related structures. By 1975 she had developed a general concept of the mode of operation of the hippocampus and related structures in selection of novel information. In order to understand better the intrinsic activity of the local neuronal systems maintained in complete afferent isolation, she proceeded with a series of studies to investigate neuronal activity in incubated brain slices, and later (1979) in nervous tissue grafted into the anterior chamber of the eye and into the brain. This new experimental approach generated a series of new questions which she addressed in later work. The first concerns neuronal mechanisms of rhythmic processes (especially the theta-rhythm) and their significance in processing sensory information, and the second addresses activity of the neurons in grafts, developing in isolation (*in oculo*) and in interaction with the host's brain, and their involvement in compensation for sensory and behavioural defects.

Viteles, Morris S.

Born: 1898, Zvanstz, Russia **Died:** n.d. **Nat:** Russian/American **Ints:** Individual differences, industrial, military **Educ:** AB University of Pennsylvania, 1918; MA University of Pennsylvania, 1919; PhD University of Pennsylvania, 1922 **Appts & awards:** University of Paris, 1922; Social Research Council, USSR, 1923; Professor of Psychology, University of Pennsylvania, 1924–74; President, International Council of Applied Psychology,

Principal publications

1921   Test in industry. *Journal of Applied Psychology*, 6, 392–401.
1926   Psychology in industry. *Psychological Bulletin*, 23, 638–88.
1932   *Industrial Psychology*. Norton.
1934   *The Science of Work*. Norton.
1945   The aircraft pilot: Five years of research, a survey of outcomes. *Psychological Bulletin*, 42, 489–526.
1953   *Motivation and Morale in Industry*. Norton.
1972   Psychology today, fact and fiction. *American Psychologist*, 27, 601–5.

Further reading

Krwegek, T.S. (1974) *The Psychologists*, vol. 2. Oxford University Press.
Murchison, C.E. (ed.) (1961) *A History of Psychology in Autobiography*. Clark University Press.

Morris Viteles was born in the small town of Zvanstz in Russia, bordering on Romania. His family emigrated to London in the same year, 1898, and then to the United States in 1904. After his PhD, he studied under James McKeen **Cattell**, and developed a keen interest in individual differences and their measurement. Like Cattell he was strongly influenced by the **Wundt**ian tradition in experimental psychology. During the 1920s his interests turned to vocational guidance. This, in turn, led him to an area which was to engulf the rest of his career, industrial psychology; probably the credit for this goes to Hugo **Münsterberg**, under whom Viteles also studied. At any rate, during the succeeding years he was a major figure in that area of psychology. One of his early contributions was the 'job psychograph', which presented the skills necessary for various kinds of vocation. Further, he discovered that intelligence as measured by current tests was not the best criterion for some kinds of occupation. For example, a bus driver with a high IQ might be bored and more careless in the execution of his or her duties.

As his career evolved, Viteles' interests turned to military psychology. In 1932 he published his most important book, *Industrial Psychology*. He called it his 'magnum opus'. During World War II he devoted his energies to aviation psychology. Here he studied transfer in the range of approaching aircraft.

In his 1953 book, *Motivation and Morale in Industry*, he presented the most comprehensive data on motivation and on factors affecting performance and morale in various jobs. He questioned the assertion that labour unions can best meet workers' needs and demands. Other social institutions might do better.

ROBERT W. LUNDIN

Vroom, Victor H.

Born: 1932, Montreal, Canada **Nat:** American **Ints:** Industrial and organizational psychology, Society for the Psychological Study of Social Issues **Educ:** BSc McGill University, 1953; MPsSc McGill University, 1955; PhD University of Michigan, 1958 **Appts & awards:** Instructor and Lecturer, Department of Psychology, University of Michigan, 1958–9; Ford Foundation Doctoral Dissertation Competition Winner, 1958–9; Assistant Professor, Department of Psychology, University of Pennsylvania, 1960–3; Ford Foundation Faculty Fellowship, 1961–2; Associate Professor, Graduate School of Industrial Administration, Carnegie Institute of Technology, 1963–6; Professor of Psychology and Industrial Administration, Graduate School of Industrial Administration, Carnegie-Mellon University, 1966–72; McKinsey Foundation Research Design Competition Winner, 1967; Fulbright Lecturer in UK, 1967–8; James McKeen Cattell Award, APA, 1970; Professor of Administrative Sciences and of Psychology, Yale University, 1972–3; John G. Searle Professor of Organization and Management, 1973– ; Professor of Psychology, Yale University, 1973– ; President, Society of Industrial and Organizational Psychology, 1980–1; Excellence in Teaching Award, Yale som Alumni Association, 1994

Principal publications

1960   *Some Personality Determinants of the Effects of Participation*. Prentice Hall.
1961   Industrial social psychology. *Annual Review of Psychology* (with N.R.F. Maier).

1962   Ego involvement, job satisfaction and job
       performance. *Personnel Psychology*, 15, 150–77.
1964   *Work and Motivation*. Wiley.
1965   Motivation in management. *American
       Foundation for Management Research*.
1967   (ed.) *Methods of Organizational Research*.
       University of Pittsburgh Press.
1968   Toward a stochastic model of managerial
       careers. *Administrative Science Quarterly* (with
       K. MacCrimmon).
1969   Industrial social psychology. In G. Lindzey
       and E. Aronson (eds), *Handbook of Social
       Psychology*, vol. 5. Addison-Wesley.
1970   (ed.) *Management and Motivation*. Penguin
       (with E.L. Deci). (2nd edn, 1992).
1973   *Leadership and Decision-Making*. University
       of Pittsburgh Press (with P. Yetton).
1976   Leadership. In M. Dunnette (ed.), *Handbook
       of Industrial and Organizational Psychology*.
       Rand-McNally.
1977   Hierarchical level and leadership style.
       Organizational Behavior and Human Performance,
       18, 131–45 (with A.G. Jago).
1978   On the validity of the Vroom–Yetton model.
       Journal of Applied Psychology, 63, 151–62 (with
       A.G. Jago).
1982   Sex differences in the incidence and
       evaluation of participative leader behavior. *Journal
       of Applied Psychology*, 67, 776–83 (with A.G.
       Jago).
1988   *The New Leadership: Managing Participation
       in Organizations*. Prentice Hall.

Further reading

Vroom, V.H. (1993) Improvising and muddling
    through. In A.G. Bedeian (ed.), *Management
    Laureates: A Collection of Autobiographic Essays*.
    JAI Press.

Victor Vroom was born and grew up in Montreal, Canada. During his youth, he was fascinated by jazz music and played the saxophone in bands. He went to the Sir George Williams College in Montreal, where he had his first contact with psychology. After one year of college study he changed to McGill University. There, he took his first course in psychology from Donald **Hebb**. Later, he concentrated on industrial psychology, and received his Master's degree in 1955.

For his PhD Vroom went to Michigan. There he was influenced by Norman Maier, social psychologists such as Ted Newcomb, Doc Cartwright, Dan Katz and Jack French, and by the ideas of Kurt **Lewin**. Vroom wrote his doctoral dissertation on 'Some personality

determinants of the effects of participation'. His study showed a positive relationship between participation and both a positive attitude towards the job and high job performance. Additionally, enhancing effects of the personality variables 'authoritarianism' and 'need for independence' were found. For this dissertation, Vroom received an award from the Ford Foundation. After having finished his dissertation, he stayed at Michigan for another two years.

Vroom joined the Department of Psychology at the University of Pennsylvania in 1960. During his time there, Vroom worked on his book *Work and Motivation* (1964). There he presented his valence–instrumentality–expectancy (VIE) theory of work motivation, which has subsequently become very influential within organizational psychology. This theory states that a person's (choice) behaviour is a function of the combination of the perceived expectancy that effort leads to specific first-order outcomes, the instrumentality of these first-order outcomes for second-order outcomes, and the valence of these second-order outcomes. A multiplicative relation between expectancy, instrumentality and valence is assumed. Thus, the theory predicts that people engage in a specific behaviour if they expect that effort leads with a high probability to a result which is closely associated with a highly valued outcome. Subsequently, the model received great attention among researchers. This attention is reflected in empirical studies supporting Vroom's assumptions as well as in critical discussions of the theoretical and methodological problems associated with the VIE theory.

In 1963, Vroom went to the Graduate School of Industrial Administration at the Carnegie Institute of Technology, where he also got involved in interdisciplinary discussions. Later, he got a professorship of psychology and industrial administration at the Carnegie-Mellon University. Together with Ken McCrimmon he was engaged in a project that aimed at the description of managerial careers by a Markov chain model. It was at Carnegie that Vroom met Edward **Deci** and Philip Yetton. Both were initially students of Vroom and with both of them Vroom collaborated for many years. Together with Deci, Vroom edited a book entitled *Management and Motivation* (1970), which has become wide-spread in subsequent years.

Together with Yetton, Vroom continued his work on participative management and decision making. Vroom and Yetton studied decision-making situations that were reported to them by managers and began to formalize these situations with the help of decision trees. Vroom's and Yetton's work resulted in a normative model of managerial decision making that was published in 1973. In this model, Vroom and Yetton differentiate between five types of decision process varying in the degree of subordinates' participation. In order to choose the most appropriate decision process for a given situation, the manager must first assess the problem on the basis of seven rules referring to availability of information, trust, structuredness of the problem, acceptance of the decision, existence of conflict, fairness and acceptance priority. By applying the seven rules, the most appropriate decision procedure can be derived. Unlike other leadership theories, the Vroom–Yetton model is prescriptive in nature and limited to a specific issue within the broad range of leadership behaviour, namely participation in decision making. Vroom's and Yetton's work on their model was not only an academic endeavour; the model was also put into practice by the authors, as well as by a company that was licensed for the rights to use it.

After having been nine years at Carnegie, Vroom left for a professorship at Yale University. Soon after his arrival at Yale he was asked to be the chairman of the Department of Administrative Sciences. He fulfilled this challenging task in a difficult financial and organizational situation until 1975. At Yale, Vroom met Arthur Jago, who was then a graduate student. Vroom and Jago did research on the descriptive aspects of participation in decision making, including sex and hierarchical differences. In 1978, they published their research on the validity of the Vroom–Yetton model. However, during the 1980s, they concentrated more on the weaknesses of that model. Their work resulted in a revised version of the original model that took into account additional situational variables and criteria, and that abandoned the concept of rules and the feasible set. Instead of the seven rules of the Vroom–Yetton model, the revised model by Vroom and Jago is based on four mathematical equations. For solving these equations managers can be provided with a software program written by Jago.

Besides his active involvement in research and administrative duties, during his career Vroom has been engaged in teaching undergraduate and PhD psychology students as well as aspiring and experienced managers. In his teaching he incorporates experiential methods including role playing and personal reflection. Vroom has held numerous editorial positions and served on the editorial boards of journals such as *Administrative Science Quarterly*, *Organizational Behavior and Human Performance*, *Journal of Conflict Resolution*, and *Leadership Quarterly*. From 1980 to 1981 Vroom was president of the Society of Industrial-Organisational Association. Additionally, Professor Vroom has consulted to over fifty major corporations, including Bell Labs, GTE, American Express and General Electric.

Although Vroom himself recently described his career in Lindbloom's terms of 'muddling through' and characterized it by the lack of long-term planning, in hindsight some general lines become apparent. They include concentration on motivational and leadership issues, with an explicit focus on the adaptive nature of leadership as well as participation in decision making. His work has been very influential in organizational psychology, and his books have been translated into other languages including Spanish, German and Korean. Both the VIE model and the Vroom–Yetton model stimulated a lot of subsequent research. Criticisms of Vroom's research have resulted in expanded or revised models by other researchers, reflecting progress in science.

SABINE SONNENTAG

Vygotsky, Lev Semeonovich

Born: 1896, Gomel, White Russia **Died:** 1934, Moscow, Russia **Nat:** Russian **Ints:** Developmental psychology, philosophical and theoretical psychology **Educ:** First State University of Moscow, 1913–17

Principal publications

1929   The problem of the cultural development of the child. *Journal of Genetic Psychology*, 36, 415–34.

1976   Play and its role in the mental development of the child. In J. Bruner *et al.* (eds), *Play – Its Role in Development and Evolution*. Penguin (1st pub. 1933).

1977   The development of higher psychological functions. *Soviet Psychology*, 15, 60–73.

1978   *Mind in Society: The Development of Higher Psychological Processes*. Cambridge University Press.

1979   Consciousness as a probem in the psychology of behavior. *Soviet Psychology*, 17(4), 3–35.

1981   The development of higher mental functions.

In J.V. Wertsch (ed.), *The Concept of Activity in Soviet Psychology*. Sharpe.

1981   The development of higher forms of attention in childhood. In J.V. Wertsch (ed.), *The Concept of Activity in Soviet Psychology*. Sharpe.

1987   *Collected Works*, vol. 1. Plenum.

1987   Diagnosis of the development and pedological clinical care of difficult children. *Soviet Psychology*, 26(1), 86–101 (1st pub. 1936).

1989   Concrete human psychology. *Soviet Psychology*, 27(2), 53–77 (1st pub. 1929).

1990   Imagination and creativity in childhood. *Soviet Psychology*, 28, 84–96 (1st pub. 1930).

Further reading

Kozulin, A. (1990) *Vygotsky's Psychology: A Biography of Ideas*. Harvard University Press.

Luria, A.R. (1935) Professor Leon Semeonovich Vygotskii. *Journal of Genetic Psychology*, 46, 224–6.

Van der Veer, R. and Valsiner, J. (1991) *Understanding Vygotsky: A Quest for Synthesis*. Blackwell.

Lev Semeonovich Vygotsky grew up in Gomel, near Belarus's borders with Russia and with the Ukraine. His early life and education were those of a well-to-do Jewish family of the time, and by merit (initially) and by luck – the Jewish quota being altered from selection to lottery at the time – he gained entry to Moscow University. Switching from medicine to law, Vygotsky read widely, including **James** and **Freud** as well as Russian and European literature. After graduation he returned to Gomel and taught at various adult institutes, meanwhile playing a major part in the literary and cultural life of the provincial town. He was able to set up a psychology laboratory at the teachers' college, and to work on the manuscript of a psychology textbook for secondary school teachers (his first published book, *Pedagogical Psychology*). His 1924 appearance at the Second Psychoneurological Congress in Leningrad, at which he presented three papers, was well prepared. Vygotsky spoke against **Pavlov**ian reflexology as a psychology of consciousness, and in support of the less mechanistic 'reactology' being applied by Kornilov, who had recently been appointed director of the Institute of Experimental Psychology at Moscow. Kornilov's invitation to Vygotsky to join the Institute cannot have been totally unexpected.

There, in Moscow, Vygotsky joined **Luria** (at that time a psychoanalytic psychologist) and others, even living for a while, with his wife and daughter, in a room in the Institute's library. The Institute was a lively place and included a kindergarten. Vygotsky followed a number of lines of investigation, also branching out into 'defectology', an interest that earned him his only foreign trip (to Berlin, Amsterdam, Paris and London) in 1925. In that year, also, his thesis 'The psychology of art' was accepted for his doctorate.

Vygotsky was involved in a vast range of teaching, consulting and research activities. He held numerous editorial posts and maintained other reviewing duties. At this time (up to 1928), Vygotsky's substantive psychology was a humanistic reactology: a version of a learning theory of human consciousness that tried to recognize the social nature of human thought and action. In conceptual issues, Vygotsky emphasized the fundamental significance of a unified methodology, for example, in 'The Historical Significance of a Crisis in Psychology' (1926). Here he attempted to sketch a truly Marxist psychology: a materialist science of human social behaviour. Neither the founding Marxists themselves (Marx, Engels) nor Vygotsky's contemporary Soviet psychologists had, in his view, made much progress in this project. Fragments or slogans from Marx, Engels and so on had been trumpeted, but this superficial and fragmentary approach failed to grasp Marx's method as a whole. Vygotsky looked forward to an account of human psychology that was scientific, based on causal laws (but not mechanistic), and established the concepts through which human activity might be described. As Vygotsky remarked, he was in effect setting himself the goal of writing his own *Capital*. The project remained programmatic and was never to be achieved by Vygotsky (nor, arguably, by any subsequent Marxist psychologist). Instead of pursuing it in its theoretical, materialist form, Vygotsky instead followed an empirical, evolutionist route in studying cultural differences in thinking, hence giving rise to the 'cultural historical' approach to psychology. This work was strongly influenced by a collaboration with Luria.

Between 1928 and 1932, Vygotsky carried out experimental work at the Academy of Communist Education, with colleagues including Luria and **Leont'ev**. Vygotsky headed the psychological laboratory, Luria heading the faculty itself. In 1930, the Ukrainian Psychoneurological Academy was founded at Kharkov, with Vygotsky, Luria and Leont'ev invited to join. Vygotsky visited frequently, but did not relocate from Moscow; indeed, he began to expand his relationships with the Institute in Leningrad. But around 1931 at least Vygotsky was very close to Luria and gave him every encouragement in his most ambitious project so far; the testing out of their joint theoretical hypotheses on the lately collectivized peasants of Uzbekistan, in Soviet Central Asia (1931–2). Vygotsky enthusiastically concurred with Luria in treating the Uzbekis as perfect subjects for their claim that people of different cultures have different forms of higher mental process.

Given that some 14 million people were killed in the course of the collectivization of Soviet agriculture, the scientific exploitation of the Uzbekis' experience seems, to put it mildly, inappropriate, at least with hindsight. A semi-nomadic, Islamic culture was being violently transformed into a clone of the Communist– Russian culture of the agricultural worker. This disgraceful episode in fact seems more consistent with the general approach of Luria (someone who could design lie-detection apparatus for use on fellow students) than that of the less opportunistic Vygotsky. Vygotsky remained at a distance from the research, although he had spent some time (in 1929) in Tashkent, near Kazakhstan's border with Uzbekistan. Vygotsky welcomed Luria's findings, which seemed to indicate that whereas some mental processes (such as susceptibility to the **Müller**–Lyer illusion) were identical in a range of adult Uzbekis – and hence 'natural' or physiological – it was only in the well-educated (Sovietized) Uzbekis that certain culturally mediated processes could be detected. Crudely put, only those Uzbekis who had received the benefit of a Soviet education showed signs of the higher mental processes typical of the Russian; and even these fortunate persons retained traces of the lower or primitive thinking characteristic of their uneducated brothers (their sisters, meanwhile, were being forcibly 'enlightened' by the ripping off of Islamic veils). It is sad that Vygotsky's only empirical test of his cultural theory should have constituted such a stark monument to ethnocentrism. Paradoxically, Luria suffered more than Vygotsky as a consequence of this research project; 'traces of primitive thinking' in the Uzbekis was a politically unacceptable diagnosis of these new citizens. Vygotsky himself appears to have escaped censure on this matter.

Political pressure was, however, building up around Soviet psychology. During the early 1930s ideological positions were focused on the issue of 'pedology'. Vygotsky was at this time attempting to establish pedology as a distinct developmental discipline, which would serve to underpin educational and teaching practice. At conferences in the early 1930s, the inter-disciplinary discussions around psychology and education were increasingly dominated by the demands of socialist correctness. Vygotsky and Luria were criticized in print on ideological grounds, although as yet in ways that encouraged accommodation rather than condemnation. The Stalinist regime was fearful of internationalism other than of the Communist variety, and was enforcing a Russian nationalism which identified any reference to European science as suspect. Such reference was always a strong point in Vygotsky's intellectual approach. It is not clear whether Vygotsky ever had to make a public defence of his work; certainly, some of his close colleagues made public retractions of their 'mistaken' views.

In the last two or three years of his life, Vygotsky focused his attention on articulating a theory of children's development. His intention was to bring together the cultural-historical approach, the desirable residue of the reactology of his earlier work, and the demands of socialism. He cannot be said to have achieved this goal, but an idea that emerged from these late efforts has proved immensely (and diversely) productive: the notion of the zone of proximal development. Vygotsky applied the notion in diverse ways himself, from a closed, quasi-psychometric measurement device to a quasi-mystical affirmation of an individual's potential in a social world. Like so much of Vygotsky's work, the notion of the zone can be unpacked in a myriad of ways. Vygotsky, however, in 1934, suffered a bout of chronic tuberculosis, was hospitalized and died.

Vygotsky was not, in his lifetime, considered by Soviet psychology as more than a very bright young thinker. Moreover, his associations with pedology – interpreted as bourgeois mental testing – led to the posthumous suppression of his work. The theoretical position of Leont'ev was to gain prominence instead, with its politically correct emphasis on physical activity rather than the 'idealistic' culture–meaning–thinking complex favoured by Vygotsky. It was therefore necessary for Vygotsky to be (re)discovered in the East as well as in the West. In the English-speaking world, Vygotsky's significance was urged by Michael Cole and his colleagues from the 1960s onwards. Jerome **Bruner** incorporated Vygotsky's claims into his cultural version of a naturalistic developmental theory; Rom **Harré** and John Shotter read Vygotsky, persuasively, as a founder of the social construction movement in psychology. Younger scholars such as James Wertsch and Jaan Valsiner, both immensely well informed about Vygotsky's claims and achievements, discerned limitations as well as great strengths in the corpus. The developmental psychology of the late 1990s – typified perhaps by the work of Valsiner and of Barbara Rogoff – is post-Vygotskian in a virtuous sense. It could not have happened without the intense, caring and deeply humanist effort of that modest lawyer-turned-psychologist from Gomel. It is perhaps idle to speculate what Vygotsky might have achieved if he had lived as long as **Piaget** (for example) or to celebrate his own centenary in 1996. He would surely have had constructive criticisms to make of neuroscience and of social construction, of psychobiology and of 'the theory of mind', and he would surely have offered his critique with a smile.

JOHN MORSS

W

Wallach, Hans

Born: 1904, Berlin, Germany **Nat:** German
Ints: Experimental **Educ:** PhD University of
Berlin, 1935 **Appts & Awards:** Emeritus Professor of Psychology, Research Psychologist,
Swarthmore College; Guggenheim Fellow;
Institute for Advanced Study, Princeton,
1954–5; APA Distinguished Scientific Contribution Award

Principal publications

1940 The role of head movements and vestibular
and visual cues in sound localization. *Journal of
Experimental Psychology*, 27, 339–68.

1948 Brightness constancy and the nature of
achromatic colors. *Journal of Experimental
Psychology*, 38, 310–24.

1949 The precedence effect in sound localization.
American Journal of Psychology, 62, 315–36
(with E.B. Newman and M.R. Rosenzweig).

1953 The kinetic depth effect. *Journal of
Experimental Psychology*, 45, 205–17 (with D.N.
O'Conell).

1955 On memory modalities. *American Journal of
Psychology*, 68, 249–57 (with E. Averbach).

1963 Modification of stereoscopic depth perception.
American Journal of Psychology, 76, 191–204
(with M.E. Moore and L. Davidson).

1963 The constancy of stereoscopic depth.
American Journal of Psychology, 76, 404–12
(with Z.C. Zuckerman).

1972 The nature of adaptation in distance perception
based on oculomotor cues. *Perception and
Psychophysics*, 11, 110–16 (with K.J. Frey and
K.A. Bode).

1975 *On Perception*. Times Books.

1977 Two kinds of adaptation in the constancy of
visual direction and their different effects on the
perception of shape and visual direction.
Perception and Psychophysics, 21, 227–42 (with
J. Bacon).

1985 Learned stimulation in space and motion.
American Psychologist, 40, 399–404.

Further reading

Kaufman, L. (1979) *Perception*. Oxford University
Press.

Murch, G.M. (1973) *Visual and Auditory Perception*.
Bobbs-Merrill.

Except for a brief period during which Wallach
worked on memory, when he published an
article with Averbach in which they first
demonstrated what is now called 'coding', his
research has been in perception. His early work
was on sound localization, and he demonstrated
how sound is localized using information derived from binaural difference. He also
discovered the precedence effect, which underlies stereophonic reproduction. Research on
lightness constancy followed, and he showed
that it is largely the result of the manner in
which achromatic colours are produced. He also
conducted investigation of the kinetic depth
effect and Benussi's stereokinetic effect.

In 1958 he started a programme of work on
perceptual learning. He altered stereoscopic
depth perception by adaptation, and demonstrated adaptation in distance perception based
on oculomotor cues. (These studies are reprinted
in Chapter 10 of *On Perception* (1975).) Some
years were spent on measuring the processes
that compensate for stimulation caused by the
relative motions that result from one's own head
movements and one's locomotion. Wallach's
major papers published on this topic before 1975
are reprinted in Chapter 11 of *On Perception*.

His later research was concerned with the
multiple stimuli that mediate motion perception
and stereoscopic depth perception. With Joshua
Bacon he found ways to alter by adaptation the
perceived motions that two of these stimuli,
ocular pursuit and configurational change,
produce. This work is summarized in 'Learned
stimulation in space and motion' (1985).
Wallach has also published important work in
other areas of perception such as size, shape and
stereoscopic depth constancy.

Wapner, Seymour

Born: 1917, Brooklyn, New York, USA **Nat:**
American **Ints:** Adult development and ageing,
developmental, experimental, population and

environmental, Society for the Psychological Study of Social Issues *Educ:* AB University College, New York University, 1939; AM University of Michigan, 1940; PhD University of Michigan, 1943 *Appts & awards:* G. Stanley Hall Professor of Genetic Psychology; Chair, Department of Psychology, Clark University; Member, NIMH Review Panel, 1960–3, 1963–7, 1967–9; Member, APA Education and Training Board, 1964–6; Board of Directors, EPA, Member, 1968–70, 1971–4, 1984–8, President, 1979–80; Member, NEPA Steering Committee, 1969–81; Member, US National Committee for Man and the Biosphere, Directorate 13, 1975– ; President, NEPA, 1979–80; Executive Board, Council of Graduate Departments of Psychology, 1981–4; Foreign Research Fellow, International Association of Traffic Safety Sciences, 1982; Editorial Board, *Journal of Environmental Psychology*, 1981–

Principal publications

1944 *The Differential Effects of Cortical Injury and Retesting on Equivalence Reactions in the Rat.* Psychological Monograph.

1949 Sensory-tonic field theory of perception. *Journal of Personality*, 18, 88–107.

1952 Toward a general theory of perception. *Psychological Review*, 59, 324–38 (with H. Werner).

1957 *Perceptual Development.* Clark University Press.

1965 *The Body Precept.* Random House (ed. with H. Werner).

1966 *Experiencing the Environment.* Plenum (ed. with S.B. Cohen and B. Kaplan).

1969 Organismic-developmental theory: Some applications and cognition. In Langer, Mussen and Covington (eds), *Trends and Issues in Developmental Psychology*. Holt, Rinehart & Winston.

1969 Sensory-tonic theory: Toward a reformulation. *Archivio di Psicologia Neurologia e Psichiatria*, 30, 493–512 (with L. Cirillo and A.H. Baker).

1971 Some aspects of the development of space perception. In J.P. Hill (ed.), *Minnesota Symposium on Child Psychology*. University of Minnesota Press (with L. Cirillo and A.H. Baker).

1983 (ed.) *Towards a Holistic Developmental Psychology*. Erlbaum (with B. Kaplan).

1983 Critical transitions through the life cycle. In S. Wapner and B. Kaplan (eds), *Toward a Holistic Developmental Psychology*. Erlbaum (with R. Ciottone, G. Hornstein, O. McNeil and A.M. Pacheco).

1986 A holistic, developmental, systems-oriented

environmental psychology: Some beginnings. In D. Stokols and I. Altman (eds), *Handbook of Environmental Psychology*. Wiley.

1988 Unifying psychology: Strategies from a holistic, developmental, systems theory. *Hiroshima Forum for Psychology*, 13, 1–15.

1991 (ed.) *Field Dependence–Independence: Cognitive Style Across the Life Span*. Erlbaum (with J. Demick).

1993 Parental development: A holistic, developmental systems-oriented perspective. In J. Demick, K. Bursik and R. DiBiase (eds), *Parental Development*. Erlbaum.

1995 Toward integration: Environmental psychology in relation to other subfields of psychology. *Environment and Behavior*, 27, 9–32.

Further reading

Wapner, S. (1990) One person in his environments. *Human Behavior and Environment Advances in Theory and Research*, 11, 257–90.

—— and Craig-Bray, L. (1992) Person-in-environment transitions: Theoretical and methodological approaches. Special issue: Transitions. *Environment and Behavior*, 24, 161–88.

The work of Seymour Wapner shows a steady movement from the biological to the socio-cultural level of organization. His earliest research was restricted to the laboratory and dealt with the effect of various physiological conditions on behaviour. This was followed by work on individual differences in space orientation, cognitive style and perception–personality relations (with H.A. **Witkin**) and long-term research on perception, cognition, affect and development, co-ordinated in terms of the sensory-tonic field theory and the organismic-developmental theory (with H. **Werner** and others at Clark University). Later he turned to the field of environmental psychology. He moved from the study of perception of isolated objects to the study of experience of and orientation in the complex macro-environment with its physical, social and cultural objects. Together with colleagues at Clark University and in Japan and Puerto Rico, he pursued this goal utilizing an organismic-developmental systems approach. This perspective is central to his research and allowed him to focus on the paradigmatic situation of critical person-in-environment transitions through the life-cycle. This involved examining changes to the person (e.g. transition to retirement), to the environment (e.g. earthquake) and to the person-environment (e.g. adolescent migration to a new country). Related research considered the development of relationships among experience, planning and action, and cross-cultural studies on values and on commitment and compliance toward carrying out actions which vary in immediacy of impact on the person-in-environmental system.

Underpinning all of his work are a number of assumptions and values, including: (1) belief that both the 'natural science' and the 'human science' perspectives can be employed profitably – the former especially when the problem focuses on the biological level of organization and the latter when the focus is on the sociocultural level; (2) belief that the person-in-environment is the most appropriate unit of analysis; (3) belief that both causal and teleological analyses are necessary because the different questions they address contribute towards fuller understanding; (4) adherence to the value that inquiry and praxis are interrelated goals; (5) belief that basic research can be done appropriately on problems which immediately touch on human needs, and conviction that good science includes precise analysis of limited problems in the laboratory; (6) rejection of reductionism, and belief that there is need for study and analysis of relations among levels of organization. Real progress, he argues, will only be made in psychology when it moves towards holistic, developmental, systems-oriented analyses.

Warr, Peter Bryan

Born: 1937, Birkenhead, England **Nat:** British **Ints:** Individual and organizational, community, health, personality and social, psychological study of social issues **Educ:** BA Cambridge University, 1960; MA Cambridge University, 1963; PhD University of Sheffield, 1963 **Appts & awards:** Fellow, BPS; BPS Spearman Medal, 1969; Manpower Services Commission, Training Research Advisory Committee, 1973–80; Director, Institute of Work Psychology, University of Sheffield; 1973– ; Ministry of Defence, Flying Personnel Research Committee, 1975–80; BPS President's Award, 1982; ESRC, Industry and Employment Committee, 1984; MRC, Neurosciences and Mental Health Board, 1984– ; Editor, *Journal of Occupation Psychology*, Organizational and Occupational Psychology series (Academic Press); Associate Editor, *British Journal of Social and Clinical Psychology*, 1969–78, *British Journal of Pychology*, 1970–9, *Journal of Occupational Psychology*, 1972–9; Editorial Board, *Leadership and Organisation Development*, 1979– ,

Industrial Relations Journal, 1970–85, Modern Psychology series (Penguin), 1968–73; *Encyclopedic Dictionary of Psychology* (Blackwell), 1980–3, *British Journal of Social Psychology*, 1980– , *Current Psychological Research and Reviews*, 1980–

Principal publications

1968   *The Perception of People and Events*. Wiley (with C.K. Knapper).
1970   *Thought and Personality*. Penguin.
1971   *Psychology at Work*. Penguin (2nd edn, 1978; 3rd edn, 1986; 4th edn, in press).
1973   Towards a more human psychology. *Bulletin of the BPS*, 26, 1–8.
1977   Retraining and other factors associated with job finding after redundancy. *Journal of Occupational Psychology*, 50, 67–84 (with D.J. Lovatt).
1981   *The Experience of Work*. Academic Press (with J.D. Cook, S. Hepworth and T.D. Wall).
1982   Paid employment and women's psychological well-being. *Psychological Bulletin*, 91, 498–515 (with G. Parry).
1983   On the independence of positive and negative affect. *Journal of Personality and Social Psychology*, 44, 644–51.
1984   Job loss, unemployment and psychological well-being. In V. Allen and E. van de Vliert (eds), *Role Transitions*. Plenum.
1984   Unemployment and psychological ill-health: The moderating role of duration and age. *Psychological Medicine*, 14, 605–14 (with P.R. Jackson).
1985   The experience of unemployment among black and white urban teenagers. *British Journal of Psychology*, 76, 75–87 (with M.H. Banks and P. Ullah).
1987   *Work, Unemployment and Mental Health*. Oxford University Press.
1993   *Training for Managers*. Institute of Management.
1994   *The Corporate Culture Questionnaire: Manual and User's Guide*. Saville & Holdsworth.
1995   Age differences in three components of employee well-being. *Applied Psychology: An International Review*, 44, 345–73 (with K. Birdi and A. Oswald).

Further reading

Dick, N. and Shepherd, G. (1994) Work and mental health: A preliminary test of Warr's model in sheltered workshops for the mentally ill. *Journal of Mental Health*, 3, 387–400.
Sevastos, P., Smith, L. and Cordery, J.L. (1992) Evidence on the reliability and construct validity of

Warr's (1990) well-being and mental health measures. *Journal of Occupational and Organizational Psychology*, 65, 33–49.

Peter Warr's contributions relate to organizational and occupational psychology generally and to the psychology of work in particular. They can be organized around three themes: psychological well-being, age and employment, and psychometrics. Warr has developed and applied a broad-ranging model of environmental determinants of mental health. He argues that mental health in these settings is determined by the same environmental characteristics. The harmful features of some jobs are also those which cause deterioration in unemployment, and the factors which are beneficial in jobs can also enhance mental health during unemployment. In both large- and small-sample studies he has shown significant decrements for people of all ages as a result of unemployment, and for middle-aged men additional effects of continuing joblessness. Research into factors mediating the harmful impact of unemployment has covered the amount of time since job loss, employment commitment, social relationships, gender, ethnic group membership, social class, local unemployment rate and personal vulnerability.

In his analysis of psychological well-being and work Warr has developed a conceptual framework within which the key features that influence mental health in both jobs and unemployment can be considered. The framework is structured around three axes of affective well-being, and particular significance is attached to environmental features (including opportunity for control, physical security and valued social position). Warr suggests that the impact of these features on mental health is analogous to the influence of vitamins on physical health, with an explicit non-linearity in the relationship. This vitamin model is extended to permit examination of the way in which individual differences can moderate environmental features.

In his investigations of age and occupational well-being, Warr has demonstrated the presence of a U-shaped relationship, as – middle-aged workers report lower well-being than do both younger and older people. For example, he has examined the relationship between employee age and occupational well-being within nine countries. A U-shaped pattern was found for job satisfaction and was inverted for job stress; however, job boredom merely declined linearly with increasing age. He showed that the positive association between age and job satisfaction can

be explained by differences in job and personal factors, as can the curvilinear association between age and job stress.

Finally, Warr has developed a number of psychometric instruments which have been used in a large number of studies throughout the world. These include the Job Aspiration Questionnaire, the Job Competence Questionnaire and the Corporate Culture Questionnaire.

Warrington, Elizabeth Kerr

Born: Elizabeth Kerr Butler *Nat:* British *Ints:* Experimental psychology, neuropsychology *Educ:* BSc University College London, 1954; PhD University of London, 1960; DSc University of London, 1975 *Appts & awards:* National Hospital for Neurology and Neurosurgery, London, 1956– ; Professor of Clinical Neuropsychology, 1982–96; Fellow, Royal Society, 1986

Principal publications

1962 The completion of visual forms across hemianopic field defects. *Journal of Neurology, Neurosurgery and Psychiatry*, 25, 208–17.

1967 Disorders of visual perception in patients with localised cerebral lesions. *Neuropsychologia*, 5, 253–66 (with M. James).

1968 New method of testing long-term retention with special reference to amnesic patients. *Nature*, 277, 972–4 (with L. Weiskrantz).

1969 The selective impairment of auditory verbal short-term memory. *Brain*, 92, 885–96 (with T. Shallice).

1970 Amnesia and the distinction between long- and short-term memory. *Journal of Verbal Learning and Verbal Behavior*, 9, 176–89 (with A.D. Baddeley).

1970 Amnesia: Consolidation or retrieval? *Nature*, 288, 628–30 (with L. Weiskrantz).

1972 Neuropsychological evidence of visual storage in short-term memory tasks. *Quarterly Journal of Experimental Psychology*, 24, 30–40 (with T. Shallice).

1973 Contribution of the right parietal lobe to object recognition. *Cortex*, 9, 152–64 (with A.M. Taylor).

1974 The effect of prior learning on subsequent retention in amnesic patients. *Neuropsychologia*, 12, 419–28 (with L. Weiskrantz).

1975 The selective impairment of semantic memory. *Quarterly Journal of Experimental Psychology*, 27, 635–57.

1978 Two categorical stages of object recognition. *Perception*, 7, 695–705 (with A.M. Taylor).

1979   Semantic access dyslexia. *Brain*, 102, 43–63 (with T. Shallice).

1980   Word form dyslexia. *Brain*, 103, 99–112 (with T. Shallice).

1982   Amnesia: A disconnection syndrome. *Neuropsychologia*, 20, 233–49 (with L. Weiskrantz).

1983   Category access dysphasia. *Brain*, 106, 859–7 (with R.A. McCarthy).

1984   Category specific semantic impairments. *Brain*, 107, 829–53 (with T. Shallice).

1985   Agnosia: The impairment of object recognition. In J.A.M. Frederiks (ed.), *Handbook of Clinical Neurology*, vol. 1: *Clinical Neuropsychology*. Elsevier.

1985   Visual deficits associated with occipital lobe lesions in man. In C. Chagas, R. Gattass and C.G. Gross (eds), *Pattern Recognition Mechanisms*. Springer-Verlag.

1987   The dissociation of visuo-spatial neglect and neglect dyslexia. *Journal of Neurology, Neurosurgery and Psychiatry*, 50, 1110–16 (with A. De Lacy Costello).

1988   Visual apperceptive agnosia: A clinico-anatomical study of three cases. *Cortex*, 24, 13–32 (with M. James).

1990   *Cognitive Neuropsychology*. Academic Press (with R.A. McCarthy).

1991   Failure of object recognition due to a breakdown of figure–ground discrimination in a patient with normal acuity. *Neuropsychologia*, 29, 969–80 (with L.D. Kartsounis).

Further reading

Grüsser, O.J. and Landis, T. (1991) *Vision and Visual Dysfunction*, vol. 12: *Visual Agnosias and Other Disturbances of Visual Perception and Cognition*. Macmillan.

Shallice, T. (1988) *From Neuropsychology to Mental Structure*. Cambridge University Press.

When Elizabeth Warrington joined the National Hospital in 1956, neuropsychology barely existed. Indeed her pioneering work there over the next fifteen to twenty years helped greatly to establish the subject within the UK not only as an emerging scientific discipline but also as an important speciality within clinical psychology, especially in relation to diagnosis and assessment. At that time psychologists had to work hard to gain respect within the neurological clinic, and Warrington found herself having to do battle with powerful figures like Macdonald Critchley at the National. Her doctoral research was on the 'visual completion' effect, in which a hemianopic patient may report seeing the

whole of a geometric form despite its being presented partly to the 'blind' hemifield (sometimes even when only one half is presented, within the good field and abutting the blind hemifield). At this early stage of her career, she collaborated with Oliver **Zangwill**, George Ettlinger and Maria Wyke, and subsequently with Marcel **Kinsbourne**. She published some nineteen papers with Kinsbourne between 1961 and 1966, on a range of topics including finger agnosia, simultanagnosia, alexia, aphasia and disorders of short-term visual memory.

The success of the next phase of Warrington's research career owed much to her collaborations with Lawrence Weiskrantz. Together they made important discoveries of intact memory capacities in severely amnesic patients, and of intact visual capacities in hemianopic patients ('blindsight'). Their series of investigations of what is now called 'implicit memory', though initially greeted with scepticism, heralded the beginning of what is now a major research area. Other discoveries of importance to understanding memory followed, with the description – in collaboration with Tim **Shallice** – of a selective disorder of auditory short-term memory. This work provided unambiguous evidence that the 'route' to long-term memory did not obligatorily pass via a short-term store, as had been generally believed. This work with Shallice can reasonably be said to have inspired the birth of the modern subdiscipline of cognitive neuropsychology. In the years since then, Warrington has published many other important studies, notably on visual recognition disorders, semantic memory disorders, and various forms of acquired dyslexia and dysphasia. Her major collaborator over much of this period has been Rosaleen McCarthy. Like her research on amnesia and short-term memory disorders, this work has been informed by the methods and theories of normal cognitive psychology, but it has in turn fed back data which have enriched those theories in critically important ways. For example, her descriptions of an impairment in recognizing unusual views of everyday objects (following damage to the parietotemporal region of the right hemisphere) strongly influenced the computational modelling of object recognition via the work of David **Marr**. Similarly, it is now generally accepted that theories of knowledge representation have to take into account her discoveries of domain-selective impairments in reading, naming and comprehension.

Elizabeth Warrington has published prolifically over the entire range of human neuropsychology, mainly in quality, peer-reviewed journals, with a recent publication count giving her a total of 184. Following her retirement from her post as Head of Clinical Psychology at Queen Square (where she has spent her whole career), she is now working with the Dementia Research Team that is currently based jointly at St Mary's Hospital and the National Hospital.

A.D. MILNER

Washburn, Margaret Floy

Born: 1871, Harlem, New York City, USA **Died:** 1939, Poughkeepsie, New York, USA **Nat:** American **Ints:** Experimental, general, personality and social, philosophical and theoretical, physiological and comparative **Educ:** BA Vassar College, 1891; MA Vassar College, 1893; PhD Cornell University, 1894 **Appts & awards:** Professor of Psychology, Vassar College, 1908–37; Advisory Editor, *Psychological Review*, 1916–30; Representative of Psychology, Division of Psychology and Anthropology, NRC, 1919–20, 1925–8; President, APA, 1921; Hon. DSc, Wittenberg College, 1927; Chairman, Section 1, Vice-President, AAAS, 1927; Festschrift, *American Journal of Psychology*, 39, dedicated to her 'in recognition of 33 years of distinguished service to psychology', 1927; Member, International Committee, 1929, Society of Experimental Psychologists, 1929; Fellow, National Academy of Sciences (second woman to receive that honour), 1931; President, New York Branch, APA, 1931; Chairman, Society of Experimental Psychologists, 1931; US Delegate, International Congress of Psychology, Copenhagen, 1932; Co-operating Editor, *American Journal of Psychology*, 1903–25, *Psychological Bulletin*, 1909–15; Associate Editor, *Journal of Animal Behavior*, 1911–17, *Journal of Comparative Psychology*, 1921–35; Co-Editor, *American Journal of Psychology*, 1926–39; Advisory Board, *Dictionary of Psychology* (ed. Howard C. Warren), 1934

Principal publications

1894   Some apparatus for cutaneous stimulation. *American Journal of Psychology*, 6, 422–6.

1908   *The Animal Mind: A Textbook of Comparative Psychology*. Macmillan (rev. and enlarged, 1917, 1926, 1936).

1909   The physiological basis of relational processes. *Psychological Bulletin*, 6, 369–78.

1914   The function of incipient motor processes. *Psychological Review*, 21, 376–90.

1916   *Movement and Mental Imagery: Outlines of a Motor Theory of Consciousness*. Houghton Mifflin.

1917   The social psychology of man and the lower animals. *Studies in Psychology: Titchener Commemorative Volume*, 11–17.

1923   A questionary study of certain national differences in emotional traits. *Journal of Comparative Psychology*, 3, 413–30.

1926   Hunger and speed of running as factors in maze learning in mice. *Journal of Comparative Psychology*, 6, 181–7.

1932   Margaret Floy Washburn: Some recollections. In C. Murchison (ed.), *A History of Psychology in Autobiography*, vol. 2. Clark University Press.

1932   Ejective consciousness as a fundamental factor in social psychology. *Psychological Review*, 39, 395–402.

1934   The effect of area on the pleasantness and unpleasantness of colors. *American Journal of Psychology*, 46, 638–40 (with K.C. McLean and A. Dodge).

1938   The comparative efficiency of intensity, perspective and the stereoscopic factor in producing the perception of depth. *American Journal of Psychology*, 51, 151–5 (with C. Wright).

Further reading

Woodworth, R.S. (1948) Margaret Floy Washburn. *Biographical Memoirs of the National Academy of Sciences*, 25, 275–95.

Margaret Washburn was one of the most prominent figures in the early days of American psychology and a lifetime proponent of equality of educational opportunity for women. An early interest in philosophy was reflected in her translation of **Wundt**'s *Ethical Systems* in 1897, and it was only in 1908 that the title of her appointment at Vassar was changed to Professor of Psychology. Her two books cover her main areas of interest in psychology: animal behaviour and sensation and perception. *The Animal Mind* (1908) was the first comprehensive survey of experimental work in comparative psychology, and subsequent revised editions in 1917, 1926 and 1936 charted the changing emphases from a review of the anecdotal method to a discussion of the behaviourist position and the incentive and drive. *Movement and Mental Imagery* (1916) marked her break with **Titchener**'s structuralist approach and the formulation of her motor theory of consciousness. This was an attempt to integrate the introspective method with an understanding of motor processes, and put forward the idea that thinking involved tentative or incipient movements. Consciousness, Washburn maintained, 'accompanies a certain ratio of excitation to inhibition in a motor discharge, and if the amount of excitation either sinks below a certain minimum or raises above a certain maximum consciousness is lessened'.

Margaret Washburn remained at Vassar for thirty-six years, and among nearly two hundred articles published was the remarkable series of sixty-six 'Minor Studies from the Psychological Laboratory of Vassar College', published in the *American Journal of Psychology* between 1905 and 1938. In 1927 she was awarded the singular honour of having a commemorative volume of this journal dedicated to her.

CLARE FULLERTON

Watson, John Broadus

Born: 1878, Greenville, South Carolina, USA
Died: 1958, Woodbury, Connecticut, USA
Nat: American *Ints:* Consumer psychology, experimental psychology, physiological and comparative psychology, psychotherapy *Educ:* MA Furman College, 1900; PhD University of Chicago, 1903 *Appts & awards:* University of Chicago, Assistant in Psychology, 1903–4, Instructor, 1904–8; Professor of Experimental and Comparative Psychology, Johns Hopkins University, 1908–20; President, APA, 1915; Staff Member and Vice-President, J.Walter Thompson Company, 1921–36; Vice-President, William Esty and Company, 1936–46; Fellow, American Academy of Arts and Sciences

Principal publications

1903 *Animal Education: An Experimental Study on the Psychical Development of the White Rat.* University of Chicago Press.
1907 Kinaesthetic and organic sensations: Their role in the reactions of the white rat to the maze. *Psychological Monographs*, 8, no. 33.
1908 The behavior of noddy and sooty terns. *Carnegie Publications*, 103, 187–255.
1908 Orientation of the white rat. *Journal of Comparative Neurology and Psychology*, 18, 27–44.
1913 Psychology as the behaviorist sees it. *Psychological Review*, 20, 158–77.
1914 *Behavior: An Introduction to Comparative Psychology.* Holt.
1919 *Psychology from the Standpoint of a Behaviorist.* Lippincott.
1920 Conditioned emotional reactions. *Journal of Experimental Psychology*, 3, 1–14 (with R. Rayner).

1924 *Behaviorism.* Norton.
1928 *The Psychological Care of Infant and Child.* Norton (with R.R. Watson).

Further reading

Boakes, R.A. (1984) *From Darwin to Behaviorism: Psychology and the Minds of Animals.* Cambridge University Press.
Cohen, D. (1979) *J.B. Watson: The Founder of Behaviourism.* Routledge & Kegan Paul.
O'Donnell, J.M. (1985) *The Origins of Behaviorism: American Psychology, 1870–1920.* New York University Press.
Samelson, F. (1981) Struggle for scientific authority: The reception of Watson's behaviorism. *Journal of the History of the Behavioral Sciences*, 17, 399–425.

Watson described himself as a rough and unruly child and a lazy student, who preferred carpentry, cobbling shoes and milking cows. Even when he entered Furman University at the age of 16 he found little to interest him, and if he passed his exams it was because of last-minute swotting or the kindness of the examiners. After Furman he taught for a time at a rural school, where he entertained his pupils with trained rats. He discovered an interest in philosophy and psychology, and went to Chicago to take a PhD in these subjects. He had gone there intending to study philosophy with John **Dewey**, but he found himself more interested in Jacques Loeb, the mechanistic biologist famous for his work on tropisms, and in the psychology laboratory.

At that time the Chicago psychology department was the only one in the States with a rat colony. This was supervised by Henry Donaldson, who gave Watson a part-time job as an animal technician. Eventually he carried out his research on the rats, supervised by Donaldson and James Angell. Angell had studied with William **James**, and together with James and Dewey was one of the founders of functionalism, which viewed the mind as a result of evolution and a function of the environment, rather than as an independent entity to be studied only in controlled isolation. This was a move away from traditional mind–body dualism, and already in 1904 William James had asked 'Does consciousness exist?' and answered 'No', a rejection echoed in the work of his students, R.B. Perry and E.B. Holt. In the same year, James McK. **Cattell** gave a speech in St Louis (attended by Watson) calling for an objective psychology. To complement these theoretical developments, Loeb's work showed how behaviour can in principle be studied without postulating mental processes, and this had been continued by his student H.S. Jennings, later Watson's colleague at Johns Hopkins. Watson was also friendly with G.H. **Mead**, another critic of dualism, and they spent hours together watching his rats. Presumably they discussed them, but as with Dewey, Watson claimed not to understand Mead. Nevertheless it must have been obvious to anyone in Chicago that the traditional dualist view of consciousness was in a state of crisis.

After obtaining his PhD Watson stayed on at Chicago, building up the laboratory and continuing his own research on sensory cues used by rats in maze learning. In 1905 he went to Johns Hopkins University in Baltimore to learn surgical techniques, and returned to study the effects of removing the peripheral sense organs on the rat's maze learning. He found little effect, and after the famous 'kerplunk' experiment with Harvey Carr, in which well-trained rats ran into the ends of maze arms when they were shortened, he felt confident that the basis of maze learning is kinaesthetic feedback, rather than guidance from external stimuli. He also set up a primate laboratory to study visual discrimination, and he and Robert **Yerkes**, who was at Harvard, prepared a report on methods of studying visual discrimination. In 1907 he began the first of his visits to study noddy and sooty terns on the Dry Tortugas islands. He was an acute and painstaking observer, and carried out pioneering work on their behaviour, especially on their sense of orientation. In 1908, James **Baldwin**, whom he had impressed during his visit to Johns Hopkins, invited him there as Professor of Psychology to start up a comparative psychology laboratory. Within a year of Watson's arrival Baldwin was asked to resign following a scandal, and he arranged to hand over to Watson not only chairmanship of the department, but also editorship of several journals, including the already influential *Psychological Review*. So at the age of 31 he became a power in the land of psychology, with sufficient control over the relevant media to bring about a revolution.

He had around him an impressive group of close colleagues, all at odds with the reigning dogma of introspectionism, and moving towards biological approaches to psychology. They included Jennings in the biology department, who in 1911 recruited Karl **Lashley**; Knight Dunlap, who had been in the psychology department since 1906 and had argued consistently for a practical psychology based on action rather than introspection; and Adolf Meyer, the founder and director of the Phipps Clinic in Baltimore, who believed that mental illness is the result of faulty habits, and who looked for environmental rather than genetic causes – his attempt to classify according to 'reaction types' was an influential outcome of these views. For all these men there was a conflict between what they tried to do and a psychology which paid lip-service to introspection as the primary source of data.

The conflict was especially acute for animal psychology. As long as the essence of psychology was to study the workings of the mind directly through introspection, animal psychology could only take second place to human experimental psychology. Its practical implications were uncertain, and Watson had not found it easy to defend himself against charges of useless cruelty in ablating sense organs in his maze experiments. However impressive the work of Yerkes, Watson, Carr, Lashley and others, how could they get money and students if animal psychology was regarded as peripheral, and unsuitable training for anyone contemplating a career in the subject? Watson himself found this low status of animal psychology extremely irksome, and a disadvantage in his efforts to establish psychology at Johns Hopkins. At times both he and Yerkes wondered if they had better call themselves physiologists. Watson's genius was to push ahead with an alternative strategy, to redefine psychology so that the animal work was given a central place and the practical implications were clear. So it was that Watson came to publish 'Psychology as the behaviorist sees it', and to define psychology as the 'control and prediction of behavior'. This 1913 paper was a fine revolutionary manifesto. It is well written, shamelessly selective in its use of historical context, brutally simple and uncompromising in its dismissal of opponents (notably **Titchener**'s introspectionism), and carried a clear and prescient programme for the future.

It did not radically change the thinking of sympathetic psychologists like Lashley, Yerkes, Mead, Dunlap and Holt, but behaviourism became a rallying point for them, and after 1913 psychologists all over the country gradually started to define themselves by their support or opposition to it. None was more influenced than Watson himself, who was now committed to consolidating the revolution. He drew on his earlier belief in the importance of kinaesthesis in his theory of subvocal responses to explain the undeniable fact that human beings can think to themselves silently. In his presidential address to the APA in 1915 he welcomed **Pavlov**'s work on conditioned reflexes as an experimental foundation for behaviourism. He wrote sympathetically on **Freud**, whose work had thoroughly undermined reliance on subjective reports; he even detected in Freud a behavioural definition of unconscious processes as the 'unverbalized'. At the same time he looked for behaviourist alternatives to psychoanalysis. The much-publicized conditioned phobia of Little Albert has often been cited as a starting point of behaviour therapy, even though the 'phobia' seems in fact to have been short-lasting, and no attempt was made to remove Little Albert's fear. The later work with Mary Cover Jones, starting in 1923 and described in *Behaviorism* (1924), was the real beginning of behaviour therapy.

In 1920 Watson was forced to resign from Johns Hopkins following the publicity given to some letters written to his lover and co-worker, Rosalie Rayner. The sensational details of the divorce that followed made another university post unlikely, and Watson began a successful career in advertising. He continued to publish in psychology journals for a few years, and his book *Behaviorism* was based on lectures given at the New School for Social Research in New York. This was when Watson's science of behaviour without mind became psychology's most famous 'ism', and his extreme claims on behalf of nurture rather than nature achieved wide publicity (his celebrated guarantee to 'take anyone at random and train him to become any type of specialist I might select' comes from the 1924 book). He and Rayner published their influential book on child rearing in 1928, which circulated widely amongst parents eager for scientific guidance. Behaviourism was fiercely debated in the press, and it became a long-lasting source of challenge and argument in all the human sciences. But after the 1920s Watson was busy with his new career and played little part in the fate of his brainchild.

To understand the full impact of Watson's behaviourism, it is necessary to recognize its several aspects: (1) observation of behaviour, replacing introspection; (2) 'prediction and control' rather than theoretical understanding; (3) avoidance of mentalistic terms; and (4) an atomistic, stimulus–response view of behaviour. The last of these was traditional and had already been effectively criticized in a well-known paper by Dewey on the reflex arc nearly twenty years earlier. It was the behaviourist equivalent of Titchener's atomistic view of the mind. Just as Titchener refused to accept the findings of the Würzburg psychologists on imageless thought, so Watson did not at first believe in the results of delayed response experiments. In both cases there were inexplicable and unacceptable breaks in the succession of observable events.

Amongst the heirs to the behaviourist tradition, **Tolman** in the 1920s accepted only (1). In the 1930s Clark **Hull** and his many followers accepted (1) and (4); they were atomistic stimulus–response theorists, and developed Watson's notion of implicit responses to bridge the gaps between observable events. **Skinner** made control and behaviour (2) his goal, and acknowledged Watson as his source, while developing his own non-atomistic version of behaviourism. Modern cognitive psychology often prides itself at having rejected behaviourism, but this is as unhistorical a view as Watson's own. In most cases the atomism remains, with the gaps now bridged by theoretical entities grounded in the 'effective procedures' of computer science. These entities are given traditional mentalistic labels like memory and attention, but experiments are designed around observable inputs and outputs, and there has been no lasting reversal of Watson's ban on introspective reports as the primary source of data.

ARTHUR STILL

Watson, Robert I.

Born: 1909, New Jersey, USA **Died:** 1980, Florida, USA **Nat:** American **Ints:** Developmental psychology, history of psychology, personality and social psychology **Educ:** BA Dana College, 1934; PhD Columbia University, 1938 **Appts & awards:** Professor of Psychology and Director of the Clinical Programme, Northwestern University, 1953–67; Professor and Director of the History of Psychology Programme, University of New Hampshire, 1967–75; Adjunct Professor, University of Florida, 1975–80

Principal publications

1951 *The Clinical Method in Psychology*. Harper.
1960 The history of psychology: A neglected area. *American Psychologist*, 15, 251–5.
1963 *The Great Psychologists: From Aristotle to Freud*. Lippincott (4th edn, 1979).
1967 Psychology: A prescriptive science. *American Psychologist*, 22, 435–43.

1971 A prescriptive analysis of Descartes'
psychological views. *Journal of the History of the
Behavioral Sciences*, 7, 223–98.
1975 The history of psychology as a speciality: A
personal view of its first fifteen years. *Journal of
the History of the Behavioral Sciences*, 11, 5–14.
1978 *The History of Psychology and the Behavioral
Sciences: A Bibliographical Guide.* Springer-Verlag.
1979 *Basic Writings in the History of Psychology.*
Oxford University Press.

Further reading

Benjamin, L.T. Jr (ed.) (1988) *A History of
Psychology: Original Sources and Contemporary
Research.* McGraw-Hill.

Robert I. Watson was educated at Dana College
and Columbia. He specialized at first in clinical
psychology, publishing several books on clinical
topics, including *The Clinical Method in Psychology* (1951). He is, however, better known as
one of the founding fathers of the history of
psychology movement. He was Professor and
Director of the History of Psychology programme at the University of New Hampshire
from 1967 to his retirement in 1975 and continued his work as Adjunct Professor at the
University of Florida until his death in 1980. He
was the first editor of the *Journal of the History
of the Behavioral Sciences* (1965–75) and
remained on the editorial board. He also played
a leading role in the establishment of the
Cheiron Society, devoted to the history of the
behavioural and social sciences. He was responsible in large part for the success of both the
Journal and the Society.

Watson was much influenced by the historical
work of E.G. **Boring** (Boring authored the first
paper to appear in the *Journal*) but he also
thought deeply about the role history might
play in psychology. At that time the work of
Thomas Kuhn (e.g. *The Structure of Scientific
Revolutions*, 1962) was a central topic of discussion among historians and philosophers of
science. Kuhn had suggested that sciences pass
through periods of revolution which eventually
resolve into an agreed paradigm, accepted by
everyone working in the area. The paradigm
specifies appropriate questions and appropriate
methods for their solution, and persists until
anomalies accumulate and force another period
of revolution, followed by another agreed paradigm, and so on. Watson concluded that either
psychology did not conform to this model or it
had not yet emerged from an initial period of
revolution and showed no sign of being about to

do so. Since there was no agreed paradigm in
psychology it was not possible to write what
used to be called 'Whig' history, in which
events are portrayed in a regular sequence
progressing towards some agreed goal. What
was required was, in Watson's view, a means of
specifying precisely where any given psychological theorist stood on a number of issues
on which psychologists characteristically disa-
gree. In 1967 he proposed a set of eighteen
opponent-pairs of dimensions, ranging from
'Conscious mentalism–Unconscious mentalism'
to 'Staticism–Dynamicism', in terms of which
he believed it was possible to categorize the
views of any psychologist; thus making possible
a valid comparison between any one of them
and any other. He applied his 'Prescriptive'
analysis to a number of theorists in psychology,
including Descartes.

So far as I know, Watson's prescriptive
analysis has not yet been adopted by any other
historian of psychology, though it seems to
have much to recommend it as a framework
principle. Watson finally devoted himself to
necessary spadework on the sources available to
the historian, and his last publications are
concerned with bibliography and the reprinting
of source materials that would otherwise be
difficult to find for consultation. For this work
future historians of psychology will remain in
his debt.

N.E. WETHERICK

Weber, Ernst Heinrich

Born: 1795, Wittenberg, Germany **Died:** 1878,
Leipzig, Germany **Nat:** German **Ints:** Experi-
mental psychology **Educ:** MD University of
Wittenberg, 1815 **Appts & awards:** Professor,
University of Leipzig, 1818–78

Principal publications

1834 *De pulsu, resorptione, auditu et tactu:
Annotationes anatomicae et physiologicae.* Koehler.
1846 Der Tastsinn und das Gemeingefühl. In R.
Wagner (ed.), *Handworterbuch der Physiologie*,
vol. 3. Vieweg.

Further reading

Watson, R.I. and Evans, R.B. (1991) *The Great
Psychologists: A History of Psychological Thought.*
HarperCollins.

Weber was appointed Dozent at the University
of Leipzig in 1817, the same year Gustav **Fechner** enrolled as a medical student. The following

year Weber was appointed Professor of Anatomy and later Professor of Physiology. His most important contribution to psychology relates to his investigations of the small discriminable difference a person can sense – the just noticeable difference (JND). Working with weights he found that it was not absolute differences in weight that led to discriminations, but the ratio of the JND to the standard weight. For example, on each trial a person lifts two weights, one of which is a standard weight and the other a comparison weight. On subsequent trials the weight of the comparison is increased in small amounts until the person reports a noticeable difference in weight. If the standard weight were 40 ounces it would take a comparison weight of 41 ounces to be discriminated as heavier. If the standard weight were 80 ounces it would take a comparison weight of 82 ounces (not 81) before a JND was reported. The ratio is 1/40. If the standard weight were lower, say 20 ounces, one would predict a comparison weight of 20.5 ounces to be just noticeably different (i.e. 1/40 of 20 ounces). This is in fact what happens. Weber observed constant ratios for other senses too (for judgements of the length of lines and the pitch of tones), except at the extremes. His findings might have gone unnoticed had Fechner not formulated the ratio as: $dR/R = K.dR$ is the just noticeable stimulus increment, K is a constant and R is the standard stimulus magnitude. The ratio is referred to as Weber's law or Weber's fraction. Weber's law works well except at the extremes. It was later developed and refined by Fechner.

Wechsler, David

Born: 1896, Romania *Died:* 1981 *Nat:* American *Ints:* Clinical, developmental, educational, evaluation and measurement, military, school *Educ:* AB City College of New York, 1916; MA Columbia University, 1917; PhD Columbia University, 1925 *Appts & awards:* University of Paris Fellowship, 1920–2; Bureau of Child Guidance (New York City), 1922–4; Acting Secretary, Psychological Corporation, 1925–7; Private practice, 1927–32; Chief Psychologist, Bellevue Psychiatric Hospital and Professor, New York University College of Medicine, 1932–67; APA Clinical Psychology Division Distinguished Contributions to Psychology Award, 1960; APA Division of School Psychology Tribute, 1973; APA Distinguished Professional Contribution Award, 1973; numerous other honours

Principal publications

1935 *The Range of Human Capacities* (updated 1971).
1939 *The Measurement of Adult Intelligence.* Williams & Wilkins.
1949 *Manual for the Wechsler Intelligence Scale for Children.* Psychological Corporation.
1955 *Manual for the Wechsler Adult Intelligence Scale.* Psychological Corporation.
1958 *The Measurement and Appraisal of Adult Intelligence* (4th edn). Williams & Wilkins.

Further reading

Anastasi, A. (1982) *Psychological Testing.* Macmillan.
Matarazzo, T. (1972) *Wechsler's Measurement and Appraisal of Adult Intelligence.* Oxford University Press.

Wechsler was the youngest of seven children. When he was 6 his family emigrated to New York City, where Wechsler later completed his first degree, at a time when clinical psychology as we know it today was not imagined. He worked with R.S. **Woodworth** for his MA (on retention in Korsakoff's psychosis), and while awaiting induction into the army he worked under E.G. **Boring** at an army camp on Long Island, where he administered and scored the Army Alpha, an offshoot of the Stanford–**Binet**. He was assigned to the psychology unit at Fort Logan, Texas, where he was involved in individual assessment. There he became acutely aware of the limitations of conventional group tests of assessment for adults with limited reading and writing skills and for whom English was a second language. He was then assigned to a position in France, and in 1919 studied as an army student at the University of London, where he came under the influence of **Pearson** and **Spearman**. After his discharge from the army he studied at the University of Paris (with Henri Pieron and Louis Lapique) and gathered psychogalvanic response data which he used for his PhD, again under the supervision of Woodworth.

Wechsler is associated with developing and disseminating a set of scientifically credible techniques for clinical practice and research that accommodated a humanistic philosophy in their use – the idea that assessment is different from and better than testing. He made considerable contributions to psychology in two main areas: the development and standardization of tests of intelligence that bear his name, and the introduction of a deviation quotient (as a substitute for Binet's Mental Age) in which an individual's test score was interpreted with respect to his or her age-peer reference group. Wechsler's early experiences of group tests of intelligence (Stanford–Binet and the Army Alpha test) highlighted a fundamental limitation when used with adults of diverse social and cultural backgrounds and low levels of literacy, and he came to regard these tests as unreliable. This stimulated a period of experimentation with a variety of other published tests of adult intelligence, and led to the publication of the Bellevue–Wechsler Scale (1939). Moreover, whereas Spearman (University of London) and **Thorndike** (Columbia University) were conducting their investigations with very large samples of students and 'normal' individuals, Wechsler was working with special groups of individuals considered to be not normal. He was acutely aware that the notion of a 'normal IQ' was a fairly limited indicator of a broad range of important psychological processes (e.g. motivation, personality, emotionality, etc.). He wanted to develop tests that could measure intelligence defined as the capacity of a person to understand the world around him or her, and his or her resourcefulness in meeting its varied and complex challenges. He felt that the ten verbal and performance subtests of the Bellevue-Wechsler were collectively capable of yielding important clinical insights that could be used for differential diagnosis (in clinical neuropsychological investigations) as well as measuring a broad range of complex psychological functioning. Thus, he went on to develop the Army Wechsler (1942), WISC (1949, revised 1981), WAIS (1955, revised 1974) and Wechsler Preschool and Primary Scale of Intelligence (1967), and the WISC and WAIS have been standardized in many countries and still enjoy considerable professional respect. In this respect there are few psychologists whose work has impinged so directly on the lives of so many people.

Weiner, Bernard

Born: 1935, Chicago, USA **Nat:** American **Ints:** Educational, personality and social **Educ:** AB University of Chicago, 1955; PhD University of Michigan, 1958 **Appts & awards:** Professor of Psychology, University of California at Los Angeles; 1965– ; Guggenheim Fellow, 1970–1; Consulting Editor, *Journal of Research in Personality*, 1973–8, *Journal of Educational Psychology*, 1975– , *Journal of Personality and Social Psychology*, 1978–9

Principal publications

1971 Perceiving the causes of success and failure. In E.E. Jones, D. Kanouse, H.H. Kelley, S. Valins and B. Weiner (eds), *Attribution: Perceiving the Causes of Behavior*. General Learning Press (with I. Frieze, A. Kukla, L. Reed, S. Rest and R.M. Rosenbaum). (reprinted, 1972).

1972 *Theories of Motivation*. Rand-McNally.

1974 (ed.) *Achievement Motivation and Attribution Theory*. General Learning Press.

1974 (ed.) *Cognitive Views of Human Motivation*. Academic Press.

1974 Achievement motivation as conceptualized by an attribution theorist. In B. Weiner (ed.), *Achievement Motivation and Attribution Theory*. General Learning Press.

1979 A theory of motivation for some classroom experiences. *Journal of Educational Psychology*, 71, 3–25.

1980 A cognitive (attribution)–emotion–action model of motivated behavior: An analysis of judgements and help-giving. *Journal of Personality and Social Psychology*, 39, 186–200.

1980 *Human Motivation*. Holt.

1982 *Personality*. Heath (with S. Feshbach).

1982 The emotional consequences of causal ascriptions. In M.S. Clark and S.T. Fiske (eds), *17th Annual Carnegie Symposium on Cognition: Affect and Cognition*. Erlbaum.

1986 *An Attributional Theory of Motivation and Emotion*. Springer-Verlag.

1992 *Human Motivation: Metaphors, Theories and Emotion*. Springer-Verlag.

1995 *Judgments of Responsibility: A Foundation for a Theory of Social Conduct*. Guilford Press.

Further reading

Sorrentino, R.M. and Higgins, E.T. (eds) (1986) *Handbook of Motivation and Cognition: Foundation of Social Behaviour*. Guilford.

Bernard Weiner's main concern has been with the development of a theory of motivation in which emotions and cognitions play a major role. His theoretical perspective is that of an attribution theorist, believing that answers to 'why' questions are central to the field of psychology. Hence, he investigates how causal ascriptions relate to both emotion and action and how these may have determined the relationship in the tripartite division in psychology between thinking, feeling and doing. To some extent he succeeded in this goal. For example, it is quite evident that if the reason for a failure is the intentional interference of another, then anger is often evoked and aggressive behaviour tends to follow. Or, as another example, if one fails because of lack of aptitude, then humiliation and shame are elicited and there is behavioural withdrawal. These are the kinds of attribution–affect–action sequence that he has examined from a systematic theoretical position, and his ideas have had considerable influence in understanding work behaviour, health behaviour and education.

Weinert, Franz E.

Born: 1930, Komotau, Germany *Nat:* German *Ints:* Adult development and ageing, developmental psychology, educational psychology, experimental psychology *Educ:* MA Teacher College Bamberg 1953, PhD University of Erlangen 1958 *Appts & awards:* Teacher and Principal, public schools, Germany, 1953–9; Research Assistant, University of Bonn, 1960–7; Professor, Teacher's College, Bamberg, 1967–8; Professor and Director, Psychological Institute, University of Heidelberg, 1968–81; Director, Max Planck Institute for Psychological Research, Munich, 1981–

Principal publications

1964 Experimentelle Untersuchungen über Formen und Bedingungen des kognitiven Lernens bei Kindern (Experimental investigations on forms and conditions of cognitive learning in children). *Archiv der Gesamten Psychologie*, 116, 126–64.

1975 Untersuchungen zur differentialpsychologischen Analyse von Rechenleistungen. (Differential analysis of arithmetic capacities.) *Zeitschrift für Entwicklungspsychologie und Pädagogische Psychologie*, 7, 153–69.

1982 School socialization and cognitive development. In W.W. Hartup (ed.), *Review of Child Development Research*, vol. 6. University of Chicago Press (with B. Treiber).

1983 *Metakognition, Motivation und Lernen.* Kohlhammer (with R.H. Kluwe).

1985 *Gute Schulleistungen für alle? (Good School Performance for All?)* Ashendorff (with B. Treiber).

1988 Individual difference in cognitive development: Does instruction make a difference? In M. Heatherington, R. Lerner and M. Perlmutter (eds), *Child Development in Life-Span Perspective*. Erlbaum (with A. Helmke).

1989 Individual differences in learning performance and in school achievement: Plausible parallels and unexplained discrepancies. In H. Mandl, E. de Corte, N. Bennett and H.F. Friedrich (eds), *Learning and Instruction*. Pergamon (with A. Helmke and W. Schneider).

1990 (with M. Waldmann) *Intelligenz und Denken: Perspektiven der Hochbegabungsforschung.* (*Intelligence and Thinking: Perspective of Research Giftedness*). Verlag für Psychologie.

Further reading

Knopf, M. and Schneider, W. (eds) (1990) *Festschrift für Frank E. Weinert.* Hogrefe.

From the very beginning of his career, Weinert's scientific interests were focused on the anaysis of human learning. This long-lasting commitment stems from his earlier experiences as a school teacher and from a fascination with a variety of learning theories. His scientific work has been concerned with two lines of research, which at the level of daily empirical work are relatively independent of each other, but are connected in their theoretical conception.

One of Weinert's research approaches has concerned experimental studies of learning and memory development across the life-span. These studies aimed to describe universal changes and individual variations in performance at a great variety of learning and memory tasks. Clearly related to this investigation was the development of local reasoning – domain-specific knowledge and the acquisition and use of encoding and retrieval strategies. The conceptualization of metacognitive competencies was the link between this field of study and the research of motivation and action control.

Weinert's second approach has consisted of field studies of the learning process and of academic achievement, with a special focus on mathematics in grades five and six. It has been the primary goal of Weinert's research to develop models capable of predicting and explaining differences in achievement across student and classes. His approach has given emphasis to the individual capabilities of students and the quality of teaching. It has also examined various situational variables, such as parental influence and class composition. It is Weinert's long-term goal to combine the instructional approach in development psychology with the developmental approach in instructional psychology.

FRANK WESLEY

Welford, Alan T.

Born: 1914, London, England *Nat:* British *Ints:* Adult development and ageing, ergonomics, experimental psychology, psychology of religion

Educ: BA Cambridge University, 1935; MA Cambridge University, 1939; MA Princeton University, 1946; ScD Cambridge University, 1964; DSc Adelaide University, 1969 **Appts & awards:** Professor Emeritus of Psychology, University of Adelaide; Fellow, ASSA; Hon. Member, Ergonomics Society, Formerly Chairman of Council; Fellow, BPS, APS, Gerontology Society of America, and Ergonomics Society of Australia and New Zealand (President, 1972–4); Editor, *Ergonomics*, 1956–63; Editorial Boards: *Ergonomics, Journal of Genetic Psychology, Genetic Psychology Monographs, Journal of Motor Behavior, Perceptual and Motor Skills, Perception, Mechanisms of Aging and Development, Aging and Human Development, Journal of Human Movement Studies, Journal of Gerontology, Gerontologia, Vita Humana, Developmental Neuropsychology*

Principal publications

1952　The 'psychological refractory period' and the timing of high speed performance – a review and a theory. *British Journal of Psychology*, 43, 2–19.

1958　*Ageing and Human Skill*. Oxford University Press.

1960　The measurement of sensory-motor performance: Survey and reappraisal of twelve years' progress. *Ergonomics*, 3, 189–230.

1962　On changes of performance with age. *Lancet*, 194, 365–6.

1966　The ergonomic approach to social behavior. *Ergonomics*, 9, 357–69.

1967　Single-channel operation in the brain. *Acta Psychologica*, 27, 5–22.

1968　*Fundamentals of Skill*. Methuen.

1971　*Christianity: A Psychologist's Translations*. Hodder & Stoughton.

1975　Display layout strategy and reaction time: Tests of a model. In P.M.A. Rabbitt and S. Dormie (eds), *Attention and Performance V*. Academic Press.

1976　*Skilled Performance: Perceptual and Motor Skills*. Scott Foresman.

1978　Mental work load as a function of demand, capacity, strategy and skill. *Ergonomics*, 21, 151–67.

1980　*Reaction Times*. Academic Press.

1981　Signal, noise, performance and age. *Human Factors*, 23, 97–109.

1984　Between bodily changes and performances: Some possible reasons for slowing with age. *Experimental Aging Research*, 10, 73–88.

Further reading

Pashler, H. (1992) Attentional limitations in doing two tasks at the same time. *Current Directions in Psychological Science*, 1, 44–8.

Patrick, J. (1992) *Training: Research and Practice*. Academic Press.

Schmidt, R.A. (1991) *Motor Learning and Performance: From Principles to Practice*. Human Kinetics Books.

Having spent the war as Chaplain and Junior Bursar of St John's College, Cambridge, Welford went for the year 1945–6 to Princeton University as a visiting Procter Fellow to rehabilitate his psychology. In 1946 he became Director, under Frederick **Bartlett**, of the Nuffield Unit for Research into Problems of Ageing at the Psychological Laboratory of Cambridge University, and in the following year he became a university lecturer in experimental psychology. The Nuffield Unit had been set the task of examining the potentiality of older people for industrial work, and was a pioneer in the study of performance in relation to age. Its work included laboratory experiments and field studies in industry, all conceived within the skills approach for which the laboratory was then famous. When the Unit was disbanded, he became a Fellow and Tutor of St John's, while continuing to hold the lectureship. The next few years allowed time for the starting of the journal *Ergonomics*, for the writing and editing of several books, and for attempts to extend the concepts of skill to social interaction. A visiting professorship to the University of Adelaide in 1964 was productive, and when invited to return there in 1968 as a Professor of Psychology, he accepted. The time from then until retirement in 1979 was busy with writing and with research on reaction times, especially in relation to age. From 1979, his interest in ageing has continued and broadened to include changes of learning and memory.

Werner, Heinz

Born: 1902, Vienna, Austria *Died:* 1964, Worcester, Massachusetts, USA *Nat:* American *Ints:* Developmental psychology, experimental psychology, psychology and the arts, philosophical and theoretical psychology, physiological and comparative psychology *Educ:* PhD University of Vienna, 1914 *Appts & awards:* Trebitsch Prize, 1913; Clark University, G. Stanley Hall Professor of Genetic Psychology, 1948–60 Chair, Department of Psychology, 1948–60, Chair, Board of Directors, Institute of Human Development, 1960; AAA&S, 1956;

reinstated Ordenlicher Professor Emeritus, University of Heidelberg, 1957; Co-Editor, *Zeitschrift für Psychologie, A History of Psychology in Autobiography*

Principal publications

1919 *Die Ursprunge der Metapher*. Barth.
1926 *Einfuhrung in die Entwicklungspsychologie*. Barth.
1932 *Grundfragen der Sprachphysiognomik*. Barth.
1937 Process and achievement. *Harvard Educational Review*, 7, 353–68.
1942 Disorders of conceptual thinking in the brain-injured child. *Journal of Nervous and Mental Disorders*, 96, 153–72 (with A. Strauss).
1945 Motion and motion perception: A study on vicarious functioning. *Journal of Psychology*, 19, 317–27.
1952 Toward a general theory of perception. *Psychological Review*, 59, 324–38 (with S. Wapner).
1952 *The Acquisition of Word Meanings: A Developmental Study*. Child Development Publications (with E. Kaplan).
1956 Microgenesis and aphasia. *Journal of Abnormal and Social Psychology*, 52, 347–53.
1956 The developmental approach to cognition: Its relevance to the psychological interpretation of anthropological and ethnolinguistic data. *American Anthropologist*, 58, 866–80 (with B. Kaplan).
1957 The concept of development from a comparative and organismic point of view. In D.B. Harris (ed.), *The Concept of Development: An Issue in the Study of Human Behavior*. University of Minnesota Press.
1963 *Symbol Formation: An Organismic-Developmental Approach to Language and the Expression of Thought*. Wiley (with B. Kaplan).
1967 An experimental approach to body perception from the organismic-developmental point of view. In S. Wapner and H. Werner (eds), *The Body Percept*. Random House.

Further reading

Franklin, M.B. (1990) Reshaping psychology at Clark: The Werner era. *Journal of the History of the Behavioral Sciences*, 176–89.
Kaplan, B. (1992) Strife of systems: Tension between organismic and developmental points of view. *Theory and Psychology*, 2, 431–43.

Werner provided a comparative-developmental, organismic approach to the understanding of psychological phenomena in all their variety and complexity. The general developmental principles he described were applicable to all life sciences and his work was truly interdisciplinary, having implications for aesthetics, anthropology, biology, education, linguistics and medicine. Development was empirically investigated in the phenomena of ontogenesis, phylogenesis, neuropathology, psychopathology, microgenesis and the various levels of functioning (consciousness, reverie states, dreams) of the mature individual. His modes of inquiry ranged from highly controlled experimental designs to phenomenological methods. They encompassed structural (part–whole), as well as dynamic (means–ends) analyses, and focused on processes rather than achievement. His comparative developmental orientation was co-ordinated with a holistic orientation into a unitary organismic-developmental framework. Werner carried out creative programmatic research in diverse areas, including: mental retardation (e.g. disorders of conceptual thinking in the brain-injured child, with A.A. Strauss); perceptual experience (e.g. spatial, physiognomic, motion, body, auditory perception and sensory-tonic field theory of perception, with S. Wapner); and language and symbolization (e.g. metaphor, expressive language, microgenesis, aphasia and symbol formation, with B. Kaplan).

SEYMOUR WAPNER

Werry, John Scott
Born: 1931, Christchurch, New Zealand *Nat:* New Zealander *Ints:* Child and family services, teaching, developmental, physiological, adult development and ageing *Educ:* BMedSc University of New Zealand, 1952; MBChB University of New Zealand, 1955; DipPsychiat McGill University, 1962; MD University of Otago, 1975 *Appts & awards:* New Zealand Research Fellow, Canadian Mental Health Association, 1962–5; Professor of Psychiatry, School of Medicine, University of Auckland, 1970– ; Corresponding Fellow, American Psychiatric Association, 1971– ; New Zealand MRC, 1979–85; Royal Australian and New Zealand College of Psychiatrists Organon Research Award, 1980; Chairperson, Standing Committee on Therapeutic Trials, New Zealand MRC, 1984– ; Associate Editor: *Journal of Abnormal Child Psychology, Applied Research in Mental Retardation*; Editorial Boards: *Journal of Child Psychology and Psychiatry, Australian and New Zealand Journal of Psychiatry, American Journal of Ortho-psychiatry, Journal of the American Academy of Child Psychiatry*

Principal publications

1968   Studies on the hyperactive child IV: An empirical analysis of the minimal brain dysfunction syndrome. *Archives of General Psychiatry*, 19, 9–16.

1970   Methylphenidate and thoridazine learning, reaction time and classroom behavior in emotionally disturbed children. *American Orthopsychiatric Association Journal*, 40, 615–28 (with R. Sprague and K. Barnes).

1971   The hyperactive child VIII: Five year follow-up. *Archives of General Psychiatry*, 24, 409–18 (with G. Weiss, K. Minde, V. Douglas and E. Nemeth).

1972   (ed.) *Psychopathological Disorders of Childhood*. Wiley (with H.C. Quay).

1974   Methylphenidate in children: Effect of dosage. *Australian and New Zealand Journal of Psychiatry*, 8, 9–19 (with R.L. Sprague).

1975   Methylphenidate and haloperidol in children. *Archives of General Psychiatry*, 32, 790–5 (with M.G. Aman).

1978   (ed.) *Pediatric Psychopharmacology*. Brunner/Mazel.

1980–4   (ed.) *Advances in Human Psychopharmacology* (3 vols). JAI Press (with G.D. Burrows).

1981   Psychopharmacology in children. In S. Arieti and H.K.H. Brodie (eds), *American Handbook of Psychiatry*, vol. 7. Basic Books.

1983   Rhythmic motor activities (stereotypes) in children under five: Etiology and prevalence. *Journal of the American Academy of Child Psychiatry*, 22, 329–36 (with J. Carlielle and J. Fitzpatrick).

1983   The inter-rater reliability and validity of the DSM III diagnostic system in children. *Journal of Abnormal Child Psychology*, 11, 341–54 (with R.J. Methven, J. Fitzpatrick and H. Dixon).

1989   Behavior therapy with children and adolescents: A twenty-year overview. *Journal of the American Academy of Child and Adolescent Psychiatry*, 28, 1–18 (with J.P. Wollersheim).

1992   Child psychiatric disorders: Are they classifiable? *British Journal of Psychiatry*, 161, 472–80.

1994   Clinical features and outcome of child and adolescent schizophrenia. *Schizophrenia Bulletin*, 20, 619–30 (with J.M. McClellan, L.K. Andrews and M. Ham).

Further reading

Barkley, R.A. (1988) Child behavior rating scales and checklists. In M. Rutter, A.H. Tuma and I.S. Lann (eds), *Assessment and Diagnosis in Child Psychopathology*. Guilford.

Mash, E.J. and Terdal, L.G. (eds) (1988) *Behavioral Assessment of Childhood Disorders*. Guilford Press.

Matson, J.L. (eds) (1993) *Handbook of Hyperactivity in Children*. Allyn & Bacon.

Werry has been concerned with the scientific analysis of clinical problems, especially in children, and with teaching these principles to medical students and psychiatric residents. Because of his medical background, he has focused primarily on those areas where this background seemed most relevant. In the early 1960s this was in the brain and behaviour area. With Gabrielle Weiss, he researched hyperactivity and psychopharmacology, and the effects of brain factors in child psychopathology. This research had a number of novel components : an emphasis on behaviour rather than internal events, properly controlled designs, and statistical analysis of variables. Werry and Weiss also recognized the importance of cognitive factors in the aetiology, symptomatology and pharmacology of childhood disorders, and asked Virginia Douglas to assist. Though ultimately diversifying in their work, all three have made major early and continuing contributions to the study of 'hyperactivity', now called, as a result of Douglas's work, Attention Deficit Disorder. Werry recognized early on the limitations of psychiatric training and sought out training in psychology. He was for several years a member of the Psychology Department of the University of Illinois at Urbana, where he strengthened an interest in behaviour modification and developed two very profitable professional relationships, one with H.C. **Quay** and the other with R.L. Sprague, both of whom greatly influenced his work and thinking. His work has changed somewhat to an interest in the validity of diagnostic taxonomies in child psychiatry, though an interest in psychopharmacology and behaviour modification have continued.

Werry has made a significant impact on clinical child psychology, principally through his work on hyperactivity, psychopharmacology, behaviour modification, brain damage and nosology. Some of this is less substantive as to content than as to setting a standard of clarity and methodological rigour in a difficult area. Latterly he has begun to interest himself in ageing or medical gerontology, where the parallels between interests in brain damage, cognition and pharmacological variables are striking. As Foundation Head of Psychiatry at the Medical School in Auckland (since 1970), Werry has sought to teach and project psychiatry as an applied bio-social science, with a low tolerance for loose thinking and untestable theorizing.

Wertheimer, Max

Born: 1880, Prague, Austria **Died:** 1943, New Rochelle, New York, USA **Nat:** German **Ints:** Experimental psychology, military psychology, philosophical and theoretical psychology, psychological study of social issues, psychology and law **Educ:** PhD University of Würzburg, 1904 **Appts & awards:** Berlin Psychological Institute, 1916–29; Professor, University of Frankfurt, 1929–33; Professor, New School of Social Research, New York, 1933–43; Wilhelm Wundt plaque, 1980

Principal publications

1904 Psychologische Tatbestandsdiagnostik (Psychological evidence diagnostic). *Archiv für Kriminalanthropologie*, 15, 72–113.

1912 Über das Denken der Naturvolker. (Thought processes of sound directions). *Preussische Akademie der Wissenschaft*, 61, 161–265

1920 Über Wahrnehmung der Schallrichtungen (The perception of sound directions). *Preussische Akademie der Wissenschaft*, 20, 388–96.

1922 Untersuchungen zur Lehre von der Gestalt (Investigations of the study of Gestalt). *Psychologische Forschung*, 1, 47–58.

1923 Untersuchungen zur Lehre von der Gestalt (Investigations of the study of Gestalt). *Psychologische Forschung*, 4, 301–50.

1925 Über Gestalttheorie (On Gestalt theory). *Philosophische Zeitschrift*, 1, 39–60.

1934 On truth. *Social Research*, 1, 135–46.

1935 Some problems in the theory of ethics. *Social Research*, 2, 353–67.

Further reading

Köhler, W. (1944) Max Wertheimer 1880–1943. *Psychological Review of Psychology*, 51, 143–6.

Newman, E.B. (1944) Max Wertheimer 1880–1943. *American Journal of Psychology*, 57, 428–35.

Max Wertheimer is considered to be one of the founders of Gestalt psychology, one of psychology's major schools. He studied law and philosophy at Charles University in Prague and philosophy and music with **Stumpf** and Schumann in Berlin, before obtaining his PhD degree summa cum laude in psychology under Külpe in Würzburg. His earliest work concerned the psychology of testimony and also the music and language of native cultures.

Wertheimer's main contribution to psychology was his demonstration of the phi-phenomenon, the optical illusion of movement of two stationary lights. The *Gestalt* School used this phenomenon to emphasize that the psychological experience, here the motion, is different from the sensory elements which did not move. In general, the Gestaltists disapproved of examining detailed elements in order to understand human thoughts and actions.

Wertheimer emphasized that an examination of the whole is of primary importance for a meaningful understanding of its parts. Together with **Koffka**, Goldstein and Grule he founded a new journal, the *Psychologische Forschung*, to publish the research emanating from the new *Gestalt* School. He consolidated his views in his 'Law of Prägnanz', which subsumes such phenomena as proximity, similarity, closure and symmetry. He thought that these phenomena are perceived mainly because the mind imposes certain organizational principles on sensations.

Political events in German made Wertheimer's professorship at the University of Frankfurt untenable. After emigrating to New York in 1934, he became instrumental in establishing the New School of Social Research, where he lectured and wrote on the subjects of social values, truth and *Gestalt* ethics.

FRANK WESLEY

Wertheimer, Michael

Born: 1927, Berlin, Germany **Nat:** American **Ints:** Experimental and clinical, history, teaching **Educ:** BA Swarthmore College, 1947; MA Johns Hopkins University, 1949; PhD Harvard University 1952; MA Worcester State Hospital 1952 **Appts & awards:** Professor, Department of Psychology, University of Colorado at Boulder; APA, Fellow, 1966– , President, Division 2, 1965–6, President, Division 1, 1975–6, President, Division 24, 1976–7, 1984–85, President, Division 26, 1977–8; Chair, numerous APA Committees; APA Council, Division 26, 1966–9, Division 24, 1975–7, 1981–3, Division 1, 1986–8; President, Rocky Mountain Psychological Association, 1981–2; APA G. Stanley Hall Lecturer, 1983; APF Distinguished Teaching in Psychology Award, 1983; Editorial Consultant, *Contemporary Psychology*, 1963–71; Editorial Boards: *Gestalt Theory*, 1980– , *Zeitschrift für Psychologie*, 1981– , *Computers in Human Behavior*, 1984–

Principal publications

1953 An investigation of the 'randomness' of threshold measurements. *Journal of Experimental Psychology*, 45, 294–303.

1954 Constant errors in the measurement of figural aftereffects. *American Journal of Psychology*, 67, 543–6.

1957 Perception and the Rorschach. *Journal of Projective Techniques*, 21, 209–16.

1958 The relation between the sound of a word and its meaning. *American Journal of Psychology*, 71, 412–15.

1959 *Productive Thinking*. Harper (reprinted 1978, 1982).

1962 Auditory-oculomotor reflexes at birth. *Science*, 135, 989–99.

1967 Some determinants of associations to French and English words. *Journal of Verbal Learning and Verbal Behavior*, 6, 574–81 (with B. Davis).

1972 *A Brief History of Psychology*. Holt, Rinehart & Winston (reprinted 1979, 1986).

1972 *Fundamental Issues in Psychology*. Holt, Rinehart & Winston.

1978 Humanistic psychology and the humane but tough-minded psychologist. *American Psychologist*, 33, 739–45.

1979 *Psychology Teacher's Resource Book: First Course*. APA (with M. Johnson).

1982 *Gestalt* theory, holistic psychologies and Max Wertheimer. *Zeitschrift für Psychologie*, 90, 125–40.

1987 Some implicit assumptions of modern psychology. *Zeitschrift für Psychologie*, 95, 311–23.

Further reading

American Psychological Foundation Award (1984) Michael Wertheimer. *American Psychologist*, 39, 311–13.

O'Roark, A.M. (1979) Humanistic psychology: The ultimate singularity in the behavioral science universe. *American Psychologist*, 34, 552–3.

Michael Wertheimer was born in Berlin, a son of Max **Wertheimer**. The family emigrated to the USA in 1933 and Michael was educated in New York. His PhD in experimental psychology brought him under the influence of B.F. **Skinner**, S.S. **Stevens** and E.G. **Boring**. Wertheimer has worked principally in perception, cognition, the psycholinguistics of multilingualism, and the history and philosophy of psychology. His primary contributions are in two main areas. First, he is recognized as an outstanding teacher of psychology who has consistently enthused and inspired those who have studied under him.

Many of his students have gone on to distinguished careers in psychology. He has written or co-authored several introductory texts, a book on research methodology and a history of psychology (published in several languages). Thus, he has occupied an influential role in the 'cultural transmission' of psychology from generation to generation. His second contribution has been in developing and promoting the teaching of psychology as a professional activity in its own right. He led the effort to promote national guidelines and standards for placing the teaching of psychology in high schools in the USA.

Whiting, Beatrice Blyth

Born: 1914, New York City, USA **Nat:** American **Ints:** Comparative psychology, psychological anthropology **Educ:** AB Bryn Mawr, 1935; PhD Yale University, 1942 **Appts & awards:** Professor (Emeritus) of Anthropology and Education, Harvard Graduate School of Education; Distinguished Scholar, Henry A. Murray Center for the Study of Lives; President, Society for Cross-Cultural Research, 1968–70; Fellow, Center for Advanced Studies in the Behavioral Sciences, 1978–9; Sigma Xi, Phi Beta Cappa, Distinguished Service Award, 1982; President, Society for Psychology and Anthropology, 1983–4; Award for Contribution to Science of Human Development, 1987; Society for Research in Children Development; Fellow, American Academy of Arts and Science; Editor, Adolescence in a Changing World series (Rutgers) (with J.W.M. Whiting)

Principal publications

1963 Contributions of anthropology to the methods of studying child rearing. In P.H. Mussen (ed.), *Handbook of Research Methods in Childhood Development*. Wiley (with J.W.M. Whiting).

1965 Sex identity conflict and physical violence: A comparative study. *American Anthropologist*, 67, 123–40.

1966 (ed.) *Six Cultures: Studies of Child Rearing*. John Urley.

1973 Cross-cultural analysis of sex differences in the behaviour of children aged 3–11. *Journal of Social Psychology*, 91, 171–88 (with C. Edwards).

1973 Altrustic and egotistic behaviour in six cultures. In L. Nader and T.W. Maretzki (eds), *Cultural Illness and Health: Essays in Human Adaptation*. American Athropological Society (with J.W.M. Whiting).

1974 The Kenyan career women: Traditional and

modern. In R.B. Kundsin (ed.), *Women and Success: The Anatomy of Achievement*. Morrow.

1974   Folk wisdom and child rearing. *Merrill-Palmer Quarterly of Behavior and Development*, 20, 9–19.

1975   *Children of Six Cultures: A Psycho Cultural Analysis*. Harvard University Press (with J.W.M. Whiting).

1976   The problem of the packaged variable in the developing individual in a changing world, vol. 1. In K.F. Riegel and J.A. Meacham (eds), *Historical and Cultural Issues*. Aldine.

1980   *Handbook of Comparative Human Development*. Garland Press.

1988   *Children of Different Worlds: The Formation of Social Behaviour*. Harvard University Press (with C.P. Edwards).

Further reading

Handel, G. (ed.) (1988) *Childhood Socialization*. Aldine de Gruyter.

The research of Beatrice Whiting is cross-cultural and based on the collaborative work of anthropologists and psychologists who have done fieldwork in various parts of the world. The work seeks to identify culturally defined experiences that shape human development. She argues that all generalizations that purport to describe principles of human development should apply to individuals growing up in all societies. If findings derived from psychological studies conducted in the United States and Europe do not hold up when replicated in other societies, there is a high probability that there are hidden variables that have been overlooked because of cultural blindness. Cross-cultural studies, she contends, make it possible to study child development under culturally approved conditions that are different from normative experiences in our society, and to identify these hidden variables.

Examples of the types of contextual variable that she and her colleagues have found to influence human development are: (1) household arrangements, settlement patterns and family structure; (2) mother's workload; (3) tasks assigned to children; (4) schooling; and (5) examples of behaviour consequences studied.

Whiting's publications include the analysis of the interpersonal behaviour of children between the ages of 2 and 11. It compares similar types of social interaction observed in twelve societies as they relate to the types of companion a child has during the early years. In the area of cross-cultural research, she worked with the Harvard Adolescent Project on the experiences of adolescent boys and girls growing up in Arctic Canada, Nigeria, Kenya, Australia, Morocco, Romania and Thailand. She is one of a small number of psychologists who have contributed to the emergence and growth of psychological anthropology as a discipline in its own right.

Wickens, Delos Donald

Born: 1909, Rochester, New York, USA **Nat:** American **Ints:** Engineering, experimental physiological and comparative, general, history **Educ:** BA Centre College of Kentucky, 1931; MA University of North Carolina, 1933; PhD University of North Carolina, 1937 **Appts & awards:** Distinguished Visiting Professor, Colorado State University; President, APA Division 1, APA Division 3, Mid-Western Psychological Association; Chairman and Board Member, Psychonomics Society; Chairman, Society of Experimental Psychologists; Vice-President, AAAS; APA Council; Warren Medal, Society of Experimental Psychologists; APA Distinguished Teaching Award; Distinguished Research Award, Ohio State University; Distinguished Alumnus Award, University of North Carolina; Associate Editor, *Journal of Experimental Psychology*, 1957–8, 1966–73; Publication Board, Psychonomic Society; Consulting Editor, *Journal of Experimental Psychology*, 1950–7, 1959–65, Merrill Press

Principal publications

1938   The transference of conditioned excitation and conditioned inhibition from one muscle group to the antagonistic muscle group. *Journal of Experimental Psychology*, 22, 101–23.

1940   A study of conditioning in the neonate. *Journal of Experimental Psychology*, 26, 94–102 (with C. Wickens).

1949   *Experimental Foundations of General Psychology*. Rinehart (with W.L. Valentine).

1955   *Psychology*. Dryden (with D.R. Meyer). (Holt, Rinehart & Winston, 1961).

1956   Retroactive inhibition as a function of the temporal position of the interpolated learning. *Journal of Experimental Psychology*, 51, 149–54 (with J.M. Newton).

1959   Conditioning to complex stimuli. *American Psychologist*, 7, 180–8.

1963   Proactive inhibition and item similarity in STM. *Journal of Verbal Learning and Verbal Behavior*, 2, 440–5 (with D.G. Born and C.K. Allen).

1970   Encoding categories of words: An empirical

approach to meaning. *Psychological Review*, 77, 1–15.

1973   Stimulus selection as a function of CS1 and CS2 lower 1 and 2 interval in compound classical conditioning of cats. *Journal of Comparative and Physiological Psychology*, 85, 295–303 (with A.F. Nield, D.S. Tuber and C.D. Wickens).

1977   Memory for the conditioned response: The effects of potential interference before and after original conditioning. *Journal of Experimental Psychology: General*, 106, 47–70 (with D.S. Tuber, A.F. Nield and C.D. Wickens).

1981   The nature and timing of the retrieval process and interference effects. *Journal of Experimental Psychology: General*, 110, 1–20 (with M. Moody and R. Dow).

1983   Memory for the conditioned response: The proactive effect of preexposure to potential conditioning stimuli and context change. *Journal of Experimental Psychology: General*, 112, 41–57.

Further reading

Brannelly, S., Tehan, G. and Humphreys, M.S. (1989) Retrieval plus scanning: Does it occur? *Memory and Cognition*, 17, 712–22.

Eberts, R.E. and Posey, J.W. (1990) the mental model in stimulus-response compatibility. In R.W. Proctor and T.G. Reeve (eds) *Stimulus-Response Compatibility: An Integrated Perspective*. North-Holland.

Gorfein, D.S. and Hoffman, R.R. (eds) (1987) *Memory and Learing: The Ebbinghaus Centennial Conference*. Erlbaum.

Working with his PhD advisor J.F. Dashiell, who obtained his PhD under John **Dewey**, the father of functionalism, Delos Wickens was an advocate for the experimental method as the basis of knowledge and for the field of psychology. From the beginning he was fascinated by **Pavlov**'s work and the field of experimental psychology in general, but especially by learning and eventually memory. His list of principal publications reflects the development of these interrelated interests through his professional career. His dissertation (published 1938) was designed to test **Guthrie**'s statement that the response that is learned is the response which is made. It was well received then and is still cited. The 1940 publication occurred because his first job was at Ohio State University. It had a laboratory for studying infant behaviour, and, collaborating with his wife, he took advantage of an unusual opportunity. The 1956 article was his first significant venture into the field of human memory. Its importance lies in the fact

that he found interference where, according to the theory of the day, there should be none. The 1963 publication resulted from a reaction to a highly debated question of the day: do short- and long-term memory obey different laws? Its findings suggested an extension into measurement of distance in semantic memory (1970). The 1977 and 1983 articles represent a confluence of interests in conditioning and memory, while that for 1981 was designed to analyse the locus of the interference effect reported in earlier publications.

Winocur, Gordon

Born: 1941, Winnipeg, Manitoba, Canada **Nat:** Canadian **Ints:** Adult development and ageing, clinical neuropsychology, experimental, physiological, comparative **Educ:** BA University of Manitoba, 1962; MA University of Manitoba, 1964; PhD University of Waterloo, 1966 **Appts & awards:** Professor of Psychology, Trent University; Member, NSERC Grant Review Committee, 1977–80; Ontario Mental Health Foundation, 1979–84; Gerontology Research Council, 1981– ; President, Ontario Mental Health Foundation, John Dewan Award, 1984; Canadian Psychological Association, Fellow, Board of Directors, 1984– , President, Brain and Behaviour Section 1986

Principal publications

1976   An investigation of paired associate learning in amnesic patients. *Neuropsychologia*, 14, 97–110 (with L. Weiskrantz).

1978   Effects of context manipulation on memory and reversal learning in rats with hippocampal lesions. *Journal of Comparative and Physiological Psychology*, 92, 312–21 (with J. Olds).

1978   Contextual cueing as an aid to Korsakoff amnesic patients. *Neuropsychologia*, 16, 671–82 (with M. Kinsbourne).

1981   The effect of cueing on release from proactive interference in Korsakoff amnesic patients. *Journal of Experimental Psychology: Human Learning and Memory*, 7, 56–65 (with M. Kinsbourne and M. Moscovitch).

1982   Learning and memory deficits in institutionalized and non-institutionalized old people: An analysis of interference effects. In F.I.M. Craik and S. Trehub (eds), *Aging and Cognitive Processes*. Plenum.

1982   Radial arm maze behavior by rats with hippocampal lesions: Effects of cueing. *Journal of Comparative and Physiological Psychology*, 96, 155–69.

1983 Learning and memory deficits in aged populations: An analysis of interference effects. *Journal of Gerontology*, 38, 455–64 (with M. Moscovitch).

1984 Amnesia in a patient with bilateral lesions to the thalamus. *Neuropsychologia*, 22, 123–43 (with S. Oxbury, R. Roberts, V. Agnetti and C. Davis).

1984 The effects of retroactive and proactive interference on learning and memory in young and old rats. *Developmental Psychobiology*, 17, 537–45.

1984 Memory localization in the brain. In L. Squire and N. Butters (eds), *Neuropsychology of Memory*. Academic Press.

1990 Anterograde and retrograde amnesia in rats with dorsal hippocampal or dorsomedial thalamic lesions. *Behavioural Brain Research*, 38, 145–54.

1993 High-fat diets impair conditional discrimination learning in rats. *Psychobiology*, 21, 286–92 (with C.E. Greenwood).

Further reading

Craik, F.I.M. and Salthouse, T.A. (eds) (1992) *Handbook of Aging and Cognition*. Erlbaum.

Squire, L.R. and Butters, N. (eds) (1992) *Neuropsychology of Memory*. Guilford.

Gordon Winocur is a physiological psychologist with a long-standing interest in brain function and behaviour. Much of his research has been concerned with the effects of brain damage on cognitive function, with a particular interest in the role of limbic system and diencephalic structures. His early work with animals was important in implicating the hippocampus in an information-processing function that is particularly significant in learning and memory situations in which stimulus cues lack salience. Analogous experiments conducted with patients known to have similar brain damage yielded similar results. Among brain structures, the hippocampus is one of the most susceptible to the ageing process and, since the elderly frequently complain of and indeed suffer from memory loss, he studied age-related memory change from a neuropsychological perspective. His studies of old animals and elderly people show a pattern of memory loss that is reminiscent of that seen in hippocampus-damaged subjects. However, the larger emerging picture with respect to cognitive decline indicates a complex interaction involving age and physiological and environmental factors, and in more recent work Winocur has addressed the nature of this interaction.

Witkin, Jeffrey M.

Born: 1953, Washington, DC, USA *Nat:* American *Ints:* Drug and alcohol dependence, experimental psychology, neuroscience, psychopharmacology *Educ:* BS University of Maryland, 1975; PhD University of North Carolina, 1979 *Appts & awards:* Research Assistant, Professor, Uniformed Services University of Health Sciences, 1983–6; Research Associate Professor, Department of Psychiatry, Uniformed Services University of Health Sciences, Walter Reed Army Research Institute, 1986– ; Army Achievement Medal for work on the development of anticholinergic compounds, 1987; Head, Drug Development Group, Psychobiology Laboratory, Addiction Research Centre, 1990– ; Joseph Cochin Young Investigator Award – College on Problems of Drug Dependence, 1992; Member: American Society for Pharmacology and Experimental Therapeutics, Society for Neuroscience, American Association for the Advancement of Science; Grant and Fellowship External Review Committee, National Science Foundation, Human Frontier Science Program, International Science Foundation; Board of Editors, *Journal of the Experimental Analysis of Behaviour*, 1987–9, 1991–3; Editoral Advisory Board, *Journal of Pharmacology and Experimental Therapeutics*, 1993–97; Guest Reviewer: *Pharmacology, Biochemistry and Behaviour*, *Psychopharmacology*, *Physiology and Behaviour*, *Behavioural Pharmacology*, *Neuropsychopharmacology*, *Brain Research*, *Life Sciences*, *Pharmacology Communications*, *Drug and Alcohol Dependence*, *Experimental and Clinical Psychopharmacology*, *Alcohol*

Principal publications

1976 Effects of pentobarbital on punished behaviour at different shock intensities. *Pharmacology, Biochemistry and Behaviour*, 5, 535–8 (with J. Barret).

1980 Discriminative stimulus properties of *d*-amphetamine-pentobarbital combinations. *Psychopharmacology*, 68, 269–76 (with R. Carter and L. Dykstra).

1983 Modification of behavioural effects of morphine, meperidine and normeperidine by naloxone and morphine tolerance. *Journal of Pharmacology and Experimental Therapeutics*, 225, 275–83 (with J. Leander and L. Dykstra).

1984 Effects of some volatile sedative-hypnotics on punished behaviour. *Psychopharmacology*, 84, 16–19.

1986 Differential antagonism of diazepam-induced

loss of the fighting response. *Pharmacology, Biochemistry and Behaviour*, 24, 963–5. (with J. Barret, J. Cook and P. Larscheid).

1986   Pharmacological optimisation of military response: Antianxiety agents. *Psychology in the Department of Defense, Tenth Symposium Proceedings* (USAFA-TR-86-1), 76–80 (with F. Jones).

1987   Comparison of in vitro actions with behavioural effects of antimuscarinic agents. *Journal of Pharmacology and Experimental Therapeutics*, 242, 796–803 (with R. Gordon and P. Chiang).

1989   Lethal effects of cocaine are reduced by the dopamine-1 receptor antagonist SCH 23390 but not by haloperidol. *Life Sciences*, 44, 1285–91 (with S. Goldberg and J. Katz).

1989   Physostigmine-insensitive behavioural excitatory effects of atropine in squirrel monkeys. *Pharmacology, Biochemistry and Behaviour*, 32, 309–15 (with R. Markowitz and J. Barret).

1990   Analysis of the behavioural effects of drugs. *Drug Development Research*, 20, 389–409 (with J. Katz).

1990   Stereoselective effects of cocaine. *Behavioural Pharmacology*, 1, 347–54 (with J. Katz and E. Tirelli).

1991   Genetic factors influence changes in sensitivity to the convulsant properties of cocaine following chronic treatment. *Brain Research*, 542, 1–7 (with R. Marley and S. Goldberg).

1992   Preclinical assessment of cocaine toxicity: Mechanisms and pharmacotherapy. *Acute Cocaine Intoxication: Current Methods of Treatment*, NIDA Research Monograph, 123, 44–69 (with J. Katz).

1993   Transduction of a discriminative stimulus through a diazepam-insensitive $GABA_A$ receptor. *Journal of Pharmacology and Experimental Therapeutics*, 266, 570–6 (with G. Wong, P. Skolnick and J. Katz).

1994   Pharmacotherapy of cocaine abuse: Preclinical development. *Neurosciences and Biobehavioural Reviews*, 18, 121–42.

1995   Role of N-methyl-D-asparate receptors in behaviour and behavioural effects of drugs. In T.W. Stone (ed.), *CNS Neurotransmitters and Neuromodulators*, vol. I: *Glutamate*. CRC Press.

Further reading

Barrett, J.E., Thompson, T. and Dews, P.B. (eds) (1990) *Advances in Behavioral Pharmacology*, vol. 7. Erlbaum.

Professor Witkin is both a psychologist and a neurobiologist, who has devoted his career to the study of drugs and their effects. The import-ance of this work and its applications is reflected in the awards and research contracts that he has received.

He was awarded his PhD in 1979 for his dissertation 'Behavioural effects of drugs: The role of the stimulus-reinforcer contingency'. He then became a Neurobiology Postdoctoral Fellow at the University of North Carolina, where he produced a great deal of animal research with David Leander. Since then he has held a number of research and teaching positions throughout Maryland, and has produced an impressive body of research relating to the effects of a wide variety of drugs on a range of behaviours. In recent years he has turned much of his attention to the behavioural effects of cocaine. He is currently head of the Drug Development Group at the Addiction Research Centre in Baltimore.

MOIRA MAGUIRE

Wohlwill, Joachim F.

Born: 1928, Hamburg, Germany **Died:** 1987, State College, Pennsylvania, USA **Nat:** German/American **Ints:** Cognitive development, developmental methodology and theory, developmental psychology, environmental psychology, life-span development **Educ:** Harvard University, 1949; PhD University of California at Berkeley, 1957 **Appts & awards:** Assistant Professor to Professor in Psychology, Clark University, 1958–70; Fellow, Centre for Advanced Study in the Behavioral Sciences, 1963–4; Visiting Research Fellow, Educational Testing Service, 1968–9; Research Fellowship, Social Science Research Council, 1968–9; Professor of Man–Environment Relations, Pennsylvania State University, 1970–9; Professor of Human Development in the Programs in Individual and Family Studies and Man–Environment Relations, Pennsylvania State University, 1979–87; Fellow, American Society for the Advancement of Science, 1975–82; Beatrice Ferrand Fellow, Department of Landscape Architecture and Institute for Urban and Regional Development, University of California at Berkeley, 1977; Fellow, APA Divisions 3, 7 and 10

Principal publications

1962   An experimental analysis of the development of the conservation of number. *Child Development*, 33, 153–67 (with R. Lowe).

1962   From perception to inference: A dimension of cognitive development. *Monographs of the Society for Research in Child Development*, 27, no. 2 (whole no. 83).

1966   Man's response to the physical environment. *Journal of Social Issues*, 22, whole no. 4 (with R. Kates).

1966   Perceptual learning. *Annual Review of Psychology*, 17, 201–32.

1969   Formal and functional aspects of cognitive development. In D. Elkind and J.H. Flavell (eds), *Studies of Cognitive Development*. Oxford University Press (with J.H. Flavell).

1970   The age variable in psychological research. *Psychological Review*, 77, 49–64.

1970   The emerging discipline of environmental psychology. *American Psychologist*, 25, 303–12.

1973   The concept of experience: S or R? *Human Development*, 16, 90–107.

1973   *The Study of Behavioral Development*. Academic Press.

1976   Environmental aesthetics: The environment as a source of affect. In I. Altman and J.F. Wohlwill (eds), *Human Behavior and Environment: Advances in Theory and Research*, vol. 1. Plenum.

1977   Environmental psychology. In B.B. Wolman (ed.), *International Encyclopaedia of Psychiatry, Psychology, Psychoanalysis and Neurology*. Van Nostrand Reinhold/Aesculapius.

1980   The confluence of environmental and developmental psychology. In D. Magnusson and V.J. Allen (eds), *Personality Development as Person Environment Interaction*. Academic Press.

1983   Physical and social environment as factors in development. In D. Magnusson and V.L. Allen (eds), *Personality Development as Person Environment Interaction*. Academic Press.

1983   Relationships between exploration and play. In T.D. Yawkey and A.D. Pellegrini (eds), *Child's Play: Developmental and Applied*. Erlbaum.

1984   Psychology and the environmental disciplines. In M.H. Bornstein (ed.), *Psychology and its Allied Disciplines: The Social Sciences*. Erlbaum.

Further reading

Heft, H. (1988) Joachim F. Wohlwill (1928–87): His contributions to the emerging discipline of environmental psychology. *Environment and Behavior*, 20, 259–75.

—— (1996) Toward a functional ecology of behavior and development: The legacy of Joachim F. Wohlwill. In D. Gorlitz, H. Harloff, G. May and J. Valsiner (eds), *Children, Cities and Psychological Theories: Developing Relationships*. De Gruyter.

Downs, R.M., Lynn, S.L. and Palermo, D.S. (eds) (1991) *Visions of Aesthetics, the Environment and Development: The Legacy of Joachim F. Wohlwill*. Erlbaum.

Joachim Wohlwill was born in Hamburg, Germany, on 27 September 1928. In 1933, his family fled Nazi Germany and moved to Portugal. Fearful of an invasion of Portugal during World War II, his family sent him to the United States in 1949, where he was mentored by Gordon **Allport** and majored in social relations. Following graduation, he spent two years in the US Army, following which he began his graduate work at the University of Chicago in 1952–3, completing his PhD at the University of California at Berkeley in 1957. He spent a postdoctoral year in Geneva with **Piaget**, after which he joined the Department of Psychology at Clark University and soon assumed the role of the Director of the Developmental Psychology Training Program. Through the Clark years (1958–70), Wohlwill developed an international reputation as a developmental psychologist and published a number of significant papers on perceptual development and developmental theory. Also during these years he began writing *The Study of Behavioral Development* (1973), one of his most widely regarded books, in which he examined developmental methodologies, particularly in life-span development. During this period, too, Wohlwill's interest in environmental psychology began to emerge. In his early years, his interest in environmental correlates of perceptual experience reflected the influence of Egon Brunswick, a mentor during his time at Berkeley. Wohlwill's concern about societal and environmental problems and the role that psychology might play in addressing them were developed when he accepted an invitation to spend a year as Fellow in the Center for Advanced Study in the Behavioral Sciences in 1963. At about this time, he published with Robert Kates 'Man's response to the physical environment' in a special issue of the *Journal of Social Issues* (1966). This work had a powerful impact on environmental psychology and served as an impetus for Wohlwill's leadership in developing the area at Clark in the late 1960s.

He left Clark in 1970 to become Professor of Man–Environment Relations at the Pennsylvania State University. This move enabled him to focus his efforts on environmental psychology for a number of years. His academic work while affiliated with the department was quite diverse and consistent with the interdisciplinary nature of the programme. During this time, one of his concerns was with developing empirically validated objective descriptions of the environment. He counselled that the objective characteristic of the environment could be understood independent of the individual's experiences.

In a series of articles, he attempted to identify the stimulus correlates of environmental aesthetic preference. His publications in this area including works on stimulus complexity, and on the compatibility between natural and built features in an environmental scene. His published articles on environment and behaviour, however, covered a wide range of additional areas, including the relationship between recreational area use and pressures for further development, attitudes towards conservation, analysis of land use, and the effect of noise in the environment, among others. Also related to this research line was his long-standing interest in the psychology of the arts and in the work of Daniel **Berlyne** on exploration, curiosity and arousal. In 1979, with a reorganization at Penn State, he became Professor of Human Development in the Programs in Individual and Family Studies and Man–Environment Relations. With this move, he sought to combine his interest in the physical environment and human development. The move to integrate his two major interests focused on research on environments fit for the developing child. By this time he had already published his influential article 'The concept of experience: S or R ?' (1973), in which he analysed ways psychologists could conceptualize the relationship between environment and development. He drew the distinction between viewing the environment as a source of stimulation for the developing individual and as a context for the expression of behaviour. More specifically, he argued that the child would benefit most from increasing opportunities with age for voluntary rather than passive exploration of the environment, and for the development of environments that provide feedback for the child's actions. Other developmental questions explored in his later years examined exploration and curiosity in development, and children's artistic and creative development. Wohlwill emerged as a leading contributor, shaper and proponent in the fields of developmental and environmental psychology. In the course of much of this work he offered a distinctive approach that departs from the mainstream thinking in both areas.

D. THOMPSON

Wolpe, Joseph

Born: 1915, Johannesburg, South Africa **Nat:** South African **Ints:** Clinical psychology, psychotherapy, psychiatry **Educ:** MB University of Witwatersrand, 1939; BCH University of Witwatersrand, 1939; MD University of Witwatersrand, 1948 **Appts & awards:** Member, APA, 1961–

Principal publications

1949   An interpretation of the effect of combinations of stimuli (patterns) based on current neurophysiology. *Psychological Review*, 56, 277–83.

1950   Need-reduction, drive reduction and reinforcement: A neurophysiological view. *Psychological Review*, 37, 19–26.

1952   Experimental neuroses as learned behavior. *British Journal of Psychology*, 43, 243–68.

1953   Learning theory and 'abnormal fixations'. *Psychological Review*, 60, 111–16.

1958   *Psychotherapy by Reciprocal Inhibition*. Stanford University Press.

1964   Behavior therapy in complex neurotic states. *British Journal of Psychiatry*, 110, 28–34.

1966   *Behavior Therapy Techniques: A Guide to the Treatment of Neuroses*. Pergamon (with A. Lazarus).

1967   *Learning Theory Approaches to Psychotherapy*. Forest Hospital Foundation Monograph.

1969   *The Practice of Behavior Therapy*. Pergamon.

1976   *Theme and Variation: A Behavior Therapy Casebook*. Pergamon.

1978   Cognition and causation in human behavior and its therapy. *American Psychologist*, 33, 437–46.

1980   The Eysenck and the Wolpe theories of neurosis. *Behavioral and Brain Sciences* (invited article).

Further reading

Crown, S. and Freeman, H.L. (eds) (1994) *The Book of Psychiatric Books*. Jason Aronson.

Freedheim, D.K. *et al.* (1992) *History of Psychotherapy: A Century of Change*. American Psychological Association.

O'Donohue, W.T. and Krasner, L. (eds) (1995) *Theories of Behavior Therapy: Exploring Behavior Change*. American Psychological Association.

Joseph Wolpe was the eldest of four children. His parents had arrived in South Africa from Lithuania shortly after the turn of the century. His father was a freelance bookkeeper who, anticipating the educational needs of his children, had purchased the 1909 edition of *Webster's New International Dictionary* and the twenty-five-volume *Historian's History of the*

World. On his mother's side there was a long and strong tradition of intellectual achievement. Wolpe went to school in Johannesburg, and his ambition to become a chemist was tempered by the argument that, by becoming a physician, he would be better off financially while retaining the option of doing chemical research.

Wolpe began his medical training in 1933 and took no university courses in psychology. His interest in psychology arose relatively late in a clinical context. As a medical student he had been taught the **Freudian** theory of neuroses. In 1942, having volunteered for the South African medical corps, he was posted to a camp that received numerous cases of war neurosis. Narcoanalysis was a popular treatment for war neuroses at that time, but it quickly became apparent to Wolpe that this kind of treatment was not having long-term benefits. In looking for an alternative approach, he heard of the work of Russian psychologists and particularly that of **Pavlov**. In 1945, a chance meeting with James G. **Taylor**, an ardent follower of **Hull**, led Wolpe to read Hull's *Principles of Behavior*.

In the middle of 1946 Wolpe was accepted for an MD degree (equivalent to an American PhD in medicine) in the Department of Psychiatry in the University of Witwatersrand. In 1947 he began working on the production and elimination of experimental neuroses in cats. The experiments showed that animal neuroses were, as he suspected, a matter of learning. The following year he began a private practice in which he applied to human neuroses the principles of reciprocal inhibition that he had used successfully in his animal work. In animal studies, feeding had been the behaviour that was competitively successful in the weakening of anxiety. However, a number of attempts to counterpose feeding behaviour with human anxiety produced no beneficial effects. Wolpe then tried to encourage his clients to express ongoing emotions such as anger and defiance, verbalizing their thoughts and feelings. In 1949 he started work using calmness procedures, in the hope that these might inhibit his clients' anxieties. He tried a series of experiments which involved weak disturbing stimuli to the imagination of a deeply relaxed client. He noted that if a scene evoked weak anxiety, successive repetitions produced less and less anxiety, and, finally, none at all. This was in fact the discovery of systematic desensitization. In later work he found that a relatively large number of other bodily responses could be used to compete with anxiety. These included the comforting feelings

that all psychologists inadvertently arouse in all their clients, and he concluded that this was an important explanation for the fact that more than 40 per cent of clients improved greatly with any form of therapy. News of Wolpe's new behaviour therapy spread very quickly, and led to the therapy's widespread use in clinical settings around the world.

In 1957 Wolpe returned to South Africa, but remained for just three years before returning to America, this time to the University of Virginia School of Medicine. In 1962 the first conference on behaviour therapy was held at Virginia. Wolpe found Virginia less enjoyable than he had hoped, and took a year's unpaid leave of absence (1962–3) to go to London and explore with Hans **Eysenck** the possibility of establishing a behaviour therapy centre at the University of London. They pursued this idea vigorously but without success. Wolpe returned to Virginia in 1963 and remained there until 1965, when he was offered a position in the Department of Psychiatry at the Temple University School of Medicine. There he established the world's first Behavior Therapy Unit.

Wolpe has made fundamental and far-reaching contributions to our understanding of abnormal behaviour and in particular to the development of behaviour modification techniques that led to the establishment of behaviour therapy. His therapeutic methods, especially desensitization, have been used successfully to reduce anxiety, fear and distress in tens of thousands of people throughout the world.

Woodworth, Robert S.

Born: 1869, Belchertown, Massachusetts, USA **Died:** 1962, New York, USA **Nat:** American **Ints:** Experimental, general, history, personality and social, physiological and comparative **Educ:** AB Amherst University, 1891; AB Harvard University, 1896; AM Harvard University, 1897; PhD Columbia University, 1899 **Appts & Awards:** Vice-President, AAAS, 1909, 1929; President, APA, 1914, Psychological Corporation, 1929; Gold Medal, American Psychological Foundation, 1956; numerous consultantships; five honorary degrees; Editor, *Archives of Psychology*, 1906–45

Principal publications

1900 The influence of special training on general ability. *Psychological Review*, 7, 140–1 (with E.L. Thorndike).

1901 The influence of improvement in one mental

function upon the efficiency of other functions. *Psychological Review*, 8, 247–61 (with E.L. Thorndike).

1910   Racial differences in mental traits. *Science*, 31, 171–86.

1915   A revision of imageless thought. *Psychological Review*, 22, 1–27.

1918   *Dynamic Psychology*. Columbia University Press.

1921   *Psychology*. Holt (with D.G. Marquis) (5th edn, 1947).

1927   Dynamic psychology. In C. Murchison (ed.), *Psychologies of 1925*. Clark University Press.

1931   *Contemporary Schools of Psychology*. Ronald (with M. Sheehan) (rev. 1948, 1964).

1938   *Experimental Psychology*. Holt (with H. Schlosberg) (rev. 1954).

1943   The adolescence of American psychology. *Psychological Review*, 50, 10–32.

1958   *Dynamics of Behavior*. Holt.

Further reading

Murphy, G. (1963) Robert Sessions Woodworth. *American Psychologist*, 18, 131–3.

Poffenberger, A.J. (1962) Robert Sessions Woodworth. *American Journal of Psychology*, 75, 677–89.

Woodworth studied with William **James** and Josiah **Royce** at Harvard before taking his PhD under James McKeen **Cattell** at Columbia in 1899. After briefly holding positions at NYU and Liverpool, he returned to Columbia in 1903 and remained until his retirement in 1942. His first influential research was done with his long-time Columbia colleague E.L. **Thorndike**, on the transfer of learning. Showing that training in one function often had little carry-over to another, this work helped overthrow the 'doctrine of formal disciplines' in education. At the 1904 St Louis Exposition, Woodworth collected anthropometric data on some 1100 individuals of differing racial backgrounds, and published an important report showing that within-population variation outweighed any differences between races in significance. As he became interested in more systematic psychological issues, Woodworth stressed the importance of motives, and popularized (and perhaps coined) the expression 'dynamic psychology'. In analysing stimulus–response (S–R) relationships, he emphasized the importance of an active and predisposed organism intervening between the two, altering the formula to S–O–R. His introductory textbook, *Psychology* (1921), went through five editions and outsold all others for many years:

his *Experimental Psychology* (1938) was a virtual bible for several generations of advanced students; and his *Contemporary Schools of Psychology* (1931) was one of the earliest histories of the field. Throughout his career, Woodworth advocated moderation and eclecticism, decrying the narrow, rigid approaches of such 'bogeymen' as **Titchener** and **Watson**. He entitled the final chapter of his *Contemporary Schools* 'The middle of the road', and this was the position he unabashedly and effectively endorsed. Woodworth was active almost until his death in 1962, and his quiet leadership placed him among the handful of figures to have been commonly called the 'dean' of American Psychology. He published more than two hundred papers and ten major books.

Wundt, Wilhelm Max

Born: 1832, Neckarau, Baden, Germany ***Died:*** 1920, Grossbathen, Leipzig, Germany ***Nat:*** German ***Ints:*** Attention, apperception, experimental psychology, sensation, perception ***Educ: Appts & awards***

Principal publications

1873–4   *Principles of Physiological Psychology*. Engleman (6 editions).

1894   *Lectures on Human and Animal Psychology* (trans. J.E. Crighton and E.B. Titchener). Macmillan.

1896   *Outlines of Psychology* (trans. C.H. Judd). Engleman (1907).

1900–20   *Volkerpsychologie* (10 vols). Engleman.

1920   Erlebtes und Erkanntes.

Further reading

Blumenthal, A.L. (1975) A re-appraisal of Wilhelm Wundt. *American Psychologist*, 1081–8.

Reiber, R.W. (ed.) (1980) *Wilhelm Wundt and the Making of Modern Psychology*.

Titchener, E.B. (1921) Wilhelm Wundt. *American Journal of Psychology*, 32, 161–78.

Wilhelm Wundt is credited with being the 'father of experimental psychology' and the 'founder of modern psychology'. He was educated at Tubingen and had studied physiology at Berlin with Johannes Muller and Du-Bois Reymond before qualifying at Heidelberg with the degrees of PhD and MD. At Heidelberg he became a Docent in Physiology shortly before Hermonn von **Helmholtz**'s arrival as Professor and Head of the Physiology Department, and it is believed that he was for a short time a laboratory assistant to Helmholtz. In 1874 he went to the University of Zurich, and shortly after to Leipzig as Professor of Philosophy, where he remained until his death.

Wundt was appointed Professor of Physiology at Leipzig in 1875, and in the same year he established the first laboratory dedicated to experimental psychology. This was officially declared the Institute for Experimental Psychology by the University of Leipzig in 1882. This laboratory became a focus for those who held a serious interest in psychology, at first mainly those who had studied philosophy and psychology in other German universities, but soon graduates of several American and a few British universities. All subsequent psychological laboratories were closely modelled in their early years on the Wundt model.

There has been some contention regarding this. Some have claimed that, in so far as as a space for housing demonstration equipment may be called a laboratory, William **James** held a small room in Harvard as early as 1875. Wundt himself had space for storage of physiological and psychophysical equipment at Heidelberg in in 1865. G. Stanley **Hall** alleged in 1894 that the laboratory he founded at Hopkins in 1881 was the first significant psychological laboratory. Distinctions about the precise historical record of these events are, however, less important than they are reflective of the expression of scientific forces prevalent at the time.

Up to that point, the study of psychology had remained in the provinces of philosophy and the natural sciences. From philosophy had come (theories of) interactionism, empiricism and materialism, theories hypothesizing the nature of the mind, mind–body interaction and the acquisition of knowledge. From the natural sciences, the work of Johannes Müller presaged a different approach to the study of human physiology. Müller adopted a more direct and precise exploration of the human body, employing systematized experimental procedures to the study of physiology. It was these methods that inspired Wundt's work and his most important book, *Grundzüge der physiologische Psychologie* (*Principles of Physiological Psychology*). Published first in 1873–4, it laid the foundation for much of his later work and ultimately ran to six editions. Its emphasis lay in psychological investigation employing the method of the physiological laboratory. To Wundt, the essence of all total adjustments of the organism was a psychophysical process, an organic response mediated by both the physiological and the psychological. He pioneered the concept of stating mental events in relation to objectively knowable and measurable stimuli and reactions. Physiological psychology was concerned with the process of excitations from stimulation of the sense organs, through sensory neurones to the lower and higher brain centres, and from these centres to the muscles. Parallel with this process ran the events of mental life, known through introspection.

Introspection became, with Wundt, a primary tool of the experimental psychologist. His subjects or observers were usually adults who had undergone training in the technique as he understood it. The observers were presented with controlled stimuli and reported their introspections about covert mental processes while perceiving them. The theoretical approach of introspection was based on the assumption that all human mental experience, no matter how complex, could be viewed as combinations of simple processes or elements. The elements of experience were categorized into three main types: sensations, images and feelings. Sensations were ultimate or elementary forms of experience, representing a one-to-one correspondence between an excitation of the cerebral cortex and a sensory experience. They were classified according to their modality, vision, audition, etc., or by other features such as intensity and duration. Images were not fundamentally different from sensation, and were thought to be associated with local excitation in the cortex. Feelings included all qualities of experience that did not come from the sense organs or from the revival of sensory experiences and were classifiable. In the fourth edition of the *Physiological Psychology* (1893), Wundt published the 'tridimensional theory of feeling': feelings were classified as pleasant or unpleasant, tense or relaxed, excited or depressed. A given feeling might be at the same time a combination of one of each of the categories, e.g. pleasant, tense and depressed.

Wundt's structuralist approach proposed a cumulative process whereby sensations, carrying with them feeling qualities, combined to form more complex states, whereupon a certain feeling quality resulted from the total. This might again combine with another such quality and become arranged in various patterns or cross-sections of experience in time. Emotions were comprised of characteristic sequences of feelings resulting in a temporal pattern specific to each emotion. Will, like emotion, was ascribed a temporal pattern of feelings but allied with ideas. Particular feelings of resolution ensued, resulting in the overt act of will.

Wundt used the term apperception to describe the creative synthesis of elements of experience. This synthesis has been called the 'law of psychic resultants', similar in sense to the *Gestalt* idea that the whole is greater than the sum of its parts. Apperception in the original interpretation, dating back to Leibniz, referred to a phase of perception where there is recognition or comprehension of what has been perceived. With Kant and Herbart, apperception had been the process of assimilating and interpreting new impressions. Wundt used the term with emphasis on the active mental process by which individuals select and structure internal experience and focus clear introspective consciousness. He directed his experimental psychology towards the extension and systematization of existing problems. His work was concentrated principally in the psychology and physiology of vision and hearing. He was also concerned with reaction time experimentation in the manner of Helmholtz and Donders. With this methodology he believed that he could show experimentally the three stages he held to be present in all responses to stimulus, namely perception, apperception and will, subsequently leading to muscle innervation.

Continuing the quantitative approach to the study of association, following **Galton**, Wundt worked on the analysis of association. With his pupils, he developed devices for the uniform presentation of one-word stimuli in visual and auditory form, and measured the response time between stimulus word and response word. He classified all word associations into two categories, inner and outer. Inner associations defined word relationships where the meaning of the response word was identical or similar to the stimulus word. Outer associations described extrinsic or accidental relationships between stimulus and response (e.g. fire—toast). The fifth edition of *Physiological Psychology* (1902) describes the role of association in the higher mental processes. Associations are regarded as passive experiences, as they do not engage activity characteristic of the processes of volition and attention. Associations can arouse volitions but are not directly influenced by them. They are passive because they must be 'added to'. However, the apperceptive combinations are seen to be superior to the automatic associative processes. They imply a consciousness of the internal state, of active sensation or feeling from which arises attention, and thus constitute a higher class of mental function.

Wundt assigned the role of the complementary phsyiological centre of the process of apperception to the frontal lobe region of the cortex, which he agreed with a number of eminent physiologists of the period was connected with the functions of intelligence. He thought that the physiological substrate of the apperception process was necessarily an inhibitory process, as it stopped other excitations not directly involved with the process. He sought throughout his work to associate the physiological with the psychological, to integrate the body—mind complex that is the human being.

Wundt was a prolific writer and established the journal *Philosophische Studien* (*Philosophical Studies*) in 1883. It contained some theoretical articles but largely reported on the the problems and methodology of the laboratory. More than 50 per cent of all the research work published in the first years of the journal was concerned with the four principal areas of experimental research in the Leipzig laboratory: the psychophysiology of the senses, reaction time, psychophysics and the association experiment. In 1900, the first of ten volumes of *Volkerpsychologie* (*Folk Psychology*) was published. Wundt devoted a great deal of time to philosophical and sociological issues of psychology and the higher levels of mental development expressed in language, myth, art forms and social customs. He conducted studies in the psychological interpretation of language, with emphasis on the interrelation of psychical and physiological factors in the development of linguistic structure. He also supported the approach of understanding a social group through the analysis of its language, believing that the language and vocabulary of a people gave an insight into their psychology. The scope of Wundt's work in folk psychology included human and animal psychology, hypnotism and spiritualism, among other areas. He also undertook a systematic psychological interpretation of the data of anthropology and history.

Wundt became increasingly preoccupied with philosophical and psychological issues, and for many years held lectures on psychology directed primarily at students of philosophy. His students came from all over the world and included many famous names, e.g. from America, G. Stanley Hall and James **Cattell** (Cattell worked as Wundt's assistant *c*.1885). From Europe, the students who worked in his laboratory included Oswald **Külpe**, Alfred Lehman, Ernst Meumann,

Theodor Lipps, Felix Krueger and Edward **Titchener** (Titchener later translated some of Wundt's work into English).

Perhaps Wundt's greatest achievement was to found psychology as an independent scientific discipline, complementary to anatomy and physiology though in no sense reducible to them. Although he succeeded in firmly establishing empiricism in the study of psychology, he did not himself believe that experimental method is applicable to all aspects of human psychology. With particular reference to language and its development, he sought understanding through the study of history and culture rather than through experimental analysis. He himself wrote voluminously on such issues in his later years, though very little of this work has appeared in English. His greatest strength was, through his own work and that of his pupils, the systematization and synthesis of work that had preceded him, thus preparing the foundation for experimental psychology.

Y

d'Ydewalle, Gery

Born: 1946, Bruges, Belgium **Nat:** Belgian **Ints:** Experimental psychology, vision, psycholinguistics **Educ:** Diplomas in Music in Schools of Music of Bruges, Ghent, and Cologne; PhD in Psychology, University of Louvain, 1974; Baccalaureus Philosophy, University of Louvain, 1976 **Appts & awards:** Félicien Cattier Fellow, Francqui Foundation and CRB Fellow of the Belgian American Educational Foundation, Indiana University, 1972–3; Deputy Secretary-General 1974–8, Secretary-General 1978–87; Psychology Award of the Royal Academy, 1977; Fulbright-Hayes and NATO Fellow, Rockefeller University, 1977–8; Director of the Laboratory of Experimental Psychology, University of Louvain, 1980– ; Invited Professor, Birkbeck College, University of London, 1983–4; Professor, University of Louvain, 1984– ; President, International Committee for Social Science Information and Documentation, 1985–9; Invited Professor, London School of Economics, 1986–7; Vice President 1987–90, President, 1993– , Belgian Psychological Society; Secretary-General, National Committee of Psychology of the Belgian Royal Academy of Sciences; Deputy Secretary-General 1987–92, Secretary-General 1992– ; International Union of Psychological Science; President, 1992, XXV International Congress of Psychology, Brussels; Francqui Award, 1992; Francqui Chair, University of Liège; Corresponding member, Belgian Royal Academy of Sciences, 1992– ; Vice President, International Social Sciences Council, 1994–

Principal publications

1975 Repetition and recall of 'Right' and 'Wrong' responses in incidental and intentional learning. *Journal of Experimental Psychology: Human Learning and Memory*, 104, 429–41 (with P. Eelen).

1981 Test expectancies in free recall and recognition. *Journal of General Psychology*, 105, 175–95.

1982 (ed.) *Cognition in human motivation and learning*. *Hillsdale*, Erlbaum (with W. Lens).

1984 Personality and attribution in subjects' impression outcomes. In H.C.J. Bonarius, G.L.M. van Heck and N.G. Smid (eds), *Personality Psychology in Europe: Theoretical and Empirical Developments*. Swets & Zietlinger.

1985 (ed.) *Cognition, Information Processing, and Motivation*. North-Holland.

1986 Motivation and information processing in learning experiments. In S.E. Newstead, S.H. Irvine and P.L. Dann (eds) *Human Assessment: Cognition and Motivation*. Kluwer.

1990 Tachistoscopic presentation of verbal stimuli for assessing cerebral dominance: Reliability data and some practical recommendations. *Neuropsychologia*, 28, 443–55 (with M. Brysbaert).

1991 A mathematical analysis of the convenient viewing hypothesis and its components (pp. 331–40); Visual and linguistic processes in children with reading disabilities (pp. 491–502). In R. Schmid and D. Zambarbieri (eds), *Oculomotor Control and Cognitive Processes: Normal and Pathological Aspects*. Elsevier.

1991 Watching subtitled television: Automatic reading behavior. *Communication Research*, 18, 650–66.

1991 Detection of symmetry in tachistoscopically presented dot patterns: Effects of multiple axes and skewing. *Perception and Psychophysics*, 50, 413–27.

1991 Orientational effects and component processes in symmetry detection. *Quarterly Journal of Experimental Psychology*, 44A, 475–508.

1992 Simultaneous effects of multiple reference points in spatial stimulus-response compatibility. *Acta Psychologica*, 92, 115–30.

1992 Local and global contextual constraints on the identification of objects in scenes. *Canadian Journal of Psychology*, 46, 490–509.

1992 *Cognitive Modelling and Interactive Environments in Language Learning*. Springer-Verlag.

1993 *Perception and Cognition: Advances in Eye Movement Research*. Elsevier.

1994 *Visual and Oculomotor Functions: Advances in Eye Movement Research*. Elsevier.

1994 An affine group model and the perception of orthographically projected planar random polygons. *Journal of Mathematical Psychology*, 38, 59–72.

1994 Stroop-like interference in sorting for intrinsic color: A test of the Glaser and Glaser (1989) model. *Acta Psychologica*, 85, 123–37.

Further reading

Brogan, D. (ed.) (1990) *Visual Search.* Taylor and Francis.

Gerbino, W. (1989) From categorization and amodal completion: A reply to Wagemans and d'Ydewalle. *Acta Psychologica.* 72, 295–300.

A leader in European experimental psychology, Gery d'Ydewalle has been active in organizations that foster psychology's growth through international collaborations. After early training in music both in his native Belgium and in Germany, d'Ydewalle pursued the study of philosophy and psychology at the University of Louvain, where he completed the PhD in 1974. Part of his graduate training was done at Indiana University. He has continued his affiliation with the University of Louvain and was appointed Full Professor in 1984. He has held visiting appointments at the Rockefeller University and Birkbeck College of the University of London, and he was named a corresponding member of the Belgian Royal Academy of Sciences in 1992.

d'Ydewalle's research centres on the cognitive processes underlying visual perception. He has advocated a levels-of-processing approach to the study of perception and memory, which attempts to accommodate variables that concern structure, meaning and relations. He has conducted programmatic experiments that examine information processing in advertising messages, particularly through television. While this approach has been criticized for its reductionism, d'Ydewalle's work is recognized for its precision and prescriptive value. In recent years he has studied visual transformations of shape and colour and related his findings within a mathematical model that effectively predicts human visual perception of orthographically projected random polygons.

In addition to his productive research program, d'Ydewalle is an impressive advocate of European psychology and the importance of international cooperation for psychology. He serves on a number of editorial boards of European journals. He has also held leading positions in professional organizations in Bel-

gium and internationally, including the presidency of the XXV International Congress of Psychology in 1992.

JAMES F. BRENNAN

Yela, Mariano Granizo

Born: 1921, Madrid, Spain **Died:** 1994, Madrid, Spain **Nat:** Spanish **Ints:** Experimental psychology, evaluation and measurement, industrial and organizational psychology, philosophical and theoretical psychology **Educ:** BSc University of Madrid, 1940; Cicenciado en Filosofia University of Madrid, 1945; PhD University of Madrid, 1957 **Appts & awards:** Professor, University Compulsensis Campus Somosaguas; Co-Founder and Executive Secretary, Psychological Research Council, 1948–69; Secretary, SPA, 1952–8, Vice-President, 1968–73, President, 1973–83; Secretary, Institute of Applied Psychology, University of Madrid, 1953–75, President, 1973–83; Madrid Royal Academy, Social Sciences, Plaza Villa, Madrid Spanish Psychological Association (SPA) Prize, 1954; President, International Association of Experimental Psychology and Animal Behaviour, 1958; International Francqui Prize (Belgium), 1961; University of Louvain Prize, 1962; Executive Member, French Language Association of Scientific Psychology, 1962; Simarro Foundation of Psychological Research, 1964; International Association of Audiophonology, 1975; Research Council, Human Sciences Division, 1976; National Scientific Research (Spain) Prize, 1977; Spanish Communications, UNESCO, 1979; Spanish National Research Committee, 1979; Editorial Boards: *Revue Psicologia General y Aplicada*, 1948– , *Revue Educacion*, 1953– , *International Journal of Psychology*, 1966–9, *Analisis y Modificacion de Conducta*, 1974– , *Revue Neurologia, Neurocirugia y Psiquiatria*, 1976– , *German Journal of Psychology*, 1977, *Interdisciplinaria*, 1979–

Principal publications

1949 The application of the principle of simple structure to Alexander's data. *Psychometrika*, 2, 121–35.

1952 Phenomenal causation. *Quarterly Journal of Experimental Psychology*, 4, 139–54.

1956 *Psicologia de las Aptitudes*. Gredos.

1956 *Psicometria y Estadistica*. Universidad de Madrid.

1956 Role of auditory cortex in discrimination requiring localization of sound in space. *Journal of Neurophysiology*, 19, 500–12.

1957   *La Tecnica del Analisis Factorial.* Bibloteca
Nueva.
1963   Concencia, cuerpo y conducta. *Revue
Universidad de Madrid*, 41, 7–39.
1968   La estructure factorial de la inteligencia
tecnica. *Revue Psicologica General y Aplicada*, 94,
705–70 (with M. Pascual).
1973   Entropia homeostasis y equilibrio: El proceso
fundamental de la motivacion. *Revue Psychologica
General y Aplicada*, 123, 621–53.
1974   *La Estructura de la Conducta.* Real Academia
de Ciencias Morales y Politicas.
1980   La evolucion del conductismo.
Interdisciplinaria, 1, 43–65.
1981   Ambiente, herencia y conducta. In *Psicologia
y Medio*. Ministerio de Obras Publicas.

Further reading

Yela, M. (1983). Autobiography and other papers.
Anthropos Monograph, 23.
Carpintero, H. (1995) Mariano Yela-Granizo
(1921–1994). *American Psychologist*, 50, 1097.

The Spanish Civil War (1936–9) interrupted
the development of psychology in Spain, and
after Yela graduated from Madrid he spent
several years of study and research at the University of Washington (with Moore), Chicago
(with **Thurstone**, Neff, **Rogers**), Edinburgh
(with Thomson), London (with **Burt**), Paris (with
Pieron), Louvain (with **Michotte**) and Freiberg
(with Heidegger). He returned to Spain and
became actively involved in founding the basic
institutions for psychological research, teaching,
professional work, associations and publishing.

Yela's research work is organized themati-
cally around the concepts of epistemology and
history and has led him to a position he terms
biological and personal behaviourism. He argues
that behaviour is not simply a stimulus–
response (S–R) physical event but a physical
pattern of biological and/or personal meaningful action. Psychology should be concerned with
elucidating the processes, structures, systems
and laws of psycho-organic activity. Working
from this perspective, he has sought to clarify
the history of psychology and the epistemological meaning of stimulus, situation, response and
action. His work has included investigations of
the psychophysiology of the perception of
sound, the perception of functional relations
(such as phenomenal causation), and the structure and processes of intelligence and thinking,
especially in the domains of spatial and verbal
action. He has developed a theory of the heterogenous continuum of intelligence and applied

his ideas to the theoretical and practical study of
human work, education and health.

Yerkes, Robert Mearns

Born: 1876, Breadysville, Pennsylvania USA
Died: 1956, New Haven, Connecticut, USA
Nat: American **Ints:** General psychology,
evaluation and measurement, physiological and
comparative, military psychology **Educ:** AB
Ursinus College, 1897; AB Harvard University,
1898; AM Harvard University, 1899; PhD
Harvard University, 1902; **Appts & awards:**
Instructor, 1902–08, and Assistant Professor of
Comparative Psychology, 1908–17, both at
Harvard University; President, APA, 1916–17;
Professor of Psychology, University of Min-
nesota (in absentia), 1917–19; Chief, Division
of Psychology, Office of the Surgeon General,
1917–18; Chairman, Research Information
Service, National Research Council, 1919–24;
Hon. LLD Ursinus College, 1923; Hon. DSc
Wesleyan University, 1923; Member, National
Academy of Science, 1923; Professor of Psy-
chobiology, Yale University, 1929–44;
Director, Yale Laboratories of Primate Biology,
1929–41; Hon. MA Yale University, 1931;
Member, American Philosophical Society 1936;
President, American Society of Naturalists,
1938; Fellow, American Academy of Arts and
Sciences and AAAS; Member, American Phy-
siological Society; Gold Medal, New York
Zoological Society, 1954

Principal publications

1907   *The Dancing Mouse: A Study in Animal
Behavior.* Macmillan.
1908   The relation of strength of stimulus to rapidity
of habit formation. *Journal of Comparative
Neurology and Psychology*, 18, 459–82 (with J.D.
Dodson).
1911   Methods of studying vision in animals.
Behavior Monographs, 1, 96 (with J.B. Watson).
1916   The mental life of monkeys and apes: A study
of ideational behavior. *Behavior Monographs*, 3,
149.
1920   (ed.) *Mental Tests in the American Army.* Holt
(with C.S Yoakum).
1929   *The Great Apes: A Study of Anthropoid Life.*
Yale University Press (with A.W. Yerkes).
1943   *Chimpanzees: A Laboratory Colony.* Yale
University Press.

Further reading

Boakes, R. (1984) *From Darwinism to Behaviourism.*
Cambridge University Press.

Yerkes, R.M. (1932) Robert Mearns Yerkes: Psychobiologist. In C. Murchison (ed.) *A History of Psychology in Autobiography*, vol. 2. Clark University Press.

Although Yerkes is normally classified as a pioneer of comparative psychology (or psychobiology, to use his later, preferred description), equally important contributions to psychology came through his work as an organizer and committee man, and as an academic entrepreneur who founded laboratories, and arranged funding for, and ran, large-scale practical projects.

As an academic, however, Yerkes was happy to study animal intelligence in an unashamedly ninteenth-century fashion (including himself among 'the students of consciousness'), adopting an essentially phylogenetic stance over how intelligence expressed itself. His experimental work also recapitulated phylogeny, with the earliest research on crustacea, and ending with the group most closely associated with his name, primates, particularly chimpanzees and gorillas. His theorizing was equally anthropomorphic, involving extensive cross-references between, say, the intellectual development of the chimpanzee and the child. This was, in a sense, almost pure **Darwin**, emphasizing upward continuity between species, but downward interpretation of the phenomena, particularly when *Homo sapiens* figured in the list.

Yerkes's almost reactionary approach to animal behaviour proved entirely antithetical to the revolutionary behaviourism of his friend and colleague, J.B. **Watson**. This attitude almost certainly excluded Yerkes from the intellectual company of the behaviourist Young Turks whose number and influence were to grow rapidly from the 1920s onward. It is, however, a matter of considerable historical dispute as to whose approach, in the end, proved to be the more successful, Yerkes or Watson. Certainly there are few ascetic animal behaviourists around today.

But it was his indefatigable work on his many committees and as the driving force behind many large-scale projects that helped ensure his place in psychology. For instance, he set up the comparative psychology facilities at Harvard in the early years of this century (a period which also saw him attempting with Watson to standardize aspects of the practice of comparative psychology) and, during the First World War, launched the mass programme of psychometric testing for the American Army. He held a full-time post as chairman of several influential committees of the National Research Council in Washington from 1919 until 1924, when he was invited to Yale as research professor with the remit of establishing a full-scale primate laboratory. Yerkes also became director of the laboratory when it was eventually found a permanent site in Florida, a post he relinquished only shortly before his retirement from Yale. During the Second World War and for several years afterwards, Yerkes continued his beloved committee work with the NCR, the APA and many other bodies. From all of this we can perhaps begin to appreciate just how great was Yerkes's influence on the direction of American psychology during the first half of this century.

A.D. LOVIE AND PATRICIA LOVIE

Z

Zajonc, Robert B.

Born: 1923, Lodz, Poland *Nat:* Polish *Ints:* General psychology, personality and social psychology *Educ:* PhD University of Michigan, 1955 *Appts & awards:* Fulbright Scholar, 1962–3; APA Division 8, Executive Board, 1966–9; NSF Review Panel, Social Psychology, 1968–70; APA Board of Scientific Affairs, 1973–6; AAAS Prize for Social Psychology (with G. Markus), 1975; Fellow, Center for Advanced Study in the Behavioral Sciences, 1975–6; NH Research Review Panel, 1977–9; APA Distinguished Scientific Contribution Award, 1978; APA Committee on Scientific Awards, Chairman, 1979– ; NAS Committee on Basic Research in the Social Sciences, 1980; Society for Experimental Social Psychology, President, 1980–1; APA Council of Representatives, 1981–2; Fellow, Divisions 1 and 8, AAA&S, New York Academy of Sciences; APA Division 1, President, 1983; University of Michigan, Director, Research Center for Group Dynamics, 1983– ; Hon. D, University of Louvain, 1984; Editorial Boards: *Human Relations*, 1956, *Annual Review of Psychology*, 1978–84, *European Journal of Social Psychology*, 1978–86, *Population*, 1978, *British Journal of Social Psychology*, 1979, *Social Cognition*, 1980, *Current Issues and Research in Advertising*, 1981, Pergamon Psychology Software, 1985, *Revue de Psychologie Sociale*, 1986; Consulting Editor: *Contemporary Psychology*, 1956–60, *Journal of Experimental Social Psychology*, 1968; Associate Editor, *Journal of Abnormal and Social Psychology*, 1960–7; Editorial Consultant, *Motivation and Emotion*, 1981

Principal publications

1962 *Methods in Small Group Processes*. Stanford University Press.
1964 Perception, drive, and behavior theory. *Psychological Review*, 71, 273–90 (with D.D. Dorfman).
1966 *Social Psychology: An Experimental Approach*. Wadsworth.

1966 Cognitive consequences of a person's position in a formal organization. *Human Relations*, 19, 139–50 (with D.M. Wolfe).
1968 Attitudinal effects of mere exposure. *Journal of Personality and Social Psychology*, monograph supplement, 9, 1–27.
1969 *Animal Social Psychology*. Wiley.
1975 Birth order and intellectual development. *Psychological Review*, 82, 74–88 (with G.B. Markus).
1980 Feeling and thinking: Preferences need no inferences. *American Psychologist*, 35, 151–75.
1982 Exposure effects in person perception; Familiarity, similarity, and attraction. *Journal of Experimental Social Psychology*, 18, 395–415 (with R.L. Moreland).
1983 (ed.) *Emotions, Cognition and Behavior*. Cambridge University Press (with C.E. Izard and J. Kagan).
1983 Validating the confluence model. *Psychological Bulletin*, 93, 457–80.
1985 The cognitive perspective in social psychology. In G. Lindzey and E. Aronson (eds), *Handbook of Social Psychology*. Random House (with H. Markus).
1985 Emotion and facial expression. *Science*, 230, 608–87.
1987 *Principles of Psychology Today*. Random House (with G.H. Bower and R.R. Bootzin).
1989 Styles of explanation in social psychology. Special issue: Controversies in the Social Explanation of Psychological Behaviour. *European Journal of Social Psychology*, 19, 345–68.
1993 The confluence model: Differential or difference equation. *European Journal of Social Psychology*, 23, 211–15.
1993 Affect, cognition, and awareness: Affective priming with optimal and suboptimal stimulus exposures. *Journal of Personality and Social Psychology*, 64, 723–39 (with S.T. Murphy).
1994 Emotional expression and temperature modulation. In S.H.M. van Goozen, N.E. Van de Poll and J.A. Sergeant (eds), *Emotions: Essays on Emotion Theory*. Erlbaum.

Further reading

Barbut, M. (1993) Comments on a pseudo-mathematical model in social psychology. *European Journal of Social Psychology*, 23, 203–10.

Geen, R.G. (1989) Alternative conceptions of social facilitation. In P.B. Paulus (ed.), *Psychology of Group Influence*. Erlbaum.

Lazarus, R.S. (1981) A cognitivist's reply to Zajonc on emotion and cognition. *American Psychologist*, 36, 222–3.

Lemaine, G. (1989) Styles of explanation in social psychology: Comment on Zajonc. *European Journal of Social Psychology*, 19, 369–70.

Schwanenberg, E. (1990) World of probability and world of meaning: Cognition and affect in perspective. *Social Science Information*, 29, 249–77.

Zajonc is principally associated with two major contributions to social psychology: the drive theory of social facilitation, and a theory of emotion. Social facilitation refers to the ways the mere presence of others affects individual performance. This presence influences our level of arousal, causing improvements on simple tasks and decrements on complex tasks. Zajonc conducted a classic study of mere presence effects using cockroaches. With colleagues Heingartner and Herman, he built a simple maze with a bright light and a 'viewing gallery' in which other roaches could be placed. Bright light is a noxious stimulus for cockroaches and in this device they could avoid it by scurrying down the maze and into a darkened box. Cockroaches run the simple maze faster when other roaches are watching, but the results are reversed when the complexity of the maze is increased (i.e. mere presence impairs performance in the complex maze). Zajonc offered an elegant explanation for the effect. First, the mere presence of others increases physiological arousal, and second, under conditions of heightened arousal it is easier to perform simple tasks better but harder to do something complex. Stated another way, the presence of others will facilitate the performance of strong, well-learned responses but may interfere with the performance of new, as yet unmastered ones. But why should the mere presence of others cause physiological arousal? Zajonc prefers an explanation which states that the presence of other people (or other roaches, if you are a cockroach) increases the complexity of the situation – others are unpredictable and, being unlike static elements in the environment, induce a mild level of arousal. Competing explanations suggest: (1) the presence of others is distracting and this increases arousal; and (2) people are more complex than other animals and the arousal is due to evaluation apprehension – i.e. apprehension about being judged.

Zajonc's explanation for social facilitation is situated in the context of a broader theory of emotion. According to his theory, a person person can have an emotional reaction to a stimulus without any corresponding cognitive reaction. Zajonc suggests that emotional responses may be produced by a system that is completely independent from cognitive processes. This is different from the two-factor theory of emotion, which posits a two-step self-perception process: people first experience physiological arousal and seek an explanation for it, and it is this labelling of the arousal that is experienced as the emotion. Empirical support for Zajonc's theory comes from several sources. For example, people have emotional responses to subliminal presentations of stimuli that have been repeatedly encountered, but are not consciously detectable.

More generally, Zajonc argues that the study of emotions holds the best promise for a solution to the mind–body problem in psychology, since research on emotions deals with data that are directly observable. He suggests that one way to examine the interrelationships between mind and body is to determine what it is that culture and past experience contribute to variance in subjective experience, expression and physiological process. Another avenue is the examination of how facial action changes affect. In support of his argument he points to research suggesting that this occurs via brain temperature (e.g. in the hypothamalus). Studies on the correspondence between feeling states and bodily states suggest that negative affect is associated with the right hemisphere and positive affect with the left. Subjective emotional states can be produced by emotional efference governed by changes in hypothalamic temperature. In Zajonc's view, outward behavioural actions, and especially facial efference associated with an emotional episode, may modulate the hypothalamic temperature. His theoretical analyses and his ingenious experimental manipulations have stimulated a controversial debate and will continue to so do.

Zangwill, Oliver Louis

Born: 1913, Littlehampton, England **Died:** 1987, Little Paxton, England **Nat:** British **Ints:**

Experimental psychology, clinical neuropsychology **Educ:** BA University of Cambridge, 1935; MA University of Cambridge, 1939 **Appts & awards:** Assistant Director, Institute of Experimental Psychology, Oxford, 1945–52; Visiting Psychologist, National Hospital for Nervous Diseases, Queen Square London, 1947–79; Senior Lecturer in General Psychology, University of Oxford, 1948–52; Professor of Experimental Psychology, and Head of the Psychological Laboratory, University of Cambridge, 1952–81; Fellow, King's College Cambridge, 1955; President, Experimental Psychology Society, 1962–5; Hon. Foreign Member, Société Française de Neurologie, 1971; President, BPS 1974–5; Fellow, Royal Society, 1977; Kenneth Craik Award, St John's College Cambridge 1977–8; Hon. DSc University of St Andrews, 1980.

Principal publications

1950   *An Introduction to Modern Psychology.* Cambridge University Press.

1960   *Cerebral Dominance and its Relation to Psychological Function.* Oliver & Boyd.

1961   (ed.) *Current Problems in Animal Behaviour.* Cambridge University Press (with W.H. Thorpe).

1983   Disorders of memory. In M. Shepherd and O.L. Zangwill (eds), *Handbook of Psychiatry*, vol. 1: *General Psychopathology.* Cambridge University Press.

Further reading

Jeeves, M. (1988) Obituary. *The Psychologist*, 1, 59.

Weiskrantz, L. (1988) Obituary. *Quarterly Journal of Experimental Psychology*, 40A, 1–4.

Oliver Louis Zangwill was educated at University College London School and King's College Cambridge, where he read Natural and Moral Sciences, achieving a starred First, and stayed on as a research student until 1940. He worked during World War II in the Brain Injuries Unit in Edinburgh, encountering the problems of rehabilitation of soldiers with head injuries. In 1952, he succeeded Sir Frederick **Bartlett**, under whom he had trained, to the Chair in Psychology at Cambridge University. He introduced animals into the Psychological Laboratory and, together with W.H. Thorpe, fostered inter-disciplinary research into animal behaviour. While welcoming the influences of applied psychology and cultural anthropology (if not social psychology) on his subject, his own bent was to look to the integration of psychology and physiology, albeit stressing the value of verbal report.

Following Sherrington and Hughlings **Jackson**, he appreciated the significance of loss of hierarchical integration in the nervous system for explaining the effects of brain lesions. This was a point of departure for much of his clinical work, in research associations with the Radcliffe Infirmary, Oxford, the National Hospital for Nervous Diseases, London and the United Cambridge Hospitals. Zangwill was particularly associated with the analysis of parietal lobe syndromes, describing the resulting defects in the perception of spatial relations following right hemisphere damage (and thus confirming Hughlings Jackson's neglected hypothesis as to laterality). He contributed signally to the understanding of the relations between cerebral dominance and handedness, arguing that certainly the latter, and possibly the former, were graded characteristics, and also that left-handers were more likely to be left- than right-dominant for speech. He carried out work on amnesic syndromes, in particular on Korsokoff's psychosis. In 1941 he drew attention to a previously unrecorded deficit, the inability to respond to identity. He later (1983) elaborated the distinction between the classical Korsokoff syndrome and the amnesia associated with medial temporal lobe lesions. Zangwill's inaugural lecture, his introductory textbook, and his many contributions to the *Oxford Companion to the Mind* illustrate his wide-ranging knowledge. His capacity for careful analysis, offering perspective while avoiding over-generalization, is exemplified in his essay on the development and range of application of **Lashley**'s concepts of mass action and equipotentiality, and by his papers with Oldfield on the concepts of the schema employed by Head, Bartlett and Wolters.

As a public figure, Zangwill was, in an unobtrusive manner, influential both nationally and internationally within his discipline. He was instrumental in founding the Experimental Psychology Group in Cambridge in 1946 (from 1958 called the Experimental Psychology Society), an association for the study of basic scientific issues in psychology. To publish the results of relevant research, the *Quarterly Journal of Experimental Psychology* was founded, which he edited for eight years. His other major influence, as both an experimentalist and a clinician, was on the growing discipline of neuropsychology. According to Weiskrantz, the founding of the journal *Neuropsychologia*, edited by Zangwill for some twenty years, drew heavily on his advocacy. The inspiration for the EPS Bartlett Lectureship was also his. He had a substantial influence on the development of clinical neuropsychology in benign and profitable association with cognitive psychology.

E.R. VALENTINE AND MARY J. PICKERSGILL

Zeigarnik, Bluma Vulfowna

Born: 1900, Prenai, Russia *Died:* 1988, Moscow, Russia *Nat:* Russian *Ints:* Pathopsychology, clinical psychology, psychology of personality *Educ:* Berlin University, graduated 1927 *Appts & awards:* Professor, Department of Psychology, Moscow State University, 1959–88; D Pedagogical Sciences (on Psychology), Moscow State University, 1959; Winner of Lomonosov Prize and Kurt Levin Award, 1983

Principal publications

1965   *The Pathology of Thought*. Consultants Bureau.

1971   *Personality and Pathology of Activity*. Moscow University Press (in Russian).

1972   *Experimental Abnormal Psychology*. Plenum.

1973   *Foundation of Pathopsychology*. Moscow University Press (in Russian).

1976   *Pathopsychology*. Moscow University Press (in Russian).

1982   *Theory of Personality in Foreign Psychology*. Moscow University Press (in Russian).

Further reading

Zeigarnik, B.W (1961) *Denkstörungen bei psychiatrischen Krankheitsbildern; eine experimentalpsychologische Untersuchung*. Akademie Verlag.

—— (1980) *Outline of Psychology of Abnormal Personality Development*. Moscow University Press (in Russian).

—— (1981) *Kurt Lewin's Theory of Personality*. Moscow University Press (in Russian).

Bluma Vulfovna Zeigarnik was born in small town of Prenai in the former Vilen region of Russia (Lithuania now) on 9 November 1900. She was educated at the university of Berlin (graduating in 1927). This period was a climax of German experimental psychology. She heard lectures by Max **Wertheimer**, **Köhler** and other great psychologists. Her first experimental investigation, done as diploma work under the supervision of Kurt **Lewin**, was devoted to remembering unfinished actions. It was found that people involved in some tasks requiring them to remember things (names, figures etc.) related to these tasks much better when the task is interrupted than when it is completed. This effect, now known as the Zeigarnik phenomenon, brought world fame to Zeigarnik. Joint work and fruitful scientific communication with other students and followers of K. Lewin (such as T. Dembo, F. Hoppe, G. Birenbaum) during this 'Berlin period' had a strong influence on her further scientific interests. Another influence on Zeigarnik came from the remarkable Soviet psychologist **Vygotsky**, with whom Zeigarnik worked from 1931 at the Institute of Experimental Medicine on the so-called culture-historical approach to the pathology of the mental activity of patients.

During World War II Zeigarnik worked in the hospital at Ural together with other well known Soviet psychologists (**Leont'ev**, **Luria**, Zaporozhetz and others) on the rehabilitation of soldiers suffering from brain damage. In Soviet psychology Zeigarnik was known for establishing a new branch of science, 'pathopsychology', which differed from both clinical and medical psychology as these were understood in the West. Pathopsychology was considered as an experimental science whose object was claimed to be the mental processes of mentally ill people, considered from the point of view of general psychology. It was not aimed directly at helping a patient having some behaviour or mental disorder to find better adjustment and self expression.

Belonging to the so-called Moscow school in Soviet psychology (Vygotsky, Leont'ev, and Luria), Zeigarnik built pathopsychology on the principles of the activity theory as it was formulated in the works of A.N. Leont'ev. She developed the principles of conducting pathopsychological experiments taking into account the effect of the patient's motivation and his/her attitude to the particular situation of the experiment on performing an experimental task.

Zeigarnik and her followers described specificity in thinking and personality of people suffering from schizophrenia, epilepsy, alcoholism and some other mental illness. By these studies they corroborated Leont'ev's theory of personality as a hierarchy of motives, having shown that mentally ill people had this hierarchy essentially restructured. Furthermore, Soviet pathopsychologists revealed changes in other types of the individual's mental activity (e.g. thinking, perception, personality). They have shown that cognitive disorder in patients is mediated by their motivation disorder. As a result, they claimed to have established a principle of studying personality through investigating restructuring cognitive activity.

Zeigarnik has developed a system of pathopsychological examination of mentally ill people and made great efforts to foster the whole generation of Soviet pathopsychologists who now work successfully in psychiatric clinics in Russia using the works of their teacher. Zeigarnik wrote six books and more than 120 articles which were translated in USA, Germany, Italy, Spain, Portugal, Poland and Yugoslavia.

A. LOGVINENKO AND T. SOKOLSKAYA

Zigler, Edward

Born: 1930, Kansas City, USA **Nat:** American **Ints:** Child, youth and family services, developmental, mental retardation, psychotherapy **Educ:** BS University of Missouri, 1954; PhD University of Texas at Austin, 1958 **Appts & awards:** Yale University, Seeling Professor of Psychology, Director, Bush Center in Child Development and Social Policy; Hon. MA, Yale University, 1967; Hon. Commissioner, National Commission on the International Year of the Child, 1979; Hon. D, Boston College, 1985; Aldrich Award, American Academy of Paediatrics; APA National Achievement Award, Association for the Advancement of Psychology; APA Seymour B. Sarason Award, 1993; APA Nicholas Hobbs Award; APA Distinguished Contribution to Psychology Award; G. Stanley Hall Award; Merril Palmer Citation Award; Research Award, AAMD Dale Richmond Memorial Award, American Academy of Paediatrics; Gunnar Dybwad Award, NARC; Associate Editor: *Children and Youth Services Review*; Consulting Editor: *Merril-Palmer Quarterly*, *Young Children*; Editorial Boards: *American Journal of Orthopsychiatry*, *Applied Research in Mental Retardation*, *Family Violence and Pathology*, *Journal of Applied Developmental Psychology*, *Journal of Developmental Psychopathology*

Principal publications

1976   A developmental psychologist's view of Operation Babylift. *American Psychologist*, 31, 329–40.

1976   Mainstreaming: The proof is in the implementation. *American Psychologist*, 34, 993–5 (with S. Muenchow).

1978   IQ, social competence, and evaluation of early childhood intervention programs. *American Psychologist*, 33, 789–98 (with P. Trickett).

1979   (ed.) *Project Head Start: A Legacy of the War on Poverty*. Free Press (with J. Valentine).

1979   Controlling child abuse in America: An effort doomed to failure? In R. Bourne and E. Newberger (eds), *Critical Perspectives on Child Abuse*. Lexington.

1981   A plea to end the use of the patterning treatment for retarded children. *American Journal of Orthopsychiatry*, 51, 388–90.

1982   (ed.) *Socialization and Personality Development*. (2nd edn). Oxford University Press, (with M. Lamb and I. Child).

1982   (ed.) *Day Care: Scientific and Social Policy Issues*. Auburn House (with E. Gordon).

1983   *Children, Families and Government: Perspectives on American Social Policy*. Cambridge University Press (with S.L. Kagan and E. Klugman).

1983   Discerning the future of early childhood intervention. *American Psychologist*, 38, 894–906 (with W. Berman).

1984   On the definition and classification of mental retardation. *American Journal of Mental Deficiency*, 89, 215–30 (with D. Balla and M. Hodapp).

1984   Paranoid schizophrenia: An unorthodox view. *American Journal of Orthopsychiatry*, 54, 43–70 (with M. Glick).

1984   How to influence social policy affecting children and families. *American Psychologist*, 39, 415–20 (with S. Muenchow).

1986   *Understanding Mental Retardation*. Cambridge University Press (with R. Hodapp).

1989   Addressing the nation's child care crisis: The school of the twenty-first century. *American Journal of Orthopsychiatry*, 59, 484–91.

1989   The Head Start Synthesis Project: A critique. *Journal of Applied Developmental Psychology*, 10, 267–74 (with T.J. Gamble).

1993   Adolescent suicide prevention: Current research and social policy implications. Special issue: Adolescence. *American Psychologist*, 48, 169–82 (with A.F. Garland).

1994   Reshaping early childhood intervention to be a more effective weapon against poverty. *American Journal of Community Psychology*, 22, 37–47.

1995   Developmental differences in the symptomatology of psychiatric inpatients with and without mild mental retardation. *American Journal on Mental Retardation*, 99, 407–17 (with M. Glick).

Further reading
Greenspan, S. (1980) Is social competence synonymous with school performance? *American Psychologist*, 35, 938–9.
Lee, L.C. (1979) Is social competence independent of cultural context? *American Psychologist*, 34, 795–6.
Menolascino, F.J. and Stark, J.A. (1990) Research versus advocacy in the allocation of resources: Problems, causes, solutions. *American Journal on Mental Retardation*, 95, 21–5.
Ramey, S.L. (1990) Staging (and re-staging) the trio of services, evaluation, and research. *American Journal on Mental Retardation*, 95, 26–9.

After completing research for a dissertation on factors affecting the performance of retarded children, Zigler worked as a clinical intern in a state psychiatric hospital. These two interests started to converge into what he describes as a developmental similarity among these two atypical groups and their non-deviant counterparts. Familial retarded children behaved much like their non-retarded peers of like mental age when certain socioemotional factors were controlled. Psychiatric patients with higher-level disorders employed higher-level coping mechanisms, which put them at a prognostic disadvantage. While continuing to explore the developmental approach to psychopathology, more of his professional work centred on retardation, culminating in a recent effort to redefine this intellectual classification. A natural extension of this research on how experiential factors influence retarded individuals was to study how they influence non-retarded children who also have deviant social histories, e.g. economically disadvantaged children. He became involved in the design, implementation and assessment of early pre-school interventions for poor and at-risk children. Zigler was responsible for all these elements of the Nation's Head Start programme in the US when he served as the first Director of the Office of Child Development.

In a 1994 review of the accomplishments and difficulties of the Head Start programme, he outlined the Head Start Transition Project as a new approach to early intervention. The three-stage intervention includes child care for infants and toddlers, a pre-school component, and a transition component in the school environment through the primary grades. Health care and nutrition, social and educational experiences, and parenting education to help families and children are other programme components. While continuing to be deeply involved with Head Start, his role as a child advocate expanded greatly. He continues to work to establish social policies to institute family-support systems and to alleviate some of the many problems facing American children and families, such as child abuse, infant mortality, single-parent and dual families, and the availability, quality and effects of day care. His experiences as a clinician, researcher and academic, policy analyst and advocate has convinced Zigler that professionals must direct their expertise towards improving the situations that they so painstakingly detail and investigate.

Zimbardo, Philip G.

Born: 1933, New York City, New York USA ***Nat:*** American ***Ints:*** Personality and social, psychological study of social issues, teaching ***Educ:*** AB Brooklyn College, 1954; MS Yale University, 1955; PhD Yale University, 1959 ***Appts & awards:*** Director, Stanford University Social Psychology Research Training Program, Stanford University; 1970–88; Fellow, Center for Advanced Study in the Behavioral Sciences, 1972; National Media Award, American Psychological Foundation, 1973; Fellow, APA Divisions 2, 8, 9, AAAS; Gordon Allport Intergroup Relations Prize, Society for the Psychological Study of Social Issues, 1974; APF Distinguished Teaching Award, 1975; California State Psychological Association, Distinguished Research Contribution Award, 1977; President, Western Psychological Association, 1982

Principal publications
1965 The effect of effort and improvisation on self-persuasion produced by role-playing. *Journal of Experimental Social Psychology*, 1, 103–20.
1970 Modifying the impact of persuasive communication with external distraction. *Journal of Personality and Social Psychology*, 16, 669–80 (with M. Snyder, J. Thomas, A. Gold and S. Gurwitz).
1972 The tactics and ethics of persuasion. In E. McGinnies and B. King (eds), *Attitudes, Conflict and Social Change*. Academic Press.
1972 *The Ecological Orientation: Its Implications for Psychology*. Scott Foresman.
1972 A study of prisoners and guards in a simulated prison. *Naval Research Reviews*, 9, 1–17 (with C. Haney and C. Banks).
1974 The psychology of imprisonment: Privation, power and pathology. In Z. Rubin (ed.), *Doing Unto Others: Explorations in Social Behavior*. Prentice Hall.

1976 A social-psychological anaysis of vandalism:
Making sense of senseless violence. In E.P.
Hollander and R.G. Hunt (eds), *Current
Perspectives in Social Psychology*. Oxford
University Press.

1978 *Psychology and You*. Scott Foresman (with D.
Dempsey).

1979 The affective consequences of inadequately
explained physiological arousal. *Journal of
Personality and Social Psychology*, 37, 970–88
(with G. Marsall).

1979 The psychology of evil: On the perversion of
human potential. In T.R. Sarbin (ed.), *Challenges
to the Criminal Justice System: The Perspectives of
Community Psychology*. Human Sciences Press.

1981 *The Shy Child*. McGraw-Hill (with S.L. Radl).

1981 Modifying shyness-related social behavior
through symptom misattribution. *Journal of
Personality and Social Psychology*, 41, 437–49
(with S.E. Brodt).

1983 Transforming experimental research into
advocacy for social change. In H.H. Blumberg,
A.P. Hare, V. Kent and M. Davies (eds), *Small
Groups and Social Interaction*. Wiley.

1985 *Working with Psychology*. Scott Foresman
(with S.C. Fraser).

1991 *The Psychology of Attitude Change and Social
Influence*. McGraw-Hill (with M.R. Leippe).

1992 *Psychology and Life* (13th edn). Stanford
University Press.

Further reading

Banuazizi, A. and Movahedi, S. (1975) Interpersonal
dynamics in a simulated prison: A methodological
analysis. *American Psychologist*, 30, 152–60.

Thayer, S. and Saarni, C. (1975) Demand
characteristics are everywhere (anyway): A
comment on the Stanford prison experiment.
American Psychologist, 30, 1015–6.

Being in the presence of others can cause deindividuation, i.e. a feeling of anonymity and a
reduced sense of ourselves as individuals. Under
these circumstances, people appear to experience a sense of reduced accountability – a
perceived reduction in the likelihood that they
will be held responsible for their actions. Philip
Zimbardo is credited with a series of ingenious
experiments which examined social accountability. For example, in one study participants were
invited to put on lab coats and hoods as soon as
they arrived. Names were not used and the room
was darkened to preserve anonymity. In a comparison condition the participants wore their
normal clothes, wore large name tags and sat in
a well-lit room. All of the participants were then

instructed to deliver (supposed) electric shocks
to another person. Those in the anonymous
condition behaved considerably more aggres-
sively towards the person, delivering more and
longer shocks.

Zimbardo extended his research beyond
highly contrived laboratory contexts in a
famous, but controversial, study known as the
Stanford Prison Experiment.. Students who had
volunteered for a psychological study of prison
life were 'arrested' and confined to a simulated
prison in the basement of the Stanford University psychology building. The 'guards' were
also paid volunteers. In time, subjects came to
act more and more like actual prisoners and
actual guards in real prisons. In fact the change
was so great that the study, scheduled for two
weeks, was halted after six days. In effect,
Zimbardo and his colleagues had demonstrated
that people would use implicit and explicit
social norms concerning the roles they were
occupying and allow these to shape their behaviour. It has been argued that people who
participated in the study were merely behaving
as they thought they were expected to behave,
but Zimbardo and others have countered that
even if they were simply 'playing the roles',
they were in effect no different from others
occupying those roles for the first time in real
prisons.

Zuckerman, Marvin

Born: 1928, Chicago, USA ***Nat:*** American ***Ints:***
Clinical, evaluation and measurement, personal-
ity, psychopharmacology ***Educ:*** BA New York
University, 1949; PhD New York University,
1954 ***Appts & awards:*** Professor of Psychology,
University of Delaware; DE USA 1971– ;
President, International Society for the Study of
Individual Differences, 1985–7; Fellow, APA
Divisions 8, 12; Editorial Boards: *Personality
and Individual Differences*, *Journal of Psycho-
pathology and Behavioral Assessment*

Principal publications

1960 The development of an Affect Adjective
Check List for the measurement of anxiety. *Journal
of Consulting Psychology*, 24, 457–62.

1964 Development of a sensation seeking scale.
Journal of Consulting Psychology, 28, 477–82
(with B.A. Kolin, L. Price and I. Zoob).

1965 *Test Manual for the Multiple Affect Adjective
Check List*. Educational and Industrial Testing
Service (with B. Lubin). (rev. 1985).

1968 Experimental and subject factors determining

responses to sensory deprivation, social isolation and confinement. *Journal of Abnormal Psychology*, 73, 183–94 (with H. Persky, K.E. Link and G.K. Basu).

1969   Theories of sensory deprivation. In J.P. Zubek (ed.), *Sensory Deprivation: Fifteen Years of Research*. Appleton-Century-Crofts.

1971   Dimensions of sensation seeking. *Journal of Consulting and Clinical Psychology*, 36, 45–72.

1971   Physiological measures of sexual arousal in the human. *Psychological Bulletin*, 75, 297–329.

1974   Sensation seeking and cortical augmenting-reducing. *Psychophysiology*, 11, 535–42 (with T. Murtaugh and J. Siegel).

1976   (ed.) *Emotions and Anxiety: New Concepts, Methods and Applications*. Erlbaum (with C.D. Speilberger).

1980   Sensation seeking and its biological correlates. *Psychological Bulletin*, 88, 198–214 (with M.S. Buchsbaum and D.L. Murphy).

1984   Sensation seeking: A comparative approach to a human trait. *Behavioral and Brain Sciences*, 88, 198–214.

1984   The neurobiology of some dimensions of personality. In J.R. Smythies and R.J. Bradley (eds), *International Review of Neurobiology*. Academic Press (with J.C. Ballinger and R.M. Post).

1990   The psychophysiology of sensation seeking. *Journal of Personality*, 58, 313–45.

1991   Five (or three) robust questionnaire scale factors of personality without culture. *Personality and Individual Differences*, 12, 929–41 (with D.M. Kuhlman, M. Thornquist and H. Kiers).

1993   A comparison of three structural models for personality: The Big Three, the Big Five, and the Alternative Five. *Journal of Personality and Social Psychology*, 65, 757–68 (with D.M. Kuhlman, T.J. Joireman, P. Teta *et al.*).

1993   Sensation seeking, risk appraisal, and risky behavior. *Personality and Individual Differences*, 14, 41–52 (with P. Horvath).

Further reading

Zuckerman, M. (1983) *Sensation Seeking: Beyond the Optimal Level of Biological Bases of Sensation Seeking, Impulsivity and Anxiety*. Erlbaum.

Marvin Zuckerman describes the most abiding interest in his career as being in personality research, theory and assessment. Although he has been side-tracked at times into purely methodological issues of assessment, such as response sets and the trait–state distinction, his primary contribution has been in developing instruments that can be used in the investigation of important applied and theoretical problems. He constructed the first trait–state version of the Affect Adjective Check List (AACL) in order to investigate changes in anxiety levels during natural and experimental stress conditions. The first version of the Sensation Seeking Scale (SSS) was devised to investigate the relevance of the optimal level of stimulation theory for experiments in sensory deprivation (1958–69). The SSS was developed (1961–4) as an incidental part of a major experimental programme in sensory deprivation. In 1969 Zuckerman became more fully involved in the investigation of this personality dimension, apart from its relevance to sensory deprivation. He commenced correlational studies of the SSS with phenomena in the 'real' world, such as drug abuse and sexual experience. The research showed that the dimension of sensation seeking was centrally involved in many types of life experience and could predict such behaviour as volunteering for experiments and different types of risk taking. With colleagues, he began the first studies of the biological bases of sensation seeking, using the electrodermal orienting reflex. Later Zuckerman and colleagues used a more direct measure of cortical reactivity, the cortical evoked potential (EP). In the mid-1970s his interests began to be directed more into the biochemical area, spurred on by the discoveries that gonadal hormones and the enzyme monoamine oxidase (MAO) were related to sensation seeking. Since MAO is a regulator of the monoamine systems, centred largely in limbic brain, a revised biological model was devised (1979) and collaborative investigations with psychopharmacologists were undertaken to test the theory.

d'Zurilla, Thomas Joseph

Born: 1938, Carteret, New Jersey, USA **Nat:** American **Ints:** Clinical, health and community, psychotherapy (cognitive-behavioral) **Educ:** BA Lafayette College, 1960; MA University of Illinois, 1962; PhD University of Illinois, 1964 **Appts & awards:** Associate Professor of Psychology, Department of Psychology, State University of New York at Stony Brook

Principal publications

1969   A behavior-analytic model for assessing competence. In C.D. Spielberger (ed.), *Current Topics in Clinical and Community Psychology*. Academic Press (with M.R. Goldfried).

1971   Problem solving and behavior modification. *Journal of Abnormal Psychology*, 78, 107–26 (with M.R. Goldfried).

1973 Cognitive processes, problem solving, and effective behavior. In M.R. Goldfried and M. Merbaum (eds), *Behavior Change through Self-control*. Holt, Rinehart & Winston (with M.R. Goldfried).

1975 Behavioral approaches to marital discord and conflict. *Journal of Marriage and Family Counselling*, 1, 299–315 (with S. Greer).

1979 An experimental evaluation of the decision-making process in social problem solving. *Cognitive Therapy and Research*, 3, 269–77 (with A. Nezu).

1980 A study of the generation-of-alternatives in social problem solving. *Cognitive Therapy and Research*, 4, 67–72 (with A. Nezu).

1981 Effects of problem definition and formulation on decision making in the social problem-solving process. *Behavior Therapy*, 12, 100–6 (with A. Nezu).

1981 Effects of problem definition and formulation on the generation of alternatives in the social problem-solving process. *Cognitive Therapy and Research*, 5, 265–72 (with A. Nezu).

1983 Problem-solving therapy. In K.S. Dobson (ed.), *Handbook of Cognitive-Behavioral Therapies*. Guilford Press.

1990 Problem-solving training for effective stress management and prevention. *Journal of Cognitive Psychotherapy*, 4, 327–54.

1990 Development and preliminary evaluation of the Social Problem-Solving Inventory. *Psychological Assessment*, 2, 156–63 (with A.M. Nezu).

1991 Relation between social problem-solving ability and subsequent level of psychological stress in college students. *Journal of Personality and Social Psychology*, 61, 841–6 (with C.F. Sheedy).

1994 Assessing the dimensionality of optimism and pessimism using a multimeasure approach. *Cognitive Therapy and Research*, 18, 143–60 (with E.C. Chang and A. Maydeu-Olivares).

Further reading

Dobson, K.S. (ed.) (1988) *Handbook of Cognitive-Behavioral Therapies*. Guilford Press.

Nezu, A.M. and Nezu, C.M. (eds) (1989) *Clinical Decision Making in Behavior Therapy: A Problem-Solving Perspective*. Research Press.

d'Zurilla's work has focused on the development and evaluation of a prescriptive model of social problem solving, and the applications of this model to clinical intervention and prevention. Social problem solving is the cognitive-affective-behavioral process by which an individual (or group) attempts to identify or discover effective means of coping with problematic situations encountered in everyday living. Social problem solving is at the same time a social learning process (it results in a change in human performance), a self-control strategy, and an active, versatile coping process which can produce generalized improvements in social competence. The clinical application of problem-solving training (PST) has come to be known as 'problem-solving therapy'. Since the goal of PST is to facilitate general social competence, it has important implications not only for treatment, but also for treatment maintenance, generalization and prevention. The prescriptive social problem-solving model which d'Zurilla developed with the help of associates such as Marvin Goldfried and Arthur Nezu has five components: (1) problem orientation (i.e. beliefs and expectations which make up a problem-solving 'set'); (2) problem definition and formulation; (3) generation of alternative solutions; (4) decision making; and (5) solution implementation and verification. d'Zurilla's conceptualization of social problem solving has been influenced strongly by the work of Richard **Lazarus** on stress and coping. Lazarus's work helped identify the parallels between social problem solving and the stress-and-coping process, and led d'Zurilla to conclude that social problem solving is best conceptualized within a transactional framework. He has pursued these ideas through the development of a transactional/problem-solving model of stress and coping and a problem-solving approach to stress management based on this model. This has been followed by comparative evaluations of the problem-solving approach to stress management and other stress-management strategies, including relaxation training, cognitive restructuring and social-performance skill training.

INDEX OF NAMES

This index lists those entrants whose names also appear in the text of other main entries, whether they have worked with the other entrants, hold theories in common, influenced or been influenced by them, or some other association.

INDEX OF INTERESTS

This index is linked to the **Ints:** field in the main entry, and gives the special area(s) of interest for each psychologist. These include the APA subject divisions.

Dollard
Dreikurs
Ellis, A.
Frank
Fromm
Garfield
Kazdin
Kelly, G.A.
Korchin
Laing
Lazarus, A.A.
Locke
Meehl
Merei
Minami
Münsterberg
O'Leary
Rank
Reich
Rogers
Sahakian
Schafer
Singer
Sullivan
Watson
Wolpe
d'Zurilla
Zigler

race psychology
Garth
Porteus

rehabilitation psychology – APA Division 22
Barker
Byrne
Golden, C.J.

religion, psychology of – APA Division 36
Allport, G.W.
Jung
Mailloux
Rosch
Thouless
Welford

school psychology – APA Division 16
Ames
Bardon
Burt
Corsini
Dewey
Gagné
Harré
Lambert, N.
Montessori
Terman
Thorndike, E.L.
Thorndike, R.

Torrance
Wechsler

sex therapy
Ellis, A.

science of man
Combe

social issues, psychological study of – APA Division 9
Allport, F.
Altman
Aronson
Barker
Bem, D.
Bem, S.
Campbell
Converse
Crutchfield
Deaux
Denmark
Deutsch
Dohrenwend
Eagly
Ekman
Endler
Eysenck
Farrington
Feather
Feshbach
Frank
Galton
Hackman
Hollander
Hunt, J.M.
Iritani
Jackson, J.S.
Jahoda, M.
Kelman
Klineberg
Korchin
Langer
Latane
Lefcourt
McClelland
McDougall
McGuire
Milgram
Murphy, G.
Neisser
Osgood
Pheterson
Polanyi
Proshansky
Rapoport
Rodin
Rubin
Sarbin
Scarr
Schein
Sherif

Slovic
Snyder
Sullivan
Tajfel
Tizard
Tobach
Triandis
Vroom
Wapner
Warr
Wertheimer, Max
Zimbardo

sociology
Antonovsky
Crutchfield

teaching of psychology - APA Division 2
Adler
Allport, F.
Allport, G.W.
Boring
Carmichael
Chiland
Crutchfield
Day
Decarie
Denmark
Guilford
Haber
Krech
Murrell
Snyder
Stevens
Werry
Wertheimer, Michael
Zimbardo

theoretical and philosophical psychology – APA Division 24
Allport, F.
Apter
Arnheim
Back
Baldwin
Bar-Tal
Barker
Barron, F.X.
Bateson
Baumrind
Bickhard
Bisiach
Block
Boden
Bohr
Boring
Brainerd
Bromley
Bruner
Bühler, K.

INDEX OF INSTITUTIONS

This gives the psychologists associated with particular institutions (universities, colleges, seminars, institutes, research units, hospitals).

INDEX OF KEY TERMS

Lists the key concepts of psychology and the psychologists associated with them.